LET'S GO
Ireland

■ Let's Go writers travel on your budget.

"Guides that penetrate the veneer of the holiday brochures and mine the grit of real life."
—*The Economist*

"The writers seem to have experienced every rooster-packed bus and lunar-surfaced mattress about which they write."
—*The New York Times*

"All the dirt, dirt cheap."
—*People*

■ Great for independent travelers.

"The guides are aimed not only at young budget travelers but at the independent traveler, a sort of streetwise cookbook for traveling alone."
—*The New York Times*

"Flush with candor and irreverence, chock full of budget travel advice."
—*The Des Moines Register*

"An indispensable resource. *Let's Go*'s practical information can be used by every traveler."
—*The Chattanooga Free Press*

■ Let's Go is completely revised each year.

"Only *Let's Go* has the zeal to annually update every title on its list."
—*The Boston Globe*

"Unbeatable: good sight-seeing advice; up-to-date info on restaurants, hotels, and inns; a commitment to money-saving travel; and a wry style that brightens nearly every page."
—*The Washington Post*

■ All the important information you need.

"*Let's Go* authors provide a comedic element while still providing concise information and thorough coverage of the country. Anything you need to know about budget traveling is detailed in this book."
—*The Chicago Sun-Times*

"Value-packed, unbeatable, accurate, and comprehensive."
—*Los Angeles Times*

Let's Go Publications

Let's Go: Alaska & the Pacific Northwest 1999
Let's Go: Australia 1999
Let's Go: Austria & Switzerland 1999
Let's Go: Britain & Ireland 1999
Let's Go: California 1999
Let's Go: Central America 1999
Let's Go: Eastern Europe 1999
Let's Go: Ecuador & the Galápagos Islands 1999
Let's Go: Europe 1999
Let's Go: France 1999
Let's Go: Germany 1999
Let's Go: Greece 1999 **New title!**
Let's Go: India & Nepal 1999
Let's Go: Ireland 1999
Let's Go: Israel & Egypt 1999
Let's Go: Italy 1999
Let's Go: London 1999
Let's Go: Mexico 1999
Let's Go: New York City 1999
Let's Go: New Zealand 1999
Let's Go: Paris 1999
Let's Go: Rome 1999
Let's Go: South Africa 1999 **New title!**
Let's Go: Southeast Asia 1999
Let's Go: Spain & Portugal 1999
Let's Go: Turkey 1999 **New title!**
Let's Go: USA 1999
Let's Go: Washington, D.C. 1999

Let's Go Map Guides

Amsterdam	Madrid
Berlin	New Orleans
Boston	New York City
Chicago	Paris
Florence	Rome
London	San Francisco
Los Angeles	Washington, D.C.

Coming Soon: Prague, Seattle

Let's Go
Publications

Let's Go
Ireland
1999

Jenny Weiss
Editor

Brina Milikowsky
Associate Editor

Researcher-Writers:
Kathleen Conroy
Daniel Horwitz
Christopher Leighton
Deirdre O'Dwyer

St. Martin's Press ✹ New York

HELPING LET'S GO

If you want to share your discoveries, suggestions, or corrections, please drop us a line. We read every piece of correspondence, whether a postcard, a 10-page email, or a coconut. Please note that mail received after May 1999 may be too late for the 2000 book, but will be kept for future editions. **Address mail to:**

> **Let's Go: Ireland**
> **67 Mount Auburn Street**
> **Cambridge, MA 02138**
> **USA**

Visit Let's Go at **http://www.letsgo.com**, or send email to:

> **feedback@letsgo.com**
> **Subject: "Let's Go: Ireland"**

In addition to the invaluable travel advice our readers share with us, many are kind enough to offer their services as researchers or editors. Unfortunately, our charter enables us to employ only currently enrolled Harvard-Radcliffe students.

Contents

List of Maps

How to Use This Book

Welcome, gentle Reader, to *Let's Go: Ireland 1999*, a multi-splendored yet tasty little book intended to bring out the best *bodhrán*-banging, Guinness-guzzling, sheep-loving budget traveler in you.

As we begin our collective journey, let us, for a moment, take time out from the high-speed thrills of travel and get to know one another. Let us attempt to escape the dry, business-like relationship most often achieved between book and reader. Let us have a drink. After all, what is *Let's Go* but a publican of sorts, that clear, reliable, identifiable figure who serves you what you want when you want it. No frills—ok, a few frills—but we're here to answer crucial questions with accuracy, honesty, and precision. Stout, lager, whiskey, whatever your preferred method of getting drunk off Irish culture—our pub is stacked and waiting for you to explore its cozy snugs, its hearty grub, and its odd cast of characters.

Of course, as we pour your pint and wait for it to settle, we'll take the opportunity to ask *you* some questions, to see just what kind of a drinker you are, to see how much and in what way you will cherish the creamy goodness of the blonde in the black skirt. Are you Reader enough to deal with our legion hints for beating the travel industry, included in our **Essentials** chapter? Are you Reader enough to cope with a country that includes both Peatland Park and Peatland World? We cover 'em both if you're ready, and, even better, in our **Life and Times** section, we attempt to make sense of the history and culture of the country that spawned them. Are you Reader enough to hike the 89,000 miles of hiking trails we include? Are you Reader enough to quaff Guinness from jam jars, part of our extensive pub coverage that includes carefully mapped pub crawls in Dublin (p. 94) and Belfast (p. 388)? Are you Reader enough to stare down the terrifying four-horned sheep of the Isle of Man, Reader enough to deal with the worldly ways of London, which we considerately include as a convenience to aid your travel?

Before the dark stuff gets to your head, you might want to familiarize yourself with some organizational tactics. In cities and larger towns, an **Orientation** section provides a rudimentary verbal map, laying out the city and the relative locations of key points. **Practical Information** provides hard data on things like transportation, tourist offices, financial services, emergency contacts, internet access, and telephone info. **Accommodations, Food,** and **Pubs** listings feature **ranked entries;** those establishments we feel provide the highest quality at the lowest price can be found at the top. **Sights** and **Entertainment** highlight the places we recommend you visit and the festivals we recommend you debauch.

Well, we hope that you've enjoyed the first of a many sweet, sweet pints. Remember that a good drink becomes every so much tastier when shared among a community of drunkards, fools, friends, or fellow travelers. So drain the dregs of our cumulative wisdom and let us go to your head, dear Reader. Go forth and enjoy.

To peat!

A NOTE TO OUR READERS

The information for this book was gathered by *Let's Go*'s researchers from May through August. Each listing is derived from the assigned researcher's opinion based upon his or her visit at a particular time. The opinions are expressed in a candid and forthright manner. Other travelers might disagree. Those traveling at a different time may have different experiences since prices, dates, hours, and conditions are always subject to change. You are urged to check beforehand to avoid inconvenience and surprises. Travel always involves a certain degree of risk, especially in low-cost areas. When traveling, especially on a budget, always take particular care to ensure your safety.

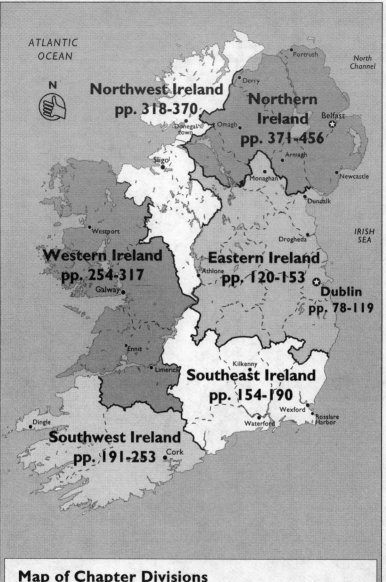

ATLANTIC
OCEAN

N

Northwest Ireland
pp. 318-370

Portrush

North
Channel

Derry

Northern
Ireland
pp. 371-456

Belfast

Omagh

Donegal town

Armagh

Newcastle

Sligo

Monaghan

Dundalk

IRISH
SEA

Westport

Drogheda

Western Ireland
pp. 254-317

Eastern Ireland
pp. 120-153

Athlone

Dublin
pp. 78-119

Galway

Ennis

Kilkenny

Southeast Ireland
pp. 154-190

Limerick

Dingle

Wexford

Rosslare Harbor

Waterford

Southwest Ireland
pp. 191-253

Cork

Map of Chapter Divisions

Eastern Ireland
Counties: Monaghan, Cavan, Louth, Meath, Longford, Westmeath, Offaly, Laois, Kildare, and Wicklow.

Southeast Ireland
Counties: Tipperary, Kilkenny, Carlow, Wexford, and Waterford.

Southwest Ireland
Counties: Cork and Kerry.

Western Ireland
Counties: Limerick, Clare, Galway, and Mayo.

Northwest Ireland
Counties: Roscommon, Leitrim, Sligo and Donegal.

Northern Ireland
Counties: Derry, Antrim, Tyrone, Fermanagh, Armagh, and Down.

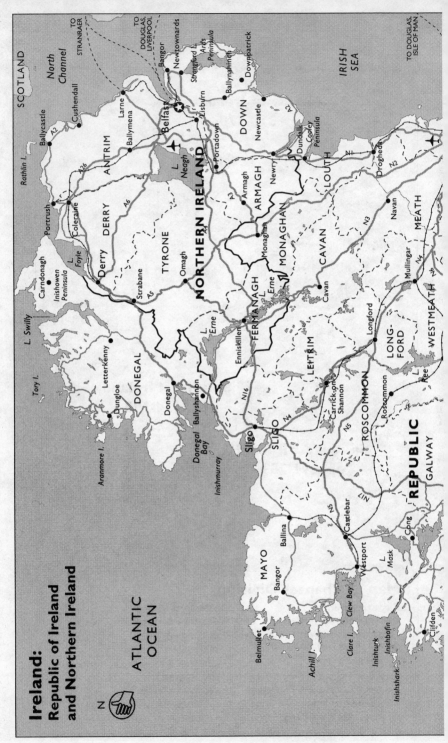

Ireland:
Republic of Ireland
and Northern Ireland

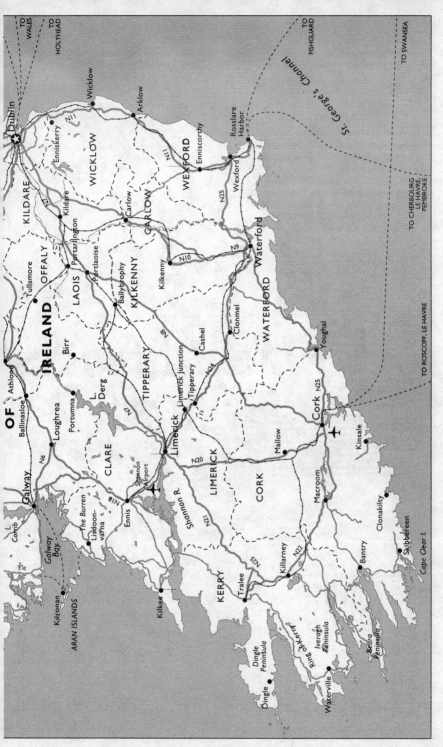

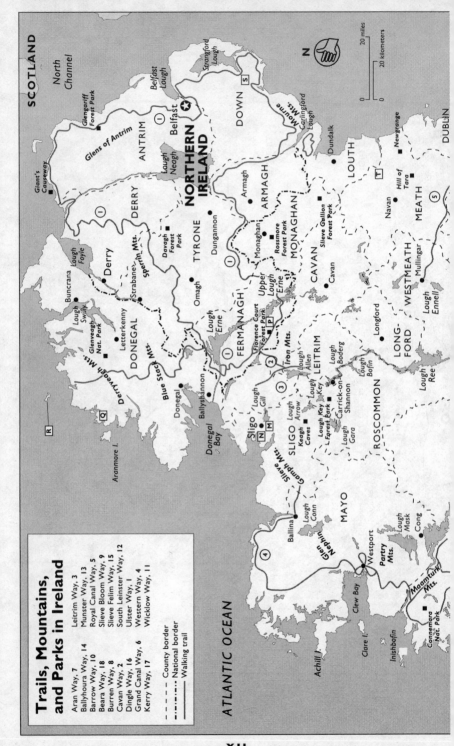

Trails, Mountains, and Parks in Ireland

Aran Way, 7	Leitrim Way, 3
Ballyhoura Way, 14	Munster Way, 13
Barrow Way, 10	Royal Canal Way, 5
Beara Way, 18	Slieve Bloom Way, 9
Burren Way, 8	Slieve Felim Way, 15
Cavan Way, 2	South Leinster Way, 12
Dingle Way, 1	Ulster Way, 16
Grand Canal Way, 6	Western Way, 4
Kerry Way, 17	Wicklow Way, 11

– – – – County border
·–··–·· National border
·····—···· Walking trail

ATLANTIC OCEAN

SCOTLAND

North Channel

NORTHERN IRELAND

Belfast

ANTRIM

DERRY

TYRONE

DONEGAL

DOWN

ARMAGH

MONAGHAN

FERMANAGH

CAVAN

LEITRIM

SLIGO

MAYO

ROSCOMMON

LONGFORD

LOUTH

MEATH

WESTMEATH

DUBLIN

Giant's Causeway

Glenariff Forest Park

Glens of Antrim

Lough Neagh

Belfast Lough

Strangford Lough

Carlingford Lough

Mourne Mts.

Dundalk

Newgrange

Hill of Tara

Navan

Mullingar

Lough Ennell

Lough Ree

Longford

Lough Bofin

Lough Boderg

Carrick-on-Shannon

Lough Key Key Forest Park

Lough Allen

Lough Arrow

Lough Gara

Keogh Caves

Sligo

Lough Gill

Slieve Gamph (Ox) Mts.

Iron Mts.

Upper Lough Erne

Florence Court Forest Park

Lough Erne

Omagh

Dungannon

Davagh Forest Park

Sperrin Mts.

Strabane Mts.

Derry

Lough Foyle

Buncrana

Lough Swilly

Glenveagh Nat. Park

Derryveagh Mts.

Aranmore I.

Donegal

Ballyshannon

Donegal Bay

Blue Stack Mts.

Letterkenny

Armagh

Monaghan

Rossmore Forest Park

Cavan

Slieve Gullion Forest Park

Ballina

Lough Conn

Nephin Mts.

Westport

Clew Bay

Achill I.

Clare I.

Inishbofin

Partry Mts.

Lough Mask

Cong

Maamturk Mts.

Connemara Nat. Park

N

20 miles
20 kilometers

XII

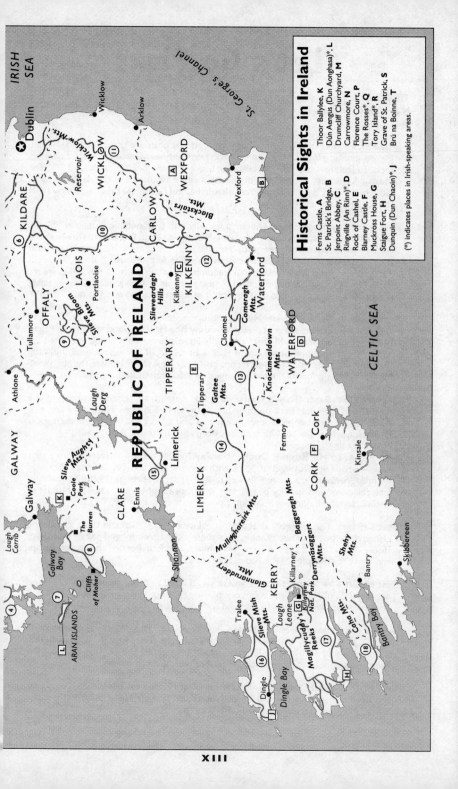

Historical Sights in Ireland

Ferns Castle, A
St. Patrick's Bridge, B
Jerpoint Abbey, C
Ringville (An Rinn)* D
Rock of Cashel, E
Blarney Castle, F
Muckross House, G
Staigue Fort, H
Dunquin (Dun Chaoin)*, J

Thoor Ballylee, K
Dun Aengus (Dun Aonghasa)* L
Drumcliff Churchyard, M
Carrowmore, N
Florence Court, P
The Rosses*, Q
Tory Island*, R
Grave of St. Patrick, S
Brú na Bóinne, T

(*) indicates places in Irish-speaking areas.

Let's Go Picks

These are the places we loved and the places we'd run back to. Of course, subjective is as subjective does. How about a Readers' Picks 2000? Send us a postcard of your favorite finds.

Best Pints: Mulligan's, Dublin, where exceptional pints are pulled in a so-unexciting-it's exciting locals' hangout (p. 97). The **Guinness Brewery** is not as convenient to Dublin's nightlife as Mulligans, but it is at the heart of it all (p. 104). **Yer Mans,** Killarney, is officially licensed to serve Guinness in jam jars (p. 230). **Gaughan's Bar,** Ballina, serves remarkable natural Guinness, bringing a new twist to the dark goodness (p. 314).

Best Pubs: The Stag's Head, Dublin, a friendly pub with notable pints that will fulfill your every Irish pub fantasy. So good-looking it's been featured in Guinness ads (p. 96). Locals pack **The Liverpool Bar,** Belfast, a 150-year-old building for the best trad on the island (p. 391). **Buskar Browne's/The Slate House,** Galway, a perfect compromise for guilty drinkers in a building that was a convent for 300 years (p. 290). **Matt Molloy's,** Westport, with so many people in such a small place you may not be able to get your face to your beer, but the craic is too good to miss (p.307).

Best Places to Stay: Mainistir House, Inishmore, haven for writers, musicians, and the wandering backpacker (p. 280). **Wicklow Bay Hostel,** Wicklow, a former beer bottling factory that now boasts a friendly atmosphere and amazing sea views (p. 122). **Maria's Schoolhouse,** Union Hall, a beautiful (if unconventional) building with big skylights that offers rare comfort (p. 212). **Avalon House,** Dublin, possibly the most comfortable, most friendly, and safest hostel in the country (p. 87).

Backpackers' Best: Giant's Causeway, Co. Antrim, an "eighth wonder of the world" that definitely lives up to its billing (p. 433). **Killarney National Park,** gorgeous hiking and biking around mountains and lakes (p. 230). **Benbulben,** near Drumcliff, where the land inexplicably drops five thousand feet (p. 325).

Best Places to Hit Besides Dublin: Galway (p. 283), a hip university town that knows what's up. **Donegal** (p. 331), with majestic sea cliffs, beautiful beaches, and friendly *gaeltacht* in a sprawling expanse of quiet. **Cashel** (p. 162), all the historical, religious, and spooky power you want out of an Irish town. The **Murals of Belfast,** to which our words couldn't possibly do justice (p. 395).

Best Critters: The **bilingual sheep** of Knocknarea (p. 324) retain their lead in the critter department, while coming on strong is the **three-legged cat** of Bunrower House, Killarney (p. 229). Also in the running: the **four-horned sheep,** the **rumpies,** and the **stumpies** of the Isle of Man (p. 457).

Best Music: The Crane, Galway, where you'll need to bring an instrument or you may be the only one in the room not playing (p.290). **Whelan's,** Dublin, where a cool young crowd grooves to trad and rock nightly (p. 108).

Best Literary Haunts: Thoor Ballylee, near Drumcliff: Yeats, Yeats, and more Yeats (p. 277). **McDaid's,** Dublin, one of the few pubs from which Brendan Behan wasn't banned and host to literary greats throughout the century (p. 96). On **Bloomsday,** June 16, all of Ireland explodes with Joycean revelry.

Best Mythologically Loaded Landscapes: Glen Head, near Glencolmcille, where the devil's privates were left on display (p. 343). **Fair Head,** near Ballycastle, where romance and intrigue washed ashore (p. 428).

ESSENTIALS

PLANNING YOUR TRIP

▨ When to Go

Traveling is like comedy—timing is everything. Traveling during the low or off season (mid-Sept. to May) has its benefits: airfares are less expensive, and you won't have to fend off flocks of fellow tourists. The flip side is that many attractions, hostels, bed and breakfasts, and tourist offices close in winter, and in some rural areas of west Ireland, local transportation drops off significantly or shuts down altogether.

Although festivities increase with the population during the summer, Ireland's calendar of events is continually jam-packed. A thriving music scene fills pubs all year round, with increased performances in the summer. Dublin's acclaimed theater productions tend to occur mostly during the fall and winter. Countless music, film, arts, and, above all, region-specific festivals spring up practically every week; a visit during a town festival will meet an explosive display of excitement, community, beer consumption, and perhaps free stuff. Although different festivals occur throughout the year, the summer months bear a high concentration of them. For example, a visit to Ireland in the beginning of July would coincide with, among others, a trad and storytelling festival in Cobh, the International Arts Festival in Donegal Town, the Galway Film Fleadh, the Samba Festival in Drogheda, the Ballina Street Festival, and the John Wayne/Maureen O'Hara look-alike contest in Cong. Festivals are described in regional sights sections throughout the book; see **Appendix** for a complete 1999 festivals calendar.

The infamous rainy weather of Ireland and Northern Ireland is subject to frequent changes but few extremes, with average temperatures of 60-65°F (15-18°C) in summer and 40-45°F (4-7°C) in winter. The east and south coasts are the driest and sunniest, while western Ireland is wetter and cloudier. Spring is the driest season in Ireland, especially on the east coast. May and June are the sunniest months, particularly in the south and southeast, and July and August are the warmest. December and January have the worst weather of the year: wet, cold, and cloudy. It also gets dark early in winter months; kiss the sun goodnight at 5pm or so.

▨ Useful Information

GOVERNMENT INFORMATION OFFICES

Irish Tourist Board (Bord Fáilte): tel. (1850) 230330 from Ireland; (0171) 493 3201 from the U.K.; (353) 666 1258 from elsewhere); http://ireland.travel.ie. **Australia:** Level 5, 36 Carrington St., Sydney NSW 2000 (tel. (02) 9299 6177; fax 9299 6323). **Canada** and the **U.S.:** 345 Park Ave., New York, NY 10154 (tel. (800) 223 6470 or (212) 418 0800; fax 371 9052). **New Zealand:** 87 Queen St., Auckland (tel. (09) 302 2867). **South Africa:** Everite House, 20 DeKorte St., Braamfontein, Johannesburg (tel. (002711) 339 4865; fax 339 2474). **U.K.:** 150 New Bond St., London W1Y 0AQ (tel. (0171) 518 0800; fax 493 9065).

Northern Ireland Tourist Board: Head Office: 59 North St., Belfast, BT1 1NB, Northern Ireland (tel. (01232) 246609; fax 240960; http://www.ni-tourisim.com). **Dublin:** 16 Nassau St., Dublin 2 (tel. (01) 679 1977; CallSave (1850) 230230; fax (01) 677 1587. **Canada:** 111 Avenue Rd., Ste. 450, Toronto, Ontario M5R 3J8 (tel. (416) 925 6368; fax 961 2175). **U.K.:** British Travel Centre, 12 Lower Regent St., London SW1Y 4PQ (tel. (0171) 839 8417). From elsewhere overseas, contact any British Tourist Office. Tourist boards should have free brochures as well as *Where* *to Stay in Northern Ireland 1999,* a list of all B&Bs and campgrounds (UK£4), and *Where to Eat in Northern Ireland 1999* (UK£3). **U.S.:** 551 Fifth Ave. #701, New York, NY 10176 (tel. (800) 326 0036 or (212) 922 0101; fax 922 0099).

All Ireland Information Bureau: London: British Travel Centre, 12 Lower Regent St., London SW1Y 4PQ (tel. (0171) 839 8417). Open M-F 9am-6:30pm, Sa 9am-5pm, Su 10am-4pm. **Australia:** All Ireland Board, 36 Carrington St., Sydney, NSW 2000 (tel. (02) 9299 6177; fax 9299 6323).

Isle of Man Tourist Information: Sea Terminal Building, Douglas IM1 2RG, Isle of Man (tel. (01624) 686766; fax 627443).

TRAVEL ORGANIZATIONS

Council on International Educational Exchange (CIEE), 205 E. 42nd St., New York, NY 10017-5706 (tel. (888) COUNCIL (268 6245); fax (212) 822 2699; http://www.ciee.org). A private non-profit organization, Council administers work, volunteer, academic, internship, and professional programs around the world. They also offer identity cards (including the ISIC and the GO25) and a range of publications, among them the useful magazine *Student Travels* (free).

Federation of International Youth Travel Organizations (FIYTO), Bredgade 25H, DK-1260 Copenhagen K, Denmark (tel. (45) 33 339600; fax 33 939676; email mailbox@fiyto.org; http://www.fiyto.org), is an international organization promoting educational and cultural travel for young people. Member organizations include language schools, educational travel companies, tourist boards, accommodations, and other suppliers of travel services to youth and students. FIYTO sponsors the GO25 Card (http://www.go25.org); see **Student and Teacher Identification,** p. 10.

International Student Travel Confederation, Herengracht 479, 1017 BS Amsterdam, the Netherlands (tel. (31) 204 212800; fax 204 212810; email istcinfo@istc.org; http://www.istc.org). The ISTC is a non-profit confederation of student travel organizations. Member organizations include International Student Surface Travel Association (ISSA), Student Air Travel Association (SATA), IASIS Travel Insurance, the International Association for Educational and Work Exchange Programs (IAEWEP), and the International Student Identity Card Association (ISIC).

USEFUL PUBLICATIONS

Adventurous Traveler Bookstore, P.O. Box 1468, Williston, VT 05495 (tel. (800) 282 3963; fax (800) 677 1821; email books@atbook.com; http://www.AdventurousTraveler.com). Free 40-page catalogue upon request. Specializes in outdoor adventure travel books and maps for the U.S. and abroad. Extensive website.

Blue Guides, published in Britain by A&C Black Limited, 35 Bedford Row, London WC1R 4JH; in the U.S. by W.W. Norton & Co. Inc., 500 Fifth Ave., New York, NY 10110; and in Canada by Penguin Books Canada Ltd., 10 Alcorn Ave., #300, Toronto, Ontario N4V 3B2. Blue Guides' *Ireland* and *Literary Britain and Ireland* provide invaluable and unmatched historical and cultural information as well as sightseeing routes, maps, and tourist information.

Bon Voyage!, 2069 W. Bullard Ave., Fresno, CA 93711-1200 (tel. (800) 995 9716, from abroad (209) 447 8441; fax 266 6460; email 70754.3511@compuserve.com). Annual mail order catalog offers a range of guaranteed products shipped free. Books, travel accessories, luggage, electrical converters, maps, and videos.

The College Connection, Inc., 1295 Prospect St. Ste. B, La Jolla, CA 92037 (tel. (619) 551 9770; fax 551 9987; email eurailnow@aol.com). Publishes *The Passport,* a booklet listing hints about traveling and studying abroad. This booklet is free to *Let's Go* readers; send your request by email or fax only. The College Rail Connection, a division of the College Connection, sells railpasses with student discounts.

Forsyth Travel Library, Inc., 1750 E. 131st St., P.O. Box 480800, Kansas City, MO 64148 (tel. (800) 367 7984; fax (816) 942 6969; email forsyth@avi.net; http://www.forsyth.com). A mail-order service that stocks a wide range of maps, guides for rail and ferry travel in Europe, and rail tickets and passes. Also offers reservation services. Sells *On the Rails Around Britain & Ireland* (US$15). Call or write for free catalogue.

Hunter Publishing, P.O. Box 7816, Edison, NJ 08818 (tel. (908) 225 1900; fax 417 0482; email hunterpub@emi.net; http://www.hunterpublishing.com). Has an extensive catalogue of travel books, guides, language learning tapes, and quality maps, among them the *Charming Small Hotel Guide* to Britain and Ireland (US$15) and *AA's Ireland Leisure Guide* (US$18).

Irish Books and Media (tel. (800) 229 3505) publishes *Ireland at a Glimpse,* a catalog good for hundreds of 2-for-1 entries to attractions in Ireland (US$14, postage $4).

Transitions Abroad, P.O. Box 1300, 18 Hulst Rd., Amherst, MA 01004-1300 (tel. (800) 293 0373; fax 256 0373; email trabroad@aol.com; http://transabroad.com). Magazine lists publications and resources for overseas study, work, and volunteering (US$25 for 6 issues, single copy $6.25). Also publishes *The Alternative Travel Directory,* a guide to living, learning, and working overseas (US$20; postage $4).

INTERNET RESOURCES

Along with everything else in the 90s, budget travel is moving rapidly into the information age, with the **Internet** as a leading travel resource. On today's Net you can make airline, hotel, hostel, or car rental reservations and connect personally with others abroad, allowing you to become your own budget travel planner. The forms of the Internet most useful to budget travelers are the World Wide Web and Usenet newsgroups. **Search engines** such as **Lycos** (a2z.lycos.com), **Alta Vista** (www.altavista.digital.com), **Excite** (www.excite.com), and **Yahoo!** (www.yahoo.com) can significantly aid the search process. Check out **Let's Go's** own site (http://www.letsgo.com) for an always-current list of links, or double-click on any of these sites:

Ireland Sites

Ireland's National Tourism Database (http://www.touchtel.ie) has extensive information on camping, hostels, castles, car rentals, and more; accessible by county and region. Also includes some information on Northern Ireland.

Official Guide to Northern Ireland (http://www.interknowledge.com/northern-ireland/) has regional information on sights, accommodations, transportation, and other travel tips for Northern Ireland arranged by city and county.

City.Net Ireland (http://www.city.net/countries/ireland/) provides links of interest to travelers, divided into helpful categories.

Yahoo! UK & Ireland (http://www.yahoo.co.uk). A search engine of British and Irish links; a good place to start looking for information.

General Travel Websites

Microsoft Expedia (expedia.msn.com) has everything you'd ever need to make travel plans on the web: compare flight fares, look at maps, and make reservations.

Shoestring Travel (http://www.stratpub.com). A budget travel 'zine with feature articles, links, listings of home exchanges, and accommodations information.

The CIA World Factbook (http://www.odci.gov/cia/publications/factbook) has tons of vital statistics.

Cybercafé Guide (www.cyberiacafe.net/cyberia/guide/ccafe.htm) can help you find cybercafés.

Let's Go also lists relevant websites throughout different sections of the Essentials chapter. Just a warning: the Web's lack of hierarchy often makes it difficult to distinguish between good information, bad information, and marketing.

Newsgroups

Another popular source of information are **newsgroups**—forums for discussion of specific topics. One user posts a written question or thought, to which other users respond. There is information available on almost every imaginable topic (and some unimaginable ones, too). In some cases this proliferation has become burdensome; the quality of discussion is often poor, and you have to wade through piles of non-

sense to come to useful information. Despite this inconvenience, there are still a number of useful newsgroups for the traveler.

Usenet, the name for the family of newsgroups, can be accessed easily from most Internet gateways. In UNIX systems, type "tin" at the prompt. Most commercial providers offer access to Usenet and often have their own version of Usenet.

There are a number of different hierarchies of newsgroups. For issues related to society and culture, try the "soc" hierarchy. These newsgroups allow anyone to post; **soc.culture.irish** is a high-volume forum for the discussion of all things vaguely Irish. The "rec" (recreation) hierarchy is also good for travelers, with newsgroups such as **rec.travel.air.** The "alt" (alternative) hierarchy houses a number of different types of discussion, such as **alt.politics.belfast. Moderated newsgroups** allow only certain agencies to post articles; **clari.world.europe.british_isles.ireland** is a moderated newsgroup that provides breaking news from Ireland from Reuters, the U.P., and other press agencies. **clari.world.europe.british_isles.uk.n-ireland** is a similar newsgroup covering Northern Ireland.

■ Documents and Formalities

All applications should be filed at least several weeks in advance of your planned departure date. Remember that you are relying on government agencies to complete these transactions. Demand for passports is highest between January and August, so try to apply as early as possible. A backlog in processing can spoil your plans, especially as airlines sometimes require a passport number to even book a ticket.

When you travel, always carry on your person two or more forms of identification, including at least one photo ID. A passport combined with a driver's license or birth certificate usually serves as adequate proof of your identity and citizenship. Many establishments, especially banks, require several IDs before cashing traveler's checks. Never carry all your forms of ID together, however; you risk being left entirely without ID or funds in case of theft or loss. In the event of loss, photocopies of your IDs will prove invaluable. Also carry several extra passport-size photos that you can attach to the sundry IDs or railpasses you will eventually acquire. If you plan an extended stay, register your passport with the nearest embassy or consulate.

EMBASSIES AND CONSULATES

See p. 36 for the contact information of your embassy abroad.

Ireland: Australia: 20 Arkana St., Yarralumla ACT 2600, Australia (tel. (02) 6273 3022; fax 6273 3741). **Canada:** 130 Albert St., Ste. 1105, Ottawa, Ontario K1P 5G4 (tel. (613) 233 6281; fax 233 5835). **New Zealand:** Dingwall Building, 87 Queens St., Auckland (tel. (09) 302 2867; fax 302 2420). **South Africa:** Tubach Centre, 1234 Church St., 0083 Colbyn, Pretoria (tel. (012) 342 5062; fax 342 4572). **U.K.:** 17 Grosvenor Pl., London SW1X 7HR (tel. (0171) 235 2171; fax 245 6961). **U.S.:** Irish Embassy, 2234 Massachusetts Ave. NW, Washington, D.C. 20008 (tel. (202) 462 3939; fax 232 5993). Consulates: 345 Park Ave., 17th floor, New York, NY 10154 (tel. (212) 319 2555); Rm. 911, 400 N. Michigan Ave., Chicago, IL 60611 (tel. (312) 337 1868); 44 Montgomery St., #3830, San Francisco, CA 94104 (tel. (415) 392 4214); 535 Boylston St., Boston, MA 02116 (tel. (617) 267 9330).

U.K.: Australia: British High Commission, Commonwealth Ave., Yarralumla, Canberra, ACT 2600 (tel. (02) 6270 6666). **Canada:** British Consulate-General, British Trade & Investment Office, 777 Bay St. #2800, Toronto, Ontario M5G 2G2 (tel. (416) 593 1290). **New Zealand:** British Consulate-General, 17th floor, Fay Richwhite Blvd., 151 Queen St., Auckland 1 (tel. (09) 303 2973). **South Africa:** British High Commission, Liberty Life Pl., Glyn St., Hatfield 0083, Pretoria. **U.S.:** British Consulate, 19 Obervatory Circle NW, Washington, D.C. 20008. British Embassy, 3100 Massachusetts Ave. NW, Washington D.C. 20008 (tel. (202) 462 1340).

PASSPORTS

Before you leave, photocopy the page of your passport that contains your photograph, passport number, and other identifying information. Carry one photocopy in a safe place apart from your passport, and leave another copy at home. These measures will help prove your citizenship and get you a new passport if something happens. Consulates also recommend that you carry an expired passport or an official copy of your birth certificate in a part of your baggage separate from other documents.

If you do lose your passport, immediately notify the local police and the nearest embassy or consulate of your home government. To expedite its replacement, you will need to know all information from it and show identification and proof of citizenship. A replacement may take weeks to process, and it may be valid for only a limited time. Some consulates can issue new passports within 24 hours if you give them proof of citizenship. Any visas stamped in your old passport will be irretrievably lost. In an emergency, ask for immediate temporary traveling papers that will permit you to re-enter your home country.

Your passport is a public document belonging to your nation's government. You may have to surrender it to a foreign government official, but if you don't get it back in a reasonable amount of time, inform the nearest mission of your home country. **U.K.** citizens do not need passports to travel on the island.

Australia: Citizens must apply in person at a post office, passport office, or Australian diplomatic mission overseas. An appointment may be necessary. Passport offices are located in Adelaide, Brisbane, Canberra City, Darwin, Hobart, Melbourne, Newcastle, Perth, and Sydney. Adult passports cost AUS$120 (for a 32-page passport) or AUS$180 (64-page); children's are AUS$60 (32-page) or AUS$90 (64-page). For more information, call toll-free 131232 or visit http://www.austemb.org.

Canada: Application forms in English and French are available at all passport offices, Canadian missions, many travel agencies, and Northern Stores in northern communities. Citizens may apply in person at any one of 28 regional Passport Offices across Canada. Canadian citizens residing abroad should contact the nearest Canadian embassy or consulate. Children under 16 may be included on a parent's passport. Passports cost CDN$60, plus a CDN$25 consular fee, are valid for 5 years, and are not renewable. Processing takes approximately 5 business days for applications in person; allow 3 weeks for mail delivery. For additional info, contact the Canadian Passport Office, Department of Foreign Affairs and International Trade, Ottawa, Ontario, K1A 0G3 (tel. (613) 994 3500; http://www.dfait-maeci.gc.ca/passport). Travelers may also call (800) 567 6868 (24hr.); in Toronto (416) 973 3251; in Vancouver (604) 775 6250; in Montreal (514) 283 2152. Refer to the booklet *Bon Voyage, But...*, free at any passport office or by calling InfoCentre at (800) 267 8376 (within Canada) or (613) 944 4000 for further help and a list of Canadian embassies and consulates abroad. You may also find entry and background information for various countries by contacting the Consular Affairs Bureau in Ottawa (tel. (800) 267 6788 (24hr.) or (613) 944 6788). There is no charge for re-entering Canada with an expired passport.

New Zealand: Application forms are available from travel agents and Department of Internal Affairs Link Centres in the main cities and towns. Overseas, forms and passport services are provided by New Zealand embassies, high commissions, and consulates. Applications may also be forwarded to the Passport Office, P.O. Box 10526, Wellington, New Zealand. Standard processing time in New Zealand is 10 working days. The fees are adults NZ$80, children NZ$40. An urgent passport service is also available for an extra NZ$80. Different fees apply at overseas post: 9 posts including London, Sydney, and Los Angeles offer both standard and urgent services, and a passport will be issued within 3 working days. Children's names can no longer be endorsed on a parent's passport; children must apply for their own, valid for up to 5 years. An adult's passport is valid for up to 10 years. More information is available on the Internet at http://www.govt.nz.

South Africa: Citizens can apply for a passport at any Home Affairs Office or South African Mission. Tourist passports, valid for 10 years, cost SAR80. Children under

16 must be issued their own passports, valid for 5 years (SAR60). If a passport is needed in a hurry, an emergency passport may be issued (SAR50). An application for a permanent passport (and its fee) must accompany the emergency passport application. Time for the completion of an application is normally 3 months or more from the time of submission. Current passports less than 10 years old (counting from date of issuance) may be renewed until December 31, 1999; every citizen whose passport's validity does not extend far beyond this date is urged to renew it as soon as possible, to avoid the expected glut of applications as 2000 approaches. Renewal is free, and turnaround time is usually 2 weeks. For further information, contact the nearest Department of Home Affairs Office.

United States: Citizens may apply for a passport at any federal or state courthouse or post office authorized to accept passport applications, or at U.S. Passport Agencies, located in Boston, Chicago, Honolulu, Houston, Los Angeles, Miami, New Orleans, New York, Philadelphia, San Francisco, Seattle, Stamford, or Washington, D.C. Refer to the "U.S. Government, State Department" section of the telephone directory or the local post office for addresses. Parents must apply in person for children under age 13. You must apply in person if this is your first passport, if you're under age 18, or if your current passport is more than 12 years old or was issued before your 18th birthday. Passports are valid for 10 years (5 years if under 18) and cost US$65 (under 18 US$40). Passports may be renewed by mail or in person for US$55. Processing takes 3-4 weeks. Rush service is available for a surcharge of US$30 with proof of departure within 10 working days (e.g., an airplane ticket or itinerary) or for travelers leaving in 2-3 weeks who require visas. Given proof of citizenship, a U.S. embassy or consulate abroad can usually issue a new passport. Report a passport lost or stolen in the U.S. in writing to Passport Services, 1425 K St. N.W., U.S. Department of State, Washington, D.C. 20524, or to the nearest passport agency. For more info, contact the U.S. Passport Information's 24hr. recorded message (tel. (202) 647 0518). U.S. citizens may receive consular information sheets, travel warnings, and public announcements at any passport agency, U.S. embassy, or consulate or by sending a self-addressed stamped envelope to: Overseas Citizens Services, Room 4811, Department of State, Washington, D.C. 20520-4818 (tel. (202) 647 5225; fax 647 3000). Additional information (including publications) about documents, formalities, and travel abroad is available through the Bureau of Consular Affairs homepage at http://travel.state.gov or through the State Department site at http://www.state.gov.

ENTRANCE REQUIREMENTS

Citizens of Australia, Canada, New Zealand, South Africa, and the U.S. all need valid **passports** to enter the Republic and Northern Ireland and to re-enter their own country. Some countries do not allow entrance if the holder's passport expires in under six months. U.K. citizens do not need passports to travel on the island. Citizens of Australia, Canada, New Zealand, South Africa, the U.K., and the U.S. may enter both Ireland and Northern Ireland without a visa.

Upon entering a country, you must declare certain items from abroad and must pay a duty on the value of those articles that exceed the allowance established by that country's **customs** service. Keeping receipts for purchases made abroad will help establish values when you return. It is wise to make a list, including serial numbers, of any valuables that you carry with you from home; if you register this list with customs before your departure and have an official stamp it, you will avoid import duty charges and ensure an easy passage upon your return. Be especially careful to document items manufactured abroad.

When entering the country, dress neatly and carry **proof of your financial independence** (such as an airplane ticket to depart, enough money to cover your living expenses, etc.). A letter of recommendation may be useful for dealing with officials. The standard period of admission is three months to Ireland, six months to Northern Ireland. To stay longer, you must show evidence that you can support yourself for an extended period of time, and a medical examination is often required. Admission as a visitor from a non-EU nation does not include the right to work, which is authorized only by the possession of a work permit (see **Alternatives to Tourism,** p. 21). Entering either Ireland or Northern Ireland to study does not require a special visa, but immigration officers will want to see proof of acceptance by an Irish school.

CUSTOMS: ENTERING

It is illegal to bring into the **U.K.** or **Ireland** any controlled drugs, obscene material, fireworks, meat, or plant or vegetable material (including fruit and bark). Neither country limits the amount of currency brought in, although Ireland places restrictions on the amount taken out: no more than IR£150 in Irish currency, plus no more than the value of £1200 in foreign currency.

Ireland: Citizens must declare everything in excess of IR£34 (£15 per traveler under 15 years of age) obtained outside the EU or duty- and tax-free in the EU above the following allowances: 200 cigarettes, 100 cigarillos, 50 cigars, or 250g tobacco; 2L table wine; 1L strong liquor or 2L of liquor under 22% volume; 50g perfume; and 250mL toilet water. Goods obtained duty and tax paid in another EU country up to a value of £460 (£115 per traveler under 15) will not be subject to additional customs duties. You must be over 17 to import liquor or tobacco. For more information, contact The Revenue Commissioners, Dublin Castle, Dublin 1 (tel. (01) 679 2777; fax 671 2021; email taxes@iol.ie; http://www.revenue.ie) or The Collector of Customs and Excise, The Custom House, Dublin 1 (tel. (01) 873 4555).

Northern Ireland: Citizens or visitors arriving in the U.K. from outside the EU must declare any goods in excess of the following allowances: 200 cigarettes, 100 cigarillos, 50 cigars, or 250g tobacco; 2L still table wine; 1L strong liquers over 22% volume, or 2L other liquers including fortified or sparkling wine; 60mL perfume; 250mL toilet water; and UK£145 worth of all other goods including gifts and souvenirs. You must be over 17 to import liquor or tobacco. These allowances also apply to duty-free purchases within the EU, except for the last category, which then has an allowance of UK£75. Goods obtained duty and tax paid for personal use within the EU do not require further customs duty. For more info, contact Her Majesty's Customs and Excise, Custom House, Nettleton Road, Heathrow Airport, Hounslow, Middlesex TW6 2LA (tel. (0181) 910 3744; fax 910 3765).

CUSTOMS: GOING HOME

Upon returning home, you must declare all articles you acquired abroad and pay **duty** on the value of those articles that exceed the allowance established by your country's customs service. Goods and gifts purchased at **duty-free** shops abroad are *not* exempt from duty or sales tax at your point of return; you must declare these items as well. "Duty-free" means that you need not pay a tax in the country of purchase.

Australia: Citizens may import AUS$400 (under 18 AUS$200) of goods duty-free, in addition to 1.125L alcohol and 250 cigarettes or 250g tobacco. You must be over 17 to import alcohol or tobacco. There is no limit to the amount of Australian or foreign cash that may be brought into or taken out of the country, but amounts of AUS$10,000 or more, or the equivalent in foreign currency, must be reported. All foodstuffs and animal products must be declared on arrival. For information, contact the Regional Director, Australian Customs Service, GPO Box 8, Sydney NSW 2001 (tel. (02) 9213 2000; fax 9213 4000; http://www.customs.gov.au).

Canada: Citizens who remain abroad for at least 1 week may bring back up to CDN$500 worth of goods duty-free any time. Citizens or residents who travel for a period between 48hr. and 6 days can bring back up to CDN$200. Both of these exemptions may include tobacco and alcohol. You are permitted to ship goods except tobacco and alcohol home under the CDN$500 exemption as long as you declare them when you arrive. Goods under the CDN$200 exemption, as well as all alcohol and tobacco, must be in your hand or checked luggage. Citizens of legal age (which varies by province) may import in-person up to 200 cigarettes, 50 cigars or cigarillos, 200g loose tobacco, 1.14L wine or alcohol, and 24 355mL cans/bottles of beer; the value of these products is included in the CDN$200 or CDN$500. For more information, write to Canadian Customs, 2265 St. Laurent Blvd., Ottawa, Ontario K1G 4K3 (tel. (613) 993 0534), phone the 24hr. Automated Customs Information Service at (800) 461 9999, or visit Revenue Canada at http://www.revcan.ca.

New Zealand: Citizens may import up to NZ$700 worth of goods duty-free if they are intended for personal use or are gifts. The concession is 200 cigarettes (1 carton) or 250g tobacco or 50 cigars or a combination of all 3 not to exceed 250g. You may also bring in 4.5L of beer or wine and 1.125L of liquor. Only travelers over 17 may import tobacco or alcohol. For more information, contact New Zealand Customs, 50 Anzac Ave., Box 29, Auckland (tel. (09) 377 3520; fax 309 2978).

South Africa: Citizens may import duty-free: 400 cigarettes, 50 cigars, 250g tobacco, 2L wine, 1L of spirits, 250mL toilet water, and 50mL perfume, and other consumable items up to a value of SAR500. Goods up to a value of SAR10,000 over and above the above allowance are dutiable at 20%; such goods are also exempted from payment of VAT. Items acquired abroad and sent to the Republic as unaccompanied baggage do not qualify for any allowances. You may not export or import South African bank notes in excess of SAR2000. For more information, consult the free pamphlet *South African Customs Information,* available in airports or from the Commissioner for Customs and Excise, Private Bag X47, Pretoria 0001 (tel. (12) 314 9911; fax 328 6478).

United Kingdom: Citizens or visitors arriving in the U.K. from Ireland must declare goods in excess of the following allowances: 200 cigarettes, 100 cigarillos, 50 cigars, or 250g tobacco; 2L still table wine; 1L strong liqueurs over 22% volume, 2L other liquors, or fortified or sparkling wine; 60mL perfume; 250mL toilet water; and UK£75 worth of all other goods including gifts and souvenirs. Goods obtained duty and tax paid for personal use within Ireland do not require any further customs duty. You must be over 17 to import liquor or tobacco. For more information, contact Her Majesty's Customs and Excise, Custom House, Nettleton Road, Heathrow Airport, Hounslow, Middlesex TW6 2LA (tel. (0181) 910 3602 or 910 3566; fax 910 3765; http://www.open.gov.uk).

United States: Citizens may import US$400 worth of accompanying goods duty-free and must pay a 10% tax on the next US$1000. You must declare all purchases, so have sales slips ready. The US$400 personal exemption covers goods purchased for personal or household use (this includes gifts) and cannot include more than 100 cigars, 200 cigarettes (1 carton), and 1L of wine or liquor. You must be over 21 to bring liquor into the U.S. If you mail home personal goods of U.S. origin, you can avoid duty charges by marking the package "American goods returned." For more information, consult the brochure *Know Before You Go,* available from the U.S. Customs Service, P.O. Box 7407, Washington, D.C. 20044 (tel. (202) 927 6724; http://www.customs.ustreas.gov).

STUDENT AND TEACHER IDENTIFICATION

The **International Student Identity Card (ISIC)** is the most widely accepted form of student identification. Flashing this card can procure you discounts for sights, theaters, museums, accommodations, meals, trains, ferries, buses, flights, and other services. Present the card wherever you go, and ask about discounts even when none are advertised. An ISIC allows you to get a useful **Travelsave** stamp, good for large bus and rail discounts (see **Getting Around,** p. 36). It also provides insurance benefits, including US$100 per day of in-hospital sickness for a maximum of 60 days and US$3000 accident-related medical reimbursement for each accident (see **Insurance,** p. 20). In addition, cardholders have access to a toll-free 24-hour ISIC helpline, whose multilingual staff can provide assistance in medical, legal, and financial emergencies overseas (tel. (800) 626 2427 in the U.S. and Canada; elsewhere call collect (44) 181 666 9025).

Many student travel agencies around the world issue ISICs, including STA Travel in Australia and New Zealand; Travel CUTS and via the web (http://www.isic-canada.org) in Canada; USIT in Ireland and Northern Ireland; SASTS in South Africa; Campus Travel and STA Travel in the U.K.; Council Travel, Let's Go Travel, STA Travel, and via the web (http://www.ciee.org/idcards/index.htm) in the U.S.; and any of the other organizations under the auspices of the International Student Travel Confederation (ISTC). When you apply for the card, request a copy of the *International Student Identity Card Handbook,* which lists by country some of the available discounts. You can also write to Council for a copy (see **Travel Organizations,** p. 2). The card is valid from September to December of the following year and costs US$20, CDN$15, or AUS$15. Applicants must be at least 12 years old and degree-seeking students of a secondary or post-secondary school. Because of the proliferation of phony ISICs, many airlines and some other services require other proof of student identity, such as a signed letter from the registrar attesting to your student status and stamped with the school seal or your school ID card. The **International Teacher Identity Card (ITIC)** offers the same insurance coverage and similar but limited discounts. The fee is US$20, UK£5, or AUS$13. For more information on these cards, consult the organization's web site (http://www.istc.org) or email them at isicinfo@istc.org.

The Federation of International Youth Travel Organizations (FIYTO) issues a discount card to travelers who are under 26 but not students. Known as the **GO25 Card,** this one-year card offers many of the same benefits as the ISIC and is sold by most organizations that sell the ISIC. A brochure that lists discounts is free when you purchase the card. To apply, you will need a passport, valid driver's license, or copy of a birth certificate; and a passport-sized photo. The fee is US$20. Information is available on the web at http://www.ciee.org or by contacting Travel CUTS in Canada, STA Travel in the U.K., Council Travel in the U.S., or FIYTO headquarters in Denmark (see **Travel Organizations,** p. 2).

DRIVING PERMITS AND INSURANCE

You may use an American or Canadian driver's license for one month or a U.K. license for six months in Ireland provided you've had it for one year prior to arriving. If you plan a longer stay, you must officially have an **International Driving Permit (IDP),** although most car rental agencies don't require it. Your IDP must be issued in your own country before you depart and accompanied by a valid driver's license from your home country. **Australians** can obtain an IDP by contacting their local **Royal Automobile Club (RAC),** or the **National Royal Motorist Association (NRMA)** if in NSW or the ACT, where a permit can be obtained for AUS$15. An application can be obtained by phone or on the web (tel. (08) 9421 4271; fax (08) 9221 1887; http://www.rac.com.au). Canadian license holders can obtain an IDP (CDN$10) through any **Canadian Automobile Association (CAA)** branch office in Canada by writing to CAA, 1145 Hunt Club Rd., Ste. 200, K1V 0Y3 Canada (tel. (613) 247 0117, ext. 2025; fax 247 0118; http://www.caa.ca). In **New Zealand,** contact your local **Automobile Association (AA)** or their main office at P.O. Box 5, Auckland (tel. (9) 377 4660; fax (9) 302 2037; http://www.nzaa.co.nz). IDPs cost NZ$8, plus NZ$2 for return postage if mailed from abroad. In South Africa visit your local **Automobile Association of South Africa** office, where IDPs can be picked up for SAR28.50; for information, call or write P.O. Box 596, 2000 Johannesburg (tel. (11) 799 1000; fax (11) 799 1010). In the **U.K.,** IDPs are UK£4 and you can either visit your local **AA Shop,** call (tel. (1256) 493932; if abroad, fax (44) 1256 460750), or write to AA at 5 Star Post Link, Freepost, Copenhagen Ct., 8 New St., Basingstroke RG21 7BA, and order a postal application form (allow 2-3 weeks). For further information, call (44) 0990 448866 or visit http://www.theaa.co.uk/travel. U.S. license holders can obtain an IDP (US$10) at any **American Automobile Association (AAA)** office or by writing to AAA Florida, Travel Agency Services Department, 1000 AAA Dr. (mail stop 28), Heathrow, FL 32746 (tel. (407) 444 4245; fax 444 4247). You do not have to be a member of AAA to receive an IDP.

Some credit cards cover standard **insurance.** To rent, lease, or borrow a car, you might need a **green card,** or **International Insurance Certificate,** to prove that you have liability insurance. You can obtain it through the car rental agency or dealer; most include coverage in their prices. Some travel agents offer the card; it may also be available at border crossings. Check whether your auto insurance applies abroad. Even if it does, you'll still need a green card to certify this fact to foreign officials. If

ESSENTIALS

you have a collision abroad, the accident will show up on your domestic records if you report it to your insurance company. Rental agencies may require you to purchase theft insurance in countries that they consider to have a high risk of auto theft.

■ Money

CURRENCY AND EXCHANGE

AUS$1 = IR£0.43	IR£1 = AUS$2.36
CDN$1 = IR£0.47	IR£1 = CDN$2.14
NZ$1 = IR£0.36	IR£1 = NZ$2.80
SAR1 = IR£0.11	IR£1 = SAR8.95
UK£1 = IR£1.16	IR£1 = UK£0.86
US$1 = IR£0.71	IR£1 = US$1.41
AUS$1 = UK£0.36	UK£1 = AUS$2.74
CDN$1 = UK£0.40	UK£1 = CDN$2.48
NZ$1 = UK£0.31	UK£1 = NZ$3.25
SAR1 = UK£0.10	UK£ = SAR10.39
US$1 = UK£0.61	UK£1 = US$1.63

> The information in this book was researched during the summer of 1998. Inflation and the Invisible Hand may raise or lower the listed prices by as much as 20%. The European Union's Echo Service posts daily exchange rates on the web (http://www.dna.lth.se/cgi-bin/kurt/rates?). In the chapters on the Republic of Ireland, the symbol £ denotes Irish pounds. In the chapters on the North, the Isle of Man, and London, it denotes British pounds.

Legal tender in the Republic of Ireland is the Irish pound (or "punt"), denoted £. It comes in the same denominations as the British pound (which is called "sterling" in Ireland) but has been worth a bit less recently. British small change is no longer accepted in the Republic of Ireland. The Irish punt is difficult to convert abroad.

Legal tender in Northern Ireland and the Isle of Man is the British pound. Northern Ireland has its own bank notes, which are identical in value to English, Scottish, or Manx notes of the same denominations. Although all of these notes are accepted in Northern Ireland, Northern Ireland bank notes are not accepted across the water. U.K. coins now come in logical denominations of 1p, 2p, 5p, 10p, 20p, 50p, and £1. An old "shilling" coin is worth 5p, a "florin" 10p. "Quid," popular slang for pounds sterling, derives from *cuid,* which serves as both the singular and plural in Irish. Therefore the plural of quid is "quid," not "quids."

Most banks are closed on Saturday, Sunday, and all public holidays, although more and more banks, especially in cities, have 24-hour ATMs. Most businesses close on "bank holidays," which occur several times a year in both countries. Banks in Ireland are usually open Monday to Friday 9am to 4pm. Usual bank hours in Northern Ireland are Monday to Friday 9:30am to 4:30pm. In both the Republic and the North, some close for lunch and many close early or late one day per week.

It is more expensive to buy foreign currency than to buy domestic: pounds will be less costly in Ireland than at home. However, converting some money before you go will allow you to avoid airport exchange lines. Generally, you should bring enough Irish currency to last the first 24-72 hours of a trip (exchanging currency will be difficult over a weekend or holiday). Travelers living in the U.S. can get foreign currency from the comfort of home; contact **Capital Foreign Exchange** on the East Coast (toll-free (888) 842 0880, fax (202) 842 8008), or on the West Coast, **International Currency Express** (toll-free (888) 278 6628, fax (310) 278 6410; email currencyrush@worldnet.att.net). They will deliver foreign currency or traveler's checks (see **Traveler's Checks**) overnight (US$15) or second-day (US$12) at competitive exchange rates. Observe commission rates closely and check newspapers to get the standard rate of exchange. Banks generally have the best rates, but sometimes tourist offices or exchange kiosks are better. A 5% margin between buy and sell prices is a fair deal (be sure that both are listed). Since you lose money with every transaction, convert in large sums, but not more than you'll need. Personal checks from home probably won't be accepted.

If you stay in hostels and prepare your own food, expect to spend anywhere from US$16-35 per person per day; transportation and beer will increase these figures dramatically; US$50 is a good all-around budget ballpark.

TRAVELER'S CHECKS

Traveler's checks are a safe and easy means of carrying funds, as they can be refunded if stolen. Several agencies and many banks sell them, usually for face value plus a small percentage commission. **American Express, Visa,** and **Thomas Cook** checks can be sold, exchanged, cashed, and refunded at virtually every bank in Ireland and Northern Ireland with almost equal ease. Traveler's checks are accepted at most B&Bs, shops, and restaurants, although many smaller establishments only take cash. Traveler's checks are less readily accepted in small towns than in cities with large tourist industries. Order your checks well in advance, especially if you're requesting large sums.

Each agency provides refunds **if your checks are lost or stolen,** and many provide additional services. You may need a police report verifying loss or theft. Inquire about international toll-free refund hotlines, emergency message relay services, and stolen credit card assistance when you purchase your checks. Expect a fair amount of red tape and delay in the event of theft or loss of traveler's checks. For a speedy refund, keep your check receipts separate from your checks and store them in a safe place or with a traveling companion, record check numbers when you cash them and leave a list of check numbers with someone at home, and ask for a list of refund centers when you buy your checks (American Express and Bank of America have over 40,000 centers worldwide). Keep a separate supply of cash or traveler's checks for emergencies. Never countersign your checks until you're prepared to cash them, and always bring your passport with you when you plan to use the checks.

If you will be visiting other countries in addition to Ireland and Northern Ireland, you should buy your checks in U.S. dollars. Few currencies are as easily exchanged worldwide, and you will save yourself the cost of repeatedly converting currency. If you are staying exclusively in Northern Ireland, you might wish to buy your checks in British pounds. In Northern Ireland, most branches of the Bank of Ireland and Ulster Bank and some branches of other banks will not charge a commission when changing traveler's checks if you show a student ID. The following companies offer checks in U.S. dollars, British pounds, or both:

American Express: Call (800) 251902 in Australia; in New Zealand (0800) 441068; in the U.K. (0800) 521313; in the U.S. and Canada (800) 221 7282). Elsewhere, call U.S. collect (801) 964 6665. American Express Traveler's Cheques are now available in 10 currencies, including British, but not Irish, pounds. They are the most widely recognized worldwide and the easiest to replace if lost or stolen. Checks can be purchased for a small fee (1-4%) at American Express Travel Service Offices, banks, and American Automobile Association offices (AAA members can buy the checks commission-free). Cardmembers can also buy checks at American Express Dispensers at Travel Service Offices at airports, or order them by phone (tel. (800) ORDER TC (673 3782)). American Express offices cash their checks commission-free (except where prohibited by national governments), although they often offer slightly worse rates than banks. You can also buy *Cheques for Two* which can be signed by either of 2 people traveling together. Request the American Express booklet "Traveler's Companion," which lists travel office addresses and stolen check hotlines for each European country. Visit their online travel offices (http://www.aexp.com).

Citicorp: Call 24hr. (800) 645 6556 in the U.S. and Canada; in Europe or Africa (44) 171 508 7007; from elsewhere call U.S. collect (813) 623 1709. Sells both Citicorp and Citicorp Visa traveler's checks in British pounds. Commission is 1-2% on check purchases. Citicorp's World Courier Service guarantees hand-delivery of traveler's checks when a refund location is not convenient.

Thomas Cook MasterCard: For 24hr. cashing or refund assistance: from the U.S., Canada, or Caribbean call (800) 223 7373; from the U.K. call (0800) 622101 free or (1733) 318950 collect; from anywhere else call (44) 1733 318950 collect. Offers checks in British pounds. Commission 2% for purchases; try buying the checks at a Thomas Cook office for potentially lower commissions. No commission if you cash checks at a Thomas Cook office. Thomas Cook MasterCard Traveler's Checks are also available from **Capital Foreign Exchange** (see **Currency and Exchange**).

Visa: Call (800) 227 6811 in the U.S.; (0800) 89578 in the U.K.; from elsewhere call collect (44) 1733 318949 to get the location of the nearest office.

CREDIT CARDS AND CASH CARDS

In Ireland, **credit cards** are accepted in all but the smallest businesses. Credit cards are also invaluable in an emergency. Depending on the issuer, credit cards may offer an array of other services, from insurance to emergency assistance.

Visa (tel. (800) 336 8472) and **MasterCard** are usually issued in cooperation with individual banks and allow the easiest access to ATM machines in Europe. Keep in mind that MasterCard and Visa have different names elsewhere ("EuroCard" or "Access" for MasterCard and "Carte Bleue" or "Barclaycard" for Visa). For cash advances, credit card companies get the wholesale exchange rate, which is generally 5% better than the retail rate used by banks. All such machines require a **Personal Identification Number (PIN).**

American Express (tel. (800) 843 2273) has a US$55 annual fee but offers a number of services. AmEx cardholders can cash personal checks at AmEx offices outside the U.S., and Global Assist, a 24-hour hotline with medical and legal assistance in emergencies, is also available (tel. (800) 554 2639 in U.S. and Canada; from abroad call U.S. collect (202) 554 2639). Cardholders can use the American Express Travel Service; benefits include assistance in changing airline, hotel, and car rental reservations, baggage loss and flight insurance, sending mailgrams and international cables, and holding your mail at one of the more than 1700 AmEx offices around the world. If you lose your card, call their Dublin service office at (01) 205 5111.

Cash cards, or **ATM** (Automated Teller Machine) cards, are widespread in Ireland, but international network connections are hard to make. Happily, ATMs get the same wholesale exchange rate as credit cards. Despite these perks, credit cards are more reliably accepted at ATMs than personal bank cards. Also, there is often a limit on the amount of money you can withdraw per day (usually about US$500, depending on the type of card and account), and computer networks sometimes fail. Memorize your PIN code in numeral form since machines outside the U.S. and Canada often don't have letters on their keys. The two major international money networks are **Cirrus** (U.S. tel. (800) 4 CIRRUS (424 7787)) and **PLUS** (tel. (800) 843 7587 "Voice Response Unit Locator," or http://www.visa.com). Cirrus charges US$3-5 to withdraw non-domestically, depending on your bank.

In the Republic, **Visa** and **MasterCard/Access** are accepted at some **Bank of Ireland** ATMs and at all **Allied Irish Bank (AIB)** ATMs. Many ATMs that accept Visa will also accept Plus, and many that accept MasterCard also accept Cirrus. Both banks, and **Trustee Savings Bank (TSB),** accept Visa and MasterCard at their foreign exchange desk. In Northern Ireland, **First Trust** and **Ulster Bank** accept Visa, MasterCard, Plus, and Cirrus cards at most of their ATMs: **Bank of Ireland's** ATMs in the North accept only Visa. **Isle of Man Bank** has branches in most towns on the Isle of Man. Isle of Man Banks' ATMs accept Visa, MasterCard, Plus, and Cirrus system cards. TSB ATMs on the Isle of Man accept Visa and MasterCard. For location and hours of ATMs accepting MasterCard/Cirrus or Visa/Plus in your specific town or city destination, check http://www.mastercard.com or http://www.visa.com, respectively.

GETTING MONEY FROM HOME

One of the easiest ways to get money from home is to bring an **American Express** card. AmEx allows its cardholders to draw cash from their checking accounts at any of its major offices and many of its representatives' offices, up to US$1000 every 21 days (no service charge, no interest). AmEx Express Cash (cardmembers call (800) CASH NOW (227 4669); outside the U.S. call collect (336) 668 5041) and bank ATM/debit cards linked to credit cards can withdraw cash from your checking account with good exchange rates and a small fee. Avoid cashing checks in foreign currencies; they usually take weeks and a US$30 fee to clear.

Money can also be wired abroad through international money transfer services operated by **Western Union** (tel. (800) 325 6000). In the U.S., call Western Union any time at (800) CALL CASH (225 5227) to cable money with your Visa, Discover, or MasterCard within the domestic U.S. and the U.K. The rates for sending cash are generally US$10 cheaper than with a credit card, and the money is usually available in the country you're sending it to within an hour, although this time may vary.

In emergencies, U.S. citizens can have money sent via the State Department's Overseas Citizens Service, **American Citizens Services,** Consular Affairs, #4811, U.S. Department of State, Washington, D.C. 20520 (tel. (202) 647 5225; nights, Sundays, and holidays 647 4000; fax (on demand only) 647 3000; email ca@his.com; http://travel.state.gov). For a fee of US$15, the State Department will forward money within hours to the nearest consular office, which will then disburse it according to instructions. The quickest way to have the money sent is to cable the State Department through Western Union depending on the circumstances. The office serves only Americans in the direst of straits abroad; other travelers should contact their embassies for information on wiring cash.

VAT (VALUE-ADDED TAX)

Both Ireland and Northern Ireland charge value-added tax (VAT), a national sales tax on most goods and some services. In Ireland, the VAT ranges from 0% on food and children's clothing to 17% in restaurants to 21% on other items, such as jewelry, clothing, cameras, and appliances; the VAT is usually included in listed prices. The British rate, applicable to Northern Ireland and the Isle of Man, is 17.5% on many services (such as hairdressers, hotels, restaurants, and car rental agencies) and on all goods (except books, medicine, and food). Prices stated in *Let's Go* include VAT. Refunds are available only to non-EU citizens and only for goods taken out of the country, not services. In Ireland, VAT refunds are available on goods purchased in stores displaying a "Cashback" sticker (ask if you don't see one). Ask for a voucher with your purchase, which you must fill out and present at the Cashback service desk in Dublin or Shannon airports. Purchases greater than £200 must be approved at the customs desk first. Your money can also be refunded by mail, which takes six to eight weeks. Visitors to Northern Ireland and the Isle of Man can get a **VAT refund** on goods taken out of the country through the **Retail Export Scheme.** Look for signs like "Tax Free Shopping" or "Tax Free for Tourists" and ask the shopkeeper about minimum purchases (usually £50-100) as well as for the appropriate form. Keep purchases in carry-on luggage so a customs officer can inspect the goods and validate refund forms. To receive a refund, mail the stamped forms back to the store in the envelope provided. Refunds can take up to three months to be processed. In order to use this scheme, you must export the goods within three months of purchase.

TIPPING

Many restaurants in Ireland figure a service charge into the bill; some even calculate it into the cost of the dishes themselves. The menu often indicates whether or not service is included (ask if you're not sure). For those restaurants that do not include a tip in the bill, more common in cities, customers should leave 10-15%. The exact amount should truly depend upon the quality of the service. For waiter service in a bar or lounge, 20p will do. Tipping is less common for other services, especially in rural areas, but is always very welcome. Porters, parking-lot attendants, wait staff, and hair-dressers are usually tipped. Cab drivers are usually tipped 10%. Hotel housekeepers will welcome a gratuity, but owners of establishments, including B&Bs, may be insulted by a tip. And above all, **never tip the barman.**

■ Safety and Security

PERSONAL SAFETY

Ireland and Northern Ireland are safer for the traveler than most other European countries, but theft or harassment can easily occur. To avoid unwanted attention, try to **blend in** as much as possible. Walking directly into a pub or shop to check your map beats checking it on a street corner—better yet, look over your map before leaving your hostel. Find out about unsafe areas from tourist offices, the manager of a reputable hotel or hostel, or a local whom you trust. Especially when traveling alone, be sure that someone at home knows your itinerary, and never say that you're traveling alone. Both men and women may want to carry a small **whistle** to scare off attackers or attract attention. When walking at night, stick to busy, well-lit streets and avoid dark alleyways. Do not attempt to cross through parks, parking lots, beaches, or any other large, deserted areas.

If you are using a **car**, be sure to park your vehicle in a garage or well-traveled area. **Sleeping in your car** is one of the most dangerous ways to get your rest. If your car breaks down, wait for the police to assist you. If you must sleep in your car, do so as close to a police station or a 24-hour service station as possible. Sleeping out in the open can be even more dangerous—camping is recommended only in official, supervised campsites or in wilderness backcountry. **Let's Go does not recommend hitchhiking** under any circumstances, particularly for women (see **By Thumb,** p. 40).

There is no sure-fire set of precautions that will protect you from all of the situations you might encounter when you travel. A good self-defense course will give you more concrete ways to react to different types of aggression, although it often carries a steep price tag. **Impact, Prepare,** and **Model Mugging** can refer you to local self-defense courses in the United States (tel. (800) 345 KICK (345 5425)) and Canada (tel. (604) 878 3838). Course prices vary from $50-500. Women's and men's courses are offered. Community colleges frequently offer inexpensive self-defense courses.

The **Australian Department of Foreign Affairs and Trade** (tel. 2 6261 9111) offers travel information and advisories at their website (http://www.dfat.gov.au). The **Canadian Department of Foreign Affairs and International Trade** (DFAIT) provides advisories and travel warnings at its website (http://www.dfait-maeci.gc.ca). Call them at (613) 944 6788 from Ottawa or (800) 267 8376 elsewhere in Canada; to receive their free publication, *Bon Voyage,* call (613) 944 4000. Official warnings from the **United Kingdom Foreign and Commonwealth Office** are on-line at http://www.fco.gov.uk; you can also call the office at (0171) 238 4503. For official **United States Department of State** travel advisories, call their 24-hour hotline (tel. (202) 647 5225) or check their website (http://travel.state.gov), which provides travel information; order publications such as *A Safe Trip Abroad* for a small fee by calling the Superintendent of Documents (tel. (202) 512 1800). **Travel Assistance International by Worldwide Assistance Services, Inc.** (http://www.worldwide-assistance.com) provides its members with a 24-hour hotline for travel emergencies and referrals in over 200 countries. Their Per-Trip (from US$21) and Frequent Traveler (from US$88) plans include medical (evacuation and repatriation), travel, and communication services. Call or write them at 1133 15th St. NW #400, Washington, D.C. 20005-2710 (tel. (800) 821 2828 or (202) 828 5894, fax (202) 828 5896; e-mail wassist@aol.com).

FINANCIAL SECURITY

Although Ireland is generally safe, precautions are always useful. **Don't put a wallet in your back pocket.** Never count your money in public and carry as little as is feasible. If you carry a purse, buy a sturdy one with a secure clasp, and carry it crosswise on the side, away from the street with the clasp against you. Secure packs with small combination padlocks that slip through the two zippers. A **money belt** is the best way to carry cash; you can buy one at most camping supply stores or through the Forsyth Travel Library (see **Useful Publications,** p. 2). A nylon, zippered pouch with a belt that sits inside the waist of your pants or skirt combines convenience and security. A **neck pouch** is equally safe though far less accessible. Refrain from pulling out your neck pouch in public; if you must, be very discreet. Avoid keeping anything precious in a fanny-pack (even if it's worn on your stomach): your valuables will be highly visible and easy to steal.

In city crowds and especially on public transportation, pick-pockets are amazingly deft at their craft. Rush hour is no excuse for strangers to press up against you on the bus. If someone stands uncomfortably close, move to the other end and hold your bags tightly. Also, be alert in public telephone booths. If you must say your calling-card number, do so very quietly; if you punch it in, make sure no one can look over your shoulder. **Photocopies** of important documents allow you to recover them in case they are lost or filched. Carry one copy separate from the documents and leave another copy at home. Keep some money separate from the rest to use in an emergency or in case of theft. Label every piece of luggage both inside and out.

Be particularly careful on **buses** (for example, carry your backpack in front of you where you can see it), don't check baggage on trains, and don't trust anyone to "watch your bag for a second." Thieves thrive on **trains;** professionals wait for tourists to fall asleep and then carry off everything they can. When traveling in pairs, sleep in alternating shifts; when alone, use good judgement in selecting a train compartment: never stay in an empty one, and use a lock to secure your pack to the luggage rack. Keep important documents and other valuables on your person and try to sleep on top bunks with your luggage stored above you (if not in bed with you).

Let's Go lists locker availability in hostels and train stations, but you'll need your own padlock. Lockers are useful if you plan on sleeping outdoors or don't want to lug everything with you, but don't store valuables in them. Never leave your belongings unattended; crime occurs in even the most demure-looking hostel or hotel. If you feel unsafe, look for places with either a curfew or a night attendant. When possible, keep valuables or anything you couldn't bear to lose at home.

DRUGS

If you are caught with any quantity of **illegal** or **controlled drugs** in Ireland or Northern Ireland, you will be arrested and tried under Irish or British law or be immediately expelled from the country. Your home government is powerless to shield you from the judicial system of a foreign country. If you are imprisoned, consular officers can visit you, provide you with a list of local attorneys, and inform your family and friends, but that's all. The London-based organization **Release** (tel. (0171) 603 8654) advises people who have been arrested on drug charges. If you carry **prescription drugs** while you travel, it is vital to have a copy of the prescriptions themselves readily accessible at country borders.

■ Health

In the event of sudden illness or an accident, dial **999,** the general **emergency** number for the Republic of Ireland, Northern Ireland, and the Isle of Man. It's a free call from any pay phone to an operator who will connect you to the local police, hospital, or fire brigade. "Late-night pharmacy" is an oxymoron; after 6pm, you'll often have to go to a local hospital for medical assistance, even for aspirin. EU citizens receive health care; others must have medical insurance or pay upfront. Public bathrooms exist only in larger cities and may cost 10-20p; you're better off stepping into a pub (*fir* means "men," *mná* means "women").

Common sense is the simplest prescription for good health while you travel: eat well, drink and sleep enough, and don't exert yourself too much. Travelers complain most often about their feet and their stomach. Drinking lots of fluids can often prevent dehydration and constipation, and wearing sturdy shoes and clean socks and using talcum powder can help keep your feet dry and pain-free. To minimize the effects of jet lag, "reset" your body's clock by adopting the time of your destination immediately upon arrival. Most travelers feel acclimatized to a new time zone after two or three days. The Superintendent of Documents publishes *Health Information for International Travel* (US$20); reach them at P.O. Box 371954, Pittsburgh, PA 15250-7954 (tel. (202) 512 1800; fax 512 2250; email gpoaccess@gpo.gov; http://www.access.gpo.gov/su-docs).

BEFORE YOU GO

Your **passport** should list any information needed in case of accident: the names, phone numbers, and addresses of anyone you would wish to be contacted, all allergies or medical conditions you would want doctors to be aware of (diabetes, asthma, corrective lenses, etc.), and insurance information. If you wear **glasses** or **contact lenses,** carry an extra pair and know your prescription. Allergy sufferers should find out if their conditions are likely to be aggravated by the Irish flora (or wool), and obtain a full supply of any necessary medication before the trip, since matching a prescription to a foreign equivalent is not always easy, safe, or possible. Carry up-to-date, legible prescriptions or a statement from your doctor, especially if you use insulin, a syringe, or a narcotic. While traveling, keep all medication in carry-on luggage.

A compact **first-aid kit** for minor problems should include bandages, aspirin or other pain killer, antibiotic cream, a thermometer, a Swiss Army knife with tweezers, moleskin, a decongestant for colds, motion sickness remedy, medicine for diarrhea or stomach problems, sunscreen, insect repellent, and burn ointment.

Those with potentially dangerous medical conditions may want to obtain a stainless steel **Medic Alert** identification tag (US$35 the first year, $15 annually thereafter), which identifies the problem and gives a 24-hour collect-call information number. Contact Medic Alert at Medic Alert Foundation, 2323 Colorado Ave., Turlock, CA 95382 (tel. (800) 825 3785). Diabetics can contact the **American Diabetes Association**, 1660 Duke St., Alexandria, VA 22314 (tel. (800) 232 3472) to receive copies of the article "Travel and Diabetes" and a diabetic ID card, which explains the carrier's diabetic status.

For up-to-date health data and information, the **United States Centers for Disease Control and Prevention,** an excellent source of information for travelers around the world, maintains an international fax information service for travelers. Call (888) 232 3299 and select an international travel directory; the requested information will be faxed to you. Similar information is available from the CDC website at http://www.cdc.gov. The CDC also publishes the booklet "Health Information for International Travelers" (US$20), an annual global rundown of disease, immunization, and general health advice, including risks in particular countries. This book may be purchased by calling or writing the Superintendent of Documents, U.S. Government Printing Office, P.O. Box 371954, Pittsburgh, PA 15250-7954 (tel. (202) 512 1800; fax 512 2250). For more general health information, contact the **American Red Cross,** which publishes a *First-Aid and Safety Handbook* (US$5), available for purchase by writing to or calling the American Red Cross, 285 Columbus Ave., Boston, MA 02116-5114 (tel. (800) 564 1234). In the U.S., the American Red Cross also offers many first-aid and CPR courses, which are well taught and relatively inexpensive. **Global Emergency Medical Services (GEMS)** provides 24-hour international medical assistance and support coordinated through registered nurses who have on-line access to your medical information, your primary physician, and a worldwide network of screened, credentialed, English-speaking doctors and hospitals. Subscribers also receive a pocket-sized personal medical record that contains vital information in case of emergencies. For more information, call or write to 2001 Westside Drive #120, Alpharetta, GA 30201 (tel. (800) 860 1111; fax (770) 475 0058).

ON-THE-ROAD AILMENTS

You can minimize the chances of contracting a disease while traveling by taking a few precautionary measures. **Ticks** can be particularly dangerous in rural and forested regions all over Europe. Brush off ticks periodically when walking by using a fine-toothed comb on your neck and scalp. Topical cortisones may help relieve the itching. Ticks carry the infamous **Lyme disease,** a bacterial infection marked by a circular bull's-eye rash of 2 in. or more that appears around the bite. Other symptoms include fever, headache, tiredness, and aches and pains, but travelers are prone to these symptoms anyway. Antibiotics are effective if administered early. Left untreated, Lyme can cause problems in joints, the heart, and the nervous system. Again, avoiding tick bites in the first place is the best way to prevent the disease. If you do find a tick attached to your skin, grasp the tick's head parts with tweezers as close to your skin as possible and apply slow, steady traction. Do not try to remove ticks by burning them or coating them with nail polish remover or petroleum jelly. If you remove a tick before it has been attached for 24 hours, you greatly reduce your risk of infection.

The cold, wet climate is a far greater danger than heat in Ireland, especially if you will be hiking. Overexposure to cold brings the risk of **hypothermia,** when body temperature drops rapidly, resulting in the failure to produce body heat. Warning signs are easy to detect and may include shivering, poor coordination, slurred speech, exhaustion, fatigue, hallucination, or amnesia. Do not let hypothermia victims fall asleep if they are in the advanced stages—their body temperature will drop more and if they lose consciousness they may die. Seek medical help as soon as possible. To avoid hypothermia, keep dry and stay out of the wind. Wear wool, especially in wet weather—it retains insulating properties even when soggy. Polypropylene also dries quickly when wet, allowing you to stay warm; however, nearly all other fabrics make you colder when wet. If you are in danger of hypothermia, remove all wet, non-wool clothing (especially all cotton). Make warm and protective clothing a priority. Dress in layers, and remember that you lose most of your body heat through your head— carry a wool hat with you and your body will thank you.

WOMEN'S HEALTH

Women traveling in unsanitary conditions are vulnerable to urinary tract and bladder infections, common and severely uncomfortable bacterial diseases that cause a burning sensation and frequent, painful urination. Drink cranberry and vitamin-C-rich juice (preferably without added sugar), plenty of clean water, and urinate frequently, especially right after intercourse. Untreated, these infections can lead to kidney infections, sterility, and even death. If symptoms persist, see a doctor. Women are also susceptible to vaginal yeast infections and cystitis. It's a good idea to bring medicine for yeast infections; this medicine is available only with a prescription in Ireland. Your preferred brands of tampons and pads may not be available, so it might be a good idea to take supplies along. For publications that include information on women's travel health issues, see **Women Travelers,** p. 23.

BIRTH CONTROL AND ABORTION

Contraception has been legal in the Republic of Ireland for over a decade, and condoms are now widely available in pharmacies and from vending machines in some pubs and nightclubs. Women on the pill should bring enough to allow for possible loss or extended stays and should bring a prescription, since forms of the pill vary a good deal. If you use a diaphragm, be sure that you have enough contraceptive jelly on hand. In Ireland, the age of consent for heterosexual sex is 17.

Abortion is illegal in Northern Ireland and the Republic, although recent referenda allow women to receive information about abortions and to travel from Ireland to

Britain expressly to obtain an abortion (see **Current Issues,** p. 75). Women's centers, listed in major cities, can provide advice. The **morning-after pill,** however, has recently been legalized and is readily available with a doctor's prescription. The **U.K. Family Planning Association** can provide you with information on contraception and abortion in Britain; write to 2-12 Pentonville Road, London N1 9FP (tel. (0171) 837 5432; fax (0171) 837 3026). Your embassy can give you list of ob/gyn doctors who perform abortions. For general information on contraception and abortion worldwide, contact the **International Planned Parenthood Federation,** European Regional Office, Regent's College Inner Circle, Regent's Park, London NW1 4NS (tel. (0171) 487 7900; fax 487 7950).

AIDS AND SEXUALLY TRANSMITTED DISEASES

Acquired Immune Deficiency Syndrome (AIDS) is a growing problem around the world. The World Health Organization estimates that there are around 30 million people infected with the HIV virus, which causes AIDS. Well over 90% of adults newly infected with HIV acquired their infection through heterosexual sex; women now represent 40% of all new HIV infections. The easiest mode of HIV transmission is through direct blood-to-blood contact with an HIV+ person; *never* share intravenous drug, tattooing, or other needles. The most common mode of transmission is sexual intercourse. Health professionals recommend the use of latex condoms. Casual contact (including drinking from the same glass or using the same eating utensils as an infected person) does not pose a risk. For more information on AIDS, call the **U.S. Center for Disease Control's** 24-hour hotline at (800) 342 2437. In Europe, write to the **World Health Organization,** attn: Global Program on AIDS, 20 av. Appia, 1211 Geneva 27, Switzerland (tel. (22) 791 2111), for statistical material on AIDS internationally. *Travel Safe: AIDS and International Travel,* from the **Bureau of Consular Affairs,** is available at all Council Travel offices.

Sexually transmitted diseases (STDs) such as gonorrhea, chlamydia, genital warts, syphilis, and herpes are a lot easier to catch than HIV. Warning signs for STDs include: swelling, sores, bumps, or blisters on sex organs, rectum, or mouth; burning and pain during urination and bowel movements; itching around sex organs; swelling or redness in the throat, flu-like symptoms with fever, chills, and aches. If these symptoms develop, see a doctor immediately. Condoms may protect you from certain STDs, but oral or even tactile contact can lead to transmission.

■ Insurance

Travel insurance generally covers four basic areas: medical/health problems, property loss, trip cancellation/interruption, and emergency evacuation. Beware of buying unnecessary travel coverage—your regular insurance policies may well extend to many travel-related accidents. **Medical insurance** (especially university policies) often cover costs incurred abroad. Australia has a Reciprocal Health Care Agreement (RHCA) with the UK; in Northern Ireland, Australians are entitled to many of the services that they would receive at home. The Commonwealth Department of Human Services and Health can provide more information. Your **homeowners' insurance** or your family's may cover theft during travel. Homeowners are generally covered against loss of travel documents (passport, plane ticket, railpass, etc.) up to US$500.

ISIC and **ITIC** provide basic insurance benefits, including US$100 per day of in-hospital sickness for a maximum of 60 days and US$3000 of accident-related medical reimbursement (see **Student and Teacher Identification,** p. 10). Cardholders have access to a toll-free 24-hour helpline whose multilingual staff can provide assistance in medical, legal, and financial emergencies overseas (from Europe call collect (713) 267 2525). **Council** and **STA** offer a range of plans that can supplement your basic insurance coverage, with options covering medical treatment and hospitalization, accidents, baggage loss, and even charter flights missed due to illness. Most **American Express** cardholders receive travel accident coverage of US$100,000 on flight purchases made with the card; call Customer Service (tel. (800) 528 4800); AmEx will not, however, cover automobile insurance in Ireland.

Remember that insurance companies usually require a copy of the police report for thefts, or evidence of having paid medical expenses (doctors' statements, receipts), before they will honor a claim and may have time limits on filing for reimbursement. Always carry policy numbers and proof of insurance. Check with each insurance carrier for specific restrictions and policies. Most of the carriers listed below have 24-hour hotlines.

Access America, 6600 W. Broad St., P.O. Box 11188, Richmond, VA 23230 (tel. (800) 284 8300; fax (804) 673 1491). Covers trip cancellation/interruption, on-the-spot hospital admittance costs, emergency medical evacuation, sickness, and baggage loss. 24hr. hotline (if abroad, call collect (804) 673 1159 or (800) 654 1908).

Avi International, 30 rue de la Mogador, 75009 Paris, France (tel. (33) 01 44 63 51 86; fax 01 40 82 90 35). Caters primarily to the international youth traveler, covering emergency travel expenses, medical/accident, dental, liability, and baggage loss. 24hr. hotline.

Globalcare Travel Insurance, 220 Broadway, Lynnfield, MA 01940 (tel. (800) 821 2488; fax (617) 592 7720; email global@nebc.mv.com; http://www.nebc.mv.com/globalcare). Complete medical, legal, emergency, and travel-related services. On-the-spot payments and special student programs, including benefits for trip cancellation and interruption. GTI provides coverage for the bankruptcy or default of cruise lines, airlines, or tour operators.

Wallach and Company, Inc., 107 West Federal St., P.O. Box 480, Middleburg, VA 20118-0480 (tel. (800) 237 6615; fax (540) 687 3172; email wallach_r@media-soft.net). Comprehensive medical insurance with direct payment to service providers. Other optional coverages available. 24hr. toll-free international assistance.

■ Alternatives to Tourism

STUDY

It's not difficult to spend a summer, a term, or a year studying in Ireland or Northern Ireland. Enrolling as a full-time student is more difficult. The requirements for admission can be hard to meet unless you attended an EU secondary school. American students must pay full fees—EU students go free, so Americans are a welcome source of funds—and places are few, especially in Ireland. Local libraries and bookstores are helpful sources for current information on study abroad, and the Internet has a study abroad web site at http://www.studyabroad.com. **Council** sponsors over 40 study abroad programs throughout the world. Contact them for more information (see **Travel Organizations,** p. 2). For more information, try:

Trinity College Dublin: Offers a 1-year program of high-quality undergraduate courses for visiting students. Graduates can also register as one-year students not reading for a degree. Write to The Office of International Student Affairs, Arts and Social Sciences Bldg., Trinity College, Dublin 2, Ireland (tel. (01) 608 1396; fax 677 1698; email scoyle@tcd.ie).

University College Dublin: Offers a **Junior Year Abroad** program for North American students. Contact Dr. Michael Laffen, C103 Faculty of Arts, UCD, Dublin 4, Ireland (tel. (01) 706 8548; fax 283 0328). Also offers the **Semester in Irish Studies** (tel. (01) 475 4704) every fall semester for college juniors and seniors of all majors with solid academic records. Courses in Irish history, literature, politics, and folk culture. Its **International Summer School**, Newman House, 86 St. Stephen's Green, Dublin 2, Ireland (tel. (01) 475 2004; fax 706 7211; email summer.school@ucd.ie; http://hermes.ucd.ie/summerschool) offers a 2½-week course in July on Irish tradition and contemporary culture for students over 17.

University College Cork: International Education Office, West Wing, Main Quad, Western Road, University College, Cork, Ireland (tel. (021) 902543; fax 903118).

10,000 students are living large in Ireland's college town. Call or write for application and information.

University College Galway: International Office, Galway, Ireland (tel. (091) 750304; fax 525051; email intloffice@mis.ucg.ie). Offers year and semester opportunities for junior year students who meet the college's entry requirements. **Summer school** courses offered July-Aug. include Irish Studies, Education, and Creative Writing.

Queen's University Belfast: Study Abroad for a semester or year on any of over 100 programs. There is also a new 3-week **Introduction to Northern Ireland** program that studies the political, social, and economic questions unique to the North. Contact the International Liaison Office, Queen's University Belfast, Belfast BT7 1NN, UK (tel. (1232) 335415; fax 687297; email ilo@qub.ac.uk).

Coláiste Dara: Indreabhán, Co. Galway, Ireland (tel. (091) 553480). 3-week intensive Irish-language summer courses for students ages 10-18 in the Connemara *gaeltacht,* 15mi. west of Galway (IR£290). Homestays with Irish-speaking families included.

Oideas Gael: Glencolmcille, Co. Donegal, Ireland (tel. (073) 30248; email oidsgael@iol.ie). Offers week-long courses from June until Aug. Irish language and cultural activity courses. The program offers courses at various levels, including the option of being in a bilingual activity such as hillwalking, setdancing, painting, archaeology, and weaving.

Irish Studies Summer School: Ireland in Europe, 19/21 Aston Quay, Dublin 2, Ireland (tel. (01) 602 1777). From North America, contact Ireland in Europe Summer School, USIT, New York Student Centre, 895 Amsterdam Ave., New York, NY 10025 (tel. (212) 663 5435; email usitny@aol.com). On the campus of Trinity College Dublin. Offers 2-week summer courses in Irish civilization.

Beaver College Center for Education Abroad: 450 S. Easton Rd., Glenside, PA 19038-3295 (tel. (888) BEAVER-9 (232 8379) or (800) 755 5607; fax (215) 572 2174; email cea@beaver.edu; http://www.beaver.edu/cea/). Operates study abroad programs in 10 universities in Ireland and 35 institutions in the U.K. including 2 programs in Northern Ireland. Summer and graduate study programs also available. Applicants must have completed 3 full semesters at an accredited university. Call for brochure.

Inter-Study Programs: 42 Milsom St., Bath BA1 1DN, U.K. (tel. (01225) 464769; in the U.S. call (800) 663 1999 or (781) 391 0991; http://www.interstudy.org). Offers semester- and year-long programs in Britain and Ireland. Handles all details between program institution and your home institution, including housing and credit transfer.

The Experiment in International Living: Courthouse Chambers, 27-29 Washington St., Cork (tel. (021) 275101; fax 274677; email info@eilireland.org; http://www.eilireland.org), offers a variety of programs in Ireland, including study visits, cultural tours, and individual programs that offer homestays and academic counseling for students who wish to study in Ireland.

WORK

There are precious few jobs in Ireland, even for the Irish. European Union citizens can work in any EU country, and if your parents were born in an EU country, you may be able to claim dual citizenship with Ireland or at least the right to a work permit. Commonwealth residents with a parent or grandparent born in the U.K. do not need a work permit to work in Northern Ireland. Contact your British Consulate or High Commission for details before you go and the Department of Employment when you arrive. If you do not fit into any of these categories, you must apply for a **work permit** to be considered for paid employment in the Republic, Northern Ireland, or the Isle of Man. Your prospective employer must obtain this document, usually demonstrating that you have skills that locals lack.

If you are a **U.S. citizen** and a full-time student at a U.S. university, the simplest way to get a job abroad is through work permit programs run by **Council on International Educational Exchange (Council)** and its member organizations. For a US$225 application fee, Council can procure three- to six-month work permits and help with finding accommodations, openings, and connections in Britain and Ireland. Contact Council for more information (see **Longer Stays,** p. 45).

Peterson's, P.O. Box 2123, Princeton, NJ 08543-2123 (tel. (800) 338 3282; fax (609) 243 9150; http://www.petersons.com). Their Vacation Work Series includes such titles as *Overseas Summer Jobs 1999, Work Your Way Around the World,* and *Teaching English Abroad* (US$16.95 each). Available in bookstores or call Peterson's toll-free line. 20% off the list price when you order through their online bookstore, http://bookstore.petersons/com.

Office of Overseas Schools, A/OS Room 245, SA-29, Dept. of State, Washington, D.C. 20522-2902 (tel. (703) 875 7800; fax 875 7979; email overseas.schools@dos.us-state.gov;http://www.state.gov/www/about_state/schools). Keeps a list of schools abroad and agencies that arrange placement for Americans to teach abroad.

Transitions Abroad Publishing, Inc., 18 Hulst Rd., P.O. Box 1300, Amherst, MA 01004-1300 (tel. (800) 293 0373; fax (413) 256 0373; email trabroad@aol.com; http://www.transabroad.com). Publishes *Transitions Abroad,* a bi-monthly magazine listing all kinds of opportunities and resources for those seeking to study, work, or travel abroad. They also publish *The Alternative Travel Directory,* an exhaustive listing of information for the "active international traveler." Contact them for subscriptions (US$20 for 6 issues, Canada US$30, other countries US$42).

Vacation Work Publications, 9 Park End St., Oxford OX1 1HJ, U.K. (tel. (01865) 241978; fax 790885). Publishes a wide variety of guides and directories with job listings and info for the working traveler. Opportunities for summer or full-time work in many countries. Write for a catalogue of publications.

World Trade Academy Press, 50 E. 42nd St., #509, New York, NY 10017-5480 (tel. (212) 697 4999). Publishes *Looking for Employment in Foreign Countries* (US$16.50), which gives information on federal, commercial, and volunteer jobs abroad and advice on resumes and interviews. Check your local library for their 1996 *Directory of American Firms Operating in Foreign Countries* (US$200).

VOLUNTEERING

Volunteer jobs are readily available almost everywhere. You may receive room and board in exchange for your labor; the work may be fascinating or stultifying. You can sometimes avoid the high application fees charged by placement organizations by contacting the individual workcamps directly; check with the organizations. Listings in Vacation Work Publications's *International Directory of Voluntary Work* (UK£9; postage £2.50) can be helpful (see above).

InterExchange, 161 Sixth Ave., New York, NY 10013 (tel. (212) 924 0446; fax 924 0575; email interex@earthlink.net) provides information on international work and au pair positions in Ireland and Britain.

Volunteers for Peace, 43 Tiffany Rd., Belmont, VT 05730 (tel. (802) 259 2759; fax 259 2922; email vfp@vfp.org; http://www.vfp.org). A nonprofit organization that arranges speedy placement in 2- to 3-week workcamps comprising 10-15 people. Includes 25 programs in Ireland and Northern Ireland. Most complete listings provided in the annual *International Workcamp Directory* (US$15). Registration fee US$195 includes meals and accommodations but not transportation. Some work programs are open to 16- and 17-year olds for US$225. Free newsletter.

■ Specific Concerns

WOMEN TRAVELERS

Women exploring on their own inevitably face additional safety concerns. Always trust your instincts: if you'd feel better somewhere else, move on. Stick to centrally located accommodations and well-lit streets, and avoid late-night treks. **Hitching** is particularly unsafe for lone women or even for two women traveling together.

Your best answer to verbal harassment is no answer at all; the look on your face is key to avoiding unwanted attention. The extremely persistent can sometimes be dissuaded by a firm, loud, and very public "Go away!" Wearing a conspicuous wedding band may help ward off over-friendly individuals. Don't hesitate to seek out a police officer or a passerby if you are being harassed. Again, the **emergency number** in Ireland is **999** and free. Carry change for the phone, enough extra money for a bus or taxi, and a whistle or an airhorn on your keychain. These warnings and suggestions are not meant to discourage women from traveling alone: keep your spirit of adventure, but don't take unnecessary risks. Generally, women on their own in Ireland are much more likely to experience an excess of friendliness and advice than aggression.

The following resources and books are useful:

A Journey of One's Own, by Thalia Zepatos (US$17). Interesting and full of good advice, with a bibliography of books and resources. **Adventures in Good Company,** on group travel by the same author, costs US$17. Available from The Eighth Mountain Press, 624 Southeast 29th Ave., Portland, OR 97214 (tel. (503) 233 3936; fax 233 0774; email soapston@teleport.com).

Women's Travel in Your Pocket, Ferrari Guides, P.O. Box 37887, Phoenix, AZ 85069 (tel. (602) 863 2408; ferrari@q-net.com; http://www.q-net.com), an annual guide for women (especially lesbians) traveling worldwide. Hotels, night life, dining, shopping, organizations, group tours, cruises, outdoor adventure, and lesbian events (US$14, plus shipping).

A Foxy Old Woman's Guide to Traveling Alone, by Jay Ben-Lesser (Crossing Press, US$11). Information, informal advice, and a resource list on solo travel on a low-to-medium budget.

Active Women Vacation Guide, by Evelyn Kay (US$17.95; shipping is free for *Let's Go* readers). Includes listings of 1000 trips worldwide offered by travel companies for active women and true stories of women's traveling adventures. Blue Panda Publications, 3031 Fifth St., Boulder, CO 80304 (tel. (303) 449 8474; fax 449 7525).

OLDER TRAVELERS

Senior citizens are eligible for a wide array of discounts on transportation, museums, movies, theaters, and concerts. In *Let's Go: Ireland,* the discounts on admission fees listed for students are generally also valid. The terms "concessions" and "OAPs" (old-age pensioners) indicate discounts for seniors. In the Republic, citizens on social welfare are entitled to free rail and bus travel. Unscrupulous foreigners who look older and Irish often try to slip by. Generally, proof of senior citizen status is required for many discounts listed, so prepare to get carded.

Agencies for senior group travel are growing in enrollment and popularity. Try **Walking the World,** P.O. Box 1186, Fort Collins, CO 80522 (tel. (970) 498 0500; fax 498 9100; email walktworld@aol.com), which sends trips to Europe. The following organizations and publishers may be useful:

AARP (American Association of Retired Persons), 601 E St. NW, Washington, D.C. 20049 (tel. (202) 434 2277). Members 50 and over receive benefits and services including the AARP Motoring Plan from AMOCO (tel. (800) 334 3300) and discounts on lodging, car rental, cruises, and sight-seeing. Annual fee US$8 per couple; $20 for 3 years.

Elderhostel, 75 Federal St., 3rd Fl., Boston, MA 02110-1941 (tel. (617) 426 7788; email cadyg@elderhostel.org; http://www.elderhostel.org). For those 55 or over with a spouse of any age. Programs at colleges, universities, and other learning centers in over 70 countries on varied subjects lasting 1-4 weeks.

Pilot Books, 127 Sterling Ave., P.O. Box 2102, Greenport, NY 11944 (tel. (516) 477 1094 or (800) 79 PILOT (797 4568); fax (516) 477 0978; email feedback@pilot-books.com; http://www.pilotbooks.com). Publishes a large number of helpful guides including *Doctor's Guide to Protecting Your Health Before, During, and After International Travel* (US$10, postage $2) and *Have Grandchildren, Will Travel* (US$10, postage $2). Call or write for a complete list of titles.

No Problem! Worldwise Tips for Mature Adventurers, by Janice Kenyon. Advice and info on insurance, finances, security, health, and packing. Useful appendices. US$16 from Orca Book Publishers, P.O. Box 468, Custer, WA 98240-0468.

Unbelievably Good Deals and Great Adventures That You Absolutely Can't Get Unless You're Over 50, by Joan Rattner Heilman. After you finish reading the title page, check inside for some great tips on senior discounts. US$10 from Contemporary Books.

GAY, LESBIAN, AND BISEXUAL TRAVELERS

Though not exactly welcoming, Ireland is more tolerant of homosexuality than one might expect. As is true elsewhere, people in rural areas may not be as accepting as those in cities, whose attitudes have noticeably changed since the decriminalization of homosexuality in the Republic in 1993. Dublin now supports a gay community, with growing student societies at Trinity and UCD, a gay youth group that has doubled its size over the last five years, and an ever-growing array of pubs and clubs. Belfast and, to a lesser degree, Cork also have increasingly open gay scenes. *Gay Community News* covers mostly Irish gay-related news, and its listings page covers most gay locales in all of Ireland. *Let's Go: Ireland* has gay pub and nightlife listings as well as phone numbers for gay information in Dublin, Belfast, Cork, and London. Clubs tend to be frequented by both men and women, though more men. Below are a few resources for the BGL traveler:

Ireland's Pink Pages (http://indigo.ie/~outhouse/). Ireland's web-based BGL directory. Regional info, including the Republic and the North. Helpful links.

Queer Ireland (http://homepage.tinet.ie/~nlgf/). Listings, contacts, and the *Gay Community News* online.

International Gay and Lesbian Travel Association, 4331 N. Federal Hwy., Ste. 304, Fort Lauderdale, FL 33308 (tel. (954) 776 2626 or (800) 448 8550; fax (954) 776 3303; email IGLTA@aol.com; http://www.iglta.org). An organization of over 1350 companies serving gay and lesbian travelers worldwide. Call for lists of travel agents, accommodations, and events.

The Gay Vacation Guide: The Best Trips and How to Plan Them, Mark Chesnut. Provides a complete listing of tour operators and travel companies along with advice on how to use gay-friendly businesses and how to avoid problems while traveling (US$14.95, shipping and handling US$4 for the first order, $1 for each additional title). Carol Publishing, 120 Enterprise Ave., Secaucus, NJ 07094 (tel. (800) 447 2665; fax (201) 866 8159).

Ferrari Guides, P.O. Box 37887, Phoenix, AZ 85069 (tel. (602) 863 2408; fax 439 3952; email ferrari@q-net.com; http://www.q-net.com). Gay and lesbian travel guides: *Ferrari Guides' Gay Travel A to Z* (US$16), *Ferrari Guides' Men's Travel in Your Pocket* ($16), *Ferrari Guides' Women's Travel in Your Pocket* ($14), *Ferrari Guides' Inn Places* ($16). Available in bookstores or by mail.

Gay's the Word, 66 Marchmont St., London WC1N 1AB (tel. (0171) 278 7654). The largest gay and lesbian bookshop in the U.K. Mail-order service available. No catalog of listings, but they will provide a list of titles on a given subject.

DISABLED TRAVELERS

Ireland is not particularly wheelchair accessible. Ramps, wide doors, and accessible bathrooms are less common than in the U.S., even in cities such as Dublin. Advance booking is strongly recommended; if you notify a bus company of your plans ahead of time, they will have staff ready to assist you. Those with disabilities should also inform airlines and hotels of their disabilities when making arrangements for travel; some time may be needed to prepare special accommodations. *Let's Go Ireland* lists and indexes wheelchair-accessible hostels. Not all train stations are wheelchair accessible. Guide dogs are always conveyed free, but both the U.K. and Ireland impose a six-month quarantine on all animals entering the country and require that the owner obtain an import license. In 1998, British Parliament was considering modifying the animal passports for guide dogs—consult a British or Irish Consulate for the latest information. Write to the British Tourist Authority or Bord Fáilte for free handbooks and access guides. Other helpful sources of information are:

DTour (http://www.ireland.travel.ie/gi/index.asp) is a web-based visitors' guide to Ireland for people with disabilities. Index of accommodation and transportation facilities, with links to other resources in Ireland.

Access Department, The National Rehabilitation Board, 25 Clyde Rd., Dublin 4. Offers a county-by-county fact sheet about accommodations facilities.

Disabled Drivers' Motor Club, Cottingham Way, Thrapston, Northamptonshire NN14 4PL, England (tel. (01832) 734 724; fax 733 816; email ddmc@ukon-line.co.uk). Membership (£8 per year) includes arrangements with specialized insurance brokers and discounts on ferries and other transportation in the U.K.

Graphic Language Press, P.O. Box 270, Cardiff by the Sea, CA 92007 (tel. (760) 944 9594; email niteowl@cts.com; http://www.geocities.com/Paris/1502). Comprehensive advice for wheelchair travelers, including accessible accommodations, transportation, and sight-seeing for various European cities. Their website features trip reports from worldwide disabled travelers, tips, resources, and networking.

Twin Peaks Press, P.O. Box 129, Vancouver, WA 98666-0129 (tel. (360) 694 2462; fax 696 3210; email 73743.2634@compuserve.com; http://netm.com/mall/info-prod/twinpeak/helen.htm). Publishers of *Travel for the Disabled,* which provides travel tips, lists of accessible tourist attractions, and advice on other resources for disabled travelers (US$20). Also publishes *Directory for Travel Agencies of the Disabled* ($20), *Wheelchair Vagabond* ($15), and *Directory of Accessible Van Rentals* ($10). Postage $4 for first book, $2 for each additional book.

Directions Unlimited, 720 N. Bedford Rd., Bedford Hills, NY 10507 (tel. (800) 533 5343; in NY (914) 241 1700; fax 241 0243). Specializes in arranging individual and group vacations, tours, and cruises for the physically disabled. Group tours for blind travelers.

Flying Wheels Travel Service, 143 W. Bridge St., Owatonne, MN 55060 (tel. (800) 535 6790; fax 451 1685). Arranges trips in the U.S. and abroad for groups and individuals in wheelchairs or with other sorts of limited mobility.

DIETARY CONCERNS

Let's Go lists **vegetarian restaurants** wherever we find them, which is none too often in this morass of pub grub. While vegetarian entrees may be hard to find in small towns, a tasty meal can be put together with a little ingenuity. Many Irish will be mystified by requests for **kosher** food. The following organizations can offer advice on how to meet your specific dietary needs while traveling.

The International Vegetarian Travel Guide, last published in 1991 (UK£2). Order back copies from the Vegetarian Society of the UK (VSUK), Parkdale, Dunham Rd., Altringham, Cheshire WA14 4QG (tel. (0161) 928 0793; fax 926 9182). VSUK also publishes other titles, including *The European Vegetarian Guide to Hotels and Restaurants.* Call or send a self-addressed, stamped envelope for a listing.

The Jewish Travel Guide lists synagogues, kosher restaurants, and Jewish institutions in over 80 countries. Available from Vallantine Mitchell Publishers, Newbury House 890-900, Eastern Ave., Newbury Park, Ilford, Essex IG2 7HH, U.K. (tel. (0181) 599 8866; fax 599 0984). Available in the U.S. from Sepher-Hermon Press, 1265 46th St., Brooklyn, NY 11219 (tel. (718) 972 9010; US$15 plus $3 shipping).

MINORITY TRAVELERS

The majority of Ireland's 5 million people are white and Christian (largely Catholic in the Republic, mixed Catholic and Protestant in the North). While a growing Malaysian, Indian, and Pakistani population mainly resides in and around Dublin, on the whole, the Irish have never had to address racial diversity on a large scale. Although the Irish do not perceive themselves as racist, media coverage and attitudes can sometimes take an unconsciously racist slant. Darker-skinned travelers may be the subjects of unusual attention, especially in rural areas, but comments or stares are more likely to be motivated by curiosity than ill will. Ireland's Jewish community of 1800 people is concentrated in Dublin and experiences little anti-Semitism. For more information, check out:

The Jewish Traveler, Alan M. Tigay, editor. Published by *Hadassah Magazine.* Covers Jewish history of Dublin and many other cities worldwide. Also includes accommodations, kosher restaurants, synagogues, and sights of interest. Available for purchase on the web at http://www.amazon.com.

Go Girl! The Black Woman's Book of Travel and Adventure, Elaine Lee, editor. The Eighth Mountain Press, 624 SE 29th Ave., Portland, OR 97214 (tel. (503) 233 3936; fax 233 0774). Includes 52 travelers' tales, advice on how to travel inexpensively and safely, and a discussion of issues of specific concern to black women.

TRAVELING WITH CHILDREN

Children enjoy Ireland; they should, considering how they get fussed over by enraptured strangers. Children under 16 are generally charged half the adult price on trains and buses, and three-quarters the adult price for admission to sights. Some accommodations are more child-friendly than others; when planning, it might be worth a phone call to ask. Rental car services sometimes provide car seats upon request, and papoose-style devices are often a great help for carrying babies on walking trips. Be sure that your child carries some sort of ID in case of an emergency or if he or she gets lost. You may also want to refer to:

Backpacking with Babies and Small Children (US$10). Published by Wilderness Press, 2440 Bancroft Way, Berkeley, CA 94704 (tel. (800) 443 7227 or (510) 843 8080; fax 548 1355; email wpress@ix.netcom.com; http://wildernesspress.com).

Take Your Kids to Europe, by Cynthia W. Harriman (US$17). A budget travel guide geared toward families. Published by Globe-Pequot Press, 6 Business Park Rd., Old Saybrook, CT 06475 (tel. (800) 285 4078; fax (860) 395 1418).

How to take Great Trips with Your Kids, by Sanford and Jane Portnoy (US $9.95, shipping and handling US$3). Advice on planning trips geared toward the age of your children, packing, and finding child-friendly accommodations. The Harvard Common Press, 535 Albany St., Boston, MA 02118 (tel. (888) 657 3755, fax 695 9794).

■ Packing

Plan your packing according to the type of travel you'll be doing (multi-city backpacking tour, week-long stay in one place, etc.) and the temperate drizzle of Ireland. If you don't pack lightly, your back and wallet will suffer. The larger your pack, the more difficult it is to store safely. Before you leave, pack your bag, strap it on, and imagine yourself lying on a Mediterranean beach at sunset, the waves softly caressing your toes. Just kidding—imagine yourself walking uphill on gravel roads for the next three hours. A good rule is to lay out only what you absolutely need, then take half the clothes and twice the money.

LUGGAGE

Backpack: If you plan to cover most of your itinerary by foot, a sturdy backpack is unbeatable. Many packs are designed specifically for travelers, while others are for hikers; consider how you will use the pack before purchasing one or the other. In any case, get a pack with a strong, padded hip belt to transfer weight from your shoulders to your hips. Be wary of excessively low-end prices, and don't sacrifice quality. Good packs cost anywhere from US$150 to US$500. For more info, see **Camping and Hiking Equipment,** p. 46.

Suitcase or trunk: Fine if you plan to live in 1 or 2 cities and explore from there, but a bad idea if you're going to be moving around a lot. Make sure it has wheels and consider how much it weighs even when empty. Hard-sided luggage is more durable and doesn't wrinkle your clothes, but it is also heavier. Soft-sided luggage should have a PVC frame, a strong lining to resist bad weather and rough handling, and triple-stitched seams for durability.

Duffel bag: If you are not backpacking, an empty, lightweight duffel bag packed inside your luggage will be useful: once abroad you can fill your luggage with purchases and keep your dirty clothes in the duffel.

Daypack, rucksack, or courier bag: Bringing a smaller bag in addition to your pack or suitcase allows you to leave your big bag behind while you go sight-seeing. It can be used as an airplane carry-on to keep essentials with you.

Moneybelt or neck pouch: You may choose to guard your money, passport, rail pass, and other important articles in a **moneybelt** or **neck pouch,** available at any good camping store; this will enable you to keep your valuables with you *at all times*. The moneybelt should be tucked inside the waist of your pants or skirt and hidden. See **Safety and Security,** p. 16, for more information on protecting your sexy person and your valuables.

CLOTHING AND FOOTWEAR

Clothing: Choose your clothing with the infamous Irish weather in mind. If you plan to camp, pay a little more for a lightweight poncho that unbuttons to form a groundcloth. Make sure the poncho will cover both you and your pack. Ordinary "rainproof" materials will not suffice in the eternal drizzle of the Emerald Isle. Invest in good quality rain gear that breathes and covers your upper *and* lower body; Gore-Tex® or another specialized material will make your life infinitely more pleasant. A good rain poncho runs US$20-45. Summertime is hardly warm—a wool sweater comes in handy even in mid-June. A pair of wool pants, available at a discount from army surplus stores, will keep you dry and comfortable for long bouts on the road in the non-summer months. Packing more than one pair of shorts is both needlessly optimistic and a fashion *faux pas;* you will rarely see Irish locals (other than children) wearing them. Sweatshirts and jeans soak up rain like a sponge. You should focus on warm, practical clothes even if you don't plan on spending a lot of time outside—because you will, whether you plan to or not.

Walking shoes: Well-cushioned **sneakers** are good for walking, although you may want to consider a good water-proofed pair of **hiking boots.** A double pair of socks—light silk or polypropylene inside and thick wool outside—will cushion feet, keep them dry, and help prevent blisters. Break in your shoes before you leave. Talcum powder in your shoes and on your feet can prevent sores, and moleskin is great for blisters. You may want to bring a pair of flip-flops for protection in the shower.

MISCELLANEOUS

Sleepsacks: If you plan to stay in **youth hostels,** you can avoid the linen charge by making the requisite sleepsack yourself. Fold a full size sheet in half the long way, then sew it closed along the open long side and one of the short sides. For those less textilely inclined, sleepsacks can be bought at any HI outlet store.

Washing clothes: *Let's Go* attempts to provide information on laundromats in the **Practical Information** listings for each city, but sometimes it may be easiest to use a sink. Bring a small bar or tube of detergent soap and a travel clothes line.

Electric current: In most European countries, electricity is 220 volts AC, enough to fry any 110V North American appliance. 220V Electrical appliances don't like 110V current, either. Visit a hardware store for an adapter (which changes the shape of the plug) and a converter (which changes the voltage). Don't make the mistake of using only an adapter (unless appliance instructions explicitly state otherwise), or you'll melt your curling iron.

Contact lenses: Machines that heat-disinfect contact lenses will require a small converter (about US$20). Consider switching temporarily to a chemical disinfection system, but check with your lens dispenser to see if it's safe to switch; some lenses may be damaged by a chemical system. Your preferred brand of contact lens supplies are sometimes rare or expensive. Bring enough saline and cleaner for your entire vacation, or wear glasses. In any case, always bring a backup pair of glasses.

Film: Readily and inexpensively available just about everywhere in Ireland. Despite disclaimers, airport security X-rays *can* fog film, so either buy a lead-lined pouch, sold at camera stores, or ask the security to hand inspect it. Always pack it in your carry-on luggage, since higher-intensity X-rays are used on checked luggage.

Other useful items: First-aid kit; umbrella; sealable plastic bags (for damp clothes, soap, food, shampoo, and other spillables, or to protect valuables from the insistent Irish rain); alarm clock; padlock; whistle; flashlight; waterproof matches; sun hat; moleskin (for blisters); needle and thread; safety pins; sunglasses; a personal stereo (Walkman) with headphones; pocketknife; plastic water bottle; compass; string (makeshift clothesline and lashing material); towel; cold-water soap; earplugs; insect repellant; electrical tape (for patching tears); clothespins; maps and phrasebooks; sunscreen; vitamins. However, were you to actually bring all these useful items, you wouldn't have space in your pack for a pair of undies. So before you go out and buy a Swiss army knife with corkscrew, remember: **"Money" can be used to purchase goods and services.**

GETTING THERE

■ Budget Travel Agencies

Students and people under 26 ("youth") with proper ID qualify for enticing reduced airfares. Student travel agencies that negotiate special reduced-rate bulk purchase with the airlines then resell them to the youth market. These discounts are rarely available from airlines or travel agents. Return-date change fees also tend to be low (around US$35 per segment through Council or Let's Go Travel). Most flights are on major airlines, although in peak season some agencies may sell seats on less reliable chartered aircraft. Student travel agencies can also help non-students and people over 26 but probably won't be able to get the same low fares.

Campus Travel, 52 Grosvenor Gardens, London SW1W 0AG (http://www.campus-travel.co.uk). 46 branches in the U.K. Student and youth fares on plane, train, boat, and bus travel. Skytrekker, flexible airline tickets. Discount and ID cards for students and youths, travel insurance for students and those under 35, and maps and guides. Publishes travel suggestion booklets. Telephone booking service: in Europe call (0171) 730 3402; from North America call (44) (171) 730 2101; worldwide call (0171) 730 8111.

Council Travel (http://www.ciee.org/travel/index.htm), the travel division of Council (see p. 2), is a full-service travel agency specializing in youth and budget travel. They offer discount airfares on scheduled airlines, railpasses, hosteling cards, low-cost accommodations, guidebooks, budget tours, travel gear, and international student (ISIC), youth (GO25), and teacher (ITIC) identity cards. U.S. offices include: Emory Village, 1561 N. Decatur Rd., **Atlanta,** GA 30307 (tel. (404) 377 9997); 273 Newbury St., **Boston,** MA 02116 (tel. (617) 266 1926); 1138 13th St., **Boulder,** CO 80302 (tel. (303) 447 8101); 1153 N. Dearborn, **Chicago,** IL 60610 (tel. (312) 951 0585); 10904 Lindbrook Dr., **Los Angeles,** CA 90024 (tel. (310) 208 3551); 530 Bush St., **San Francisco,** CA 94108 (tel. (415) 421 3473); 1314 NE 43rd St. #210, **Seattle,** WA 98105 (tel. (206) 632 2448); 3300 M St. NW, **Washington, D.C.** 20007 (tel. (202) 337 6464). **For U.S. cities not listed,** call (800) 2-COUNCIL (226 8624). Also 28A Poland St. (Oxford Circus), **London,** W1V 3DB (tel. (0171) 287 3337), **Paris** (01 46 55 55 65), and **Munich** (089 395022).

CTS Travel, 220 Kensington High St., W8 (tel. (0171) 937 3366 for travel in Europe, 937 3388 for travel world-wide; fax 937 9027). Kensington. Also at 44 Goodge St., W1. Specializes in student/youth travel and discount flights.

Educational Travel Centre (ETC), 438 North Frances St., Madison, WI 53703 (tel. (800) 747 5551; fax (608) 256 2042; email edtrav@execpc.com; http://www.edtrav.com). Flight information, HI-AYH cards, Eurail, and regional rail passes. Write for their free pamphlet *Taking Off.* Student and budget airfares.

Let's Go Travel, Harvard Student Agencies, 17 Holyoke St., Cambridge, MA 02138 (tel. (617) 495 9649; fax 496 7956; email travel@hsa.net; http://hsa.net/travel). Railpasses, HI memberships, ISICs, ITICs, FIYTO cards, guidebooks, maps, bargain flights, and a complete line of budget travel gear. All items available by mail; call or write for a catalogue.

Rail Europe Inc., 226 Westchester Ave., White Plains, NY 10604 (tel. (800) 438 7245; fax 432 1329; http://www.raileurope.com). Sells all Eurail products and passes, national railpasses including Brit Rail, and point-to-point tickets. Up-to-date information on all rail travel in Europe, including Eurostar and the English Channel train.

STA Travel, 6560 Scottsdale Rd. #F100, Scottsdale, AZ 85253 (tel. (800) 777 0112 nationwide; fax (602) 922 0793; http://sta-travel.com). A student and youth travel organization with over 150 offices worldwide offering discount airfares for young travelers, railpasses, accommodations, tours, insurance, and ISICs. 16 offices in the U.S. including: 297 Newbury St., **Boston,** MA 02115 (tel. (617) 266 6014); 429 S. Dearborn St., **Chicago,** IL 60605 (tel. (312) 786 9050); 7202 Melrose Ave., **Los Angeles,** CA 90046 (tel. (213) 934 8722); 10 Downing St. G, **New York,** NY 10003 (tel. (212) 627 3111); 4341 University Way NE, **Seattle,** WA 98105 (tel. (206) 633 5000); 2401 Pennsylvania Ave., **Washington, D.C.** 20037 (tel. (202) 887 0912); 51 Grant Ave., **San Francisco,** CA 94108 (tel. (415) 391 8407). In the U.K., 6 Wrights Ln., **London** W8 6TA (tel. (0171) 938 4711). In New Zealand, 10 High St., **Auckland** (tel. (09) 309 9723). In Australia, 222 Faraday St., **Melbourne** VIC 3050 (tel. (03) 349 6911).

Students Flights Inc., 5010 East Shea Blvd., #A104, **Scottsdale, AZ** 85254 (tel. (800) 255 8000 or (602) 951 1177; fax 951 1216; email jost@isecard.com; http://ise-card.com). Also sells Eurail and Europasses and international student exchange identity cards.

Travel CUTS (Canadian Universities Travel Services Limited), 187 College St., Toronto, Ont. M5T 1P7 (tel. (416) 979 2406; fax 979 8167; email mail@travelcuts.com). Canada's national student travel bureau and equivalent of Council, with 40 offices across Canada. Also in the U.K., 295-A Regent St., **London** W1R 7YA (tel. (0171) 637 3161). Discounted domestic and international airfares open to all; special student fares to all destinations with valid ISIC. Issues ISIC, FIYTO, GO25, and HI cards, as well as railpasses. Offers free *Student Traveller* magazine as well as information on the Student Work Abroad Program (SWAP).

Unitravel, 117 North Warson Rd., St. Louis, MO 63132 (tel. (800) 325 2222; fax (314) 569 2503). Offers discounted airfares on major scheduled airlines.

USIT Youth and Student Travel, 19-21 Aston Quay, O'Connell Bridge, Dublin 2 (tel. (01) 677 8117; fax 679 8833). In the **U.S.:** New York Student Center, 895 Amsterdam Ave., New York, NY, 10025 (tel. (212) 663 5435; email usitny@aol.com). Additional offices in Cork, Galway, Limerick, Waterford, Maynooth, Coleraine, Derry, Athlone, and Belfast. Specializes in youth and student travel. Offers low-cost tickets and flexible travel arrangements all over the world. Supplies ISIC and FIYTO-GO 25 cards in Ireland only.

Wasteels, 7041 Grand National Drive #207, Orlando, FL 32819 (tel. (407) 351 2537; in **London** (0171) 834 7066). A huge chain in Europe, with 200 locations. Information in English can be requested from the London office (tel. (0171) 834 7066; fax 630 7628). Sells Wasteels BIJ tickets, which are discounted (30-45% off regular fare) 2nd class international point-to-point train tickets with unlimited stopovers (must be under 26 on the first day of travel); sold only in Europe.

■ By Plane

The airline industry attempts to squeeze every dollar from customers; finding a cheap airfare will be easier if you understand the airlines' systems. Call every toll-free number and don't be afraid to ask about discounts; if you don't ask, it's unlikely they'll be volunteered. Have knowledgeable **travel agents** guide you; better yet, have an agent who specializes in the British Isles to guide you. An agent whose clients fly mostly to Nassau or Miami will not be the best person to hunt down a bargain flight to Dublin. Travel agents may not want to spend time finding the cheapest fares (for which they receive the lowest commissions), but if you travel often, you should definitely find an agent who will cater to your needs and track down deals in exchange for your frequent business.

Students and others under 26 should never need to pay full price for a ticket. Seniors can also get great deals; many airlines offer senior traveler clubs or airline passes with few restrictions and discounts for their companions as well. Sunday newspapers often have travel sections that list bargain fares from the local airport. Australians should consult the Saturday travel section of the *Sydney Morning Herald.* Outsmart airline reps with the phone-book-sized *Official Airline Guide* (check your local library; at US$359 per year, the tome costs as much as some flights), a monthly guide listing nearly every scheduled flight in the world (with fares, US$479) and toll-free phone numbers for all the airlines, which allow you to call in reservations directly. Of course, these numbers are also in the phone book. More accessible is Michael McColl's *The Worldwide Guide to Cheap Airfare* (US$15), an incredibly useful guide for finding cheap airfare.

There is also a wealth of travel information to be found on the Internet. The **Air Traveler's Handbook** (http://www.cs.cmu.edu/afs/cs.cmu.edu/user/mkant/Public/Travel/airfare.html) is an excellent source of general information on air travel. **TravelHUB** (http://www.travelhub.com) provides a directory of travel agents that includes a searchable database of fares from over 500 consolidators (see **Ticket Consolidators,** below). Edward Hasbrouck maintains a **Consolidators FAQ** (http://www.travel-library.com/air-travel/consolidators.html) that provides great background on finding cheap international flights. Groups such as the **Air Courier Association** (http://www.aircourier.org) offer information about traveling as a courier and provide up-to-date listings of last minute opportunities. **Travelocity** (http://www.travelocity.com) operates a searchable online database of published airfares, which you can reserve online, as does **Microsoft Expedia** (http://expedia.msn.com).

Most airfares peak between mid-June and early September. Midweek (M-Th morning) round-trip flights run about US$40-50 cheaper than on weekends; weekend flights, however, are generally less crowded. Traveling from hub to hub (for example, Los Angeles to London) will win a more competitive fare than from and to smaller cities. Since Ireland is mostly smaller cities, you might find it cheaper to take the plane to London and ferry across the Irish Sea (see **By Ferry,** p. 34). Return-date flexibility is usually not an option for the budget traveler; traveling with an "open return" ticket can be pricier than fixing a return date and paying to change it. Whenever flying internationally, pick up your ticket well in advance of the departure date, have the flight confirmed within 72 hours of departure, and arrive at the airport at least three hours before your flight.

COMMERCIAL AIRLINES

The airlines' published airfares should be just the beginning of your search. Even if you pay an airline's lowest published fare, you may waste hundreds of dollars. For the adventurous or the bargain-hungry, there are other, perhaps more inconvenient or time-consuming options. But before shopping around it is a good idea to find out the average commercial price in order to measure just how great a "bargain" you are being offered.

The commercial airlines' lowest regular offer is the **Advance Purchase Excursion Fare (APEX);** specials advertised in newspapers may be cheaper, but have more restrictions and fewer available seats. APEX fares provide you with confirmed reservations and allow "open-jaw" tickets (landing in and returning from different cities). Generally, reservations must be made seven to 21 days in advance, with seven- to 14-day minimum and up to 90-day maximum stay limits, and hefty cancellation and change penalties, which rise in summer. Book APEX fares early during peak season; by May you will have a hard time getting the departure date you want.

Major Irish destinations are Shannon, Dublin, Cork, and Belfast. Shannon is often cheaper for transatlantic flights, as many stop there anyway en route to other airports (until recently, airlines were required by law to do so); Belfast tends to be the most expensive destination. **Aer Lingus** (tel. (800) 474 7424; http://www.aerlingus.ie), Ireland's national airline, has direct flights to the U.S., service to South Africa, and constant flights to London. If another airline doesn't fly directly to one of the airports in Ireland, it can almost certainly get you to London. For connections to Ireland from London, see **Flights from Britain,** below.

TICKET CONSOLIDATORS

Ticket consolidators resell unsold tickets on commercial and charter airlines at unpublished fares. Consolidator flights are the best deals if you are traveling on short notice (you bypass advance purchase requirements, since you aren't tangled in airline bureaucracy); on a high-priced trip; to an offbeat destination; or in the peak season, when published fares are jacked way up. Fares sold by consolidators are generally much cheaper; a 30-40% price reduction is not uncommon. There are rarely age constraints or stay limitations, but unlike tickets bought through an airline, you won't be able to use your tickets on another flight if you miss yours, and you will have to go back to the consolidator to get a refund, rather than the airline. Keep in mind that these tickets are often for coach seats on connecting (not direct) flights on foreign airlines, and that frequent-flyer miles may not be credited. Decide what you can and can't live with before shopping.

Not all consolidators deal with the general public; many only sell tickets through travel agents. **Bucket shops** are retail agencies that specialize in getting cheap tickets. Although ticket prices are marked up slightly, bucket shops generally have access to a larger market than that available to the public and can also get tickets from wholesale consolidators. The country of your destination will provide more options and cheaper tickets. The **Association of Special Fares Agents (ASFA)** maintains a database of specialized dealers for particular regions (http://www.ntsltd.com/asfa). Look for bucket shops' tiny ads in the travel section of weekend papers; in the U.S., the Sunday *New York Times* is a good source. In London, a call to the **Air Travel Advisory Bureau** (tel. (0171) 636 50 00) can provide names of reliable consolidators and discount flight specialists. Kelly Monaghan's *Consolidators: Air Travel's Bargain Basement* (US$7 plus $2 shipping) from the Intrepid Traveler, P.O. Box 438, New York, NY 10034 (email intreptrav@aol.com), is an invaluable source for more information and lists of consolidators by location and destination.

It pays to be a smart shopper. Among the many reputable and trustworthy companies are, unfortunately, some shady wheeler-dealers. Contact the local Better Business Bureau to find out how long the company has been in business and its track record. It is preferable to deal with consolidators close to home so you can visit in person, if necessary. Ask to receive your tickets as quickly as possible so you have time to fix any problems. Get the company's policy in writing: insist on a **receipt** that gives full details about the tickets, refunds, and restrictions, and record who you talked to and when. It may be worth paying with a credit card (despite the 2-5% fee) so you can stop payment if you never receive your tickets. Beware the "bait and switch" gag; shyster firms will advertise a super-low fare and then tell a caller that it has been sold. Although this is a viable excuse, if they can't offer you a price near the advertised fare on *any* date, it is a scam to lure in customers—report them to the Better Business Bureau. Also ask about accommodations and car rental discounts; some consolidators have fingers in many pies. Mmmm, pie.

For destinations worldwide, try **Airfare Busters,** with offices in Washington, D.C. (tel. (202) 776 0478), Boca Raton, FL (tel. (561) 994 9590), and Houston, TX (tel. (800) 232 8783); **Pennsylvania Travel,** Paoli, PA (tel. (800) 331 0947); **Cheap Tickets,** with offices in Los Angeles, San Francisco, Honolulu, Seattle, and New York (tel. (800) 377 1000); **Interworld** (tel. (305) 443 4929; fax 443 0351); **Travac** (tel. (800) 872 8800; fax (212) 714 9083; email mail@travac.com; http://www.travac.com). **NOW Voyager,** 74 Varick St. #307, New York, NY 10013 (tel. (212) 431 1616; fax 334 5243; email info@nowvoyagertravel.com; http://www.nowvoyagertravel.com), acts as a consolidator and books discounted international flights, mostly from New York, as well as courier flights (see **Courier Companies and Freighters** below), for an annual fee of US$50. For a processing fee, depending on the number of travelers and the itinerary, **Travel Avenue,** Chicago, IL (tel. (800) 333 3335; fax (312) 876 1254; http://www.travelavenue.com), will search for the lowest international airfare available, including consolidated prices, and will even give you a 5% rebate on fares over US$350. **Rebel,** Valencia, CA (tel. (800) 227 3235; fax (805) 294 0981; email travel@rebeltours.com; http://www.rebeltours.com), or Orlando, FL (tel. (800) 732 3588) also books flights to Europe.

Eleventh-hour **discount clubs** and **fare brokers** offer members savings on European travel, including charter flights and tour packages. Research your options carefully. **Last Minute Travel Club,** 100 Sylvan Rd., Woburn, MA 01801 (tel. (800) 527 8646 or (617) 267 9800) is one of the few travel clubs that doesn't charge a membership fee. **Travelers Advantage,** Stamford, CT (tel. (800) 548 1116; http://www.travelersadvantage.com), has a US$49 annual fee. Study these organizations' contracts closely; you don't want to end up with an unwanted overnight layover.

STAND-BY FLIGHTS

Airhitch, 2641 Broadway, 3rd Fl., New York, NY 10025 (tel. (800) 326 2009 or (212) 864 2000; fax 864 5489) and Los Angeles, CA (tel. (310) 726 5000), will add a certain thrill to the prospects of when you will leave and where exactly you will end up. Complete flexibility on both sides of the Atlantic is necessary; flights cost US$175 each way when departing from the Northeast, US$269 from the West Coast or Northwest, $229 from the Midwest, and $209 from the Southeast. Travel within the USA and Europe is also possible, with rates ranging from US$79-129. The snag is that you buy not a ticket but the promise that you will get to a destination near where you're intending to go within a window of time (usually 5 days) from a location in a region you've specified. You call in before your date-range to hear all of your flight options for the next seven days and your probability of boarding. You then decide which flights you want to try to make and present a voucher at the airport that grants you the right to board a flight on a space-available basis. This procedure must be followed again for the return trip. Be aware that you may only receive a monetary refund if all available flights which departed within your date-range from the specified region are full, but future travel credit is always available. There are several offices in Europe, so you can wait to register for your return; the main one is in Paris (tel. (1) 47 00 16 30).

Air-Tech, Ltd., 588 Broadway #204, New York, NY 10012 (tel. (212) 219 7000, fax 219 0066; http://www.airtech.com), offers a very similar service. Their travel window is one to four days. Rates to and from Europe (continually updated; call and verify) are: Northeast US$169; West Coast $239; Midwest/Southeast $199. Upon registration and payment, Air-Tech sends you a FlightPass with a contact date falling soon before your Travel Window, when you are to call them for flight instructions. You must go through the same procedure to return—and no refunds are granted unless the company fails to get you a seat before your Travel Window expires. Air-Tech also arranges courier flights and regular confirmed-reserved flights at discount rates.

Be sure to read all the fine print in your agreements with either company—a call to the Better Business Bureau of New York City may be worthwhile. Be warned that it is difficult to receive refunds, and that clients' vouchers will not be honored if an airline fails to receive payment in time.

COURIER COMPANIES

Those who travel very light should consider flying internationally as a **courier.** The company hiring you will use your checked luggage space for freight; you're allowed to bring only carry-ons. You are responsible for the safe delivery of the baggage claim slips (given to you by a courier company representative) to the representative waiting for you when you arrive—don't screw up or you will be blacklisted as a courier. You will probably never see the cargo you are transporting—the company handles it all—and airport officials know that couriers are not responsible for the baggage checked for them. Restrictions to watch for: you must be over 21 (18 in some cases), have a valid passport, and procure your own visa if necessary; most flights are round-trip only with short fixed-length stays, usually one week; only single tickets are issued (although a companion may be able to get a next-day flight); and most flights are from New York. Round-trip fares to Western Europe from the U.S. range from $100-400 (during the off-season) to $200-550 (during the summer); flights to Dublin tend to range from $160-400. For an annual fee of US$45, the **International Association of Air Travel Couriers,** 8 South J St., P.O. Box 1349, Lake Worth, FL 33460 (tel. (561) 582 8320; email iaatc@courier.org; http://www.courier.org), informs travelers of courier opportunities worldwide via computer, fax, and mailings. **NOW Voyager,** 74 Varick St. #307, New York, NY 10013 (tel. (212) 431 1616; fax 334 5243; email info@nowvoyagertravel.com; http://www.nowvoyagertravel.com), acts as an agent for many courier flights worldwide primarily from New York and offers special last-minute deals to such cities as London, Paris, Rome, and Frankfurt for as little as US$200 round-trip plus a $50 registration fee. (They also act as a consolidator; see **Ticket Consolidators,** above.) Another agent to try is **Halbart Express,** 147-05 176th St., Jamaica, NY 11434 (tel. (718) 656 5000; fax 917 0708; offices in Chicago, Los Angeles, and London).

You can also go directly through courier companies in New York, or check your bookstore or library for handbooks such as *Air Courier Bargains* (US$15 plus $3 shipping from the Upper Access Publishing, P.O. Box 457, Hinesburg, VT 05461; tel. (800) 356 9315; fax 242 0036; email upperaccess@aol.com). *The Courier Air Travel Handbook* (US$10 plus $3.50 shipping) explains how to travel as an air courier and contains names, phone numbers, and contact points of courier companies. It can be ordered directly from Bookmasters, Inc., P.O. Box 2039, Mansfield, OH 44905 (tel. (800) 507 2665; fax (419) 281 6883).

FLIGHTS FROM BRITAIN

Airplanes fly between Dublin, Shannon, Cork, Kerry, Galway, Knock, Sligo, and Waterford (in Ireland); Belfast and Derry (in Northern Ireland); Gatwick, Stansted, Heathrow, Luton, Manchester, Birmingham, Liverpool, and Glasgow airports; and Ronaldsway on the Isle of Man. Flying to London and connecting to Ireland is often easier and cheaper. Aer Lingus (see p. 31) and several other carriers offer service on these routes. **British Midland Airways** (in the U.K. (0345) 554554; in the Republic (01) 283 8833); http://www.iflybritishmidland.com/) flies about eight times per day to London Heathrow. **British Airways** (in the U.K. (0345) 222111; in the Republic (800) 626747; in the U.S. (800) AIRWAYS or 247 9297; http://www.british-airways.com), flies about seven times per day Monday through Saturday, Sunday six per day. Prices range from UK£70-150 return but can drop from time to time. Call and inquire about specials. **Ryanair** (tel. (01) 609 7800) connects Kerry, Cork, and Knock to London and nine other destinations in England and Scotland. Flights from London to Belfast generally take 1¼hr. **Manx Airlines** (tel. (01) 260 1588) flies from the Isle of Man to Dublin and London. Book as early as you can to get the cheapest fare. The **Air Travel Advisory Bureau,** 28 Charles Sq., London N16ST, England (tel. (0171) 636 50 00) will put you in touch with the cheapest carriers out of London for free.

■ By Ferry

Ferries are popular and usually more economical than flights. Boats run from Fishguard Harbour and Pembroke Dock in South Wales to Rosslare Harbour in southeast Ireland; from Holyhead in North Wales to Dún Laoghaire (dun LEER-ee), a suburb of Dublin; from Swansea in South Wales to Cork; and from Stranraer, Scotland, to Belfast and Larne, Northern Ireland. Almost all sailings in June, July, and August are "controlled sailings," which means that you must book the crossing ahead of time (a few days in advance is usually sufficient). Low season on ferry prices runs March to May and October to December; mid-season is June to mid-July and September; and high season is mid-July to August.

Fares vary tremendously depending on time of year, time of day, and type of boat. Adult single tickets usually range from £20 to £35, and a world of discount rates is out there waiting to be explored. Some people ask car drivers to let them travel as one of four free passengers that a set of wheels gets. Students, seniors, families, and youth traveling alone should almost never pay full fare. Children under 5 almost always travel free, and bikes can usually brought on for no extra charge. **An Óige (HI)** members receive up to a 20% discount on fares from Irish Ferries and Stena Sealink. **ISIC cardholders** receive a 15% discount from Irish Ferries and an average 17% discount (variable among four routes) on StenaLine ferries. Ferry passengers from the Republic are taxed an additional IR£5; from England to Éire, there's a tax of UK£5.

BRITAIN TO IRELAND

Assorted bus tickets that include ferry connections between Britain and Ireland are also available as package deals through ferry companies, travel agents, and USIT offices. Contact Bus Éireann for information (see **By Bus,** p. 37).

Irish Ferries sails from Holyhead, North Wales, to Dublin (3½hr.) and from Pembroke, Wales, to Rosslare Harbour (4hr.). Also sails from Le Havre and Roscoff, France to Cork and Rosslare Harbour (about 22hr.); Eurailpasses grant passage on ferries from France. For specific schedules and fares contact them at: 2-4 Merrion Row, **Dublin** 2 (reservations tel. (01) 661 0511, fax 661 0743; holidays tel. (01) 661 0533, fax 661 0732); St. Patrick's Bridge, **Cork** (tel. (021) 551995); **Rosslare Harbour** (tel. (053) 33158); **Holyhead,** Wales (tel. (0990) 329129); and **Pembroke,** Wales (tel. (0990) 329543). Their after-hours information line in Ireland is (01) 661 0715. Email info@irishferries.ie; http://www.irish-ferries.ie.

Stena Line ferries go from Holyhead, North Wales, to Dún Laoghaire (1¾hr. on the HSS; 3½hr. on the Superferry); from Fishguard, South Wales, to Rosslare Harbour (3¾hr. on the Stena Lynx; 3½hr. on the Superferry); and from Stanraer, Scotland, to Belfast (2¾hr.). Offers package deals that include train service from London. Contact them at: Charter House, Park St., Ashford, Kent TN24 8EX, England (tel. (01233) 647047; fax 202231); **Dun Laoghaire Travel Centre** (tel. (01) 204 7777); **Rosslare Harbour** (tel. (053) 33115); Tourist Office, **Cork** (tel. (021) 272965); Tourist Office, Arthurs Quay, **Limerick** (tel. (061) 316259). For 24hr. recorded information, contact **Ferry Check** (tel. (01) 204 7799; email david@seaview.co.uk; http://www.seaview.co.uk/Stena.html).

Cork-Swansea Ferries sails between Swansea, South Wales, and Cork (10hr.). Contact them at 52 South Mall, Cork (tel. (021) 271166).

Hoverspeed SeaCat sails from Stranraer to Belfast (1½hr.), and the **SuperSeaCat Ferry** sails from Liverpool, England to Dublin (4hrs.). These SeaCat trips are faster than ferries but can cost as much as UK£40 more. For information and bookings, contact them at U.K. tel. (0345) 523523 or (800) 551743, fax (01776) 702355.

To Ireland via the Isle of Man

You can easily combine a ferry across the Irish Sea with a stopover on the Isle of Man. An advantage of this route is that you can ferry into Dublin and ferry out of Belfast at no extra charge. The **Isle of Man Steam Packet Co.** (Douglas tel. (01624) 645645 (information), 661661 (reservations); fax 661065; http://www.steam-packet.com) charges UK£23-33 one-way; student, senior, family, and dog rates available; bikes free. The principal ports in the British Isles are Heysham and Liverpool.

■ By Bus

Supabus (run by **Bus Éireann,** the Irish national bus company) offers connecting service from Bristol and London to Cork, Waterford, Tralee, Killarney, Ennis, and Limerick, and from Cardiff and Birmingham to Cork, Waterford, Ennis, and Limerick. Prices range from IR£10 to £25. Tickets can be booked through USIT, any Bus Éireann office, Irish Ferries, Stena Line, or any Eurolines (tel. (01582) 404511) or National Express office in Britain (tel. (0990) 808080). Inconvenient arrival and departure times mean you won't be sleeping very well. Supabus connects in London to the immense **Eurolines** network, which in turn connects with many European destinations. Contact the Bus Éireann General Inquiries desk in Dublin (tel. (01) 836 6111) or a travel agent. Take an **express bus** to London from over 270 destinations in Europe with Eurolines (U.K.) Ltd., 52 Grosvenor Gardens, Victoria, London SW1W OAU (tel. (0171) 730 8235); London to Paris UK£34; return £49.

ONCE THERE

■ Embassies and Consulates

For Irish and U.K. embassies in your country of origin, see p. 5.

Australia: Fitzwilton House, Wilton Terr., Dublin 2 (tel. (01) 676 1517).
Canada: Canadian Embassy, Canada House, 65 St. Stephen's Green, Dublin 2 (tel. (01) 478 1988). Canadian High Commission, McDonald House, 1 Grosvenor Sq., **London** W1XC 0AB (tel. (0171) 258 6600).
New Zealand: New Zealand Embassy, New Zealand House, 80 Haymarket, London SW1Y 4QT (tel. (0171) 930 8422).
South Africa: The Republic, South Africa Embassy, Alexandra House, Earlsford Terr. (tel. (01) 661 5553; fax 661 5590), Dublin 2. **U.K.,** South African High Commission, South Africa House, Trafalgar Sq., London WC2N 5DP (tel. (0171) 451 7299; fax 451 7283).
United Kingdom: British Embassy, 31 Merrion Rd., Dublin 4 (tel. (01) 269 5211).
United States: The Republic, American Embassy, 42 Elgin Rd., Ballsbridge, Dublin 4 (tel. (01) 668 7122; fax 668 9946). **Northern Ireland** Consulate General, Queens House, 14 Queen St., Belfast BT1 6EQ (tel. (01232) 328239; fax 248482).

■ Getting Around

Fares on all modes of transportation are either "single" (one-way) or "return" (round-trip). "Period returns" require you to return within a specific number of days; "day return" means you must return on the same day. Unless stated otherwise, *Let's Go* always lists single fares. Round-trip fares on trains and buses are rarely more than 30% above the one-way fare.

Roads between Irish cities and towns have official letters and numbers ("N" and "R" in the Republic; "M," "A," and "B" in the North), but most locals refer to them by destination ("Kerry Rd.," "Tralee Rd."). Signs and printed directions sometimes give only the numbered and lettered designations, sometimes only the destination. Most signs are in English and Irish; some destination signs are only in Irish. Old black and white road signs give distances in miles; new green and white signs are in kilometers. Speed limit signs are always in miles per hour.

BY TRAIN

Iarnród Éireann (Irish Rail) branches out from Dublin to larger cities, but there is limited service. For schedule information, pick up an *InterCity Rail Travellers Guide* (50p), available at most train stations. The **TravelSave stamp,** available for £8 at any USIT if you have an ISIC card, cuts fares almost in half on national rail and will let you break your journey to visit at any stop on the way to your final destination (valid for 1 month). It also provides 15% discounts on bus fares (except on fares less than £1). A **Faircard** (£8) can get anyone age 16 to 26 up to 50% the price of any InterCity trip. Those over 26 can get the less potent **Weekender card** (£5; up to a third off, valid F-Tu only). Both are valid through the end of the year. Information is available from Irish Rail information office, 35 Lower Abbey St., Dublin 1 (tel. (01) 836 6222). Unlike bus tickets, train tickets sometimes allow travelers to break a journey into stages yet still pay the price of a single-phase trip.

While the **Eurailpass** is not accepted in Northern Ireland, it *is* accepted on trains (but not buses) in The Republic. A range of youth and family passes are also available, but Eurailpasses are generally only cost-effective if you plan to travel to the Continent as well. The passes are good for travel on Irish Ferries from Rosslare to Cherbourg or Le Havre. A **BritRail+Ireland** pass with rail options and round-trip ferry service between Britain and Ireland is also an option (US$350-500). You'll find it easiest to buy a Eurailpass before you arrive in Europe; contact Council Travel, Travel CUTS,

Let's Go Travel (see **Budget Travel Agencies,** p. 29), or any of many other travel agents. The **Rail Europe Group,** 500 Mamaroneck Ave., Harrison, NY 10528 (tel. (800) 438 7245; fax (800) 432 1329 in the U.S.; and tel. (800) 361 7245; fax (905) 602 4198 in Canada; http://www.raileurope.com), also sells point-to-point tickets.

Northern Ireland Railways (Belfast tel. (01232) 899411, BritRail service tel. (01232) 230671) is not extensive but covers the northeastern coastal region well. The major line connects Dublin to Belfast (2hr., M-F 8 per day, Su 5 per day, UK£17, £26 return; student rates available). When it reaches Belfast, this line splits, with one branch ending at Bangor and one at Larne. There is also rail service from Belfast and Lisburn west to Derry and Portrush, stopping at three towns between Antrim and the coast. British Rail passes are not valid here, but Northern Ireland Railways offers its own discounts. A valid **Northern Ireland Travelsave** stamp (UK£6, affixed to back of ISIC) will get you 50% off all trains and 15% discounts on bus fares over UK£1 within Northern Ireland. The **Freedom of Northern Ireland** ticket allows unlimited travel by train and Ulsterbus and can be purchased for seven consecutive days (UK£35), three consecutive days (£25), or a single day (£10).

BY BUS

Buses in the Republic of Ireland reach many more destinations and are less expensive than trains, but they are less frequent, less comfortable, and slower. The national bus company, **Bus Éireann,** operates both long-distance **Expressway** buses, which link larger cities, and **Local** buses, which serve the countryside and smaller towns. The invaluable bus timetable book (£1) is available at Busáras Station in Dublin and at many tourist offices. A myriad of **private bus services** are faster and cheaper than Bus Éireann. *Let's Go* lists these private companies in areas they service. Most of these services link Dublin to one or two towns in the west. In Donegal, private bus providers take the place of Bus Éireann's nearly nonexistent local service.

Bus Éireann's discount **Rambler** tickets mostly aren't worth buying; individual tickets often provide better value. The Rambler ticket offers unlimited bus travel within Ireland for three of eight consecutive days (£28), eight of 15 consecutive days (£68), or 15 of 30 consecutive days (£98). A combined **Irish Explorer Rail/Bus** ticket good for unlimited travel eight of 15 consecutive days on rail and bus lines is available for £90. Purchase these tickets from Bus Éireann at their main tourist office in Dublin, Store St., Dublin 1 (tel. (01) 836 6111), or in Cork (tel. (021) 508188), Waterford (tel. (051) 879000), or Galway (tel. (091) 562000). Contact the **Irish Rail** information office at 35 Lower Abbey St., Dublin 1 (tel. (01) 836 6222).

Ulsterbus, Laganside, Belfast (tel. (01232) 320011), the North's version of Bus Éireann, runs extensive and reliable routes throughout Northern Ireland, where there are no private bus services. Coverage expands in summer, when open-top buses cover a northeastern coastal route, and full- and half-day tours leave for key tourist spots from Belfast. Pick up a regional timetable (25p but often free) at any station. Again, the bus discount passes won't save you much money: a **Freedom of Northern Ireland** bus pass offers travel for one day (UK£10) or seven consecutive days (£35).

The **Emerald Card** offers travel for eight out of 15 consecutive days (£105, children £53) or 15 out of 30 consecutive days (£180). The Emerald card allows unlimited travel on Ulsterbus; Northern Ireland Railways; Bus Éireann Expressway, Local, and City services in Dublin, Cork, Limerick, Galway, and Waterford; and intercity, DART, and suburban rail Iarnród Éireann services.

BY CAR

The advantages of car travel speak for themselves. Disadvantages include high gasoline prices, the unfamiliar laws and habits associated with driving in foreign lands, and, for Americans, the fact that in Ireland, as in Britain, **you drive on the left.** Be particularly cautious at roundabouts (rotary interchanges)—give way to traffic from the right. Irish drivers speed along narrow, twisting, pot-holed, poorly lit back roads. You will need to drive rather slowly and cautiously, especially at night.

In both countries, the law requires drivers and passengers to wear seat belts—these laws are enforced. In Ireland, children under 12 are not allowed to sit in the front seat of a car. Children under 40 lbs. should ride only in a specially designed carseat, which can be obtained for a small fee from most car rental agencies.

In the Republic of Ireland, roads numbered below N50 are "primary routes," which connect all the major towns; roads numbered N50 and above are "secondary routes," not as well trafficked but still well signposted. Regional "R-roads" are rarely referred to by number. Instead, the road takes the name of its destination. The general speed limit is 55 mph (90km per hr.) on the open road and either 30 mph (50km per hr.) or 40 mph (65km per hr.) in town. There are no major highways.

Northern Ireland possesses exactly two major highways (M-roads or motorways) connecting Belfast with the rest of the province. The M-roads are supplemented by a web of "A-roads" and "B-roads." Speed limits are 60 mph (97km per hr.) on single carriageways (non-divided highways), 70 mph (113km per hr.) on motorways (highways) and dual carriageways (divided highways), and usually 30 mph (48km per hr.) in urban areas. Speed limits are always marked at the beginning of town areas. Upon leaving, you'll see a circular sign with a slash through it, signaling the end of the speed restriction. Speed limits aren't rabidly enforced; remember, though, that many of these roads are sinuous and single-track—use common sense.

Renting (hiring) an automobile is the least expensive option if you plan to drive for a month or less, but the initial cost of renting a car and the price of gas will astound you in Ireland. People under 21 cannot rent, and those under 25 often encounter difficulties. Major rental companies include **Alamo, Avis, Budget Rent-A-Car, Murrays Europcar, Hertz, Kenning, McCausland,** and **Swan National.** Prices range from IR£100 to IR£300 (plus VAT) per week with insurance and unlimited mileage. For insurance reasons, most companies require renters to be over 23 and under 70. Some plans require sizable deposits unless you're paying by credit card. Make sure you understand the insurance agreement before you rent; some require you to pay for damages that you may not have caused. Automatics are around 40% more expensive to rent than manuals (stickshifts). Try **Budget Rent-A-Car,** 151 Lower Drumcondra Rd., Dublin 9 (tel. (01) 837 9611; £45 per day), or **Thrifty** (tel. (061) 472 649) at the Shannon Airport (£35 per day).

If you rent, lease, or borrow a car, you will need a **green card** or **International Insurance Certificate** to prove that you have liability insurance. Obtain it through the car rental agency; most of them include coverage in their prices. If you lease a car, you can obtain a green card from the dealer. Verify whether your auto insurance applies abroad; even if it does, you will still need a green card to certify this fact to foreign officials. If you have a collision, the accident will show up on your domestic records if you report it to the company. Some credit cards that generally cover insurance on rental cars will not do so in Ireland because of the high rate of accidents.

You may use an American or Canadian driver's license for 30 days in the U.K. and Ireland, provided you've had it for one year. If you plan on staying for a longer duration, you will need an **International Driver's Permit** (see p. 11). The **Irish Automobile Association** (tel. (01) 677 9481) is on 23 Suffolk St., Rockhill, Blackrock, Co. Dublin, off Grafton St. They honor most foreign automobile memberships (24hr. breakdown and road service tel. (800) 667788; toll-free in Ireland).

BY BICYCLE

Much of Ireland's and Northern Ireland's countrysides are well suited for cycling by daylight; many roads are not heavily traveled. Single-digit N roads in the Republic, and M roads in the North, are more busily trafficked; try to avoid them. Begin your trip in the south or west to take advantage of prevailing winds. Bikes can go on some trains but not all: inquire at the information desk. You'll have better luck getting your bike on a bus if you depart from a terminal, not a wayside stop. Bikes are allowed on Bus Éireann at the driver's discretion (if the bus isn't crowded) for a fee of £3-5, but this fee isn't always enforced; the fee for taking a bike on the train is at most £6. It's a pain to bring a bike on an airplane, and each airline has different rules. *Let's Go* lists bike shops and bike rental establishments wherever we can find them. The cash deposit may often be waived if you pay for the rental with a credit card.

Irish Cycle Hire, Mayoralty St., Drogheda, Co. Louth (tel. (041) 41067, 43982, or 42338; fax 35369), has offices in Dublin, Cork, Killarney, Dingle, Galway, and Donegal. They also own **Viking Rent-a-Bike** and **Railbike,** so they have many depots. The Drogheda office, which is the office to contact with any questions, is open daily from 9am to 5:30pm. Most other offices are open from May to October daily 9:30am to 6pm; some offices are closed on Sundays, although their depots stay open. All charge IR£6 per day, £30 per week, with £30 deposit. Bikes come with lock pump and repair kit. One-way rental (renting in one location and dropping off in another) is possible for IR£7. Students with ID get a 10% discount.

Rent-A-Bike, 58 Lower Gardiner St., Dublin (tel. (01) 872 5399), rents 18-speed cross-country and mountain bikes for £30 per week, plus £30 deposit. The shops will equip you with locks and repair kits. You can return your bike at a different depot for about IR£5. Used bikes, which you can sell back up to four months later for half price, are sometimes available in September or October at the Dublin shop. Rent-A-Bike depots are located in Dublin; Isaac's Hostel, Cork; An Óige Hostel, Limerick; Shannon Airport; Great Western Hostel, Galway; and Scotts Garden, Killarney. All bookings should be made through the head office in Dublin (open daily 9:30am-5pm).

Raleigh Rent-A-Bike rents for IR£7 per day, £30 per week, plus £40 deposit. The shops will equip you with locks, patch kits, and pumps, and for longer journeys, pannier bags (IR£5 per week). Their **One-Way Rental** plan allows you to rent a bike at one shop and drop it off at any of 66 others for a flat charge of IR£12. Reservations should be made through the main office at **C. Harding for Bicycles,** 30 Bachelors' Walk, Dublin 1 (tel./fax (01) 873 3622). A list of Raleigh dealers is available at most tourist offices and bike shops. You might also contact **Raleigh Ireland Limited** (tel. (01) 626 1333), 10 Raleigh House, Kylemore Rd., Dublin 10. In West Cork, the **Wheel Escapes** program provides one-way rental to a series of hostels; see p. 191).

Many small local dealers and hostels also rent bikes; rates are usually IR£6 to £9 per day and £25 to £35 per week. Tourist offices can direct you to bike rental establishments and distribute leaflets on local biking routes, as well as providing the extensive *Cycle Touring Ireland* (£7). If you plan to do much long-distance riding, you might also check a travel bookstore for other Irish cycling guides. Mountaineers Books (tel. (800) 553 4453; http://www.mountaineers.org) sells *Ireland by Bike: 21 Tours* for US$15 (plus US$3 shipping). If you are nervous about striking out on your own, **CBT Bicycle Tours** (tel. (800) 736 BIKE (736 2453) or (773) 404 1710; fax 404 1833) in the U.S. and Canada offer bicycle tours through the U.K. and Ireland that are geared toward the college-aged. One- to seven-week tours cost about US$95 per week, including accommodations and some food; CBT also arranges discounted airfares for their participants. Adequate **maps** are a necessity; Ordnance Survey maps (£4.50) or Bartholomew maps are available in most bookstores in Ireland and the U.K., and in good ones in the U.S.

BY FOOT

Ireland's mountains, fields, and heather-covered hills make walking and hiking an arduous joy. The **Wicklow Way,** a popular trail through mountainous Co. Wicklow, has hostels designed for hikers within a day's walk of each other. The best hillwalking maps are the Ordnance Survey series (IR£4.20 each). There are many other trails all over the island; consult Bord Fáilte for more information and free pamphlets.

The **Ulster Way** encircles Northern Ireland with 560 mi. of marked trails. Less industrious trekkers are accommodated by frequent subdivisions. Plentiful information is available on the numerous paths that lace Northern Ireland. For the booklet *The Ulster Way* (UK£2), contact the **Sports Council for Northern Ireland,** House of Sport, Upper Malone Rd., Belfast BT9 5LA (tel. (01232) 381 222). If you're planning a hike through the Mourne Mountains, contact the **Mourne Heritage Centre,** 87 Central Promenade, Newcastle, Co. Down BT33 OHH (tel. (013967) 24059).

For guided backpacking tours, you can try **Tír na nÓg Tours,** 57 Lower Gardiner St., Dublin 1 (tel. (01) 836 4684). The three- and six-day tours zip along the south and west coasts, and the price includes transportation, breakfast, admission to visitors centers, and accommodations along the way. 6-day tours leave weekly throughout the year (IR£159); 3-day tours run twice weekly March to October (IR£89).

BY THUMB

Let's Go strongly urges you to consider seriously the risks before you choose to hitch. We do not recommend hitching as a safe means of transportation, and none of the information presented here is intended to do so.

No one should hitch without careful consideration of the risks involved. Not everyone can be an airplane pilot, but almost any bozo or lunatic can drive a car, especially in Ireland. Hitching means entrusting your life to a random person who happens to stop beside you on the road and risking theft, assault, sexual harassment, and unsafe driving. Hitching in Ireland has a glowing reputation, but it does have sobering risks—the past few years have seen several instances of violence against hitchers. There has been a recent backlash against hitching in both parts of Ireland; the percentage of travelers hitching has declined drastically. Locals in Northern Ireland do not recommend hitching there.

In spite of these disadvantages, some find the gains are many. Favorable hitching experiences allow you to meet local people and get where you're going, especially in rural areas, where public transportation is less reliable. While we don't endorse hitchhiking, we'll tell you some ways to make it safer and how to do it right.

The **decision to pick up** a hitcher can be a difficult one for a driver, so a smart hitcher will do everything possible to make it easier. Your success as a hitcher will depend partly on **what you look like.** Successful hitchers travel light and stack their belongings in a compact but visible cluster. Most Europeans signal with an open hand, rather than a thumb; many write their destination on a sign in large, bold letters and draw a smiley-face under it. Drivers prefer hitchers who are neat and wholesome. No one stops for anyone wearing sunglasses. **Where you stand** is vital. Experienced hitchers stand where drivers can stop, have time to look over potential passengers as they approach, and return to the road without causing an accident. Hitching on hills or curves is hazardous and unsuccessful; traffic circles and access roads to highways are better. In the **Practical Information** section of many cities, we list the bus lines that take travelers to strategic points for hitching out.

You can get a sense of the amount of traffic a road sees by its letter and number: in the Republic, single-digit N-roads (A-roads in the North) are as close as Ireland gets to highways, double-digit N-roads see some intercity traffic, R-roads (B-roads in the North) generally only carry local traffic but are easy hitches, and non-lettered roads are a **hitcher's purgatory.** In Northern Ireland, hitching (or even standing) on motorways (M-roads) is illegal: you may only thumb at the entrance ramps—*in front* of the nifty blue and white superhighway pictograph (a bridge over a road).

Safety issues are always imperative, even for those who are not hitching alone. If you're a woman traveling alone, don't hitch. A man and a woman are a safer combination, two men will have a harder time, and three will go nowhere. Hitchhiking at night can be particularly dangerous; experienced hitchers stand in well-lit places and expect drivers to be leery of nocturnal thumbers. Safety-minded hitchers avoid getting in the back of a two-door car and never let go of their backpacks. They will not get into a car that they can't get out of again in a hurry. If they ever feel threatened, they insist on being let off, regardless of where they are. Acting as if they are going to open the car door or vomit on the upholstery usually gets a driver to stop.

If you are hitching a **long distance** or to a remote spot with an intervening town between your present and desired location, you would do well to make your sign for the intervening town rather than your final destination. Shorter lifts are easier to pick up because it's easier for the driver and because more cars will be going to the nearby spot than to the distant one. If the driver is not going the entire way, then you've at least covered some of the distance and probably put yourself in a better location for hitching the rest of the way.

■ Accommodations

Bord Fáilte (bored FAHL-tshah; meaning "welcome board") is the Republic of Ireland's tourism authority. Actually a government department (and a fairly important one), its system for approving accommodations involves a more-or-less frequent inspection and a fee. Approved accommodations get to use Bord Fáilte's national booking system and display its icon, a green shamrock on a white field. Approved campgrounds and bed and breakfasts are listed with prices in the *Caravan and Camping Ireland* and *Bed and Breakfast Ireland* guides, respectively, available from any Bord Fáilte office. Bord Fáilte's standards are very specific and, in some cases, far higher than what hostelers and other budget travelers expect or require. Unapproved accommodations can be better and cheaper than their approved neighbors, though, of course, some unapproved places are real dumps. Most official tourist offices in Ireland will refer *only* to approved accommodations; some offices won't even tell you how to get to an unapproved hostel, B&B, or campground. Most tourist offices will book a room for a IR£1-3 fee, plus a 10% deposit. **Credit card reservations** can be made through Dublin Tourism (tel. (1800) 668668 from Ireland, (0800) 783 5740 from the U.K., and 669 2082 from elsewhere). See **Longer Stays**, p. 45, for information on long-term accommodations.

HOSTELS

> ### A Hosteler's Bill of Rights
> There are certain standard features that we do not include in our hostel listings. Unless we state otherwise, you can expect that every hostel has: no lockout, no curfew, free hot showers, secure luggage storage, and no key deposit.

For those out for friends and a unique experience minus the expense, hostels are the place. These generally feature dorm-style accommodations with large rooms and bunk beds; some allow families and couples to have private rooms. Some have kitchens and utensils for your use, storage areas, laundry facilities, and bike rentals. Some close during daytime "lock-out" hours, have curfews, or impose a maximum stay. In Ireland more than anywhere else, senior travelers and families are invariably welcome. Some hostels are strikingly beautiful (a few are even housed in castles), while others are little more than run-down barracks. You can expect every Irish hostel to provide blankets, although you may have to pay extra for sheets (see **Packing**, p. 27). Hostels listed are chosen based on location, price, quality, and facilities.

Hostelling International is the largest hosteling organization. A membership in any national HI affiliate allows you to stay in HI hostels in any country. Nonmembers may ask at hostels for an "International Guest Card." Hosteling membership is rarely necessary in Ireland, although there are sometimes member discounts. For non-members, an overnight fee plus one-sixth of the annual membership charge buys one stamp; a card with six stamps is proof of full HI membership. In Ireland, the HI affiliate is **An Óige** (an OYJ), which operates 37 hostels countrywide. Many An Óige hostels are in remote areas or small villages and were designed mostly to serve hikers, long-distance bicyclists, anglers, and others who want to see nature rather than meet people. The North's HI affiliate is **YHANI** (Youth Hostel Association of Northern Ireland). It operates only nine hostels, all comfortable. Many HI hostels have curfews and lockouts (midday hours when everyone has to leave the building for cleaning), although they're not always strict about them; almost all have laundry facilities and kitchens. Some HI hostels operate only from March to November, April to October, or May to September. The annually updated *An Óige Handbook* (IR£1.50) lists,

Ireland.
A country of contrasts,
whose natural land-
scape remains one of
the most unspoiled in
Europe. From wild, spectacular
mountain ranges to lively, cosmopolitan
cities, Ireland demands to be explored.

Ireland.
Go your own way.

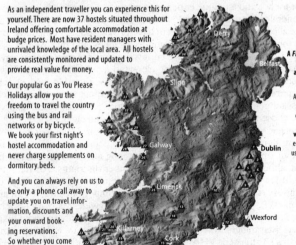

As an independent traveller you can experience this for
yourself. There are now 37 hostels situated throughout
Ireland offering comfortable accommodation at
budge prices. Most have resident managers with
unrivaled knowledge of the local area. All hostels
are consistently monitored and updated to
provide real value for money.

Our popular Go as You Please
Holidays allow you the
freedom to travel the country
using the bus and rail
networks or by bicycle.
We book your first night's
hostel accommodation and
never charge supplements on
dormitory beds.

And you can always rely on us to
be only a phone call away to
update you on travel information, discounts and
your onward book-
ing reservations.
So whether you come
as an individual or in a
group, we look forward
to your arrival.

HOSTELLING INTERNATIONAL

A *FREE* foldout information sheet
with holiday suggestions,
a map and a list of hostels is
available from An Óige.

Alternativly you can get up to the
minute information along with
on-line Hostel booking facilities
by accessing our web site on:
www.irelandyha.org or via our
e-mail: **anoige@iol.ie** or contact
us direct at the following numbers.

**Irish Youth
Hostel Association**
61 Mountjoy Street,
Dublin 7, Ireland
Tel: +353 1 830 4555
Fax: +353 1 830 5808

Hostels in Ireland 1. Dublin Int'l. - Dublin City 2. Glencree - Co.Wicklow 3. Knockree - Co.Wicklow 4. Baltyboys - Co.Wicklow 5. Glendaloch Int'l - Co.Wicklow 6. Tiglin - Co.Wicklow 7. Glenmalure - Co.Wicklow 8. Ballinclea - Co.Wicklow 9. Aghavannagh - Co.Wicklow 10. Foulksrath Castle - Co.Kilkenny 11. Rosslare - Co.Wexford 12. Arthurstown - Co.Wexford 13. Ballydavid Wood - Co.Tipperary 14. Mountain Lodge - Co.Tipperary 15. Cork - Cork City 16. Cape Clear Island - Co.Cork 17. Allihies - Co.Cork 18. Glanmore Lake - Co.Kerry 19. Loo Bridge - Co.Kerry 20. Killarney - Co.Kerry 21. Black Valley - Co.Kerry 22. Ballinskelligs - Co.Kerry 23. Valentia Island - Co.Kerry 24. Dunquin - Co.Kerry 25. Limerick - Limerick City 26. Doorus - Co.Galway 27. Galway - Galway City 28. Inverin - Co.Galway 29. Cong - Co.Mayo 30. Ben Lettery - Co.Galway 31. Killary Harbour - Co.Galway 32. Westport - Co.Mayo 33. Traenlaur Lodge - Co.Mayo 34. Ball Hill - Co.Donegal 35. Crohy Head - Co.Donegal 36. Errigal - Co.Donegal 37. Trá na Rossan - Co.Donegal locates, and describes all An Óige and YHANI hostels; its pricing system isn't always followed by all the hostels it lists.

A number of hostels in Ireland belong to the **Independent Holiday Hostels (IHH)**. The 160 IHH hostels have no lockout or curfew (with a few exceptions), accept all ages, require no membership card, and have a comfortable atmosphere; all are Bord Fáilte-approved. Pick up a free booklet with complete descriptions of each at any IHH hostel. Contact IHH at the IHH Office, 67 Lower Gardiner St., Dublin (tel. (01) 836 4700; fax 836 4710). The **Independent Hostel Organization (IHO)** is a recently formed group of a few hostels.

Lastly, if you have Internet access, check out the **Internet Guide to Hostelling** (http://hostels.com), which includes hostels from around the world in addition to oodles of information about hostelling and backpacking worldwide. Information on budget hostels and several international hostel associations can be found at **Eurotrip** (http://www.eurotrip.com/accommodation/accommodation.html). Reservations for over 300 **Hostelling International (HI)** hostels (see listing below) may be made via the International Booking Network (IBN; U.S. tel. (202) 783 6161), a computerized system that allows you make reservations months in advance for a nominal fee. Credit card bookings may be made over the phone; contact An Óige or YHANI.

HI Affiliates Worldwide

An Óige (Irish Youth Hostel Association), 61 Mountjoy St., Dublin 7 (tel. (01) 830 4555; fax 830 5808; email anoige@iol.ie; http://www.irelandyha.org). One-year memberships IR£7.50, under 18 IR£4, families IR£7.50 for each adult with children under 16 free. Prices from IR£4-9.50 a night. 37 locations.

Australian Youth Hostels Association (AYHA), Level 3, 10 Mallett St., Camperdown NSW 2050 (tel. (02) 9565 1699; fax 9565 1325; email YHA@yha.org.au; http://www.yha.org.au). Memberships AUS$44, renewal AUS$27; under 18 AUS$13.

Hostelling International-American Youth Hostels (HI-AYH), 733 15th St. NW, Ste. 840, Washington, D.C. 20005 (tel. (202) 783 6161 ext. 136; fax 783 6171; email hiayhserv@hiayh.org; http://www.hiayh.org). Maintains 35 offices and over 150 hostels in the U.S. Memberships can be purchased at many travel agencies or the national office in Washington, D.C. One year membership US$25, under 18 US$10, over 54 US$15, family cards US$35; includes *Hostelling North America: The Official Guide to Hostels in Canada and the United States.*

Hostelling International-Canada (HI-C), 400-205 Catherine St., Ottawa, Ontario K2P 1C3 (tel. (613) 237 7884; fax 237 7868; email info@hostellingintl.ca; http://www.hostellingintl.ca). Maintains 73 hostels throughout Canada. IBN booking centers in Edmonton, Montreal, Ottawa, and Vancouver. Membership packages: 1-year, under 18 CDN$12; 1-year, over 18 CDN$25; 2-year, over 18 CDN$35; lifetime CDN$175.

Youth Hostels Association of England and Wales (YHA), Trevelyan House, 8 St. Stephen's Hill, St. Albans, Hertfordshire AL1 2DY, England (tel. (01727) 855215; fax 844126; email yhacustomerservices@compuserve.com; http://www.yha.org.uk). Memberships UK£10; under 18 UK£5; UK£20 for each parent with children under 18 enrolled free; UK£10 for one parent with children under 18 enrolled free; UK£140 for lifetime membership. Overnight prices for adults UK£5.85-21.30, under 18 UK£4-17.90.

Hostelling International Northern Ireland (HINI), 22-32 Donegall Rd., Belfast BT12 5JN, Northern Ireland (tel. (01232) 324733 or 315435; fax 439699; email info@hini.org.uk; http://www.hini.org.uk). Prices range from UK£8-12. Year membership UK£7, under 18 UK£3, family UK£14 for up to 6 children; lifetime UK£50.

Youth Hostels Association of New Zealand (YHANZ), P.O. Box 436, 173 Cashel St., Christchurch 1 (tel. (643) 379 9970; fax 365 4476; email info@yha.org.nz; http://www.yha.org.nz). Annual membership NZ$24.

Hostelling International South Africa, P.O. Box 4402, Cape Town 8000 (tel. (021) 242511; fax 244119; email info@hisa.org.za; http://www.hisa.org.za). Membership SAR50, group SAR120, family SAR100, lifetime SAR250.

BED AND BREAKFASTS

"Bed-and-breakfast" means just that: a bed in a private room in a small place, often a private home with extra rooms, and a breakfast of some sort. Irish B&Bs are most savory. Singles run about IR£12-20, doubles £20-36. "Full Irish breakfasts"—eggs, bacon, bread, sometimes black or white pudding, fried vegetables, cereal, orange juice, and coffee or tea—are often filling enough to get you through until dinner. Remember that attitudes in rural Ireland can be conservative. An unmarried man and woman staying together may encounter some raised eyebrows, but usually no real problems. B&Bs displaying a shamrock are officially approved by the Irish Tourist Board, Bord Fáilte. For accommodations in Northern Ireland, check the Northern Ireland Tourist Board's annual *Where to Stay in Northern Ireland* (UK£4), available at most tourist offices. Be aware that Bord Fáilte meets at the end of the year and decides how much prices should increase in the Republic of Ireland. As our prices were researched in the summer of 1998, prices may have increased since publication.

■ Longer Stays

Unemployment in Ireland is widespread, especially in rural areas. If you're looking for a job, you'll have better luck in cities. Check the *Irish Independent* and the *Irish Times* for employment and apartment listings. Also, you might try the kiosks at Trinity College or the University Colleges. Council's work program will help with job-placement and housing (see p. 2). For more info on long-term accommodations, see **Long-Term Stays** in the Dublin and Galway sections (p. 92, p. 288) or **Work** (p. 22).

HOME EXCHANGE

Home exchange offers a traveler with a house the opportunity to live like a native and to dramatically cut down on accommodation fees—usually only an administration fee is paid to the matching service. Once the introductions are made, the choice is left to the two hopeful partners. Most companies have pictures of member's homes and information about the owners (some will even ask for your photo). A great site listing many exchange companies can be found at http://www.aitec.edu.au/~bwechner/ Documents/Travel/Lists/HomeExchangeClubs.html. Renting a home may also be a good deal for some.

Barclay International Group, 150 West 52nd St., New York, NY 10022 (tel. (800) 845 6636 or (212) 832 3777; fax 753 1139; email dawn@netgate.net; http:// www.barclayweb.com), arranges hotel-alternative accommodations (apartment, condo, cottage, or villa rentals) in Ireland and the U.K. Most are equipped with kitchens, telephones, TV, concierge, and maid service. Dublin rentals start around US$700 per week in the off-season, while suburban cottages start as low as US$300 per week. Apartments may be cheaper than comparably serviced hotels and are especially useful for families with children, business travelers, or travelers with special dietary needs.

Europa-Let/Tropical Inn-Let, 92 North Main St., Ashland, OR 97520 (tel. (800) 462 4486 or (541) 482 5806; fax 482 0660; email europalet@wave.net; http:// www.europa-let.com), offers over 100,000 private rental properties with fully equipped kitchens in 25 countries including Ireland and the U.K. Customized computer searches allow clients to choose properties according to specific needs and budget. This service may be especially advantageous for families, business people, large groups, or those planning to stay over one week.

■ Camping and the Outdoors

Camping brings you closest to the land, the water, the insects, and continued financial solvency. Ireland is gratifyingly well endowed with sites and gratifyingly not endowed at all with snakes. Most campsites are open from April to October, although some stay open year-round. While a few youth hostels have camping facilities (the charge is usually half the hostel charge), most campsites are privately owned and designed for people with caravans rather than people with tents. You can legally set up camp only in specifically marked areas unless you get permission from the person on whose land you plan to squat. It is legal to cross private land by **public rights of way;** any other use of private land without permission is considered trespassing. Remember, bogs catch **fire** easily.

Camping in State Forests and National Parks is not allowed in Ireland, nor is camping on public land if there is an official campsite in the area. It is also illegal to light fires within 2km of these forests and parks. Designated caravan and camping parks provide all the accoutrements of bourgeois civilization: toilets, running water, showers, garbage cans, and sometimes shops, kitchens, laundry facilities, restaurants, and game rooms. In addition, many have several caravans for hire at the site. Northern Ireland treats its campers royally; there are well-equipped campsites throughout, and spectacular parks often house equally mouthwatering sites.

USEFUL PUBLICATIONS

A variety of publishing companies offer hiking guidebooks to meet the educational needs of novices or experts. For information about camping, hiking, and biking, write or call the publishers listed below to receive a free catalog.

Automobile Association, AA Publishing. Orders and enquiries to TBS Frating Distribution Centre, Colchester, Essex, CO7 7DW, U.K. (tel. (01206) 255678; fax 255916; http://www.theaa.co.uk). Publishes a wide range of maps, atlases, and travel guides, including *Camping and Caravanning: Europe* and *Camping and Caravanning: Britain & Ireland* (each UK£8).

The Caravan Club, East Grinstead House, East Grinstead, West Sussex, RH19 1UA, U.K. (tel. (01342) 326944; fax 410258; http://www.caravanclub.co.uk), produces one of the most detailed guides to campsites in Europe and the U.K.

Sierra Club Bookstore, 85 2nd St., 2nd floor, San Francisco, CA 94105 (tel. (800) 935 1056 or (415) 977 5600; fax 977 5500; http://www.sierraclub.org/books). Books include *The Sierra Club Family Outdoors Guide* (US$12) and *Wild Ireland* (US$16).

The Mountaineers Books, 1001 SW Klickitat Way, #201, Seattle, WA 98134 (tel. (800) 553 4453 or (206) 223 6303; fax 223 6306; email mbooks@mountaineers.org; http://www.mountaineers.org). Many titles on hiking (the *100 Hikes* series), biking, mountaineering, natural history, and conservation.

Stanfords Ltd., 12-14 Long Acre, London, WC2E 9LP, U.K. (tel (0171) 836 2260; fax 379 4776), supplies maps of just about anywhere, especially the British Isles.

Wilderness Press, 2440 Bancroft Way, Berkeley, CA 94704-1676 (tel. (800) 443 7227 or (510) 843 8080; fax 548 1355; http://www.wildernesspress.com). Publishes over 100 hiking guides including *Backpacking Basics* (US$11) and *Backpacking with Babies and Small Children* ($11).

CAMPING AND HIKING EQUIPMENT

Purchase **equipment** before you leave. This way you'll know exactly what you have and how much it weighs. Spend some time examining catalogues and talking to knowledgeable salespeople.

Sleeping bags: Most good sleeping bags are rated by "season," or the lowest outdoor temperature at which they will keep you warm. "Summer" means 30-40°F, "three-season" usually means 0°F, and the generally unnecessary "four-season" or "winter" often means -50°F. Sleeping bags are made either of down (warmer and lighter, but more expensive, and miserable when wet) or of synthetic material (heavier, more durable). Prices vary, but range from US$65-100 for a summer synthetic to $250-550 for a good down winter bag. **Sleeping bag pads,** including foam pads ($15 and up) and air mattresses ($25-50) cushion your back and neck and insulate you from the ground. A good alternative is the **Therm-A-Rest,** part foam and part air-mattress, which inflates to full padding when you unroll it and is warmer than traditional foam pads.

Tents: The best **tents** are free-standing, with their own frames and suspension systems; they set up quickly and require no staking (except in high winds). Tents are also classified by season. Low profile dome tents are the best all-around. When pitched, their internal space is almost entirely usable, which means little unnecessary bulk. Tent sizes can be somewhat misleading: two people *can* fit in a two-person tent, but will find life more pleasant in a four-person. If you're traveling by car, go for the bigger tent; if you're hiking, stick with a smaller tent that weighs no more than 3-4 lbs. Good two-person tents start at US$150, four-person tents at $400, but you can sometimes find last year's model for half the price. Be sure to seal the seams of your tent with waterproofer, and make sure it has a rain fly.

Backpacks: If you intend to do much hiking, you should have a **frame backpack. Internal-frame packs** mold better to your back, keep a lower center of gravity, and can flex adequately to allow you to hike difficult trails that require a lot of bending and maneuvering. **External-frame packs** are more comfortable for long hikes over even terrain since they keep the weight higher and distribute it more evenly. Whichever you choose, make sure your pack has a strong, padded hip belt, which transfers the weight from the shoulders to the legs. Most backpacking requires a pack of at least 4000 cubic inches. Allow an additional 500 cubic inches for your sleeping bag in internal-frame packs. Sturdy backpacks cost anywhere from US$125-500. Backpacks are one area where it doesn't pay to economize—cheaper packs may be less comfortable, and the straps are more likely to fray or rip. Try any pack on before you buy it and imagine carrying it, full, a few miles up a rocky incline.

Boots: Be sure to wear hiking boots with good **ankle support.** Your boots should fit snugly and comfortably over one or two wool socks and a thin liner sock. Be sure that the boots are broken in—a bad blister will ruin your hiking for days.

Other necessities: Rain gear should come in two pieces, a jacket and pants, rather than a poncho. **Synthetics,** like polypropylene tops, socks, and long underwear, along with a pile jacket, will keep you warm even when wet. **Wool pants** are a great buy at army surplus stores and regulate temperature well. When camping in autumn, winter, or spring, bring along a **"space blanket,"** which helps you to retain your body heat and doubles as a groundcloth (US$5-15). Plastic **canteens** or water bottles, like the ever-popular Nalgenes, keep water cooler than metal ones do, and are virtually shatter- and leak-proof. Large, collapsible **water sacks** will significantly improve your lot in primitive campgrounds and weigh practically nothing when empty, though they can get bulky. Bring **water-purification tablets** for when you can't boil water. Although most campgrounds provide campfire sites, you may want to bring a small **metal grate** or **grill** of your own. For those places that forbid fires or the gathering of firewood (nearly every organized campground in Europe), you'll need a **camp stove.** The classic Coleman starts at about US$30. In Europe, consider the "GAZ" butane/propane stove. Its little blue cylinders can be purchased anywhere on the continent—just don't try to take them onto a plane. Campers heading to Europe should also look into buying an **International Camping Carnet,** which is similar to a hostel membership card; it's required at a few campgrounds and provides discounts at others (available in North America from the **Family Campers and RVers Association** and in the U.K. from **The Caravan Club;** see **Useful Publications,** p. 46). A **first aid kit, swiss army knife, insect repellent, calamine lotion,** and **waterproof matches** or a **lighter** are essential camping items. Other items include: a **battery-operated lantern,** a **plastic groundcloth,** a **nylon tarp,** a **waterproof backpack cover** (although you can store your belongings in plastic bags inside your backpack), and a **"stuff sack"** or plastic bag to keep your sleeping bag dry.

The mail-order firms listed below offer lower prices than those you'll find in many stores, but shop around locally first in order to determine what items actually look like and weigh. Camping equipment is generally more expensive in Australia, New Zealand, South Africa, and the U.K. than in North America.

Campmor, P.O. Box 700, Saddle River, NJ 07458-0700 (tel. (888) CAMPMOR (226 7667), outside the U.S. call (201) 825 8300; email customer-service@campmor.com; http://www.campmor.com), has a wide selection of name-brand equipment at low prices. One-year guarantee for unused or defective merchandise.

L.L. Bean, Freeport, ME 04033-0001 (tel. (800) 441 5713 in Canada or the U.S.; (0800) 962954 in the U.K.; (207) 552 6878 elsewhere; fax (207) 552 4080; http://www.llbean.com). This monolithic equipment and outdoor clothing supplier offers high quality and loads of information. Call or write for a free catalogue. The customer is guaranteed 100% satisfaction on all purchases; if it doesn't meet your expectations, they'll replace or refund it. Always open.

Mountain Designs, P.O. Box 1472, Fortitude Valley, Queensland 4006, Australia (tel. (07) 3252 8894; fax 3252 4569), is a leading Australian manufacturer and mail-order retailer of camping and climbing gear.

Mountain Safety Research Inc., P.O. Box 24547, Seattle, WA 98124 (tel. (800) 877 9677; email info@msrcorp.com; http://www.msrcorp.com), has stores in the U.S. and Canada and sells products in Australia, New Zealand, South Africa, and the U.K. They offer high-quality maintenance kits, emergency kits, stoves, water filters, and climbing gear.

Recreational Equipment, Inc. (REI) (tel. (800) 426 4840; http://www.rei.com) stocks a comprehensive selection of REI brand and other leading brand equipment, clothing, and footwear for the activities of travel, camping, cycling, paddling, climbing, and winter sports. In addition to mail order and an Internet commerce site, REI has 49 retail stores, including a flagship store in Seattle: 222 Yale Ave. N., Seattle, WA 98109-5429.

YHA Adventure Shop, 14 Southampton St., London, WC2E 7HY, U.K. (tel. (0171) 836 8541; fax 836 8541). Main branch of one of Britain's largest outdoor equipment suppliers.

CAMPERS AND RVS

Many North American campers harbor a suspicion that traveling with a **camper** or **recreational vehicle (RV)** is not "real camping." No such stigma exists in Europe, where RV camping, or "caravanning," is both popular and common. European RVs are smaller and more economical than the 40-foot Winnebagos of the American road. Renting an RV will always be more expensive than tenting or hostelling, but the costs compare favorably with the price of renting a car and staying in hotels, and the convenience of bringing along your own bedroom, bathroom, and kitchen makes it an attractive option for some, especially older travelers and families with small children.

It is not difficult to arrange an RV rental from overseas, although you will want to begin gathering information several months before your departure. Rates vary widely by region, season (July and Aug. are most expensive), and type of RV. It always pays to contact several different companies to compare vehicles and prices. **Avis** (tel. (800) 331 1084) and **Hertz** (tel. (800) 654 3001) are U.S. firms that can arrange RV rentals overseas; **Auto Europe** (tel. (800) 223 5555) and **National Car Rentals** (tel. (800) 227 3876; (800) 227 7368 in Canada) are European firms with branches in North America. *Camping Your Way through Europe* by Carol Mickelsen (Affordable Press, US$15) and *Exploring Europe by RV* by Dennis and Tina Jaffe (Globe Pequot, also US$15) are both good resources for planning this type of trip.

WILDERNESS AND SAFETY CONCERNS

Stay warm, stay dry, and **stay hydrated.** The vast majority of life-threatening wilderness problems stem from a failure to follow this advice. On any hike, however brief, you should pack enough equipment to keep you alive should disaster befall. This includes **rain gear, hat** and **mittens, a first-aid kit, a reflector, a whistle, high energy food,** and **water.** Dress in warm layers of **synthetic materials** designed for the outdoors, or **wool.** Pile fleece jackets and Gore-Tex® raingear are excellent choices (see **Camping and Hiking Equipment,** p. 45). **Extreme cold** is a far greater danger than heat in Britain and Ireland, especially for hikers. A bright blue sky can turn to sleeting rain before you can say **"hypothermia,"** which can occur even in July, especially in rainy or windy conditions or at night. Never rely on cotton for warmth; it is absolutely useless, actually hazardous in the cold, should it get wet. When camping, be sure to bring a proper tent with rain-fly and warm sleeping bags. See **Health,** p. 17, for more information about hypothermia and other outdoor ailments and **Packing,** p. 27, for more tips on clothing. A good guide to outdoor survival is *How to Stay Alive in the Woods,* by Bradford Angier (Macmillan, US$8). Whenever possible, let someone know when and where you are going hiking, whether that person is a friend, your hostel manager, a park ranger, or a local hiking organization.

■ Keeping in Touch

MAIL

Sending Mail To Ireland

In the Republic, there are no postal codes, except in Dublin, where there are 24 widely ignored ones. Northern Ireland uses the British system of six-character codes. *Let's Go* lists post offices in the **Practical Information** section for each city and most towns. Mail can be sent internationally through **Poste Restante** (the international phrase for General Delivery) to any city or town; it's well worth using and much more reliable than you might think. Mark the envelope "HOLD" and address it, for example, "Michael COLLINS, Poste Restante, Enniscorthy, Co. Wexford, Ireland." The last name should be capitalized and underlined. The mail will go to a special desk in the central post office (or, more likely, the only post office), unless you specify a post office by street address or postal code. As a rule, it is best to use the largest post office in a city; sometimes mail will be sent there regardless of what you write on the envelope. When possible, it is usually safer and quicker to send mail express or registered. When picking up your mail, bring your passport or other ID.

Generally, letters specifically marked "airmail" are faster than postcards and provide more writing room than **aerogrammes,** printed sheets that fold into envelopes and travel via airmail, available at post offices. Most post offices will charge exorbitant fees or simply refuse to send aerogrammes with enclosures. Airmail letters between American cities and the island average 6-10 days. Allow roughly two weeks to Europe from Australia, New Zealand, and South Africa. If regular airmail is too slow, there are a few faster, more expensive, options. **FedEx** (tel. (800) 247 4747 for international operator) can theoretically get a letter from Ireland to the U.S. in two days for $48; from the U.S. to Ireland costs US$29. By Express Mail, a letter from New York would arrive in Dublin in two to three days and would cost US$21.

Surface mail is by far the cheapest and slowest way to send mail and is appropriate for sending large quantities of items you won't need to see for a while. It takes one to three months to cross the Atlantic. When ordering books and materials from abroad, always include one or two **International Reply Coupons (IRCs)**—a way of providing the postage to cover delivery. IRCs should be available from your local post office as well as abroad (US$1.05).

American Express offices throughout the world will act as a mail service for cardholders if you contact them in advance. Under the free **"Client Letter Service,"** they will hold mail for 30 days, forward upon request, and accept telegrams. Again, the last name of the person to whom the mail is addressed should be capitalized and underlined. Some offices will offer these services to non-cardholders (especially those who have purchased AmEx Traveler's Cheques), but call ahead to make sure. We list AmEx office locations when they exist; a complete list is available free from AmEx (tel. (800) 528 4800) in the booklet *Traveler's Companion* or online (http://www.americanexpress.com/shared/cgi-bin/tsoserve.cgi?travel/index).

ESSENTIALS

TELEPHONES

Calling Ireland

You can place international calls from most telephones. Dial your country's international access code (011 in the USA and Canada, 0011 in Australia, 00 in New Zealand); then the country code (44 for Britain, Northern Ireland, and the Isle of Man; 08 for Northern Ireland if calling from the Republic; 353 for the Republic of Ireland); then the regional telephone code, *dropping the initial zero,* and, finally, the local number. *Let's Go* lists telephone codes in **Practical Information** sections, except when covering rural areas where more than one telephone code may apply, where we list the area code before the number. For example, when calling Irish Ferries in Dublin (telephone code 01) from the U.S. to inquire about times of sailings, you would dial 011-353-1-661-0715. Regional telephone codes range from two to five digits, and local telephone numbers range from five to seven digits.

Calling Home

From The Republic of Ireland

Operator (not available from card phones): 10.
Directory inquiries (for the Republic and the North): 1190.
Directory inquiries for Britain: 1197.
Telecom Éireann information number: (1800) 330 330.
International operator: 114.
International access code: 00.

Using Irish pay phones can be tricky. Public phones come in two varieties: **coin phones** and **card phones.** Public coin phones will sometimes make change (it depends on which order you insert coins) but private pay phones ("one-armed bandits") in hotels and restaurants do not—once you plunk in your change, you can kiss it good-bye. In any pay phone, do not insert money until you are asked to, or until your call goes through. The frightening pip, pip noise that the phone makes as you wait for it to start ringing is normal and can last up to 10 seconds.

Local calls cost 20p on standard pay phones; "one-armed bandits" can charge 30p or whatever they please. Local calls are not unlimited—one unit pays for four minutes. News agents sell **callcards** in denominations of £2, £8, or £15, which are essential for international calls. For calls direct-dialed to the U.S. during the cheapest hours, one unit lasts eight seconds, so a 100-unit (£15) card lasts for 13.3 minutes. Talk fast. Card phones have a digital display that ticks off the perilous plunge your units are taking. When the unit number starts flashing, you may push the eject button on the card phone; you can then pull out your expired calling card and replace it with a fresh one. If you try to wait until your card's units fall to zero, you'll be disconnected. Eject your card early and use that last remaining unit or two for a local call.

To make **international calls** from the Republic of Ireland, dial the international access code (00); then the country code (see **Telephone Codes,** p. 489); area code (dropping the initial zero); and local number. Alternatively, you can access an Irish international operator at 114. Note that to call the North from the Republic, you dial 08 plus the regional phone code (*without* dropping the initial zero) plus the number. Phone rates tend to be highest in the morning, lower in the evening, and lowest on Sunday and late at night. International calls from the Republic are cheapest during **economy periods.** The low-rate period to North America is Monday through Friday 10pm to 8am and Saturday and Sunday all day; to EU countries it's Monday through Friday 6pm to 8am and Saturday and Sunday all day; to Australia and New Zealand call Monday through Friday 2 to 8pm and midnight to 8am and Saturday and Sunday all day. There are no economy rates to the rest of the world. Long distance calls within the Republic are also cheapest Monday through Friday 6pm to 8am and Saturday and Sunday all day.

From Northern Ireland, The Isle of Man, and London

Operator: 100.
Directory inquiries: 192.
International operator: 155.
International directory assistance: 153.
International access code: 00.

Pay phones in Northern Ireland and the Isle of Man charge 20p for local calls. A series of harsh beeps warns you to insert more money when your time is up. The digital display ticks off your credit in 1p increments so you can watch your pence in suspense. Only unused coins are returned. You may use all remaining credit on a second call by pressing the "follow on call" button (often marked "FC"). Phones don't accept 1p, 2p, or 5p coins. The dial tone is a continuous purring sound; a repeated double-purr means the line is ringing. Northern **Phonecards,** in denominations of £2, £5, £10, and £20, are sold at post offices, newsstands, or John Menzies stationery shops. The £5 and higher denominations provide extra credit. Phone booths that take cards (the majority) are marked by yellow signs; coin booths are marked with white signs. In Belfast, British Telecom card phones, labeled in green and blue, take phonecards, credit cards (Visa or MasterCard/Access), or change. Card phones are common on the **Isle of Man,** where Manx Telecom **Smart Cards** come in £2, £3, £5, and £10 denominations, with 10% extra credit free. These cards are available at post offices and newsagents.

Reduced rates for most **international calls** from Northern Ireland and the Isle of Man apply Monday through Friday 8pm to 8am, and weekends all day. Rates are highest Monday through Friday 3 to 5pm. The low-rate period to Australia and New Zealand is daily midnight to 7am and 2:30 to 7:30pm. Rates to the Republic of Ireland go down Monday through Friday 6pm to 8am and weekends.

Collect Calls

Operators in most countries will place **collect calls** for you. It's cheaper to find a pay phone and deposit just enough money to be able to say "Call me" and give your number (though some pay phones can't receive calls). Some companies, seizing upon this "call-me-back" concept, have created callback phone services. Under these plans, you call a specified number, ring once, and hang up. The company's computer calls back and gives you a dial tone. You can then make as many calls as you want, at rates about 20-60% lower than you'd pay using credit cards or pay phones. This option is most economical for loquacious travelers, as services may include a US$10-25 minimum billing per month. For information, call **America Tele-Fone** (tel. (800) 321 5817) or **Telegroup** (tel. (800) 338 0225).

For more information, call **AT&T** about its **USADirect** and **World Connect** services (tel. (888) 288 4685; from abroad call (810) 262 6644 collect), **Sprint** (tel. (800) 877 4646; from abroad, call (913) 624 5335 collect), or **MCI WorldPhone** and **World Reach** (tel. (800) 444 4141; from abroad dial the country's MCI access number; see below). In Canada, contact Bell Canada **Canada Direct** (tel. (800) 565 4708); in the U.K., British Telecom **BT Direct** (tel. (800) 345144); in Australia, Telstra **Australia Direct** (tel. 132200); in New Zealand, **Telecom New Zealand** (tel. 123); and in South Africa, **Telkom South Africa** (tel. 0903).

Calling Card Calls

A **calling card** is a cheap alternative. Your local long-distance phone company will have a number for you to dial while traveling (either toll-free or charged as a local call) to connect instantly to an operator in your home country. The calls (plus a small surcharge) are then billed either collect or to a calling card.

If your carrier is **Australia Direct,** call (1800) 550061 in the Republic and (0800) 890061 in the North; **British Telecom** users call (1800) 550144 in Ireland; **Ireland Direct** users would call (0800) 890353 in Northern Ireland. **Telecom New Zealand** customers dial (1800) 550064 in the Republic of Ireland and (0800) 890064 in the

North, while **Telekom South Africa** kustomers kall (1800) 550027 in the South and (0800) 890027 up North. The numbers for the **AT&T Direct** service are (1800) 550000 in the Republic of Ireland and (0800) 890011 in the United Kingdom; users of **MCI World Phone** ring (1800) 551001 in Ireland and (0800) 890222 in the North.

OTHER COMMUNICATION

Between May 2 and Octoberfest, **EurAide**, P.O. Box 2375, Naperville, IL 60567 (tel. (630) 420 2343; fax 420 2369; http://www.cube.net/kmu/euraide.html), offers **Overseas Access,** a service useful to travelers without a set itinerary. The cost is US$15 per week or US$40 per month plus a US$15 registration fee. To reach you, people call, fax, or use the Internet to leave a message; you receive it by calling Munich whenever you wish, which is cheaper than calling overseas. You may also leave messages for callers to pick up by phone. (The web-site also provides Eurail time-table information, order forms for rail passes as well as making reservations on European trains.)

   Electronic mail (email) is an attractive option of staying in touch. With a minimum of computer knowledge and a little planning, you can beam messages anywhere for no per-message charges. **Traveltales.com** (http://traveltales.com) provides free, web-based email for travelers and maintains a list of cybercafés, travel links, and a travelers' chat room. Other free, web-based email providers include **Hotmail** (http://www.hotmail.com), **RocketMail** (http://www.rocketmail.com), and **USANET** (http://www.usa.net). Search through http://www.cyberiacafe.net/cyberia/guide/ccafe.htm to find a list of cybercafés around the world from which you can drink a cup of joe and email him too. *Let's Go* lists and indexes internet access, which is still not widespread in Ireland. For information on internet accessibility world-wide, contact www.nsrc.org, which has a host of connections to sites supplying further internet information on any country.

EMERGENCY

Dial **999** anywhere in Ireland, Northern Ireland, the Isle of Man, or London for police, fire, or ambulance; no coins are required. Police in the Republic of Ireland are called *garda* (GAR-da), plural *gardaí* (gar-DEE).

LIFE AND TIMES

It can be hard to see Ireland through the mist of stereotypes that surrounds the island even on the clearest of days. Although much of the country is still rural and religious, there is also a developing urban culture with links to Great Britain and the Continent. Long hiking trails, roads, and cliff walks make a chain of windy, watery, spectacular scenery around the coast of the island, while Dublin and Belfast suffuse modernity and sophistication to all in their orbits. Travelers visit the Republic of Ireland for its traditional (trad) music and unique pub culture and to study Irish language and literature. The Irish language lives in small, secluded areas known as *gaeltacht* as well as on road signs, in national publications, and in a growing body of modern literary works. Literature in English—especially poetry—thrives on this highly educated island. Northern Ireland is undergoing an increase in tourism to its remarkable natural scenery and capital city.

Although the chapters in *Let's Go: Ireland* don't mirror these divisions, it helps one's historical understanding to know that Ireland is traditionally divided into four provinces: **Leinster,** the east and southeast; **Munster,** the southwest; **Connacht,** the province west of the river Shannon; and **Ulster,** the north. Six of Ulster's nine counties make up Northern Ireland, part of the United Kingdom. Under the 1998 Northern Ireland Peace Agreement, residents of Northern Ireland may choose whether to individually identify as Irish or British, but word choice can still be sticky. "Ireland" can mean the whole island or the Republic of Ireland, depending on who's listening. "Ulster" is a term used almost exclusively by Protestants in Northern Ireland. It's best to refer to "Northern Ireland" or "the North" and "the Republic" or "the South." "Southern Ireland" is not a viable term. In any event, you shouldn't have to go out of your way in any county to encounter either Ireland's past—its castles, medieval streets, monasteries, legends, language, and music—or its equally exciting present.

■ History

Travel on this island with a strong sense of past will be more rewarding for those who take time to learn its history. *Let's Go* can provide only a very condensed account. Mark Tierney's *Modern Ireland* is a clear and comprehensive narrative covering the period from 1850 to 1968; *The Oxford History of Ireland* is a good source on earlier periods; and R.F. Foster's hefty tome *Modern Ireland: 1600-1972* is authoritative and interesting if you know a little already. For a history of Northern Ireland since Republican independence, see **Northern Ireland,** p. 371.

PRE-CHRISTIAN IRELAND (TO AD 450)

Ireland's first settlers came from Britain in about 7000 BC. The first major civilization was that of the **Neolithic** mound builders. Little is known about these mysterious, industrious, and agrarian people, but ruins of their structures can still be seen. **Dolmens** are T-shaped or table-shaped groups of three or more enormous stones, with one big flat stone as the roof or "tabletop." They might have been used for a number of things, but the best recent guess is that they're a kind of shrine. **Passage graves,** stone-roofed, ornamented, underground hallways, lead past series of rooms containing corpses or cinerary urns. **Stone circles** look like rings of pint-sized gravestones. They mark spots of religious importance, show up on top of passage graves, and sometimes track heavenly paths. Beakers (perhaps for drinking mead) and stone henges (circles) of an astronomical bent also appeared around 2500 BC.

Bronze arrived in Ireland circa 2000 BC, radically changing the island's culture over the next 700 years. The megaliths and henges disappeared, more weapons and fortifications emerged, and a new warrior aristocracy took control. When not busy fighting, the Bronze Age Irish built **ring forts** (walls around villages, made of stone or of earth), *souterrains* (underground chambers, used for storage or for hiding from marauders), and *clocháns* (mortarless beehive-shaped stone huts). The last two centuries of the Bronze Age (900-700 BC) saw a flowering of Irish culture. Ireland in the **Irish Golden Age,** dominated by hierarchical warrior-nobles, held a central position exporting bronze, copper, and gold on Atlantic trade routes stretching from Gibraltar to Sweden. **Celtic** people began arriving in Ireland from the Continent at about 600 BC and continued to arrive for the next 600 years. Complex artwork (later seen in Christian texts like the *Book of Kells*) shows their influence. The heroism prominent in the *Táin* (see **Legends and Folktales,** p. 61) and other Irish epics was inspired by this period.

The Roman armies who conquered England didn't think Ireland worth invading. The society left alone was Celtic, spoke Old Irish, lived in small farming settlements, and organized itself under a loose hierarchy of regional chieftains, who ruled a territory called a *túath,* and provincial kings, who ruled over several *túatha.* The most famous of the chieftains were the **Ulaid of Ulster,** chariot warriors who dominated La Tène culture from their capital near Armagh. These kings organized raids on Britain and established settlements in Scotland and Wales.

EARLY CHRISTIANS AND VIKINGS (450-1200)

A series of hopeful missionaries Christianized Ireland in piecemeal fashion. The foremost of these missionaries, **St. Patrick,** was dragged to the island as a boy by Irish raiders. After seven years of slavery, he escaped to England and returned (without church permission) to do God's work, landing probably in southeast Co. Down in the early 5th century. Although St. Patrick probably covered only the northwestern parts of the island, Armagh churchmen used his legendary status to claim that he had converted the whole island in order to justify their claim to authority of the Irish Church.

> *The Roman armies who conquered England didn't think Ireland worth invading*

At about this time, the mysterious freestanding monuments known as **ogham** stones were inscribed. These property-marking obelisks usually recorded a man's name and that of his father in a non-Latin script made up of dots and slashes. The highest concentration of remains is probably in the Burren, Co. Clare, where the limestone moonscape kept later settlers out (see **The Burren,** p. 273). The most famous sites are the Hill of Tara and the passage graves of Brú na Bóinne in Co. Meath (see **Brú na Bóinne,** p. 134).

Missionaries and monks brought new structures: the short *oratories* gave way to Viking-inspired **round towers,** dozens of which survive. A few now charge admission, but most are just sitting in fields and forests, in various states of disrepair. **High crosses,** or Celtic crosses, have a circle near the top, which made the cross more palatable to sun-worshipping pagans. These stone crucifixes are as tall as or taller than a person and have elaborate carvings on their sides, sometimes illustrating Bible stories or legends of saints.

As barbarians overran the Continent, monks fled to island safety. The enormous **monastic cities** of the 6th to 8th centuries later earned Ireland the name the "island of saints and scholars." From their bases in Armagh, Glendalough, Derry, Kells, Clonmacnoise, and elsewhere, the monastics of the Early Irish Church recorded the old epics, wrote long religious and legal poems in Old Irish and Latin, and illuminated gospels. The 7th century *Book of Durrow,* the earliest surviving illuminated manuscript, and the 8th or 9th century *Book of Kells* are now exhibited at Trinity College (see **Trinity College and Nearby,** p. 100). While not writing, the monks were busy proselytizing. Irish missionaries converted (and reconverted) much of Europe to Christianity, although the Early Irish Church remained decidedly independent of Rome. The monks refused pressures to adopt the Roman calendar and maintained their own method of calculating the date of Easter until 704. Monastic cities allied themselves instead with up-and-coming chieftains; Armagh, an important religious center, owed its prominence in part to the **Uí Néill** (O'Neill) clan, which had gradually spread from Meath into central Ulster.

The **Vikings,** who characteristically raided every coastline in Northern Europe in the 9th and 10th centuries, made no exception for Ireland. Those who tired of pillaging founded larger towns in the South, including Limerick, Waterford, and Dublin. Settled Vikings built Ireland's first castles, allied themselves with local chieftains, injected Scandinavian words into Irish, and left the southeast littered with Viking-derived place names.

The first decade of the new millennium saw the rise of High King **Brian Ború** of the warlike Dál Cais clan of Clare, who challenged the Uí Néill clan for control of Ireland and finally took Armagh in 1002. The Battle of Clontarf in 1014 set Leinstermen and Vikings against Brian Ború's clan. The Dál Cais won, but Brian died in battle, leaving Ireland divided. Brian's successors, including Rory O'Connor and Dermot Mac-Murrough, skirmished over who was the true "High King." Dermot made the mistake of asking English Norman nobles to help him reconquer Leinster. Richard de Clare, known popularly as **Strongbow,** was too willing to help. Strongbow and his Anglo-Normans arrived in 1169 and cut a bloody swath through south Leinster. After Dermot's death in 1171, Strongbow married Dermot's daughter, Aoife, and seemed ready to proclaim an independent Norman kingdom in Ireland, but he then affirmed his loyalty to King Henry II and offered to govern Leinster on England's behalf.

FEUDALISM (1200-1607)

Thus, ironically, began both the English hold over Irish land and the Catholic hold over Irish religion. The following feudal period saw constant power struggles between Gaelic and Norman-descended English lords. The Old English areas, concentrated in Leinster, had more towns and more trade, while Gaelic Connacht and Ulster remained agrarian. England controlled the **Pale,** a fortified domain around Dublin. Old English and Irish fiefdoms used similar castles, ate similar foods, appreciated the same poets, and hired the same mercenaries. This cultural cross-pollination worried the English crown, who sponsored the notorious 1366 **Statutes of Kilkenny.** These decrees banned English colonists (dubbed "more Irish than the Irish themselves") from speaking Irish, wearing Irish styles of dress, or marrying native Irish, and forbade the Irish from entering walled cities (like Derry). The harsh statutes had little effect. Gaelic lords kept taking land from English ones. Feudal skirmishes and economic decline lasted until the rise of the "Geraldine Earls," two branches of the FitzGerald family who fought for control of south Leinster. The victors, the Earls of Kildare, were virtual rulers of Ireland from 1470 to 1534. The 1494 **Poynings' Law,** however, threatened their authority and that of subsequent leaders by declaring that the Irish Parliament could convene only with the consent of England and that any laws passed must meet the approval of the Crown.

The English Crown's control over Ireland increased through the next century. When Henry VIII broke with the Catholic Church to create the Church of England, a newly convened Dublin Parliament passed the 1537 **Irish Supremacy Act,** which declared Henry head of the Protestant Church of Ireland and effectively made the island property of the Crown. The English neither articulated any substantive difference between the two religious outlooks nor attempted to convert the Irish masses, yet the Church of Ireland held a privileged position over Irish Catholicism. The lords of Ireland, both English and Gaelic, however, wished to remain loyal both to Catholicism and to the Crown. **Thomas FitzGerald** of Kildare sent a missive to Henry VIII stating this position. In response, Henry destroyed his power. A FitzGerald uprising in Munster in 1579 planted the idea in English heads that Irish land had to be directly controlled by Protestants if it were to be considered safe and loyal. **Hugh O'Neill,** an Ulster earl, raised an army of thousands in open rebellion in the late 1590s. Gaelic lords supported him, but the Old English lords were divided. The King of Spain promised naval assistance, which arrived in Kinsale Harbour in 1601 and then sat there with Spanish soldiers still on their boats as armies from England demolished O'Neill's forces. His power broken, O'Neill and the rest of the major Gaelic lords fled Ireland in 1607 in what came to be known as the **Flight of the Earls.** The English used their military advantage to take control of the land and to parcel it out to Protestants.

> ## Trinity College
>
> Through the late 16th century, the English toyed with the idea of an Irish university. In 1592, a small group of Dubliners obtained a charter from Queen Elizabeth to found Trinity College. The city granted the new foundation the lands and run-down buildings of a monastery just southeast of the city walls. The late-17th century brought turmoil to its hallowed halls: the Provost fled in 1641, the college had to pawn its plate in 1643, and all fellows and students were expelled in order to turn the college into a barrack for James II's soldiers in 1689.
>
> Trinity was up and running again by the beginning of the 18th century with the construction of the library underway. As the university of the Protestant Ascendancy, Trinity met few disturbances save the small number of boisterous Jacobites who unsuccessfully tried to introduce radical politics into this burgeoning intellectual aristocracy. In 1793, Trinity went avant-garde and admitted Roman Catholic students. By the late 19th century, the tumultuous political climate had finally seeped into the college grounds. The government made numerous attempts to incorporate Trinity into a federated university with several other Irish academic institutions; the college vehemently opposed and ultimately terminated such threats to its independence. In 1904, the university first admitted women, who comprised 16% of the student population only ten years later. World War I and the creation of the Republic left Trinity without resources or strength in a divided Ireland, while newer universities in the U.K. quickly gained prestige. With the help of a long-needed annual state grant finally secured in 1947, however, Trinity has continued to prosper through its fourth century.

PLANTATION AND CROMWELL (1607-1688)

The English project of "planting" Ireland with Protestants and dispossessing Catholics of their land was most successful in Ulster, where Scottish Presbyterian tenants and laborers, themselves displaced by the English, joined the expected mix of adventurers, ne'er-do-wells, and ex-soldiers. King Charles's representative in Ireland, Lord Wentworth, pursued a policy with few supporters outside England by closing off the South to the Scots while confiscating more land than there were Protestant takers. The now landless Irish revolted in Ulster in 1641 under a loose group of Gaelic-Irish leaders soon joined by the next O'Neill generation, **Owen Roe O'Neill,** who had returned from the Continent to lead the insurrection. The Catholic Church backed the rebels, who advanced south and in 1642 formed the **Confederation of Kilkenny,** an uneasy alliance of Church, Irish, and Old English lords. Some English lords considered themselves loyal to the King while rebelling against his treasonous viceroy. The arrival of the English Civil War complicated the tangle of interests, but long negotiations between the Confederation and the King ended with **Oliver Cromwell's** victory in England and his arrival in Ireland at the head of a Puritan army.

Anything Cromwell's army did not occupy it destroyed. Catholics were massacred and whole towns razed as the Confederation melted away. Entire tracts of land were confiscated and given to soldiers and Protestant adventurers. The native Irish landowners could go "to hell or Connacht," the desolate and remote western region. In practice, the richest landowners found ways to stay, while the smaller farmers were displaced. The net result was that by 1660, the vast majority of land was owned, maintained, and policed by imported Protestants. In the 1665 Act of Explanation, Charles II required Cromwellians to relinquish one-third of their land to "innocent papists"; in actuality, Catholics received little compensation.

THE PROTESTANT ASCENDANCY (1688-1801)

Thirty years later, English political disruption again meant Irish bloodshed. Catholic **James II,** driven from England by the "Glorious Revolution" of 1688, came to Ireland with his army, intending to conquer Ireland before Britain. Jacobites (James's supporters) and Williamites (supporters of new Protestant King William III) fought each other in battles that would have far-reaching political and symbolic consequences throughout Ireland. In 1689, James attempted to take the northern city of Derry, where the young band of **Apprentice Boys,** who would become heroes of Northern Protestants, closed the gates at his approach. The **Seige of Derry** lasted 105 days. In 1690, William defeated James at the **Battle of the Boyne,** and James went into exile again. This battle would be lamented by Irish Catholics and celebrated by Northen Protestants, many of whom still march on the politically charged **Orange Day,** named for William of Orange, throughout Northern Ireland. This defeat is depicted on many murals in Belfast. The disastrous Battle of Aughrim brought the war's end in the **Treaty of Limerick,** which ambiguously promised Catholics civil rights that were never delivered. The unenforceable **Penal Laws,** enacted at the turn of the 18th century, attempted to limit Catholics economically and banned the public practice of their religion. At this time, Catholics comprised 90 percent of the island's population.

The newly secure Anglo-Irish elite built their own culture in Dublin and the Pale with political parties, garden parties, talk, and architecture second only to London. The term "Ascendancy" was coined to describe a social elite whose distinction depended upon Anglicanism. Within this exclusive social structure, such thinkers as Bishop George Berkeley and Edmund Burke rose to prominence. **Trinity College** flourished as the quintessential institution of the Ascendancy. Despite their cultural ties, many of these aristocrats felt little political allegiance to England. Jonathan Swift campaigned against dependency upon England, tirelessly pamphleteering on behalf of both the Protestant Church and the rights of the Irish people. Swift was an early proponent of the limited nationalism developed by Irish Parliamentary patriots who wanted an Anglo-Irish state (under the King and excluding Catholics) free from the authority of the English Parliament. Meanwhile, displaced peasants filled Dublin's poorer quarters, creating the horrific slums that led Swift to write "A Modest Proposal" (see **Literature 1600-1880,** p. 62).

The Penal Laws made life difficult for priests but did not prevent the growth of a Catholic merchant class in places like Galway and Tralee. Early in the 18th century, Catholics practiced their religion furtively, using hidden, big, flat rocks, appropriately dubbed **Mass rocks,** when altars were unavailable. Denied official education, Gaelic-Irish teens learned literature and religion in **hedge schools,** hidden assemblies whose teachers were often fugitive priests. The hedge schools later became a powerful symbol of the poor Irish of the 18th century. Typically, landlords were Anglo-Irish Protestants and their tenants Gaelic-Irish Catholics. The cultural divide made brutal rents and eviction policies easier for some landlords to adopt, while secret agrarian societies, like the **Defenders,** formed to defend peasant holdings.

REBELLION, UNION, REACTION (1775-1848)

The American and French Revolutions inspired ideas of independence in small political organizations like the **United Irishmen,** which began as a radical Ulster debating society. When war between England and Napoleon's France seemed likely, the United Irishmen were outlawed and reorganized as a secret society. Their leader, **Theobald Wolfe Tone,** a Protestant, had hoped for a general uprising to create an independent, non-sectarian Ireland. His followers had less abstract ideals, which erupted in a bloody uprising of peasants and priests in May 1798. **Vinegar Hill,** near Enniscorthy in Co. Wexford, saw the rebels' celebrated last stand. A month later, French troops arrived and managed to hold territory there for about a month before meeting utter destruction. French soldiers were held as prisoners of war and shipped home; Irish soldiers were executed.

By relaxing anti-Catholic laws, England had hoped to make Irish society less volatile, but Wexford's rebels scared the British into abolishing Irish "self-government" altogether. The 1801 **Act of Union** abolished the Dublin Parliament and created "The United Kingdom of Great Britain and Ireland," while the Church of Ireland was subsumed by the "United Church of England and Ireland." Wolfe Tone committed suicide in captivity, while other United Irishmen escaped to France, building a secret network that would eventually link up with the Fenians (see below).

The mad gaiety of Dublin vanished. The Anglo-Irish gentry collapsed as agrarian violence escalated, and English and Continental visitors to Ireland were aghast at its rural poverty. Meantime, the Napoleonic Wars raged in Europe, and paranoid generals constructed short, thick, cylindrical structures named **Martello towers** all along the Irish coasts in fear of a Napoleonic assault that never came. The English, upon encountering them on Cape Mortella in Corsica, decided to copy these almost impenetrable towers. (Being British, they felt free to improve on the name.)

Union meant Ireland could now send representatives to the British parliament, and the electoral reforms of the 1810s and 20s lowered the property qualifications to the point where many Irish Catholic small farmers had the vote. They elected Catholic **Daniel O'Connell** to Parliament in 1829, essentially forcing Westminster into repealing the remaining anti-Catholic laws that would have barred him from taking his seat. O'Connell acquired the nickname "The Liberator," and his efforts within Parliament allotted money to improve Irish living conditions, health care, and trade. When unsympathetic Tories took power, O'Connell began to convene huge rallies in Ireland, showing popular support for repealing the Act of Union. Romantic Nationalism, imported from Germany and Italy, pervaded the intellectual air, and some felt O'Connell had not gone far enough. "Young Ireland" poets and journalists like **John Mitchel** (whom Yeats quoted: "Send war in our time, O Lord") wanted independence and would work for it through violence. They tried a revolt in 1848—but much of Ireland was starving and his efforts thus went unnoticed.

Amid this political thought arose unprecedented social reform. The 1830s brought the passage of the Irish Poor Law Act, which established workhouses to provide in-kind services for impoverished citizens. In the mean time, the police force was centralized and professionalized in 1836 under the title Royal Irish Constabulary, which later became the model for the British Empire's colonial police forces.

THE FAMINE (1845-1870)

The only crop capable of providing enough nutrients per acre to support 19th-century Ireland's population was the potato. From 1845 to 1847 a new fungal disease blackened and poisoned increasing numbers of crops. The Great Famine was far harsher than any of the dozens of smaller blights and crop failures that had befallen the island during the earlier 19th century. British authorities often forcibly exchanged what few decent potatoes peasants could find with inedible grain. Those Catholic peasants who accepted British soup in exchange for their conversion to Protestantism earned the disdainful title "Soupers," a family nickname that would last for decades. Murals in Belfast today depict British ships, full of potatoes, heading toward England (see **West Belfast and the Murals,** p. 395). The mercantilist government would not divert crops meant for exports to the starving poor, and this policy was exacerbated by English economists who considered the Famine a "Malthusian apocalypse." Some landlords were known for their efforts to help the displaced famine victims; others were notorious for their cruelty. Famine lasted roughly from 1847 to 1851 and utterly devastated rural Ireland. Of the 1841 population of eight million, an estimated 1.5 to three million people died. Another million emigrated to Liverpool, London, Australia, and America. Depopulation in Connacht in the west was particularly severe, while the number of Dublin poor swelled.

> *Of the 1841 population of eight million, an estimated 1.5 to three million people died*

Two Irish economists, in analyzing the tragedy, made major advances in political economy. **Isaac Butt,** founder of the Irish Home Rule Party (see **Parnell's Cultural Nationalism,** p. 59) argued that it was hypocritical to claim political unity but refuse economic aid. **John Elliot Cairnes** blasted the idea of *laissez faire,* which he claimed was only applicable to those countries whose economic organization and division of land imitated those in England. The remaining Irish peasants completely reorganized. The bottom layer of truly penniless farmers had been eliminated. Men married late, eldest sons inherited whole farms, and unskilled younger sons were as likely as not to leave Ireland. The Encumbered Estates Act began the 50-year process of removing the landlord class. This process was continued by a series of Land Acts and by the Congested Districts Board, which converted Ireland (except for Dublin and northeast Ulster) by 1900 into a nation of conservative, religious, culturally uniform, Catholic smallholders. The widening net of railroads—more extensive than today's— improved rural standards of living.

In 1858, James Stephens, who had previously worked with the Young Ireland movement, founded the Irish Republican Brotherhood (IRB), commonly known as the **Fenians.** The Fenians was a secret society aimed at the violent removal of the British. Fenian violence in 1867 made William Gladstone, among others, notice the Irish discontent, and he became Britain's Prime Minister a year later under the slogan "Justice for Ireland." Justice consisted in disestablishing the minority Protestant Church of Ireland and battling for land reform. Combining agrarian thinkers, Fenians, and Charles Stewart Parnell, the Land League of the 1870s pushed for reforms with O'Connell-style mass meetings.

PARNELL'S CULTURAL NATIONALISM (1870-1914)

Isaac Butt, a leading economist of the time, founded the **Irish Home Rule Party** in 1870. Its several dozen members adopted obstructionist tactics—making long dull speeches, introducing endless amendments, and generally trying to keep the rest of Parliament angry, bored, and ineffective until they saw fit to grant Ireland autonomy. **Charles Stewart Parnell** was a charismatic, Protestant aristocrat with an American mother and a hatred for everything English. Backed by Parnell's invigorated Irish party, Gladstone introduced a Home Rule Bill, which was defeated. Parnell gained more esteem when letters linking him to the **Phoenix Park Murders,** an infamous Fenian crime, turned out to be forgeries. But in 1890 allegations that Parnell was having an affair were proven true: the scandal split the Home Rulers, and all of Ireland, into Parnellites and anti-Parnellites.

While the parliamentary movement split, civil society grew. The Irish Women's Suffrage Federation was established in 1911, following the lead of the British and American suffragette struggles underway. **James Connolly,** who had made a name for himself as the leading proponent of socialism in Ireland, led strikes in Belfast. In Dublin, **James Larkin** spearheaded an enormous general strike in 1913, a short-term defeat that nevertheless established large trade unions in Ireland. Conservatives, attempting to "kill Home Rule by kindness," also pushed social reform. Most important of their efforts was the **Wyndham Land Purchase Act** of 1903, which provided huge incentives for landlord to sell their estates to the government and transferred ownership to the tenants.

Meanwhile, many groups and journals tried to revive or preserve what they took to be essential "Gaelic" culture. The **Gaelic Athletic Association** (see **Sports,** p. 69) worked to replace English sports with hurling, camogie, and Gaelic football, and the **Gaelic League** (see **The Irish Language,** p. 76) spread the use of the Irish language. Through the work of these organizations, "Gaelic" became synonymous with "Catholic." Cultural developments quickly intersected with political movements, which were increasingly causing commotion throughout Ireland. The Fenians actively involved themselves in the Gaelic cultural organizations, seeing them as means to a future mobilization. An unknown named Arthur Griffith, who advocated Irish abstention from British politics, began a tiny movement and little-read newspaper that both went by the catchy name **Sinn Féin** (SHIN FAYN, "Ourselves Alone"). As the Home Rule movement grew, so did resistance to it. Between 1910 and 1913, thousands of Northern Protestants opposing Home Rule joined mass rallies, signed a covenant, and organized into the quasi-military Ulster Volunteer Force (UVF). Nationalists led by Eoin MacNeill in Dublin responded in 1913 by creating the **Irish Volunteers,** which the Fenians correctly saw as a potential revolutionary force.

THE EASTER RISING (1914–1918)

In the summer of 1914, Irish Home Rule seemed imminent and Ulster seemed ready to go up in flames, but neither happened—World War I did. British Prime Minister Henry Asquith passed a Home Rule Bill on the condition that the Irish Volunteer and Home Rule parties would recruit Irishmen for the British army. Asquith followed with a Suspensory Act, which delayed home rule until peace returned to Ulster; meanwhile, 170,000 Irish Volunteers and 600,000 other Irishmen enlisted with the Brits. An 11,000-member armed guard remained in Ireland, led officially by MacNeill, who knew nothing of the revolt that the Fenians were planning. If there was one architect of what followed, it was poet and schoolteacher **Padraig Pearse,** who won his co-conspirators over to an ideology of "blood sacrifice." If, Pearse believed, a small cache of committed men might die publicly and violently as martyrs for Ireland, then the entire nation would mobilize to win its independence.

The Volunteers conducted a series of unarmed maneuvers and parades throughout 1915 and 1916, leaving Dublin Castle convinced of their harmlessness, while the leaders planned a shipment of German arms to be used in a nationwide revolt on Easter Sunday, 1916. But the arms arrived a day too early and were never picked up, and the British captured the man who was to meet the shipment, **Roger Casement,** and hanged him. Yet the leaders still hoped for rebellion. To muster support from the Volunteers by provoking their leader, the Fenians told MacNeill about the arms shipments and showed him proof of Dublin Castle's intention to suppress the Volunteers. Fearing the destruction of the Volunteers, MacNeill gave orders for the Easter Sunday mobilization. On Saturday he learned that the Castle order had been forged and that the arms had been captured, and he inserted in the Sunday papers a plea ordering all Volunteers *not* to mobilize.

MacNeill and most Fenian leaders had been thinking in terms of military success, which at that point was clearly impossible, but the Pearse followers wanted martyrdom. On Sunday the Pearse group met and decided to have the uprising anyway on the following Monday, April 24, although it could be organized only in Dublin. Pearse, James Connolly, and about one thousand others seized the General Post Office on O'Connell St., read aloud a "Proclamation of the Republic of Ireland," and held out for five days of firefights across downtown Dublin. Dubliners initially saw the Easter rebels as criminal annoyances, since their only tangible accomplishment was massive property damage.

The British martial-law administration in Dublin then transformed popular opinion by turning **Kilmainham Gaol** into a center of martyrdom. Over 10 days in May, 15 "ringleaders" received the death sentence, among them Pearse, Pearse's brother (executed primarily for being Pearse's brother), and James Connolly, who was shot while tied to a chair because his wounds prevented him from standing. **Éamon de Valera** was spared because the British wrongly thought him an American citizen. By June the public mood was sympathetic to the martyrs—and increasingly anti-British. In 1917 the Volunteers reorganized under master spy and Fenian bigwig **Michael Collins.** The **Sinn Féin** party, though not involved, was thought to be linked to the Rising and became the political voice of military Nationalism; Collins brought the Volunteers to Sinn Féin, and de Valera became the party president. When in 1918 the British tried to introduce a military draft in Ireland, the public turned overwhelmingly to Sinn Féin, repudiating the nonviolent plans of the Home Rule party.

INDEPENDENCE AND CIVIL WAR (1919–1922)

Extremist Volunteers became known as the **Irish Republican Army (IRA),** which functioned as the military arm of the new Sinn Féin government. The new government fought the **War of Independence** against the British, who reinforced their police with **Black and Tans,** demobilized soldiers whose nickname came from their patched-together uniforms. Both the IRA's guerrillas and the Black and Tans were notorious for committing atrocities. British Prime Minister Lloyd George, supported by U.S. President Woodrow Wilson, passed the **Government of Ireland Act** in 1920, which divided the island into Northern Ireland and Southern Ireland, two partially self-governing areas within the U.K. After the Unionist general elections for Parliament, Lloyd George felt compelled to open negotiations with de Valera, which remained a near-impossible feat when neither side would admit the other's legality. Finally, hurried negotiations produced the **Anglo-Irish Treaty,** which would recognize a 26-county Irish Free State. The treaty also imposed on Irish officials a tortuous oath of allegiance to the King of England but not to the British government. Lloyd George threatened war on Ireland if the treaty were rejected.

The Sinn Féin, the IRA, and the population split on whether to accept the treaty. Collins said yes; de Valera said no. When the representative parliament voted yes, de Valera resigned from presidency and Arthur Griffith assumed the position. The capable Collins government began the business of setting up a nation, with treasury, tax collection, a foreign ministry, and an unarmed police force, the *Garda Siochana.* Some of the IRA, led by **General Rory O'Connor,** opposed the treaty; this faction was also thought to be behind the assassination of Sir Henry Wilson, the newly appointed military advisor to the government of Northern Ireland. These Republicans occupied the Four Courts in Dublin, took a pro-treaty Army general hostage, and were attacked by the Collins's government. Two years of **civil war** followed, tearing up the countryside and dividing the population. The pro-treaty government won, but Griffith died suddenly from the strain of the struggle and Collins was assassinated before the end of 1922. The dwindling minority of anti-treaty IRA officers fled deeper into Munster in the east. Disillusioned by the loss, Sinn Féin denied the legitimacy of the free state government, and party leaders in 1999 still resist referring to the Republic by its official name, calling it instead "the 26-county state" or "the Dublin Government."

For a history of the **Republic of Ireland since 1922,** see p. 72.

■ Literary Traditions

BEFORE 1600: LEGENDS AND FOLKTALES

In early Irish society, language was equal to action. What the bard (directly from the Irish *baird*) sang about battles, valor, and lineage was the only record a chieftain had by which to make decisions. Poetry and politics of the Druidic tradition were so intertwined that the *fili,* trained poets, and *breitheamh* (BREH-huv), judges of the Brehon Laws, were often the same people. The poet-patron relationship was fairly simple and symbiotic—the poet sang long praise poems about his lord and in return received his food and a roof above his head.

Scholars have been arguing for decades about which of Ireland's legends, folktales, and epics record actual events and which ones are just good yarns. The vast repertoire includes fairy tales, war stories, revenge tales, and many tales of cattle raids. (Cattle was the ancient Celtic men's most marketable commodity—slaves and women were valued in cows.) Each story had many authors and was passed down orally through many generations before someone (most likely a medieval monk) wrote it down. The books we have now often compile surviving bits and pieces of different versions. The Christian monks sometimes altered details as they recorded the tales and created tales of historical saints by appropriating stories of pre-Christian heroes or gods. The legends aren't incredibly accurate as a record of historical events, but they do give an exciting picture of ancient Irish patriarchal culture: defensive about property (especially cows), warlike, sport-loving, and heavy-drinking.

The long, famous **Book of Invasions** (*Leabhar Gabhála;* LOWR GA-vah-lah) is a record of the cultures and armies that have invaded Ireland, from Noah's daughter, Cesair, up to the Celts. The tales locate the Irish peoples' ancestry in the Greek islands, where Nemed, a Scythian, became lost at sea after pursuing a mysterious tower of gold that rose out of the waves. After a year and a half of wandering, he and his ships landed in Ireland, until the next wave of settlers arrived...and the next, and the next, in wave upon wave of invasions. Three clans of Nemed's descendants survived, one of which was enslaved in Greece but eventually escaped, returned to Ireland as the **Fir Bolg,** and fought the **Túatha de Danann.** Each of the early waves of invaders had to deal with the fierce and mysterious indigenous people, the Formorians. These stories aren't the oldest Irish legends, but they do claim to have taken place first.

The Túatha de Danann are a race of men somewhere between gods and humans who live underground, emerging occasionally to aid their descendents, fight with the mortals, and seduce (or when all else fails, abduct) mortal beauties. The stories about the Túatha de Danann may have developed to explain the burial mounds left behind by the pre-Celtic Stone Age culture. The earliest tales of the Túatha de Danann describe them as ordinary warriors and chieftains—only when fighting other races do their supernatural powers arise. Poets living in the chieftains' households invented the art of verse satire. These poets, and sometimes ordinary folk, have the power to curse and lay a *geis,* a magic compulsion or prohibition. When the Túatha de Danann retreat to the Other World, leaving Éire to the Celts, the Celtic heroes acquire some of the gods' ways and skills.

Several "cycles," or collections, of tales narrate the entire life story of a hero. One of the largest is the **Ulster Cycle,** the adventures of King Conchobar of Ulster and his clan, the **Ulaid.** His archenemies are Queen Medbh of Connacht and her husband Ailill. Ulster and Connacht are continually raiding each other and exacting revenge. (In reality, the archenemies of the Ulaid were the Laigin of Leinster.) Ulster's champion is **Cú Chulainn** (COO-hullin), the king's nephew, whose adventures begin at the age of five. He was taught by the Amazonian warrior Scathach the arts of war and how to wield the Gae Bolga, the sun-god's destructive spear.

The central tale of the Ulster Cycle is the **Táin bo Cuailnge** (Cattle Raid of Cooley). Queen Medbh decides first to borrow, and then to steal, the most famous bull in the country, the Donn of Cooley. She assembles an army to capture the bull and invades Ulster when all the Ulster warriors are disabled by the curse of Queen Macha. Only the 17-year-old Cú Chulainn is immune. He strikes a deal with the Queen and fights her warriors in single combat one by one for an entire season. He beats them all, but the bull dies of heart failure after being held as a POW.

Other cycles include **Tales of the Traditional Kings** and the **Cycle of Finn, Ossian, and their Companions.** Finn McCool (Fionn MacCumaill) leads a group of heroes that includes his son, Ossian, and his grandson, Oscar. In some stories, he is a king or a giant with supernatural powers and saves Ireland from monsters. In others, he is more or less a mercenary.

Toward the end of the first millennium, the oral tradition of the bards ceded some ground to the monastic penchant for writing it all down. The monastic settlements of pre-Norman Ireland compiled enormous annals of myth, legend, and history. An established pagan tradition and the introduction of Christianity created a tension in Irish literature between recalling old bardic forms and incorporating a new worldview. This tension, it could be argued, exists in Irish literature to this day and is expressed fully in Sweeney Astray, the story of a pagan king who turns into a bird after being cursed by a monk.

Literati have periodically compiled Ireland's **folktales.** Some stories involve the *sí* (SHEE; sometimes spelled *side* or *sidhe*), who are residents of the Other World underground or undersea. They were sometimes believed to be members of the biblical tribe of Dan or the disempowered remnants of the Túatha de Danann. **Leprechauns** are a late, degenerate version of the *sí*. For more myths and tales, try *Folktales of Ireland,* edited by Sean O'Sullivan; Yeats's *Fairy and Folk Tales of Ireland; Ancient Irish Tales,* edited by Cross and Slover; or *The Irish Literary Tradition,* by J.E.C. Williams and P.K. Ford.

1600-1880

After the Battle of Kinsale in 1601 (see p. 55), a group of Irish writers predicted an imminent collapse of Irish language and culture. A majority of the works written in Irish at this time lament the state of Ireland and draw heavily on the trope of Ireland as a captive woman. **Daíbhí Ó Bruadhair's** "The Shipwreck" laments the Treaty of

Limerick (see p. 56). Ireland in the early 1700s had enough bilingual readers to support works like **Seán Ó Neachtain's** *The Story of Eamon Cleary*, in which unusual, often punning effects depended on a mixture of English and Irish.

Jonathan Swift (1667-1745), for decades the Dean of St. Patrick's Cathedral in Dublin, towered above his Anglo-Irish contemporaries with his mix of moral indignation, bitterness, and wit. Besides his masterpiece, *Gulliver's Travels,* Swift wrote political pamphlets and essays decrying English exploitation while defending the Protestant Church of Ireland. "A Modest Proposal" satirically suggests that the overpopulated and hungry native Irish sell their children as food. After his death, Swift's works dominated the Irish literary scene for the second half of the 18th century.

The Act of Union (1801) was a death knell for Irish writing, since the Anglo-Irish gentry could no longer afford to support the arts. Still, **Maria Edgeworth** (1768-1849) achieved Irish literary greatness as the first writer to deal with specifically Irish themes. Her most famous and lasting work, *Castle Rackrent,* published anonymously in 1800, deals with the responsibilities of landowners to their tenants. Along with Edgeworth, Gerald Griffin, John Banim, and William Carleton (who was later praised by J.M. Synge as the father of modern Irish literature) wrote still-read novels about the gentry and peasantry that attempt to define the nature of rural Irish society. Many of these books depict peasants plotting against their selfish and rich Irish masters. Almost as soon as these novelists died, however, their works were rejected by the **Young Ireland** movement, which decided that these writers had yielded, both in language and in form, to the demands of English writers and critics. They saw the authors as perpetuating a false stereotype of Irish peasants.

Maria Edgeworth achieved Irish literary greatness as the first writer to deal with specifically Irish themes

The late 19th century saw the removal of a number of talented authors to England. Many emigrated because it was easier to make a living by writing in London. Dublin-born **Oscar Wilde** (1856-1900) moved to London and set up as a cultivated aesthete to write one novel and many sparklingly witty plays, including *The Importance of Being Earnest.* While his work usually satirized society and propriety to a degree, he personally challenged Irish clichés and Victorian determinism by perfecting a stylish demeanor more English than the English themselves. Prolific playwright **George Bernard Shaw** (1856-1950) was also born in Dublin but moved to London in 1876, where he became an active socialist. *John Bull's Other Island* depicts the increasing hardships of the Irish peasant laborer. Shaw himself identified much of his writing as Irish, in form if not always in content: "When I say I am an Irishman I mean that my language is the English of Swift and not the unspeakable drivel of the mid-19th century newspapers." Shaw won the Nobel Prize for Literature in 1925 for a body of work that includes *Arms and the Man, Candida, Man and Superman,* and *Pygmalion.*

1880-1939

Following on the heels of these literary movements, a vigorous and enduring effort known today as the **Irish Literary Revival** took over the scene. For almost a century, Irish writers' central concern had been a reaction, either cultural or political, against England. The task of literature was now to discover the real Ireland, whether Gaelic or Anglicized (or both). Interest in the Irish language suddenly revived. **Peig Sayers's** *Peig,* a mournful book about a girl growing up on the Blaskets, was written during the revival and is still read in high schools today. This memoir, like others, mourns the decline of Gaelic culture and language; unlike others, Sayers's can be read as a protofeminist work.

The Irish Literary Revival began with attempts to record peasant stories through which a literary cache hoped to create a distinctively Irish literature in English. The writers of the Revival considered their own works to be chapters in a book of Irish identity. Affected by the revivalists and the Sligo of his youth, the early poems of **William Butler Yeats** (1865-1939) create a dreamily rural Ireland of loss, longing, and legend. His early work, from *Crossways* (1889) to *In the Seven Woods* (1904), won Yeats worldwide fame. In 1923, he became the first Irishman to win the Nobel Prize.

The turbulence of 1914, 1916, and after enabled Yeats to recreate himself as a poet of difficulty, power, and violence (see p. 60). "Easter 1916" described the sudden transformation that the Easter rebels brought to the Irish national self-image: "All changed, changed utterly / A terrible beauty is born." Yeats later bought and renovated a stone tower, Thoor Ballylee (see p. 277). The tower became a symbol in an idiosyncratic and mystical system that appears in his last two decades of poems. From *The Tower* (1928) to the posthumous *Last Poems* (1939) Yeats was at his peak of verbal invention. Yeats's lifelong friend and colleague, **Lady Augusta Gregory** (1852-1932), wrote 40 plays as well as a number of translations, poems, and essays. She began her career by collecting the folktales and legends of Galway's poor residents and later discovered her own skill as a writer of dialogue, creating mainly comedic plays with a staunch nationalism.

The **Abbey Theatre Movement,** spearheaded by Yeats and Lady Gregory, aimed "to build up a Celtic and Irish school of dramatic literature." But conflict almost immediately arose between various contributors. Was this new body of drama to be written in verse or prose, in the realistic or the fantastic and heroic mode? In theory, the plays would be written in Irish, but in practice they needed to be written in English. A sort of compromise was found in the work of **John Millington Synge** (1871-1909) who wrote English plays that were perfectly Irish in essence. A multi-faceted man who "wished to be at once Shakespeare, Beethoven, and Darwin," he spent much of his early years traveling and living in Paris. During one of his many stays in Ireland, Synge met Yeats, who advised that he look for inspiration on the Aran Islands. This advice, which Synge followed in 1898, led him to write *The Aran Islands,* a documentary of life on the islands (see p. 278). His experiences also gave him the subject matter for writing his black comedy *The Playboy of the Western World,* which destroys the pastoral myth about Irish peasantry and humorously portrays a rural society divided into classes. The play's first production instigated riots.

James Joyce brought a stylistic revolution to Irish literature

Sean O'Casey (1880-1964) also caused rioting in 1926 at the Abbey Theatre with *The Plough and Star,* which depicted the Easter Rebellion without mythologizing its leaders. His portrayal of urban life, however, pleased Dublin's emerging middle class. Meanwhile, poets tried their hand at various languages and forms, but none seemed totally suitable for the uniquely Irish dilemma between Irish and English

James Joyce (1882-1941), an integral force in Modernism, brought a stylistic revolution to Irish literature. This most famous of Irish authors was born and educated in Dublin, but spent much of his time after 1904 on the continent. One of his earlier and most autobiographical works, *A Portrait of the Artist as a Young Man,* remains an example of an innovative stream-of-consciousness piece. *Dubliners,* a collection of linked short stories that result in a novelesque work, is his most accessible writing. In contrast to most urban literature, most of the stories describe movement out of the city as liberating. *Ulysses,* Joyce's revolutionary novel, minutely chronicles one day in the life of the antihero, Leopold Bloom, a middle-class Jewish man living his life in a stagnating Dublin. The novel's structure follows that of Homer's *Odyssey*—hence the title. It was first published in serial form in a small American magazine in 1918 and banned for obscenity by a U.S. Court in 1920. In 1922, Sylvia Beach's Paris-based Shakespeare and Co. published the first full edition. Joyce's last book, *Finnegans Wake,* is so dependent on allusions and puns that some people find it unreadable. Those who can make sense of it often see it as his masterpiece.

After the heroism of the Civil War and Republicanism, the Republic of Ireland had suddenly become conservative. In this atmosphere, the Irish Ireland movement, provincial and Catholic in its beliefs, brought about the **Censorship of Publications Act** in 1929. This act severely restricted the development of Irish literature. In the journal which he edited, the poet **AE** fought against such repression and tried to retain pre-Civil War idealism. He envisioned a broad cultural synthesis that would include various cultures and religions, not just those that Ireland's new government accepted.

Nobel Prize winner **Samuel Beckett** (1906-89) is considered the last product of Irish Modernism, even though he wrote most of his work in French and was more influential outside Ireland. A Trinity graduate who fled for Paris and never came back, he told his family that he'd rather live in a France at war than an Ireland at peace. His three novels (*Molloy, Malone Dies,* and *The Unnameable*), world-famous plays (*Waiting for Godot, Endgame),* and bleak prose poems convey a deathly pessimism about language, society, and life. Although Beckett denounced Ireland in general and those Irish contemporaries who based their works on the Gaelic or Yeatsian traditions in particular, some critics still read his recurring character, the tramp, as a representative of the rootless Anglo-Irish middle class.

Northern Protestant poet **Louis MacNeice** (1907-63) infused his lyric poems with a Modernist concern for struggle and social upheaval, but he took no part in the sectarian politics. His "Valediction" masterfully attacks an idealized Ireland. **Patrick Kavanaugh** (1906-67) also debunked a mythical Ireland in such poems as "The Great Hunger" (1945), which was banned for its obscenities, prompting the Irish police to visit Kavanaugh's house and seize the manuscript. Censorship remained an overwhelming force through most of this century, banning writers from Edna O'Brien to F. Scott Fitzgerald. Should a citizen's complaint prove a book to be indecent, obscene, or advocating unnatural forms of birth control, the censorship board would outlaw the book indefinitely. Even classic Irish language works came under scrutiny, although *Ulysses* had escaped attack in the Republic. While the laws have been repealed, some of the banned books are still not found on the shelves.

In the 1940s, the short story was becoming a popular, successful, and sophisticated art form in Ireland. These stories frequently took the common lives of Irish people as their theme, depicting individual liberty and energy as victims of oppressive provincialism. **Flann O'Brien** (1912-66) let loose an unrestricted literary inventiveness that earned him a long-lasting international reputation. Unlike other writers of the time, he set almost all of his work in Dublin. O'Brien tried to provide a comic answer to Joyce and to set himself in opposition to a cultural and linguistic lethargy.

After 1950, Irish poetry suddenly began to flourish again. This movement involved an increased contact with the continent; playwright **Brendan Behan** and poet **John Montague,** for example, both went to Paris. Living in the backwash of the Revival and the Civil War, these new Irish poets questioned their cultural inheritance, finding a new version of Ireland that was a parody of the old one.

The struggle to bridge the gap between Gaelic and Anglo-Irish themes and languages continued. In an effort to strengthen the Gaelic traditions, authors revived Irish-language poetry. **Michael Hartnett** began to write solely in Irish. **Nuala ní Dhomhnaill** is a living poet whose public readings are generally bilingual. In contrast to the

---

Behan Alive

Northern Catholic playwright Brendan Behan was born in 1923 and, at the age of 16, was arrested in Liverpool for carrying explosives for the IRA. He was sentenced to Borstal (the juvenile prison) for 18 months, an experience that provided the basis for his 1958 novel *Borstal Boy.* After his release, he returned to the IRA; four years later he was arrested again for shooting a policeman. A tiny 1956 Dublin production of his play, *The Quare Fellow,* brought him instant acclaim, and a production in London soon thereafter brought him critical success. In addition to his plays, he often published stories in the *Irish Times* and the *Irish Press.* In the late 50s he moved to Paris, where he spent his time writing pornography and drinking heavily. He developed a reputation for his drunken performances at productions of his own plays. While Behan was in New York, comedian Jackie Gleason became his drinking buddy. Behan passed away in 1964. In early 1996, rumor had it that director Jim Sheridan was making a movie about Behan called *Bells of Hell.* Sean Penn was to play Behan but supposedly walked out of the Dublin rehearsals before shooting began.

pessimism non-speakers associate with the Irish language, her work brings refrigerators, feminism, and smart bombs into proximity with the *sí*. The younger poet **Biddy Jenkinson** refuses to authorize any translation of her work into English, although it has been translated into French. The preeminent Irish-language novel is **Maírtín Ó Cadhain's** *Cré na Cille* (Churchyard Clay), a dialogue among corpses in a graveyard.

Others tried to incorporate the English modes into the Irish tradition. **Derek Mahon** saw the poet as anthropologist rather than student of Irish inheritance or of Republicanism. He tried to focus on the common elements that people of all cultures share. Although some poets are directly political and almost propagandistic, much of contemporary poetry is intensely private. Most poets treat the political issue from a distant, mundane, every-day perspective. Contemporary poet **Frank Ornsby** writes poetry devoid of political conflict that celebrates the rituals of domestic life.

Born in rural Co. Derry, **Seamus Heaney,** who won the Nobel Prize for Literature in 1995, is the most prominent living Irish poet. Though concentrating on bogs and earth, Heaney writes in an anti-pastoral mode. His fourth book, *North* (1975), tackles the Troubles head-on. He was part of the **Field Day movement,** led by Derry poet and critic **Seamus Deane,** which produced what was billed as the definitive anthology of Irish writing, although it's come under heavy fire for its relative lack of women writers. One of Heaney's contemporaries, who also writes in a non-political vein, is **Paul Muldoon,** whose tools are a corrosive self-skepticism and an ear for weird rhymes. **Eavan Boland,** a poet, and **Medbh McGuckian,** a novelist, are two of the few modern Irish writers who have attempted to capture the experience of middle-class Irish women.

The Field Day Movement also gave its name to a successful theater company. Native playwrights include politically conscious **Frank McGuinness** and **Brian Friel,** whose *Dancing at Lughnasa* was a Broadway hit. Important critics and essayists include **Conor Cruise O'Brien,** a former diplomat who writes about history, literature, politics—hell, everything; **Denis Donoghue,** whose *We Irish* is a vigorous, skeptical lit-crit grab-bag; and the provocative **Declan Kiberd,** whose Ireland is a postcolonial society more like India than like England.

Stimulated by Flann O'Brien, the Irish novel developed. **Brian Moore's** *The Emperor of Ice Cream* (1965) is a coming-of-age story set in wartime Belfast. **Roddy Doyle** wrote the well-known Barrytown Trilogy (see **Film,** p. 68) as well as the acclaimed *The Woman Who Walked Into Doors* (1996). Doyle won the Booker Prize in 1994 for *Paddy Clarke Ha Ha Ha.* **Frank McCourt,** who was born in New York but grew up in the slums of Limerick, won the Pulitzer Prize for his 1996 memoir *Angela's Ashes.* His brother **Malachy McCourt** recently published his own best-selling memoir, *A Monk Swimming.*

■ Music

TRADITIONAL AND FOLK MUSIC

Irish traditional music is alive and well, as is Irish folk music, but the two can mean different things. "Folk music" often means singing with acoustic guitar accompaniment, whether it's Irish (the Clancy Brothers, Christy Moore, Luka Bloom) or not (Joni Mitchell). "Traditional music" or "trad," on the other hand, is the centuries-old array of dance rhythms, cyclic melodies, and embellishments that has been passed down through generations of traditional musicians. It can be written down, but that's not its primary means of transmission. Indeed, a traditional musician's training consists largely of listening to and imitating others. The tunes and forms (hornpipe, reel, etc.) are the skeletons around which the players in a trad session build the music. The same tune will produce a different result every session.

Irish traditional music is mainly encountered in two forms: impromptu evening pub sessions and recordings, which are becoming more numerous. Well-known recording artists include **Altan, De Danann,** and the **Chieftains.** Trad music is also, though rarely, performed at concerts. *Let's Go* lists many pubs with regular trad sessions, but you'll find the best music by asking local trad enthusiasts. Pubs in Cos. Clare, Kerry, Galway, and Sligo are especially strong. If you want a guarantee that you'll hear lots of traditional music, find a *fleadh* (FLAH), a big gathering of trad musicians whose officially scheduled sessions often spill over into nearby pubs. **Comhaltas Ceoltóirí Éireann,** the national traditional music association, organizes *fleadhs.* Write or call them at 32 Belgrave Sq., Monkstown, Co. Dublin (tel. (01) 280 0295).

For centuries the most common way to "listen" to trad music was to dance to it, but spontaneous traditional dancing is fading fast, replaced by formal, rigid competitions where traditional dancers are graded, like ballroom dancers. *Céilís,* where attendants participate in traditional Irish set-dancing, do still take place occasionally in many Irish towns, but they are planned in advance. The world-sweeping spectacles of *Riverdance* and *Lord of the Dance* offer loose (some would say awful) interpretations of Irish dance.

To play trad well requires tremendous practice and skill and the techniques have little in common with those of European classical music; it's often said that training in one is an impediment to playing the other. The instruments with which Irish trad music is most frequently played are the fiddle, the simple flute, the concertina or hand-held accordion, the tin whistle, and the *uilleann* pipes (elbow pipes). These pipes are similar to bagpipes but are pumped with a bellows held under the arm and are more melodic than the Scottish instrument. The harp, Ireland's national symbol, is rarely encountered in live trad music now but is frequently heard in recordings. The *bodhrán* (BOUR-ohn), a hand-held drum, wasn't seen as a legitimate instrument until the 60s, when the influential **Sean Ó Riada** of the Chieftains introduced it in an effort to drive rock and jazz drumming out. Today, the *bodhrán* has skillful specialists. It is played either with both ends of a stick or with the bare hand. To observers it looks easy, but playing this drum well takes practice and patience.

Purists get in heated arguments about what constitutes "traditional" singing. A style of unaccompanied vocals called *sean-nós* ("old-time") is more talked about than heard, although everyone says it sounds great. This style of nasal singing descends from the ancient practice of keening. It requires the vocalist to sing each verse of a song differently, either by using embellishments or varied techniques or different sounds. Sessions in pubs will sometimes alternate fast-paced traditional instrumental music with guitar- or mandolin-accompanied folk songs.

ROCK, RAP, POP, AND PUNK

In Ireland there is surprisingly little distinction between music types—above all a fine musician is a fine musician who uses material from a variety of sources. This crosspollination produces great live music and a number of successful musicians who draw on traditional elements. **John McCormack** of Athlone is considered one of the finest tenors of the early 20th century. While he was known internationally for opera, he endeared audiences to the Irish folk songs he invariably included in his recitals. Chief among this group, the inspiring and hugely popular **Christy Moore** has been called the Bob Dylan of Ireland. The ballads and anthems that Moore made popular now form something of a pub-singalong canon—hardly a late-night session goes by without someone's moving rendition of "Ride On," "City of Chicago," or the lament "Irish Ways and Irish Laws." Other popular groups include Moore's old bands, Moving Hearts and Planxty.

This lack of distinction between different genres has had mixed results. **Van Morrison's** inspirations included American soul and blues. Submerging them into Celtic "soul," he managed to make them his own. Brian Kennedy, a former backup singer for Morrison, is becoming increasingly popular in Ireland. **Horslips** became hugely popular in the 70s by trying to merge trad and rock forms but wound up shuffling uneasily between the two. **Thin Lizzy** tried to Gaelicize early heavy metal, while a succession of groups, like Clannad, started out trad and slowly became new age rockers. **Enya** used Irish lyricism and electronics to create a style of pervasive tunes you hear before Aer Lingus in-flight movies. Watercress and the Strawmen live life on the edge of the rock/trad duality. Maybe the best hybridizers were the **Pogues,** London-based Irishmen whose famously drunken, punk-damaged folk songs won a wide international audience. New York-based Irish emigrés Black 47 tried for Poguish success by fusing trad with rap to middling reviews. **The House of Pain** also incorporated Gaelic elements in a rap context, achieving some mainstream success. More recently, the **Afro-Celt Sound System** have achieved popular and critical success with their fusion of traditional Celtic and African sounds with manic rhythms of drum and bass.

The worldwide punk rock explosion, which began in the late 1970s, had brilliant effects in Belfast, where **Stiff Little Fingers** spat forth three years of excellent anthems. Most Northern punks rebelled against their over-serious parents by emphasizing the fun part of rock and roll. Through their songs, they tried to create the depoliticized youth culture that had existed in England and America since the 50s. Starjets, Rudi, Protex, Big Self, and the silly Radio Stars emphasized this approach in Belfast, but its most successful advocates were Derry's **Undertones,** which eventually evolved into the garage rock of That Petrol Emotion. With their album *1977*, the young but promising **Ash** heralded a 90s revival of the Belfast punk aesthetic.

Punk was slower to happen in Dublin, although the Boomtown Rats (fronted by future Live Aid guy Bob Geldof) tried. Slightly afterwards, the **Virgin Prunes** shocked Dublin with agitprop and goth-rock. The frontman for the band, Gavin Friday, was a good friend of the modestly named Bono, singer for Ireland's biggest rock export, **U2.** From the adrenaline-soaked promise of the 1980 *Boy,* the band slowly ascended into the rock stratosphere, culminating in world-wide fame with *The Joshua Tree.* The band found new vitality in *Achtung Baby* and *Pop,* and while fans wondered if the band had sold out or was only pretending to, the music spoke for itself. The smartest Irish popsters of the 80s, bands like the Slowest Clock and the folky Stars of Heaven, went nowhere commercially, while plenty of U2-derived bands have raced up and down British and American charts on the basis of their perceived Celtic aura. Distortionists **My Bloody Valentine** started in Ireland, but like the Pogues, John Lydon, and U2, they moved to London before becoming significant. **Sinéad O'Connor** has garnered mixed acclaim, spite, and indifference for her focus on Irish social issues. The lowercase **cranberries** from Limerick and, more recently, the Coors have cornered the U.S. cheese market; back in Ireland, country singer **Daniel O'Donnell** makes the lasses swoon and throw things. Meanwhile, the rock press has christened Cork a hot spot; its flagship bands, **Nomos, the Young Offenders,** and **Hyperborea** are not exactly revolutionary, but a hubbub of new 'zines and clubs in Cork, Dublin, and the Southeast demonstrates the vibrance of the Irish music scene.

■ Media and Popular Culture

FILM

Alfred Hitchcock filmed O'Casey's *Juno and the Paycock* with the Abbey Theatre Players in 1930, but Hollywood didn't truly discover Ireland until John Wayne's 1952 film *The Quiet Man* gave millions their first view of the country's beauty. In the years since, numerous movies set elsewhere have been filmed in Ireland; the expanses of green, appealing small towns, and comparatively low labor costs are a filmmaker's dream. American director John Huston, who lived in Ireland, made numerous films there, including his last film, *The Dead* (1987), based on Joyce's story in *Dubliners*.

In the last five-odd years, however, the Irish government has begun to encourage a truly Irish film industry. An excellent art cinema has opened in Dublin, and there's an office two blocks away to encourage budding moviemakers. Based on the Barrytown Trilogy by Roddy Doyle, *The Commitments, The Snapper,* and *The Van* followed youths from the depressed North Side of Dublin as they variously form a band, have a kid, and sell evil-looking fish and chips. **Neil Jordan,** who lives near Dublin, has become a much sought-after director thanks to the success of *The Crying Game* and *Michael Collins.* **Liam Neeson**, the star of the latter, has emerged as one of the world's great actors, winning an Academy Award for *Schindler's List* in 1993. Directors **Jim Sheridan** and **Terry George** have focused on the humanity brought out by the Troubles in 1993's *In the Name of the Father*. Independent film flourishes in Ireland; a good example is Neil Jordan and Patrick McCabe's *The Butcher Boy* (1998), which portrays the fantasy world of a young boy in the 1960s dealing with his father's alcoholism.

Ireland has an increasing number of film festivals. The **Dublin Lesbian and Gay Film Festival,** during the last week of July, will be held for the seventh year in 1999. Limerick, Galway, Foyle, Cork, and Dublin also host film festivals. The **ACCBank Dublin Film Festival** is the largest, showing more than two hundred films in 1998. Dublin also hosts the **Junior Dublin Film Festival,** showing the world's best children's films.

NEWSPAPERS AND OTHER MEDIA

The Republic and Northern Ireland together support eight national **dailies** with a combined circulation of around 1.5 million. The largest of these papers in the Republic are the *Irish Independent* and the *Irish Times* (http://www.irish-times.com). The *Independent* tends to be conservative; the *Times* is more liberal. *The Herald* is an evening daily that hovers somewhere in the middle. In the North, the *Belfast Newsletter* and the *Belfast Telegraph* (http://www.belfasttelegraph.co.uk) maintain large readerships. There are five or so island-wide Sunday papers. The *Sunday Business Post* gives the latest on the corporate world. **Tabloids** like the *Daily Mirror,* the *Irish Sun,* the *Irish Star,* and the *Sporting News* offer low-level coverage with an emphasis on stars, scandals, and sports, and the occasional topless picture. A large number of regional papers offer more in-depth local news; the largest is the Cork *Examiner*.

BBC brought radio to the Irish island when it established a station in Belfast in 1924; two years later, the Irish Free State started the radio station 2RN in Dublin. Television struck when BBC began TV broadcasts from Belfast in 1953. Ulster Television, the island's first independent channel, was established in 1959. In 1961, the Republic's national radio service made its first television broadcast, renaming itself **Radio Telefís Éireann (RTE).** Most of the island now has cable service with access to the BBC and other independent British channels. Satellite stations are available via cable in Dublin and Cork. As of 1995, televisions were in 99% of Irish households, while only 74% had a telephone.

As of 1995, televisions were in 99% of Irish households

■ Sports

Ireland is mad for two sports: hurling and Gaelic football. For many Irish, these games are the reason that spring changes into summer. Beer bellies are burned off over the last mile or two to the stadium and welded back on again after the game, win or lose. Many a day would be wasted trying to find a farmer, business exec, or sheep unaware of his or her county's progress. Attending a pub the day of that county's game will leave you happy, deaf, drunk, and counting down the days to the next round.

Most traditional Irish sports are modern developments of contests fought between whole clans or parishes across expanses of countryside. In 1884, the **Gaelic Athletic Association (GAA)** was established to promote hurling, Gaelic football, and all Irish and non-British activity. The organization's first patron was Archbishop Croke of Cashel and Emly, after whom Croke Park, the biggest Gaelic games stadium in Ireland, was named. The GAA divided the island on a club-county-province level, in which the club teams organized according to parish lines. Arranged according to the four provinces Connacht, Munster, Leinster, and Ulster, all 32 counties of the island compete in the knockout rounds of the two sports' "All Ireland" Championships, but only two make it to either final in September. Despite the fervent nationalism of its beginnings, the GAA has always included the Northern Ireland teams in these leagues, another testament to the multiple personalities of this divided island. Sectarian politics plague the GAA again, now leaving its fate uncertain. In June of 1998, the

GAA refused to delete their Rule 21, which prohibits members of the RUC from join-ing the association and participating in events. This restriction violates the Equal Sta-tus Bill, under which any organization guilty of discrimination, in this case on the basis of religion, would be ineligible for receiving public funding. In addition to losing access to public recreation facilities and their license to sell beer during games, the GAA would lose its £20 million grant for redeveloping Croke Park.

According to the GAA, "played well, **Gaelic football** is a fast, skillful game striking to the eye. Played badly, it is an unimpressive spectacle of dragging and pulling!" Gaelic football seems like a cross between soccer and rugby, although it predates both of them. The ball is shorter and fatter than a rugby ball, and it can be dribbled, punched, or kicked but not thrown. Teams of 15 each play two 30-minute periods. At each end of the field is a set of goalposts, and below the crossbar there is a net resem-bling a soccer net. One point is scored for putting the goal over the crossbar between the posts, three for netting it.

As fans like to say, if football is a game, then **hurling** is an art. This fast and danger-ous-looking game was first played in the 13th century. Perhaps best imagined as a blend of lacrosse and field hockey, the game is named after the stick with which it is played, called a "hurley," or *caman.* The hurley—like a hockey stick with a shorter and wider blade—is used to hit the ball along the ground or overhead. Sides of 15 players each try to score a point by hitting the ball over the eight-foot-high crossbar of the goalposts. A goal is worth three points and is scored by hitting the ball under the crossbar. The ball, or *sliothar,* is leather-covered and can be caught for hitting but not thrown. The ball may be carried or juggled along on the stick.

Rugby, golf, and soccer are also huge sports in both the Republic and Northern Ire-land. In 1990, Ireland's soccer team reached the quarter-finals in the World Cup for the first time ever. Horseracing maintains a devoted following in the Republic, and watersports like surfing and sailing are popular hobbies, particularly along the West-ern coast. Swimming became a source of Irish pride in 1996 when Irish swimmer Michelle Smith won three gold medals and one bronze at the Summer Olympics.

■ Food and Drink

TASTY TREATS

Food in Ireland can be fairly expensive, especially in restaurants. The basics—and that's what you'll get—are simple and filling. "Take-aways" (take-out) and "chippers" (fish 'n' chips shops) are quick, greasy, and very popular. At chippers, "fish" is a whitefish, usually cod, and chips are served with salt and vinegar—ketchup some-times costs extra. For variation, try chips with gravy, potato cakes (flat pancakes made of potato flakes), or the infamous spiceburger (a fried patty of spiced bread-crumbs). Most pubs serve food as well as drink, and **pub grub** is a good option for a quick and inexpensive meal. Typical pub grub includes Irish stew (meat, potatoes, carrots, and onions), burgers, soup, and sandwiches. *Colcannon* (a potato, onion, and cabbage dish), "ploughman's lunch," and Irish stew are essential Irish dishes.

Loud and long will the Irish bards sing the praises of the Clonakilty man who first concocted **black pudding,** or **blood pudding.** This delicacy was invented during a shortage of meat to try and make the most of the bits of the pig not usually eaten. A pinnacle of world culinary achievement, black pudding is, as one local butcher put it, "some pork, a good deal of blood, and grains and things—all wrapped up in a tube." White pudding is a similar dish but contains milk instead of blood. **Irish breakfasts,** often served all day, include eggs, sausage, white or black pudding, cereal, rashers (a salty pork similar to Canadian bacon), and fried tomato and toast. Another staple of the Irish diet is **soda bread,** a crispy, tasty cousin of the English muffin, especially yummy when fried. Seafood can be a real bargain in smaller towns, and mussels and oysters are often pictured on postcards with Guinness as "Irish breakfast." In addition to the widespread fried fish, smoked mackerel is splendid year-round and Atlantic salmon is freshest around July. Regional specialties include **crubeen** (tasty pigs' feet) in Cork, **coddle** (boiled sausages and bacon with potatoes) in Dublin, and **blaa** (sausage rolls) in Waterford. Wexford berries in the Southeast are luscious May through July. **Tea** accompanies most meals, but it has come to signify more than just that which quenches thirst or politely washes down unwanted cabbage. If the Irish drink Guinness for strength, they drink tea for everything else.

In Northern Ireland, you'll find similar culinary offerings, along with some regional specialties. Meal portions tend to be large, fried, and canopied with potatoes. A hearty Ulster Fry (fried eggs, fried bacon, fried sausage, fried potato bread, and fried tomatoes) at breakfast will tide you over until the main midday meal. Tea is often substituted for dinner around 6pm. Every town has a few enticing bakeries selling pasties (PASS-tees, meat or vegetable wrapped in a pastry) and traditional soda bread.

PUBS AND PINTS

A study released in the summer of 1998 found that Irish students spend roughly £80 a month on drinks, which is no wonder considering the centrality of pubs in Irish culture. More so in the Republic than in the North, the pub is, in a sense, the living room of the Irish household. Locals of all ages from every social milieu head to the public house for conversation, food, singing and dancing, and lively **craic** (crack), an Irish word meaning "a good time." Although the clientele of the average public house is predominantly male, women can feel comfortable here, especially on the weekends in urban areas when students swarm the town. People aren't normally looking for much other than communal talk and drink. You might have your ears talked off, however, especially by amateur *seanachaí* (SHAN-ukh-ee), traveling storytellers. In the evening, some pubs host traditional music. Local and traveling musicians, toting fiddles, guitars, *bodhráns* (a shallow, one-sided drum), and whistles, drop in around 9:30pm to start impromptu trad sessions.

Pubs in the Republic are generally open Monday to Saturday from 10:30am to 11:30pm (11pm in winter) and Sunday from 12:30 to 2pm and 4 to 11pm (closed 2-4pm due to the Holy hour). Some pubs have been granted special "early" licenses, which allow them to open at 7:30am and require an act of Parliament to revoke. Pubs almost never charge a cover price or require a drink minimum. Pubs in the North tend to be open Monday to Saturday from 11:30am to 11pm, and Sunday from 12:30 to 2:30pm and 7 to 10pm. Some pubs close for a few hours on weekday afternoons as well, particularly in rural areas. Pub lunches are usually served from Monday to Saturday, 12:30 to 2:30pm, while soup, soda bread, and sandwiches are served all day. Children are often not allowed in pubs after 7pm. The legal drinking age in Ireland and Northern Ireland is 18.

Beer is the default drink in Irish pubs. Cocktails are an oddity found mainly in American-style bars and discos, and most pubs stock only a few bottles of wine. Beer comes in two basic varieties, **lagers** (blond, fizzy brews served cold, a bit weaker than ales or stouts) and **ales** (slightly darker, more bitter, and sometimes served a bit warmer than lagers). **Stout,** a type of ale, is thick, dark-ruby colored, and made from roasted barley to impart an almost chocolaty flavor. **Guinness** stout inspires a reverence otherwise reserved for the Holy Trinity. Known variously as "the dark stuff," "the blonde in the black skirt," or simply "I'll have a pint, please," it's a rich, dark brew with a head thick enough to stand a match in. It's also far better in *Guinness!* Ireland than anywhere else. For a sweeter taste, try it with blackcurrant or cider. **Murphy's** is a similar, slightly sweeter stout brewed in Cork, as is **Beamish,** a tasty "economy" stout. Stout takes a while to pour properly (usually 3-4min.), so quit drumming the bar and be patient. **Kilkenny ale** (called Smithwicks abroad), a hoppy, English-style bitter, and **Harp** lager, made by Guinness, are both popular domestic brews. You might be surprised by the many pubs serving Budweiser or Heineken here and by the number of young people quaffing such imported lagers. In general, the indigenous brews are far worthier. Beer is served in imperial **pint glasses** (about 20oz.) or half-pints (called a "glass"). If you ask for a beer you'll get a full pint, so be loud and clear if you can only stay (or stand) for a half (or just take the pint and drink faster). A pint of Guinness costs anywhere from IR£1.90 to 2.30, and remember never to tip the barman.

Irish whiskey—which Queen Elizabeth once declared her only true Irish friend—is sweeter than its Scotch counterpart, spelled "whisky" (See **Know Your Whiskey,** p. 205). Irish whiskey is also served in larger measures than you might be used to. **Jameson** is popular everywhere. Dubliners are partial to **Powers and Sons, Bushmills,** distilled in Portstewart, is the favorite in the North, and drinkers in Cork enjoy **Paddy. Irish coffee** is sweetened with brown sugar and whipped cream and laced with whiskey—allegedly invented at Shannon Airport by a desperate bartender looking to appease cranky travelers on a layover, although others place the drink's origin in San Francisco. **Hot whiskey** (spiced up with lemon, cloves, and brown sugar) can provide a cozy buzz, as will the Irish version of **eggnog** (brandy, beaten egg, milk, and a touch of lemon juice). In the west, you may hear some locals praise "mountain dew," a euphemism for **poitín** (po-CHEEN), an illegal distillation sometimes given to cows in labor that ranges in strength from 115 to 140 proof. Bad *poitín* can be very dangerous.

THE REPUBLIC OF IRELAND (ÉIRE)

In the 77 years since independence, the Republic has worked to create a modern civic society in English based on Irish culture. Despite a centralized republican identity, strong regional distinctions and urban-rural divides continue to enrich and disrupt the national character. Similarly, the increased secularization of this traditionally religious society has complicated the social role of government and its unique relation to the church. After a history of relatively widespread poverty and unemployment, the Republic now stands to gain tremendously from the infrastructure and development of the European Union; no one knows to what extent this economic influence will Eurotrash the growing Irish cities. Surrounded by these uncertainties and contradictions, the Irish maintain a strong public life centered around music, sports, a laid-back attitude, and, of course, drinking.

Éire: An Introduction in Factoids

The average Irish drinker consumes 135.2 liters of beer a year and 12.1 liters of wine. The average French citizen drinks 40 liters of beer and 62.5 liters of wine. Only the Germans drink more beer than the Irish (139.6L). An average month in the Republic had 64 divorces; 50 were in Dublin. Four Irish writers have been awarded the Nobel Prize in Literature: Yeats, Shaw, Beckett, Heaney. The rate of literacy in the Republic of Ireland is 99%. The Irish are pretty when I'm drunk. During the summer, the number of people in Ireland doubles with tourists. The name Kennedy comes from the Irish for "Ugly-headed." The five top grossing Irish companies in 1997 were the Smurfit Group (Paper/Packaging), Intel Ireland, Cement Roadstone Holdings, Dell, and the Irish Dairy Board. Guinness was 17th, with a turnover of £703 million. For every person in the Republic, there are 1.8 cows, 1.5 sheep, and four chickens.

Source: *The Irish Almanac and Yearbook of Facts,* 1998

■ History

THE DE VALERA ERA (1922-1960)

After the Civil War (see **Independence and Civil War (1919-1922),** p. 60), the country's most prominent leaders were gone, and the remaining ministers were still in need of armed protection. Under the Anglo-Irish Treaty, the newly elected Dáil of the 26-country Irish Free State had to frame a constitution by December 6, 1922. With time running out, **W.T. Cosgrave** was elected prime minister and quickly passed a preliminary constitution. Under the influence of **Éamon de Valera,** the government ended armed resistance by May 1923, imprisoned Republican insurgents, and executed 77 of them. Cosgrave and his party Cumann na nGaedheal (which evolved into today's **Fine Gael** party) headed the first stable Free State administration until 1932. His government restored civil order, granted suffrage to women in 1923, and brought **electrical power** to much of the West by damming the Shannon River. The anti-Treaty voters at first supported abstentionist Sinn Féin (see **Parnell's Cultural Nationalism (1870-1914),** p. 59). De Valera broke with Sinn Féin and the IRA in 1927, founding his own political party, **Fianna Fáil,** to participate in government and oppose the treaty nonviolently. Fianna Fáil won the 1932 election, and de Valera held power for much of the next 20 years. His ideal Ireland was a nation of deeply Catholic small farmers. Accordingly, Fianna Fáil's economic program broke up the remaining large landholdings and imposed high tariffs, producing a trade war with Britain that battered the Irish economy until 1938. IRA hard-liners trickled out of jails in the early 30s and resumed violence.

In 1937, de Valera and the voters approved what is still the **Irish Constitution.** It begins "In the name of the most Holy Trinity," declares the state's name to be Éire, and establishes the country's legislative structure. The legislature consists of two chambers. The **Dáil** (DAHL), the powerful lower house, is composed of 166 seats directly elected in proportional representation. The less important upper house, the **Seanad** (SHA-nud), has 60 members, who are chosen by electoral colleges. Terms in both houses last five years. The **Taoiseach** (TEE-shuch; Prime Minister) and **Tánaiste** (tah-NESH-tuh; Deputy Prime Minister) lead a Cabinet, while the **President** (Douglas Hyde was the first) is the ceremonial head of state, elected to a seven-year term. Article 2 says the state's authority extends over "the whole island of Ireland," but article 3 admits that this claim is "pending the reintegration of the national territory." The original constitution referred to the special role of the **Catholic Church** in Ireland. Although Ireland remains overwhelmingly Catholic, the "special position" clause was deleted by a constitutional amendment in 1972.

Ireland was neutral during World War II, despite German Air raids on Dublin in 1941 and pressure from U.S. President Franklin Roosevelt. Some Irish, especially Northern Nationalists, privately supported the Nazis on the grounds that they, too, were fighting England, but far more Irish citizens (around 50,000) served in the British army. **"The Emergency,"** as the war was known, meant strict rationing of basic foodstuffs and severe censorship of newspapers and letters. Éire expressed its neutrality in such a way as to effectively assist the Allies; for example, downed American or British airmen were shipped north to Belfast, while downed German pilots were detained in P.O.W. camps. After the firebombing of Belfast in 1941, Northerners cheered the arrival of Dublin's fire brigade. De Valera, on the other hand, demonstrated what he thought neutrality meant by delivering official condolences to the German ambassador on the death of Hitler—the only head of government in the world to do so.

Éire expressed its neutrality in such a way as to effectively assist the Allies

A Fine Gael government under John Costello in 1948 had the honor of officially proclaiming "the Republic of Ireland," ending the supposed British Commonwealth membership of the previous decade. Britain recognized the Republic in 1949 but declared that the U.K. would maintain control over Ulster until the Parliament of Northern Ireland consented to join the Republic. Costello's government was plagued with problems. There were many controversies between the new coalition government and the church, one of which was the proposed reforms of the health care plan. Dr. Noel Browne, appointed Minister of Health to the Dáil, proposed a **Mother and Child Scheme** to improve a health bill passed by the Fianna Fáil in 1947. Emphasizing a need to clarify the position of women in the health scheme, Browne suggested additions to the health bill that included free maternity care to all mothers, childcare up to the age of 16, and an education plan. Browne's plan was innovative but was criticized for containing aspects of a socialized medical care system reminiscent of the British National Health Service. It was indicted by the Catholic Church for running counter to church teachings "in direct opposition to the rights of the family and of the individual and…liable to very great abuse."

The last de Valera government, in office from 1951 to 1959, and its successor under **Sean Lemass** finally boosted the Irish economy by ditching protectionism in favor of attempts to attract foreign investment. In place of the skirmishes—verbal and military—over constitutional issues that had dominated the 20s, Irish politics had become a contest between two ideologically similar parties, Fianna Fáil and Fine Gael, who vied with each other to provide local benefits and constituent services.

RECENT HISTORY (1960-1998)

The 1960s brought Ireland into unprecedented contact with the outside world, which meant economic growth and a slowdown in emigration. The government developed the economy, improved education, and bolstered tourism. In 1967, the government introduced free secondary education, including state grants for privately owned schools; in 1968, it introduced free university education for those below a certain income level. Tourism became a major industry: Shannon Airport and Bord Fáilte expanded tremendously. In 1969, the Troubles in the North disturbed everyone but didn't alter the Republic's political or economic trends. While politicians still expressed nationalist sentiments, few Irish citizens cast votes based on Northern events (see **History and Politics,** p. 373). Ireland entered the European Economic Community (now the **European Union**) in 1972.

Entering a European community and welcoming international visitors inevitably produced a more secular Ireland. **Garret FitzGerald** revamped Fine Gael partly under that banner. During the late 70s and early 80s, he and **Charlie Haughey,** Fianna Fáil's leader, alternated as Taoiseach, producing a bewildering set of economic programs and initiatives periodically interrupted by scandal and events in the North. Recession in the mid-80s inspired a new wave of emigration and produced more complex economic problems for Fianna Fáil. FitzGerald had the honor of signing the 1985 **Anglo-Irish agreement,** which gave Éire an official but not legal role in Northern negotiations. EU membership and EU funds are crucial to Ireland's economy, and greater involvement in the Continent's culture and economy saves the Irish from having to choose between isolation and the United Kingdom.

In September of 1993, Ireland elected a coalition between Fianna Fáil and the newer, smaller, leftist **Labour Party.** The latter's enormous success in the November '92 election surprised even the party leaders, who had not yet fielded a full slate of candidates. Newly elected Taoiseach **Albert Reynolds** declared that stopping violence in Northern Ireland was his highest priority. Almost miraculously, Reynolds announced the August 1994 cease-fire agreement with Sinn Féin leader **Gerry Adams** and the IRA.

Albert Reynolds was forced to resign in December, 1994, due in part to a scandal involving his appointee for President of the High Court, Attorney General **Harry Whelehan.** Whelehan had been heavily criticized for his lack of action in a case involving a pedophiliac priest, **Father Brendan Smyth.** Other scandals in the Church implicated the conservative government for protecting priests from legal charges of sexual misconduct and abuse. During the week following the appointment, Fine Gael, led by **John Bruton,** introduced a no-confidence motion against the government in Parliament. After Reynold's resignation, the Labour Party formed a new coalition with Fine Gael, and John Bruton became Taoiseach in mid-December. In June 1997, Fianna Fáil won the general election, making **Bertie Ahern,** the 45-year-old party leader, the youngest Taoiseach in the history of the state. Ahern joined the Northern Ireland peace talks, which led to the Northern Ireland Peace Agreement in April of 1998 (see **History and Politics,** p. 373). On May 22, in the first island-wide election since 1918, 94% of voters in the Republic voted for the enactment of the Agreement. Among other things, the Agreement created a North-South Ministerial Council, a cross-border authority to focus on such issues as education, transportation and urban planning, environmental protection, tourism, and EU programs.

CURRENT ISSUES

Social reform was a major issue for the Labour Party and its coalition government. Although the **women's movement** has been historically tied to political activism, it has become a movement of its own. The election in 1991 of President **Mary Robinson** was a surprise; it marked a public turning point in the Republic's progressive liberalism for a forward-looking activist to be elected to a typically figurehead position. Robinson, the first woman and first non-Fianna Fáil candidate elected, took a vigorous approach to elevate her office above the purely ceremonial role it had become.

Ireland's High Court horrified many people in February 1992 by ruling that a 14-year-old girl (called **X** in court papers) who said she had been raped could not leave the country to obtain an **abortion**. In 1983 voters had approved a constitutional amendment endorsing "the right to life of the unborn." In November 1992, voters still said no to legalizing abortion but did approve a measure to provide "right to information." In May 1995, the High Court made it legal for centers to give advice on where to go abroad. A November 24, 1995, referendum legalized **divorce** by a margin of 50.3% to 49.7%, the closest vote in Irish history. The newly passed Divorce Bill, which closely follows the terms of the referendum, allows divorce if spouses have lived apart for four years with "no reasonable prospect of a reconciliation." In 1986 two out of three voters had chosen to keep divorce illegal.

The **gay and lesbian rights** movement has been slowly gaining legal ground. In 1980, the first legal challenge to laws against homosexuality was brought before the High Court. Lawyer Mary Robinson, later President, represented David Norris, a gay lecturer of Trinity College who challenged the tacit discriminatory laws. While their challenge lost in both the High Court and Supreme Court of Ireland, an appeal to the European Court of Human Rights in Strasbourg in 1988 was fruitful. The European court ordered Ireland to change its laws; in June 1993, the age of consent between gay men was set at age 17. Dublin especially has developed a large and relatively open gay scene, and colleges are becoming more aware of gay issues. A pamphlet offering advice to third-level students about "coming out" at college was recently distributed nationwide, and many colleges support gay student groups.

Travellers

Travellers, Ireland's distinct itinerant population, traditionally roamed the countryside peddling tinware and handmade crafts, trading horses and donkeys, and performing seasonal labor. Post-World War II industrialization eliminated the demand for their wares and services as roads, transportation, and machines improved. Many migrated to urban areas in the 50s, while others still live in rural areas in caravans along the roadsides, in fields, or in "halting sites." There are an estimated 4000 traveller families in Ireland today. Many are concerned with securing safe housing, as many halting sites lack such services as water, sewers, and electricity. Travellers have infant and adult mortality rates twice that of "settled" Irish and an average life expectancy of 50. Many are illiterate since few participate in public education.

Many "settled" Irish stereotype travellers, perjoratively called "tinkers," as criminal, intemperate, and lazy, and vigilante groups try to keep travellers out of their neighborhoods by constructing roadblocks and burning caravans. In the "new Ireland," however, travellers can no longer be ignored. Pressure from such groups as the Irish Traveller Movement prompted the government to create a task force on travellers that recently unveiled a five-year plan to provide 3100 accommodation units. Travellers are routinely denied service in pubs and 32 hotels recently refused to host a traveller wedding reception, but the passage of the Equal Access Bill would curb discrimination. Travellers may now file job-discrimination claims under the Employment Equality Bill.

Crime is an increasingly difficult issue in Ireland. Drugs have become a significant problem over the past few years, and recent government elections have focused on increasing public safety and reforming prisons.

The Irish **economy** boomed in 1996 and 1997, thanks to generous economic aid from the European Union, causing some to dub Ireland the "Celtic tiger." Unemployment is comparatively low; industry has been expanding at an unprecedented pace, outstripping Britain. Few regulations and huge incentives have drawn foreign investors, boosting Ireland's economy at a faster rate than that of any other European country. Tourism remains one of the most profitable portions of the Republic's economy. EU funding was so successful that the organization cut off aid to Ireland, as its economy was doing better than that of most of Europe. By the summer of 1998, however, the inflation rate had reached a three year high, placing it well above that of the rest of the EU. Economists now fear an overheating of the economy. The euro, the new EU currency of Ireland and ten other European countries, officially begins circulation in 1999, but Irish economists don't expect it to affect the Republic for another few years. Although prices will begin to be listed in both punts and euros, people will not be required to pay in euros until 2000.

Ireland continues to make its presence felt in Europe and the world. In recognition of her work for human rights, President Mary Robinson was appointed U.N. High Commissioner of Human Rights. In October 1997, **Mary McAleese**, a law professor, became the first Northern resident to be elected president. The Republic's Constitution allows Northern residents to run for this office, but it also requires governmental permission every time the president leaves the country. President McAleese, however, regularly visits her family in the North without appealing to the legislature. McAleese was elected claiming that she would rather resign from the presidency than sign into law a bill liberalizing abortion policies.

As more Irish young people spend time abroad and as more international travelers spend time here, the culture's conservatism slowly cracks. The short-term result is an enormous generation gap and growing disparity between rural and urban areas. "New Ireland" is an oft-used term, but few can agree on its meaning as the country continues to cringe under stress between a historically religious conservatism and an increasingly secular human rights movement.

■ The Irish Language

Irish is the corpse that sits up and talks back.

Nuala Ní Dhomhnaill

The constitution declares Irish to be the national and the first official language of the Republic. Irish is a Celtic language closely related to Scottish Gaelic and Manx and more distantly to Breton and Welsh. Although the language is called *Gaeilge* by its speakers, the English word "Gaelic" generally refers to the Scottish version. Irish is spoken exclusively in only a few isolated parts of Ireland, called **gaeltacht** (GAYL-tacht). Some prominent areas are on the Dingle Peninsula, on Cape Clear Island, in the Aran Islands, around the Ring in Co. Waterford, in Connemara in Co. Galway, and in patches of Co. Donegal. Even in the *gaeltacht*, all but a few elderly people *can* speak English—they'd just rather not. Ulster, Munster, and Connacht each have dialects of Irish. Ulster Irish, like Donegal's traditional music, has been altered by contact with Scotland and Scottish Gaelic.

Until the 12th century, even the Viking settlers learned to speak Irish

The oldest vernacular literature and the largest collection of folklore in Europe are in Irish. Until the 12th century, even the Viking settlers learned to speak Irish. In 1600 there were as many speakers of Irish worldwide as of English. The Anglophones, however, had more money and better armies; over the next 250 years, more Irish speakers had to learn English to conduct business and their children grew up speaking English only. Mid-19th-century British efforts to introduce systematic schooling in rural areas resulted in the further spread of English. The Famine hit Irish-speaking areas hardest, and the number of Irish speakers continued to decline.

The **Gaelic League,** founded by **Douglas Hyde** (who later became the first president of Éire) in 1893, was created to inspire enthusiasm for Irish among people who didn't grow up speaking it. The League aimed to spread the everyday use of Irish as part of a project to de-Anglicize the island, just as the Gaelic Athletic Association aimed to overpower English sports. Placing political importance in cultural nationalism, Hyde believed that cultural change was more important than political revolution, although many Gaelic Leaguers disagreed. Gaboodles of adults whose first language was English took to the study of Irish, and the League ballooned, becoming almost trendy. Writers who were bilingual from birth enjoyed Douglas Hyde's famous mispronunciations. O'Brien's *An Béal Bocht* ("the poor mouth") satirized these new language enthusiasts.

The revolutionaries of 1916 and the political leaders of the 20s were almost without exception excited about reinvigorating the Irish language, and they tried to use the government to strengthen it: the civil service exam included an Irish test, and Irish became a compulsory subject in school. Preoccupied with economic development, the people and governments of the postwar Republic resented these policies and felt little commitment to their elementary-school language courses. The *gaeltacht* shrank, although a government department was "maintaining" them.

The last 15 years have seen a renewed interest in all things Celtic and more controversy over the fate of Irish. Adults who hated Irish in their youth regret having let it atrophy and now attend classes. As Irish students increasingly travel abroad and are often mistaken as English, they feel the need to assert the distinctiveness of their own culture. All schoolchildren are still required to take extensive Irish courses, and many Republican and Northern Catholic parents are sending their children to increasingly common and chic *gaelscoileanna* (GAYL-kol-AH-nuh; Irish immersion schools). The modern Irish-literature community, which produces dozens of novels, poetry collections, and critical essays every year, has finally begun to influence the Irish language curriculum, once only filled with antiquated traditional novels. All Irish universities require a knowledge of the language for admission, although many teens and twenty-somethings resent being forced to learn a language that is essentially useless in the broad, EU market in which they are now immersed. A Connemara-based Irish radio station and a new Irish language television station, *Telifís na Gaelige* (T na G [TEE NUH JEE] to locals), expand Irish-hearing opportunities.

Long-term trends in most *gaeltachta* still point to depopulation and dispersal, but nearly 32% of the current population claims some knowledge of the language. While most Irish do not want to see their language die, some also see the appropriation of money to Irish programs as a waste. The paradox leaves the language's fate in the air, but Irish is still showing signs of life.

Peruse the **Glossary** (p. 490) for a list of Irish words and phrases.

COUNTY DUBLIN

Dublin and its suburbs form one economic and commercial unit, most of which can be reached by DART (Dublin Area Rapid Transit), suburban rail, or Dublin buses. On weekends, Dublin's city center teems with suburbanites looking for a good time. Despite the homogenizing effects of a booming economy and suburban sprawl, Dublin's suburbs offer no less excitement for visitors, but undoubtedly more crowds, than do Ireland's romanticized rural villages. Between the area's beautiful beaches, literary history attractions, imposing castles, and monastic ruins, some towns—notably Howth, Bray, and Dún Laoghaire—deserve a day devoted to their exploration. If time allows for only one suburban jaunt, heather-crammed Howth is the incontestable choice. If monastic ruins and historical monuments are what you're looking for, check out the towns of the Boyne Valley, a little farther north.

■ Getting Around the Transportation Hublin

Rail lines, bus lines (both state-run and private), and the national highway system radiate from Ireland's capital. Major highways N5 and N6 lead to N4. N8, N9, and N10 all feed into N7, pumping buses and cars into Dublin's vehicular sphere. Because intercity transport is so Dublin-centric, you may find it more convenient in the long run to arrange your travel in other parts of the Republic while you're in the capital. Students may wish to get a **TravelSave** stamp for bus and rail discounts (see **Practical Information**, p. 85); for more information on national and international transportation, see the **Essentials** section (p. 29).

BY BUS

The lime-green **Dublin Buses,** *Bus Átha Cliath* (ATH-ah CLEE-ath), are fantastically useful. The buses, sporting "db" logos, run from 6am to 11:30pm and comprehensively cover the city of Dublin and its suburbs: north to Balbriggan, Rush, Malahide, and Donabate; west to Maynooth and Celbridge; and south to Blessington, Dún Laoghaire, and Bray. Buses are cheap (55p-£1.50), but some routes run infrequently (8am-6pm generally every 8-20min., other times every 30-45min.). Most bus routes end or begin at the city center, defined by Christ Church, the Trinity facade, St. Stephen's Green, and the top of O'Connell St. The yellow bus timetables along the quays have insets of the city center that indicate route termini with a box around the route number. It's easiest to figure out bus routes by using the *Map of Greater Dublin* (£4.10) in conjunction with the accurate **Dublin Bus Timetable** (£1.20). Both are available from newsagents and the Dublin Bus office, which also has free pamphlets detailing each route (see **Dublin: Transportation,** p. 81). The **NiteLink** service runs express routes to the suburbs (Th-Sa midnight, 1, 2, and 3am, £2.50, no passes valid). Tickets for the NiteLink are sold from a van parked on the corner of Westmoreland and College St. next to the Trinity College entrance. Some shops also carry tickets; look for the NiteLink sign in windows. Dublin runs a **wheelchair-accessible** bus service around the downtown area called **OmniLink** (M-Sa 8am-11pm, 30p).

Travel passes were not designed for the casual traveler. Except for the 10 Journey bus pass, all have time limits that require constant movement to be worth their price. There are three pass options: the **One Day Travel Wide** (Dublin buses only, £3.50); the **One Day Bus/Rail** (valid on buses, DART, and rail service anywhere between Kilcoole, Balbriggan, and Maynooth, £4.50); and the **Four Day Explorer** (same service as the One Day Bus/Rail, £1). Tourists can also buy a **weekly adult bus pass** (valid Su-Sa; £11) or a **weekly adult bus/rail pass** (valid Su-Sa; £14.50). With a **TravelSave** stamp on their ISIC cards, **students** can buy £9 weekly bus passes. Groups may want

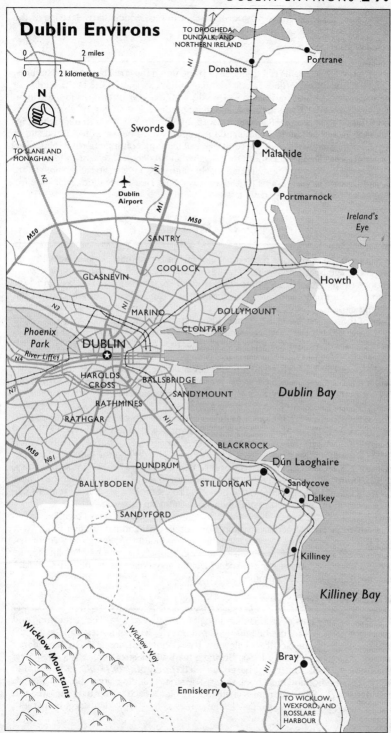

Dublin Environs

0 ___ 2 miles
0 ___ 2 kilometers

N

TO SLANE AND
MONAGHAN

N2

TO DROGHEDA,
DUNDALK, AND
NORTHERN IRELAND

N1

Donabate

Portrane

Swords

Malahide

Dublin
Airport

N1

M1

M50

Portmarnock

Ireland's
Eye

SANTRY

M50

GLASNEVIN

COOLOCK

N3

MARINO

DOLLYMOUNT

Howth

Phoenix
Park

River Liffey

DUBLIN

CLONTARF

N4

HAROLDS
CROSS

BALLSBRIDGE

N7

RATHMINES

SANDYMOUNT

Dublin Bay

RATHGAR

N11

M50

W81

DUNDRUM

BLACKROCK

BALLYBODEN

STILLORGAN

Dún Laoghaire

SANDYFORD

Sandycove

Dalkey

Killiney

Killiney Bay

Wicklow Mountains

Wicklow Way

Bray

N11

Enniskerry

TO WICKLOW,
WEXFORD, AND
ROSSLARE
HARBOUR

to consider the transferable **10 Journey ticket books,** which allow 10 trips of the same price and produce savings of 50p to £2.

BY TRAIN

The electric **DART** trains run frequently up and down the coast to serve the suburbs. From Connolly, Pearse, and Tara St. stations in the city center, the DART shoots all the way south to Bray and north to Howth; within a year or two, its range will be even greater. DART trains are faster and more predictable than comparable bus rides and suburban rail. The DART runs every 15 minutes from 6:30am to midnight (75p-£2). Tickets are sold in the station and theoretically must be presented at the end of the trip. The orange trains of the **suburban rail** network continue north to **Malahide, Donabate,** and **Drogheda;** south to **Wicklow** and **Arklow;** and west to **Maynooth.** These trains leave from Connolly Station, although the southern line also stops at Tara St. and Pearse Stations. Trains to **Kildare** leave from Heuston Station. Trains are frequent on weekdays (30 per day), less so on Sundays.

DUBLIN

In a country known for its relaxed pace of life and rural quiet, Dublin is stylish and energetic. The Irish who live outside of Dublin worry that it has taken on the characteristics of big cities everywhere: crime, rapid social change, and a weakness for short-lived international trends. The truth is that Ireland is changing, and that Dublin, holding close to one-third of the country's population in its environs, is at the forefront of those changes. Dublin's fast cultural and economic growth has been fueled by the EU and international and rural immigration. The old Ireland is still present in castles, cathedrals, and fine pubs that saturate the city. The friendliness of the Irish people, the love of good craic, and the willingness to befriend a stranger are all certainly legendary—whether you'll find them amid the urban bustle is another issue. While not cosmopolitan in the same sense as London or New York, Dublin is more European than either and boasts vibrant theater, music, and literary productions.

Dublin has been a port since the winter of 840-1, when Vikings built a longship port downstream from the older Celtic settlement of Áth Cliath. After years of visiting, the Vikings eventually set up a permanent town, Dubh Linn ("Black Pool"), around the modern College Green. The Viking Thingmote, or hill of assembly, stood there as the administrative center for both Viking powers and the Norman Pale until William III's 1690 victory at the Battle of the Boyne (see **The Protestant Ascendancy,** p. 56). During the ensuing Protestant Ascendancy, the Irish Parliament House sprang up near the old Viking center. The period's Protestant English culture remains evident today in the architecture of Dublin's tidy Georgian squares.

The capital of Ireland since the late 17th century, Dublin has seen a blending of cultures that has occasioned an extraordinary intellectual and literary life. From Swift and Burke to Joyce and Beckett, Dublin has produced so many great writers that nearly every street contains a literary landmark. Pubs shelter much of Dublin's public life and a world-renowned music scene. Dublin may not embody the "Emerald Isle" that the tourist brochures promote, but it charms and excites in its own way.

ORIENTATION

The **River Liffey** cuts central Dublin in half from west to east. The better food and more famous sights are on the **South Side,** although plenty of hostels and the bus station sprout up on the North Side. Beware that several main streets in Dublin undergo a name change every few blocks. Buying a map with a street index is a good idea. Dundrum publishes the invaluable color-coded *Handy Map of Dublin* (£4), available at the tourist office and most book stores. The streets running alongside the Liffey are called quays (KEYS); their names change every block. Each bridge over the river also has its own name, and all streets change names as they cross. If a street is split into

"Upper" and "Lower," then the "Lower" part of the street is always closer to the mouth of the Liffey.

The core of Dublin is circumscribed by North and South Circular Rd. Almost all the sights are located within this area, and you can walk from one end to the other in about 40 minutes. **O'Connell St.,** three blocks west of the central bus station, links north and south Dublin. South of the Liffey, O'Connell St. becomes Westmoreland St., passes Fleet St. on the right, goes around Trinity College Dublin on the left, then becomes Grafton St. Fleet St. becomes Temple Bar running west. **Temple Bar** is a street, but the term usually refers to an area. Dublin's version of Soho, this area is Dublin's liveliest nightspot, with tons of students, visitors, and excellent pubs. Its eclectic array of funky restaurants and a set of art museums and workshops ensure a crowd throughout the day as well. Dame St., running parallel to Temple Bar from Trinity College, defines the southern edge of the area. **Trinity College Dublin** functions as the nerve center of Dublin's cultural activity, drawing legions of bookshops and student-oriented pubs into its orbit. At the base of **Grafton St.** you'll find the more expensive, tourist-oriented shops and restaurants. Grafton St. passes **St. Stephen's Green** on the left.

Merchandise and services on the north side of the Liffey are more affordable than their southern counterparts. **Henry/Talbot St.** is a pedestrian shopping zone that runs perpendicular to O'Connell just after the General Post Office (GPO). The **North Side** has the reputation of being a rougher area. This reputation may not be wholly deserved; avoid walking in unfamiliar areas on *either* side of the Liffey at night, especially if you're alone. Phoenix Park is extremely shady at night and should definitely be avoided.

PRACTICAL INFORMATION

Transportation

For more on national and international transportation, see **Getting Around,** p. 36.

Airport: Dublin Airport (tel. 844 4900). Dublin buses #41, 41A, and 41C run to Eden Quay in the city center with stops along the way (every 20min., £1.30). **Airport Express** buses (tel. 704 4222) go to Busáras Central Bus Station and sometimes to Heuston Station (40min., M-Sa 6:40am-11pm, Su 7:10am-11pm, departs every 15-30min., £2.50). A cab from the airport to the city center costs £13-15. Wheelchair-accessible cabs may be available; call ahead (see Taxis below).

Trains: Irish Rail, *Iarnród Éireann* (EER-ann-road AIR-ann), 35 Lower Abbey St. (tel. 836 6222), spews data on its own InterCity services as well as on DART, suburban trains, international train tickets, and ferries. Open M-F 9am-5pm, Sa 9am-1pm; phones open M-Sa 9am-6pm, Su 10am-6pm. 24hr. "talking timetables" recite info on trains to **Belfast** (tel. 855 4477), **Cork** (tel. 855 4400), **Galway/Westport** (tel. 855 4422), **Killarney/Tralee** (tel. 855 4466), **Limerick** (tel. 855 4411), **Sligo** (tel. 855 4455), **Waterford** (tel. 855 4433), and **Wexford/Rosslare** (tel. 855 4488). **Connolly Station,** Amiens St. (tel. 836 3333), north of the Liffey and close to Busáras Bus Station. Buses #20, 20A, and 90 at the station head south of the river, but it's faster to walk. Trains to **Belfast** (2½hr., 10 per day, Su 7 per day, £16.50), **Sligo** (3¼hr., 4 per day, Su 3 per day, £12), and **Wexford per Rosslare** (3hr., 5 per day, Su 2 per day, £10). **Heuston Station** (tel. 703 2132), south of Victoria Quay, well west of the city center, a 25min. walk from Trinity College. Buses #26, 51, and 79 go from Heuston to the city center. Trains to **Cork** (3¼hr., 16 per day, Su 11 per day, £32), **Galway** (3hr., 6 per day, Su 3 per day, £14, F-Sa £24), **Limerick** (2¾hr., 9 per day, Su 7 per day, £25), **Tralee** (4hr., 3 per day, Su 2 per day, £34), and **Waterford** (3hr., 4 per day, Su 3 per day, £11.50). Any of the Dublin buses heading east will take you into the city. **Pearse Station,** just east of Trinity College on Pearse St. and Westland Row, receives southbound trains from Connolly Station. Bus #90 (every 10min., 80p) makes the circuit of Connolly, Heuston, and Pearse Stations and Busáras. Connolly and Pearse are also DART stations serving the north and south coasts (see **Getting Around the Transportation Hublin,** p. 78).

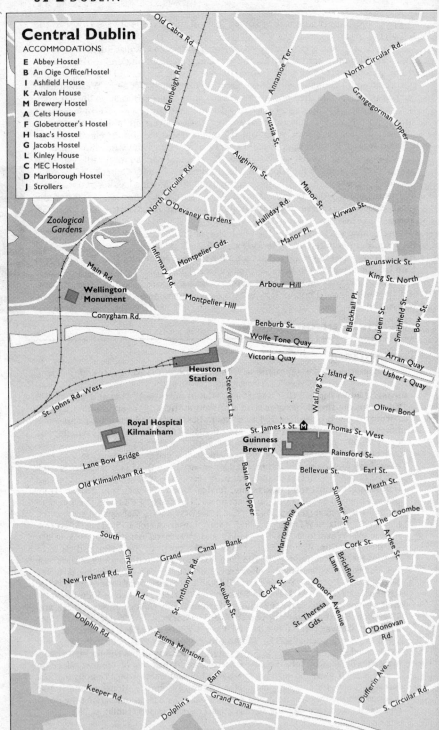

Central Dublin

ACCOMMODATIONS

- **E** Abbey Hostel
- **B** An Oige Office/Hostel
- **I** Ashfield House
- **K** Avalon House
- **M** Brewery Hostel
- **A** Celts House
- **F** Globetrotter's Hostel
- **H** Isaac's Hostel
- **G** Jacobs Hostel
- **L** Kinley House
- **C** MEC Hostel
- **D** Marlborough Hostel
- **J** Strollers

Old Cabra Rd.
Glenbeigh Rd.
North Circular Rd.
Annamoe Ter.
Grangegorman Upper
Prussia St.
Aughrim St.
Manor St.
Kirwan St.
North O'Devaney Gardens
North Circular Rd.
Halliday Rd.
Manor Pl.
Brunswick St.
Montpelier Gds.
Arbour Hill
King St. North
Infirmary Rd.
Zoological Gardens
Main Rd.
Wellington Monument
Montpelier Hill
Benburb St.
Blackhall Pl.
Queen St.
Smithfield St.
Bow St.
Conygham Rd.
Wolfe Tone Quay
Victoria Quay
Arran Quay
Usher's Quay
St. Johns Rd. West
Heuston Station
Steevens La.
Island St.
Watling St.
Oliver Bond
Royal Hospital Kilmainham
St. James's St.
Thomas St. West
Guinness Brewery
Rainsford St.
Lane Bow Bridge
Bellevue St.
Earl St.
Old Kilmainham Rd.
Meath St.
Basin St. Upper
Marrowbone La.
Summer St.
The Coombe
South
Circular
Rd.
Grand Canal Bank
Bellevue St.
Cork St.
Ardee St.
New Ireland Rd.
St. Anthony's Rd.
Reuben St.
Cork St.
Brickfield Lane
Donore Avenue
St. Theresa Gds.
O'Donovan Rd.
Dolphin Rd.
Fatima Mansions
Barn
Dufferin Ave.
S. Circular Rd.
Keeper Rd.
Dolphin's
Grand Canal

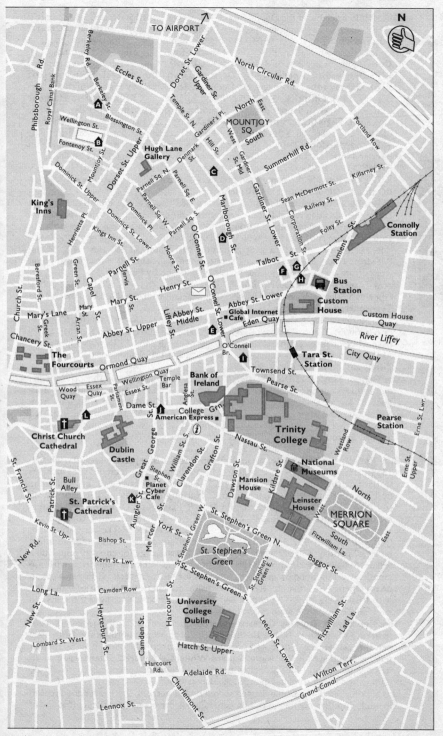

Buses: Info available at the Dublin Bus Office, 59 O'Connell St. (tel. 873 4222 or 872 0000), open M-Sa 9am-6pm. Inter-city buses to Dublin arrive at **Busáras Central Bus Station,** Store St. (tel. 836 6111), directly behind the Customs House and next door to Connolly Station. Buses run to **Belfast** (3hr., 7 per day, Su 3 per day, £11), **Cork** (4½hr., 4 per day, Su 3 per day, £12), **Derry** (4½hr., 4 per day, Su 3 per day, £10), **Dingle** (7hr., 1 per day, £16), **Donegal Town** (4hr., 4 per day, Su 3 per day, £10), **Galway** (4hr., 8 per day, Su 4 per day, £8), **Killarney** (6hr., 5 per day, Su 3 per day, £14), **Limerick** (3¼hr., 5 per day, Su 7 per day, £10), **Rosslare Harbour** (3hr., 6 per day, Su 5-6 per day, £8), **Shannon Airport** (4½hr., 6 per day, Su 5 per day, £10), **Sligo** (4hr., 3 per day, £8), **Tralee** (6hr., 5 per day, £14), **Waterford** (2¾hr., 8 per day, Su 5 per day, £6), **Westport** (5½hr., 3 per day, Su 1 per day, £11), and **Wexford** (2¾hr., 6 per day, Su 5-6 per day, £7). For more information on inter and intra-city buses, see **Getting Around the Transportation Hublin,** p. 78. **PAMBO** (Private Association of Motor Bus Owners), 32 Lower Abbey St. (tel. 878 8422), can provide the names and numbers of private bus companies serving particular destinations. Open M-F 10am-5pm.

Ferries: Bookings in Irish Rail office (above). **B&I** docks at the mouth of the River Liffey, just outside central Dublin. From there, buses #53 and 53A run past Alexandra Rd. and arrive near the Custom House (80p). **Stena-Sealink** ferries arrive in Dún Laoghaire (p. 116), from which the DART shuttles passengers to Connolly Station, Pearse Station, or Tara St. Station in the city center (£1.30). Buses #7, 7A, and 8 go from Georges St. in Dún Laoghaire to Eden Quay (£1.30). For information on ferries from England, Wales, and the Isle of Man, see **By Ferry,** p. 34.

Local Transportation: Dublin Bus, 59 O'Connell St. (tel 873 4222 or 872 0000). Open M 8:30am-5:30pm, Tu-F 9am-5:30pm, Sa 9am-1pm. See **Getting Around the Transportation Hublin,** p. 78.

Taxis: National Radio Cabs, 40 James St. (tel. 677 2222). **Co-op Taxi** (tel. 677 7777 or 676 6666). **Central Cabs** (tel. 836 5555) and **City Group Taxi** (tel. 872 7272) have wheelchair-accessible taxis (call in advance). All 24hr. £1.80 plus 80p per mi.; £1.20 call-in charge. It's easiest to pick up cabs at taxi stands, located in front of Trinity and on Lower Abbey St.

Car Rental: Thrifty, 14 Duke St. (tel. 679 9420). Another office at the airport. Summer from £35 per day, £210 per week; in winter £30, £175. Ages 23 and over. **Budget,** 151 Lower Drumcondra Rd. (tel. 837 9611), and at the airport. Summer from £36 per day, £250 per week; winter £30, £175. **Argus,** 59 Terenure Rd. East (tel. 490 4444; fax 490 6328). Offices also in the tourist office on O'Connell St. and the airport. From £38 per day, £225 per week for ages 26-64; prices vary by season. Special arrangements for drivers 23-26 or 64-70.

Bike Rental: see **By Bicycle,** p. 38. **Raleigh Rent-A-Bike,** Kylemore Rd. (tel. 626 1333). Limited one-way rental system (£12 surcharge; deposit credit card) includes C. Harding (below). Bikes £8 per day; £35 per week; deposit £40. In Dublin, the best selection and advice comes from **C. Harding for Bikes,** 30 Bachelor's Walk (tel. 873 2455; fax 873 3622). Open M-Sa 8:30am-6pm. Other Raleigh dealers include **McDonald's Cycles,** 38 Wexford St. (tel. 475 2586), and **Little Sport,** 3 Merville Ave. (tel. 833 2405), off Fairview Rd. **Rent-A-Bike,** 58 Lower Gardiner St. (tel. 872 5931 or 872 5399; fax 836 4763), offers cross-country and mountain bikes. £7 per day; £30 per week; deposit £35. Extra charge for one-way rental. Bike repair. Sells bikes for about £100 and buys them back for half-price within 6 months. Cycling holidays in An Óige hostels for £82 per week, £135 per week in B&Bs. Open M-Sa 9am-6pm. **RailBike,** Heuston Station (tel. (041) 41067), affiliated with **Irish Cycle Hire.** £7 per day; £30 per week; deposit £30. Return the bike to RailBike depots in the main rail stations.

Bike Repair and Storage: C. Harding, 30 Bachelor's Walk (tel. 873 2455). Turn right off O'Connell St. before the bridge. Has bike storage north of the Liffey. 50p per 4hr.; £1 per day, students £3.50 for 6 days; overnight parking £1.50. Repair service. Open M-Sa 8:30am-6pm. **Square Wheel Cycleworks,** Temple Lane South (tel. 679 0838), off Dame St. below the Well-Fed Café. Excellent advice on bicycle touring and expert repair. Open M-F 8:30am-6:30pm.

Hitchhiking: Since Co. Dublin is well served by bus and rail, there is no good reason to hitch. Hitchers coming to Dublin generally ask drivers to drop them off at one of the myriad bus and DART stops outside the city. Those leaving Dublin ride a bus to the city outskirts where the motorways begin. Buses #25, 25A, 66, 66A, 67, and 67A from Middle Abbey St. travel to Lucan Rd., which turns into N4 (for Galway and the West). To find a ride to Cork, Waterford, and Limerick (N7), hitchers usually take bus #51, 51B, or 69 from Fleet St. to Naas (NACE) Rd. N11 (to Wicklow, Wexford, and Rosslare) can be reached by buses #46 and 84 from Eden Quay or #46A from Fleet St. toward Stillorgan Rd. N3 (to Donegal and Sligo) can be reached on buses #38 from Lower Abbey St. or #39 from Middle Abbey St. to Navan Rd. Buses #33, 41, and 41A from Eden Quay toward Swords send hitchers on their way to N1 (Belfast and Dundalk).

Tourist and Financial Services

Tourist Information: Main Office, Dublin Tourist Centre, Suffolk St. (tel. (1850) 230330 in Ireland; 666 1258 outside Ireland). From Connolly Train Station, walk left down Amiens St. and right on Abbey St. Lower past Busáras until you come to O'Connell St. Turn left, cross the bridge, and walk past Trinity College; Suffolk St. will be on your right (office signposted). The Centre is in a converted church. Accommodation service with £1 booking fee and 10% deposit; £2 charge to book outside Dublin. Bookings by phone (tel. (1800) 668668 in Ireland; 669 2082 outside Ireland). The monarchs among the billions of pamphlets are the *Map of Greater Dublin* (£3.90) and the *Handy Map of Dublin* (£4). **American Express** maintains a branch office with currency exchange here (tel. 605 7701). **Bus Éireann** and **Stenalink** have representatives on hand to provide info and tickets. **Argus Rent-a-Car** has a desk here, and a free list of car rental agencies is also available. Credit card reservations (tel. 605 7777; from overseas fax 605 7787). Open mid-June to mid-Sept. M-Sa 8:30am-7:30pm, Su 9am-5:30pm; mid-Sept. to mid-June M and W-Sa 9am-5:30pm, Tu 9:30am-5:30pm.

Branch Offices: Dublin Airport, open daily 8am-10pm. **Dún Laoghaire Harbour,** Ferry Terminal Building, open daily 8am-10:30pm (subject to ferry arrivals). **Tallaght,** The Square Towncentre, open daily 8am-10:30pm. **Baggot Street,** open daily 8am-10:30pm. The latter three branches are well stocked and less crowded than the airport and Suffolk St. branches. All telephone inquiries are handled by the central office.

Northern Ireland Tourist Board: 16 Nassau St. (tel. 679 1977 or (1800) 230230). Much more extensive info on the North than the Dublin Tourism Centre. Books accommodations. Open M-F 9am-5:30pm, Sa 10am-5pm.

Temple Bar Information Centre: 18 Eustace St. (tel. 671 5717). Heading away from Trinity College, make a right off Dame St. where it intersects both Eustace and Great Georges St. Info on the artsy Temple Bar, better arts information than the Dublin Tourist Office, and more time to answer questions. The center publishes the useful, bimonthly *Temple Bar Guide* (free), which lists all upcoming events, many of which are free, and distributes *Gay Community News* (free). Open June-Sept. M-F 9am-6pm, Sa 11am-4pm, Su noon-4pm; Oct.-May M-F 9am-6pm, Sa noon-6pm.

Community and Youth Information Centre: Sackville Pl. (tel. 878 6844), at Marlborough St. A library with a wealth of resources on careers, culture, outings, travel and tourist information, accommodations (no bookings), camping, sporting events, counseling, and referrals. Bulletin boards advertise youth and special-needs groups. Open M-W 9:30am-1pm and 2-6pm, Th-Sa 9:30am-1pm and 2-5pm.

An Óige Head Office (Irish Youth Hostel Association/HI), 61 Mountjoy St. (tel. 830 4555), at Wellington St. Follow O'Connell St. north, continuing through all its name changes. Mountjoy St. is on the left, about 20min. from O'Connell Bridge. Book and pay for HI hostels here. Also sells package bike and rail tours. The *An Óige Handbook* (£1.50) lists all HI hostels in Ireland and Northern Ireland. Membership £10, under 18 £4. Open Apr.-Sept. M-F 9:30am-5:30pm, Sa 10am-12:30pm; Oct.-Mar. M-F 9:30am-5:30pm.

Budget Travel: USIT (Irish Student Travel Agency), 19-21 Aston Quay (tel. 679 8833), near O'Connell Bridge. The place to seek Irish travel discounts. ISIC, HI, and EYC cards; **TravelSave** stamps £8. £3 photo booths. Big discounts, especially for people under 26. They will book you into Kinlay House (see below), a hostel run by USIT, for a £1 deposit. Open M-F 9am-6pm, Sa 10am-5:30pm.

Embassies: Australia, 2nd fl., Fitzwilton House, Wilton Terr. (tel. 676 1517). Open M-Th 8:30am-12:30pm and 1:30-3:30pm, F 9am-noon. **Canada,** 65 St. Stephen's Green South (tel. 478 1988). Open M-F 9am-noon and 1-4:30pm. **New Zealand's** embassy is in London: New Zealand House, Haymarket, London SW1Y 4QT. From Ireland, dial 00 44 (171) 930 8422. **South Africa,** 2nd fl., Alexander House, Earlsford Centre (tel. 661 5553; fax 661 5590). Open 9am-12:30pm and 2-4pm. **U.K.,** 29 Merrion Rd. (tel. 269 5211). Open M-F 9am-12:45pm and 2-5pm. **United States,** 42 Elgin Rd., Ballsbridge (tel. 668 8777). Open M-F 8:30am-5pm.

Banks: Bank of Ireland, AIB (Allied Irish Bank), and **TSB (Trustees' Savings Bank)** branches with bureaux de change and **ATMs** cluster on Lower O'Connell St., Grafton St., and in the Suffolk and Dame St. areas. Most bank branches are open M-F 10am-4pm. **Bureaux de change** also found in the General Post Office and in the tourist office main branch.

American Express: 116 Grafton St. (tel. 677 2874), up the street from Trinity College gates. Traveler's Check refunds (tel. (1800) 626000). Client mail held; currency exchange (no commission for AmEx Traveler's Cheques). Non-members can also change currency here. Open June-Sept. M-Sa 9am-5pm, Su 11am-4pm; Oct.-May M-Sa 9am-5pm. There's a second smaller branch on Suffolk St. inside the tourist center.

Local Services

Luggage Storage: Connolly Station, £1 per item. Open M-Sa 7:30am-9:30pm, Su 9:15am-1pm and 5-10pm. **Heuston Station,** £1 per item. Open M-Sa 7:15am-8:35pm, Su 8am-3pm and 5-9pm. **Busáras,** £1.50 per item, rucksacks £2. Open M-Sa 8am-7:45pm, Su 10am-5:45pm.

Library: New Central Library, ILAC Centre, Moore St. (tel. 873 4333). Video and listening facilities and a children's library. Telephone directories on shelves for EU countries and on microfilm for U.S. and Canada. Open M-Th 10am-10pm, F-Sa 10am-5pm.

Women's Resources: Women's Aid (tel. (1800) 341 900 or 860 0033). Open M-F 10am-10pm, Sa 10am-6pm. **Dublin Well Woman Centre,** 73 Lower Leeson St. (tel. 661 0083 or 661 0086), a professional health center for women.

Gay, Lesbian, and Bisexual Information: See **Gay, Lesbian, and Bisexual Dublin,** p. 112.

Laundry: The Laundry Shop, 191 Parnell St. (tel. 872 3541). Closest to Busáras and North Side hostels. Wash £2.40, dry £1.30, soap 60p. Open M-Sa 8am-7pm. **All-American Launderette,** Wicklow St. (tel. 677 2779). Wash and dry £3.50, £4.60 serviced, powder 50p. Open M-Sa 10am-10pm, Su 10am-6pm.

Pharmacy: O'Connell's, 55 Lower O'Connell St. (tel. 873 0427). Convenient to city bus routes. Open M-Sa 8:30am-10pm, Su 10am-10pm.

Hospital: Meath Hospital, Heytesbury St. (24hr. tel. 453 6555, 453 6000, or 453 6694). Served by buses #16, 16A, 19, 19A, 22, 22A, and 55. **Mater Misericordiae Hospital,** Eccles St. (tel. 830 1122), off Lower Dorset St. Served by buses #10, 22, 38, and 120. **Beaumont Hospital,** Beaumont Rd. (tel. 837 7755). Served by buses #27A, 51A, 101, and 103. **St. James Hospital,** James St. (tel. 453 7941). Served by buses #17, 19, 19A, 21A, 78A, and 123.

Emergency and Communications

Emergency: Dial 999; no coins required.

Garda: Dublin Metro Headquarters, Harcourt Sq. (tel. 732 2222). Store St. office (tel. 873 2222 or 478 1822), Fitzgibbon St. office (tel. 836 3113). **Garda Confidential Report Line:** tel. (1800) 666 111.

Counseling and Support: Samaritans, 112 Marlborough St. (tel. (1850) 609 090 or 872 7700), for the depressed, lonely, or suicidal. 24hr. **Tourist Victim Support:** Parliament St. (tel. 679 8673). If you are robbed, this organization will help find accommodations and put you in contact with your Embassy or family. **Rape Crisis Centre,** 70 Lower Leeson St. (tel. 661 4911; freefone (1800) 778 888). **Cura,** 30 South Anne St. (tel. 671 0598), Catholic-funded support for women with unplanned pregnancies. **AIDS Resource Centre,** 14 Haddington Rd. (tel. 660 2149), off Baggot St. Advice, counseling, and anonymous HIV testing. **Alcoholics**

Anonymous, 109 South Circular Rd. (tel. 453 8998 or 453 7677). **Narcotics Anonymous** (tel. 830 0944), 24hr. phone service.

Post Office: General Post Office (G.P.O.), O'Connell St. (tel. 705 7000), on the left from the Liffey. Big. Dublin is the only city in Ireland with postal codes (24 of them). Even-numbered postal codes are for areas south of the Liffey, odd-numbered are for the north; the numbers increase with distance from the city center. *Poste Restante* pick-up at the bureau de change window, which closes 15min. early. Open M-Sa 8am-8pm, Su 10am-6:30pm. **Postal Code:** Dublin 1.

Internet Access: Internet cafés tend to be busiest in the late afternoon and early evening. **Cyberia Café,** Temple Ln. South (tel. 679 7607), provides sustenance for the email starved. Telnet, ftp, the web, and basic wordprocessing services await you in the cheerful jungle of computer cable. Grab some java from the friendly, alternative staff. Open M-Sa 10am-11pm, Su noon-8pm. £1.50 per 15min., students £1.25. **Global Internet Café,** 8 Lower O'Connell St. (tel./fax 878 0295), a block north of the Liffey and on the right. The most professionally run café with the widest array of services. Fill your ears with techno as you video conference, surf, or just check email, but you might have to wait. £1.25 per 15min., students £1. Open M-Sa 10am-11pm, Su noon-10pm. **Planet Cyber Café,** 23 South Great Georges St. (tel. 679 0583; fax 677 1463). This black sci-fi den offers the full range of computer and internet services, as well as toasties. £1.50 per 15min. Open Su-W 10am-10pm, Th-Sa 10am-midnight.

Phones: Telecom Éireann (inquiries and phonecard refunds, tel. 671 4444). Public payphones are on every corner. For more info, see **Keeping in Touch,** p. 49.

Directory Inquiries: tel. 1190 for all of Ireland. No charge.

Phone Code: Dear, dirty 01.

ACCOMMODATIONS

Dublin has a host of marvelous accommodations, but the ever-flowing glut of visitors ensures that real dumps stay open as well. Reserve as early as possible to be sure that you've got a bed, particularly during Easter weekend, bank holiday weekends, sporting weekends, and July and August. Private hostel rooms and B&B singles are especially hard to come by. The tourist offices books local accommodations for £1, but they only deal in Bord Fáilte-approved B&Bs and hostels, which aren't necessarily better than unapproved ones. Dublin hostels that pay the fee to be plugged into Bord Fáilte's system are Abraham House, Ashfield House, Avalon House, An Óige, Brewery Hostel, Globetrotter's Tourist Hostel, Goin' My Way, Isaac's, Jacobs Inn, Kinlay House, the Marlborough Hostel, and Morehampton House.

Phoenix Park may tempt the desperate, but camping there is a really, really bad idea. If the Garda or park rangers don't get you to leave, the threat of thieves and drug dealers should. Dublin is big—the accommodations listed here are not the only ones. If these places are full, consult Dublin Tourism's annually updated *Dublin Accommodation Guide* (£3), or ask hostel and B&B staff for referrals.

Hostels

There's a dearth of hostels in Dublin; the ones south of the river fill up fastest as they are closest to the city's sights and nightlife. Dorm prices range from £7 to £12 per night. Always **reserve ahead** in the summer and on weekends throughout the year, especially for private rooms. Call as early as possible, even if it's a few hours before you'll arrive. **The Old School House Hostel** in Dún Laoghaire (p. 116), only a DART ride away, is a hosteler's alternative to busy city life. All listed hostels have 24-hour reception. For a list of standard hostel features, see **A Hosteler's Bill of Rights,** p. 41.

Avalon House (IHH), 55 Aungier St. (tel. 475 0001; fax 475 0303; email info@avalon.ie). Turn off Dame St. onto Great Georges St.; the hostel is a 10min. walk down on your right. Temple Bar is within stumbling distance. Completely refurbished in 1998, Avalon boasts a new kitchen, email access, and top-notch security. The rooms are a joy to return to: groovy comforters and clean bathrooms. Co-ed showers, toilets, and dorms (all non-smoking). Dorms are split-level; the beds on each level are connected by a circular stairway. The result is B&B-level privacy at dorm prices. 24hr. luggage storage access. Bike rack. TV room. In-house café (all meals under £5, open noon-10pm). June-Sept. large dorms £11; 4-bed dorms £13.50; doubles £32. Oct. and Mar.-May £9; £12.50; £30. Nov.-Feb. £8; £11.50; £28. Singles also available. Continental breakfast included. Towels £1 with £5 deposit. Safety deposit boxes £1 per night. Many rooms wheelchair accessible.

Abbey Hostel, 29 Bachelor's Walk, O'Connell Bridge (tel. 878 0700 or 878 0719; email info@abbey-hostel.ie). From O'Connell Bridge, turn left to face this emphatic yellow addition to Dublin's hostel scene. Clean, comfy, and well kept. Do your laundry in the cool but spooky winecellar/crypt out back. Great location. June-Sept. big dorms £12; 6-bed dorms £15; 4-bed dorms £17. Oct. and Mar.-May £10; £13; £15. Nov.-Feb. £8; £11; £13. Pricey doubles £40-60.

Barnacle's Temple Bar House (tel. 671 6277; fax 671 6591; email templeba@barnacles.iol.ie). On the corner of Cecilia St. and Temple Ln. Literally "the burning hot center of everything." A brand new, well-kept hostel right in Temple Bar. All rooms with bath. June-Sept. 10-bed dorms £11; 6-bed dorms £13; 4-bed dorms £15; doubles and twins £19; Mar.-May and Oct. about £1 cheaper; Nov-Feb. about £2-3 cheaper.

Isaac's Hostel, 2-5 Frenchman's Ln. (tel. 855 6215 or 855 6574; email isaacs@indigo.ie), off the lower end of Gardiner St. behind the Customs House. The most basic of a biblical chain that includes plusher Jacob's nearby. Simple, clean rooms and a split log-furnished common area for a rough-hewn feel. Occasional live music. Café. Apr.-Oct. big dorms £8; small dorms £9.25; singles £18.95; doubles £32; triples £43.50. Nov.-Mar. £1 cheaper per person. Laundry £5.

Jacobs Inn, 21-28 Talbot Pl. (tel. 855 5660; fax 855 5664; email jacob@indigo.ie). On a narrow north-south street 2 blocks north of the Customs House and down the street to the right of the Garda Station. Bright and airy reception area with café is grand; rooms, though all with bath, are standard hostel issue. Apr.-Oct. 6- to 8-bed dorms £10.95; 4-bed dorms £15.50; 3-bed dorms £16.50; doubles £39. Nov.-Mar. £2 cheaper per person. Towels £1. Bed lockout 11am-3pm. Wheelchair accessible.

Abraham House, 82 Gardiner St. Lower (tel. 855 0600; fax 855 0598; email abraham@indigo.ie). Bright white washed cinderblocks give a slightly antiseptic feel to this well-kept hostel. **Bureau de change.** July-Sept. 12-bed dorms £8.50; 6-bed dorms £11; 4-bed dorms £12.50; singles £18; doubles £32. Oct.-June £1-2 cheaper per person. Light breakfast and towels included. Laundry £5.

Celts House, 32 Blessington St. (tel. 830 0657; email res@celtshouse.iol.ie). 38 comfy, solid wooden bunk beds in a brightly painted, friendly atmosphere. A bit secluded from the city center. Dorms £8-11; double £32. Sheets £1.50.

M.E.C., 42 North Great Georges St. (tel. 878 0071; meccles@iol.ie). Walk up O'Connell to Parnell St., turn right, then take the first left. The hostel is ¾ block down on the right. A former convent and sometimes teachers college, this boxy Georgian edifice seems impossibly large inside. A bit worn but serviceable. The street is refreshingly quiet. Kitchen and 24hr. TV lounge. Dorms £7.50-12; doubles £24-£32; quads £34-53. Free luggage storage and car park.

Marlborough Hostel (IHH), 81-82 Marlborough St. (tel. 874 7629; fax 874 5172; email marlboro@internet-ireland.ie), up the street from the Protestant cathedral, just 2 quick turns off a main drag. Large rooms, mediocre showers, and exciting barbecue area. Bike shed. Kitchen with microwave. 4- to 10-bed dorms £7.50; doubles £26. Continental breakfast included. Sheets 50p. Check-out 10:30am.

Dublin International Youth Hostel (An Óige/HI), 61 Mountjoy St. (tel. 830 1766; fax 830 1600; email anoige@iol.ie). O'Connell St. changes names 3 times before reaching the turn left onto Mountjoy St. Welcome to the mothership. A convent with stained-glass windows and confessional boxes converted into an institutional, 420-bed hostel. Large rooms, squeaky wooden bunks. Guard possessions closely and keep the door to your room shut; security isn't great. **Bureau de change.** Secure parking. 24hr. kitchen. Café has cheap meals (£3.50) and packed lunches (£2). Big dorms £10, non-members £10.50; 4- to 6-bed dorms £11; double £25. Oct.-May £2 cheaper. Breakfast included. Luggage storage 50p. Sheets £1.50. Self-service laundry £5.

Globetrotter's Tourist Hostel (IHH), 46 Gardiner St. Lower (tel. 873 5893). Comfortable beds in high bunks. Tastefully decorated. Smoking room, TV room, civilized kitchen. Excellent bathrooms and superb showers. Free luggage storage. July to mid-Sept. dorms £15. Mid-Sept. to June £11 or £25 for 3 nights. Great breakfast included. Safety deposit boxes £1.50. Towels 50p.

Strollers, 58 Dame St. (tel. 677 5614 or 677 5422; fax 839 0474). In the middle of Temple Bar action, a short walk from Trinity. Super location and bright rooms, though cars whiz by at all hours. Live music 4 nights a week. Dorms £12-14.50; doubles £34. Breakfast and discounts at the attached café (dinners £5; open daily 9am-11pm). Wheelchair accessible.

The Brewery Hostel, 22-23 Thomas St. (tel. 453 8600). Follow Dame St. past Christ Church through its name changes (High and Cornmarket). Next to Guinness and a 20min. walk to Temple Bar. Hope you like Guinness, because distinct odors of its production waft through the whole neighborhood. Barbecue area and patio make it easy to meet other hostelers. Free tea/coffee available all day. All rooms with bath. Carpark. TV lounge area with VCR; full kitchen and small dining area (with microwave) open 24hr. Free luggage storage. Dorms £9-13; singles £20. Breakfast buffet. Laundry service £3.50.

Morehampton House Tourist Hostel, 78 Morehampton Rd., Donnybrook (tel. 668 8866; fax 668 8794). On buses #10, 46A, and 46B. Though out of the way (10min. bus ride, 20min. walk from city center), this refurbished Victorian building provides comfortable accommodations. Luggage storage. Bike park and rental. Kitchen, TV room, and laundry. 10-bed dorms £9; 6- to 8-bed dorms £12; doubles £32. Oct.-May £1-2 cheaper. Add £2 for rooms with bath.

Baggot University Centre, 114 Baggot St. (tel. 661 8860). Sean and Moira Fitzgerald make their hostel a welcoming place. The mattresses are thin and some rooms get overcrowded, but the breakfast is unique for Dublin hostels: yogurt, fresh brown bread, and orange juice. Carpark. Small kitchen. Free luggage storage. 5- to 8-bed dorms £11.50; doubles £28.

Ashfield House, 19-20 D'Olier St. (tel. 679 7734; email ashfield@indigo.ie). Great location steps away from Trinity, Grafton St., and Temple Bar. This hostel boasts new beds with thick mattresses and bright, airy rooms. From time to time the traffic is noisy, so you might want to request a quiet room. Full kitchen with microwave. **Bureau de change.** Dorm beds around £10; doubles £32; triples £48. Discounts in winter. All rooms with bath. Breakfast included. Free luggage storage. Serviced laundry £4. Wheelchair accessible.

Kinlay House (IHH), 2-12 Lord Edward St. (tel. 679 6644; fax 679 7437), the continuation of Dame St. Protestant country boys who came to work in the city once slid down the beautifully carved oak banisters in the lofty entrance hall. Today, tired backpackers trudge upstairs to collapse on comfortable beds. One can gaze out at Christ Church Cathedral across the street from the soft couches in the TV room. **Bureau de change.** Wake-up calls. 10-bed dorms £9.50; 4- to 6-bed dorms £13; singles £18; doubles £28, with bath £32. Oct.-June prices £1 less. Breakfast and towel included. Lockers. Free luggage storage. Laundry £5.

If you're still without a room, you may want to try **Gogarty's Temple Bar Hostel,** 18-21 Anglesea St. (tel. 671 1822; dorms £14 in summer), or **Goin' My Way,** 15 Talbot St. (tel. 878 8484 or 874 1720; dorms £10). Either way, you get what you pay for. Also worth considering is university housing, available in the summers. These accommodations tend to be modern, comfortable, and expensive. **Dublin City University,** Glasnevin (tel. 704 5736), can be reached on bus #11, 13, or 19A from the city center (singles with bath around £23; rooms available June 18-Sept. 22). Other options are **USIT,** which operates University College Dublin dorms in Belfield (tel. 269 7111), and **University of Dublin** dorms in Rathmines (tel. 497 1772).

Bed and Breakfasts

A blanket of quality B&Bs covers Dublin and the surrounding suburbs. Those with a green shamrock sign out front are registered, occasionally checked, and approved by Bord Fáilte. B&Bs without the shamrock haven't been inspected but may be cheaper and better located. B&B prices stretch from £15 to £25 per person. Near the city center, inexpensive B&Bs cluster along Upper and Lower Gardiner St., on Sheriff St., and near the Parnell Sq. area. This area, however, is not the best to walk though at night; exercise caution. The B&Bs listed below are warm and welcoming standouts in this neighborhood.

Suburban B&Bs are often spare rooms in houses emptied of children. They tend to be close to the city; Clonliffe Rd., Sandymount, and Clontarf are no more than a 10- or 15-minute bus ride from Eden Quay. Suburbs offer more calm and a greater chance of finding decent B&Bs, especially for those without a reservation. B&Bs in Howth (p. 113) and Dún Laoghaire (p. 116) are just as accessible (by DART) to Dublin as many of the B&Bs listed below. Maynooth (p. 130) and Malahide (p. 115), accessible by suburban rail, are also good places to stay. Aside from the regions covered below, you can also find large numbers of B&Bs within the city limits in Rathgar (Dublin 6), Drumcondra (Dublin 9), Templeogue (Dublin 6W), and Santry Rd. (Dublin 9, close to the airport). Dublin Tourism's annually updated *Dublin Accommodation Guide* (£3) lists all approved B&Bs and their rates.

Near O'Connell St.: Parnell, Blessington, and Gardiner Streets

The B&Bs in this area can be a budget-traveler's hell. Many travelers arrive late at night and, knowing no better, are plundered here. Choose wisely, or choose a suburban B&B. Lower Gardiner and Upper Gardiner St. are within walking distance, but buses #41, 41A, 41B, and 41C from Eden Quay are convenient to the farther parts of the road. Those who are walking should head north up O'Connell St. and take a right onto Parnell St. to reach Gardiner St.

Glen Court, 67 Gardiner St. Lower (tel. 836 4022), 1 block west of Busáras, 2 blocks east of O'Connell. An old Georgian house with high ceilings and mismatched furniture, but it's clean, cheap, and well located. Singles £18; doubles £30; triples £42; quads £49.

Parkway Guest House, 5 Gardiner Pl. (tel. 874 0469). Rooms are plain but comfortable, and the location just off Gardiner St. is excellent. Friendly, young proprietor offers discerning advice on restaurants and pubs and could talk for hours about Irish sports—his hurling scars brand him as an authority. Singles £21; doubles £35, with bath £42.

Kingfisher B&B, 166 Parnell St. (tel. 872 8732 or 825 9277), 2 blocks west of the top of O'Connell St. Self-contained clean, sunny apartments with TV, full kitchen, and bath. Singles £25; doubles £40. Weekly discounts.

Leitrim House, 34 Blessington St. (tel. 830 8728), on the final stretch of what was O'Connell St. after it crosses Mountjoy, 1 block past the false teeth repair shop. Bus #10 drops you off nearby at the top of Mountjoy St. Lilac walls and flowers on the windowsill result in flowery and pleasant-smelling rooms. Pampering proprietor really makes the place. £15.

Clonliffe Road

This modest, respectable neighborhood has several friendly empty-nests-turned-B&Bs. This area is an ideal place to stay if you're planning to attend an event at Croke Park or if you want to listen to the concerts there for free. Take bus #51A from Lower Abbey St. or make the 20-minute walk from the city center: up O'Connell St., right on Dorset St., across the Royal Canal, and right onto Clonliffe Rd.

Mrs. M. Ryan, 10 Distillery Rd. (tel. 837 4147), off Clonliffe Rd., on the left if you're coming from city center. Yellow paint trims this gingerbread-like house, attached to #11. The oft-dyed proprietor welcomes all with firm beds and warm comforters. Singles £15; doubles £28.

Mona B&B, Mrs. Kathleen Greville, 148 Clonliffe Rd. (tel. 837 6723). Firm beds and clean rooms kept tidy by a warm proprietor who is also an avid sports fan. Fresh homemade bread, tea, and cakes are always on hand to welcome guests. Singles £16; doubles £30. Open May-Oct.

St. Aiden's B&B, Mrs. Brid Creagh, 150 Clonliffe Rd. (tel. 837 6750). The healthy plants, non-smoking rooms, and green, gurgling fountain create a comfortable atmosphere. Singles £16, doubles £30. Open Apr.-Sept.

Sandymount

Sandymount is a peaceful seaside neighborhood near Dublin Port, 1¾ mi. south of city center. Take bus #3 from O'Connell St. or the DART to Landsdowne Rd. or Sandymount stops (10min.).

Mrs. R. Casey, Villa Jude, 2 Church Ave. (tel. 668 4982), off Beach Rd. Bus #3 or DART (Lansdowne Rd. stop). Mrs. Casey has nourished 7 children and countless others with her homemade bread and strapping Irish breakfasts. The parlor overflows with family photos, fresh flowers, and lace doilies. Every room is immaculate and TV-equipped. Singles £14; doubles £26.

Mrs. Bermingham, 8 Dromard Terr. (tel. 668 3861). Bus #3 from O'Connell St. or DART to Sandymount stop. Old-fashioned rooms, one with a bay window overlooking the garden, and a TV in the sitting room. Soft beds with great, fluffy comforters. Owner is lots of fun. Singles £15; doubles £28.

Mrs. Dolores Abbot-Murphy, 14 Castle Park (tel. 269 8413). Friendly owner is as sweet as candy. Each cheerful room has a TV and the dining room adds elegance to every meal. Singles £15; doubles £28. Open May-Oct.

Clontarf Rd.

Clontarf Rd. runs along Dublin Bay across from the Dublin Port facility north of the city center. Behind it rise the startlingly pretty hills of Howth. Houses with addresses in the 200s face directly onto the Irish Sea; those with addresses in the 90s face it through a maze of smokestacks. Sea breezes and a waterfront park almost make up for the lively sight of car ferries chugging into dock. Take bus #30 from Lower Abbey St. to Clontarf Rd. (15min.).

Ferryview Guest House, 96 Clontarf Rd. (tel. 833 5893). Thick carpets, fluffy comforters, friendly family—you won't want to leave. Nautical objects abound in the cheerful, non-smoking rooms. Singles £20; doubles £34.

Mrs. Patricia Barry, Bayview, 98 Clontarf Rd. (tel. 833 3950). Beds with pink bows in recently refurbished, fresh, airy rooms. Piano in sitting room. Super showers. Singles £18; doubles £32.

Mrs. Geary, 69 Hampton Ct. (tel. 833 1199). Comfortable rooms made special by friendly proprietors. Hampton Ct. connects Vernon St. with Castle St. off Clontarf Rd. Singles £16; doubles £30.

Camping

Most campsites are far from the city center, but camping equipment is available in the heart of the city. **The Great Outdoors,** Chatham St. (tel. 679 4293), off the top of Grafton St., has an excellent selection of tents, backpacks, and cookware. (10% discount for An Óige/HI members. Open M-W and F-Sa 9:30am-5:30pm, Th 9:30am-8pm.) **O'Meara's,** 26 Ossory Rd. (tel. 836 3233), off North Strand Rd., sells camping equipment and rents tents (£28 per week; open M-Th and Sa 10am-1pm and 2-6pm, F 10am-9pm, Su 2:30-5:30pm). Tempting as it may be, Phoenix Park is not at all safe for camping.

Backpackers EuroHostel, 80/81 Lower Gardiner St. (tel. 836 4900). Not really a campsite, but a big room behind the hostel has mattresses where diehard budget travelers can camp out (£4) and still use all of the hostel facilities. No toilet seats, few showers—by no means plush, but good location.

Comac Valley Caravan & Camping Park, Corkagh Park, Naas Rd., Clondalkin (tel. 462 0000; fax 462 0111). Peaceful, modern campground accessible by buses #77, 77A, 49, and 65 (30min. from city center). Food shop, laundry, and kitchen facilities; electricity included. Lounge with cable TV. Tents £3.50-4.50 plus £1 per adult, 50p per child. Caravans £9.

Shankill Caravan and Camping Park (tel. 282 0011). The DART and buses #45, 45A, 46, and 84 from Eden Quay all run to Shankill. Middle-aged tourists in campers alternate with shrubs and tents. Not the ideal accommodation for seeing Dublin.

The views of the hills and 20min. walk to the beach are much more convenient. £4.50-5 per tent plus £1 per adult, 50p per child. Showers 50p.

North Beach Caravan and Camping Park (tel. 843 7131 or 843 7602), in Rush. Bus #33 from Eden Quay (runs every 45min.) and the suburban train go here. Peaceful, beach-side location in a quiet town just outside Dublin's sphere of urbanity. Kitchen; indoor beds for emergencies. £4.50, children £1.75. Electricity £1.

Long-term Stays

Solo travelers expecting to spend several weeks in Dublin may want to consider a bedsit, or sublet. Long stays are often most economical when sharing the cost of renting a house or apartment with others. Rooms in outer-city locations like Marino and Rathmines fetch about £32-50 per week (ask whether electricity, phone, and water are included). B&Bs sometimes give reduced rates (£70 per week) for long-term stays but are reluctant to do it in the summer. Dublin's countless university students are often looking for roommates, usually for the summer but also on a weekly basis. The most up-to-date, comprehensive postings of vacancies are at USIT, 19-21 Aston Quay (see **Practical Information,** p. 85). Trinity College has a **noticeboard** near the guard's desk. Also check in the Student Union and the main entrance to Trinity College.

A group looking to rent a house or apartment for a few months should consult the *Dublin Accommodation Guide* (£3), which lists affordable abodes (£45-100 per week per person). Ballsbridge (Dublin 4) and Rathmines (Dublin 6) are popular, upscale neighborhoods with pubs, restaurants, and stores of their own. Classified ads in the *Evening Herald,* the *Irish Times,* and the *Irish Independent* can also help in finding cheap housing, often at weekly rates. If you want someone else to do the legwork, **Relocators,** 38 Dame St. (tel. 679 3511), opposite the Central Bank, arranges accommodation in Dublin and the suburbs. The company has set deals with landlords to get reduced rates on flats, apartments, B&Bs, and Irish cottages. Bedsits may be as little as £25 per week, but there is a service charge of £45 (open M-F 9am-7:30pm, Sa 10am-4:30pm, Su 11am-3:30pm). Trinity is really the place to rent without a middleman.

FOOD

Dublin's **open-air markets** sell fresh and cheap fixings. Vendors with thick Dublin accents hawk fruit, fresh Irish strawberries, flowers, and, most of all, smelly fish from their pushcarts. Actors head to **Moore St. Market** to try to perfect a Dublin Northsider's accent and get fresh veggies to boot (open M-Sa 9am-5pm). Moore St. runs between Henry and Parnell St. The **Thomas St. Market,** along the continuation of Dame St., is a calmer alternative for fruit and vegetable shopping (open F-Sa 9am-5pm). The cheapest **supermarkets** around Dublin are the **Dunnes Stores,** which are at St. Stephen's Green Shopping Centre, ILAC Centre off Henry St., and on North Earl St. off O'Connell. (All open M-W and F-Sa 9am-6pm, Th 9am-8pm.) **Quinnsworth** supermarkets are also widespread. The **Runner Bean,** 4 Nassau St. (tel. 679 4833), vends wholefoods, homemade breads, veggies, fruits, and nuts for the squirrel in you (open M-F 8am-6pm, Sa 9am-6pm). **Down to Earth,** 73 South Great Georges St. (tel. 671 9702), stocks health foods, herbal medicines, and a dozen varieties of granola (open M-Sa 10am-6pm). **Padania Gastronomic Emporium** (tel. 679 2458), at Crow and Cecilia St., Temple Bar, offers "the largest selection of exclusive Italian delicacies in Ireland." Cook this food in hostel kitchens and watch your popularity increase three-fold.

Temple Bar

This neighborhood is ready to implode from its mass of inexpensive and creative eateries. The Temple Bar has more ethnic diversity in its restaurants than the combined counties of Louth, Meath, Wicklow, and Longford (probably Offaly, too). Be sure to pick up a **Temple Bar Passport** for a 5-10% discount at area stores and restaurants (available at the Temple Bar Information Centre, Eustace St., and most hostels).

La Mezza Luna, 1 Temple Ln. (tel. 671 2840), corner of Dame St. Stars and half-moons twinkle from a midnight-blue ceiling. The food is celestial, too. You can't upstage *paglia*—smoked ham with a mushroom, cream, and wine sauce (£5.50). Daily £5 lunch specials noon-4pm. Delicious desserts £2-5. Open M-Sa 12:30-11pm, Su 4-10:30pm.

Bad Ass Café, Crown Alley (tel. 671 2596), off Temple Bar. Burned down in 1994 but, like phoenixes, Bad Asses rise from the ashes. Colorful, touristy café atmosphere. The food fits right in. Sinéad O'Connor once worked here, so you can't go wrong. Lunch £3-5. Medium pizza £5.15-7.75. Student menu (with ISIC): coleslaw, scone and butter, "magic mushrooms," medium pizza, and beverage £5.75. Open daily 9am until "late" (past midnight). —

The Well Fed Café, 6 Crow St. (tel. 677 2234), off Dame St. Inventive vegetarian dishes served by a worker's cooperative in a stripped-down, bohemian atmosphere. Peace and protest posters on the walls; idealists and disenchanteds at the tables. Ads for indie band gigs and leaflets for liberal causes in lobby. Popular with the gay community. Main courses £2.50-3.50. Open M-Sa noon-8pm. Wheelchair accessible.

Old New Orleans, 3 Cork Hill (tel. 670 9785), across from Dublin Castle. The least expensive Cajun restaurant in town, it's spicy enough to satisfy even expatriate Louisianians, and candlelit besides. High booths ensure privacy. Liam may read your palm with eerie accuracy. Entrees £3.50-6. Open Tu-F 12:30pm-12:30am, Sa 6pm-12:30am, Su 2-10pm.

Poco Loco, 32 Parliament St. (tel. 679 1950), between Grattan Bridge and City Hall. Where else can you get a Dos Equis in Dublin? Enchiladas, burritos, chimichangas, or tacos £4.75, combo of 2 £7. Open M-F noon-midnight, Sa 5pm-midnight, Su 5-10pm.

Gogarty's Hotel Café, 18-21 Anglesea St. (tel. 671 1822). Much more reasonable price-wise to eat than to stay here. Big breakfast £3; pastas £3.50; sandwiches £1.30; Irish dish of the day £3.50. Open daily 8am-9:30pm.

Grafton Street and South Great Georges Street

Marks Bros., 7 South Great Georges St. (tel. 667 1085), off Dame St. Thick sandwiches (£1.30-1.70) and high salads for starving artists and punks. 2 levels allow for solitary contemplation of James Joyce or of the causes of social stratification. Next door to the George. Just for fun, tally up the total number of pierced body parts among the waitstaff. Legendary cinnamon buns 40p; choice of 10 herbal teas 50p; salads 95p. Open daily 11am "til late."

The Stag's Head, 1 Dame Court (tel. 679 3701), via an alleyway off Dame St. at Stanley Racing #28. Marked by the Stag's Head logo in tile on the sidewalk. A great pub with even better grub. Boiled cabbage and potatoes £4.25; lovely cheese sandwiches (£1.50). Food served M-F 12:30-3:30pm and 5:30-7:30pm, Sa 12:30-2:30pm.

Cornucopia, 19 Wicklow St. (tel. 677 7583). This vegetarian horn of plenty overflows with huge portions. Sit down for a meal (about £5) or just a snack (about £1.50) and people-watch. Open M-W and F 9am-8pm, Th 9am-9pm, Sa 9am-6pm.

Wed Wose Café, Exchequer St. off South Great Georges St., near the red brick market. Lovely breakfasts served all day in Dublin's slickest greasy spoon. Irish breakfast £3; sandwiches £1.50. Open M-Sa 7am-7pm.

Metro Café, 43 S. William St. (tel. 679 4515). New wave café with a fine coffee selection and homemade breads. Simple but scrumptious. *Ciabatta* (Italian roll) £3; caesar salad £4; cappuccino £1. Open M-Sa 8am-8pm.

Leo Burdock's, 2 Werburgh St. (tel. 454 0306), uphill from Christ Church Cathedral. Take-out only. Eating Burdock's fish and chips is a religious experience from which walking shouldn't distract. Dubliners' pick for best fish and chips in the universe. Haddock or cod £3; large chips 95p. Open M-F 11am-11pm, Sa 2-11pm.

La Cave, 28 South Anne St. (tel. 679 4409), off Grafton St. An underground wine-bar replete with Frenchness. Elegant, romantic, soothing. Wines served by every measure. On Sunday nights, poets, musicians, and aesthetes gather for readings and repartee. *Table d'hôte* (complete meal; say "TAH-bluh DOTE" to fit in) £12.50. Open daily 12:30-3pm and 6pm-2am or later. Gnoshes £4-6, entrees £6 and up.

Chez Jules, 16a D'Olier St. (tel. 677 0499). Often pumping with people of all ages. Mainly seafood and pasta dishes. Mussels in garlic £5; veggie dish of the day £5.75.

Special 3-course lunch £7, 3-course dinner £12. Open M-F noon-3pm and 6pm-11pm, Sa 1-4pm and 6-11pm, Su 5-10pm.

Harrison's, Westmoreland St. (tel. 679 9664). Romance that special someone without spending a fortune. 3-course meal (£7) served 5-7pm on candlelit tables as piano music floats through the air. Prices still reasonable after 7pm. Entrees £6-9. Open daily noon-10:30pm.

North of the Liffey

Eating here is undoubtedly less interesting than it is south of the river. O'Connell St. sports blocks of neon fast-food chains, and side streets filled with fish-and-chips shops and newsagents hawking overpriced groceries.

Flanagan's, 61 O'Connell St. (tel. 873 1388). "A well-regarded establishment whose tourist trade occasionally suffers from being too close to a McDonald's," describes Tom Clancy in *Patriot Games.* Close, but better. Veggie dishes £6; calzone £4.90. Special deals at pizzeria upstairs. Open daily 8am-midnight.

Clifton Court Hotel, Eden Quay (tel. 874 4535). Excellent pub grub served with cigars in a convivial atmosphere. Trad music nightly at 9pm, no cover. Chicken and mushroom *vol au vent* £5; salmon steak £6.45. Open daily noon-9pm.

The Winding Stair Bookshop and Café, 40 Lower Ormond Quay (tel. 873 3292), near Bachelor's Walk. Café overlooking the river shares 2 floors with bookshelves. Contemporary Irish writing, periodicals, and soothing music decrease the pace even more. Salads and sandwiches £2-3. Open M-Sa 10:30am-5:30pm.

Throughout Dublin

Bewley's Cafés (tel. 677 6761). A Dublin institution. Dark wood paneling, marble table tops, and mirrored walls complete the look. Wildly complex pastries (£1) and outstanding coffee. Meals are plain but inexpensive. 4 branches at: 78 Grafton St., the largest (open Su-Th 7:30am-1am, F-Sa 7:30am-2am); 12 Westmoreland St., once frequented by James Joyce (open M-Sa 7:30am-9pm, Su 9:30am-8pm); 13 South Great Georges St. (open M-Sa 7:45am-6pm); and Mary St., past Henry St. (open M-W 7am-9pm, Th-Sa 7am-2am, Su 10am-10pm).

Beshoff's. Provides almost-as-good chip bliss named after the cook in *Battleship Potemkin.* Branches on O'Connell and Westmoreland. Open M-F 10am-11pm, Sa 9am-11:30pm.

PUBS

"Good puzzle would be cross Dublin without passing a pub," wrote James Joyce. A local radio station once offered £100 to the first person to solve the puzzle. The winner explained that you could take any route—you'd just have to visit them all on the way! Dublin's pubs come in all shapes, styles, specialties, and subcultures. Dublin is the place to hear Irish rock and, on occasion, trad. Ask around or check *In Dublin, Hot Press,* or the *Event Guide* for pub music listings.

Many heated debates stem from the postulate that Guinness tastes slightly different from every tap. In-depth *Let's Go* research continues to fuel the rivalry between two pouring heavyweights. Multiple trips and dozens of tastings have failed to pick out a clear-cut winner. The **Guinness Hop Store** (see p. 104), behemoth of stout production, shares its pedestal with **Mulligan's** (p. 97). Honorable mention goes to **The Stag's Head** (p. 96). Do your part to contribute to this growing field of research. The **Dublin Literary Pub Crawl** (tel. 454 0228) traces Dublin's liquid history in reference to literary history, spewing snatches of info and entrancing monologues. (Meet at The Duke, 2 Duke St. June-Aug.M-Sa 3 and 7:30pm, Su noon and 3pm; May and Sept. daily 7:30pm; Oct.-Apr. F-Sa 7:30pm, Su noon. £6, students £5.)

The **Let's Go Dublin Pub Crawl Map** aids in discovering the city and researching the best pint of Guinness. We recommend that you begin your crawl at the gates of Trinity College, then stroll up Grafton St., teeter to Camden St., stumble to South Great Georges St., and triumphantly drag your soused self to Temple Bar. Start early (say, noon). The pubs are listed below by their position in the pub crawl.

COUNTY DUBLIN

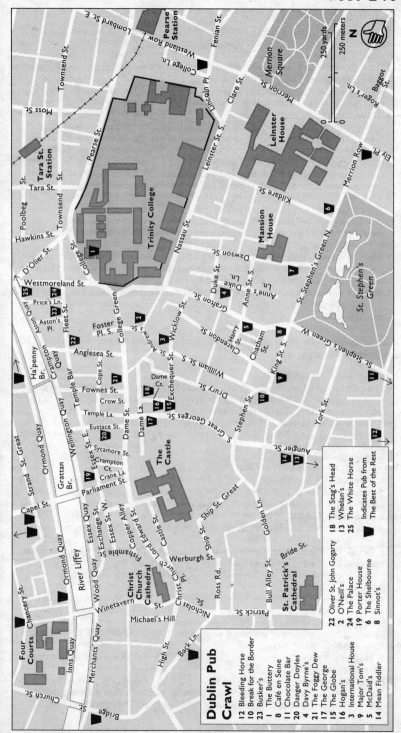

Dublin Pub Crawl

12 Bleeding Horse
10 Break for the Border
23 Busker's
1 The Buttery
8 Café en Seine
11 Chocolate Bar
20 Danger Doyles
4 Davy Byrne's
17 The Foggy Dew
15 The George
16 The Globe
16 Hogan's
3 International House
5 Major Tom's
5 McDaid's
14 Mean Fiddler

22 Oliver St. John Gogarty
2 O'Neill's
19 The Palace
24 Porter House
6 The Shelbourne
8 Sinnot's

18 The Stag's Head
13 Whelan's
25 The White Horse
▼ Indicates Pub from The Best of the Rest

Grafton Street and Vicinity

1. **The Buttery,** Trinity College, in the front arch on the left. Dark, smoky, no-frills, and crammed with students. People come here to talk and drink. Renovations are coming; who knows what the future may bring. Open M-F noon-11pm.

2. **M. J. O'Neills,** Suffolk St. Quiet by day, but a fun, crowded meeting spot by night.

3. **The International Bar,** 23 Wicklow St. (tel. 677 9250), off Grafton St. on the corner of South William St. Excellent improv comedy Mondays and stand-up Wednesdays. All other nights blues at 9pm (cover £3.50). Ballads and trad Su 12:30pm.

4. **Davy Byrne's,** 21 Duke St. (tel. 677 5217), off Grafton St. A lively, middle-aged crowd gathers in the comfortable seats that Joyce once wrote about, though the velvet backdrop behind the bar indicates some redecorating since Joyce's time.

5. **McDaid's,** 3 Harry St. (tel. 679 4395), off Grafton St. across from Anne St. The center of Ireland's literary scene in the 50s. Old books adorn the walls, enclosing a young, packed crowd downstairs and a more sedate set above. Wednesdays feature contemporary ballads; Sundays blues and jazzier tunes.

6. **Café en Seine,** 40 Dawson St. (tel. 677 4151). Built to impress. A chic café with dainty pastries occupies the front of the shop, while a very long bar stretches through a high-ceilinged hall hung with tapestries and zany paintings. A large crowd of mixed ages packs in, apparently indifferent to the fact that the Seine is not at all nearby.

7. **Sinnott's,** South King St. (tel. 478 4698). Classy crowd of 20-somethings gather in this basement pub with a wooden beam ceiling. Portraits of Irish writers crowd the walls. Music and beer are churned out daily noon-2am.

8. **Major Tom's,** South King St. (tel. 478 3266). Screw Ground Control; this pub with a club feel wants to rock. Packed with rock 'n' roll memorabilia. A DJ keeps it rolling Th-Sa nights.

If in the interests of time or your liver you need to shorten the crawl, skip 9 and 10 and head to Whelan's.

Harcourt and Camden St.

9. **The Chocolate Bar,** Hatch St. (tel. 478 0225), at Harcourt St. No special attractions like music or a literary past, but hugely popular. Young, lively group of clubbers drink here until **The Pod,** the attached nightclub, opens (see p. 98).

10. **The Bleeding Horse,** 24 Camden St. Upper (tel. 475 2705). Wood-paneled hive; standing room only. Bring mobile phone or other phallus substitute. Open Su-W until 11:30pm, Th-F 1:30am, Sa 12:30am.

Wexford St. and South Great Georges

11. **Whelan's,** 25 Wexford St. (tel. 478 0766). Continue down South Great Georges St. One of the hot spots for live rock despite a dark, dismal interior and uncomfortable pews. Nightly Irish indie rock or blues (cover £2-4).

12. **The Mean Fiddler,** Wexford St., next door to Whelan's. Live music regularly with a hip crowd. At 11pm the gates of the attached nightclub open (cover £5; see p. 98). Bar open daily noon-2am.

13. **Break for the Border,** Lower Stephen's St. (tel. 478 0300). With a restaurant, bars, and a nightclub, this "entertainment complex" is always buzzing, usually with an older crowd. Su-Tu late bar and DJs, W-Sa live rock and dance music. Open noon-2am. Dance club cover £5-8.

14. **The Globe,** 11 South Great Georges St. (tel. 671 1220). Music issues forth from the Roman busts on the walls. Guinness and frothy cappuccinos fuel the young clientele of this café/pub. It is indeed pretentious, and yet so relaxed that you can appreciate the modernist paintings next to the bust of Julius Caesar. **Rí Rá** nightclub attached (see p. 98).

15. **Hogan's,** 35 South Great Georges St. (tel. 677 5904). Attracts a trendy crowd despite its basic name.

16. **The Stag's Head,** 1 Dame Ct. (tel. 679 3701). The entrance is marked by "Stag's Head" written in tile on the sidewalk. Beautiful Victorian pub with stained glass, mirrors, and brass. Shiny. Huge mounted whiskey kegs. Truly excellent grub.

Temple Bar

17. The Porter House, 16-18 Parliament St. (tel. 679 8850). Dublin's only micro-brewery brews 6 different kinds of porter, stout, and ale, including Wrasslers 4X Stout, "Michael Collins' favorite tipple—a stout like your grandfather used to drink." If you're up for it, try *An Bratnblásta*—7% alcohol by volume. Their excellent sampler tray includes a sip of ale brewed with mussels and other oddities (£6).

18. Danger Doyles, Eustace St. (tel. 670 7655). This large pub with celestial painted walls and blaring dance music is packed with the young and beautiful. Don't forget your halter top, ladies. M-Th from 5-7pm pints £1.75 and 2 for 1 cocktails. Open daily from 11pm "'til late" (2am or so).

19. The Foggy Dew, Fownes St. (tel. 677 9328). Like a friendly, mellow neighborhood pub, but twice as big. The Foggy Dew makes a great spot for a pint or two without the artsy flash of other Temple Bar pubs. Classic rock Sunday nights.

20. Oliver St. John Gogarty (tel. 671 1822), at Fleet and Anglesea St. Lively and convivial atmosphere in a traditionally decorated pub. Named for Joyce's nemesis and once roommate, who appears in *Ulysses* as Buck Mulligan. Good food and trad sessions nightly 7:30pm. Always crowded. Open Th and F until 1am, Sa until midnight.

21. Buskers, Fleet St. Large bar with a small dance floor in the back. Sway to the dance music while you swill your pint. Open daily 11pm-2am.

22. The Palace, 21 Fleet St. (tel. 677 9290), behind Aston Quay. This classic neighborly Dublin pub has old-fashioned wood paneling and close quarters. The favorite of many a Dubliner.

In the morning, make the **White Horse** your last stop for the night and your first for the day.

23. The White Horse, 1 Georges Quay (tel. 679 3068). For those mornings when you just *need* a pint with your muesli, the White Horse opens at 7:30am every day. A small, low-key bar, frequented by regulars who come for the trad and rock (starts around 9:30pm).

The following pubs are a bit too far for the pub crawl but are worth visiting. All are on the north side of the Liffey except The Brazen Head, Mulligan's, and The Horseshoe.

The Best of the Rest

Mulligan's, 8 Poolbeg St. (tel. 677 5582), behind Burgh Quay off Tara St. Big rep as one of the best pints of Guinness in Dublin. The crowd consists mainly of middle-aged men. A taste of the typical Irish pub: low key and nothing fancy. Really.

The Horseshoe Bar, the Shelbourne Hotel at the corner of Kildare St. and St. Stephen's Green North. The center of Ireland's media culture. Political cartoons decorate the walls; journalists chat it up. The best place for cocktails in Dublin—their Bloody Mary is a divine hangover remedy.

The Brazen Head, 20 North Bridge St. (tel. 679 5816), off Merchant's Quay. Dublin's oldest pub, established in 1198 as the first stop after the bridge on the way into the city. The courtyard is quite the pickup scene on summer nights.

Lanigans, Clifton Court Hotel, Eden Quay (tel. 874 3535). Imagine a pub with Irish folk singers that actually attracts more Dubliners than tourists: this happy pub is it. Live music nightly at 9pm breaks down generational barriers.

Fibber MaGee's, 80 Parnell St. (tel. 874 5253). A young crowd dances to indie rock in this big pub. You can rest your pint on tree-stump tables outside. The antithesis of a "classy" pub, Fibber's has pints for only £1.65 10:30am-5pm every day and pints for only £1.80 every Wednesday evening. Local rock bands play on Sa afternoons (cover £3). Open until 2am every night, so you can avoid the dreaded 11:30pm bar call. Prices go up to £2 per pint after the other pubs close.

The Grattan, 165 Capel St. (tel. 873 3049), on the corner of Little Strand St. Cushy blue velvet seats envelop international ears attuned mostly to jazz, but also blues, folk, and rock. Separate rock venue upstairs often features French rock bands whose mettle draws a Euro-slick, urbane crowd. Music starts at 9pm. Cover £2.

Slattery's, 129 Capel St. (tel. 872 7971). The pub best known for traditional Irish music and set dancing. Rock and blues, too. Music nightly 9pm: trad downstairs (free), rock and blues upstairs (cover £4).

Hughes, 19 Chancery St. (tel. 872 6540), behind the Four Courts. A delightful venue for trad (nightly) and set dancing (M and W 9pm).

CLUBLIN

In recent years, clubs have displaced rock venues as the home of Dublin's nightlife. As a rule, these spots open at 10:30 or 11pm, but the action gets moving only after 11:30pm when the pubs close. Clubbing is not the least expensive evening entertainment, since covers runs £4-8 and pints are a steep £3. The last four clubs listed are a bit cheaper but not a full-night's entertainment. "Concessions" provide discounts of varying amounts and with varying restrictions. The best place to get them is Stag's Head around 11pm. A cheaper option than clubbing is to go to a pub with late closing, like **Major Tom's, The Bleeding Horse,** or **Fibber MaGees** (see **Pubs,** above). There are also a number of small clubs on Harcourt and Leeson St. that can be fun, if austere. Most clubs close at 2 or 3am, but a few have been known to last until daybreak. To get home after 11:30pm when Dublin Bus stops running, dancing fiends take the **NiteLink bus** (1 per hour Th-Sa midnight-3am, £3), which runs designated routes from the corner of Westmoreland and College St. to Dublin's outer city and its suburbs. **Taxi** stands are located in front of Trinity, the top of Grafton St. by St. Stephen's Green, and on Abbey St. Lower. Be prepared to wait 30-45 minutes on Friday and Saturday nights. Those hoping to catch the gay/lesbian scene should also check out **Gay and Lesbian Dublin,** p. 109.

The Kitchen, The Clarence Hotel (tel. 662 3066), Wellington Quay, Temple Bar. With 2 bars and a dance floor, this U2-owned club is the coolest spot in town. Half of it is impossible to get into on Fridays and Saturdays because it's filled with "VIPs." Dress to fit in with the rocker/model crowd. Cover £8, students £3 on Tu.

Rí-Rá, 1 Exchequer St. (tel. 677 0485), in the Central Hotel, pumps Top 40 music with old and new favorites. 2 floors, several bars, and more nooks and crannies than an English muffin. Open daily 11pm-2:30am. Cover £6.

Club M, Blooms Hotel, Anglesea St. (tel. 679 0277), Temple Bar. One of Dublin's largest clubs, attracting a crowd of diverse ages and styles, with multiple stairways and a few bars in the back. Another place to go up and down the charts all night. Cover around £6.

The Mean Fiddler, Wexford St. Live music and DJs; indie as well as charts. Cover £4. (See **Pubs,** p. 96.)

Pod, 35 Harcourt St. (tel. 478 0225). Spanish-style decor meets hardcore dance music. A trendy club where people go to press flesh and be seen. The truly brave venture upstairs to the **Red Box,** where a warehouse atmosphere with brain-crushing music and an 8-person deep crowd winnows out the weak at the bar. Cover £8.

UFO, upstairs at Columbia Mills, Sir John Rogerson's Quay. A mind-bogglingly intense club with heavy dance music. Cover £6.

The Turk's Head (tel. 679 2606), beneath the bar on Parliament St. Its choice selection of 70s and 80s classics will remind you of bygone days. Open nightly 10:30pm-2am. Su-Th free, F-Sa cover £4.

Republica, Kildare St., in the bottom of the Kildare Hotel. A funny little place that plays charts, is quite cheap, and has a variety of good drink deals. Cover £4.

Temple of Sound, in the Ormond Hotel on Ormond Quay, pumps out serious dance grooves Th-Su nights. Open 8:10pm-late. Cover £5.

Club Paradiso, at the Irish Film Centre, has an appropriately cinematic decor. Open 11:30pm-late. Cover £4.

TOURS

Self-Guided Walking Tours

Dublin is definitely a walking city. Most major sights lie within a mile of O'Connell Bridge. The tourist office sells *Visitor Attractions in Dublin,* which lists the main sights (£2.25). **The Cultural Trail,** starring James Joyce and Sean O'Casey, zips among the Four Courts, the Custom House and King's Inn, the Municipal Gallery, and the Dublin Writers' Museum and touches on most of the important historical and political sights. The **Old City Trail** begins on College Green and weaves its way through the Liberties, the markets, and Temple Bar. It's mostly a gathering of miscellaneous "here-once-stoods." The more tangibly gratifying **Georgian Heritage Trail** connects some of the better preserved Georgian streets, terraces, and public buildings south of the Liffey. All three walking tours are in *Heritage Trails: Signpost Walking Tours of Dublin* (£3 at the tourist office). The disturbingly worshipful **Rock 'n' Stroll Trail** brochure (£2 at the tourist office), accompanied by a cassette tape, makes a circuit of significant sights in Dublin's recent musical history. The highlights include Sinéad O'Connor's waitressing job at the Bad Ass Café and U2's Windmill Lane Studios. For Joyce fans, the tourist office provides a **Ulysses map of Dublin** (£1) that details some of Leopold Bloom's haunts and retraces his literary actions, beginning with kidneys for breakfast. The entire walk inevitably takes 18 hours (including drinking and debauching).

Guided Walking

If you lack the discipline to follow a self-guided walking tour in its entirety, you might consider a guided one. Tours generally last about two hours, but entertaining anecdotes and continuous movement preclude boredom. The **Historical Walking Tour** (tel. 845 0241) is a two-hour crash course in Dublin's history from the Celts to the present, stopping at nine points of historical interest and laying great emphasis on the "gritty" lives of ordinary Dubliners. *(June-Sept. M-Sa at 11am, noon, and 3pm, Su also at 2pm; Oct.-May Sa-Su at noon. Meet at Trinity's front gate. £5, students £4.)* The witty and irreverent **Trinity College Walking Tour** also touches on Dublin's history, but it concentrates on University lore. *(30min. Leaves every 15min. from the Info Booth inside the front gate. £5, students £4, includes admission to the Old Library and the Book of Kells.)*

    Dublin Footsteps (tel. 496 0641 or 845 0772) runs an "early morning" tour of Dublin's main attractions as well as tours with literary and medieval themes. *(2hr. M-Sa literary tour 11am; medieval tour 2:30pm. Meet at the Grafton St. Bewley's. £5. Free coffee at the end.)* Those yearning for guidance in the matters of *céilí* and Guinness should try the **Traditional Music Pub Crawl,** which meets at Oliver St. John Gogarty's on the corner of Fleet and Anglesea St. *(May-Oct. daily 7:30pm, Nov.-Apr. F-Sa 7:30pm. £6, students £5.)* (See also the **Dublin Literary Pub Crawl,** p. 94).

Bicycle Tours

If you want to be eco-friendly, get more exercise, and cover more ground, **Dublin Bike Tours** (tel. 679 0899) offers an alternative to the walking tours. Tours visit a mix of cultural and historical sights while taking advantage of quieter back streets. *(July-Oct. daily 10am, 2, and 6pm. Meet 15min. early at Darkey Kelly's Bar, Fishamble St., beside Christ Church. £12 includes bike and insurance.)* There's also a Dublin at Dawn Tour on Saturdays. Book ahead.

Bus Tours

The **Dublin City Sightseeing Tour** (tel. 873 4222) stops at Dublin's major sights, including the Writers Museum, Trinity, and the Guinness Brewery, and allows you to get on or off all day. *(1¾hr. Departs Apr.-Sept. daily every 30min. 9:30am-5pm. £6.)* The **Dublin Grand Tour** (tel. 872 0000) covers a larger area and includes more sights, but does not stop. *(2½hr. Departs every 30min. 9:30am-5pm. £8.)* Both tours depart from the Dublin Bus office, 59 O'Connell St. Tours often change, so call Dublin Bus for the latest offering. The **hop-on/hop-off tourist buses** offer easy access to the city's sights.

SIGHTS

South Side

Trinity College and Nearby

Trinity College (tel. 677 2941) sprawls within its ancient walls between Westmoreland and Grafton St. in the very center of Dublin, fronting the block-long traffic circle now called College Green. Pearse St. runs along the north edge of the college, Nassau St. to its south. Inside, stone buildings, a cobblestone walk, and spacious green grounds give the campus an illusory seclusion and allow for the occasional white-suited game of cricket. The British built Trinity in 1592 as a Protestant religious seminary that would "civilize the Irish and cure them of Popery." The college became part of the accepted path that members of the Irish Anglican upper class trod through on their way to high government and social position. The Catholic Jacobites who briefly held Dublin in 1689 used it as a barracks and prison, but for the next 100 years it was again a focus of Anglo-Irish society. Jonathan Swift, Robert Emmett, Thomas Moore, Edmund Burke, Oscar Wilde, and Samuel Beckett are just a few of the famous Irish Protestants who studied here. Bullet holes from the 1916 uprising scar the stone near the main entrance (see **History,** p. 60). Until the 1960s, the Catholic church deemed it a cardinal sin to attend Trinity. Once the church lifted the ban, the size of the student body more than tripled.

The 1712 **Old Library** holds Ireland's finest collection of Egyptian, Greek, Latin, and Irish manuscripts, including the **Book of Kells.** *(Open M-Sa 9:30am-5pm, Su noon-4:30pm. £3.50, students £3.)* Around 800, Irish monks squeezed multicolored ink from insects to make the famous book, a four-volume edition of the Gospels. Each page holds a dizzyingly intricate lattice of Celtic knotwork and scrollwork into which animals and Latin text are interwoven. In 1007 the books were unearthed in Kells, where thieves had apparently buried them. In order to enhance preservation, the display is limited to two volumes, of which one page is turned each month. For amusement, ask the Trinity librarians why they won't return the *Book of Kells* to the town of Kells. The line to see the *Book of Kells* is often lengthy, and visitors are herded onward by fastidious librarians. Trinity owns other illuminated books, some of which are periodically put on display, including the *Book of Durrow,* Ireland's oldest manuscript. Visitors should also check out the ever-changing science and history exhibits. Upstairs, in the Library's Long Room, are "Ireland's oldest harp"—the Brian Ború harp (the design model for Irish coins)—and one of the few remaining 1916 proclamations of the Republic of Ireland.

In Trinity's Davis Theatre, the **Dublin Experience** movie takes visitors on a 45-minute historical tour of Dublin, reminiscent of grade-school educational films. *(Mid-May to Oct. 10am-5pm, on the hour. £3, students £2.75. Combination ticket to Library and Dublin Experience £6, students £5.)* **The Douglas Hyde Gallery,** on the south side of campus, exhibits the works of modern Irish artists. *(Open M-Sa 10am-5pm. Free.)* During the academic year, Trinity bulges with events, which are listed on bulletin boards under the front arch or by the Nassau St. entrance. Concerts and plays are also posted.

Staring down Trinity from across College Green is a monolithic, Roman-looking building, the **Bank of Ireland** (tel. 677 6801). *(Open M-W and F 10am-4pm, Th 10am-5pm. 45min. guided tours Tu 10:30, 11:30am, and 1:45pm. Free.)* Built in 1729, the building originally housed the 18th-century Irish Parliament, a body that represented the Anglo-Irish landowning class. Its members envisioned a semi-independent Irish "nation" under the British crown made up of the privileged Protestants of the Pale. After the Act of Union, the British sold the building to the bank on the condition that the bank blot out any material evidence of the parliament. The enormous curved walls and pillars were erected *around* the original structure to make the whole thing look more impressive; the bank inside is actually much smaller. Tourists can still visit the former chamber of the House of Lords, where the gold mace of the old House of Commons hangs beneath a huge antique chandelier. The last Speaker of the House refused to hand the mace over, saying he would keep it until an Irish assembly

---

The Phil

Founded in 1684, Trinity College's University Philosophical Society is the oldest undergraduate student society in the world. With a current membership of 2000 students, "the Phil" counts Jonathan Swift, Oscar Wilde, Bram Stoker, and Samuel Beckett among its alumni. Throughout the past three centuries, the Society has held debates and read papers every Thursday evening at 7:30pm, even through times of trouble. After several members murdered the dean in a pistol shoot-out in the 18th century, the society was expelled from the college for a century of penance. This century's greatest prank was sabotaging a formal debate organized by the Historical Society, the Phil's greatest rival. "The Hist" invited a prominent black South African dissident to speak about apartheid; he accepted. The college administration, academics, press, and the public attended the much-anticipated event. The South African speaker arrived, gave his speech, debated, and answered questions. All in attendance clapped politely, although they were surprised by his pro-apartheid, rather racist views. At the end of the meeting, he revealed that he was a white South African member of the Phil covered in boot polish.

---

returned. Also on display is Maundy Money: special coins once given to the poor on the Thursday before Easter and legal tender only for that day.

South of College Green run the three or so blocks of **Grafton Street,** off-limits to cars and ground zero for shopping tourists and residents alike. This crowded pedestrian street provides some entertaining observations but nothing much to do or even to buy besides a Big Mac. Upstairs at the Grafton St. branch of Bewley's is the **Bewley's Museum,** located in the coffee chain's former chocolate factory. *(Open daily 10am-7pm. Free.)* Tea-tasting machines, corporate history, and a display on Bewley's Quaker heritage are among the fun curiosities.

Merrion Square and St. Stephen's Green

Leinster House, south of Trinity College, off Leinster St. between Kildare St. and Merrion Square, was once the house of the Duke of Leinster. When he built it, most of the urban upper-crust lived north of the Liffey. By erecting his house so far south, where land was cheaper, he was able to front it with an enormous lawn. The first Irishman to ride in a balloon ascended from this lawn in 1785. The airman had neglected to bring enough ballast, however, and drifted out over the Irish Sea, where well-aimed gunfire from the Dún Laoghaire barge brought him down. Now Leinster House provides chambers for the Irish parliament, holding both the Dáil (DOIL), which does most of the government work, and the Seanad (SHAN-ad), the less-powerful upper house. Together, these two houses make up the parliament, called An tOireachtas (on tir-OCH-tas). When the Dáil is in session, visitors can view the proceedings by contacting the Captain of the Guard (tel. 678 9911; passport necessary for identification). The Dáil meets, very roughly, Wednesday through Friday from January to July from 10:30am to 5pm. The Captain's office also conducts some **tours** of the Dáil's galleries. *(Tours Sa 10:30am-12:45pm and 1:30-4:50pm.)*

Near Leinster House, a passel of museums pops up. The **National Museum** (tel. 677 7444), now next to Leinster House, looks as though it may be bidding the square adieu. *(Open Tu-Sa 10am-5pm, Su 2-5pm. Free.)* By the summer of '99, curators hope to move most of the collection to the Gallery's new location at Colin's Barracks (the oldest purpose-built barracks in the world) across from the train station. The museum focuses on legendary ancient Ireland and the equally epic Easter Rising. One room gleams with the Tara Brooch, Ardagh Chalice, and other Celtic goldwork. Another, devoted to the Republic's founding years, offers plenty of historical information for the curious and shows off the bloody vest of nationalist hero James Connolly to pique the interest of the morbid. Other chambers collect musical instruments and, oddly, Japanese ceramics.

Connected to the National Museum, the **Natural History Museum** specializes in stuffed Irish wildlife. *(Same hours and number as the National Museum. Free.)* The collection is a tightly packed proliferation of dead animals in menacing poses, a bit like Narnia on crack. Mounted on the walls are beasts from the noble, extinct Great Irish elk to leeches and tapeworms. On the other side of Leinster House, the **National Library** (tel. 661 2523) chronicles Irish history and exhibits literary objects in its entrance room. *(Open M-W 10am-9pm, Th-F 10am-5pm, Sa 10am-1pm. Free, but academic reasons necessary to obtain a library card and entrance to the reading room.)* Down the street on Merrion Square West, the **National Gallery** (tel. 661 5133) holds 2400 canvases, including paintings by Brueghel, Goya, Rembrandt, and El Greco. *(Open M-Sa 10am-5:30pm, Th 10am-8:30pm, Su 2-5pm. Free.)* The works of Irish artists compose a major part of the collection. Portraits of Lady Gregory, Eliza O'Neill, James Joyce, George Bernard Shaw (who willed a third of his estate to the gallery), and William Butler Yeats (by his father, John Butler Yeats) stare at one another in the four-story staircase.

Dublin may remember its Viking conquerors more fondly than its British ones, but the British had much more influence on the appearance of the capital today. **Merrion Square** and **Fitzwilliam Street** (near the National Museum) are plum full of Georgian buildings and their elaborate rows of colored doorways. W.B. Yeats moved from 18 Fitzwilliam St. to 82 Merrion Sq. Farther south on Harcourt St., playwright George Bernard Shaw and Dracula's creator, Bram Stoker, were once neighbors at #61 and #16, respectively. **#29 Lower Fitzwilliam Street** (tel. 702 6165) tries to give tourists an impression of late 18th-century Dublin domestic life. *(Open Tu-Sa 10am-5pm, Su 2-5pm. £2.50, students £1.)* The prim Georgian townhouses continue up **Dawson Street,** which connects St. Stephen's Green to Trinity College one block west of Leinster House. A few small and endearing churches line this street, along with **Mansion House,** home of the Lord Mayors of Dublin since 1715. The house's various facades and additions give it an interesting but eclectic appearance. The Irish state declared independence here in 1919, and the Anglo-Irish truce was signed here in 1921.

Kildare, Dawson, and Grafton St. all lead south from Trinity to **St. Stephen's Green.** *(Gates open M-Sa 8am-dusk, Su 10am-dusk.)* The 22-acre park was a private estate until the Guinness clan bequeathed it to the city. Today the park is a center for activity, crowded with arched bridges, an artificial lake, flowerbeds, fountains, gazebos, pensioners, punks, trees, couples, strollers, swans, ducks, and a waterfall. On sunny days, half of Dublin seems to fill the lawns. During the summer, even the ducks enjoy the outdoor theatrical productions near the old bandstand. Edging the green, **Newman House,** 85-86 St. Stephen's Green South (tel. 706 7422), was once the seat of University College Dublin, the Catholic answer to Trinity. *(Open June-Sept. Tu-F noon-5pm, Sa 2-5pm, Su 11am-2pm. £2, students £1.)* Joyce's years here are chronicled in *Portrait of the Artist as a Young Man.* The poet Gerard Manley Hopkins spent the last years of his life teaching classics at the new college. Inside Newman House, the range of restored rooms has less kitsch than that at #29 Fitzwilliam.

The **George Bernard Shaw House,** 33 Synge St. (tel. 475 0854), between Grantham and Harrington St. off Camden Rd. near the Grand Canal Bridge, bills itself both as a period piece and as a glimpse into Shaw's childhood. *(Open May-Oct. M-Sa 10am-1pm and 2-6pm, Su 11:30am-1pm and 2-6pm. £2.40, children £1.15. Joint ticket with Dublin Writer's Museum and the James Joyce Tower at Kilinney £6, children £5.)* Mrs. Shaw held recitals, sparking little George's interest in music, and kept a lovely Victorian garden, sparking George's interest in landscape painting. So how did he get into socialism in London? If it's too wet to walk, take bus #16, 19, or 22 from O'Connell St. The **Irish Jewish Museum,** 3-4 Walworth Rd., off Victoria St. (tel. 676 0737), lies even farther from the city center. *(Open May-Sept. Tu, Th, and Su 11am-3pm, Oct.-Apr. Su 10:30am-2:30pm.)* South Circular Rd. runs to Victoria St., and from there the museum is signposted. A restored, former synagogue houses a large collection of artifacts, documents, and photographs chronicling the history of the very small Jewish community in Ireland from 1079—five arrived and were duly sent away—through the waves of European migration. The most famous Dublin Jew is, predictably, Leopold Bloom, hero of *Ulysses.* He's covered here, too.

Temple Bar, Dame Street, and Cathedrals

West of Trinity between Dame St. and the Liffey, the **Temple Bar** neighborhood wriggles with activity. Narrow cobblestone streets link cheap cafés, hole-in-the-wall theaters, rock venues, and used clothing and record stores. In the early 1980s, the Irish transport authority intended to replace the neighborhood with a seven-acre transportation center, but they decided to lease the land for the short term while they acquired all of the necessary property. The artists and transient types who moved into Temple Bar started a brouhaha about being forced into homelessness; in 1985 they circulated petitions and saved their homes and businesses from the rapacious transit project. Government-sponsored Temple Bar Properties has since spent over £30 million to build eight arts-related tourist attractions. Among the cultural attractions are the **Irish Film Centre** (tel. 679 5744); four contemporary art galleries; **The Ark** (tel. 670 7788), a cultural center aimed at seven- to fourteen-year olds; and the **Temple Bar Music Centre** (tel. 670 9202). Call each venue directly, or consult the Dublin Event Guide (tel. 677 7349). Next to the Temple Bar area is the **Dublin Viking Adventure,** Essex St. West (tel. 679 6040). (Open Th-M 9:30am-4pm. £4.75, students £3.95.) Walk through the Dublin of the 9th and 10th century and talk with the Dubliners of long ago. For added fun, try to get the actors to break character.

South of the Temple Bar across Dame St. awaits an inviting shopping district (see **Shopping,** p. 110). The **Dublin Civic Museum,** South William St. (tel. 679 4260), seems a bit out of place in the middle of all those shops. (Open Tu-Sa 10am-6pm, Su 11am-2pm. Free.) The pint-size, two-story townhouse holds photos, antiquities, and knick-knacks relating to the whole range of Dublin life, from the comparatively small-toed Vikings to the shoes of Patrick Cotter, the 8'6" "giant of Ireland."

At the west end of Dame St., where it meets Parliament and Castle St., sits **Dublin Castle** (tel. 677 7129). King John built the castle in 1204 on top of an old Viking fort. For the next 700 years Dublin Castle was the seat of British rule in Ireland. The present Dublin Castle structure actually dates mostly from the 18th and 19th centuries. Fifty insurgents died at the castle's walls on Easter Monday, 1916 (see **History,** p. 60). Since 1938 the presidents of Ireland have been inaugurated here. The **State Apartments,** once home to English viceroys, now entertain EU representatives and foreign heads of state. (State Apartments open M-F 10am-12:15pm and 2-5pm, Sa-Su and holidays 2-5pm, except during official functions. £2, students £1.) The Visitors Centre exhibits photos of many of Dublin's architectural showpieces and of the castle itself. Next door, the **Dublin City Hall,** designed as the Royal Exchange in 1779, boasts an intricate inner dome and statues of national heroes like Daniel O'Connell.

Dublin's ecclesiastical beauties stand west of the castle. All are owned by the Church of Ireland, none by the Catholic Church. As Ireland is overwhelmingly Catholic and the Anglo-Irish aristocracy no longer exists, the cathedrals and churches are now considered works of art more than centers of worship. **Christ Church Cathedral** (tel. 677 8099) looms at the end of Dame St., uphill and across from the Castle. (Open daily 10am-5pm except during services. Choral evensong Sept.-May Th 6pm. £1; free with Dublinia, below.) Sigtyggr Silkenbeard, King of the Dublin Norsemen, built a wooden church on this site in 1038, and Strongbow rebuilt it in stone in 1169. Further additions were made in the following century and again in the 1870s. Stained glass sparkles above the raised crypts (one of them supposedly Strongbow's own). The cavernous crypt once held shops and drinking houses, but now cobwebs hang down from the ceiling, fragments of ancient pillars lie about like bleached bones, and a mummified cat is frozen in the act of chasing a mummified mouse. Christ Church also hosts **Dublinia** (tel. 679 4611), a charming recreation of medieval Dublin with life-size reconstructions of a merchant's house and of Wood Quay circa 1200. (Open Apr.-Oct. daily 10am-5pm; Sept.-Mar. 11am-4pm. £4, students and children £3, includes admission to Christ Church.) Less charming is the buboe-covered mannequin in the Black Death display. Take buses #50 from Eden Quay or 78A from Aston Quay.

From Christ Church, Nicholas St. runs south and downhill, becoming Patrick St. and passing **St. Patrick's Cathedral** (tel. 475 4817). (Open M-F 9am-6pm, Sa 9am-5pm, Su 10-11am and 12:45-4:30pm. £1.20.) The body of the church dates to the 12th century, although Sir Benjamin Guinness remodeled much of the church in 1864. Measuring 300 ft. from stem to stern, it's Ireland's longest church. St. Patrick allegedly baptized converts in the park next to the cathedral. Artifacts and relics from the Order of St. Patrick show up inside. Jonathan Swift spent his last years as Dean of St. Patrick's, and Sir Walter Scott said of his visit to St. Patrick's that "one thinks of nothing but Swift there…The whole cathedral is practically his tomb." His crypt rises above the south nave. Take bus #50, 54A, or 56A from Eden Quay.

Marsh's Library, St. Patrick's Close (tel. 454 3511), beside St. Patrick's Cathedral, is Ireland's oldest public library. *(Open M and W-F 10am-12:45pm and 2-5pm, Sa 10:30am-12:45pm. £1 donation expected.)* A peek inside reveals its elegant wire alcoves, or "cages," and an extensive collection of early maps. Farther west, along High St., stands **St. Audoen's Church** (Church of Ireland), the oldest of Dublin's parish churches, which was founded by the Normans (and not to be confused with the completely separate Catholic St. Audoen's Church). *(Open Sa-Su 2:30-5pm.)* Papal Bulls were read aloud here during the Middle Ages. **St. Audoen's Arch,** built in 1215 next to the church and now obscured by a narrow alley, is the only gate that survives from Dublin's medieval **city walls.** During the 16th century, the walls ran from Parliament St. to the Dublin Castle, along the castle walls to Little Ship St., along Francis St. to Bridge St., and then along the Liffey.

Guinness Brewery and Kilmainham

From Christ Church Cathedral, follow High St. west (away from downtown) through its name changes—Cornmarket, Thomas, then James—to reach the giant **Guinness Brewery,** St. James Gate (tel. 453 6700; fax 408 4965). Take bus #68A or 78A from Ashton Quay or bus #123 from O'Connell St. **The Hop Store,** on Crane St. off James St., is Guinness's way of perpetuating the legend of the world's best stout. *(Open Apr.-Sept. M-Sa 9:30am-5pm, Su 10:30am-4:30; Oct.-Mar. M-Sa 9:30am-4pm, Su noon-4pm. £3, students £2, children £1.)* The building still smells of the hops that were stored there for 200 years. Farsighted Arthur Guinness signed a 9000-year lease at the original 1759 brewery nearby. There are exhibits on the historical and modern processes of brewing, a short promotional film, and art exhibits that showcase local talent. Best of all is the bar, where visitors get two complimentary glasses of the dark and creamy goodness. Some believe this glass to be the best Guinness in Dublin and, as such, the world's best beer. Don't even ask if it's "good for you." Drink, silly tourist.

The Royal Hospital and Kilmainham Gaol lie farther to the west, a 20-minute walk from the city center. "The cause for which I die has been rebaptized during this past week by the blood of as good men as ever trod God's earth," wrote Sean MacDiarmada in a letter to his family while he awaited his execution for participation in the 1916 Easter Rising (see **The Easter Rising (1914-1918),** p. 60). He, along with most of the rebels who fought in Ireland's struggle for independence from 1792 to 1921, was imprisoned at **Kilmainham Gaol** (tel. 453 5984). *(Open Apr.-Sept. daily 9:30am-4:45pm; Oct.-Mar. M-F 9:30am-4pm, Su 10am-4:45pm. £2, students and children £1.)* Take bus #51 from Aston Quay, #51A from Lower Abbey St., or #79 from Aston Quay. The jail's last occupant was Éamon de Valera, the future Éire leader who had been imprisoned by his own countrymen. Today the former prison is a museum that traces the history of penal practices over the last two centuries. The tour, which lasts 1½ hours, begins in the prison chapel, where Easter Rebel Joseph Plunkett was married to his betrothed hours before his execution. The reception was a subdued affair.

The **Royal Hospital Kilmainham** began in 1679; it wasn't a "hospital" in the modern sense but a hospice for retired or disabled soldiers. *(Tours Su noon-4:30pm and by request. £1.)* The facade and courtyard copy those of Les Invalides in Paris; the baroque chapel looks cool, too. Since 1991 the hospital has held the **Irish Museum of Modern Art** (tel. 671 8666), which took some heat over its avant-garde use of this historic space. *(Call for changing exhibits, artist talks, or concerts. Museum and building open Tu-Sa 10am-5:30pm, Su noon-5:30pm. Free. Guided tours W and F 2:30pm, Sa 11:30am.)* Modern Irish artists are intermixed with others as the gallery builds up a permanent collection in its capacious, brightly colored galleries.

North Side

O'Connell St. and Parnell Square

Rising from the river to Parnell Square, **O'Connell St.** is the commercial center of Dublin, at least for those who can't afford to shop on Grafton St. It's also said to be the widest street in Europe, though it's hard to imagine anyone traveling to Madrid with a yardstick to compare. In its Joycean heyday, it was known as Sackville St. After independence, the name was changed in honor of "The Liberator" (see **Independence and Civil War (1919-1922)**, p. 60). Smaller avenues leading off O'Connell St. retain the old name. The center traffic islands are monuments to Irish leaders Parnell, O'Connell, and James Larkin, who organized the heroic Dublin general strike of 1913. O'Connell's statue faces the Liffey and O'Connell Bridge; the winged women aren't angels but Winged Victories, although one has a bullet hole from 1916 in a rather inglorious place.

Farther up the street, the newer statue of a woman lounging in water is officially named the Spirit of the Liffey or "Anna Livia," unoffically and scathingly called "the floozy in the jacuzzi," "the whore in the sewer" (in Dublin, that rhymes, too), or "Anna Rexia." The even newer statue of Molly Malone, of ballad fame, on Grafton St. gets called "the tart with the cart." Decide for yourself whether Dubliners are mocking the city, the monument-making mentality, or the popular. One monument you won't see is **Nelson's Pillar,** a tall freestanding column that remembered Trafalgar outside the GPO for 150 years. The IRA blew it up in 1966 in commemoration of the 50th anniversary of the Easter Rising. Nelson's English head rests safely in the Dublin Civic Museum.

The **General Post Office** presides over O'Connell St. Not just a fine place to send a letter, the Post Office was the nerve center of the 1916 Rising. Patrick Pearse read the Proclamation of Irish Independence from its steps. When British troops closed in, mailbags became barricades. Outside, some bullet nicks are visible; inside, a glass case exhibits pennies fused together by the British army's incendiary bombing. Turn right on Cathedral St., a few blocks up O'Connell St., to find the inconspicuous **Dublin Pro-Cathedral,** the city's center of Catholic worship, where tens of thousands once gathered for Daniel O'Connell's memorial service. "Pro" means "provisional"— Dublin Catholics want Christ Church Cathedral returned (see p. 103).

The **Hugh Lane Municipal Gallery,** Parnell Sq. North (tel. 874 1903), holds modern art within the Georgian walls of Charlemont House. *(Open Tu-F 9:30am-6pm, Sa 9:30am-5pm, Su 11am-5pm. Free.)* When Lane offered to donate his collection of French Impressionist paintings to the city, he did so on the condition that the people of Dublin contribute to the gallery's construction. Because his collection and the architect chosen to build the gallery were foreign, Dubliners refused to lend their support; Yeats lamented their provincial attitudes in a string of poems. Lane's death aboard *Lusitania* in 1915 raised decades of disputes over his will, resolved by a plan to share the collection between the gallery in Dublin and the Tate Gallery in London.

Next door, the **Dublin Writers' Museum,** 18 Parnell Sq. North (tel. 872 207), introduces visitors to the city's rich literary heritage. *(Open June-Aug. M-F 10am-6, Sa 10am-5pm, Su 11am-5pm; Sept.-May M-Sa 10am-5pm, Su 11am-5pm. £2.95, students £2.50. Combined ticket with either Shaw birthplace or James Joyce Centre £5, student £3.80.)* Rare editions, manuscripts, and memorabilia of Swift, Shaw, Wilde, Yeats, Beckett, Brendan Behan, Patrick Kavanagh, and Sean O'Casey blend with caricatures, paintings, and an incongruous Zen Garden. Adjacent to the museum, the **Irish Writer's Centre,** 19 Parnell Sq. North (tel. 872 1302), is the center of Ireland's writing community, providing working and meeting space for today's aspiring Joyces. Frequent poetry and fiction readings present current writings to the public. The center is not a museum, but if you ring the doorbell you can get information about Dublin's literary happenings. Just past Parnell Sq., the **Garden of Remembrance** eulogizes the martyrs who took the GPO. A cross-shaped pool is plugged at one end by a statue representing the mythical Children of Lir, who turned from humans into swans. They proclaim, in

COUNTY DUBLIN

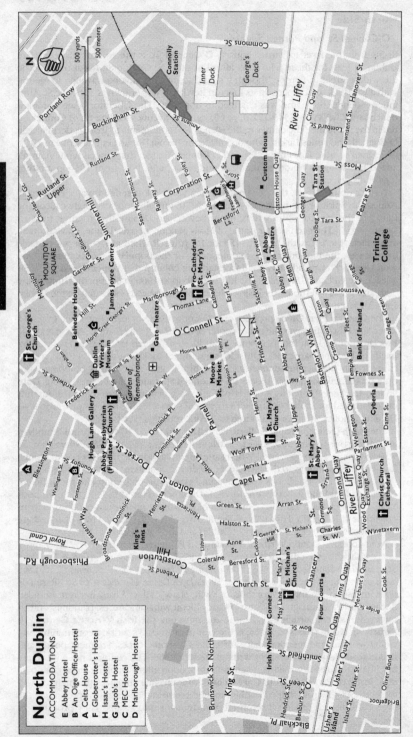

North Dublin

ACCOMMODATIONS

- E Abbey Hostel
- B An Oige Office/Hostel
- A Celts House
- F Globetrotter's Hostel
- G Isaac's Hostel
- H Jacob's Hostel
- C MEC Hostel
- D Marlborough Hostel

N

500 yards
500 meters

Royal Canal
Phisborough Rd.
Portland Row
Buckingham St.
Connolly Station
Inner Dock
George's Dock
Commons St.
River Liffey
Amiens St.
Rutland St.
Rutland St. Upper
Charles St. Gt.
Summerhill
Gardiner's Ln.
Sean McDermott St.
Railway St.
Foley St.
Corporation St.
Store St.
Custom House
Custom House Quay
City Quay
Lombard St.
Hanover St.
Townsend St.
Moss St.
Tara St. Station
Pearse St.
Talbot St.
Beresford La.
Frenchman's La.
George's Quay
Poolbeg St.
Tara St.
Trinity College
Pro-Cathedral (St. Mary's)
Cathedral St.
Earl St.
Marlborough St.
Thomas Lane
Gate Theatre
O'Connell St.
Sackville Pl.
Abbey St. Lower
Abbey St. Old Theatre
Abbey St.
Eden Quay
Burgh Quay
Westmoreland St.
College St.
College Green
Bank of Ireland
Fleet St.
Aston Quay
Crampton Quay
Temple Bar
Fownes St.
Dame St.
Cyberia
Essex St.
Parliament St.
Wellington Quay
Essex Quay
Wood Quay
Christ Church Cathedral
Winetavern St.
Merchant's Quay
Cook St.
Bridge St.
Oliver Bond
Bridgefoot St.
Usher's Quay
Usher's Island
Island St.
Usher St.
Blackhall Pl.
Queen's St.
Hendrick St.
Benburb St.
Smithfield St.
King St.
Brunswick St. North
Arran Quay
Bow St.
Inns Quay
Four Courts
Church St.
Chancery St.
May Lane
Irish Whiskey Corner
St. Michan's Church
Mary's La.
George's Hill
Cuckoo La.
St. Michan's St.
Charles St. W.
Ormond Quay
Strand St.
Ormond Quay
Capel St.
St. Mary's Abbey
St. Mary's Church
Abbey St. Upper
Liffey St. Lower
Jervis St.
Wolf Tone
Jervis La.
Henry St.
Great. Henry St.
Bachelor's Walk
Prince's St. N.
Moore Lane
Moore St.
Moore St. Market
Sampson's La.
Parnell St.
Bolton St.
Dorset St.
Loftus La.
Dominick La.
Dominick St.
Dominick Pl.
Garden of Remembrance
Parnell Sq. E.
Parnell Sq. W.
Hugh Lane Gallery
Dublin Writer's Museum
Abbey Presbyterian (Findlater's Church)
North Great George's St.
James Joyce Centre
Belvedere House
Hardwicke St.
Frederick St.
Gardiner St.
Hill St.
Mountjoy Square
Mountjoy St.
St. George's Church
Blessington St.
Wellington St.
Fontenoy St.
Western Way
Broadstone
Dominick
King's Inns
Constitution Hill
Henrietta Pl.
Henrietta St.
Halston St.
Green St.
Anne St.
Lisburn St.
Beresford St.
Coleraine St.
Prebend St.
Arran St.

Irish, their faith in a vision of freedom: "In the winter of bondage we saw a vision. We melted the snows of lethargy and the river of resurrection flowed from it."

One block east of Parnell Sq. East lies the new **James Joyce Centre,** 35 North Great Georges St. (tel. 873 1984), up Marlborough St. across Parnell St. *(Open Apr.-Oct. M-Sa 9:30am-5pm, Su noon-5pm; Nov.-Mar. Tu-Sa 10am-4:30pm, Su 12:30-4:30pm. £2.50, students £1.75, children 70p.)* If you only visit one of Dublin's many Joycean institutions, this restored 18th-century Georgian house should be it. Run by his nephew, this museum features documents, photos, and manuscripts that make Joyce come alive. Feel free to mull over his works in the library or the tearoom, whose walls are lined with a *Ulysses* mural depicting each of the book's chapters. Call for info on lectures, walking tours, and Bloomsday events.

Along the Quays

East of O'Connell St. at Custom House Quay, where Gardiner St. meets the river, is one of Dublin's architectural triumphs, the **Custom House.** It was designed and built in the 1780s by James Gandon, who gave up the chance to be St. Petersburg's state architect to settle in Dublin. The building's expanse of columns and domes suggests the mix of Rome and Venice that the 18th-century Anglo-Irish wanted their city to become. Carved heads along the frieze represent the rivers of Ireland; the Liffey is the only woman of the bunch. Several quays to the west, on Inn's Quay, stands another of Gandon's works, the **Four Courts.** From the quay or across the river, the building appears monumentally impressive, but the back and sides reveal 20th-century ballast. On April 14, 1922, General Rory O'Connor seized the Four Courts on behalf of the anti-Treaty IRA; two months later, the Free State government of Griffith and Collins attacked the Four Courts garrison, starting the Irish Civil War. The building now houses the highest court in Ireland.

Mummies! Just up Church St., the dry atmosphere has preserved the corpses in the vaults of **St. Michan's Church,** which inspired Bram Stoker's *Dracula. (Open mid-Mar.-Nov. M-F 10am-12:45pm and 2-4:45pm, Sa 10am-1pm; Dec. to mid-Mar. Sa 10am-1pm. £1.20, under 16 50p. Church of Ireland services on Su 10am.)* Of particular interest in this creepy place is a 6'6" crusader (dead) and the hanged, drawn, and quartered bodies of two of the 1759 rebels (very dead).

The **Irish Whiskey Corner,** Bow St. (tel. 872 5566), is located in a whiskey warehouse off Mary St. *(Tours May-Oct. M-F 11am, 2:30, and 3:30pm, Sa 3:30pm; Nov.-Apr. M-F 3:30pm. £3.50, students £2.)* From O'Connell St., turn onto Henry St. and continue straight as the street becomes Mary St., then Mary Ln., then May Ln.; the warehouse is on a cobblestone street on the left. Learn how science, grain, and tradition come together to create the golden fluid with "the coveted appellation, whiskey." The film recounts the rise, fall, and spiritual renaissance of Ireland's favorite spirit. The experience ends with a glass of the Irish whiskey of your choice. Feel the burn.

Distant Sights

Take bus #10 from O'Connell St. or #25 or 26 from Middle Abbey St. west along the river to **Phoenix Park,** Europe's largest enclosed public park. The "Phoenix Park murders" mentioned in *Ulysses* happened in 1882; the Invincibles, a tiny nationalist splinter group, stabbed the Chief Secretary of Ireland, Lord Cavendish, and his Under-Secretary 200 yd. from the Phoenix Column. A British Unionist journalist forged a series of letters linking Parnell to the murderers. The Phoenix Column, a Corinthian column capped with a phoenix rising from flames, is something of a pun—the park's name actually comes from the Irish *Fionn Uisce,* "clean water." The 1760-acre park incorporates the President's residence *(Áras an Uachtaráin),* the U.S. Ambassador's residence, cricket pitches, polo grounds, and grazing red deer and cattle. The deer are quite tame and not to be missed; they usually graze in the thickets near Castleknock Gate. The park is usually peaceful during daylight hours but very unsafe at night. **Dublin Zoo** (tel. 677 1425), one of the world's oldest zoos and Europe's largest, is nearby. *(Open June-Aug. M-Sa 9:30am-6pm, Su 10:30am-6pm; Sept.-May M-F 9:30am-4pm, Sa 9:30am-5pm, Su 10:30am-5pm. £5.50, students £4, children £3, families £15.)* It contains 700 animals and a discovery centre that features the world's biggest egg. Bus #10 from O'Connell St. passes the zoo.

Casino Marino, Malahide Rd. (tel. 833 1618), is an architectural gem and house of tricks. *(Open daily mid-June to Sept. 9:30am-6:30pm; Oct. 10am-5pm; Nov. and Feb.-Apr. Su-W noon-4pm. £2.50, students £1.50, children £1.)* You can certainly gambol here, but you can't gamble; it's a casino only in the sense of "small house," built for the Earl of Charlemont in 1758 as a seaside villa. Funeral urns on the roof are chimneys, the columns are hollow and serve as drains, the casino has secret tunnels and trick doors, and the lions standing guard are actually made of stone. Speaking of tricks: since then, the house's ocean view has vanished! Take bus #20A or B from Eden Quay, or #27 or 27A from Lower Gardiner St.

ENTERTAINMENT

Be it Seamus Heaney or the Pogues you fancy, Dublin is equipped to entertain you. The *Dublin Event Guide* (free), available at the tourist office, Temple Bar restaurants, and the Temple Bar Info center, comes out every other Friday with ads in the back, fawning reviews in the front, and reasonably complete listings of museums and literary, musical, and theatrical events in between. Hostel staff are often good, if biased, sources of information. *In Dublin* (£1.50) comes out every two weeks with feature articles and listings for music, theater, art exhibitions, comedy shows, clubs, and movie theaters.

Music

Dublin's music world attracts performers from all over the country. Pubs are the scene of much of the musical action, since they provide musicians with free beer and a venue. There is often a cover charge of £3-4 on better-known acts. *Hot Press* (£1.50) has the most up-to-date music listings, particularly for rock. Its commentaries on the musical scene are usually insightful, and its left-leaning editorials give a clear impression of what the Dublin artistic community is thinking. *In Dublin* comes out less often and thus isn't quite so up-to-the-minute, but its listings are more comprehensive and it has a wider range of information. Record store clerks and habitués are valuable fonts of knowledge on the current Irish rock scene. Tower Records on Wicklow St. has reams of leaflets. Bills posted all over the city also inform of coming attractions. Scheduled concerts tend to start at 9pm, impromptu ones later.

Traditional music (trad) is not a tourist gimmick but a vibrant and important element of the Irish culture and the Dublin music scene. Some pubs in the city center have trad sessions nightly, others nearly so: **Hughes', Slattery's, Oliver St. John Gogarty,** and **McDaid's** are all good choices for trad (see **Pubs,** p. 94).

The best place for live music, from rock to folk, is **Whelan's,** 25 Wexford St. (tel. 478 0766), the continuation of South Great Georges St., with music nightly. Covers vary; look for posters around the city. Next door, **The Mean Fiddler,** Wexford St., has shows regularly. Big deal bands frequent the **Baggot Inn,** 143 Baggot St. (tel. 676 1430). U2 played here in the early 80s; some people are still talking about it. **An Béal Bocht** often hosts rock acts (see **Theater,** below). Big, big acts play to huge crowds at **Tivoli Theatre,** Francis St. (tel. 454 4472), and will be not only well publicized but also quite often sold out. **The Waterfront Rock Bar,** Sir John Rogerson's Quay (tel. 677 8466), was the big pub featured at the end of *The Commitments* ("Tour of Irish Rock" nightly 8pm; open Su-Th until 11:30pm, Th-Sa until late). Customers mellow at **Rudyard's Wine Bar,** 15 Crown Alley (tel. 671 0846), to the sound of live jazz sessions. **McDaid's,** 3 Henry St. (tel. 679 4395), hosts blues acts on Sundays at 8:30pm.

The **National Concert Hall,** Earl's Fort Terr. (tel. 671 1533), provides a venue for classical concerts and performances. July and August bring nightly shows (8pm; tickets £8-15, students half-price). A summer lunchtime series makes a nice break from work on occasional Tuesdays and Fridays (tickets £2.50-3). Programs for the National Symphony and smaller local groups are available at classical music stores and the tourist office. Sunday afternoon jazz is a common phenomenon. *In Dublin* has listings. The biggest names in rock and pop play at **Croke Park,** Clonliffe Rd. (tel. 836 3152), and the R.D.S. in Ballsbridge.

Theater

Dublin's curtains rise on a full range of mainstream productions, classic shows, and experimental theater. Showtime is generally 8pm. Off Dame St. and Temple Bar, smaller theater companies thrive, presenting new plays and innovative interpretations of classics.

Abbey Theatre, 26 Lower Abbey St. (tel. 878 7222), was founded by Yeats and his collaborator Lady Gregory in 1904 to promote Irish cultural revival and modernist theater, which turned out to be a bit like promoting corned beef and soy burgers—most people wanted one or the other. J.M. Synge's *Playboy of the Western World* was first performed here in 1907. The production occasioned storms of protest and yet another of Yeats' political poems. (See **Literary Traditions,** p. 63.) Today, the Abbey, like Synge, has become respectable. As part of the National Theatre, it receives government funding. Box office open M-Sa 10:30am-7pm. Tickets £10-25; student standby M and Th 1hr. before show, £8.

Peacock Theatre, 26 Lower Abbey St. (tel. 878 7222), downstairs from the Abbey and more experimental. The usual evening shows plus occasional lunchtime plays, concerts, and poetry (£8, students £5). Box office open M-Sa at 7:30pm for that night's performance only; advance booking at the Abbey Theatre box office.

Gate Theatre, 1 Cavendish Row (tel. 874 4045), produces everything from Restoration comedies to Irish classics. Box office open M-Sa 10am-7pm. Tickets £10-12; student standby M-Th £6 at curtain time.

Project Arts Centre, 39 East Essex St. (tel. 671 2321), presents not just theater but all the performing arts, including dramatic readings, comedy, and dance. Box office open daily 10am-6pm; tickets £8, with concession £6. The gallery hosts rotating visual arts exhibitions (open same time as box office; free).

Gaiety, South King St. (tel. 677 1717), provides space for modern drama, ballet, pantomime, music, and the Dublin Grand Opera Society. Box office open M-Sa 11am-7pm; tickets £7.50-12.50.

Olympia Theatre, 72 Dame St. (tel. 677 7744). Old standbys like *The Sound of Music.* Box office open M-Sa 10am-6:30pm; tickets £8-15; ½-price student standby tickets after 7pm.

Andrews Lane Theatre, Andrews Ln. (tel. 679 5720), off Dame St. Dramatic classics, old and new—Shakespeare, Molière, Brecht.

An Béal Bocht, 58 Charlemont St. (tel. 475 5614), hosts traditional Irish-language theater W at 9pm. £4.

City Arts Centre, 23-25 Moss St. (tel. 677 0643), parallel to Tara St. off Georges Quay. Avant-garde exploration of sexual and political issues. £8, students £5.

Samuel Beckett Theatre, Trinity College (tel. 478 3397). Inside the campus. Hosts anything that happens by.

Cinema

Ireland's well-supported film industry got a kick in the pants with the arrival of the **Irish Film Centre,** Eustace St. (tel. 679 3477), Temple Bar. The IFC mounts tributes and festivals, including a French film festival in October and a gay and lesbian film festival in August. A variety of classic and European arthouse films appear throughout the year. You must be a "member" to buy tickets. (Weekly membership £1; yearly membership £10, students £7.50. Membership must be purchased at least 20min. before start of show. Each member can buy only 4 tickets per screening. Matinees £2; 5pm showing £2.50; after 7pm £4, students £3.) Other artsy cinemas are the **Light House Cinema,** Middle Abbey St. (tel. 873 0438; £3 before 5pm, £5 after), and **The Screen,** D'Olier St. (tel. 671 4988 or 872 3922). First-run movie houses cluster on O'Connell St., the quays, and Middle Abbey St. The **Savoy,** O'Connell St. (tel. 874 6000) and **Virgin,** Parnell St. (tel. 872 8400) offer the widest selection of new releases, primarily American films.

Sports and Recreation

Dubliners, probably because they have more to distract them, aren't as sports-centered as their country cousins tend to be. Sports are still a serious business, though, as attested to by the frequency of matches and events and the amount of money spent on them. The seasons for **Gaelic football** and **hurling** (the national sports of Ireland) run from mid-February to November (see **Sports,** p. 69). Both are games of skill, stamina, and strength that have evolved from ancient origins. Action-packed and often brutal, these games are entertaining for any sports-lover. Provincial finals take place in July, national semifinals on Sundays in August (hurling the first week, football the 2nd and 3rd weeks), and All-Ireland Finals in September. Games are played in **Croke Park** and **Phibsborough Rd.** (tickets available at the turnstiles; All-Ireland Finals tickets sell out quickly). Home games of the Irish **rugby** team are played in **Lansdowne Road Stadium** (Oct.-Mar.). **Camogie** (women's hurling) finals also take place in September. For sports information, check the Friday papers or contact the Gaelic Athletic Association (tel. 836 3232). Formal and pick-up games of **cricket** also spring up on Trinity's sports fields. **Greyhound racing** continues all year. Races start at 8pm and end around 10pm (M and Sa at Shelbourne Park, tel. 668 3502; Tu, Th, and F at Harold's Cross, tel. 497 1081). **Horses** race at Leopardstown Racetrack, Foxrock, Dublin 18 (tel. 289 2888). On the first or second weekend of August the **Royal Dublin Horse Show** takes place at the RDS in Ballsbridge.

Festivals and Events

The tourist office's *Calendar of Events* (£1; info on events throughout Ireland) and bimonthly *Dublin Events Guide* (free; biweekly) describe Dublin's many festivals, provincial parades, mayor's balls, concerts, dances, and art shows. Ask about *fleadhs* (FLAHS), traditional day-long musical festivals. The **World Irish Dancing Championships** are held in late March or early April. The **Festival of Music in Irish Houses,** held during the second and third weeks of June, organizes concerts of period music in local 18th-century homes. The **Dublin Film Festival** (tel. 679 2937) in March features Irish and international movies and a panoply of seminars. The **Temple Bar Blues Festival** is a three-day blues extravaganza in mid-July. Bluesmen come from all over. Past guests have included Robert Cray and B.B. King. (Contact Temple Bar Information Centre for information, tel. 671 5717; most acts free; program guides available in July.) **St. Patrick's Day** (Mar. 17) occasions enormous parades, drunken carousing, and closed banks. Pubs offer special promotions, contests, and extended hours. Don't expect corned beef and cabbage for dinner though—that's more of an Irish-American tradition.

Dublin returns to 1904 each year on **Bloomsday,** June 16, the day on which the action of Joyce's *Ulysses* takes place. Festivities are held all week long. The **Joyce Centre** (tel. 873 1984) sponsors a mock funeral and wake, a lunch at Davy Byrne's, and a breakfast with Guinness, all as part of its Bloomstime program. On the day itself, a Messenger Bike Rally culminates in St. Stephen's Green with drink and food. Many bookstores have readings from *Ulysses.* Some of the better ones are Hodges Figgis and Waterstone's (p. 111). Check out the June issue of *In Dublin* and the *Dublin Event Guide* for year-to-year details.

The **Dublin Theatre Festival** in late September and early October is a premier cultural event. Tickets may be purchased all year at participating theaters and at branches of the Irish Life Building Society (main office on Lower Abbey St., tel. 704 2000). As the festival draws near, tickets are also available at the Festival Booking Office, 47 Nassau St., Dublin 2 (tel. 677 8439; tickets £8-14, £2 student discount; student standby tickets £3-5).

SHOPPING

Dublin is not really a center for international trade, and consumer goods are generally expensive. Your time may be better spent in pubs and castles. That said, if something is made anywhere in Ireland, you can probably find it in Dublin. Stores are usually open from 9am to 6pm Monday through Saturday, with later hours on Thursdays (until 7-8pm). Tiny shops pop up everywhere along the streets both north and south of the Liffey, but Dublin's major shopping is on **Grafton** and **Henry St.** On pedestrianized Grafton St., well-dressed consumers crowd into boutiques and restaurants, and buskers aplenty lay out their caps for money. At the top of Grafton St., **St. Stephen's Green Shopping Centre** is, well, a mall. Nearby, Lord Powerscourt's 200-year-old townhouse on Clarendon St., now the **Powerscourt Townhouse Centre,** has been converted into a string of chic boutiques carrying Irish crafts. GenX shoppers can head to **Georges St. Market Arcade** on South Great Georges St. near Dame St. The arcade includes a number of vintage clothing, jewelry, and used record stalls as well as a fortune teller. (Nose-piercing with stud £1.50. Open M-Sa 8am-6pm, Th 8am-7pm.) **Wild-Child,** 61 South Great Georges St. (tel. 475 5099), has Dublin's largest selection of vintage and secondhand goods, including clothes, jewelry, accessories, make-up, and posters (open M-Sa 10am-6pm, Th 10am-7pm). The **Festival Market,** at the corner of Nicholas St. and Back Ln. off High St. (just past Christ Church), is better known for inexpensive clothing and jewelry than for produce (open F-Su 9am-5pm).

Teens and barely-twenties buy their used clothes and punk discs in the **Temple Bar.** A **Temple Bar Passport** entitles you to discounts at stores and restaurants (available at hostels or the Temple Bar Info Centre, 18 Eustace St.). Across the river, Henry and Talbot St. sport shops for those on a tighter budget. **Henry St.,** off O'Connell, has cheaper goods, in price and quality, to suit a less finicky clientele. **ILAC,** another mall, lurks just around the corner on Moore St. (behind a rainbow facade), where street vendors sell fresh produce at very low prices. **Clery's** (tel. 878 6000) on Upper O'Connell St. is Dublin's principal department store. They pride themselves on quality goods to meet every need. Get great deals on high quality Irish linens to give to the folks at home. (Open M-W and F-Sa 9am-5:30pm, Th 9am-8pm.)

Dublin's Literary Shopping

Waterstone's, 7 Dawson St. (tel. 679 1415), off Nassau St. 5 floors of well-stacked books and an informed reference staff. Open M-F 9am-8:30pm, Sa 9am-7pm, Su noon-7pm.

Hodges Figgis, 56-58 Dawson St. (tel. 677 4754). Part of an English chain, this large bookstore has a good selection for those with eclectic tastes. Open M-F 9am-7pm, Sa 9am-6:30pm, Su noon-6pm.

Eason's, 40-42 Lower O'Connell St. (tel. 873 3811). The biggest game in town. Lots of serious tomes and an extensive "Irish interest" section. Wide selection of local and foreign magazines and newspapers. Special bargain section in the basement. Open M-Sa 8:30am-6:15pm.

Fred Hanna's, 27-29 Nassau St. (tel. 677 1255), across from Trinity College at Dawson St. Second-hand books mingle with new ones under the watchful eye of an intelligent staff. Any questions about contemporary Irish writing are best answered here. Open M-Sa 9am-5:30pm.

Books Upstairs, 36 College Green (tel. 679 6687), near Trinity Gate. Dublin's alternative bookshop. Extensive sections on gay literature and women's studies. The principal distributor for *Gay Community News.*

Winding Stair Bookstore, 40 Ormond Quay (tel. 873 3292), on the North Side. 3 atmospheric floors of good tunes, great Liffey views, and cheap café food. Used books, contemporary Irish literature, and literary periodicals. Open M-Sa 10:30am-6pm.

An Siopa Leabhar, 6 Harcourt St. (tel. 478 3814). Varied selection of Irish historical and political books, as well as tapes and books on traditional music. Specializes in literature and resources in Irish.

Records, Tapes, and CDs

Besides **Tower** (tel. 671 3250), the megastores in Dublin are **HMV,** Grafton St. (tel. 679 7817), and **Virgin,** 14 Aston Quay (tel. 677 7361). Megastores are stocked mostly with CDs, but the smaller places are more balanced between CDs and cassettes. Cassettes run £6-12, CDs £11-16.

Celtic Note, Nassau St. Specializes in Irish traditional and classical music.

Claddagh Records, 2 Cecilia St. (tel. 677 0262), Temple Bar, between Temple Ln. and Crow St. Best selection of trad and a variety of music from other countries. Open daily June-Sept. 10:30am-5:30pm; Oct.-May 12:30-5:30pm.

Freebird Records, 1 Eden Quay (tel. 873 1250), on the North Side facing the river. Slick, crowded basement shop below a newsstand proves its name with a good selection of indie rock, probably Dublin's best. Proprietors are refreshingly honest about which local bands they actually like. Open M-Sa 10:30am-6pm.

Comet Records, 5 Cope St. (tel. 671 8592), Temple Bar. Much like Freebird, but smaller and open later. More info on current groups and gigs, used LPs, and new indie CDs. Punk, metal, techno, and t-shirts, too. Open M-Sa 10am-6:30pm.

Smile, 59 South Great Georges St. (tel. 478 2005). Good selection of American soul and jazz. Also has a wall of used books, some of which expound on rock. "Shoplifters will be reincarnated as snails," they warn. Don't let it happen to you, sluggo. Open M-Sa 10am-6pm.

GAY, LESBIAN, AND BISEXUAL DUBLIN

Dublin's progressive (for Ireland) thinking translates into a tolerance that has been exemplified by the success of PRIDE, an annual, week-long festival in July celebrating gay identity. This attitude has encouraged the development of a small but lively gay scene punctuated by organized events. *Gay Community News* offers the most comprehensive and up-to-date information on gay life and nightlife in Dublin (free; available at Books Upstairs Bookstore, Temple Bar Information Centre, and the Well Fed Café). *In Dublin*'s gay page lists pubs, dance clubs, saunas, gay-friendly restaurants, bookshops, hotlines, and organizations. The listings are comprehensive but sometimes outdated. Copies of *Out* and *Advocate* magazines, when they make it here, can be found at Eason's bookstore. Visit **Books Upstairs,** 36 College Green (tel. 679 6687), for your copy of the pricey *Irish Scene Gay Guide* (£7), which lists gay hotlines and venues throughout Ireland, or *The English Gay Times,* a monthly magazine that addresses social and political issues.

Gay Switchboard Dublin is a good resource for events and updates and sponsors a hotline (tel. 872 1055; Su-F 8-10pm, Sa 3:30-6pm). **Lesbian Line** offers similar services (tel. 661 3777; open Th 7-9pm). **The National Gay and Lesbian Federation,** Hirschfield Centre, 10 Fownes St. (tel. 671 0939), in Temple Bar, publishes *Gay Community News* and offers counseling on legal concerns. It is not an information service but can provide advice. The lesbian community meets at **LOT** (Lesbians Organizing Together), 5 Capel St. (tel. 872 7770). The drop-in resource center and library is open Tuesdays and Thursdays 10am to 5pm. **Outhouse,** 65 William St. (tel. 6706377), is a gay community and research centre. Tune into local radio FM103.8 for a gay talk show, **Out in the Open** (Tu 8-10pm).

Out on the Liffey is Dublin's best gay pub. **The Front Lounge,** Parliament St. (tel. 679 3369), is a classy pub that stays open until 1am on Thursdays and Fridays. **The George** rocks every night in the attached disco, ruling the gay club scene. Most gay dance venues occur one night per week.

The George, 89 South Great Georges St. (tel. 478 2983). This throbbing, purple man o' war is Dublin's first gay bar. A mixed-age crowd gathers throughout the day to chat, sip, and admire the "artistic" pictures of men wearing nothing but white athletic socks. Lesbian night generally Wednesdays. Gay men Th-Su. Cover £4-7. Look spiffy—no effort, no entry. Periodic theme nights.

Out on the Liffey, 27 Upper Ormond Quay (tel. 872 2480). Ireland's second gay bar. The name is a deliberate play on words aimed at the traditional Inn on the Liffey down the street. Rather small and a hike from the city center. Lesbians are welcome but rarely appear. A small disco on the weekend offers bump and grind opportunities.

Stonewall, Griffth College, South Circular Rd., is large and lively. Dancing, a video screen, and pool tables make this club worth the trip. Some nights are male or female only—check *In Dublin* for details. Bus #19, 19A, or 22. Cover £5.

The Mean Fiddler, Wexford St., hosts **Heaven,** a gay night on Sundays.

The Candy Club, at the Kitchen, Essex St., draws in an artsy crowd of gays and lesbians. Open M 11pm-2:30am. Cover £4.

Gosh, at **Rí Rá,** 1 Exchequer St., hosts serious, well-dressed gays and lesbians. Open M 11pm-2:30am. Cover £6, concession £4.

DUBLIN'S SUBURBS

Strung along the Irish Sea from Donabate in the north to Killiney in the south, Dublin's suburbs offer a calmer alternative to the human tide on Grafton Street. Two standouts in the uniform suburban sprawl are Dún Laoghaire in the south, a port town that bulges into Dublin bay, and quiet, homey Howth in the north. DART and suburban rail are by far the best way to travel—single tickets are never more than £1.50. Buses, however, can be confusing and unreliable. Any of these towns north or south of Dublin can be seen in an afternoon, and all share Dublin's **phone code,** 01.

North of Dublin, castles and factories are surrounded by planned estates, all clamoring for a view of the rocky shore. The Velvet Strand, a plush stretch of rock and water, is Dublin's best beach (see **Malahide,** p. 115). Dublin's **southern** suburbs are tidy and a bit posh. The suburb/beach/port hybrids from Dún Laoghaire to Killiney form a nearly unbroken chain of snazzy houses and bright surf. The whole area is technically the "Borough of Dún Laoghaire." The individual towns are best considered neighborhoods within this larger area. A set of paths called the "Dún Laoghaire Way," "Dalkey Way," and so on connects the towns by what someone once decided was the best walking route. The separate parts combine into a trail three miles long. Getting from one town to the next is easy enough as long as you stay within 10 blocks of the sea, on the path or off. For those who don't want to invest the shoe leather, the DART also makes for great (and less exhausting) coastal views between Dalkey and Bray. An entertaining ramble would begin with a ride on bus #59 from the Dún Laoghaire DART station to the top of Killiney Hill and proceed along the path through the park and down into Dalkey.

■ Howth

Only 9 mi. from Dublin and quite DARTable, hilly Howth (rhymes with "both") gives a quick look at Ireland's highlights: scenery, pubs, history, literature, a castle, an abbey, and fresh fish all in one town. Dangling from the mainland, Howth looks out to sea from the north shore of Dublin Bay. Fish are inescapable here, in the sea, in the boats, in the restaurants, and sometimes in the air.

PRACTICAL INFORMATION

The easiest way to reach Howth is by **DART.** Take a northbound train to the end of the line (30min., 6 per hr., £1.10). **Buses** bound for Howth leave from Dublin's Lower Abbey S. Bus #31 runs every hour to the center of Howth, near the DART station, and #31B climbs Howth Summit. The *Guide to Howth Peninsula,* a hand-drawn map with sights and walking trails clearly labeled, is posted at the harbor entrance across from the St. Lawrence Hotel.

There is an ATM at **Bank of Ireland** (tel. 839 0271), 1 Main St. (open M-F 10am-4pm, Th 10am-5pm). Down the street is **C.S. McDermott's Pharmacy** (tel. 832 2069), 5 Main St. (open M-Sa 9am-6pm, Su 10:30am-1pm). The **post office,** 27 Abbey St. (tel. 831 8210), also exchanges currency.

ACCOMMODATIONS

Howth's B&Bs are all located on or near Thormanby Rd., which runs parallel to the beach one block from the coast.

Gleann na Smól (tel. 832 2936), on the left at the end of Nashville Rd. off Thormanby Rd. This full-service B&B is the most convenient in Howth. Weary travelers are spared the long trek other places require, and the cliff walk begins practically at the back door. Mrs. Rickard's satellite dish pulls in MTV and CNN for the benefit of the post-literate, while a generous supply of books suits wormier guests. Huge bathrooms and lip-smackin' homemade bread with fresh rhubarb jam. £20, all rooms with bath. Ask about ISIC discounts.

Highfield (tel. 832 3936), a 20min. walk up Thormanby Rd. Highfield's sign is obscured by its hedges, but it's on the left as you go up the hill. Honeysuckle tumbles onto the lawn during the spring and summer. Inside, beautiful floral prints spill onto the bedspreads and wallpaper. Comfortable lounge with cable TV. £19.50, all rooms with bath.

Hazelwood (tel. 839 1391), in the Thormanby Woods estate off Thormanby Rd. Peace and quiet in an already demure town. £19.50, all rooms with bath.

FOOD AND PUBS

Quash your monstrous traveler's appetite with fabulous pizza and sundaes at **Porto Fino's** (tel. 839 3054), Harbour Rd. (open M-F 6-10:45pm, Sa-Su 1pm-midnight). **Caffè Caira**, Harbour Rd. (tel. 839 3823), is a better-than-average chipper, and its tables soothe the Howth youth (burgers or fish £3, chips 95p). Hungry shoppers run to **Spar Supermarket** on St. Laurence Rd. off Abbey St. (open M-Sa 8am-11:30pm). Book a seat in advance to hear trad at **Ye Olde Abbey Tavern,** Abbey St. (tel. 832 2006 or 839 0282), or stand and regret it (cover £4). If you're not up for battling the crowd at ye tavern, the **Lighthouse,** Church St. (tel. 832 2827), offers a mellower atmosphere and has trad Wednesday, Thursday, and Sunday at 9pm.

SIGHTS

Maud Gonne, Yeats's unyielding beloved, described her childhood in Howth in *A Servant of the Queen:* "After I was grown up I have often slept all night in that friendly heather... From deep down in it one looks up at the stars in a wonderful security and falls asleep to wake up only with the call of the sea birds looking for their breakfasts." A one-hour **cliff walk** rings the peninsula and trails through just such heather and past the nests of thousands of seabirds. Among the sights along the trail are a cairn reputed to be the grave of Griffan (the last pre-Christian King) and a cleft in Puck's Rock marking the spot where the devil fell when St. Nessan shook a Bible at him. To get to the trailhead from Howth, turn left at the DART and bus station and follow Harbour Rd. around the corner and up the hill (about 20min.). The footpath begins where the cul-de-sac ends, at the top of the long, long ascent. The trail is not only unmarked but also uncleared in places. Regardless, the views, and especially the springtime blooms of the slopes, are inspiring. For the less hearty, bus #31B cruises from Lower Abbey St. in Dublin to the cliffs' summit.

The town of Howth itself occupies this hill. The ruins of **St. Mary's Abbey** stand peacefully surrounded by a cemetery at the bend in Church St. The walls and arches of this 13th-century abbey are still quite sound. The courtyard, though cordoned off, is nonetheless visible; get the key from the caretaker, Mrs. O'Rourke, at 13 Church St. The more modern **Howth Harbour** bustles with fishermen. A strip of fresh-fish shops lines West Pier. Fishing boats come in on Thursday; get 'em while they're slippy.

Just offshore, **Ireland's Eye** once provided both religious sanctuary and strategic advantage for monks, as attested to by the ruins of **St. Nessan's Church** and one of the coast's many **Martello towers** (see **History,** p. 58), both located on the island. The monks eventually abandoned their refuge when pirate raids became too frequent. The island's long beach is now primarily a bird haven. **Frank Doyle & Sons** (tel. 831 4200) jet passengers across the water. *(15min., £4 return, children £2. Call ahead to schedule departure times.)* Their office is on the East Pier, toward the lighthouse.

Howth has its own castle on the outskirts of town. To reach **Howth Castle,** take a right on Harbour Rd. as you leave the DART station. The castle turn-off, ¼ mi. down the road, is marked by signs for the Deer Park Hotel and the National Transport

(take in a rock show)

and use **AT&T Direct**[SM] Service
to tell everyone about it.

It's all within   **AT&T**   your reach.

Exploring lost cultures? You better have an

AT&T Direct^{SM} Service wallet guide.

It's a list of access numbers you need to call home fast and clear from

around the world, using an AT&T Calling Card or credit card.

What an amazing planet we live on.

For a list of **AT&T Access Numbers,**
take the attached wallet guide.

It's   all   within      your   reach.

w w w . a t t . c o m / t r a v e l e r

For your calling convenience tear off and take with you!

AT&T Direct℠ Service

WALLET GUIDE

Inside you'll find simple instructions on how to use AT&T Direct Service to place calling card or collect calls from outside the U.S.

All you need are the AT&T Access Numbers when you travel outside the U.S., because you can access us quickly and easily from virtually anywhere in the world. And if you need any further help, there's always an AT&T English-speaking Operator available to assist you.

www.att.com/traveler

Special Features

Just dial the AT&T Access Number for the country *you are in* and follow the instructions listed below.

● To call U.S. 800 numbers: Enter the 800 number you are calling. (Note: Based upon the 800 number dialed, calls may be toll-free or AT&T Direct℠ Service charges may apply for the duration of the call; some numbers may be restricted.)

● To set up conference calls: Dial AT&T TeleConference Services at 800 232-1234. (Note: One conferee must be in the U.S.)

● To access language interpreters: Dial AT&T Language Line® Services at 408 648-5871.

● To record and deliver messages: Dial #123 if you get a busy signal or no answer, or dial AT&T True Messages® Service at 800 562-6275.

Here's a time-saving tip for placing additional calls: When you finish your conversation, or if there is a busy signal or no answer, don't hang up – press # and wait for the voice prompt or an AT&T Operator.

To Call the U.S. and Other Countries Using Your AT&T Calling Card* or credit card°°, Follow These Steps:

1. Make sure you have an outside line. (From a hotel room, follow the hotel's instructions to get an outside line, as if you were placing a local call.)

2. If you want to call a country other than the U.S., make sure the country *you are in* is highlighted in blue on the chart like this:

3. Enter the AT&T Access Number listed in the chart for the country *you are in.*

4. When prompted, enter the telephone number you are calling as follows:

   ● For calls to the U.S., dial the Area Code (no need to dial 1 before the Area Code) + 7-digit number.

   ● For calls to other countries,† enter 01+ the Country Code, City Code, and Local Number.

5. After the tone, enter your AT&T Calling Card* or credit card number (not the international number). If you need help or wish to call the U.S. collect, hold for an AT&T Operator.

* You may also use your AT&T Corporate Card, AT&T Universal Card, or most U.S. local phone company cards.
† The cost of calls to countries other than the U.S. consists of basic connection rates plus an additional charge based on the country you are calling.
°° Credit card billing subject to availability.

Calling From Specially Marked Telephones

Throughout the world, there are specially marked phones that connect you to AT&T Direct℠ Service. Simply look for the AT&T logo. In the following countries, access to AT&T Direct Service is *only* available from these phones: Ethiopia, Mongolia, Nigeria, Seychelles Islands.

Public phones in Europe displaying the red 3C symbol also give you quick and easy access to AT&T Direct Service. Just lift the handset and dial ✱60 (in France dial M60) and you'll be connected to AT&T.

Pay phones in the United Kingdom displaying the New World symbol provide easy access to AT&T. Simply lift the handset and press the pre-programmed button marked AT&T.

Customer Care

If you have any questions, call 800 331-1140, Ext. 707.

When outside the U.S., dial the AT&T Access Number for the country *you are in* and ask the AT&T Operator for Customer Care.

108-25   © AT&T 6/98

Printed in the U.S.A. on recycled paper.

AT&T Access Numbers (Refer to footnotes before dialing.) From the countries highlighted in blue below, like this ☐, you can make calls to virtually any location in the world; and from *all* the countries listed, you can make calls to the U.S.

It's all within your reach.

Albania ●	00-800-0010
American Samoa	633 2-USA
Angola	0199
Anguilla +	1-800-872-2881
Antigua +	1-800-872-2881
(Public Card Phones)	#1
Argentina ●	0-800-54-288
Armenia ● ▲	8●10111
Aruba	800-8000
Australia ●	1-800-881-011
Austria ○	022-903-011
Bahamas	1-800-872-2881
Bahrain	800-001
Bahrain +	800-000
Barbados +	1-800-872-2881
Belarus ✕ ↪	8●800101
Belgium ●	0-800-100-10
Belize ▲	811
(From Hotels Only)	555
Benin ●	102
Bermuda +	1-800-872-2881
Bolivia ●	0-800-1112

Bosnia ▲	00-800-0010
Brazil	000-8010
British V.I. +	1-800-872-2881
Brunei ●	800-1111
Bulgaria ● ▲	00-800-0010
Cambodia ✱	1-800-881-001
Canada	1 800 CALL ATT
Cape Verde Islands	
Cayman Islands +	
	1-800-872-2881
Chile	800-800-311
	or 800-800-311
(Easter Island)	800-800-311
China, PRC ▲	10811
Colombia	980-11-0010
Cook Island	09-111
Costa Rica	0-800-0-114-114
Croatia ▲	99-385-0111
Cyprus ●	080-90010
Czech Rep. ▲	00-42-000-101
Denmark	8001-0010
Dominica +	1-800-872-2881

Dom. Rep. ✱ ▲ ☐	1-800-872-2881
Ecuador ▲	999-119
Egypt ● (Cairo)	510-0200
(Outside Cairo)	02-510-0200
El Salvador ○	800-1785
Estonia	8-00-800111-0010
Fiji	004-890-1001
Finland ●	9800-100-10
France	0800 99 00 11
French Antilles	0800 99 00 11
French Guiana	0800 99 00 11
Gabon ●	00●001
Gambia ●	00111
Georgia ▲	8●0288
Germany	0130-0010
Ghana	0191
Gibraltar	8800
Greece ●	00-800-1311
Grenada +	1-800-872-2881
Guadeloupe + ☀	0800 99 00 11
(Marie Galante)	

Guam	1 800 CALL ATT
Guantanamo Bay ↑ (Cuba)	935
Guatemala ○ ☀	99-99-190
Guyana ✱	165
Haiti	183
Honduras	800-0-123
Hong Kong	800-96-1111
Hungary ●	00●800-01111
Iceland ●	800 9001
India ✕ , ▸	000-117
Indonesia ↪	001-801-10
Ireland ●	1-800-550-000
Israel	1-800-94-94-949
Italy ●	172-1011
Ivory Coast ▲	00-111-11
Jamaica	1-800-872-2881
Jamaica ☐	872
Japan KDD ▲	005-39-111
Japan IDC ▲ , ▲	0066-55-111
Kazakhstan ▲	8●800-121-4321
Korea → ² 0072-911 or 0030-911
Korea → 550-HOME or 550-2USA

Kuwait	800-288
Latvia (Riga)	7007007
(Outside Riga)	8●27007007
Lebanon ● (Beirut)	426-801
(Outside Beirut)	01-426-801
Liechtenstein ●	0-800-89-0011
Lithuania ✕ , ↪	8●196
Luxembourg †	0-800-0111
Macao ●	0800-111
Macedonia, F.Y.R. of ● ○	99-800-4288
Malaysia ○	1800-80-0011
Malta	0800-890-110
Marshall Isl.	1 800 CALL ATT
Mauritius	73120
Mexico ▽ ¹	01-800-288-2872
Micronesia	288
Monaco ●	800-90-288
Montserrat +	1-800-872-2881
Morocco	002-11-0011
Netherlands Antilles ○ ☀	001-800-872-2881

Netherlands ●	0800-022-9111
New Zealand	000-911
Nicaragua	174
Norway	800-190-11
Pakistan ▲	00-800-01001
Palau	02288
Panama	109
(Canal Zone)	281-0109
Paraguay ■ , ▲	
(Asunción City)	008-11-800
Papua New Guinea 0507-12880
Peru ●	0-800-50000
Philippines ●	105-11
Poland ▲	0♦0-800-111-1111
Portugal ▲	05017-1-288
Qatar	0800-011-77
Reunion Isl.	0800 99 0011
Romania ●	01-800-4288
Russia ● , ▲	01-801-0151
(Moscow)	755-5042
(Outside Moscow)	8-095-755-5042

Russia ● , ↪ , ▲ (St. Petersburg)	325-5042
(Outside St. Petersburg)	8-812-325-5042
St. Kitts/Nevis & St. Lucia +	1-800-872-2881
St. Pierre & Miquelon	0800 99 0011
St. Vincent △ , ■	1-800-872-2881
Saipan △	1 800 CALL ATT
San Marino ●	172-1011
Saudi Arabia ◇	1-800-10
Senegal	3072
Sierra Leone	1100
Singapore ●	800-0111-111
Slovakia ▲	00-42-100-101
Solomon Isl.	0811
So. Africa	0-800-99-0123
Spain	900-99-00-11
Sri Lanka ■	430-430
Sudan	800-001
Suriname △	156

Sweden ●	020-795-611
Switzerland ●	0-800-890011
Syria	0-801
Taiwan	0080-10288-0
Thailand ▲	001-999-111-11
Trinidad/Tob. +	1-800-872-2881
Turkey ●	00-800-12277
Turks & Caicos + , ■	01-800-872-2881
Uganda	800-001
Ukraine ●	8●100-11
U.A. Emirates ●	800-121
U.K. ▲ , ÷	0800-89-0011
	or 0500-89-0011
Uruguay	000-410
U.S. ▼	1 800 CALL ATT
Uzbekistan ◇	641-7440010
Venezuela	800-11-120
Vietnam ●	1-201-0288
Yemen	00 800 101
Zambia	00-899
Zimbabwe ▲	110-98990

● Public phones require coin or card deposit. ✱Press red button. ▲ Additional charges apply when calling outside of Moscow. ■ AT&T Direct℠ calls cannot be placed to this country from outside the U.S. ✕ Not available from public phones. ✱ Phnom Penh and Siem Reap only. ✕ Not available from pay phones. ÷ From St. Maarten or phones at Bobby's Marina, use 1-800-872-2881.

◇ From this country, AT&T Direct℠ calls terminate to designated countries only. ▽ From U.S. Military Bases only. ☀ Await second dial tone. ▲ May not be available from every phone/public phone. † Collect calling from public phones. ▸ Available from phones with international calling capabilities or from most Public Calling Centers. ✓ From Northern Ireland use U.K. access code.

★ Collect calling only. ○Public phones require local coin payment through the call duration. ▼ When calling from public phones, use phones marked "Lenfon." † If call does not complete, use 001-800-462-4240. ▲ Available from public phones and select hotels. ✕ When calling from public phones use phones marked Lenso.

☐ Calling Card calls available from select hotels. ← Use phones allowing international access. ▼ Including Puerto Rico and the U.S. Virgin Islands. ⚬ AT&T Direct℠ Service only from telephone calling centers in Hanoi and post offices in Da Nang, Ho Chi Minh City and Quang Ninh. ÷ If call does not complete, use 0800-013-0011.

WE GIVE YOU THE WORLD...AT A DISCOUNT

LET'S GO®

TRAVEL

MERCHANDISE CATALOG FOR 1999

LET'S GO Travel Gear

World Journey

Equipped with Eagle Creek Comfort Zone Carry System which includes Hydrofil nylon knit on backpanel and lumbar pads. Parallel internal frame. Easy packing panel load design with internal cinch straps. Lockable zippers. Detachable daypack. Converts into suitcase. 26x15x9", 5100 cu. in., 6 lbs. 12 oz. Black, Evergreen, or Blue. $30 discount with railpass. **$225.00**

Continental Journey

Carry-on size pack with internal frame suspension. Comfort Zone padded shoulder straps and hip belt. Leather hand grip. Easy packing panel load design with internal cinch straps. Lockable zippers. Detachable daypack. Converts into suitcase. 21x15x9", 3900 cu. in., 4 lbs. 5 oz. Black, Evergreen, or Blue. $20 discount with railpass. **$175.00**

Security Items

Undercover Neckpouch Ripstop nylon with a soft Cambrelle back. Three pockets. 5 1/2" x 8 1/2". Lifetime guarantee. Black or Tan. **$10.50**

Undercover Waistpouch Ripstop nylon with a soft Cambrelle back. Two pockets. 12" x 5" with adjustable waistband. Lifetime guarantee. Black or Tan. **$10.50**

Travel Lock Great for locking up your World or Continental Journey. Two-dial combination lock. **$5.25**

Hostelling Essentials

Hostelling International Membership
Cardholders receive priority, discounts, and reservation privileges at most domestic and international hostels.

Youth (under 18)..................... free
Adult (ages 18-55)................$25.00
Senior (over 55).....................$15.00

European Hostelling Guide
Offers essential information concerning over 2500 European hostels. **$10.95**

Sleepsack
Required at many hostels. Washable polyester/cotton. Durable and compact. **$14.95**

International ID Cards 1999

Provide discounts on airfares, tourist attractions and more. Includes basic accident and medical insurance. **$20.00**

International Student ID Card (ISIC)
International Teacher ID Card (ITIC)
International Youth ID Card (GO25)

1-800-5LETSGO
http://www.hsa.net/travel

— Prices are in US dollars and subject to change.—

LET'S GO® Order Form

Last Name*	First Name*	Home and Day Phone Number* (very important)	
Street*	(Sorry, we cannot ship to Post Office Boxes)		
City*		State*	Zip Code*
Citizenship‡§¤ (Country)	School/College§	Date of Birth‡§	Date of Travel*

Qty	Description	Color	Unit Price	Total Price

Shipping and Handling

2-3 Week Domestic Shipping	
Merchandise value under $30	$4
Merchandise value $30-$100	$6
Merchandise value over $100	$8
2-3 Day Domestic Shipping	
Merchandise value under $30	$14
Merchandise value $30-$100	$16
Merchandise value over $100	$18
Overnight Domestic Shipping	
Merchandise value under $30	$24
Merchandise value $30-$100	$26
Merchandise value over $100	$28
All International Shipping	$30

Total Purchase Price	
Shipping and Handling	+
MA Residents add 5% sales tax on gear and books	+
TOTAL	

☐ Mastercard ☐ Visa

Cardholder name:

Card number:

Expiration date:

When ordering an International ID Card, please include:

1. Proof of birthdate (copy of passport, birth certificate, or driver's license).
2. One picture (1.5" x 2") signed on the reverse side.
3. (ISIC/ITIC only) Proof of current student/teacher status (letter from registrar or administrator, proof of tuition, or copy of student/faculty ID card. FULL-TIME only).

* Required for all orders
‡ Required in addition for each Hostelling Membership
§ Required in addition for each International ID Card
¤ Required in addition for each railpass

Prices are in US dollars and subject to change.

Make check or money order payable to:
Let's Go Travel
17 Holyoke Street
Cambridge, MA 02138
(617) 495-9649

1-800-5LETSGO

Hours: Mon.-Fri., 10am-6pm ET

Amazing Grace

Howth Castle is a private residence, belonging to the St. Lawrence family, which has occupied it for four centuries, but you might try knocking if your surname is O'Malley. In 1575, the pirate queen Grace O'Malley paid a social call but was refused entrance on the grounds that the family was eating. Not one to take an insult lightly, Grace abducted the St. Lawrence heir and refused to hand him back until she had word that the gate would always be open to all O'Malleys at mealtimes.

Museum. The castle itself is a patchwork of different architectural styles, which gives its exterior an awkward charm. The castle is unfortunately not open to the public.

At the end of the road on which the castle perches is the **National Transport Museum** (tel. 848 0831), a dusty graveyard of tired, green buses. You can't even climb on them or toot the horns. *(Open June-Aug. M-F 10am-6pm, Sa-Su 11am-6pm; Sept.-May Sa-Su noon-5pm. £1.50, children 50p.)* Farther up the hill, an uncertain path leads around the Deer Park Hotel to the fabulous **Rhododendron Gardens,** in which Molly remembers romance at the end of Joyce's *Ulysses. (Always open. Free.)* At the top of the forested path, you emerge into an astounding floral panorama overlooking Howth and Dublin to the south. The flowers bloom in June and July. The management of the hotel strongly discourages picking any of the flowers.

■ Malahide

Eight miles north of Dublin, rows of prim and proper shops smugly line the main street in Malahide, a perennial coastal contender in Ireland's cutthroat Tidy Town competition. The gorgeous parkland and castle at Malahide Demesne somewhat justify the town's pride.

PRACTICAL INFORMATION Turn left from the rail station onto Coast Rd. to reach Malahide's center and all its facilities at the intersection of Church Rd. and New St., called The Diamond. Bus #42, which leaves from behind the Custom House (Beresford Place) in Dublin, drives right up to the Malahide Demesne entrance. Suburban rail to Malahide leaves Connolly, Tara, and Pearse stations infrequently (£1.10). You can also take the DART to Sutton Station (a stop before Howth) then take bus #102 to Malahide (M-Sa, 3 per hr.). Malahide distributes brochures and maps at the **Citizens Information Centre** (tel. 845 0627), behind the library on Main St. Ask for the Malahide Tourist Guide, with a town map, and bring those lovely people some flowers.

ACCOMMODATIONS & FOOD Malahide hosts a number of inexpensive B&Bs along Coast Rd. and its tributaries, particularly Biscayne St. (20min. walk from The Diamond). Since Malahide is only a 10-minute ride from the airport (bus #230 runs back and forth throughout the day, £1.10), it's convenient for travelers who lack the energy to drag themselves to Dublin. **Aishling,** Mrs. Noreen Handley, 59 Biscayne St. (tel. 845 2292), one block off Coast Rd., has pink carpets and curtains and firm, comfortable beds (£16, with bath £17; open Mar.-Nov.). Hair dryers! Big breakfast includes fruit, yogurt, and homemade bread. **Pegasus,** Mrs. Betty O'Brien, 56 Biscayne St. (tel. 845 1506), impresses with welcoming, well-appointed rooms that boast elegant channel views (£17, with bath £18; open Mar.-Nov.). The full Irish breakfast includes smoked kippers for the daring. For those un-schooled in Irish *haute cuisine,* kippers are herring cooked in tea. Beware the pricey, predatory restaurants newly arrived in Malahide. For friendly commotion and old favorites, dine at **Smyths** (tel. 845 0960) on New St. (off The Diamond), which has entrées for about £5 and nightly trad. For more economical fare and a quieter meal, eat where the locals do: **Duffy's** (tel. 845 0735) on Main St., a dark wood pub with frequent trad. The sandwiches are cheap, delicious, and filling (£2-3).

SIGHTS   Left off Main St. (a 10min. walk heading north, past the railroad tracks), Malahide Demesne envelops **Malahide Castle** (tel. 846 2184), the town's main attraction. *(Open Apr.-Oct. M-F 10am-5pm, Sa-Su 11am-6pm; Nov.-Mar. M-F 10am-5pm, Sa-Su 2-5pm. No tours 12:45-2pm. £2.95, students £2.45.)* The castle luxuriates in 250 acres of sweeping lawns and densely foliated paths. Publicly owned, the well-preserved mansion houses a collection of Irish period furniture and part of the National Portrait Collection inside its regal walls. The Malahide Demesne also surrounds a church, a playground, and stunning botanical gardens. *(Demesne/park open daily June 10am-9pm; July-Aug. 10am-8pm; Oct. 10am-7pm; Nov.-Jan. 10am-5pm; Feb.-Mar. 10am-6pm.)*

Between Malahide and **Portmarnock** (2 mi. down the coastal road toward Dublin) lies the **Velvet Strand.** This stretch of soft, luxurious beach makes a fantastic stop on a sunny day and can almost hold its own with any Caribbean beach. Due to the climate, though, any Venus you see here will likely be wearing furs.

■ Dún Laoghaire

As Dublin's major out-of-city ferry port, Dún Laoghaire (dun-LEER-ee) is the first peek at Ireland for many tourists. Fortunately, it is a pleasant, well-developed town and a good spot to begin a ramble along the coast south of Dublin. Summer evenings are the best time to visit, when couples stroll down the waterfront and the whole town turns out for sailboat races on Tuesdays and Thursdays.

PRACTICAL INFORMATION

Reach Dún Laoghaire on the **DART** south from Dublin (£1.10) or on **buses** #7, 7A, 8 or 46A from Eden Quay. The **tourist office** (tel. 280 6600) in the ferry terminal is a gold medal office, accustomed to dealing with delirious travelers and equipped with copious maps and pamphlets on all of Dublin and the Borough of Dún Laoghaire. (Open in summer daily 9am-5pm; in winter M-F 9am-5pm.) Ferry travelers can change money at the **bureau de change** in the ferry terminal, or they can wait for the **Bank of Ireland** on Upper George's St. (Bank open M-W and F 10am-4pm, Th 10am-5pm, and at ferry arrival times. 24hr. ATM.) From the tourist office, Royal Marine Rd. climbs up to the center of town. George's St., at the top of Marine Rd., holds most of Dún Laoghaire's shops, many in the **Dún Laoghaire Shopping Centre** at the intersection (open M-W and Sa 9am-6pm, Th-F 9am-9pm). Patrick St., which continues Marine Rd.'s path uphill on the other side of George's St., offers cheap eateries.

ACCOMMODATIONS

As the port for the Stena-Sealink ferries and convenient DART stop from Dublin, Dún Laoghaire is prime breeding ground for B&Bs, some more predatory than others.

Old School House Hostel (IHH), Elbana Ave. (tel. 280 8777), right off Royal Marine Rd. Full-service hostel sports a TV lounge, an eager, 24hr. staff, and a friendly atmosphere. A café enhances hostel life. 6-bed dorms £6; doubles £24; quads £40. Safety deposit boxes at reception and innovative lockers built into the beds. 24hr. kitchen. Add 50p for rooms with bath. Sheets included. Towels £1. Laundry £3. Wheelchair access.

Marleen, 9 Marine Rd. (tel. 280 2456). Fall off the DART or ferry, and you'll be here. Great location on the first block of Marine Rd. just west of the harbor. Marleen's is a venerable Dún Laoghaire institution. Friendly owners; TV and tea facilities in every room. £17.

Avondale, 3 Northumberland Ave. (tel. 280 9628), next to Dunnes Stores. A crimson carpet leads honored guests to pampering rooms with high ceilings and big beds. Singles £25; doubles £38.

FOOD AND PUBS

Stock up on provisions at **Quinnsworth Supermarket** (tel. 280 8441) in the Dún Laoghaire shopping center or at fruit stands and delis (supermarket open M-W and Sa 9am-6pm, Th-F 9am-9pm). Fast-food restaurants and inexpensive coffee shops line George's St. **The Coffee Bean,** 88b Upper George's St. (tel. 280 9522), virtually rolls customers out, filled to the brim with quiche (£4), soup and brown bread (£1.20), and scrumptious desserts (£1-1.50; open M-Sa 8am-6pm). A full Irish breakfast is served until noon (£2.45). **Bits and Pizzas,** Patrick St., gives a good return on your money (lunch special of pizza, cole slaw, and tea £4; open M-Sa noon-6pm).

The Purty Kitchen, Dunleary Rd., is a lively pub. Upstairs, the **Purty Loft** (tel. 284 3576) livens Dún Laoghaire weekends with groovy disco action (cover £4). From the harbor, turn right down Crofton Rd. (a 15min. walk; the pub is actually closer to the Monkstown DART station than to Dún Laoghaire's). **Smyth's Pub,** Callaghan's Ln. (tel. 280 1139), at the corner of George's St., is a pleasant old pub with tasty entrées (hot open sandwiches £2.50) and some cozy snugs. Live music (contemporary or trad) Thursday through Sunday nights.

SIGHTS

The **harbor** itself is a sight, filled with yachts, boat tours, car ferries chugging to Wales, and fishermen on the west pier. Boat races Tuesday and Thursday evenings in summer draw most of the town. On a clear day, head down to the piers to soak up the ambience, the sun, or the fishy smells. Samuel Beckett's *Krapp's Last Tape* is set on one of the piers.

For more organized sightseeing, try the **National Maritime Museum,** Haigh Terr. (tel. 280 0969). (*Open May-Sept. Tu-Su 1-5pm; Apr. and Oct. Sa-Su 1-5pm. £1.50, children 80p.*) From the tourist office, turn left on Queen's Rd. to the stone steps that lead up to Haigh Terr. The museum is in the Mariners' Church. A giant lens has been moved here from its home in the Bailey Lighthouse in Howth. In the center of the museum stretches a longboat (like a rowboat, but better) sent by revolutionary France to support the United Irishmen in 1796.

The sights of dandy **Sandycove,** at the end of upper George's St., and tiny **Killiney** are also accessible from Dún Laoghaire via DART. Sandycove is pretty enough in a Victorian way, but its real allure is the **James Joyce Tower,** Sandycove Ave. W. From the Sandycove DART station, go left at the green house down Islington Ave. and then right along the coast to Sandycove Point; or take bus #8 from Burgh Quay in Dublin to Sandycove Ave. W. James Joyce stayed in the Martello tower (see **History,** p. 58) for six days in August 1904 as a guest of Oliver St. John Gogarty, a Dublin surgeon, poetic wit, man-about-town, and first civilian tenant of the tower. Unfortunately, Gogarty's other guest was an excitable Englishman with a severe sleepwalking problem. One night, as the foreigner paced, Gogarty shouted "leave him to me" and fired his shotgun into a row of saucepans. Joyce took the hint and left in the morning. Part I of *Ulysses* is set in and near the tower, with Gogarty transformed into Buck Mulligan, the Englishman into "an Englishman," and Joyce into Stephen Daedalus, who meditates on the wine-dark sea from the gun platform at the top of the tower. Another scene takes place at the Forty Foot Men's Bathing Place (see below). Sylvia Beach, Joyce's publisher, opened the tower as a **museum** (tel. 280 9265) in 1962. (*Open Apr.-Oct. M-Sa 10:30am-1pm and 2-5pm, Su 2-6pm; Nov.-Mar. by appointment. £2.40, seniors and students £2, children £1.15.*) The two-room museum contains Joyce's death mask, his bookshelves, some of his correspondence, clippings of Ezra Pound's rave reviews, and lots of editions of *Ulysses,* including one illustrated by Henri Matisse. One letter to Italo Svevo mentions a briefcase "the color of a nun's belly." Genius! Upstairs, the Round Room reconstructs Joyce's bedroom; from the gun platform, you can stand in his shoes to see "many crests, every ninth, breaking, plashing, from far, from farther out, waves and waves."

Juicy Joycean Tidbits

Though Stephen Daedulus' adventures tend to capture major moments of Joyce's life, lesser-known and often equally intriguing, facts about the luminary's life have been left off the bookjackets. But any self-respecting Bloomsday buffs should add the following information to their repertoire of fun facts. Joyce was a blood relation of Daniel O'Connell, "the Liberator." In 1909, Joyce helped found the Volta, Ireland's first cinema. His trademark white suit became a habit while writing *Ulysses*—he refused to wear stronger glasses as his eyesight deteriorated, but the suit reflected sunlight onto his page. He and his family only spoke Italian at home, and he suffered from a rather exaggerated superstitious fear of thunder.

At the foot of the tower lies the infamous **Forty Foot Men's Bathing Place.** A wholesome crowd with plenty of toddlers splashes in the shallow pool facing the road. But behind a wall, on the rocks below the battery and adjacent to the Martello Tower, men traditionally skinny-dip year-round—they don't even seem to mind that they're tourist attractions. The pool rarely contains 40 men, and even more rarely 40-foot men. Instead, the name derives from the Fortieth regiment of British foot soldiers, who made it their semi-private swimming hole. Joyce's host, Oliver St. John Gogarty, once took the plunge here with a reluctant George Bernard Shaw in tow.

"Europe was exhausting. Everything's at the top of a hill," joke the Kids in the Hall. You won't be laughing if you take the DART to Killiney (kill-EYE-nee), a posh suburb that's really just a DART stop on the beach rather than an actual town. The easiest route is to get off at the Dalkey DART stop. Pick up the Heritage map of Dún Laoghaire for details on the seven area walks and historical anecdotes. From Castle St. take a left onto Dalkey Ave. and proceed to climb Dalkey Hill, which leads to **Killiney Hill Park.** From the obelisk at the top, the views are breathtaking—that dark smudge on the horizon is called Wales. A path runs from the obelisk to Dalkey Hill. The **wishing stone** is on the way. If you walk around each level from base to top and then stand facing Dalkey Island and make a wish, it's bound to come true. Beware that this process works only if you walk in a clockwise direction; in earlier times, women wishing to acquire the power of witchcraft walked naked in a counter-clockwise direction. The Heritage guide states that "visitors should not do this on Killiney Hill!"—sorry to disappoint. The path slips off Dalkey Hill onto Torca Rd. **Shaw's Cottage,** up the road on the left, was the home of George Bernard Shaw during a fraction of his childhood. Steps descend from Torca Rd. to coastal Vico Rd., which runs to Dalkey. Killiney itself has a bonny beach. Refreshments after the hard climb are sold across from the Killiney Hill Park entrance next to atmospheric **Druid's Chair Pub** (tel. 285 7297), where you can down a pint in calm surroundings before finally committing to trek to the obelisk.

■ Bray

Despite its official location in Co. Wicklow, Bray's function as a beach town for fugitive Dubliners makes it one of the suburbs. If you're looking for rural Irish charm, you won't find it here, but Bray is the southernmost stop on the DART and a jumping off point to north Wicklow.

PRACTICAL INFORMATION Bray is a 45-minute **DART** ride from Connolly Station (£2.50 return). Buses #45 and #84 leave from Eden Quay. Bray has good connections to Enniskerry, Co. Wicklow. Bus #85, from the DART station in Bray to Enniskerry (£1), runs more frequently than the Enniskerry-Dublin bus. The **tourist office** (tel. 286 4000) is the first stop south of Dublin that can give you info on Co. Wicklow. (Open June-Sept. M-Sa 9:30am-5pm; Oct.-May M-Sa 10am-4pm.) The office, which has a free history trail brochure, is adjacent to the Heritage Centre, downhill on Main St. next to the Royal Hotel. Several half-day bus tours depart from the Heritage Center to local sights at 10am and 2pm (£5-10). **David's Market** (tel. 287 6989) in the DART station rents **bikes** for those who snub their noses at the bus to Enniskerry (£10 per day;

deposit £20). **Scotman's Hut,** 5 Albert Walk (tel. 286 9178), in a pedestrian alley by the station, is the ideal Army-Navy store for hikers, providing equipment for Wicklow hikes (open M-Sa 9:30am-6pm). The **Cyber Left,** 89 Main St. (tel. 205 0003), has email and internet access (£5 per hr.) as well as games. Friendly management lets you help yourself to coffee or snacks as you add to your jpeg collection (open M-Sa 10am-10pm, Su 1-10pm).

ACCOMMODATIONS AND FOOD
Seafront **B&Bs** line the Strand. The cheaper ones are on Convent and Sidmonton Ave., both off the Strand. **St. Judes,** Convent Ave. (tel. 286 2534), entices customers with a comfortable atmosphere and colorful comforters (£17; open June-Sept.). **Sans Souci,** Meath Rd. (tel. 282 8629), next to Convent Ave., helps travelers forget their worries in well-decorated rooms. Only the luckiest guests get to sleep in the bed that once cushioned Sting's bones (July-Aug. £18; low season £16).

The shelves overflow with groceries at **SuperQuinn** market on Main St. north of the tourist center (open daily 8am-6pm). The surrounding shopping center also houses fruit stands and sandwich shops. On the Strand, **Porter House** (tel. 286 0668) serves food until 8pm and boasts what is "probably the largest selection of beers in Ireland"—Chimay, Grolsch, and (if you honestly crave American beer) Rolling Rock. Trad happens nightly in summer and on Wednesday, Friday, and Sunday nights in winter. The best meal in town is waiting for you at **Escape,** Albert Ave. (tel. 286 6755), where heaping portions of creative vegetarian dishes please any appetite. Lunches are around £4, dinner specials are £5.25, and a new menu appears daily (open M-Sa 9am-10:30pm, Su noon-8:30pm).

SIGHTS
Bray's history since the Neolithic Age is on display in a small but well-designed **Heritage Centre** (tel. 286 7128), on Main St. in the same building as the tourist office (same hours as tourist office; donations requested). Joe Loughman, local historian and phone repairman, gathered the center's artifacts by exchanging them with the local populace for working phones. The floor is a giant map of Bray. Along the **Esplanade** (tel. 286 4450), grim amusement palaces and B&Bs cater to a dwindling crowd of Dublin beachgoers (open daily 10am-7pm). Low-confidence gamblers can try 2p slot machines in the **Fun Palace** on the seafront. Kiddie rides, dodgems, and video games promise to entertain children on rainy afternoons.

At the far end of the sea-front near Bray Head is the spanking new **Natural Sea Life Center.** *(Open daily 10am-6pm. £5, children £3.50. Wheelchair accessible.)* Part of an international organization that promotes understanding of local ecology, the Bray Sea Life Center is the latest franchise in a chain open across the continent. Go ahead and touch the manta rays and other fish—they'd appreciate the affection.

Enough with these silly amusements; climb the rocky outcrop that is **Bray Head** and glory over the Irish Sea. The trailhead is clearly marked at the end of the promenade. **Brandy Hole,** a cave at the foot of Bray Head, was once a smugglers' warehouse. Inland, the ruins of **Raheen A Cluig,** a 13th-century Augustinian church, look very small and very old. The climb to Bray Head takes a good 45 minutes.

COUNTY DUBLIN

EASTERN IRELAND

Woe to the unfortunate tourists whose exposure to eastern Ireland is limited to what they see out of the window on a bus headed to the west. Although less-frequented by foreign visitors, the eastern towns offer many interesting and unusual places to visit. The monastic city at Clonmacnoise and the ruins in Co. Meath, which are older than the pyramids, continue to mystify archaeologists. The mountains of Wicklow offer spectacular views, and tired hikers can rest along the beaches of the nearby shoreline. The tiny lakeland towns of Co. Monaghan, really a part of the Fermanagh Lake District in the North, harbor the warmest waters in the northern half of Ireland. And where else but Kildare can you find a horse farm run according to the laws of metaphysics or a theme-park based on bogs? Counties Meath, Louth, Wicklow, and Kildare all hold goodies fit for daytrips from Dublin.

County Wicklow

Mountainous Co. Wicklow allows wilderness fans to lose themselves on deserted back roads, zoom down seesaw ridges by bicycle, and still be back in Dublin by nightfall. Wild as parts of it are, the whole county is in the capital's backyard. Its major sights are accessible by one bus or another from downtown Dublin, but traveling within the county is often best done by bike or car. The Wicklow Way hiking trail is an excellent reason for your feet to come to the county.

Co. Wicklow was once so incredibly rich in gold that lumps of gold could be casually gathered on the surface. Unfortunately, the Irish traded it in vast quantities for meager amounts of Cornwall tin to make bronze—it was the bronze age, after all. Later, 9th-century Vikings settled at present-day Wicklow and Arklow and used them as bases while raiding Glendalough and other monasteries. Norman invaders in the 1100s followed the same pattern, building defenses on the coast while leaving the mountains to the Gaelic O'Toole and O'Byrne clans. English control was not fully established until the 1798 rebellion, when military roads and barracks were built through the interior so that the British Army could hunt down the remaining guerrillas (see **History**, p. 57). The mountains later produced a mining industry in the southern part of the county. Bray is in Co. Wicklow, but since it's on the DART, *Let's Go* covers it as a suburb of Dublin (see **Bray**, p. 118).

WICKLOW COAST

The natural sights and uncrowded towns of Wicklow coast seem a world away from urban Dublin. As a route to the southeast, it lacks the heavy-hitting historical sites of the inland route through Glendalough and Kilkenny, but its natural offerings are intriguing. It is also faster by any means of transport and leads to Rosslare Harbor, your ticket to the Continent or the UK should you want a change of pace.

■ Wicklow

Wicklow Town is touted both for its coastal pleasures and for its usefulness as a departure point into the Wicklow Mountains. Wicklow also makes a good resting point on your journey should you wish to spend a relaxing night out, with a wider selection of restaurants than the surrounding area and plenty of accommodations within walking distance of pubs. Long, skinny Main St. snakes past the Grand Hotel

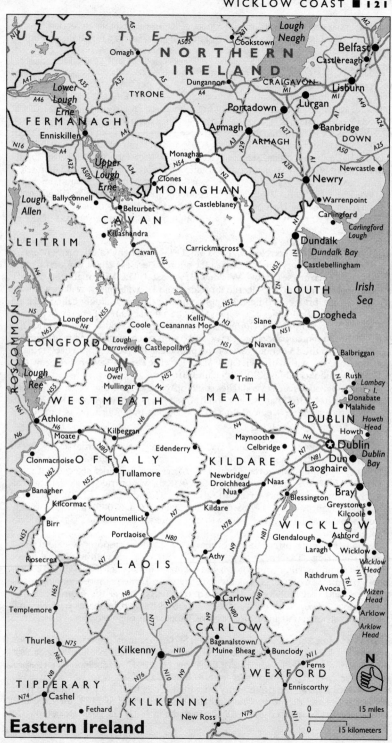

Eastern Ireland

and the grassy triangular plot by the tourist office to its terminus in Market Square. While the town itself doesn't have any extraordinary charms, a few hours spent biking along the nearby coastal road can pleasantly occupy an afternoon.

PRACTICAL INFORMATION Trains run to **Dublin's** Connolly Station (1hr., £4) and to **Wexford** (1hr., £3) via **Rosslare** (both run M-Sa 4 per day, Su 2 per day). The station is a 15-minute walk east of town on Church St. **Bus Éireann** leaves for Dublin from the street uphill from the Billy Byrne monument and from the Grand Hotel at the other end of Main St. (M-Sa 9 per day, Su 7 per day). **Wicklow Tours Ltd.** (tel. 67718) runs a van to **Rathdrum** (£6) and **Glendalough** (£5) from the Bridge Tavern on Bridge St. (July-Aug. M-Sa 10:35am, 1:05, and 3:35pm, Su 10:45am, 1:35, and 4:05pm.) The **tourist office**, Main St., Fitzwilliam Sq. (tel. 69117; fax 69118), can fill you in on the Wicklow Way and other county attractions. Their book and map selection is excellent. (Open June-Aug. M-Sa 9am-6pm; Sept.-May M-F 9:30am-1pm and 2-5:30pm.) An **AIB**, with a 24-hour **ATM**, conducts business on Main St. **Bikes** can be rented from **Wicklow Hire** (tel. 68149), on Abbey St., the continuation of Main St. (£7 per day, £30 per week; deposit £30; open M-Sa 8:30am-5:30pm). Wicklow's **phone code** is 0404.

ACCOMMODATIONS Travelers will be content in almost any of the many B&Bs on Patrick Rd., uphill from Main St. and past the church. Besides being a wonderful place to stay with amazing sea views, **Wicklow Bay Hostel,** The Murrough (tel. 69213), appears in *The Nephew,* with Pierce Brosnan. From Fitzwilliam Sq., walk toward the river, cross the bridge, and head left until you see the big building called "Marine House." (Dorms £8; doubles £20. Open Mar.-Oct.) It takes a bit of energy to hike up Patrick Rd. to friendly Mrs. H. Gorman and son's **Thomond House,** Upper Patrick Rd. (tel. 67940). Veranda, panoramic views, and rooms as comfortable as your own are certainly worth the 15-minute walk or the phone call for pick-up, however. (Singles £20; doubles £30, with bath £35. Open Mar.-Oct.) The **Bridge Tavern,** Bridge St. (tel. 67718), has snooker tables (£20, with bath £30).

Two **campgrounds** are several miles south of Wicklow. **Johnson's** (tel. 48133) and **River Valley** (tel. 41647) are similar (both £7; showers 50p; open Mar.-Sept.). From Wicklow, turn right off Wexford Rd. (N11) at Doyle's pub. Johnson's is 1 mi. down the road, River Valley 2½ mi.

FOOD AND PUBS Main St. is lined with greasy take-aways and fruit stands. **Fresh Today,** Main St. (tel. 68322), stocks stacks of fruits and vegetables (open M-Sa 8:30am-6:30pm). **Quinnsworth,** Church St., offers an even wider selection of nutriments. The **Coffee Shop,** Fitzwilliam Sq. (tel. 68006), will provide a quick shot of caffeine before your hike and serve you salads (85p), sandwiches (£1.50), and baked goods after. Plant yourself in **Pizza del Forno,** Main St. (tel. 67075), to enjoy a variety of foods (3-course lunch £4.50, sandwiches £1, unique desserts £1.70-4; open daily 10am-11:30pm).

A number of pubs offer musical evenings for the delectation of Wicklow's residents. The **Bridge Tavern,** Bridge St. (tel. 67718), resounds with traditional music (Th-Su in summer, Th only in winter) and is known to have informal concertina sessions on summer nights to complement the snooker. Those not satisfied with just listening should visit **Mulvihill's,** Market Sq. (tel. 68823), near the monument. The comfortable little bar with plenty of seats advertises that "roving bards are welcome" and throws its own trad and ballad sessions Thursday through Monday.

SIGHTS Market Square, at the end of Main St. farthest from the train station, holds open-air markets and displays a pike-less monument to local hero Billy Byrne, a Protestant landowner who fought against the Crown in the 1798 rebellion (see **History,** p. 57). The first left past Market Sq. leads to **Black Castle.** Although only a few wind-worn stones remain, the promontory on which it was built is a great vantage point above the sea and meadows. The Normans built the castle in 1169; the local Irish lords immediately attacked and finally destroyed it in 1301. The staircase cut into the

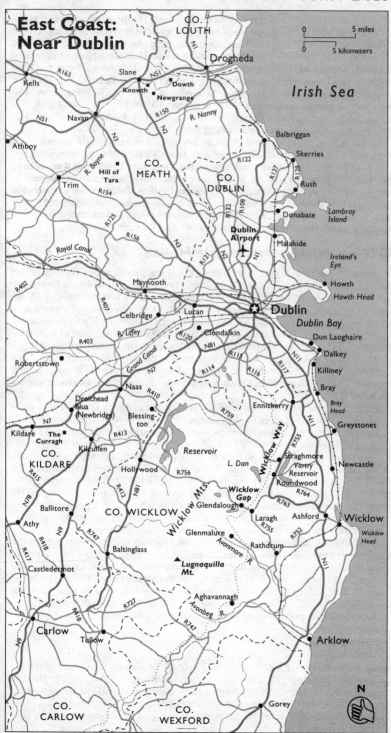

East Coast: Near Dublin

0 — 5 miles
0 — 5 kilometers

Irish Sea

CO. LOUTH

N1

R163 Kells

Slane N51

Knowth Dowth
Newgrange

Drogheda

N51 Navan

N3 Athboy

R. Boyne Hill of Tara

Trim R154

R125

R156

Royal Canal

R402

Maynooth

R407

Celbridge

R403

R. Liffey

Robertstown

Naas

Droichead Nua (Newbridge)

Kildare The Curragh

CO. KILDARE

Kilcullen

Ballitore

Athy

Castledermot

Carlow

Tullow

CO. CARLOW

R. Nanny

CO. MEATH

R150

N2

R122

CO. DUBLIN

R172 R108

R121

N2

R127 Balbriggan

Skerries

R128

Rush

Donabate

Lambray Island

Dublin Airport

Malahide

Ireland's Eye

Howth

Howth Head

Dublin

Dublin Bay

Lucan

Clondalkin

Dun Laoghaire

Dalkey

Killiney

Grand Canal

N7

R410

R413

Blessington

Hollywood

Reservoir

R759

R756

Wicklow Mts.

CO. WICKLOW

Glendalough

Glenmalure

▲ *Lugnaquilla Mt.*

Aghavannagh

Avonbeg R.

R747

R727

N81

R114

R113

R116

R117

Enniskerry

Bray

Bray Head

Greystones

Straghmore

Vartry Reservoir

Roundwood

R764

R763

Laragh

Ashford

R755

R752

Rathdrum

Wicklow Way

R755

Wicklow Gap

L. Dan

Avonmore R.

N11

Newcastle

Wicklow

Wicklow Head

N11

Arklow

Gorey

CO. WEXFORD

N

seaward side of the remains reputedly accesses a tunnel to the nearby convent. At the other end of Main St., an **abbey** keeps company with the remnants of a 13th-century **Franciscan Friary.** The abbey was founded at the same time as Black Castle and destroyed along with it. It was subsequently rebuilt and became a place of retirement for both Normans and native Irish, who considered it neutral ground. A cliff trail leads to **St. Bride's Head,** where St. Patrick landed on Travilahawk Strand in 432. The local population greeted him by knocking the teeth out of one of his companions, who was later assigned to convert the local residents. The trail itself is only slightly less threatening, leading past cannons before arriving at St. Bride's Head (1hr.). The heights of the cliff walk provide smashing views.

At the Billy Byrne monument, Main St. becomes Summer Hill, the coastal road, from which beaches extend south to Arklow. From Wicklow, the closest strips of sun and sand are **Silver Strand** and **Jack's Hole.** The most popular is **Brittas Bay,** midway between Wicklow and Arklow, where you can buy ultra-cheap crabs in summer. In the last week of July, Wicklow hosts its **Regatta Festival,** the oldest such celebration in Ireland. The two-week festival features a race of barges made of barrels and timber and includes the street music, drama performances (£4), and extended bar hours required for true Irish fun. Contact the tourist office for more information.

■ Near Wicklow: Avondale House

Avondale House (tel. 46111), the birthplace and main residence of political leader Charles Stewart Parnell, is now a Parnell museum where restorers have turned the clocks back to the 1850s. *(Open daily in summer 11am-5pm, in winter 11am-4pm. £3, students and seniors £2.)* The walls are decked with transcriptions of Parnell's love letters to his mistress, Kitty O'Shea. The 20-minute biographical video is a well-produced, illuminating glimpse into Parnell's life and his role in the development of Irish independence. Flora fanatics will faun over the 500 acres of **forest** and parkland that surround the house and spread along the west bank of the Avonmore River. *(Same hours as Avondale House.)* The diverse tree species of Avondale's grounds stretch out and blossom along the **Great Ride,** a meandering grassy expanse that was once an avenue for horse riding.

Avondale House is on the road from Wicklow Town to Avoca, one mile after Rathdrum (see below) and before the Meeting of the Waters. From Rathdrum, take Main St. heading toward Avoca and follow the signs. **Buses** arrive in Rathdrum from **Dublin** (M-Sa 2 per day, Su 1 per day, £5.50, £7.50 return), as do trains (M-Sa 3 per day, £7.50). The **tourist office** (tel. 46262), in the center of town, will help you locate one of the many B&Bs around Rathdrum should you wish to stay (open in summer M-F 9am-5:30pm, Sa-Su 1-6pm). The cheapest option in town is **The Old Presbytery Hostel** (tel. 46173), a clean hostel built in an old Presbyterian monastery (6-bed dorms £9; singles £10; wheelchair accessible). The **post office** (tel. 46211) is concealed within "Smith's Fancy Goods" on Main St., where you can take care of your stamp and candy needs at the same time. The **phone code,** 0404, had an anvil dropped on it.

Rathdrum now serves mostly as a convenient place for visitors to Avondale House to eat or chill out. The **Cartoon Inn** (tel. 46774), on Main St., a pub with wacky cartooned walls, refers to the International Cartoon Festival that Rathdrum held until recently. For less animated fare, check out the **Woolpack Pub** (tel. 46574), also on Main St. This pub dishes out scrumptious servings (main courses £2-8), devious homemade desserts, and discos on weekend nights (no cover). Hollywood groupies will appreciate the pub as one of the settings for *Michael Collins.*

■ Arklow

When St. Kevin visited Arklow in the 5th century, he blessed the town's fishermen and guaranteed prosperity. The Anglo-Irish government bestowed a more tangible blessing in the 18th century by building a modern harbor, and Arklow has blossomed into a strapping and well-known port and shipbuilding center. The town is an increasingly popular weekend spot for Dubliners yearning for a break from the big city.

ORIENTATION AND PRACTICAL INFORMATION Arklow is 40 mi. south of Dublin on N11 (Dublin/Wexford Rd.). The town follows the gentle turns of the Avoca River, with shops and restaurants resting on the river's banks. The harbor, beaches, and potteries are located slightly southeast of the town center. **Trains** run to Arklow from **Dublin** on their way to **Rosslare** (M-Sa 4 per day, Su 2 per day). **Bus Éireann** passes through on its way to **Rosslare** and **Wexford**, stopping at the chocolate shop on Main St. (M-Sa 5 per day, Su 3 per day). The Arklow **tourist office** (tel. 32484), actually a trailer parked in the town center, is at the end of St. Mary's Rd. and Main St. (open M-F 9:30am-5:30pm). **Bank of Ireland** (tel. 32004) and **AIB** on Main St. both have 24-hour **ATMs. Black's Cycle Center,** Upper Main St. (tel. 31898), repairs and rents bikes (£8 per day, £35 for 5 days; open in summer M-Sa 9:30am-6pm, winter hours vary). The **phone code** is a fishy 0402.

ACCOMMODATIONS AND FOOD Those who can't resist Arklow's siren call head to Coolgreany Rd., which houses a passel of B&Bs. From the tourist trailer, walk along Main St. up the hill and through the roundabout; Main St. becomes Upper Main St. and then Coolgreany Rd. **Vale View** (tel./fax 32622) boasts huge, charmingly decorated bedrooms. From one of the glass-roofed suites on the top floor, you can gaze at the stars or listen to the patter of raindrops. (£15.50, with bath £17.50; singles £5 extra). **Dunguaire** (tel. 32774), run by friendly Mrs. Fennel, is another comfortable B&B on Coolgreany Rd., with cozy rooms and a lovely view from the dining room (singles with bath £20).

   The River Walk Restaurant (tel. 31657), on the Avoca River, serves hearty fare at low prices (special bargain entrees under £5). The **New Delhi** deli (tel. 39889), on Upper Main St., offers an assortment of fresh food at reasonable prices (entrees £2-3, sandwiches £1.50) available for take-away or sit-down (open M-Sa 9am-6pm).

SIGHTS About one mile from town, both the north and south **beaches** are safe for swimming but gray and rocky. A walk along the Avoca River is lovely, but why walk when you can paddle? Paddleboats, rowboats, and canoes can be hired next door to the River Walk Restaurant (£2 per person for 30min.). **St. Savior's Church,** Coolgreany Rd. (tel. 32439), at the roundabout, is a beautiful building with an international reputation for campanology (bell-ringing). The ringers sound their stuff on Sunday mornings. The Arklow and Wicklow Vale **pottery outlets** along the quays sell glassware and ceramics straight from the kiln. If you're not impressed with the selection in the outlets, the hundreds of freshly baked ceramic toilets in the Quality Ceramics storage yard across the street might do the trick. The seafoam-green **Arklow Maritime Museum** froths on St. Mary's Rd. between the train station and the Catholic church. *(Open daily 10am-1pm and 2-5pm. £2, students £1, families £3.)* If you like ships, set sail for this one-room museum, nearly all that remains of Arklow's maritime past. A piece of the first transatlantic cable, laid by an Arklow captain, is proudly displayed. In addition, a new video fills visitors in on all aspects of Arklow's history.

WICKLOW MOUNTAINS

Over 2000 ft. high, covered by heather, and pleated by rivers rushing down wooded glens, the Wicklow summits are home to grazing sheep and a few villagers. Glendalough, in the midst of the mountains, draws a steady summertime stream of coach tours from Dublin. The stunning Powerscourt Waterfall in Enniskerry also draws tourists to the area. The towns of Enniskerry, Ashford, Rathdrum, Avoca, and Blessington, all in the Wicklow Mountains, are on the tourist trail and are covered separately below. The area is a bit difficult to navigate; Bray, Wicklow Town, Arklow, and Rathdrum all have free maps in the tourist offices.

■ Glendalough

In the 6th century, a vision told St. Kevin to give up his life of ascetic isolation and found a monastery. Reasoning that if you've got to be a monk, you'd might as well be a monk in one of the most spectacularly beautiful valleys in Ireland, he founded Glendalough (GLEN-da-lock, glen of two lakes). During the great age of Irish monasteries—563 to 1152—monastic schools were Ireland's religious and cultural centers, attracting pilgrims from all over Europe to the "land of saints and scholars." Supported by lesser monks who farmed and traded, the privileged brothers inscribed and illuminated religious texts and collected jewels and relics for the glory of God.

PRACTICAL INFORMATION Most pilgrims to Glendalough come by car; a few hike the Wicklow Way into town. The rest take buses run by the private **St. Kevin's Bus Service** (tel. (01) 281 8119). The buses run from St. Stephen's Green W., **Dublin** (M-Sa at 11:30am and 6pm, Su 11:30am and 7pm. £6, £10 return). They also leave from **Bray,** just past the Town Hall (M-Sa 12:10 and 6:30pm, Su 12:10 and 7:30pm, £6 return). Buses return from the glen in the evening (M-F 7:15am and 4:15pm, Sa 9:45am and 4:15pm, Su 9:45am and 5:30pm). **Bus Éireann** (tel. (01) 836 6111 to book) also runs **tours** to Glendalough Friday through Sunday in March, daily from April to September, and Wednesday and Friday through Monday in October. Buses leave Busáras Station in Dublin at 10:30am, travel along the coast, pass through Avoca, stop in Glendalough, and return to Dublin by 5:45pm. The driver is the tour guide, and admission fees are included in the cost (£16, children £8). **Wicklow Tours** (tel. 67671) runs a van to **Rathdrum** (Avondale) and **Wicklow** daily. (Departs from Glendalough hotel M-Sa 11:20am and 4:40pm, Su 11:45am and 4:55pm. To Wicklow £6 return, to Rathdrum £4 return.) **Mary Gibbons** (tel. (01) 283 9973) offers an afternoon tour of Powerscourt Waterfall and Glendalough leaving from Dublin. (Leaves Suffolk St. tourist office Tu, Th, and Sa-Su 12:45pm, returns at 6pm. £18 includes admission.) **Hitching** is a bit difficult, since most drivers going to Glendalough are tourists coming on the buses. Hitchers starting at the beginning of N11 in southwest Dublin (see p. 84) make it as far as the juncture of N11 with Glendalough's R755. In Laragh (see below), **bike rental** is available from the **post office/video rental store** (tel. 45236; £6 per day, £24 per week, deposit £20; open daily 9am-10pm). The **phone code** wakes for matins at 0404.

ACCOMMODATIONS, FOOD, AND PUBS The **Glendalough Hostel (An Óige/HI)** (tel. 45342) lies five minutes up the road past the Glendalough visitors center. The hostel was undergoing reconstruction in 1998 but promises to be one of the more modern places to stay in the area. Glendalough town consists of the monastic site, a hostel, and an overpriced hotel/restaurant—all within a ¼ mi. radius. For more affordable food, B&Bs, and groceries, travelers should depend on **Laragh** (LAR-a), a village 1 mi. up the road (signposted, 10min. walk from the Wicklow Way; 15 mi. from Powerscourt, 7 mi. from Roundwood). The bus leaves from the phone booth across from the post office. In Laragh, the **Wicklow Way Hostel** (tel. 45398) is relatively new and has sturdy beds with warm comforters. The kitchen has a microwave and is open from 7am to 10pm, and there's a TV in the lounge. An attached coffeehouse serves inexpensive breakfasts (co-ed dorms £8; sheets £1). The older, more cramped **Old Mill Hostel** (tel. 45156) offers beds and kitchen facilities 10 minutes down the road (signposted; dorms £6.50, private rooms £14; sheets 75p). You can also **camp** there for £4.50 per person. **B&Bs** abound in Laragh. One of the most welcoming is **Gleannailbhe** (tel. 45236), next to the post office (inquire there). Gleannailbhe offers tea and coffee facilities, a TV lounge, and a choice of breakfasts (£14, with bath £16).

The **Laragh Inn** (tel. 45345) piles plates high with hot edibles (entrees £5-7; open daily noon-9pm). Attached **Lynahanam's Pub** attracts hostelers and locals alike with its ballad sessions and trad most nights from 9:30pm to midnight.

SIGHTS Today only the **visitors center** (tel. 45352) and a handful of tourist trappings mark Glendalough's ancient monastic spot. *(Center open daily June-Aug. 9am-*

6:30pm; Sept. to mid-Oct. 9:30am-6pm; mid-Oct. to mid-Mar. 9:30am-5pm; mid-Mar. to May 9:30am-6:30pm. £2, students and children £1. Wheelchair accessible.) The center shows a film on the history of monasteries and conducts tours of the local ruins, the center-piece of which is **St. Kevin's tower,** once a landmark for approaching pilgrims.

The present ruins were only a small part of the monastery in its heyday, when wooden huts for low-status laborer monks were plentiful. Monks once hid in the 100 ft. round tower, built in the 10th century as a watchtower and belltower. The entrance is 12 ft. from the ground. When Vikings approached, the monks would climb the inside of the tower floor by floor, drawing up the ladders behind them. Nearby **St. Kevin's Cross** is an unadorned high cross (see **Early Christians,** p. 54). The **Cathedral,** constructed in a combination of Greek and Roman architectural styles, was once the largest in the country. **St. Kevin's Church** is also casually known as St. Kevin's Kitchen because its stone roof and round tower give the appearance of a chimney for cooking. Built in the 11th century, it was used as a church for 500 years. It lay derelict until the 19th century, when locals once again used it as a church until the newer St. Kevin's Church was built a mile away.

The **Upper and Lower Lakes,** across the bridge and to the right, are a rewarding sidetrip from the monastic site. A five-minute walk from the site, the Lower Lake is serene. Near the spectacular Upper Lake, a half-hour walk from the site, **St. Kevin's Bed** is the cave where he prayed. Local chieftains are buried in a church nearby. Leg-end says that when St. Kevin prayed, his words ascended in a vortex of flame and light that burned over the Upper Lake's dark waters with such intensity that none but the most righteous monks could witness it without going blind.

Climbing a Stairway to Kevin

Kevin was apparently an angelically beautiful man who wasn't interested in women. A lascivious local gal named Kathleen made advances on Kevin, forcing him to retreat to his hermitage to Glendalough. Still she pursued him, so he with-drew to his cave near the Upper Lake. Kathleen scoured the area until Kevin's dog gave him away. When she followed the dog to Kevin's cave, she found him asleep and began to take advantage of the situation. Kevin awoke and angrily flung her from the rocky ledge now called "Lady's Leap" into the lake, where she drowned. Kevin felt guilty, lived a life of atonement, and prayed that none might ever drown in the lake again. Lest this tale lead one to judge harshly this pious man, those that recount this legend add that despite his lack of interest in women, St. Kevin was known for his kindness to the local animals.

■ The Wicklow Way

The lonely mountain heights reach westward and upward along established trails negotiable by foot or horse. The 70 mi. Wicklow Way, Ireland's best-known long-dis-tance path, starts a few miles south of Dublin and heads south along the crests all the way to Clonegal in Co. Carlow. Parts of it are well graded and even paved. Although the path is well marked with yellow arrows, hikers should get the *Wicklow Way Map Guide* (£5). Since the path is mostly out of sight- and hearing-range of the lowlands, traveling alone can be dangerous. Drinking water from the streams is also not a good idea, and lighting fires within 1 mi. of the forest is illegal.

Although some people choose to leave from Bray and more quickly encounter the real wilderness, the more popular northern 45 mi. of the path (from Dublin to Agha-vannagh) have the best scenery and offer better access to hostels. To reach the north-ern end of the path, take bus #47B from Hawkins St. in Dublin's city center to its terminus at Marlay Park in Rathfarnham, a Dublin suburb. Bus #47 also stops nearby. If you hike seven to eight hours a day, the northern section will take about three days, and the entire trail will take about six. Bikers cover virtually the same mileage by sticking to roads—it is not advisable to take a bike on the Way itself.

From its start in Marlay Park, the Wicklow Way piggybacks on **Kilmashogue Forest Trail,** which gives great views of Dublin and the distant Mourne Mountains. Farther on, the trail passes the 400 ft. **Powerscourt Waterfall** in Enniskerry. (Open daily mid-May to mid-Oct. 9:30am-7pm; late Oct. to early May 10:30am to dusk. £1.50, seniors and students £1, under 16 80p.) Unfortunately, you have to pay to get a close look, but the view is worth it. The Knockree hostel is between the trail and Enniskerry, while the Glencree hostel is off the trail in the opposite direction from Knockree and Enniskerry (see below). A "Greatest Hits" excerpt of the Wicklow Way would start in Enniskerry and end in Glendalough. Between the two, the trail climbs to the summit of **White Hill** (2073 ft.), from which you can see the mountains of North Wales on a clear day. Soon after White Hill, the trail passes Annamoe, where a road and trail lead to Ashford, Devil's Glen, and the Tiglin Hostel.

The trail then descends to Roundwood, a stop for **St. Kevin's Bus** (see **Glendalough,** p. 126), and runs alongside Glenmacnass Rd. to Glendalough's impressive monastic ruins. The trail rises to visit **Poulanass Waterfall** and then climbs a forest track toward 2300 ft. **Mullacor,** the highest point of the Way. The trail then drops into **Glenmalure,** with another hostel and Mt. Lugnaquilla nearby, crosses another mountain ridge, and finally tiptoes across the **Dun River** over an iron bridge, 1½ mi. southeast of the hostel at Aghavannagh. A detour east off the Way between Glendalough and Aghavannagh leads to bus and rail stations in Rathdrum. Past Aghavannagh, the trail makes smaller climbs amid mellower scenery, ending in Co. Carlow with views of antenna-topped Mt. Leinster. Long-distance hikers can connect here to the **South Leinster Way.** Bus Éireann serves the southern section of the Wicklow Way at Aughrim, Tinahely, Shillelagh, and Hackettstown.

An Óige prints a list of suggested stages for a six-day walk along the Way, with mileage and expected walking time, available at their main office or any of their nearby hostels. Walking times between the hostels are: Tiglin to Glendalough, five hours; Rathdrum to Aghavannagh, four hours; Aghavannagh to Glenmalure, five hours; Aghavannagh to Glendalough, seven hours. Other trails, with other accommodations, meander every which way through the Wicklovian wilderness.

ACCOMMODATIONS

Several hostels lie within 5 mi. of the Wicklow Way; these places fill up in July and August. Book An Óige hostels ahead through the An Óige Head Office, 61 Mountjoy St., Dublin (tel. (01) 830 4555). The hostels are listed here north to south, with distances from the Way included. **Wicklow Way, Old Mill,** and **Glendalough hostels** are reviewed under Glendalough (see p. 126).

Knockree (An Óige/HI), Lacklan House, Enniskerry (tel. (01) 286 4036), on the Way. A reconstructed farmhouse 4mi. from the village and 2mi. from Powerscourt Waterfall. From Enniskerry, take the left fork road leading from the village green, take a left at Buttercups Newsagent, and begin a steep walk, following signs for Glencree Dr. Alternatively, take the DART to Bray and bus #85 to Enniskerry, which drops you off 2 mi. from Knockree. Spacious kitchen and dining area with fireplace. Simple, single-sex dorms £5.50, Oct.-May £4.50. Lockout 10:30am-5:30pm (unless it's raining).

Tiglin (An Óige/HI), a.k.a. **Devil's Glen,** Ashford (tel. (0404) 40259), 5mi. from the Way near the Tiglin Adventure Centre. From Ashford, follow Roundwood Rd. for 3mi., then follow the signs for the Tiglin turnoff on the right, a hilly 8mi. from Powerscourt. 50 beds in a basic accommodation. Dorms £7, Oct.-May £6.

Wicklow Way Hostel (tel. (0404) 45398), on the Way. Dorms £8. Sheets £1.

Old Mill Hostel (tel. 45156). Signposted 10min. down the road from the Wicklow Way Hostel. Dorms £6.50, private rooms £14; sheets 75p. **Camping** £4.50 per person.

Glendalough (An Óige/HI) (tel. (0404) 45342), 1½mi. from the Way. From Dublin, take bus #65 from Eden Quay, which brings you to Donard 3mi. to Ballinclea Youth Hostel and 7mi. by mountain track to Glenmalure. West of Glenmalure is an army range in the Glen of Imaal where military exercises are conducted. Stay out. Dorms £6.50, Oct.-May £5.50. Open July-Aug. daily; Sept.-June weekends only.

WESTERN WICKLOW

Squatter, lumpier, and less traveled, western Wicklow offers scenic hikes for the misanthropic. You won't find picnicking families from the suburbs here. Don't try to hike between western Wicklow and the Wicklow Way—the straight shootin' Irish Army allegedly maintains a shooting range at the Glen of Imaal. There are hostels in Blessington (see below), Baltinglass, and Donard.

Two buses run every day from Busárus in Dublin to **Baltinglass.** The Baltinglass **tourist office** in Weavers Sq. (tel. (0508) 81615) dispenses West Wicklow hiking info (open July-Sept. M-Sa 9am-5pm; Oct.-June M-F 9am-1pm and 2-5pm). **Rathcoran House (IHH)** (tel. (0508) 81073; fax (01) 453 2183) is an easy hiking destination since you won't have to make a huge detour around the Army. Easy car access via Tullow to N81 road between Dublin and Wexford makes this hostel a good starting or ending point for western Wicklow hikers. (Dorms £8.50; doubles £19. Camping £3.50 per person. Open May to mid-Sept.) To reach **Donard** from Dublin, take bus #65 from Eden Quay (Sa-Su 1 per day, £1.10). **Ballinclea (An Óige/HI)** (tel. (045) 404657) is near the forest and Blessington Lake but cut off from Glenmalure Hostel on the Wicklow Way by the Glen of Imaal. Though clean and simple, the hostel is a bit less accessible than Baltyboys (see below). (Dorms £6.50. Lockout 10am-5:30pm. Open Mar.-Nov. daily; Dec.-Feb. F-Sa.)

■ Blessington

Since the Liffey was dammed to make a reservoir for Dublin's teeming, thirsty masses, Blessington in West Wicklow has become a popular recreation center. A pretty lake embellishes art-filled **Russborough House** (tel. (045) 865239), built in 1741 for Joseph Leeson, a member of the Anglo-Irish parliament. *(Open daily June-Aug. 10:30am-5:30pm; Apr.-May and Sept.-Oct. M-Sa 10:30am-5:30pm, Su 10:30am-5:30pm. 45min. tour of main rooms and paintings £3, students £2, ages 12-18 £1. 30min. tour of the bedrooms £1.)* The architect was Richard Cassells, also responsible for Dublin's Leinster House and many of Trinity College's Georgian marvels. The house is Palladian, like those at Powerscourt and Castletown, its central block flanked by colonnades and wings. Lavish trim is spread throughout the house like tinsel. The house holds paintings by Goya, Velasquez, and Rubens, and the National Gallery of Ireland sometimes mounts exhibits here. The house is 2½ mi. down the main road toward Ballymore.

Blessington is served by **bus #65** hourly from Eden Quay in **Dublin** (£1.25). On Saturday and Sunday, one bus continues on to **Donard** and the Ballinclea Hostel there (see above). **Bus Éireann** passes through Blessington on its **Dublin/Waterford** route (3 per day), connecting it with **Baltinglass** and its hostel. Blessington is on both N81, which runs from Dublin to Enniscorthy, and R410, which connects it to Naas. Turn to the Blessington **tourist office** (tel. (045) 865850), in the town square, for ideas on outdoor pursuits (open June-Aug. M-Sa 10am-6pm, Su noon-6pm). **Baltyboys (An Óige/HI)** (tel. (045) 867266), a.k.a **Blessington Lake Hostel,** provides cozy accommodation in a refurbished schoolhouse near Russborough House with excellent fishing. Co-ed dorms feature basic bunks and hot showers. (June-Sept. dorms £6.50, Oct.-May £5.50. Lockout 10am-5pm. Open Mar.-Nov. daily; Dec.-Feb. F-Sa.)

County Kildare

The towns immediately west of Dublin in Co. Kildare are still well within the city's orbit: the best sights—Kildare's horses and Lullymore's Heritage Park—are easily seen as daytrips from Dublin. Only a bit farther from Dublin, though, the towns become shockingly tiny communities. The county is linked to Dublin by more than just highways—half of Kildare was included in the Pale, the region of English dominance centered around Dublin. From the 13th to the 16th century, the FitzGerald Earls of Kildare had effective control over all of eastern Ireland. Today, mansions and the big-money Irish Derby evoke Kildare's former prominence.

■ Maynooth

Carton House on one end of Main St. and Maynooth Castle and St. Patrick's College on the other side make Maynooth (ma-NOOTH) a dignified and religiously significant sandwich worth a day trip from Dublin. In 1795, King George III granted permission for St. Patrick's College, the first Catholic seminary in Ireland, to open out of concern that priests educated in Revolutionary France (the only other option) would acquire dangerous notions of independence. He later said that opening St. Patrick's "cost me more pain than the loss of the colonies." The Maynooth Seminary was the only site for training Irish Catholic priests during much of the 19th century. Although other centers exist today, many of today's priests, both in Ireland and abroad, are still ordained here.

PRACTICAL INFORMATION Maynooth is 12 mi. west of Dublin on N4. Suburban **trains** run from Connolly Station in **Dublin** (30min., M-Sa 14 per day, Su 4 per day, £1.80). **Bus** #66 runs directly to Maynooth twice an hour from Middle Abbey St., **Dublin** (50min., £1.75); #67A, also twice an hour from Middle Abbey St., takes the long way through **Celbridge** (£1.75). **Hitchers** from Dublin stand on Chapelizod Rd., between Phoenix Park and the Liffey, or even farther west where Chapelizod becomes Lucan Rd. The **Citizens Information Centre,** Main St. (tel. 328 5477), is a volunteer-staffed center that answers questions about the area (open M-F 10am-4pm). The St. Patrick's visitor's center (see below) also provides helpful information about the town and area. 01 walks the Path of **Phone Codes.**

ACCOMMODATIONS, FOOD, AND PUBS The **Leinster Arms,** Main St. (tel. 628 6323), is mainly a pub, but it's also a great B&B value for groups as guests pay a flat £30 per room. Reserve ahead in summer, especially for the room with an attached kitchen. The pub downstairs serves snacks and entrees (vegetables £2.50, entrees about £5; food served 10:30am-10pm). **St. Patrick's College** rents out singles and doubles in student apartments (B&B £17, available mid-June to Sept; contact Bill Tinley at the conference center, tel. 708 3726). Enjoy light fare for two or three pounds at **Elite Confectionery,** Main St. (tel. 628 5521; open M-Sa 8:30am-6:30pm).

SIGHTS The powerful Fitzgerald family controlled their vast domains from **Maynooth Castle,** built in 1176. (*Pick up key from Mrs. McTernan, 1 Parson St., the road across from the castle.*) However, it was dismantled in 1647 and now lies in ruins in a sun-dappled field right off Main St. Hundreds of birds will take off when you climb the staircase to the roofless Great Hall to become the sole, if temporary, resident of the castle.

The least visited but most worthy of Maynooth's sights is St. Patrick's College, recently renamed the **University of Maynooth.** The sculpted gardens and austere architecture put students in the right frame of mind to study at Ireland's oldest Catholic seminary. Walk the Path of Saints or the Path of Sinners in the garden just beyond the first courtyard and you may drink at the Font of Faith or gaze meditatively at the Apocalypse carved in 5000-year-old bog wood. Don't worry—both paths lead to "Christhood," a 12 ft. font in the center of a pool. A small cemetery lies at the end of a long line of interwoven trees behind the garden and to the left. Ancient Celtic crosses that mark 18th- and 19th-century graves lie beside freshly dug ones. The **Visitor's Centre** (tel. 708 3576) is on the left under the arch as you enter the college grounds. (*Open M-Sa 11am-5pm, Su 2-6pm.*) Its collection of Christian paraphernalia and video presentation are mediocre, but the model of the grounds is useful for planning walks and they offer a worthwhile 45-minute tour of the college (£2, students £1). The college also has an **Ecclesiastical Museum** that oddly combines items from religious rituals with 19th-century scientific equipment. At the other end of Maynooth's main drag, the Georgian **Carton House** impresses visitors with its imposing facade at the end of a long, beautifully landscaped drive. Tourists must crowd at the gate like paupers of yesteryear; the privately owned house isn't open to the public.

■ Near Maynooth: Celbridge

The raison d'être of Celbridge (SELL-bridge) is **Castletown House** (tel. (01) 628 8252). As of summer 1998, the raison d'être was undergoing renovations and scheduled to reopen some time in the indefinite near future. The estate's driveway extends for a full half mile, spilling past its entrance gates to become Main St. The grounds overlook the Liffey, and a shaded, bubbling creek is popular with young lovers. William Conolly, once the Speaker of the Irish House of Commons, built himself this magnificent home, touching off a nationwide fad for Palladian architecture. Edward Lovett Pearce, who also designed the Parliament House/Bank of Ireland in Dublin (see **Trinity College and Nearby,** p. 100), finished the house after Conolly's death. From a central block, two wings and rows of colonnades stretch out in graceful arcs to hide the stables behind. Inside, sumptuous furnishings and baroque wallpaper show off the lifestyles of the rich and obscure Anglo-Irish gentry. Particularly noteworthy are the print room (the only one of its kind surviving in Ireland) and some garish chandeliers in the den. The devil allegedly visited the dining room one afternoon for tea. (He wasn't served.) Outside, the Obelisk, also known as **Conolly's Folly,** is an unruly stack of arches and towers conceived as a make-work project during the severe winter of 1739. Americans may be surprised that the original plans for the Washington Monument looked like this, only bigger. Down Main St. from the house's entrance, **Celbridge Abbey** provides an opportunity for picnicking. *(Open Mar.-Oct. Tu-Su noon-6pm. £2, students £1.50.)* The abbey has also been undergoing renovations. Elegantly manicured gardens spread out behind the house, laced with two trails that tell stories about Jonathan Swift. There's also a neat model railway.

 Buses #67 and 67A run to Celbridge from Middle Abbey St., **Dublin.** (#67A also goes to Maynooth.) The suburban rail has an infrequent service to Celbridge from Dublin's Heuston Station.

■ Kildare

Kildare is Ireland's horse-racing mecca. Carefully bred, raised, and raced here, purebloods are the lifeblood of the town, providing the logic for bookies all over the country to cover their establishments with pictures of Kildare thoroughbreds. Kildare seems imbued with some of the nervous energy and natural grace of their racing beauties, especially in contrast with the town's mule-like neighbors. While Kildare's present religion centers around horses, its past was more influenced by Christianity; it grew up around a church founded here in 480 by St. Brigid. The sacred lass founded the church next to an oak tree that she saw in a vision, giving the town its original name *Cill Dara,* "Church of the Oak." Despite Kildare's grounding in thoroughbreds, quirky and unusual sights abound here and in neighboring towns.

PRACTICAL INFORMATION Kildare lies on the busy, harrowing N7 (Dublin-Limerick) and is well connected by **train** to **Dublin's** Heuston Station (40min., M-Sa 30 per day, Su 12 per day, £6). **Bus Éireann** also hits big, bad **Dublin** (1½hr., 1 per hr.), and if you play your hand right you may even land in **Cork** (3 per day, Su 2 per day, £8.50) or **Limerick** (4 per day, Su 3 per day, £7.50). The Kildare **tourist office** (tel. 522 696), in The Square, offers basic information and free maps (open June-Sept. M-Sa 10am-1pm and 2-6pm). Rent a **bike** in Kildare at **Kieran's Bike Shop** (tel. 522 354) on Claregate St. The **phone code,** 045, won in a photo finish.

ACCOMMODATIONS, FOOD, AND PUBS Accommodation in Kildare isn't very forthcoming. Toward the outskirts of town, **Fremont,** Tully Rd. (tel. 521604), has firm beds, well-decorated rooms, and a quasi-rural setting on the way to the Japanese Gardens that allow visitors to dream of racehorses (singles £18; doubles £32). In town, the **Lord Edward Guest House B&B,** Dublin St. (tel. 522389), is more hotel than B&B, with professional staff and a TV in every room (singles £18; doubles £30). **The Shell House** (tel. 521293) on Dublin Rd. is worth a stop just to gawk. Once a thatched cottage with a bizarre form of weatherproofing, the house was sold on the condition that the shells covering all the outside walls of the house must be maintained. They are arranged to form pictures of local attractions, like the round tower and cathedral steeple. Inside, the beds are firm, and the breakfast is light. (Singles £16; doubles £30.)

Good pubs are plentiful. **The Silken Thomas,** The Square (tel. 522232), has locally renowned food, ranging from bar snacks (locally famous pork loin with apple sauce £4.50) to serious entrees (£5-7). Lunch, lounge, and dinner menus are variously served between 11am and 10pm. The pub's name isn't a euphemism but a reference to "Silken Thomas" FitzGerald, who raised a revolt against the British in Dublin in 1534. **Li'l Flanagan,** in the back of The Silken Thomas (tel. 522232), is a small, delightfully scruffy, old-time pub (trad W, Th, and Su 9:30pm; rock F-Sa). **Nolan's,** The Square (tel. 521528), is a low-key pub that was once a hardware store. Sadly, the saws are gone, but Nolan's compensates with trad Tuesday through Thursday nights.

SIGHTS The **Round Tower,** just off The Square, was originally built in the 10th century and now stands testimony to Kildare's rich cultural heritage. *(Open M-Sa 10am-1pm and 2-5pm, Su 2-5pm. £2, children 50p.)* This round tower is one of the few in Ireland that visitors can actually enter and climb—most of the others have no floors inside. **St. Brigid's,** currently a Church of Ireland cathedral, lies in the shadow of the tower. *(Open May-Oct. M-Sa 10am-1pm and 2-5pm, Su 2-5pm. Free tours available upon request.)* The cathedral, an imposing building with old stonework, rests on the site where St. Brigid founded one of Ireland's first churches in 480. She was one of the first powerful women in the Catholic church, even holding power over bishops. Next to the church is **St. Brigid's Fire Temple,** a site of pagan rituals that Brigid repossessed for Christianity. Only female virgins were allowed to tend the fire, which burned continually for 1000 years. There is an unadorned high cross on the site.

More exciting is **The Irish National Stud,** "where strength and beauty live as one," about 1 mi. from Kildare in Tully (tel. 521617), which does its best to make the town's horse fever contagious. *(Irish National Stud, Irish Horse Museum, and Japanese Gardens open Feb. 11-Nov. 10 daily 9:30am-6pm. Joint admission £5, students and seniors £3.50, under 12 £2.)* Don't use the gold and wrought-iron gates on the Dublin Rd.; instead, follow the plentiful signs for the turnoff on Tully Rd. Colonel William Hall-Walker, the mystical son of a Scottish brewer, started to breed thoroughbreds at Tully in 1900. Every time a foal was born, the Colonel would cast its horoscope; if it was unfavorable, the foal would be sold, regardless of how well it was bred. The "system" has proved remarkably successful. Astrology aside, the whole place is still eccentric. The horses quaff naturally sparkling mineral water from the Tully River; its water is carbonated and has 260 parts per million of calcium, which is said to promote good bone formation. Hall-Walker stressed that the moon and stars should exercise their maximum influence on the horses, so lanterns were incorporated into the roofs of all stables. Sky lights in the stallion boxes, built after Hall-Walker's death, continue his policy. A visit to the "Irish National Stud" sign is worthwhile even if you're not a horse freak.

As the sights lose any practical purpose, things grow steadily weirder. The small **Irish Horse Museum** is housed in a converted groom's house and stallion boxes. It tells the history of the horse from its origins in *Hyracotherium* to modern times, most vividly with the skeleton of Arkle, Ireland's greatest steeplechaser, a noble horse, even in death. Why focus on death, though—every ten minutes you can see a video on the birth of a foal. **The Japanese Gardens,** also part of the Stud, are beautiful and truly bizarre, like a walk-through boardgame. Devised by Hall-Walker and built by two Japanese gardeners between 1906 and 1910, the gardens purport to tell "the story of the life of man" on a guided-by-numbers trail.

■ Near Kildare Town: The Curragh

Entertainment in Kildare is understandably equinocentric. Between Newbridge and Kildare on N7 lies **The Curragh**, 600 acres of what are perhaps the greenest fields in Ireland. Thoroughbred horses graze and train, hoping one day to earn fame and money at The Curragh racecourse (tel. (045) 541205), which hosts the **Irish Derby** (DAR-bee) on the first Sunday in July. The race, sponsored by horse-crazy Budweiser, is Ireland's premier sporting and social event and one of the most prestigious races in the world. The atmosphere on race day is grand, with everyone dressing like royalty. The Derby race itself is at 4pm. Other races are held from late March to early November. (Irish Rail timetable lists dates; trains stop at The Curragh on racedays. £9 to Derby, £7.50 to other events; students and seniors get 50% off by purchasing tickets at the Enquiries booth, opposite the racecourse's VIP entrance.) The Curragh was once a headquarters for the British military presence in pre-1916 Ireland. In the important but hushed-up "Curragh mutiny" of 1914, British army officers who incorrectly thought they were about to be ordered north stated that they would rather be fired than act against the Unionists.

■ Peatland World and Lullymore

When times get tough in the bogs, the boglanders know who to turn to—their friend peat. Nine miles from Kildare in Lullymore, **Peatland World** (tel. (045) 860133 or 860193) explains this phenomenon. *(Open M-F 9:30am-5pm, Sa-Su 2-6pm. £3, students £2.50, children £2.)* Located in a mineral island in the immense Bog of Allen, Peatland World comprises a museum and a natural history gallery. The natural history component expounds on the ecological diversity of the bogs and some of its eco-friendly post-peat-production uses. The museum explains the evolution of turf production from community activity to big business, with some attention given to the social impact of turf over the centuries. On display are bog-preserved prehistoric artifacts, a model of an Irish cottage with a turf fire, and trophies from turf-cutting competitions. The museum displays their achievements: a model of a peat briquette factory and a peat-fueled power station, as well as a range of peat-based products, including boxed chunks of the old sod itself (£4). Those bitten by the bog bug should certainly take a bog tour on the West Offaly Railway (see **Clonmacnoise**, p. 151).

Anyone interested in early-Christian Ireland should not miss **Lullymore Heritage Park** (tel. (045) 870 238). *(Open M-F 9:30am-6pm, Sa-Su noon-6pm. 1hr. tour. £3, students £2, children £1.50.)* Surrounded by bogland and farms, the park offers a realistic depiction of Irish life in the pre-famine years and shows relics and ruins from Lullymore's 5th-century heyday. To reach Lullymore from Kildare, take Allenwood Rd. to Rathangan Rd. It's a tricky hitch; your best bet is to bike. Buses drive to nearby Allenwood from Dublin (1¼hr., M-Sa 6 per day, Su 3 per day).

County Meath

Meath is a quiet, peaceful county, which makes it an appropriate home for the crypts of ancient, creeping terror that lurk among its hills. In pre-Norman times, after the builders of these crypts had faded into stony memory, Meath was considered Ireland's fifth province; Tara was the political and spiritual center of Ireland. Vikings sailing up the Boyne built Drogheda, which today serves as a base for exploring the county's pleasantly morose charms.

BOYNE VALLEY

The thinly populated Boyne Valley safeguards Ireland's greatest historical treasures. (They're too big to cart back to Dublin anyway, but they make perfect daytrips from the city.) The massive passage tombs of **Newgrange, Knowth,** and **Dowth** predate the pyramids, and even after so long, archaeologists have failed to unpuzzle the strange symbols carved on their faces or even guess the purpose of their existence. Once upon a time, he who possessed ownership of the Celtic **Hill of Tara** was granted Kingship of Ireland. Today, the hill sucks in tourist revenue from legions of visitors who come for a wonderfully soggy walk and multi-media presentations of clashing swords. **Slane** and **Trim** both boast well-preserved medieval castles. Every so often, farmers plow up artifacts from the 1690 Battle of the Boyne (see **The Protestant Ascendancy,** p. 56).

Buses from Dublin and Drogheda hit the major Boyne towns, but service between towns is spotty and many famous sights are miles off the main roads. Bus fares from Dublin run £3-6 return. The several N-roads criss-crossing the valley make it possible to **hitch,** but the grand tour requires a fair degree of hiking. Bikers will find the terrain between the sights welcoming: mostly flat, with hills gentle enough to conquer without stopping but steep enough to boost one's ego. Several tours herd visitors through the circuit of sights. **Celtic Twilight** (tel. (088) 54787) offers a full sight-seeing "Tour of the Royal Meath" on Sundays in the summer (£14). The coach leaves the Nassau St. entrance to Trinity College Dublin at 10am and returns to Dublin at 5:30pm. **Sightseeing Tours** (tel. (01) 283 9973) visits Newgrange and Knowth on its Boyne Valley tour. The bus leaves from the Dublin Tourist Office (June-Sept. daily at 1:20pm, return at 6pm, £14).

■ Brú na Bóinne

The area southeast of the town Slane, Brú na Bóinne (brew na BO-in-yeh, Palace of the Boyne), is saturated not with palaces but with prehistoric tombs: Newgrange, Knowth, Dowth, and 37 more. The tombs were made by an indigenous pre-Celtic neolithic culture with mind-boggling engineering talents. The tombs are older than the pyramids or Stonehenge. On a July or August afternoon, you may grow old yourself waiting in the long lines to see them, especially at Newgrange. But the prehistoric architectural ingenuity will prove worth the wait. Brú na Bóinne is well-signposted: all three of the passage-tombs are reached from the turnoff on N51, 3 mi. from Slane and 7 mi. from Drogheda. Follow the turnoff road for about a half mile, then take a right at the intersection for Knowth, a left for Newgrange and Dowth. The road is very well traveled, and **hitchers** report an easy trip to and from the tombs. Follow signs for Slane (west down West St.) and then Dowth for a more scenic (and no longer) route. Most hitchers stick to the well-traveled Slane Rd. until they come to the intersection at which signs direct travelers to Knowth and Newgrange. Bikers in search of the easiest ride should follow the road to Dowth on their way to the tombs and take Slane Rd. back to Drogheda. The **phone code,** 041, has mind-boggling engineering talents.

■ Newgrange

Newgrange (tel. 24488; fax 24798), the most spectacular, most well restored, and most visited of the sites, is the prime example of a passage-tomb. Built by a highly organized religious society over 5000 years ago, using stones believed to have been carted from Wicklow 40 mi. away, Newgrange is covered with elaborate patterns and symbols that mystify archaeologists. The inner chamber's roof was cobbled together without the use of mortar and has stood since about 3200 BC. The 30-minute **tour** is one part information and nine parts wild speculation, but it's the only way to see the inside of the one-acre tomb. *(Tours begin every 30min. daily June-Sept. 9:30am-7pm; Mar.-*

Apr. and Oct. 10am-5pm; Nov.-Feb. 10am-4:30pm; May 9:30am-6pm. £3, seniors £2, students £1.25.) The highlight of the tour is the re-creation of a moment that actually occurs five days each year around the winter solstice, when the sun's rays enter at just the right angle to illuminate the inner chamber. Although this function was only recently discovered, for thousands of years the natives have told stories of how the people of the mound could stop the sun. Antique graffiti was left by visitors to Newgrange since the rediscovery of its passage in 1699. Bring a coat or sweater; it gets chilly inside even in summer. The **tourist office** (tel. 24274) is just before the entry to the site, near the parking lot (open Apr.-Oct. daily 9am-7pm). Next door, visitors are welcome to feed and pet animals at **Newgrange Farm** (tel. 24119) or just get caffeinated at the coffee shop (farm open in summer daily 10am-5pm, £2.50).

■ Knowth and Dowth

One mile west of Newgrange is the less-frantic and less-impressively restored site of **Knowth** (rhymes with "mouth"). Knowth was inhabited continuously from 3000 BC until the Battle of the Boyne, so the site today is a mishmash of Stone Age tombs, early Christian subterranean refuge tunnels, and Norman grain ovens. Among those who made use of the mounds were the "beaker people." These mysterious people were not muppets but pre-Celtic tribes known only for their drinking flasks. They may have worshipped mead (who doesn't?). The **tour** here is more informative and entertaining than the one at Newgrange, and it's usually less crowded. *(30min. tours daily May to mid-June and mid-Sept. to Oct. 10am-5pm; mid-June to mid-Sept. 9:30am-6:30pm. £2, students £1.)* Because people lived on top of the tomb for so many years, it's not safe to go inside, but guests are welcome to crawl through short, underground tunnels. There is no tourist office, but the **admission office** (tel. 24824) sells booklets about Knowth's history. One mile east of Newgrange is **Dowth** (rhymes with "Knowth"), the third of the great passage tombs. Unfortunately, Dowth is not open to the public. Signs past Dowth lead to the more-scenic and less-traveled route back to Drogheda. Everyone will enjoy the subtle humor of farmer Willie Redhouse, who can take you on a tour of his 400-acre **farm,** pausing by a chuckling river and prehistoric mounds on his property. *(Contact Willie through Newgrange Farm, tel. 24119. Open July-Aug. daily 10am-5pm; Apr.-June and Sept. Su-F 10am-5pm. £2.25.)* Newgrange tour guides may attribute such grassy wonders to religious origins, but Willie invites more imaginative speculation: where else would leprechauns bury their gold and the tooth fairy store everyone's teeth?

■ Hill of Tara

From prehistoric times until at least the 10th century, Tara was the political and sometime religious center of Ireland. The hill is home to a Stone Age tomb, an Iron Age fort, and the principal late Celtic royal seat. The combination has guaranteed Tara's popularity with tourists and archaeologists alike. Control of Tara, seat of the powerful Uí Néill family, theoretically entitled a warlord to be High King. Ownership of the hill was understandably disputed until the 10th century, but the arrival of St. Patrick (traditionally held to be in 432, more likely closer to 400) deposed Tara from its position as the Jerusalem of Ireland. The overlapping of Bronze Age, High King, and early Christian civilizations at Tara has confused historians and archaeologists for centuries, and today the historical functions of many of the hill's structures remain unknown. Tara's symbolic importance remains even in modern times. In 1843, Daniel O'Connell gathered a million people here for a Home Rule rally.

The enormous site is about halfway between Dublin and Navan on the N3. Take any Navan-bound **bus** from **Dublin** (1hr., M-Sa 13 per day, Su 5 per day) and ask the driver to let you off at the turnoff. The site is about a mile straight uphill. The actual buildings—largely wattle, wood, and earthwork—have long been buried or destroyed; what you'll see is mostly a set of concentric and overlapping earthen rings and walls, whose traditional names correspond to the buildings the mounds were thought to cover. The whole history of Tara decamps at the **visitors center** (tel. (046)

25903), in an old church at the site. *(Open daily May to mid-June 10am-5pm, mid-June to mid-Sept. 9:30am-5:45pm, mid-Sept. to Oct. 10am-5pm. £1.50, seniors £1, students and children 60p.)* The center displays aerial photos of Tara, essential for making sense of the place, and a good 20-minute flick about Tara's history, complete with warrior-kings, pagan priestesses, and scary sound effects. After the film, an excellent guided tour (25min.) circles the site. The full site encompasses 100 acres of many smaller mounds and ring forts, although the tour usually covers only the sites at the top of the hill.

■ Trim

A series of enormous, well-preserved Norman castles and abbeys that thrill even the most jaded tourist overlook this charming town on the River Boyne. It's definitely worth a trip from Dublin.

PRACTICAL INFORMATION Bus Éireann stops on Castle St. in front of the castle en route to **Dublin** (6 per day, £6 return) and **Athlone** (1 per day). Trim's **tourist office,** Mill St. (tel. 37111), has meaty information on Meath and a useful self-guided walking tour of Trim (£1.50; open daily 9:30am-6pm). The **Bank of Ireland** (tel. 31230) surveys Market St. (open M 10am-5pm, Tu-F 10am-4pm). Trim's **phone code,** 046, is undergoing continual renovations.

ACCOMMODATIONS, FOOD, AND PUBS The new **Bridge House Tourist Hostel** (tel. 31848), perched next to the River Boyne, offers small, comfortable rooms (all with bath) and a cool stone-walled lounge (dorms £10; doubles £24; breakfast included; curfew 11:30pm; open June-Aug.). A handful of B&Bs makes a night in Trim an enticing possibility. In the heart of town, **Brogan's,** High St. (tel. 31237), offers a hotel-like B&B (singles £25; doubles £40; all with bath) and a three-course meal for £4. Floral comfort blooms in **O'Briens,** Friars Park (tel. 31745), off Dublin Rd. The rooms are both spacious and neat (singles £22; doubles £36; all with bath).

The Pastry Kitchen, Market St. (tel. 36166), puts sturdy breakfasts and luscious pastries on the table (sandwiches £2; open M-Sa 7:30am-6pm, Su 10am-6pm). **The Abbey Lodge,** Market St. (tel. 31549), presents a tremendous plate of prime roast with potato and vegetables (£3.95) with your pint. **McCormack's** (tel. 31963), across from the castle on Castle St., may show cricket on TV, but it's all Irish on Sunday nights when the *bodhrán,* tin whistle, and a fiddle or two liven things up (cover £1). **The Bounty** (tel. 31640), across the Bridge St. bridge, is bedecked with spinning wheels, old umbrellas, and bulls' horns. In The Square off Market St., the **Judge and Jury** offers an excellent pint of Guinness and frequent live bands in the evenings.

SIGHTS Norman invader Hugh de Lacy first built **Trim Castle** in 1172, but the unruly O'Connors of Connacht trashed the place a year later. *(Tours July-Aug. daily 9:30, 11am, 2, and 6pm. £2.)* A new castle was constructed in the 1190s, and it was this structure that Mel Gibson sacked for *Braveheart* 800 years later. King John of England dropped by long enough to rename it King John's Castle. For a few hundred years, the castle was an important fortification for all of Meath and defended a walled town with separate gates and battlements. The castle, which locals say is the largest in Ireland and has the thickest wall—the outer curtain wall is nine yards all around—stands above the center of town and can be easily reached through the gate on Castle St. Walking tours offer access to parts of the castle (others are still undergoing renovations). A few ancient abbeys open for interesting exploration crumble across the river from the castle.

Across the river stand the 12th-century remains of **St. Mary's Abbey,** destroyed by Cromwell's armies. You can still see the **Yellow Steeple,** so called because of the yellowish gleam it gives off at twilight. In front of the Yellow Steeple is what's left of **Talbot's Castle,** a 15th-century manor built by John Talbot, Viceroy of Ireland. Outside the two ruins lies the **Sheep Gate,** the only surviving medieval gate of the once walled town. You can rid yourself of unwelcome warts at the **Newtown Cemetery,** far behind the Castle, at the site of two tomb figures mistakenly called the **Jealous**

Man and Woman. The name comes from the sword between them, which conventionally signified not resentment but chastity. Put a pin between the two figures; when the pin rusts (which shouldn't take long in this damp country) your warts should disappear.

For more spicy Trim history, the **Meath Visitors Centre** (tel. 37227), next to the tourist office, educates and frightens with a multimedia presentation, an exhibit, and an excellent, dramatic slideshow. *(Open daily 10am-5pm. £2, students and seniors £1.25, children £1.)* Decapitations, the villainous Hugh de Lacy, and hideous plague rats—maybe Trim isn't so charming after all. For one week each June (usually the last), the **Scurlogstown Olympiad Town Festival** fills Trim with horse and dog shows, carnival rides, traditional music concerts, and herds of sheep and pigs for sale.

BEYOND THE VALLEY OF THE BOYNE

■ Kells

The name of Kells (Ceanannas Mór) is known far and wide, thanks to a book that wasn't written there. The monastery at Kells was founded by St. Columcille (also known as St. Columba) in 559, before the saint went on to found the more important settlement of Iona on an island west of Scotland. It was at Iona that the famous *Book of Kells,* an elaborately decorated Latin gospel, was begun. It came to Kells in some form of development in 804 when the Columbans fled Iona. In 1007, the book was stolen, its gold cover ripped off, and the pages buried under sod, from which they were rescued two months later. It remained in Kells until 1661, when Cromwell carted it off to Trinity College, where it is now recovering. Kells is trying to get the book back, which Trinity finds amusing.

Even without the book, Kells can boast of some of Ireland's best-preserved monastic ruins, including an oratory, a round tower, and four high crosses. The fifth and largest cross, Market Cross, which had stood with relatively little mishap for a thousand years, was knocked off its pedestal last year by a school bus driver. The cross has been moved to Trim, where it is now recovering...and has been for over a year. In the meantime, several housing estates are being built as Dublin's sphere of suburbia grows.

PRACTICAL INFORMATION Most maps refer to Kells in Irish, as *Ceanannas Mór,* but no one in the region uses the Irish in speech. **Bus Éireann** stops outside of O'Rorke's Bar on Lower John St. on its way to Dublin (1hr., M-Sa 17 per day, Su 8 per day, £6 return). **AIB** bank (tel. 40610; fax 41222) is on John St. (open M 10am-5pm, Tu-F 10am-4pm), and the **post office** (tel. 40127) is on Farrel St. (open M-Sa 9am-5:30pm). Kells's **phone code,** 046, hasn't been swiped or toppled. Yet.

ACCOMMODATIONS, FOOD, AND PUBS Kells has the area's only real hostel. **Kells Hostel** (tel. 40100; fax 40680), on the Dublin-Donegal Rd., has clean dorms, usually with available beds. There are also squash courts and a gym downstairs that offers a special £2 per session rate for hostelers. If you would rather not break a sweat, you can play snooker in the common room for 50p. Check in at Monaghan's Bar next door to the hostel. (Dorms £7, self-service laundry £2.) **Camping** is available behind the hostel, with full use of the indoor hostel facilities (£3 per person). **Latimor House** (tel. 40133), half a mile down Oldcastle Rd., provides B&B in a pretty, rustic setting. From Market Square, go down Cross St. and take the first right onto Canon St. The house is full of antiques, and the beds are firm with thick comforters (£15).

Penny's Place, Market St. (tel. 41630), is a pink paradise that serves excellent food for a pittance (open M-Sa 9am-6pm). **O'Shaughnessey's,** Market St. (tel. 41110), has good pub grub (£1-4) and live music Wednesday through Sunday evenings. If you're hankering for country cuisine, scrape the muck off your boots and head to **The Buttery** on Farrel St., a late-night restaurant that stews old favorites (entrees £3.50).

The best nightclub in all Meath is a short hop away in **Athboy.** If you're up for some ragin', head over to Farrel St. and ask one of the private minibuses if they're heading to **Buck Mulligan's** (£3 return, but no cover). If you're more in the mood for a 'disco bar,' **The Ranch** is right next door.

SIGHTS Despite (or because of) its centuries-long tradition as a center of Christian learning, the monastery at Kells kept getting burned down by rival monasteries. The current structure, with the exception of the 12th-century belltower, dates only to the 1700s. Inside **St. Columba's Church** (tel. 40151), there's a replica of the Book with copies of selected pages enlarged for your viewing pleasure. The door should be open during daylight hours; if not, ask at the gate outside. Four large **high crosses** covered with Bible scenes, some better preserved than others, are scattered on the south and west side of the church. The church was surrounded by a wall dating from the 12th century until the County Council began building a path alongside it that undermined its foundations and toppled the whole thing. The 100 ft. **round tower** sheltered the monks, the relics of St. Columcille, and (less successfully) the would-be High King Murchadh Mac Flainn, who was murdered there in 1076.

The most satisfying of the sights, however, is **St. Columcille's House,** Church Ln., where the *Book of Kells* may have been finished. When facing the gates of the churchyard from Market St., walk up the lane on the right of the yard; you can't miss the only 8th-century house on the block, even if it's dwarfed by the new Death Star-like Garda station behind it. The key is available from Mrs. Carpenter, 100 yd. down the hill from Columcille's House on Church Ln. The place looks almost exactly as it would have in St. Columcille's day, except that the present above-ground door was originally part of a secret underground passageway from the churchyard; the original entrance began 8 ft. above the present ground level. Climb the ladder to the three tiny attic rooms for a glimpse of the sleeping quarters where entire families sometimes lived in centuries past.

Two miles down Oldcastle Rd., within the People's Park, is the **Spire of Lloyd,** a 150 ft. viewing tower erected by the old Headfort landlords. Constructed as a make-work project for the poor, its ostensible purpose was letting the Headfort women watch the hunt comfortably and safely. From the top, behold spectacular Irish countryside and Northern Ireland in the distance. Next to the spire is the **Graveyard of the Poor,** where the area's huge pauper population buried its dead in mass graves. The plot was a chaotic cow pasture until a few years ago, when the town scraped together the money to restore it. Now the grass is cut regularly and there's a high sign reading: "1838-1921, Erected to the poor interred here during the operation of the English Poor Law System. R.I.P."

Louth, Monaghan, and Cavan

Farther north in Co. Louth, the Cooley Peninsula contains hills and water for bikers and sailors to enjoy. When traveling toward Cooley, the boat trip is much more enjoyable and interesting than the dull land routes. The teeny towns of Co. Cavan and Co. Monaghan make fine stopovers on the way to the Northwest or to Northern Ireland's Fermanagh Lake District, especially since crossing the border has become so easy and painless. Belturbet, though in Co. Cavan, is covered under the Fermanagh Lake District in Northern Ireland.

■ Drogheda

Drogheda (DRA-hed-a) perches on steep slopes astride the Boyne river. The waterfront's drab, functional industrialness bursts into crowded streets and cheerful pubs on the streets north of and parallel to the Boyne, while remnants of Drogheda's Viking past linger in the city's gates and crumbling walls. Most sights in Co. Meath are bikable from Drogheda.

PRACTICAL INFORMATION

Trains: (tel. 38749) east out of town on the Dublin road. Follow John St. south of the river. To **Dublin** (1hr., express 30min., M-Sa 26 per day, Su 4 per day, £8, £12 return) and **Belfast** (2hr., M-Sa 9 per day, Su 4 per day, £12).

Buses: Station on John St. (tel. 35023). Inquiries desk open M-F 9am-6:30pm, Sa 8:30am-1:30pm. To **Athlone** (2½hr., M-Sa 3 per day, Su 1 per day, £9), **Belfast** (2hr., M-Sa 6 per day, Su 3 per day, £8), **Dublin** (50min., M-Sa 18 per day, Su 7 per day, £4.80), **Dundalk** (40min., M-Sa 11 per day, Su 6 per day, £4.40), **Galway** (4hr., M-Sa 2 per day, Su 1 per day, £12), and **Mullingar** (2hr., M-Sa 2 per day, Su 1 per day, £8).

Tourist Office: Donore Rd. (tel. 37070), in the bus station off Dublin Rd., opposite the McDonald's. Offers the *Drogheda Town Map* (£1), which has all the sights in Drogheda and nearby as well as a map of the region and copious advertising. Open June-Sept. M-Sa 10am-1pm and 2-5:30pm.

Banks: AIB, West St. (tel. 36523). Open M-W and F 9:30am-5pm, Th 9:30am-7pm. 24hr. **ATM. TSB,** West St. (tel. 38703). Same hours as AIB.

Bike Rental: Bridge Cycles, North Quay (tel. 34526), is the best place to rent bikes. £7 per day, £30 per week; deposit £30. Helmet rental £5. Open M-Sa 9am-1pm and 2-6pm. 10% discount with ISIC card, another 10% with *Let's Go.*

Emergency: Dial 999; no coins required. **Garda:** West Gate (tel. 38777).

Hospital: Our Lady of Lourdes, Cross Lanes (tel. 37601).

Post Office: West St. (tel. 38157). Open M-Sa 9am-5:30pm.

Phone Code: A blackened, shriveled 041.

ACCOMMODATIONS

Drogheda's accommodations, like most things in the town, are north of the River Boyne. **Harpur House,** William St. (tel. 32736), is a small hostel in a big townhouse. Follow Shop St. up the hill, continue up Peter St. and take a right onto William St.; the hostel is on the right. The house is old and it shows, but the rooms are airy and the beds are not bunks. Simple B&B rooms provide additional privacy. (9-bed dorms £7, with full breakfast £10. B&B £15. Kitchen available.) Buses from Harpur House do half-day sightseeing tours of the Boyne Valley (£13). Well-kept and backpacker-friendly, **Abbey View House,** Mill Lane (tel. 31470), defines B&B courtesy. Head west on West St. and take the first left after it crosses over to Trinity St. Sitting pretty on the River Boyne, the house has parking, bikes, canoes, a tunnel to Monasterboice, and big rooms with patchwork quilts (£15). High ceilings and elegant wallpaper make **St. Laurence's Lodge,** King St. (tel. 35410), seem more like a hotel than the old Christian Brothers school that it is. The rooms are pleasant, with firm beds, tea-makers, and TVs. (Singles £23; doubles £37. All with bath.)

FOOD AND PUBS

Groceries can be found on West St. at **Dunnes Stores** and **Quinnsworth** (both open M-Tu and Sa 9am-6:30pm, W 9am-8pm, and Th-F 9am-9pm). **The Pizzeria,** Peter St. (tel. 34208), cooks all kinds of Italian specialities (pasta £7) and 13 types of pizza (£5.40). It's also very popular, so make reservations or arrive before 9pm if you want a seat. (Open M-Tu and Th-Su 6-11pm.) **Birdie Mac's,** West St. (tel. 33861), supplies everything from bus snacks (£2) to full meals (£7) to live music (food served daily 3-9pm; music Th-F and Su 9:30pm). You can grab a light meal for about £2 at **The Cop-**

per Kettle, 1 Peter St. (tel. 37397), a hole-in-the-wall café just up from the junction with West St. The offerings are simple but scrumptious. (Open M-Sa 9:30am-5:30pm.)

The largest town in the area, Drogheda has a pretty active nightlife. Dark wood engulfs **Peter Matthews,** 9 Laurence St. (tel. 37371), also known as McPhail's, a very old, very likable pub (live rock and blues Th-Su nights). **The Weavers,** West St. (tel. 32816), is renowned for its lunchtime and dinner grub. There's more wood and darkness at this destination for well-dressed businesspeople. (DJs spin top 40 tunes F-Su; no cover). **Carberry's,** Back Strand, is the only place in town with trad (Th and Su). **The Trinity Arms** at the intersection of George and West St. is polished and cheerful and generally draws a young crowd, particularly on weekends.

Drogheda has a happening disco that brings dancers from miles around. **The Earth,** Stockwell Ln. (tel. 30969), is a Flintstones-meet-techno sort of place, with fossils embedded in the walls and bar, rock-themed bathrooms, and not a single straight wall. (Open Th-Su 11pm-3:30am. Cover £5, £3 with concession Su and before midnight Th-Sa. Techno F-Sa, 70s disco Th and Su.)

SIGHTS

Encounter a blackened, shriveled head in the imposing, neo-Gothic **St. Peter's Church** on West St. *(Open daily 8:30am-8:30pm.)* Most of the town's medieval churches (at one time there were as many as seven) were sacked or burned, some with people taking refuge inside, by Cromwell, a deeply religious man. Built in the 1880s, St. Peter's safeguards what's left of the martyred saint Oliver Plunkett. Pious visitors light candles to pay homage. Plunkett is at the end of the left-hand aisle, along with the door of his London prison cell. The church also has one the few **cadaver stones** in Ireland. These elaborate funerary monuments, popular in the 16th century, were meant to show that decay corrupts the flesh of rich and poor alike. In the graveyard outside the church lies Joseph Duggan, one of the survivors of the **Light Brigade.**

At the end of West St. stand the four-story twin towers of **St. Laurence Gate,** a 13th-century fortification outside the town walls that is no less impressive for never having faced a serious attack. At the top of the hill on Saint Peter's St., the mossy **Magdalen Steeple,** dating from 1224, is all that remains of the Dominican Friary that once stood on the spot. On Saturday mornings, an open-air market is held in Bolton Square, as it has been every week since 1317. The **Millmount Museum** (tel. 33097) occupies a Martello tower on the southern hill overlooking Drogheda's center (see **Rebellion, Union, and Reaction,** p. 57). *(Open Apr.-Oct. Tu-Sa 10am-6pm. £1.50, children 75p.)* The museum displays artifacts from the Civil War period, antique household appliances, and a geological collection. On Old Abbey Ln. south of West St., the few remains of the 5th-century **Priory of St. Mary** perch among the urban refuse. During the second week of July, locals swagger through the streets to the Latin rhythms of the **Samba Festival.**

The Battle of the Boyne raged at **Oldbridge,** 5 mi. west of Drogheda. *(For information and tours, contact Paul McAuley (tel. (041) 41644). M-F 9am-5pm, Sa 10am-6pm, Su noon-6pm.)* On July 1, 1690, Protestant forces under William of Orange (King William III of England) defeated the Irish Catholic armies supporting the ousted Stuart king of England, James II, who fled the country. The battle gave William control of Dublin, and James's flight made it clear that English Protestants would continue to control at least the eastern half of Ireland. Catholics and English Jacobites remembered the Battle of the Boyne as a momentous tragedy for centuries; for Ulster Protestants, it became an occasion for celebration. Calendar reform has moved the battle's anniversary to July 12, Orange Day, when Protestants march throughout Northern Ireland. (See **The Protestant Ascendancy,** p. 56.)

■ Mellifont Abbey and Monasterboice

What were once two of the most important monasteries in Ireland crumble 5 mi. north of Drogheda. Turn off Drogheda-Collon Rd. at Monleek Cross and follow signs to either one. The more interesting of the two, **Mellifont Abbey** (tel. (041) 26459), has served as a grand setting for many of Ireland's tragedies. *(Open daily 9:30am-6:30pm, last admission 5:45pm. £1.50, students 60p, seniors £1.)* Founded in 1142 by St. Malachy, a friend of Bernard of Clairvaux, Mellifont was the first Cistercian abbey in Ireland. The 1152 Senate of Mellifont weakened the independent Irish monastic system with a papal legate that confiscated the monasteries' tithes, divided Ireland into four bishoprics, and established Armagh as primate. Subsequently, the monastic centers declined, as did the traditions of scholarship within their walls. Three years later, Cistercian pope Adrian IV issued a bull giving the English King authorization to "correct" Ireland, which served as approval for the Norman invasion of the 1170s. In 1603, the last of the O'Neills, who had once ruled Ulster, surrendered to the English here and then skipped Ireland for the Continent (see **History,** p. 55). Most of the grandeur of the place has disappeared as well, although a trace remains at the **old lavabo,** where monks once cleansed themselves of sins and grime. This bath of past ages offers a glimpse of the original structure's impressiveness.

Just off N1, the monastic settlement of **Monasterboice** (MON-ster-boyce) is well known for its 9th-century high crosses and round tower. *(Always open. Free.)* The monastery was one of Ireland's most wealthy from its founding in 520 until its sacking by Vikings in 1097. **Muiredach's Cross,** the first high cross you'll see upon entering, is one of Ireland's most impressive. A frenzy of sculpted Bible scenes, from Eve tempting Adam to the Judgement Day, cover the cross, the top of which is carved in the shape of a reliquary. At nearly 7 yd. high, the timeworn West Cross is the tallest High Cross in Ireland.

▨ Dundalk

If you want to see the natural wonders of the Cooley Peninsula, you don't need to come to Dundalk. If you're looking for a hopping nightlife, though, Dundalk is the place to be. Located at the mouth of Dundalk Bay, this relatively industrial town has information on the rest of Co. Louth and Cooley Peninsula, making it a good place to stay while exploring these areas. Otherwise, it has little to attract tourists other than a youthful atmosphere, the Harp Brewery, and a few monuments.

ORIENTATION AND PRACTICAL INFORMATION The main street in Dundalk is Clanbrassil St., with Park St. as runner-up. Both are lined with the shops and pubs that are Dundalk's attractions. Dundalk's streets have great transformative powers; Clanbrassil becomes Market Square, then Earl St. as it heads south. Earl St. intersects Park St., which becomes Francis St., then Roden Pl., then Jocelyn St. if you head left from Earl St. To the right, Earl St. becomes Dublin St. The N1 highway zips south to Dublin and north to Belfast, becoming A1 at the border. The **train station** is on Carrickmacross Rd. From Clanbrassil St., turn right on Park St. then right on Anne St., which becomes Carrickmacross. Trains run to **Belfast** (1hr., M-Sa 7 per day, Su 4 per day, £9) and **Dublin** (1hr., M-Th 10 per day, F 11 per day, Sa 9 per day, Su 5 per day, £11). **Buses** stop at the Bus Éireann station (tel. 34075) on Long Walk, which is parallel to Clanbrassil, and run to **Belfast** through **Newry** (1½hr., M-Sa 9 per day, Su 3 per day, £6.70), and **Dublin** (1½hr., M-F 16 per day, Sa 13 per day, Su 7 per day, £6). The **tourist office,** Jocelyn St. (tel. 35484), hands out the free *Dundalk Town Guide,* which includes maps marked with the city's sights. From the bus stop, take Clanbrassil St. down to Park and turn left to reach Jocelyn St.; the office is on the right after the cathedral. (Open June-Oct. M-F 9am-6pm, Sa 9:30am-1pm and 2-5:30pm; Nov.-May M-F 9:30am-1pm and 2-5:30pm, Sa 10am-1pm and 2-6pm.) **Banks** (including the **AIB, Bank of Ireland,** and **Ulster Bank**) are scattered within a block of each other on Clanbrassil St.; most have 24-hour **ATMs. FonaCab,** Francis St. (tel. 74777), has 24-hour taxi service for those late clubbing nights. The **post office** (tel. 34444) is on Clanbrassil St. (open M and W-Sa 9am-5:30pm, Tu 9:30am-5:30pm). Life, the universe, and the **phone code** sum to 042.

ACCOMMODATIONS, FOOD, AND PUBS In town, **Oriel House,** 63 Dublin St. (tel. 31347), is well located and inexpensive, with dim but serviceable rooms and a warm proprietress (singles £12; doubles £20). **Glen Gat House,** 18-19 The Crescent (tel. 37938), around the corner from Dublin St. near the train station, is pricier, but the exquisite garden might justify the mark-up. Rooms are very private and well maintained (£18). Restaurants and late-night fast food cluster on the main streets in town. For a more upscale bite that's still cheap and quick, try **Adrienne's Deli** (tel. 32460), next to the tourist office on Jocelyn St., which serves sandwiches for under £2 while more elaborate dishes wink at you from beneath the long counter-glass (open M-Sa 9am-6pm). Fashionable types go to **Café Metz,** Francis St. You, too, can afford to be seen in its art deco halls if you order from their nicely priced yet filling sandwich menu (around £3; open M-Sa 8:30am-6pm, dinner 7pm, Su 9:30am-8:30pm).

Only the truly trepidatious will need guidance in seeking out pub life in Dundalk, but here are a few picks. The locals' pub, **Windsor Bar,** Dublin St. (tel. 38146), is convenient to Oriel House and serves particularly tasty pub grub (£1.20-4 for a full meal; food served 12:30-3pm). At least get a look at it, because it was the winner of the Board Fáilte 1997 National Traditional Shop Front Contest. **Jockey's** (tel. 34621), on the corner of Anne and Dublin St., also tempts passersby with its alluring front and serves good, cheap pub grub during the day (breakfast daily 10am, lunch noon-2:30pm; trad F 10pm). **Seanachaí,** 12 Park St. (SHAN na kee; tel. 35050), has trad and lots of character (live music Tu and Th-Sa; cover varies). For pints and disco, head to one of the spacious bars in the **Imperial Hotel** (tel. 32241): **Rockwell's,** a gilt-and-mirrored pub, or the **Arc Nightclub,** with late-night dancing. (Bar open daily 11:30am-11:30pm. Club open Th-Su 10:30pm-2:15am. Cover varies.)

SIGHTS The gothic **St. Patrick's Cathedral,** Francis St. (tel. 34648), was modeled after King's College Chapel in Cambridge. *(Open daily 7:30am-5pm.)* Next door to the tourist office, the **County Museum** (tel. 26578) caters to those with a particular interest in "Louth's industrial legacy"—perfect for that research paper on Louth's tractors. *(Open M-Sa 10:30am-5:30pm, Su 2-6pm. £2, students and seniors £1, children 60p, families £5.)* A new wing on the history of Co. Louth is slated to open during the autumn of 1998 and will feature displays on Louth's pre-history and natural environment. In the far northwest corner of town, the 12th-century **Cúchulainn's Castle** (off Mount Ave.) supposedly stands on the birthplace of Cúchulainn, the hero of the **Ulster Cycle** of myths (see **Literary Traditions,** p. 61). The seven-story high **Seatown Windmill** was once one of the largest in Ireland, but the wind has been taken out of its sails: the sails necessary for the propeller to work were removed in 1885. Balmy beaches beckon from **Blackrock,** 3 mi. south on R172.

COOLEY PENINSULA

According to proud locals, little Cooley Peninsula is the "best bit of Ireland." The numerous trails in the surrounding mountains are a hiker's paradise, and Carlingford Lough has the warmest waters in the northern half of the island. Moreover, the area is steeped in intriguing historical myths. It was the setting for part of the most famous Irish epic, the *Táin bo Cuailnge,* or "The Cattle Raid of Cooley" (see **Literary Traditions,** p. 61). Although little material evidence remains of these legendary feats, medieval settlements, built about 1300 years after the epics supposedly took place, are remarkably well preserved in their stone remnants. Cooley's **phone code** is a dastardly cow thief named 042.

■ Carlingford

Situated at the foot of Slieve Foy, the highest of the Cooley Mountains, the coastal village of Carlingford displays a hodge-podge of various epochs in Irish history since the 1300s. Carlingford was not always the sleepy town that tourists see today—its mercantile heyday lasted from the 14th to the 16th centuries. Now it's a little pile-up of buildings and ruins at the foot of the mountain with the lough beneath.

PRACTICAL INFORMATION **Buses** (tel. 34075) stop along the waterfront on their way to **Dundalk** (50min., M-Sa 5 per day, £3.20) and **Newry** (30min., M-Sa 2 per day). **Teach Eoalais** (CHOCK OAL us), Old Quay Ln. (tel. 73888), next to PJ's Anchor Bar, offers tourist information (open mid-June to Aug. daily 9:30am-7pm; Sept to mid-June M-F 9:30am-5pm). An **AIB** (tel. 73105) sub-office is located on Newry St. (open Tu and Th 10:30am-12:30pm and 1:30-2:30pm). For **taxi** service call **Gally Cabs** (tel. 73777) or **K&F Cabs** (tel. 76316); a ride to Dundalk goes for £15.

ACCOMMODATIONS, FOOD, AND PUBS At the **Carlingford Adventure Centre and Hostel (IHH)**, Tholsel St. (tel. 73100), the friendly staff leads adventurers down long cement-block corridors to dark rooms with wooden bunks. In May and June, the hostel is often filled with groups of school children. (8-bed dorms £8.50; 4-bed dorms £9.50; doubles £21. Open Feb.-Nov., all year for groups. Wheelchair accessible.) **B&Bs** in Carlingford tend to be posh and expensive. You can dance the hora all the way to the **Shalom B&B,** Ghan Rd. (tel. 73151), signposted from the waterfront. Each spacious and modern room has a TV, hotpot, and bathroom, and if you're a guest, you can play the "Shalom Crazy-Putt" miniature golf course for free (£17). **Viewpoint** (tel. 73149), at Omeath Rd. just off the waterfront beyond King John's castle, provides motel-style rooms with baths and private entrances. Its highlights are—surprise!—incredible views of the mountains and the lough (£20).

Carlingford contains a handful of pubs and eateries, and their offerings range from traditional Irish hospitality to supernatural phenomena. Particularly good craic is on tap at **Carlingford Arms,** Newry St. (tel. 73418). Look for daily specials. (Food served 12:30-9:30pm. Folk music Sa 9:30pm.) **PJ's Anchor Bar,** across the street from the hostel (tel. 73106), is barely larger than a breadbox but has big windows; tight quarters and daily sunshine make close friendships. During good weather, the backyard provides a refreshing and less crowded alternative. The real magic is inside where the publicans proudly display the clothes of a leprechaun caught in the nearby hills several years ago (see below).

SIGHTS The **Holy Trinity Heritage Centre,** Church Yard Rd. (tel. 73454), housed in a renovated medieval church squeezed between several recent centuries' worth of buildings, will educate visitors on the history of Carlingford from the 9th century to the present. (Open Sa-Su and bank holidays noon-5pm. £1, children 50p.) **King John's Castle,** by the waterfront, is the largest and most foreboding of Carlingford's five medieval remains. Built in the 1190s and named for King John, who visited briefly in 1210, the castle is now locked. **Taaffe's Castle,** toward town along the quay, was built in the 16th century as a merchant house on what was then the waterfront, and it contains classic Norman defensive features. You can't go in—now, as then, the castle is privately owned. In a tiny alley off Market Square, the turret-laden 16th-century **Mint** is fenestrated with five ornate limestone windows; it might—or might not—be open to the public in the near future. At the end of the street, one of the old 15th-century town gates, the **Tholsel** (TAH sehl), survives, leaving only a narrow path underneath for cars. Most impressive (and most accessible) is the mammoth **Dominican Friary** at the south end of town. The recently renovated ruins are open for exploration. You can pretend that you're a Dominican friar and Cromwell is oppressing you. The **Adventure Centre** (see above), Tholsel St. (tel. 73100), gives instruction in canoeing, windsurfing, kayaking, *currach* building, and sailing (all £28 per day, children £16). Skipper Peadar Elmore's **MV Slieve Foy** (tel. 73239) goes sea angling.

For those seeking more group-oriented (or booze-oriented) recreation, Carlingford hosts several festivals throughout the year. The late August **Medieval Oyster Fair** supposedly increases everyone's fecundity for a week; it definitely makes for a great lunch (call tel. 21805 for details). The season ends on Heritage Day in late September with a **medieval banqueting weekend** that brings parades, costumes, and indigestion along with a weekend **folk festival** that draws musicians from all over the Republic.

The Leprechaun of Slieve Foy

One misty morn about a decade ago, PJ (the late owner of PJ's Anchor Bar) was going about his usual morning work—painting murals over the windows of abandoned houses—when he heard a high-pitched yell. On his way to investigate the source of the noise, he met a school teacher who had also heard the scream. The men's keen ears soon led them to the place where the yell had originated. About halfway up Slieve Foy was a "fairy ring" of trampled grass with bones and a wee leprechaun suit at its center. The men picked up the leprechaun's remains and returned to Carlingford with their amazing discovery in hand. Further investigation determined that the bones were from a sheep. However, as PJ later commented, everyone knows that leprechauns are changelings, and this one had probably turned into a sheep on the men's approach. The story soon reached the ears of national and international reporters, and for a short time afterwards, Carlingford was known worldwide as the town that had seen a leprechaun.

■ Monaghan

Indifferently pleasant, Monaghan (MOH-nah-han) is a busy market town of 6000 in the center of the country encircled by tiny, egg-shaped hills called drumlins. At its best, Monaghan is a tourist-free rural town where visitors can become absorbed in authentic local life. Pity the authentic local life is a bit mundane.

PRACTICAL INFORMATION The **bus** depot (tel. 82377) is north of Market Sq. (open M-Sa 8:30am-8pm, additional phone hours Su 10am-2pm and 4-8:30pm). Buses run to **Dublin** (2hr., M-Sa 7 per day, Su 3 per day, £6) and **Belfast** (1½hr., M-Sa 5 per day, Su 2 per day, £5.50). From Church Square, walk up the Market St. hill to find the **tourist office** (tel. 81122; open June-Sept. M-Sa 9am-6pm, Su 10am-2pm; call for winter hours). **AIB,** The Diamond, has an **ATM. Tommy's** (tel. 84205) runs **taxis,** and you might be able to rent bikes at **Clerkin's,** Park St. (tel. 81113; £5 per day; open M-W and F-Sa 9am-1pm and 2-6pm). Just north of Church Square lies the **post office,** Mill St. (tel. 82131; open M-Sa 9am-6pm). **Spyderbyte,** off The Diamond, is the only wired café between Dublin and Belfast (open M-F 11am-11pm, Sa 11am-8pm, Su 2-10pm. £3 per 30min., cheaper after 6pm). To call the **hospital,** dial 81811; for the **Garda,** call 82222. The **phone code** is surrounded by tiny, egg-shaped hills called 047.

ACCOMMODATIONS, FOOD, AND PUBS Monaghan has no hostels, but **Ashleigh House,** 37 Dublin St. (tel. 81227), has rosy rooms decorated in floral prints and "whatever you want" for breakfast (£16, with bath £20). Two doors down, **Argus Court,** 32 Dublin St. (tel. 81794), provides basic, no-frills B&B upstairs from your basic no-frills pub (singles £18; doubles £32). If all else fails, call Monaghan's **Ancestor Research Center** (tel. 82304) and stay with a distant relative.

Pizza D'Or, 23 Market St. (tel. 84777), behind the tourist office, is a town institution. It stays open until after the discos close, and your *Let's Go* book buys a £1 discount on a pizza. (Pizzas from £3.50. Open M-F 5pm-1am, Sa-Su 5pm-3am.) **Tommy's** (tel. 81722), around the corner from the Squealing Pig, has burgers and grease. The diner furniture was new in the fifties and hasn't died yet. Yes, they serve pizza. (12in. pies from £3. Open M-Sa 10am-8pm.) There's a **SuperValu** supermarket (tel. 81344) on Church Square (open M-Th 9am-7pm, F 9am-9pm, Sa 9am-6pm).

Pubs crowd around the tourist office off Church Sq. and down Dublin St. from The Diamond. **The Squealing Pig,** The Diamond (tel. 84562), with its barn-like wooden floor and large-screen TV, gets the vote for the most popular pub in town (ages 21 and up). **McKenna's Pub,** Dublin St. (tel. 81616), books mostly blues acts for its upstairs stage (music Th-Sa). The floor, dating from 1934, is far newer than the tables, which were once distillery barrels. **Patrick Kavanaugh's,** off Church Square (tel. 81950), is an intimate old kitchen that's been a pub since before anyone can remember. It draws a young crowd with trad Wednesday and Sunday evenings. **Jimmy's** (tel.

81694), a classy 1950s pub on Mill St. off Church Sq., serves up trad on Thursdays and jazz on Sunday mornings.

SIGHTS In the center of town, the **Monaghan County Museum,** Hill St. (tel. 82928), across from the tourist office, painstakingly chronicles Co. Monaghan's history. *(Open Tu-Sa 11am-1pm and 2-5pm. Free.)* A 14th-century Cross of Clogher looks on. The comprehensive and detailed **St. Louis Heritage Centre,** Market Rd. (tel. 83529), which traces the St. Louis Order of nuns, occupies a red-brick building in the convent school grounds. *(Open M-Tu and Th-F 10am-noon and 2:30-4:30pm., Sa-Su 2:30-4:30pm. £1, children 50p. Wheelchair accessible.)* Past sisters' hairshirts and cutlery are on display, while Barbie dolls model the evolution of nun fashion. The 1895 **St. Macartan's Cathedral** on the south side of town is Monaghan's most impressive building and offers panoramic views of the town. The Monaghan pub scene goes into overdrive during the first weekend in September with the **Jazz and Blues Festival** (contact Somhairle McChongaille, tel. 82928, for details).

■ Castleblayney

Twenty miles southeast of Monaghan on the bus route to **Dublin,** Castleblayney has everything a backpacker could want: a street, a hostel, a big lake, an adventure center, a supermarket, and a nightclub. To the right, **Lough Muckno Leisure Park** has 900 acres of forest and Lough Muckno (Lake of the Swimming Pig), where large numbers of perch, trout, and pike live until caught. The **Adventure Centre** offers all manner of land and water sport to the energetic. (Open June-Sept. Tu-F 2-7pm, Sa-Su noon-7pm. Windsurfing £20 per 4hr., tennis £2 per hr.) If you liked summer camp, you'll love Castleblayney's **hostel (IHH)** (tel. (042) 46256), in the same building as the adventure center (dorms £7, with continental breakfast £10, with full breakfast £13; open Apr.-Oct.). **Camping** space is available (£4 per tent plus £1 per person; open St. Patrick's Day to mid-Oct.). The **White House** B&B (tel. (047) 49550) outside the park is a classier alternative, with bright, friendly rooms (£14, with bath £16).

Fast food at **Barney's,** Main St. (tel. (042) 40120) is the cheapest of the town's few options (open M-Sa noon-1am, Su 3pm-1am). The best desserts are at **Deirdre's Home Bakery** two doors down. Better yet, pack a picnic at **Spar Supermarket** (tel. 40137), on the way to the park (open M-Sa 8am-10pm, Su 9am-10pm). 'Blaney is a wee bit hipper since the **Hale-Bopp** nightclub (tel. (042) 49550) opened above **The Comet Bar** in 1998, two decades after space funk imploded. They host occasional disco nights with £1 pints. (Cover £5. Thursday blues, Friday trad, Saturday DJ. Open Th-Su midnight-2:30am.) A pint in the beer garden behind **Tiny's Pub** (tel. (042) 40510) will warm your liver.

Westmeath, Offaly, Laois, and Longford

These central counties are often passages rather than destinations. Co. Westmeath, with nineteen lakes, is sometimes called the Land of Lakes and Legends; it's something like Minnesota, but smaller. Farther south in famously soggy Co. Offaly, small towns and the impressive ruins of Clonmacnoise civilize the peatland. Co. Laois (LEESH) benefits a lot from its central location. Portaoise, the county's largest city, boasts a central mail-sorting facility, shopping centers, a peat-powered generator with cooling towers, and a prison. The Slieve Bloom Mountains, between Mountrath, Kinitty, and Roscrea, are unfairly neglected, however. And no, we didn't forget forlorn Co. Longford: it's mostly harmless.

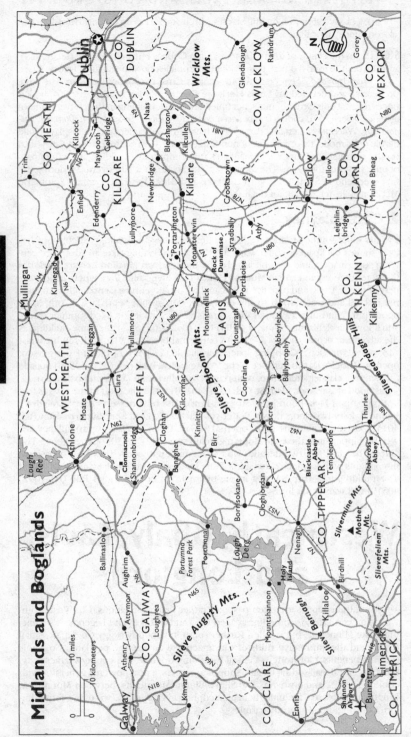

EASTERN IRELAND

Midlands and Boglands

■ Mullingar

Mullingar, plumb in the center of Co. Westmeath, serves most travelers as a hub for transit between Dublin and Galway or Sligo. If your stay is a little longer, you can explore the nearby trails by day and discos by night.

PRACTICAL INFORMATION From the train station, follow the road to the green bridge and turn right onto Dominick St. to reach the town center. The station is open 6:30am to 8:30pm (**luggage storage** £1 per item). **Trains** (tel. 48274) chug to **Dublin** (1½hr., M-Sa 5 per day, Su 3 per day, £8) and **Sligo** (2hr., M-Th and Sa-Su 4 per day, F 5 per day, £8.50). **Bus Éireann** stops at Miss Fitz's Hair Salon on Castle St. and runs to **Athlone** (1hr., 3 per day), **Dublin** (1½hr., 5 per day), **Galway** (3hr., 1-2 per day), and **Sligo** (2½hr., 7 per day). Note that three of the buses to Sligo leave from the train station. **O'Brien's Bus Co.** (tel. 48977) sends buses to **Dublin** (M-Sa 5 per day, Su 3 per day); they stop in front of the post office on Dominick St. The **Chamber of Commerce Tourist Information Centre** (tel. 44044 or 44285), in Market Sq. at the corner of Pearse and Mount St., is more convenient than the tourist office and almost as well stocked with information, including the monthly *Calendar of Events* (open M-F 9:30am-5:30pm). The **tourist office** (tel. 48650; fax 40413) is half a mile from town on Dublin Rd. (open M-Sa 9am-6pm). **TSB,** Oliver Plunkett St., has the longest hours of area banks (open M-W and F 9:30am-5pm, Th 9:30am-7pm). The **post office** (tel. 48393), is on Dominick St. (open M-Sa 9am-5:30pm). The **phone code** is 044.

ACCOMMODATIONS **Auburn B&B** (tel. 40507) is opposite the park on Auburn St. Head down Mount St. and turn left onto Sunday's Well Rd. Call ahead for rooms and access to the private sauna. (Singles £20; doubles £30, with bath £34.) The **Midland Hotel,** Mount St. (tel. 48381), hides rooms above the ground-floor pub (£20). Palm trees shade the fish pond at **Grove House,** Grove Ave. (tel. 41974). From Oliver Plunkett St., turn right onto Dominick Pl., which leads directly to the front door. The B&B was temporarily closed in summer of 1998; call the tourist office for prices.

The **Kitchen Fare Deli,** Mount St. (tel. 41294), is a great place to lunch on delicious, meat-filled salads (£1) and fruit scones (65p; open M-Th 7:30am-6pm, F-Sa 7am-11pm, Su 11am-4pm). **The Greville Arms Hotel,** Pearse St. (tel. 48563), serves restaurant meals at coffeeshop prices to Mullingar residents in a luxuriously red pub (entrees £5; open daily 9am-7pm). The most youthful and popular pub in town is **Hughes'** (tel. 48237), on the corner of Pearse and Castle St. Candlelit trad sessions draw big crowds on Wednesday nights (variety of music F-Sa). **The Final Fence,** Oliver Plunkett St. (tel. 48688), hosts a nightclub (F-Su 11pm; cover £5).

SIGHTS If you've been wondering, "How did Mullingar get its name?" or "What was James Joyce doing here?" then you should join a **Forgotten Heritage Guided Walking Tour** (tel. 44044), departing from the information center in Market Sq. *(M-Tu and Th-F 10:30am and 2:30pm. 1hr. £1, students 50p.)* Crowned with two spires, the **Cathedral of Christ the King** towers over Mary St. Inside, an **ecclesiastical museum** (tel. 44625) displays penal crosses and the vestments of St. Oliver Plunkett, Ireland's most recently canonized saint. *(Cathedral and museum open Th and Sa-Su 3-4pm or by appointment. £1.)* The **Military Museum,** Colomb Barracks (tel. 48391), is south across the canal bridge, an immediate right, then left. *(Open by appointment. Free.)* It's chilling to learn that some Irishmen privately fought for the Nazis in WWII out of pure hatred for England. Anglers and aquaphiles can rent boats from Mrs. Doolan (tel. 42085) to head to **Lough Owel** (£10 per day, £22 with engine) or from Eileen Hope (tel. 40807) for **Lough Ennell** (£10 per day, £20 with engine). **Sam's Tackle,** Castle St. (tel. 40431) sells fishing gear (open M-Sa 9:30am-6pm).

EASTERN IRELAND

▓ Near Mullingar

Heading north of Mullingar, the **Fore Trail** first follows N4 to Coole, then turns east onto R395, and finally swoops back down to Mullingar on R394. The **Belvedere Trail,** which covers the area south of Mullingar, follows N52 to N6 and then takes Kilbeggan Rd. back to Mullingar. Either of these trails is an easier alternative to the Wicklow Way and other more arduous and more famous hikes.

■ The Fore Trail

The first stop on the Fore Trail is the little village of **Multyfarnham,** 6 mi. north. At a 15th-century **Franciscan friary,** life-size figures in a peaceful garden depict the stations of the cross. Tommy Newman (tel. (044) 71111; £25 per day) rents out **boats,** and hiking trails lace the area. Four miles north on N4, the trail brings travelers to **Coole** and **Turbotstown House.** The 200-year-old Georgian mansion is privately owned (open May-Sept.). Some of the Midlands' famous bogs border Coole on the west. One mile before Castlepollard to the east, the Gothic Revival Towers of romantic **Tullynally Castle** (tel. (044) 61159) are surrounded by 30 acres of gardens. *(Castle open mid-June to mid-Aug. daily 2-6pm. Gardens open May-Sept. daily 2-6pm. Castle and gardens £5, students and seniors £3.)* Black Australian swans swim proudly in the pond.

With a little marketing, the lakeshore town of **Fore** could be the next Glendalough. Fore was known for its seven wonders: water that flows uphill, water that won't boil, a tree that won't burn, a tree with only three branches (representing the Holy Trinity), a monastery that should have sunk into the bogs, a mill without a source of water to turn its wheel, and a saint encased in stone (he had vowed never to leave his cell). **Fore Abbey** was founded in 630 by St. Fechin and rebuilt during the 11th, 13th, and 15th centuries. Today, it is the most extensive set of Benedictine ruins in Ireland. **St. Fechin's Church,** in the graveyard, is the oldest standing building. The abbey is on the **Shamrock Experience** tours (tel. (046) 40127) based in Kells (see **Kells,** p. 137). The Fore Trail continues along R395 to R394 then turns south to reach Collinstown. From the village, the trail turns east onto Kells Rd. toward **Delvin,** where a golf course abuts the ruins of the 12th-century castle that once marked the western boundary of the British-controlled Pale. Returning to R394 along Kells Rd., the trail carries on to **Crookedwood,** where a well-preserved 14th-century church sits in front of a ring fort. The trail continues south and returns to Mullingar.

■ The Belvedere Trail

Four miles south of Mullingar, the 18th-century **Belvedere House and Gardens** (tel. (044) 42820) pompously promenade along the shore of Lough Ennel. The house seems to strive for imperial grandeur, with Roman gods frescoed along the ceiling. Robert Rochford, Lord Belvedere, for whom the house was built, also commissioned the fake and expensive "ruins" of a nonexistent abbey in order to obstruct his own view of his brother's superior rose garden. The ruin is now called **"the Jealous Wall"** in his dishonor. (Open daily July-Aug. noon-6pm; Apr.-June and Sept. noon-5pm. £1, students 50p.)

As the trail turns off N52 and onto N6, it passes **Tyrellspass Castle** (tel. (044) 23105), built in 1411 and restored in 1979. (Open daily 9am-7pm.) The small town of **Kilbeggan** appears at the next major intersection east on N6 (Dublin-Galway). **Locke's Distillery** (tel. (0506) 32134), a former firewater factory, has been converted into a museum. The zany anecdotes about workers' experiences on the job make a visit here worthwhile. (Open daily Apr.-Oct. 9am-6pm; Nov.-Mar. 10am-4pm. £3, students and seniors £2, children £1.) From Kilbeggan, the trail turns right heading northeast toward **Lough Ennell,** a major bird sanctuary favored by trout fishermen (try local tackle shops for permits). On the shore of the lough await **Lilliput House,** sadly life-size, and **Jonathan Swift Park,** with trails and fishing piers. Swift supposedly conceived *Gulliver's Travels* during a visit to Lough Ennell in the 1720s, and the surrounding area was renamed Lilliput shortly after the book's publication in 1726. The Belvedere Trail continues northeast and returns to Mullingar along N52.

■ Athlone

Plopped down in the pastures of Roscommon and Westmeath, Athlone is the center of everything in the middle of nowhere. Lying at the intersection of the Shannon River and the Dublin-Galway road, the city is sort of a transportation hub, but the dearth of any other cities nearby or famous attractions has relegated Athlone to backwater status. A castle and several large churches, however, attest to Athlone's past strategic importance. Athlone is divided by the Shannon, which also divides Leinster from Connacht; the bus and train station and the hostel are on the right bank, while the left bank teems with restaurants.

PRACTICAL INFORMATION Athlone's **train and bus depot** (tel. 73322) is on Southern Station Rd., which runs parallel to Church St. **Trains** leave for **Dublin** (2hr., 8 per day, M-Th and Sa £9, F and Su £12.50) and **Galway** (1hr., 4 per day, M-Th and Sa £7, F and Su £11). **Buses** shuttle off to **Dublin** (9 per day, £7), **Galway** (M-Sa 9 per day, Su 8 per day, £7), **Tullamore** (1 per day, £5.50), **Rosslare** (1 per day, £14), **Cahir** (1 per day, £9.70), and **Cork** (1 per day, £13). The **tourist office** (tel. 94630), in the castle, has free copies of the *Athlone and District Visitors Guide* (open Easter-Oct. M-Sa 10am-6pm). **Bank of Ireland** (tel. 75111) and **AIB** (tel. 72089), on Church St., have 24-hour **ATMs** (banks open M 10am-5pm, Tu-F 10am-4pm). The **post office** (tel. 83544) is on Barrack St. (open M-Tu and Th-Sa 9am-5:30pm, W 9:30am-5:30pm). Athlone's **phone code** is 0902.

ACCOMMODATIONS Undoubtedly, the best place to stay in Athlone is the **Athlone Holiday Hostel** (tel. 73399; fax 73833; email athhostl@iol.ie), conveniently located next to the train station. The common area has a TV, a pool table, and murals painted by a local artist depicting Irish tales. The kitchen and spacious dining area are open 8am to 11:30pm. Ask Seámus Mac Aogáin to tell you about Clonmacnoise and other Irish legends. (Single-sex 10-bed dorms £8, with full breakfast £11. Showers 50p. Laundry. 24hr. reception. **Internet access. Bike rental** £10 per day.) B&Bs inhabit Inishtown Rd. and its continuation toward Dublin. Closer to town is Mrs. Devaney's **Shannon View,** Church St. (tel. 78411), near the church, offering crisp rooms with big beds and TVs (£16). **The Thatch** (tel. 94981) opposite the castle also provides B&B, although the street gets noisy as pubs close (doubles with bath £36). **Lough Ree Caravan and Camping Park** (tel. 78561) awaits 3 mi. northeast on N55 (Longford Rd.). Follow signs for Lough Ree (£2.50 per person; open May-Sept.).

FOOD AND PUBS The shelves overflow at the **Quinnsworth Supermarket,** Athlone Shopping Centre, Dublin Rd. (tel. 72465; open M-W and Sa 9am-6pm, Th-F 9am-9pm). Restaurants on the left bank are more expensive but more convenient than elsewhere in town. **Branburry's,** across the street from the church on Church St., is where locals go for cheap, delicious breakfast and lunch (scones 25p, sandwiches £1.50; open M-F 8am-5pm, Sa 9am-4pm). **The Left Bank,** Bastion St. (tel. 94446), serves delicious meals and homemade desserts in a bohemian atmosphere on the winding medieval streets by the Seine—no, wait, that's Paris (entrees £5-7; lunch served M-Sa 10:30am-5:30pm, dinner M-Sa 6-10pm.) **The Crescent Restaurant** (tel. 73456), at the hostel, serves fresh meals in a café atmosphere (entrees £4; open July-Aug. 8am-10:30pm; Sept.-June 8am-7pm). **The Hooker Tackle Shop,** Custume Pl. (tel. 74848), provides fishing equipment for getting lucky.

    Sean's Bar, Main St. (tel. 92358), behind the castle, goes trad five nights per week and has been known to feature the accordion, banjo, and fiddle. The bar traces its ancestry back to 1654; ask for the history lesson. Dim and wood-paneled, the **Keg,** Barrack St. (tel. 93031), hosts musicians Fridays and Saturdays and Irish dancing Thursdays. The crowd at the **Palace Bar,** Market Sq. (tel. 92229), gathers for trad Tuesday, Saturday, and Sunday nights but is sparsely populated other times. The only club in town is **BoZo's,** at Conlon's on Dublingate St. (£5 cover; open Th-Su 11:30pm-2am). *The Westmeath Independent* has entertainment listings.

SIGHTS Athlone's fame, such as it is, comes from a single, humiliating defeat. During the siege of Athlone in 1691, a Jacobean army foolishly ensconced in Athlone Castle discovered that defending an ugly hunk of stone against gunpowder and more than 12,000 cannon balls is a strategic mistake. The Jacobites folded and ceded control of Athlone to the Williamite army across the river. (For background on the conflict, see **History**, p. 56). **The Athlone Castle Visitor Centre** (tel. 92912) tells the story with stiff models and a noisy 45-minute audio-visual show. *(Open May-Sept. daily 10am-6pm, multimedia show and museum 1-4:30pm. £2.60, students £1.75. Museum only half-price.)* The **museum** inside the castle has phonographs, uniforms from the Civil War, and other oddities. Poking around **Athlone Castle,** however, with its grand Shannon views, is free. *(Open May-Sept. daily 9:30am-6pm.)* **Athlone Town Walks** gives the inside scoop on Athlone's history. *(Call Mary at 72466 or Jean at 75184. 1½hr. £1.50.)* The **Athlone Crystal Factory,** 28 Pearse St. (tel. 92867), has one glass-cutter; you can take a free tour and covet goods in the small factory shop. *(Open Tu-F 10am-6pm.)*

    Rossana Cruises (tel. 73833) departs from the strand across the river from the castle and sails a Viking ship up the Shannon to Lough Ree. *(1½hr., 2 per day, £5, students £4.)* Faster **Hovercraft Tours,** Monksland (tel. 92658 or 74593), shows you Lough Ree at 40 mph. *(From £6. Departs every 30min. from Hudson Bay Hotel.)*

    The last week in June brings the **Athlone Festival,** which includes parades, exhibits, and free concerts. Aspiring singers head to Athlone in late autumn for the **John McCormack Golden Voice** opera competition, named for Athlone's most famous tenor (see **Music,** p. 66). Contact the Athlone Chamber of Commerce (tel. 73173).

■ Clonmacnoise

Isolated 14 mi. southwest of Athlone and surrounded by the intense green of fields and marshes, Clonmacnoise (clon-muk-NOYS) is one of the few monastic ruins yet to be devoured by tourism. St. Ciaran (KEER-on) founded the monastery in 545 overlooking the eastern (Leinster) shore of the gently curving Shannon, and his settlement grew into a city and important scholastic center. The precious *Book of the Dun Cow* was written here by monks around 1100, supposedly on vellum (skin) from St. Ciaran's cow, which traveled everywhere with St. Ciaran and miraculously produced enough milk for the whole monastery. Seamus Heaney's *Seeing Things* retells a vision of manned ships passing through the air above the city in 748, described in the monastery's *Annals.*

    The site itself is impressive for its lonely grandeur, with crumbling buildings rising amid hills, bog, river, and sheep. The **cathedral** was destroyed by Vikings and rebuilt several times; the current structure dates from about 1100. The last High King of Ireland, Rory O'Connor, was buried inside in 1198. **O'Connor's Church,** built in 1000, still has Church of Ireland services on the fourth Sunday of the month at 10am. Peaceful **Nun's Church** is left off the path through the main site, about a quarter mile away. The finely detailed chancel, arc, and doorways are some of the best Romanesque architecture in Ireland. One of the doorways of the cathedral is known as the **whispering arch.** When young Irish sweethearts of long ago were too poor to get married, they would come here to exchange their vows. By standing on either side of the arch and whispering into the hollowed-out space, lovers can discreetly convey their steamiest private thoughts. The second archway, seven stones up, is believed to have a Sí Le na Gig (SHE-la na gig; see **Sí Le na Gig**). The **visitors center** (tel. (0905) 74195) craves attention for its wheelchair-accessible displays. Entrance to the ruins is through the visitors center. (Open in summer daily 9am-5pm; in winter 10am-5pm. £3, students and seniors £1.50.) The **tourist office** (tel. (0905) 74134), at the entrance to the Clonmacnoise car park, gives local information and sells Kenneth MacGowan's excellent *Clonmacnoise* (£2.50), a guide to the monastic city (open daily in summer 9am-6pm; in winter 9am-5pm).

    If you have a car, the easiest way to reach Clonmacnoise from Athlone or Birr is to take N62 to Ballynahoun, then follow signs. Paddy Kavanaugh's **Minibus Service** (tel. (0902) 74839 or (087) 407706) departs daily at 11am from the Athlone Castle and

EASTERN IRELAND

Sí Le na Gig

The men who led ancient Irish tribes supposedly had many wives. When a woman went through puberty, she would be married to the chief, often an older man no longer sexually potent. Because the young wives did not become pregnant, they were thought to be infertile. The cure for this condition was touching the **Sí Le na Gig** sculpted in the archway of the Nun's Church. By touching the Sí Le na Gig, goddess of fertility, the young woman would become impregnated. The birth was attributed to the touch of the carving though more likely due to the touch of some fetching young man on the pilgrimage. Sí Le na Gig is sometimes a source of embarrassment, as she is often depicted as a smiling woman with her legs drawn up behind her head.

will pick up from the hostel or any of the B&Bs with advance notice. *(£15, students £11, includes admission.)* Tours run to both Clonmacnoise and the **Clonmacnoise** and **West Offaly Railway** and return around 4pm. Special visits to Clonmacnoise can be arranged at other times. Clonmacnoise is accessible by bike, but it's 14 mi. of hilly terrain. Hitchers first get a lift to Ballynahoun on heavily trafficked N62, then get a ride from there to Clonmacnoise.

The best accommodation is run by **Mr. and Mrs. Augustin Claffey** (tel. (0905) 74149), on Shannonbridge Rd. near town. The couple restored the cute cottage across the road, which dates back to 1843. Two double beds, a lambskin rug in the bedroom, and peat fire in the sitting room are charming beside the large modern bathroom, cooker, and refrigerator. Reserve far in advance. (£12.) Another good spot is **Kajon House** (tel. (0905) 74191), past the Claffeys on the Shannonbridge Rd. Along with great bog views, Kajon House serves reasonably priced breakfast and dinner (£15). You can pitch a **tent** in the field next to the house (£2 per person) or, with permission, in the fields of local farmers.

■ Birr

William Petty labelled Birr *"Umbilicus Hiberniae,"* the belly button of Ireland. Who knows why; it's not the center of Ireland—maybe he was drunk. Birr makes a decent starting point for exploring the Slieve Bloom mountains to its east; unfortunately, Birr is 9 mi. from minuscule Kinitty at the base of the mountains. If you don't have a car, your best bet is to bike there (not enough cars go by to make hitching practical). Even if you're not going to the Slieve Bloom mountains, however, Birr Castle provides a good enough reason to visit.

ORIENTATION AND PRACTICAL INFORMATION The *umbilicus* of Birr is Emmet Sq. Most shops and pubs are in Emmet Sq. or south down O'Connell St.; the areas north and west of the square down Emmet and Green St. are residential. Buses stop by the post office in the square. **Bus Éireann** runs to **Dublin** (2hr., M-Sa 3 per day, Su 1 per day, £10), **Cahir** (2hr., 1 per day, £12), and **Athlone** (40min., 3 per day, £6). To reach the sleek, Danish-modern **tourist office** (tel. 20110) from Emmet Sq., walk down O'Connell and Main St. and then make a right onto Castle St.; the office is on the right. (Open May-Sept. daily 9:30am-1pm and 2-5:30pm.) They sell hiking maps of the Slieve Blooms (£1) and can put you in touch with guides. **P.L. Polan,** Main St. (tel. 20006) rents **bikes** (£8 per day, £35 per week; deposit £30; open M-W and F-Sa 9:30am-6:30pm). **AIB** (tel. 20069) offers a 24-hour **ATM** in Emmet Sq. The **phone code** is 0509.

ACCOMMODATIONS, FOOD, AND PUBS The Irish are known for their hospitality, and **Kay Kelly** (tel. 21128) defines it. Her B&B rests atop the toy store on Main St. and boasts comfortable rooms with playground out back. (£13-15, all with bath.) **Spinners Town House,** Castle St. (tel. 21673), offers beautiful, simply decorated rooms with framed antique postcards on the walls. In addition, there's a charming bistro downstairs and breakfast options like scrambled eggs with smoked salmon. One room and bathroom are wheelchair accessible. (£15-17.50, all with bath.) The highly recommended and cheap **Kong Lam** cooks Chinese take-away at the end of Main St. **Kelly's** pub on Green St. welcomes all for a pint and friendly banter. **Craughwell's** (tel. 21839) on Castle St. has an amicable atmosphere and turf fires.

SIGHTS You're welcome to tread on the Earl of Rosse's front lawn at **Birr Castle** (tel. 20336), which remains his private home. *(Grounds open daily 9am-6pm. £3.50, students and seniors £2.50, children £1.50.)* A babbling brook, a tranquil pond, the tallest box hedges in the world, and acres of lush woods and gardens make Birr Castle stand out. Don't miss the immense telescope, whose 72-in. mirror was the world's largest for 72 years. The third Earl of Rosse used this instrument to discover the Whirlpool nebula; the fourth Earl used it to measure the heat of the moon. A new historical science museum is set to open on the grounds in early 1999. The **Slieve Bloom Environmental Display Center** (tel. (0509) 7299), which explains the mountain flora and fauna, is moving from Kinitty, 9 mi. from Birr at the foot of the mountains, to somewhere closer to Birr; check with the tourist office. **Birr Vintage Week,** which takes place in mid-August, involves a parade, a car rally, an antique and art fair, and people dressing up in Georgian costume.

■ Slieve Bloom Mountains

Though only 2000 ft. at their highest, the Slieve (SHLEEVE) Bloom Mountains give the illusion of great height, bursting up from plains between Birr, Roscrea, Portlaoise, and Tullamore. **Ard Erin** was once mistakenly thought to be the tallest peak in Ireland and named accordingly. **The Slieve Bloom Way** is a circular walking trail that passes mountain bogs, Ard Erin, waterfalls, and heaps of scenery and is marked along the way by signs explaining geological features. From the peaks of the moutons, all of Ireland is at your feet.

The tourist office in **Birr** (see above) makes the best pre-mountain stop; it sells maps and can also put you in touch with a guide if you like. *New Irish Walk Guides,* found in bookstores, has more information on Bloom walks. Remember, bogs are highly flammable: it is illegal to light fires anywhere on the Way (smokers beware!). Closer than Birr is **Coolrain,** where **The Olde Schoolhouse** B&B (tel. (087) 456477) makes an excellent starting point. The amiable owners will meet visitors at the Ballybrophy railroad stop, arrange **bike rentals** (£8 per day), and provide picnic baskets for day hikes. (Singles £20; doubles £38.) **Mountrath,** southeast of the mountains in Co. Laois, and **Kinitty,** to the northeast in Co. Offaly, also make good springboards for hiking, and it's possible to trek from one to the other.

■ Roscrea

Picturesque Roscrea (ross-CRAY), actually in Co. Tipperary, poses 10 mi. south of Birr and southwest of the Slieve Blooms. The medieval remains hide among the shops and pubs. On Castle St., a 13th-century castle surrounds the **Damer House,** the best preserved example of Queen Anne architecture in Ireland, with an amazing vaulted ceiling. *(Castle tours £2.50, students £1.)* The other highlight of Damer House is its spectacular **Bog Butter,** a 1000-year-old chunk of dairy heroically rescued from the bog. The **Roscrea Heritage Centre** (tel. (0505) 21850) in the castle is the closest thing to a tourist office. In addition to tours of the castle, it has the useful and free *Roscrea Heritage Walk* map. *(Open daily 9:30am-6:30pm. Last admission 5:45pm.)*

Bus Éireann stops at Christy Maker's pub on Castle St., just downhill from the castle. Buses go to and from **Dublin** (2hr., 3 per day), **Limerick** (1hr., 3 per day), **Cork** (3hr., 1 per day), and **Athlone** (1½hr., 1 per day). **Bank of Ireland** (tel. (0505) 21877) on Castle St. sports a 24-hour **ATM** (open M-W and F 10am-4pm, Th 10am-5pm). Mrs. Fogarty will take good care of you in the elegant rooms of the **White House,** Castle St. (tel. (0505) 21516; £16). Groceries abound at **Quinnsworth** in the Roscrea Shopping Centre, Castle St. (open M-W and Sa 9am-7pm, Th-F 9am-9pm). **Mick Delahunty's,** Main St. (tel. (0505) 22139), offers pub grub (burgers £3.25).

■ Portlaoise

Mostly famous for its large prison and as the center of Ireland's cement industry, Portlaoise (port-LEESH) also boasts a major highway running right through the center of the city. The one sight Portlaoise does have is the **Rock of Dunamase.** Take Stradbally Rd. east 4 mi.; the Rock is on the left (follow the sign to Athy/Carlow at the big, red church). The truly ancient fortress, recorded by Ptolemy, passed between Irish and Viking hands many times and still bristles with fortifications. The Rock is a fantastic vantage point for viewing the Slieve Bloom Mountains.

The **train station** (tel. 21303) is in a tall gray building at the curve on Railway St. (open daily 7:30am-9pm). **Trains** run to **Dublin** and points south (1hr., 8 per day, £12). **Bus Éireann** stops at Egan's Hostelry on Main St. and on Lawlor Ave. on the way to **Dublin** (1½hr., 10 per day, £9). The **tourist office,** Lawlor Ave. (tel. 21178), can help you find your way somewhere else, providing information on the Slieve Blooms and the Midlands. Lawlor Ave. runs parallel to Main St. on the left if you're facing uphill. (Open July-Aug. M-Sa 10am-1pm and 2-6pm; Sept.-June M-F 10am-1pm and 2-6pm.) **AIB** (tel. 21349) graces Lawlor Ave. with a 24-hour **ATM.** There's a **laundromat** in the mini-mall across from the public library (wash and dry £4; open M-Sa 9am-6pm). The regional **post office** (tel. 22339) is inside the shopping center on Lawlor Ave. (open M-F 9am-5:30pm, Sa 10am-1pm and 2-5pm). The **phone code,** 0502, is slightly reminiscent of Houston.

The most affordable accommodations are left at the top of Main St., where an oasis of green survives. **O'Donoghue's B&B,** Kellyville Park (tel. 21353), a large, beautifully kept B&B with flower gardens and a friendly proprietor, makes a stay in town worthwhile. (Singles £19; doubles £32, with bath £36.) For psycho groceries, head to **Crazy Prices,** in the shopping mall on Lawlor Ave. **Dowlings,** half way up Main St. on the left (tel. 22770), offers the best deal on fresh meals (entrees £3-4; open M-Th 8:30am-6pm, F-Sa 8:30am-7pm, Su 10am-6pm). **Sally Gardens,** Main St. (tel. 21658), hosts frequent impromptu sessions and live music Mondays and Thursdays to ensure a supply of good craic. Grab a stool in the cave—it's the most desirable point.

SOUTHEAST IRELAND

The power base of first the Vikings and then the Normans, Southeast Ireland reveals the most foreign influence. Any invasions these days consist of Irish people on holiday storming the beaches along the sunny southern coast from cozy Kilmore Quay to tidy Ardmore. Wexford is a charismatic town, packed with historic sites and convenient to many of the Southeast's finest attractions, while Waterford has the resources and the grit of a real city. Cashel boasts a superbly preserved cathedral complex, and Ring is the region's sole *gaeltacht.* Heading to the south coast from Dublin, you can take in the rocking nightlife of a route through Carlow, Kilkenny, and Waterford, or enjoy the pretty paths through Glendalough, Wicklow, Enniscorthy, and Wexford. Continental youth and families driving stuffed autos speed to and from Europe via Rosslare Harbor in the southeastern tip of the island.

Kilkenny and Carlow

The counties of Kilkenny and Carlow, northwest of Wexford and Waterford, are lightly populated hills and plains characterized by small farming villages and the occasional medieval ruin. The city of Kilkenny is the exception, a popular destination for both tourists and young Irish on the move. The town of Carlow, though much smaller, is also lively, especially at night and during the mid-June arts festival.

▓ Kilkenny

Suave young couples are moving here in droves. As as the money rolls in, Kilkenny, already touted as the best-preserved medieval town in Ireland, has launched an historial preservation campaign to draw more visitors and net a few more Tidy Town awards. Visitors find both excitement and history in Kilkenny, where ancient architecture houses rocking nightlife and nine churches share the streets with 78 pubs.

ORIENTATION AND PRACTICAL INFORMATION

From McDonagh Station, turn left on John St. and continue straight to reach The Parade, dominated by the castle. Most activity takes place in the triangle formed by Rose Inn, High, and Kieran St. Hitchhikers take N10 to Waterford, Freshford Rd. to N8 toward Cashel, and N16 toward Dublin. Patience is a virtue.

> **Trains: McDonagh Station,** Dublin Rd. (tel. 22024). Open M-Sa 8am-8pm, Su 10am-noon, 3-5pm, and 6:30-8:30pm. Always staffed, although ticket window is open only around departure times. Kilkenny is on the main Dublin-Waterford rail route (M-Sa 4 per day, Su 3 per day). To **Dublin** (2hr., £10), **Waterford** (45min., £5.50), and **Thomastown** (15min., £3). Connections to western Ireland at the Kildare station 1hr. north on the Dublin-Waterford line.
>
> **Buses: McDonagh Station,** Dublin Rd. (tel. 64933), and on Patrick St. in the city center. Buses leave for **Clonmel** (M-Sa 5 per day, Su 4 per day), **Cork** (3hr., 3 per day), **Dublin** (M-Sa 5 per day, Su 4 per day), **Galway** (daily mid-June to mid-Sept.), **Rosslare Harbour** (daily mid-June to mid-Sept.), **Thomastown** (1 per day), and **Waterford** (5 daily). **Buggy's Buses** (tel. 41264) run from Kilkenny to **Castlecomer** (M-Sa 2 per day, £1.50) with stops at **Dunmore Cave** (20min.), and the An Óige hostel (15min.).

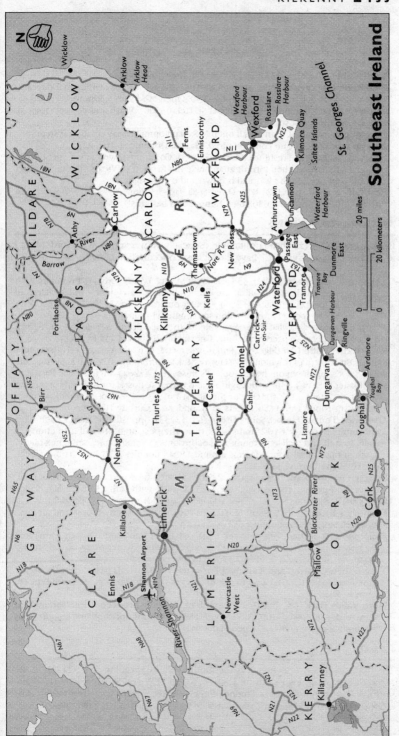

Southeast Ireland

Tourist Office: Rose Inn St. (tel. 51500; fax 63955). Free maps! Open June-Sept. M-Sa 9am-6pm, Su 11am-5pm; Oct.-May M-F 10am-5:30pm, Sa 10am-2pm.

Banks: AIB, The Parade (tel. 22089), at the intersection with High St. Open M 10am-5pm, Tu-F 10am-4pm; 24hr. **ATM. TSB,** High St. (tel. 22969). Open M-W and F 9am-5:30pm, Th 9am-7pm.

Taxi: K&M Cab (tel. 61333). £3 max. within the city.

Bike Rental: J.J. Wall Cycle, Maudlin St. (tel. 21236). £7 per sentimental day, £30 per effusive week; tear-jerking deposit £30. Open M-Sa 9am-5:30pm.

Laundry: Brett's Launderette, Michael St. (tel. 63200). Wash and dry £6. Open M-Sa 8:30am-8pm; last wash 7pm.

Pharmacy: Several on High St. All open M-Sa 9am-6pm; Sunday rotation system.

Emergency: Dial 999; no coins required. **Garda:** Dominic St. (tel. 22222).

Hospital: St. Luke's, Freshford Rd. (tel. 21133). Continue down Parliament St. to St. Canice's Cathedral, then turn right and take the first left to Vicars St., then another left on Gowran Rd. The hospital is down and on the right.

Post Office: High St. (tel. 21879). Open M-Sa 9am-5:30pm.

Phone Code: Oh my god, 056 killed Kenny! You bastards!

ACCOMMODATIONS

B&Bs average £17; call ahead in summer, especially on weekends. Waterford Rd. and more remote Castlecomer Rd. have the highest concentration of beds.

Kilkenny Town Hostel (IHH), 35 Parliament St. (tel. 63541). Always brimming with activity as people bustle about in the kitchen, lounge on couches, and socialize on the front steps. Directly across from popular pubs and next to the brewery. Clean, light, and bare rooms. Friendly, non-smoking environment. Kitchen (7am-11pm) with microwave. Cyclist maps available. 6- to 8-bed dorms £8; doubles £18. 50p discount to *Let's Go* users Sept.-June. Check-out 10:30am. Laundry £3.

Foulksrath Castle (An Óige/HI), Jenkinstown (tel. 67674). Awesome 16th-century castle 8mi. north of town on N77 (Durrow Rd.). Turn right off N77 at signs for Connahy; it's ¼mi. down on the left. Buggy's Buses (tel. 41264) run from The Parade to the hostel M-Sa at 11:30am and 5:30pm and leave the hostel for Kilkenny at 8:25am and 3pm (20min., £1.50). One of the nicest hostels in Ireland. TV room. Kitchen open 8am-10pm. Dorms £6. Sheets £1. Laundry £4. Curfew 10:30pm.

Ormonde Tourist Hostel, Johns Green (tel. 52733), opposite the train station. This enormous hostel is a 10-15min. walk from the best nightlife and attractions. A friendly staff and well-kept rooms and bathrooms maintain a pleasant atmosphere. Kitchen open until 10pm. Dorms around £8.50; doubles £22. Laundry £4. Check out 10:30am. Curfew 3am.

Bregagh House B&B, Dean St. (tel. 22315). Handsome wood furniture, floral comforters and pristine rooms. Singles £20-25; doubles with bath £36; Nov.-May £34.

Daly's B&B, 82 Johns St. (tel. 62866). Quiet, plain, tidy rooms. £17. Breakfast £2.

Fennelly's B&B, 13 Parliament St. (tel. 61796). Large, orderly rooms and an ideal location. Singles £22; doubles £32, with bath £36.

Philomena Heffernan, Dean St. (tel. 64040). Basic, clean rooms. A sign warns that the house is guarded by an attack housewife, but don't worry, she's actually rather charming. Singles £22; doubles £32. Higher weekend rates.

Tree Grove Caravan and Camping Park (tel. 70302). 1mi. past the castle on the New Ross road (R700). Close to the town center. Free showers. 2-person tent £6. Caravan £8.

Nore Valley Park (tel. 27229), 6mi. south of Kilkenny between Bennetsbridge and Stonyford, signposted from Kilkenny. A class act, with hot showers, laundry, and TV room. 2-person tent £5. Open Mar.-Oct.

FOOD

The biggest grocery selection is at the mothership **Superquinn** (tel. 52444), in the Market Cross shopping center off High St. (open M-W and Sa 9am-6pm, Th-F 9am-9pm). A smaller but still large **Dunnes Supermarket** is steps away from the tourist office (open M-Tu and Sa 9am-7pm, W-F 9am-9pm, Su and bank holidays noon-6pm).

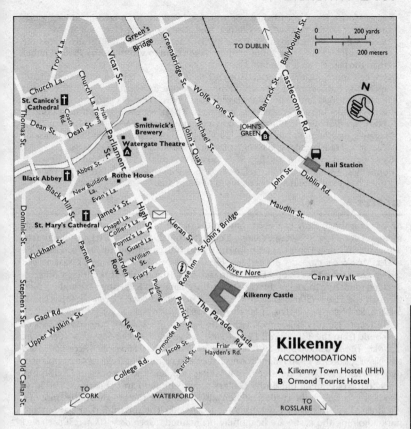

Kilkenny

ACCOMMODATIONS
A Kilkenny Town Hostel (IHH)
B Ormond Tourist Hostel

Butterslip Restaurant, Butterslip Ln., between Kieran and High St. Fresh food made to order at great prices with daily specials.

Edward Langton's, 69 John St. (tel. 65133). Voted the country's best pub food 3 times and perpetually expanding. Lunch £4-6, served daily noon-3pm. Dinner menu reaches double digits (served daily 4:30-11pm).

Italian Connection, 38 Parliament St. (tel. 64225). Italian food in a mahogany, carnation-laden setting. Lunch specials daily noon-3pm. Open daily noon-11pm.

Lautrec's Wine Bar, 9 St. Kieran St. (tel. 62720). Tex-Mex and other cuisines; pours wine even after pubs have closed. Open M-Th 5:30pm-midnight, F-Sa 5:30pm-1am.

Doors, on High St. near Kieran St. Come to this café to smoke and smoke some more in a trendy atmosphere. Light food (sandwiches £2). Open daily noon-11:30pm.

Rinnucinni's, on Castle Rd. before Friar. Couples sit and enjoy mood lighting, good service, and romantic music while sucking face. Entrees £7.

PUBS

Kilkenny is known as the "oasis of Ireland."

Matt the Miller's, John St. across the river half a block before the rail station. Huge, thronged, and friendly. It'll suck you in and force you to dance to silly Euro pop.

Caisleán Uí Cuain (cash-LAWN ee COO-an), 2 High St. (tel. 65406), at The Parade. A local crowd settles in for pints and the zany atmosphere. Music Monday nights and Sunday afternoons.

Pump House Bar, 26 Parliament St. (tel. 63924). Remains a favorite among locals and many hostelers. Loud, easy to find, and always packed. Live rock M-Th.

Cleere's Pub, 28 Parliament St. (tel. 62573). Thespians from the theatre across the street converge here for a pint at intermission (and to watch *Monty Python* rather than the game). Trad Mondays.

Kyteler's Inn, St. Kieran St. (tel 21064). This historical pub has a witch in the basement and butcher-blocks for tables; the wine cellar dates back to 1324. Mixed ages gather for food and craic in a relaxed atmosphere. Trad occasionally in summer; enjoy drinks in the beer garden. Late night Th-Su, transfer yourself next door to **Nero's,** a nightclub that's burning down the house (cover £5; open 11:30pm-2am).

Maggie's, St. Kieran St. (tel. 62273). Busy, with an older group than Pump House or Cleere's. Trad Tuesdays, live contemporary Wednesdays.

Ryan's, on Friary St. just off High St. Good old trad mixed with African and Beat.

Fennelly's, 13 Parliament St. (tel. 64337), hosts an older crowd in its homey confines. Trad Friday and Sunday nights in July and Aug.

SIGHTS

All of central Kilkenny is a sight, since most of the buildings have preserved their medieval good looks. **Tynan Walking Tours** (tel. 65929) offers a brief introduction to Kilkenny's history. Tours depart from the tourist office on Rose Inn St. *(Tours mid-Mar. to Oct. M-Sa 6 per day, Su 4 per day; Nov.-Feb. Tu-Sa 3 per day. 1hr.-1½hr. £3, students and seniors £2.)* At the **City Scope Exhibition** (tel. 51500), upstairs at the tourist office, a detailed miniature model of the city shows the changes in Kilkenny's life and housing through the years. *(30min. show M-F 9am-12:45pm and 2-6pm, Sa 9am-12:45pm and 2-5:30pm, Su 11am-1pm, 2-5pm. £1.50, students 75p.)*

Thirteenth-century **Kilkenny Castle,** The Parade (tel. 21450), housed the Earls of Ormonde from the 1300s until 1932. *(Castle and gallery open June-Sept. daily 10am-7pm; Oct.-Mar. Tu-Sa 10:30am-5pm, Su 11am-5pm; Apr.-May daily 10:30am-5pm. Access by guided tour only. £3, students £1.50.)* Many rooms have been restored to their former opulence; ogle the Long Room, reminiscent of a Viking ship, and the portraits of English bigwigs. In the basement, the **Butler Gallery** mounts modern art exhibitions. This level also houses a **café** in the castle's kitchen and shelters the castle's **ghost,** the spirit of a girl burned at the stake by witchphobic townsfolk. The formal **flower garden** and park adjoining the castle are beautifully maintained. *(Open daily 10am-8:30pm. Free.)* The internationally known **Kilkenny Design Centre** (tel. 22118) fills the castle's old stables with fine but expensive Irish crafts. *(Open Apr.-Dec. M-Sa 9am-6pm, Su 10am-6pm; Jan.-Mar. M-Sa 9am-6pm.)* **Rothe House,** Parliament St. (tel. 22893), a Tudor merchant house built in 1594, is now a small museum of local archaeological finds and Kilkennian curiosities. *(Open Apr.-Oct. M-Sa 10:30am-5pm, Su 3-5pm; Nov.-Mar. M-Sa 1-5pm, Su 3-5pm. £2, students £1.50.)* The tour introduces you to the lifestyles of the 16th-century rich and famous. Exhibits change throughout the year.

Kilkenny is well endowed with religious architecture. The finest example is 13th-century **St. Canice's Cathedral** on Dean St. *(Open daily 10am-6pm, except during services. Donation requested.)* The stone-step approach from Inishtown is lined with fragments of old sculpture from the cathedral itself, which was sacked by Cromwell's merry men(aces). The name "Kilkenny" itself is derived from the Irish *Cill Chainnigh,* "Church of St. Canice." Medieval tombstones are embedded in the floor and walls of the church. The 100 ft. tower near the south transept is a relic of the earlier 6th-century Church of St. Canice. For an additional £1, you can climb the series of six steep ladders inside for a panoramic view of the town and its surroundings. **The Black Abbey,** off Abbey St., was founded in 1225 and got its name from the black habits of its Dominican friars. The fiery, modern stained-glass window contrasts with older, subtler ones and the heavy stone structure. Nearby **St. Mary's** stands testament to the incredible religious faith of the Irish people, who built the cathedral in 1849 during the darkest of the Famine days.

It is rumored that crafty 14th-century monks brewed a light ale in St. Francis' Abbey on Parliament St.; the abbey is in ruins but its industry survives in the abbey's yard at the **Smithwicks Brewery.** *(Tours July-Aug. M-F 3pm. Tickets free at the tourist office.)* Smith-wicks Brewery offers an audio-visual show and ale tasting. Smithwicks itself, called Kilkenny in Ireland, is a tasty brew naturally best in Kilkenny and easier on the palate than Guinness, but the company profanes the abbey by brewing Budweiser there.

ENTERTAINMENT

The Kilkenny People is a good source for arts and music listings. **The Watergate Theatre,** Parliament St. (tel. 61674), puts on traditional Irish plays. *(Tickets usually £5, students £3. Booking office open daily 10am-8pm.)* During the first two weeks of August Kilkenny holds its annual **Arts Festival,** which has a daily program of theater, con-certs, recitals, and readings by famous European and Irish artists. *(Event tickets free to £7; student tickets available. 1-week ticket £75; before July 31 £65. Student discounts available.)* Buy tickets from Kilkenny Arts Week at Rothe House, Parliament St. (tel. 63663), or the tourist office. Kilkenny's population increases by 10,000 in early June for the **Cat Laughs** (tel. 51254), a week-long festival featuring Irish, English, and American come-dians. The cat referred to is the Kilkenny mascot, culled from the famous poem:

> There once were two cats from Kilkenny
> Each thought there was one cat too many.
> So they fought and they fit,
> And they scratched and they bit,
> 'Til excepting their nails and the tips of their tails,
> Instead of two cats there weren't any.

■ Near Kilkenny

Beautiful Jerpoint Abbey, south of Kilkenny, and the eery Dunmore Caves to the north provide intriguing reasons to leave Kilkenny for an afternoon.

■ Thomastown and Jerpoint Abbey

Thomastown, a tiny community perched on the Nore River, is picturesque, but one would mainly come to visit **Jerpoint Abbey** (tel. 24623), 1½ mi. away. (Open mid-June to Aug. daily 9:30am-6:30pm; Sept. to mid-Oct. daily 10am-1pm and 2-5pm; Apr. to mid-June Tu-Su 9:30am-6:30pm. £3, students and seniors £1.50, families £6.) Founded in 1180, the abbey is one of the most beautiful Cistercian ruins in Ireland, with remarkable etchings and tombs. Free tours, given on request, are incredible; only with the guidance of the employees are most people able to see the unique com-bination of Christian and Celtic imagery.

Bus Éireann stops by Kavanagh's in Thomastown between **Waterford** and **Kilk-enny** (M-Sa 7 per day, Su 4 per day). Those in need of cash should head for **AIB** (open M 10am-12:30pm and 1:30-5pm, Tu-F 10am-12:30pm and 1:30-3pm). **Barrett's Phar-macy** (tel. 24216) has a free **tourist information** pamphlet (open M-Sa 9am-6pm, Su 10:30am-noon). **Gary's Minibus** (tel. 24102) can take you to points of historical inter-est. **Simon Treacy Hardware** (tel. 24291) rents **bikes** (£6 per day, £25 per week; deposit £20), sells fishing tackle and salmon licenses, and can put you in touch with horse manure distributors (£2 per bag; open M-Sa 9am-6pm). Thomas goes to town with a **phone code** of 056.

SuperValu, around the corner on Marshes St., can handle your grocery needs (open M-W 8am-7pm, Th-F 8am-9pm, and Su 8am-12:30pm), but the serene **Water-garden** (tel. 24690) on Ladywell St., signposted from Market St., serves an amazing lunch. Members of the Camphill Community, an organization that supports and employs the mentally handicapped, serve cheap, tasty food in a cozy café with lovely gardens out back (open 10am-6pm). **O'Hara's** pub (tel. 24597) has 200-year-old walls and fireplaces and offers **B&B** upstairs. It's not particularly quiet (the pub *is* down-stairs), but the rooms are comfy and clean. (Singles £22; doubles £36.)

At one end of Market St. rests the remains of **St. Mary's,** a church built in the early 13th century. Among the gravestones lies a rare stone with ancient ogham writing as well as part of a Celtic cross and the weathered effigy of a 13th-century man. At **Jerpoint Glass** (tel. 24350), visitors may watch Keith Leadbetter as he sculpts glass.

■ Dunmore Cave

North of Kilkenny on the road to Castlecomer lurks the massive **Dunmore Cave** (office tel. (056) 67726), known as "the darkest place in Ireland," which contains fascinating limestone formations. Recently unearthed human bones show that 40 people died underground here in 928, probably while hiding from marauding Vikings. *(Open mid-June to mid-Sept. daily 10am-7pm; mid-Sept. to Oct. daily 10am-6pm; Nov.-Feb. Sa-Su 10am-5pm; mid-Mar. to mid-June Tu-Sa 10am-4pm, Su 2-4pm. £2, students £1.)* There is no direct public transport to the cave, but **Buggy's Buses** (tel. (056) 41264) runs a bus between Kilkenny and Castlecomer that stops nearby on request (4 per day). If you're driving, take N78 (Dublin Rd.) from Kilkenny; the turn-off for the cave is on the right after the split with N77 (Durrow Rd.).

■ Carlow

A small, busy town with surprisingly good nightlife, Carlow sits on the eastern side of the River Barrow on N9 (Dublin-Waterford). Despite its modern placidity, Carlow has hosted several of the most gruesome historic battles between Gael and Pale. During the 1798 rising (see **History,** p. 57), 417 Irish insurgents were ambushed in the streets of Carlow; they were buried across the River Barrow in the gravel pits of Graiguecullen (greg-KULL-en). Part of the gallows from which they were hanged is now displayed in the county museum.

PRACTICAL INFORMATION Trains run through Carlow from Heuston Station in **Dublin** on their way to **Waterford** (1¼hr., M-Th and Sa 4 per day, Su 3 per day, £12). From the train station, it's a 15-minute walk to the center of town; head straight out of the station down Railway Rd., turn left onto Dublin Rd., and make another left at the Court House onto College St. The cheapest **buses** to **Dublin** depart from Doyle's by the Shamrock D.I.Y.—you can go to the Custom House for as little as £3.50 return. **Bus Éireann** bounces from Carlow to **Athlone** (2¼hr., 1 per day), **Dublin** (1¾hr., M-Sa 8 per day, Su 4 per day), and **Waterford** via **Kilkenny** (1¼hr., 6 per day). **Rapid Express Coaches,** Barrack St. (tel. 43081), runs a bus through **Tramore-Waterford-Carlow-Dublin** and back (M-F 7 per day, Su 5 per day). The Carlow **tourist office,** Kennedy Ave. (tel. 31554), tucked in Hadden's car park by the Dinn Rí, hands out photocopied maps of the town as well as the Carlow Town Trail pamphlet, which introduces the town's historical and architectural highlights (open M-F 9:30am-12:45pm and 2-5:30pm, Sa 10am-5:30pm). Rent **bikes** from **Coleman Cycle,** 19 Dublin St. (tel. 31273; £5 per day, £25 per week; deposit £40; open M-Sa 8:30am-7:30pm). The **post office** mails your post or posts your mail (open M and W-Sa 9am-5:30pm, Tu 9:30am-5:30pm). The **phone code** is 0503.

ACCOMMODATIONS The **Otterholt Riverside Hostel** (tel. 30404; fax 41318), on the banks of the River Barrow, is by far the best place to stay in Carlow and much nicer than the hostel in Athlone. It's a half a mile from the center of town on Kilkenny Rd., but you can request a stop at RTC, the college across the street, on the bus to or from Kilkenny. Rooms are bright with comfortable beds; amenities include washing machines, carpark, bike storage, and a lovely garden. (Dorms £8; doubles £20; **camping** £4.) The **Redsetter Guest House,** 14 Dublin Rd. (tel. 42837), next to the Royal Hotel in the center of town, offers phones and bath in every room and cable in some, with the friendliness of a B&B. (Single £20; doubles £38.)

FOOD AND PUBS Superquinn (tel. 30077), in the Carlow shopping mall, supplies groceries and fresh fruit. **Scragg's Alley,** 12 Tullow St. (tel. 42233 or 40407), fills you with cheap, hearty lunches in an old Irish kitchen through an arched tunnel (served daily noon-2:30pm). **The Bradburry,** 144 Tullow St., serves a variety of inexpensive dishes in a clean, quiet atmosphere (open M-Sa 9am-6pm). **Buzz's Bar,** 7 Tullow St., jams its shelves with books and its patrons' bellies with victuals.

The hippest spot in town is the **Dinn Rí,** Kennedy St., a three-pubbed Cerberus that fits 800 people. Carlow grooves to live rock and trad at **Scragg's Alley,** Tullow St. (music W, Su). Friday and Saturday nights, the music continues at the **Nexus Nightclub** upstairs, one of the best clubs in Ireland (cover Friday £5, Saturday £6). **Tully's,** 149 Tullow St. (tel. 31862), is friendly and offbeat, with occasional live bands. The good-looking people come here accompanied by their cell phones. **O'Loughlin's,** 53 Dublin St. (tel. 32205), is dark and velvety with typewriters strewn about—no music, but a lively, young crowd trying desperately to be bohemian. You'd better go home and read *Ulysses* first.

SIGHTS In the middle of a cow field about a 10-minute drive from Carlow lies the rather big and six- or seven-millennia-old **Brownshill Dolmen,** believed to mark the grave of an ancient king. Follow Tullow St. through the traffic light and straight through the roundabout; the dolmen is 2 mi. away in a field on the right. The stone on top weighs approximately 150 tons, a fact that raises the question of how it got there. **The Carlow Museum,** Haymarket (tel. 40730), behind Town Hall through the carpark, looks like somebody's attic. *(Open Tu-F 11am-5pm, Sa and Su 2-5pm. £1.50, students 75p.)* An old bar and blacksmith shop are tritely reconstructed; on the plus side, there's an informative exhibit on the 1798 massacre. **Carlow Castle** lurks behind the storefronts on Castle St. Sadly, the castle ruins are closed to the public. The castle's current condition can be blamed on one Dr. Middleton, who intended to convert the castle into an asylum but wanted to enlarge the windows and thin the walls. He used dynamite to make his modifications—not the greatest engineering decision ever made. Carlow's other big attraction is the local **cross-training fanatic,** with a red beard and crazed eyes. He cycles up hills then carries the bike back down. He does push-ups in the street. He races the trains that pass through the town on foot. He loses. He should probably not be interrupted during his workouts.

The best time to visit Carlow is during the first two weeks of June, when the town hosts **Éigse** (AIG-sha, "gathering"), a 10-day festival of the arts. Artists from all over Ireland come to present visual, musical, and theatrical works; some events require tickets. Call the Eigse Festival office (tel. 40491) for more information.

County Tipperary

To the south of Kilkenny and west of Waterford lies the medieval sprawl of south Tipperary, where Clonmel, Cahir, and Cashel air their fancifully crumbling castles in idyllic countryside. North Tipperary is a long way from the beaten tourist track, and for good reason; the fertile region has more spud farmers than visitor centers. South of the Cahir-Cashel-Tipperary triangle stretch the underrated Comeragh, Galtee, and Knockmealdown Mountains. Although Lismore is actually located in Co. Waterford, it is covered under Co. Tipperary with the nearby Knockmealdown Mountains.

■ Tipperary Town

> *Good-bye to Piccadilly/Farewell to Leicester Square.*
> *It's a long way to Tipperary/And my heart lies there.*

This famously named town is perhaps less exciting for today's travelers than the World War I marching song would imply. "Tipp Town," as it's affectionately known, is primarily a market town for the fertile Golden Vale farming region. Compared with the soft rolling hills of the surrounding area and the much acclaimed **Glen of Aher-**

low to the south, Tipp Town doesn't tend to impress. The **tourist office,** James St. (tel. 51457), just off Main St., is a useful resource for trips into the glen and the nearby mountains (Glen of Aherlow walking trail maps 50p; open May-Oct. M-Sa 10am-6pm). An **AIB** is on Main St. (open M-W and F 10am-4pm, Th 10am-5pm; **ATM**). The **post office** hides on Davis St. (open M-F 9am-5:30pm, Sa 9am-noon and 1-5:30pm). Tipp's **phone code** is 062.

The best B&B in Tipp is the aptly named **Central House B&B,** 45 Main St. (tel. 51117), which has a welcoming owner and seemingly endless number of mostly spacious rooms (£16, with bath £17). Other B&Bs are on Emly Rd. about a half mile west of town off Main St. Tipp features a full-scale **SuperValu** on Main St. (open M-W and Sa 9am-6pm, Th and F 9am-9pm). For simple bistro fare you're sure to get lucky at the **Seamróg,** Davis St. (tel. 33881; open M-Sa 8am-6pm, Su 4-8pm). **The Brown Trout,** Abbey St. (tel. 51912), one block down Bridge St. from Main St., has surprisingly reasonable lunchtime prices (£5-7) considering its chandelier, swanky red tablecloths, and multiple sets of flatware (open daily 12:30-3pm and 6-9:30pm). Youths congregate in the **Underground Tavern,** James St., where wine barrels now function as tables and provide the atmosphere. Tipp's oldest tavern, **Corny's Pub** (tel. 33036), on Davitt St. (which moonlights as both Limerick Rd. and Church St.) plays trad that attracts an older crowd (trad Wednesday and F-Sa).

■ Cashel

The town of Cashel lies inland, halfway between Limerick and Waterford, tucked behind a series of mountain ranges on N8 from Cork to Dublin. Airy and magical when seen from the northern plains, the commanding **Rock of Cashel** looms 300 ft. above the town. The dark limestone hill bristles with an elaborate complex of medieval buildings and exudes an eerie power surpassing other Irish ruins. **Bus Éireann** (tel. 62121) leaves from Bianconi's Bistro on Main St., serving **Dublin** (3hr., 4 per day, £9), **Cork** (1½hr., 4 per day, £8), **Limerick** (4 per day, £8.80), and **Cahir** (15min., 4 per day, £2.40). Bus transport to **Waterford** is available via Cahir. Hitching to Cork or Dublin along N8 is a common occurrence; thumbing west to Tipp and Limerick on N74 is also feasible. Cashel's efficient **tourist office** (tel. 62511) shares space with the Heritage Centre in the recently renovated Cashel City Hall, Main St. (open daily May-Sept. 9am-8pm; Oct.-Apr. 9:30am-5:30pm). **McInerney's,** Main St. (tel. 61366), next to SuperValu, rents bikes (£7.50 per day, £30 per week; open M-Sa 9am-6pm). **AIB,** Main St., has a **bureau de change** and an **ATM** (open M-W and F 10am-12:30pm and 1:30-4pm, Th 10am-12:30pm and 1:30-5pm.) The **post office** (tel. 61418) is also on Main St. (open M and W-F 9am-1pm and 2-5:30pm, Tu 9:30am-1pm and 2-5:30pm, Sa 9am-1pm). The **phone code** rocks the Cashel at 062.

ACCOMMODATIONS Cashel is graced with two excellent hostels that contribute greatly to the town's appeal as a backpackers' base. The plush **Cashel Holiday Hostel (IHH),** 6 John St. (tel. 62330; email cashel@iol.ie), just off Main St., has a gorgeous kichen crowned with a glass pyramid skylight and spacious and interestingly named bedrooms (the "big fellows' room" has extra-long beds). The gregarious staff offers hints on the area's natural and archaeological sights that have been known to keep backpackers in Cashel for an extended stay. Guests can receive messages at the hostel's email address. (4- to 8-bed dorms £7; 4-bed dorms with bath £8; private rooms £10 per person. Laundry £3.50. Key deposit £3. Email access £2.50.) **O'Brien's Farmhouse Hostel** (tel. 61003), a five-minute walk from Cashel on Dundrum Rd., has spotless rooms, fluffy beds, and an unbelievable location. This stunning hostel boasts one of the best views of the Rock and overlooks one of Hore Abbey's picture-postcard cow pastures. Although Mrs. O'Brien has sort of upscale hostel facilities, her new, cheerful, pine-floored private rooms are worthy of guest-house status. (6-bed dorm £8; private room from £10 per person. **Camping** £4 per person. Laundry £5.) The high quality (and high price) of local B&Bs reflect the number of tourists drawn to the Rock. Just steps from the Rock on Moor Lance is **Rockville House** (tel. 61760), which does credit to its outstanding location with crisp bedrooms; turn behind the tourist office and pass the model village museum (£16 with bath).

FOOD AND PUBS The **Bake House** (tel. 61680), across from the Heritage Centre on Main St., is the town's best spot for scones, coffee, and light meals. It also provides pseudo-elegant upstairs seating. (Open M-Sa 8am-9pm, Su 10am-7pm.) **Bailey's,** Main St., has hearty fare at passable prices (soup £2, sandwiches £3-4, dinner entrees £8-10; open noon-10:30pm, dinner served 5:30-10:30pm). The **Spearman Restaurant,** 97 Main St. (tel. 61143), offers a delicious but costly break from the brown-bread diet (sandwiches £1.60, dinner entrees £7-13; open M-Sa noon-2:30pm and 5:30-9:30pm, Su noon-3pm and 6-9pm). **Pasta Milano,** Lady's Well St. (tel. 62729), a vast and entertainingly tacky wonderland of drippy candles, fountains, and Greco-Roman statues, has an extensive and affordable menu (pizza £5-9, pasta £6-10; open M-Th noon-11am, F-Su noon-midnight). **SuperValu Supermarket,** Main St., offers the biggest selection of groceries (open M-Sa 8am-9pm, Su 9am-6pm); **Centra Supermarket,** Friar St., is open latest (open daily 7am-11pm).

Good craic and nightly music entice locals to the most popular pub in Cashel, **Feehan's,** Main St. (tel. 61929; trad 3 nights a week). The bartenders at staid and well-appointed **Dowling's,** 46 Main St. (tel. 62130), make it their best (and only) business to pour the best pint in town. Innocuous-looking **Ryan's,** Main St. (tel. 61431), hides a softly lit, music-filled parlor and a mighty multilevel beer garden. The **Fox's Den,** 42 Main St. (tel. 62428), fills up with, as one patron said, "fucking footballers and hurlers" the night after big matches. This is the place to ask your questions about the fastest field game in the world.

SIGHTS The **Rock of Cashel** (also called **St. Patrick's Rock**) is a huge limestone outcropping topped by a stunning complex of medieval buildings. *(Rock open daily mid-June to mid-Sept. 9am-7:30pm; mid-Sept. to mid-Mar. 9:30am-4:30pm; mid-Mar. to mid-June 9:30am-5:30pm. Last admission 45min. before closing. £3, students £1.25.)* The Rock itself is attached to a number of legends, some historically substantiated and others more dubious. The one-hour tour explains the legends in detail but threatens the magical potential of the Rock through its dearth of humor and excess of self-importance. Over the next few centuries, local political and ecclesiastical powers subsequently added to the construction on the Rock, creating a Gothic cathedral crammed between a round tower and a Romanesque chapel that, incredibly enough, fails to look incongruous. On the Rock stands the two-towered **Cormac's Chapel,** consecrated in 1134. The interior displays semi-restored Romanesque paintings, disintegrating stone-carved arches, and a barely visible, ornate sarcophagus once thought to be in the tomb of King Cormac. A highlight of Cashel's illustrious history was the reported burning of the cathedral by the Earl of Kildare in 1495—when Henry VII demanded an explanation, the Earl replied, "I thought the Archbishop was in it." Henry made him Lord Deputy. The 13th-century **Cashel Cathedral** survived the Earl and remains unequalled in its grandeur, whether because of or despite the fact that its vaulted Gothic arches no longer buttress a roof. Next to the cathedral, a 90 ft. **round tower,** probably dating from just after 1101, is the oldest part of the Rock. The **museum** (tel. 61437) at the entrance to the castle complex preserves the 12th-century **St. Patrick's Cross.** A stirringly narrated film on medieval religious structures is shown every 30 minutes or so. Far from the maddening crowd and down the cow path from the Rock, the ruins of **Hore Abbey,** the last Cistercian monastery established in Ireland, put out with a striking view of the Rock. *(Always open. Free.)*

The small but brilliantly executed **Heritage Centre,** Main St. (tel. 35362), features permanent exhibitions, including "Rock: From 4th to 11th Century" and the scintillatingly titled "Rock: 12th-18th Century," and temporary exhibitions on such themes as Hore Abbey, Cashel Palace, and life in Cashel. *(Open July-Aug. daily 9:30am-8pm; Sept.-Feb. M-Sa 9:30am-5:30pm, Su noon-5:30pm; Mar.-June daily 9:30am-5:30pm. £1, students 50p.)* The **GPA-Bolton Library,** John St. (tel. 61944), past the hostel, displays a musty collection of books and silver that formerly belonged to an Anglican archbishop of

Cashel, Theophilus Bolton. *(Open M-Sa 9:30am-5:30pm, Su 2:30-5:30pm. For a tour, call tel. 61232 or the tourist office (tel. 62511). £2.50, students £1.50.)* The collection harbors ecclesiastical texts and rare manuscripts, including a 1550 edition of Machiavelli's *Il Principe,* the first English translation of *Don Quixote,* and what is locally reputed to be the smallest book in the world. The **Brú Ború Heritage Centre** (tel. 61122), at the base of the Rock, performs Irish traditional music, song, and dance to international acclaim. *(Performances June 15-Sept. 15 Tu-Sa at 9pm. £6.)* Brú Ború also has access to genealogical records for South Tipperary county. A name, approximate dates of birth and/or location, and £15 will get you info on whether they have information. For another £25, you can get your hands on the info. In the town of **Golden,** 5 mi. west of Cashel on Tipperary Rd., stand the ruins of lovely **Althassel Abbey,** a 12th-century Augustinian priory founded by the Red Earl of Dunster.

■ Cahir

Like any spot in Ireland that sports a set of public toilets, Cahir (CARE) is a fairly heavily touristed town. Its well-preserved and enthusiastically shown castle certainly justify the visitors' attention. Though not as well stocked with hostels as its northern neighbor Cashel, Cahir makes for a good afternoon of let's-play-castle and a sedate stopover; the nightlife is largely maintained by locals.

PRACTICAL INFORMATION Trains leave from the station off Cashel Rd., just past the church, for **Limerick** and **Rosslare** (M-Sa 2 per day). **Bus Éireann** runs from the tourist office to **Limerick** via **Tipperary** (1hr., M-Th and Sa 4 per day, F 5 per day, £7.30), **Waterford** (1¼hr., M-Th and Sa 5 per day, F 6 per day, £7.70), **Cork** (1½hr., 4 per day, £7), **Dublin** (3hr., 4 per day, £10), and **Cashel** (15min., £2.50). **Hitchers** to Dublin or Cork station themselves on N8, a 20-minute hike from the center of town. Those hoping to hitch to Limerick and Waterford wait just outside of town on N24 (Limerick/Waterford Rd.), which passes through the town square. The well-sign-posted **tourist office,** Castle St. (tel. 41453), knows less about the mountains than the town, but they do give out free town maps (open July-Aug. M-Sa 9:30am-6pm and Su 11am-5pm; mid-Apr. to Sept. M-Sa 9:30am-6pm). Backpackers can stow their bags free for a time at the **Crock O' Gold,** across from the tourist office. The **phone code** is a cahiring and nurturing 052.

ACCOMMODATIONS, FOOD, AND PUBS There are two hostels in the countryside relatively close to Cahir. **Lisakyle Hostel (IHH)** (tel. 41963), 1 mi. south on Ardfinnan Rd., is the more accessible of the two; if coming from the bus station, walk up the hill and make a right at Cahir House. Though the exterior is beautiful and the flower garden is gorgeous, the accommodations are extremely basic and the beds are thin. The hostel is about 1¼ mi. from the nearest walking trail. Reserve a bed with the hostel's superfriendly owners at **Condon's Shop** on Church St., across from the post office. Condon's will also arrange lifts to the hostel from town. (Dorms £7; private rooms £8.50 per person; families max. £30. Sheets 50p. **Camping** £4.) The **Kilcoran Farm Hostel (IHH)** (tel. 41906 or (088) 539185) promises to be an education in rural living, with vocal sheep out back and an impressive collection of rusting farm tools. From Cahir, take Cork Rd. for 4 mi., turn left at the Top Petrol Station, and then, after a quarter mile, veer right at the T-shaped junction. Call for pickup from town. (Dorms £7. Free **bike rental.**) One of the closest B&Bs to Cahir is **The Rectory,** Cashel Rd. (tel. 41406), which provides old-fashioned enormous rooms and unbeatable charm (£18). **Killaun** (tel. 41780), a quarter mile from town along Clonmel Rd., provides comfortable, airy rooms and a hostess who can pull out her Irish charm when necessary (£15, with bath £17).

The best bet for groceries is **SuperValu Supermarket,** Bridge St. (tel. 41515), across the bridge from the castle (open M-W 8:30am-6:30pm, Th 8:30am-8pm, F 8:30am-9pm, Sa 8:30am-7pm, Su 9am-1pm). The **Italian Connection,** Castle St. (tel. 42152), spares no olive oil to fatten you up Mediterranean style (pasta £5-6; fish, veal, and chicken £8-12; open daily noon-11pm). **Castle Arms,** Castle St. (tel. 42506), serves up cheap grub in an atmosphere that could only be called "pub" (hot entrees £3.95). A local favorite is the **Galtee Inn**, The Square (tel. 41247), where lunch costs £4.85 (lunch daily noon-3pm, dinner 5-10:30pm).

For an innocuous-looking town that panders to tourists, Cahir has an inexplicably large biker following. Consequently, it contains biker bars, something of a rarity in this country. Compare tattoos at **Black Tom's** (tel. 42539), on Limerick Rd. past SuperValu, a favorite among Tipperary's leather set that occasionally features live rock on weekends. **J. Morrissey,** Castle St. (tel. 42123), across from the tourist office, hosts folk sessions every Thursday night. **Galtee Inn,** Church St., The Square (tel. 42147), and the **Castle Arms,** Castle St. (tel. 42506), attract fewer Harleys and more well-dressed locals of all ages. (They probably drive mopeds.)

SIGHTS Cahir is often defined by **Cahir Castle** (tel. 41011), one of the larger and better preserved castles in Ireland. *(Open daily mid-June to mid-Sept. 9am-7:30pm; Apr. to mid-June and mid-Sept. to mid-Oct. 9:30am-5:30pm; mid-Oct. to Mar. 9:30am-4:30pm. £2, students £1. Last admission 30min. before closing.)* It is exactly what every tourist envisions a castle to be—heavy, lots of battlements, and gray—which must be why so many people come to reinforce their preconceptions. Built in the 13th century to be all but impregnable to conventional military attack, the castle's defenses were rendered obsolete by the advent of the age of artillery. In 1599, the Earl of Essex forced its surrender by tossing some cannonballs its way, one of which is still visibly stuck in the wall. Note the 11,000-year-old preserved head of the long-extinct Irish Elk; the noble beast's antlers span nearly an entire wall. Climb the towers for an unparalleled view of the tourist office and parking lot. There is a free, one-hour guided **tour** of the castle that points out the numerous and interesting ways of doing horrid things to people trying to get in; none of them succeed in keeping the tourists out.

The broad River Suir that flows into Waterford Harbour is still a mere stream in Cahir. The wildly green **river walk** follows it from the tourist office to the 19th-century **Swiss Cottage** (tel. 41144), a half-hour walk from town, and beyond. *(Access by 30min. guided tour only. Last admission 45min. before closing. Open May-Sept. daily 10am-6pm; Apr. Tu-Su 10am-1pm and 2-5pm; Mar. and Oct.-Nov. Tu-Su 10am-1pm and 2-4:30pm. £2, students £1.)* A charming jumble of architectural styles, the cottage was built in the early 19th century so that the Butlers of Cahir Castle could fish, hunt, and generally pretend to be peasants. Gorgeously restored, it is a delight for anyone who fancies building, decorating, or being rich. **Fishing** opportunities abound along the river walk past the Swiss Cottage. Fishing licenses are required, and can be obtained at the Heritage cornerstone (tel. 42730) on Church St. *(Open daily 7am-11pm.)*

■ Near Cahir: Caves, Mountains, and Glen

The **Mitchelstown Caves** (tel. (052) 67246) drip 8 mi. off the Cahir-Cork road in the town of **Burncourt,** about halfway between Cahir and Mitchelstown. The perfunctory tour lasts only 30 minutes, but that's plenty of time for the rippled, gooey subterranean formations to leave you awestruck. (Open daily 10am-6pm; last tour 5:30pm. £3.)

The **Galtee Mountains** rise abruptly from the flatlands due west of Cahir. The purplish range boasts Galtymore, Ireland's third highest peak at 3654 ft. The north climb is most difficult. Serious hikers should invest in one of the excellent Ordnance Survey maps at the tourist office or local bookstore (£3.90). The *New Irish Walk Guides* have maps and routes for the Galtees as well as all the other mountains in the region (available in bookstores; about £3). Tourist offices in Tipp Town, Cahir, and Cashel also sell a four-walk series of trail maps, each containing a map and written directions detailing a "classic" and a less strenuous "family walk" (50p). The walks wind through the Glen of Aherlow, Lake Muskry, Lake Borheen, Glencush, Lake Curra, and Duntry League Hill. Glenbarra is a popular base camp, reached by driving west from Cahir toward Mitchelstown.

The **Glen of Aherlow (Ballydavid Wood) Youth Hostel (An Óige/HI)** (tel. (062) 54148), 6 mi. northwest of Cahir off Limerick Rd. (signposted) is a renovated old hunting lodge that makes a good start for cavorting around the Galtees (June-Sept. dorms £7, Mar.-May and Oct.-Nov. £6). On occasion, dedicated hikers make the 10 mi. trek across the mountains to the **Mountain Lodge (An Óige/HI),** Burncourt (tel. (052) 67277), a gas-lit Georgian hunting lodge in the middle of the woods. From Cahir, follow the Mitchelstown Rd. (N8) 8 mi., then turn right at the sign for another 2 mi. on an unpaved path. (Dorms £6.50.) The **Kilcoran Farm Hostel** (tel. (052) 41906) also makes a convenient hiking home (see **Cahir,** p. 164). The campsite in the Glen of Aherlow, **Ballinacourty House** (tel. (062) 56230), is excellent, and the staff provides detailed information on the Glen. (£8 per tent, off-season £7; plus £1 per person. Meals and cooking facilities available. Open Apr. to mid-Sept.) They also operate a pleasant **B&B** and restaurant (doubles with bath £34). To reach Ballinacourty House, take R663 off the Cahir-Tipperary road (N24) in Bansha and follow the road for 8 mi. to the signposted turnoff.

■ Clonmel

Clonmel (pop. 16,000) derives its name from the Irish *Cluain Meala,* "the honey meadow." This medieval town on the banks of the River Suir (SURE) does have something sweet about it in the fall, when locally produced Bulmer's cider fills the air with apple scents. Co. Tipperary's economic hub, the town maintains much more of a commercial focus than its neighbors. Lest industrial centers strike fear in the hearts of idyllic Ireland seekers, be reassured that Clonmel is also a good place to rest after exploring the nearby Comeragh Mountains, especially if your stay involves one of the gems in Clonmel's "heaps of pubs."

ORIENTATION AND PRACTICAL INFORMATION

Clonmel's central street runs parallel to the Suir. From the station, follow Prior Park Rd. straight into town. Prior Park Rd. becomes businesslike Gladstone St., which intersects the main drag, known successively as O'Connell St., Mitchell St., Parnell St., and Irishtown. Sarsfield and Abbey St. run toward the river from the main street.

Trains: Prior Park Rd. (tel. 21982), about 1mi. north of the town center. Trains chug here on their way to **Limerick** (50min., M-Sa 2 per day, £11) and **Waterford** on the way to **Rosslare Harbour** (1¼ hr., M-Sa 2 per day, £6.50).

Buses: Bus information is available at **Rafferty Travel,** Gladstone St. (tel. 22622). Open M-Sa 9am-6pm. Buses head to Clonmel from **Cork** (3 per day, £8), **Dublin** (3 per day, £8), **Galway** (M-F 5 per day, Su 3 per day, £12), **Kilkenny** via **Carrick-on-Suir** (M-Sa 4 per day, Su 3 per day, £3.50), **Limerick** via **Tipperary** (5 per day, £8.80, students £5), **Rosslare** (2 per day, £10), and **Waterford** (M-Sa 7 per day, Su 5 per day, £5.90).

Tourist Office: Sarsfield St. (tel. 22960), across from the Clonmel Arms Hotel. Pick up the extensive *Southeastern Holiday Guide* (free) and the 6 self-guided walking tours of Clonmel and the Nire Valley (50p). Open M-F 9:30am-7pm, Sa 10am-5pm.

Bank: AIB (tel. 22500) and **Bank of Ireland,** both with **ATMs,** are neighbors on O'Connell St. Both open M 10am-5pm, Tu-F 10am-4pm.

Pharmacy: Joy's, 68 O'Connell St. (tel. 21204). Open M-Sa 9am-6pm.

Emergency: Dial 999; no coins required. **Garda:** Emmet St. (tel. 22222).

Hospital: St. Joseph's/St. Michael's, Western Rd. (tel. 21900).

Post Office: Emmet St. (tel. 21164), parallel to Gladstone St. Open M-F 9am-5pm, Sa 9am-1pm.

Internet Access: FAS Clonmel Multi-Media Center, Parnell St. (tel. 28520). £2.50 per 30min. Open in summer M-Sa 9am-9pm; sometimes shorter hours in winter.

Phone Code: Sweet nectar of Bulmer's youth, 052.

ACCOMMODATIONS

Not the most backpacker-friendly town in Ireland, Clonmel caters more to the hotel and B&B crowd. The only hostel is well outside of town, but committed hostelers explore Clonmel by day and then head to the gorgeous **Powers-the-Pot Hostel and Caravan Park,** Harney's Cross (tel. 23085). To reach the hostel, follow Parnell St. east out of town, turn right at the first traffic light (not N24), cross the Suir, and continue straight for 5½ mi. of arduous mountain road to the signposted turnoff. Niall and Jo run the hostel out of their large 19th-century house majestically perched atop the Comeragh Mountains and offer huge fluffy beds and a bar/restaurant under a thatched roof (breakfast £3.50, dinners £7.50-10). (Dorms £6; private rooms £7. **Camping** £3.50 per person. Laundry £2. Open May to mid-Oct. Maps and walking guides for the Munster Way. Freezing and smoking facilities for anglers.)

In Clonmel, the area past Irishtown along the Cahir and Abbey Rd. is graced with numerous **B&Bs.** If you're willing to walk a mile or two to town, your options are relatively extensive. In Clonmel proper, gracious **Riverside House** (tel. 25781), on New Quay overlooking the Suir, entertains its guests with large rooms, in-room BBC, and Max the Wonderdog (£14).

FOOD AND PUBS

Grocery shopping is a surreal experience at **Crazy Prices,** Gladstone St. (tel. 27797; open M-Tu and Sa 9am-7pm, W-F 9am-9pm, Su 11am-4pm). **The Honey Pot,** Abbey St. (tel. 21457), sells health foods and bulk grains. Organic vegetable vendors parade their wares here on Friday mornings. (Open M-Sa 9:30am-6pm.)

Catalpa, Sarsfield St. (tel. 26821), next to the tourist office. This Italian restaurant is so good that diners sometimes fall into a coma of bliss after tasting the *penne Arrabiata* (pasta £4.80-6.75; pizza £4.20-5; meat dishes £7-13). Unconsciousness is safe here, though—the building used to be both a bank vault and a barracks during the war for independence. Open Tu-Su 12:30-2:30pm and 6:30-11pm.

Tom Skinny's Pizza Parlor, 4 Gladstone St. (tel. 26006). Pizza made fresh right before your eyes. £4.30 lunch special comprises a small 2-topping pizza, tea or coffee, and soup or ice cream. Most pizzas £4-8. Open daily noon-midnight.

Niamh's (NEEVS), Mitchell St. (tel. 25698). Locals love this cozy and efficient deli/restaurant. Niamh herself is just plain funny. Hot lunches, sandwiches, and Irish breakfast served all day. Pita the Great £2.60. Open M-F 9am-5:45pm, Sa 9am-5pm.

Angela's Wholefood Café, Abbey St. (tel. 26899), off Mitchell St. Well-prepared and creative vegetarian and meat wholefood dishes served on country pine tables. Salads, specials £5-6. Open M-F 9am-5:30pm, Sa 9am-5pm.

Tierney's, O'Connell St. (tel. 24467), is resplendent with wood paneling and polished brass. With a restaurant upstairs and meals served all day, it feels less like a pub than a cushy club. The trendy younger set favors **Phil Carrol's,** 16 Parnell St. (tel. 25215), known to pull the best pint in town—don't blink, you might miss it. Watch the barman write your name in Guinness foam. **Mulcahy's,** Gladstone St. (tel. 22825), is by far the biggest and most elaborate pub in town. On Wednesday, Friday, and Sunday nights, it hosts **Danno's,** the disco that lures the over-18s from miles around (cover £5, concession £3; nightclub entrance on Market St.). The Clonmel Arms also hosts a disco, **The Riveroom** (tel. 21233; F-Sa, cover £2-5). Check the *Nationalist* for entertainment listings.

SIGHTS

Clonmel could win the best-signposted tourist-trail award, but it wouldn't do quite as well in the content or eloquence portions of the pageant. The best approach to the town's sights might be to take a guided **tour** from the tourist offfice, but you may end up seeing more than you bargained for. *(Stop in or call to arrange times. £2.)* One of the best stops on the walk is the **WestGate** that straddles the west end of O'Connell St., the 1831 reconstruction of the gate that separated Irishtown from the much more prosperous Anglo-Norman town in the medieval era. Built in 1204, the 84 ft. octagonal tower of **Old Mary's Church,** Mary St., is also not to be missed. In the 19th century, **Hearn's Hotel,** Parnell St., was the center of Clonmel Mayor Bianconi's vast horsecart business empire, which competed successfully with the railways in the 1850s. The **Franciscan Friary,** Abbey St., between Parnell St. and The Quay, has housed the tomb of the Lords of Cahir since the 13th century, although most of the current structure dates from the 1880s. Several walks in the area and in the nearby Nire Valley are described in the tourist office's glossy leaflets *Clonmel Walk #1* and *#2* (50p each). See **Comeragh Mountains,** p. 168, for day hike info.

The **Tipperary S.R. County Museum,** Parnell St. (tel. 25399), hosts small but interesting traveling art exhibitions. *(Open Tu-Sa 10am-1pm and 2-5pm. Free.)* The well-documented but inexplicable upstairs gallery concentrates on somewhat esoteric facets of local history—including a thousand-pound skull of the long-extinct giant Irish elk.

■ The East Munster Way

The East Munster Way footpath starts in Carrick-on-Suir, hits Clonmel, skirts the Comeragh Mountains, and runs into the Knockmealdowns full-force, ending at mile 43 in Clogheen. The best **maps** to use are sheets 74 and 75 of the 1:50,000 Ordnance Survey series. In addition, the *East Munster Way Map Guide* (£4), available at the Clonmel tourist office and at Powers-the-Pot Hostel, provides a written guide and an accurate but less detailed map (as an added bonus, it points out all the pubs along the way!). The route contact is the Tipperary Co. Council in Clonmel (tel. (052) 25399), but Powers-the-Pot is the best information center for hiking in and around the Comeragh and Knockmealdown Mountains.

■ Comeragh Mountains

The Comeragh "mountains" are more like large hills; not even the highest peaks are very steep. The ground is almost always soft and wet. Hiking boots are obviously best, but most of the terrain is manageable in sneakers. If you'd rather expend your energy admiring the view instead of worrying about shoes, consider doing the Comeragh Mountains on horseback (inquire in Clonmel). The technical term for the mountain hollows so common in the mild Comeraghs is "cwms" (KOOMS). Borrowed from the Welsh, it's the only word in the English language without a vowel.

Nire Valley Walk #1 to *12* (50p each at the Clonmel tourist office and Powers-the-Pot Hostel) are excellent waterproof maps explaining Comeragh day hikes from Clonmel. For more extensive hikes, begin from **Powers-the-Pot Hostel,** ½ mi. off the Munster Way (see **Clonmel,** p. 166). The best **map** for exploring the Comeraghs is sheet 75 of the Ordnance Series. If you want to wing it, head east from Powers-the-Pot and follow the ridges south. The land is mostly open, and in good weather it's relatively hard to get lost (still, make sure that someone knows you're out there).

■ Knockmealdown Mountains

Straddling the Tipperary/Waterford border 12 mi. south of Cahir, the Knockmealdown Mountains roll against the sky. *Knockmealdown Walks 1* to *4* (50p) are available at local tourist offices, including those in Clonmel and Clogheen. All four start at Clogheen (although walks 2 and 4 assume transportation to nearby carparks that mark the true beginnings of these walks). As an alternative, many hikers prefer to begin in the town of **Newcastle,** where tiny but locally renowned **Nugent's Pub** stands. For guided **tours,** contact Helen McGrath (tel. (052) 36359). Tours depart at noon on Sundays from the Newcastle Car Park (£5, other days available on request). If you wish to chart your own path, the best **map** to use is sheet 74 of the Ordnance Series. Sights to head for include the spectacular **Vee Road** south from Clogheen, which erupts with purple rhododendrons on its way to the **Knockmealdown Gap.** Just before the **Vee,** in the town of **Graigue,** thirsty pilgrims can stop in at **Ryan's Pub,** a charming little thatched building in the middle of a farm yard. At the pass of the Knockmealdown Gap, about two-thirds of the way to the top of the gap, the pines give way to heather and bracken, and a parking lot marks the path up to the top of **Sugarloaf Hill.** The walk takes about an hour and, on a clear day, affords a panorama of patchwork fields. From there, you can continue on to the Knockmealdown Peak, the highest in the range at 2609 ft. Beautiful (and supposedly bottomless) **Bay Loch,** on the road down to Lismore, is the stuff of legend. The affable and decidedly unofficious **tourist office** in Clogheen (tel. (052) 65258; across from the Vee Rd. turnoff) is generous with local maps and lore (open M-Sa 10am-6pm). Five minutes from the village on Cahir Rd., **Parsons Green** (tel. (052) 65290), part gardens and part **campsite,** offers river walks, boat rides, and pony rides (£6 per 2-person tent; kitchen; laundry £2). The idyllic **Kilmorna Farm Hostel** (tel. (058) 54315) in Lismore makes a far more luxurious if somewhat less convenient base for hiking in the range (see below).

■ Lismore

The disproportionate grandeur of Lismore's castle and cathedral reminds visitors of the once-thriving monastic scholarship of this sleepy little town. Lismore, actually in Co. Waterford, straddles the Blackwater River at the end of Vee Rd., across the Knockmealdown Mountains from Cahir.

PRACTICAL INFORMATION Bus Éireann stops at O'Dowd's Bar on West St. and runs to **Dungarvan** (1½hr., M, Th, and Sa 2 per day), **Waterford** (1¼hr., M-Sa 1 per day, F 2 per day), and **Cork** (1¼hr., F 1 per day). The best way to get to Lismore is by foot or bike over the Vee or along the Blackwater River. Hitching to Dungarvan is common. To get to Cork, hitchers first ride east to Fermoy, then head south on N8. Lismore's extremely helpful **tourist office** (tel. 54975) shares the old courthouse building with the **heritage center** (open June-Aug. daily 9am-6pm; Apr.-May and Sept.-Oct. M-Sa 9:30am-5:30pm, Su noon-5:30pm). The **phone code** is 058.

ACCOMMODATIONS, FOOD, AND PUBS One mile from Lismore, the **Kilmorna Farm Hostel** (tel. 54315) is the city-dweller's dream of a farm hostel. From town, walk up Chapel St. to the left of the Interpretive Centre, take the first left, and follow the signs (or call for a lift). Occasionally the family isn't around, but registered guests are welcome to head out and let themselves in. The 18th-century coach house is completed by gingham curtains, fluffy duvets, and solid wood beds built by a local craftsman. The working farm provides fresh eggs and supports cows, chickens, horses who line up straight in their stone stable, and no fewer than six dogs. There's also a common room with TV and a perfectly appointed kitchen. (3- to 6-bed dorms £8; doubles £19. Continental breakfast £3. Laundry £4. **Camping** £3 per person.) Cheerful rooms open up behind unpromising doorways in the **Red House Inn** (tel. 54248) across from the Interpretive Centre on Main St. (£15).

Lismore is less impressive on the restaurant front than on the hostel one. Stock up on supplies at **Londis,** Main St. (tel. 54279; open M-W and Sa 9am-6:30pm, Th 9am-7:30pm, F 9am-8:30pm). **Eamonn's Place,** Main St. (tel. 54025), is probably the best spot for a well-prepared Irish meal, served in their gorgeous, stone-walled beer garden (lunch entrees from £5, dinners £7-8; open for lunch M-F 12:30-2pm, dinner M-Su 6-9pm). **Madden's Bar,** East Main St. (tel. 54148), serves tasty, elegant lunches at similar prices (£4-6) and many a pint in their renovated pub. The **Red House Inn** (tel. (058) 54248) has occasional trad sessions on Fridays and a variety of music on Saturdays much anticipated by Lismore's younger crowd.

SIGHTS Swathed in foliage and looming grandly over the Blackwater River, **Lismore Castle** is stunning. Once a medieval fort and bishop's residence, the castle was extensively rebuilt and remodeled in the 19th century into an imaginative romantic's idea of what a castle should be. In 1814, the Lismore Crozier and the *Book of Lismore,* priceless artifacts thought to have been lost forever, were found hidden in the castle walls. The castle, a former home of Sir Walter Raleigh, was also the birthplace of 17th-century scientist Robert Boyle (of PV=nRT fame). The castle is privately owned, although the owners occasionally accommodate guests at an estimated £7,000 per week. Admire the castle from the bridge over the Blackwater River, because its **gardens** (tel. 54424) are not worth their admission fee. *(Open Apr.-Sept. daily 1:45-4:45pm. £2.50, under 16 £1.50.)* The bridge is also the starting point for the shady and peaceful **Lady Louisa's Walk** along the tree-lined Blackwater.

Locals whisper that a secret passage connects the castle to the Protestant **Lismore Cathedral,** Deanery Hill. Built in 1633 by Richard Boyle, Robert's father, the cathedral contains Ireland's only Edward Burne-Jones stained-glass window. Outside the cathedral, a large number of tombs are sealed with stone slabs in the ancient graveyard. These graves are a relic of Lismore's infamous past as a center for bodysnatching—the slabs ensured that the stiffs wouldn't be stolen. The cathedral did better at retaining historical markers. A collection of 9th- to 10th-century engraved commemorative stones and their ancient mass are set into one wall of the cathedral. For those who haven't tired of standing to read the history, the cathedral has one of the most interesting and even-handed accounts of the famine on display.

Lismore's **Heritage Centre** (tel. 54975), in the town square, includes a video presentation and a cursory exhibit highlighting the 1000-year-old *Book of Lismore,* a survey of Lismorian history, and local sites of interest. *(Open June-Aug. daily 9am-6pm, Apr.-May and Sept.-Oct. M-Sa 9:30am-5:30pm, Su noon-5:30pm. £2.50, students £2.)* Included in the admission price is a guided tour of the town. *(Tour only £1.50. Self-guided tour booklet £1.)* Those hankering for a break from the Guinness diet should stop in at the **West Waterford Vineyards** (tel. 54283), 5 mi. from Lismore off Dungarvan Rd. *(Open daily 10am-8pm; call ahead for wine tastings.)* The Vineyard produces a dry white wine in addition to seasonal fruit wines like pear and strawberry and will send you on your way armed with any local information you wish. Two miles from Lismore is a car park for the locally loved **Towerswalk.** From the castle, cross the bridge back and make a left. The towers and entrance gate to a grand castle were begun by Keily-Ussher, a local landlord, in the mid-19th century (see **The Fall of the House of Ussher**). Today there is a woodsy walk to "the Folly," which takes about one hour total from the car park.

The Fall of the House of Ussher

Rather Keily was the notoriously mean landlord of a huge piece of property near Lismore. During the mid-19th century, his most common management technique was forcing successful tenant farmers to abandon their land, then moving them higher in the mountains to enrich yet-unworked soil. When he married, his wife wanted a castle as elegant as the one at Lismore. Keily, or, rather, Keily Ussher—the second name added for an aristocratic ring—started to build a grand castle several miles from Lismore. Poor planning and keeping-up-with-the-Joneses, however, got the best of Keily Ussher, and he got only as far as the grand entrance arch before exhausting his funds. Perhaps his "Folly" was a learning experience; he is said to have warmed up a bit during the Famine, even granting leniency to tenants who pulled down their *own* house after he evicted them.

Wexford and Waterford

Geography makes Co. Wexford the front door to Ireland for anyone coming from France, Wales, or England. Ireland's invaders—from Vikings to Normans, Christians to modern backpackers—have begun their island-conquering business in Co. Wexford. Naturally, with so many people passing through, Wexford has been particularly prone to foreign influences. The county doesn't seem to mind lying prostrate under foreign invaders; they're used to it. The one time it did take a stand—in 1798 against the Brits—is much remembered and exaggerated. Away from the salty pubs and crowded streets of Wexford town, thin beaches stretch from dismal Rosslare Harbour and pop up again at the county's southwest edge, along Waterford Harbour and Tramore. County Waterford is dedicated to the production of industrial and agricul-

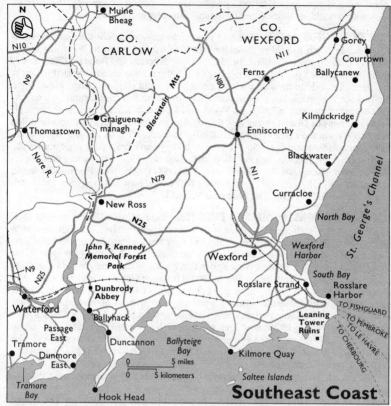

N

CO. CARLOW

CO. WEXFORD

N10

N9

Muine Bheag

Graiguenamanagh

Blackstairs Mts

Thomastown

Nore R.

N80

Ferns

Gorey

Courtown

Ballycanew

Kilmuckridge

Enniscorthy

Blackwater

N79

Curracloe

New Ross

N25

N11

North Bay

St. George's Channel

John F. Kennedy Memorial Forest Park

Wexford

Wexford Harbor

N9

N25

Dunbrody Abbey

Waterford

Ballyhack

Passage East

Tramore

Dunmore East

Duncannon

Ballyteige Bay

Rosslare Strand

South Bay

Rosslare Harbor

Leaning Tower Ruins

TO FISHGUARD

TO PEMBROKE

TO LE HAVRE

TO CHERBOURG

0   5 miles

0   5 kilometers

Kilmore Quay

Tramore Bay

Hook Head

Saltee Islands

Southeast Coast

SOUTHEAST IRELAND

tural goods. The commercial and cultural core of the Southeast is Waterford City, where thriving crystal and other sootier industries create an urban environment that is worlds apart from the sheep-speckled fields of the inner county. New Ross, with its fine hostels and urban amenities, is a good base for exploring the Southeast.

Slí Charman (SHLEE KAR-man), a.k.a. "An Slí," is a pathway that runs 135 mi. along Wexford's coast from the Co. Wicklow border through Rosslare and Wexford to Waterford Harbour, but it is not as rewarding as hiking the Wicklow Way. Maps hang out at major Bord Fáilte offices in Wexford and Waterford. Major roads in the region are the east-west N25 (Rosslare-Wexford-New Ross-Waterford), the north-south N11 (Wexford-Enniscorthy-Arklow-Dublin), and the N30 from Enniscorthy to New Ross.

■ Enniscorthy

The welcoming town of Enniscorthy perches on a hill 14 mi. north of Wexford. Much of the hilltop activity is hidden from view by the river below. The town is exceptionally conscious of its Republican history: in 1798, rebels, led by a local priest and their whiskey-induced courage, held the British at bay for 12 days and then suffered defeat at nearby Vinegar Hill (see **Rebellion, Union, Reaction (1775-1848)**, p. 57). Enniscorthy was one of the only towns to join Dublin's 1916 Easter Rising and the last to surrender (see **The Easter Rising (1914-1918)**, p. 60). Today, Enniscorthy sprawls across the river with roads recently refurbished courtesy of the E.U. Its comelier west side incorporates a cluster of historic buildings, including a 13th-century Norman castle with an eclectic museum inside. Although the introduction it provides to the political conflicts of Ireland's past may be a sobering experience, the 20 or so pubs within walking distance greatly diminish the chances of that.

PRACTICAL INFORMATION The N11 motorway passes straight through Enniscorthy, heading north to Arklow, Wicklow, and Dublin and south to Wexford. **Trains** connect Enniscorthy to **Dublin** (2hr., £10) in one direction and **Rosslare** (50min., £7) in the other (M-Sa 3 per day, Su 2 per day). From the railway station, cross the river at the Slaney Dr. bridge then take a left to reach the main shopping area. **Buses** leave the Bus Stop Shop on Templeshannon Quay, opposite the castle, running south to **Waterford** (2 per day, £7.50) and **Wexford** (4 per day, £3.50) and north through **Ferns** (10min.) to **Dublin** (4 per day, £7.50). The moderately informed **tourist office** (tel. 34699) is in the castle off Castle Hill Rd. (Directions? It's the big gray stone structure. Open M-Sa 10am-6pm, Su 2-5:30pm). If they can't help you, walk across the room and ask the folks in the craft shop. **AIB** Bank (tel. 33184) dispenses cash (open M-W and F 9:30am-4pm, Th 9:30am-5pm; 24hr. **ATM**). The **Irish Permanent Bank,** Market Sq. (tel. 35700), also has a 24-hour **ATM.** The **post office,** Abbey Quay (tel. 33545), is off Mill Pack Rd. The **phone code** is 054.

ACCOMMODATIONS, FOOD, AND PUBS Don Carr House, Bohreen Hill (tel. 33458), is well worth the five-minute walk from Market Square. Turn right past Murphy's Hotel then left on Bohreen Hill. Don Carr has a clean, homey feel and two sumptuous sunrooms where breakfast is served. (£16, with bath £17.50.) At **Aldemar,** Summerhill (tel. 33668), Mrs. Agnes Barry's hospitality and pleasant company justify the 15-minute walk from Main St. Go up Bohreen Hill, then look for signs. (Singles £17; doubles £30. Open June-Sept.) **P. J. Murphy's B&B,** Main St. (tel. 33522), not to be confused with Murphy's Hotel, is just steps away from Market Sq. Rooms are small but have TVs, and you won't have to walk far for a pint—Murphy's Pub is right downstairs. (Singles £15-18; doubles £30, with bath £34.) The nearest hostels are in New Ross and Courtown; the latter makes a good stopover for the Dublin-bound. The **Anchorage Hostel,** Poulshone, Courtown Harbour (tel. (055) 25335), is a former B&B with great beaches nearby (dorms £7.50; private rooms £9; open May-Oct.).

Food eagerly awaits you at various pubs or at the **L&N Supermarket** (tel. 34541) in the shopping center on Mill Park Rd. off Abbey Sq. (open M-W and Sa 9am-6pm, Th-F 9am-9pm). Vegetarians or those seeking home-baked goodies should try **The Baked Potato,** 18 Rafter St. (tel. 34085), for hot, inexpensive food (open M-Sa 9am-6pm). Just across the street at **Karen's Kitchen,** 11 Rafter St. (tel. 36488), you can delve into delicious dishes (most entrees £2.50-4.50). Twice-awarded Wexford County "pub of the year," **The Antique Tavern** (tel. 33428) is crammed with artifacts from the depths of Enniscorthy's Republican past. The sign out front of this cozy spot explicitly forbids "three card tricksters" and bandits (you know who you are). **Rackards,** 23 Rafter St. (tel. 33747), with its mellow atmosphere, is currently the hippest spot in Enniscorthy. Zesty lunch is served noon to 3pm (prawns in rich Marie Rose sauce with chips £4.60). **Kileen's,** Slaney St. (tel. 35935), dishes up roast chicken, potatoes, and vegetables (£4). They also have trad sessions on Saturday nights.

SIGHTS The **Walking Tour of Enniscorthy,** given by the fabulous Maura Flannery, is fun and informative. (*Tours in English, French, or Spanish leave from the craft shop at 10am and 1pm. £2.50, children £1.25. Ask for senior discounts; mention Let's Go for more savings. Info available at the tourist office.*) The one-hour tours reveal the town's dirty little secrets of its prestigious past. Find out about the time in 1649 that Enniscorthy women got Cromwell's soldiers drunk and killed them, or how John P. Holland, a native son, invented the submarine—kind of the way Da Vinci did. The Norman castle houses the tourist office, but the **Wexford County Museum** (tel. 35926) fills the bulk of the building. (*Open June-Sept. M-Sa 10am-1pm and 2-6pm, Su 2-5:30pm; Oct.-Nov. and Feb.-May daily 2-5:30pm; Dec.-Jan. Su 2-5pm. £2, ages 13-18 £1, under 13 50p.*) The museum chronicles Co. Wexford's collective stream of consciousness rather than an historical narrative. Initially a 13-object display in 1960, curators have stuffed the castle from eaves to dungeon with such odd bits as ship figureheads and a collection of international police patches. The exhibits feature original letters and belongings of the principle players of the 1798 and 1916 risings.

St. Aiden's Cathedral, Cathedral St., uphill from Murphy's Hotel, was built in 1860 under the close supervision of architect Augustus Pugin, who littered Ireland's towns with his neo-Gothic creations. In Market Sq., a statue commemorates Father Murphy, who led the town in rebellion in 1798. The priest had been something of a Loyalist before an angry mob threatened to burn down his church. He was instantly affected with revolutionary zeal and promptly put himself at the head of the rowdy crowd.

If you're around until the last weekend in June, you'll harvest the annual **Strawberry Fair.** Ten days of festival and fructose redden Enniscorthy's streets. Pub theater performances draw the literati, while "Lego Competitions" attract the child in each fair-goer. The **Blues Festival** in mid-September features three days of entertainment by locally and internationally renowned musicians. Contact Maura Flannery (tel. 36800) for information.

■ New Ross

New Ross's greatest advantage is its location as an ideal point from which to base excursions around Ireland's southeast. Waterford, the Hook, Wexford, and Kilkenny are all within easy reach. New Ross also has a tidy list of sights to tick off, most involving the Irish exodus and favored great-grandson John F. Kennedy. The Dunbody, a coffin ship replica cum genealogical center, is a must-see.

ORIENTATION AND PRACTICAL INFORMATION Most of the activity bubbles along the water on The Quay. The other major thorough fares are Mary St., which extends uphill from the bridge, and South St., which runs parallel to The Quay one block inland. New Ross is on N25 (Wexford-Cork Rd.) and N30 (Enniscorthy-Waterford Rd.). Hitchers can find plenty of rides on either but have the best luck in the morning or late afternoon. **Bus Éireann** runs from The Mariners Inn, The Quay, to **Dublin** (3hr., M-Sa 3 per day, Su 2 per day, £8), **Rosslare Harbour** (1hr., 3 per day, £7), and **Waterford** (35min., M-Sa 7 per day, Su 5 per day, £3). The New Ross **tourist office,** 22 The Quay (tel. 421857), just down the street from the SuperValu, is small but informative and offers the free *New Ross Town and Area Guide* with map. (Open June-Aug. M-F 9am-8pm, Sa 10am-8pm, Su noon-6pm; Sept.-May M-F 9am-5pm.) The **Bank of Ireland,** The Quay (tel. 421267), is just steps away from the bus stop and tourist office (open M and W-F 10am-5pm, Tu 10am-4pm, Sa 10am-4pm). The **AIB** on South St. has a 24-hour **ATM** (bank open M 10am-5pm, Tu-F 10am-4pm). The **post office** (tel. 421261) delivers on Charles St., off The Quay (open M-F 9am-5:30pm, Sa 10am-4pm). The **phone code** is 051.

ACCOMMODATIONS **Mac Murrough Farm Hostel** (tel. 421383; email machostel@tinet.ie) is an idyllic reason to be in (well, near) New Ross. Follow Mary St. uphill to the end. Turn left, then make the first right down the wide street. Pass the cross and take a left at the supermarket, then a right at the Statoil Station; from there, follow the signs for a mile to the hostel. Call if you need to be picked up. If you've never stayed in a hostel, now is the time. The sheep give a rowdy greeting and the owner gives a hoot. This is the best place to stay in New Ross and the best value (dorms £7). In case you really must stay closer to town and pay more, **Inishross House,** 96 Mary St. (tel. 21335), offers well-kept, 70s-style rooms in the center of town (singles £18; doubles £32). **Riversdale House,** William St. (tel. 422515), provides comfort just a short walk out of the center of town. Follow South St. all the way to William St., then turn left up the hill. Friendly owners take pride in their commanding view of town. (Singles £21; doubles £34.)

FOOD AND PUBS **L&N SuperValue,** The Quay (tel. 421963), is your generic grocer (open M-W and Sa 9am-6pm, Th-F 9am-9pm). **The Sweeney,** Mary St. (tel. 421963), is a cozy deli with a room full of palm trees and a menu full of sandwiches (£1.25; open M-Tu and Th-Sa 9am-6pm and 6:30-9:30pm, W 9am-2pm and 6:30-9:30pm, Su noon-

8pm). **The Mariner's Inn,** 16 The Quay (tel. 421 325), is an early house, unofficial tourist office, bus agent, and, last but not least, a fun pub. It's a mellow place where people talk, play chess, nibble sandwiches (£1.50), gaze at the huge collection of foreign money, and drink (trad Fridays, also Sa-Su in summer). **John V's,** 5 The Quay (tel. 425188), has an extensive menu (entrees £4), karaoke Tuesdays, and belly wobble Wednesdays. The pub is bright and airy with a strong group of regulars who, if the afternoon is particularly slow, can sometimes be caught watching *Sesame Street* on the big screen. You can travel in Barrow style on **The Galley** (tel. 421723), which runs daily restaurant cruises from New Ross to Waterford. Eat lunch (2hr.; £11, £5 for cruise only; Apr.-Oct. at 12:30pm), tea (2hr.; £5, £4 for cruise only; June-Aug. at 3pm), or dinner (2-3hr.; £20, £9 for cruise only; April-Sept. at 7pm).

SIGHTS New Ross isn't much of a city for museums, and most of its historical sights are unimpressive. The site of the **Tholsel** ("toll stall"), South St., originally held a Norse tollbooth. The original structure collapsed in the mid-1700s, and the current Tholsel, which now serves as the town hall, was built in 1749. Strongbow's grandson founded **St. Mary's Church,** off Mary St., in the 13th century. Even if you don't go in, at least hang out with the crows in the eerily beautiful graveyard. Mrs. Culleton, at 6 Church St., four doors down from the church, can provide the key and give you a booklet detailing the significance of the stone structures inside. Irish-Americans and Irish locals wanted to further honor the memory of JFK and decided to say it with flowers. They found 4500 different ways, which are displayed in a 400-acre thesaurus of flora, **The John F. Kennedy Arboretum** (tel. 388171), 7 mi. south of New Ross on the Ballyhack Rd. *(Open daily May-Aug. 10am-8pm; Apr. and Sept. 10am-6:30pm; Oct.-Mar. 10am-5pm. Last admission 45min. before closing. £2, seniors £1.50, children £1, family £5. Tours £1.50.)* The park packs preposterous proportions of trees and shrubs (all labeled) and 500 different rhododendrons, all dedicated to the memory of Ireland's favorite U.S. President. A small café doubles as a gift shop, and a playground entertains children.

New Ross's greatest sight is the **Dunbrody,** an exact replica of a coffin ship that sailed from New Ross in 1849 carrying huddled and starving Irish as human ballast. Docked in New Ross Harbour, this impressive sight is 176 ft. in length, with two decks and three masts. The Dunbrody will spend much of 1999 on a voyage to American ports but should return home before 2000.

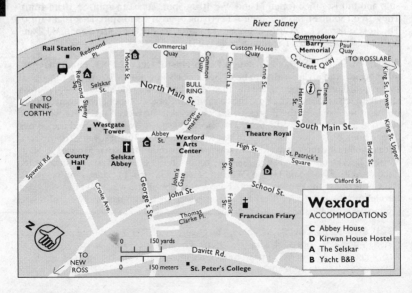

Wexford
ACCOMMODATIONS
C Abbey House
D Kirwan House Hostel
A The Selskar
B Yacht B&B

■ Wexford

The sidewalks of densely populated Wexford are so narrow that everyone mills around on Main St. or in the numerous alleys that twist upward from the quays. Cars have to bow to the flocks of mothers pushing baby carriages down the middle of Main St. by noon. The Twin Churches punctuate the skyline of the huddled harbor city. Excellent pubs and restaurants now fill the stone passageways built in the 12th century when the Normans conquered the Viking settlement of *Waesfjord*. The prominent Bull Ring and surrounding Norman ruins remain visual reminders of the history that features the likes of Henry II and Oliver Cromwell.

ORIENTATION AND PRACTICAL INFORMATION

The quays hum with the construction of the town's new **marina**—the dark water-front pubs and ambitious tourist office that now sit here look forward to increased consumer, not construction worker, foot traffic. One block inland, lively **Main St.** twists and turns. Although they seem to careen off in different directions, North and South Main St. are joined by the **Bull Ring** at the town's center. Just off the water on the northern edge of town is the bus and rail station. The Franciscan Friary, tall and inviolate at the top of the hill, surveys the older city and train station to its right. Hitchers out of Wexford town recommend extending one's digit before noon when the odds of getting a lift are higher. Hitchhikers to Dublin (N11) stand at the Wexford Bridge off the quays; those bound for Rosslare head south along the quays to Trinity St. Hitchers heading to Cork, New Ross, or Waterford continue down Westgate and turn left onto Hill St. then right onto John St. Upper (N25). N11 and N25 merge near the city, so savvy hitchers make a point of specifying either the Dublin Rd. (N11) or the Waterford Rd. (N25). Hitching is rarer these days; as always, be wary.

Trains: North Station, Redmond Sq. (tel. 22522), a 5min. walk along the quays from Crescent Quay. Booking offices open around departure times; buy tickets on the train when the office is closed. Information available from 7am until last departure. Trains hustle to Connolly Station in **Dublin** (3hr., M-Sa 3 per day, Su 2 per day, £11) and to **Rosslare Harbour** (30min., M-Sa 4 per day, Su 3 per day, £3).

Buses: At the train station. Buses run to **Dublin** (2½hr., 6 daily) and to **Rosslare Harbour** (20min., M-Sa 7 per day, Su 5 per day, £1.25). Buses to and from **Limerick** (2 daily) connect with Irish Ferries and Stena-Sealink sailings. From mid-July to Aug., buses run directly to **Galway** (6hr.) and other western points via **Limerick** (3½hr.) and **Waterford** (1hr.).

Tourist Office: Crescent Quay (tel. 23111), in the Chamber of Commerce building. Scars and blemishes attest to the centuries of sailors who have sharpened their knives on the windowsills of the building. The free, ad-packed *Wexford: Front Door to Ireland* and *Welcome to Wexford* offer handy maps. Open July-Aug. M-Sa 9:30am-6pm, Su 11am-5pm; Sept.-June M-Sa 9:30am-6pm.

Banks: AIB, South Main St.; 24hr. **ATM. TSB,** 73-75 Main St. (tel. 41922). Both open M 10am-5pm, Tu-F 10am-4pm.

Taxi: P.K. Cabs, 9 William St. (tel. 47999, mobile (088) 509420), and **Jim's Cabs,** 2 Slaney St. (tel. 47108). Both open 24hr. and have a £2.50 max. fare within the city.

Bike Rental: Hayes Cycle Shop, 108 South Main St. (tel. 22462), Raleigh touring bikes £7 per day, £35 per week; £40 or ID deposit. Open M-Sa 9am-6pm. **The Bike Shop,** North Main St. (tel. 22514), £6 per day, £35 per week; £30 deposit; extra charge and deposit to drop off elsewhere in the country. Open M-Sa 9am-6pm.

Laundry: My Beautiful Launderette, St. Peter's Sq. (tel 24317), up Peters St. from South Main St. Wash £1.85, dry 80p, soap 40p. Open in summer M-Sa 10am-6pm; in winter M-Sa 10am-9pm. Access via video store next door Su and holidays 3-8pm.

Pharmacy: Seven pharmacies along Main St. rotate Sunday and late hours. All open M-Sa 9am-1pm and 2-6pm.

Emergency: Dial 999; no coins required. **Garda:** Roches Rd. (tel. 22333).

Hospital: Wexford General Hospital, New Town Rd. (tel. 42233), on N25.

Post Office: Anne St. (tel. 22587). Open M and W-F 9am-5:30pm, Tu 9:30am-5:30pm.

Phone Code: 053.

ACCOMMODATIONS

There are a number of nice B&Bs in town as well as a hostel. If the B&Bs listed are full, ask the proprietors for recommendations or look along N25 (Rosslare Rd.).

Kirwan House Hostel, 3 Mary St. (tel. 21208; email kirwanhostel@tinet.ie). Small common room, but the sleeping quarters are nifty. Staying here will save you enough money for a few pints, and it's within post-pub stumbling distance. Launderette next door. **Internet access** £2 per 20min. Dorms £7.50-8; doubles £20.

Abbey House, 34 Abbey St. (tel. 24409), flaunts a fantastic location and comfy quarters. Doubles with bath and TV £34.

The Selskar (tel. 23349), corner of North Main and Selskar St. Ideal location. A double and twin on each floor share a bathroom, kitchen, and sitting area with TV. Be delicate with the showers, and don't wait for breakfast—they don't serve it. Bread and cereal are left out for you to prepare your own grub. Doubles £30.

The Yacht B&B, 2 Monck St. (tel. 22338), offers clean, cushy rooms above the Yacht Pub overlooking the River Slaney. Singles £19; doubles £30.

Carraig Donn, Mrs. Daly, New Town Ct. (tel. 42046), off New Town Rd. (Waterford Rd.). Call from town for pick up, or trek 15min. from Main St. Large rooms and Brady Bunch-decor. Singles £18; doubles £30. Wheelchair accessible.

Ferrybank Caravan and Camping Park (tel. 44378 or 43274). On the eastern edge of town, across from Dublin Rd. Take the bridge and continue straight to the camping site. Beautiful ocean view, clean area. £6 per 1-person tent; £8 per 2-person tent. Showers £1. Laundry £1.50. Open Easter-Oct.

FOOD

Dunnes Store, Redmond Sq. (tel. 45688), has a wide selection of meats and sells clothes, too (open M-Tu and Sa 9am-6pm, W-F 9am-9pm, Su noon-6pm). **L&N Superstore** (tel. 22290), on Custom House Quay, and **Crazy Prices** (tel. 24788), on Crescent Quay, are large supermarkets. **Greenacres,** 56 North Main St. (tel. 24788), is Wexford's gourmet grocery. In general, restaurant prices start to go up after 6pm.

The Sky and the Ground, 112 South Main St. (tel. 21273). This pub serves superb sandwiches (most main courses £4-5; food served noon-9pm). Music most nights: trad M, Th; blues Tuesdays; acoustic W, Su; DJ F-Sa. If you feel like splurging a bit, head upstairs and feast at new **Heavens Above** (most entrees £6-8.50).

Tim's Tavern, 51 South Main St. (tel. 23861), offers only the finest pub grub, but they only offer it Th-Su. The menu is a short list of hits. Tim's has won national awards for dishes like avocado, pear, and crab, stuffed loin of pork, and bacon and cabbage—all served with vegetables and potatoes. Entrees £5-6.50. Similar food (more veggies, more sauces, more expensive) for dinner. Lunch served daily noon-5pm, dinner 6-10pm. Trad Wednesday and Saturday at 9:30pm.

La Cuisine, 80 North Main St. (tel. 24986). The glass jars gently stacked on wooden shelves give this bakery and restaurant an old school feel. A quiet spot for a quick cuppa' and scones. Entrees £4.50-6. Open M-Sa 9am-6pm.

PUBS

The Centenary Stores, Charlotte St. (tel. 24424). "The Stores," a pub and dance club housed within the brick walls and soaring ceilings of a former warehouse, caters to a classy crowd of twentysomethings. Excellent trad on Sunday mornings as well as Tu-W nights. Blues and folk on Monday nights. A DJ spins dance music and top 40 Th-Su nights 11pm-2am. Cover £5.

The Sky and the Ground (tel. 21273) is a solid pub as well as a restaurant (see above). Thump the hardwood furniture to make your point to a buzzing crowd of mixed ages. Trad and acoustic sessions.

The Tackroom, The Bull Ring. Muted voices, soft pine, and friendly people sometimes spill outside on cool evenings. Sorry, you can't borrow the fishing rods.

O'Faolain's (oh PHWAY lawns), 11 Monck St. (tel. 23877). The most raucous of Wexford's pubs. A crowd of all ages mingles here without generational strife. In case you have one too many and lose your sense of direction, there's a signpost inside directing you to all nearby towns. The *bodhrán* and *uilleann* appear on Sundays (12:30-2pm) and Monday nights. Mixed music Tu, Su.

SIGHTS

The historical society (tel. 22311) runs free **walking tours** departing from White's Hotel at 8:15pm. Tours depend on weather and interest—it's best to call around 6pm for availability. *Welcome to Wexford* (free from the tourist office) details a 45-minute self-guided walking tour. The remains of the Norman **city wall** run the length of High St. **Westgate Tower,** at the intersection of High and Westgate St., is the only one of the wall's six original towers that still stands. You can even see the barred and blackened cell that served as a lock-up for renegades. The tower gate now holds the **Westgate Heritage Centre** (tel. 46506), where an audio-visual show that recounts the history of Wexford with fire and canon special effects will blow your mind. *(Open July-Aug. M-Sa 10am-2pm and 2:30-5:30pm, Su 2-6pm; Sept.-June M-Sa 10am-2pm and 2:30-5:30pm. £1, children 50p.)* The center also offers walking **tours** of Wexford. *(1½-2hr. Call ahead to book or join a group. £2.50.)* Next door, the **Selskar Abbey,** site of King Henry II's extended penance for Thomas Becket's murder, now acts as a windowbox for lush wildflowers. *(Same hours as the center.)* Enter through the tall, narrow wicket gate by the center. The dark and frightening tower stairwell leads up to a precarious view of the town and the bay.

An open area between North and South Main St. marks the Bull Ring. Bull baiting was inaugurated in 1621 by the town's butcher guild as a promotional device. The mayor got the hide while the poor got the meat. "The Pikeman," a statue of a stalwart peasant fearlessly brandishing a sharp instrument, commemorates the 1798 uprising (see **History,** p. 56). Get your stuffed Harvey the Friendly Rebel, a smiling bunny holding a pike and draped in the tricolor, at the tourist office, the exclusive distributor. The bottom of Crescent Quay, which held ship repair yards until the early 1900s, is reputed to be cobblestoned, although nobody has gone down to check. Facing the sea stands the statue of Commodore John Barry, Wexford-born founder of the U.S. Navy. The **Friary Church** in the Franciscan Friary, School St., houses the "Little Saint." This creepy effigy of young St. Adjutor shows the wounds inflicted by the martyr's Roman father. Franciscan monks have lived in town since 1240—keep a lookout for peaceful fellows in brown robes.

ENTERTAINMENT

Many of the pubs in town offer nightly music. For more detailed information, check *The Wexford People* (85p), which lists events for all of Co. Wexford immediately after the "Farm Scene" section. The funky **Wexford Arts Centre,** in the Cornmarket (tel. 23764 or 24544), presents free visual arts and crafts exhibitions; evening performances of music, dance, and drama also take place in the center throughout the year. "Open mic" night features poetry readings and songs. (Open M-Sa 10am-6pm. Performances June-Aug. W 8:30pm. £2.) The **Theatre Royal,** High St. (tel. 22400; box office tel. 22144), couched inconspicuously off Main St., produces performances throughout the year, specializing in the acclaimed **Wexford Festival Opera** during the last two weeks in October. For these festivities, three obscure but deserving operas are rescued from the artistic attic and performed in an intimate setting. (Open M-F 11am-5pm. Opera tickets £36-48, available from early June. Afternoon, late-night, and operatic scenes £5-10.) **St. Iberius's Church,** Main St. (tel. John Bayley 22936), offers lunchtime opera concerts during the festival and free lunchtime concerts throughout the year. Call or stop by for a schedule.

■ Near Wexford: The Slobs

The **North and South Slobs** are messy, but in a delightful way: "slob" is the term for the cultivated mudflats to the north and south of Wexford Harbour that are protected from flooding rivers by dikes. The Slobs are internationally famous for the rare geese who winter there at the **Wexford Wildfowl Reserve** (tel. 23129). Ten thousand of Greenland's white-fronted geese (one-third of the world population) descend on the Slobs from October to April, cohabiting with other rare geese, some from as far away as Siberia and Iceland. Resident Irish birds arrive in the summer and mellow the Slobs (although mating along the channels still manages to generate some excitement). The **Reserve Centre** will help visitors spot specific species. *(Open daily mid-Apr. to Sept. 9am-6pm; Oct.-Apr. 10am-5pm. Free.)* The Reserve is on the North Slob, 2 mi. north of Wexford town. Take Castlebridge/Gorey Rd. to well-signposted Ardcavan Ln.

■ Rosslare Harbour

Rosslare Harbour refers to the over-equipped village from which the ferries to France and Wales depart; Rosslare is the less important town between Rosslare Harbour and Wexford on N25. Rosslare Harbour's primary purpose is to receive or bid farewell to Ireland's visitors and voyagers, and it is best seen from the porthole of a departing ferry. Ferries from Rosslare Harbour run daily to Britain and every other day to France. **Hitching** anywhere around the ferry port can be very difficult. Neither locals surfeited with tourists nor a foreign family of four in an overstuffed car are likely to pick you up; the road ends in Rosslare Harbour anyway.

PRACTICAL INFORMATION

Trains: Office (tel. 33114 or 33592) open daily 6am-9:30pm. Trains run from the ferry port to **Dublin** (2hr., M-Sa 3 per day, Su 2 per day, £10.50), **Limerick** (2¾hr., M-Sa 2 per day, £12), **Waterford** (1¼hr., M-Sa 3 per day, £6), and **Wexford** (20min., M-Sa 3 per day, Su 2 per day, £2).

Buses: Buses stop at J. Pitt's Convenience Store by the ferry port in Kilrane and at the Catholic church in Rosslare Harbour. Buses run twice per day via **Waterford** to **Galway** (£16), **Killarney** (£15), and **Tralee** (£16). Also to **Cork** (M-Sa 3 per day, £13), **Limerick** (M-Sa 2 per day, Su 3 per day, £12), **Waterford** (M-Su 3 per day, £8.80), **Dublin** (3hr., M-Sa 6 per day, Su 5 per day, £9), and **Wexford** (20min., M-Sa 9 per day, Su 8 per day, £2.50).

Ferries: Trains and buses often connect with the ferries. **Bus Éireann** and **Irish Rail** have desks in the terminal (tel. 33592). Open daily 6:30am-9:45pm. There is also a **bureau de change** in the ferry port. **Stena Sealink/Sea Lynx** (tel. 33115, recorded info 33330; fax 33534; office open daily 7am-10pm) and **Irish Ferries/Britain and Ireland line** (tel. 33158; fax 33544) serve the ferry port. Open daily 7am-10pm. For info on ferries from Rosslare Harbour to England and France see **By Ferry,** p. 34.

Tourist Office: The Rosslare area has 2 tourist offices. The manic-panic **ferry office** (tel. 33623) offers free, photocopied maps covered with strange, meaningless numbers and **TravelSave** stamps. Open 10am-8pm. The **Kilrane office** (tel. 33232), 1mi. from the harbor on Wexford Rd. in Kilrane, is really a large souvenir shop, with only a single fuzzy, copied map of Rosslare Harbour for office use. Open May to mid-Sept. daily noon-8pm.

Bank: Currency exchange at the **Bank of Ireland** (tel. 33304), on Kilrane Rd. Open M-F 10am-12:30pm and 1:30-4pm; **ATM.**

Taxis: To get to B&Bs outside of town, call **Paddy's Taxis** (tel. 33533).

Emergency: Dial 999; no coins required.

Post Office: (tel. 33207) in the **SuperValu,** between produce and checkout. **Bureau de change.** Open M-F 9am-1pm and 2-5:30pm, Sa 9am-1pm.

Phone Code: 053.

ACCOMMODATIONS

The nature and function of Rosslare Harbour makes accommodations here convenient but inevitably mercenary. Exhausted ferry passengers fill both good and mediocre beds, while the better places to stay in Kilmore Quay and Wexford go untenanted. B&Bs swamp N25 just outside of Rosslare Harbour. There is a noticeable difference between approved and non-approved B&Bs on N25—in Rosslare, more than anywhere in Ireland, take the Bord Fáilte shamrock as a measure of quality.

Mrs. O'Leary's Farmhouse, Killilane (tel. 33134), off N25 in Kilrane, a 15min. drive from town. Set on a gloriously rural 100-acre farm, Mrs. O'Leary's place is a holiday unto itself. A grassy lane leads to a secluded beach. Call for pickup from the ferry or the train station. £15, with bath £17.

Marianella B&B (tel. 33139), off N25 across from the pharmacy. Rosemarie Sinner's house lacks a great view, but she welcomes you with tea and cookies in each room. Singles £19; doubles £32, with bath £36. Spacious family room available.

Clifford House, Michael Delaney (tel. 33226; email cliffordhouse@tinet.ie), Barryville. Nestled on a quiet cul-de-sac, Clifford's conveniently located house boasts bright, comfortable rooms. As you sip your tea, gaze out at the sea and watch the ferries arrive and depart. £16, with bath £17. Open Apr.-Sept.

Rosslare Harbour Youth Hostel (An Óige/HI), Goulding St. (tel. 33399; fax 33624). Take a right at the top of the steps on the hill opposite the ferry terminal, then head left around the far corner of the Hotel Rosslare; the hostel is down the street across from the supermarket. Offers decent showers, cramped bunks, cinderblock walls, and a collection of continental youth. Michelle, the wonderwoman who runs the place by herself, may remind you of Basil Fawlty at times. June-Aug. dorms £7.50; Sept.-May £6.50. Sheets £1.50. Midnight curfew.

FOOD

The restaurants in Rosslare Harbour tend to be expensive. The **SuperValu supermarket** (tel. 33107), a tastefully laid out grocery store with a nice selection, is opposite the Rosslare Harbour Youth Hostel and popular with the hostel crowd (open M-W and Sa 8am-6pm, Th-F 8am-7pm, Su 9am-1pm). The pub in the **Devereux Hotel** (tel. 33216), just up from the ferry terminal, has good pub grub for reasonable prices. A large lunch can be gulped down for £4.

■ Kilmore Quay and The Saltee Islands

Thirteen miles southwest of Rosslare Harbour on Forlorn Point, the small fishing village of Kilmore Quay charms with its beautiful beaches, thatched roofs, and whitewashed seaside cottages. Information is available at the **Stella Maris Community Centre** (tel. 29922), which also has private showers (£1), a game room, and a wonderful coffee shop with huge meals for about £3.50 (open daily 9am-2pm; center open daily 9am-10pm). The village berths its **Maritime Museum** (tel. 29655) in the lightship *Guillemot* (light because it has no motor) by the community center. The tour, offered in English, French, and German, encompasses Irish naval history and the history of the town. (Open June-Sept. daily noon-6pm. £2, students, seniors, and children £1.) **Dick Hayes** (tel. 29704) offers to bring you aboard for deep-sea angling and reef-fishing. The **Kilmore Seafood Festival** (tel. 26959) runs around the second week of July with loads of cheap seafood, music, and dancing.

To reach Kilmore Quay from Rosslare Harbour, take Wexford Rd. to Tagoat and turn left; from Wexford, take Rosslare Rd., turn right at Piercetown, and continue 4 mi. to town. **Bus Éireann** runs between Wexford and Kilmore Quay (30min., M-Sa 3-4 per day, £4 return). **Doyle's Hackney & Bus Hire** (tel. 29624) runs a shuttle into Wexford leaving at 11am and returning at 2pm (Tu, Th, F). He is also available for hackney service 24 hours. (A hackney is similar to a taxi; see **Getting Around,** p. 36). Bike rental is available at **Kilmore Quay Bike Hire** (tel. 29781) at Island View House (£7 per day, £30 per week). The **phone code** is 053.

For the freshest of fresh seafood, take yourself across from the Maritime Museum to the **Silver Fox** (tel. 29888; open M-Sa 12:30-9:30pm, Su 12:30-9pm; lunch specials 12:30-2:50pm). **The Haven** (tel. 29979), 100 yd. down from the first right after the post office, has a water view, several kinds of tea and coffee, and an elegant and friendly proprietor, Betty Walsh (doubles with bath £30). Mrs. Deirdre Brady's **Castle View** (tel. 29765) has friendly and bright surroundings right on Wexford Rd. and within a stone's throw of a random castle that was plopped down here some time ago (doubles £30). The budget traveler dead set on passing up the wonderful B&Bs might want to try the **Kilturk Independent Hostel** (tel. 29883), 1 mi. from town on Wexford Rd., between Kilmore Quay and Kilmore Town. The hostel is very basic but clean. (Dorms £6.50; private room £8. Sheets £1.) Bus Éireann stops at the hostel by request on its way from Wexford to Kilmore Quay.

Kilmore Quay sends boat trips out to the two **Saltee Islands,** formerly pagan pilgrimage sites and now Ireland's largest bird sanctuary, with a winged population nearing 50,000. These puffin palaces and razorbill refuges are owned by Prince Michael Salteens (who bears no likeness to the cracker). A narrow ridge of rock once connected the smaller island to the mainland. This land bridge, called **St. Patrick's Bridge,** was used for driving cattle to the island for pasture. Due to natural erosion, the land bridge is now submerged. Weather permitting, boats leave the mainland each morning, stranding you for picnics, ornithology, and bonding with gray seals. **Declan Bates** (tel. 29682) heads out daily at around 11am for the half-hour trip and will pick you up at 4pm (Apr.-Oct., £12). Call ahead. If you're really nuts for puffins, he'll do longer cruises, too.

THE HOOK

Locals refer to the coastal region between Ballyhack and Tramore as the Hook, a peaceful area notable for its historic abbeys, forts, and lighthouses. Sunny landscapes draw travelers for deep-sea angling in Waterford Harbour and Tramore Bay. Although stretches of scenery make for quiet, if challenging, bike rides, the Hook is perhaps best explored with a car.

■ Ballyhack and Arthurstown

The profile that Ballyhack shows its cross-channel neighbor, Passage East, is dominated by 15th-century **Ballyhack Castle** (tel. 389468 or 389164). Built by the Crusading Order of the Knights Hospitalers in the 1450s, the castle was recently restored by the town and now houses an unimpressive heritage center. The heritage center is the only good place to get information on The Hook, but the Crusader exhibit warrants only a few minutes of your time. (Open mid-June to Sept. daily 10am-1pm and 2-6pm. £1, students 70p, senior 40p.) The repulsive face set in the seaward wall of the castle had been stolen from nearby Tintern Abbey and is locally known as Cromwell's face.

Dunbrody Abbey (tel. 388603), 2 mi. from Ballyhack on New Ross Rd. (although the road from Arthurstown is better maintained), is a magnificent Cistercian ruin dating from 1190. Go through the turnstile on the left side of the road, cross the field, and climb on in. Almost wholly intact, this abbey lets you wander through staircases and little rooms ideal for a game of medieval hide-and-seek. (Open daily 10am-6pm. £1.50, children £1, families £3.) Across the road, the **visitor's center** (tel. 389468) sits among the ruins of a castle once associated with the abbey. The center features a dollhouse replica of what the castle would have looked like fully furnished and intact. An increasingly impressive **hedge-row maze,** planted in 1992, began with only 2 ft. high bushes, making it difficult to get lost. They now stand 6 ft., however, and should grow to 15. (Open July-Aug. 10am-7pm; Sept.-June 10am-6pm. £1.50, children £1.)

As you exit the ferry, take a right and follow the *Slí Charman* (SHLEE KAR-man), a coastal walking path to reach **Arthurstown.** The trail leads almost all the way to Dublin, but long before Dublin (in fact, just a few minutes from the ferry) you'll find the town, which offers accommodations, a pub, opulent ocean views, and little else. **SuperValu,** just outside town on Duncannon Hill, is the only grocery store (open M-Sa 9am-6pm, Su noon-6pm). The only affordable competition is the prepared grub at the **King's Bay Inn** (tel. 389173), the local pub, which also sports a **bureau de change.** The first left coming from Ballyhack, across from Marsh Mere House, is the entrance to the **Arthurstown Youth Hostel (An Óige/HI)** (tel. 389441), which was built to the exacting specifications of the English coastguard and stayed that way for two centuries. Stand in front of the first house to see perspective in action. The gentleman warden has a fascination for and encyclopedic knowledge of all things naval, and he's stayed in virtually every hostel in the country. Rooms are small but clean. (Dorms £6.50, under 18 £4.50. Curfew 10:30pm. Lockout 10:30am-5pm. Kitchen open 7:30-10am. Open June-Sept.) **Glendine House** (tel./fax 389258), on Duncannon Hill, is a large, Georgian-style house surrounded by acres of green grass. Glendine is hard to miss and it's recognizable by the horses prancing in the front lawn. The rooms are huge, beautifully decorated, and very comfortable—you'll be tempted to move in. The owners can arrange **bike rentals.** (Singles £20; doubles £36.)

■ Duncannon and Hook Head

South of Arthurstown, the sunny and scenic **Hook Head Peninsula** begins. A circuit of the towns, ruins, and sea views of the peninsula is best done by car, but it's possible for brave bikers. From Arthurstown, head east on Duncannon Rd. and keep an eye out for the sharp right labeled "Duncannon." One mile will bring you to town.

    Duncannon Fort (tel. 325208) perches on the cliffs at the edge of the village. The fort was attacked by the Spanish Armada in 1588, Cromwell in 1649, William of Orange in 1690, and the United Irishmen rebels in 1798. The original Elizabethan structures were used right up to the abandonment of the fort in 1945. The Irish army took it over and refitted it during World War II, and it served as their summer camp until 1986. Today, the tired site is being restored and turned into a museum. Most rooms are still just empty, but the **tourist office** (tel. 389454) holes up there. Tours are given on demand (or you can just ask). (Open mid-May to Oct. daily 10am-5:30pm. £1.50, seniors £1, children 50p.)

    Horse rides on the Hook (usually for children) can be arranged through the **Hook Trekking Centre** (tel. 389166), 1 mi. from Duncannon on the New Ross Rd. (£5 per 30min., £9 per hr.; open daily July-Aug.). The **Duncannon Festival** runs the first week in July, offering cod pieces, cheap tarts, and other inexpensive delectables. Call Eileen Roche (tel. 389188) for details. **The Strand Stores,** also in Duncannon, sells groceries (open daily 9am-10pm). Next door is the **Strand Tavern** (tel. 389109), home to a groovy mug collection and a meditative ocean view.

    From Duncannon, the **Ring of Hook** road goes down to **Hook Head,** the tip of the peninsula. Welsh missionary St. Dubhan founded the first **Hook Lighthouse** in the 5th century, making it one of Europe's oldest. On the eastern side of the peninsula is Ireland's version of **Tintern Abbey** (tel. (051) 362321), founded in the 13th century and now minutes from the Ballycullane stop on the Waterford-Rosslare train line (£1, students 50p). **Wexford Festival Tours** (tel. 397124) can arrange for a bus to take you around the Hook to get up close and personal with the sights.

■ Waterford Harbour

East of Waterford City, Waterford Harbour straddles the Waterford-Wexford county line. It is here that Oliver Cromwell coined the phrase "by hook or by crook"; he had plotted to take Waterford City from either Hook Head or the opposite side of the harbor at Crooke. Both sides of the harbor are host to historic ruins, friendly fishing villages, and breathtaking ocean views. Although the area is peaceful and quiet, it's not the place to go if you're looking for the amenities of an urban center. The scenic harbor can be thought of as A-shaped: popular beach destination Dunmore East is on the left slope of the A while thin Hook Head is on the right slope. The crossbar represents

SOUTHEAST IRELAND

the **Passage East Car Ferry** (tel. 382488 or 382480), which carries coastal explorers between Passage East on the west side of the harbor and Ballyhack on the east side, bypassing a 37 mi. land route between them. (Continuous sailings Apr.-Sept. M-Sa 7:20am-10pm, Su 9:30am-10pm; Oct.-Mar. M-Sa 7:20am-8pm, Su 9:30am-8pm. Pedestrians 80p, £1 return; cyclists £1.50, £2 return.) It's a nice bike ride to Passage East from Waterford and then around the Hook, but there's no place to get a bike in the harbor area so rent one in Waterford. The road between Passage East and Dunmore East is a bit hilly and should be used only by those looking to increase their heart rate significantly. From Wexford, follow signs for Ballyhack to reach the ferry. The **phone code** for these towns is 051.

■ Dunmore East

Dunmore East is a tiny village southeast of Waterford. The **Suirway** bus service (tel. 382209) runs the 9½ mi. from **Waterford** to Dunmore East (3 per day, £1.80). The **Murphy's Gold Classic Golf Tournament** is held here each April, drawing over 500 international golfers. When the town's attention is turned away from the tee, tourists and townsfolk head to the beach. The sandy strand attracts bathers and tanning frogs on the rare days when the sun is shining. At several points, trails descend to the isolated coves below, offering more secluded swimming opportunities. At **Badger's Cove,** facing the docks, dozens of seagulls perch on the rocky cliff face and produce a frightening cacophony of echoing cries. The nests here are possibly the closest seagull nesting site to human habitation. For an even more dramatic view, follow the gravel road past Dock Rd. to see the ocean crashing onto rocky shores. There's no ATM in Dunmore, but **Powers** (tel. 83202), the convenience store on Dock Rd., has a **bureau de change** (open M-Sa 9am-9pm, Su 10am-7pm). At the end of Dock Rd., behind the pink Harbour House, Irish surfer dudes at the **Dunmore East Adventure Centre** (tel. 383783) will teach you to snorkel, sail, surf, kayak, or ride a horse. Bring a towel and swimsuit; they provide the equipment. Space fills quickly, so call ahead to reserve a spot (July-Aug. £15 per ½day; Sept.-June £12).

The elegant **Dunmore Harbour House,** Dock Rd. (tel. 83218), offers convenient rooms and new hostel accommodations, some with an ocean view (dorms £13; B&B doubles with bath £39). For a special treat, stay across the road at **Harbour View B&B** (tel. 383198). Miriam Shipsey doesn't joke about eating off a silver platter; she serves your breakfast on it. Antique china and furniture adorn every room of this 19th-century house (£18). Down the road, the **Dunmore Caravan and Camping Park** (tel. 383200) has offices in the Park Shop. The park is packed with trailers, but you can pitch a tent (£8). Groceries abound at **Londis Supermarket** (open M-F 8:30am-8:30pm, Sa-Su 9am-8pm). The **Bay Café,** Dock Rd. (tel. 383900), serves all homemade food, sit-down or take-away (sandwiches £1.50, entrees £4-8; open daily 9am-8:30pm). **Lucy's Kitchen** (tel. 383350), on the Strand, dishes up standard take-away (entrees £2-5; open daily 8am-1am). Farther up the road, the **Ocean Hotel Restaurant** (tel. 383136) has an assortment of curry dishes, steaks, veggie dishes, and more (£5 and up; open M-Sa 10am-10pm, Su 12:30-3 and 4-9pm). Dunmore citizens gather at the **Strand Inn** (tel. 383783) to enjoy the pool table and live music.

■ Passage East

Passage East is just that; from here, people hop on the ferry (see above) that crosses the River Suir to the Wexford side. Passage is a small, friendly fishing village oriented around two quiet squares. The cheerful, community-run **Discover East Waterford Tourism Enterprise** office (tel. (051) 382677) offers well-informed advice about the area and a **bureau de change** (open Mar.-Oct. M-F 9:30am-5pm; in Aug. also open Sa 10am-4pm). **Cois Abhainne B&B** is, as the name says, just beside the river (£15). There aren't many B&Bs in town; if they're all full, try the **Seaview Guest House** (tel. 382638) on the quay. Paddy and Maureen Conden will fill you up with a gut-busting breakfast. (Doubles with bath £32.) Travelers often stop at regionally famous **Jack Meade's Pub** (tel. (051) 873187), halfway between Waterford and Passage, which has been in operation for almost 300 years and owned by the same family for half that time. Antiques adorn the walls and a close-knit band of locals claims their own corner, but frequent entertainment attracts a wide audience. For a drink and some trad in town, stop in at **The Fairleigh** (tel. 382240; open daily 10:30am-midnight). During the third weekend in September, Passage East has mollusk mania during the annual **Mussel Festival,** which features exhibitions, cooking demonstrations, fishing tips, and mussel tasting. The **Suirway** bus service (tel. 382209) goes to Passage from opposite the **Waterford** tourist office (30min., 1 per day, £1.50).

■ Tramore

Tramore tempts all those in the Waterford area with its smooth 3 mi. strand. *Trá Mór* means "big beach" in Gaelic; those crazy Celts had an eye for the obvious. The cliffs that rise above the beach offer beautiful coastal views and great places to stay. Despite the amusements that line the promenade in classic seaside-resort style, Tramore retains its small-town character and low prices. In the summer, the beach and boardwalk bustle with music and bathers, but Tramore resumes its quiet coastal town status during the rest of the year.

PRACTICAL INFORMATION Bus Éireann stops on Strand St. en route from **Waterford** (15min., at least 1 per hr., £1.50). The very professional **tourist office,** Strand Rd. (tel. 381572), can help you see past the tourist traps (open June to mid-Sept. M-Sa 10am–6pm). An **AIB** 24-hour **ATM** is next door. **Flanagan's,** Market St. (tel. 381252), rents **bikes,** but Tramore is so darn hilly that cycling might not be much fun (£3 per hr., £8 per day, £35 per week; no deposit). Tramore's **phone code** is a beachin' 051.

ACCOMMODATIONS The Cliff, Church St. (tel. 381363), owned by the YWCA, looks out on the ocean from a prime cliffside location. The newly refurbished rooms (all with bath) are closer to B&B status, and the small kitchenette has a fridge, a microwave, and tea-making facilities. (Singles £17; doubles £34. Breakfast included.) Tramore is bursting with B&Bs, especially along Church Rd. **Ard More House,** Doneraile Dr. (tel. 381716), has a beautiful view of the water and a gorgeous garden at your feet. Walk down Gallway's Hill toward the Church of Ireland and make your first left. (Singles £18; doubles £36; all with bath.) **Turret House,** Church Rd. (tel. 386342), has huge rooms, some with ocean views, all with TV, tea and coffee facilities, and bath (singles £18-25; doubles £36). **Venezia,** Church Road Grove (tel. 381412), signposted off Church Rd., is immaculate and glossy, with top-notch, firm beds (singles £18; doubles £36). Small but bright and clean rooms await at **Church Villa,** Church Rd. (tel. 381547; £15). Located between the golf course and the Metal Man (a monument to shipwreck victims) 1½ mi. from town off Dungarvan Coast Rd., the family-style **Newtown Caravan and Camping Park** (tel. 381979) is the best of several nearby campsites. (July-Aug. £4 per person; Easter- June and Sept. £3. Showers 50p. Open Easter-Sept.)

FOOD, PUBS, AND WATER Tourist traps line up next to Splashworld and the amusement park; walk into town instead for regionally famous **Cunningham's Fish and Chips,** Main St. It's well worth the wait. (Fish and chips £2.10. Open daily 5pm-midnight.) **The Sea Horse,** Strand St. (tel. 386091), has great pub grub, fancy coffee, and a friendly atmosphere (entrees £3-5; food served noon-9pm). To combine your eating and ocean-viewing time, check out **Emo's Café,** Strand Rd. **Londis Supermarket** (tel. 381217) provides groceries right off Main St. (open daily 8am-10pm). As for watering holes, locals love to be hip and abbreviate their faves. **The Victorian House ("The Vic"),** Queens St. (tel. 390338), offers trad several nights a week during the summer, usually on Tuesdays. The younger crowd prefers **The Hibernian** or **"Hi B"** (tel. 386396), which has bar extension during the summer (W-Su) and a disco nightly (10:30pm-2am; cover £4). Most locals congregate at **O'Neill's** (tel. 381088) on Summer Hill at the top of Strand St. If the beach doesn't provide you with enough action, head to **Splashworld,** The Promenade (tel. 390176), which has heated bubble pools, water slides, and wave machines. Besides white-knuckle rides, whirlpools, and water-cannons, the park also has new private flotation rooms where you can float in epsom salt solution. Welcome to the Dead Sea, Irish style. (Open Mar.-Oct. daily 11am-8pm; Nov.-Feb. M-F noon-8pm, Sa-Su 11am-6pm. £4.95, students £3.25, children £3.95.)

■ Waterford

Huge metal silos and storage facilities greet the first-time visitor to Waterford. Fortunately, behind this industrial facade lies a wonderfully complex city. Waterford dates back to 1003, when Vikings built Reginald's Tower to defend their longships; they called their settlement *Vadrafjord*. Over the years, Waterford has endured sieges by Strongbow and Cromwell. The town remains a commercial center, although massive freighters have since replaced the longships and shops and amiable pubs have filled the winding, narrow streets. Waterford's accessibility and amenities are a relief from the small towns that dot the area.

ORIENTATION AND PRACTICAL INFORMATION

Waterford is a mix of narrow Viking streets and broad English thoroughfares. The various quays on the River Suir and Barranstrand St. (through its many name changes) form a crooked T where most activity takes place.

   Airport: tel. 875589. Served by **British Airways** and **Suckling Airlines.** Follow The Quay, turn right at Reginald's Tower then left at the sign. 20min. from town.

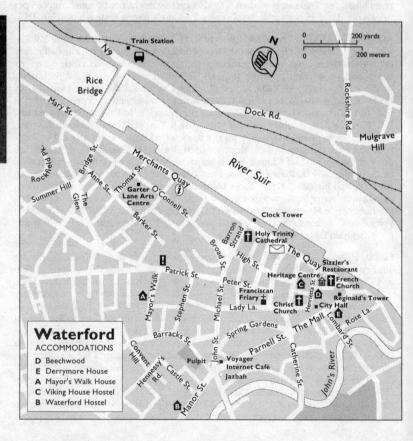

Waterford
ACCOMMODATIONS

D Beechwood
E Derrymore House
A Mayor's Walk House
C Viking House Hostel
B Waterford Hostel

Trains: Plunkett Station, across the bridge from The Quay. For information, call M-F 9am-5pm tel. 873401, after hours M-F tel. 873402, Sa 9am-6pm tel. 873403; 24hr. recorded timetable tel. 873401. Train station staffed M-Sa 9am-6pm, Su at departure times. JFK's ancestors grew up in Waterford, and the city is still well connected. Trains chug to **Limerick** (2¼hr., M-Sa 2 per day, £11.50), **Kilkenny** (40min., M-Sa 4 per day, £6), **Dublin** (2½hr., M-Sa 4 per day, Su 3 per day, £12), and **Rosslare Harbour** (1hr., M-Sa 3 per day, £7.50).

Buses: Plunkett Station (tel. 879000). Office open M-Sa 9am-5:30pm, Su 2-5:30pm. To **Dublin** (3½hr., M-Sa 5 per day, Su 3 per day, £8.50), **Kilkenny** (1hr., 2 per day, £5), **Limerick** (2½hr., 4 per day, £9.70), **Cork** (2½hr., M-Sa 8 per day, Su 6 per day, £8), **Galway** (4¾hr., M-Sa 4 per day, Su 3 per day, £13), and **Rosslare Harbour** (1¼hr., 3 per day, £8).

Local Transportation: City buses leave from the Clock Tower on The Quay. 75p for trips within the city. Check the tourist office for details.

Hitching: The rare hitchers place themselves on the main routes, away from the tangled city center. To reach N24 (Cahir, Limerick), N10 (Kilkenny, Dublin), or N25 (New Ross, Wexford, Rosslare), they head over the bridge toward the train station. For the N25 (Cork), they continue down Parnell St.; others take a city bus out to the Waterford Crystal Factory before they stick out a thumb.

Tourist Office: 41 Merchant's Quay (tel. 875788), between Hanover and Gladstone St. Ask for a map of Waterford and the free, ad-packed *Ireland's South East* guide. *The Waterford Touring Guide* (£2) has good county-wide info. Open June and Sept. M-Sa 9am-6pm; July-Aug. M-Sa 9am-6pm, Su 11am-1pm and 2-5pm; Oct.-Feb. M-F 2-5pm; Mar.-Apr. M-Sa 9am-1pm and 2-6pm.

Budget Travel: USIT, 36-37 Georges St. (tel. 872601; fax 871723). Near the corner of Gladstone St., 1 block east of Barronstrand St. As knowledgeable as the Dublin office. ISICs, **Travelsave** stamps, student deals for daily flights and bus/ferry packages from Waterford to London (see **Getting There,** p. 29). Open M-F 9:30am-5:30pm, Sa 11am-4pm.

Banks: 24hr. **ATM** at **AIB,** just off The Quay on Barronstrand Rd. **Bank of Ireland,** Merchants Quay (tel. 872074). Open M 10am-5pm, Tu-F 10am-4pm; **ATM. TSB,** O'Connell St. (tel. 872988). Open M-W and F 9:30am-5pm, Th 9:30am-7pm.

Luggage Storage: Plunkett Station. £1 per item. Open M-Sa 7:15am-9pm.

Bike Rental: Wright's Cycle Depot, Henrietta St. (tel. 874411). £7 per day, £30 per week; deposit £40. Open M-Th and Sa 9:30am-1pm and 2-6pm, F 9:30am-1pm and 2-9pm.

Laundry: Rainbow Laundrette, Thomas St. (tel. 855656). Serviced wash and dry (no self-service) £5.90. Open M-F 8:45am-6pm, Sa 9am-5:30pm.

Emergency: Dial 999; no coins required. **Garda:** Patrick St. (tel. 874888).

Counseling and Support: Samaritans, 13 Beau St. (tel. 872114). 24hr. hotline. **Rape Crisis Centre** (tel. 873362). Call M 10am-noon, Tu-W and F 10am-noon and 2-4pm, Th 10am-noon, 2-4pm, and 8:30-10pm. **Youth Information Centre:** 130 The Quay (tel. 877328). Information on work, travel, health, and a variety of support groups (including gay and lesbian support groups). Photocopy and fax service. Open to all. Open M-F 9:30am-5:30pm.

Hospital: Ardkeen Hospital (tel. 873321). Follow The Quay to the Tower Hotel; turn left, then follow signs straight ahead to the hospital.

Post Office: The Quay (tel. 874444), the largest of several. Open M-Tu and Th-F 9am-5:30pm, W 9:30am-5:30pm, Sa 9am-1pm.

Internet Access: Voyager Internet Café, Parnell Court Shopping Center (tel. 843843). Follow Barronstrand St. up from The Quay through its name changes to John St. Voyager is on the left opposite Eddie Rockets before John St. crosses Parnell St. Keep your eyes peeled; the shopping center is almost invisible. No food, no drink—just computers. £1.50 per 15min., students £1.25. Open M-Sa 11am-11pm, Su 3-11pm.

Phone Code: 051.

ACCOMMODATIONS

Most B&Bs in the city are unimpressive; those on the Cork Rd. are a better option.

Viking House Hostel (IHH), Coffee House Ln. (tel. 853827; email pjreddy@iol.ie). Follow The Quay east past the Clock Tower and another block past the post office; the hostel is on the right, behind another building. Comfortable spacious lounge, shiny clean kitchen, and a friendly and informed staff. Just don't try to wash your clothes; they'll never dry. Free luggage storage and secure lockers. Kitchen accessible 10am-noon and 3-10pm. June-Sept. 14-bed dorm £8; 4- to 6-bed dorm £9.50-12; doubles £27. Add £1 for room with bath and £2 for TV. Prices £1 less Mar.-May and £2 less Oct.-Feb.

Waterford Hostel, 70 The Manor (tel. 850163). From the Quay, walk down John St. and turn right onto The Manor. The hostel is on your right before the traffic lights. Not as big or as nice as Viking House, but clean and comfortable. Small lounge and kitchen, but there are real bathrooms—not stalls like most hostels. Dorms £8.

Derrynane House, 19 The Mall (tel. 875179). Walk down the Quay away from the bridge. When it swings into The Mall, so should you. This beautiful house built in the 1820s flaunts heavenly high ceilings and bright spacious rooms. Ask about the famous prisoner/politician who stayed here. £15.

Mayor's Walk House, 12 Mayor's Walk (tel. 855427). A 15min. mayoral walk from the train station. Mrs. Ryder offers advice, biscuits, and an endless pot of tea. Simple, quiet rooms. Singles £15; doubles £28. Open Mar.-Nov.

Beechwood, 7 Cathedral Sq. (tel. 876677). From the Quay, go up Henrietta St. Mrs. Ryan invites you into her charming home, located on an ideal quiet pedestrian street. Singles £17; doubles £30.

FOOD

Despite the overwhelming presence of fast food chains, there are some real restaurants with reasonable prices. You might want to try Waterford's contribution to Irish cuisine, the *blaa* ("blah"), a floury white sausage roll of Huguenot origins. Besides the *blaa*, Waterford gave the world the modern process of bacon curing. To satisfy your pork products cravings (and pick up some cheap groceries while you're at it) visit **Dunnes Stores** in the City Square Mall (open M-W and Sa 9am-6pm, Th-F 9am-9pm). **Treacy's,** The Quay (tel. 873059), has a very large selection for a late-night grocery, even a small deli (open daily 9:30am-11pm). **The Late, Late Shop** (tel. 855376), farther up The Quay, gives you an extra, extra hour to shop but a smaller and more expensive selection (open daily 7:30am-midnight).

Sizzlers Restaurant (tel. 85211), on The Quay toward Reginald's Tower. Chat with the locals sharing your table over delicious fried entrees (£3-5). Open 24hr.

Café Luna, 53 John St., offers cheap food with a trendy touch. Open Su-Th until 2:30am and F-Sa until 4am.

Haricot's Wholefood Restaurant, 11 O'Connell St. The vegetarian and the carnivore live in harmony with Haricot's tasty, innovative dishes as peacemakers. Most entrees £3.50-5.50. Open M-F 9:30am-8pm, Sa 9:30am-5:45pm.

Chapman's Pantry Restaurant, 61 The Quay (tel. 873833). Homefare served in a friendly, casual atmosphere. Sandwiches £2. Open M-Sa 8:30am-5:30pm.

The Reginald, The Mall (tel. 855087). You can't miss Reginald's with its faux castle facade nestled behind the real Reginald's Tower. This bar/restaurant serves rich, delicious food in a classy environment. Dinner is expensive, but lunch is reasonable. Lunch special £5, vegetarian specials £5.50. Lunch daily noon-3pm, dinner 5:30-10:30pm.

Crumbs, Michael St. (tel. 854323). Good food served quickly in a coffee shop atmosphere. Breakfast foods served all day plus a variety of main courses. Entrees about £4. Open M-Sa 9am-6pm.

Gino's, John St. (tel. 879513), at the Apple Market. Busy family restaurant serves pizza made right before your eyes. Reservations recommended on F-Sa nights. Individual pizza £2.25 plus 50p per topping. Open daily noon-midnight.

PUBS

The Quays are loaded with pubs, and there are even more as you travel up Barron-strand St. into town. The pubs, however, constitute the extent of the town's nightlife.

T&H Doolan's, George's St. (tel. 841504). Waterford's oldest and best drinking establishment. One of the city's medieval walls runs through the pub (history *and* beer!). Trad nightly. No cover.

The Pulpit, John St. (tel 879184). The church-like wooden detail may make you want to kneel down and pray. Instead, grab a seat and a pint and enjoy the hip crowd. **Preachers,** the upstairs nightclub, opens at 10:30pm, playing tunes from the 70s, 80s, and 90s. Amen! Cover £3 before 10:30pm, £6 after.

Geoff's Pub, 9 John St. (tel. 874787). Most locals will tell you that Geoff's is the place to see and be seen. If you have a cell phone (even if it doesn't work), bring it to enhance your hipness while you sip your pint and laugh a bit too loudly.

The Jazbah (tel. 858128), at Parnell and John St. This swanky new bar with 1920s decor is a classy joint, ideal for a mellow pint with friends. Live jazz F-Sa nights.

Muldoon's, John St. (tel. 873693). Although it has a generic sports bar feel and a loud crowd of older 20s to 30s, the late bar hours (Th-Su until 2am) and cheap food (£1.95 daily specials) make it worthwhile. Free food between 11pm-1am.

Mullane's, 15 Newgate St. (tel. 873854), off New St. Famous for its hard-core trad sessions. A sprinkling of the young, a dash of tourists, and the older regular crowd results in the perfect mix. Call ahead for session times; the pub is almost empty when there isn't one.

SIGHTS

You can cover all of Waterford's sights in a day, but only if you move quickly. The **Waterford Crystal Factory** (tel. 373311), 1 mi. out on N25 (Cork Rd.), is the city's highlight. *(Tours and audio-visual shows every 10min. Apr.-Oct. daily 8:30am-4pm, showroom open 8:30am-6pm; Nov.-Mar. tours daily 9am-3:15pm, showroom open 9am-5pm. £3.50, students £1.75. Tours wheelchair accessible. Book ahead via telephone or through the tourist office.)* Forty-minute tours allow you to witness the transformation of molten glass into polished crystal. Many of the people taking the tour intend to buy something sparkly and expensive at its end; don't feel bad if you don't. Admire the finished products—and their outrageous prices—in the gallery. The least expensive item, a crystal heart (£16), seems like the real thing. City bus #1 (Kilbarry-Ballybeg) leaves across from the Clock Tower every 30 minutes and passes the factory (75p). The City Imp (basically a mini-bus) also stops at the factory by request.

Reginald's Tower (tel. 873501), at the end of The Quay, has guarded the entrance to the city since the 12th century. *(£2, children 75p.)* Its 12 ft. thick Viking walls were almost impossible for invaders to penetrate. The tower has housed a prison, a mint, and the wedding reception of Strongbow and Aoife (see **Vikings,** p. 54). Climb the stone spiral staircase for bits of local history, old maps of Waterford, and a view of the city. Just down the street, the **Waterford Heritage Centre,** Greyfriars St. (tel. 871227), off The Quay, displays a wealth of Viking artifacts snatched from the jaws of bulldozers. *(Open July-Aug. M-F 9am-8:30pm, Sa-Su 9am-5pm; Mar.-June and Sept.-Oct. M-F 10am-5pm, Sa 2-5pm. £1.50, students £1, children 50p, 25% off with walking tour ticket.)* The collection includes Viking swords, jewelry, pottery, decorative tools, and shoes. A beautiful collection of charters dates back to 1215.

After your visit to the Heritage Centre, ask at the reception for the key to the ruins and wide-open tombs of the **French Church** at the corner of New and Greyfriars St., a Dominican monastery built in 1240. The monastery was given to Huguenot refugees in the 17th century. Many of Waterford's more recent monumental edifices were the brainchildren of 18th-century architect John Roberts. The **Theatre Royal** and **City Hall,** both on The Mall, are his secular masterpieces. He also designed both the Roman Catholic **Holy Trinity Cathedral** on Barronstrand St. and the Church of Ireland **Christ Church Cathedral** in Cathedral Square up Henrietta St. from the Quay, making Waterford the only Irish town to have the faiths united by a common architect. Christ Church Cathedral has the rather unique tomb of Bishop Tunes Rice that depicts vermin chewing on his decaying corpse: a gruesome posthumous sermon on the ephemeral nature of human life. Other highlights include a 2000-year-old sword from the Bronze Age and a 1681 version of the New Testament written in Irish. Scattered throughout town are remnants of the town's medieval **city walls;** the biggest blocks are behind the Theatre Royal on Spring Garden and Patrick St., extending to Bachelor's Walk.

Unfortunately, much of Waterford's history has been converted into retail space. Because the city hasn't expanded outward since 1790, Viking, Victorian, and modern structures are piled on top of each other. One way to get a feel for the city is to take a **Walking Tours of Historic Waterford.** *(Mar.-Oct. daily at noon and 2pm. £3.)* These 45-minute tours depart from the Granville Hotel (tel. 873711) on the Quay and provide a thorough introduction to Waterford's mongrel history.

ENTERTAINMENT

The Munster Express (80p), a local newspaper, has entertainment listings. The **Waterford Show** (tel. 358397 or 875788) at City Hall is an entertaining performance of Irish music, stories, and dance in a historical setting. (Th and Sa-Su at 9pm. £6. Call for reservations or make them at the tourist office.) The **Garter Lane Arts Centre,** Garter Lane 2, 22a O'Connell St. (tel. 877153), stages dance, music, and theater in an old Georgian building. In July and August, the **Summer Arts and Crafts Fair** fills the exhibition space, displaying handmade objects for sale. Down the street **screen/ space,** at Garter Lane 1, 5 O'Connell St. (tel. 857198), strikes a lower-case balance between art and capitalism. The result is a mix of smart second-run movies and cheap tickets. Information about Waterford's theater scene is available here. (Double features W-Th at 8pm. You must buy a membership in order to buy a ticket. Yearly memberships £2, tickets £1.50.)

■ Dungarvan

This busy market town is a regional transportation hub with a vibrant pub scene. Main St. (also O'Connell St.) runs through the central square; Emmet St. (also Mitchell St.) runs parallel to Main St. one block uphill and is home to the hostel and a number of B&Bs. The road to Cork veers off Emmet St. at the Garda station.

PRACTICAL INFORMATION Buses (tel. (051) 79000) run from Davitt's Quay east to **Waterford** (1hr., M-Su 9 per day, £5), west to **Cork** (M-Sa 7 per day, Su 5 per day, £7), and north to **Lismore** (daily). The unreservedly helpful **tourist office** (tel. 41741) on The Square is a good resource for information on Dungarvan and the nearby Ring *gaeltacht* (open June-Aug. M-Sa 9am-9pm, Su 9am-6pm; Sept.-May M-Sa 9am-6pm). The best villages in West Waterford are inaccessible by bus; bikes can be rented at **Murphy's Cycles,** 68 Main St. (tel. 41376; open M-Sa 9am-6pm), a **Raleigh Rent-A-Bike** depot (£5 per day, £25 per week; insurance included). **Bank of Ireland,** The Square, has a 24-hour **ATM** that accepts all major cash networks, as does **AIB,** just steps away on Meagher St. (both open M 10am-5pm, Tu-F 10am-4pm). The **post office** (tel. 41210) sits on Bridge St. just outside The Square (open M-F 9am-5:30pm, Sa 9am-3pm). The **phone code** is 058.

ACCOMMODATIONS, FOOD, AND PUBS The **Dungarvan Holiday Hostel (IHH),** Youghal Rd. (tel. 44340), just off Emmet St. opposite the Garda Station, is completely adequate, suffering only from an excess of concrete and a lack of comfort, with tightly packed rooms and few kitchen supplies (4- to 6-bed dorms £7; doubles £16; **bike rental** £7 per day; wheelchair accessible). **Santa Antoni,** Mitchell St. (tel. 42923), and its gregarious owner are appreciably more welcoming (£10 per person with continental breakfast; with full breakfast singles £13; doubles £24). Two doors down the road, **Amron** (tel. 43337) nearly bursts with the energetic hospitality of its proprietress, who lets out her basic rooms (from £13).

Ormond's Café, The Square (tel. 41153), a few doors down from the tourist office, serves outstanding desserts and a huge variety of meals to precede them in its stone–walled, skylit café (sandwiches £2-3, hot meals £4-5; open daily 8am-6pm). **An Bialann** (AHN be-LEEN), 31 Grattan Sq. (tel. 42825), is a neat little café with vinyl booths and inexpensive standard Irish fare (open M-Sa 9:30am-8:30pm, Su 9:30am-7pm). There's an **L&N Superstore** (tel. 41628) on Main St. (open M-W and Sa 9am-6pm, Th-F 9am-9pm).

The **Gows,** 13 Main St. (tel. 41149), is probably the best pub in town, even though their sign is upside-down (incredible trad Tu-W). **Davitt's Pub,** Davitt's Quay (tel. 44900), is huge and usually packed (disco Th-Su; cover £5; open nightly 11pm-2:15am). **The Anchor** (tel. 41249), down the quay a bit, is popular among the younger crowd and hosts trad on Thursdays and Saturdays. **Lady Belle,** Grattan Sq. (tel. 44222), invites you to sing along with the big boys Tuesday and some Friday nights. If you have transportation, try **The Seanachie** (tel. 46285) on N25 to Cork, about 10 miles from Dungarvan. The food is terrific though rather expensive (dinner about £12). They pump out marathon trad sessions nightly and craic all day.

SIGHTS The tourist office offers one-hour **Walking Tours** of medieval and Georgian Dungarvan. (*£2, students 50p.*) Surprise them by asking. They also give out the Town Trail brochure (free), which takes you to all of Dungarvan's seven or eight sights—not all of them thrilling. **King John's Castle,** presiding over Davitt's Quay, has 7 ft. thick walls but has nevertheless been in disrepair since 1299. It's not open to the public, but the Office of Public Works has its hands on it, so it's bound to end up a heritage center soon. The **Dungarvan Museum** (tel. 41231), at the end of Lower Main St. above the library, spares nothing in its breathless and well-mounted story of Dungarvan. (*Open M-F 11am-1pm and 2-5pm. Free.*) From the Ice Age to Vikings, Cromwell, and maritime trade, it's in there for those who like to stand and read.

There's not much else to see in Dungarvan itself, but the deep-sea and in-shore **fishing** is excellent just off the coast. Book a boat at **Gone Fishin',** 42 Lower Main St. (tel. 43514), a professional outfit with plenty of experience guiding less professional anglers to a catch. (*£25, rod and tackle hire £5. Open M-Sa 9am-6pm.*) **Baumann's,** 6 St. Mary St. (tel. 41395), dispenses tackle, licenses, and a wealth of inside information.

Dungarvan is home to several annual festivals. **Féile na nDéise** packs The Square with free concerts during the first weekend in May. Valentine's weekend brings the **Dungarvan Jazz Weekend,** a futuristic romp through the ruins of downtown Tokyo. The **Motorsport Weekend** pulls in vintage and race car enthusiasts in mid-July.

If you make it out to the local *gaeltacht*, **An Rinn** (ahn RINE, anglicized as **Ringville**), 6 mi. down the coast west of Dungarvan, you can treat yourself to the **Féile na nOisirí** (Oyster Festival). Locals and sportsmen from all over Ireland come to compete in oyster shucking and presenting competitions (or maybe they just come for the booze and music, both of which abound). Locals also crown their local Venus on the half-shell, the Oyster Queen. Stop in at the best pub in town, **Tigh an Cheoil** (tel. 46455), where the trad sessions are famous. Brush up on your Irish—it's the *teanga an tí* (language of the house) here.

■ Ardmore

Pastel houses and thatched cottages line this Ardmore's Main St., which eventually disappears into the sea. Besides having a satisfyingly picturesque beach, Ardmore claims to be the oldest Christian settlement in Ireland, and it has the ruins to back its claim. St. Declan christianized the area around the fourth century. His feast day, "Pattern Day," July 24, is a big deal in Ardmore, featuring a midnight mass and religious vigils and processions.

PRACTICAL INFORMATION Buses run to Cork (1½hr., M-Sa 3 per day, Su 1 per day, £7.30), **Dungarvan** (40min., July-Aug. M-Th 2 per day, F-Sa 1 per day, Sept.-June F-Sa 1 per day, £3.10), and **Waterford** (2hr., July-Aug. M-F 2 per day, Sa 1 per day, Sept.-June Sa 1 per day, £7.70). The **tourist office** (tel. 94444), in the carpark by the beach, is housed in what appears to be a demonic sandcastle. The office dispenses information about the local beaches as well as an excellent leaflet outlining a **walking tour** of town. (Open daily Easter-Sept. 10am-8pm, Sept.-Easter 11am-7pm.) Ardmore is a 3 mi. detour off Cork-Waterford Rd. (N25). **Hitching** from the junction can be slow. The **phone code** is 024.

ACCOMMODATIONS, FOOD, AND PUBS Ardmore's tranquil seaside location has finally been exploited by a hostel. The **Ardmore Beach Hostel,** Main St. (tel. 94501), has simple accommodations perked up by yellow gingham comforters and back-patio beach access. (Dorms £8; private rooms £10 per person; add 50p in winter for heating. Laundry £4.60.) A beautiful new chalet out back offers a romantic escape for two (from £30). Ardmore is home to several **B&Bs** with breathtaking sea views. **Byron Lodge,** Middle Rd. (tel. 94157), has literary aspirations and rooms with sunny alcoves. From Main St., take the street that runs uphill between the town's two thatched cottages. Don't make the mistake of thinking there's a single non-Georgian item. (Singles £21.50; doubles £30, with a view £34. Open Easter-Sept.) **Camping** in Ardmore is available along the beach at **Healy's** (tel. 94181; £5 per tent; £6 with car), but some travelers just pitch their tents in local fields.

Ardmore's food offerings are not extensive but yummy nonetheless. **Quinn's Food-store** (tel. 94250), in the town center, has the best selection of groceries (open daily 8am-10pm). The local favorite is **Cup and Saucer,** Main St. (tel. 94501), which has a delightful flower garden out back for sunny days (open daily 10am-8pm). **White-horses,** Main St. (tel. 94040), cooks up interesting and varied dishes, but don't forget your credit card (entrees £7-10; open 5:30-10pm). **Paddy Mac's,** Main St. (tel. 94166), is vast and warehouse-like but serves tasty smoked salmon on brown bread (£3.75) and has live music every night. Though seemingly run-down, **Riley's** pub, Main St., has more character than it knows what to do with. **Keever's Bar,** Main St. (tel. 94141), is another favorite of the older Ardmore crowd.

SIGHTS The all-encompassing must-do in Ardmore is the **cliffwalk,** a windy 3 mi. path with great views of the ocean and stops at all of Ardmore's various historic sites. The free map and guide pamphlet is available at the tourist office and the hostel. At one end of the walk is the **cathedral,** built piecemeal between 800 and 1400, which covers the site of St. Declan's monastery. He is said to be buried here, and the faithful avow that soil from the saint's grave cures diseases. The cathedral and its graveyard are marked unmistakably by the 97 ft. high **round tower,** whose door is a monk-protecting 12 ft. above the ground. Farther along the St. Declan pilgrimages, the **St. Declan's Stone** is perched at water's edge, just right from Main St. along the shore. Devotees would sometimes wedge themselves under the stone during prayers on Pattern Day. Down past the Cliff House hotel at the other end of the cliffwalk is **St. Declan's Well,** whose water is said to cure illness and affliction. Ardmore is one end of the 56 mi. **St. Declan's Way,** which runs up to Cahir in Co. Tipperary.

SOUTHWEST IRELAND

Even more difficult than deciphering the bus schedule is conceptualizing the scale of things in Ireland. The city of Cork's population of 146,000 doesn't sound like a lot, but, then again, grand architecture, loads of music, and a little pollution go a long way toward making the city a cosmopolitan center. On the barren southwest coast, it's hard to imagine that there are enough people for a proper mass, but a glance around any village will tell you that there are, at very least, a few publicans. All of this remoteness has been a vehicle for rebellion in the southwest's history; more recently it's been a lure. Nowhere in Ireland has signs in as many languages as Killarney, all of them screaming "buy me," and the land in west Cork is steadily being bought by investors and the occasional movie star. If you're short on time, it might be best to skip Cork and frolic on the coast, splitting your time between the quiet Beara peninsula and the understandably trafficked Dingle and Ring of Kerry.

County Cork

Historically, Eastern Cork's superb harbors have made it a prosperous trading center, while its distance from Dublin and the Pale gave the English less leverage over it. Perhaps as a result, Cork was a center of patriotic activity during the 19th and early 20th centuries. Headquarters of the "Munster Republic" controlled by the anti-Treaty forces during the Civil War, the county produced patriot Michael Collins, as well as the man who assassinated him in 1922 (see **Independence and Civil War (1919-1922),** p. 60). The energies of today's Cork City are directed toward industry and culture, while the sea towns of Kinsale and Cobh gaily entertain tall ships and stooped backpackers. "West Cork," the southwestern third of the county, was once the "badlands" of Ireland; its ruggedness and isolation rendered it lawless and largely uninhabitable. Ex-hippies and antiquated fishermen have replaced the outlaws, and now do their best to make the villages laid-back and ultra-hospitable. Roaringwater Bay and wave-whipped Mizen Head mark Ireland's land's end. The lonely beauty here is a stately solitude unmarred by the polyester shamrock-shlock brigades raining down on other parts of Ireland. Ireland's rich archaeological history is particularly visible in Cork. Celtic ring forts, mysterious stone circles, and long-ruined abbeys dot the sheep-speckled hills.

The new **Wheel Escapes** program provides an excellent way to traverse the wilds of West Cork while burning off those fatty lipids that are an essential part of most Irish cuisine. You can rent a bike at any of the hostels listed below (£7 per day, £35 per week, helmet, lock, toolbag, and panniers included) and drop it off at any other hostel on the list. For more info, call one of the following participating hostels: Maria's Schoolhouse, Union Hall (p. 212); Russagh Mill Hostel and Adventure Center, Skibbereen (p. 212); Rolf's Hostel, Baltimore (p. 214); Schull Backpacker's Lodge, Schull (p. 217); Bantry Independent Hostel, Bantry (p. 219); Shiplake Mountain Hostel, Dunmanway (p. 207); and Murphy's Village Hostel, Glengarriff (p. 222).

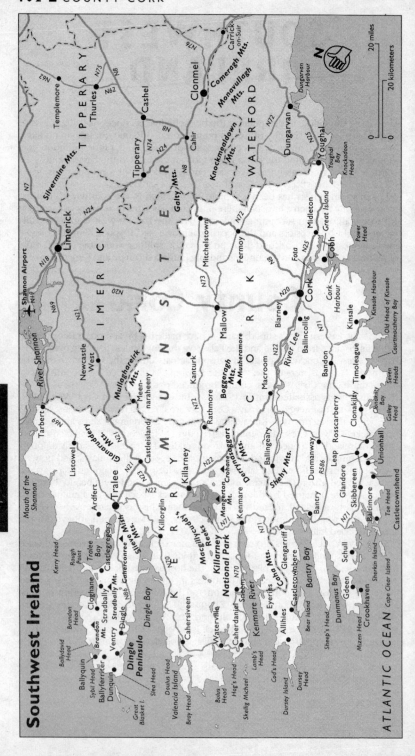

SOUTHWEST IRELAND

Southwest Ireland

CORK

As Ireland's second largest city, Cork (pop. 146,000) is the center of the southwest's sports, music, and arts. Unfortunately for the visitor, behind every cultural site is its ugly but dependable twin, commerce. Indeed, what older charms industry has not blackened, the English have blighted. The old city burned down in 1622, Cromwell expelled half its citizens in the 1640s, the English Duke of Marlborough laid siege to Cork in 1690, and the city was torched again in 1920 during the Irish War of Independence. Wise visitors will more politely exploit the city's resources and use Cork as a place to eat, drink, shop, and sleep well while filling their lungs with fresh country air. Lovely pseudo-pastoral walks unravel out to the Mardyke area and across the University College of Cork campus.

ORIENTATION AND PRACTICAL INFORMATION

Downtown Cork is the tip of an arrow-shaped island in the River Lee. Many central north-south streets were Venice-style canals until the 1700s, when Cork discovered pavement. Today the river separates Cork's residential south side from its north side, which includes the poorer but sight-filled Shandon district. Downtown action concentrates on Oliver Plunkett St., Saint Patrick St., Paul St., and the north-south streets that connect them. Heading west from the Grand Parade, Washington St. becomes Western Rd. and then N22 to Killarney; to the north of the Lee, MacCurtain St. flows east into Lower Glanmire Rd., which becomes N8 and N25. Cork is compact and pedestrian-friendly. City buses crisscross the city and its suburbs. From downtown, catch the buses (and their schedules) at the bus station on Merchant's Quay or on St. Patrick St., across from the Father Matthew statue.

Transportation

Airport: Cork Airport (tel. 313131), 5mi. south of Cork on Kinsale Rd. **Aer Lingus** (tel. 327155), **Manx Airlines** (tel. (01) 260158), **British Airways** (tel. (800) 626747), and **Ryanair** (tel. 313091) connect Cork to Dublin, the Isle of Man, various English cities, and Paris. A taxi (£5-6) or bus (18 per day, £2.50) will deliver you from the airport to the bus station on Parnell Place in Cork City.

Trains: Kent Station, Lower Glanmire Rd. (tel. 506766), across the river from the city center in the northeast part of town. Open M-Sa 7am-8:30pm, Su 7am-8pm. Train connections to **Dublin** (3hr., M-Sa 9 per day, Su 6 per day, £32), **Limerick** (1½hr., M-Sa 8 per day, Su 4 per day, £15.50), **Killarney** (2hr., M-Sa 5 per day, Su 3 per day, £13.50), and **Tralee** (2½hr., M-Sa 5 per day, Su 3 per day, £18). Best prices with advance booking.

Buses: Parnell Pl. (tel. 508188), 2 blocks east of Patrick's Bridge on Merchants' Quay. Inquiries desk open Apr.-Sept. M-F 9am-6pm, Su 9am-5pm; Oct.-Mar. M-F 9am-6pm. Bus Éireann goes to all major cities: **Bantry** (2hr., M-Sa 3 per day, Su 2 per day, £8.80), **Galway** (4hr., M-Sa 5 per day, Su 4 per day, £12), **Killarney** (2hr., M-Sa 7 per day, Su 5 per day, £8.80), **Limerick** (2hr., M-Sa 6 per day, Su 5 per day, £9), **Rosslare Harbour** (4hr., M-Sa 3 per day, Su 2 per day, £13), **Tralee** (2½hr., M-Sa 7 per day, Su 5 per day, £9.70), **Waterford** (2¼hr., M-Sa 6 per day, Su 5 per day, £8), **Dublin** (4½hr., M-Sa 4 per day, Su 3 per day, £12), **Belfast** (7½hr., M-Sa 2 per day, Su 1 per day, £17), **Sligo** (7hr., 3 per day, £16), and **Donegal Town** (9hr., 1 per day, £17).

Ferries: Ferries to England dock at **Ringaskiddy Terminal** (tel. 378111), 9mi. south of the city. The 30min. bus ride from the terminal to the bus station in Cork costs £3. For 24hr. ferry information, call (01) 661 0715. See **By Ferry**, p. 34.

Local Transportation: Downtown **buses** run every 20 to 40min. (reduced service Su), from about 7:30am-11:30pm. Fares from 70p. Bus Éireann Kiosk, Patrick St., near the bridge (open M-Sa 7:30am-11:15pm, Su 9:30am-11:15pm).

Car Rental: Great Island Car Rentals, 47 MacCurtain St. (tel. 503536). £40 per day, £90 for 3 days, £160 per week for subcompact standard. Min. age 23. **Budget**

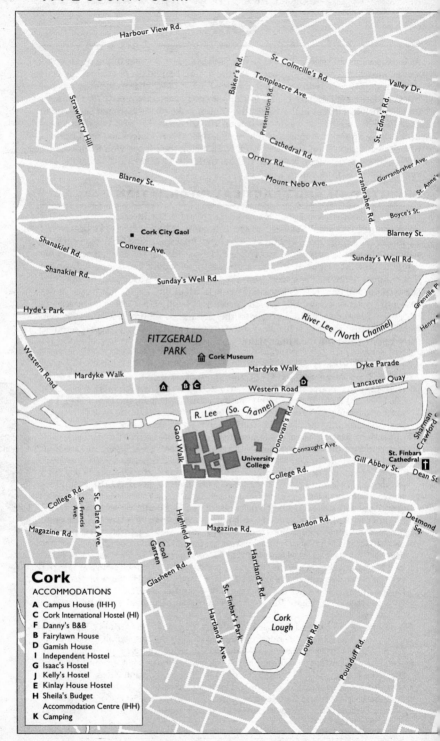

Harbour View Rd.

St. Colmcille's Rd.

Valley Dr.

Baker's Rd.

Templeacre Ave.

Presentation Rd.

St. Edna's Rd.

Cathedral Rd.

Orrery Rd.

Gurranbraher Ave.

Mount Nebo Ave.

Gurranbraher Rd.

St. Anne's

Boyce's St.

Strawberry Hill

Blarney St.

Blarney St.

■ **Cork City Gaol**

Convent Ave.

Sunday's Well Rd.

Shanakiel Rd.

Shanakiel Rd.

Sunday's Well Rd.

Hyde's Park

River Lee (North Channel)

Grenville P

Henry

FITZGERALD PARK

Western Road

🏛 **Cork Museum**

Mardyke Walk

Mardyke Walk

Dyke Parade

Ⓐ   Ⓑ Ⓒ

Lancaster Quay

Western Road

Ⓓ

R. Lee (So. Channel)

Donovan's Rd.

Shandon

Crawford

Gaol Walk

Connaught Ave.

St. Finbars Cathedral ✝

University College

College Rd.

Gill Abbey St.

Dean St

College Rd.

St. Francis Ave.

St. Clare's Ave.

Highfield Ave.

Magazine Rd.

Bandon Rd.

Desmond Sq.

Magazine Rd.

Cool Garten

Glasheen Rd.

St. Finbar's Park

Hartland's Rd.

Hartland's Ave.

Cork Lough

Lough Rd.

Pouladuff Rd.

Cork

ACCOMMODATIONS

A Campus House (IHH)
C Cork International Hostel (HI)
F Danny's B&B
B Fairylawn House
D Gamish House
I Independent Hostel
G Isaac's Hostel
J Kelly's Hostel
E Kinlay House Hostel
H Sheila's Budget
    Accommodation Centre (IHH)
K Camping

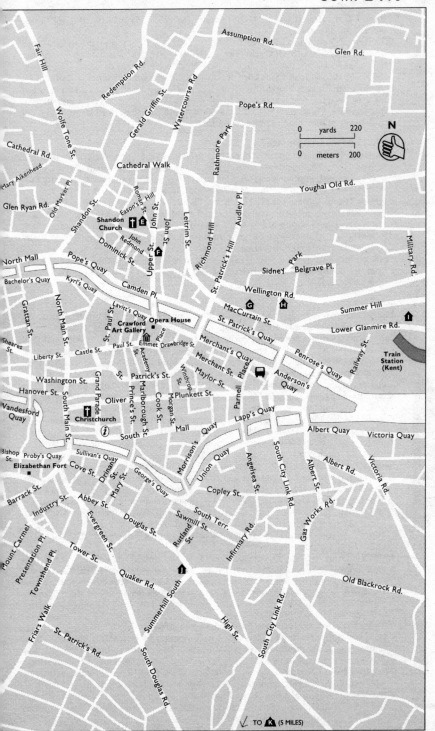

Fair Hill
Glen Rd.
Assumption Rd.
Redemption Rd.
Wolfe Tone St.
Gerald Griffin St.
Watercourse Rd.
Pope's Rd.
Cathedral Rd.
Rathmore Park
Mary Aikenhead
Cathedral Walk
Youghal Old Rd.
Glen Ryan Rd.
Old Market Pl.
Leitrim St.
Richmond Hill
St. Patrick's Hill
Audley Pl.
Military Rd.
Shandon St.
Easton's Hill
Roman St.
John St.
Shandon Church
John Redmond
Upper John St.
Dominick St.
Sidney Park
Belgrave Pl.
North Mall
Pope's Quay
Wellington Rd.
Bachelor's Quay
Kyrl's Quay
Camden Pl.
MacCurtain St.
Summer Hill
Grattan St.
North Main St.
Lavitt's Quay
St. Paul St.
Opera House
St. Patrick's Quay
Lower Glanmire Rd.
Sheares St.
Crawford Art Gallery
Emmet Place
Drawbridge St.
Merchant's Quay
Penrose's Quay
Railway St.
Train Station (Kent)
Liberty St.
Castle St.
Paul St.
Academy St.
Merchant St.
Patrick's St.
Winthrop St.
Maylor St.
Anderson's Quay
Washington St.
Grand Parade
Oliver Plunkett St.
Prince's St.
Marlborough St.
Cook St.
Morgan St.
Parnell Place
Lapp's Quay
Hanover St.
South Main St.
Christchurch
South Mall
Morrison's Quay
Albert Quay
Victoria Quay
Vandesford Quay
Union Quay
Angelsea St.
South City Link Rd.
Albert St.
Albert Rd.
Victoria Rd.
Bishop St.
Proby's Quay
Sullivan's Quay
Cove St.
Elizabethan Fort
Douglas St.
Copley St.
Gas Works Rd.
Barrack St.
Industry St.
Abbey St.
Dunbar St.
Mary St.
George's Quay
South Terr.
Sawmill St.
Rutland St.
Infirmary Rd.
Mount Carmel
Presentation Pl.
Tower St.
Evergreen St.
Quaker Rd.
Old Blackrock Rd.
Townshend Pl.
Friars Walk
St. Patrick's Rd.
Summerhill South
High St.
South City Link Rd.
South Douglas Rd.
TO (5 MILES)

0 yards 220
0 meters 200
N

Rent-a-Car, Tourist Office, Grand Parade (tel. 274755). £39 per day, £175 per week. Min. age 21.

Bike Rental: Tents and Leisure, York St. (tel. (021) 500702), rents bikes for £7 per day, £35 per week. **Irish Cycle Hire** (tel. (021) 551430) rents hybrids and mountain bikes at £6 per day, £30 per week; £30 deposit. One-way rental system (tel. (800) 298100) to Irish Cycle Hire depots in Killarney, Dingle, Ennis, and others.

Hitching: Hitchhikers headed for West Cork and County Kerry walk down Western Rd. past both the An Óige hostel and the dog track to the Crow's Nest Pub, or take bus #8 there. Those hoping to hitch a ride to Dublin or Waterford stand on the hill to the train station along Lower Glanmire Rd.

Tourist and Financial Services

Tourist Office: Tourist House, Grand Parade (tel. 273251), near the corner of South Mall and Grand Parade downtown. Offers a Cork city guide and map (£1.50), booking, car rentals, and advice. The office runs an open-top bus tour of the city (£7, students £6). Open in summer M-Sa 9am-6pm; in winter M-Sa 9:30am-5pm.

Budget Travel Office: USIT, 10 Market Parade (tel. 270900), in the Arcade off Patrick St. Large, helpful travel office sells **TravelSave** stamps, Rambler tickets, and Eurotrain tickets. Open M-F 9:30am-5:30pm, Sa 10am-2pm. A second office (tel. 273901) is at University College across from Boole Library. Open M-F 9:30am-5:30pm. See **Getting Around,** p. 36.

Banks: TSB, 4-5 Princes St. (tel. 275221). Open M-W and F 9:30am-5pm, Th 9:30am-7pm. **Bank of Ireland,** 70 Patrick St. (tel. 277777). Open M 10am-5pm, Tu-F 10am-4pm. 24hr. **ATM.**

Local Services

Luggage Storage: Lockers £1 at the **train station.** Storage at the **bus station** £1.30 per item, 80p each additional day. Open M-F 8:35am-6:15pm, Sa 9:30am-6:15pm.

Bookstores: Collins Bookshop, Carey's Ln. (tel. 271346), between Patrick and Paul St. Small but well-stocked. Open M-Sa 9am-6pm. **Waterstone's,** 69 Patrick St. (tel. 276522). Monstrously huge. Open M-Th 9am-8pm, F 9am-9pm, Sa 9am-7pm, Su noon-7pm. **Mercier Bookstore,** 18 Academy St. (tel. 275040), off Patrick St. Specializes in Irish interest books. Open M-F 9:30am-6pm, Sa 9:30am-5:30pm.

Camping Supplies: Outside World and the Tent Shop, Parnell Pl. (tel. 278833), next to the bus station. 2-person nylon tent £17 per week; deposit £10. Extensive stock of camping supplies, including boots and clothing. Open M-F 9:30am-6pm, Sa 9:30am-5:30pm. **Tents and Leisure,** York St. (tel. 500702). Smaller selection but bigger (and pricier) tents. 3- to 4-person tent £16 per night, family-sized tent £10 per night; no deposit.

Bisexual, Gay, and Lesbian Information: The Other Place, 8 South Main St. (tel. 278470), is a resource center for gay and lesbian concerns in Cork and hosts a gay mixed disco (F and Sa 11pm-2am) and a gay coffeehouse (open M-Sa 10am-6pm). **The Other Side Bookshop** (tel. 317660) upstairs sells new and second-hand gay and lesbian publications. Open M-Sa 10am-5:30pm. **Gay Information Cork** (tel. 271087) offers a telephone helpline W 7-9pm and Sa 3-5pm. Lesbian line Th 8-10pm. The second weekend of May is **Cork Women's Fun** weekend. Contact The Other Place for info.

Laundry: Duds 'n Suds, Douglas St. (tel. 314799), around the corner from Kelly's Hostel. Provides dry-cleaning services, TV, and even a small café. Wash £1.50, dry £1.80. Open M-F 8am-9pm, Sa 8am-8pm. **College Launderette,** Western Rd. by the University. Large load, full service £5.20. Open M-F 8am-5:30pm, Sa 10am-5pm.

Emergency and Communications

Emergency: Dial 999; no coins required. **Garda:** Anglesea St. (tel. 313031).

Crisis and Support: Rape Crisis Centre, 5 Camden Pl. (tel. (800) 496496). 24hr. counseling. **AIDS Hotline,** Cork AIDS Alliance, 16 Peter St. (tel. 276676). Open M-F 10am-5pm. **Samaritans** (tel. 271323) offers a 24hr. support line for depression.

Hospital: Mercy Hospital, Grenville Pl. (tel. 271971). £20 fee for access to emergency room. **Cork Regional Hospital,** Wilton St. (tel. 546400), on bus #8.

Pharmacies: Regional Late Night Pharmacy, Wilton Rd. (tel. 344575), opposite the Regional Hospital on bus #8. Open M-F 9am-10pm, Sa-Su 10am-10pm. **Phelan's**

Late Night, 9 Patrick St. (tel. 272511). Open M-Sa 9am-10pm, Su 11am-6pm.
Boots, 71-2 Patrick St. (tel. 270977). Open M-Th and Sa-Su 9am-6pm, F 9am-9pm.
Post Office: Oliver Plunkett St. (tel. 272000). Open M-Sa 9am-1pm and 2-5:30pm.
Internet Access: Cyberstation (tel. 273000) at Jumpin' Jacks Pub on unmarked
Sheare St., one block west of Liberty St. £1.40 per 15min., £5.60 per hr. Open M-F
10am-8pm, Sa 10am-9pm, Su 4pm-9pm. **The Favorite,** 122 Patrick St. (tel.
272646), at the top of Patrick St. near Merchant Quay. Internet access in video-
game-like stalls at the rear of the store. Bring £1 coins. Open daily 9am-10:30pm.
Phone Code: is all grown up at 021.

ACCOMMODATIONS

Cork's eight hostels range from the drearily adequate to the brilliantly beautiful. B&Bs
are clustered along Western Rd. near University College. The other concentration of
accommodations is in the slightly more central area along MacCurtain St. and Lower
Glanmire Rd., near the bus and train stations. For a list of standard features in Irish
hostels, please see **A Hosteler's Bill of Rights,** p. 41.

Hostels

●**The Cork City Independent Hostel,** 100 Lower Glanmire Rd. (tel. 509089). From
the train station, turn right and walk 100yd.; the hostel is on the left. The friendly
guests, staff, and long-time residents relax together in the laid-back atmosphere of
this creaky but very entertaining hostel. The multicolored and eclectic interior
gives this place the most character of any hostel in Cork. Kitchen. Dorms £6; doubles £17. Laundry £3.50.

Sheila's Budget Accommodation Centre (IHH), 3 Belgrave Pl. (tel. 505562), by
the intersection of Wellington Rd. and York St. Scones? A room? Sauna? Positively
packed with perks (and generally packed tight), Sheila's features a huge kitchen, a
barbecue, a sauna (£1.50 for 40min.), a new internet access system, and video
rental (£1). 24hr. reception desk doubles as a small general store, and its family of
staff can guide you to local sights. Non-smoking rooms. 6-bed dorms £6.50; 4-bed
dorms £8; singles £18; doubles £20. Rooms available with bath. Free luggage storage. Sheets 50p. Key deposit £5. Check-out 10:30am.

Kinlay House (IHH), Bob and Joan Walk (tel. 508966), down the alley to the right of
Shandon Church. Located in less-than-luxurious but convenient Shandon, Kinlay
House is large, welcoming, and clean. Each of the modern rooms has a locker and
wash basin. Kitchen with microwave. Video library. Dorms £7.50; singles £11; dou-
bles £25. 10% discount with ISIC. Continental breakfast included. Laundry £3.60.
Internet access £5 per hr.

Cork International Hostel (An Óige/HI), 1-2 Redclyffe, Western Rd. (tel. 543289),
a 15min. walk from the Grand Parade, or take bus #8. Immaculate and modern
bunkrooms in a stately brick Victorian townhouse. **Currency exchange.** Dorms
£8.50; doubles £12.50. All rooms with bath. Continental breakfast £2. Check-in
8am-midnight. **Bike rental** £5 per day, £30 per week.

Isaac's (IHH), 48 MacCurtain St. (tel. 500011). Follow Patrick St. across the North
Channel and take the second right. This large and modern hostel is conveniently
located near the bus and train stations, though it's a bit institutional. Kitchen available and café open for breakfast and lunch. 9- to 16-bed dorms £7; 4- to 8-bed
dorms £8.50. Continental breakfast £1.75, Irish £2.50. 24hr. reception. Dorm lockout 11am-5pm.

Kelly's Hostel, 25 Summerhill South (tel. 315612). Go down Angelsea St. and turn
right on Langford Row, which leads to Summerhill South. Each room is named
after a famous Irish poet, and hand-inscribed poems share the walls with intricate
decorations. Lockers in every room. Full kitchen, cable TV, videos. Free coffee and
tea. Dorms £6.50; singles £10; triples with bath £8. Laundry £2.50.

Campus House (IHH), 3 Woodland View, Western Rd. (tel. 343531). From the
Grand Parade turn onto Washington St. (which later becomes Western Rd.) and
continue for 15min., or take bus #8. Adequate and clean. Dorms £6.50-7.50. Sheets
50p. Reception daily 9am-10pm.

Bed and Breakfasts

Garnish House, Western Rd. (tel. 275111). Prepare to be pampered. Gorgeous rooms, fluffy comforters, fruit, and flowers. Fresh scones when you arrive. A new complimentary breakfast menu features 28 choices. Singles from £20; doubles from £40, with jacuzzi (!) from £50. Free laundry service.

Fairylawn House, Western Rd. (tel. 543444). The spacious rooms are somewhat bare, but the gardens out front are lovely. Elegant living room with piano. £10. Continental breakfast £2.

Danny's B&B, St. John's Terrace, Upper John St. (tel. 503606). Cross the North Channel by the Opera House, make a left on John Redmond St., and then bear right onto Upper John St. Cork's gay B&B, Danny's is all luxury, with colorful decorating that one might call "homobaroque." Complimentary breakfast (catering to vegetarians) is served in a cozy nook by the fire. Washbasins, TVs, oversized armchairs, and tea and coffee-making facilities in every room. Singles £20; doubles £36.

Camping

Bienvenue Ferry Camping (tel. 312711), very near the airport, 5mi. south of town on Kinsale Rd. Airport buses (18 per day) will take you there from the bus station. Tent £5 plus £1 per person. Open year-round.

FOOD

Don't attempt to explore the center of Cork on an empty stomach; intriguing restaurants and cafés are abundant. Particularly appealing are the lanes connecting Patrick St., Paul St., and Oliver Plunkett St. The **English Market,** accessible from Grand Parade, Patrick St., and Prince St., hops with a mesmerizing display of fresh fruit, meat, fish, and cheese. One stand is exclusively devoted to olives and olive oils. (Market open M-Sa 9am-5pm. W and Sa are the best days to visit.) Cork's historic role as a meat-shipping center meant that Corkonians often got stuck eating the leftovers: feet, snouts, and other delectable goodies. Cork's local specialties include *crubeen* (pig's feet), *drisheen* (blood sausage; its texture is a cross between liver and Jell-O), and Clonakilty black pudding (an intriguing mixture of blood and grain). For the less carnivorous, there's a scone or a vegetarian restaurant around every corner. **Tesco,** Paul St. (tel. 270791), is the biggest grocery store in town (open M-W and Sa 9am-6pm, Th-F 9am-9pm). The **Quay Co-op** stocks health and specialty vegetarian foods (see listing below).

The Gingerbread House, Paul St. (tel. 276411). Huge windows, cool jazz, and heavenly breads, pastries, and quiche. Open in summer M-Th 8am-10:30pm, F-Sa 8am-11pm, Su 8am-6pm; in winter M-Th 8am-9:30pm, F-Sa 8am-10:30pm, Su 8am-6pm.

Kafka's, 7 Maylor St. (tel. 270551). Don't let the name put you off; after one taste of these cheap and delicious dishes, you'll undergo a metamorphosis. Interesting Euro-American hybrid cuisine. Sandwiches £3-4. Open M-Sa 8am-6pm. Breakfast 8am-noon.

Polo's Gourmet Café, Washington St. (tel. 277099). Innovative Irish foods, fabulous breakfasts, and coffee choices to keep you buzzing. Open M-W 8am-1am, Th-Su 9am-4am.

Scoozi, Winthrop Ave. (tel. 275077). Follow the tomato signs to this expansive and airy brick-and-wood lined establishment, a perfect spot for enjoying burgers, pizza, and pasta with wild abandon. Most entrees £6. Open M-Sa 9am-11pm, Su 4-10pm.

Quay Co-op, 24 Sullivan's Quay (tel. 317660). A cow's delight: nary a creature was sacrificed for the scrumptious vegetarian delights served in this classy establishment. Excellent soups. Inexpensive wine list; you can also bring your own (£2 corkage fee). Open M-Sa 7-10:30pm; M-Sa 9am-9pm for takeaway. The store downstairs caters to all organic/vegan needs. Store open M-Sa 9am-6:15pm.

Gino's, 7 Winthrop St. (tel. 274485), between Patrick and Oliver Plunkett St. Super fresh (and super cheap) pizza made to order. £4.50 lunch special includes pizza, drink, and ice cream. Open daily 11:30am-midnight.

Truffles Restaurant, 6 Princes St. (tel. 270251). A cozy little bistro right off Patrick's St. that won't break your wallet. Small, intimate tables on the second floor look over the busy shopping street below. 3-course lunch special £4.95. Open M 10am-6pm, Tu-Su 10am-10pm.

Bully's, 40 Paul St. (tel. 273555). Enjoy sinfully good Italian specialties while sitting at candle-lit tables surrounded by fiery scarlet walls. Pizzas from £4. Lasagna £5. Extensive wine list. Open M-Sa noon-11:30pm, Su 1-11pm.

Tony's Bistro, 69 N. Main St. (tel. 270848). Friendly staff, colorful decor, and cheap eats (chicken basket meal £3.50). An inexplicable and bizarre "Stars on Parade" Hollywood theme in the menu adds spice to the Tony's experience. Open M-Sa 9am-6pm.

The Delhi Palace, 6 Washington St. (tel. 276227). Consume like a maharajah. Vegetarian dishes around £6, meat dishes around £7. Dinner daily 5:30pm-midnight.

PUBS

Cork's pubs have all the variety of music and atmosphere you'd expect to find in Ireland's second-largest city. Pubs compete for pint-guzzlers along Oliver Plunkett St., Union Quay, and South Main St. Cork is the proud home of **Murphy's,** a thick, sweet stout that sometimes, and especially in Cork, tastes as good as Guinness. **Beamish,** a cheaper stout, is also brewed here.

An Spailpín Fánach, 28 South Main St. (tel. 277949), across from the Beamish brewery. One of Cork's most popular pubs and probably the oldest (it opened in 1779). The name (uhn spal-PEEN FAW-nuhk) means "the wandering potato picker." The crowd tucks itself into the brick-walled, wood-trimmed nooks for conversation and great music. Live music (Su-F) ranges from bluegrass to traditional. Pub grub (Irish stew £3.75) served M-F noon-3pm.

The Lobby, 1 Union Quay (tel. 311113). The largest of the Quay pubs and arguably the most famous venue in Cork, the Lobby has given some of Ireland's biggest folk acts their start. Live music nightly at 9:30pm, ranging from trad to acid jazz. Occasional cover £4-5.

Charlie's, Union Quay (tel. 965272). Art by local student artists decks the walls of the smallest of the Quay pubs. Live music ranging from acoustic blues to rock/pop nightly in summer, 3-4 times per week during the rest of the year.

The Old Oak, Oliver Plunkett St. (tel. 276165). The hardwood floors and stained-glass cathedral ceilings strain to contain the huge mixed crowd that files in here nightly. Live music 3-4 times per week.

The Donkey's Ears, Union Quay (tel. 964846). Deceptively quaint, Donkey's Ears is the most "alternative" of the Quay pubs.

An Phoenix, 3 Union Quay (tel. 964275). Music (folk, trad, rock, or R&B) nightly in this smoky multi-leveled pub. The balcony attracts a younger group, while the wine-cask-embedded walls of the lower level contain a more mixed crowd.

The Thirsty Scholar, Western Rd. (tel. 276209), across the street from Jury's Hotel. Steps from campus, this congenial pub is proof that students will walk no farther for a pint than they have to. Live summer trad sessions.

O'Rearden's Pub, Washington St. Quite lively with a late-night bar (open until 1am). Extremely popular with mid-twenties local crowd.

The Western Star, Western Rd. (tel. 543047). The recent favorite for UCC students, this pub is under new ownership and doing fantastic things. If you're staying nearby in summer, enjoy the outdoors bar on the patio by the Lee River. Free barbecue Fridays. Trad twice a week (call for details). Buses to the discos after the bar closes. Lunch served M-F (sandwiches £1.80).

Loafer's, 26 Douglas St. (tel. 311612). Cork's sole gay and lesbian pub is jam-packed nightly by people of all ages. Good conversation makes this bar a cozy spot.

MUSIC AND CLUBS

Cork is home to several popular bands, but what is hip one week can be passé the next. Check out *List Cork,* a free weekly schedule of music available at local stores. The **Lobby** and **Charlie's Bar** (see Pubs) are consistently sound choices for live music. **Nancy Spain's,** 48 Barrack St. (tel. 314452), is one of the city's most popular venues, often featuring live rock and blues. (DJ Th-Sa, nightclub upstairs. Call for live music schedule. Cover £3-8.) Cork is also full of trendy nightclubs that suck up the sloshed and swaying student population once the pubs have closed. Before you fork over your £3-5 cover charge, remember that all clubs close at 2am.

Club FX and **The Grapevine,** Gravel Ln. (tel. 271120). Follow the tropical fish to these twin clubs. From Washington St., make a right on Little Hangover St. and then a left onto Gravel Ln. Club FX features two levels with plenty of pulsating lights, while The Grapevine sports an odd Mediterranean interior and a young, self-conscious crowd. Open W-Su 10:30pm-2am. Cover £3-6.

Sir Henry's, South Main St. (tel. 274391). Arguably the most popular club in Cork, and also the most intense. Prepare to wedge yourself between sweaty, semi-conscious bodies and throb to raging techno and house W-Sa. Cover £2-11.

City Limits, Coburg St. (tel. 501206). A pleasant, mixed-age crowd. No dance music here—DJs spin anything from the 60s to the 90s Th and Su 11pm-2am. Comedy Nites F-Sa 9pm-2am.

Zoës, Oliver Plunkett St. (tel. 270870), with its infernal red interior, draws in a similar crowd to City Limits with a mixture of club music nightly 11pm-2am. Cover £3-5. On Thursday and Friday, the adjoining **Black Bush** pub stays open until 2am.

Klüb Kaos, Oliver Plünkett St. Ascend the lit staircase at this chik klüb for poünding dance and tekhno müsic nightly 11pm-2am. Küver £3-5.

Gorby's, Oliver Plunkett St. (tel. 270074). A broad range of music. Cover £2-4.

The Other Place, South Main St. (tel. 278470). Cork's gay and lesbian disco rocks every Friday and Saturday 11:30pm-2am. Dance floor and a bar/café upstairs. Attracts the majority of Cork's gay population, especially the younger set, on weekend nights. The first Friday of the month is ladies night.

The Half Moon Club (tel. 274308), tucked behind the Opera House on Half Moon St. Delights with jazz, blues, and trad (Th-Sa). Check the Opera House box office for listing. Bars open at 11:30pm.

An Sráidbhaile (uhn SRAIJ-why-luh), Grand Parade (tel. 274391), in the Waterside Hostel. Traditional Irish set dancing June-Sept. nightly 9:30pm-midnight. Cover £4.

SIGHTS

Cork has a smattering of sights that can be reached easily by foot. For guidance, pick up *The Cork Area City Guide* at the tourist office (£1.50).

The Old City

You might start seeing Cork from Christ Church Ln. in the center of the city, off the Grand Parade just north of Bishop Lucey Park. Walk down the lane (keeping the park on your left) to emerge on South Main St., once the city's main drag. To the right is the steepleless **Christ Church,** now the Cork Archives (closed to tourists). The church is an emblem of the persistence of Catholicism in Cork; it has been burned to the ground three times since its 1270 consecration and was rebuilt promptly each time, most recently in 1729.

The small but dynamic **Triskel Arts Centre,** Tobin St. (tel. 272022), is the first right down a narrow lane. *(Open M-W and F-Sa 10am-5:30pm. Free.)* The center maintains two small galleries with rotating contemporary exhibits. It also runs a brilliant café (check out the innovative blue-back room) and organizes a wide variety of cultural events, including music, film, literature, theater, and the visual arts. *(café open M-F 8am-5:30pm, Sa 9am-5:30pm.)* On a nice day, you can get a decent view of Cork (and a much too good view of Beamish Brewery) from **Keyser Hill.** Follow South Main St. away from Washington St., cross the South Gate Bridge, and turn right onto Proby's Quay and then left onto obscure Keyser Hill. At the top of the stairs is **Elizabethan Fort,** a star-shaped, ivy-covered remnant of English rule in Cork. *(Always open. Free.)* Built in 1601 after the Elizabethan English clobbered Hugh O'Neill's forces at the Battle of Kinsale, the fort (rather, what's left of it) now sequesters the Garda station. To access the fort's strategically valuable view, climb the stairs just inside the main gate. Farther down Proby's Quay, **St. Finbarr's Cathedral,** Bishop St. (tel. 963387), is a testament to the Victorian love of Gothic bombast. *(Open daily Apr.-Sept. 10am-5:30pm, Oct.-Mar. 10am-1pm and 2-5pm. Free.)* St. Finbarr allegedly founded his "School of Cork" here in 606, but no trace of the early foundation remains. Although the present cathedral was built between 1735 and 1870, its Gothic style makes it appear much older.

Shandon and Emmet Place

On the other side of the Lee, North Main St. becomes Shandon St., heart of the Shandon neighborhood. It's less affluent than the rest of Cork and has more neighborhood pride. To get to Cork's most famous landmark, **St. Anne's Church** (tel. 505906), walk up Shandon St. until you see Donnelly's Diner on the left, then take a right down unmarked Church St. and go straight. *(Open in summer M-Sa 10am-5pm, in winter M-Sa 10am-4pm.)* Most people call it **Shandon Church,** since the steeple is Shandon Tower. The now barely visible red and white (sandstone and limestone) strips on the steeple inspired Cork's ubiquitous "Rebel" flag; the salmon on top of the church spire represents the River Lee. Like most of Cork, the original church was ravaged by 17th-century pyromaniacal English armies; construction of the current church began in 1722. Four clocks grace the four sides of Shandon's tower. Notoriously out of sync with each other, the clocks have been held responsible for many an Irishman's tardy arrival at work and have earned the church its endearing nickname, "the four-faced liar." For £1.50, visitors can subject the city to their experiments in bell-ringing (sheet music provided). Just opposite the church is the **Shandon Craft Centre,** Church St., where artisans practice weaving, crystal-cutting, and pottery. **Under the Golden Fish** (tel. 302303), a small café in the center, has glorious pastries and an enclosed garden (open M-Sa 7:30am-2pm). The circular **Firkin Crane Centre** (tel. 507487), a performance hall, is next door. Also adjacent is the new **Cork Butter Museum** (tel. 300600), an attractive museum that comes closer than one might think to making Cork's cans, commerce, and preserved butter interesting. *(Open May-Sept. M-Sa 10am-5pm. £2.50, children £2.)*

Down the other side of the hill and across the north fork of the Lee sits the monstrous cement **Opera House,** erected 20 years ago after the older, more elegant opera house went down in flames. The adjacent **Crawford Municipal Art Gallery,** Emmet Pl. (tel. 273377), boasts a permanent collection of 18th-century Irish art and features contemporary traveling exhibitions. *(Open M-Sa 10am-5pm. Free.)*

Western Cork

Cork's other major sights are on the western edge of the city. From Grand Parade, walk down Washington St., which soon becomes Western Rd. The main entrance to **University College Cork (UCC),** built in 1845, is on Western Rd. *(Campus always open for self-guided touring. Tours by prior arrangement. £15 for group.)* Gothic windows, grassy expanses, and long, stony corridors make for a fine, secluded afternoon walk or picnic along the Lee. Tours of the campus tell the story of George Boole, the Cork professor of mathematics (and the mastermind behind Boolean logic) upon whom Sir Arthur Conan Doyle based his character Prof. James Moriarty, Sherlock Holmes's nemesis. Across the street from the college entrance, signs point to the **Cork Public Museum** (tel. 270679), set in the splendid gardens of **Fitzgerald Park.** *(Open June-July M-Sa 8:30am-10pm, Su 10am-10pm; May-Aug. M-Sa 8:30am-9pm; Apr. and Sept. M-Sa 8:30am-8pm; Oct.-Mar. M-Sa 8:30am-5pm. M-Sa free; Su 75p, students free.)* The museum's astoundingly esoteric exhibits feature such varied goodies as 17th- and 18th-century toothbrushes and the 1907 costume worn by James Dwyer, chief sheriff of Cork.

If time's tight in Cork, you might go directly to the **Cork City Gaol.** *(Open daily in summer 9:30am-6pm; in winter M-F 10:30am-2:30pm, Sa-Su 10am-4pm. £3.50, students and seniors £2.50, children £2, family £9. Last tour 1hr. before closing.)* The museum is a reconstruction of the jail as it appeared in the 1800s. It's an easy walk from Fitzgerald Park; cross the footbridge at the western end of the park, turn right on Sunday's Well Rd., and then follow the signs. A tour of the jail tells the story of individual Cork prisoners and the often miserable treatment they endured. For example, prisoners ran for hours on a "human treadmill" used to grind grain. At the end of the tour is a captivating film that explains "why some people turned to crime."

ENTERTAINMENT

Cork is easy to enjoy. If you tire of drinking, take advantage of Cork's music venues, dance clubs, theaters, and sports arenas, or just explore the innumerable cafés and bookshops.

Theater and Film

The **New Granary,** Mardyke Quay (tel. 904275), stages performances of new scripts by local and visiting theater companies. **Triskel Arts Centre,** Tobin St. (tel. 277300), simmers with avant-garde theater and performance art and hosts regular concert and film series. **Everyman's Theatre** (a.k.a. "the Palace"), MacCurtain St. (tel. 501673), stages big-name musicals, plays, operas, and concerts (box office open M-Sa 10am-5pm, 7pm on show dates; tickets £6-15). The **Opera House,** Emmet Pl. (tel. 270022), next to the river, presents an extensive program of dance and performance art (open M-Sa 10:15am-5:30pm). The **Irish Gay and Lesbian Film Festival** happens in mid-October. For a fix of mainstream American celluloid or the occasional Irish or arthouse flick, head to the **Capitol Cineplex** (tel. 272216), at Grand Parade and Washington St. (£4, students £3.50, matinees £2.50). Tickets are only available before 8pm, even for later shows.

Sports

Cork is sporting-mad. Its soccer, hurling, and Gaelic football teams are perennial contenders for national titles (see **Sports,** p. 69). **Hurling** and **Gaelic football** take place every Sunday afternoon at 3pm from June to September at the stadium in Blackrock (bus #2); for additional details, call the GAA (tel. 385876) or consult *The Cork Examiner.* Be cautious when venturing into the streets on soccer game days (especially during championships), where screaming, jubilant fans will either bowl you down or, worse, force you to take part in the revelry. Tickets to big games are £13-15 and scarce, but Saturday, Sunday, and Wednesday evening matches are cheap (£1-4) to free. You can buy tickets to these local games at the **Pairc Uí Chaoimh** (park EE KWEEV), the Gaelic Athletic Association stadium. For more interactive fun, **Jumpin' Jacks** features pool, snooker, an arcade, bowling, internet "cyberstations" (see **Internet Access,** p. 197), and a high-speed monorail ride (open daily 10am-11pm).

Festivals

The **Cork Choral Festival** (tel. 308308) fills city churches with international singing groups the first weekend in May, while the **Cork Folk Festival** (tel. 317271), held in various pubs and hotels, jams in September. The **Sense of Cork Festival** (tel. 310597), a cornucopia of local crafts, arts, and theater, is held the last week in June. Also popular is the **International Film Festival** during the first week of October at the Opera House and the Triskel Arts Centre. Documentaries and shorts elbow the features for attention (contact the Triskel Arts Centre, tel. 271711). See the big names for free in local pubs during the three-week **Guinness Jazz Festival** (tel. 273946) in October. Book well ahead at all hostels.

■ Near Cork

Love, tragedy, and free drinks await you just outside Cork City. A kiss is no longer just a kiss at the Blarney Stone, the ultimate Irish tourist attraction. Cameron-inspired *Titanic* aficionados can get their fix at Cobh, the ship's final stop before her doomed journey. Sweet, sweet Jameson is distilled in nearby Midleton, where visitors learn themselves why Queen Elizabeth I once called Irish whiskey her one true Irish friend.

■ Blarney (An Bhlarna)

Whether you're in the mood for the ideal Irish countryside view or you're simply dying to stand in a damp castle passageway, **Blarney Castle** (tel. 385252), with its **Blarney Stone,** is the quintessential tourist spot. *(Open June-Aug. 9am-7pm, Su 9:30am-*

5:30pm; Sept. M-Sa 9am-6:30pm, Su 9:30am-sundown; Oct.-Apr. M-Sa 9am-sundown, Su 9:30am-sundown; May M-Sa 9am-6:30pm, Su 9:30am-5:30pm. £3, seniors and students £2, children £1.) Unfortunately, not only are the stone's origins obscure (some say it was brought from Jerusalem during the Crusades, others say it was a chip off the Scottish Stone of Scone) but the stone itself is a bit vague too—it's just a slab of limestone among others in the castle wall. Still, with everyone else doing it, you might just find yourself leaning over backward to kiss the stone in hopes of acquiring the legendary eloquence bestowed on those who smooch it. The term "blarney," meaning smooth-talking b.s., was supposedly coined by Queen Elizabeth I during her long and tiring negotiations over control of the castle. The owner, Cormac McCarthy, Lord of Blarney, followed the 16th-century practice of royal making-nice, writing grandiose letters in praise of the Queen, but he never relinquished the land. Ruffling her royal feathers, the Queen was heard to say, "This is all blarney!" The Irish consider the whole thing a bunch of blarney; they're more concerned with the sanitary implication of so many people kissing the same rock. More impressive than the stone is the castle itself, built in 1446.

Adjacent to the castle lies the **Rock Close,** an extensive and impressive rock-and-plant garden built on the sacred grounds of the Druids. If you remembered to bring along a small goat, you could offer it to their ancient gods at the **sacrificial altar.** The crowds tend to confine themselves to the castle, making the Rock Close and adjacent fields a perfect place to wander. The limestone cave near the castle also merits exploration for those who love the dark (remember to bring a flashlight). The **Blarney Woolen Mills** (tel. 385280), across from the castle, are the other main attraction of Blarney. *(Open daily 9am-6pm.)* The outlet sells Aran sweaters (from £25; much more for the handknit variety), Waterford crystal, china, and the standard tourist fare in the renovated building of the former mill. *(Open M-Sa 9:30am-5pm.)*

Bus Éireann runs buses from **Cork** to Blarney (M-Sa 16 per day, Su 10 per day, £2.60 return). From June 16 to September 6, they also offer the **Cork Tourist Trail bus,** which trundles from the Cork bus station to the City Gaol, the Ballincollig Powder Mills, Blarney Castle, and back to Cork (2 per day £5). The **phone code** in Blarney is a rock-solid 021.

Blarney is a short and pleasant bike ride from Cork, or 25 minutes by bus, so there is no reason, practical or otherwise, to stay overnight. Should you fall madly in love with the Blarney Stone after giving it a wet-lickery one, you can rent functional beds at the **Blarney Tourist Hostel** (tel. 385580 or 381430), 2 mi. from town on the Killarney Rd. in a converted farmhouse (£6). Closer to town but more expensive, the **Rosemount B&B** offers comfortable beds just up the hilly lane from the bus stop (follow the signs; £15, with bath £17). On the town square, **St. Helen's Restaurant** (tel. 385571), serves cheap sandwiches starting at £1.60 (open daily 9am-6pm), while **The Blarney Stone** (tel. 385482) cooks up Irish specialties (£5-6; open M-Sa 10:30am-10pm, Su 11am-9:30pm). Pub fare is served at the **Muskerry Arms** (tel. 385066), along with trad and cabaret (music nightly 9:30-11:30pm).

■ Cobh

Though a pleasant village today, Cobh (KOVE) was Ireland's main transatlantic port until the 1950s. For many of the emigrants who left Ireland between 1848 and 1950, the steep hillside and multi-colored houses were the last glimpse of their country. In keeping with Irish tradition, Cobh has some sad stories to tell (again and again). Cobh was the *Titanic*'s last port of call before the "unsinkable" ship met with her unfortunate iceberg. Later, when the Germans torpedoed the *Lusitania* during World War I, most survivors and some of the dead were taken back to Cobh in lifeboats. There is a Lusitania Memorial in Casement Square and a mass grave of 150 victims. In remembrance of its eminent but tragic history, Cobh recently established a museum called **The Queenstown Story** (tel. 813591), adjacent to the Cobh railway station. *(Open daily 10am-6pm, last admission 5pm. £3.50, students £2.50.)* The museum's flashy multimedia exhibits trace the port's eventful history, with sections devoted to emigration, the

Lusitania, the *Titanic,* and the peak of transatlantic travel. In June 1995, the Cork-Cobh train ran into the museum, hurtling through two walls and the ceiling—not an auspicious start in this accident-prone town.

St. Colman's Cathedral towers over Cobh. *(Open daily 7am-8pm. Free.)* Its ornate Gothic spire dominates the town's architectural landscape and provides a great view of the harbor. Completed in 1915, the cathedral boasts the largest carillon in Ireland, consisting of 47 bells weighing over 7700 pounds. The small **Cobh Museum** (tel. 813591), housed inside the Scots Church on High Rd., deals almost exclusively with Cobh's maritime history. *(Open M-Sa 11am-6pm, Su 2-6pm. 50p.)* You'll laugh, you'll cry, you'll find your ancestors through the center's "Geological Record Finder" (email cobher@indigo.ie). Twenty minutes and £15 will get you locations of church records, gravestone inscriptions, and estate records.

Cobh revels in its aquatic heritage. The tourist office occupies the recently restored site of the Royal Cork Yacht Club, built in 1854 and reputed to be the world's first yacht club. Today's visitors take advantage of the harbor for all types of water sports. **International Sailing** (tel. 811237) on East Beach teaches sailing and canoeing and rents canoes (£8 per 3hr.), sailing dinghies (from £24 per 3hr.), and windsurfing equipment (£18 per 3hr.; open daily 9:30am-6pm). The second week in July brings **Seisiún Cois Cuan Festival,** a celebration of traditional Irish music and storytelling. During the second week of August, the **Cobh People's Regatta** and visits from many cruise liners, including the QE2, draw crowds to Cobh. From June to September, tours of Cobh harbor operate daily from Kennedy Pier.

Cobh is best reached by **rail** from **Cork** (25min., M-Sa 12 per day, Su 5 per day, £2.50 return). Pick up the *Cobh Tourist Trail Map* at the **tourist office** (tel. 813301), down the hill from the train station, on the right (open M-Sa 9:30am-5:30pm, Su 11am-5:30pm). The **phone code** docks at 021.

Should you feel the call of the sea and want to stay in Cobh, try the charming **Beechmont House Hostel** (tel. 812177), run out of a family home a steep climb up Bond St. Call ahead. (£7.50 includes breakfast.) Pubs, restaurants, and B&Bs face Cobh's harbor from Beach St. **The River Room,** on West Beach (tel. 813293), grills "ciabattas," large (by Irish standards) sandwiches on tasty bread, and lunchtime quiche (open daily 9am-6pm). **The Queenstown Restaurant** will offer you a sandwich (£2.95), shepherd's pie, or a daily special while you mull over the town's disasters in the pretty entrance hall to the Queenstown Story Heritage Center (open daily 10am-6pm). Alternatively, buy a picnic at **SuperValu supermarket** (tel. 811586) on West Beach and eat it seaside at John F. Kennedy Park near the waterfront (supermarket open M-W 9am-6pm, Th-F 9am-9pm). A young and aloof crowd sits in the smoky atmosphere of Cobh's Euro-café bar, **Rob Roy,** Pearse Sq. The **Rotunda,** 14 Casement Sq. (tel. 811631), across from the Lusitania Memorial, is more sedate, with plush banquettes of crimson velvet.

Ten minutes from Cobh by rail lies **Fota Island,** where penguins, peacocks, cheetahs, and giraffes roam, largely free of cages, in the **Fota Wildlife Park** (tel. (021) 812678). *(Open Apr.-Oct. M-Sa 10am-6pm, Su 11am-6pm. Last admission 5pm. £3.70, students £3.30.)* Resist *Jurassic Park* flashbacks should a pack of small squirrel monkeys surround you. The 70-acre park houses 70 species of animals from South America, Africa, Asia, and Australia. The **Fota Arboretum** adjacent to the park houses a diverse range of plants and trees as exotic as the beasts next door. *(Always open. Free.)* Fota is an intermediate stop on the **train** from Cork to Cobh; if you buy a ticket from Cork to Cobh or vice versa, you can get off at Fota and reboard free.

■ Midleton

A short drive or bus ride from Cork or Cobh on the main Cork-Waterford highway, Midleton beckons pilgrims of the water of life (Irish for whiskey) to the **Jameson Heritage Centre** (tel. 613594). *(Open Mar.-Nov. daily 10am-6pm. £3.50, children £1.50, family £9.50.)* The center rolls visitors through a one-hour tour detailing the craft and history of whiskey production. Better yet, they give you a glass of the potent stuff at the end—for demonstration, of course. After all, "the story of whiskey is the story of Ireland." The highlight of Midleton (aside from the whiskey, of course) is its hostel, **An Stór (IHH)** (tel. (633106). From Main St., turn onto Connolly St. and then take your first left. The hostel's name means the "the treasure" in Irish. New, clean, and full of window boxes and bedrooms with bath, the hostel teaches visitors the Irish names of several birds—each room is named after one. (Fortunately, they are also listed in English so that you can find your room if you have a drop too much at the Heritage tour.) The friendly proprietor can direct you to local activities ranging from castle visits to scenic bike rides. (Dorms £7; private rooms £10 per person. Laundry £3.) For hearty Irish food to soak up the whiskey, try **Finin's** (tel. 631878), on Main St. **Mr. Dee's Chinese Takeaway,** Connolly St. (tel. 633197), boasts 105 dishes (most £7-8). Head to **The Meeting Place,** Connolly St. (tel. 631928), for a pint and excellent live music on Tuesday nights (occasional £2.50 cover). **Wallis's,** 74 Main St. (tel. 631155), is another excellent live music venue (most Tu and Su nights).

Know Your Whiskey

Anyone who drinks his whiskey as it's meant to be drunk—"neat," or straight—can tell you that there's a huge difference between Irish whiskeys (Bushmills, Jameson, Power and Son, and the like), Scotch whiskys (spelled without an e), and American whiskeys. But what makes an Irish whiskey *Irish?* The basic ingredients in whiskey—water, barley (which becomes malt once processed), and heat from a fuel source—are always the same. It's the quality of these ingredients, the way in which they're combined, and the manner in which the combination is stored that gives each product its distinct flavor. The different types of whiskey derive from slight differences in this production process. American whiskey is distilled once and is often stored in oak, bourbon is made only in Kentucky, scotch uses peat-smoked barley, and Irish whiskey is triple distilled. After this basic breakdown, individual distilleries will claim that their further variations on the theme make their product the best of its class. We could get more technical, but at *Let's Go* we realize that the best way to understand the distinctions between brands is to taste the various labels in close succession to one another. Line up those shot glasses, sniff and then taste each one (roll the whiskey in your mouth like a real pro), and have a sip of water between each brand. **"But I don't have the money to buy a shot of each brand,"** our budget-traveling readers murmur. Well, then, get thee to a distillery tour and when the tour guide asks for volunteers, stick your hand in the air and squeal, "Me! Me!" If you're lucky, you'll be selected to be an "Irish Whiskey Taster," trying no less than five kinds of Irish, two scotch, and one bourbon whiskey under the supervision of your highly trained tour guide. Sure, the certificate is nice, but the haze is even better (up to a point, of course).

■ Youghal

Thirty miles east of Cork on N25, beach-blessed Youghal (YAWL, or "Y'all" for cute Southerners) can be a stopover on the way to Waterford and points east. If you've seen the movie *Moby Dick* with Gregory Peck, you've seen Youghal—it was filmed here in 1954. A popularly tacky beach and the much more upscale ruins of what claims to have once been "Europe's leading walled port" keep Youghal a little interesting even after its brief flirtation with stardom.

PRACTICAL INFORMATION Buses stop in front of the public toilets on Main St. across from Dempsey's Bar and travel to **Cork** (50min., M-Sa 13 per day, Su 9 per day, £5.50) and **Waterford** (1½-2hr., M-Sa 7 per day, Su 5 per day, £8.80). **Hitching** to Cork or Waterford along N25 is possible. The helpful **tourist office,** Market Sq. (tel. 92390), on the waterfront behind the clocktower, distributes a useful "tourist trail" booklet (free) and can steer you to trad sessions in the town's pubs. (Open June-Aug. M-F 9am-1pm and 2-6pm, Sa-Su 10am-1pm and 2-6pm; May and Sept. M-Sa 9:30am-1pm.) Call me **phone code** 024.

ACCOMMODATIONS, FOOD, AND PUBS The spanking-new **Stella Mara** hostel opened in July 1998. Call the tourist office for details. **Hillside** (tel. 92468), just across the street, is a puzzling cross between a hostel and a B&B, but it is by far the cheapest place to stay in town. All the antiques that once graced the house were sold off, so now you'll have to make do with knit afghans on spongy beds (£7.50). **Devon View,** Pearse Sq. (tel. 92298), is considerably nicer, if slightly garish, with antique furniture and silver in the dining and sitting rooms and airy apartments with bath, TV, and phone (singles £20; doubles £32). Campers sometimes set up their tents on the beach for a night.

Youghal may have more chip fryers per capita than any other town in Cork, but it does have a few proper restaurants to round out the diet. **The Perfect Blend** (tel. 91127), next to the Clock Tower on North Main St., serves up standard Italian food at substandard prices (pasta £5, pizza £4-6, entrees £6-8). The **Coffee Pot,** 77 North Main St. (tel. 92523), is extremely popular among locals, serving pastries, soup, and light meals (most entrees £4-6, set lunch £8; open daily 9:30am-7:30pm). Should Youghal not tempt the tastebuds, head to **SuperValu** (tel. 92150) in the town center on Main St. (open M-Th 9am-6pm, F 9am-9pm, Sa 9am-8pm, Su 10am-6pm).

Local youth converge nightly on the blue and orange **Yawl Inn,** North Main St. (tel. 93024), to fill up on pints and thumping techno. **The Nook** (tel. 92225), next door, is arguably the most popular and pleasantly mixed pub in town (trad Wednesdays). Other good pubs include **The Clock Tavern,** South Main St. (tel. 93052), with nightly music and good bands on Fridays and Saturdays, and the **Central Star,** North Main St. (tel. 92419), where locals gather to play darts and croon weekend sing-alongs.

SIGHTS Enjoyably informative historical **walking tours** of the town leave from the tourist office. *(1½hr. June-Aug. M-F 11am and 3pm, Sa 11am. £2.50.)* The huge **Clock-gate,** built in 1777, straddles narrow, crowded Main St. From here you can see the old city walls, built on the hill sometime between the 13th and 17th centuries. The tower served as a prison and low-budget gallows (prisoners were hanged from the windows). On Church St. off Main St., **St. Mary's Church** and **Myrtle Grove** stand side-by-side. St. Mary's Church is possibly the oldest operating church in Ireland; parts of it remain from the original Danish-built church constructed in 1020. A well-preserved portion of the old city walls lurks at the back of the church's overgrown graveyard. Myrtle Grove was the residence of Sir Walter Raleigh when he served as mayor here in 1588-89. Pay due respect to the corner of the garden where he is said to have planted the first Irish potatoes and gawk or groan according to your taste at the window where Raleigh's buddy Edmund Spencer is said to have finished his hefty *Faerie Queen.* For an encapsulated version of Youghal's history since the 9th century, drop by the tourist office's **Heritage Centre.** *(Same phone and hours as the tourist office. £1.)* Across the street from the tourist office and up a little alley is **Fox's Lane Folk Museum** (phone the tourist office, tel. 92390). *(Open Tu-Sa 10am-1pm and 2-6pm. Last tour at 5:30pm. £2.)* The museum's collection, dedicated to illustrating the history and social context of "domestic bygones" between 1850 and 1950 (including a moustache cup and a cucumber straightener), has been lovingly and single-handedly assembled over 30 years.

The **Youghal Carnival** rages in mid-July with a different theme each year. Youghal also throws a **Busking Festival** during the first weekend of August, which fills the streets with puppet theater, street theater, nightly open-air music, and plenty of food. **Ceolta Sí** (KYOL-ta SHEE; "fairy music") reaps the talent of local youth in an enjoyable semi-professional program of traditional dance, music, and storytelling throughout the summer. *(July-Aug. Th 8:30pm. £2.50.)*

WEST CORK

From Cork City, there are two routes to Skibbereen and West Cork: an inland route and a coastal route through Kinsale. Two major **bus routes** begin in Cork City and serve West Cork: a coastal bus runs from Cork to **Skibbereen,** stopping in **Bandon, Clonakilty,** and **Rosscarbery** (M-Sa 3 per day, Su 2 per day). An inland bus travels from Cork to **Bantry,** stopping in **Bandon** and **Dunmanway** (M-Sa 3 per day, Su 2 per day). **Hitchers** are reported to have few problems in these parts.

■ The Inland Route

Cyclists and drivers wishing to save time or avoid crowds should consider one of the inland routes from Cork to Skibbereen, Bantry, the Beara, or Killarney. Popular routes are Cork-Macroom-Killarney, Cork-Macroom-Ballingeary-Bantry/Glengarriff, and Cork-Dunmanway-Bantry/Skibbereen. The views at sunset through the Shehy Mountains around Dunmanway and Ballingeary are breathtaking—celestial orange and red. The main attraction of the area is the abundance of interesting walks and bike rides.

■ Dunmanway and Ballingeary

South of Macroom on R587, **Dunmanway** is less a town than a single busy main square. **Bus Éireann** voyages to Dunmanway from **Cork** (4 per day, Su 2 per day, £6.30) and from Dunmanway to **Glengarriff** via **Bantry** (3 per day, Su 2 per day). Buses stop in front of the News Basket on The Square. The best place to stay and one of the best reasons to come to Dunmanway is the **Shiplake Mountain Hostel (IHH)** (tel. (023) 45750), in the hills 3 mi. from town. Feel free to call for a ride from Dunmanway, or follow Castle St. (next to Gatzby's Nightclub) out of town toward Coolkelure and then turn right at the hostel sign. Shiplake, which commands a view of the lakes and mountains, has heaps of information on local hiking and cycling and proprietors with contagious enthusiasm for this spectacular area. They also rent bicycles (£7 per day, part of the **Wheel Escapes** program) and cook what is perhaps the best hostel food in Ireland. A romantic and extremely popular gypsy caravan of cozy, refurbished trailers painted in bright colors accommodates couples or families behind the hostel. (Dorms £6.50-7; caravan £7.50-8 per person. **Camping** £4 per person. Wholefood groceries available. Vegetarian meals and healthy breakfasts £2.50-6.) Dunmanway's 8,500 people support 23 pubs. The most traditional, both musically and atmospherically, is the **West End Pub** (tel. (023) 45120). Filled with a younger crowd, **An Toísín,** Main St. (tel. (023) 45954), 200 yd. from The Square, rings with live music on the weekends. The **Shamrock Bar** on Main St. has recently brought trad to Dunmanway. Dunmanway's most popular club, **Gatzby's** (tel. (023) 55275), offers dance music until 2am. Eminently explorable **Castle Donovan** is an easy bike ride from Shiplake Hostel. (Ask at the hostel for details.)

Northwest of Dunmanway on R584, **Ballingeary,** with the quiet, very basic **Tig Barra Hostel (IHH)** (tel. (026) 47016), makes a good base for exploring the lush **Gougane Barra Forest,** the adjacent church marking the site of St. Finnbar's monastery, the **Shehy Mountains,** or your budding interest in the Irish language. Ballingeary is in the heart of one of West Cork's *gaeltachts,* and Tig Barra's owner is a native speaker. (Dorms £6; **camping** £3 per person. Laundry £2. Open mid-Mar. to Sept.)

■ Coastal Route

From Kinsale, southerly R600 stands watch over farming valleys before hugging the coast and wide, deserted beaches on the way to Clonakilty. From Cork, N71 purringly stretches its tough asphalt skin all the way to Clonakilty via Bandon. Past Clonakilty, the population starts to thin out. Mountains rise up inland, rocky ridges replace smooth hills, and sunset-laden shoals proliferate as Ireland's southern coast starts to

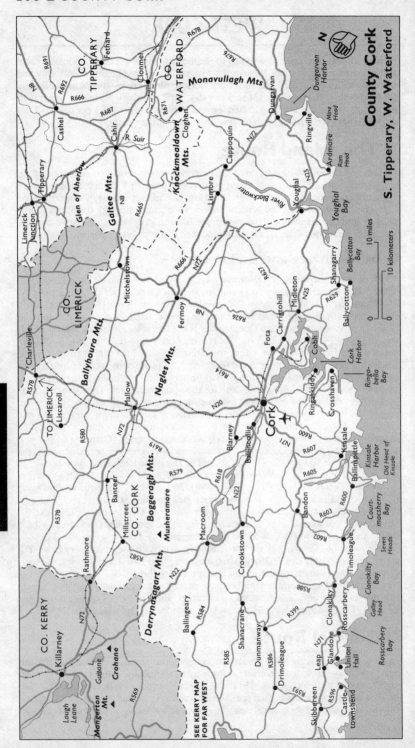

County Cork
S. Tipperary, W. Waterford

N

10 miles
10 kilometers

SEE KERRY MAP
FOR FAR WEST

look like its west. Crossroads along N71 link mellow tourist towns and hardworking fishing villages. "Blow-ins," refugees from America and Northern Europe, have settled in the area by the hundreds, though not increasing the populations so much as replacing the area's dwindling Irish population. They are usually kick-back expats who appreciate the quiet pace and extraordinary scenery of the southwest but have shaped its culture to their own tastes. Trad music thrives in these small towns, attracting long-time locals and artsy foreigners alike.

The islands in the stretch of ocean between Baltimore and Schull may be the wildest, remotest human habitations in all of southern Ireland. High cliffs plunge into the sea, accounting for a harrowing parcel of local shipwrecking tales. The O'Driscoll clan of pirates informally ruled the bay for centuries, sallying into the Atlantic for raids, off-loading brandy from Spanish galleons, then speeding home through secret channels between the islands.

▓ Kinsale

Upscale Kinsale (Cionn tSáile) is mobbed with people and money every summer, when its population temporarily quintiples. Visitors come to swim, fish, and eat at Kinsale's famed "Good Food Circle" (of 12 expensive restaurants). Luckily, Kinsale's best attractions—its pubs, forts, and pretty seaside location—don't require much money to enjoy. Kinsale has played a grimmer role in history than its pleasant present suggests. In the 1601 Battle of Kinsale, Elizabethan English armies destroyed the native Irish followers of Ulster chieftain Hugh O'Neill, while O'Neill's supposed allies from Spain watched the action from ships stationed nearby. (See **History,** p. 55.) For almost two centuries after the English victory, Kinsale was legally closed to the Gaelic Irish. In 1688, the freshly deposed King James II of England, trying to gather Catholic Irish support for a Jacobite invasion of Scotland, entered Ireland at this very spot; for his efforts, James had a fort named after him. The attention of the outside world turned here again in 1915, when the *Lusitania* was torpedoed and sank just off the Old Head of Kinsale.

ORIENTATION AND PRACTICAL INFORMATION Kinsale is a 30-minute drive southwest of Cork on R600. The city lies at the base of a U-shaped inlet. Facing the water, Charles Fort and the Scilly Walk (silly, like the Ministry) are to the left; the piers, Compass Hill, and James Fort are to the right; the town center is behind you. **Buses** to and from **Cork** stop at the Esso station on the Pier (in summer M-Sa 10 per day, Su 5 per day; in winter M-Sa 6 per day, Su 3 per day). The **tourist office,** Emmet Pl. (Mar.-Nov. tel. 772234; Dec.-Feb. tel. 774026), in the black-and-red building on the waterfront, gives out free maps (open June-Aug. daily 9am-6pm). **Bank of Ireland,** Pearse St. (tel. 772521), has a 24-hour **ATM** (bank open M 10am-5pm, Tu-F 10am-4pm). Rent **bikes** (£6 per day) and fishing poles (£10 per day) at **Deco's,** 182 Main St. (tel. 774884; open June-Aug. M-Sa 9am-6pm, Su 10am-6pm; Sept.-May M-Sa 9am-6pm.) The **phone code** is 021.

ACCOMMODATIONS Although Kinsale's hotels and plush B&Bs caters to an affluent tourist crowd, there are two hostels nearby. The **Castlepark Marina Centre** (tel. 774959) sits across the harbor, a 40-minute walk from town. From the bus depot, walk along the pier away from town for 10 minutes, turn left to cross large Duggan Bridge, and then take another left just past the bridge; follow this road back toward the harbor. **Ferries** leave the Trident Marina for the hostel June through August (call the hostel for a schedule). This stone-fronted building stands just below the James Fort and offers marvelous views of Kinsale. Rooms are large, airy, and bright, with bay windows that open out onto the harbor and have beach access. Castlepark's newly opened restaurant features intimate tables and a gourmet menu (baked goat cheese £4.75). (Dorms £8. Laundry £5. Safe-deposit box 50p. Open Mar.-Nov.) Closer to town, **Dempsey's Hostel (IHH),** Cork Rd. (tel. 772124), offers clean, pleasant rooms and an industrial kitchen (dorms £5; sheets 50p; shower 50p). Reasonably priced accommodations can also be found at **O'Donnovan's B&B,** Guardwell Rd. (tel. 772428; £14, with bath £16). The nearest **campground** is **Garrettstown House Holiday Park** (tel. 778156), 6 mi. west of Kinsale on R600 in Ballinspittle. A bus goes there occasionally (30min., Th 3 per day, F 2 per day, Su July-Aug. only 2 per day). (£3.50 per person, 2-person tent with car £8; open May-Sept.)

FOOD AND PUBS Kinsale is Ireland's gourmet food capital—locals claim it's the only town in Ireland with more restaurants than pubs. The **Good Food Circle** has 12 restaurants that uphold both Kinsale's well-deserved culinary reputation and its notoriety for tourist-scalping expense. The budget-conscious fill their baskets at the **SuperValu,** Pearse St. (tel. 772843; open M-Sa 9:30am-9:30pm, Su 10:30am-9:30pm). **Café Palermo,** Pearse St. (tel. 774143), serves delicious Italian food, fresh salads, and rich desserts (lunch about £5; open daily 10am-11pm; closed Tu and Su nights). **1601,** Pearse St. (tel. 772529), has high-quality pub grub (amazing soup £2.50, burgers £6).

On a weekend night, a stroll through Kinsale's small maze of streets will magically lead you to great trad. **The GreyHound,** Market Sq. (tel. 772889), attracts a young crowd, while **1601** serves trad in addition to its classy grub. Harder to hear from a distance, but worth the effort, **The Spaniard** (tel. 772436) rules over the Kinsale pub scene from the hill on the Scilly Peninsula (follow the signs to Charles Fort for ¼mi.). Stone walls, dark wood paneling, low-beamed ceilings, and a bar the length of the Shannon create its atmosphere (lively trad W, other nights vary). Downhill from The Spaniard and farther on the Scilly Walk, **The Spinnaker** (tel. 772098) presides over the harbor, playing loud American rock. Those who make the walk to Charles Fort are rewarded at the inviting **Bulman Bar** (tel. 772131), a picturesque spot for downing a pint of Ireland's own black gold.

SIGHTS The half-hour trek up **Compass Hill,** south of Main St., rewards with a view of the town and its watery surroundings. More impressive is the view from **Charles Fort** (tel. 772263), a classic 17th-century star-shaped fort that remained a British naval base until 1921. *(Sack the fort mid-June to mid-Sept. daily 9am-6pm; mid-Apr. to mid-June and mid-Sept. to mid-Oct. M-Sa 9am-5pm, Su 9:30am-5:30pm. £2, students and children £1. Guided tours on request.)* Reach Charles Fort by following Scilly Walk, a sylvan path along the coast at the end of Pearse St. (30min.).

In 1915, the *Lusitania* sank off the Old Head of Kinsale, a promontory south of the town; over 1000 civilians died. As either your history book or your Irish vacation has taught you, a German torpedo was to blame, and the resulting furor helped propel the United States into World War I. Hearings on the *Lusitania* case took place in the Kinsale Courthouse, now a low-key but interesting **Regional Museum,** Market Sq. (tel. 772044), home to the "Holy Stone" of Kinsale. *(Sporadic hours; call ahead. £1, children 30p.)* In town, up the hill from Market Square, the west tower of the 12th-century **Church of St. Multose** (tel. 772220), patron saint of Kinsale, has been restored into a very visit-worthy church. *(Open daylight hours. Free.)* Its ancient graveyard bewitches visitors, but a planning project has sent waves of controversy through the town. **Desmond Castle,** Cork St., a 15th-century custom house, served as an arsenal during the 100-day Spanish occupation in 1601. *(Open June-Sept. daily 9am-5pm. £3, students £1.50.)* It was put to use in the 18th century as a prison for salty French and American soldiers and has been recently upscaled into a random but charming wine museum.

Across the harbor from **Charles Fort,** the ruins of star-shaped **James Fort** delight casual explorers with secret passageways and panoramic views of Kinsale. *(Always open. Free.)* To reach the fort, follow the pier away from town, cross the bridge, then turn left. After exploring the ruins and the rolling heath, descend to Castlepark's hidden arc of beach behind the hostel. The **Kinsale Outdoor Education Centre** (tel. 772896) rents windsurfing equipment, kayaks, and dinghies. Full-day deep-sea fishing trips and scuba diving excursions can also be arranged at **Castlepark Marina** (tel. 774959; fishing £25, rod rental £5).

■ Clonakilty

Once a linen-making town with a workforce of over 10,000 people, Clonakilty ("Clon," pop. 3000) lies between Bandon and Skibbereen on N71. Military leader, spy, and organizational genius Michael Collins was born near Clonakilty in 1890 (see **The Easter Rising,** p. 60); a bit earlier, so was Henry Ford. The area is peppered with monuments to Republicans and their bitter ends. Appearing almost as frequently are monuments to nearby **Inchydoney Beach** in the form of shops devoted to large inflatable sharks and other beach goodies. However, tidy Clon also reaps the benefits of this vacation-spot status with animated streets, a vibrant pub scene, and glorious flowers everywhere. Clon is known for its live music, which can be sampled in pubs nightly. In the last weekend in August, the **Country and Bluegrass Festival** literally takes over the streets. **Buses** from **Skibbereen** (3 per day, £4.30) and **Cork** (5 per day, £5.90) stop in front of Lehane's Supermarket on Pearse St. The **tourist office** (tel. 33226) vacations at 9 Rossa St. (open June-Sept. M-F 9am-6pm, Sa 9am-1pm). You can walk the 3 mi. to Inchydoney or rent a **bike** at **MTM Cycles,** 33 Ashe St. (tel. 33584; £6 per day, £30 per week). The **phone code** is a sausage-like mix of blood and 023.

ACCOMMODATIONS Sparkling clean **Clonakilty Hostel,** Emmet Sq. (tel. 33525), sports a beautiful kitchen, comfortable new beds, and a slightly dour atmosphere. Coming from Asche St., make a left at the church, then a right before Emmet Sq. and go down a block. (Dorms £7; doubles £18. Wheelchair accessible.) Just east of town is Mrs. McMahon's **Nordav,** 70 Western Rd. (tel. 33655), a right turn after the museum. Set back from the road behind a well-groomed lawn and splendid rose gardens, this B&B features gloriously huge 3-room suites and smaller, but still lovely, double rooms. (£16-20 per person.) The unnamed **Hostel and B&B,** Wolfe Tone St. (tel. 33157), is much less luxurious but a few steps closer to town (dorms £7; B&B £15). **Desert House Camping Park** (tel. 33331) is a half mile southeast of town on a dairy farm. Follow the signs toward Ring. (£6 per family tent, 50p per person; £4 per small tent. Showers 50p. Open May-Sept.)

FOOD AND PUBS Clonakilty is famous (or infamous) for its style of **black pudding,** a sausage-like concoction made from blood and grains, obtainable at any local market (see **Tasty Treats,** p. 70). Luckily, Clonakilty offers other culinary options. **Fionnuala's Little Italian Restaurant,** 30 Ashe St. (tel. 34355), has commendable food in an atmospheric old Irish house (£7-9). **Betty Brosnan,** 58 Pearse St. (tel. 34011), specializes in friendly behavior and homemade baked goods, lasagna, and sandwiches (£2-5). **The Copper Kettle,** Pearse St. (tel. 33456), serves pastries and simple sandwiches (£1-3; open daily 9am-6pm). Brown-bag it at **Lehane's Supermarket,** Pearse St. (open M-Th 8am-6:30pm, F-Sa 8am-9pm, Su 9am-1:30pm).

There's music aplenty in Clonakilty. The most popular pub is **De Barra's,** Pearse St. (tel. 33381), with folk and trad nightly all year. Though the pub is huge (3 rooms, 2 bars, and a beer garden), come early if you want to sit down. **An Teach Beag** (tel. 33250), nestled behind O'Donovan's Hotel on Recorder's Alley, features trad and storytelling sessions nightly at 9:30pm. Around the corner from De Barra's, **Shanley's,** 11 Connolly St. (tel. 33790), juggles folk and rock nightly in summer and winter. Nationally known stars have played here. For a game of darts or pool, stop by **Bernie's Bar,** Rossa St. (tel. 33567).

SIGHTS To fill the hours before the pubs pick up, join the locals at **Inchydoney Beach,** billed as one of the nicest beaches east of Malibu. (Camping here is legal but rare.) On Inchydoney Rd. you'll pass the **West Cork Model Village** (tel. 33224), where 1940s-era West Cork has been replicated in miniature, complete with model railways and smokestacks. *(Open daily 11am-5pm, phone for special summer hours. £2.50, students £1.50.)* Back in town, the **Clonakilty Museum,** Western Rd., displays the first minute book of the Cloghnikilty Corporation (dated 1675) and other historical Clon minutiae. *(Open May-Oct. M-Sa 10:30am-6pm, Su 2:30-6pm. £1, students 50p.)* The **Michael Collins Tour Bus** visits various places of interest from a certain Irish patriot's life. *(Leaves from Emmet Sq. June-Aug. at 2:30pm Tuesdays and some Fridays. Inquire at the tourist office. £5, children £2.50.)* For more ancient history, explore the **Templebryan Stone Circle** or the **Lios na gCon Ring Fort,** 2 mi. east. The fort has been "fully restored" based on excavators' clues.

■ Union Hall and Castletownshend

A subtly beautiful countryside lurks between Clonakilty and Skibbereen. Pastures and rolling hills give way to forests as the landscape gets too rocky for farming. Sleepy towns dot the hills, each with a few rows of pastel houses, a couple of B&Bs, and the eight requisite pubs. Just across the water from the picturesque but unexciting hamlet of Glandor sits the fishing village of **Union Hall,** once a hangout for Jonathan Swift and family. Now it's home to legendary **Maria's Schoolhouse (IHH)** (tel. (028) 33002). Formerly the Union Hall National School, Maria's hostel is resplendently redecorated and refitted with a cathedral ceiling and a peat fire in the huge common room, big skylights in the bedrooms, and delightful scones at a healthy breakfast spread. This hostel is reason enough for a detour en route to Skibbereen. (Dorms £7; doubles £20-30. Breakfast £3.50. Dinner and occasional Sunday evening music £10-15. Laundry £4. Canoeing and sea kayaking lessons £15 per 2hr. Wheelchair accessible.) To get to Maria's, turn right in the center of Union Hall, left at the church, and go half a mile, or call Maria for a lift. Back in town, **Dinty's Bar** (tel. (028) 33373) serves up seafood-geared grub (12:30-2:30pm and 6-9pm), while **Nolan's Bar** (tel. (028) 33589) supplies a few bites and civilized gossip. **Casey's Bar** (tel. (028) 33590) provides a waterside patio beer garden on which to enjoy your fresh seafood or less expensive pub grub (food served daily noon-8:30pm). Pterodactyl teeth, rubber bullets, and old meteorites reside in the **Ceim Hill Museum** (tel. (028) 36280), about 3 mi. outside town. The museum's proprietress, who is both older and more interesting than most of her exhibited items, found many of these prehistoric artifacts in her backyard. (Open daily 10am-6:30pm. £2.) You can call **Atlantic Sea Kayaking** (tel. 33002) for a variety of kayaking lessons and expeditions.

From Union Hall, the most scenic route to Skibbereen is via **Castletownshend,** an Anglo-Irish hamlet that makes its way down to the sea. On the way, you'll pass **Raheen Castle,** built around 1580 using the latest grouting technique (a grisly mortar of blood, horsehair, sand, and lime), and **Rineen Forest.** The castle is almost intact, except for the cannonballs that Cromwell's army embedded in its walls. **Knockdrum Fort,** just west of town, is a typical ring fort. Celts built the tribal center in the early Iron Age and then fortified it with walls and ditches. **Mary Ann's Bar and Restaurant** (tel. (028) 36146) serves cream-laden pub grub and seafood dishes (food served noon-2:30pm and 6-9pm).

■ Skibbereen

The biggest town in West Cork, Skibbereen (pop. 2,100) unites blue-collars and blow-ins within its varied landscape: there are as many hardware stores here as cafés. When Algerian pirates sacked Baltimore in 1631, the survivors moved inland, establishing Skibbereen as a sizable settlement. The town is now the gateway for land-lubbers to Roaringwater Bay and the Beara Peninsula and consequently something of a tourist haunt. The best day to visit is Friday, when farmers tote in plants, fresh produce, and pies for the weekly market on Bridge St. (early afternoon). Or treat yourself to a new heifer at the cattle market on Wednesdays, also on Bridge St. (11am-4pm). Many stores in Skibbereen close on Thursday afternoons.

ORIENTATION AND PRACTICAL INFORMATION

Comely Skibbereen is L-shaped, with North St. standing as the base and Main and Bridge St. comprising the height (Main St. turns into Bridge St. at the small bridge). The clock tower, tourist office, and stately "Maid of Erin" statue are at the elbow. Hitchers typically stay on N71 to go east or west but switch to R595 to go south.

Buses: At Calahane's Bar, Bridge St. To Baltimore (June-Sept. M-Sa 5 per day, Oct.-May 4 per day, £2.10), Cork (M-F 5 per day, Sa 3 per day, Su 2 per day, £8.80), and Clonakilty (M-F 3 per day, Sa 2 per day, £4.40).

Tourist Office: Town Hall, North St. (tel. 21766). Open in summer M-Sa 9am-6pm, Su 9am-7pm; in winter M-Sa 9:15am-5:30pm.

Banks: AIB, 9 Bridge St. (tel. 21388; **ATM**). **Bank of Ireland,** Market St. (tel. 21700). Both open M-Tu and Th-F 10am-4pm, W 10am-5pm.

Bike Rental: Roycroft Stores (tel. 21235), Ilen St. off Bridge St. £7 per day, £30 per week. Return at Rolf's Hostel or the Diving Center in Baltimore or in Schull £1. Also part of Raleigh One-Way Rent-A-Bike; call for details. Open M-W and F-Sa 9:15am-1:10pm and 2:15-6pm, Th 9am-1pm.

Laundry: Bubble and Suds Laundry, 18 North St. (tel. 22621). Wash and dry 50p per lb. Open M-Sa 10am-6pm. **Hourihane's Laundrette,** Ilen St. (tel. 22697), behind Busy Bee fast food. £3.50 per load. Open daily 10am-10pm.

Emergency: Dial 999; no coins required. **Garda:** tel. 21088.

Post Office: The Square. Open M-Sa 9am-5:30pm.

Phone Code: 028.

ACCOMMODATIONS

Russagh Mill Hostel and Adventure Center (IHH) (tel. 22451). An extremely laid-back hostel about 1mi. out of town on Castletownshend Rd. This renovated 200-year-old mill with defunct machinery still in place offers huge rustic common rooms and a glassed-in parlor. Special rates on canoeing, rock climbing, and hiking. Dorms £7; private rooms £10 per person.

Bridge House, Bridge St. (tel. 21273). The proprietress could be a set designer for Victorian period films. Bridge House is a visual experience, with lavish canopy beds, ornate satin-laced rooms, and the biggest bathtub in West Cork. £16.50. Vegetarian breakfast option.

Mont Bretia B&B (tel. 33663), tucked among the rolling hills 4mi. from town on Drinagh Rd. Call for directions or a lift from Leap or Skibbereen. Maps of local sights, vegetarian food, and free bikes. Gay and lesbian friendly. £15; dinner £6.50, 2-course dinner £8.

Ivanhoe, North St. (tel. 21749). Big beds and bathrooms. Singles £20; doubles £30.

The Hideaway Campground, Castletownshend St., just outside of town. £2 per tent, £1 per car. Showers 50p.

FOOD AND PUBS

The cafés that cluster on Main and North St. make a handful of inviting options. Skib's **SuperValu market** (tel. 21400) does its stuff on Main St. (M-Sa 9am-6:30pm).

⊗**Kalbo's Bistro,** 48 North St. (tel. 21515). Easily the best café in Skibbereen and probably one of the best in Co. Cork. Meals are innovative, fresh, and satisfying. The delicious desserts are rumored to be outlawed in 6 counties. Lunch £4-6, dinner £7-11. Open M-Sa 11am-4:30pm and 6:30-10pm, Su noon-2:30pm and 6:30-10pm.

O'Donovan's, 12 Bridge St. (tel. 21163), has a window full of awesome baked goods. Scone-lovers munch away on the terrace out back. Hot lunch £4. Open 8am-6pm.

The Stove, Main St. (tel. 22500). Serves copious breakfasts and Irish specialties for lunch (£4-5). Open M-Sa 8am-6pm.

The Wine Vaults, Bridge St. (tel. 23112). All the excuses for a midday pub stop: delicious sandwiches, pizzas, and salads. Food served noon-12:30pm and 5-8pm.

Bernard's, Main St. (tel. 21772), behind O'Briens Off License. Above-average pub grub in a large, beautiful bar/restaurant. Most dishes £7-10. Food served 9am-6pm.

Follow the live music (blues or folk) and join the crowds at the **Wine Vaults** Wednesday evenings, when locals and tourists mingle for slightly alternative craic. Traditional music is generally featured at **Bernard's** on Friday and Sunday nights. **Seán Óg's,** Market St. (tel. 21573), hosts contemporary folk and blues on some Saturday nights and features an outdoor beer garden. **Kearney's Well,** 52-53 North St. (tel. 21350), attracts a young, lively crowd, while the **Cellar Bar,** Main St. (tel. 21329), has a collegiate atmosphere and a disco (disco 11:30pm-1am; cover £5).

SIGHTS

The **West Cork Arts Centre,** North St. (tel. 22090), across from the town library, hosts about 12 exhibits per year by Irish artists and craftsfolk. *(Gallery open M-Sa 10am-6pm. Free.)* It also draws poetry readings, concerts, dance performances, and other cultural events to West Cork. Get wired into the local arts scene with a free copy of *Art Beat,* a guide to the arts in West Cork, available at the Centre. The **gardens** at **Liss Ard Experience** (tel. 22368), down Castletownshend Rd. toward the hostel, promise to "induce new perceptions of light and sky." *(Open M-F 11am-6pm, Su 1:30-6pm. £5, students £3.)* Created as a unique attempt at conservation, the nonprofit organization's 50 acres include a waterfall garden, a wildflower meadow (with over 100 species of butterflies), and the surreal "Irish sky garden," designed by American artist James Turrell. Three and a half miles west of town on the Baltimore Rd., the well-maintained **Creagh Gardens** (tel. 22121) contrast with their woodland setting. *(Open daily 10am-6pm. £3, children £1.50.)* During the end of July, Skibbereen celebrates **Welcome Home Week,** which features street entertainment and live bands.

■ Baltimore

The tiny fishing village of Baltimore (pop. 200) and its harbor serve as a point of departure for Sherkin Island and Cape Clear Island. In the center of the village stand the stone remains of *Dún na Sead,* "The Fort of the Jewels," one of nine 16th-century O'Driscoll castles. Even today, your best bet at stopping a man in the street is to shout, "Mr. O'Driscoll!" Since some of the clan has left the area, the O'Driscoll family congregates here annually to elect a chieftain and to stage a family gathering, complete with live music, jammed pubs, and inebriated Irishmen. Artists, like seagulls, come to Baltimore in spring and fall for bright, dramatic seascapes.

ORIENTATION AND PRACTICAL INFORMATION Baltimore's main road runs about a mile through town and out to the Beacon, a hilariously suggestive white lighthouse perched on a magnificent cliff with views over the ocean and across to Sherkin Island. The window of the post office has a full schedule of the **buses** running from **Cork** and on to **Glengarriff** (M-F July-Aug. 5 per day, Sept.-June 4 per day, £2). The **tourist office** (tel. 20441), halfway up the steps from the ferry depot, is non-Bord Fáilte and keeps sporadic hours. Next door, **Islands Craft** (tel. 20347) dispenses helpful information on Sherkin and Cape Clear, including ferry schedules and historical accounts of the islands. All the crafts in the shop were handmade on one of the islands. (Open M-Sa 11am-5:30pm, Su 12:30-5:30pm.) The **post office** is inside the small general store above the craft shop (open M-F 9am-5:30pm, Sa 9am-1pm). The **phone code** is 028.

ACCOMMODATIONS, FOOD, AND PUBS A visit to Baltimore requires a stay at **Rolf's Hostel (IHH)** (tel. 20289), run by a charming German family. The 300-year-old complex of stone farmhouses is a 10-minute walk up the turnoff immediately before the village on Skibbereen Rd. Comfortable pine beds (brass in the private rooms) and a dining room with stunning views and delicious food are hard to resist. (Dorms £7-8.50; doubles £23. **Camping** £3.50 per person. Laundry £4. **Bike rental** £7 per day.) Rolf's also runs a café, which serves delicious pasta, fresh fish, and Malaysian munchies (£4-6). **Café Opus,** next door, offers an exquisite menu, elegant ambience, and rotating art exhibits for those who want to splurge a bit (main courses £9.50-11.50). The **Lifeboat Restaurant** (tel. 20143), in the post office building, serves cheap soup, sandwiches, and pizza in a glass room on the harbor's edge (entrees £3.50-5; open daily 10am-5:30pm). Stock up on food for the islands at **Cotter's** (tel. 20106), on the main road facing the harbor (open year-round M-Sa 9:30am-8pm; in peak season also Su 10:30am-8pm). All of Baltimore's pubs offer food. **Declan McCarthy's,** just above the pier (tel. 20159), is the liveliest pub, with trad and folk three to four nights a week in summer (occasional cover £3-5). The comfortable stools and tables outside **Bushe's Bar** (tel. 20125) are prime spots for scoping out the harbor, while cozy **Algiers Inn** (tel. 20145), just around the corner, draws a younger crowd (food served M-Sa 5:30-9:30pm).

SIGHTS A number of shipwrecks offshore await divers willing to brave the icy waters. To arrange dives or rentals, contact the **Baltimore Diving & Watersports Centre** (tel. 20300), down the road from Rolf's. (Scuba experience not required. Full set of equipment with wetsuit £30 per day, £100 per week. Boat trips from £15.) **Atlantic Boating Service** (tel. 22734), located at the end of the pier, offers waterskiing (starting at £20 per 30min.) and boat rental (£8 per hr.). Inquire at **Algiers Inn** (tel. 20145) for information about deep-sea angling. Explorers equipped with bicycles or cars head east to circle **Lough Hyne** (EYEN), Northern Europe's only saltwater lake, where clear rapids change direction with the tide. The lough, originally a freshwater lake, was inundated when sea levels rose after the last ice age. It is now a stomping ground for marine biologists, who search out the dozens of sub-tropical species it shelters. A 30-minute ascent through moss-strewn **Knockomagh Wood** (adjacent to the lough; trails leave from the carpark) affords a view of nine towns and the Mizen Head.

■ Sherkin Island

Just a hop on the ferry, Sherkin Island (pop. 90) offers sandy, cliff-enclosed beaches, wind-swept heath, and a sense of unhurried ease. **Ferries** come from **Baltimore** (in summer 8 per day, in winter 3 per day, £4 return). Ferry schedules are posted outside the Island Craft office in Baltimore (see above), and Vincent O'Driscoll (tel. 20125) can provide information. Ferries also run from **Schull** (1hr., July-Aug. 3 per day, June and Sept. 2 per day, £6 return). For information, call Kieran Molloy (tel. 28138).

If you're looking for solitude, **Island House** (tel. 20314), 15 minutes from the ferry landing on the main road, is ideal. The old farmhouse provides mesmerizing views from large and charming (if rustic) rooms, occasional strains of cool jazz, and splendid breakfasts (£14; open Apr.-Sept.). As far as views go (and they go pretty far here), the cows who live at **Cuina House** (tel. 20384) are some of the luckiest bovines around. To reach the B&B, take the road behind the Jolly Roger. The rooms are new and spacious. (£16, with bath £18.) **Murphy's Bar** (tel. 20116), close to the ferry landing and next to Dún-na-Long ruins, serves a mean pint and expansive views of the bay. The **Islander Restaurant** (tel. 20116) next door offers an informal atmosphere and a fine view of the harbor (dinner served 6-9:30pm; open June-Sept.). Amiable **Jolly Roger** (tel. 20379) across the street has spontaneous music sessions nearly every night in summer and quite dependable pub grub until late. The **Abbey** (tel. 20181), on the main road, is the only food store on the island and stocks only the basics (open in summer M-Sa 9am-6pm, Su noon-6pm).

When you get off the ferry, you'll encounter the ruins of a 15th-century **Franciscan abbey** founded by Fineen O'Driscoll. Vengeful troops from Waterford sacked the abbey in 1537 to get back at the O'Driscolls for stealing Waterford's wine. The ruins are currently undergoing renovation and are closed to the public. Unimpressive **Dún-na-Long Castle** ("fort of the ships"), also built by the buccaneer clan and sacked in the same raid, lies in ruins north of the abbey behind Murphy's Bar (castle always open; free). Stay straight on the main road from the ferry dock and you'll pass the blue-green **Kinnish Harbour** and Sherkin's yellow one-room schoolhouse, where the island educates its children. The beaches on Sherkin are sandy, gradually sloped, and great for swimming. **Trabawn Strand, Cow Strand,** and the bigger **Silver Strand** are all on the west side of the island (follow the main road and bear right after the Island House B&B). The defunct **lighthouse** on Horseshoe Harbour stares across the channel toward the giggle-eliciting Beacon, affording some of the best views on the island.

■ Cape Clear Island (Oileán Chléire)

The rough landscape seen from the bumpy ferry docking at Cape Clear Island seems appropriate to its sparse population. But the island shows its capacity every summer when the population quadruples with the arrival of Irish College attendees, secondary school students who come here to brush up on their Irish. The main industry of this wild and beautiful island, however, is still farming; the landscape of patchwork fields separated by low stone walls hasn't changed much since the Spanish galleons stopped calling here hundreds of years ago. Life is leisurely and hours are approximate. The island's stores and pubs keep flexible hours, and B&Bs rise and decline according to the residents' inclination to host guests. For an updated version of opening hours and general island information, check the bulletin board at the end of the pier. **Ferries** run to and from **Baltimore** (June and Sept. 2 per day; July-Aug. M-Sa 3 per day, Su 4 per day; Oct.-Apr. M-Th and Sa-Su 1 per day, F 2 per day; May M-F 2 per day, Sa-Su 1 per day; £8 return). Call Capt. Conchúr O'Driscoll (tel. 39135) for more information. Ferries to the island from **Schull** leave daily in June at 5:30pm and in July and August at 10am, 2:30, and 4:30pm.

ACCOMMODATIONS Cléire Lasmuigh (An Óige/HI) (tel. 39144), the Cape Clear Island Adventure Centre and Hostel, is about a 10-minute walk from the pier (keep left on the main road). Now under new management as an adventure center, the once less-than-welcoming hostel has been replaced by a staff waiting to take you and your army snorkeling, kayaking, or on an overnight survival trip. (They are equally happy to leave you alone if you prefer.) The hostel resides in a drafty but picturesque stone building only steps from the south harbor. The song of the pounding surf just outside the window lulls guests to sleep. Reception hours are limited, but the hostel is always open for you to put down your bag. (June-Sept. £7; Apr. and Sept.-Oct. £6. Sheets 60p.) The proprietors of Ciarán Danny Mike's (below) run the hospitable **Cluain Mara B&B** (tel. 39153) in a house adjacent to the pub (£15, with bath £16; self-catering apartment across the road £25). The island's **campsite** (tel. 39136), on the south harbor, is a five-minute walk from the harbor: go up the main road, turn right at the yellow general store, then bear left. Campers get the same breathtaking views as hostelers. (Open June-Sept. £2.70 per person, under 15 £1.50.)

FOOD AND PUBS The one grocery store, **An Siopa Beag** (tel. 39119), stocks the essentials in a white building a few hundred yards down the pier to the right (open M-Sa 10am-1pm, 2:30-6:30pm, and 7:45-8:45pm, Su 2-5pm). The island **craft shop** sells everything from ice cream to warm sweaters but gives information for free (open daily 2-6pm). Food on Cape Clear is mediocre, but perhaps it will see improvement from a new restaurant at **Ciarán Danny Mike's** (tel. 39172), just up the hill from North Harbour. Currently, **Cistin Chéire** (tel. 39145) serves sandwiches, soup, and the same old Irish specialities harborside (open daily 11am-8pm).

What the Cape Clear pub scene lacks in variety it makes up for in stamina. The island has no resident authorities to regulate after-hours drinking, and if any have the impudence to sail over from the mainland, their lights give publicans plenty of time to close up shop. The island's 150 people support three pubs. **The Night Jar** (tel. 39102) opens at noon and is liveliest in the afternoon and early evening, while **Club Chléire** (tel. 39184), above the café, has live sessions most weekend nights, often lasting until 4am or later. Those feeling spontaneous should bring their ukuleles to **Ciarán Danny Mike's** for good spirits and song.

SIGHTS About a 25-minute walk up a steep hill from the pier is the island's **Heritage Centre,** half a room containing everything from an O'Driscoll family tree to a deck chair from the equally ubiquitous *Lusitania. (Open June-Aug. daily 2-5:30pm. £1.50, students £1, under 18 50p.)* Since over half of the exhibits are in Irish, it's a quick trip for the Irish-challenged. On the road to the center, **Cleire Goats** (tel. 39126) sells goat's milk ice cream (65p) and even raises the animals responsible. In case Cape Clear has inspired romance and you need a profession to earn your keep there, Cleire Goats offers two- and five-day goat-keeping courses. A right turn past the heritage center leads to the **windmills** that until recently generated three-quarters of the island's electricity. On a misty day you'll hear the eerie keening noise of their motion long before you see them. Cape Clear also shelters gulls, stormy petrels, cormorants, and ornithologists. The **bird observatory,** the white farmhouse on North Harbour, is one of the most important in Europe. Cape Clear hosts an annual **International Storytelling Festival** (tel. 39157) in late August, featuring puppet workshops, music sessions, and a weekend's worth of memorable tales.

■ The Mizen Head Peninsula

If you've made the mistake of skipping Cape Clear Island, you'll have to take the land route to Schull, Crookhaven, and Mizen Head. Whatever the route, however, the destination is the same: the craggy, windswept, beach-laden, and gloriously unspoiled southwest tip of Ireland. The **phone code** masts the Mizen at 028.

■ Schull

A jovial seaside hamlet 45 minutes by ferry from Cape Clear and 4 mi. west of Ballydehob on R592, Schull (SKULL) is the last glimpse of culture and commerce on the peninsula, with its one busy street, a great hostel, and excellent eateries. It makes the best base for exploring the Mizen Head Peninsula.

PRACTICAL INFORMATION Buses to **Cork** (3 per day) and **Goleen** (2 per day) stop in front of Griffin's Bar on Main St. From June to September, there is also bus service between Schull and **Killarney** (1 per day). Inquire at the Backpacker's Lodge for information on school bus service between Schull and **Bantry. Ferries** connect Schull to **Cape Clear** and **Sherkin** (June and Sept. 1 per day, July-Aug. 3 per day, £8 return) and to **Baltimore** (June to mid-Sept. 3 per day, £6 return). Contact Capt. O'Driscoll (tel. 39135) for more information. The Schull **tourist office** has occasional existential dilemmas. Look for it on Main St., or pick up the prosaic and lengthy *Schull Guide* in any store (£1.50). Either sing on a street corner or get cash at **AIB,** 3 Upper Main St. (tel. 28132; open M-F 10am-12:30pm and 1:30-4pm; 24hr. **ATM**). Although many of Schull's attractions are aquatic, terrestrial types can rent bikes at **Freewheelin',** Cotter's Yard, Main St. (tel. 28165; £8 per day, £45 per week; open M-Sa 10am-noon). A cheaper and more convenient option is the **Wheels Escapes** program (see p. 191), available at the hostel in Schull. The **post office,** Main St. (tel. 28110), is across from the Courtyard Coffeeshop and Pub.

ACCOMMODATIONS Schull's appeal for budget travelers is immeasurably enhanced by the presence of the **Schull Backpackers' Lodge (IHH),** Colla Rd. (tel. 28681). The wooden lodge is bright and immaculate, with fluffy comforters, a sparkling kitchen, and the best showers in West Cork. (Peak season big dorms £7; 4-bed dorms £8; doubles £20, with bath £24. Laundry £4. **Bike rental** £7 per day, £35 per week.) **Adele's B&B,** Main St. (tel. 28459), warms you up with small fireplaces and dark wooden floors (£12.50 includes continental breakfast). Three miles from town on the way to Goleen, **Jenny's Farmhouse** (tel. 28205) offers a friendly, quiet "home away from home." (£10, with breakfast £12-14. Ideal for travel by car or bike, but call for possible pick up in Schull.)

FOOD AND PUBS Schull is known for its upscale shopping and eateries. The town is a treat for scone and brown bread connoisseurs. **Adele's Restaurant** (tel. 28459) bakes decadent cakes and pastries and dishes up tasty soups, salads, and sandwiches in a proper tea room. She opens again in the evening for scrumptious, if pricey, dinners (£8-10). (Open May-Oct. for lunch and tea daily 9:30am-6pm, dinner W-Su 7-10pm.) Not to be outdone, multi-talented **Courtyard** (tel. 28390) down the street bakes eight types of bread (85p-£1) and sells a variety of gourmet foods, wholefoods, soups, and sandwiches (open M-Sa 10am-4pm). Plentiful dinners, fish, pasta, and meat are served daily (6:30-9:30pm). On Mondays, Fridays, and some Sundays, the adjacent **pub** features trad, jazz, and blues. The **Bunratty Inn** (tel. 28341), up the hill on Main St., prepares, as proclaimed on a sign outside, some of West Cork's finest pub fare (£5.50; food served M-Sa noon-7pm, Su 12:30-2pm). The **Bunratty Inn** and

An Tigín (tel. 28337) both host live folk and rock one night a week during the summer. **The Galley Inn** (tel. 28733) concocts a mean bowl of soup and pricey meat and fish dinners as well as rollicking tunes Thursday nights and during some long weekends (food served noon-3pm and 5:30-8:30pm). Before leaving, stock up for Mizen forays at one of Schull's **grocery stores** on Main St.: **Spar Market** (tel. 28236; open daily 7am-9pm) or smaller **Hegarty's Centra** (tel. 28520) across the street (open M-Sa 7:30am-10:30pm, Su 7:30am-9:30pm).

SIGHTS Schull is a great spot from which to explore the walking and biking trails that snake along the water and up the nearby hills. Inquire at the Backpacker's Lodge for maps and information. The Republic's only planetarium, the **Schull Planetarium,** Colla Rd. (tel. 28552), offers extraterrestrial diversions for rainy days. *(Open June Tu, Th, and Sa 3-5pm; July-Aug. Tu-Sa 2-5pm and M-Th 7-9pm; Apr.-May Su 3-5pm. Most starshows at 4 or 8pm. £1, star show £3.)* A calm harbor and numerous shipwrecks make Schull a diver's paradise. The **Watersports Centre** (tel. 28554) on the pier rents dinghies, sailboards, wetsuits, and scuba air tanks at decent rates. *(Open M-Sa 9:30am-8:30pm.)*

■ Farther On: Crookhaven and Mizen Head

The Mizen becomes more scenic and less populated the farther west one goes from Schull. The peninsula continues to lose its native population, with reinforcements coming in the form of European house-buyers. Accordingly, the Mizen is mobbed during peak season weekends, as water-worshippers pack sandy beaches. The most reliable transit is **Betty's Bus Hire** (tel. 28410), which will take you on a tour of the Mizen via the scenic coast road (£5). The tour includes bits of local history and runs to the **Mizen Vision** (see below). Betty leaves from Schull at 11am on Tuesdays and Thursdays in June, July, and August; other times can be arranged. **Bus Éireann** only goes as far as **Goleen** (2 per day; inquire in Schull or Ballydehob for schedule). **Hitching** is convenient if it is high-traffic season for camping, and confident cyclists can make a daytrip to Mizen Head (36mi. return from Schull).

The block-long town of **Goleen** seems to move at half-pace with only half-charm. Just up the hill from town is **The Ewe** (tel. 35492), a surprising and wonderfully eccentric "art retreat." Accommodations are available in bright, comfortable rooms (£100 per week in peak season; rooms rented by the night if available). The intricate gardens surrounding the retreat are not to be missed. Art courses are £11.50 per session. If you can't get a room at The Ewe, try **Heron's Cove B&B** (tel. 35225), down the hill from Goleen on the water (£20). The **restaurant** downstairs serves excellent seafood, although catching the fish out back yourself would be a good deal cheaper (sandwiches from £4, 3-course dinner with wine £16.50).

Slightly longer than the main road, but tremendously worthwhile, the coast road winds to Barley Cove Beach and Mizen Head. Tiny **Crookhaven** (pop. 37), a 1 mi. detour off this road, is perched at the end of its own peninsula. You can meet half of the population as they work at running **O'Sullivans** (tel. 35319), which serves sandwiches, soups, desserts, and cold pints on the water's edge (food served noon-8:30pm); and the **Crookhaven Inn** (tel. 35309), which provides similar fare (sandwiches £1.70, meals £5-7) in a lovely outdoor café overlooking the bay (food served daily noon-8pm). **Barley Cove Caravan Park** (tel. 35302), 1½ mi. from Crookhaven, offers camping on the edge of the wind-swept peninsula. (£6.50 per tent, £1 for extra person July to mid-Aug. Showers 50p. Mini-market and laundry available. **Bikes** £5 per ½-day, £8 per day; deposit £20 for campers, £40 for non-campers. Open May 7-Sept. 11.) A cheaper (free) and infinitely more romantic option is to camp *near* the **Barley Cove Beach,** a gorgeous quarter mile of sand whose warm, shallow coves satisfy bathers who won't brave the frigid sea.

Three miles past Barley Cove, Ireland ends at spectacular **Mizen Head,** whose cliffs rise to 700 ft. **The Mizen Head Lighthouse,** built in 1909, was recently automated and electrified, and the buildings nearby were turned into a small museum, the **Mizen Vision** (tel. 35115). To get to the museum, you'll have to cross a suspension bridge only slightly less harrowing than the tale and rendering of shipwreck that are its centerpiece. The museum also assembles lighthouse paraphernalia and sheds light on the solitary lives of lighthouse keepers. The small and very windy viewing platform is the most southwesterly point in Ireland. (Open June-Sept. daily 10am-6pm; Apr.-May and Oct. 10:30am-5pm; Nov.-Mar. 11am-6pm. £2.50, students £1.75.)

BEARA PENINSULA

Untold numbers of visitors traveling up and down Ireland's southwest coast skip the Beara altogether. This region has a more wild and romantic majesty than the Ring of Kerry and a more profound sense of tranquility. The spectacular **Caha** and **Slieve Miskish Mountains** march down the center of the peninsula, separating the Beara's rocky southern coast from its lush northern coast. West Beara remains remote—travelers traverse treacherous single-track roads of the stark Atlantic coastline, dodging mountains, rocky outcrops, and the occasional herd of sheep. For unspoiled scenery and solitude the Beara is superb; if you're looking for pubs, people, and other signs of civilization, you might be happier on the Iveragh or Dingle Peninsulas. The dearth of cars west of Glengarriff makes cycling the Beara a joy (weather permitting), but **hitchhikers** will find themselves admiring the same views for longer than their sanity can bear.

■ Bantry

According to the *Book of Invasions,* the first humans landed in Ireland just a mile from Bantry (see **Legends and Folktales,** p. 61). Historians are more clear on Bantry's second invasion, in which English settlers seized Bantry and drove out the Irish in the 17th century. Patriot Theobald Wolfe Tone tried to return the favor by attacking the town in 1796 (see **History,** p. 57). While a day or two in today's more civilized and quite elegant Bantry may pay off with a cruise round the bay, an afternoon visit to Wolfe Tone Square, or an expedition to the Armada exhibit, the night might be more pleasantly spent elsewhere.

PRACTICAL INFORMATION

Bantry sits at the east end of Bantry Bay. If your back is to the water, the road that leads out of the square to the right is New St., which becomes Bridge St. Williams St. branches off New St. to the right. Barrack St. intersects New St. a bit farther up. Sheep's Head stretches due west and the Beara Peninsula is northwest. Cars, cyclists, and hitchers stay on N71 to get in or out of town.

Buses: Buses stop outside of Lynch's Pub in Wolfe Tone Sq., several doors from the tourist office toward the pier. **Bus Éireann** heads to **Cork** and **Bandon** (M-Sa 3-5 per day, Su 2-4 per day, £8.80) and **Glengarriff** (M-Sa 3 per day, Su 2 per day, £2.25). June-Sept. only, buses go to **Skibbereen** (2 per day), **Clonakilty** (1 per day), **Killarney** via **Kenmare** (2 per day), and **Schull** (1 per day). **Berehaven Bus Service** (tel. 70007) stops in Bantry on the way to and from **Cork.**

Tourist Office: Wolfe Tone Sq. (tel. 50229). Open M-Sa June-Sept. 9am-7pm, Oct.-May 9am-6pm. **Bureau de change** and general Bantry and Sheep's Head maps for sale. The best guide to Sheep's Head, *The Sheep's Head Way,* is sold at the **Craft Shop,** Glengarriff Rd. (tel. 50003), in a bright yellow house.

Banks: AIB, Wolfe Tone Sq. (tel. 50008); **ATM. Bank of Ireland,** Wolfe Tone Sq. (tel. 51377). Both open M-W and F 10am-4pm, Th 10am-5pm. The AIB **bureau de change** is up the street. Open M-Sa 9:30am-5:30pm.

Bike Rental: Kramer's, Glengarriff Rd., Newtown (tel. 50278). Open M-Sa 9am-6pm. £7 per day, £42 per week; deposit credit card, license, or passport. The **Bantry Independent Hostel,** closer to town, rents bikes as part of **Wheel Escapes** (see p. 191). £7 per day, £35 per week.

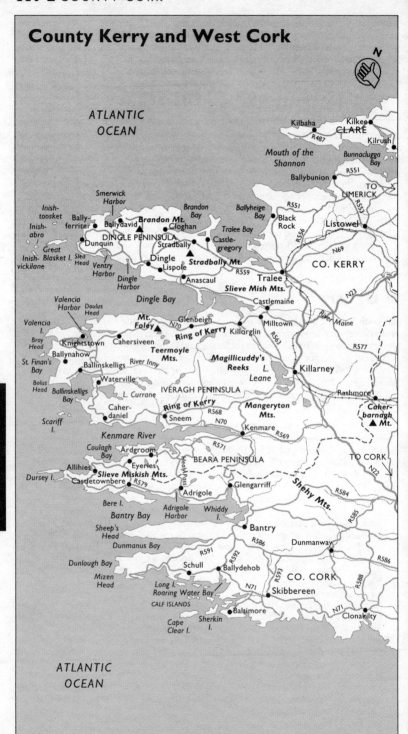

County Kerry and West Cork

N

ATLANTIC
OCEAN

Kilbaha
Kilkee
CLARE
R487
Kilrush

Bunnaclugga
Bay

Mouth of the
Shannon

Ballybunion
R551

TO
LIMERICK
R553

Smerwick
Harbor
Brandon
Bay
Ballyheige
Bay
R551
Inish-
tooske
Inish-
abro
Bally-
ferriter
Ballydavid
Brandon Mt.
Cloghan
Black
Rock
Listowel
DINGLE PENINSULA
Tralee Bay
N69
Great
Blasket I.
Dunquin
Slea
Head
Stradbally
Castle-
gregory
CO. KERRY
Inish-
vickilane
Dingle
Stradbally Mt.
R556
Ventry
Harbor
Lispole
Castlemaine
N23
Dingle
Harbor
Anascaul
Tralee
R559
Slieve Mish Mts.
R577
Dingle Bay
Castlemaine
Valencia
Harbor
Doulus
Head
Mt.
Foley
Glenbeigh
N70
Ring of Kerry
Milltown
River Maine
Valencia
I.
Killorglin
R563
Bray
Head
Knightstown
Cahersiveen
Teermoyle
Mts.
St. Finan's
Bay
Ballynahow
Magillicuddy's
Reeks
Killarney
Ballinskelligs
River Inny
L. Leane
Bolus
Head
Waterville
IVERAGH PENINSULA
Rathmore
Caher-
barnagh
Mt.
Ballinskelligs
Bay
L. Currane
Ring of Kerry
Caher-
daniel
Sneem
R568
N70
Mangerton
Mts.
Scariff
I.
Kenmare River
Kenmare
R569
TO CORK
N22
Coulagh
Bay
Ardgroom
R571
BEARA PENINSULA
Shehy Mts.
R584
Allihies
Eyeries
Healy Pass
R585
Dursey I.
Castletownbere
R579
Adrigole
Glengarriff
R586
Bere I.
Adrigole
Harbor
Whiddy
I.
Slieve Miskish Mts.
Bantry Bay
Sheep's
Head
Dunmanway
R586
Dunmanus Bay
Bantry
R586
Dunlough Bay
R591
R592
CO. CORK
R588
Mizen
Head
Schull
Ballydehob
R593
Long I.
Roaring Water Bay
N71
Skibbereen
N71
CALF ISLANDS
Baltimore
Clonakilty
Cape
Clear I.
Sherkin
I.

ATLANTIC
OCEAN

Laundry: The Wash Tub, Wolfe Tone Sq. Wash and dry £4. Open M-Sa 10am-6pm.
Pharmacy: Coen's Pharmacy, Wolfe Tone Sq. (tel. 50531). Open M-Tu and Th-Sa
  9:30am-1pm and 2-6pm, W 9:30am-1pm.
Emergency: Dial 999; no coins required. **Garda:** Wolfe Tone Sq. (tel. 50045).
Hospital: Bantry Hospital, Dromleigh (tel. 50133), ¼mi. past the library.
Post Office: 2 William St. (tel. 50050). Open M-Tu and Th-Sa 9am-5:30pm, W
  9:30am-5:30pm.
Phone Code: 027.

ACCOMMODATIONS

Bantry Independent Hostel (IHH), Bishop Lucey Pl. (tel. 51050), not to be confused
with the "small independent hostel" on the square, is the better of Bantry's two
unglamorous hostels. Head away from town on Glengarriff Rd. (Marino St.), take the
left fork, and walk a quarter mile. It has adequate bunks, a pretty common room, and
lots of fluorescent lighting. (6-bed dorms £6.50; private rooms £9 per person. Open
mid-Mar. to Oct.) **Harbour View Hostel (Small Independent Hostel),** Harbour View
(tel. 51313), to the left of the fire station along the water, provides drearily basic
accommodations (dorms £6.50; private rooms £7.50 per person). Four miles from
town in Ballylickey, the **Eagle Point Camping and Caravan Park,** Glengarriff Rd. (tel.
50630), has private beach and tennis courts, a TV room, and free showers. (£4 per
person. Laundry £3. Open May-Sept.)

FOOD AND PUBS

SuperValu is on New St. (open M-Th 8:30am-6:30pm, F 8:30am-9pm, Sa 8:30am-
6:30pm), and **Organico,** Glengarriff Rd. (tel 51391), stocks health food. Bantry has a
number of inexpensive lunch restaurants. Pub fare at the **Snug** or the **Wolfe Tone**
may be the best value for an evening meal. **O'Siochain,** Bridge St. (tel. 51339), serves
well-prepared food in a comfy, if kitschy, coffeehouse (sandwiches £1.50, pizza and
entrees £3.50-5; open daily 9am-10pm). Satisfy your lunchtime seafood cravings at
O'Connor's, Wolfe Tone Sq. (tel. 50221), which has eight variations on the mussel
theme (entrees £5-10; dinner prices much higher; lunch served daily noon-5pm,
open until 9:30pm). Vegetarians need not apply at **Peter's Steak House,** New St. (tel.
50025). They serve a £5 quick grill. (Most entrees £6-12. Open daily 10am-12:30am.)
The 5A Café, Barrack St., serves savory vegetarian selections at laughably low prices
to a kick-back café crowd (lunch £1.50-2.50; evening meals £6-8; open M-W 10am-
4:30pm, Th-Sa 10am-4:30pm and 6-10pm).

Bantry nightlife has kicked into overdrive thanks to **1796** (The Bantry Folk Club; tel.
52396), Wolfe Tone Sq. They host live music most nights with either nationally
known musicians or impromptu sessions and serve food (pasta £4-5, meat dishes
£10; served noon-9pm). **The Wolfe Tone,** Wolfe Tone Sq. (tel. 50900), has music (in
summer Tu and Th-Su) and cooks excellent pub grub (sandwiches £1.30-4). **The
Snug,** Wolf Tone Sq. (tel. 50051), aside from being an exceedingly popular pub, also
serves up grub at great prices (burgers and entrees £4-6). As any good seaside town
should, Bantry sports its **Anchor Bar,** New St. (tel. 50012). Drop yours next to their
miniature lighthouse and listen to rock on Thursdays. For those looking for a little
techno with their seafood, **Amadeus** (tel. 50062), in the Bantry Bay Hotel, keeps it
rolling Friday and Saturday nights (11:30pm-1:30am). Lonely Yankees should stop by
the **Kilgoban Pub** on the way to the hostel—it was won by an American couple in the
Guinness "win your own pub in Ireland" contest.

SIGHTS

Bantry's biggest tourist draw is **Bantry House** (tel. 50047), a Georgian manor with an
imposing garden overlooking Bantry Bay. *(Open mid-Mar. to Oct. daily 9am-6pm. House
and garden £5.50, students £4. Garden £1.50.)* The long and shaded driveway to the
house is a 10-minute walk from town on Cork Rd. Although the interior of the tired
mansion is in a sad state, the contents include some impressive art and furnishings.

The former seat of the four Earls of Bantry (and the current residence of the same, though now less wealthy, family), the house was transformed into a hospital during Ireland's Civil War and again during the "Emergency" (neutral Éire's term for World War II). Much more impressive than the house are the manicured gardens and the view of the bay from the grand lawn.

Bantry House still displays several delicately colored, carefully lettered statements expressing the gratitude of Irish tenants for the protection of their English landlords. The same earls, however, had a bit of scrambling to do when Irish rebel Theodore Wolfe Tone successfully borrowed a bit of France's anti-English sentiment for his own anti-English insurrection (see **History,** p. 57). Wolfe Tone's idea and campaign, as well as the 1970s discovery of one Armada ship that had been scuttled in the harbor, is thoroughly and interestingly documented in the museum of the **1796 Bantry French Armada Exhibition Centre** (tel. 51796). *(Open Mar.-Nov. daily 10am-6pm. £3, students £1.75.)* Enjoy the irony of its location next to Bantry House, home of Richard White, who mobilized British resistance to Wolfe Tone's invasion. **Sea trips** (tel. 50310) circumnavigate the harbor or drop you at **Whiddy Island,** a prime spot for repressed ornithologists and Crazygolf players. *(Trips depart every hr. July-Sept. daily 10am-7pm. £4 return.)*

Bantry is home to the **West Cork Chamber Music Festival** (tel. 61105) during the last week of June. The heart of the festival is the **RTE Vanburgh String Quartet.** For two festive weeks in August (usually beginning on the second weekend), the **Bantry Bay Regatta** employs the best sailors in Ireland.

■ Sheep's Head

Largely ignored by tourists passing through Skibbereen, Bantry, and Glengarriff, narrow Sheep's Head is best explored on a daytrip by bike or on foot. The **Sheep's Head Way** across the middle of the peninsula affords great mountain views. The **Craft Shop** in Bantry has a book detailing the walk (see above). Hitchers may find it difficult to get a ride to or from the peninsula, since it's the most sparsely populated part of West Cork. Cyclists head west along the cove-filled southern shore and return by the barren and windswept northern road, while hikers explore the spine of hills down the middle. Sheep's Head itself is marked by the requisite lighthouse and its spectacular (and untouristed) clifftop vistas. If you're lucky, you might see the tide change in Bantry Bay, where incoming breakers meet the outgoing tide to create a mini-maelstrom. For a snack on the way out, try the highly recommended **Tin Pub** in **Ahakista,** on the southern road; the corrugated iron "shack" serves gratifying sandwiches. There is also a Japanese restaurant nearby, **Shiro** (tel. 67030).

■ Glengarriff and Garinish Island

Glengariff identifies itself as a gateway to the Beara peninsula, and an attractive entrance it is, with a few pubs and restaurants and ringed by green mountains. The bizarre gardens at Garinish Island are a short ferry ride away. Although Glengarriff gives way to an untouched countryside beyond, there are more Aran sweaters here than natives. Castletownbere has much more local flavor, if fewer amenities.

PRACTICAL INFORMATION Buses stop in front of Casey's Hotel on Main St. **Bus Éireann** runs to Glengarriff from **Bantry** (25min., M-Sa 3-5 per day, Su 2-3 per day, £2.25). Another route runs between **Killarney** and Glengarriff via **Kenmare** (Kenmare 45min., Killarney 1¾hr., June to mid-Sept. M-Sa 2 per day, £3.70). In the summer, buses also run to **Castletownbere** daily (£2.25). **Berehaven Bus Service** (tel. 70007) serves **Cork** (2¾hr., M-Sa 3 per day, Su 2 per day, £7) and **Bantry** (M 2 per day, Tu and Th-Sa 1 per day, £3). Glengarriff is graced with two friendly **tourist offices.** The large, privately run office is in "the village" next to the public bathrooms and offers typical shamrock schlock (open daily 9am-6pm). The smaller Bord Fáilte office (tel. 63084) is on Bantry Rd. next to the Eccles Hotel (open June-Aug. M-Sa 10am-1pm and 2:15-6pm). The **post office** (tel. 62001) is inside O'Shea's Market on Main St. The **phone code** is 027.

ACCOMMODATIONS, FOOD, AND PUBS The best place to stay in Glengarriff is the new and very friendly **Murphy's Village Hostel** (tel. 63555), in the middle of the village on Main St. Feel the staggeringly powerful showers or lounge in the convenient café munching Mrs. Murphy's popular banana muffins. (Dorms £7-8; private rooms £10.50 per person. Laundry £4.50.) The **Hummingbird Rest** (tel. 63195), a 10-minute walk from town along Kenmare Rd., has cramped, private rooms (£6) and **camping** (£3.50). In the center of town, **Maureen's,** Main St. (tel. 63201), offers comfortable rooms from £13.50. Two **campsites, Dowling's** (tel. 63154) and **O'Shea's** (tel. 63140), are neighbors on Castletownbere Rd. 1½ mi. from town (both £4-5 per tent; open mid-Mar. to Oct.). **The Coffee Shop,** Main St. (tel. 63073) has cake, sandwiches, and hot meals (£2-5), while **Johnny Barry's** (tel. 63315) and **The Blue Loo** (tel. 63167), also on Main St., serve standard pub grub. Johnny Barry's has live folk and trad Monday through Saturday; the Blue Loo has ballads most summer nights.

SIGHTS Glengarriff's kindest attraction is its proximity to the lush **Glengarriff National Forest,** where hiking trails allow you to meander among giant rhododendrons and moss-strewn evergreens. Walking trails in the area range from pebbled paths for the most sedentary, scone-snarfing walkers to rugged climbs for serious hikers. *Let's Walk Around Glengarriff,* available at hostels in town and at the tourist office, outlines several walks in the park, but hikers seeking more intense thrills should pick up maps at the tourist office in town. The **Caha Walking Festival** in early May offers guided walks for all levels of hiking expertise; contact Laurie Craggs (tel. 63445). Glengarriff is also good starting point for the 130 mi. **Beara Way** walking path, obviously geared toward the truly committed.

The town's popularity, however, really comes from **Garinish Island,** a small island in Glengarriff Harbour. *(Open July-Aug. M-Sa 9:30am-6:30pm, Su 11am-7pm; Apr. and June-Sept. M-Sa 10am-6:30pm, Su 1-7pm; Mar. and Oct. M-Sa 10am-4:30pm, Su 1-5pm. Last landing 1hr. before closing. £2.50, students £1.)* Three companies along the main Glengarriff Rd. run **ferries** to the island (£4-5 return). Be all the tourist you can be at this "second oldest tourist spot in Ireland." Garinish was only a rocky outcrop inhabited by gorse bushes until 1900, when Annan Bryce dreamed up a fairyland for his family: a mansion and exotic garden on the island. A million hours of labor and countless boatloads of topsoil later, he had the garden, but his money disappeared in a Russian oil company before the mansion was built. Opening the island to the public became an obvious way to keep things blooming. The name of nearby **Lake Eekenohoolikeaghaun** ("Lake of Twelve Cows") doesn't compare to that place in Wales (see Llanfair P.G. in *Let's Go: Britain & Ireland 1999*). Upper and Lower Lough Avaul are stocked with brown and rainbow trout, but you need a fishing permit to catch 'em. Barley Lake, nearby rivers, and the ocean do not require permits. For more details, pick up *Fishing in Glengarriff* (free) and ask around by the piers.

The breathtaking **Healy Pass** branches north off R572 near Adrigole; it's a narrow, winding road that takes you through the green and rocky Caha Mountains to **Lauragh.** The **Glanmore Lake Youth Hostel (An Oíge/HI)** (tel. (064) 83181) makes a good base for hiking or fishing in the little-explored mountains near Lauragh. The prim and immaculate hostel is housed in a stately former schoolhouse with great mountain views. Follow signs from town; it is located 3 mi. from Lauragh on a dead-end road. (Dorms £6.50, Open Easter-Sept.)

■ Castletownbere

The fishing town of Castletownbere is a quiet relief next to Glengarriff. The largest town on the Beara Peninsula reverberates with the sounds of ferry engines, cars, and wind over the world's second-largest natural harbor, Berehaven Bay. During the summer, the town supports street musicians, festivals, and long-distance cyclists who stop here for a pint. The summer culminates with the regatta at the **Festival of the Sea** during the first weekend in August. In winter the town reverts to its true calling—plucking the fruits of the sea.

PRACTICAL INFORMATION Bus Éireann operates a summer service between Castletownbere and **Killarney** via **Kenmare** (June 26-Sept. 2 M-Sa 2 per day, £8.80). **Berehaven Bus Service** (tel. 70007) leaves from the parking lot next to O'Donoghue's and heads to **Bantry** via **Glengarriff** (M 2 per day, Tu-Sa 1 per day; Glengarriff 45min., £2.70; Bantry 1½hr., £4) and to **Cork** (3hr., Th only, £8). Two **minibus** services leave **Cork** for Castletownbere (M-Sa 6pm and Su 8pm); phone **Harrington's** (tel. 74003) or **O'Sullivan's** (tel. 74168) for mandatory reservations (both £8, £14 return). The bathroom-sized **tourist office** (tel. 70054), behind O'Donoghue's by the harbor, gives away heaps of maps (open June-Sept. M-Sa 10:30am-5pm). The **AIB** has an **ATM**, Main St. (tel. 70015; open M 10am-12:30pm and 1:30-5pm, Tu-F 10am-12:30pm and 1:30-4pm). **Bike hire** is available at **SuperValu,** Main St. (tel. 70020; £7 per day, deposit £20; open M-Sa 9am-7pm, Su 9am-1pm). The **phone code** is 027.

ACCOMMODATIONS, FOOD, AND PUBS Two miles west of town on Allihies Rd., just past the fork to Dunboy Castle, the **Beara Hostel** (tel. 70184) has a pleasantly rural location and adequate rustic rooms, although you might consider bringing your parka to stay warm at night (their blankets aren't much help). (Dorms £7; private rooms £8 per person. Camping £3.50 per person.) The clean and spacious **Seapoint B&B** (tel. 70292), about a mile outside of town toward Glengariff, has spectacular views (singles £20; doubles £32; laundry £5). **Castletown House,** Main St. (tel. 70252), above the Old Bank Seafood Restaurant, offers lovely rooms and lots of info (£15, with bath £17). Six miles west of Castletownbere and a good deal more isolated is the euphoria-inducing **Garranes Farmhouse Hostel (IHH)** (tel. 73147). Stay on the Allihies Rd. and look for the sign; a taxi from Castletownbere costs £7. This luxurious and intimate cottage perched above the sea has a view worthy of a pilgrimage. Phone ahead to confirm that all the space hasn't been absorbed by the Buddhist center next door (see below). (Dorms £6.50; doubles £16. Laundry £3.)

SuperValu, Main St. (tel. 70020), sells the largest selection of foodstuffs (open M-Sa 9am-9pm, Su 9am-6pm). Seafood spawns in almost all of Castletownbere's restaurants. One exception is **The Old Bakery,** Main St. (tel. 70901), which serves piping-hot pizzas and an extensive menu of top-quality curries, sandwiches, and pasta (£4-6) in a charming building that was, not surprisingly, once a bakery. It is now a great spot to sit around on a rainy day (live trad and jazz most Saturday nights; open daily 9am-7pm). **Jack Patrick's,** Main St. (tel. 70319), serves enormous fish platters and affordable lunch specials (£3.50; set 3-course dinner £13.50; open in summer M-Sa 10:30am-9pm, Su 12:30-7pm; in winter M-Sa 10:30am-9pm). Across the street, **Niki's** (tel. 70625) expands the seafood options with grilled garlic mussels (£3.25; open daily 10am-3pm and 7-9:30pm). For the less gourmet, the **Cronin's Hideaway,** Main St. (tel. 70386), serves reasonable food fast and fresh (entrees £3-7.50; open M-Sa 6-10pm, Su 1-10pm). **MacCarthy's,** Main St. (tel. 70014), the most popular pub in town and a well-stocked grocery, serves food all day (all sandwiches under £2) and belts out live trad and ballads on the weekends. Get the local dirt from Ms. MacCarthy, charming proprietress and granddaughter of the original owner, who has her father's dramatic life story displayed round the bar. **O'Donoghue's** pub, Main St. (tel. 70007), on The Square, lures a younger catch with its pool table and sunny (or starry) tables outside. **Lynch's,** Main St. (tel. 70363), is also popular, hosting sporadic live music in summer.

SIGHTS Castletownbere's seat at the foot of awe-inspiring **Hungry Hill** (3414ft.) makes it a fine launch pad for daytrips up the mountain (inquire in the tourist office). In addition, the huge harbor is a joy for watersports enthusiasts. **Beara Kayaks** (tel. 70692) offers one- and two-hour classes in Castletownbere, Bere Island, Glengarriff, and Schull. *(£5 per hr., all equipment included. Call for bookings.)* The **Beara Sheepdog Centre** (tel. 70287) has capitalized on city mice by showing off their obedient sheep in a daily roundup. Two miles southwest of Castletownbere on the Allihies Rd., **Dunboy Castle** shelters two separate ruins. Cows roam the crumbling Gothic-style halls of its 18th- and 19th-century mansion. Three quarters of a mile past the gate stand the ruins of the 14th-century **O'Sullivan Bere** fortress (50p). The road that runs past the castle becomes a shady trail that passes a number of sheltered coves perfect for swimming (as long as you don't mind jellyfish). Six miles west of town, the **Dzogchen Buddhist Centre** is perched on the same clifftop as the Garranes Hostel. The views from the meditation room are inspiration in themselves. A very respected Tibetan Buddhist teaching site, the center offers a beginning **meditation session** every day. Phone the hostel (see above) for details.

■ Near Castletownbere: Bere Island

Though lacking both the grandeur and amenities of Cape Clear, Bere Island provides views of the Beara Peninsula, which stretches out next to it. The spectacular ferry ride to this fishing community makes a quiet daytrip. Two **ferries** chug to Bere Island. **Murphy's Ferry Service** (tel. 75004) leaves from the pontoon 3 mi. east of Castletownbere off the Glengarriff Rd. but lands you much closer to the island's "center," **Rerrin Village** (4 per day, £4 return, students £3). The other company, **Bere Island Ferry** (tel. 75009), leaves from the center of Castletownbere but drops you inconveniently on the western end of the island (June 21-Sept. 2 5 per day, Su 4 per day, £3 return). As return times tend to be uncertain, it's a good idea to discuss your return plans with the driver.

Bere Island used to be a British naval base; forts and military remnants are still scattered around the island. The Irish Army now uses the island for training. If you plan to stay the night, you can check out the island's **self-catering accommodation** (tel. 75028) or dock at **Mrs. O'Sullivan's Harbour View B&B** (tel. 75011), a half hour walk from the Bere Island Ferry on the west end of the island; you can call for a lift. (£14, with bath £16.) **Kitty Murphy's Café** (tel. 75004), a pretty little café, serves the only affordable food on the island. Kitty herself may be the best source of information on the Bere. Next door, **Desmond O'Sullivan's** will pamper you with Guinness.

■ Dursey Island

The best scenery on the Beara is on **Dursey Island,** reached by Ireland's only cable car (tel. (027) 73017). The car has a small copy of the 91st Psalm posted inside for nervous perusal during the exciting 10-minute aerial trip. (Car runs continuously M-Sa 9-11am, 2:30-5pm, and 7-8pm; Sunday hours vary depending on which church has mass that morning. £2.50 return.) The whole of Dursey Island is best seen by bike, but call ahead to ensure that there is room for your bike on the cable car. The English Army laid waste to Dursey Fort in 1602 after raiding the unarmed garrison and callously tossing many soldiers over the cliffs to their doom. A trip to the western tip provides a stunning view over these cliffs of the sea and a chance to observe the island's much-vaunted migrant bird flocks. There is no accommodation on the island, but camping is legal. Besides, the island's seven residents could use the company.

▓ Northern Beara Peninsula

Past Castletownbere, the Beara Peninsula stretches determinedly out into the Atlantic, supporting craggy knolls, cliff-lined coasts, and desolate villages. A remarkable dearth of trees increases the harshness of the peninsula and the expanse of the views out to sea. The stark isolation of this part of the Ring is both an attraction and a frustration for hitchers, who report success only during the mid-afternoon beach traffic in July and August. Biking is the way to go.

■ Allihies

The blunt northern head of the peninsula is choked with cultural relics. Children's gravestones crumble outside the **Celtic Church,** two miles from Allihies and marked on some maps and signs as Point Nadistiert. The collapsing entrance to a series of caves stands nearby. **Mass rocks** dot the fields surrounding the village, as steadfast as the Catholics who once practiced their forbidden religion at these makeshift altars.

Evidence of a booming mid-19th-century mining industry, fences forbids entry to Allihies's abandoned copper mine shafts. Popular **Ballydonegan Strand** is just short of town on Castletownbere Rd. More pristine and secluded are the white sands of **Garnish Strand,** a few miles down the road toward Dursey (follow the signs to the right at the fork) across from the post office on Dursey Rd. The **Windy Point House** (tel. (027) 73017), at the cable car a few minutes away, sustains scone-deprived beachgoers admirably with their full midday menu and tempts some to stay the night with its amazing views of Dursey Sound (sandwiches under £2; food served 11am-6pm; B&B £17 with bath and unbeatable sea views).

Surrounded by the Slieve Mountains, the only street in teeny Allihies dangles on the Atlantic, west of Castletownbere as the gannet flies but on the northern loop of R575. **The Village Hostel (IHH),** Main St. (tel. (027) 73107), next to the very red O'Neill's pub, is an excellent stop for exploring the nearby coastline. Lavender walls, a sun-drenched kitchen, and warm showers take the starkness off of Allihies. (Dorms £7; doubles £18. **Camping** £4.50 per person. Laundry £3.50. Open May-Oct.) One mile south of the village (and well marked by signs) lies the sparse **Allihies Youth Hostel (An Óige/HI)** (tel. (027) 73014), which, despite remarkable views, threatens to compound the sense of bare isolation in Allihies (dorms £6.50, under 18 £5; sheets 50p; open June-Sept.; reception 9-11am and 4-7pm). No-frills **camping** is available behind the beach at **Kathleen's** (£2). To reach the site, stay on the road toward the beach (don't turn right toward the pier). **Anthony's,** next door, has more amenities with a correspondingly higher price (£6 per tent). Turn right at the beach, look for signs that say "Campground." From Anthony's, the view back up to town is as picturesque as the one out to sea; the campground owners can tell you who owns each building on the horizon. **O'Neill's Bar and Restaurant** (tel. (027) 73008), next to the Village Hostel, offers a varied menu of pub grub (sandwiches £1.40-5; warm food £5-8; evening menu £4.50-12.50, served daily 6-9pm). The sponge-painted orange walls at **Jackie's** (tel. 73283) are almost as cheery as Jackie herself; her limited menu is the gateway to nonetheless good food (sandwiches £1.30; open daily 11am-7pm). **The Atlantic,** Main St. (tel. (027) 73072), at the bottom of the town, prepares modest seafood right off the boat (plaice £6; open daily 9am-10pm). **O'Sullivan's** (tel. (027) 73004) sells everything necessary for a first-class picnic on Dursey and even rents **bikes** to get you there (mountain bikes £6 per day; open daily 9am-9pm). Allihies's four pubs cater mostly to locals. Usually one pub—seemingly chosen by tacit consensus among the villagers—is quite lively each night. **O'Neill's** is a safe bet, usually hosting trad and ballads on Wednesdays. **The Lighthouse** is a popular spot on Fridays and Sundays, as are the **Oak Bar's** trad sessions on Thursdays.

■ Eyeries and Ardgroom

Through some of the most barren land and some of the most exciting roads in Ireland lies the colorful hamlet of Eyeries. The **beach** here is a lovely stop, or ask for directions to **Ballycrovane,** where the tallest *ogham* stone in Ireland stands. This 17 ft. stone is on private property but well signposted, since the owners collect £1 from each visitor. Five minutes east of the village, the **Ard Na Mara Hostel** (tel. (027) 74271) makes you feel like a friend of the family (dorms £7; private rooms £8; laundry £3; **camping** £3.50).

The only other thing to see on the northern side of the Beara (except for more mountains, more forests, and more sea) are the **Derreen Gardens** (tel. (064) 83103), half a mile north of Lauragh on the coast road, where you can lose yourself in the mossy tunnels that run through evergreens and massive rhododendrons. These rhododendrons, taller than most buildings in Ireland, originally occupied almost the entire garden because of their readiness to grow. (Open Apr.-Sept. daily 11am-6pm. £2.50.) Heading east past Eyeries, you pass through **Ardgroom** (a-GROOM), a small village with…drum roll please…a good pub. **The Holly Bar** (tel. (027) 74082) hosts live trad on most Tuesdays, Fridays, and Sundays and serves up a mean bowl of seafood chowder (£3.50).

County Kerry

Various places in Co. Kerry claim to be Europe's westernmost inhabited land. They're all wrong (the honor goes to Hellisandur, Iceland), but the ubiquitous mistake reveals a Kerry paradox. The county's small towns, vast beaches, and mountain roads feel distant from the rest of Ireland. Residents of (relatively) large Dingle talk of things being brought in from "the outside"—usually meaning Tralee, only 30 mi. away. Yet the economy of Kerry, famous for its natural beauty, revolves around tourism, and the Kerry identity incorporates the belief that this attention is well deserved. From soft, emerald Dingle to tough, mountainous Killarney to the strands of the Iveragh peninsula, Kerry is unlike anywhere else in Ireland; Kerryites will make sure you know it.

The Iveragh Peninsula, colloquially equated with the Ring of Kerry road, has the lake-filled Killarney National Park at its base, Bray Head near its tip, and noxious tour buses traveling between the two. Even so, the views are incomparable. The Dingle Peninsula is slightly less visited; narrow roads protect Slea Head, the West Dingle *gaeltacht,* and the Blasket Islands from tour bus madness. Summer bus transport throughout Kerry is quite available. In the off season, however, public transportation grows sparse along coastal routes.

■ Killarney

With something for everyone, Killarney seems to have just about everyone at once. And with an economy based on tourism, Killarney sometimes celebrates tourism itself rather than its extraordinarily beautiful national park or well-preserved heritage.

ORIENTATION AND PRACTICAL INFORMATION

Killarney packs into three crowded major streets. **Main St.**, in the center of town, begins at the Town Hall, then becomes High St. **New** and **Plunkett St.** both intersect Main St., each heading in different directions. New St. heads west to the Knockreer Estate toward Killorglin. Plunkett St. becomes College St. and then Park Rd. on its way east to the bus and train stations. **East Avenue Rd.** connects the train station back to town hall and then bends, becoming Muckross Rd. on its way to the Muckross Estate and Kenmare.

Trains: Killarney Station (tel. 31067), off East Avenue Rd. near the intersection with Park Rd., past the Great Southern Hotel. Open M-Sa 7:30am-12:30pm and 2-6:20pm, Su 30min. before train departures. Trains run until 6:20pm to **Cork** (1½hr., 5 per day, £13.50), **Dublin** (3½hr., 4 per day, £33.50), **Galway** (6hr., 3 per day, £30), and **Limerick** (2hr., M-Sa 4 per day, Su 3 per day, £15).

Buses: off East Avenue Rd. (tel. 34777), across from the Great Southern Hotel. Open M-Sa 8:30am-5:45pm. Buses rumble to **Cork** (2hr., 6-7 per day, £8.80), **Dingle** (2hr., 3-6 per day, £8.80), **Dublin** (6hr., 3-4 per day, £14), **Galway** (7hr., 5-7 per day, £13), **Limerick** (2hr., 4-5 per day, £9.30), and **Sligo** (7½hr., 2-3 per day, £17). Buses leave daily June-Sept. for the **Ring of Kerry Circuit,** with stops in **Killorglin, Glenbeigh, Kells, Cahersiveen, Waterville, Caherdaniel, Sneem,** and **Moll's Gap.** £8 if booked at a hostel; return with 1-night stop £12 for students. **Bus Éireann** also runs a no-frills Ring of Kerry circuit in the summer (2 per day, see p. 233). The June to mid-Sept. **Dingle/Slea Head** tour (M-Sa 2 per day) stops in **Inch, Annascaul, Dingle, Ventry, Slea Head, Dunquin,** and **Ballyferriter** (£9.70).

Tourist Office: Beach St. (tel. 31633), off New St. Exceptionally helpful and deservedly popular. Open July-Aug. M-Sa 9am-8pm, Su 9am-1pm and 2:15-6pm; June and Sept. M-Sa 9am-6pm, Su 10am-5pm; Oct.-May M-F 9:15am-5:30pm, Sa 9:15am-1pm.

Banks: TSB, 23-24 New St. (tel. 33666). Gives Visa and Mastercard cash advances at the counter but not from the **ATM.** Open M-W and F 9:30am-5pm, Th 9:30am-7pm. **AIB,** Main St. (tel. 31922), next to the town hall. Open M-Tu and Th-F 10am-

4pm, W 10am-5pm. **Bank of Ireland,** New St. (tel. 31050). Open M-Tu and Th-F 9am-4pm, W 9am-5pm. Their **ATM,** at the corner of Main and New St., accepts most major cards.

American Express: International Hotel, East Avenue Rd. (tel. 35722). Moneygrams, traveler's checks, card or traveler's check replacement, and client mail service. Open June-Sept. M-F 9am-8pm, Sa-Su 10am-7pm; Oct.-May M-F 9am-5pm, sort of.

Bike Rental: Crafts and Curios Rent-a-Bike, Bishop's Ln. (tel. 31282), next to Neptune's Hostel. £6 per day, £30 per week. Free panniers, locks, and park maps. Open M-Sa 9am-7pm, Su 9am-6:30pm.

Laundry: J. Gleeson's Launderette (tel. 33877), next to Spar Market on College St. £4.50 per load. Open M-W and Sa 9am-6pm, Th-F 9am-8pm.

Pharmacy: Sewell's Pharmacy (tel. 31027), corner of Main and New St. Open M-Sa 9am-6:30pm. No snake-bite kits, but that's usually not a problem around here.

Emergency: Dial 999; no coins required. **Garda:** New Rd. (tel. 31222).

Hospital: District Hospital, St. Margaret's Rd. (tel. 31076). Follow High St. 1mi. from the town center. Nearest emergency facilities are in Tralee.

Post Office: New St. (tel. 31288). Open M and W-F 9am-5:30pm, Tu 9:30am-5:30pm, Sa 9am-1pm.

Internet Access: PC Assist (tel. 37288), at the corner of High St. and New Rd. (not New St.). £1.50 per 15min., £5 per hr.

Phone Code: 064.

ACCOMMODATIONS

With every other house a B&B, it's easy to find cushy digs in Killarney. The town is also home to some excellent hostels—six lie within easy walking distance of the town center, while four are in rural settings near the National Park. Camping is not allowed in the National Park.

In Town

◉**The Súgán (IHH),** Lewis Rd. (tel. 33104), 2min. from the bus or train station. Make a left onto College St.; Lewis Rd. is the first right. Late nights spent in the stone common room with a glowing turf fire, candlelight, and groovy music give the hostel an incomparable ambience. Small, ship-like bunk rooms blur the distinction between intimacy and claustrophobia. 4- to 8-bed dorms £8.

Neptune's (IHH), Bishop's Ln. (tel. 35255), the first walkway off New St. on the right. Large and clean with good showers and solid mattresses. The staff is friendly and professional. 8-bed dorms £7; 4- to 6-bed dorms £8.50; doubles £20; 10% ISIC discount. Breakfast £1.50-3.50. Free luggage storage; £5 locker deposit. Laundry £4.50. **Tour booking** (Dingle tour £12, Ring of Kerry £8). **Bike rental** £5 per day.

The Railway Hostel (IHH), Park Rd. (tel. 35299), across the street from the bus and train stations. Big, bright building with skylights, a modern kitchen, and a pool table. Friendly staffers tread new hardwood floors at this recently renovated hostel. 4- to 9-bed dorms £7.50-8.50; doubles £20. Breakfast £2-3. **Bike rental** £6 per day.

The Four Winds Hostel (IHH), 43 New St. (tel. 33094). Situated in town but very close to the entrance to the National Park. Adequate and well located, although cinder-block architecture makes it a little dreary. Large dorms £8; small dorms £9; doubles £18. Breakfast £2. **Camping** £3.50 per person.

Atlas House, Park Rd. (tel. 36144). An unscenic 10min. walk from town. Take College St. past the bus station until it turns into Park Rd.; turn left at the first traffic light. Atlas House, which bills itself as a "budget accommodation," is in a huge, spanking-new building and will comfort those suffering Holiday Inn withdrawal. Big kitchen and luxuriously institutional sitting room with satellite TV. 6-bed dorms £9; doubles with bath £30; triples £37.50. Continental breakfast included.

◉**Orchard House,** Fleming's Ln. (tel. 31879), off High St. Tasteful, immaculate, friendly, and centrally located. Hard to beat. A goldfish pool—what more could you want? Singles £16; doubles £32; most rooms with bath.

Sunny Bank B&B (tel. 34109). A 5min. walk from the town center on Park Rd. Cheerful and downright luxurious with bath and TV in all rooms. Specially modified showers with serious water pressure. June-Sept. £18-20; Oct.-May £16-17.

Outside Town

Bunrower House (IHH), Ross Rd. (tel. 33914). Follow Muckross Rd. out of town and take a right at the Esso station onto Ross Rd. The hostel is about ¾mi. down the road on the left. Free minibus to and from train and bus stations on request. A sister hostel to the Súgán, the "Bun" has a common room with wood fire, spacious bunk-rooms, sky-lit toilets, outstanding showers, a golden retriever, and a three-legged cat. Dorms £7-8.50; doubles £20. **Camping** in the quiet yard is the closest you can legally get to sleeping in the National Park (£3.50). **Bike rental** £6.

Peacock Farms Hostel (IHH; tel. 33557). Take Muckross Rd. out of town and turn left at Muckross Village just after the hotel. Take that road 2mi. and follow the sign-posts—if you think you're nearly there, you haven't gone far enough. As a less tax-ing alternative, call for a ride from the bus station. Overlooking Lough Guitane and surrounded by Killarney's slopes, this hostel is home to a friendly family of pea-cocks and a collection of homing pigeons. Skylights, hand-painted showers, and comfy rooms. Dorms £6. Open May-Sept. Wheelchair accessible.

Aghadoe Hostel (An Óige/HI; tel. 31240). In Aghadoe, 3mi. west of town on the Killorglin Rd. Call for free van to and from bus and train stations. A grandiose and comfortable hostel in a stone mansion with magnificent views of the mountains. Offers outdoor activities, including canoeing and climbing, and day-long classes on Celtic heritage, storytelling, and local lore (class £20, including lunch). Dorms June-Sept. £7.50, Oct.-May £6.50. Continental breakfast £2; café food £1.50-3.50. Laundry £4. Reception 8:30am-midnight. **Bike rental** £6 per day.

Black Valley Hostel (An Óige/HI; tel. 34712), 12mi. from town on Gap of Dunloe Rd. This spare but spotless hostel, one of the last places in Ireland to receive elec-tricity, is conveniently located on the Kerry Way. Buy food in town or eat at the hostel. Dorms £6.50, off-season £5.50. Sheets 80p. Midnight curfew.

Fossa Caravan and Camping Park (tel. 31497), 3½mi. west of town on the Killorg-lin Rd. Kitchen, laundromat, tennis courts, shop, and restaurant. £4 per person. Showers 50p. Wash £1.50, dry 50p per 20min. Open mid-Mar. to Oct.

Flesk Caravan and Camping (tel. 31704), 1mi. from town on Muckross Rd. £4 per person. Laundry £3.50. Showers 20p. Open Mar.-Oct.

FOOD

Food in Killarney is affordable at lunchtime, but prices skyrocket in the evening. **Quinnsworth,** in an arcade off New St., is the town's largest grocer (open M-W and Sa 8am-8pm, Th-F 8am-10pm, Su 10am-6pm). A number of fast-food joints and take-aways stay open until 2-3am nightly to satisfy the post-Guinness munchies.

Teo's, 13 New St. (tel. 36344). Tired of Ireland? Get away from Shepherd's pie *and* trad music in this marvelous Mediterranean restaurant. Salads, pasta, fresh fish, and flamenco dancing. Open noon-4:30pm and 5:30-11pm.

The Green Onion Café, Flemings Ln. (tel. 34225), off High St. Sandwiches and plen-tiful salads are served up in this small, skylit restaurant. Open daily noon-5:30pm.

O'Meara's Restaurant, 12 High St. (tel. 36744), above O'Meara's bar. Lunch or dine on eclectic and high-quality cuisine from around the world. Lunch £6-8; 3-course earlybird dinner 6-7:30pm £12. Open Tu-Su noon-10pm.

Charlie Nelligan's, High St. (tel. 31441). This cheap, friendly coffee house serves New York-style doughnuts, an excellent fried breakfast (£4), and sandwiches (£2).

A Taste of Eden, Bridewell Ln. (tel. 33083), on the left off New St. Fresh and cre-ative vegetarian dishes with an international flair. Lunch £4-6. Dinner entrees £8-10. Open 12:30-3:30 and 6:30-10pm.

Robertino's, 9 High St. (tel. 34966). Eat *bruschetta* and *antipasti* in the company of plaster Greco-Roman goddesses; be aware that the quality of the food demands that your wallet take on mythic proportions as well. 3-course lunch £10-13. **Allegro's** next door is for the plebes. Pizza and burgers £3-4.50. Open daily noon-10:30pm.

PUBS AND CLUBS

Battalions of jig-seeking tourists have influenced Killarney's pubs, but plenty have managed to withstand the rising tide of shamrock-mania. During the summer, trad can be heard nightly around town.

⚜Yer Mans, Plunkett St. (tel. 32688). Uncontestedly the best pub in town and frequented by a young, mixed crowd actually from Killarney. Serves Guinness in jam jars on request (£1.25); Yer Mans is the only pub in Ireland licensed by Guinness to do so. Trad nightly in summer, singer/songwriter nights every other Friday.

O'Connor's Traditional Pub, 7 High St. (tel. 32496). Tourists and locals mingle in this upbeat, comfortable pub. Trad Mondays and Thursdays.

Fáilte Bar, College St. (tel. 33404). A large, relaxed crowd gathers at this dark and woody pub. Singer/songwriter sessions every night, DJ on weekends.

Buckley's Bar, College St. (tel. 31037). Locals and visitors warm themselves by the peat fire. Lack of atmosphere compensated for by some of the best acoustic trad in town (nightly at 9:30pm).

Mustang Sally's, Main St. (tel. 35790). A young crowd of locals flocks to loud rock.

Several **nightclubs** simmer from 10:30pm until 1:30 or 2am. Most charge £4-5 cover but often offer discounts before 11pm. Smallish **Rudy's Nightclub** (tel. 32688), above Yer Mans on Plunkett St., plays alternative music for Killarney's ruthlessly hip element. The scrutiny at the door can be ruthless as well; dress sharp (shows Tuesday and Th-Su). **Revelles,** East Avenue Rd. (tel. 32522), in the East Avenue Hotel, clogs with rave and club kids on Friday through Sunday nights, while **Scoundrels** (tel. 31640) in the Eviston House Hotel on New St. attracts a slightly older crowd. (Monday 60s-80s music, Tu-Th mixed music, Friday dance, Sa-Su mixed and often live music. Discounts before 11pm. Closes 1:30am.) Check the *Killarney Advertiser* (free) for happenings around town and the *Kingdom* (70p) for county events.

SIGHTS AND ENTERTAINMENT

In a town congested with bureaux de change, souvenir shops, and disoriented foreigners, Killarney's charm is elusive at best. The glories of Killarney are really located in the National Park just beyond city limits. The neo-Gothic **St. Mary's Cathedral** on New St., with three huge altars, seats 1400 in its rough limestone structure. (*Always open.*) Killarney's festivals are worth exploration: locals take them quite seriously and come out en masse. In mid-March, Killarney hosts the **Guinness Roaring 1920s Festival,** in which pubs, restaurants, and hostels bust out in jazz, barbershop singing, and flapper regalia. In mid-May and mid-July, horses run in the **Killarney Races** in the racecourse on Ross Rd. (tickets available at gate; £3-5). The **Killarney Regatta,** the oldest regatta in Ireland, draws rowers and spectators to Lough Leane in early to mid-July. **Gaelic football matches** are held in Fitzgerald Stadium on Lewis Rd. most Sunday afternoons and some weekday evenings (tickets £2-5). Kerry's fanatical rivalry with Cork comes to a head when Cork's team comes to town. For more information, inquire at Sheahan's Pharmacy on Main St. The Killarney area has excellent salmon and trout fishing, especially in late summer and September; call **O'Neill's Fishing Shop** (tel. 31970) for details.

▓ Killarney National Park

The Ice Ages had a dramatic impact around Killarney, scooping out a series of glens and scattering ice-smoothed rocks and precarious boulders. The 37 sq. mi. park, stretching west and south of Killarney toward Kenmare, incorporates a string of forested mountains and the famous **Lakes of Killarney:** huge **Lough Leane (Lower Lake),** medium-sized **Middle (Muckross) Lake,** and small **Upper Lake,** 2 mi. southwest and connected by a canal. Ireland's last indigenous herd of red deer, numbering about 850, roams the glens that surround the lakes.

Kenmare Rd. curves along the southeastern shores of the lakes between park sites but misses some woodland walks and bike rides. With many more tourists than Irish driving these sections, hitching can be difficult. These paths are also frequented by droves of horse-drawn buggies. Be forewarned—there's more *cac capall* (Irish for what's left on a road after dozens of roughage-eating horses have traveled it) than any sane person would want to smell in a lifetime. The park's size demands a map, available at the Killarney tourist office or the **Information Centre** (tel. 31440) behind Muckross House. Serious hikers should buy the 1:25,000 Ordnance Survey map (open daily June-Sept. 9am-7pm).

The most frequented destinations are the **Ross Castle/Lough Leane** area, **Muckross House** on Middle Lake, and the **Gap of Dunloe** just west of the park area, bordered on the southwest by **Macgillycuddy's Reeks,** Ireland's highest mountain range (most of the peaks are under 3000ft.). The Gap of Dunloe is a full-day excursion, but the others can be managed in several hours or stretched over a full day, depending on your mode of transport. Hikers and bikers should take the necessary precautions whether alone or in groups (see **Camping,** p. 45).

The best way to see almost all of the park in one day is to bike to the Gap of Dunloe (see p. 233). If the idea of a 14 mi. bike excursion fills you with trepidation, there are several short, well-marked, and well-paved walking trails closer to the Killarney side of the park. The park is also a perfect starting point for those who plan to walk the 129 mi. **Kerry Way**—essentially the Ring of Kerry on foot. Do not attempt the Kerry Way from October to March, when rains make the uneven terrain dangerous. The **Old Kenmare Road,** the first (or last) leg of the walk, passes through the spectacular Torc and Mangerton Mountains and can be managed in one day. From Killarney, fol-

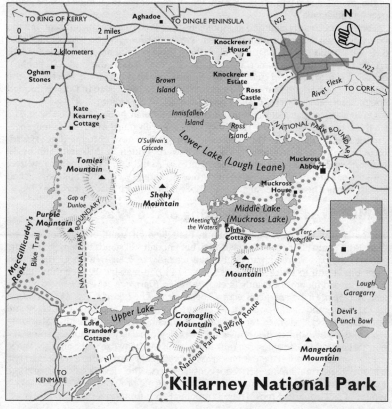

Killarney National Park

low the Kenmare Rd. 4 mi. and turn left just beyond the main entrance to Muckross House—the path leaves from the carpark on this side road. The Killarney bookstore sells a *Kerry Way* guide, with topographic maps of the Way. The excellent 1:50,000 Ordnance Survey maps (unfortunately, far from waterproof) of the Iveragh include minor roads, trails, and archaeological points of interest (£4.60).

■ Ross Castle and Lough Leane

From town, **Knockreer Estate** is a short walk down New St. The original mansion housed Catholic Earls of Kenmare and, later, the Grosvenor family of *National Geographic* fame. The current building, dating only from the 1950s, is unimpressive and not open to the public, but provides great views of the hills. You can drive or walk out to **Ross Castle** (tel. 35851), a right on Ross Rd. off Muckross Rd. 2 mi. from Killarney, but the numerous footpaths from Knockreer are more scenic (15min. walk). *(Admission by guided tour only. Open daily June-Aug. 9am-6:30pm, May-Sept. 10am-6pm; Oct. 9am-5pm. Last admission 45min. before closing. £2.50, students £1.)* The castle, built by the O'Donaghue chieftains in the 14th century, was the last in Munster to fall to Cromwell's army (see **History,** p. 56). In the last two decades the castle has been completely renovated, and it shows: the gleaming limestone and fresh wooden beams are much nicer looking than the castle could have been in its own day. Tales of a drippy, claustrophobic castle life and the O'Donoghue's incessant, if ultimately futile, attempts to repel intruders can be very therapeutic. Past the castle, paths lead to the wooded and relatively secluded **Ross Island**—not an island at all, but a peninsula shaped like a lobster claw that stretches out into Lough Leane. Ross Island is the site of the green-colored copper pools from which copper has been mined for probably over four millennia.

The view of Lough Leane and its mountains from Ross Island is magnificent, but the best way to see the area is from the water. Two **waterbus services,** Pride of the Lakes (tel. 32638) and Lily of Killarney (tel. 31068), leave from behind the castle for lake cruises (5-6 per day in summer, £5). You can hire rowboats by the castle (£2 per hr.), or take a **motorboat trip** (tel. 34351) to Innisfallen Island (£3), the Meeting of the Waters through Lough Leane and Muckross Lake (£5), or the Gap of Dunloe through Lough Leane, Muckross Lake, and Upper Lake (£7.50, £10 return).

On Innisfallen Island sit the stoic remains of **Innisfallen Abbey,** founded by St. Finian the Leper around AD 600. The abbey was eventually transformed into a university during the Middle Ages. The *Annals of Innisfallen,* now entombed at Oxford, recount world and Irish history. The annals were written in Irish and Latin by 39 monastic scribes and supposedly finished in 1326. At the abbey's center is a yew tree; yew and oak groves were sacred to the Druids, so abbeys were often built among and around them. The separate Augustinian abbey is so ruined it's barely recognizable.

■ Muckross and the Meeting of the Waters

The remains of **Muckross Abbey,** built in 1448, lie 3 mi. south of Killarney on Kenmare Rd. Cromwell tried to burn it down, but enough still stands to demonstrate the grace of the part-Norman, part-Gothic cloisters. *(Always open. Free.)* From the abbey, signs direct you to **Muckross House** (tel. 31440), a massive 19th-century manor whose garden blooms brilliantly in early summer. *(Open daily July-Aug. 9am-7pm; Sept.-June 9am-6pm. House and farms each £3.80, students £1.62; joint tickets £5.50, students £2.75.)* The grand and proper house, completed in 1843, reeks of aristocracy and commands a regal view of the lakes and mountains. Upon first visiting Muckross House, the philosopher Bishop George Berkeley proclaimed: "Another Louis XIV may make another Versailles, but only the hand of the Deity can make another Muckross." Outside the house lie the **Muckross Traditional Farms,** where traditional cottages recreate rural life in early 20th-century Kerry. The view is fantastic, and the expansive lawns are perfect for a mid-afternoon picnic or nap. The gorgeous flora is typical of sub-tropical climes. There is no direct path from Ross Castle to Muckross;

the only road veers off Muckross Rd. back in Killarney. Therefore, accomplishing both in one day requires a bicycle, a car, or a spirit willing to walk about ten miles.

From Muckross House, it's a 2 mi. stroll to the **Meeting of the Waters;** walk straight down the front lawn and follow the signs. The paved path is nice, while the dirt trail through the **Yew Woods** is more secluded and not accessible to bikes. The Meeting of the Waters is the natural sight that justifies the trip, but the real focus for tourists is **Dinis Cottage** (tel. 31954), which serves homemade pizza, drinks, and pastries (open June-Sept. daily 10:30am-6pm). If you're coming from the cottage, the roaring influx of water straight ahead is Upper Lake; the forks to the left and right lead to Middle Lake and Lough Leane, respectively. The path returns to the main (Kenmare/Killarney) road; from here, turn left toward Killarney and continue about a mile to **Torc Waterfall.** A short walk through mossy woods brings you to the cascading 60 ft. drop. Past the waterfall, the trail makes its way up **Ford Mountain,** which affords dramatic views of the lakes.

■ Gap of Dunloe

A pilgrimage to the Gap of Dunloe guarantees misty mountain vistas and significant calorie expenditure. There are plenty of organized trips to the Gap that can be booked from the Killarney tourist office (£13). These trips, designed to be combination walking tour and boat-trip, shuttle visitors to the foot of the Gap, effectively cutting the 7 mi. from Killarney. After walking over the Gap and down to **Lord Brandon's Cottage** (tel. 3430), trippers pause for a bite (sandwiches £2-3.50) and meet a boat, which takes them across the lake to Ross Castle (open June-Sept. daily 9am-6pm); a bus returns them to Killarney. Walking the Gap in this direction, however, is a trek up the long side of the mountain. Far better, and potentially less expensive, is to attack the Gap by bike from the opposite direction. Take a **motorboat** trip to the head of the Gap from Ross Castle (£7; book ahead at the tourist office). From Lord Brandon's Cottage on the Gap, turn left over the stone bridge and continue for about 2 mi. to the hostel and church. A right turn up a road with sincere hairpin turns will bring you to the top of the Gap a breathtaking 1½ mi. later. Beyond is a well-deserved 7 mi. downhill coast through the park's most breathtaking scenery.

At the foot of the Gap, you'll pass **Kate Kearney's Cottage** (tel. 44116). Kate Kearney was an independent mountain-dwelling woman famous for brewing the near-poisonous *poitín.* Now her former home is a pub and restaurant that sucks in droves of tourists. (Open daily 9am-midnight; restaurant open until 9pm. Live trad often.) The 8 mi. ride back to Killarney passes the entirely ruined **Dunloe Castle,** an Anglo-Norman stronghold demolished by Cromwell's armies. Bear right after Kate's, turn left on the road to Fossa, and turn right on Killorglin Rd. There is also a set of *ogham* stones from about AD 300 (see **History,** p. 54).

RING OF KERRY

The Southwest's most celebrated peninsula has been a visitor attraction for so long that the history of tourism can be easier to grasp than the tough, romantic spirit the visitors hope to see. A lucky few travelers spend days out on the peninsula, soaking up the great sea spray, grand views, and pervasive quiet, except for during the time each day when the buses pass through a given location—locals can give you almost the exact time. Find a good hostel in a small town on a windy day by the sea, and you may achieve a state of serious bliss.

The term "Ring of Kerry" is often used to describe the entire Iveragh Peninsula, but it more correctly refers not to a region but to a set of roads: N71 from Kenmare to Killarney, R562 from Killarney to Killorglin, and the long loop of N70 west and back to Kenmare. If you don't like the prepackaged private bus tours based out of Killarney, **Bus Éireann** does a summer circuit through all the major towns on the Ring (2 per day), allowing you to get off anywhere and anytime you like. Unfortunately, you will have to pay in increments for the trip, since they don't offer one single Ring package that allows you to get on and off. You can, however, pay the round-trip fare, get off the first bus, and then pick up the later bus, as long as it's all done in one day. Buses travel around the Ring counterclockwise, from Killarney to Killorglin, west along Dingle Bay, east along Kenmare River and north from Kenmare to Killarney. In summer, other Bus Éireann buses also travel clockwise from Waterville back to Killarney (2 per day). Biking is best in the afternoon and during other non-prime tour bus times, and bikers may want to avoid the traffic by doing the Ring clockwise. Drivers are forced to choose between lurching behind large tourbuses or meeting them face-to-face on narrow roads.

The Ring of Kerry traditionally commences in Killorglin. If you are traveling clockwise around the Ring on N70, stop at the **Quarry in Kells** (tel. 77601), a restaurant/craft shop/convenience store with magnificent views and dark green benches. The shop is particularly inviting to haggard bikers cycling against hurricane-like winds. (Open daily 9am-8pm.)

■ Killorglin

Thirteen miles west of Killarney, Killorglin lives in the shadow of Iveragh's mountain spine and of its own tourist industry. Killorglin's placid pass-through tourism is interrupted every year from August 10 to 12, when it holds the riotous **Puck Fair**, a celebration of the crowning of a particularly virile he-goat as King Puck. The pubs stay open for 72 straight hours to refresh the exuberant musicians, dancers, and singers. Be forewarned that the town's hostel and B&Bs operate on a first-come, first-served basis during the Puck Fair. During the rest of the year, residents show off their mountains, entertain the Ring crowd, and plan the next fair. The sights of Killorglin, except for the town's mountain views, are generally a few miles from town and best explored by car or bike.

ORIENTATION AND PRACTICAL INFORMATION Killorglin's **Main St.** runs uphill from the water and widens to form The Square. At the top of The Square to the right, Upper Bridge St. climbs to the tourist office at the intersection of Iveragh Rd. The Ring of Kerry **bus** stops in Killorglin next to the tourist office (June-Sept. 2 per day; **Cahersiveen** 50min., £5; **Waterville** 1¼hr., £5.90; **Sneem** 3hr., £8.80). The eastbound bus from Cahersiveen goes more directly to **Killarney** (Sept.-June M-Sa 1 per day, July-Aug. M-Sa 2 per day). The spiffy, octagonal **tourist office** (tel. 61451) hands out armfuls of relevant information (open May-Sept. M-Sa 9:30am-6pm, Su 10am-3pm). **AIB** (tel. 61134) is at the corner of Main St. and New Line Rd. (open M and W-F 10am-4pm, Tu 10am-5pm; **ATM**). **O'Shea's** (tel. 61919) on Main St. rents **bikes** (£7.50 per day, £40 per week; open M-Sa 9am-6pm). Clothes sparkle at **Starlite Cleaners,** Langford St., to the left from the top of The Square (£5 per load; open M-Sa 9am-6pm). The **post office** (tel. 61101) is on Main St. (open M-F 9am-5:30pm, Sa 9am-1pm). The **phone code,** 066, is a particularly virile he-goat.

ACCOMMODATIONS Laune Valley Farm Hostel (IHH) (tel. 61488), 1½ mi. from town off Tralee Rd., is bright and beautiful and hosts a local population of cows, chickens, dogs, and ducks—save your table scraps. Fresh milk and eggs from the farm are for sale. (Dorms from £6; doubles from £16. Camping £3 per person. Wheelchair accessible.) **Orglan House** (tel. 61540), atop a steep hill on Killarney Rd. a three-minute walk from town, proffers grand views from immaculate rooms and relieves you from brown bread delirium with its delicious, individually tailored breakfasts (£15-17). **Laune Bridge House** (tel. 61161), a few doors down from Orglan, opens its florid and comfortable rooms (£16 with bath). Sleep in the fresh Kerry air at **West's Caravan and Camping Park** (tel. 61240), 1 mi. east of town on Killarney Rd. Pool table, TV, tennis (racket 75p), fishing (rods from £5 per day), and laundry (£4) are available. They also have mobile homes to let on a weekly or nightly basis. (July 9-Aug. 20 £3.50, off season £3. Showers 50p. Open Easter to late Oct.)

FOOD AND PUBS The **Bianconi Restaurant** (tel. 61146) on Lower Main St. is pricey and unabashedly touristy, but the salads are famous, and the "early dinner menu" offers some reasonable choices. (Salads £7, entrees £9.50-12; served 5:30-9pm. Open M-Sa 11am-9pm, Su 12:30-2pm and 5:30-9pm.) Good budget food comes at the expense of ambience at the **Starlite Diner,** The Square (tel. 61296). Burgers are all under £3.20, and a complete breakfast (available all day) is £4. Take your food upstairs for a more dignified dining experience. (Open daily 9:30am-11pm.) Across from the tourist office hunkers **Bunker's** (tel. 61381), a red-faced restaurant/café/take-away (café open daily 9:30am-11pm; restaurant open daily 6-10:30pm). Their regal purple pub lies next door, where live music is performed on Sundays. A young, local crowd satisfies all its Guinness needs at **Old Forge,** Main St. (tel. 61231), a lively stone pub (music nightly, trad M-W). An older and more subdued crowd watches football at the **Laune Bar,** Lower Main St. (tel. 61158), on the water, which hosts folk sessions on Thursday nights. For those who like to sing once they've had a few, there's always **Nick's Piano Bar,** Lower Main St. (tel. 61219).

SIGHTS The **Cappanalea Outdoor Education Centre** (tel. 69244), 7 mi. southwest of Killorglin off the Ring of Kerry road, offers canoeing, rock-climbing, windsurfing, sailing, hillwalking, fishing, and orienteering. *(£10 per ½ day, £18.50 per day. Open daily 10am-5pm. Overnight programs with accommodations available. Book a few days in advance.)* **Cromane Beach** is only 4 mi. west of town; take New Line Rd., which branches off Main St. south of The Square. Five miles off Killarney Rd., the 16th-century **Ballymalis Castle** lies on the banks of the River Laune in view of Macgillycuddy's Reeks. Play a round at the **Killorglin Golf Club** (tel. 61979), 1½ mi. from town on Tralee Rd., whose green fees are much more affordable than those in Killarney. *(18-hole greens fee £14 weekdays, £16 weekends.)*

■ Cahersiveen

Good hostels, decent food, and an eminently explorable surrounding countryside make Cahersiveen (car-si-VEEN) an enjoyable place to put down your pack. And with nearly 30 pubs, there's certainly no shortage of nightlife.

PRACTICAL INFORMATION The Ring of Kerry **bus** stops in front of Banks Store on Main St. (June-Sept. 2 per day) and continues on to **Waterville** (25min., £2.70), **Caherdaniel** (1½hr., £3.10), **Sneem** (2hr., £6.30), and **Killarney** (2½hr., £9). One route heads directly east to **Killarney** (M-Sa 1-2 per day). Cahersiveen's official **tourist office** (tel. 72589) is housed in the former barracks on the road to Ballycarbery Castle (open June to mid-Sept. M-Sa 10am-6pm, Su 1-6pm). A **craftshop** (tel. 72996) in the old Protestant church on Main St. is another good source of local information (open May-Sept. daily 10am-7pm). Main St. is home to **AIB** (tel. 72022; open M 10am-5pm, Tu-F 10am-3pm; Visa-friendly **ATM**) and **Bank of Ireland** (tel. 72122; open M 10am-12:30pm and 1:30-5pm, Tu-F 10am-12:30pm and 1:30-4pm). Cahersiveen's **post office** (tel. 72010) is on Main St. (open M-F 9:30am-1pm and 2-5:30pm, Sa 9:30am-1pm). Cahersiveen's **phone code** is 066.

ACCOMMODATIONS The **Sive** (rhymes with "hive") **Hostel (IHH),** 15 East End, Main St. (tel. 72717), is comfortable and friendly with magnificent views from its third-floor balcony. (Dorms £7-7.50; doubles £18. **Camping** £4 per person. Wash £2, dry £2.) Behind its charming bay window and flowerpot facade, **Mortimer's Hostel** (tel. 72338), Main St., competes with the Sive in friendliness. Mortimer's features a large, comfortable common room and a great garden. (Dorms £6. Key deposit £1.) At the west end of town, the **Mannix Point Caravan and Camping Park** (tel. 72806), one of the best camping parks in the country, adjoins a waterfront nature reserve and faces across the water toward the romantic ruins of Ballycarbery Castle. Mannix Point's common area, complete with turf fire, is like that of a relaxed hostel. The camping fee includes hot showers and use of a cooker-less kitchen. (£3.25 per person. Open mid-Mar. to mid-Oct.)

FOOD AND PUBS **Au Cupán** (tel. 73011), in the yellow building across from the bank, has Irish breakfasts for £4, a slightly cheaper and exceedingly yummy vegetarian option, and plenty of sandwiches and salad to keep you sitting in their cheerful café all day. **Shebeen** (tel. 72361), near the Sive Hostel on Main St., gives great pub grub (entrees £4-6; open daily 9:30am-10:30pm). Tasty **Grudle's,** Main St. (tel. 72386), serves up scrumptious pizza and pasta and artful salads, but this simple restaurant can be deceptively expensive (pizza, pasta, salads £6-9; open daily 9am-10pm). Up and coming **Teach Chulann** (tel. 72400) cooks an affordable lunch menu by day and ambitious delights by night. Unfortunately, their prices are up and their quality still coming (dinner entrees £8-13; open noon-3pm and 6-10pm). Those with wheels can roll out to the **Point Bar,** Reenard Point (tel. 72165), 3 mi. from Cahersiveen, famous for its fresh fish (£5-9; open daily 10:30am-midnight).

Cahersiveen's long Main St. still has several **original pubs.** Common in rural Ireland during the first half of this century, these establishments were a combination of watering hole and the proprietor's "main" business, general store, blacksmith, leather shop, and farm goods store. The **Anchor Bar** (tel. 72049), toward the west end of Main St. next to Kerry's Fast Food, is one of the best. Don't come before 10pm, and take your drink into the kitchen for an unforgettable night. **Mike Murt's** (tel. 72396) brims with Irish character. If you come here to chat in the afternoon, be prepared to tell your life story to the entire pint-clutching ensemble. A younger set hangs out in the Fertha Bar, across from the Anchor Bar, where live music occasionally combusts. The warm and newly renovated **Central Bar** (tel. 72441), a favorite with laid-back natives, features a charmingly effervescent hostess. You may have to sing a few songs with the crowd. For live music, the **East End Bar** and the **Shebeen** can be good choices, but ask around town for pointers.

SIGHTS Every schoolchild in Ireland knows that Cahersiveen is the birthplace of Daniel O'Connell; the Catholic Church in town that bears his name is the only one in Ireland named for a layperson. O'Connell, "the Liberator," is celebrated at the **Heritage Centre** (tel. 72589), housed in the town's former guard barracks (see tourist office, above). *(Open M-Sa 10am-6pm, Su 1-6pm. £2.50.)* The center is an engrossing introduction to the life of O'Connell, complete with sections devoted to the Famine and Irish rebellions. Two miles northwest of town across the bridge and to the left, the ruins of the 15th-century **Ballycarbery Castle,** once held by O'Connell's ancestors, command great views of mountains and sea. Two hundred yards past the castle turnoff lie two well-preserved stone forts. You can walk atop the 10 ft. thick walls of **Cahergal Fort** or visit the small stone dwellings of **Leacanabuaile Fort.** A few minutes walk beyond the second fort, **Cuas Crom** beach, known as the best swimming spot in the area, stretches out. The first weekend in August, Cahersiveen hosts the **Celtic Music Weekend,** featuring street entertainment, fireworks, pub sessions, and numerous free concerts.

■ Valentia Island

Valentia Island provides an appealing respite from the Ring of Kerry pilgrimage. The expansive views of the mainland from the quiet country roads could be reason enough to come to Ireland. Connected to the mainland at opposite ends of the island by both bridge and ferry, Valentia is a very feasible bicycle daytrip from Cahersiveen, and there are several hostels on the island should you choose to stay a while. Valentia Island is archaeologically and historically rich; the first transatlantic telegraph cable infused Valentia with cable operators and sent some of the island's families to cable stations around the globe. A parcel of bee-hive huts, ogham stones, and small ruins are well-spaced resting points on a hike of the island.

PRACTICAL INFORMATION The comically short **car ferry** trip departs from Reenard Point, 3 mi. west of Cahersiveen off the Ring of Kerry Rd. The walk to Reenard Point can be slightly difficult with cars passing, and a taxi from Cahersiveen runs about £4. The ferry drops you off at **Knightstown,** the island's population center. (Ferries depart every 10min. Apr.-Sept. M-Sa 7:30am-10:30pm, Su 8:30am-10:30pm. Cars £4 return, pedestrians £2, cyclists £3.) The bridge ties Valentia to the mainland at Portmagee, 10 mi. west of Cahersiveen, but hitching there is difficult. To get to Portmagee, go south from Cahersiveen or north from Waterville (a longer trip), then west on R565. Hard-core bikers can also make a worthwhile trip following the "loop" (Waterville to Ballinskelligs, Portmagee to Knightstown to Cahersiveen). Just up from the pier, the **tourist office** sell maps (£1) of Valentia with track walks marked, but the bulk of the marked walking is on the other side of the island, several miles from Knightstown.

ACCOMMODATIONS AND FOOD There are two hostels in Knightstown, but the best accommodations on Valentia are just outside of town at **Coombe Bank House** (tel. 76111). Follow the main road and turn right just past the Pitch & Putt. This hostel/B&B occupies a grand stone house with lovely views across the island back to the mainland. Wonderful private rooms with bath and bunkrooms are so tastefully decorated that they do justice to the house. (Dorms £10, continental breakfast £3; B&B £15. Laundry £3.) A mile and a half down the main road from Knightstown lies tiny **Chapeltown,** home to the **Ring Lyne Hostel** (tel. 76103), which has basic but comfortable rooms (dorms £6.50; private rooms £7). The large **Royal Pier Hostel (IHH)** (tel. 76144) in Knightstown was built for Queen Victoria but retains little of its aged grandeur and even less of its mattresses' firmness (dorms £7; private rooms £10 per person; B&B £20). A few blocks up the hill from the pier, **Altazamuth House** (tel. 76300) has basic, pretty rooms and a sunny breakfast room (£14, with bath £15). **Spring Acre** (tel. 76141) across from the pier has bedrooms with huge waterfront windows (£16 with bath). The **Gallery Kitchen** (tel. 76105), on the main road in Knightstown, serves creative meals amid scandalous sculptures and drawings of half-clothed people (entrees £6-8; open daily 1-4pm and 6:30-9:30pm).

SIGHTS The road from town to the **old slate quarry** offers some of Valentia's best views across Dingle Bay. The large and impressive quarry, supplier of the slate that roofed the Paris Opera House and the British Parliament, is marred by an astoundingly tacky "sacred grotto." At the opposite end of the island, you can hike up to the ruins of a Napoleonic lookout tower with views to the Skelligs at **Bray Head.** On the way there from Knightstown, you'll pass the turnoff for **Glanleam Subtropical Gardens** (tel. 76176), which features such luminaries as the 50 ft. tall Chilean Fire Bush. *(Open daily 11am-5pm. £2.50, students £1.50.)*

■ The Skellig Rocks

Eight miles off the shore of the Iveragh Peninsula, the **Skellig Rocks** and their centuries old, dry-stone, vertigo-inducing 650 steps break the ocean's surface. The almost completely white Little Skellig appears to be snow-covered, but as your boat chugs close enough to make out the surface of the island, the white reveals itself as 22,000 calling, flying, nest-wetting gannets. Moving downwind of the island you can sense the presence of the inevitable consequence of this population, which is much larger than that of most Irish towns. The island **bird sanctuary** is not open to the public, but the larger Skellig Michael makes an exciting and awe-inspiring, if expensive, trip. Christian monks founded an austere **monastery** in the 6th century along the craggy faces of the 714 ft. high rock that George Bernard Shaw once called "not after the fashion of this world." Their beehive-like dwellings are still intact and admirably explained by eloquent guides from the Irish heritage service. Your ferryman will drop you on the pier, leaving you to a 45-minute climb toward the top. **Christ's Cradle,** the grass valley between the island's two peaks, is the only lush place for miles and unparalleled as a picnic spot. The old steps and walls of the island now shelter 40,000 gannets, petrels, kittiwakes, and quirky puffins.

The fantastic and stomach-churning **ferry voyage** takes up to 1½ hours, depending on where you begin; from Ballinskelligs, it's only 45 minutes (see **Waterville,** below). Mrs. Walsh (tel. 76115) sails from **Valentia Island,** Reenard Pier (3 mi. from

Cahersiveen), and **Portmagee,** and she offers the longest time on the rocks (3hr., £20). Joe Roddy (tel. 74268) and Sean Feehan (tel. 79182) depart from **Ballinskelligs** (£20), and Michael O'Sullivan (tel. 74255) and Mr. Casey (tel. 72437) leave from **Portmagee** (£20). Roddy and O'Sullivan will give you a lift from **Waterville,** and Casey will pick you up from your hostel in **Cahersiveen.** The boats run mid-March to October, depending on the weather; phone ahead for reservations and to confirm that the boats are operating. They usually leave between 9:30am and noon and land for at least two hours on the island. The grass-roofed **Skellig Experience** visitor center (tel. 76306) is just across the Portmagee Bridge on Valentia Island. Videos and models engulf visitors in virtual Skellig, and for an extra (steep) charge you can sail from the center to the islands themselves, although the boats do not dock. The video is a good diversion on a rainy day, provided you ignore the dramatic rhetorical questions. (Open daily Apr.-Sept. 9:30am-6pm. £3, with cruise £15; students £2.70, with cruise £13.50.)

■ Waterville

Waterville suffers from a dearth of quaintness, but, as the name implies, it's got a fine beach. Hotels dominate the small strip of town, originally planned as a cluster of summer homes for wealthy English vacationers, but, strangely, most of the tour buses clear out of town at an early hour. One is left with Waterville's gently lapping waves and the sun setting over the hills on the other side of the beach.

PRACTICAL INFORMATION The Ring of Kerry **bus** stops in Waterville in front of the Bay View Hotel on Main St. (June-Sept. 2 per day), with service to **Caherdaniel** (20min., £2.20), **Sneem** (50min., £4.30), and **Killarney** (2hr., £8.60). In the off season, **Dero's** (tel. (064) 31251) fills in with a Ring of Kerry bus all its own (1 per day, £10, reservations required). **Bus Éireann** travels to **Cahersiveen** Monday through Friday at 8:20am (June-Sept. also Sa). The **tourist office** soaks up sea spray across from Butler Arms Hotel on the beach (open June-Sept. daily 9am-6pm). The **phone code** is 066.

ACCOMMODATIONS Like the town itself, the hostel situation has its ups and downs. The good news is that the town's one established hostel is beachfront and expanding as fast as its wiry owner can put it together. The bad news is that one has to put up with a bit of dirt, noise, and hyperactivity to stay at **Peter's Place.** Still, cozy and full of surprises, Peter has candles and peat fires continually burning. In addition to making brown bread that is the base of his free continental breakfast, Peter is a *seanachaí* (Irish storyteller), spinning yarns that are the best reason to come to Waterville. (Dorms £6.50. **Camping** £3.) Rumor has it that a new hostel may open its doors in Waterville well before the 1999 season. Check with the tourist office, or avail yourself of the smorgasbord of B&Bs. Track down **The Huntsman** (tel. 74124) for gorgeous seaside B&B accommodations (singles £30; doubles £40).

FOOD AND PUBS The self-described "purple passion house of food," **An Corcán** (tel. 74711), across from the Butler Arms Hotel, is intimate and affordable, adding good atmosphere to otherwise standard food (breakfast £3-5, lunch and dinner entrees £5-7; open daily 8am-10:30pm). Up the hill from the tourist office, the **Beach Cove Café** (tel. 74733) offers café cuisine and take-away overlooking the beach. This quasi-fast food place also practically overlooks your wallet (entrees £2-4). The **Lobster Bar and Restaurant,** Main St. (tel. 74255), is worth a visit just for the icon outside—a giant lobster clutching a Guinness—but stay for the food (seafood-sprinkled pub grub £5). The Lobster stays lively into the evening, with a pool table and folk or trad most nights. **Mick O'Dwyer** (tel. 74248) is a quintessential do-it-all Irishman running a musical pub as well as a nightclub at the Strand Hotel down the road. (DJed "Piper" nightclub Wednesday and Saturday; cover £4. Bands Sundays, cover £5). The **Bay View Hotel** (tel. 74510) follows suit with their own disco, and an older crowd drinks it up in their **Back Bar** (turn left at the toilets inside the hotel). **The Fisher-**

men's **Bar** (tel. 74205), Charlie Chaplin's old haunt, is linked to the Butler Arms Hotel (sing-along F-Sa; open July-Sept.).

SIGHTS Two miles from town (turn inland at the AIB), **Lough Currane** lures anglers, boaters, and divers with its several picnic-friendly islands and its submerged castle ruins. **Waterville Boats** (tel. 74255) rents rowboats (£10 per day), motorboats (£24 per day), and fishing poles (£5 per day).

The Irish-speaking hamlet of **Ballinskelligs** between Waterville and Bolus Head isn't worth a special trip, but if you're there to catch a Skellig-bound boat, check out the ruins near the pier of the **Ballinskelligs Monastery.** It was here that the monks moved from their lofty heights to start Europe's first "university." The quiet **Prior House Youth Hostel (An Óige/HI)** (tel. 79229) overlooks the bay and offers basic hostel accommodations (dorms £7; open May-Oct.). Two miles south of Ballinskelligs, **Bolus Head** affords great views of the Skelligs and the bay on clear days.

■ Caherdaniel

There's delightfully little in the village of Caherdaniel to attract the Ring's drove of travel coaches, but this hamlet (two pubs, a grocer, a restaurant, and a take-away) has the benefit of proximity to one of Ireland's best beaches and one of the region's finest hostels. Derrynane Strand, 2 mi. of gorgeous beach ringed by picture perfect dunes, is 1½ mi. from Caherdaniel in Derrynane National Park. Although the tour groups haven't put this spot on their route, many wealthy Irish have; the road to the beach is traversed by any number of fancy cars bringing people to their holiday homes.

PRACTICAL INFORMATION The **bus** stops in Caherdaniel twice per day at the junction of the Ring of Kerry road and Main St. for **Sneem** (1½hr., June-Sept. 2 per day, £2.90) and **Killarney** (1½hr., June-Sept. 2 per day, £7.30). The new **tourist office** is 1 mi. east of town at the Wave Crest Camping Park (open daily 8am-10pm). Information is also dispensed at **Mathius Adams Junk Shop** (tel. 75167) in the center of town (open 10am-5pm). Caherdaniel's **phone code** is 066.

ACCOMMODATIONS, FOOD, AND PUBS The **Traveller's Rest Hostel** (tel. 75175) looks and feels more like a B&B than a hostel, with its turf fire in the sitting room, tasteful flowerboxes, and small but comfortable rooms upstairs. (Dorms £7; private rooms £8.50 per person.) The **Caherdaniel Village Hostel** (tel. 75277), across the street from Skellig Aquatics, resides in the first English police building to be deserted in the Civil War. The hostel offers basic accommodation and may have private rooms available for 1999. The managers can also arrange climbing trips and diving holidays; see Skellig Aquatics listing for rates. (Dorms £7. Open Mar.-Nov.) A mile west of town on the Ring of Kerry road is the intimate and charmingly friendly seven-bed **Carrigbeg Hostel** (tel. 75229), which features expansive views of the surrounding hills and the beach and bay; call for pick-up from Caherdaniel. (Dorms £6; private rooms available. Laundry £3.50.) Campers get their beauty sleep 1 mi. east of town on the Ring of Kerry road at **Wave Crest Camping Park** (tel. 75188), overlooking the beach. The well-stocked shop (open 8am-10pm) and self-service laundry (£4 per load) are handy. (£3 per cyclist or hiker. Showers 50p. Open Apr.-Sept.)

The **Courthouse Café** (tel. 75422), which serves the most affordable food in town, has both a sit-down menu and take-away (sandwiches under £2; open daily noon-10pm, take-away until 1am). **Freddy's Bar** (tel. 75400) sells groceries (daily 8:30am-9pm) and serves pints to locals. In summer, the bright yellow **Blind Piper** (tel. 75126) attracts a lively crowd with pub grub and trad on Wednesday and Saturday nights.

SIGHTS Derrynane House (tel. 75113), signposted just up from the beach, was the cherished residence of Irish patriot Daniel "The Liberator" O'Connell, who won Catholic representation in Parliament in 1829 (see **History**, p. 57). *(Open May-Sept. M-Sa 9am-6pm, Su 11am-7pm; Apr. and Oct. Tu-Su 1-5pm; Nov.-Mar. Sa-Su 1-5pm. Last admission 45min. before closing. £2, students and children £1.)* Inside the house, you can check out the dueling pistol that O'Connell used to kill challenger d'Esterre and the black glove he wore to church for years afterwards to mourn his victim. The half-hour film on O'Connell presents an engrossing and refreshingly multi-faceted image of the acerbic barrister.

If you can motivate yourself for several miles of uphill hiking or pedaling to get there, the pre-Christian **Staigue Fort** (tel. 75288), 6 mi. west of town, will make you feel tall and powerful. The largest and one of the best-preserved forts in Ireland, Staigue Fort stands high on a hill overlooking the sea. Skip the **heritage center** devoted to the fort, which runs the danger of being an over-hyped tourist attraction. *(Heritage center open Easter-Oct. daily 10am-10pm. £2, students £1.50.)*

Offshore lies a shipwreck rumored to have been a smuggling ship. It's worth a look for divers. Contact **Skellig Aquatics** (tel. 75277) for rental information (½day dive for experienced diver £30; 4½-day training course £285!). **Derrynane Sea Sports** (tel. 75266) handles the sailing and windsurfing in this affluent vacation spot.

■ Sneem

Tourists make Sneem their first or last stop along the Ring, and the town has adapted to please them. Canned Irish music rolls out of the Irish music shop, entertaining both those shopping at Quills and those heading off to expensive dinners. With its two public squares and its unique sculpture collection, Sneem has a quirky charm.

PRACTICAL INFORMATION The Ring of Kerry **bus** leaves for **Killarney** via **Kenmare** (1hr., June-Sept 2 per day, £5.50). Sneem's **tourist information center** (tel. 45270) is across the street from Murphy's Pub (open daily 11am-6pm). Rent a bike at **M. Burns' Bike Hire,** The North Square (tel 45140; £5.50 per day, £33 per week; open 9:30am-9:30pm). If Sneem's **phone code** took out a personal, it would read "attractive 064 likes long walks, leather, and Sneem."

ACCOMMODATIONS The closest hostel to Sneem, the **Harbour View Hostel** (tel. 45276), a quarter mile from town on Kenmare Rd., used to be a motel and still looks like one, with ranch-style units in a gravel lot. (4-bed dorms £8; doubles or twins £20. **Camping** £3.) More comfortable accommodations are 5 mi. out of town on Caherdaniel Rd. at the **Cozy Hostel** (tel. 45151; dorms £7.50). **Old Convent House,** Pier Rd. (tel. 45181), a right off The South Square just after Erin Co. Knitwear, has charming rooms with mountain views (£17). They also offer picturesque **camping** next to the sculpture garden by the river (£3 per person; laundry £4.50). **The Green House** (tel. 45565), next to the bridge on The South Square, has well-decorated, light-filled rooms with TV (£16 with full Irish breakfast, £15 with continental breakfast).

FOOD AND PUBS Check out the **Riverain Restaurant** (tel. 45245) for low-fat and vegetarian meals with a view of the river (early-bird 3-course dinner 5:45-8:30pm £9.50; open May-Sept. noon-9:30pm). The **Sacré Coeur Restaurant** (tel. 45186) dishes up seafood at reasonable prices. The lunch and snack menus offer the best value. (Light meals £5-7, dinners £9-14. Open Apr.-Oct. 12:30-3pm and 5-9:30pm.) On the north side of town, **The Village Kitchen** (tel. 45281) serves seafood and sandwiches in a comfortable café setting (sandwiches under £2, entrees £4-7; open 9:30am-8:30pm). For the best fish and chips on the Ring, gallop down to **The Hungry Knight,** The North Square (tel. 45237; £2.75). The **Blue Bull** (tel. 45382), next to the wool shops, is a pub noted for its seafood (pub grub £4-6, served noon-8:30pm) and hosts ballad sessions (M, Th, and Sa). **O'Sheas Bar,** on The North Square, is recognizable from postcards of a previous era. Its dependable, old-school trad several nights weekly makes it very popular. The **Fisherman's Knot** pub (tel. 45224), across the bridge on Caherdaniel Rd., reverberates with trad a few nights each week.

SIGHTS Sneem's first claim to fame came with Charles de Gaulle's visit to the town in 1969. The town was so honored that they erected a monument to commemorate the event: a bronze sculpture of de Gaulle's head mounted on a boulder of local stone. And thus a tradition was born. Today, Sneem's **sculpture park** is home to no less than three modern sculptures celebrating the late President Cearbhaill O'Dalaigh, the Egyptian Goddess Isis, and the terribly strange set of cave buildings on the banks of the river. It can be difficult to decide whether they or their collective name "Where the Fairie Went" is more bizarre. Pick up the *Sneem Guide* in the tourist office for details (25p). Frankie Jim (tel. 82904) leads **boat trips** from the pier (gear provided), and Jackie O'Shea (tel. 45369) runs **deep-sea angling** trips from Ross-dohan Pier.

■ Kenmare

A bridge between the Ring of Kerry and Beara, Kenmare has adapted to a continuous stream of visitors. Everything to be seen in a classic Irish town is here in spades, with travelers' amenities as well. Colorful houses, flower boxes, nice mountain views, and great restaurants overshadow the Irish music vendors and sweater stalls.

ORIENTATION AND PRACTICAL INFORMATION

Kenmare's streets form a triangle: **Henry St.** is the lively base, while **Main** and **Shelbourne St.** form the other two sides. The intersection of Henry and Main St. forms **The Square,** which contains a small park and the tourist office. Main St. then becomes N71 to Moll's Gap and Killarney; N70 to Sneem and the Ring of Kerry also branches off this road. From Kenmare, cunning travelers take N70 west (not N71 north) to do the Ring clockwise and avoid tour bus traffic.

Buses: Leave from Brennan's Pub on Main St. for **Killarney** (1hr., M-Sa 3 per day, Su 2 per day), **Tralee** (2hr., M-Sa 3 per day, Su 2 per day), **Sneem** (35min., June-Sept. M-F 2 per day), and **Cork** via **Bantry** (4hr., June-Sept. 2 per day).

Tourist Office: The Square (tel. 41233). Open July-Aug. daily 9am-7pm; May-June and Sept. M-Sa 9am-6pm.

Bank: AIB, 9 Main St. (tel. 41010). Open M-Tu and Th-F 10am-4pm and W 10am-5pm. **ATM** takes all major cards.

Bike Rental: Finnegan's (tel. 41083), on the corner of Henry and Shelbourne St. £7 per day, £40 per week. Open M-Sa 9:30am-6:30pm.

Laundry: The Pantry Launderette, Market St., just off The Square. Wash and dry £4.50. Open M-F 9:30am-1:30pm and 2:30-6:30pm, Sa 9:30am-7pm.

Pharmacy: Sheahan's, Main St. (tel. 41354). Open M-Sa 9am-6pm. **Brosnan's,** Henry St. Open M-Sa 9:30am-6:15pm, Su 12:30-1:30pm.

Emergency: Dial 999; no coins required. **Garda:** Shelbourne St. (tel. 41177).

Hospital: Old Killarney Rd. (tel. 41088). Follow Henry St. past The Square.

Post Office: Henry St. (tel. 41490), at the corner of Shelbourne St. Open M and W-F 9am-1pm and 2-5:30pm, Tu 9:30am-1 and 2-5:30pm, Sa 9am-1pm.

Phone Code: 064.

ACCOMMODATIONS

Fáilte Hostel (IHH; tel. 41083), corner of Henry and Shelbourne St. Not the white building that says "private hostel," but the one across the street. The proprietors make certain that the only thing loud about this hostel is its 70s decor. All the same, it is a stately house featuring a common room with a VCR, ideal for a rainy day. Huge kitchen with an antique coal-burning stove to satisfy adventurous cooks. Dorms £7.50; doubles £20. 1am curfew.

La Brasserie, Henry St. (tel. 41379), above the bistro. The best B&B bargain in town offers surprising luxury and a great location. Singles £15; doubles £28.

Keal Na Gower House B&B, The Square (tel. 41202). Sleep comfortably in this small B&B within earshot of a brook. One room has bathtub; the other two have brook views. Singles £16; doubles £32.

Ring of Kerry Caravan and Camping Park, Sneem Rd. (tel. 41648), 2½mi. west of Kenmare. Overlooks mountains and a bay. £3.50 per person. Open May-Sept.

FOOD AND PUBS

Good food is plentiful, if pricey, in Kenmare. Stick to the smaller cafés, which tend to close around 9 or 10pm, for the lowest prices. **SuperValu** (tel. 41037) is on Main St. (open M-Th 8am-8pm, F 8am-9pm, Sa 8am-7pm, Su 8:30am-5pm). **The Pantry,** Henry St. (tel. 42233), sells wholefoods and organic produce (open M-Sa 10am-6pm).

Mickey Ned's, Henry St. (tel. 41591). A popular spot for lunchtime treats. Sandwiches £2-5, hot meals £4-5. Open M-Sa 9am-5:30pm.

La Brasserie Bistro, Henry St. (tel. 41379). Reasonably priced meals all day long in a spacious dining area. Hideously tempting desserts. Lunch £4-6, dinner £7-10. Open daily 9am-9pm.

The New Delight. All of the veggies you never had in Ireland, a few at unbeatable prices. Just don't ask for meat or a cola. Lunches £3-6, dinner £7-9. Open daily July-Aug. 10am-10pm; Sept.-June 10am-4pm.

An Leath Phingin, 35 Main St. (tel. 41559). Italian masterpieces served up in an old stone townhouse. They even make their own pasta and smoke their own salmon. Splurge a little, it's well worth it. 10" pizza £6-9.50. Open daily 6-10pm.

Virginia's Restaurant, Henry St. (tel. 41021). Sit back and enjoy the relaxed atmosphere of this well-attended little restaurant. Set dinner £11, a la carte £8-13. Open M-Sa at 5pm, Su at 12:30pm.

Kenmare's pubs attract a hefty contingent of tourists. Native Guinness guzzlers, however, hear too much good music to quibble over "Kiss me, I'm a leprechaun" hats. **Ó Donnabháin's,** Henry St. (tel. 42106), is a favorite among natives, with a pleasant beer garden out back. Huge **Murty's,** New Rd. (tel. 41453), just off Henry St., features live bands (Wednesday and F-Sa) and disco (Thursday and Sunday). **Brennan's,** Main St. (tel. 41011), serves great pub grub and live music three or four nights a week. There's great music at **The Square Pint. Crowley's,** Henry St. (tel. 41472), asks: "When you've got frequent trad sessions, why bother with interior decorating?"

SIGHTS

There are plenty of good hikes in the country around Kenmare, but few sights in the town itself. The ancient **stone circle,** a two-minute walk from The Square down Market St., is the largest of its kind in southwest Ireland (55ft. diameter), but it ain't no Stonehenge. *(Always open. £1.)* The stone circle is one stop on Kenmare's tourist trail, a well-marked route with several even less glamorous historical points (maps at the tourist office). The new **Kenmare Heritage Centre,** in the same building as the tourist office, has a model of the stone circle and historical exhibits. *(Same hours as the tourist office. Cassette self-tour £2, students £1.50.)* The **Kenmare Lace Centre** has demonstrations of the Kenmare lace-making technique, invented in 1862 by nuns at the Kenmare convent and once on the cutting edge of lace. *(Open M-Sa 10am-1pm and 2-6pm. Free.)* Presently, local artisans are working to resurrect the craft.

Seafari Cruises (tel. 83171) explores Kenmare Bay and its colonies of otters, seals, and whales. *(1½-2hr., 3 per day, £9.50, students £8.)* The cruises depart from the pier; follow Glengarriff Rd. and turn right just before the bridge. You can fish at the **Ardtully Castle Salmon Fishery** on Roughty Rd. *(£10 per day, £30 per week. Open daily 9am-7pm. For permits contact Mr. John O'Hare, 21 Main St.)*

DINGLE PENINSULA

For years, the Dingle Peninsula had been the undertouristed counterpart to the Ring of Kerry. The word has finally gotten out about the peninsula's beautiful beaches and stunning views and the Killarney and Ring of Kerry tourist blitz has recently begun to encroach upon this scenic, Irish-speaking peninsula. **Slieve Mish** and the flat farming country of **East Dingle** are not as convenient for backpackers as **Dingle Town,** the charming, if increasingly touristy and pricey, regional center. The coast to the west of town combines striking scenery with *gaeltacht* communities. Locating the grocery store among Irish signs may be a challenge, but, thankfully, Guinness signs still mark the pubs. Dingle's *bohareens* (side roads) are best explored by bike: the entire western circuit, from Dingle out to Slea Head, up to Ballydavid, and back, is only a daytrip, although bikers should be prepared to share the road with cars and buses. The **Cloghane/Brandon** area in the north remains most free of foreigners; **Slea Head, Dunquin,** and the **Blasket Islands** are the most inspiring spots. Maps available in area tourist offices describe **The Dingle Way,** a 95-mile walking trail that circles the peninsula.

While Dingle Town is well connected to Killarney and Tralee, public transport within the peninsula is scarce. **Buses** to towns in South Dingle run daily in July and August but only two or three times per week the rest of the year. There is no direct bus service to towns on the peninsula north of Dingle Town. Hitchers along the **Connor Pass** find unspoiled hamlets. For detailed bus information, call the Tralee station (tel. (066) 23566). The **phone code** for the entire peninsula is 066.

■ Dingle

For now, the craic in Dingle is still home-grown, but foreigners are talking about the fabulous pubs, smart cafés, and gregarious dolphin, Fungi, who charms the whole town from his permanent residence in Dingle Bay. Hostels, restaurants, and souvenir shops are all multiplying with the population. After scouring the deserted parts of the peninsula for vistas and *ogham* stones, you can return to town in the evening for great music and quality time with your publican.

ORIENTATION AND PRACTICAL INFORMATION

Dingle dangles in the middle of the southern coast of Dingle Peninsula. R559 heads east to Killarney and Tralee and west to Ventry, Dunquin, and Slea Head. A narrow road running north through the Connor Pass leads to Stradbally and Castlegregory. The streets of downtown Dingle approximate a grid pattern, although it's just a bit more confusing than you'd expect. The lack of street signs in English complicates matters. Strand and Main St. run parallel to Dingle Harbour. The Mall, Dykegate St., and Green St. run perpendicular to the shore uphill from Strand St. to Main St. On the eastern edge of town, Strand St., The Mall, and Tralee Rd. converge in a roundabout.

Buses: Buses stop on Ring Rd., behind Garvey's SuperValu. Bus information is available from the Tralee bus station (tel. (066) 23566). **Bus Éireann** runs to **Ballydavid** (Tu and F 3 per day, £3.15 return), **Dunquin** and **Ballyferriter** (summer M and Th 4 per day, Tu-W and F-Sa 2 per day, Su 1 per day, £2.30), **Killarney** (1½hr., June-Sept. 3 per day, Su 2 per day, £7.30), and **Tralee** (1¼hr., June-Sept. 6 per day, Su 5 per day, Oct.-May 6 per day, Su 4 per day, £5.90). From June-Sept. additional buses tour the south of the peninsula from Dingle (M-Sa 2 per day).

Tourist Office: Corner of Main and Dykegate St. (tel. 51188). Great if you like lines and Bord Fáilte propaganda. Open July-Aug. M-Sa 9am-7pm, Su 9am-1pm and 2:15-7pm; Apr.-June and Sept.-Oct. daily 9:30am-6pm.

Banks: AIB, Main St. (tel. 51400). Open M 10am-12:30pm and 1:30-5pm, Tu-F 10am-12:30pm and 1:30-4pm. **Bank of Ireland,** Main St. (tel. 51100). Same hours. Both have multi-card tolerant **ATMs.**

Bike Rental: Paddy's Bike Shop, Dykegate St. (tel. 52311), rents the best bikes in town. £5 per day, £25 per week. Open daily 9am-7pm.

Camping Equipment: The Mountain Man, Strand St. (tel. 52400). Open daily July-Aug. 9am-9pm; Sept.-June 9am-6pm. No tent rental. Offers a 2hr. coach tour to Connor Pass (£7) and a shuttle to the Blasket ferry (£6) in addition to the very informative "Guide to the Dingle Peninsula," including a proper walking map (£5).

Laundry: Níolann an Daingin, Green St. (tel. 51837), behind El Toro. Medium wash and dry from £5.50. Open M-Sa 9am-5:30pm.

Pharmacy: O'Keefe's Pharmacy Ltd. (tel. 51310). Open M-W and F-Sa 9:30am-6pm, Th 9:30am-1pm, Su 9:30am-12:30pm.

Emergency: Dial 999; no coins required. **Garda:** The Holy Ground (tel. 51522), across from Tig Lise.

Post Office: Upper Main St. (tel. 51661). Just the place for mailing Fungi postcards. Open M-F 9am-1pm and 2-5:30pm, Sa 9am-1pm.

Phone Code: 066.

ACCOMMODATIONS

There are good hostels in Dingle, although some are a fairly long walk from town. B&Bs along Dykegate and Strand St. and hostels in town tend to fill up fast in summer; call ahead.

Ballintaggart Hostel (IHH) (tel. 51454), a 25min. walk east of town on Tralee Rd. Ballintaggart is set in the grand stone mansion where the Earl of Cork poisoned his wife in an upstairs room that her ghost supposedly now haunts. Gloriously renovated with enormous bunk rooms, many private rooms with bath, an enclosed cobblestone courtyard, a crystal chandelier, and a high-quality, fairly reasonable restaurant (dinners £7-9). Free shuttle to town. Horse-riding lessons (£7 per 30min.) and wetsuit rental (£10 per 4hr.). Kitchen locked after 10pm. 10- to 12-bed dorms £7; 4-bed dorms £8; private rooms from £13 per person. Laundry service £4. Bike hire £7 per day. **Camping** £3.50 per person.

Rainbow Hostel (tel. 51044; email rainbow@iol.ie), 15min. west of town on Strand Rd. and worth the hike. Bear right and inland at the corner of Dunquin Rd. The huge kitchen is a gourmand's dream and the spacious bunkrooms are chummy. Free lifts to and from town. July-Aug. dorms £7; doubles £18. June-Sept. £6; £16. **Camping** £3.50. Laundry £4. **Bike rental** £6 per day.

Grapevine Hostel, Dykegate St. (tel. 51434), off Main St. Smack in the middle of town and just a short stagger from Dingle's finest pubs, the Grapevine features close but comfortable bunk rooms with baths. The common room has a peat fire, a CD player, and dangerously cushy chairs. Dorms £8-9.

An Caladh Spáinneach (un KULL-uh SPINE-uck; the Spanish Pier), Strand St. (tel. 52160). This comfortable hostel offers basic and friendly lodging across from the marina. Open June-Aug. Dorms £8.

Lovett's Hostel, Cooleen Rd. (tel. 51903). Turn opposite the Esso Station past the roundabout, right on the bay. Small and cozy, this hostel perches on the outskirts of town, away from most of the hustle and nearly all of the bustle. Dorms £6.50; doubles £17. Laundry £2 (no dryer).

Old Mill House, Dykegate St. (tel. 51120; email verhoul@iol.ie). The comfort of the new pine beds in this charming house can be outdone only by its vivacious owner and her magnificent breakfast menu. Crepes suzette, anyone? From £15.

Kirrary House (tel. 51606), across from Old Mill House. With good cheer and pride, Mrs. Collins puts guests up in her delightful rooms. Book your archaeological tours here with *Sciuird* Tours, offered by Mr. Collins (see **Sights** below). £16 with bath. **Bike rental** £6 per day.

The Marina Inn B&B, Strand St. (tel. 51660), upstairs from the pub. Very basic rooms are a bargain. Doubles with breakfast £24; off-season beds only £7.

Phoenix Hostel (tel. 66284), on the Dingle-Killarney road (R561), 4mi. west of Castlemaine, 20mi. east of Dingle. This multi-faceted hostel can be a destination of its own. On the Dingle-Killarney bus route (via Castlemain), the Phoenix's colorfully decorated country house and garden are also the site of a vegetarian, organic, and reasonably priced restaurant (most entrees £4). Inquire about the belly-dancing lessons. 8-bed dorms £8; doubles £23, with bath £27. Breakfast £3.50. Sheets £1. Laundry £4. **Bike rental** (reserve evening before) £6 per day. **Camping** £3.50. Also offers rides from Kerry airport (£10) or from Killarney (£18).

FOOD

Dingle is home to every conceivable (in Ireland) sort of eatery, from gourmet seafood restaurants to the hot dog and doughnut stand by the marina. **SuperValu supermarket,** The Holy Ground (tel. 51397), stocks a SuperSelection of groceries and juicy tabloids (open M-Sa 9am-9pm, Su 9am-6pm). **An Grianán,** Dykegate St. (tel. 51090), near the Grapevine Hostel, offers a selection of crunchy wholefoods and an organic vegetable and cheese deli counter (open M-F 9:30am-6pm, Sa 10am-6pm).

Greany's, Bridge St. (tel. 52244). Hearty, well-prepared breakfasts (£2.50-4.50) and seafood and meat dishes (dinner £8-11) in a crowded but pleasantly modern café. Open daily 9am-10pm.

The Oven Door, The Holy Ground (tel. 51056), across from SuperValu. Crispy pizzas (£3.50-7), yummy sundaes (£3), and a gleaming counter of light food lure crowds to this simple café. Open daily 10am-11pm.

The Forge, The Holy Ground (tel. 51209). This large green-and-red family restaurant serves a rich 3-course early bird dinner for £10 (before 6:30pm). Open daily noon-3pm and 5:30-10:30pm.

Danno's, Strand St. (tel. 51855). The railroad theme may send purists chugging away, but this popular restaurant/bar can't be beat for pints and burgers on a cold, wet night. Burgers £6-7, other entrees £5-9. Food served noon-8:30pm.

An Café Liteartha, Dykegate St. (tel. 51388), across the street from the Grapevine. This café/bookstore was one of the first Irish language cafés in the Republic, and Irish speakers still frequent the place. Great for a scholarly scone, but don't bring your full appetite. Open M-F 10am-5:30pm, Sa-Su 11am-5:30pm. Bookstore open until 6pm.

An Sméara Dubha (tel. 51465), off Strand St. near the traffic circle for Dunguin Rd.; follow the signs uphill. Artfully assembled vegetarian meals in a cozy bistro that occupies the front parlor of the owner's house. Her ranch-style windows grant great Dingle views. Main courses £8. Open daily 6-10pm.

PUBS

Though only 1500 people live in Dingle permanently, the town maintains 52 pubs. In theory, every inhabitant could hoist a pint simultaneously without anyone having to scramble for a seat. Many pubs are beginning to cater to tourists, but the town still produces copious craic. The **Dingle Storytelling Pub Crawl** (tel. 52161) presents a literary tour of Dingle's pubs and "other sacred sights." Tours meet outside the post office on Main St. (July-Aug. Th-M 7-8:30pm; £3 per person, £5 per couple).

An Droichead Beag (The Small Bridge), Lower Main St. (tel. 51723). The most popular pub in town is nearly always crowded but still unleashes the best trad around—401 sessions a year.

O'Flaherty's Pub, The Holy Ground (tel. 51983), a few doors up from the traffic circle. Memorable, varied jam sessions most nights in this well-decorated pub. The great atmosphere is no secret; get here by 9pm if you want a seat.

Dick Mack's, Green St. (tel. 51070), opposite the church. A leather bar—"Dick Mack's Bar, Boot Store, and Leather Shop," that is. The proprietor leaps between the bar and his leathertooling bench. Shoeboxes and whiskey bottles line the walls. Though featured on some postcards, the pub has a genuine local following; spontaneous singing is a great treat.

McCarthy's, Upper Main St. (tel. 51205), across the street and a few doors up from the post office. Quiet, intimate, local pub. Good craic when there's music (Th-Sa). Also features Irish drama on Thursdays in a venue behind the pub—stop in to ask.

An Connair, Green St. Delightful, intense trad keeps this pub mixed and crowded.

Murphy's, Strand St. (tel. 51450). Classic, crowded, smoky pub by the marina. Trad and ballads nightly.

Jack Neddy's, on the corner of Green and Strand St. The sign outside the green-trimmed building says simply "Bar." The bartender is older than the hills, and he sure pours a mean pint. Frequented by locals who, if you're lucky, will break into a spontaneous singing chorus. If you return the next night the crowd might feel strangely familiar.

SIGHTS

Fungi the Dolphin swam into Dingle Bay one day in 1983 with his mother, and the pair immediately became local celebrities. Dolphins are common in the bay, but

Fungi particularly liked it around Dingle, cavorting with sailors and swimmers, flirting with TV cameras, and jumping in and out of the water for applause. Mom has gone to the great tuna can in the sky, but egomaniacal Fungi remains fond of humans. Wet-suited tourists incessantly swarm around him, and much of the tourist industry here sinks or swims with the delightful dolphin. **Boat trips** to see the dolphin leave from the pier constantly in summer. Most cost around £6 and guarantee that you'll see the dolphin. A cheaper option (it's free) is to watch Fungi from shore as he chases the boats in a little cove east of town. To get there, walk two minutes down Tralee Rd., turn right at the Skellig Hotel, and then follow the beach away from town for about 10min. The small beach on the other side of a stone tower will probably be packed with Fungi-seekers. Anti-dolphinites can be lured along by the promise of great views on the walk (£10 for 1½hr., £14 for 3hr.). The best times to see him are 8-10am and 6-8pm. You can rent a **wetsuit** from **Flannery's** (tel. 51967), just east of town off Tra-lee Rd. (£14 per 2hr., £22 overnight), or just jump in as you are. Ballintaggart Hostel rents suits cheap to its guests (see **Accommodations**, above).

Deep-sea angling trips (tel. 51337) leave daily in summer at 10am and 6pm from the pier. Full (£40, lunch included) and half-day (£15) sailing also available (book ahead at tel. 59882). For a closer look at marine matters, **Dingle Ocean World**, Strand St. (tel. 52111), features 160 species of fish, a huge tank with a walk-through tunnel, and a petting-zoo tank where rays and skates swim up to have their fins scratched or poked in disbelief. *(Open daily July-Aug. 9am-9:30pm; Apr.-July and Aug.-Sept. 10am-6pm; in winter 10am-5pm. £4.50, students £3.50.)* While the aquarium can pass some time on a rainy day, the uncaged Dingle is much better when the weather's fine.

The Dingle area has some interesting historical sites. The information office at the Mountain Man sells *The Easy Guide to the Dingle Peninsula* (£5), which details walking tours, cycling tours, and local history and includes a map. **Sciúird Archaeology tours** (tel. 51606) take you from the pier on a three-hour whirlwind bus tour of the area's ancient spots. *(2 per day. £7. Book ahead.)* The same company also coordinates historic walking tours of Dingle Town. *(2 per day. £2.50.)* Summer festivals periodically turn the town into a carnival. The **Dingle Races** (second weekend in August) are geared more for children than for horses, while the **Dingle Regatta** (usually the third Sunday in August) hauls in the salty mariners.

■ Slea Head and Dunquin

Glorious **Slea Head** inspires with jagged cliffs and crashing waves. *Ryan's Daughter* and parts of *Far and Away* were filmed around here, and it's easy to see why. Green hills, interrupted by rough stone walls and occasional sheep, lead down to plunging cliffs lashed by a foam-flecked sea. There's plenty of space on the head to **camp**, though in high season you'll have some neighbors. For some, the hundreds of teddy bears holding court at the **Enchanted Forest Café** may seem a product of the febrile ravings of some diseased imagination. Upstairs, the teddy-bear orgy of a museum creatively depicts the four seasons and Celtic pagan holidays (£2, under 12 £1). Downstairs, a satisfying lunch can be had with striking views of the Head (brown bread sandwiches from £2.10; teddy bear scones £1.10).

The road from broad horseshoe-shaped **Ventry Beach** out to Slea Head passes several Iron Age and early Christian stones and ruins. **Dunbeg Fort** (£1, students 80p) and the less impressive **Fahan Group** (£1) of oratories, beehive-shaped stone huts built by early monks, cluster on hillsides over the cliffs. The view from Dunbeg is worth the price of admission.

North of Slea Head, the scattered settlement of **Dunquin** (Dún Chaoin) consists of stone houses, a pub, and plenty of spoken Irish, but no grocery store. Stock up in Dingle or in Ballyferriter if you're going to stay here or on Great Blasket. **Kruger's** (tel. 56127), purportedly the westernmost pub in Europe, features pub grub (entrees around £5), frequent spontaneous music sessions, and fantastic views. Its adjacent **B&B** has pretty and comfortable rooms (£15). Along the road to Ballyferriter, **An Óige Hostel (HI)** (tel. 56121) provides clean, adequate bunkrooms and a spacious, window-walled sitting and dining room that look out onto the sea. (June-Sept. dorms £7-8; doubles £18; Oct.-May £6-7; £16. Showers closed 9am-5:30pm. Breakfast £1.75. Sheets 80p. Lockout 10:15am-5pm. Midnight curfew.)

The striking architecture of the **Blasket Centre** (tel. 56444), just outside of "town" on the road to Ballyferriter, enhances the museum's outstanding exhibits. Writings and photographs of the Great Blasket authors recreate the lost era of the islands and describe their own literary achievements (see **Blasket Islands,** p. 247). The museum also shows a 20-minute film on the islanders and presents exhibits on the past richness and current status of the Irish language. (Open daily July-Aug. 10am-7pm, Easter-June and Sept. 10am-6pm. £2.50, students £1. Last admission 45min. before closing.)

About a mile past Dunquin, parked cars and an occasional stopped coach indicate that there must be something grand to see at this non-signposted spot. A path that snakes seaward up to a clifftop affords even more sweeping views of green-carpeted cliffs and the seemingly endless ocean. Two miles past Dunquin, about halfway to Ballyferriter, **Tig Áine** (tel. 56214), a gallery and café, charms visitors with views of the cliffs. Stop in for scones and tea, or enjoy the huge and affordable dinners with home-grown vegetables (£4-8).

■ Blasket Islands

The Blaskets (*Na Blascaodaí*) comprise six islands: Beginish, Tearaght, Inishnabro, Inishvickillane, Inishtooskert, and Great Blasket. Evacuated in 1953, the Blasket Islands were once inhabited by poet-fishermen, proud but impoverished and aging villagers, and memoirists reluctantly warning that "after us, there will be no more." Blasket writers themselves helped produce and publicize the story of their isolated *gaeltacht* culture in English and Irish and its memorable decline. The well-known memoirs *Twenty Years a-Growing* (Maurice O'Sullivan), *The Islander* (Thomas O'Crohan), and *Peig* (Peig Sayers, recently published in English) are obscure outside Ireland but required reading for Irish students. Mists, seals, and occasional fishing boats may continue to pass the Blaskets, but the simpler ways of life once exemplified there are gone forever.

Days on somnolent Great Blasket are long and meditative: wander through the mist down to the white strand, follow the grass paths of the island's 10 mi. circumference, explore the stone skeletons of former houses in the village, and observe the puffins and seals that populate the island. Those spending the night can enjoy fresh fish and wholefood dinners for £5 in the **café** near the old village. The portions are massive and the seaweed is choice (open daily 10am-6pm when there are customers). **Campers** can pitch their tents anywhere for free. There's no hot water, food (other than in the café), or electricity, so if you plan to stay, stock up on supplies in Dingle or Ballyferriter. Keep in mind that if the weather is bad, the boats don't run—people have been stuck here for two weeks during gales. **Boats** (tel. 56455) for the Blaskets depart from Dunquin May to September daily, every half-hour from 10am to 3pm, weather and ferry operator's mood permitting (£10 return). A shuttle bus runs from Dingle to the Blasket ferry and back (2 per day, £6; ask at the Mountain Man for details). **Sail cruises** (tel. 56455) departing from Dingle Town encircle and stop on the Great Blasket. (10am departure. Full day including lunch £40; cruise without a stop on islands £12.).

The Last Islander

The famous autobiographers of the Blasket Islands described 19th- and early 20th-century Irish life on the island and voiced concern over the possible eradication of Irish culture. By 1953, most of Great Blasket's residents were old, with the exception of a 19-year-old who represented "the future" to everyone else on the island. He came down with meningitis during weather so severe that no boats could leave for the mainland's hospital. The sea calmed only two days after his death. By the end of that year, everyone had moved to the mainland.

■ Ballyferriter

Ballyferriter *(Baile an Fheritéaaigh)* is West Dingle's closest approximation to a town center. In contrast to the Blasket Centre, which eulogizes the almost extinct Irish oral tradition, Ballyferriter, an authentic *gaeltacht*, stands as a testament to the language's continued existence—even the Guinness signs are in Irish. Many people are lured to Ballyferriter by the musical strains and prosaic voices inside **Tigh Pheig** (Peig's Pub), Main St. (tel. 56433), with two pool tables and frequent evening trad sessions. Peig's makes a welcoming spot for an appetizing meal (including vegetarian options; daily specials £5.50). Across the street, **Tig ú Mhurchú** (Murphy's; tel. 56224) pours pints to the rhythm of their nightly music. **Ócatháin** (tel. 56359) offers pub grub and sandwiches and occasionally lures local musicians on weekends.

The **Heritage Centre** (tel. 56333) brims with photos and text relating to the area's wildlife, archaeology, and folklore (open June-Sept. M-F 10am-noon and 2-4pm; £1). The Heritage Centre is a noble attempt at making the area's history accessible, but the actual ancient sites aren't far. From Ballyferriter, follow the signs to **Dún An Óir** (the Fort of Gold), an Iron Age fort where, in 1580, the English massacred over 600 Spanish, Italian, and Irish soldiers who openly supported the Irish Catholics' rebellion against Queen Elizabeth. From the main road, signposted roads branch to **Riasc**, a puzzling monastic site with an engraved standing slab, and to the **Dillon Stone**, a monument erected by early British settlers and flocked to by Protestants every year on January 7.

The largest grocery in town is **O Shcilleaghán Market** (tel. 56157), in the town center (open in summer daily 9am-10:30pm, winter daily 9am-8pm). Five minutes outside town on Dunquin Rd., the very simple **An Cat Dubh** (Black Cat Hostel; tel. 56286) crosses your path in a tacky but friendly sort of way (£6; **camping** £3 per person). The B&B next door, **An Spéice** (tel. 56254), provides quiet rest (£15, with bath £16).

■ North Dingle

The Northern coast of the Dingle peninsula is good hiking territory; while the few smallish towns here hold little of enduring interest, they all make good staging points for assaults on the various peaks and passes of the region. Hiking maps are available in Dingle Town at the tourist office or the Mountain Man. From Dingle Town, a winding cliffside road runs north by way of the 1500 ft. **Connor Pass** and affords tremendous views of the valleys and the bays beyond. Buses won't fit on the road, but automobiles will squeeze through. A slight detour west on the north side of the Connor Pass (watch for the signs) leads to the quiet hamlet of **Cloghane**. From here you can hike north along the scenery-splashed main road to **Ballyquin Strand** and **Brandon Point** or west (and up) to 3127 ft. **Mt. Brandon** and its surrounding lakes. **The Saint's Road** to the summit was cleared by St. Brendan. While it may have been easy for someone who crossed the Atlantic in a leather boat, for most people it's quite a hike. Climb on the west side from Ballybrack, or try the more impressive ascent from the Cloghane side, which begins between Brandon Point and Cloghane.

Back toward Tralee in **Stradbally**, narrow beds proliferate in the friendly **Connor Pass Hostel (IHH)** (tel. 39179; dorms £6.50; open mid-Mar. to Nov.). The hostel makes a good base for hikes in the **Slieve Mish Mountains** to the east. The 2713 ft. ascent to **Cáherconree** culminates with views of the peninsula, the ocean, and the Shannon Estuary. Stradbally is also an excellent place from which to do the **Loch a'Duín** nature and archaeology walk. Inquire at the friendly, multi-faceted **Tomásin's Pub** (tel. 39179) across the street from the hostel for info packets (£3). The pub also serves mean grub (shrimp, plaice, and other warm food £3.50-7 at lunch, served noon-4:30pm; dinners £7-11, served 6-9pm). A trip to Stradbally is far from complete without walking the three-quarters of a mile downhill to the beach. Beyond the dune lies a surreally magnificent strand, especially so at low tide.

Castlegregory, with a tourist office and a grocery store, may make the best home base for exploring north Dingle. From Castlegregory, head north up the sandy **Maharees Peninsula** where you can play a round of golf at the **Castlegregory Golf Club** (tel. 39444; 9 holes £9, 18 holes £12), rent sailboards from **Focus Windsurfing** (tel. 39411; from £10 per hr., with wetsuit), or swim at numerous strands. Castlegregory's **Summer Festival** wakes up the town a bit in mid-July. A **bus** to Tralee runs erratically (July-Aug. M, W, and Sa 2 per day, Tu and Th 2 per day, all year F 3 per day, £3.80). The small but informative **tourist information center** (tel. 39422) is open daily 10am to 8pm (off season until 5pm). **Spar Market** (tel. 39433) is open daily 8:30am to 10pm. The quiet **Lynch's Hostel** (tel. 39128) is the better of the two hostels in town (dorm £7; **bike rental** £7 per day). If you're stuck, try **Fitzgerald's Euro-Hostel** (tel. (066) 39133) above the pub (dorms £6; showers 50p). The small **Milesian Restaurant,** Main St., hosts frequent poetry readings and an ever-changing menu with cheap vegetarian options in a restored stone cottage (open Easter-Nov. daily noon-9:30pm, weekends in winter). **Ferriter's Pub** (tel. 39494) serves food all day and plays trad and ballads on weekends (open 9am-9pm). Their spanking-new B&B across the road allows them to be an all-in-one service (£17 with bath). **Ned Natterjack's** (tel. 39491), named for the rare and quite vocal Natterjack toad that resides in this area, presents trad Tuesday through Friday and Sunday, live rock on Saturday, and a glorious beer garden too.

■ Tralee

While tourists tend to identify Killarney as the core of Kerry, residents correctly see Tralee (pop. 20,000) as the county's economic center. Despite the presence of industry and traffic that make Tralee the hub it is, stately Georgian architecture and a surprisingly cosmopolitan flair provide energized atmosphere that doesn't pander only to tourists. On the other hand, there's plenty for tourists to do here these days; local effort and buckets of EU development funds have gone toward building new, splashy attractions. Precious minutes are most wisely spent at Kerry the Kingdom museum, the folk theater next door, and the radiant rose gardens.

SOUTHWEST IRELAND

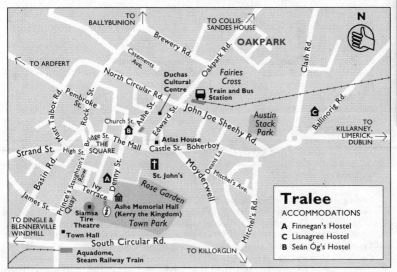

ORIENTATION AND PRACTICAL INFORMATION

Tralee's streets are hopelessly knotted; it's wise to find the tourist office immediately and arm yourself with a free map. The main street in town—variously called The Mall, Castle St., and Boherboy—is a good reference point, as is wide Derry St.

Airport: Kerry Airport (tel. 64644), off N22 halfway between Tralee and Killarney. **Manx Airlines** (tel. (01) 260 1588) flies to London.

Trains: Edward St. and John Joe Sheehy Rd. (tel. 23522). Ticket office open sporadically. Phone inquiries taken M-F 9am-12:30pm and 1:30-5:30pm. Trains tie Tralee to **Cork** (2½hr., M-Sa 5 per day, Su 3 per day, £17), **Killarney** (40min., M-Sa 5 per day, Su 4 per day, £5.50), **Galway** (3 per day, £33.50), **Dublin** (4hr., M-Sa 4 per day, Su 3 per day, £33.50), **Waterford** (4hr., M-Sa 2 per day, £33.50), and **Rosslare Harbour** (5½hr., M-Sa 1 per day, £33.50).

Buses: Edward St. and John Joe Sheehy Rd. (tel. 23566). Station open in summer M-Sa 8:30am-6pm, Su 11am-6pm; in winter M-Sa 8:30am-5:10pm, Su 11am-5:10pm. Buses rumble off to **Cork** (2½hr., M-Sa 6 per day, Su 4 per day, £9.70), **Dingle** (1¼hr.; July-Aug. M-Sa 9 per day, Su 6 per day; Sept.-June M-Sa 4 per day, Su 2 per day; £5.90), **Killarney** (40min.; June-Sept. M-Sa 14 per day, Su 8 per day; Oct.-May M-Sa 5 per day, Su 6 per day; £4.40), **Limerick** (2¼hr., M-Sa 5 per day, Su 4 per day, £9), and **Galway** (M-Sa 5 per day, Su 4 per day, £13).

Tourist Office: Ashe Memorial Hall (tel. 21288), at the end of Denny St. From the station, go into town on Edward St., and turn right on Castle St. and then left onto Denny St. The staff is extremely kind and helpful. Open M-Sa 9am-7pm, Su 9am-6pm; off season Tu-Sa 9am-5pm.

Banks: Bank of Ireland, Castle St. Open M 10am-5pm, Tu-F 10am-4pm. **AIB,** corner of Denny and Castle St. Open M 10am-5pm, Tu-F 10am-4pm. Both have **ATMs.**

Taxi: Kingdom Cabs, 48 Boherboy (tel. 27828), or **Call-A-Cab** (tel. 20333). Cabs park on Denny St. at the intersection with The Mall and charge £1 per mile, less for longer distances.

Bike Rental: O'Halloran, 83 Boherboy (tel. 22820). Sometimes, you've just got to ride. £6 per day, £30 per week. Open M-Sa 9:30am-6pm.

Camping Equipment: Landers, Courthouse Ln. (tel. 26644), has an extensive selection. No tent rental. Open M-Sa 9am-6pm.

Laundry: The Laundry, Pembroke St. (tel. 23214). 50p per lb. Open M-F 9am-6pm.

Pharmacy: Kelly's Chemist, The Mall (tel. 21302), indulges your pharmaceutical fancies. Open M-F 9am-8pm, Sa 9am-6pm.

Emergency: Dial 999; no coins required. **Garda:** High St. (tel. 22022).

Counseling and Support: Samaritans, 44 Moyderwell (tel. 22566). 24hr. hotline.

Hospital: Tralee County General Hospital, off Killarney Rd. (tel. 26222).

Post Office: Edward St. (tel. 21013), off Castle St. Open M and W-Sa 9am-5:30pm, Tu 9:30am-5:30pm.

Phone Code: by any other name would still be 066.

ACCOMMODATIONS

Though not at the top of everyone's must-do lists, Tralee has a remarkable supply of good hostels. A number of pleasant B&Bs line Oakpark Rd., while a smattering of others sit on Boherboy by the traffic circle.

Finnegan's Hostel (IHH), 17 Denny St. (tel. 27610). At the end of the city's most dignified street, this majestic 19th-century townhouse contains part of the old town castle. The hostel's location is brilliant, as is its common room: grand doorways, oriental rugs, and velvet furniture. Spacious, wood-floored bunk rooms are named after Ireland's literary heroes. Dorms £7.50; doubles £18.

Collis-Sandes House (IHH) (tel. 28658). Near-perfect, but far from town. Follow Edward St./Oakpark Rd. 1mi. from town, take the first left after Halloran's Foodstore, and follow signs another ½mi. to the right. This stately stone mansion, built in 1857, has beautiful high ceilings and unexpected but impressive Moorish arches and sits right next to a golf course and tennis courts. Bunk rooms vary from spacious and sunny to quite basic; two kitchens and a TV with VCR. Free lifts to town and pubruns. Dorms £6.50; doubles from £18. Laundry £3. Wheelchair accessible.

Lisnagree Hostel (IHH), Ballinorig Rd. (tel. 27133). On the left fork just after the traffic circle before the Maxol garage (follow Boherboy away from town), 1mi. from town center and close to the bus/train station. Small, pretty, relaxed hostel perfect for families or couples, but a bit remote for anyone who wants to hit the pub at night. Bike and walking tours. 4-bed dorms with bath from £7.50; doubles from £17. **Bike rental** £7 per day, £30 per week; deposit £40.

Atlas House, Castle St. (tel. 20722). More like a Holiday Inn than a hostel. Satellite TV, large kitchen, continental breakfast included. Non-smoking rooms. 8-bed dorms £7.50; 4-bed dorms with bath £10; twins from £26.

The Hostel, Church St. (tel. 27199), formerly Seán Óg's. Walk up Barrack Ln., the pedestrian walkway off The Mall opposite Denny St., and make the first right. Small, downtown hangout with a cozy, warm sitting room and a skylit kitchen. It risks approximating a damp Irish cottage, but will most likely be renovated for the 1999 season. Dorms £7.

Dowling's Leeside, Oakpark Rd. (tel. 26475). About ½mi. from town center on Edward St./Oakpark Rd. Pamper yourself at this cheerful B&B, decorated with gorgeous Irish pine antique furniture, cushy chintz chairs, and fresh flowers. The lovely hostess will make you want to move in. Glass-enclosed dining room makes breakfast bright. Singles £18; doubles £32.

FOOD

Tralee's culinary landscape has definitely improved over the past few years, although it's still not great. For the chefs, there's a **Quinnsworth Supermarket** (tel. 22788) in The Square (open M-Tu 9am-7pm, W-F 9am-9pm, Sa 9am-6pm, Su 10am-6pm) and a health food store/bakery, **Sean Chara** (tel. 22644), across the street (open M-W and Sa 9am-6pm, Th 9am-8pm, F 9am-9pm). **Counihans Newsagent** on the corner of Prince's St. and Ivy Terrace sells expensive groceries until 11pm.

Finnegan's (tel. 27610), below the hostel on Denny St. Savor the delicacies prepared in this candle-lit, shadowy bistro. A fireside meal could last for hours. Dinners are in the upper range of budget eats, but large and unbelievably tasty (entrees £9-15).

The Old Forge, Church St. (tel. 28095), just down from The Hostel (formerly Seán Óg's). A Tralee institution, with fine Irish fare. Beef and Guinness casserole £6.75, Irish breakfast £3.50. Open July-Sept. M-Sa 9am-10pm; Oct.-June M-Sa 9am-6pm.

Brat's Place, 18 Milk Market Ln., pedestrian walkway off The Mall. Tasty, conscientiously prepared vegetarian food with mostly local and organic ingredients. Specializes in low-cal, low-fat, and gluten-free meals. Soup £1.50; warm entrees £4.50. Delicious desserts £1-1.50. Open M-Sa 12:30-2:30pm, perhaps later if food lasts.

Snackers, The Mall (tel. 26024). An unassuming diner known for its tasty burgers (£2.55 with chips). Everything under £3.05. Open 10am-6pm.

Roots, 76 Boherboy (tel. 22665). An ever-changing, though limited, menu of vegetarian food with gargantuan portions (£3-4). Open M-Tu 11am-3pm, W-F 11am-3pm and 7-9pm.

The Skillet, Barrack Ln. (tel. 24561), off The Mall. If the pizza doesn't exhilarate you, the photos of Mt. Everest will—the owner was on the first Irish expedition to climb it. Lunch is reasonable; dinner (£5.90-9) is a bit overpriced for what you get. Open in summer daily 9am-10pm; in winter M-Sa 9am-10pm.

PUBS

Baily's Corner Pub (tel. 23230), at Ashe and Castle St. This mellow pub has music Sundays through Thursdays and an especially great session on Tuesdays. Kerry's Gaelic football legacy hangs on the walls while real-life players join an older crowd at the bar.

Paddy Mac's, The Mall (tel. 21572). A Tralee favorite with the only old-style pub decor around. Many a trad session.

Val O'Shea's, Bridge St. (tel. 21559). Extremely popular among locals, Val's draws in a mixed crowd for craic, but no live music.

Seán Óg's (tel. 28822). With its impressive fireplace (hand-built by the owner) and lots of trad, year-old Seán Óg's has already generated a lively following. It's easier just to list when they don't have music: Wednesdays.

Abbey Inn, The Square (tel. 22084). Tough crowd comes to hear live rock, especially the bands F-Sa. Bono swept here! When U2 played here in the late 70s, the manager made them sweep the floors to pay for their drinks because he thought they were so bad. Open Su-F until 1am.

SIGHTS

Tralee is home to Ireland's second-largest museum, **Kerry the Kingdom,** Ashe Memorial Hall, Denny St. (tel. 27777). (*Open daily July-Aug. 9am-7pm, Su 10am-6pm; Mar.-June and Sept.-Oct. 9am-6pm; Nov.-Mar. 9am-5:30pm. £5.50, students £4.75.*) Named one of Europe's top 20 museums in 1994, the Kingdom marshals all the resources of display technology to tell the story of Co. Kerry from 8000 BC to the present. Although the rise and fall of the Kerry Gaelic football league gets disproportionate attention, some temporary exhibits are world-class. "Geraldine Tralee" downstairs is a reconstruction of Tralee in 1450 seen from a small moving cart. You even get the old city's stench! Across from the museum, the **Roses of Tralee** bloom each summer in Ireland's second-largest town park. The gardens, designed in 1987, could convert even floraphobes into rose-sniffers. The gray carpeting in **St. John's Church,** Castle St., dampens the echo and the Gothic mood, but the stained glass is worth a look.

The building on the Prince's Quay traffic circle that looks like a cross between a Gothic castle and a space-age solarium is actually Tralee's £4.5-million **Aquadome** (tel. 28899), complete with whirlpools, steam room, sauna, and gym. (*Open daily 10am-10pm. July £6, students £5; Aug.-June £4, £3.*) A wave pool, river rapids, and speedy waterslide are all substantially warmer than the Atlantic.

Just down Dingle Rd. (N86/R559) whir the arms of the **Blenneville Windmill and Visitor Centre** (tel. 21064). (*Open Apr.-Oct. daily 10am-6pm. £2.75, students £2.25.*) Blenneville's is the largest operating windmill in the British Isles, and you can climb to the top. Recalling Blenneville's status as Kerry's main port of emigration during the Famine, a small **museum** focuses on the "coffin ships" that sailed from Ireland during the Famine. The restored **Tralee & Dingle Railway** (tel. 21064) runs the 2 mi. between the aquadome and the Blennerville complex. (*Trains run July-Aug. 10:30am-5:30pm, Sept.-June 10:30am-5pm, except 2nd Su and M of each month. £2.75, students £2.25.*) Trains leave the aquadome every hour on the hour and leave the windmill on the half hour.

ENTERTAINMENT

The **Siamsa Tíre Theatre** (tel. 23055), at the end of Denny St. next to the museum, is Ireland's national folk theater. It mounts brilliant summer programs depicting traditional Irish life through mime, music, and dance. (Productions July-Aug. M-Sa; May-June and Sept. M-Th and Sa. Shows start at 8:30pm. Box office open M-Sa 9am-10:30pm. £9, students £8.) The **Dúchas Cultural Centre,** Edward St., produces dance and musical performances (July-Aug. Tu 8:30pm; £4). Less culturally elite entertainment is available in Tralee's two nightclubs. The Brandon Hotel's club **Spirals,** Prince's Quay (tel. 23333), discos (Wednesday and F-Su), while **Horan's,** Boherboy (tel. 21933), blasts country-western and disco (Th-Su). Both stay open until 1:45am (cover £4-5).

Lovely Irish lasses from around the world come to town during the last week of August for the **Rose of Tralee International Festival.** A maelstrom of entertainment surrounds the main event, a personality competition to earn the coveted title "Rose of Tralee." Rose-hopefuls or spectators can call the Rose office, in Ashe Memorial Hall (tel. 21322). For other local goings-on, check *The Kerryman* (85p).

■ Tarbert

Little more than a peaceful seaside spot on the N69, Tarbert would be unremarkable were it not for a fabulous hostel and convenient ferry service between Co. Kerry and

Clare. **Bus Éireann** stops outside the hostel on its way from **Tralee** to **Doolin** and **Galway** (mid-June to Sept. M-Sa 3 per day, Su 2 per day, Galway to Tralee £13). During the rest of the year, the nearest stop to Tarbert is in Kilrush. Hitchers report mid-afternoon success from Killimer, the ferry port 1 mi. from Tarbert, to Kilrush (see p. 267). **Shannon Ferry Ltd.** (tel. (065) 53124) makes the 20-minute ferry trip across the Shannon between Tarbert and Killimer. (June-Aug. every 30min. from both sides, every hr. on the half hour from Tarbert and on the hour from Killimer Apr.-Sept. 7am-9:30pm; Oct.-Mar. 7am-7:30pm; Su from 9am. £8 per carload, £2 per pedestrian or biker.) Tarbert's **tourist office** (tel. (068) 36500), in the 1831 Bridewell Jail and Courthouse, is a small but surprisingly interesting look at Irish prison history and the rest of Tarbert's past (open Apr.-Oct. daily 10am-6pm; jail admission £3, students £2). The nearest **ATM** is 15 mi. away in Listowel. The **Ferry House Hostel** (tel. (068) 36555) is a two-year-old occupant of a 200-year-old building in the center of town (dorms £7; doubles £18; laundry £1-4). As if comfy wide mattresses, cushy Victorian chairs, stone hallways wide enough for a truck, and hot showers with unbelievable water pressure weren't enough, a great **coffeeshop** is in the same building (sandwiches about £1.50). (Open May-Sept. 8am-7pm.) Recently revamped **Coolhan's** is the most notable of Tarbert's five pubs. A few hundred meters from the ferry stands **Tarbert House** (tel. (068) 36198), the home of the family of Signeur Leslie of Tarbert since 1690. (Open daily 10am-noon and 2-4pm. £2. Tours given by Mrs. Leslie herself.) The recently restored exterior rivals the period pieces and priceless art it protects.

WESTERN IRELAND

Even Dubliners will tell you that the west is the "most Irish" part of Ireland. Yeats agreed: "For me," he said, "Ireland is Connacht." For less privileged Irish, Connacht has sometimes meant poor soil, starvation, and emigration. When Cromwell uprooted the native Irish landowners in Leinster and Munster and resettled them west of the Shannon, he was giving them a raw deal. The West was also hardest-hit by the potato famine—entire villages emigrated or died. Today, every western county has less than half of its 1841 population. But from Connemara north to Ballina, hikers, cyclists, and hitchhikers enjoy the isolation of boggy, rocky, or brilliantly mountainous landscapes.

The city Galway is a different story, a successful port that's now a boomtown for the young. The rest of Co. Galway draws summer tourists to its rugged scenery and Irish-speaking villages. Farther south, the barren moonscape of the Burren, the Cliffs of Moher, and a reputation as the center of the trad music scene attracts travelers to Co. Clare. Western Ireland's gorgeous desolation and enclaves of traditional culture are now its biggest attractions. The river itself has provided subsistence and tourism for generations, and the thriving Limerick town is even becoming a tourist haven. With *Angela's Ashes* as testament to the phenomenon, even Ireland's tragic history can be a compelling part of travel.

Limerick and Clare

The Dál Cais (later O'Brien) clan invaded Clare around AD 744, ruthlessly exterminated the natives, and prepared themselves for a 300-year rise to power and high-kingship. Counties Limerick and Clare are substantially less violent today. With convenient Shannon Airport and a host of quintessential Irish attractions located in the immediate vicinity, Limerick is showing off its rolling hills and marketing shrewdness. Ironically enough, the historic poverty of Limerick City has become more famous in recent years while the economy has ridden the tide of its EU boom. Geology defines Co. Clare: fine sands glisten on the beaches of Kilkee, skyscraper-high limestone slabs mark the Cliffs of Moher, and 100 sq. mi. of exposed limestone form Ireland's most perculiarly alluring landscape, the Burren.

■ Limerick

Despite a flourishing trade in off-color poems, Limerick has never had much status as a tourist town. While a sagging economy and its buddies "dirt" and "crime" gave Limerick a bad name in the past, the lack of tourists today seems both surprising and refreshing. The republic's third largest city sports a top-notch museum and a developing art scene, truly fantastic food, and pubs with all of the diversity of character that a city of this size demands. And, although Limerick has its share of depressing history, it did get great architecture along the way; 12th-century St. John's castle is visible from the smart 19th-century Georgian section down the river.

Though it hardly deserves its sinister nickname "Stab City," Limerick has historically been a fairly contentious place. The Vikings settled around Limerick in 922, presaging a millennium of turbulent hullabaloo. During the English Civil War, Limerick was the last stronghold of Royalist support against Cromwell's army. When the city finally did break, it took Cromwell's commander, Henry Ireton, with it. Forty years later, the Jacobites made their last stand here against the Williamites. The battle resulted in the infamous Treaty of Limerick, a promise of limited civil rights for Cath-

Western Ireland

ATLANTIC OCEAN

DONEGAL
TYRONE
N. IRE.
Donegal
N56
N15
Donegal Bay
Ballyshannon
Bundoran
Lower
Lough Erne
A46
FERMANAGH
Lough Melvin
Drumcliff
Manor hamilton
Enniskillen
A4
Killala Bay
Easky
Sligo Bay
Sligo
Dromahair
CAVAN
Belmullet
Ballycastle
Inishcrone
Ballysadare
Colooney
Riverstown
Lough Allen
Bangor
Ballina
SLIGO
Tober-curry
Ballymote
Drumshanbo
LEITRIM
Blacksod Bay
Lough Conn
Boyle
Carrick-on-Shannon
Keel
Achill Island
MAYO
Castlebar
Knock
ROSCOMMON
Castlerea
Longford
Clare Island
Clew Bay
Westport
Claremorris
Roscommon
LONGFORD
Inishturk
Louisburgh
CONNACHT
Lough Ree
Inishbofin
Lough Mask
Ballinrose
WESTMEATH
Inish-shark
Leenane
Cong
Tuam
Athlone
CONNEMARA
Lough Corrib
Oughterard
GALWAY
Ballinasloe
Clifden
Roundstone
Galway
N64
OFFALY
Aran Islands
Galway Bay
Loughrea
Inishmore
Kinvara
Portumna
Birr
Inishmaan
Inisheer
Ballyvaughan
Gort
Doolin
Lisdoonvarna
Rosecrea
LAOIS
Cliffs of Moher
Corofin
Lough Derg
Lahinch
CLARE
0   20 miles
0   20 kilometers
Milltown Malbay
Ennis
Nenagh
N
Kilkee
Shannon Airport
TIPPERARY
Thurles
Kilrush
Limerick
Mouth of the Shannon
Tarbert
MUNSTER
Cashel
Listowel
LIMERICK
Rathkeale
Tipperary
Clonmel
Abbeyfeale
Newcastle West
Kilmallock
Tralee Bay
Tralee
Dingle Peninsula
Kanturk
Mallow
Fermoy
WATERFORD
Dingle Bay
Killarney
Dungarvan
KERRY
CORK

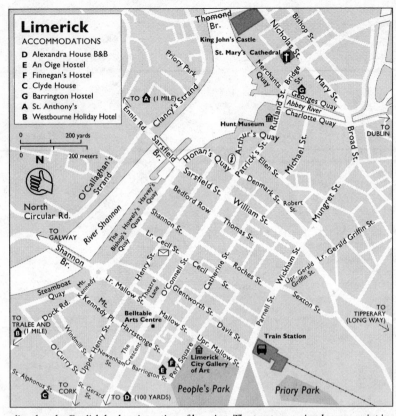

Limerick
ACCOMMODATIONS
D Alexandra House B&B
E An Oige Hostel
F Finnegan's Hostel
C Clyde House
G Barrington Hostel
A St. Anthony's
B Westbourne Holiday Hotel

olics that the English had no intention of keeping. The treaty remained a sore point in British-Irish relations for the next 150 years (see **The Protestant Ascendancy (1688-1801),** p. 56).

ORIENTATION AND PRACTICAL INFORMATION

Limerick's streets form a grid pattern, bounded by the River Shannon on the west and by the Abbey River on the north. The center of most of the city's activity stretches around a few blocks of **O'Connell Street** (sometimes called Patrick's or Rutland St.). Follow O'Connell St. north and cross the Abbey River to reach **King's Island,** which is dominated architecturally by St. Mary's Cathedral and King John's Castle. The city itself is easily navigable by foot, but to reach the suburbs, catch a **city bus** (75p) from Boyd's or Penney's on O'Connell St. (buses run M-Sa 2 per hr. 8am-11pm, Su 1 per hr.). Buses #2, 5, and 8 access the university, while bus #6 follows Ennis Rd. A one-week pass for a week of unlimited city bus travel is available at the bus station for £8.

Trains: Colbert Station (tel. 315555), off Parnell St. Inquiries desk open M-F 9am-6pm, Sa 9:30am-5:30pm. Trains from Limerick to **Dublin** (2hr., M-Sa 10 per day, Su 8 per day, £25), **Waterford** (2hr., M-Sa 2 per day in summer, 1 per day in winter, £17), **Rosslare** (3½hr., M-Sa 1 per day, £23), **Ennis** (M-Sa 2 per day, £5.50), **Cork** (2½hr., M-Sa 7 per day, Su 6 per day, £13.50), **Killarney** (2½hr., M-Sa 4 per day, Su 3 per day, £15), and **Tralee** (3hr., M-Sa 6 per day, Su 3 per day, £15).
Buses: Colbert Station, just off Parnell St. (tel. 313333 or 418855; 24hr. talking timetable tel. 319911). Open June-Sept. daily 8:45am-6pm; Oct.-May M-Sa 8am-6pm, Su 3-7pm. Most buses leave from the station, but some depart from Penney's

or Todd's downtown on O'Connell St. Limerick sends buses to **Cork** (2hr., 6 per day, £9), **Dublin** (3hr., M-Sa 8 per day, Su 5 per day, £10), **Galway** (2hr., 7 per day, £9), **Ennis** (1hr., 7 per day, £5), **Killarney** (2½hr., M-Sa 6 per day, Su 3 per day, £9.30), **Sligo** (6hr., 4 per day, £14), **Tralee** (2hr., 6 per day, £9), **Waterford** (2½hr., M-Th and Sa 5 per day, F 6 per day, Su 5 per day, £9.70), and **Wexford** and **Rosslare Harbour**, with some departures timed to meet the ferries (4hr., 4 per day, £12).

Tourist Office: Arthurs Quay (tel. 317522), in the space-age glass building. From the station, walk straight down Davis St., turn right on O'Connell St., then left just before Arthurs Quay Mall. Handy city maps £1. **Bureau de change** and a Bus Éireann info booth. Open July-Aug. M-F 9am-7pm, Sa-Su 9am-6pm; Mar.-June and Sept.-Oct. M-Sa 9:30am-5:30pm; Nov.-Feb. M-F 9:30am-5:30pm, Sa 9:30am-1pm.

Budget Travel Office: USIT, O'Connell St. (tel. 415064), across from Ulster Bank. Issues ISICs and **TravelSave** stamps. Open M-F 9:30am-5:30pm, Sa 10am-1pm. Also located at University of Limerick (tel. 332073).

Taxi: Top Cabs, Wickham St. (tel. 417417). Takes you most places in the city for under £3 and to the airport for about £14.

Bike Rental: Emerald Cycles, 1 Patrick St. (tel. 416983; email emarldalp@tinet.ie). £7 per day, £30 per week; deposit £40. £12 for return at other locations. Open M-Sa 9:15am-5:30pm. **McMahon's Cycleworld,** 25 Roches St. (tel. 415202). £7 per day, £30 per week.

Luggage Storage: in Colbert Station. Lockers £1 per day, 24hr. limit.

Laundry: Laundrette (tel. 312712) on Mallow St. Wash, dry, and fold £5. Open M-F 9am-6pm, Sa 9am-5pm.

Camping Equipment: River Deep, Mountain High, 7 Rutland St. (tel. 400944), off O'Connell St. Open M-Th and Sa 9:30am-6pm, F 9:30am-9pm.

Pharmacy: Arthurs Quay Pharmacy, Arthurs Quay Centre (tel. 416662). Open M-W 9am-7pm, Th-F 9am-9pm, Sa 9am-6pm.

Emergency: Dial 999; no coins required. **Garda:** Henry St. (tel. 414222), at Lower Glentworth St.

Post Office: Main office on Lower Cecil St. (tel. 315777), just off O'Connell St. Open M and W-Sa 9am-5:30pm, Tu 9:30am-5:30pm.

Internet Access: Webster's, Thomas St. (tel. 312066). Full web and email access costs £2.50 per 30min. Bring your *Let's Go* and get 30min. free. Food and cider for online consumption are available from the adjoining pub. Open M-Sa 10am-10pm, Su 2pm-10pm.

There once was a **phone code** *named 061*...Damn, nothing rhymes with 061.

ACCOMMODATIONS

Limerick has three "real" hostels and several budget accommodation centers geared toward term-time university students. These dorm-like establishments are usually large and in very good condition but are slightly more expensive and less homey than the average hostel. Although Limerick is not the place to find cozy cottage hostels with peat fires, several hostels take advantage of the very lovely city architecture. For those seeking refuge from the bustle of the city, Ennis St. is a B&B bonanza, most priced around £16 per person.

✒**Finnegan's (IHH),** 6 Pery Sq. (tel. 310308). This new hostel is located in a grand old Georgian mansion overlooking People's Park. From the bus station, cross Parnell St. and head up Daris St. for 1 long block. Take a left on Pery St. and walk 2 blocks to Harstoye St.; the hostel is on the corner. Elegant high-ceilinged common rooms, bright and spacious dormitories, and positively torrential showers make Finnegan's one of the best hostels in Limerick. Dorms £7.50; private rooms £10 per person. Laundry £3-4.

Barrington Hostel (IHH), George's Quay (tel. 415222). Far from the train and bus station, but very close to sights, restaurants, and pubs. Barrington compensates for its large size by offering relatively private dorms. Hand-painted flower decorations brighten up the common rooms. 2 kitchens and a resplendent front garden. 4-bed dorms £7.50; 3-bed dorms £8.50; singles £10; doubles £20. Laundry £5.

An Óige Hostel (HI), 1 Pery Sq., (tel. 314672). Around the corner from Finnegan's. A pleasant, old Georgian house and a cheerful staff help ease the usual An Óige restrictions and dreariness. Rather tightly packed metal bunks in rooms, some with splendid views of People's Park. With 2nd- and 3rd-floor dorms and a basement kitchen, this hotel is not for the stair-haters of the world. June-Sept. dorms £8.75, Oct.-May £7.75; £1.25 less for HI members. Sheets £1. Midnight curfew.

Westbourne Holiday Hostel (IHH), Courbrack Ave. (tel. 302500), off Dock Rd. From Colbert Station, make a left on Parnell St. then a right on Upper Mallow St. by the park. Follow Mallow St. to the traffic circle, make a left, and continue for 1 rather unscenic mile. The hostel is on the left after the Shell Station. Although it suffers from an institutional character and requires a long walk from the city center, this student housing masquerading as a hostel is incredibly equipped. Carpeted hallways, a huge kitchen and dining room, a lounge and TV, and no bunks. 3-bed dorms £8; singles £13; twins £22. Continental breakfast included. Wash £1, dry £1.

Clyde House, St. Alphonsus St. (tel. 314727), right off Henry St. Budget student accommodations/hostel in a clean and comfortable but institutional setting. Without a common kitchen, Clyde House does not exactly cater to backpackers. However, rooms with interior kitchens are available. 3 pool tables. Dorms £7.50; singles £20; doubles £32; triples £37.50; quads £46. All dorms include continental breakfast. Substantial discounts for longer stays.

St. Anthony's, 8 Coolraine Terr., Ennis Rd. (tel. 452607), 1mi. from city center; best route via Sarsfield Bridge. Pleasant rooms look out onto a flourishing garden. Homemade brown bread and jam await in the morning. £16, with bath £17, but the friendly proprietress usually gives a *Let's Go* discount.

Alexandra House, O'Connell St., several blocks south of the Crescent. Large, comfortable, and pleasantly decorated, although its proximity drives prices up. £18, with bath £22.

FOOD

Limerick probably has more fast-food joints than all the truck stops in Ohio combined, but there are also some top-notch eateries with reasonable prices. Otherwise, stock up at **Quinnsworth Supermarket** (tel. 412399) in Arthurs Quay Mall (open M-W 8:30am-7pm, Th-F 8:30am-9pm, Sa 8:30am-7pm) or at **Eats of Eden,** Henry St. (tel. 419400), a well-stocked health food store (open M-F 9am-6pm, Sa 9am-5:30pm).

The Green Onion Café, 3 Ellen St. (tel. 400710), just off Patrick's St. Crimson-splashed walls etched with writing surround diners. Elite bistro fare at egalitarian prices (lunch entrees and sandwiches £4-6). Stick to the lunch menu; dinners after 6pm skyrocket in price (£10-12). Open daily noon-10pm.

Dolmen Gallery and Restaurant, Honan's Quay (tel. 417929), across from the tourist office. Enjoy massive portions of admirably prepared Irish specialities while critiqueing the current exhibit. Your views of ham, salad, and dessert will never be the same. Entrees £5. Open M-Sa 10am-5:30pm.

Moll Darby's, 8 Georges Quay (tel. 411511), just across the Abbey River. Delicious and artfully prepared international cuisine is served up in this popular, if borderline pricey, quay-side restaurant. Open daily 6-11pm.

Java's, 5 Catherine St. (tel. 418077). Flavored coffees, herbal teas, café food, and desserts please a steady stream of Limerickites. Possibly the only bagels available in Limerick. Sandwiches £1.20-3.20. Open M-Su 8am-8pm.

O'Grady's Cellar Restaurant, O'Connell St. (tel. 418286). Maroon walls and faux thatch abound in this cozy little subterranean place. Soup, lunch entree, and tea or coffee £4.95; 3-course dinner £9.95. Open daily 8:30am-11pm.

O'Flaherty's Basement Restaurant, 74 O'Connell St. (tel. 316311), at Hartstoye St. The stone walls of this tasteful restaurant are lined with bits and pieces of Irish history, and the atmosphere is uncomparatively seductive. Excellent hearty food but quite expensive (main courses £9-14); call ahead for student deals.

Paul's Restaurant, 59 O'Connell St. (tel. 316600), between Glentworth and Mallow St. The spacious, modern interior of this cool new restaurant may induce you to spend more than you want, but fantastic and reasonable meals can be found. Lunch entrees £5-6.50, dinner £7-9.

PUBS AND CLUBS

Trad is played nightly around town. You can pick up the tourist office's *Guinness Guide to Irish Music* for schedules or you can opt for one of the local gig *"Guides"* for more detailed information and local gossip. A large student population ensures plenty of more raucous musical options.

🏅**Dolan's,** Dock Rd. (tel. 314483). This warm and extremely popular dockside pub attracts a mixed crowd with its nightly trad sessions. Its keen proprietor recently opened a beautiful music venue out back that hosts big-name bands on weekend for a £3-5 cover.

Nancy Blake's, Denmark St. (tel. 416443). One of the better pubs in town and insanely popular. A mature crowd packs itself into the large store rooms, which actually have sawdust on the floor, while the younger set revels in the outdoor "outback." Prim, sharp Nancy will tell you that there is trad inside every M-W, rock and blues outside nightly.

Doc's, Michael St. (tel. 417266), at the corner of Charlotte's Quay in the Granary. Spacious, interesting pub in a former warehouse with arched brick ceilings. Large outdoor beer garden, complete with palm trees and waterfalls, is invariably packed with rollicking youth. Tu and Th live music, Saturdays DJ.

Locke Bar, Georges Quay (tel. 413733). Hip, but without the grunge atmosphere of Doc's. Pleasant, quay-side seating with festive Christmas lights. Owner Richard Costello, who used to play rugby for Ireland's national team, now plays trad Tuesday and Sunday nights.

The Old Quarter, Denmark St. (tel. 401190). Modern and colorful, this bar risks over-decoration. Its adjoining café will please travelers who are sick of the endless parade of "traditional Irish pubs."

Tom Collins, Cecil St. (tel. 415749). There's no music here, since it would interrupt the pub's true calling. Described as a "palace of conversation" for "all walks of life." Even the mayor is a frequent visitor. Unsuspecting American tourists have come here, asking for a "Tom Collins" (you know, the cocktail). They fetched the owner.

The White House (tel. 412377), the corner of O'Connell and Glentworth St. A sophisticated and artsy crowd gathers at this relaxed pub. Trad sessions often arise in a burst of *bodhrán* and spontaneity.

Limerick has a nightclub scene worthy of the Republic's third-largest city. Most social events congregate according to word of mouth, but a few nightclubs are safe bets. **Doc's** (see **Pubs,** above) revels in a rave-like disco Thursday through Sunday nights. **The Works,** on Bedford Row next to the Cinema, opens its club seven nights a week. **Ted's,** O'Connell St. (tel. 417412), provides a classier alternative nightly (no sneakers; cover £3-6). Watch out for concession stubs in the pub. **Baker's Place,** Dominick St. (tel. 418414), a few doors down from the Clock Tower on Davis St., has live music nightly, with a club pumping music Tuesday through Sunday nights.

SIGHTS

Limerick City Bus Tours (tel. 313333) focus primarily on the old English city on King's Island. *(Tours depart from the tourist office June-Aug. M-Sa 11am and 2:30pm. £5, students £4.)* **Walking tours** (tel. 318106) depart from St. Mary's Action Centre on Nicholas St. *(Tours M-F 11am and 2pm. Weekends and evenings by appointment. £2.)* The tours skip the area around the Daniel O'Connell monument on **O'Connell St.,** dominated by red-brick Georgian townhouses with brightly painted, stately doorways. The elegant, if slightly decrepit, buildings are indicative of careful town planning during the late 18th and early 19th centuries.

McCourt Mania

Until recently, the only thing that most people knew about Limerick was its reputed penchant for raunchy poetry. Now anyone who knows nothing about Limerick can comment on its unfortunate days, thanks to Limerickian-Frank McCourt's bestselling and Pulitzer Prize-winning novel *Angela's Ashes*. Although Limerick residents have taken a generally dim view of McCourt's humorous but terrible acount of his childhood during the 30s and 40s, the work has launched Limerick enough into the limelight to generate the tourism it deserves. Some residents are proud to have grown up with McCourt (a treat, no doubt) or to see their heritage gain international recognition. Many others, however, resent the dreary depiction of Limerick and all the money McCourt's made off it. For better or worse, McCourt mania continues to grow; in addition to countless fan clubs, a movie version by Alan Parker *(Evita, Mississippi Burning)* is in the works. McCourt territory—and there's a lot of it because the family moved so often—is largely concentrated in the Georgian part of town around Windmill St. and Pery Sq.; the actual slum buildings, however, have long been cleared. The path of the "Angela's Ashes Tour" is not yet marked, but walking tours of the city will gladly show you all you want to see.

A few decades after the Normans displaced the O'Brien dynasty from the Limerick area, extremely unpopular Norman King John ordered a castle built for his much-needed protection, but he never actually visited the castle. In fact, this untrusted leader, who signed the Magna Carta against his will, made only one trip to Ireland, during which he supposedly pulled the beards of his subjects for kicks. **King John's Castle,** Nicholas St. (tel. 411201), still defends Limerick, although the ranks of prospective invaders have dwindled somewhat. *(Open daily 9:30am-6pm. Last admission 5pm. £3.80, students £2.10.)* Walk across the Abbey River and take the first left after St. Mary's Cathedral. With well-prepared exhibits that supply a survey of history from the Vikings to the present, the castle today is more educationally than physically impressive. The history of military strength remains evident outside where the **mangonel** is displayed. Easily recognizable from its use in *Monty Python's Quest for the Holy Grail,* the mangonel was used to catapult pestilent animal corpses into enemy cities and castles. Do not lick it. The rough exterior of nearby **St. Mary's Cathedral** (tel. 416238) was built by the O'Briens in 1172. *(Open M-Sa 9am-1pm and 2-5pm.)* Fold-down seats, built into the wall on the side of the altar, are covered with elaborate carvings that depict the struggle between good and evil. They are called *misericordia,* Latin for "acts of mercy," for good reason—they were places to rest one's arse during long services, in which sitting was prohibited.

Across the river, in the city proper, you can critique Irish paintings for free at the **Limerick City Gallery of Art,** Pery Sq. (tel. 310633). *(Open M-W and F 10am-1pm, Th 2-6pm, Sa 10am-1pm. Free.)* The building was undergoing construction in 1998-9; phone ahead. More modern and abstract art decks the walls at the very small and very busy **Belltable Arts Centre,** O'Connell St. (tel. 319866). *(Open M-Sa 9am-7pm. Free.)* The fascinating **Hunt Museum,** Custom House, Rutland St. (tel. 312833), houses the largest collection of medieval, Stone Age, and Iron Age artifacts outside the national museum in Dublin, as well as a clay copy of the supposedly perfect Leonardo da Vinci's four "Rearing Horses." *(Open Tu-Sa 10am-5pm, Su 2-5pm. £3.90, students £2.50.)* The collection was compiled in the 1930s and 40s by the Hunt family, who personally displayed many of the items in their home before setting up the museum. Other highlights of the collection include the personal seal of Charles I and a coin reputed to be one of the infamous 30 pieces of silver paid to Judas by the Romans. The impressive collection is appreciably enhanced by an excellent guided tour (call ahead to arrange times). Should you venture to the University, stop by the **National Self-Portrait Collection** (tel. 333644) that exhibits itself in Plassey House. *(Open M-F 10am-5pm. Free.)*

ENTERTAINMENT

The **Belltable Arts Centre,** 69 O'Connell St. (tel. 319866), stages excellent, big-name productions year round (box office open M-Sa 9am-6pm and prior to performances; tickets £5-7). The **Theatre Royal,** Upper Cecil St. (tel. 414224), hosts any large concerts that come to town. The **University Concert Hall** (tel. 331549), on the university campus, attracts opera, dance, and classical and traditional music (tickets £8-14). **Greyhounds** race every Monday, Thursday, and Saturday night at the **Market's Field** (tel. 316788) on Mulgrave St., several blocks up William St. Races start at 8pm and cost £3. The free *Calendar of Events and Entertainment,* available at the tourist office, has details on events.

■ Near Limerick: Adare

Adare's well-preserved medieval architecture and meticulous rows of thatched cottages have earned it a reputation as one of the prettiest towns in Ireland. With that distinction came busloads of tourists. An older, well-heeled set crowds the town's award-winning restaurants and grand hotels, sometimes making the backpackers who stop for the monuments feel out of place. Adare is worth a daytrip, but the charm is easily exhausted in a few hours.

The medieval Fitzgerald family endowed Adare with several thriving monasteries of three different orders. The **Trinitarina Abbey,** which survives on Main St., was established in the 13th century by an order of monks who liberated Christian prisoners during the Crusades. Renovated in the 19th century, the priory now serves as the town's Catholic Church. Farther down Main St. toward Limerick, the 14th-century **Augustinian Priory** stands, having been restored as a Protestant church. The **Franciscan Friary,** adjacent to the grounds of Adare Manor, lies in crumbling disarray. Slightly farther down Main St. on the banks of the River Maigue lies the 13th-century **Desmond Castle,** which has been declared a national monument but has been closed to the public. **Walking tours** of the town start from the tourist office on request (£3.50). Back in the village, the **Adare Heritage Centre** (tel. 396666), in the same building as the tourist office, traces Adare's history, filled with earls, monks, knights, monks, lords named "Fitz," and monks (open daily 9am-7pm; £2.50, students £2). Five miles from Adare, nature trails wind through the 600-acre **Curraghchase Forest Park.** The **Adare Jazz Festival** kicks off in mid-March. **Horse trials** and **country fairs** are scheduled in the area around Adare in March, May, and October.

Buses travel to Adare from **Limerick** (20min., M-Sa 6 per day, Su 7 per day, £3.50) and **Tralee** (1¾hr., M-Sa 6 per day, Su 7 per day). The **tourist office** (tel. 396255) is located on Main St. (Open June-Sept. M-F 9am-7pm, Sa-Su 9am-6pm; earlier closings Mar.-May and Oct.-Nov.; open Dec. Sa-Su 9am-6pm.) The **AIB,** just off Main St., has an **ATM. Bikes** can be rented from **Eddie Daly** (tel. 396091); try to call 24 hours in advance (£10 per day). The **phone code** is 061.

Although there is no hostel here, Adare is B&B central. Many people touring the Shannon region or awaiting flights at the airport prefer to stay here rather than in Limerick. Good choices include the clean, modern rooms at **Riversdale,** Manorcourt, Station Rd. (tel. 396751; singles £22, with bath £25; doubles £32, with bath £34), and the charming 160-year-old cottage **Murphy's Cross** (tel. 396042), one mile outside town on the Killarney Rd. (singles £16; doubles £28, with bath £32). Food is generally expensive in Adare. **The Blue Door** (tel. 396481), a 200-year-old thatched cottage with roses blooming outside, offers reasonable lunches (£3-5 for delicioius sandwiches, soups, and main courses) and pricey dinners (open daily 10am-9:30pm). A similar lunchtime value can be found at **The Arches Restaurant** (tel. 396246), where a main course and coffee is £6.50. Pub grub awaits those who wish to eat after 3pm with their funds unpillaged. **Pat Collin's Bar** (tel. 396143), next to the post office on Main St., is the best bet for sandwiches and soups. **Shean Collin's Bar,** around the corner, hosts live music Tuesday nights during the summer.

▨ Lough Derg

Lough Derg, the lake region northeast of Limerick, plays host to affluent middle-aged tourists, or "cruisers," who navigate boats upriver from Limerick to the small towns of **Killaloe, Mountshannon,** and **Portumna.** Younger, personal vehicle-free travelers are much rarer here than they are farther west. Archaeological attractions are not the main draw; visitors come to the lake for swimming, windsurfing, and other recreational activities. The **Lough Derg Way** walking path starts in Limerick, follows the western bank of the Shannon up to Killaloe, then crosses over to Ballina. The trail traces the eastern shore of the lake beneath Arra Mountain. The Neolithic tombs known as the "Graves of the Leinstermen" mark the refuge of Fintan the White, legendary consort of Cesair.

Killaloe lies along the Lough Derg Drive northeast of Limerick. Commuter **buses** run to and from **Limerick** (M-F 1 per day), but the thrice-weekly bus (Tu, F, and Sa) will be more conveniently timed for sightseers based in the city. Hitchhikers report an easy time getting to Killaloe from Limerick or from Dublin Rd., where hitchers station themselves on R494 and hitch to Ballina, just across the river.

■ Killaloe

The pleasant hills and lakeside orientation of Killaloe (KILL-a-loo), fifteen miles out of Limerick along the Lough Derg Dr. and just south of the lake, feel very distant from the industry of the city. Old churches and oratories remember the town as a 7th-century religious center, and Killaloe's twin (tourist) town is **Ballina,** Co. Limerick, just across a picturesque, if treacherously narrow, bridge.

PRACTICAL INFORMATION The **tourist office** (tel. 376866), in the former Lock House on the Killaloe side of the bridge, provides free maps of the town and the lake and information on several rural walks around Killaloe (open mid-May to Sept. daily 10am-6pm). Main St. is home to an **ATM**-blessed **AIB** bank (tel. 376115; open M and W-F 10am-4pm, Tu 10am-5pm) and, farther uphill, the **post office** (tel. 376111; open M-F 9:30am-12:30pm and 1:30-5:30pm, Sa 9:30am-12:30pm). The **phone code** is 061.

ACCOMMODATIONS, FOOD, AND PUBS Killaloe is an easy daytrip from Limerick, but several nice B&Bs near town make it a pleasant stopover. The very hospitable **Kincora House,** Main St. (tel. 376149), across from Crotty's Pub, is filled with well-maintained antiques and serves a healthy breakfast on request (£16). The best place to stock up for a luau is **McKeogh's** (tel. 376249), on Main St. in Ballina. (Open M-W 9am-7:30pm, Th-F 9am-9pm, Sa 9am-8:30pm, Su 9:30am-1pm.) Super-fresh seafood makes the **Dalcassian,** Main St. (tel. 376762), near the cathedral, a local favorite (dinner entrees £7-9; open daily 11am-5pm and 6-9:30pm; bar menu until 5pm). Another immensely popular pub, **Crotty's Courtyard Bar** (tel. 376965) serves up eclectic tunes Saturdays and hearty grub (£5-8) on a patio decorated with antique ads. Next to the bridge in Ballina, **Molly's** serves elevated pub grub (Irish stew £4) and pleasant lake and river views (with *al fresco* pints if the weather allows; food served from 12:30-10pm). Check out the **Seanachaoi Pub** (tel. 376913). The Irish name means "storyteller," but Seanachaoi specializes in live music of all types (F-Su).

SIGHTS At the base of the town on Royal Parade lies **St. Flannan's Cathedral,** built between 1195 and 1225 and still in use. Visitors can climb the tower for £1. Although the view is not spectacular, the climb has merit, especially if the guard who accompanies you is cute. Inside the Cathedral, the Thorgrim Stone is inscribed in both Scandinavian characters and the monks' *ogham* script, with a prayer for the conversion of Thorgrim, a Viking, to Christianity. Market Sq. may have once held the Kincora palace of High King Brian Ború, who lived here from 1002 to 1014. The other candidate for the coveted site-of-Ború's-palace award is the abandoned fort known as **Beal Ború,** 1½ mi. out of town toward Mountshannon and unfortunately not much to see. The legends of Ború continue at the **heritage center,** where interactive displays doc-

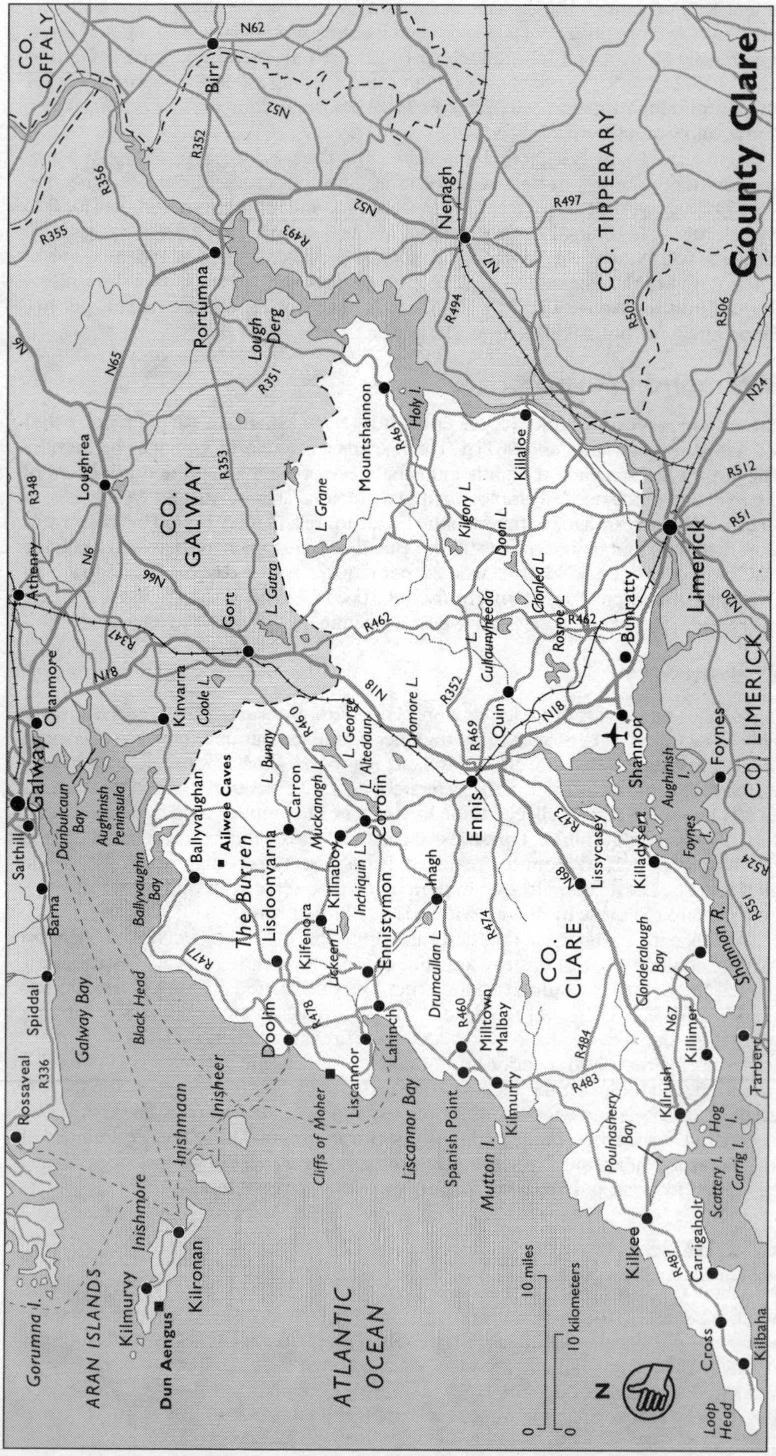
County Clare
CO. OFFALY
CO. GALWAY
CO. TIPPERARY
CO. CLARE
CO. LIMERICK
ARAN ISLANDS
ATLANTIC OCEAN
Galway
Salthill
Oranmore
Athenry
Loughrea
Portumna
Birr
Nenagh
Gort
Kinvarra
Barna
Spiddal
Rossaveal
Ballyvaughan
Ailwee Caves
The Burren
Lisdoonvarna
Kilfenora
Doolin
Carron
Corofin
Killnaboy
Ennistymon
Lahinch
Liscannor
Cliffs of Moher
Inagh
Ennis
Quin
Bunratty
Shannon
Limerick
Killaloe
Mountshannon
Lough Derg
Holy I.
L Grane
L Gutra
Coole L.
L Bunny
L George
L Altedaun
Muckanagh L
Inchiquin L
Lickeen L
Dromore L
Drumcullan L
Kilgory L
Doon L
Clonlea L
Rosroe L
L Cullaunyheeda
Milltown Malbay
Spanish Point
Kilmurry
Mutton I.
Liscannor Bay
Lissycasey
Killadysert
Clonderalough Bay
Killimer
Kilrush
Poulnasherry Bay
Hog I.
Scattery I.
Carrig I.
Tarbert
Kilkee
Carrigaholt
Cross
Kilbaha
Loop Head
Foynes
Foynes I.
Aughinish I.
Shannon R.
Galway Bay
Dunbulcaun Bay
Aughinish Peninsula
Ballyvaughn Bay
Black Head
Inisheer
Inishmaan
Inishmore
Kilronan
Kilmurvy
Dun Aengus
Gorumna I.
N18
N6
N65
N66
N62
N52
N7
N24
N20
N68
N67
N69
R355
R356
R352
R348
R347
R353
R351
R493
R497
R494
R503
R506
R512
R511
R462
R461
R460
R469
R473
R474
R476
R477
R478
R483
R484
R487
R524
R551
R336
10 miles
10 kilometers
N
0
0

ument Killaloe's much busier years at the beginning of the century, when its luxurious hotels were popular vacation spots and its canal was still a central point of trade. (Open daily 10am-6pm. £1.50, students £1.) In early July, the **Irish Chamber Orchestra** (tel. 202620) plays several concerts in the cathedral; ask at the tourist office for info. In mid-July, Killaloe celebrates **Féile Brian Ború,** four days of music, watersports, and various Ború-based activities.

Lough-related activities abound in Killaloe. The **Derg Princess** (tel. 376364) leaves from across the bridge in **Ballina** for relaxing one-hour cruises (£5). **Whelan's** (tel. 376159) stations itself across from the tourist office and rents out motorboats for fishing or cruising (£10 first hr., £5 per additional hr.). A boat (and a bit of navigational prowess) will allow you access to the eminently picnickable **Holy Island.** A couple of miles north of Killaloe, you can indulge in an afternoon of watersports at the **University of Limerick Activity and Sailing Centre** (tel. 376622; windsurfing £8 per hr., canoeing £3 per hr., sailboats from £10 per hr.).

■ Shannon Airport

Fifteen miles west of Limerick off Ennis Rd. (N18), **Shannon Airport** (tel. (061) 471444; Aer Lingus info tel. (061) 471666) sends jets to North America and Europe. The airport has spawned unsightly industrial development along the north shore of the river and much-needed employment in the coastal areas north and west of Limerick. Until a few years ago, all transatlantic flights to Ireland were bound by Irish law to stop first at Shannon, and many still do. **Bus Éireann** stops here between Limerick and Ennis (to Limerick 45min., M-Sa 22 per day, Su 13 per day, £3.50) and runs to Dublin (4½hr., 5 per day, £10). **Thrifty** (tel. (061) 472649) is the cheapest of many **car rentals** (£35 per day, £190 per week; 3-day min. rental; min. age 23; call ahead).

■ Bunratty

Eight miles northwest of Limerick along Ennis Rd., **Bunratty Castle** and **Bunratty Folk Park** (tel. (061) 361511) bring together a jumbled but unforgettable collection of historical attractions from all over Ireland. *(Open daily July-Aug. 9am-6:30pm; Sept.-June 9:30am-5:30pm. Last admission 1hr. before closing. Castle closes at 4:15pm. £5, students £3.60.)* Bunratty Castle is alleged to be Ireland's most complete medieval castle, with superbly restored furniture, tapestries, and stained-glass windows. The castle derives much of its popularity from the medieval feasts that it hosts nightly for deep-pocketed tourists. Local lasses dressed in period costume serve wine and meat to would-be chieftains (5-course meal with wine £31 per lord or lady).

The folk park originated in the Bord Fáilte-approved 60s, when builders at Shannon Airport couldn't bear to destroy a quaint cottage for a new runway. Instead, they moved the cottage to Bunratty. Since then, reconstructions of turn-of-the-century houses from all over Ireland and a small village of old-fashioned stores (now catering to modern tourist tastes) have been added. Peat fires are lit in the cottages each morning by occupationally and period-appropriate costumed "inhabitants." Try not to visit in mid-afternoon during the high season, as the thick line of visitors on the narrow castle stairways is annoying and treacherous. The Bunratty complex also claims one decent but still tourist-friendly pub. The first proprietress at **Durty Nelly's,** founded in 1620, earned her name by serving Bunratty soldiers more than just beer. **Buses** between **Limerick** and **Shannon Airport** (see above) pass Bunratty.

■ Ennis

Narrow, cobblestone streets line the small city of Ennis (pop. 16,000), 20 mi. northwest of Limerick. The merchants of Ennis vend fruit from makeshift stands along the river, and pubs shake nightly with trad. Ennis's reputations for safe streets, city-caliber nightlife and down-home friendliness have drawn enough migrants in the past 10 years to double the population. Ennis may never pack in the tourists with its scenery, but its proximity to Shannon Airport and the Burren makes it a likely stop.

ORIENTATION AND PRACTICAL INFORMATION

Ennis's layout is quite confusing, but the city center is navigable enough that you'll eventually find what you need. The center of town is **O'Connell Square**; to reach it from the stations, head left down Station Rd., turn right on O'Connell St., and go down a few blocks. From O'Connell Sq., **Abbey** and **Bank St.** lead across the river to the burbs, and **High St.** runs perpendicular to O'Connell St. through the center of town. **Market Place** is between O'Connell and High St.

Trains: The station (tel. 40444) is a 10min. walk from the town center on Station Rd. Open M-Sa 7am-5:30pm, Su 15min. before departures. Trains leave for **Dublin** via **Limerick** (M-Sa 2 per day, Su 1 per day, £16).

Buses: The station (tel. 24177) is next to the train station. Open M-F 7:15am-5:30pm, Sa 7:15am-4:45pm. To **Limerick** (40min., M-Sa 18 per day, Su 6 per day, £5), **Galway** (1¼ hr., 5 per day, £7.70), **Dublin** via **Limerick** (4hr., 5 per day, £10), **Cork** (3hr., 5 per day, £10), **Kilkee** (1hr., M-Sa 2-3 per day, Su 1-2 per day, £6.90), **Doolin** (1½hr., M-Sa 3 per day, Su 1 per day, £5.50), and **Shannon Airport** (40min., M-F 13 per day, Sa 9 per day, Su 10 per day, £3.50). A **West Clare** line (7 per day) goes to various combinations of **Lisdoonvarna, Ennistymon, Lahinch, Miltown Malbay, Doolin, Kilkee,** and **Kilrush.** The crowded post bus runs from the post office to **Liscannor** and **Doolin** (M-Sa 2 per day, £2.50 to Doolin). Arrive early to get a seat.

Tourist Offices: Ennis Tourist Office, O'Connell Sq. (tel. 41670), in the Upstairs Downstairs shop, answers questions and provides bus and train information. Open June-Sept. daily 9am-9pm; Oct.-May M-Sa 9am-6pm, Su 10am-6pm. **Shannon Region Tourist Office** (tel. 28366) looks like a highway rest stop and seems designed to serve the car-equipped. From the bus station, take a left and follow Clonakilty Rd., then take a left onto Clare Rd. They book rooms in Bord Fáilte B&Bs, hostels, and hotels (local bookings £1, national £2). Open June-Sept. daily 9am-7pm; Oct.-May Tu-Sa 9am-6pm.

Banks: Bank of Ireland, O'Connell Sq. (tel. 28615). Open M-Tu and Th-F 10am-4pm, W 10am-5pm; **ATM. AIB,** Bank Pl. (tel. 28089). Same hours; **ATM.**

Bike Rental: Michael Tierney Cycles and Fishing, 17 Abbey St. (tel. 29433, after 6pm tel. 21293). Rentals and repair. Tierney helpfully suggests routes through the hilly countryside. £4 per afternoon, £7 per day, £30 per week; deposit £30 or credit card. Open M-Sa 9:30am-6pm. **Irish Cycle Hire/Railbike,** Ennis Train Station (tel. (041) 41067). £6 per day, £30 per week; deposit £30. Open daily 9am-6pm.

Luggage Storage: At the bus station. Lockers 50p. Open M-Sa 7:30am-6:30pm, Su 10am-7:15pm.

Laundry: Like cows in Doolin, laundrettes in Ennis are ubiquitous, quiet presences who watch blandly as you walk by and occasionally moo. **Parnell's,** High St. (tel. 29075). Wash and dry £4-6. Open M-Sa 9am-6pm.

Pharmacy: O'Connell Chemist, Abbey St. (tel. 20373). Open M-Sa 9am-6:30pm, Su 11am-1pm. **Michael McLoughlin,** O'Connell St. (tel. 29511), in Dunnes Supermarket. Open M-W 9am-6pm, Th-F 9am-9pm, Sa 9am-6pm.

Counseling and Support: Samaritans (tel. (1850) 609090). 24hr.

Emergency: Dial 999; no coins required. **Garda:** tel. 28205.

Internet Access: MacCool's Internet Café (tel. 21988), hidden in an alley behind Abbey St. £3 per 30min., £5 per hr.

Post Office: Bank Pl. (tel. 21054). Open M-F 9am-5:30pm, Sa 9:30am-2:30pm.

Phone Code: 065.

ACCOMMODATIONS, FOOD, AND PUBS

A new, purpose-built hostel, the **Clare Hostel** (tel. 29370) has great potential. All rooms are modern with bath and wide mattresses, but there's no kitchen, laundry is £7, and all dorm beds are £10, a good value for the two-bed rooms but pricey for the 14-bed barracks. Follow High St. away from O'Connell Sq., then turn left on Cornmarket St. The hostel is on the left. (Dorms £10; doubles £25.) On the river's edge, across Club Bridge from Abbey St., the **Abbey Tourist Hostel (IHH)** (tel. 22620) is a 300-year-old labyrinth on Harmony Row with a somewhat alternative staff. The hostel is clean, with wide mattresses and fluorescent lighting. (Dorms July-Aug. £6.50; Sept.-June £6. Private rooms £8-8.50. Laundry £2.50.) **Mary Conway's Greenlea B&B** (tel. 29049) on Station Rd. between the cathedral and the station, has comfy rooms and very helpful management (£12-13.50; open Mar.-Oct.). **Derrynane House** (tel. 28464), in The Square, will put a roof over your head right in the middle of town (£18, all with bath).

Food and pubs go hand in hand, but there are a few alternatives. **Dunnes supermarket** (tel. 40700) lurks in the mall on O'Connell St. (open M-Tu and Sa 9am-6:30pm, W-F 9am-9pm, Su noon-6pm). **Pearl City,** O'Connell St. (tel. 21388) serves dozens of Chinese dishes late into the night (open daily until 1am). **Upper Crust,** off Market Sq. (tel. 43261), sells high-class helpings for low prices (open M-Th 8am-8pm, F-Sa 8am-6pm, Su 8:30am-2:30pm). **Considine's,** Abbey St. (tel. 29054), serves huge, salad-surrounded sandwiches (£3.50) and tempting chicken plates (£4.50). **Cruises Pub,** Abbey St. (tel. 41800), next to the Friary, is a dimly lit oldie whose uneven stone floor gives a premature feeling of intoxication (trad nightly and Sunday afternoons in summer, £4). **Brandon's Bar,** O'Connell St. (tel. 28133), serves huge plates of spuds, meat, and veggies (entrees £3.50) alongside its pints (trad W-Su). **Brogan's,** O'Connell St. (tel. 29859), supplies Irish stew (£5.50) in the afternoon or early evening. It becomes packed and smoky in the evening as young people flock here (trad Tu-W). Ennis has its fair share of dark and woody pubs serving dark and frothy pints, the darkest and woodiest being **The Usual Place,** 5 Market St. (tel. 20515). The *Clare Champion* has music listings.

There's no shortage of nightlife in Ennis. **Queen's** (tel. 28963), next to the Friary on Abbey St., has two swanky clubs, the bigger of which was just refurbished at the end of 1998 (Sa rave, Su 60s-80s, charts otherwise). The member's bar at the back serves until 2am (open W-Su, cover £5). **The Boardwalk,** above Brandon's, plays some indie music; regulars get their faces depicted on a gigantic Sgt. Pepper mural (open F-Sa, cover £3 before midnight, £4 after).

SIGHTS

Daniel O'Connell watches over the town from his square. The original O'Connells were Catholic landowners dispossessed by Cromwell (see **History,** p. 56). In 1828, almost 200 years later, Ennis residents elected Catholic barrister Daniel O'Connell, soon to become "The Liberator," to represent them at Westminster (see p. 58). A 10-minute walk from the town center on Mill Rd. leads to the **Maid of Erin,** a life-size statue remembering the "Manchester Martyrs," three nationalists hanged in Manchester in 1867 (see also **Kilrush,** p. 267). Abbey St. leads northeast to the ruined and roofless 13th-century **Ennis Friary** (tel. 29100), famous for the slender panes and peaked points of its east window. *(Open mid-May to Sept. daily 9:30am-6:30pm. £1, students 40p.)* In 1375 the seminary became one of Ireland's most important pre-Reformation theological schools. Inside, depictions of the Passion adorn the 15th-century **McMahon tomb.** Across from the Friary, a block of sandstone inscribed with part of Yeats's "Easter 1916" remembers the Easter Rising (see p. 60). A few doors down from the Abbey House Hostel on Harmond Row, the **de Valera Library and Museum** (tel. 21616) adds a door from the Spanish Armada to its collection of the ex-Taoiseach's stuff, which includes his private car. *(Museum and library open M and Th 11am-5:30pm, Tu-W and F 11am-8pm. Free.)* IRA weapons and Land League banners recall Ennis's political life. Saturday is **Market Day** in Market Sq., where all conceivable wares are sold beneath a statue of crafty Daedalus.

■ Corofin

The small village of Corofin enjoys the water of seven lakes and the River Fergus, but it's only a few miles to the barren Burren. Tourists eager to reach Ennis or Doolin usually overlook Corofin's quiet charm. **Buses** travel to **Ennis** (M-Sa 1 per day, £6) and **Lahinch** (M-Sa 1 per day, £4.20). The **tourist office,** Church St. (tel. 37955), is in the

Clare Heritage Centre (open June-Sept. daily 10am-6pm). The **post office** is on Main St. (open M-F 9am-1pm and 2-5:30pm, Sa 9am-1pm). The **phone code** is 065.

The **Corofin Village Hostel and Camping Park,** Main St. (tel. 37683), offers clean, modern facilities, **bike rental** (£6 per day), internet access (£1 per hr.), and **bureau de change,** plus friendly and helpful hosts who can arrange bird watching trips (dorms £7.50, private rooms £9; camping £4, £10 per family; laundry £5; wheelchair accessible). The invisible hand doles out food from **Spar Market** on Main St. at reasonable prices (open daily 9am-8pm). The kids come to **Cahir's Bar** (tel. 37238) for live rock on weekends, pool, and murals of local folks (music 9:30pm; no cover). The **Corofin Arms** (tel. 37373), up the hill from the hostel, also has music (3 nights per week), but their guitars are tuned to trad and folk. On Thursday evenings from June to August, the **Teác Celide,** on Main St., near the post office, puts Clare heritage into action with organized music, song, set dancing, poetry, and the obligatory brown bread and tea—beware: visitors are often asked to share something from their own folk tradition (starts at 9pm; £3).

You can find a "microcosm of 19th-century Ireland" at the **Clare Heritage and Genealogical Research Centre,** Church St. (tel. 37955). The Genealogical Centre caters to the thousands of people whose ancestors emigrated from Clare, providing birth, marriage, and death certificates. The **Heritage museum** across the street houses artifacts from the potato famine, emigration, and landowner days—all in an old, decaying Protestant church (£2, students £1.50). A history trail that stays within 2 mi. of the center leads you to Corofin's sights. The trail visits well-preserved 12th-century **St. Tola's Cross** and the battlefield where, in 1318, Conor O'Dea defeated the intruding Normans and put off English domination for another two centuries. Three miles south of Corofin, **Dysert O'Dea Castle and Archaeology Centre** (tel. 37722), housed in a restored 15th-century tower, uncovers the more distant past and explains the archaeological features of the surrounding lands (open May-Sept. daily 10am-6pm; £2.50). The **Dromore National Nature Reserve** and its peaceful, swan-inhabited lakes are about 8 mi. west of Corofin. Follow signposts to Ruan Village; the reserve is signposted from there. Guided tours are available, but the trails allow you to ramble. Fishing is rampant in the lakes and rivers around. At **Burke's** (tel. 37677) you can hire a gillie (a fishing guide, £35-40) or a boat with a day's notice.

CLARE COAST

Those traveling between Co. Clare and Co.–Kerry should take the 20-minute **Tarbert-Killimer car ferry** across the Shannon estuary, avoiding an 85 mi. drive by way of Limerick (see **Tarbert,** p. 252).

■ Kilrush

The route to the Clare Coast from either Tarbert or Limerick passes through Kilrush (pop. 2900), a colorful market town with wide streets, the coast's only marina, and a strong sense of its history.

PRACTICAL INFORMATION Bus Éireann (tel. 24177 in Ennis) stops in Market Sq. on its way to **Ennis** (M-Sa 3-5 per day, Su 2-3 per day) and **Kilkee** (M-Sa 2-4 per day, Su 1-2 per day). The tourist information office is in the **Kilrush Heritage Centre,** Town Hall, Market Sq. (tel. 51577; open May-Sept. M-Sa 9am-1pm and 2-5pm, Su noon-4pm). You can hear the town's bitter memories of the Great Famine on "Kilrush in Landlord Times," a self-guided cassette tour (£2) of the town's history. The tourist office changes money; there is also an **ATM** at **AIB,** Frances St. (tel. 51012; open M 10am-6pm, Tu-F 10am-3pm). **Bike rental** is available at **Gleesons,** Henry St. (tel. 51127), which is affiliated with Raleigh Rent-A-Bike (£7 per day, £30 per week). Anthony Malone's **pharmacy,** Frances St. (tel. 52555), has what you need (M-Sa 9am-6pm, Su 11am-1pm). The **Internet Bureau** (tel. 51061), beside the marina, provides access to the web (£2.50 per hr; call for hours). The **post office** is on Frances St. (open M-Sa 9am-5:30pm). The **phone code** is 065.

ACCOMMODATIONS, FOOD, AND PUBS Katie O'Connor's Holiday Hostel (tel. 51133), next to the AIB on Frances St., provides decent quarters. Before you go to bed, read the history of your room; it dates back to 1797. (Dorms £7; doubles £18; quads £25.) The **Kilrush Creek Lodge** (tel. 52855), in the cyan and red building across from the marina, is a large, clean, group-oriented accommodation with an affiliated adventure center next door (dorms £13, doubles £30; full Irish breakfast included; laundry £4). **B&Bs** are plentiful and expensive.

You can stock your larder at the **Mace Supermarket** (tel. 51885), on the first floor of the hostel. The **Central Restaurant** (tel. 52477), on Market Sq., prepares light fare at the right price. Sandwiches, pastries, quiche: everything but the Coke is made on the premises (M-Sa 9am-6pm, Su 11am-3pm). Fresh-baked bread is waiting for you at **Cosidines** (tel. 51095), across the street from the hostel, a 150-year-old bakery that still uses the same ovens and mixers that it used in the 1850s (open M-Sa 8am-6pm). Of Kilrush's 15 or so pubs, at least one has music each night during the summer. Kilrush's musical history is celebrated every night but Monday and Friday in **Crotty's Pub** (tel. 52470), Market Sq. It was here in the 1950s that Lizzy Crotty helped repopularize trad. Crotty's also cooks up pub grub and offers beautifully restored rooms for an elegant escape (£15).

SIGHTS If you're really interested in the nitty gritty details of historical Kilrush, pick up Paul Gleeson's *Kilrush: A Walking Tour* at the tourist office for £2.50. In town, a monument facing the Town Hall remembers the Manchester Martyrs of 1867 (see also **Ennis**, p. 264). Just outside town on the ferry road, the dirt paths of 420-acre **Kilrush Forest Park** promise adventure, romance, and an ultimate return to town. They may not deliver, but they're pretty and not long enough that you can't backtrack to town. Kilrush's real attraction, however, is offshore **Scattery Island,** where monastic ruins, deserted churchyards, and a round tower could use some company; the island has been uninhabited since the 1970s. Boats depart regularly in summer (June-Sept. 4-5 per day, £4.50 return) and irregularly in other seasons. The tourist office books tours, and transportation can be arranged with **Gerald Griffen** (tel. 51327) or **Martin Brennan** (tel. 52031). Both also embark on two- or three-hour dolphin watching and fishing expeditions during the summer (£9). On the mainland, the **Scattery Island Centre,** Merchant's Quay (tel. 52139), explains the island's history and ecology. *(Open mid-June to mid-Sept. daily 9:30am-6:30pm. Free.)* The **Éigse Mrs. Crotty** ("Rise up Mrs. Crotty!") festival celebrates the glory of the traditional Irish concertina with lessons, lectures, and non-stop trad August 13-15, 1999.

■ Kilkee

Three years ago, Kilkee was a quiet, small-time beach resort on the southwest tip of Co. Clare. A few rows of stately Victorian houses overlooked a perfect crescent of white sand, while gorgeous cliffs cut islands out of the coast nearby. But curious government tax incentives in the past three years have produced a massive building spree. The numer of homes tripled, prices tripled, and dozens of ugly, connected, cinderblock housing units were packed into formerly grand old estates overnight. Still, the surrounding cliff scenery remains spectacular and the pub scene is as lively as ever. If your greatest ambitions are to eat, drink, and lounge on Irish beaches, you could live your whole life between the beach and O'Curry St.

PRACTICAL INFORMATION Bus Éireann (tel. 24177 in Ennis) leaves from Kett's Bar for **Limerick** (2hr., 3-4 per day) via **Ennis** (1hr.) and for **Galway** with an hour-long stop at the **Cliffs of Moher** (4hr. total, 2-3 per day). The **tourist office** (tel. 56112) pops up in the central square next to the Stella Maris Hotel (open June-Sept. daily 10am-6pm). The brand-new **ATM** at the **Bank of Ireland,** O'Curry St. (tel. 56053), puts cash in your pocket (open M 10am-12:30pm and 1:30-5pm, Tu-F 10am-12:30pm and 1:30-4pm). Rent **bikes** and get your greens from **Rosarie's** (tel. 56622), O'Curry St. (£6 per day, £32 per week; deposit £20; open May-Sept. daily 9am-11pm). **Williams** (tel. 56041), opposite the post office on Circular Rd., also rents bikes (£7 per day; deposit £30). The **post office** (tel. 56001) is on Circular Rd. (open M-F 9am-5:30pm, Sa 9am-12:30pm). Kilkee's **phone code** is 065.

ACCOMMODATIONS AND FOOD The family-run **Kilkee Hostel (IHH),** O'Curry St. (tel. 56209), creates an atmosphere of fellowship among travelers and itinerant geology students who gather in the large living room (dorms £7; sheets 50p; laundry £4). **Dunearn House B&B** (tel. 56545) sits atop high cliffs on the coastal road left of the bay (singles £23.50; doubles £34). **Cunningham's** (tel. 56430) neatly arranges a battalion of caravans; turn left onto the coast road and take the first turnoff behind the pink building (tents £7-8; open Easter-Sept.).

A **Central Stores** supermarket (tel. 56249) vends victuals on the corner of O'Curry St. and Circular Rd. (open in summer M-Th 9am-8:30pm, F-Su 9am-9pm; in winter daily 9am-8pm). **The Pantry,** O'Curry St. (tel. 56576), is a culinary oasis in a desert of fast food (lunches £4-5, dinners £8-10; open June-Sept. daily 9:30am-noon, 12:30pm-5pm, and 6:30-9:30pm). In the alley behind The Pantry, the **Country Cooking Shop** makes desserts for the decadent traveler. A good bet for breakfast or tea, **Eats & Treats** (tel. 56866) also serves snacks to hungry beach bums (open June-Oct. daily 9am-7pm). **Purtills** (tel. 56900), O'Curry St., is a full restaurant—a rare breed in these parts (open Easter-Sept. daily 6-10pm, Oct.-Mar. Sa-Su 6-10pm).

PUBS Kilkee's pub crawl is famously fun. The palatial bar and large stage of **The Strand Bar** (tel. 56177), on the beach near the tourist office, is a good place to start. From there, head to **Michael Martin's Pub,** opposite the tourist office. If you're still standing (get up!), the next stop is the **Central Bar** (tel. 56103), O'Curry St., which offers a pool table, dark red wood, and plenty of seating. The handy Limerick chef who rebuilt the **Old Bistro** (tel. 56898) with his wife three years ago decorated it with choice farm tools. Don't be alarmed if you see twice as many going out as you did going in—you're drunk. **Richie's,** O'Curry St. (tel. 56597), has an informal setting. The **Myles Creek Pub** (tel. 56670), also on O'Curry St., has both a bar and a lounge, although it is often hard to tell which is which (especially when you're drunk! Trad Mondays). **O'Mara's** (tel. 56286) is a traditional Irish bar: old men with little pints of Guinness for teeth. After last call, clubbers head to **Waterfront,** O'Curry St. (tel. 56838), above the amusement center. Music pumps from 11pm to 2am (cover £3).

SIGHTS The spectacular **Westend Cliff Walk** begins at the end of the road to the left of the seafront and climbs easily up to the top of the cliffs. Poets can bring their notebooks, but it will take much scribbling to capture this sea-hewn beauty in words. Two sets of **Diamond Rocks** lie on the coast: the original is a slippery, kelp-coated mussel bed next to the harbour to which locals bring nets at low tide; the "new" Diamond Rocks are quartz rocks farther up the coast. A gravel path from the car park leads to the original rocks. Four **Pollock Holes** provide natural rock pools for swimming. The fourth is known as a men's nudist bathing spot, although a far more popular one is Burns' Cove, past the golf course on the other side of the coast. The path out to the new Diamond Rocks leads into **Loop Head Drive,** which runs through small villages, ruined farmhouses, and plenty of pasture to the Loop Head Lighthouse at the very tip of Co. Clare. On the way, it passes through **Carrigaholt,** a village 7 mi. south of Kilkee on the Shannon Estuary. Boat trips (tel. (088) 584711) geared for dolphin sighting "with 100% success" shove off from Carrigaholt into waters where approximately 60 bottle-nosed dolphins have made their home (£10).

■ Milltown Malbay

Milltown Malbay, 20 mi. north of Kilkee, is what Doolin was in the early 80s: the place to be for music. While Doolin moved from impromptu sessions to paid concerts long ago, Milltown is the real deal, and as superb musicians continue to move here from all over the country, things are only getting better. The high point of the year is a large music festival hosted by the Willie Clancy School of Traditional Music (tel. 84148). During **"Willie Week,"** July 3-10, 1999, thousands of musicians, instrument-makers, fans, tourists, and craic addicts will flock here from all corners of the globe to celebrate the famous Irish piper who was born here. Participants pay £50 for the week's lectures, lessons, and recitals, while the musically challenged are given a wide variety of set-dancing classes. The incessant trad sessions in the town's packed pubs are free but range in quality. Accommodations are booked months in advances but the notice board at the community center in town can provide some leads. As there are no hostels and little transportation, Milltown doesn't get many tourists the rest of the year. Two miles to the west, a vague sprawl of B&Bs surrounds the clean beach at Spanish Point, where 60 survivors of the 1588 Armada swam to shore only to be executed by the local sheriff.

The **Bank of Ireland** (tel. 84018) is next to O'Friels (open M-W and F 10am-12:30pm and 1:30-4pm, Th 10am-12:30pm and 1:30-5pm). **Byrne's** on Ennis Rd. (tel. 84079) rents and repairs **bikes** and has a limited supply of camping equipment (bikes £7 per day, £30 per week; deposit £40; open M-Sa 9:30am-6:30pm). Marie Kelly's **pharmacy** (tel. 84440) is on Main St. (open M-Sa 9:30am-6pm, W 9:30am-7pm). Milltown Malbay's **phone code** booms 065 on its *bodhrán*.

Right in the center of town, **Ward's B&B** (tel. 84684) has beautiful rooms in a tastefully renovated old house run by a likeable and expanding young family (in summer £13, in winter £12). The affordable **Station House** (tel. 84008) at the old railway station, five minutes down the road from Cleary's (below), has huge beds and is run by friendly twins (£15). **Campers** take refuge above the Spanish Point beach. **Spar Supermarket & Bakery,** Main St. (tel. 84093), sells super groceries (open M-Sa 9am-9pm, Su 9am-1:30pm). **Mary's Place Restaurant & Pizzeria,** Ennis Rd. (tel. 84551), is a little bit of heaven in Milltown (open July-Aug. M-Sa 10am-8pm, Su noon-8pm; Sept.-June M-Sa 10:30am-6pm.)

Milltown squeezes 15 pubs into two blocks; on any given night, several of them host sessions. At **Cleary's** (tel. 84201), an easy-going, busy bar just off the main street on the Ennistymon road, musicians often outnumber listeners. It's locally known as "The Blond's" after a former proprietor. **Clancy's** (tel. 84077) also has excellent music and occasionally opens up a tent out back for bigger concerts. The sign above **O'Friel's** (tel. 84275) still says "Lynch's" after all these years; "a local favorite with decent grub" would be more accurate.

■ Lahinch

The tiny resort town of Lahinch lies in a corner of the mile-wide strand of smooth sand deposited by the Inagh River. World-class golf courses add to the area's natural attractions, while surfers, swimmers, and beachcombers flock here to frolic in the Atlantic. Those seeking the tacky arcades, bars, and discos one usually finds in seaside retreats will not be disappointed. **Buses** (tel. 24177) roll in two to three times a day during the summer from Cork, Galway, Limerick, Ennis, and Doolin to the edge of town near the golf courses. There's a **bank** and **ATM** in Ennistymon, about 2 mi. east, and an **ATM** is due to open in town in 1999. The **bureau de change** (tel. 81743) is at the top of Main St. (open M-Su 9am-10pm). The **post office** (tel. 81001) is on Main St. (open M-F 9am-1pm and 2-5:30pm, Sa 9am-1pm). Cito Gaston hits the **phone code** under par at 065.

Clean, comfortable bunkrooms and a waterfront location score a birdie at the **Lahinch Hostel (IHH)** (tel. 81040), on Church St. in the town center (dorms £7.50; doubles £22; laundry £2; **bike rental** £7 per day). **The Village Hostel (IHH)** (tel. 81550), a 2 mi. bus ride west in Liscannor, features a huge echoing kitchen, locally mined foscilite stone floors, and a laid-back way of life. (Dorms £7; private rooms £9, with packed lunch and dinner £15. Sheets 50p. **Camping** £4 per person.) The **Lahinch Caravan & Camping Park** on N67 (tel. 81424) has plenty of space for camping (£3 per tent; open Easter-Sept.) and rents bikes (£7 per day; open daily 9am-9pm). **B&Bs** line the Milltown Malbay Rd.

Mrs. O'Brien's Kitchen, Main St. (tel. 81020), serves stomach-soothing breakfasts all day in addition to a varied lunch and dinner menu and hosts a wine bar from 9pm to 1am for those seeking an alternative to the usual pub scene (open Mar.-Sept. daily 8am-1am). **Kenny's Bar,** Main St. (tel. 81433), resounds most nights with ballads, trad, and rock. Its tasty Irish stew (£4.85) was once written up in the *New York Times.* The crowded, woody interior of **O'Looneys Bar & Restaurant** (tel. 81414) serves decent food and looks out at the crashing waves and the surfers they carry. After the 18th hole, try **The Nineteenth Pub** (tel. 81440), the best place to swap golf stories and hear music nightly at 9:30pm. Two discos rock this tiny town: **The Claremont Hotel** on Main St. (open F-Su) has a popular 60s, 70s, and 80s music night on Sundays (cover £4), while **O'Looneys** hosts its own beachside disco on Thursdays and Saturdays (cover £4).

The arcades, rides, and general amusements along the beach should provide at least an evening of entertainment. **Seaworld** (tel. 81900), off the beach, has a swimming pool and a mediocre collection of live fish (£3.80, students £2.75; open 10am-8pm). For excellent deals on locally knitted sweaters, visit **Kenny Wollen Mills** on Main St. The Cliffs of Moher are a mere 15 minutes away by bus, and ferries leave from nearby Liscannor (Lahinch-Doolin bus route) for the Aran Islands (see p. 278).

■ Cliffs of Moher

The Cliffs of Moher are justifiably one of Ireland's most famous sights. The view from the edge leads 700 ft. straight down into the open sea. These cliffs are so high that people actually see gulls whirling below them. Tour groups cluster where the road ends at the cliffs, although better views await a bit farther off the road. Occasionally marked paths wander along the cliffs; most tourists drop away after the first curve. American poet Wallace Stevens based his poem "The Irish Cliffs of Moher" on photographs, as he'd never been here—you shouldn't miss the chance.

Three miles south of Doolin, the Cliffs brush against R478; cars pay £1 for use of the parking lot. **Bus Éireann** clangs by on the summer-only Galway-Cork route (M-Sa 3 per day). The 26-mile **Burren Way** and several non-linear bike trails more elusively weave through raised limestone and beds of wildflowers from Doolin (3hr.) and Liscannor (3½hr.). Hitchers report mixed success in finding rides here. The **tourist office** (tel. (065) 81171) houses a bureau de change (open Apr.-Oct. 9:30am-5:30pm), and a teashop rejuvenates weary travelers. **O'Brien's Tower,** built in 1835 as a viewing tower for tourists, marks Clare's first attempt at promoting local tourism yet adds nothing to the thrilling cliffside view (open Apr.-Oct. daily 9am-7:30pm; £1, students 60p). **Aran Ferries** (tel. 81368) operates a fantastic cruise that leaves from the pier in nearby Liscannor and sails along right under the cliffs (55min., 1 per day, £10).

■ Doolin

Ireland sees Doolin much as Europe views Ireland—as a small, beautiful, windy, rural, musical, depopulated, overtouristed place where life revolves around pubs. Most of Doolin's two hundred or so permanent residents run its four hostels, countless B&Bs, and three pubs famous for their traditional music and incomparable craic. The remaining residents farm the land and, in their spare time, wonder how so many backpackers ended up in their small corner of the word. But not even the crowds can stop the streams from bubbling through the fields or dent the pervasive sense of peace.

The 8 mi. paved and bicycle-friendly segment of the **Burren Way** links Doolin to the Cliffs of Moher. The steep climb along the road from Doolin to the Cliffs earns you the thrilling glide back down and the anticipation of another night of carousing at the pubs. For those who prefer two feet to two wheels, the walk to the Cliffs is manageable (approximately 2hr. each way). Boats leave the pier on the other end of town for the Aran Islands, but boats from Galway and Rossaveal are cheaper under almost any circumstances (see **Galway City,** p. 283).

ORIENTATION AND PRACTICAL INFORMATION

Doolin is shaped like a barbell, made up of two villages about a mile apart from each other. **Fisherstreet**, the **Lower Village**, is closer to the shore than **Roadford**, which is farther up the road and separated from Fisherstreet by a stretch of farmland. A traveling **bank** comes to Lower Village every Thursday from 11am to 2pm, but there's a permanent **bureau de change** at the post office. The nearest **ATM** is in Ennistymon, 5 mi. to the southeast. The **Doolin Bike Store** (tel. 74260), outside the Aille River Hostel, will set you up with a bike (£7 per day; open M-Sa 9am-8pm). **Simply Cycling** (tel. 74429) rents healthy bikes (£5 per day; deposit £40) and repairs the afflicted (open Apr.-Oct. daily 9:30am-9:30pm; call Nov.-Mar.). The **post office** (tel. 74209) operates from the Upper Village (open M-F 9am-1pm and 2-5:30pm, Sa 9am-1pm). Doolin's **phone code** is 065.

ACCOMMODATIONS

Tourists pack Doolin in the summer, so book ahead for hostels. B&Bs are common, but those along the main road tend to be expensive.

⍟**Aille River Hostel (IHH)** (tel. 74260), halfway between the villages, in a cute cottage by the river. Small, relaxed hostel with groovy ambience. Local musicians often stop by the Aille to warm up before gigs in the pubs. Free laundry! No phone. Dorms July-Aug. £7, Sept.-May £6.50; doubles £16; triples £24. **Camping** £3.50. Open mid-Mar. to mid-Nov.

Flanaghan's Village Hostel (tel. 74564), ½mi. up the road from the Upper Village. This brand-new hostel boasts spacious sunny rooms, a modern kitchen, mammoth leather couches, and floors with a story. Plus, you'll have plenty of time to sober up on the long walk home. Dorms £7, off season £6.50. Laundry £1.50.

Rainbow Hostel (IHH) (tel. 74415), Upper Village. Just a few steps from those pubs of legend, McGann's and McDermott's. Small, with pastel rooms and a casual atmosphere. Free 1½hr. guided walking tours of the Burren for hostelers. Dorms July-Aug. £7.50, Sept.-June £7; doubles July-Aug. £16. Laundry £3.

Doolin Hostel (IHH) (tel. 74006), Lower Village. Run by "Paddy," as he is affectionately known to visitors, this quiet, modern hostel offers more than the average budget accommodation: a shop, a **bureau de change,** free tennis (and rackets), and bus ticket sales. Very clean and comfortable. All buses stop outside their door daily. Dorms £7.50; doubles £18. Sheets 50p. Laundry £2.50. Reception 8am-9pm. Bikes £6 per day for hostelers. MC, Visa.

⍟**Westwind B&B** (tel. 74227), Upper Village, behind McGann's, in the same driveway as the Lazy Lobster. Quentin Tarantino stayed here in '92, just before making *Reservoir Dogs*. The sane find it relaxing, pleasant, friendly, and clean, and they report no threats to their ears. Vegetarian or meaty breakfasts available. Helpful advice for spelunkers and other Burren explorers. £12.

Doolin Cottage (tel. 74762), one door down from the Aille. Run by a friendly young couple and often used by backpackers when the Aille River Hostel is full. One reader called to say that "Carol Spencer rocks." Thanks, kind reader—we think so too. Doubles £22, with bath £24. Open Mar.-Nov.

Campsite (tel. 74458), near the harbor, has a kitchen, laundry facilities, and a view of the Cliffs of Moher. £4 per tent plus £1.50 per person. Showers 50p. Laundry £3.

FOOD AND PUBS

Doolin has many excellent but costly restaurants, and all three pubs serve excellent grub. In addition, the **Doolin Deli** (tel. 74633), near O'Connor's in the Lower Village, packs overstuffed sandwiches (£1.30) and stocks groceries (open June-Sept. M-Sa 8:30am-9pm, Su 9:30am-9pm). The **Doolin Café** (tel. 74795), Upper Village, emits positive karma, feeding and caring for meat lovers, vegetarians, and vegans alike. Talented chefs use local ingredients. (Sandwiches £2-4; dinners pricy. Open daily Apr.-Oct. 10am-10pm). **Bruach na h Aille** (tel. 74120) has a working antique phonograph player and delicious, creative home-grown dishes; the three-course early-bird special

(£10) will make your stomach purr (early-bird special until 7:30; open daily St. Patrick's day-Oct. 6-9:30pm).

The pubs of Doolin are well known for their musical brilliance. Both O'Connor's and McGann's have won awards for the best trad music in Ireland, but many prefer McDermott's. **McGann's** (tel. 74133), Upper Village, has music nightly at 9pm in the summer, weekends at 9pm in the winter, and figgety Irish stew year round (£5). **McDermott's** (tel. 74328), Upper Village, with its warming fireplace, ranks right up there with McGann's (entrees around £5; music nightly in summer, weekends in winter). Most summer standing-room-only sessions start at 9:30pm. **O'Connor's** (tel. 74168), Lower Village, is the busiest of the three, with drink, song, and music nightly and Sunday afternoons all year. The pub also runs a B&B (tel. 74242; £16 with bath).

Why Worry?

There are only two things to worry about: either you are well or you are sick. If you are well then there is nothing to worry about. If you are sick there are only two things to worry about: either you will get better or you will get worse. If you get better, you have nothing to worry about. If you get worse, you have only two things to worry about: either you will go to heaven or hell. If you go to heaven, you will have nothing to worry about, and if you go to hell, you will be so busy shaking old friends' hands that you won't have time to worry. —*Irish saying*

THE BURREN

The Burren comprises nearly 100 square miles and almost one third of Co. Clare's coastline. Visitors who go to the Burren as they would to the Blarney Stone or the Cliffs of Moher may find themselves disappointed and confused. Much like good craic, the Burren's beauty is both legendary and elusive. Jagged gray hills resemble skyscrapers turned to rubble, hidden depressions open up into labyrithian caves, and wildflowers found nowhere else in the world pepper the landscape. As Oliver Cromwell complained, "There is not wood enough to hang a man, nor water enough to drown him in, nor earth enough to bury him in." He shouldn't have worried, though; there are more than enough rocks to bash a man's skull in with and plenty of cliffs to throw him off of.

The best way to see the Burren is to walk or cycle in it. George Cunningham's *Burren Journey* series is worth a look (£4.50), as are Tim Robinson's meticulous maps (£5). The *Burren Rambler* maps (£2) are extremely detailed. All of the surrounding tourist offices (at Kilfenora, Ennis, Corofin, the Cliffs of Moher, or Kinvara) are bound to stock these maps and any other information on the Burren that you might need.

Bus service in the Burren is passable. **Bus Éireann** (tel. (065) 24177) connects **Galway** to towns in and near the Burren a few times a day during summer but infrequently during winter. Every weekday in summer (June-Oct.) some of those buses continue over the Shannon car ferry at Killimer to Killarney and Cork. Bus stops are the Doolin Hostel in **Doolin** (p. 271), Burke's Garage in **Lisdoonvarna** (p. 274), Linnane's in **Ballyvaughan** (p. 275), and Winkles in **Kinvara** (p. 276). Other infrequent but year-round buses run from some individual Burren towns to **Ennis**. Brian's **West Clare Shuttle** (tel. (091) 767801 or (088) 517963) supplies a door-to-door Galway to Doolin service every morning with stops at hostels in **Fanore** and **Lisdoonvarna** if arranged. Brian arrives in Doolin around noon and then turns around (£5; book ahead). Full-day bus tours from Galway are another popular way to see the Burren (see **Galway**, p. 291). **Hitchhiking** requires patience.

■ Kilfenora

A small town 5 mi. southeast of Lisdoonvarna along R478, Kilfenora, too, calls itself "the heart of the Burren." It's certainly a useful stopover, providing one-stop shopping for any trek into the Burren. Tourists, most of them on bicycles, delay here for a pint, some grub, and a walk through the **Burren Centre** (tel. 88030), which presents a lecture on the natural history of the region and shows an excellent film on Burren biology. (Open daily June-Sept. 9:30am-6pm; Mar.-May and Oct. 10am-5pm. Lecture and film £2.50, students £1.85.) The adjacent tea room serves cheap lunches, and the tourist office sells the helpful Burren Rambler map series for £2. Across from the grocery store on Main St. is the **post office** (tel. 88001; open M-F 9am-5:30pm, Sa 10am-1pm). The **phone code** is 065.

Bridgid and Tony's B&B (tel. 88148) has airy rooms, helpful information, and veggie breakfasts (singles £13; doubles £26). **Ms. Mary Murphy,** Main St. (tel. 88040), runs a central B&B with snug comforters (£14 with bath; open June-Sept.). Kilfenora has only three pubs. **Vaughan's** (tel. 88004) offers varied entertainment nightly (June-Sept.). The festivities include set dancing in the adjacent thatched cottage on Thursday and Sunday nights and open-air dancing on Sunday afternoons. For expat Texans, Vaughan's has a barbecue on Fridays and Sundays (£5; 7-9pm). **Linnane's** (tel. 88157) feels tourist lethargy in the afternoons but revives at night with trad sessions (nightly in summer, weekends in winter, supersession Wednesday). Red vinyl covers everything in **Nagle's** (tel. 88011) except the locals who flock here after work. No, there aren't any half-size people to go with the half-size door behind the bar (music F-Su).

Next to the Centre, Church of Ireland services are still held in the nave of the **Kilfenora Cathedral** (1st and 3rd Su of the month, 9:45am). The rest of the Cathedral and its graveyard stand open to the sky. The structure itself dates from 1190, but the site has held churches since the 6th century. (Tours July-Aug. £2.50, students £1.85. Ask at the tourist office.) West of the church is the elaborate **Doorty Cross,** one of the "seven crosses of Kilfenora" built in the 12th century. Although time and erosion have taken their toll, carved scenes of three bishops and Christ's entry into Jerusalem still adorn the cross. Odd birds and menacing heads cover its sides.

■ Lisdoonvarna

Four miles east of Doolin, Lisdoonvarna is a small, not quite picturesque, and not quite interesting collection of hotels and B&Bs. Originally a spa town, Lisdoonvarna's relative fame comes from its hot springs. During its **Matchmaking Festival,** by far the most well known of its kind, farm boys of all ages—their crops safely harvested, but with wild oats yet to sow—gather together to pick their mates (and, one hopes, vice versa). Matchmaker Willie Daley from Ennistymon presides over the five-week-long festival each September. Festival-goers and others take advantage of Lisdoonvarna's mineral springs at the **Spa Wells Health Centre,** Sulfur Hill Rd. (tel. 74023), at the bottom of the hill south of town. Lisdoonvarna began to boom when the springs were discovered in the early 1700s. If you can't stay for a bath, at least savor their aromatic sulfur water. (30p per glass; sulphur bath £8, full massage £18, sauna £5. Open June-Oct. daily 10am-6pm.) **Buses** head to Doolin and Lahinch daily from the main square during summer (1-3 per day). Lisdoonvarna's **phone code** is 065.

There are no hostels in Lisdoonvarna. To find a decent B&B for £15-16, close your eyes, point your finger, spin around until confused, open your eyes, et voilà! Or you can dream of that special someone under the foot-high comforters at **Mrs. O'Connor's Roncalli House** (tel. 74115; singles £16, doubles £25; all with bath). Colossal breakfasts are guaranteed at **The Banner Country Lodge** (tel. 74340), on Galway Rd., just off the main square (singles £15, doubles £30). The **Roadside Tavern,** Doolin Rd. (tel. 74494), looks more like an antique shop than a bar, but the nightly trad gives it away (Mar.-Sept. nightly at 9:30pm; Oct.-Feb. Sa only). The tavern also serves yummies (soup so light that it nearly floats off your spoon £1.30; serving noon-8:45pm). The **Hydro Hotel** (tel. 74005) does disco on Saturday nights (cover £5).

■ Carron

Imagine a mile-wide, five-yard-deep puddle in the middle of the Burren, with a pub high above and a hostel across the road. Don't worry, Carron is not just your imagination. The disappearing lake, called a turlough, is the largest in Europe. Carron is off a small road connecting Bellharbor to Killnaboy; to get there, drive (8min.), bike (25min.), or hike (1½hr.) south from Bell Harbor. Hitching odds approach zero. The hostel, called **Clare's Rock Hostel** (tel. (065) 89129), composes half the town. It opened in 1998 with brand new, clean, comfortable rooms with bath, tastefully decorated interior spaces, and handy management. (Dorms £7; private rooms £9. Laundry £5. Open May-Oct.) The pub, **Croide Na Boirne** (tel. (065) 89109), has a cold tap for tourists and a warm tap for locals; a warm pint takes longer to pour but tastes like nothing else. Gourmet grub specializes in cooked, broiled, and shredded local kids (kid burger £3.75; food served Apr.-Dec. noon-9:30pm). Four miles west and north of Carron, off the side of the road, is the **Poulnabrane Dolmen,** a well-known, photogenic group of Irish rocks. About 5000 years ago, over 25 people were put to rest with their pots and rocks under the five-ton capstone, only to be dug up by curious archaeologists in 1989. The rocks themselves predate the first humans. Two miles east of Carron, Ireland's only **perfumery** (tel. (065) 89102) makes some scents of the Burren's wildflowers.

■ Ballyvaughan

Along the jagged edge of Galway Bay, eight miles west of Kinvara on N67, Ballyvaughan is bona-fide Burren. Unfortunately, the Burren's natural desolation is interrupted by the man-made desolation of identical rows of "holiday cottages." A cute harbor, fine cake shops, and decent trad sessions partially redeem Ballyvaughan's aesthetic butt. The **phone code** is 065.

There's no hostel in Ballyvaughan, but the **Bridge Hostel** (tel. 76134) is an 8 mi. bus ride west to Fanore. Isolated in the fingers of the Burren, the Bridge is best for hikers, bikers, drivers, and lovers of open peat fires and home-cooked meals. (Dorms £6; doubles £17. Breakfast £3; dinner £4. Wash £2. Bikes £5. **Camping** £4 per person. Open Mar.-Oct.) B&B is available at **Gentian Villa** (tel. 77042), on the main road on the Kinvara side of town (£16 with bath; open Easter-Oct.), and at seaside **Oceanville** (tel. 77051), next door to Monk's on the pier (£16).

Spar Supermarket (tel. 77077) sells fresh bread from their bakery (open daily 9am-8pm). **An Féar Gorta** ("the hungry grass"; tel. 77023) by the pier serves tea and a mouth-watering array of wonderful cakes (£2) in a flourishing garden. You can read *The Legend of the Hag of Loughrask* while you wait for food. (Open June-Sept. M-Sa 11am-5:30pm). The **Tea Junction Café** (tel. 77289) tempts you to ruin your appetite with their famous rhubarb pie (£2). (Open daily 9am-6pm.) Helen remembers the vegetarians (veggie entrees around £5) and will provide breakfast and take-away. Down by the pier at **Monk's Pub** (tel. 77059), fishermen unload their catch right into the kitchen, while minstrels croon inside on Tuesday, Wednesday, and Saturday nights in summer. Back in town, **Greene's** (tel. 77147) is a small, card-playing locals' pub with an older crowd that knows where the Guinness runs best. Huge helpings of their one daily special (around £5) are hot from noon to midnight.

Prehistoric bears once inhabited the two million-year-old **Aillwee Cave** (I'LL WEE; tel. 77036), 2 mi. south of Ballyvaughan and almost 1 mi. into the mountain. The 30-minute tour is all about bears and fancy lighting effects, but most find the myriad of waterfalls and rocks more interesting than the average bear. (Open daily July-Aug. 10am-6:30pm; mid-Mar. to June and Sept. to early Nov. 10am-5:30pm. £4.25, students £3.50.) One mile out of Ballyvaughan on N67 is the turnoff for **Newtown Castle and Trail** (tel. 77216), where you can find the restored 16th-century home of the O'Loghlens, the princes of the Burren. The hour-long tour includes ancient Clare manuscripts and Bardic Poetry recitals. Another hour-long guided tour covers about a half-mile of beautiful hillside terrain, discusses the geology and archaeology of the Burren, and visits a Victorian folly "gazebo" (a children's miniature castle) and an 18th-century military waterworks system. (Open Easter-early Oct. daily 10am-6pm. Castle or trail tour £2, both £3.50.)

■ Kinvara

Despite the lines of cars that plow right through it every day on their way from Galway to the Burren, Kinvara (pop. 2300 and growing rapidly) is a fairly well-kept secret. If they knew that this fishing village has an excellent music scene, a vibrant artistic community, pubs of character, a well-preserved medieval castle, intriguing history, and lively locals, the drivers might stop. **Bus Éireann** connects Kinvara to **Galway** (£3.80) and **Doolin** (June-Sept. M-Sa 4 per day, Su 2 per day, £5.50). Would-be poets on their way to Yeats's summer homes (see **Coole Park and Thoor Ballylee,** p. 277) can rent a bike at **McMahon's** (tel. 637577), just up the street from the hostel on the Ballyvaughan Rd. (£5 per day, £25 per week; ID deposit). **Kinvara Pharmacy,** Main St. (tel. 637397), soothes your blisters (open M-Sa 9:30am-6pm). Mail your postcards at the **post office** (tel. 637101; open M-F 9am-1pm and 2-5:30pm, Sa 9am-1pm). The **phone code** is 091.

ACCOMMODATIONS AND FOOD Johnston's Hostel (IHH), Main St. (tel. 37164), uphill from the Quay, is a relaxing retreat, with fireplaces in the colorful eight-bed rooms. Cupid seems to have pitched camp on the roof: the owner, his sisters, and over a dozen others have met their mates here, as many others did back when the gigantic common room was a dance hall. (Dorms £7.50. **Camping** £4.50. Sheets £1. Showers 50p. Laundry £4. Lockout 12:30-7am. Open June-Sept.) The blossoming gardens of Mary Walsh's **Cois Cuain B&B** (tel. 637119), on the Quay, complement the carefully decorated rooms inside (doubles £36; open Apr.-Nov.). Right in town, the fabulous **Fallons** (tel. 637483) maintain an elegant B&B above their Spar with the help of their seven beautiful kids, ages 12 to 26 (doubles £36).

The **Londis** supermarket (tel. 637508) does its grocery thing on the main road (open M-Sa 9am-9pm, Su 9am-8pm). **Partners** (tel. 637503) makes hunger disappear with style (open M and W-Sa 10am-11pm, Su 12:30-10pm). Patrons of **Keogh's,** Main St. (tel. 637145), assure wary travelers that its Saturday and Sunday evening trad sessions are "the best in the West." The menu, served until 9:30pm, is a bit pricey, but daily specials are down to earth.

PUBS Kinvara has many more pubs of note than most towns its size. Across the street from the hostel is **Tully's** (tel. 637146), where a grocery and bar keep company in smoky surroundings. U.S. license plates of all things provide the atmosphere for the best impromptu trad sessions in Kinvara. The evening view of the bay from the candle-lit **Pierhead** (tel. 638188) is enough to set your heart aflutter. If that doesn't work, perhaps the lively trad (Tu, Th, and Sa) or the delicious dishes (£4-6) from the adjoining café will. **Greene's** (tel. 637110) is Kinvara's most traditional pub (established 1873) and has the sagging shelves, concrete floors, and friendly local patrons to prove it. **Winkle's** (tel. 637137) has music and set dancing Wednesday through Saturday, although Friday draws the most dancers (lessons Friday in winter 9pm, £2). Pots, pans, and pictures of Kinvara's yesteryear hang from **Connolly's** (tel. 637131) elaborately decorated walls, while a wall of flowers obscures the entrance. The small, intimate interior will nurture your relationship with your pint. **Ould Plaid Shawls** (tel. 637400) draws its energy and its name from the Irish Folk tradition. It features a younger, more exclusive crowd, spontaneous trad sessions whenever, and championship darts Tuesday at 10:30pm (£2 to play).

SIGHTS Dunguaire Castle (tel. 37108), 10 minutes from town on Galway Rd., is an excellent example of a Tower House, a popular type of dwelling for country gentlemen of the 16th century. *(Open May-Sept. daily 9:30am-5pm. £2.75, students £1.90.)* The narrow, winding staircase weaves its way to the battlements, which provide an expansive view of the town, sea, and countryside. Three small rooms with limited exhibits on the castle's history break up the ascent. From May to September, huge medieval banquets are held at 5:30 and 8:45pm, in which lords and ladies are entertained with music and a literary pageant during their meal (four course meal and wine £29). The first weekend in May, the town comes to a full boil with the **Cuckoo**

Fleadh, which brings over 200 musicians into town. The **Cruinniu Na Mbad** festival (Gathering of the Boats) is a lively early August event when Galway hookers come down to Kinvara for a racy weekend.

■ Doorus Peninsula

Next to Kinvara, the Doorus Peninsula reaches out into Galway Bay. The house that Yeats and Lady Augusta Gregory inhabited while planning the Abbey Theatre (see p. 64) and collaborating on plays is now the isolated **Doorus House Hostel (An Óige/ HI)** (tel. 637512). Originally the country seat of an expatriate French aristocrat, this well-appointed hostel sits gracefully among old oak trees and peers out on the great expanse of a tidal estuary. (June-Sept. dorms £7; Oct.-May £5.50. Sheets 80p. Reception 5-10:30pm.) For those not enamored of nature, it's probably best to stay in Kinvara, but for families with cars, hikers, and bikers, Doorus is righteous. Three castles, several holy wells, a handful of ringforts, a cave, winged critters, panoramic views, and boggy islands await the rambler; most are detailed in *Kinvara: A Rambler's Map and Guide*, available in town for £2. A 10 mi. round trip west from the hostel to the **Aughinish Peninsula** offers views of the Burren across the bay accompanied by splashing waves. The more convenient blue-flag **Traught Strand** is just a five-minute walk from the hostel. Campers can pitch a tent in the field nearby and wake to the slosh of surf. After a hike, the **Traveller's Inn** (tel. 637116) pub and grocery at Knockgarra, in the middle of the peninsula, is a great place to relax over an old-school pint (open for groceries daily 9am-10pm). The **Galway-Doolin bus** does not pass through Doorus but will stop on request at the turnoff on Ballyvaughan Rd. (June-Sept. M-Sa 4 per day, Su 2 per day; Oct.-May M-Sa 1 per day). From there the hostel is 2 mi. (follow the signs toward the beach).

■ Coole Park and Thoor Ballylee

W. B. Yeats's two best-known residences are about 20 mi. south of Galway near Gort, where N18 meets N66. One is now a ruin and national park; the other has been restored to reflect its condition when Yeats lived there. Neither is accessible by bus; biking from Kinvara is the best option.

Located west off the N18 one mile north of Gort, the **Coole Park** nature reserve was once the estate of Lady Augusta Gregory, a friend and collaborator of Yeats (see **Literary Traditions,** p. 64). To Yeats, the estate represented the beautiful aristocratic order, which crass industrialists and the wars of the 1920s were destroying: "ancestral trees/Or gardens rich in memory glorified/Marriages, alliances and families/And every bride's ambition satisfied." Although the house was ruined by the 1922 Civil War (see p. 60), the yew walk and garden have been preserved. The famous great copper beech "autograph tree" in the picnic area bears the initials of some important Irish figures: George Bernard Shaw, Sean O'Caseld, Douglas Hyde (first president of Ireland), and Yeats himself. The **Coole Park's Visitors Centre** (tel. (091) 631804) is in the right place, but it eschews Yeats in favor of local rocks, trees, and furry wildlife. *(Open mid-Apr. to mid-June Tu-Su 10am-5pm; mid-June to Aug. daily 9:30am-6:30pm; Sept. daily 10am-5pm. Last admission 45min. before closing. £2, students £1.)* **Coole Lake,** where Yeats watched nine-and-fifty swans "all suddenly mount/And scatter wheeling in great broken rings/Upon their clamorous wings," is about a mile from the garden. The swans are still here in winter.

Three miles north of Coole Park, a road turns off Galway Rd. and runs a mile to **Thoor Ballylee.** In 1916, Yeats bought this 13th- and 14th-century tower for £35, renovated it, and lived here with his family off and on from 1922 to 1928. While he was cloistered here writing "Meditations in Time of Civil War," Republican forces blew up the bridge by the tower. In Yeats's account, they "forbade us to leave the house, but were otherwise polite, even saying at last 'Good-night, thank you.'" A film on Yeats's life informs visitors in the **Visitors Centre** (tel. (091) 631436) while a coffee shop feeds them. *(Open Easter-Sept. daily 10am-6pm. £3, students £2.50.)*

ARAN ISLANDS

The three Aran Islands (Oileáin Árann)—Inishmore, Inishmaan, and Inisheer—rise up out of Galway Bay 15 mi. southwest of Galway City. Once the islands were stark slabs of limestone much like the Burren in Co. Clare, but with centuries of toil, farmers piled the fields of stones into mazes of walls, mixed a thin soil from seaweed, sand, and manure, and managed to eke out a secluded existence. For the most part, however, the islands have been left to themselves. Iron age peoples liked the isolation and built awesome ring-forts on the edges of precipices to ensure it. Early Christians, too, found spiritual inspiration in the Arans' solitary, rugged terrain and left ruins of ancient churches and monasteries to prove it. Clans sought to control the islands during medieval times, and Elizabeth I set up a garrison here. The islands' dominant position in the mouth of the Galway Bay for a time gave the islands some strategic military and commercial importance, but fishing and farming long occupied most of the islanders.

Although the jagged cliffs, pristine beaches, abandoned fields pocked with wildflowers, and rocky coves create a startling landscape, the islands are more famous for their cultural isolation. Dublin-born writer John Millington Synge met with Yeats in 1894 looking for some creative criticism. Yeats told him to go to the Arans, learn Irish, and write plays about the islanders. Synge did and became instantly famous (see **Literary Traditions,** p. 63). Robert Flaherty's groundbreaking film *Man of Aran* (1934) added to the islands' fame. Helped by this artistic attention, the islands' reputation for harboring traditional ways of life has stimulated a small tourist industry.

During July and August, crowds of curious visitors surround every monument and fill every pub on Inishmore. The empty spaces between the sights are still deserted, however. Visitors are rarer on Inishmaan and Inisheer, the two smaller islands, but their numbers are rising as the inter-island ferries become larger and more frequent. The scenery remains awe-inspiring, regardless of the number of people who see it. The lifestyle also remains traditional—locals still make *curraghs* (small boats made from curved wicker rods tied with string and covered with cowskin and black tar). Some retain local styles of dress, footwear, and fishing, and almost all speak Irish. Many foreign visitors express a sense of "invading" the island, and there is certainly a tangible difference in attitude toward natives—and even outsider-natives—from that generally found on the mainland. The islands are where many of the Irish go to explore their own roots. The **phone code** for all three islands is partying like it's 099.

GETTING THERE

Three ferry companies—**Island Ferries, O'Brien Shipping/Doolin Ferries,** and **Liscannor Ferries**—operate boats to the Aran Islands. They reach the islands from four points of departure: **Galway** (1½hr. to Inishmore), **Rossaveal** several miles west of Galway (30min. to Inishmore), **Doolin** (30min. to Inisheer), and **Liscannor** (30min. to Inisheer). Ferries serving Inishmore are reliable (always leaving daily) and generally on time. Even in the summer, ferries to the smaller islands are less certain. There is no charge to bring bicycles on board. If the ferry leaves from Rossaveal, the company making the trip will provide a shuttle bus from Galway City to Rossaveal, usually for £3. The hitch is difficult. Flying with **Aer Árann** is double the cost, double the fun, and a fraction of the time.

  Island Ferries (tel. (091) 561767, after hours 72273), based in the Galway Tourist Office. The Aran Sea Bird serves all 3 islands year-round from Rossaveal (35min., £15 return). A bus connects the tourist office in Galway with the ferry port (departs 1½hr. before sailing time, £4 return). The Sea Sprinter connects Inishmore with Inisheer via Inishmaan (£10 return per island). They also offer a package deal: the bus from Galway, return ferry to Inishmore, and one night's accommodation at the Mainistir House Hostel with breakfast for £21, with B&B instead for £24.

Aran Islands

Brannock
Islands

Inishmore (Inis Mór)

The Seven Churches
(Na Seacht d'Teampaill)

Clochán na
Carraige

Onaght
(Eoghanacht)

Dún
Eoghanachta

Kilmurvy
(Cill Mhuirbhigh)

Dún Aengus
(Dún Aonghasa)

*Blind
Sound*

Oatquarter

Teampall I Chiaráin

Heritage Center
(Ionad Árann)

Kilronan
(Cill Rónáin)

Killeany
Port

*Killeany
Bay*

Black Fort
(Dún Dúchathair)

Temple Benan
(Teampall Bheanáin)

*Clinewalee
Point*

Puffing Holes

Synge's Chair
(Cathaoir Synge)

*Gregory's
Sound
(Sunda Ghrídra)*

Dún Chonchúir

Dún Fearbhaí

*Dog's
Head*

Lighthouse
*Straw
Island*

Museum (Museam)

Port

Loch Ceann Gainimh

Loch Mhuirbhigh

Leaba Dhairmada 'is Ghráinne
(Bed of Diarmuid and Bráinne)

Baile an Mhothair

Trá Leitreach

An Córa

Cill
Cheannannach

Port

An Sunda
Salach

An Baile
Thíos

Baile an Lurgáin

Tobar Éinne

*Inishmaan
(Inis Meáin)*

Cnoc Raithni

Baile an Chaisleáin

St. Kevin's Church
(Teampall Chaomháin)

Formna

Plassy Wreck

Dún Formna

Cill na Seacht nInion

Lighthouse

Inisheer (Inis Oirr)

*South Sound
(An Sunda ó Dheas)*

Walking Trails

N

0 —— 3 miles

0 —— 3 kilometers

O'Brien Shipping per Doolin Ferries (tel. (065) 74455 in Doolin, (091) 567283 in Galway; after hours (065) 71710). Year-round service connects Doolin and Galway to the Aran Islands. Galway to any island £12 return. Doolin to Inishmore £20 return, to Inishmaan £18 return, and to Inisheer £15 return. ISIC discount £3. Galway-Aran-Doolin £25. All trips from Doolin include inter-island travel; otherwise, inter-island trips £5 return. Cars always £100.

Liscannor Aran Ferries (tel. 065) 81368). Ferries depart twice per day from Liscannor and stop at Inishmaan and Inisheer. £17 return.

Aer Árann (tel. (091) 593034), 19mi. west of Galway at Inverin, flies to all three islands. Amazing photo ops. Reservations accepted over the phone or in person at the Galway Tourist Office. 10min. to Inishmore. In summer 20-25 per day; in winter 4 per day. £18; £35 return. Bus from Galway tourist office leaves 1hr. before departure (£2.50).

■ Inishmore (Inis Mór)

The archaeological sites of Inishmore (pop. 900), the largest of the Aran Islands, are among the most impressive in Ireland, even to those normally allergic to history. Of the dozens of ruins, forts, churches, and "minor sites" (holy wells and kelp kilns), the most amazing is the Dún Aengus ring fort, where a small semicircular wall surrounds a sheer 300 ft. drop off the craggy cliffs of the island's southern edge. Crowds disembark at Kilronan pier on the center of the island, spread out to lose themselves amid the stone walls and stark cliffs, then coalesce again around major sights. Minivans and "pony traps" traverse the island, encouraging anyone on foot to climb aboard and pay up. Exactly 437 kinds of wildflowers rise from the stony terrain and over 7000 miles of stone walls divide the land. Kilronan (Cill Rónáin), above the pier on the north shore, is the only place to buy supplies; the tiny Killeany and the airstrip are to the east, while Kilmurvy and most of the major sites lie to the west. Though touristy compared to Inisheer and Inishmaan, Inishmore is still quite isolated.

PRACTICAL INFORMATION **Ferries** land in Kilronan. The **Minibuses** roaming the island can be flagged down for a ride (£5 return to Dún Aengus). The buses also organize two-hour tours of the island for about £5. The **tourist office** in Kilronan (tel. 61263) changes money, holds bags during the day (75p), and sells several maps (open Feb.-Nov. daily 10am-6:45pm). The *Inis Món Way* (£1.50) is ideal for daytrippers. Anyone spending a few days on the islands should invest in the Richardson map (£5), which meticulously documents every nook and cranny of the three islands. **Aran Bicycle Hire** (tel. 61132) rents bikes; just don't lose your receipt (£5 per day, £21 per week; deposit £9; open Mar.-Nov. daily 9am-7:30pm). Strangely enough, bike theft here is a problem—lock it up, hide it, or don't ever leave it. **Internet access** is sporadically available at the heritage center. The **post office** (tel. 61101), up the hill from the pier, past the Spar Market, has **bureau de change** (open M-F 9am-5pm, Sa 9am-1pm).

ACCOMMODATIONS A free bus to the hostels meets all of the ferries at the pier. **Mainistir House (IHH)** (tel. 61169) has developed an international reputation as a haven for writers and musicians, but regular backpackers are welcome too. Joël has overcome a Yale education and now dishes up fabulous, creative, organic, all-you-can-eat "vaguely vegetarian" buffet dinners (£7). He also gets up at 6:30am to make porridge and fresh scones for all. The rooms are packed, so book ahead, especially during July and August. (Dorms £8; singles £11; doubles £24. Laundry £4. **Bikes** £5.) **Dún Aengus Hostel** (tel. 61318) hides 4 mi. west in Kilmurvey; take the first turnoff to the right from the beach. This hostel, a 10-minute walk from Dún Aengus, is a great outpost for outdoorsy types. (Dorms £7. Laundry £2.) The **Kilronan Hostel** (tel. 61255) offers clean, modern rooms just seconds from the pier (July-Aug. £9; Sept.-June £8). Wile the nights away in front of a peat fire at the family home turned hostel, **An Aharla** (tel. 61305). Take the turnoff across from Joe Watt's on the main road; it's the first building on the left (£6). **St. Kevin's** (tel. 61485), a 40-bed hostel in a musty old house behind the Kilronan Hostel, is a great alternative to sleeping out on the beach if you can't find anywhere else to stay (£7.50).

Bed down in style at Mrs. G. Tierney's ivy-covered **St. Brendan's House** (tel. 61149), across the street from the ocean (Apr.-Oct. £13, with continental breakfast £11; Nov.-Mar. £10 and £8). Three miles west of Kilronan, Mrs. B. Conneely's **Beach View House** (tel. 61141) lives up to its name and more. It also offers views of Dún Aengus and framed versions of the Alps. (Singles £18; doubles £26. Open May-Sept.)

FOOD, PUBS, AND ENTERTAINMENT **Spar Market** (tel. 61203), past the hostel in Kilronan, seems to be the island's social center (open M-Sa 9am-8pm, Su 10am-6pm). **Teach Nan Phaidt** (tel. 61330), the thatched restaurant at the turnoff to Dún Aengus, specializes in home-cooked bread with home-smoked fish (smoked salmon sandwich £4.50; open daily July-Aug. 10am-9pm, Mar.-June and Sept.-Dec. 10am-5pm). For wonderful organic lunches and desserts in an historic setting, try **The Man of Aran Restaurant** (tel. 61301), located just past Kilmurvey Beach to the right. (Toasties £2, cakes £1.70; dinner prices considerably higher. Open daily 12:30-3:30pm for lunch.) They also run perhaps the most beautiful B&B on the island, and they know it (doubles £40; open Mar.-Oct.). West of the harbor on the main road, **Joe Watty's** offers food, music, and conversation to accompany thick pints. The **American Bar** (tel. 61303) attracts younger islanders and droves of tourists with music most summer nights. Traditional musicians occasionally strum on the terrace at **Tí Joe Mac** (tel. 61248). On Friday, Saturday, and Sunday nights in summer, the first steps of a *céilí* begin at midnight at the dance hall (cover £3). The *Man of Aran* is still screened daily at the community center (£3).

SIGHTS The sights themselves are crowded, but the paths between them are desolate and unmarked. While some people travel by minibus, cycling or walking is more fun. The tourist office's £3 maps correspond to yellow arrows that mark the trails, but the markings are frustratingly infrequent and can vanish in fog. The island's most impressive (and best known) monument, dating from the first century BC, is magnificent **Dún Aengus**, 4 mi. west of the pier at Kilronan. The fort's walls are 18 ft. thick and form a semi-circle around the sheer drop of Inishmore's northwest corner. One of the better-preserved prehistoric forts in Europe, Dún Aengus commands a sublime view of miles of ocean from its hill. **Be very careful:** the strong winds have blown tourists off the edge to their deaths on the rocks below. Many visitors have been fooled by an imaginary island that sometimes appears on the horizon. The vision was so realistic that it appeared on maps until the 20th century. Down the side of the cliff, **Worm Hole** is a saltwater lake filled from the limestone aquifer below the ground. The bases of the surrounding cliffs have been hollowed by mighty waves to look like pirate caves. If you follow the cliffs to the left of Dún Aengus for about a mile, you can actually climb down to the level of the Worm Hole. The sound of the waves crashing under the rock is worth the 30-minute walk. Two roads lead to the fort from Kilronan, an inland one and a more quiet coastal one. Left off the main road a half mile past Kilmurvey is **Dun Eoghanachta,** a huge circular fort with 16 ft. walls. To the right past Eoghanachta are the **Seven Churches.** These scattered groupings of religious remains stimulate speculation about the island's former inhabitants. The island's best beach lies flat at Kilmurvey.

Uphill from the pier in Kilronan, the new **Aran Islands Heritage Centre** (Ionad Árann; tel. 61355) caters to inquisitive tourists. *(Open Apr.-Oct. daily 10am-7pm. £2, students £1.50.) Curraghs,* soil and wildlife exhibits, old Aran clothes, and a cliff rescue cart combine for a surprisingly fascinating introduction to the natural and human life of the island. The **Black Fort** (Dún Dúchathair), 1 mi. south of Kilronan over eerie terrain, is even larger than Dún Aengus and a millennium older.

■ Inishmaan

The seagulls on Inishmaan (Inis Meáin; pop. 300) plead with you to stay a little longer on the cliffs, while goats stand on stone walls looking for signs of life in the nearby fields of limestone. For those who find beauty in solitude, a walk along the rocky cliff-top is bliss. With the rapid and dramatic changes on the other two islands over the last three years, Inishmaan remains a fortress, quietly avoiding the hordes of barbarians invading from the east via Doolin and Galway. The ferry now runs regularly to the island, but it is difficult to find a budget bed for the night.

An Cora (tel. 73010), a small coffeeshop inside an old Irish cottage at the pier, dispenses food and **tourist information** on one plate (open July-Aug. daily 9am-6pm). For more comprehensive information, as well as a chance to buy a variety of local crafts, try the **Inishmaan Co-op** (tel. 73010). Take the turn-off for the knitware factory, continue straight and then make a right turn after the factory. The **post office** (tel. 73001) is in Inishmaan's tiny village, which spreads out along the road west of the pier to divide the island in half. **Mrs. Faherty** (tel. 73012) also runs a B&B, signposted from the pier, and fills you up with an enormous dinner (doubles £26; dinner £10; open mid-Mar. to Nov.). **Tig Congaile** (tel. 73085), on the right-hand side of the first steep hill from the pier, offers B&B (£16). Its restaurant concentrates on perfecting seafood (lunch under £5, dinner from £8.50; open June-Sept. daily 9am-9pm). The **An Dún Shop** (tel. 73067) sells some food at the access to Dún Chonchúir. The center of life on the island, **Padraic Faherty's** thatched pub, serves pub grub all day.

The **Inishmaan Way** brochure (£1.50) describes a 5 mi. walking route to all of the island's sights. The thatched cottage where Synge wrote much of his Aran-inspired work from 1898 to 1902 is a mile into the island on the main road. Across the road and a bit farther down is **Dún Chonchúi** (Connor Fort), an impressive 7th-century ringfort that looks over the entire island. At the western end of the road is **Synge's Chair,** where the writer came to think and compose. The view of splashing waves and open seas is remarkable, but an even more dramatic landscape awaits a bit farther down the path where the coastline comes into view. To the left of the pier, 8th-century **Cill Cheannannach** church left its remains on the shore. Islanders were buried here for ages under simple stone slabs, until the mid-20th century. One mile north of the pier is Inishmaan's safest beach, **Trá Leitreach.** Entering the **Knitwear factory** (tel. 63009) is like stepping into a Madison Ave. boutique (except not really). The company sells its sweaters internationally, but you can get them here right off of the sheep's back at nearly half the price. (Open M-Sa 10am-5pm, Su 10am-4pm.)

■ Inisheer

The Arans have been described as "quietness without loneliness," but Inishmore isn't always quiet and Inishmaan can get lonely. Inisheer (Inis Oírr, pop. 300), the smallest Aran, best fulfills the promise of the famous phrase. Islanders and stray donkeys seem to be present in even proportions on this island less than 2 mi. in diameter and traced by labyrinthine stone walls

Inisheer's town **tourist information** (tel. 75008) is cheerfully given in English or Irish from the small wooden hut on the beach near the main pier (open July-Aug. daily 10am-6pm). **Rothair Inis Oírr** (tel. 75033) rents **bikes** (£5 per day, £25 per week). The **post office** (tel. 75001) is farther up the island to the left of the pier in the cream house with turquoise trim (open M-F 9am-1pm and 2-5:30pm, Sa 9am-1pm).

The **Brú Hostel (IHH)** (tel. 75024), visible from the pier, is clean and spacious. Upper-level rooms have skylights for stargazing. Call ahead in July and August. (4- to 6-bed dorms £7; private rooms £9 per person, with bath £10. Continental breakfast £2, Irish breakfast £3.50. Sheets £1. Laundry £2.) A list of Inisheer's 19 B&Bs hangs on the window of the small tourist office next to the pier. **Bríd Póil's B&B** (tel. 75019) is booked all summer six months in advance due to the reputation of its beautiful view and the amazing gourmet meals (£10). It is worthwhile to call for that one-in-a-hundred chance that there has been a last-minute cancellation. (£14, with bath £16.) **Sharry's** B&B (tel. 75024) is behind the Brú Hostel (£16). The **Ionad Campála Campground** (tel. 75008) stretches its tarps near the beach for campers who don't mind chilling ocean winds (£2 per tent, £10 per week; showers 50p; open May-Sept.).

Marb Gan é (tel. 75049) serves coffee and treats by the pier (open June-Sept. daily 10am-6pm) and offers **B&B** (£16). Monkfish leap from the sea into the kitchen of **Fisherman's Cottage** (tel. 75703), 350 yd. to the right of the pier, where they are then killed, cooked, and expertly served (catch of the day £7, open daily 11am-9.30pm). **Tigh Ned's** pub lies next to the Brú Hostel and caters to a younger crowd, while the pub at the **Ostan Hotel** (tel. 75020), just up from the pier, is exceptionally crowded, dark, and mellow (food served daily 11am-9:30pm). **Tigh Ruairí** (tel. 75002), an unmarked pub/shop in a white building just up the road, is your best bet for groceries on the island. (Shop open July-Aug. daily 9am-8:30pm; Sept.-June M-Sa 9am-7:30pm, Su 10:45am-12:30pm.)

You can see the sights of the island on foot or from a **pony cart** island tour (tel. 75092). The **Inis Oírr Way** covers the island's major attractions in 4 mi. The first stop is in town at **Cnoc Raithní,** a bronze-age tumulus (stone burial mound) 2000 years older than Christianity. Walking along the An Trá shore leads to the romantic over-grown graveyard of **St. Kevin's Church** (Teampall Chaomháin). This St. Kevin, patron saint of the island, was believed to be a brother of St. Kevin of Glendalough. Each year on June 14, islanders hold mass in the church's ruins in memory of St. Kevin; lately, a festival has been tacked on. His grave nearby is said to have great heal-ing powers. Below the church, a pristine, sandy beach stretches back to the edge of town. Farther east along the beach, a grassy track leads to **An Loch Mór,** a 16-acre inland lake where wildfowl prevail. The stone ringfort **Dún Formna** is above the lake. Continuing past the lake and back onto the seashore is the **Plassy wreck,** a ship that sank offshore and washed up on Inisheer in 1960. The Inisheer lighthouse is nicely visible from the wreck. The walk back to the center leads through Formna Village and on out to **Cill na Seacht nInion,** a small monastery with a stone fort. The remains of the 14th-century O'Brien castle, razed by Cromwell in 1652, sit atop a nearby knoll. On the west side of the island, **Tobar Einne,** St. Enda's Holy Well, is said to have healing powers.

County Galway

Lots of people visit both Galway City and the terrain to its west, but they do so for dis-parate reasons. The city is the world headquarters of craic, especially during its many festivals. The area to the west of Galway, on the other hand, offers peaceful, rugged scenery for terrific hiking and biking opportunities. Clifden has a thriving nightlife, while Inishbofin is an intense dose of nothingness. Cong, a popular hamlet just over the Mayo border (listed in Co. Galway), boasts grassy natural attractions and ruined stony ones.

■ Galway

In the past few years, the city's reputation as Ireland's cultural capital has brought young Irish flocking to Galway (pop. 60,000) like Elvis freaks to Graceland. Mix in the over 13,000 students at Galway's two major universities, a large transient population of twentysomething Europeans, and waves of international backpackers, and you have a small college town on craic. It might be the setting that draws the crowds: casinos and amusement parks overlook the mile-long beachfront promenade in neighboring Salthill, while buskers work the cobblestoned medieval streets strad-dling the Corrib River. It might be the historical importance of the city, which was once a commercial hub: legacies of the famous 14 tribes who rebuilt Galway after a conflagration in 1490 and ruled for 170 years dot the town. Galway hookers once har-vested the ocean for fish and trade, bringing in Spanish and English goods and export-ing produce from the fertile interior. It might be Galway's cultural attractions: numerous theater companies and proximity to the Connemara *gaeltacht* make it a

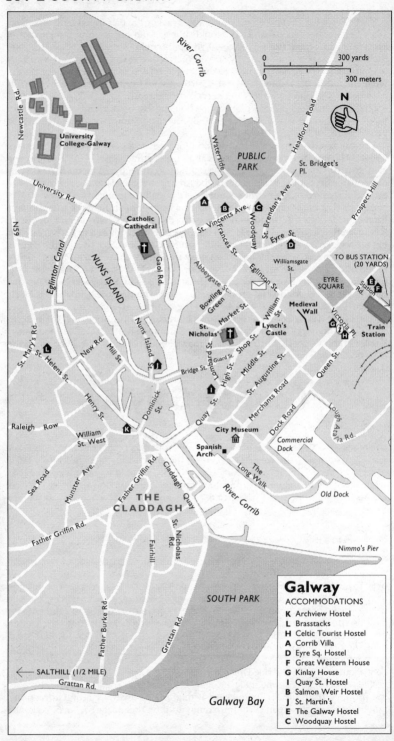

Galway

ACCOMMODATIONS

- **K** Archview Hostel
- **L** Brasstacks
- **H** Celtic Tourist Hostel
- **A** Corrib Villa
- **D** Eyre Sq. Hostel
- **F** Great Western House
- **G** Kinlay House
- **I** Quay St. Hostel
- **B** Salmon Weir Hostel
- **J** St. Martin's
- **E** The Galway Hostel
- **C** Woodquay Hostel

center of Irish artistic tradition. Galway's arts, film, and horse-racing festivals follow one another in rapid succession during the summers, drawing still larger crowds. Sightseers find Galway a convenient base for trips to the Clare coast or the Connemara, while backpackers appreciate the disproportionate number of fine hostels and pubcrawlers find inspiration in its wondrous variety of drinking establishments. But most of all, young people come here for each other, in huge numbers, making vibrant, cosmopolitan Galway Europe's fastest-growing city.

ORIENTATION

Bus or rail to Galway will deposit you in **Eyre Square** (officially Kennedy Park), a central block of lawn and monuments with the train and bus station on its east side. To the northeast of the square along Prospect Hill, a string of lonely B&Bs begs for business, but the town's commercial zone spreads out to the south and west. West of the square, **Woodquay** is an area of quiet commercial and residential activity. Williamsgate St. descends southwest into the lively medieval area around High, Shop, Cross, and Quay St. Flashy pubs, restaurants, shops, and youths dominate this area, which was recently pedestrianized. Fewer tourists venture over the bridges into the more bohemian **left bank** of the Corrib, where those in the know enjoy fantastic music in Galway's best pubs. Just south is **The Claddagh**, Galway's original fishing village. A path and a road stretch west past the quays to **Salthill**, a long stretch of tacky beachfront resort with row houses and skyrocketing property values. To the north of the west bank are the university areas of **Newcastle** and **Shantallow**, quiet suburbs where students and families live in inexpensive sublets. Galway's Regional Technical College is a mile east of the city center in suburban **Renmare**, which dozes peacefully by its bird sanctuary, on the path along the railroad tracks.

PRACTICAL INFORMATION

Transportation
  Airport: Carnmore (tel. 755569). 3 small Aer Lingus planes jet to Dublin daily.
  Trains: Eyre Sq. (tel. 561444). Open M-Sa 7:40am-6pm. Trains to **Dublin** (3hr., M-F 5 per day, Sa-Su 3-4 per day, M-Th and Sa £15, F and Su £21) stop in **Athlone** (M-Th and Sa £7.50, F and Su £11); transfer at Athlone for all other lines.
  Buses: Eyre Sq. (tel. 562000). Station open July-Aug. M-Sa 8:30am-7pm, Su 8:30am-6pm; Sept.-June M-Sa 8:30am-6pm, Su 8:30am-noon and 1:40-6pm. Private bus companies specialize in the run to **Dublin. P. Nestor Coaches** (tel. 797144) leaves from Imperial Hotel, Eyre Sq. (M-Th and Su 2 per day, F 7 per day, Sa 5 per day, £5 single or day return, £8 open return). **Citylink** (tel. 564163) leaves from Supermac's, Eyre Sq. (5 per day, last bus at 5:45pm, same prices as Nestor's). A **West Clare Shuttle** to **Doolin, Lisdoonvarna,** and **Fanore** leaves various Galway hostels on request (June-Sept. 1 per day, £5). **Michael Nee Coaches** (tel. 51082) drives from Forester St. through **Clifden** to **Cleggan**, meeting the **Inishboffin** ferry (M-Sa 2-4 per day, £5 single, £7 return). **Bus Éireann** heads to **Belfast** (2-3 per day, Su 1 per day, £16.30), **Cork** (5 per day, £12), **Dublin** (8-9 per day, Su 7-8 per day, £8), and the **Cliffs of Moher** (May 24-Sept. 19, 3-4 per day, Su 1-2 per day, £8.20) by way of **Ballyvaughan** (£5.90).
  Ferries: Two companies ferry folks to the **Aran Islands;** both have ticket and information booths in the tourist office. **Island Ferries** (tel. 568903) goes from Rossaveal, west of Galway on the R336, to Inishmore (Apr.-Oct. 3 per day, May-Sept. 1 per day) and to Inisheer and Inishmaan (1 per day, £12 return). A bus runs to Rossaveal (£4, £2 discount at Mainistir House hostel). **O'Brian Shipping** (tel. 567283) leaves from the Galway docks with possible connection to **Doolin** (daily June-Sept., 3 per week off-season, £12 return). See **Aran Islands,** p. 278.
  Local Transportation: City buses (tel. 562000) leave Eyre Sq. every 20min. (70p). Buses go to each area of the city: #1 to **Salthill**, #2 to **Knocknacarra** (west) or **Renmare** (east), #3 to **Castlepark,** and #4 to **Newcastle** and **Rahoon**. Service M-Sa 8am-9pm, Su 11am-9pm. Commuter tickets £8 per week, £29 per month.

Taxis: Big O Taxis, 21 Upper Dominick St. (tel. 585858). **Galway Taxis,** 7 Mainguard St. (tel. 561111), around the corner from McSwiggan's Pub. 24hr. service. Taxis can usually be found at Eyre Sq. **Hackneys** are considerably cheaper than taxis due to differences in licensing and use fixed-price service; they are run by **MGM** (tel. 757888), **Claddagh** (tel. 589000), and **Eyre Square** (tel. 569444). There's a waiting station 3 doors down from the tourist office.

Car Rental: Budget Rent-a-Car, Eyre Sq. (tel. 566376).

Bike Rental: Europa Cycles, Hunter Buildings, Earls Island (tel. 563355), opposite the cathedral. £3 per day, £5 per 24hr., £25 per week; deposit £30. Open M-F 9am-6pm. **Celtic Cycles,** Queen St., Victoria Pl. (tel. 566606), next to the Celtic Hostel. £7 per day, £30 per week; deposit £40 or ID; remote dropoff charge £12. Open daily 9am-6pm.

Hitching: While *Let's Go* does not recommend hitchhiking, dozens of hitchers at a time wait on Dublin Rd. (N6) scouting rides to Dublin, Limerick, or Kinvara. Most catch bus #2, 5, or 6 from Eyre Sq. to this main thumb-stop. University Rd. leads drivers to the Connemara via N59.

Tourist and Financial Services

Tourist Office: Victoria Pl. (tel. 563081). A block southeast of Eyre Sq. The bright, industrious staff and Aran Islands info booth make the pamphlet mania more exciting than ever. History buffs note *The Medieval Galway Map* (£3.50). Open July-Aug. daily 8:30am-7:45pm; May-June and Sept. daily 8:30am-5:45pm; Oct.-Apr. M-F and Su 9am-5:45pm, Sa 9am-12:45pm. The **Salthill** office (tel. 520500) is in a funny round metallic building visible from the main beach. Open daily 9am-5:45pm.

Travel Agency: USIT, Kinlay House, Victoria Pl., Eyre Sq. (tel. 565177), across from the tourist office. **Travelsave** stamps £8. Open May-Sept. M-F 9:30am-5:30pm, Sa 10am-3pm; Oct.-Apr. M-F 9:30am-5:30pm, Sa 10am-1pm.

Banks: Bank of Ireland, 19 Eyre Sq. (tel. 563181). Open M-W and F 10am-4pm, Th 10am-5pm. **ATM. AIB,** Lynch's Castle, Shop St. (tel. 567041). Exactly the same hours, but much more attractive. **ATM. Bank of Ireland** (tel. 522455), in Salthill. Open M-W and F 10am-4pm, Th 10am-5pm. **ATM.**

American Express: 7 Eyre Sq. (tel. 562316). Open May-Sept. M-F 9am-9pm, Sa 9am-7pm, Su 10am-7pm; Oct.-Apr. M-Sa 9am-5pm.

Local Services

Camping Equipment: River Deep Mountain High, Middle St. (tel. 563968). Open M-Th and Sa 9:30am-6pm, F 9:30am-9pm.

Bookstores: Eason & Son, Ltd., 33 Shop St. (tel. 562284), has a huge selection of books and international periodicals. Open M-Th and Sa 9am-6:15pm, F 9:30am-9pm. **Kenny's** (tel. 562739) between High and Middle St., has the country's largest collection of Irish interest books and an art gallery in the back. Open M-Sa 9am-6pm. **Charlie Byrne's Bookshop,** Middle St. (tel. 562776), has a massive stock of secondhand, discounted, and remaindered books. Open July-Aug. M-Sa 9am-8pm, Su noon-6pm, Sept.-June M-Th and Sa 9am-6pm, F 9am-8pm.

Library: St. Augustine St. (tel. 561666). Open Tu-Th 11am-8pm, M and F-Sa 11am-5pm. Overrun with small, loud children.

Bisexual, Gay, and Lesbian Information: P.O. Box 45 (tel. 566134). Recorded information on meetings and events; gay line Tu and Th 8-10pm, lesbian line W 8-10pm. The *Gay Community News* is available at Charlie Byrne's Bookshop (above).

Laundry: The Bubbles Inn, 18 Mary St. (tel. 563434). Wash and dry £4. Open M-Sa 9am-6:15pm; last wash 2pm. **Prospect Hill Launderette,** Prospect Hill (tel. 568343). Wash and dry £4. Open M-Sa 8:30am-6pm; last wash 4:45pm.

Pharmacies: Flanagan's, Shop St. (tel. 562924). Open M-Sa 9am-6pm. **McGoldrick's,** 218 Upper Salthill (tel. 562332). Open daily July-Aug. 9am-9pm, Sept.-June 9am-7pm.

Emergency and Communications

Emergency: Dial 999; no coins required. **Garda:** Mill St. (tel. 563161).

Counseling and Support: Samaritans, 14 Nuns' Island (tel. 561222). 24hr. phones. **Rape Crisis Centre,** 3 St. Augustine St. (tel. (1 850) 355355). Limited hours.

Hospital: University College Hospital, Newcastle Rd. (tel. 524222).

Post Office: Eglinton St. (tel. 562051). Open M and W-Sa 9am-5:30pm, Tu 9:30am-5:30pm.
Internet Access: Cyberzone, Eyre Sq. (tel. 561415), above Supermac's. £2 per 30min., £3 per hr. Open daily 7am-midnight.
Phone Code: 091.

ACCOMMODATIONS

In the last few years, the number of hostel beds in Galway has nearly tripled to almost a thousand. Nevertheless, most of them sag under sleeping backpackers during July and August, so reserve one before you arrive. Galway's hostels come in two species: large, expensive, custom-built ones with lots of facilities gather around Eyre Square near the station, while smaller, softer, furrier ones clump five minutes west at Woodquay or across the river around Dominick Street. Rates are 10-20% higher in the summer. Large numbers of B&Bs are in Salthill a mile to the west, in and around the city center, and along the approach roads to town. B&B should cost £12-18 a night.

Hostels and Camping

⊛**Kinlay House (IHH),** Merchants Rd. (tel. 565244), across from the tourist office. Modern, spotless, and friendly, though a little sedate. Washcloths, blue duvets, and closet space in uncrowded rooms approach luxury. Awesome medieval mural in the spacious dining room. Gigantic security monitors at reception remind you they're watching. **Bureau de change.** 24hr. internet access £5 per hr. No single-sex dorms. July-Sept. and special events 8-bed dorms £8.50; 6-bed dorms with bath £10; 4-bed dorms £11.50, with bath £12.50; singles £20; doubles £28, with bath £32. Oct.-June dorms 50p-£1 cheaper, private rooms £2 cheaper. 10% discount with ISIC. Small breakfast included. Laundry £3.50. Wheelchair accessible.

⊛**Salmon Weir Hostel,** St. Vincent's Ave., Woodquay (tel. 561133). Newcomers are quickly sucked into the fun-loving, comfortable atmosphere of this small hostel. Many come for a weekend and stay for months, passing the good vibes on to new arrivals. Free tea, coffee, washing powder, and peace of mind. No smoking. June-Aug. 4-6 bed dorms £7.50; doubles £20. June-Aug. dorms £7; doubles £18. Laundry £3. Curfew 2am, in summer 3am. **Bike rental** £5 per day, £3.50 per half day.

Quay Street Hostel (IHH), Quay St. (tel. 568644). Shop St. becomes Quay St. A dark wood common room with a fireplace, tidy dorms, and a peerless location in the city center make this hostel the place to be, especially for pub-crawlers. Excellent security and kitchen space add value, while the labyrinthine floorplan adds challenge. Rates vary seasonally: big dorms £7-8.50; 8-bed dorms £7.50-9; 6-bed dorms £8-9.50; 4-bed dorms with bath £9.50-12; doubles with bath £24-29. Laundry £3.50.

The Galway Hostel, Eyre Sq. (tel. 566959), across from the station. Burren Shale tiles lead up past the soft yellow walls to attractive, airy dorms with super-clean bathrooms. The small kitchen fills fast in this 80-bed hostel. June-Sept. 14-bed dorms £8; 8-bed dorms £8.50; 4-bed dorms £11, with bath £13; doubles £28. Sept.-May dorms £1 cheaper, doubles £2 cheaper.

Eyre Sq. Hostel, 35 Eyre St. (tel. 568432). A small, cozy hostel with giant windows. Quiet, yet central, location. High season big dorms £8; 4-bed dorms £10; doubles £24. Off season £7, £9, and £22, respectively.

Great Western House (IHH), Eyre Sq. (tel. 561150 or FreeFone (800) GALWAY (425929)), is a mammoth building across from the station. With sauna, pool room, large kitchen, extra-wide bunks, and satellite TV, it has the facilities of a great hostel. It might feel like one too, were it not for the dim fluorescent lighting and threadbare common areas. **Bureau de change.** July-Aug. and bank holidays 8- to 12-bed dorms £9.50; 4- to 6-bed dorms with bath £12.50; singles £18; doubles with bath £32. Off season £1.50-3 cheaper. Small breakfast included, full breakfast £1. Laundry £5. 24hr. reception. **Bike rental** £6 per day. Wheelchair accessible.

An Óige Galway Hostel (tel. 527411). Follow Dominick St. to the west and turn left onto St. Mary's Rd. St. Mary's secondary school for boys, an imposing building surrounded by playing fields, puts bunks in its classrooms and gyms in the summer to form a 180-bed hostel. Close to Galway's best bars, but far from the station. Big dorms £9; 4-bed dorms £10; twins £11. Breakfast included. Open late-June to Aug.

Archview Hostel, Dominick St. (tel. 586661). The cheapest, most laid-back accommodations in town, in the heart of Galway's bohemian district. Dorms are clean, comfortable, and well lit, and you can sleep in. Dorms £6, off-season £5.

Corrib Villa (IHH), 4 Waterside (tel. 562892). Just past the courthouse, about 4 blocks down Eglinton St. from Eyre Sq. The spacious Georgian townhouse has high ceilings and clean rooms but gets a little chilly in poor weather. Interior is freshly painted in patriotic hues. July to mid-Sept. dorms £8.50, mid-Sept. to June £7.50.

Celtic Tourist Hostel, Queen St., Victoria Pl. (tel. 586606; night 521559), around the corner from the tourist office. Sit back, relax, and gaze out the windows in the sitting room. Big, bright kitchen. Large dorms can get crowded. July-Aug. dorms £8.50; private rooms £11 per person. Sept.-June £7.50, £10. Sheets £1. **Bike rental** £7 per day.

Woodquay Hostel, 23-24 Woodquay (tel. 562618). Cute exterior, interior covered with signs proclaiming "Dorms £6.50-£8. Twin £8.50-10. 4-bed with bath £10-12," "50p for sheets," "Laundry £5," "Reception 9am-11pm," "No curfews," and other maxims.

Bed and Breakfasts

St. Martin's, 2 Nuns' Island (tel. 568286), on the west bank of the river at the end of Dominick St. (visible from the Bridge St. bridge). Gorgeous riverside location with a grassy lawn. Singles £18; doubles £32.

Brasstacks, 3 Saint Helen's St. (tel. 524728), on the continuation of Henry St. Amicable comfort. £16.

Mrs. E. O'Connolly, 24 Glenard Ave. (tel. 522147), Salthill, off Dr. Mannix Rd. Bus #1 from Eyre Sq. is easiest. Excellent B&B for an excellent price. £10 with continental breakfast, £12 with full Irish breakfast.

Mrs. Ruth Armstrong, 14 Glenard Ave. (tel. 522069), Salthill, lies just down the road and serves a full Irish breakfast with friendly chatter. £15, off-season £12-13.

Camping

Camping: Salthill Caravan and Camping Park (tel. 523972 or 522479). On the bay, ½mi. west of Salthill. Crowded in summer. £3 per hiker or cyclist. Open May-Oct.

Long-term Stays

Galway has a large population of young, transient foreign nationals who visit, fall in love, find jobs, stay for a few months, and move on. Most share apartments in and around the city, where rents run from £30 to £50 per week. The best place to look is the *Galway Advertiser*. Apartment hunters line up outside the *Advertiser*'s office on Church St. (the small alley off Shop St. behind Eason's) on Wednesdays at around 2pm and when the classified section is released at 3pm, dash to the nearest phone box (one block up on Shop St.). "Professionals" (i.e., people with jobs), women, and non-smokers find it easiest to snag apartments. An ideal time to start looking for jobs or apartments is the third week of May, when the university lets out. **Corrib Village** (tel. 527112), in Newcastle, offers housing for the summer. Some hostels have cheap weekly rates (£30-35) in winter. Jobs aren't too hard to come by in Galway either. The Thursday morning *Galway Advertiser* is the place to look. Others find service jobs simply by asking. A four-month student visa or other work permit helps a great deal, although some are hired without them. The **Galway Chamber of Commerce** (tel. 563536), on Merchant's Rd. near the docks, will put those seeking more permanent jobs in touch with recruiters.

FOOD

The large student population in Galway guarantees plenty of excellent cheap eats. Many restaurants have been set up recently by graduates of the culinary arm of Galway's Regional Technical College. The east bank has the greatest concentration of restaurants; Abbeygate St. has a large selection, and the short blocks around Quay, High, and Shop St. are filled with good values. The **Supervalu** (tel. 567833) in the Eyre Square mall is a chef's playground (open M-W and Sa 9am-6:30pm, Th-F 9am-9pm). **Evergreen Health Food,** 1 Mainguard St. (tel. 564215), offers food from its shelves as well as from a menu (open M-Th and Sa 9am-6:30pm, F 9am-8pm). **Health-**

wise, Abbeygate St. (tel. 568761), promises better living through conscientious consumption (open M-F 9:30am-6pm, Sa 9:30am-5:30pm). On Saturday mornings, a **market** sets up in front of St. Nicholas Church on Market St. (8am-1pm). Fishermen sell cups of mussels fresh from the bay (about £1). Buy. Eat. Go mussel mad.

Java's, Upper Abbeygate St. (tel. 565086). 20 varieties of flavored cappuccino jolt clubgoers unwilling to go home. Angels grace the ceiling of the elegant ground floor, while the dark-wood nooks upstairs absorb cavorting groups. Baps £4. Java's is busiest at 2:30am but doesn't close until 4.

Anton's (tel. 582067). A bit off the beaten path, 3min. walk up Father Griffin Rd. over the bridge near the Spanish Arch. The salads, cornucopia of vegetables, fruits, and meats, are right on target. Prepared in view by Anton himself. Salad and bread £3; sandwiches £2.50. Open Tu-Sa 11am-6pm.

The Long Walk (tel. 561114), next to the Spanish Arch and a hell of a lot more interesting. This café and wine bar magically creates a warm and relaxed atmosphere on the first floor of a medieval battlement. The food is as epic as the setting. Food served M-Sa 12:30-4pm and 7-10:30pm, Su 7-10:30pm.

Get Stuffed Olive, Saint Anthony's Pl., Woodquay (tel. 564445). Voluptuous wholefood vegetarian and vegan dishes, murals on the barn-like ceiling, and gargantuan servings for the crowd inherited from O'Shakespeare's, its predecessor. Smoothies £1.50; sandwiches under £2. Open daily 11:30am-10pm.

Pierre's, Quay St. (tel. 566066). The 3-course meal (£10.90) may be slightly out of range for most budget travelers, but if you are going to break the bank (or at least a tenner) it ought to happen at this Quay St. favorite. Delicious lunches under £5.

Food for Thought, Lower Abbeygate St. (tel. 565854). Coffeeshop and wholefood restaurant serves an interesting variety of vegetarian dishes (£2.50) and mind-bogglingly big baps (from £2.50). Open M-Sa 8am-6pm.

Scotty's Casual Gourmet, 1 Middle St. (tel. 566400). Scotty casually beams you down to foot-long subs and fresh salads. Subs around £2.50. Open M-Sa noon-8pm.

The Couch Potatas, Upper Abbeygate St. (tel. 561664). Visitors to Ireland really should experience the potatoes. Huge stuffed spuds with side salads. "Hawaii 5-0" is a baked potato with ham, cheese, pineapple, and onion (£4.85). Crowded at lunchtime with all types. Spuds & butter £1.75. Open M-Sa noon-10pm, Su 1-10pm.

The Home Plate, Mary St. (tel. 561475). Expect a wait between noon and 3pm, when the whole city lines up to bat. Colossal servings include a humongous beverage. Entrees £4-6, large sandwiches £2.50. Open M-Sa noon-9:30pm.

McDonagh's, 22 Quay St. (tel. 565001). A world-class chipper. Certificates, newspaper clippings, and magazine articles line the wall to prove its popularity. The pride and joy of the collection is an official recognition from the former Soviet fleet naming McDonagh's the best chipper at any port of call. Especially crowded after the pubs close. Cod fillet and chips £3.50. Open M-Sa noon-midnight, Su noon-11pm. Restaurant (open daily noon-11pm) is pricier than take-away.

Café Du Journal, Quay St. (tel. 568428). Enter and instantly relax. Regulars doze in dark corners despite the best efforts of high-powered coffee, exhausted by the huge sandwiches. Open M-Sa 9am-10pm.

Fat Freddy's, Quay St. (tel. 567279). Galway's youth give high marks to the large pies rolling down the pipe at this pizza joint, although the wait can be a drag. Large pizza £5. Students 10% off M-F 3-6pm. Open daily 9am-11:30pm.

Apostasy, Dominick St. (tel. 561478). New-age regulars fill this small, obviously hip coffee shop, talking art until 4am each morning. Poetry readings Monday nights, chess and backgammon boards available. Cappuccino £1.

PUBS

Galway's pub scene is exploding along with its population. They come in all flavors, from the fantastical to the traditional, so there's no excuse for staying in one that doesn't suit you. Fast-paced trad usually blazes in several pubs each night; unfortunately, second-rate musicians exist alongside the good ones. Good and bad versions of rock, folk, country, blues, and metal also rear their heads. Dominick St. is the best place to hear music, Quay St. is where all the fabulously beautiful pubs are, and Eyre

WESTERN IRELAND

Sq. pubs are bigger and badder. Very broadly speaking, Quay St. pubs cater more to tourists, while patrons of Dominick St. pubs are more likely to have a Galway permanent address. Only big gigs have cover charges. Check *The List,* free and available at most pubs and newsstands.

Dominick Street

La Graal, 38 Lower Dominick St. (tel. 567614). A candle-lit wine bar and restaurant in the heart of Galway's Arab quarter, La Graal draws a crowd of beautiful continentals and other sophisticates. Exquisite staff. Salsa dancing Th, (gay friendly) disco Su, and a married priest reading mass Sunday mornings. Open until 1am.

The Crane, 2 Sea Rd. (tel. 587419), a bit beyond the Blue Note. The place to hear trad in Galway. Enter in the side and hop up to the 2nd floor loft. 2 musicians quickly become 6, 6 become 10, 10 become 20. Trad "whenever."

Roisín Dubh ("The Black Rose"), Dominick St., (tel. 586540). Old bicycles and dead branches decorate the walls, but big name Irish and international musicians light up the stage. Primarily rock, but folk and trad as well. This pub is where Irish record labels send new artists they are trying to promote in Galway. Cover £5-10 only for biggest Monday and Tuesday night gigs.

The Blue Note, William St. West (tel. 589116). With its finger firmly on the pulse of the European acid jazz scene, the Blue Note throbs every night of the week with guest DJs.

Aras Na nGael, Dominick St. (tel. 526509). A bar for Irish speakers, this club nonetheless welcomes all sorts (kind of). Absorb the rhythms of the Irish language as Guinness drowns your own imperfect voice box.

Taylor's, Dominick St. (tel. 589385). A holdover from another age, Taylor's is overlooked by tourists seeking flashier new venues of entertainment. The locals who proclaim it the best pint in town don't mind much. Trad M, W, Sa, and Su nights.

The Quay

Buskar Browne's/The Slate House (tel. 563377), between Cross St. and Kirwin's Ln. A perfect compromise for guilty drinkers, the Slate House was a nunnery for 300 years before it became a pub. Its fantastic 3rd floor Hall of the Tribes is the most spectacular lounge in Galway.

The Quays, Quay St. (tel. 568347). Popular with the younger crowd and scamming yuppies. The massive, multi-floored interior was built with carved wood taken from the balconies and stained-glass windows of an old church. It's worth a visit simply to see the intriguing interior. Cover bands electrify the equally impressive upstairs extension nightly 10pm-1:30am. £5 cover.

The Front Door, Cross St. (tel. 563757). Beams of light criss-cross the dark interior of this seemingly small pub. As it gets busier, more rooms open, moving up 3 stories and sprouting appendages all over the block. Rooms range from skylit vantage points to pint-size snugs.

Seaghan Ua Neachtain (called **Knockton's**), Quay St. (tel. 568820). One of the oldest and most genuine pubs in the county. Mixed crowd trades personal space for warmth and energy. Trad nightly.

The King's Head, High St. (tel. 566630). This historic building has recently been renovated in medieval style so that pub-goers can enjoy pints while talking to a suit of armor. Amplified trad on Wednesday; other nights vary in form, but aim to entertain. Lunchtime theater M-Sa 1-2pm (£2). Popular jazz brunch Su noon-1:45pm.

Taffee's, Shop St. (tel. 564066). Everyone from tweed-capped men to platform-shoed mods comes here for daily quality trad at 5 and 9pm, despite the tight conditions. The bartender explains that there is "no useless bric-a-brac to distract from the job of drinking here."

The Lisheen, 5 Bridge St. (tel. 563804). Outstanding and ceaseless trad nightly and Su morning. Musicians and pool shooters welcome.

Padraig's, (tel. 563696), at the docks. Opens at 7:30am daily for the die-hards. You know who you are.

Eyre Square

McSwiggin's, Eyre St. (tel. 568917), near Eglington St. A sprawling mess of small rooms and stairwells spanning 3 stories, McSwiggin's holds hundreds of tourists at a time. The craic is good, though, and so is the food.

The Skeffington Arms, Eyre Sq. (tel. 563173). A grand, splendidly decorated, newly converted, multi-storied hotel with 6 different bars, the Skeff is a well-touristed pub crawl unto itself.

CLUBS

Between 11pm and midnight, the pubs empty out, and the tireless go dancing. Unfortunately, Galway's clubs lag far behind its pubs. However, those who arrive at the clubs between 11:30pm and 12:15am are legally assured of a free meal with their entrance fee. **Monroe's Tavern,** Dominick St. (tel. 583397), has Irish set dancing on Tuesdays, while **Le Graal** nearby has salsa on Thursdays. **GPO,** Eglinton St. (tel. 563073), may not be attractive but draws a high-energy crowd nonetheless. It hosts Murphy's Comedy Club on Sunday evenings (£5 includes nightclub cover). Bank holiday Mondays are "Sheight Night"—dress your worst and listen to Abba's greatest flops. **The Alley,** behind the Skeff, draws a young local crowd with its unimaginative music and decor (cover £3-6). The more adventurous and mobile head out to the **Liquid Club,** King's Hill (tel. 522715), in Salthill (open Th-Su, cover £6). Expect a provocative mix of dance and odd indie that should fire your rage until well into morning. A hackney service is the best (and for groups, the cheapest) way to get there and back.

TOURS

Half- or full-day group tours are often the best way to see the sights of Galway, the Burren, and the Connemara. Some offer excellent values, with lower prices than bus tickets. For hour-long tours in and around the city, hop on one of the many buses that line up outside the tourist office; most charge £5 (students £4). Several lines depart from the tourist office once a day for both Connemara and the Burren (about £10, students £8), including **Gaeltacht Tours** (tel. 593322), **Connemara Tours** (tel. 562905), **Bus Éireann** (tel. 562000), and **Healy Tours** (tel. 770066). **Western Cultural and Heritage Tours** (tel. 521699) leave from the tourist office at 2:30pm daily June through August. **Arch Heritage Tours** (tel. 844133) explore the flora, fauna, and archaeology of the Burren. The **Corrib Princess** (tel. 592447) sails from Galway's Woodquay on a tour of Lough Corrib to the north (1½hr., June-Aug. daily 2:30pm and 4:30pm, £5). Energetic types can hire a rowboat to visit the ruins of Menlo Castle, seat of the Blake family. **Frank Dolan,** 13 Riverside, Woodquay (tel. 565841), will have you away from the madding crowd and up the river for £1.50 per hour.

SIGHTS

The commerce and culture of Galway overshadow its historic aspects, but those digging for interesting sights usually find enough to last an afternoon. In the middle of **Eyre Square** is a rusty sculpture built to celebrate the Galway Hooker. A careful examination of the sidewalk outside of the Great Southern Hotel on the square's east side exposes two footscrapers, small cast iron implements once used by Galway's gentry to scrape the muck off their feet. Just on the south side of the square is the Eyre Square Shopping Center, a large indoor mall that encloses a major section of Galway's medieval town wall. The wall was originally built in the 13th century and stood unnoticed until the construction of the shopping development eight years ago.

The mall emerges on Shop St. just up from **Lynch's Castle,** an elegant stone mansion originally constructed in 1320. *(Exhibit room open M-W and F 10am-4pm, Th 10am-5pm. Free.)* The Lynch family ruled Galway from the 13th- to the 18th-century. Exhibits inside the edifice analyze the castle's architecture and heraldry and relate a dubious family legend. In the late 1400s, Lynch Jr. killed a Spaniard whom he suspected of liking his girlfriend. The son, sentenced to hang, was so beloved by the populace that not one man would agree to be the hangman. Lynch Sr., the lord of the castle, was so determined to administer justice that he hanged his own son. The window behind St. Nicholas Church is supposedly the one from which Lynch Sr. lynched Lynch Jr. A skull and crossbones engraved in the glass remembers the deed. The castle now houses the Allied Irish Bank.

Many Lynches lie together in the **Church of St. Nicholas,** Market St., behind the castle. *(Open May-Sept. daily 9am-5:45pm. Free. Unnecessary tour £1, students 50p.)* The church, full of oddities from many sources, devotes some of its attention to a heritage project. A stone marks the spot where Columbus stopped to pray before hitting the New World. Note the three-faced clock on the exterior; local folklore claims that the residents on the fourth side failed to pay their church taxes. Glorious stained glass and relics from the Connacht Rangers provide more distractions. Around the corner, tiny **Nora Barnacle House,** 8 Bowling Green (tel. 564743), exposes a few letters and photos relating to James Joyce and his wife. *(Open mid-May to mid-Sept. M-Sa 10am-1pm and 2-5pm. £1.)* Nora reputedly inspired much of Joyce's writing. The table where he composed a few lines to Nora draws the admiration of Joyce addicts.

Galway's Catholic Cathedral, officially known as the **Cathedral of Our Lady Assumed into Heaven and St. Nicholas,** looms above the Salmon Weir Bridge where Gaol and University Rd. meet across the river from most of the city. *(Excellent tours M-F 9:30am-4:30pm. Mood-setting organ practice M-F 3:30-5:30pm. Open Su for mass.)* The boring exterior reveals none of the controversy that assailed its eclectic design 25 years ago, centering around the great bare walls of Connemara stone intersecting with elaborate mosaics in the impressive interior. Across the University Rd. bridge from the cathedral is the **National University of Ireland at Galway,** founded 159 years ago during the Great Famine, which now enrolls some 6,000 students a year.

By the river, the Long Walk makes a pleasant stroll, bringing you to the **Spanish Arch,** the only surviving gateway to the old trading town. Built in 1584 as a defensive bastion for the port, this worn, one-story stone curve is revered by townspeople despite its unimpressive stature. The **Galway City Museum** (tel. 567641), in Tower House next to the arch, can show you up the stairs to the top of the arch. *(Open May-Oct. daily 10am-1pm and 2:15-5:15pm; check at the tourist office for Nov.-Apr. opening times. £1, students 50p.)* A knife-sharpener by a peat fire and some fishy statistics next to the one that didn't get away are the highlights of this small museum. Intriguing old photographs of the Claddagh line the walls.

Across the river south of Dominick St. lies the **Claddagh.** Until the 1930s, this area was an independent, Irish-speaking, thatched-cottage fishing village. The cottages were long ago replaced by stone bungalows, but a bit of the small-town appeal and atmosphere still persists. The famous Claddagh rings, traditionally used as wedding bands, are mass-marketed but still remarkable examples of Celtic metalworking. The rings depict the thumb and forefingers of two hands holding up a crown-topped heart. The ring should be turned around upon marriage; once the point of the heart faces inward, the wearer's heart is no longer available.

From the Claddagh, the waterfront road leads west to **Salthill.** The coast here alternates between pebbles and sand; when the ocean sunset turns red, it's time for some serious beach frolicking. Two casinos, a swimming pool, and an amusement park join the ugly new hotels that dominate the esplanade.

ENTERTAINMENT

Arts, Theater, and Film

Culture crowds into Galway proper and music of all varieties barrages pubs and clubs. The *Advertiser* and *Galway Guide* (free) provide listings of events and are available at most pubs and newsagents. The **Galway Arts Centre,** 47 Dominick St. (tel. 565886), will give you a good idea of what's going on in town (open M-Sa 10am-5:30pm). The center also hosts rotating art or photography exhibits and frequent workshops on dance, writing, and painting.

The **Town Hall Theatre,** Courthouse Sq. (tel. 569777), hosts everything from the Druid Theatre Company's Irish-themed plays and original Irish films to *Little Shop of Horrors* (programming daily in summer; tickets £5-15, student discounts most shows; most performances 8pm). Founded in 1928 by a group of academics from University College, the mostly Irish-language theater **An Taibhdhearc** (TIVE-yark), Middle St. (tel. 562024), has launched quite a few Irish actors into the limelight.

Poetry readings, musicals, and other events alternate with full-blown plays (7 per year; box office open M-F 10am-6pm, Sa 1-6pm; tickets £6-9). Along different lines, the **Omniplex** seven-screen cinema (tel. 567800) shows the usual mainstream flicks 10 minutes from town on Headford Rd.

Events

Festivals rotate through Galway's revolving door all year long, with the greatest concentration during the summer months. Reservations during these weeks are essential. At the **Galway Poetry and Literature Festival** (tel. 565886), or the **Cúirt,** the very highest of the nation's brows gather in the last week of April. Past guests have included Nobel prize-winner and Caribbean poet Derek Walcott and reggae star Linton Johnston. Hookers can be seen in Galway all year round, but the fourth weekend in June, they set off for Portaferry, Northern Ireland, in the **Galway Hooker Festival and Traditional Boat Regatta** (see p. 405). Fish nets, not fishnets, characterize these boating beauties with heavy, black hulls and billowing sails. July starts off with the **Galway Film Fleadh,** Ireland's biggest film festival, which features independent Irish and international filmmakers. American F-15s, Irish choppers, wing walkers, stunt pilots, army parachuters and many others jet in for the spectacular beachside **Salthill Air Show,** to be held on July 4, 1999. For two crazed weeks in July (July 10-25, 1999), the **Galway Arts Festival** (tel. 583800), the largest of its kind in Ireland, reels in famous trad musicians, rock groups, theater troupes, filmmakers, and comedians. The highlight of the festival is the Big Day Out, held on the first Saturday, when big-name bands come into town for a massive concert; 1998's lineup included Pulp, Cornershop, the Beastie Boys, and Radiohead. The famous **Galway Races** (tel. 753870) commence at the end of July. Those attending the races celebrate horses, money, and stout, not necessarily in that order (tickets £8-10 at the gate). The grandstand bar at the 23,000 capacity Ballybrit track holds the Guinness Book world record for the longest bar in Europe, measuring over 70 yards from end to end. The major social event is Ladies' Day, where those with the best hats and overall dress are officially recognized. Competition is notoriously stiff. Galway's last big event of the year is the **Galway International Oyster Festival** (tel. 566490), taking place September 23-26, 1999. Street theater, parades, and free concert surround this 45-year-old Galway tradition, which culminates in the Guinness World Oyster Opening Championship.

LOUGH CORRIB

Three hundred and sixty-five islands dot Lough Corrib, one for every day of the year. The eastern shores of Lough Corrib and Lough Mask stretch quietly into fertile farmland. The western shores slip into bog, quartzite scree, and the famously rough Connemarma country. The island of Inchagoill, in the middle of the lough, is the site of the second oldest existing Christian monuments in Europe.

■ Oughterard

Tourists seldom stop in Oughterard (OOK-ter-ard), perhaps because it is little more than a small population center along the N59 between Galway and Clifden. Still, those looking to escape the tourbuses find salvation in a relaxing canoe trip on Lough Corrib or a hike into the Maam Turk Mountains. The ruins on Inchagoill island are only a ferry ride away, which adds to the town's appeal. While everyone else hurries to Clifden and the sea, you can stop to sample the lake and islands as an appetizer.

PRACTICAL INFORMATION Bus Éireann coaches from **Galway** to **Clifden** stop in Oughterard (30min. to Galway, 1½hr. to Clifden; Jul.-Aug. M-Sa 4-6 per day, Su 1-2 per day; Sept.-June 1 per day). **Hitchers** report easy going, at least in summer, between Galway and anywhere west or northwest. An independent **tourist office** (tel. 552808) sells the useful *Oughterard Walking & Cycling Routes* handbook for £2 (open May-Aug. M-Sa 9am-5:30pm, Su 10am-2pm; Sept.-Apr. M-F 9am-5pm). The **Bank of Ireland,** Main St. (tel. 552123), has an **ATM** (open M-W and F 10am-4pm, Th 10am-5pm). **Corrib Laundrette** (tel. 552042), on Main St. toward Clifden, does the real work of washing and drying (from £4; open M-Sa 9am-6pm). Frances **Geoghe-gan's Pharmacy,** Main St. (tel. 552348), fills prescriptions (open M-Tu and Th-Sa 9:30am-1:45pm and 2:15-6pm, W 9:30am-1pm). The **post office** (tel. 552201) is also on Main St. (open M-F 9am-1pm and 2-5:30pm, Sa 9am-1pm). **Clearview Solutions,** Camp St. (tel. 552351), has **internet access** (£5 per 30min). The **phone code,** 091, has been making legends for years.

ACCOMMODATIONS Cranrawer House (IHH), Station Rd. (tel. 552388), is a beauti-ful hostel with superior facilities in a quiet spot. Walk 10 minutes toward Clifden and turn left. The owner is a professional angler and will guide day expeditions onto the lough. (May-Sept. 8- to 10-bed dorms £7.50; 5-bed dorms with bath £8.50; private rooms with bath £9. Oct.-Apr. £6.50-£8.50. **Camping** £5. Continental breakfast £2.50. Laundry £4.50.) Friendships are forged quickly at the **Lough Corrib Hostel (IHH)** (tel. 552866) on Camp St. The walls are lined with snapshots of backpackers who have come and gone but left their mark. Ed and his merry pranksters look after each hosteler, introducing them to the comedy and intrigue of Oughterard nightlife. How could you miss it? (Dorms £7; private rooms £8. **Camping** £4. Sheets 50p. **Bike rental** £7.50. Open Apr.-Nov.) **Cregg Lodge B&B,** Station Rd. (tel. (095) 552493), knows how to lodge (£14, with bath £16; open Apr.-Sept.).

FOOD AND PUBS Keogh's Grocery, The Square (tel. 552583), sells food, fishing tackle, and hardware (open in summer M-Sa 8am-10pm; in winter M-Sa 8am-8pm, Su 9am-9pm). The selection of eateries covers all tastes. **Corrib County,** Main St. (tel. 552678), serves all three meals, although lunch is the most affordable (sandwiches about £3; open Apr.-Oct. daily 8:30am-10pm). Good pub grub, music of all kinds, and brilliant craic hover around the hull at **The Boat Inn,** The Square (tel. 552196; Irish stew £4.95; food served 10:30am-10pm). Thatched **Power's Bar** (tel. 552712), a few doors down, is a local favorite (music F-Su). **Keogh's Bar** (tel. 552222) across the street encourages people to eat, drink, and be merry (music Tu-Su in summer, F-Su in winter). **The Mayfly** (tel. 552179) is an essential stop on the teenybopper pub crawl.

SIGHTS One mile south of town, a turn-off from N59 leads to 16th-century **Aughna-nure Castle** (tel. 82214), where a river red with peat curves around a fortified tower. *(Open mid-June to mid-Sept. daily 9:30am-6:30pm. £2, students £1.)* The secret chamber, feasting hall, and murder hole are highlights of the high-quality tour. The view from the castle roof is tremendous (key available at the ticket booth). Glann Rd. covers the 9 mi. from Oughterard to the infamous **Hill of Doon,** where the pre-Celtic Glann peo-ple annually sacrificed a virgin to the panther goddess Taryn. It is said that the prac-tice continued in secret until the 1960s, when they ran out of virgins. The 16 mi. **Western Way Walk** begins where Glann Rd. ends and passes along the lake shore to Maam at the base of the Maam Turk mountain range.

Competitors from all over Ireland assemble in June for the **Currach Racing Cham-pionships.** Anglers worldwide know of Lough Corrib and the mayfly bait that miracu-lously arises from it. The tourist office and the Fuschia Craft Shop sell tickets for **Corrib Cruises** (tel. 82644), with two to three boats running daily between Cong, Oughterard, Ashford Castle, and Inishagoil (£6-12, bikes £3). Equestrian hopefuls can start their careers by **Pony Trekking** (tel. 55212).

■ Cong

Cozy little Cong (pop. 300), a pastoral, romantic village in the lake-filled hills of Co. Mayo, has all one could ask of rural Ireland. Bubbling streams and shady footpaths criss-cross the surrounding forests, a ruined abbey crumbles gracefully on the edge of the forests, a majestic castle towers over the choppy waters of Lough Corrib, and vil-lagers cheerfully mix with outsiders in the town's pubs. Cong was once the busy market center of a far more populous region, and Cong's abbey was a tower of learning with 3,000 students. Cong was bypassed by the main roads, however, and were it not for two recent events, Cong might have slumbered into peaceful obscurity. In 1939, Ashford Castle was turned into a £500 per night luxury hotel, bringing the rich, famous, and powerful to Cong from around the world. Later, during the hot and humid summer of 1951, John Wayne and Maureen O'Hara shot *The Quiet Man* here. Thousands of fans come each year to find the location of every shot while locals look on, amused and bewildered.

PRACTICAL INFORMATION **Buses** leave for **Westport** (M-Sa 1 per day) from Ashford gates, **Clifden** (M-Sa 1 per day) from Ryan's Hotel, and **Galway** (M-Sa 1-2 per day) from both (all £6). The town's **tourist office,** Abbey St. (tel. 46542), will point you toward Cong's wonders, listed in *The Cong Heritage Trail* (£1.50). *Cong: Walks, Sights, Stories* (£2.80) describes good hiking and biking routes and is necessary for educated wandering. (Open Mar.-Oct. daily 9:30am-6pm.) **O'Connor's Garage,** Main St. (tel. 46008), is the friendliest renter of bikes (£7 per day, students £5 per day; £30 per week; ID or £40 deposit; open daily 8am-9pm). Get your fix at **Daly's Pharmacy,** Abbey St. (tel. 46119; open M-F 10am-5pm). The **post office** (tel. 46001) is on Main St. (open M-Tu and Th-Sa 9am-1pm and 2-5:30pm, W 9am-1pm). The **phone code** starred in *The Quiet* 092.

ACCOMMODATIONS, FOOD, AND PUBS The Quiet Man Hostel and the Cong Hostel, owned by the same charming family, are perfect if you're in the mood for a bit of company. Both screen the "legendary" film nightly in mini-theaters, have a **bureau de change** and laundry service (£5), rent **bikes** (£6 per day, £4 per ½-day), and will lend fishing rods, guidebooks, and rowboats for free. The **Quiet Man Hostel (IHH),** Abbey St. (tel. 46511, reservations 46089), across the street from Cong Abbey, is central, spotless, sociable, and spacious, with a large kitchen. The rooms are all named after *The Quiet Man's* characters. Guests may also use the Cong Hostel facilities down the road (playground!). (Dorms £6. Continental breakfast £2.50.) **Cong Hostel (IHH),** Quay Rd. (tel. 46089), a mile down the Galway Rd., is clean and comfortable, with skylights in every room. The playground, picnic area, game room, and piano are sure to keep you entertained. (Dorms £6; doubles with bath £17. Continental breakfast £2.50, full Irish breakfast £4. Extensive **camping** facilities £3.) The clean and fresh **Courtyard Hostel (IHH),** Cross (tel. 46203), will allow you peace of mind off the beaten track several miles east of Cong. (Dorms £6. Private rooms £7.50. **Bike rental** £5 per day. **Camping** £3.) As usual, B&Bs are everywhere. Smothered in geraniums and ivy, **White House B&B,** Abbey St. (tel. 46358), across the street from Danagher's Hotel, offers TV, coffee-maker, and bath in every room. (£16, off-season £15.) Not even the ghosts will stop you from camping on **Inchagoill Island** (see p. 296).

Cooks can go crazy at **O'Connor's Supermarket,** Main St. (tel. 46008; open daily 8am-9pm). Just across the street from the White House B&B, young locals and Ashford Castle staffers down mammoth meals (roast of the day, vegetables, and potatoes £6) and countless pints at **Danagher's Hotel and Restaurant** (tel. 46494). Occasional second-rate bands yawn the crowds, although Oasis put in a memorable cameo in 1997. **Lydon's,** on Main St. across from the supermarket, has the most trad. **The Quiet Man Coffee Shop,** Main St. (tel. 46034), is obviously obsessed. A dark dining room at the back overlooks a river. (Soup and sandwich £2.70; open mid-Mar. to Oct. daily 10am-6:30pm.) The nearest nightclub, **The Valkenburg,** is in Ballinrobe; a bus picks groups up outside Danagher's weekend nights at around 11:30pm and drops them back off at 3am (cover £5, bus £3).

SIGHTS From 1852 to 1939, the heirs to the Guinness fortune, Lord and Lady Ardilaun, lived in Ashford Castle, a structure as impressive as the lake itself. Today, big-deal diplomatic visitors stay in the castle, a £500 per night hotel. *The Quiet Man* was shot on the extensive grounds. The castle is closed to anyone who asks permission to visit, but you can see the **gardens** (£3). Oscar Wilde once informed Lady Ardilaun that she could improve them by planting petunias in the shape of a pig, the family crest.

Though lacking such clever designs, the grounds do hold exotic floral delights. A walk from the castle along Lough Corrib leads to a monument bearing Lady Ardilaun's message to her lost Lord: "Nothing remains for me/What does remain is nothing."

The sculpted head of its last abbot keeps watch over the ruins of the 12th-century **Royal Abbey of Cong**, near Danagher's Hotel in the village. *(Always open. Free.)* The last High King of a united Ireland, Ruairi ("Rory") O'Connor, retired to the abbey for his final 15 years after repeatedly leading Gaelic armies in futile battles against Norman troops. Ironically, it was General Rory O'Connor who disunited the 26 counties and sparked the Irish Civil War in 1922 (see p. 60). Across the abbey grounds, a footbridge spans the River Cong. Past the Monk's Fishing House and to the right, the footpath leads to **Pigeon Hole, Teach Aille,** and **Ballymaglancy** caves and to a 4000-year-old burial chamber, **Giant's Grave.** (The hostels lend out detailed cave maps.) Spelunkers have access to the caves, but Kelly's Cave is locked and the key held at the Quiet Man Coffee Shop. Safe spelunking requires a friend who knows when to expect you back, two flashlights, waterproof gear, and caution.

The **Quiet Man Heritage Cottage** (tel. 46089), a replica of a set from the film with a local history display on the second floor, tries to make up for the fact that the film was actually shot in a Hollywood lot. *(Only worth the £2.50, students £2, for fanatics. Open daily 10am-6pm.)* "The quiet man will never die," the center's video promises. Contestants come from all over Ireland for the extraordinary John Wayne/Maureen O'Hara look-alike contest at the annual **Cong Midsummer Ball.**

Water Water Everywhere...

Clonbur, where Mount Gable rises up above the flatness, was the site of a 19th-century engineering disaster. The Dry Canal is a deep, empty 4 mi. groove in the earth just east of Cong off the Galway road, near the Cong Hostel. Locks punctuate the useless canal as if water were flowing through it. While there is water aplenty in Ireland, not even the leprechauns could make it stay in the porous chalk bed. The canal-opening ceremony in the 1840s was a surprising failure, as water that was let into the canal from Lough Mask promptly vanished into the absorbent walls. The canal could have been sealed and made useful, but by the 1850s trains had already replaced canals as the most efficient means of commercial transport, leaving the canal as hapless as its engineers.

■ Near Cong: Inchagoill

Inchagoill (INCH-a-gill), a forested island in the middle of Lough Corrib, has been uninhabited since the 1950s. Two churches, about which very little is known, hide quietly down the right-hand path from the pier. **St. Patrick's Church,** built in the 5th century, is now only a stack of crumbling stone. The famous Stone of Lugna, supposedly the tombstone of St. Patrick's nephew and navigator, stands 3 ft. high among the stones surrounding the church. The inscription on the stone reads "LIE LUGUAE-DON MACCI MENUEH," or "stone of Luguaedon the son of Menueh." It is the earliest known instance of the Irish language written in Roman script, and probably the second-oldest inscribed Christian monument in Europe (the oldest are the catacombs of Rome). **The Church of the Saint** dates back to the 12th century. On the south side of the island is a coffee house built by the Guinness. Inchagoill's only current full-time residents are a colony of wild rats. They're civilized and proper (i.e., invisible) during the day but can be surly at night. Campers should take these furry fellows into consideration. Ed Hickey at Lough Corrib Hostel in Oughterard can take you out to Inchagoill or bring you back "any time" (4-person min., £6 return). Several other hostels in Oughterard also run boats out to the island (see p. 293). The **Corrib Queen** (tel. (092) 46029) sails daily from Lisloughrea Quay on the Quay Rd. in Cong and offers a brief but enlightening tour of the island (1½hr., June-Aug. 4 per day, £8 return). Those interested in more extensive exploration should take a morning ferry out and return in the afternoon.

THE CONNEMARA

The Connemara is composed of a lacy net of inlets and islands along the coast, a rough gang of inland mountains, and some bogs in between. This thinly populated but geographically varied western arm of Co. Galway, which harbors some of Ireland's most breathtaking and solitary scenery, seldom fails to impress. The jagged southern coastline of the Connemara teems with safe beaches ideal for camping, sinuous estuaries, and tidal causeways connecting to rocky offshore islands. The relatively uninteresting developed strip from Galway to Rossaveal soon gives way to pretty fishing villages such as Roundstone and Kilkieran. Ireland's largest *gaeltacht* stretches along the coast; Connemara-based Irish-language radio, *Radio na Gaeltachta,* broadcasts from Costelloe. Colorful **Clifden,** Connemara's largest town, also hosts its largest crowds. Squishy old bogs spread between the coast and two major mountain ranges, the **Twelve Bens** and the **Maamturks,** which rise up like little green hills that just forgot to stop growing. Northeast of the Maamturks is **Joyce Country,** an area known for its large numbers of live Joyces. Tom Joyce, the original Welsh settler of the region, was said to be 7 ft. tall, and many of his descendents share his uncommonly high vertical elevation.

Cycling is a particularly rewarding way to absorb the Connemara. The 60-mile rides from Galway to Clifden via Cong or to Letterfrack are common routes, although the roads become a bit difficult toward the end. The seaside route through Inverin and Roundstone to Galway is another option, and each of the dozens of loops and backroads in north Connemara is as spectacular as the next. **Hiking** through the boglands and along the coastal routes is popular. The **Western Way** footpath offers dazzling views as it winds 31 miles from Oughterard to Leenane through the Maamturks. **Buses** regularly service the main road from Galway to Westport, with stops in Clifden, Oughterard, Cong, and Leenane. N59 from Galway to Clifden is the main thoroughfare; R336, R340, and R341 make more elaborate coastal loops. **Hitchers** report that friendly locals are likely to stop and give interesting tours of the region. Watching the Connemara go by through the tinted windows of a **bus tour** (see **Galway,** p. 283) is a better way to see the Connemara than sitting at home and looking at someone else's photo album.

■ South Connemara

N59, the direct route from Galway to Clifden, passes through bare mountainous scenery, while the coastal route weaves in and out of the peninsulas and islands of South Connemara. A barren, boggy, lake-ridden frontier with few roads spans the large distance between the two highways. Drive-through territory runs straight along the Galway coast through the Irish-speaking suburbs of **Barna, Spiddal,** and **Inverin;** although Spiddal does have a small beach, far better ones await farther west. Boats leave for the Aran Islands from nearby **Rossaveal** (see **Aran Islands,** p. 278), west of which the landscape morphs into a lively and complicated mesh of intertwined estuaries, peninsulas, and islands. When the tides fall, bays become ponds, islands become peninsulas, and beaches grow wider. The first turnoff after Rossaveal leads to **Carraroe,** an Irish-speaking hamlet notable for its strand of coral beaches.

Seven miles from Spiddal is the **Indreabhán Youth Hostel (An Óige/HI)** (tel. (091) 593154; fax 593638). The building, which was once a school, was undergoing renovation in 1998 and due to open sometime in early 1999. (June-Sept. £7, under 18 £5.50; Oct.-May £6, under 18 £5. Sheets 75p.)

At Gortmore, a detour through **Rosmuck** leads to the cottage of **Padraig Pearse** (tel. (091) 574292), which squats in a small hillock overlooking the northern mountains. Pearse and his brother spent their summers here learning Irish and dreaming of an Irish Republic (see the **Easter Rising,** p. 60). The Republic-come-true declared the cottage a national monument. (Open mid-June to mid-Sept. daily 9:30am-1:30pm and 2:30-6:30pm. £1, students 40p.) Farther along the coast, the little fishing village of

Counties Galway, Mayo, and Sligo

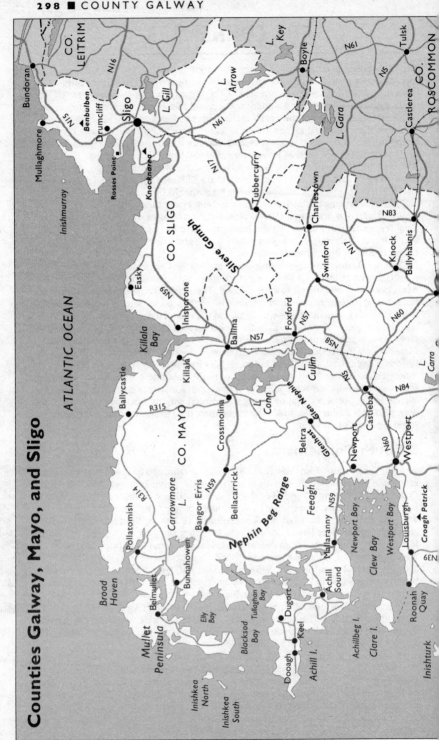

N

0 _____ 10 miles

0 _____ 10 kilometers

ATLANTIC OCEAN

ARAN ISLANDS

Inishmore

Inishmaan

Kilronan

Inisheer

Gorumna I.

Lettermore I.

Bertraghboy Bay

Roundstone

Ballyconneely

Mannin Bay

Cleggan

Clifden

Inishark

Inishbofin

Killary Harbor

Letterfrack

Connemara National Park

Twelve Bens

Connemara

Maamturk Mts.

Joyce Country

Leename

Doo L.

Mweelrea ▲

Partry Mts.

Toutmakeady

Ballinrobe

L. Mask

Cong

Cross

Inchagoill

L. Nafooey

Inagh L.

Maam Cross

N59

Oughterard

Gortmore

Rosmuck

Carraroe

Rossaveal

R336

Inverin

Spiddal

Barna

L. Corrib

Headford

N84

Tuam

N83

N17

Claregalway

Athenry

Moylough

CO. GALWAY

R362

N60

Roscommon

Shannon R.

Ballinasloe

Aughrim

N6

N65

Portumna

L. Derg

Mountshannon

N41

Loughrea

99N

Slieve Aughty Mts.

Thoor Ballylee

Gort

N18

Kilcolgan

Oranmore

Galway

Salthill

Galway Bay

Doorus

Kinvarra

Coole Park

Ballyvaughan

Ballyvaughan Bay

Carran

CO. CLARE

The Burren

N67

Lisdoonvarna

Kilfenora

Corofin

N18

Ennistymon

Doolin

Inisheer

Cliffs of Moher

Liscannor

Lahinch

Roundstone curves along a colorful harbor. From the bay, one can see a few striking Bens rising in the distance. Errisbeg Mountain overlooks Roundstone's main street, and the two-hour hike up culminates in a panoramic view of the Connemara. **Round-stone Musical Instruments** (tel. (095) 35875) is the only full-time *bodhrán* maker in the world (see **Traditional Music,** p. 66; open Mar.-Aug. daily 8am-7pm; Sept.-Feb. M-Sa 8am-7pm). Where there are musical instruments, there is music, and **An galún Taoscta** is where you're likely to find it (trad Wednesdays, Sunday lunch session). Afterwards, bang your *bodhrán* in the direction of **Wits End B&B** (tel. (095) 35951; July-Aug. £16 with bath, Sept.-June £15). Two miles along the coast from Round-stone, the beaches between Dog's Bay and Gorteen Bay fan out to a small nobby island. On a bog near **Ballyconneely,** the last town before Clifden, John Alcock and Arthur Brown landed the first nonstop transatlantic flight in 1919.

■ Clifden

Clifden (An Clochán) is the largest town in the Connemara, but as a busy, brightly colored English holiday town in an poor Irish-speaking region, it is hardly representative. Although its main draw remains its proximity to the scenic bogs and mountains of the Connemara, Clifden has recently become something of an attraction in its own right. Two high spires overlook its tiny center, a wad of hotels, restaurants, pubs, and souvenir shops. Clifden slumbers in the winter but explodes in peak season as crowds of international visitors fill its five hostels, tourbuses bring traffic to a standstill, and musicians shake the town's pubs nightly. Yuppie shoppers come to hunt in its ubiquitous art and crafts studios, young people for the liveliest pub scene this side of Galway.

ORIENTATION AND PRACTICAL INFORMATION

Market St. meets Main St. and Church Hill at The Square. The buildings on the south side of Market St. hide a surprising cliff drop. N59 makes a U-turn at Clifden; most traffic is from Galway, 1½ hours southeast, but the road continues northeast to Letterfrack and Connemara National Park. Hitchers usually wait at the Esso station on N59.

Buses: Bus Éireann rolls from Cullen's Coffeeshop on Market St. to **Galway** via **Oughterard** (2hr., June-Aug. M-Sa 6 per day, Su 2 per day, Sept.-May 1 per day, £6.50) and **Westport** via **Leenane** (1½hr., late June-Aug. 1-2 per day). **Michael Nee** (tel. 51082) runs a private bus from The Square to **Galway** (June-Sept., £5, £7 return) and **Cleggan** (June-Sept. 1-2 per day, Oct.-May 2 per week, £3, £4 return).

Tourist Office: Market St. (tel. 21163). Friendlier than most. Open July-Aug. M-Sa 9:45am-5:45pm and Su noon-4pm; May-June and Sept. M-Sa 9am-5:45pm.

Banks: AIB, The Square (tel. 21129). Open M-Tu and Th-F 10am-12:30pm and 1:30-4pm, W 10am-5pm. **ATM. Bank of Ireland,** Sea View (tel. 21111). Open M-F 10am-12:30pm and 1:30-5pm.

Taxi: Joyce's (tel. 21076).

Bike Rental: Mannion's, Bridge St. (tel. 21160, after hours 21155). £5 per day, £30 per week; deposit £10. Open M-Sa 9:30am-6:30pm, Su 10am-1pm and 5-7pm.

Boat Rental: John Ryan, Sky Rd. (tel. 21069). Prices negotiable.

Laundry: The Shamrock Washeteria, The Square (tel. 21348). Wash and dry £3.80. Open M-Sa 9:30am-6pm.

Pharmacy: Clifden Pharmacy (tel. 21821). Open M-F 9:30am-6:30pm, Sa 9:30am-5:30pm.

Emergency: Dial 999; no coins required. **Garda:** tel. 21021.

Hospital: tel. 21301 or 21302.

Post Office: Main St. (tel. 21156). Open M-F 9:30am-5:30pm, Sa 9:30am-1:30pm.

Phone Code: 095 is your chance to do the hump.

ACCOMMODATIONS

B&Bs litter the streets; the going rate is £16-18. In July and August, early reservations are a must.

The Clifden Town Hostel (IHH), Market St. (tel. 21076). Great facilities, spotless rooms, near-pub location, and a friendly, yet quiet, atmosphere. Old stone walls poking through the tasteful, modern decor serve as a reminder that the house is 180 years old. Sean has lived on this street his whole life and will cheerfully divulge its deepest secrets. Two kitchens. Dorms £7; doubles £20; triples £27; quads £32.

Leo's Hostel (IHH), Sea View (tel. 21429), straight on Market St. past The Square. This big old house is showing its age, but the turf fire, good location, and astounding "loo with a view" outweigh other considerations. Dorms £7; private rooms £8. Laundry £3. **Camping** £3 per person. **Bike rental** £5 per day.

Brookside Hostel, Hulk St. (tel. 21812), straight past the bottom of Market St. Spacious living room and kitchen. Dorms look over innocuous sheep loitering in the backyard. Owner will painstakingly plot a hiking route for you. June-Sept. dorms £7-8; Oct.-May £6. Rates of private rooms vary. Laundry £4.

Ard Rí Bay View, Market St. (tel. 21866), behind King's Garage. No-frills and proud of it. Nice views, central location, and a different color scheme for each room. July-Aug. dorms £6; Sept.-June £5. Private rooms £8 year-round.

Blue Hostel, Sea View (tel. 21835), beyond Leo's. This family home may not provide much elbow room, but with free wash and dry, at least everyone's clean. Dorms £6; private rooms £7.

White Heather House, The Square (tel. 21655). Great location and panoramic views from four of the six rooms, all with bath. £16-18.

Kingston House, Mrs. King, Bridge St. (tel. 21470). Spiffy rooms with a partial view of the church. Singles £18; doubles £32, with bath £36.

Shanaheever Campsite, (tel. 21018), a little over a mile outside Clifden on Westport Rd. The tranquility of this spot compensates for its distance from the pubs. Game room, hot showers, and kitchen. £6 for a tent and 2 people; £3 per additional person. Laundry £4.50.

FOOD AND PUBS

Finding a good restaurant or café in Clifden requires little effort; fitting the prices into a tight budget is more difficult. **O'Connor's SuperValu,** Market St., may be the best place to score some victuals (open M-F 8:30am-8pm, Su 9am-7pm).

An Tulan, Westport Rd. (tel. 21942), offers wonderful homecooked meals at down-to-earth prices. A black sheep in this town. Sandwiches from £1.20, entrees around £4. Open daily 10am-6pm.

Mitchell's Restaurant, The Square (tel. 21867). A cozy, candlelit restaurant serving hearty plates for all palates to traditional Irish muzak. Open daily noon-10:30pm.

Derryclare Restaurant, The Square (tel. 21440). Dark wood adds class. Lunch specials are a particularly good value (6 oysters £4.50). Dinner, of course, is priced a bit higher (pasta around £7). Open daily 8am-10:30pm.

Walsh's, The Square (tel. 21283). This bakery plus looks tiny but actually has quite a large seating area, and there's nothing small about the sandwiches (£2). Open M-F 8am-9pm (July-Aug. until 10pm), Sa 8am-6:30pm, Su 9am-6:30pm.

E.J. King's, The Square (tel. 21330). Crowded bar serves incomparable fare on exceptionally old wood furniture. Open daily 6-10pm. Pub downstairs serves a limited menu daily noon-9pm.

PUBS AND CLUBS

Mannion's, Market St. (tel. 21780). Bring your own instruments or just pick up some spoons when you get there. Music nightly in summer, F-Sa in winter.

King's, The Square (tel. 21800). The town's best pint by consensus; locals vote with their feet.

Malarkey's, on Church Hill, is perpetually packed and jiggity jammin' on Thursdays.

E.J. King's, The Square (tel. 21330), is a talking, laughing, shouting, touristy pub that rocks the casbah.

Its name is **Humpty's** (tel. 21511). The crowd with the boom is stepping tall at this crazy wack funky bar. On weekends, there's no stopping it from getting busy, from the panoramic back window seats to the bathrooms. Rumor alleges that it even has its own dance.

Clifden House (tel. 21187), in Smuggler's Lodge at the bottom of Market St. The best and only place to be for booty-shaking disco. Off-peak Sa, peak Th-Su. Cover £4-5.

SIGHTS

There are no cliffs in Clifden itself, but 10 mi. Sky Road, looping around the head of land west of town, paves the way to some dizzying cliffs and makes an ideal cycling route. One mile down Sky Rd. stand the ruins of **Clifden Castle,** once home to Clifden's founder, John D'Arcy. Farther out, a peek back at the far side of the bay reveals the spot where U.S. pilots Alcock and Brown landed after crossing the ocean in a biplane. One of the nicer ways to acquaint yourself with Connemara is by hiking south to the Alcock and Brown monument, situated just off the Ballyconnelly road 3 mi. past Salt Lake and Lough Fadda.

An archaeologist leads inspiring tours from the **Connemara Walking Center,** Market St. (tel. 21379), that explore the history, folklore, geology, and archaeology of the region. *(Open Mar.-Oct. M-Sa 10am-6pm. One full-day or two half-day tours per day from Easter to Oct.; call for a schedule. £8-24.)* Walks investigate the bogs, the mountains, and Inishbofin and Omey islands. The office sells wonderful maps and guidebooks.

Irish night hits **Clifden Town Hall** every Tuesday at 9pm (July-Aug.), reviving an ancient culture of traditional music, dance, and song. Clifden's artsy pretensions multiply in late September (Sept. 19-26, 1999) during the annual **Clifden Arts Week** (tel. 21295), featuring dozens of free concerts, poetry readings, and storytellings. On the third Thursday of August (Aug. 19, 1999), attractive, talented contenders come to Clifden from miles around to compete for top awards at the **Connemara Pony Show.**

Tiny **Cleggan,** 10 mi. northwest of Clifden, serves tourists mainly as a useful jumping-off point for the isle of Inishbofin. **Michael Nee** and **Bus Éireann** go to Cleggan from Clifden. **Omey Island,** just offshore of Claddaghduff a few miles south of Cleggan, has rolling sandhills and minor ruins for exploration. But this island's true gift is its accessibility—a beautiful white beach connects it to the mainland at low tide. Bareback riding along the Cleggan Strand makes for more good stories (£12 per hr.; contact the Master House in Cleggan, tel. (095) 44746).

■ Inishbofin

Seven miles from the western tip of the Connemara, the island of Inishbofin (pop. 200) keeps time according to the ferry, the tides, and the sun, and visitors easily slip into a similar habit. There's little to do on the island other than scramble up the craggy hills, sunbathe on a secluded white strand, commune with the seals, watch birds fishing among the coves, and sleep under a blanket of bright stars. A fishing boat that ran aground years ago still lies tilted on its side in the harbor. The smattering of tourists suggests that the island isn't completely removed from the universe, but Inishbofin seems to be part of another world.

PRACTICAL INFORMATION Ferries leave for Inishbofin from **Cleggan,** a tiny village 10 mi. northwest of Clifden (see above). Two ferries service the island: the **Island Discovery** (tel. 44642) is larger, steadier, faster, and more expensive (30min., July-Aug. 3 per day, Apr.-June and Sept.-Oct. 2 per day, £12), but the **M.V. Dun Aengus** (Paddy O'Halloran, tel. 45806) runs year-round (45min., July-Aug. 3 per day, Apr.-June and Sept.-Oct. 2 per day, Nov.-Apr. 1 per day, £10). Both ferries carry bikes for free. Tickets are most conveniently purchased on the ferry itself. Drivers can leave cars parked free of charge at the Cleggan Pier. Stock up at the **Spar** (tel. 44750; open daily 9am-10pm) before you go, especially if you're taking a later ferry. **Two-wheeled contraptions** can be rented at the Inishbofin pier (tel. 45833) for £5 per day, and four-legged contraptions can be hired from **Inishbofin Pony Trekking** (tel. 45853) for £12 per hour, but the island is best explored on foot. The **phone code** is Day's 095.

ACCOMMODATIONS, FOOD, AND PUBS Kieran Day's excellent **Inishbofin Island Hostel (IHH)** (tel. 45855) is a 10-minute walk from the ferry landing; take a right at the pier and head up the hill. Visitors are blessed with pine bunks, a large conservatory, and entertaining views. People come for a night and stay for weeks. (Dorms £6.50; private rooms £9-10 per person. Sheets £1. Laundry £4. **Camping** £4 per person.) **Remote Horseshoe B&B** (tel. 45812) sets itself apart on the east end of the island (£13). The **Emerald Cottage** (tel. 45865), a 10-minute walk west from the pier, offers gracious B&B living (£13). There is no camping allowed on the east end beach or the adjacent dunes. Close to the pier, **Day's Pub** (tel. 45829) serves food from noon to 5pm. **Day's Shop** (tel. 45829) is behind the pub and has what you'll need for relaxing in the sun or picnicking in the hills (open M-Sa 11:30am-1:30pm and 3-5pm, Su 11:30am-12:30pm). The island's nightlife is surprisingly vibrant, with frequent music performances during the summer. The smaller and more sedate **Murray's Pub,** a hotel-bar 15 minutes west of the pier, is the perfect place for conversation, slurred or otherwise.

SIGHTS Visitors to Inishbofin perhaps most enjoy meandering through the rocks and wildflowers of the island's four peninsulas. Paths are scarce; each peninsula usually warrants a two- to four-hour walk. Most items of historical interest are on the southeast peninsula. East of the hostel lie the ruins of a 15th-century **Augustinian Abbey,** built on the site of a monastery founded by St. Colman in 667. A well and a few gravestones remain from the 7th-century structure. A conservation area stretches east past the abbey and harbors long pristine beaches and a picturesque village. Swimming in the clear waters is safe, but, please, no eroding the dunes. The most spectacular views of the island reward those who scramble up nearby **Knock Hill. Bishop's Rock,** a short distance off the mainland, becomes visible at low tide. Cromwell supposedly once tied a recalcitrant priest to the rock and forced his comrades to watch as the tide drowned him. On the other side of the island, to the west of the pier, is the imposing **Cromwellian fort,** which was built for defense but used to hold prisoners before transporting them to the West Indies.

The ragged northeast peninsula is fantastic for bird watchers: gulls, cornets, shags, and a pair of perigrine falcons fish among the cliffs and coves while gannets wet their nests. Inishbofin provides a perfect climate for those trees hospitable to the corncrake, a bird near extinction everywhere but in Seamus Heaney's poems; two pairs of corncrakes presently call Inishbofin home. Fish swim in the clear water of two massive blowholes, while a dramatic group of round seastacks called **The Stags** towers offshore. The tidal causeway that connects The Stags to the mainland during low tide is **extremely dangerous**—do not venture out onto it. **Trá Gheal** ("Silvery Beach"), Inishbofin's most beautiful strand, stretches along the northwest peninsula, but swimming here is dangerous. Off to the west is **Inishark,** an island inhabited by sheep and gray seals (most visible during mating season in September and early October). Inspirational archaeologist Michael Gibbons, at the Connemara Walking Center in Clifden (see above), offers tours focusing on Inishbofin's history, archaeology, and ecology. Leo Hallissey's fantastic **Connemara Summer School** (tel. 41034), held during the first week in July, centers on the island's archaeology and ecology.

■ Inishturk

Inishturk (pop. 90) is where Inishbofiners go to get away from the stress of modern life. A small, rounded peak rising 600 ft. out of the ocean between Inishbofin and Clare Island, Inishturk has more spectacular walks and views than either. Those attempting an expedition to Inishturk, which remains relatively undiscovered, are advised to bring adequate supplies. Perhaps someone will discover **Concannon's B&B** (tel. (098) 45610) above a fish restaurant on the pier (£13). Another intrepid explorer might find **Paddy O'Toole's B&B** about a mile from the harbor on the west village road (£15). Who knows, explorers just might find a beautiful beach perfect for camping. **John Heanue's Caher Star** (tel. (098) 45541) discovers the island twice a day (from Cleggan Tu-Th, from Roonah F-M, £15 return). Anything can happen in this brave new world.

■ Clifden to Westport

The area to the east and northeast of Clifden hunches up into high hills and then collapses into grass-curtained bogs interrupted only by the rare bare rock. The landscape of the Connemara National Park conceals a number of curiosities, including hare runs, orchids, and roseroot.

■ Connemara National Park

Outside Letterfrack, Connemara National Park (tel. (095) 41054) occupies 7¾ sq. mi. of mountainous, bird-filled countryside. The far-from-solid terrain of the park is composed of bogs thinly covered by a screen of grass and flowers. Be prepared to dirty your shoes and pants. (*Open daily June 10am-6:30pm; July-Aug. 9:30am-6:30pm; May and Sept. 10am-5:30pm. £2, students £1.*) Guides lead free two-hour walks over the hills and through the bogs (July-Aug. M, W, and F at 10:30am) and give lectures on the region's history and ecology (July-Aug. W 8:30pm; free). The **visitors center** excels at explaining blanket bogs, raised bogs, turf, and heathland.

The **Snuffaunboy Nature Trail** and the **Ellis Wood Trail** are the perfect routes for easy hikes and pony-rides. The Snuffaunboy features alpine views while the Ellis wood submerges walkers in ancient forest; both teem with beautiful wildflowers. A guidebook mapping out 30-minute walks (50p) is available at the visitors center, where the staff helps plan longer hikes. Experienced hikers often head for the **Twelve Bens** (*Na Benna Beola*, a.k.a. the Twelve Pins), a rugged range that reaches 2400 ft. heights and is not recommended for single or beginning hikers. There are no proper trails, but Jos Lynam's guidebook (£5) meticulously plots out 18 fantastic hikes through the Twelve Bens and the Maamturks. Hikers often base themselves at the **Ben Lettery Hostel (An Óige/HI)** (tel. (095) 51136) in Ballinafad; the turn-off from N59 is 8 mi. east of Clifden (June-Aug. £6.50; Easter-May and Sept. £5.50). A hike from this institutional but friendly hostel through the park to the Letterfrack hostel can be done in one day. A tour of all 12 Bens takes experienced walkers about 10 hours. Biking the 40 mi. circle through Clifden, Letterfrack, and the spectacular Inagh valley is breathtaking, especially for the out-of-shape.

■ Letterfrack

Despite its three pubs and legendary hostel, Letterfrack, located at the crossroads of the Connemara National Park, hasn't quite achieved town status. The **Galway-Clifden** bus (M-Sa late June-Aug. 11 per week; Sept. to mid-June 4 per week) and the summertime **Clifden-Westport** bus (M and Th 2 per day, Tu-W and F-Sa 1 per day) stop at Letterfrack. Hitchers report medium-length waits on N59. The **phone code** is 095.

Uphill from the intersection, the **Old Monastery Hostel** (tel. 41132) is one of Ireland's finest, beautifully decorated and furnished with the philosophy of camaraderie. Sturdy pine bunks, desks, and couches fit the spacious high-ceilinged rooms, a peat fire burns in the lounge, and framed photos of jazz greats hang in the cozy basement café. Steve, the owner, cooks mostly organic vegetarian buffet dinners in the summer (buffet £7, plate £4) and fresh scones for breakfast. (8-bed dorms £7; 6-bed dorms £8; 4-bed dorms £9. Breakfast included. Laundry £3. **Bike rental** £6 per day. **Internet access** £2.50 per hr.) Good pub grub, groceries, pints, and locals are available at **Veldon's** (tel. 41046), which fills at 10:30am and empties late, sometimes after a trad session (grocery open daily June-Aug. 9:30am-9pm, Sept.-May 9:30am-7pm). **The Bard's Den** (tel. 41042), across the intersection, caters to tourists with its skylight and large open fire. Photos of long-gone local characters dignify the walls of **Paddy Coyne's,** a few miles north of Letterfrack in Tully Cross. Jackie Coyne's Wednesday night lessons in the Irish broom dance dignify nothing at all, but they sure are fun. At **Ocean's Alive** (tel. 43473), a new tourist magnet at Derryinver, 1½ mi. north of Letterfrack, you can reach into the touching aquarium and fondle the crabs (open May-Sept. 9:30am-7pm, Oct.-Apr. 10am-4:30pm; £3, students £2.50). Letterfrack hosts two environmentally oriented festivals a year. During **Bog Week,** the last week in October, and **Sea Week,** the first week in May, world-famous environmentalists gather to discuss current bog- and sea-related issues while musicians go out and jam in the bog.

The road from Letterfrack to Leenane passes **Kylemore Abbey** (tel. (095) 41146), a castle dramatically set in the shadow of a rocky outcrop. (Open Apr.-Oct. 9am-6pm, Nov.-Mar. 10am-4pm. £3, students £2; gardens and abbey £5, students £4.) Built in 1867 by an English industrialist, the castle has been occupied since 1920 by a group of Benedictine nuns, who cheerfully pass on the message of St. Benedict to interested tourists. Visitors mill about a small neo-Gothic church a few hundred feet down from the abbey. A rocky path winds up above the castle, under trees and over streams, to a ledge with a view of the lake that you'll be loath to leave. A statue with arms aloft welcomes you from your half-hour climb. In the spring of 1999, £3,000,000 later, the newly restored six-acre **Victorian Walled Garden** is scheduled to open; the garden gate is a mile west of the abbey (open Easter-Nov.; £3, students £2.50).

■ Leenane

Farther east along N59, **Killary Harbour,** Ireland's only fjord, breaks through the mountains to the wilderness outpost of Leenane (pop. 47), which wraps itself in the skirts of the Devilsmother Mountains. This once populous region was reduced to a barren hinterland during the famine; remnants of farms cover the surrounding hills. Epic melodies floating from the Cultural Centre provide the perfect backdrop for contemplating the desolate scenery. *The Field* was filmed here in 1989, and no one in town will ever forget it. The murder scene was shot at Aasleagh Falls. At **Leenane Cultural Centre** (tel. (095) 42323), on the Clifden-Westport Rd., spinning and weaving demonstrations reveal the fate of wool from the sheep grazing in the backyard (open Apr.-Oct. daily 10am-7pm; £2, students £1.50). **Killary Harbour Hostel (An Óige/HI)** (tel. (095) 43417) perches on the very edge of the shore 7 mi. west of Leenane. Although the hostel boasts an unbeatable waterfront location, the cramped dorms and the once-modern design lean towards the institutional. A hostel shop sells baked beans and other necessities. (Dorms £7, off-season £6. Open Jan.-Nov.) **Bay View House** (tel. (095) 42240), on the northern side of town along N59, boasts a bizarre dining room that was once a chapel (singles £20-24; doubles £29). Catching a lift from Leenane feels like winning the lottery; you won't even have a chance to play with the locals.

County Mayo

Co. Mayo fills a large expanse of northwestern Ireland with a truly remarkable emptiness occasionally interrupted by bog and beach. Towns and cities sporadically pop up out of nowhere: Westport is somewhat upscale and popular, Ballina is best known for its Moy fisheries, and old sea resorts such as Achill Island and Enniscrone line the seaboard. Mayo's fifteen minutes of fame occurred in 1798, "The Year of the French," when General Humbert landed at Kilcummin. Combining French soldiers, Irish revolutionaries, and rural secret societies into an army, Humbert seduced half the county, from Killala to Castlebar. The English retaliated and won at Ballina and Ballinamuck. The village of Cong, Co. Mayo, is covered under **Co. Galway** (p. 294).

■ Westport

In the summer, Westport draws more visitors than it knows what to do with. Some stay in its four excellent hostels, others heartily contribute to its thriving pub life, and some spend their days strolling along its four crowded streets, drinking tea in dapper cafés, shopping for commemorative keychains, and admiring the fresh coats of paint on the newest rash of B&Bs. The rest, realizing that there is little to see, quickly move on to Connemara or Mayo's islands to the northwest.

ORIENTATION AND PRACTICAL INFORMATION

The tiny Carrowbeg River runs through Westport's Mall with Bridge and James St. extending south. Shop St. connects Bridge St. to James St. on the other end. Westport House and ferries to Clare Island are on Westport Quay, a 45-minute walk west of town. The N60 passes through Clifden, Galway, and Sligo on its way to Westport. Hitchers proclaim it to be an easy route.

Trains: Trains arrive at the Altamont St. Station (tel. 25253 or 25329 for inquiries), a 5min. walk up on North Mall. Open M-Sa 9:30am-6pm. The train goes to **Dublin** via **Castlebar** and **Athlone** (M-Th and Sa 3 per day, £15; F and Su 2 per day, £20).

Buses: For Westport bus info, call the tourist office. Buses leave from the Octagon and travel to **Ballina** (M-Sa 1-3 per day, Su 1 per day, £6.70), **Castlebar** (M-Sa 5 per day, £2.50), **Louisburgh** (M-Sa 2 per day, £3.20), **Galway** (M-F 2 per day, £8.80), and **Knock** (M-Sa 3 per day, Su 1 per day, £6.70).

Tourist Office: North Mall (tel. 25711). Open Apr.-Oct. M-Sa 9am-12:45pm and 2-5:45pm, Su 10am-6pm.

Travel Agency: Westport Travel, 4 Shop St. (tel. 25511). USIT prices for students; Western Union Money Transfer point. Open M-Sa 9:30am-6pm.

Banks: Bank of Ireland, North Mall (tel. 25522), and **AIB,** Shop St. (tel. 25466), have **ATMs** and are both open M-W and F 10am-4pm, Th 10am-5pm.

Taxis: Brendan McGing, Lower Peter St. (tel. 25529). 50p per mi.

Bike Rental: Breheny & Sons, Castlebar St. (tel. 25020). £7 per day; ID deposit. Bikes can be dropped off in Galway.

Laundry: Westport Washeteria, Mill St. (tel. 25261), near the clock tower. Full service £4, self-service £2.50, powder 40p. Open M-Tu and Th-Sa 9:30am-6pm, W 9:30am-1pm.

Pharmacy: O'Donnell's, Bridge St. (tel. 25163). Open M-Sa 9am-6:30pm. Rotating Sunday (12:30-2pm) openings are posted on the door.

Emergency: Dial 999; no coins required. **Garda:** Fair Green (tel. 25555).

Post Office: North Mall (tel. 25475). Open M-Sa 9am-noon and 2-5:30pm.

Internet Access: Dunning's Cyberpub, The Octagon (tel. 25161). Dunning's thinks different. £5 per 30min. Open daily 9am-11:30pm.

Phone Code: gives props to the class of 098.

ACCOMMODATIONS

Westport's B&Bs are easily spotted on the Castlebar and Altamont Rd. off North Mall. Most charge between £16 and £18.

Old Mill Holiday Hostel (IHH), James St. (tel. 27045), between The Octagon and the tourist office. Firm pine beds line up in a renovated mill and brewery. Character and comfort live happily side by side. Kitchen and common room lockout 11pm-8am. Dorms £6.50. Sheets 50p. Laundry £3.

Club Atlantic (IHH), Altamont St. (tel. 26644 or 26717), a 5min. walk up from the mall across from the train station. This massive 140-bed complex has a pool table, ping-pong, video games, Irish videos, a shop, an elephantine kitchen, and an educational exhibition on Croagh Patrick. Guests can use sauna and swimming pool facilities at the nearby Westport Hotel for £6. Hidden away from all the action, the beds are quiet and comfortable. June-Sept. dorms £6.50; singles £9; doubles £13.80.

Mid.-Mar. to May and Oct. dorms £5.50; singles £9; doubles £11.80. Sheets £1. Laundry £2. **Camping** £4.

Slí na h-Óige (HYI), North Mall. (tel. 28751). Appropriately named "the way of the young", this family-run hostel features comfortable timber beds, free internet access, and two small kitchens. Frequent trad in the lounge and Gaelic lessons on request. Dorms £7. Open June-Sept.

The Granary Hostel (tel. 25903), 1mi. from town on Louisburgh Rd., near the main entrance to Westport House. A garden and conservatory flank this beautiful old converted granary. If you don't mind the cramped quarters or the short walk to the outdoor (enclosed and hot) showers, you're guaranteed to enjoy a night within its rugged walls. Dorms £6. Open Jan.-Nov.

Dunning's Pub, The Octagon (tel. 25161). A unique B&B. Perfect location, with a rare instance of matching carpets, curtains, and bedsheets. Also has an internet café downstairs. £15.

Altamont House, Altamont St. (tel. 25226). 30 years of B&B. Roses peep in the windows of spacious rooms. The garden is a modern Eden. £16. Open Mar.-Dec.

FOOD

Country Fresh (tel. 25377) sells juicy produce (open M-F 8am-6:30pm, Sa 8am-6pm; closes early on W during winter). The **country market** by the Town Hall at The Octagon vends farm-fresh vegetables, eggs, and milk (open Th 10:30am-1:30pm). Processed foods are abundant at the **SuperValu** supermarket (tel. 27000) on Shop St. (open M-W and Sa 8:30am-7:30pm, Th-F 8:30am-9pm, Su 10am-6pm).

McCormack's, Bridge St. (tel. 25619). Pastries, teas, and simple meals on floral tablecloths. Praised by locals as an exemplary teahouse. Open July-Sept. M-Sa 10am-6pm; Oct.-June Tu-Sa 10am-6pm.

Cafolla, Bridge St. (tel. 25168). Eat-in or take-away, the food is incredibly cheap. 7in. cheese pizza £1.75. Open June-Sept. M-Sa 11am-1am, Su noon-11pm; Oct.-May M-Sa 11am-11pm, Su 5-11pm.

The Continental Health Food Shop and Café, High St. (tel. 26679). Enjoy succulent sandwiches (under £3) by the fireplace. Open Tu-Sa 10am-6pm.

Bernie's High Street Café, High St. (tel. 27797). Soft light, ecru walls, and comfortingly healthy plants. Sausage, bacon, and mushroom pancake £4.75. Open daily noon-10pm.

The Urchin, Bridge St. (tel. 27532). A menu full of old favorites. Lunch is inexpensive (sandwiches about £3); dinner isn't. Open daily 10am-10pm; lunch noon-3pm.

PUBS AND CLUBS

Westport is blessed with good craic. Search Bridge St. to find a scene that suits you. The only disco in town is in the **Castlecourt Hotel** on Castlebar St. The guitars on the walls give an uninspired nod to the Hard Rock café, but the computerized lighting effects are pretty cool. (Open F-Su. Cover £5. Ages 18+.)

Matt Molloy's, Bridge St. (tel. 26655). Owned by the flautist of the Chieftains. All the cool people, including his friends, go here. Trad sessions nightly at 9:30pm, but can spontaneously erupt whenever the craic is good. Go early and don't flout the back room if you like yours sitting down.

Henehan's Bar, Bridge St. (tel. 25561). A run-down exterior hides a vibrant pub. 20-somethings fight 80-somethings for space at the bar. Music nightly in summer, on weekends in winter.

O'Malley's Pub, Bridge St., across from Matt Molloy's. Techno blares and Guinness flows.

The West (tel. 25886), at Bridge St. and South Mall, on the river. Choose between the light and creamy outside and the dark and woody inside. The teenage crowd is firmly in control of both. Live rock most summer nights.

Pete McCarthy's, Quay St. (tel. 27050), uphill from the Octagon. Old, dark, and smoky pub attracts regulars. Trad on weekends in summer.

The Towers (tel. 26534), down The Quay 1mi. from town center. Fishing nets and excellent grub hook lots of customers. Beef in Guinness, a uniquely Irish specialty, goes for £5-10. Music F-Su in summer, F-Sa in winter.

SIGHTS

The current commercial uses of **Westport House** (tel. 25430) must be a bitter pill to swallow for its elite inhabitant, Lord Altamont, the 13th great-grandson of Grace O'Malley (see **Amazing Grace,** p. 115). *(Open May and early Sept. daily 2-5pm; June and late Aug. daily 2-6pm; July to mid-Aug. M-Sa 10:30am-6pm, Su 2-6pm. May-June and Sept. £5; July-Aug. £6.)* The zoo and train ride may entertain children, but the carnival and terrifying bog butter in the museum are hardly worth the entrance fee. The grounds, however, are beautiful and free. To get there, take James street above the Octagon, bear right, and follow the signs to the Quay (45min.). More interesting is the **Clew Bay Heritage Centre** (tel. 26852), at the end of the Quay. *(Open July-Sept. M-F 10am-5pm, Sa-Su 2-5pm; Oct.-June M-F noon-3pm. £1.)* The narrow interior crams together a pair of James Connolly's gloves, a sash belonging to John MacBride, and the stunning original photograph of Maud Gonne that graces her biographies. A genealogical service is also available.

Conical **Croagh Patrick** rises 2510 ft. over Clew Bay. The summit has been revered as a holy site for thousands of years. Perhaps because of its height, it was sacred to Lug, sun god, god of arts and crafts, and one-time ruler of the Túatha de Danann (see **Literary Traditions,** p. 61). St. Patrick prayed and fasted here for 40 days and nights in 441 before banishing the snakes from Ireland. The deeply religious climb Croagh Patrick barefoot on the last Sunday in July, also Lug's holy night, Lughnasa. Others climb the mountain just for the exhilaration and the view. It takes about four hours total to climb and descend the mountain. Be warned that the ascent can be quite steep and the footing unsure. Well-shod climbers start their excursion from the 15th-century **Murrisk Abbey,** several miles west of Westport on R395 toward Louisburgh. Buses go to Murrisk (July-Aug. M-F 3 per day, Sept.-June M-Sa 2 per day), but a cab (tel. 27171) is cheaper for three people and more convenient. Pilgrims and hikers also set out for Croagh Patrick along the Tóchar Phádraiga path from **Ballintubber Abbey** (tel. (094) 30709), several miles south of Castlebar and 22 mi. from Croagh Patrick. Founded in 1216 by King of Connacht Cathal O'Connor, the abbey still functions as a religious center. On September 19-28, 1999, Westport celebrates the annual **Westport Arts Festival** (tel. 28833) with dozens of free concerts, poetry readings, and theatrical productions.

■ Louisburgh

Louisburgh (LOOSE-burg; pop. 150), a small but well-planned village 13 mi. west of Westport, is a worthwhile stop for Grace O'Malley fans, Clare Island-bound folks looking for groceries, and few others. The loop from Westport to Louisburgh to Killary Harbour and back to Westport covers 40 mi.; cars are few and far between. **Bus Éireann** runs between Louisburgh and Westport (2-3 per day). Near the square, the **Granuaile Heritage Centre** (tel. 66341) honors Grace O'Malley, 16th-century Pirate Queen of Clew Bay (see **Amazing Grace,** p. 115). (Open June-Sept. daily 10am-6pm. £2, students £1.) Wax figures depict Gaelic chieftains, Queen Elizabeth, and the graceful pirate queen, while a 30-minute film details some of her history. The many O'Malleys in town willingly relate a spicy version of Grace's life. Shocking pictures at the center's **tourist information** desk reveal that Ireland is occasionally sunny. The **phone code** is 098.

Mary O'Malley's riverside farmhouse, **Rivervilla** (tel. 66246), is in Shraugh, half a mile from Louisburgh; signs mark the way (£15, with bath £16; open Apr.-Oct.). Two miles down Westport Rd., **Old Head Forest Caravan and Camping Park** (tel. 66021 or 66455) helps guests enjoy tennis and clean laundry (£6.50-8 per tent; open mid-May to mid-Sept.). **Durkan's Foodstore,** Bridge St. (tel. 66394), is your place for groceries. Bread and beer sustain customers at **Durkan's Weir House,** Chapel St. (tel. 66140; entrees £4-6; food served daily noon-10pm).

Old Head Strand, 2 mi. northeast of town, is one of the finer beaches in the Clew Bay area, although **Carramore Strand** is twice as close. True beach connoisseurs head to **Silver Strand,** 10 mi. down the coast from Louisburgh. Fifteen miles south of town, calm **Doolough** ("Black Lake") offers a choice of several heart-pounding climbs up the Sheffrey Hills, the Mweelrea Mountains, or Ben Gorm. The south end of the lake leads into a wooded dell that falls into the River Bundarragh. Cars and bikes can head back to Westport on a scenic route that bends left at the south end of the lough.

■ Clare Island

An isolated, scenic dot in the Atlantic, Clare Island (pop. 170) is not so scenic as Inishbofin, nor as isolated as Inishturk. Rather, it feels like a contemporary rural village that just happens to be out in the ocean. **Ferries** provide a dolphin-sighting opportunity and dock by the blue-flag beach on the eastern end of the island. **O'Malley's store** (tel. 26987; open daily 11am-6pm), the school, and the church are 1½ mi. straight along the harbor road. Grace O'Malley (known locally as Granuaile) ruled the 16th-century seas west of Ireland from her castle above the beach. Her notorious galley fleet exacted tolls from all ships entering and leaving Galway Bay (see **Amazing Grace,** p. 115). Granuaile died in 1603 and was supposedly laid to rest here under the ruins of the **Clare Island Abbey,** near the shop. Hiking around the deserted island is fun when it's clear; a leaflet with five walks is available at the hotel or souvenir shop. You can search for buried treasure on the west coast of the island, where the cliffs of **Knockmore Mountain** (1550ft.) rise from the sea. **Ozzy** (tel. 45120) runs two-hour off-road tours of the island out of his dockside souvenir shop (£5, 4-person min.).

Charlie O'Malley's **Ocean Star Ferry** (tel. 25045) and the **Clare Island Ferry** (tel. 26307) leave from **Roonah Point,** 4 mi. west of Louisburgh (25min., July-Aug. 5 per day, May-June and Sept. 3-5 per day, Oct.-Apr. call to schedule, £10 return, bikes free). There are no buses to Roonah Point, but you can take a taxi from Louisburgh (see above). The **phone code** is 098. **O'Leary's bike hire** is near the harbor (£5 per day); if no one's there, knock at **Beachside B&B** (tel. 25640). Their clean ensuite rooms and warm hospitality are yours for £15. Just past the beach, the **Sea Breeze B&B** (tel. 26148) offers similar comforts for the same price. **O'Malley's Cois Abhain** (tel. 26216) is 3 mi. from the harbor, but the proprietor will pick you up (singles £18; doubles £32). Clare's only pub, in the **Bay View Hotel** (tel. 26307), to the right along the coast from the harbor, serves until 2am.

ACHILL ISLAND

Two decades ago, Achill (AK-ill) Island was Co. Mayo's most popular holiday refuge. Although its popularity inexplicably dwindled, Ireland's biggest island is still one of its most beautiful. Ringed by glorious beaches and cliffs, Achill's interior consists of bog, mountain, bog-like surface, bog, bog, spam, and bog. Hardly an acre is arable. The town Achill Sound, the gateway to the island, has its nicest hostel, while the island's life centers around the old-school seaside resorts of Keel, Pollagh, and Dooagh, which form a flat, connected strip of buildings along Achill's longest beaches. Dugort, in the north, is less busy. Its most potent vistas are farther west in Keem Bay and at Croaghaun Mountain. Achill is large, so visitors will find it easiest to travel by bike or car. Achill hosts the **Scoil Acla** traditional music and art festival (tel. 45284) during the first two weeks of August.

Buses run infrequently over the bridge from Achill Sound, Dugort, Keel, and Dooagh to **Westport, Galway,** and **Cork** (in summer M-Sa 5 per day, in winter M-Sa 2 per day, £6 return), and to **Sligo, Enniskillen,** and **Belfast** (in summer M-Sa 3 per day, in winter 2 per day). Hitchers report relative success during July and August, but cycling is more reliable. The island's **tourist office** (tel. 45385) is next to Ted Lavelle's Esso station in Cashel, on the main road from Achill Sound to Keel (open 10am-5:30pm M-Sa). True island explorers will pay £3.35 for Bob Kingston's map and guide, but there's a freebie for the rest. There's no bank on the island, so change money on the mainland or suffer rates worthy of Grace O'Malley. The **phone code** is 098.

■ Achill Sound

Achill Sound sits at the gateway to the island. The high concentration of shops and services reflects the fact that all who visit the island must pass through town twice. The town is full of quirky local characters; one of the more prominent is a famous stigmatic and faith healer who draws thousands to her House of Prayer each year. About 6 mi. south of Achill Sound and left at the first cross roads on the road onto the island, two sets of ruins stand near each other. The ancient **Church of Kildavnet** was founded by St. Dympna when she fled to Achill Island to escape her father's incestuous desires. The remains of **Kildownet Castle,** really a fortified tower house dating from the 1500s, proudly crumble nearby. Grace O'Malley, the swaggering, seafaring pirate of medieval Ireland, once owned the castle. The spectacular Atlantic Drive, which roams along the craggy south coast past beautiful beaches to Dooega, makes a fantastic bike ride.

The town holds a **post office** and **bureau de change** (tel. 45141; open M-F 12:30pm and 1:30-5:30pm, Sa 9am-1pm), a **SuperValu** supermarket (open daily 9am-7pm), and a **pharmacy** (tel. 45248; open July-Aug. M-Sa 9:30am-6pm; Sept.-June Tu-Sa 9:30am-6pm). **Achill Sound Hotel** (tel. 45245) rents **bikes** (£6 per day, £30 per week; deposit £40; open daily 9am-9pm). The **Wild Haven Hostel** (tel. 45392), a block left past the church, glows with polished floors, antique furniture, and a turf fire in the sitting room. (Dorms £7.50; private rooms £10 per person. **Camping** £4. Breakfast £3.50; candle-lit dinner £12.50. Sheets £1. Laundry £5. Lockout 11am-3:30pm, except on rainy days.) The **Railway Hostel,** just before the bridge to town, is a simple, multi-kitchened, casual affair in the old station (the last train arrived in the 1930s). The proprietors can be found at Mace Supermarket (tel. 45187) in town. They have all the info you could possibly need for any length stay in one massive volume. (Dorms £6; private rooms with bath £7 per person. Sheets £1. Laundry £1.50.) Opposite the Railway Hostel, **Alice's Harbour Inn** (tel. 45138) does more than its share for the tourist industry. The owners allow **camping** and provide tourist info if the office is closed. The inn also feeds hungry souls (10am-10pm). Eric Clapton was once caught, in the words of locals, "slobbering over a guitar" here during an impromptu jam session.

■ Keel

Keel is a pleasantly dated sea resort on the bottom of a flat, wide valley. The sandy Trawmore Strand sweeps 3 mi. eastward, flanked by cliffs. Encouraged by a government tax scheme, hundreds of holiday developments have popped up like zits across the forehead of the valley within the past three years. Two miles north of Keel on the road looping back to Dugort, the self-explanatory **Deserted Village** is populated only by stone houses closely related to early Christian clocháns. They were used until the late 1930s as pasture and shelter for fattening cattle. Some of these "booleying" houses are scheduled for restoration. The site is used in the summer months for an **Archaeological Summer School** (call Theresa McDonald, tel. (0506) 21627), which sponsors evening lectures at the Warecrest Hotel (tel. 43153) in Dooagh (see below; mid-July to Aug. Tu 8:30pm; £5).

O'Malley's Island Sports (tel. 43125) rents **bikes** (£7 per day, £30 per week; open daily 9am-6pm). The **Wayfarer Hostel (IHH)** (tel. 43266) offers clean, comfortable beds in white rooms. (Dorms £6; private rooms £6.50 per person. Sheets 50p. Laundry £2.50. Open mid-Mar. to mid-Oct.) A comfortable, though more expensive, option is **Mrs. Joyce's Marian Villa** (tel. 43134), a 20-room hotel/B&B with a veranda that looks onto the sea (rooms with TV and bath start at £20). **Roskeel House** (tel. 43537) has spacious, airy suites a block behind the Annexe Inn (£18-25; open Easter-Oct.) Considered a blight on the landscape by locals, **Keel Sandybanks Caravan and**

Camping Park (tel. 43211) does provide a sandy spot to drive in your tent stakes (July-Aug. £6.50 per tent, late May to June and Sept. £5).

Although there are numerous decadent chippies, more nutritious food is available at the **Beehive Handcrafts and Coffee Shop** (tel. 43134), where sweaters alternate with wooden tables. Any local will tell you that the Beehive has the island's cleanest bathrooms. (Open daily 10am-6:30pm.) **Calvey's** (tel. 43158), next to the Spar Supermarket (open M-Sa 9:30am-9pm, Su 9am-6pm), whips up hearty meals (catch of the day £6; open daily 10am-10pm). Inspired drinking is encouraged at the very vinyl **Annexe Inn** (tel. 43268). The pub has nightly trad sessions in July and August (Saturdays only off season) and pictures of dead sharks. The large **Mináun View Bar** (tel. 43120), across from the caravan park, is legendary for its Republican fervor; history lessons are dispensed alongside pints.

■ Dooagh

Corrymore House (tel. 43333), 2 mi. up the road from Keel in Dooagh (DOO-ah), was one of several Co. Mayo estates owned by Captain Boycott, whose mid-19th-century tenants went on an extended rent strike that verbed his surname. The **Folklife Centre** displays household utensils, furniture, and farm implements from the turn of the century (open daily 10:30am-5pm; free). **The Pub** (tel. 43120), on the main street, is managed by the beloved mistress of the house. Don Allum, the first man to row both ways across the Atlantic, made his first stop upon landing in Ireland at The Pub after 77 days at sea.

A grueling bike ride over the cliffs to the west of Dooagh leads to the blue-flag **Keem Bay** beach, the most beautiful spot on the island, wedged between the seas and great green walls of weed, rock, and sheep. Basking sharks, earth's second-largest fish, were once fished off Keem Bay, but bathers who don't look like plankton have nothing to fear. A river of amethyst runs through the Atlantic and comes up in **Croaghaun Mountain,** west of Keem Bay. Most of the accessible crystals have been plundered, but Frank Macnamara, a cantankerous old local, still digs out the deeper veins with a pick and a shovel and sells them from his store in Dooagh. The mountains, climbable from Keem Bay, provide bone-chilling views of the **Croaghaun Cliffs,** Europe's highest sea-cliffs according to the *Guinness Book of Records*.

■ Dugort

A right turn after Cashel leads to the northern part of the island, where Dugort, a tiny hamlet perched atop a sea-cliff, has slept through the 20th century and may sleep through the 21st as well. Mist-shrouded Slievemore Mountain looms to its east. Curious Germans come here to see the former cottage of Heinrich Böll, now a retreat for artists-in-residence. His favorite pub, **The Valley,** serves pints to literary pilgrims. Modern-looking cemeteries and abandoned buildings west of Dugort are the result of a futile mid-1800s effort to convert the islanders to Protestantism by sending in Irish-speaking missionaries. On the other side of Slievemore Mountain gapes the chambered tomb known as **Giant's Grave,** easily accessible from Dugort. Other megalithic tombs lurk nearby. The main signposted tomb, after McDowell's Hotel toward Keel 1 mi. straight up from the road, is easiest to find. Boats leave for the seal caves from the pier at Dugort up the road from the Strand Hotel daily at 11am and 6pm.

A soft pillow for your head awaits at **Valley House Hostel** (tel. 47204). The 100-year-old house is furnished in a paroxysm of fading splendor with antique furniture, massive windows, and an open turf fire. An in-house pub is the most luxurious amenity. (£7. Open Easter-Oct.) The brutal killing of the woman who once owned the house was the basis of Synge's *Playboy of the Western World* and the 1998 film *Lynchahaun,* shot on the premises. The road to the hostel turns left off the main road 2 mi. east of Dugort at the valley crossroads. Nearby, self-proclaimed seafood specialist **Atoka Restaurant** (tel. 47229) feeds hearty portions to applauding locals (entrees £6-12; open May to late Sept. daily 8:30am-11pm). Those who stay for **B&B** get a big breakfast, too (£13, with bath £15). **Seal Caves Caravan and Camping Park** (tel.

WESTERN IRELAND

43262) lies between Dugort Beach and Slievemore Mountain. Check in up the road at the blue house. (July-Aug. £3 per hiker or biker; Apr.-June and Sept. £2.50 per person. Open Apr.-Sept.)

■ Mullet Peninsula

Besides anglers ogling the 38 varieties of fish off the west coast, few visitors make it out to the Mullet Peninsula. The blue-flag beaches are therefore empty, and outsiders are welcomed with genuine Irish hospitality, not resented as a necessary evil. Cold Atlantic winds rip into the barren western half and soggy moorland covers the middle. Budget accommodations are scarce. Remote **Belmullet,** with most of the amenities, occupies the isthmus between Broad Haven and Blacksod Bay. Irish is spoken farther down, where farms and small white cottages dot the rugged bogland.

PRACTICAL INFORMATION An infrequent **bus** service runs the length of the peninsula from **Ballina** (July-Aug. M-Sa 2 per day, Sept.-June M-Sa 1 per day, £7.50). The **Erris Tourist Information Centre** (tel. 81500) is amazingly helpful, dispensing mounds of info to detectives savvy enough to find their hideout of the month (open daily June-Sept. 9:30am-7:30pm; Oct.-May 9am-5:30pm). **Lavelle's Bar** (tel. 81372) provides solid, unofficial info to everyone else. The **Bank of Ireland** (tel. 81311) has an **ATM** (open M-W and F 10am-12:30pm and 1:30-5pm). **Belmullet Cycle Centre,** American St. (tel. 81424), provides pedal power (£7 per day, open M-Sa 10:30am-6pm). The **Centra Supermarket** (open M-Sa 9am-9:30pm) is across Main St. from **Lavelle's Pharmacy** (tel. 81053; open M 11am-2pm, Tu-F 9:30am-6:30pm, Sa 10am-7pm), but meat is easier to find at the **Anchor Bar's** nightclub (£5). The **post office** (tel. 81032) is at the end of Main St. (open M and W-Sa 9am-5:30pm, Tu 9:30am-5:30pm). The **Garda** can be reached at tel. 81038. The **phone code** is 097.

ACCOMMODATIONS The relaxing **Kilcommon Lodge Hostel** (tel. 84621) is in Pollatomish, 10 miles northeast of Belmullet. Its hearty German owners advise outdoors types on hiking routes. (Dorms £6; private rooms £7 per person.) Just after the hostel, the new **Cuan na Farraige** dive center (tel. 97900) provides B&B, dinner, and water sports (dorms £16.50). **Mairín Murphy** (tel. 81195) runs Belmullet's nicest B&B from her turquoise house 350 yd. up the hill from Padden's; one of the rooms is a beautiful studio apartment suite (singles £23.50; doubles £34). Half a block down from the square, the **Mill House B&B,** American St. (tel. 81181), near the bridge, has cute rooms (singles £13; doubles £26). The **Western Strands Hotel** (tel. 91096), Main St., is close to the pubs and provides breakfast and bath for all (singles £17; doubles £30).

FOOD AND PUBS Padden's Family Fare, Carter Sq. (tel. 81324), offers somewhat dignified family dining at low prices (entrees £3-5; open Tu-Su noon-10pm). **The Appetizer** (tel. 82222) sells sandwiches and desserts (open daily 9am-6pm). Belmullet's pub scene is local and buzzing, with hinterland farmfolk congregating in town nightly. **Lavelle's** (tel. 81372) has the town's best pint and hippest crowd. Portraits of Mayo hurlers adorn the walls of **Lenehan's** (tel. 81098), the first and last stop on the old men's gossip circuit. **Clan Lir,** Main St., popular with the young, gets rowdy during football games. Knock if the doors are closed. Birdwatchers flock to the **Anchor Bar,** Barrack St. (tel. 81007), which records ornithological sightings; the nightclub out back opens on weekends (£5 cover).

SIGHTS The **Ionad Deirbhle heritage center** in Aughleam at the end of the peninsula explores items of local interest, including the history of the whaling industry and the Inishkey (Inis Gé) islands. *(Open Easter-Oct. 10am-6pm. £2.)* **Josephine and Matt Geraghty** (tel. 85741) run boat trips to the islands, which were inhabited until a disastrous fishing accident in 1935. *(1 per day in summer, 3 per week in winter. £12 per person, 6-person min.)* Fly fishing abounds in nearby **Cross Lake,** with both shore and boat angling available; contact **George Geraghty** (tel. 81492). *(Open 9am-dusk. Rod £8; boat £20.)* The **Belmullet Sea Angling Competition** (tel. 81076), in mid-July, awards

£2 per pound for the heaviest halibut as well as money prizes for most variety and a life jacket for the best specimen. The **Feille Iorras** peninsula-wide music festival (tel. 81147) will be held August 27-31, 1999.

■ Ballina

What Knock is to the Marian cult, Ballina (bah-lin-AH) is to the religion of bait and tackle. Hordes of pilgrims in olive green waders invade the town each year during the fishing season from February to September. Some anglers fish without pause for three days and three nights when the salmon are biting, paying up to £80 a day to cast in the best pools. The town, however, has non-ichthyological attractions as well, including its lovely vistas of river walks and a raging weekend pub scene. Almost everyone in a 50 mi. radius, from sheep farmers to college students, packs into town on Saturday nights. Former Irish President Mary Robinson grew up in Ballina and refined her political skills in the town's 40-odd pubs (see **Current Issues,** p. 75.)

ORIENTATION AND PRACTICAL INFORMATION

Ballina's commercial center is on the west bank of the river Moy. A bridge crosses over to the cathedral and tourist office on the east bank. The bridge connects to Tone St., which turns into Tolan St. This strip intersects Pearse and O'Rahilly St., which run parallel to the river, to form Ballina's navel.

Trains: Station Rd. (tel. 71818), near the bus station. Open M-F 7:30am-6pm, Sa 9am-1pm and 3:15-6pm. Service to **Dublin** via **Athlone** (M-Su 3 per day, £15). From the station, go left, bear right and walk 4 blocks to reach the town center.

Buses: Station Rd. (tel. 71800 or 71825). Open M-Sa 9:30am-6pm. Buses to **Athlone** (1 per day, £11), **Dublin** via **Mullingar** (4hr., 3 per day, £8), **Galway** (3hr., M-Sa 9 per day, Su 5 per day, £9.70), **Donegal** (M-Sa 3 per day, Su 1 per day, £10), **Sligo** (2hr., M-Sa 3-4 per day, £7.30), and **Westport** (1½hr., M-Sa 3 per day, Su 1 per day, £6.30). From the bus station, turn right and take the first left; the city center is a 5min. walk.

Tourist Office: Cathedral Rd. (tel. 70848), on the river by St. Muredach's Cathedral.

Banks: Bank of Ireland, Pearse St. (tel. 21144). Open M-W and F 10am-4pm, Th 10am-5pm. **ATM. Irish Permanent Building Society,** Pearse St. (tel. 22777). Open M-F 9:30am-5pm. **ATM.**

Taxis: Mulherin Taxi Service, The Brook (tel. 22583, 21783).

Bike Rental: Gerry's Cycle Centre, 6 Lord Edward St. (tel. 70455). £7 per day, £30 per week; collection service available. Open M-Sa 9am-7pm..

Bookstore: Keohane's (tel. 21475), stocks the best regional guidebooks. Open M-Sa 8am-6:30pm, Su 8am-1:30pm.

Laundry: Moy Laundrette, Cathedral Rd. (tel. 22358). Wash and dry £4.50. Open M-Sa. 9am-6pm.

Pharmacy: S. Quinn and Sons, Pearse St. (tel. 21365). Open M-Sa 9am-6pm.

Emergency: Dial 999; no coins required. **Garda:** Walsh St. (tel. 21422).

Post Office: Casement St. (tel. 21498). Open M-Sa 9am-5:30pm.

Internet Access: Moy Valley Resources, in the same building as the tourist office. Open Easter-Sept. M-Sa 10am-1pm and 2-5:30pm.

Phone Code: Has amazing natural 096.

ACCOMMODATIONS

Ballina's only hostel closed in 1998 to make way for a new Catholic University, sending rumors of a new hostel flying around. They haven't landed, but it's worth checking to see if they've reached the tourist office. **Hogan's American House Hostel** (tel. 70582), a comfy, family-run place with a dated but dignified interior, has low rates and a convenient location just up from the bus station (singles £15; doubles £25 for *Let's Go* readers; breakfast £5). Dozens of nearly identical B&Bs line the main approach roads into town; turn right from the station for one such trove. Next to the post office on John St., the **Crescent** bar has B&B upstairs (singles £25; doubles £36).

The advantages of living in a bar speak for themselves. The river, the lake, and seafishing are just a cast away from Ms. Corrigan's **Greenhill** (tel. 22767), on Cathedral Close behind the tourist office (£16, with bath £18; £5.50 extra for single). Two doors down, Breda Walsh's **Suncraft** (tel. 21573) is a good second option (doubles with bath £34). **Belleek Camping and Caravan Park** (tel. 71533) is 2 mi. from Ballina toward Killala on R314, behind the Belleek Woods (£4 per hiker with tent; laundry and kitchen available; open Mar.-Oct.).

FOOD AND PUBS

Aspiring gourmets can prepare for a feast at the **Quinnsworth** supermarket (tel. 21056) on Market Rd. (open M-W 9am-7pm, Th-F 9am-9pm, Sa 9am-6pm). Pubs and restaurants tend to go hand in hand in Ballina; get the same food for half the price by sitting in the pub. **Cafolla's** (tel. 21029), just up from the bridge, is fast, cheap, and almost Italian (open M-Sa 10am-12:30pm). **Tullio's,** Pearse St. (tel. 70815), exudes elegance, with pleasantly surprising prices (restaurant open daily noon-3pm and 6-10pm; bar serves food noon-10pm). **Humbert's Restaurant,** Pearse St. (tel. 71520), is a local coffee and tea shop that also provides cheap eats. **Brogan's Bar and Restaurant** (tel. 21961), five blocks up from the bridge, has some of the best meat in town, but you have to pay well for it (fisherman's platter £9; food served till 9pm).

    Gaughan's has been pulling the best pint in town since 1936; ask for the house special natural Guinness. No music or TV—just conversation, snugs, great grub, and homemade snuff. Jolly drinkers are fixtures of **The Parting Glass** (tel. 72714) on Tolan St., where they cheerfully sing along to music provided by proprietor David McDonald himself (Tu trad). Down by the river on Clare St., the **Murphy Bros.** (tel. 22702) serve pints to twentysomethings settled into the dark wood furnishings. They also dish out superb pub grub. The restaurant upstairs is Ballina's best (and priced accordingly). The rest of the town's twentysomethings crowd the expansive **Broken Jug** (tel. 72379) on O'Rahilly or **The Loft** (tel. 21881) on Pearse St., where the dark, intimate cellar bar serves dark, intimate pints (music Tu-F and Su; high-class B&B £22). **Doherty's** (tel. 21150), by the bridge, revels in the angling lifestyle, and great trad (Th and Sa) bridges any generation gap. **An Bolg Bui** (tel. 22561) next door is Irish for "the yellow belly." The pub calls itself a "young fisherperson's pub" and sells tackle and licenses along with pints. Of Ballina's four clubs, **Longneck's** (tel. 22702), behind Murphy's, is the most attractive and the most popular, both perhaps due to its adobe and sombrero motif (open July-Aug. Th-Su; cover £3-5; ages 21+). **The Pulse,** behind the Broken Jug, is a close second (open W and F-Su; cover £3-5).

SIGHTS

The bird-rich **Belleek Woods** (bah-LEEK) around Belleek Castle is a fairytale forest with an exquisite bird-to-tree-to-stream ratio. To reach the Belleek Woods entrance, cross the lower bridge near the cathedral on Pearse St. and keep Ballina House on your right. You can enjoy the woods all night at **Belleek Caravan and Camping Park** (£2.50 per person). Belleek Castle is an expensive hotel, but its **Armada Bar,** built from an actual 500-year-old Spanish wreck, is accessible and affordable. Downstairs, another bar carouses in a medieval banquet hall. Owner Marshall Doran gives tours of the castle and even allows a look at his own fossil collection and **armory museum** (tel. 22400) with exhibits dating as far back as the 16th century. *(Tours by appointment only. £2.50 per person; 10-person min.)*

    At the back of the railway station is the **Dolmen of the Four Maols,** locally called "Table of the Giants." The dolmen, which dates back to 2000 BC, is said to be the burial site of four Maols who murdered Ceallach, a 7th-century bishop. They were hanged at Ardaree, then commemorated with a big rock.

    The lonely **Ox Mountains** east of Ballina are best seen by bike. Dirt and asphalt trails criss-cross their way up the slopes under trees and around tiny lakes. The 44 mi. Ox Mountain Drive traces the scenic perimeter of the mountains and is well sign-posted from Tobercurry (21mi. south of Sligo on the N17). The **Western Way** footpath begins in the Ox mountains and winds its way past Ballina through Newport and Westport, ending up in the Connemara. Tourist offices sell complete guides. Equestrian enthusiasts can ride at the **Ardchuan Lodge** (tel. 45084), 5 mi. north of Ballina on the Sligo road. *(Pony trekking £10 per hr.)*

From July 11-19, 1999, catch the annual **Ballina Street Festival** (tel. 70905), which has been swinging since 1964. All of Co. Mayo is hooked for the festival's **Heritage Day** (Wednesday, July 15, 1999) when the streets are closed off and life reverts to the year 1910. All aspects of traditional Irish life are staged: greasy pig contests, a traditional Irish wake, and donkey-driven butter churns.

■ Near Ballina

N59 and N26 puncture Ballina; R297 off N59 northwest runs to Enniscrone, the quintessential Irish seaspot. Cute Killala, boggy Ballycastle, and the archaeological extravaganza of Ceide Fields are threaded onto R314 north. Odd little **Bellacorick** sits 18 mi. west of Ballina on N59. Though ugly, Bellacorick's hyperbolic power station is a welcome break from the bleak nothingness of the stretch of road between Ballina and Bangor. Nearby, a seemingly innocuous stone bridge, known as the **Musical Bridge,** fords the Owenmore River. Curious marks run the length of the stone walls on either side, and a pile of small stones sits on each end. To play the bridge, run full speed from end to end, dragging a stone across the top of the handrail; the successive blocks play a tune. Trust us, it's fun.

■ Enniscrone

Eight miles northeast of Ballina on scenic Quay Rd. (R297), the gorgeous Enniscrone (Inishcrone) Strand stretches along the east shore of Killala Bay. On a sunny summer day you'll have to fight Irish weekenders for towel space. On most days, however, you're likely to have miles of sand to yourself. Zillions of new holiday homes surround the town sprawling behind the long beach. Across from the beach, the dreamy family-run **Kilcullen's Bath House** (tel. 36238) simmers and steams, leaving you weak all over. Steam baths in cedarwood cabinets that leave only the head exposed and cool seaweed baths can relax even the most tense of travelers. (No time limits, towels supplied. Seaweed bath £7, with steam bath £8. 30min. massage £20.) A tea room with views of the strand awaits post-soak. (Open daily July-Aug. 10am-10pm; May-June and Sept.-Oct. 10am-9pm; Nov.-Apr. 11am-8pm.) **Fishing** enthusiasts should contact John McDonagh (tel. 45332) for guidance and equipment.

An unofficial **tourist office** hides off Pier Rd. (open M-F 11am-7pm). The **phone code** is 096. **Gowan House B&B,** Pier Rd. (tel. 36396), boasts big beautiful rooms. Set just back from the sea, the bedrooms are sparingly decorated in bright colors (with bath £17). Maura O'Dowd's **Point View House,** Main St. (tel. 36312), serves a home-style dinner (£9) before sending you to a comfortable night's sleep (with bath £15). **The Atlantic Caravan Park** (tel. 36132) puts some grass under your tent or caravan and has laundry facilities (£4 per tent; £6 per caravan). **Walsh's Pub,** Main St. (tel. 36110), serves great pub grub all day (dinner served 6-9pm) and music Tuesday nights. **Harnett's Bar,** Main St. (tel. 36137), cooks good but pricey food amid walls covered with old matchboxes (food served 1-2:30pm and 6-8pm).

■ Ballycastle, Ceide Fields, and Killala

Ballycastle is a small village with a decreasing population bordered by rich farmland and holiday cottages on one side and bog on the other. The single strip of houses, shops, and pubs on an incline gives the impression that Ballycastle was formed when people walking what would be R314 decided they were too tired to go up the hill. Bus Éireann has a service to **Killala** and **Ballina** (M-Sa 1 per day, £5). By offering housing and studio space, the Ballinglen Arts Foundation has brought several prominent and emerging artists into residency in Ballycastle; its new building, scheduled to open in 1999, will house exhibition space and a new **tourist office. Ulster Bank** opens its mini-office Tuesdays (10am-noon).

Opulent—nay, palatial—digs (with bath), huge meals, and potpourri under the pillow grace **Mrs. Chambers' Suantai B&B** (tel. 43040), on the Killala road (£16, singles £20). **Ceide House B&B** and **restaurant** (tel. 43105), has Mayo cuisine (entrees £5-7; open daily 9am-9pm) and comfortable lodgings (£13, with bath £15). **Mary's Bakery** (tel. 43361), whips up baked goods and scrumptious lunch specials (open daily 10am-6pm). **McNamee's Supermarket** (tel. 43057) sells peanut butter, jelly, and more (open daily 9am-10pm). Dark, low-ceilinged **Katie Mac's** (tel. 43031) wears its blackened floorboards and ancient walls with pride (trad Saturdays).

A small brochure from the tourist office (20p) outlines three walks around the area. One follows a bucolic path to the ocean, the **Dun Briste** seastack, and stoic **Downpatrick Head.** The multi-layered rock formation supposedly broke off from the mainland during a dispute between St. Patrick and a pagan king; St. Patrick used the geological disturbance to prove God's power. More recently, a car manufacturer helicoptered one of its vehicles onto Dun Briste to prove the advertising power of nature. The **North Mayo Sculpture Trail** follows the R314 from Ballina to Belmullet. Fifteen modern sculptors were invited to produce site-specific installations of earth and stone to celebrate the rugged wilderness of north Mayo. Their works range from inspired to not inspired at all; brown "Tír Sáile" signs mark the trail.

Five miles west toward the Mullet Peninsula, the **Ceide** (KAYJ-uh) **Fields** are open to visitors through an **interpretive center** (tel. 43325), which offers exhibits, films, and guided tours of the largest excavated neolithic landscape in the world. The ancient farming settlements buried in the surrounding bog have been an abundant source of archaeological insight. The center itself, a tall, incongruous pyramid of peat and glass, was constructed around a 5000-year-old Scotch pine that had been dug out of the bog. If all the muck gets you down, the 350 million-year-old **Ceide Cliffs** rise 365 ft. high nearby. The excellent film and tour provide the same information. (Tours every hr., film every 30min. £2.50, students £1. Open daily June-Sept. 9:30am-6:30pm; mid-March to May and Oct. 10am-5pm; Nov. 10am-4:30pm.)

Eight miles south of Ballycastle along the Ballina road is **Killala,** a charming seaport best known as the site of the French Invasion of 1798 (see **History,** p. 57). 1067 French soldiers landed at Killala to join the United Irishmen under Wolfe Tone in a revolt against the British. Instead of finding a well-armed band of revolutionaries, the French found a smattering of poor, Irish-speaking peasants. Undeterred, they pressed on with the revolution, winning a significant victory at Castlebar before they were soundly hammered by crack British forces at Ballnamuck.

■ Knock

At 8pm on August 21, 1879, St. Joseph, St. John, and the Virgin Mary appeared at Knock with a cross, a lamb, an altar, and a host of angels. The visions materialized before at least 15 witnesses, who stood in the rain for two hours watching the apparitions and chanting the Rosary. The Catholic hierarchy endorsed the miracle, and Knock quickly developed into a major pilgrimage site, with over 1.5 million pilgrims visiting each year. The streets overflow with entrepreneurs hawking anything (keychains, ashtrays, Knock-knacks, etc.) emblazoned with the Knock label. While the blatant commercialism may be annoying or amusing, the holy atmosphere of the town is sincere.

PRACTICAL INFORMATION Knock lies between Galway and Sligo on N17 and makes a good roadside stop for folks hopping between the two. The **Horan Cutríl Airport** (tel. 67222), 11 mi. north of town near Charlestown, is the subject of a tune by Christy Moore and attracts pilgrim cash with direct flights to the U.K. **Bus Éireann** stops at Coleman's and Lennon's; buses depart for **Dublin** (2 per day, Su 1 per day, £10), **Westport** (Su 1 per day, £9), and **Sligo** (Su 3 per day, £7.70) and arrive from **Athlone, Ballina, Castlebar, Galway, Roscommon, Sligo,** and **Westport** (all M-Sa 2-3 per day). Knock's **tourist office** (tel. 88193) is suitably central (open May-Sept. daily 10am-5pm) and contains an ATM-less **Bank of Ireland** (open May-Oct. M and Th

10:15am-12:15pm; Nov.-Apr. M 10:15am-12:15pm). The **shrine office** (tel. 88100), across the street, sells Knock literature, official calendars, and the *Knock Pilgrim's Guide* (10p), which has prayers and a useful map (open daily June-Oct. 9am-8:30pm, Nov. 10am-6pm). The **post office** (tel. 88209) is in the Spar by the traffic circle (open Tu-Sa 9am-5:30pm, M 9am-1pm). The **phone code** is 094.

ACCOMMODATIONS, FOOD, AND PUBS "Hostels" in town are for the sick or elderly, but B&Bs line the approach roads. Mrs. Kelly's **Cara** (tel. 88315), on Kiltamagh Rd., is particularly welcoming (singles £14; doubles £28). **Knock Caravan and Camping** (tel. 88223) is five minutes from the church on the Claremorris side. (July-Aug. £6 per tent, 25p per person; single backpacker £4. Mar.-June and Sept.-Oct. £5.50 per tent, 25p per person; single backpacker £3.50. Laundry £3.50.) The **Knock International Hotel,** Main St. (tel. 88466), has clean, centrally located rooms, but they're as scarce as Albanian tourists in July and August (from £12; B&B from £16). Food is priced for the masses; try **Beirne's Restaurant** (tel. 88161), on the main road (3-course lunch £6.75 until 3pm; open daily noon-6pm). **Ard Mhuire's** (tel. 88459) is an enticing split-level restaurant on Main St. (everything under £4; open Apr.-Oct. 10am-7:30pm).

SIGHTS Knock's religious sights cluster around the shrine built over the site of the Apparition. Numerous healings are said to have occurred in the courtyard. The hefty **Church of Our Lady** holds 20,000 people but remains peaceful and cozy. Mass times are posted in the processional square. *(Services M-Sa at 8, 9, 11am, noon, 3, and 7:30pm; Su 8, 9:30, 11am, noon, 3, and 7pm.)* Free holy water is dispensed near the shrine. The **Knock Folk Museum** (tel. 88100) to the right of the basilica portrays rural 19th-century life. *(Open daily July-Aug. 10am-7pm; May-June and Sept.-Oct. 10am-6pm. £2, students £1.50.)* The eyewitness accounts of the apparition and the old photographs of Irish life are the best reasons to visit. Knock's biggest festival is August 21, the **Feast of Our Lady of Knock.**

NORTHWEST IRELAND

The farmland of the upper Shannon gradually gives way to Sligo, where the town is surrounded by the landscapes and monuments that were close to the heart of William Butler Yeats. A mere sliver of land connects Co. Sligo to Co. Donegal, the most remote and most foreign of the Republic's counties. Donegal's windy mountains and winding coasts are a dreamlike landscape, and the counties' *gaeltacht* reveal pure examples of genuine, unadulterated Irish tradition. Don't leave the country before seeing the inspiring Inishowen Peninsula, from which Derry, in Northern Ireland, is readily accessible. Hitchhikers report that the upper Shannon region is difficult to thumb through and that they often end up relying on trucks. Drivers in Donegal are said to be much friendlier.

County Sligo

If William Butler Yeats had never existed, Co. Sligo would be merely a pretty coastal stretch of hills, low cliffs, and choppy waves between boggy north Mayo and mountainous Donegal. As it is, the county is something of a literary pilgrimage site. The poet divided his preadolescent time between London and Sligo. That he set many of his poems in the windswept landmarks near Sligo Bay is hardly surprising, given the almost lyric beauty and unforgettable form of the place. Fortunately, you needn't have read a word of Yeats to join the crowds gawking reverently at his grave. It's easiest and most exciting to spend the nights in Sligo; everything else can be seen either on daytrips or on the way to Enniskillen or Donegal.

▓ Sligo

Grey and relentless, the Garavogue River gurgles through the commercial, industrial, and market center of Sligo Town (pop. 18,000). During business hours, traffic is locked in place in the downtown maze of Sligo's one-way streets while cargo ships come and go from the busy pier. This urban carnival is immediately surrounded on all sides by a more natural pageant. Two imposing hills, Knocknarea and Benbulben, loom in the mist beyond train windows like possessive guardians competing for prominence in Sligo's stormy seaside landscape. William Butler Yeats spent extended summer holidays here with his mother's family, the Pollexfens, who owned a mill over the Garavogue. It was those early visits, and the exposure they provided to the superstitions of the local people, that first interested Yeats in the supernatural world. Most of Sligo can (and does) boast some connection to Yeats. Now busy streets flow with a steady stream of people during the day and with the beer from some 70 pubs and discos in the evening. *The Sligo Guardian*, available at newsagents, has local news and useful listings.

ORIENTATION AND PRACTICAL INFORMATION

Trains and buses pull into McDiarmada station on Lord Edward St. To reach the main drag from the station, take a left and follow Lord Edward St. straight onto Wine St., and then turn right at the post office onto O'Connell St. More shops, pubs, and eateries beckon from Grattan St., left off O'Connell St.

Northwest Ireland

ATLANTIC OCEAN

Malin Head
Glengad Head
Malin
Culdaff
Inishowen Head
Stroove
Greencastle
Moville
Ballyliffin
R238
Clonmany
Carndonagh
INISHOWEN PENINSULA
R238
Lough Foyle
Farad Head
Rinmore Point
Lough Swilly
Portsalon
Downings
Buncrana
Muff
Limavady
A77
Tory Island
Horn Head
Sheep Haven
Rathmullen
Inch Island
Inch
CO. DERRY
Inishbofin
Carrigart
Dunfanaghy
Milford
A2
Derry
A6
Bloody Foreland
GWEEDORE Creeslough
Falcarragh
Grainon of Aileach
Tory Sound
Errigal Mt.
Derryveagh Mts.
Rathmelton
N13
Derrybeg
Bunbeg
Glenveigh National Park
NORTHERN IRELAND
Gola I.
Crolly
Dunlewy
Churchill
Letterkenny
N14
Owey I.
Kincasslagh
Lifford
Carricktinn Airport
THE ROSSES
Burtonport
CO. DONEGAL
Strabane
A5
Aranmore Island
Dungloe
Stranorlar
N15
Newtownstewart
Crohy Head
N56
CO. TYRONE
Gweebarra Bay
Dawros Head
Maas
Glenties
N15
Blue Stack Mts.
Omagh
A5
A505
Loughros Point
Ardara
Lough Eske
Lough Derg
A32
Fintona
Mountcharles
N56
Donegal
Pettigoe
A35
Killybegs
Glencolmcille
Rasson Point
Carrick
Kilcar
St. John's Point
Ballyshannon
Beleek
A47
Lower Lough Erne
CO. FERMANAGH
A4
Rathlin O'Birne I.
N15
A46
Enniskillen
Upper Lough Erne
Donegal Bay
Bundoran
Mullaghmore
Lough Melvin
Lough Allen
A4
A32
A509
N
Inishmurray
N15
Lough Glencar
N16
N16
CO. CAVAN
0   10 miles
0   10 kilometers
Drumcliff
Rosses Point
Manor-hamilton
Lough Gill
Easky
Sligo Bay
Strandhill
Sligo
N4
Dromahair
CO. LEITRIM
Lenadoon Point
Knocknarea
Ballysadare
Collooney
Drumshanbo
Killala Bay
CO. SLIGO
Ox Mountains
N17
Riverstown
N4
Carrick-on-Shannon
N59
Ballymote
Lough Arrow
Lough Key
N4
Tobercurry
Boyle
N58
Ballina
N57
CO. MAYO
N5
N61
CO. ROSCOMMON

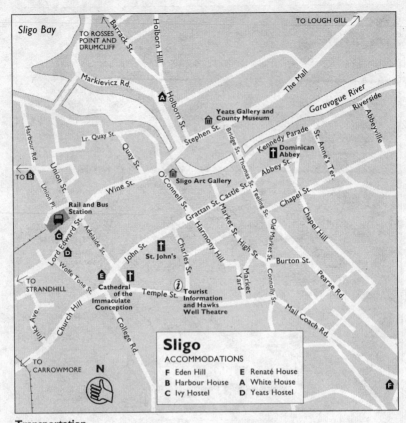

Sligo Bay

TO ROSSES POINT AND DRUMCLIFF

TO LOUGH GILL

Barrack St.

Holborn Hill

Markievicz Rd.

Holborn St.

Yeats Gallery and County Museum

Stephen St.

The Mall

Garavogue River

Riverside

Abbeyville

Lr. Quay St.

Bridge St.

Kennedy Parade

St. Anne's Ter.

Dominican Abbey

Harbour Rd.

Quay St.

Wine St.

O'Connell St.

Sligo Art Gallery

Abbey St.

Chapel St.

Old Market St.

Chapel Hill

TO B

Union St.

Union Pl.

Rail and Bus Station

Grattan St.

Castle St.

Market St.

Teeling St.

High St.

Lord Edward St.

Adelaide St.

Harmony Hill

Burton St.

Connolly St.

Pearse Rd.

Wolfe Tone St.

John St.

St. John's

Charles St.

Market Yard

TO STRANDHILL

Cathedral of the Immaculate Conception

Temple St.

Tourist Information and Hawks Well Theatre

Mail Coach Rd.

Jinks Ave.

Church Hill

College Rd.

TO CARROWMORE

N

Sligo

ACCOMMODATIONS

F Eden Hill   E Renaté House
B Harbour House   A White House
C Ivy Hostel   D Yeats Hostel

Transportation

Airport: Sligo Airport, Strandhill Rd. (tel. 68280). Open daily 9am-8pm.

Trains: McDiarmada Station, Lord Edward St. (tel. 69888). Open M-Sa 7am-6:30pm, Su 20min. before each departure. Trains to **Dublin** via **Carrick-on-Shannon** and **Mullingar** (3 per day, £13.50, students £9.50).

Buses: McDiarmada Station, Lord Edward St. (tel. 60066). Open M-F 9:15am-6pm, Sa 9:30am-5pm. Buses fan out to **Belfast** (4hr., 1-3 per day, £12.40), **Derry** (3hr., 3-6 per day, £10), **Dublin** (4hr., 3 per day, £9), **Galway** (2½hr., 3-4 per day, £11), and **Westport** (2½hr., 1-3 per day, £9.70).

Local Transportation: Frequent buses to **Strandhill** and **Rosses Point** (£1.65).

Taxis: Cab 55 (tel. 42333); **Finnegan's** (tel. 77777, 44444, or 41111 for easy dialing when you're drunk). At least £3 in town, 50p per mi. outside.

Bike Rental: Flanagan's Cycles (tel. 44477; after hours tel. 62633), Connelly and High St. £7 per day, £30 per week; deposit £35. Open M-Sa 9am-6pm, Su by prior arrangement. **P.J. Coleman,** Stephen St. (tel. 43353), repairs bikes.

Tourist and Financial Services

Tourist Office: Temple St. (tel. 61201), at Charles St. From the station, turn left along Lord Edward St., then follow the signs right onto Adelaid St. and around the corner to Temple St. to find the Northwest regional office. *The Sligo Monthly Guide* (50p) has some useful listings. Open June M-Sa 9am-6pm; July-Aug. M-Sa 9am-8pm, Su 9am-2pm; Sept. M-F 9am-8pm, Su 9am-1pm; Oct.-May 9am-5pm. The **info booth** on O'Connell St. in Quinnsworth arcade is more helpful. Open M-Tu 10am-7pm, W-F 10am-9pm, Sa 10am-6pm.

Travel Agency: Broderick's Travel, O'Connell St. Arcade (tel. 45221). Open M-Sa 9am-6pm.
Bank: AIB, 49 O'Connell St. (tel. 41085). **ATM.** Open M-W and F 10am-4pm, Th 10am-5pm.

Local Services

Luggage Storage: At bus station. Open M-F 9:30am-1:30pm and 2:30-6pm. £1.50 per bag.
Bookstore: The Winding Stair, Hyde Bridge (tel. 41244). Fiction, Irish interest, used books, and the extremely helpful *Exploring Sligo and North Leitrim,* which details walks in the area (£7).
Laundry: Pam's Laundrette, 9 Johnston Ct. (tel. 44861), off O'Connell St. Wash and dry from £5. Open M-Sa 9am-7pm.
Camping Supplies: Out & About, 20 Market St. (tel. 44550). All your outdoor needs met indoors. Open M 2-6pm, Tu-Sa 9:30am-6pm.
Pharmacy: E. Horan, Castle St. (tel. 42560), at Market St. Open M-Sa 9:30am-6pm. Local pharmacies post schedules of rotating Sunday openings.

Emergency and Communications

Emergency: Dial 999; no coins required. **Garda:** Pearse Rd. (tel. 42031).
Crisis Line: Samaritans (tel. 42011). 24hr.
Hospital: The Mall (tel. 42161).
Post Office: Wine St. (tel. 42593), at O'Connell St. Open M and W-Sa 9am-5:30pm, Tu 9:30am-5:30pm.
Internet Access: Futurenet, Pearse Rd. (tel. 50345). £6 per hr., students £5. Open M-Sa 10am-10pm.
Phone Code: The unpurged images of day recede to 071.

ACCOMMODATIONS

There are plenty of hostels in Sligo, but they fill quickly, especially during the Yeats International Summer School weeks in mid-August. If you're staying a few days with a group of people, getting a cottage can be cheaper and more fun. Contact the tourist office for more info. Over a dozen B&Bs, many of them very nice, cluster on Pearse Rd. on the south side of town; others are near the station.

Harbour House, Finisklin Rd. (tel. 71547). The sedate stone front hides this Taj Mahal of hostels. Big pine bunks with custom mattresses, skylights in the upstairs rooms, sitting rooms with TVs in each dorm, and more showers than an Irish afternoon. **Bike rental** £7. Dorms £8; private rooms £10 per person. Irish breakfast £3, continental £1.50.

The White House Hostel (IHH), Markievicz Rd. (tel. 45160 or 42398), first left off Wine St. after the bridge. Spacious dorms, some with river views, and a comfortable, if outmoded, common room make this hostel a fine choice. Dorms £6.50. Sheets £1. Key deposit £1.50.

The Ivy Hostel, 26 Lord Edward St. (tel. 45165), left from the bus station. A cozy cottage downtown holds overflow. Kitchen available. Pleasant, cozy doubles £13. Free laundry. Open June-Aug.

Yeats County Hostel, 12 Lord Edward St. (tel. 45165), across from the bus station. Spacious rooms and the attentions of a one-time butler recommend this convenient roost. Friendly company, private backyard. Dorms £6.50. Key deposit £2.

Eden Hill Holiday Hostel (IHH), Pearse Rd. (tel. 43204). Entrance via Marymount or Ashbrook St., 10min. from town. Cozy rooms and a Victorian sitting parlor in a grand but aging house. 2-microwave kitchen and a common room with VCR. Laundry facilities. Dorms £6.50; private rooms £8. **Camping** £3.50.

Renaté House, Upper Johns St. (tel. 62014). From the station, go straight one block and left half a block. Businesslike and spotless, with elegant burgundy furnishings. Singles £23, with bath £25; doubles £32, with bath £36.

FOOD

"Faery vats / Full of berries / And reddest stolen cherries" are not to be found in Sligo today. **Quinnsworth Supermarket,** O'Connell St. (tel. 62788), sells neatly packaged berries as well as an assortment of other neatly packaged things (open M-Tu 9am-7pm, W-F 9am-9pm, Sa 9am-6pm). The demands of international visitors have induced culinary development here. Good restaurants and dinners are expensive; the best values tend to end around 6pm, so eat early or pay.

The Cottage, Castle St. (tel. 45319). Sip coffee amid paper butterflies one flight up from busy Castle St. Sundry kebabs £4.50. Open M-Sa 9am-6pm.

Ho Wong, Market St. (tel. 45718). Cantonese and Szechuan take-out with Irish-Asian flair. Open daily 4-11pm.

Lyon's Café, Quay St. (tel. 42969). Tucked away upstairs, this cute café brews Bewley's coffee and bakes a selection of cakes. Lunch special of soup, entree, and cake £4.35. Open M-Sa 9am-6pm; lunch served 12:30-2pm.

Kate's Kitchen, Market St. (tel. 43022), is not quite a restaurant, but this combination deli/wholefood shop varies its take-away menu each day. Homemade soups £1. Open M-Sa 9am-6:30pm.

Abracadabra, Grattan St., serves up whatever you want fried until 3:30am.

PUBS AND CLUBS

Sligo loves its pubs, and its pubs love Sligo. Over seventy crowd the main streets, filling the town with live music during the summer. Events and venues are listed in *The Sligo Champion* (75p). Clubbers shake it at **Toff's** (tel. 62150), on the river behind the Belfry, which pumps out disco beats from Thursday to Saturday. The well-lit but crowded dance floor reveals that local clubgoers drink better than they dance. (Cover £4.50, Sa £5; £1 off with card from the Belfry, below. 21+.) Up Teeling St., sprawling **Equinox** is darker, with newfangled neon lights, zebra striped stools, and identical club music (open W-Su, cover £4.50).

Hargadon Bros., O'Connell St. (tel. 70933). Open fires, old Guinness bottles, poitín jugs, the passage of time inscribed in the tangle of dark, and intimate nooks that embrace its patrons. Here, one can enjoy philosophical conversations and contemplate the perfect pint unfettered by the modern audio-visual distractions found elsewhere. A pub the way it ought to be, just as it was when it first opened in 1868.

Shoot the Crows, Castle St., but clean up after yourself. Naked men carouse with snakes on the mural outside. An apt introduction to this epicenter of social gatherings for the modern cool person. Music Tu and Th 9:30pm.

McGarrigle's, O'Connell St. (tel. 71193). 18th-century lanterns light the cave-dark wooden interior. Upstairs is just as dark, but the walls and ceilings, covered by new-age-meets-Georgia-O'Keefe murals, enclose blaring techno and young faces. Live trad Th and Su.

McLynn's, Old Market St. (tel. 60743). The *International Pub Guide* ranks McLynn's as the best pub for music in Sligo. A wood divider separates locals from tourists. Enter through the unmarked door on the left of the building and tear down social barriers. Music F.

The Belfry (tel. 62150), off the bridge on Thomas St. The medieval castle decor dates back to 1998, and the 30-item Irish malt whiskey menu (unique outside Dublin) is even older. Lunch entrees £3-5.

SIGHTS AND ENTERTAINMENT

Yeats praised peasants and aristocrats and disdained modern middle-class merchants and industrialists. Appropriately, most of the Yeatsian sights are at least a mile from the mercantile town center. In town, the 13th-century **Sligo Abbey,** Abbey St., is very well preserved. *(Open daily in summer 9:30am-6:30pm; last admission 45min. before closing. If it's closed, ask for the key from Tommy McLaughlin, 6 Charlotte St. £1.50, students 60p.)* The Dominican friary boasts cloisters and ornate coupled pillars that, though old, can hardly be called ruins. A defaced monument stone, which bore the names of a mother and her child, graces the sacristy. Tradition claims that the mother's descendents, not wanting a public reminder of their forbearers' illegitimacy, hired a stonemason to chisel the names away in secret. Next door, the 1874 **Cathedral of the Immaculate Conception,** John St., is best visited at dawn or dusk, when the sun streams through 69 magnificent stained-glass windows. Farther down John St., the **Cathedral of St. John the Baptist,** designed in 1730, has a brass tablet dedicated to Yeats's mother, Susan Mary. The 1878 **courthouse,** on Teeling St., was built on the site of the previous one. Note the sign across the street for the famed law firm "Argue and Phibbs."

The **Yeats Art Gallery,** Stephen St., houses one of Éire's finest collections of modern Irish art, including a number of works by Jack Butler Yeats (William Butler's brother) and contemporaries Nora McGinness and Michael Healy. *(Open Tu-Sa 10am-noon and 2-5pm. Free.)* Among the museum's other treasures are some first editions by William Butler Yeats and the original publications by the Dun Emer Press and Cuala Press. The gems of the collection are a few illustrated broadside collaborations between father and son. The **Sligo County Museum** preserves small reminders of Yeats, including pictures of his funeral and Countess Markeivicz's prison apron. *(Open June-Sept. M-Sa 10:30am-12:30pm and 2:30-4:30pm; Apr.-May and Oct. M-Sa 10:30am-12:30pm. Free.)* The **Sligo Art Gallery,** Yeats Memorial Building, Hyde Bridge (tel. 45847), rotates exhibitions of Irish art with an annual northwest Ireland exhibit in November. *(Open daily 10am-5pm.)*

Hawk's Well Theatre, Temple St. (tel. 61526 or 61518), beneath the tourist office, presents modern and traditional dramas, ballets, and musicals. *(Box office open M-Sa 9am-6pm. Shows £7-10, students £4.)* The **Blue Raincoat Theatre Company,** Lr. Quay St. (tel. 70431), is a traveling troupe covering a wide range of material from the Renaissance to the modern in their Quay St. "factory space" 16 weeks a year. Look for flyers or call for show dates. *(Tickets £5-7.)*

A monthly *Calendar of Events,* available and free at the tourist office, describes the festivals and goings-on in the Northwest region. The **Sligo Arts Festival** (tel. 69802) takes place May 27 to June 7, 1999. Along with its usual fantastic events, the final weekend will focus on world music. From July 31 through August 15, 1999, the internationally renowned **Yeats International Summer School** opens some of its poetry readings, lectures, and concerts to the public. International luminaries like Seamus Heaney are regular guests. *(For an application, contact the Yeats Society, Yeats Memorial Building, Douglas Hyde Bridge, Sligo (tel. 42693), M-F 10am-1pm and 3-5pm. Tuition £690.)*

■ Near Sligo Town

Daytrippers from Sligo have so many options; Lough Gill, Carrowmore, Strandhill, Rosses Point, and Drumcliffe are all within a few miles. Small brown signs with quill and ink mark the Yeats trail, which covers the Yeats beat. These sites can be hard to get around without a car. Early risers can catch the **Bus Éireann** coach tour (tel. (071) 60066), which drives from the station to **Glencar, Drumcliffe,** and **Lough Gill** (3½hr., July-Sept. Tu and Th 9am, £6). **John Howe's** bus company (tel. (071) 42747) runs daily coach tours from the tourist office in July and August through Yeats country (3½hr., £6.50) and to **Lough Gill** (3hr., £5.50). **Peter Henry's Blue Lagoon** (tel. 42530) rents out rowboats (£15 per day) and motorboats (£30 per day). The **Wild Rose Water-Bus** (tel. (071) 64266) tours Sligo, Parke's Castle, Innisfree, and Garavogue (3 per day, £4-5); a night lough cruise departs from Parke's Castle (F 9pm).

■ The Strandhill Peninsula

Best known for its two miles of dunes, windy Strandhill ducks under solemn Knocknarea on the edge of Sligo Bay. Surfing is great; swimming, with the dangerous currents, is not great at all. At low tide, a causeway connects the beach to Coney Island, but don't get stuck. **Bus Éireann** circles to Strandhill and the turnoff to Carrowmore (M-F 6 per day, Sa 3 per day, £1.65). The **Knocknarea Holiday Hostel** (tel. 68777) is peaceful if a bit cramped (dorms £7; laundry £1; sheets £1).

A fantastic assortment of passage graves spooks visitors 3 mi. southwest of Sligo. **Carrowmore** is a great big playground where the toys are megalithic monuments and the children swarming all over them are actually middle-aged tourists who can't understand why their kids are bored by the ancient boulder piles (it's because they're not real toys, they're rocks). It had over 100 tombs and stone circles before modern folks quarried and cleared many away. Of the 60 remaining, about 30 can still be visited, some dating back to 4840 BC. Excavation is ongoing. The small but excellent **interpretive center** (tel. 61534) explains their meaning. *(Open May-Sept. daily 9:30am-6:30pm. Tours available. £1.50, students 60p.)* From Sligo, follow the signs west from John St.

The 1078 ft. Knocknarea Mountain faces Benbulben on the south shore of Sligo Bay. Queen Mebdh, also Maeve, the villain of the *Táin bo Cuailnge* (see **Literary Traditions**, p. 61), is reputedly interred in the 11 yd. high, 60 yd. wide cairn on the summit. Her notoriety is evident from the size of the cairn. She is buried standing up to face her enemies in Ulster. Decades ago, tourists started taking stones from the cairn as souvenirs; to preserve the legendary monument, local authorities created a "tradition" that anyone who brought a stone down the mountain would be cursed, while an unmarried man or woman who brought one up the mountain and placed it on the cairn would be married within a year. The plot succeeded; both the cairn and the institution of marriage survive. The stunning mountain also makes a cameo appearance in Yeats's "Red Hanrahan's Song about Ireland": "The wind has bundled up the clouds high over Knocknarea/And thrown the thunder on the stones for all that Maeve can say."

The climb takes about 45 minutes and the reward is a stunning view of the misty bay and heathered hills. Animal enthusiasts will delight in the bilingual sheep shouting insults (in cow) at the less intelligent cows and tourists stumbling up the near-vertical path. Trails crisscross the forested park on Knocknarea's eastern slopes. There are several ways up. The main path is from the car park, which is an hour's walk west from Carrowmore (turn left, take a right at the church, then the first left to the sign Mebdh Meirach) and half an hour from Strandhill (turn left from the hostel and keep to the left). Another path ascends from Strandhill, while a third begins in Glen Rd. a mile east of the car park. Eliot's **taxi** (tel. 69944) runs all day and night.

■ Lough Gill

The forested 24-mile road around Lough Gill, just southeast of Sligo, runs past woody nature trails, Yeatsy spots, an old castle, and several small towns. It's flat enough to make a wonderful bike ride from Sligo, but leave early. Take Pearse Rd. and turn off to the left at the Lough Gill signs. The first stop is **Holywell**, a leafy, flower-strewn shrine with a well and a waterfall. During the Penal Law years, secret masses were held at this site. If by chance the British military approached, the congregation would disband and pretend to be enjoying a football game. The main road itself reaches Dooney Rock, on the south shore of Lough Gill near Cottage Island. Here, Yeats's "Fiddler of Dooney" made "folk dance like a wave of the sea." Nature trails around the rock lead to views of the isle of Innisfree, a perfectly round bump in the lake that a young Yeats wrote about. If you want to arise and go now, and go to Inisfree, John O'Connor (tel. 64079) will ferry you out for £3.50; his house is next to the jetty 2½ mi. down the Inisfree turnoff on the main road.

The next town past the Inisfree turnoff along the same route is **Dromahair,** which still shelters **Creevelea Abbey.** Founded in 1508 as the Friary of Killanummery, its active days ended in 1650 when Oliver "Religious Freedom" Cromwell expelled monks from the confiscated monastery. It has been a burial site since 1721. Dromahair is the farther point of the Lough Gill route. From here, turn left onto R286 to head back to Sligo Town.

On the route back stands **Parke's Castle** (tel. (071) 64149), a recently renovated 17th-century bawn (enclosed castle). *(Open June-Sept. daily 9:30am-6:30pm; mid-Apr. to*

May Tu-Su 10am-5pm; Oct. daily 10am-5pm. £2, students £1. Tours, included in admission, leave on the hour.) Built by Anglo Parkes in the 1620s to protect himself from dispossessed Irish landowners, the castle stands on the visible foundation of an earlier stronghold of the O'Rourke family where its waterfront location enables a quick getaway across the lough. The manor house and turret walk are open for visitors and an excellent 45-minute video highlights all nearby attractions. Two miles before town, a left turn leads to Hazelwood, the park where Yeats walked "among long dappled grass" in "The Song of Wandering Aengus." The sculpture trail is particularly interesting.

Sink or Sin

Stand by the shore of Lough Gill and listen carefully. What do you hear? The lapping of the waves? The wind rustling in trees? The soft peal of a pure silver bell, sounding distantly from the bottom of the lake? No? That's because you're a sinner. When Sligo's Dominican Friary was wrecked during the Ulster rebellion of 1641, worshippers saved its bell and hid it on the bottom of Lough Gill. Legend insists that only those free from sin can still hear it. Don't worry, neither can we.

■ Yeats, Yeats, Yeats

> *Under Bare Ben Bulben's head*
> *In Drumcliffe churchyard Yeats is laid*
> *An ancestor was rector there*
> *Long years ago, a church stands near,*
> *By the road an ancient cross.*
> *No marble, no conventional phrase;*
> *On limestone quarried near the spot*
> *By his command these words are cut;*
>> *Cast a cold eye*
>> *on life, on death.*
>> *Horsemen pass bye!*

Yeats composed this poem a year before his death in France in 1939. After the delays caused by World War II, his wife George carried out his wish in 1948 and was later buried by his feet. The road Yeats refers to is the N15; the churchyard is 4 mi. northwest of Sligo. His grave is to the left of the church door. On summer Sunday evenings, the church sponsors concerts (tel. (071) 56629). **Buses** from Sligo toward Derry stop at Drumcliff (10min., in summer M-Sa 3 per day, Su 1 per day, in winter M-Sa 3 per day, £2.60 return). Hitching is reportedly painless. A few miles northeast of Drumcliff, **Glencar Lake,** mentioned in Yeats's "The Stolen Child," is the subject of more literary excursions. Stunning views of Knocknarea and Benbulben and the smashing Glencar Falls add natural beauty to literary genius. The lake is marked by a sign about 1 mi. north of Drumcliff on N15.

Farther north of Drumcliff, eerie **Benbulben,** rich in mythical associations, protrudes from the landscape like the keel of a foundered boat. In 574, St. Columcille founded a monastery on top, and it continued to be a major religious center until the 16th century. The climb up the 1729 ft. peak is rather windy, and the summit can be downright gusty. However, if you can keep from being blown away, standing at the very point of Benbulben, where the land inexplicably drops 5000 ft., can be a watershed experience for even the most weathered of hikers. Marks of old turf cuttings on the way up give evidence of one of the mountainside's historic uses. Signs guide travelers to Benbulben from Drumcliff Rd. Ask at the gas station in Drumcliff for detailed directions to trailheads.

Four miles west of Drumcliff is **Lissadell House** (tel. 63150), where poet Eva Gore-Booth and her sister Constance Markiewicz, second in command in the Easter Rising (see **History,** p. 60) and later the first woman elected to the Dáil, entertained Yeats and his circle. *(Open June to mid-Sept. M-Sa 10:30am-12:15pm and 2-4:15pm. £2.50. Grounds open year-round. Free.)* The gaunt house has lost some of its luster, and the carpets are wearing thin, but Constance's great-nephew still lives here and allows tours. Henry Gore-Booth was an Arctic explorer and avid hunter. His harpoons and stag heads create a macho atmosphere, but the real trophy, a ferocious brown bear, was actually shot by the butler. Take the first left after Yeats Tavern Hostel on Drumcliff Rd. and follow the signs. Near Lissadell in the village of Carney, just past Orchard Inn, the excellent food, nightly entertainment, and beer garden at **Laura's Pub** (tel. (071) 63056) justify the prices.

■ Inishmurray and Mullaghmore

Mullaghmore, 15 mi. north of Drumcliff, is one of the departure points for faraway Inishmurray, a tiny monastic island that looks like a hill fort with no hill. Founded around 600, pounded by Vikings around 800, and finally abandoned in 1948 when the turf supply ran out, the windswept island is now a deserted maze of stone walls and altars. The power of the **Clocha Breaca** (cursing stones) found on the islands can be unleashed on your worst enemies. **Lomax Boats** (tel. (071) 66124) cross from Mullaghmore (£75 per 8 people). Mullaghmore itself is a beautiful fishing village with two long miles of sheltered blue-flag beach, a headland, and **Classiebawn Castle**, where the Queen's brother-in-law, the Lord Mountbatten, lived and was assassinated by the IRA. B&Bs are expensive here, but dinner at **Eithne's Restaurant** (tel. (071) 66407), behind the funky blue mural on Main St., is worth the splurge. The meal will keep you fed for an entire day or more (pigeon pie £10.95; open summer M and W-Su 6:30-9:30pm). You can feasibly visit Mullaghmore on a daytrip from Sligo, but you may be happier doing so from Bundoran, just 5 mi. away in Donegal (see p. 333).

Roscommon and Leitrim

Rivers and lakes meander through quiet counties Roscommon and Leitrim, which span a diamond-shaped area from Sligo and Donegal to the middle of the island. The sights of Parke's Castle, Dromahair, and Crevelea Abbey are in Co. Leitrim but are covered in Sligo (see p. 324). The name of Drumshanbo, a small town in Co. Leitrim, does not mean "an old cow's ass" but is from Drom Seanbo, "ridge of the old hut."

■ Carrick-on-Shannon

Coursing slowly through the green hills of Leitrim on its way to the sea, the Shannon River pauses when it reaches the rows of white yachts moored at Carrick-on-Shannon's marina. Life is relaxed here in this proud seat of Ireland's most depopulated county. Anglers fish for pike during the day while merry drinkers fill the pubs with song in the evening. The few sights in town won't sustain the visitor, but nearby parks and lakes make wonderful daytrips. A bridge spans from Co. Roscommon over the Shannon and into town, leading to the clock tower and Main St.

PRACTICAL INFORMATION

Trains: The station (tel. 20036) is a 10min. walk southwest of town. Trains to **Sligo** (1hr., 3 per day, £7) and **Dublin** (2½hr., 3 per day, £11.50).

Buses: Buses leave from **Coffey's Pastry Case** (tel. (071) 60066) for **Boyle** (15min., 3 per day, £3.20— a taxi's cheaper), **Sligo** (1hr., 3 per day, £5), and **Dublin** (3hr., 3 per day, £8).

Tourist Office: (tel. 20170), on the Marina. Their encyclopedic knowledge of the town's history is yours for the asking. Open July-Aug. M-Sa 9am-1pm and 2-8pm, Su 10am-2pm; June and Sept. M-Sa 9am-1pm and 2-5pm.

Bank: AIB, Main St. (tel. 20055). **ATM.** Open M 10am-5pm, Tu-F 10am-4pm.

Taxis: P. Burke, Bridge St. (tel. 21343). 50p per mi.

Taxes: 28% on first £20,000, 40% beyond that.

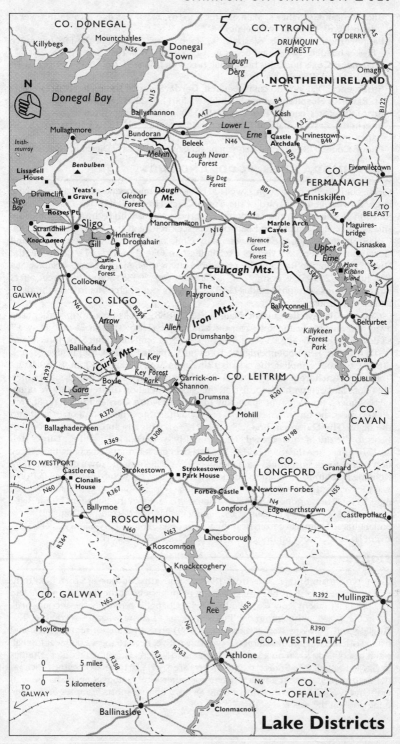

Lake Districts

Bike Rental: Geraghty's, Main St. (tel. 21316). £7.50 per day, £15-25 per week; deposit £10. Open daily 9am-9pm.

Laundromat: McGuire's Washeteria, Main St. (tel. 20339), in the FBS Insurance Broker building. Douse and desiccate £4.50. Open M-Sa 10am-6pm.

Pharmacy: Cox's hocks his bottles and boxes on Bridge St. (tel. 20158). Open M-Th 9:30am-6pm, F-Sa 9:30am-7pm.

Emergency: Dial 999; no coins required. **Garda:** Shannon Lodge (tel. 20021).

St. Patrick's Hospital: Summerhill Rd. (tel. 20011 or 20287; nights 20091).

Post Office: St. George's Terr. (tel. 20020). Open M-Sa 9am-5:30pm.

Internet Access: Upstairs at **Gartlan's,** Bridge St. (tel. 21735). £4.50 per hr., £3.50 after 6pm. Open M-Sa 9:30am-7pm.

Phone Code: 078 is so phat that you might gain weight, says Diggable Planets.

ACCOMMODATIONS, FOOD, AND PUBS

Clean, comfortable bunk rooms, well-fed birds, and a microwave organize around the large, flower-filled courtyard of the **Town Clock Hostel (IHH)** (tel. 20068), at the junction of Main and Bridge St. (dorms £6; private rooms with bath £8.50 per person; sheets 50p). Sick animals and backpackers seek refuge at the **An Óige Hostel** (tel. 21848), upstairs from the local veterinary clinic on Bridge St. Spacious rooms and "insta"-hot shower have visitors exclaiming "An Óige!" (dorms £7). B&Bs line the Dublin road, Station Rd., and the manicured lawns of St. Mary's Close. **Ariadna,** Station Rd. (tel. 20205), is homey (£15). **Villaflora** (tel. 20338) across the street offers more luxurious accommodations (£18). **Campers** can pitch tents free on the riverbank by the bridge.

Chung's Chinese Restaurant, Main St. (tel. 21888), cooks up a storm. Order takeaway and save big; eat in and savor the candlelight. (Entrees about £5 take-away, £7 sit-down. Open July-Aug. M-Th and Su 6-11pm, F-Sa 6pm-midnight; Sept.-June M and W-Th 6-11pm, F-Sa 6pm-midnight.) To eat at **Coffey's Pastry Case,** Bridge St. (tel. 20929), without sampling the cake is a sin (open M-Sa 8:30am-8:30pm, Su 10:30am-7pm). **The Anchorage,** Bridge St. (tel. 20416), is the town's most popular and venerable pub. Move in with the locals and the Next Generation (in Ireland they're drinking Guinness, not Pepsi) in splendidly furnished **Flynn's Corner Pub,** Main St. (tel. 20003), near the tiny town clock. Its fast food outlet next door stays open well into the night. **The Oarsmen,** Bridge St. (tel. 21733), with a beautiful raised wood bar, plays to the out-of-town crowd. That would be you. (Rock Th and F.) **Ging's** (tel. 21054), just across the town bridge, boasts a beer garden on the River Shannon. They don't serve food, "just drink—and plenty of it." A mile from the town center, **Rockin' Robbins** lives up to its claim to be the town's nearest nightclub. Minibuses (£1 one-way) leave from The Anchorage on weekends. (Open F-Su. Cover £3, students £2. Ages 21+.) A more popular option is a booze-cruise down the Shannon; **Moon River Cruises** (tel. 21777) is a bargain at £5. Summer sailings at 2:30 and 4:30pm and weekend nights at 11pm leave from near the tourist office. For trad, try **Glancy's** across the river (Th-Su), **Cryan's** on Bridge St. (Tu and F-Su), or **Burke's** (Th).

SIGHTS

The town's main **bridge** dates from 1846, as does the **Old Barrel Store** next to it, where Guinness kept its beer for collection by publicans. At the intersection of Main and Bridge St., teeny, tiny **Costello Memorial Chapel** is reputedly the second-smallest in the world, although no one in town seems to know what it's second to. The **Angling and Tourism Association** (tel. 20489) gives the line on rentals, sites, and fishing-oriented accommodations. To go truly native, head to the 12,000-seat football pitch just outside town on a Sunday afternoon to watch Leitrim battle other counties in Gaelic football (see **Sports,** p. 69). Tickets are £3-5, £10 for playoff games. Pick up the *Leitrim Observer* at any newsagent for other local listings. Carrick has several craft and workshops farther down Main St., as well as a sports complex and swimming pool on the east end of town.

Four miles northwest of Carrick-on-Shannon on the road to Boyle, the **Lough Key Forest Park** (tel. (079) 62363) bursts with rhododendrons in the springtime, but its 850 acres and 33 forested islands are worth exploring any time of the year. *(Park always open. Admission collected 10am-6pm. £2 per car.)* The park was once the center of the Rockingham Estate, which covered most of the surrounding area. Although the estate's classical mansion burned down in 1957, the stables, church, and icehouse still stand. The distractions provided include underground servants' chambers, "bog gardens," and boat tours. Numerous signposts won't let you miss the round tower, fairy bridge, and wishing chair. The **Lough Key Campground** (tel. (079) 62212) on is the road to the lake (£3 per person). North of the lough lies the site of Ireland's most important pre-human battle, in which the Túatha De Danann defeated Ireland's indigenous demons, the Formorians (see **Literary Traditions,** p. 61 and **How Poison Glen Got Its Name,** p. 350).

The Earls of Leitrim once roamed the **Lough Rynn Estate** (tel. (078) 31427), just outside Mohill 15 mi. east of Carrick on N4 toward Dublin. *(Open late-Apr. to Aug. daily 10am-7pm. £1.50 per person, £3.50 per car. Tours £1. Last tour 4:30pm on weekends.)* Once a massive 90,000 acres, the estate has been whittled down to a mere 100. The century-old walled Victorian garden and turret house overlook 600 acres of lake. A pleasant weekend walking tour will guide you into the beautiful parklands, which include angling spots and the country's oldest monkey-puzzle tree. On weekdays, a 50p map/guide will provide you with the basics. The **Lough Rynn Caravan Park** (tel. (078) 31054) hosts campers on the shores of Lough Rynn (£2 per tent; £5 per caravan; open May-Sept.).

■ Strokestown

Fifteen miles south of Carrick, where R368 meets N5 from Longford, rises the 18th-century **Strokestown Park House,** Main St. (tel. (078) 33013). *(Tours £3, students £2.40. Gardens £2.50.)* This former family estate, once massaging 27,000 acres, has been heavily restored. The family's history of great Irish blunders includes fighting as mercenaries for Oliver Cromwell, evicting 3006 tenants during the Famine, and subsidizing a number of coffin-ships, the infamous emigration boats. By 1847, the worst year of the Famine, the tenants had had enough and shot the landlord. Although the house has not been occupied since 1979, a casual, unforced grandeur remains. Following 10 years of restoration, the 4-acre **Pleasure Garden,** an exact replica of the original, was opened in 1998. The **Famine Museum,** in the old stables next to the house, sits in stark opposition to the wealth and privilege of the great house. *(Open Apr.-Oct. daily 11am-5:30pm. £3.)* An elaborate and detailed exhibit documents the history of the Potato Famine and conscientiously explores its connection with present-day social problems (see **Famine,** p. 58).

■ Boyle

Squeezed on a river between the two lakes southeast of the Curlieu mountains, Boyle is an inevitable crossing point for anyone trying to get anywhere in the northwest. The clever shopkeepers who started the town realized this fact, as did the clans and troops who later used Boyle as a strategic base. The modern explorer would do well to follow their example. Boyle offers convenient access to nearby mountains, lakes, and parks, as well as numerous historical sites. As if that weren't enough, in August of 1999, carefully selected men of Boyle will don funky medieval battlegear and re-create the 1599 Battle of Curlieu Pass as part of a quatrocentennial celebration.

ORIENTATION AND PRACTICAL INFORMATION

Boyle lines both sides of the river. From the train station, make a left and walk five minutes to reach the town.

Trains: tel. 62027. To **Dublin** (2½hr., 3 per day, £11.50) and **Sligo** (40min., 4 per day, £4.50).

Buses: The stop is outside the Royal Hotel on Bridge St. Service to **Dublin** (3½hr., 3 per day, £8) and **Sligo** (45min., 3 per day, £5).

Tourist Office: Main St. (tel. 62145), inside the main gates of King House. Open May-Sept. 10am-6pm. Also, an unofficial town historian, jeweller **Richard McGee** (tel. 62386), in his shop on Bridge St., can point history buffs in the right direction.

Banks: **National Irish Bank** (tel. 62058), at Bridge and Patrick St. **ATM.** Open M 10am-5pm, Tu-F 10am-3pm.

Laundromat: The Washing Well, Main St. (tel. 62503). Wash and dry £4.50, including detergent. Open M-Sa 9:30am-6:30pm.

Bike Rental: Sheerin Cycles, Main St. (tel. 62010). £7 per day, £30 per week; deposit £40 or ID. Open M-Sa 9:30am-1pm and 2-6pm.

Taxi: McKenna's (tel. 62119). 50p per mi.

Pharmacy: Ryan's, Patrick and Main St. (tel. 62003). Open M-Sa 9am-6pm.

Emergency: Dial 999; no coins required. **Garda:** Military Rd. (tel. 62030).

Post Office: Carrick Rd. (tel. 62029 or 62028). Open M and W-F 9am-5:30pm, Tu 9:30am-5:30pm, Sa 9am-1pm and 2-5:30pm.

Phone Code: 079 has been known to bubble over.

ACCOMMODATIONS, FOOD, AND PUBS

The only hostels in the area are in nearby **Carrick-on-Shannon** (see p. 326). However, lavish beds can be procured in Boyle's B&Bs. Every visitor to the **Abbey House** (tel. 62385), on Abbeytown Rd. behind the old abbey (see below), gets an individually decorated room (£16, with bath £17). **Avonlea** (tel. 62538), on the Carrick road just before you enter Boyle, traffics in satisfying slumber (£16, with bath £17). The **Lough Key Forest Caravan & Camping Park** (tel. 62212) and its laundry facilities are just a five-minute drive from Boyle on the Carrick road. (£3 per person, £8 per tent; open Easter-Aug. See p. 329.)

D. H. Burke, Main St. (tel. 62208), fulfills the duties of a supermarket (open M-Th 9:30am-6pm, F 9:30am-8pm, Sa 9:30am-7pm). **Una Bhán Restaurant** (tel. 63033), within the gates of the King House, is the place to go for breakfast and lunch (salmon salad £3.95; open daily 9:30am-6:30pm). **Chung's Chinese Restaurant,** Bridge St. (tel. 63123), has bunches of bean sprouts and a mean mushroom chicken (take-away £4.50, sit-down £6; open Th-F 12:30-2:30pm, Sa-Su 5-11:30pm). For perfect pints and rousing music (trad W), everyone heads to **Kate Lavin's** (tel. 62855), on Patrick St.

SIGHTS AND ENTERTAINMENT

Gothic arches curve over the green lawns of magnificent **Boyle Abbey** (tel. 62604; on A4), built in 1161 by Cistercian monks. *(Open mid-June to mid-Sept. daily 9:30am-6:30pm. Guided tours on the hour 10am-5pm. Key available from Mrs. Mitchell at the Abbey House B&B in the off season. £1, students 40p.)* The central arched walls, though lacking a roof, are perfectly preserved.

King House, Main St. (tel. 63242), recently reopened its doors and four Georgian floors to superb historical exhibits. *(Open May-Sept. daily 10am-6pm, Apr. and Oct. Sa-Su 10am-6pm. £3, students £2.50. Last admission 5pm).* Built by Sir Henry King around 1730 for entertaining VIPs, it served as a family home for forty years and an army barracks for a hundred and forty. The house is now decked out in 3-D displays and excellent interactive exhibits chronicling the history of the King family and the Connacht Rangers. It also houses the Boyle Civic Art Collection. **Frybrook House** (tel. 62170), next to the bridge, was built in 1752 and restored to its Georgian glory in 1994. *(Open June-Aug. daily 2-6pm. Tours £3, students £2.50.)*

From August 19 to 22, 1999, Boyle will celebrate the 400th anniversary of the 1599 **Battle of Curlieu Pass,** remembered as the final victory of the united Gaelic clans before they were thoroughly routed by crack Elizabethan forces. In what looks to be a good bit of fun, local townsmen will dress their streets and selves in medieval garb, launch fireworks, and stage a grand recreation of the battle at Lough Key. In the second week of July, the **Gala Festival** (info tel. 62469) brings busking in the streets, soccer in the fields, and all-nighters in the pubs. The last week of July rings in the **Boyle Arts Festivals** (tel. 64085). There are no bar exemptions, but the myriad recitals, workshops, and exhibitions should leave any arts aficionado delirious (tickets £2-5). The *Roscommon Herald* has other local events listings.

County Donegal

Although its name means "fort of the foreigner," tourists are still likely to feel a bit out of place in this most remote and least Anglicized of Ireland's "scenic" provinces. Among Ireland's counties, Donegal (DUN-ay-GAHL) is second to Cork in size and second to none in glorious wilderness. Donegal escaped the widespread deforestation of Ireland; vast wooded areas engulf many of Donegal's mountain chains, while the coastline alternates beautiful beaches with majestic cliffs. The tallest sea-cliffs in Europe are around Slieve League. Inishowen makes the best cycling or driving route. In between the larger pockets of civilization, distance from all things English has preserved the biggest *gaeltacht* in the country.

Donegal's decent harbors and their remoteness from London made it a stronghold for Gaelic chieftains, especially the Northern Uí Néill (O'Neill), Ó Domhnaill (O'Donnell), and McSwain (McSweeney) clans, until the Flight of the Earls in 1607, when the English forcibly gained control of the region (see **Feudalism (1200-1607)**, p. 55). After years of English occupation, during which few English actually lived in this barren "wasteland," Donegal was given to the Irish state in 1920, as its largely Catholic population would have put at risk Northern Ireland's Protestant majority. Today, cottage industries, fishing boats, and the underwear factory occupy the locals' time by day, while a pure form of trad keeps them packed into the pubs at night. The tourist industry is just starting up in Donegal, but be assured that you'll encounter fewer camera-toting tourists here than anywhere else in the country.

Session Houses

A "session house" is a Celtic tradition going back to the days of itinerant storytellers and musicians. These traveling bards would serve as one of the only sources of news for an area in olden days and were therefore held in high regard. In exchange for their services, "session houses" would provide the newsbearers with food to eat and a bed for the night. The session house tradition is still observed in Donegal—hence the County's reputation for truly stellar craic and trad.

GETTING THERE AND GETTING AROUND

Donegal has the public transportation to get you where you want to go, but only if you're willing to wait. No trains reach Donegal, and buses tend to hit smaller towns only once per day, sometimes in the early morning or late at night. Some towns, including major towns like Letterkenny, Donegal Town, and Dungloe, rent bikes. **Hitchers** report very short waits and friendly drivers on the main roads, especially those north of Donegal Town. Byways are largely devoid of drivers, leaving hitchers to rely on the same patience that they might with the buses—a kind driver will come at some point in the day.

Bus Éireann (tel. (01) 836 6111) connects **Dublin** with **Letterkenny** (tel. (074) 21309; 4hr., 3-4 per day) and **Donegal** town (4¼hr., 3-5 per day) and connects these two towns with some of the smaller villages in the southern half of the region. Private buses replace Bus Éireann on most of the major services in Donegal. Their prices are reasonable and their drivers more open to persuasion if you want to be let off on the doorstep of a remote hostel. The flexibility of their routes also means that the buses aren't always quite on time. **Lough Swilly Buses** (Derry tel. (01504) 262017; Let-

County Donegal

NORTHWEST IRELAND

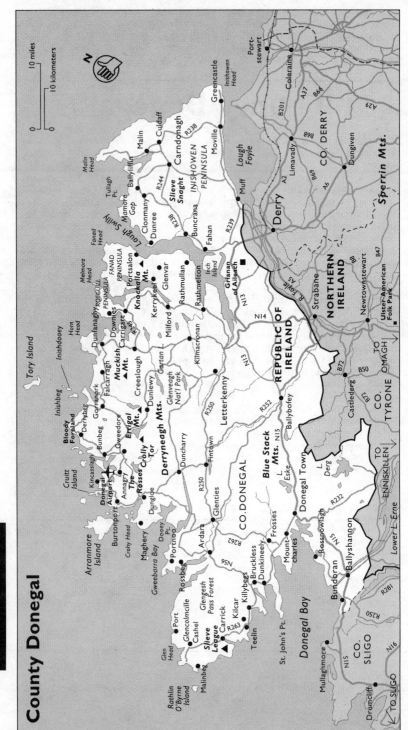

N

10 miles

10 kilometers

0

0

Tory Island

Inishdooey

Inishbeg

Inishbofin

Crutt Island

Arranmore Island

Rathlin O'Byrne Island

Malin Head

Melmore Head

Horn Head

Fanad Head

Dunfanaghy

Downies

Carrigart

Port-salon

Knockalla Mt. ▲

Kerrykeel

Glenvar

Rathmullan

Rathmelton

Milford

FANAD PENINSULA

ROSGUILL PENINSULA

Tullagh Pt.

Ballyliffin

Malin

Culdaff

Carndonagh

Moville

Greencastle

Inishowen Head

Portstewart

Coleraine

Limavady

Dungiven

CO. DERRY

Sperrin Mts.

Slieve Snaght

INISHOWEN PENINSULA

Clonmany

Dunree

Buncrana

Fahan

Inch Island

Muff

Lough Foyle

Derry

NORTHERN IRELAND

Strabane

Newtownstewart

Ulster-American Folk Park

Omagh

CO. TYRONE

Castlederg

Grianan of Aileach

Kilmacrenan

Letterkenny

Ballybofey

REPUBLIC OF IRELAND

Muckish Mt. ▲

Creeslough

Dunlewy

Errigal Mt. ▲

Gortahork

Derrybeg

Bunbeg

Gweedore

Crolly

Tor

Bloody Foreland

Kincasslagh

Annagry

The Rosses

Dunglow

Dungloe

Dooey Pt.

Portnoo

Rossbeg

Ardara

Maghery

Crohy Head

Burtonport

Donegal Airport

Gweebarra Bay

Derryveagh Mts.

Gartan L.

Glenveagh Nat'l Park

R250

R251

Dooey

Duncharry

Fintown

Glenties

CO. DONEGAL

Frosses

Mountcharles

Dunkineely

Bruckless

Killybegs

Kilcar

Carrick

Teelin

St. John's Pt.

Glencolmcille

Cashel

Port

Glen Head

Malinbeg

Glengesh Pass Forest

Slieve League ▲

Blue Stack Mts.

L. Eske

Donegal Town

Rossnowlagh

Ballyshannon

Bundoran

Mullaghmore

Drumcliff

CO. SLIGO

L. Derg

Lower L. Erne

Ballintra

N15

N56

N13

N14

N15

N13

N56

R250

R252

R262

R263

A2

A6

A5

A37

A29

B201

B898

B69

B68

B64

B47

B50

B72

R238

R244

R238

R239

R229

R245

R250

R251

R232

R281

R250

N16

N15

Mamore Gap

Fanad Head

Melmore Head

terkenny tel. (074) 22863) fan out over the northern area, connecting Derry, Letterkenny, the Inishowen Peninsula, the Fanad Peninsula, and western coastal villages as far south as Dungloe. Swilly also offers a **Runabout** ticket good for eight days of unlimited travel (£18). **McGeehan's Bus Co.** (tel. (075) 46101 or 46150) runs to and from Dublin each day, passing through almost every intervening town (Donegal to Dublin £11). **Feda O'Donnell** (tel. (075) 48114; in Galway tel. (091) 761656) runs up and down the Donegal coast, connecting northwest Ireland with **Galway** (from **Letterkenny,** M-Th and Sa 2 per day, F and Su 3 per day, £9), and carries bikes for free. Bus prices on the main routes like Letterkenny-Dublin fluctuate due to competition.

■ Bundoran

At the mouth of Dobhran River, Bundoran is the first stop in Donegal for visitors from Sligo or Leitrim. In 1777, Bundoran was the summer residence of Viscount Enniskillen, but it has since moved from the classes to the masses. The resort's clear beaches, hopping nightlife, championship surfing, water sports, and horseback riding now attract an large crowd of vacationers from Northern Ireland. In recent years, tax break-fueled development has been rapid and haphazard—the population of the town swells from 2000 to 20,000 during the summer.

PRACTICAL INFORMATION Bus Éireann (tel. 51101) leaves from the Main St. depot for **Dublin** (2 per day), **Galway** via **Sligo** (M-Sa 6 per day, Su 3 per day), and **Donegal** (3 per day). **Ulsterbus** runs to Enniskillen (in summer M-Sa 7 per day, Su 3 per day, in winter M-F 3 per day, Su 1 per day). **Feda O'Donnell** (tel. (075) 48356) serves **Galway** and **Letterkenny.** Heaping portions of information are available from the new **tourist office** (tel. 41350) over the bridge on Main St. (open May-Aug. M-Tu and Th-Sa 10am-8pm, W 10am-6pm, Su noon-6pm). **AIB** is on Main St. (open M 10am-4:30pm, Tu-F 10am-3pm; **ATM**). **Raleigh Rent-A-Bike** (tel. 41526) is on East Main St. (£6 per day, £30 per week; open M-Sa 8.30am-6pm). The **phone code** is 072.

ACCOMMODATIONS Every other house in Bundoran seems to be a B&B; the cheaper and quieter ones are farther down Main St. away from the bridge. **Homefield Hostel (IHH),** Bayview Ave. (tel. 41288), is right on Main St.; from the bus stop, head left up the hill between the Church of Ireland and the Bay View Guest House. A spacious sitting room and friendly, artsy owners have a great location. (Dorms £10; doubles £20, with bath £24. Continental breakfast included.) At **Ceol-Na-Mwa B&B,** Tullanstrand (tel. 41287), beach stretches out before you and horse pasture behind you. Walk out Ballyshannon Rd. and turn left at the KFC to the end. (Rooms up to £18.) **St. Edna's B&B,** West Main St. (tel. 42096), blesses visitors with impeccable rooms in a flower-draped pink home (£15 with bath).

FOOD AND PUBS The best restaurant in town is **La Sabbia** (tel. 42253), a first-rate Italian bistro connected to the hostel. Cheap and impeccable food is served in a cool, cosmopolitan atmosphere tempered by a roaring fire and trad (open M and W-Su 7-10pm). The **Kitchen Bake,** Main St. (tel. 41543), interrupts the string of industrial Main St. storefronts. Housed in a renovated old church, this café serves lovely light sandwiches and lunch specials that are unique in a town of fast food take-out. (Entrees £3-5. Open daily 9:30am-8:30pm, lunch until 6pm.) The **Ould Bridge Bar,** Main St. (tel. 42050) draws Bundoran's best trad players on weekends and a friendly, happily tipsy crowd nightly. **Brennans,** Main St. (tel. 41810), is a real old pub experience; it's been in the same family for over 100 years and hasn't changed much. After pub closing, 21+ clubbers dance over to **Peppies,** Main St. (tel. 41460; open nightly in summer, weekends in winter; cover £3-4).

SIGHTS The **Aughross Cliffs** ("headlands of the steeds") were once a grazing ground for war horses. A leisurely stroll past the Northern Hotel affords an impressive view of mighty Atlantic waves on your left. Curious sights include the **Fairy Bridges,** the **Wishing Chair,** and the **Puffing Hole,** where water spouts up volcano-style through a bed of rock. Farther along are the golden beaches of **Tullan Strand,** a surfers' mecca. **Fitzgeralds Surfworld,** Main St. (tel. 41223), reports conditions, while **Donegal Surf Co.,** The Promenade (tel. 41340), will rent you a wetsuit and board (£5 per hr.). The **Stracomer Silver Strand Equestrian Centre,** Tullan Strand (tel. 41288), will have you galloping across the dunes and beaches. All levels of ability are welcome. *(Open Apr.-Oct. £10 per hr.; private lessons £15 per hr.)* The annual **Bundoran Music Festival,** held over the October bank holiday weekend, attracts "big names."

■ Ballyshannon

Ballyshannon's annual musical moment comes the first weekend in August, when the **Ballyshannon Music Festival** (tel. 51088) presents a renowned mix of Irish folk and trad. If that's not enough, the entire weekend costs £25 for performances, workshops, and a jammed campsite. If that's not enough either, go ahead and skip it. During the rest of the year, Ballyshannon twiddles its thumbs by the River Erne, which splashes over the **Falls of Assaroe** (Ess Ruaid) just west of the bridge. The falls are one of Ireland's most ancient pagan holy sites, but there's little to see other than water and symbolism.

ORIENTATION AND PRACTICAL INFORMATION **Allingham's Bridge** connects the town's two halves and honors the Ballyshannon poet William Allingham, who inspired Yeats to study the mythic traditions of Co. Sligo. Most of the town lies north of the river, where Main St. splits halfway up a hill. This hill, named Mullach na Sídh ("Hill of the Fairies") is believed to be the burial site of the legendary High King Hugh, who supposedly drowned in the Assaroe Falls. **Buses** (tel. (074) 31008) leave the depot just beside the bridge for **Sligo** (1hr., M-Sa 11 per day, Su 5 per day, £5.70) and **Donegal Town** (25min., M-Sa 10 per day, Su 3 per day, £3.40). If you need cash ASAP, the **AIB,** Castle St. (tel. 51169), has an **ATM** (open M-W and F 10am-4pm, Th 10am-5pm). The **Gardaí** (tel. 51155) are watching. The **post office** (tel. 51111) settles halfway up Castle St. (open M-F 9am-1pm and 2-5:30pm, Sa 9am-1pm). **Internet access** is at **The Engine Room** (tel. 52960) up on Market St. (£3.50 per 30min.; open M-F 9am-6pm, Sa 10am-5:30pm). The **phone code** is 072.

ACCOMMODATIONS, FOOD, AND PUBS **Duffy's Hostel (IHH)** (tel. 51535) is a small bungalow-turned-hostel just north of town on Donegal Rd. The wonderfully friendly owners maintain a second-hand bookshop out back, but rooms are small and the toilets are on the dingy side. (Dorms £6.50. **Camping** £3.50. Open Mar.-Oct.) Ten minutes down Belleek Rd., the **Assaroe Lake Side Caravan & Camping Park** (tel. 52822) has a beautiful location and brand-new facilities (2-person tent £8, 4- to 6-person tent £10). A Yeats quote graces the door of the **Dead Poets Café,** 3 Main St. (tel. 52770), where bookshelves and bronzed tree branches line the forest-green walls. Speak softly, Nwanda. (Mysterious "poet's pasta" £3.50. Open M-Sa 9am-7pm, Su 11am-4pm.) **Shannon's Corner Bistro** (tel. 51180) at the top of Main St. combines airy, modern decor with home-cooked food (entrees £3-5; open M-Sa 8am-6pm) and lets predictably spotless, modern rooms upstairs (£15, with bath £17). **Spar** grocers at the end of Tirconaill St. (open daily 9am-8pm). **Finn McCool's,** Main St. (tel. 52677), is the most popular pub in town, with reputedly the best trad sessions around (M-Th 10pm). Get here early; the pub is tiny and the Guinness bottles take up as much space as the people. The **Cellar,** Bundoran Rd. (tel. 51452), opens only on summer weekends, but great trad and spirit keep the tourists coming. **Dino's Nite Club,** in the Allingham hotel on Main St., rocks Friday to Sunday (cover £2-3).

SIGHTS From the left fork of Main St., a left turn past the Imperial Hotel leads to **St. Anne's Church,** where William Allingham is buried. His grave lies on the south side of the church with all the other Allinghams. Back by the river, a fish pass near the power station allows tourists to watch the ancient biological cycle of salmon and trout struggling upstream during spawning season, which is around June. Trying to distinguish the sun-god in salmon form (believed to swim past every night after dip-ping into the western ocean) is tricky, but don't let us stop you from trying. The barely visible 12th-century **Cistercian Abbey of Assaroe** sits by the meandering river. From town, go up the left fork of Main St. past the Thatched Pub and take the second left. The Cistercians put a canal in the river, harnessing its hydraulic power for a water mill that still operates. A tiny path outside leads to the **Abbey Well,** blessed by St. Patrick (what hasn't been?). Pilgrims bless themselves with its water each year on August 15, although they avoid the cursed river. To the right of the bridge and 120 yd. down the riverbank, a tiny cave harbors a mass rock used during Penal Days and two hollow stones that once held holy water.

■ Donegal Town

Donegal Town's name comes from the Irish *Dun na nGall,* meaning "fortress of the foreigners." Like the invaders then, many travelers now begin their tour of Co. Donegal here, and some turn the town into a base for exploring the county due to the helpful tourist office and many bus routes. Marvelous trad sessions, the peaceful setting on Donegal Bay, and majestic ruins of past kingdoms that still define the town's landscape are other attractions of Donegal.

ORIENTATION AND PRACTICAL INFORMATION

The center of town is The Diamond, a triangular area bordered by Donegal's main shopping streets. At the top of the hill lies Main Street, which leads to Killybegs Rd. The bottom point of The Diamond leads to the tourist office along Sligo Rd.

Buses: Bus Éireann (tel. 21101) runs to **Dublin** (4hr., M-Sa 6 per day, Su 3 per day, £10) via **Ballyshannon** (25min., £3), to **Galway** (4hr., M-Sa 3 per day, Su 2 per day, £13), and to **Sligo** (1hr., M-Sa 6 per day, Su 4 per day). Buses stop outside the Abbey Hotel on The Diamond, where timetables are also posted. **McGeehan Coaches** (tel. (075) 46150) go to **Dublin** via **Enniskillen** and **Cavan** (Tu-Th at least 1 per day, F-M 2 per day); they also drive to **Killybegs, Ardara, Glenties,** and **Dungloe. Feda O'Donnell** (tel. (091) 761656 or (075) 48114) leaves for **Galway** from the tourist office (M-Sa 9:45am and 5:15pm, additional stops F and Su).

Tourist Office: Quay St. (tel. 21148), south of The Diamond on Sligo Rd. Brochures galore on Co. Donegal, reservations for accommodations throughout the Republic, information on the North, and a free map of the city. One of a few tourist offices in the county, it's a good stop before heading north. Open July-Aug. M-F 9am-8pm, Sa 9am-6pm, Su 9am-5pm; Sept.-Oct. and Easter-June M-F 9am-5pm, Sa 10am-2pm.

Banks: AIB (tel. 21016), **Bank of Ireland** (tel. 21079), and **Ulster Bank** (tel. 21064) in The Diamond. All open M-W and F 10am-4pm, Th 10am-5pm; all have 24hr. **ATMs.**

Taxis: Several companies, including: **Johnston Jim** (tel. 21349), **Pierce McGroary** (tel. 556098), and **Peter McGroary** (tel. 21159).

Bike Rental: C.J. O'Doherty's, Main St. (tel. 21119). £6 per day, £30 per week; panniers £4 per week; £40 deposit. One-way rental with Raleigh Rent-a-Bike dealers. Open M-Sa 9am-1pm and 2-6pm. **The Bike Shop,** Waterloo Pl. (tel. 22515), the first left off Killybegs Rd. from The Diamond. £6 per day, £30 per week; £30-40 deposit; panniers £1 per day, £5 per week. Trip-planning info free. Open M-Sa 9am-6pm, maybe Su. Both shops provide locks and repair equipment.

Laundry: Derma's Launderette & Dry Cleaning, Mill Ct., The Diamond (tel. 22255). Wash only £2; wash and dry £4.50-5; powder 50p. Open M-Sa 9am-7pm. **Eleanor's Launderette,** Upper Main St. (tel. 21414). Wash £1.80, dry 30p per 5min., powder 50p. Open M-Sa 9am-6pm. Last wash 4:30pm.

Pharmacy: Begley's Chemist, The Diamond (tel. 21232). Open M-F 9am-6pm, Sa 9am-7pm.

Emergency: Dial 999; no coins required. **Garda:** tel. 21021.

Hospital: Donegal District Hospital (tel. 21029).

Post Office: Tirconaill St. (tel. 21007), past Donegal Castle and over the bridge. Open M 9:30-10:30am and 3:30-4:30pm, Tu 11:30am-12:30pm and 3:30-4:30pm, W

11:15am-12:15pm and 3:30-4:30pm, Th 9:45am-10:45am and 3:30-4:30pm, F 3:30-4:30pm, Sa 9-10am and 2:30-3:30pm.
Phone Code: 073.

ACCOMMODATIONS

◉**Donegal Town Hostel (IHH)** (tel. 22805), ½mi. out on Killybegs Rd. In true IHH form, this hostel presents a family of fellow travelers to the road-weary backpacker. Bright rooms (some with murals) and a large kitchen. Owners will pick up travelers in town if the hostel isn't too busy. Very popular and rather small, so make reservations. Dorms £7; doubles £16. Sheets 50p. Laundry (wash and powder) £4.50. **Camping** £4. Separate kitchen and showers for campers.

Ball Hill Youth Hostel (An Óige/HI) (tel. 21174), 3mi. from town; go 1½mi. out of Donegal on the Killybegs Rd., turn left at the sign, and head another 1½mi. toward the sea. Buses leaving from the Abbey Hotel (£1) often go as far as Killybegs Rd. This hostel, an old coast guard station on a cliff, has airy, spacious rooms. Ask for a tour of the various semi-comic "shrines" surrounding the building. You probably won't bother going into town with all there is to do around the hostel: horseback riding, swimming, day hikes, boat trips, bonfires with sing-songs, or relaxation with owners Kevin and Áine in the "uncommon" room. June-Aug. £6.50, Sept.-May £5; youth discounts. 3-course dinner available for £6 at nearby Mountcharles Hotel.

Cliffview, Coast Rd. (tel. 21684), a 2min. walk along the Killybegs Rd. Spotless, agreeable rooms with bunkbeds and a private bathroom in a 3-year-old building that is a hybrid of Irish B&B aesthetics and Highway 66 motels. Kitchen. July-Aug. dorms £9; doubles £15. Sept.-June dorms £7.50; doubles £13. Continental breakfast included. Laundry £4.

Drumcliffe House (tel. 21200), next to Cliffview and owned by the same family. Beautifully decorated rooms and a large, communal breakfast table lend to the homey nature of this B&B. £14, with bath £16.

Atlantic Guest House, Main St. (tel. 21187). Unbeatable location. Despite being on the busiest street in town, this 17-room guest house offers the undisturbed privacy of a fancy hotel. Each room has plush carpets, TV, coffee/teapot, telephone, and sink. £14, with bath £17.50; single prices negotiable.

Aranmore House (tel. 21242), a 3min. walk along Killybegs Rd. 7 clean, comfortable rooms line up like peas in a pod in Mrs. Keeny's large, rhododendron-fortified home. Large, olive green common room. All rooms have tea/coffee and bathrooms. Above average breakfast portions. Singles £18; doubles £30.

FOOD

A good selection of £4-5 cafés and take-aways occupy The Diamond and the streets nearby. Other than that, your best bet is at the **Foodland Supermarket,** The Diamond (tel. 21006; open M-W 9am-7pm, Th-F 9am-8pm, Sa 9am-7:30pm). **Simple Simon's,** The Diamond (tel. 22687), sells fresh baked goods, local cheeses, homeopathic remedies, and (inedible) crafts from around the world for the organic farmer in you (open M-Sa 9am-6pm).

The Blueberry Tea Room, Castle St. (tel. 22933). Justifiably popular, with white porcelain geese and teapots. Sandwiches, daily specials, and all-day breakfast (entrees around £4). Open daily 9am-6pm.

Errigal Restaurant, Main St. (tel. 21428). "Donegal's most famous chipper." This local hangout has the cheapest dinner in town. Take-away or sit-down in their fashionably retro blue and white interior. 7 types of fish, served with chips and coffee or tea (around £3.50, sandwiches £1.10-2.50). Open in summer daily 11:30am-11pm; in winter M-Sa 11:30am-11pm and Su 3-11pm.

Sam's Deli, Main St. The rare spot where you can just relax with a cup of tea and read the paper for hours. But don't miss out on their delicious sandwiches (around £2). The colorful interior and abundance of scrumptuous baked goods will make you think you're in a gingerbread house. Open M-Sa 9am-5pm.

Harbour Restaurant, Quay St. (tel. 21702). A family restaurant with a menu ranging from pizza (£3-6) to veggie lasagna (£3.75) to steaks (£5-9). Open daily 11am-10:30pm.

PUBS AND CLUBS

Donegal puts on a good show at night, especially in the summertime. Almost every bar has live music nightly, and many pubs host Irish dancing and big name bands during the late June International Arts Festival (see **Sights,** below).

Schooner's, Upper Main St. (tel. 21671). The best trad and contemporary sessions in town—and they happen every night. A great mix of hostelers and locals all aboard on this dark wood bar. Exquisite pub grub (mussels and Guinness £4).

The Voyager Bar, The Diamond (tel. 21201). This pub keeps its patrons happy, but ask the jovial proprietor about its name and bring a tear to his eye. "Everyone has a voyage to make in life." Celebrate yours here. Live music on weekends.

The Cellar Bar, Upper Main St. (tel. 22855). Opens its doors nightly at 9pm for trad and ballads. Confident musicians and singers are invited to join in. White plaster walls and exposed wooden beams give it a rough feel. Cover £1.

The Coach House, upstairs from the Cellar Bar. Spontaneous sing-alongs are known to break out at any point during the day in this locals' hangout.

Charlie's Star Bar, Main St. (tel. 21158), sparkles with live rock, country, and blues (Th-Su in summer, F-Su in winter). The younger crowd's last stop before the discos.

The Olde Castle Bar and Restaurant, Castle St. Old stone walls and corbel windows for that recently renovated medieval feel. Excellent Guinness for an older crowd. Open in summer until 11:30pm, in winter until 11pm.

The Abbey Hotel, The Diamond (tel. 21014). The multi-talented Folk Cabaret and a lively disco (Su 10:30pm-2am; cover £5) draw tourists and locals to the Abbey lounge nightly. 1500 people join in the dancing each week—why not be 1501?

Nero's Nite Club, Main St. (tel. 21111), plays the fiddle while Donegal burns. Known for its excellent dance floor, late hours (until 2:30am), and good pick-up scene. Occasional unadvertised theme nights; ask around. Cover £3-4. Open Th-Su.

SIGHTS

During the daylight hours, Donegal Town's main tourist attractions are the ruins from the tumultuous 15th and 16th centuries. Originally the seat of regional Irish kings, Donegal was torn apart by strife during the Irish-English conflicts around the turn of the 17th century. Evidence of this turmoil remains in **Donegal Castle,** Castle St. (tel. 22405), the former residence of the O'Donnell clan (and, later, of various English nobles). *(Guided tours on the hr. Open Apr.-Oct. daily 9:30am-5:30pm. £2, children and students £1, families £5.)* The ruins of the O'Donnell clan's castle of 1474 stand adjacent to the recently refurbished manor built by English rulers in 1623. The O'Donnell's felt compelled to ruin their own treasures before the English could, but the manor's ornaments remind visitors that the English still got their way. The stones and doorways of the grand manor were taken from the ruins of the 15th-century Franciscan Friary, known as the **Old Abbey,** just a short walk from the tourist office along the river south of town. Gorgeous scenery, old grave slabs, and still-standing stairways are only a few of the delights that remain at the abbey. The abbey had been abandoned nearly a century before the English arrived; four of the monks who fled the abbey went on in their exile to write the *Annals of the Four Masters,* the first narrative history of Ireland. The narrative is the source of many still-told myths and much 16th-century Irish history. An **obelisk** built on The Diamond in 1937 pays homage to the four holy men, as does **St. Patrick's Church of the Four Masters,** a stolid Irish Romanesque church about a half mile up Main St. *(Open M-F 9am-5pm. Free.)*

Just a half mile south of Donegal Town on Sligo Rd., eight craftspeople open their workshops to the public at the **Donegal Craft Village.** *(Open July-Aug. M-Sa 9am-6pm, Su 11am-6pm; Sept.-June M-Sa 9am-6pm.)* The work of an Invereske potter (tel. 22053), a batik artist (tel. 22015), two jewelry designers (tel. 21742 and 22053), an *uileann* pipe maker (tel. 23311), a jewelry metalworker (tel. 22225), a handweaver (tel. 22200), and a porcelain crafter (tel. 22200) make great gift alternatives to the mass-produced leprechauns sold in stores. The **Donegal Drama Circle** presents summer theater at the slightly derelict Old Cinema, Main St. *(Tickets £4, students £2.)* Posters all over town give details. The **Donegal Railway Heritage Centre** (tel. 22655), a block past the post office on Tirconaill St., features a few old train cars, an informative video on narrow-gauge railways, and a handmade model of Donegal's former rail system that took 40 years to build. *(Open June-Sept. M-Sa 10am-5:30pm and Su 2-5pm; Oct.-May M-F 10am-4pm. £1, students and children 50p.)* If you're a railroad buff, it's worth a visit. The **International Arts Festival,** held during three days in the last week of June or the first week of July (call the tourist office for details), brings such diverse activities as parachuting, storytelling, theater, and trad, turning the town into a summertime center of entertainment. To join in on the three-day party, be sure to call ahead for a room, as the town doubles in size for the weekend.

Station Island

Donegal's **Lough Derg** (there's another Lough Derg along the Shannon) encircles **Station Island.** One of Ireland's most important pilgrimage sites, Station Island witnesses a three-day religious ordeal every summer, the subject of Seamus Heaney's long poem of the same name. Although St. Patrick never visited Lough Derg, he is said to have visited nearby Saints Island, where he temporarily descended into Purgatory. The pilgrimage, which can be made any time between June 1 and August 13, involves three days of similarly hellish fasting and circling the island barefoot. **Lough Derg soup** is an island delicacy; the pilgrims, who aren't allowed to eat, snack on this concoction of boiled water flavored with salt and pepper. Some scowl at a recent addition to the pilgrim's calendar—a special one-day retreat to the island that some pilgrims think is too easy. Those hoping to descend should bring nothing but warm clothing and a repentant heart. Contact the Prior of St. Patrick's Purgatory (tel. (072) 61518; email lochderg@iol.ie) for information. The **Lough Derg Journey** (tel. (072) 41546) in Pettigoe, just over the border 5 mi. south of Lough Derg, has a new exhibit on the Celtic origins of the pilgrimage. (Open May-Oct. M-Sa 10am-5pm, Su noon-5pm, Nov.-Apr. Sa 10am-5pm, Su noon-5pm. £2, students £1.50.)

■ Near Donegal Town: Lough Eske

The most worthwhile of Donegal Town's daytime attractions actually lies a few miles outside of town at Lough Eske ("fish lake"), an idyllic lake set among a fringe of trees and ruins. For a beautiful and easy two-hour hike, follow signs for "Harvey's Point" (marked from Killybegs Rd.); after about 3 mi. you will come to a stone building on your right with a gate and single stone pillar. If you take a left after the gate, you will come upon the crumbling majesty of **Lough Eske Castle** after about five minutes. Continue following the Lough Eske road and take the first path on your left after the castle to find a Celtic high cross surrounded by breathtaking gardens. If driving, follow signs from Mountcharles Rd. to Lough Eske and a 15 mi. loop around the lake.

SLIEVE LEAGUE PENINSULA

To the west of Donegal Town lies the Slieve League Peninsula, which lays claim to some of the most stunning scenery in the Republic. The region has scarcely felt the taming touch of human habitation, and its beauty remains in its rugged, wild appearance. The few villages on the peninsula all lie along busy N56, which leads from Donegal town and turns into R63 as it approaches the western tip of the peninsula. The best plan is probably to work your way up N56, stopping by its several accommodations sites on the way to **Glencolmcille.** Each bend in the road brings new views of windswept fields of heather, lonely thatched cottages, and the stark Donegal coastline. **Ardara** and **Glenties** make pleasant stops on N56 on the way back. Though most easily covered in a car, the peninsula is a spectacular opportunity for cycling. Limited bus service goes by the hostels on N56. The Peninsula's **phone code** baits its hook with 073.

■ The Eastern Peninsula

A handful of villages, each consisting of several storefronts along the coast road, lie to the west of Donegal Town. The first is **Mountcharles**, about 3 mi. from Donegal Town, where you can go **deep-sea fishing** in Donegal Bay (contact Michael O'Boyle, tel. 35257; fishing daily 11am-5pm; £20). In July and August, there is a Saturday market at **The Tannery** (tel. 35533) on the coast road to Killybegs, that features home-grown, homebaked, and organic foods. Throughout the warmer months of the year, The Tannery's **craft shop and tea room** provide a happy diversion for the wanderer on Killybegs Rd. (open July-Aug. M-F 10:30am-7pm, Apr.-June M-F 11am-6pm). About 10 mi. past Mountcharles is the tiny **Dunkineely**, surrounded by megalithic tombs, holy wells, and small streams; all are accessible by walks of 4 mi. (round-trip) or less. For information on these walks, continue another 1½ mi. to, or have the bus drop you in, the town of **Bruckless**, where **Gallagher's Farm Hostel** (tel. 37057) sits about a quarter mile off the main road. Their accommodations will certainly leave you breathless: Mr. Gallagher has turned his 17th-century barn into a wonderfully clean, well-outfitted hostel in the midst of very pleasant pastoral farmscapes. Two kitchens (and a third for campers), a huge fireplace, and a ping-pong table may make your stay longer than expected. (Dorms £7. All-you-can-eat continental breakfast with fresh baked bread and scones £3. Laundry £3. Bikes £5. **Camping** in a well-kept 3-acre field £4.) Between the hostel and Bunkineely, a turn-off leads to **St. John's Point,** which has fantastic views across the Sligo coastline.

■ Killybegs

Killybegs offers sensory overload: the smell of the fishing industry, the sight of the multi-colored fishing boats, and the taste of the endless pints at one of Killybegs's many late-licensed pubs. Cyclists enjoy rewarding views (but hilly terrain). Bus Eireann runs **buses** from **Donegal Town** to Killybegs (late-June to Aug. M-Sa 4 per day, Sept. to early-June M-Sa 3 per day). There is also an evening bus to **Glencolmcille** (late-June to Aug. M-Sa 5 per day, Sept. to early-June M-Sa 2 per day). **McGeehan Coaches** (tel. (075) 46150) also has service (at least 1 per day) to **Donegal Town** and **Dublin** from **Dungloe, Ardara, Glenties,** and several other towns on the peninsula. Killybegs has some of the only services in the area. **Ulsterbank** is on the southern end of Main St. (open M-W and F 10am-4pm, Th 10am-5pm), and **AIB** is a little farther north (open M-W and F 10am-12:30pm and 1:30-4pm, Th 10am-12:30pm and 1:30-5pm). **Bank of Ireland** is at the Kilcar end of town (open M-W and F 10am-12:30pm and 1:30-4pm, Th 10am-12:30pm and 1:30-5pm); their **ATM** accepts the widest range of foreign bank cards. **McGee's Pharmacy,** Main St. (tel. 31009), sells a full cargo of medicines and toiletries (open M-Sa 9:30am-6pm). The **post office** (tel. 31060) sorts mail on Main St. (Open M-W 10am-noon and 3:30-5:30pm, Th 11am-noon and 3:30-5:30pm, F 11am-noon and 4-5pm, Sa 10am-noon.)

The residents of Killybegs work hard and play hard: because Killybegs's pubs all have late licenses, the last call isn't until 12:30am (which means no one leaves until 2am). Whether or not you've come to Co. Donegal to hear the fiddling, a stop at the **Sail Inn,** at the far end of Main St. from the pier, is a must. The pub is owned by the famous fiddler Martin McGinley, and other renowned musicians are likely to turn up any time for the nightly sessions. **The Harbour Bar,** across from the pier, is notorious for its late hours and lively nightlife. **The Pier Bar** (tel. 31096), on the other side of the car park, is where fishermen-maties hang out and has excellent pub grub during the day (hot lunches £3.50; sandwiches under £2). **Hughie's Bar** (tel. 31095), a "small world feel and a big time bar" on the northern end of Main St., stays hopping with impromptu music sessions most nights and a weekend disco (open until 2am; disco cover £2). For those who stay overnight, Mrs. Tully puts up guests in her new B&B, **Tullycullion House** (tel. 31842), one mile south off N56, which has panoramic views of Killybegs Harbour and delicious rooms (£14).

■ Kilcar

A breathtaking 8 mi. past Killybegs along N56 is tiny **Kilcar,** the gateway to Donegal's *gaeltacht* and a commercial base for many Donegal tweed weavers. Many tweed sellers lie along Kilcar's main street, which is also the coast road that leads down to Killybegs and up to Carrick and most local accommodations. **Studio Donegal** (tel. 38194) sells handwoven tweeds fresh off the loom. Visitors are invited to watch the cloth being woven, the yarn being spun, and the jackets being sewn. (Most throws £27-54; gloves £15; watching free. Open year-round M-F 9am-5:30pm, June-Sept. also Sa 9am-5:30pm). Other companies' factory shops dot the streets. If you're interested in providing comfort to the interior as well as the exterior of your person, stop by the **Tweed Factory Craft Shop and Tea Room** below Studio Donegal, which offers, in addition to the usual assortment of fabrics, books, and postcards, homemade soups and sandwiches (£1.20) and friendly locals' advice on the area (open June-Sept. M-F 9am-6pm, Sa 10am-4pm). Still in the same building, on the same floor as Studio Donegal, is **Áistan Cill Cartha** (ASH-lahn kill KAR-ha). This marvelous community organization provides genealogical information, compendiums of residents' oral histories, and local history collections. They will open a **heritage center,** complete with craft shops, language classes, exhibitions, and computerized databases on the area, by June 1999. If you're interested in **deep-sea fishing,** a local (like your hostel or B&B proprietor) can direct you to a boat. Locals can also give you directions to any of the prehistoric and natural wonders that surround Kilcar. Kilcar's **International Sea Angling Festival** (contact Seamus McHugh, tel. 38337) takes place the first weekend in August, followed directly by the **Kilcar Street Festival** (contact Kevin Lyons, tel. 38433), a week of sports competitions, music, dance, tomfoolery, and craic.

At the **Piper's Rest Pub & Restaurant,** Main St. (tel. 38205), well-seasoned musical instruments adorn the rough stone walls, pleading with the wandering minstrel to pull them down and fill the place with music and song. Although trad is scheduled for Wednesday and Friday nights and folk ballads for Saturdays and Sundays, impromptu performances happen whenever enough local musicians gather here. Poetry and storytelling abound, too, whenever those types stop in, and great food is always in the house. Huge turreens of soup are a mere £1.50, and in the summer they serve fresh-off-the-boat seafood (food served daily 11am-9pm). Just down the street, **John Joe's** (tel. 38015) spins disco for the less traditionally inclined. **Spar Market** on Main St. sells groceries and fishing tackle (open M-Sa 9am-9:50pm, Su 9am-7:10pm).

About 1 mi. out along the coast road from Kilcar to Carrick, **Dun Ulun House** (tel. 38137) is a luxurious alternative to hostel life at virtually the same price, especially for groups of three or more. Sleep in a large, flowery bed at night and wake in rooms with hardwood floors and gorgeous views. Call ahead to book in July and August. (Rooms with at least 3 beds July-Aug. £25, Sept.-June £22; B&B July-Aug. £15, Sept.-June £14.50; all rooms with bath. Rooms in cottage across road £5, with linens £6.50. Laundry £5. Will get **bikes** delivered for you from Carrick. **Camping** £3, with separate facilities.) A mile and a half down the road past Dun Ulun and five minutes from the beach, Shaun at the **Derrylahan Hostel (IHH)** (tel. 38079) welcomes guests like long-lost cousins—don't even think about refusing the initial cup of tea. You'll be counting your blessings when you stay in this 200-year-old former church that doubles as a working farm, where the on-premise grocery shop stays well stocked and the chicken never actually peck at your feet. Campers have separate showers and kitchen facilities. Call for pick up from Kilcar or Carrick. Buses pass daily on the way to Killybegs and Glencolmcille. Calling ahead to book a bed in July and August is a good idea, but coming in the spring during lambing season is an even better one. (Dorms £6; private rooms £8. Laundry £3.50. **Bike** rental £8 per day. **Camping** £3.)

■ Carrick, Teelin, and Slieve League

Most Slieve League hikers stay in Kilcar, from which they can comfortably drive, bike, or walk (about 6 hr. return) to the mountain and the highest sea cliffs in Europe. From Kilcar, the coast road to the mountain passes the tiny village of **Carrick.** Although for most of the year Carrick is but a brief stopping point for travelers seeking refreshment, the village scene is different around late October and early November when Carrick hosts the annual **Carrick Fleadh,** which offers barrels of refreshment of the creamy, foaming variety with trad accompaniment. **Fishing** is fabulous and rewarding around Teelin Bay, particularly in an area called **Salmon Leap** (remember that salmon fishing is illegal without a license). The **Glen River** is best for trout. Tackle can be bought at the Spar Markets in Kilcar or Carrick. The Carrick area also offers several practical amenities for the local explorer. **Little Acorn Farm** (tel. 39386), located off the main Kilcar-Carrick road approximately one mile before Carrick, offers **horses** for guided trail rides or (for the experienced rider) self-guided rides (rates vary). About one mile past Carrick is the even smaller village of **Teelin,** where Mrs. Maloney at **Teelin Bay House** (tel. 39043), the third B&B on the road to Teelin, is deservedly famous for the care she bestows upon her guests. It's a bit of a hike, but the view just keeps getting better. Booking well ahead is a must (£13).

In clear weather it'd be unconscionable *not* to visit **Slieve League,** a 2000 ft. mountain set in the midst of a precipitous, beautiful coastline of 1000 ft. cliffs. To reach the mountain, turn left halfway down Carrick's main street and follow signs for Teelin. At the **Rusty Mackerel** (tel. 39101), a small and intimate pub best known for its frequent spontaneous sing-songs, you can turn left for the inland route to Slieve League. Alternatively, a turn to the right (the most popular decision) leads along the sea cliffs on the way up to Bunglass. At the end of the road at Bunglass sits a car park with fantastic views. From here, a cliff path heads west along the coast. It should take 1½ hours to walk from Carrick to the car park, and at about a half hour along the path from the car park the clifftop narrows to 2 ft. On one side of this pass—called **One Man's Pass**—the cliffs drop 1800 ft. to the sea. On the other side, the cliffs drop a measly 1000 ft. to a rocky floor. There are no railings, and the suddenly phobic sometimes slide across the 30m pass on their butts or hands and knees. (You can still enjoy a steep climb by walking along the inland face of the mountain.) The path then continues all the way along the cliffs to **Rossarrel Point,** near Glencolmcille. The entire Slieve League way usually takes six to seven hours to walk. **Never go to Slieve League in poor weather.** Use extreme caution if you plan to cross the pass. People have died here under poor conditions; several hikers have been blown off the pass by the strong winds. It's always a good idea to ask a local expert for advice.

▨ Glencolmcille (Gleann Cholm Cille)

The parish on the western top of the Slieve League peninsula, Glencolmcille (glen-kaul-um-KEEL) encompasses several tiny towns and many huge natural wonders; its land consists of rolling hills and sandy coves that lie between two huge sea cliffs. Named after St. Colmcille, who founded a monastery here, this Irish-speaking area and pilgrimage site centers around the street-long village of Cashel, which lies just off N56 on, not surprisingly, Cashel Street. This small road leads past the village's several storefronts and down to the coast, where most of the area's accommodations and attractions are located. Buses of tourists head for the Folk Village, but few venture beyond it to the desolate, wind-swept cliffs. Though less dramatic than the mountain paths, N56 is the convenient route to most of Glencolmcille. **McGeehan's buses** leave from Biddy's Bar to go to **Kilcar, Killybegs, Ardara, Glenties,** and **Letterkenny** once a day, twice from July to mid-September. **Bus Éireann** has services to **Kilcar** and **Killybegs** (ask at the hostel or tourist office for details). Glencolmcille's tiny **tourist office** (tel. 30116) is on Cashel St. (open July-Aug. M-Sa 9:30am-9pm, Su noon-6pm; Apr.-June and Sept. to mid-Nov. M-Sa 10am-6pm, Su 1-5pm). The Folk Village's

bureau de change has exchange rates that compete with those of the **post office** east of the village center (post office open M-F 7:30am-1pm and 2-5:30pm, Sa 9am-1pm).

ACCOMMODATIONS, FOOD, AND PUBS The **Dooey Hostel (IHO)** is the oldest independent hostel in Ireland, with rock walls reminiscent of ancient ring forts. To reach the hostel, turn left at the sign about halfway through the village and follow the signs three quarters of a mile uphill. Several kitchens grace the hostel, which houses guests in two- to eight-bed dorms, most with stunning views of the sea. (Dorms £6; doubles £13. **Camping** £3.50. Wheelchair accessible.) Campers share hostel facilities. Mrs. Ann Ward's **Atlantic Scene** (tel. 30186), the next house after the hostel, lives up to its name. You'll stay up just to admire the view longer. (£13. open May-Sept.) There are also B&Bs surrounding the Folk Village.

The **Lace House Restaurant and Café,** above the tourist office on Cashel St., is a chipper with a large menu of fried foods and a second story view of the sea cliffs (entrees £3-4; open Easter-Sept. daily 10am-9pm). **An Chistan** (AHN KEESHT-ahn, "the kitchen"; tel. 30213), at the Foras Cultúir Uladh, is especially affordable at lunch (seafood chowder £2.50; open M-Sa 9:30am-9:30pm). The **teashop** in the Folk Village tempts with delicious sandwiches (£1) and Guinness cake (80p). **Byrne and Sons Food Store** on Cashel St. supplies the basics in solids, liquids, and printed matter (open M-Sa 9:30am-10pm, Su 9:30am-1pm and 7-9pm). Cashel's pubs have a dark, dusty 1950s Ireland feel to them: imagine plastic-covered snugs, spare rooms, metal advertising placards on the walls, and, for once, a minimal amount of wood paneling. Although the pubs are primarily a haven for locals, they have grown an affinity for visitors during July and August. Most famous among them is the unassuming **Biddy's** (tel. 30016), at the mouth of Carrick Rd., with its iron benches out front and 110-year history. Since it's the favorite of the older crowd and the official host bar for the Foras Cultúir Uladh (see below), you'll meet lots of Irish speakers (live trad 3 times a week during the summer). **Roarty's,** the next pub down Cashel St., gathers the biggest crowd during the summer, probably because it promises blood-stirring trad seven nights a week. Last on the road is **Glen Head Tavern** (tel. 30008), the largest and youngest of the three pubs. Practically the whole village could fit into its recently redone lounge, which hosts legendary impromptu trad sessions.

SIGHTS Glencolmcille's craft movement began in the 1950s under the direction of the omnipresent **Father James McDyer,** who was also responsible for getting electricity in Glencolmcille, founding the Folk Village, and building the local football field. Today, the town is renowned for its handmade products, particularly sweaters, which are on sale at numerous little "jumper shops" on the roads surrounding the town. Close to town is the **Foras Cultúir Uladh** (FOHR-us KULT-er U-lah; "The Ulster Cultural Institute"; tel. 30248), which runs the Oideas Gael institute for the preservation of the Irish language and culture and houses the **Taipeis Gael,** a center for Irish tapestry weaving and exhibition. *(Open daily 9am-6pm.)* The Foras offers regular courses on such varied pursuits as hill walking, tapestry weaving, traditional music, and Gaelic (call for details). It also has frequently changing exhibitions on local history and concerts and performances on a regular basis.

A bit past the village center is Father McDyer's **Folk Village Museum and Heritage Centre** (tel. 30017), the town's attraction for non-hiking or Irish-speaking tourists. *(Open Easter-Sept. M-Sa 10am-6pm, Su noon-6pm. Tours July-Aug. every 30min., Apr.-June and Sept. every hr. £1.50, ask about student rates.)* The museum comprises stone replicas of old buildings with immaculately thatched roofs. Houses date from 1700, 1850, and 1900. The 1850s schoolhouse is open to the general public. Along with descriptions of furniture and tools from each of these eras in Irish history, the guided tours provide the only access to the insides of the houses. A short nature trail from the village leads up a hill past various reconstructed remains, including a Mass rock, a sweat house, and a lime kiln. The **craft shop** stocks a good assortment of sweaters, books, and postcards and is probably the only place in the world where you can buy rosary beads made from seaweed. The **sheeben** (the old name for an illegal drinking establishment) sells homemade heather, fuschia, and seaweed wines (free samples with tour) and whiskey marmalade, and the **tea shop** offers physical succor. The beginning of July brings the **Glencolmcille Folk Festival,** a lively and occasionally raucous celebration (ask at the tourist office or hostel for details).

Fine beaches and cliffs make for excellent hiking in all directions. A 5 mi. walk southwest from Cashel leads to **Malinbeg,** a winsome hamlet at the edge of a sandy cove. This coastal area was once notorious for smuggling *poitín* through tunnels, some of which may still be in use. **Silver Strand** is now ideal for those seeking tranquility, as long as it's not raining, in which case it's a good place for imagining an adventurous life on the high seas. From here, you can walk up and along the Slieve League coastline by the longest route possible (see **Carrick, Teelin, and Slieve League,** p. 341). A sandy beach links the cliffs on the south and north sides of Glencolmcille. North of Glencolmcille, **Glen Head,** easily identifiable by the Martello tower at its peak, is an hour's walk from town through land rich in prehistoric ruins and St. Colmcille's stations of the cross. The tourist office and hostel in town each have a map that shows the locations of major sites. A third walk from town begins at the Protestant church and climbs over a hill to the ruins of the ghostly "famine village" of **Port** in the valley on the other side (3hr. walk). Supposedly haunted by crying babies, this eerie village has been empty since its inhabitants emigrated during the Famine. The only current resident, according to local rumor, is an eccentric artist who lives by the isolated bay without electricity or water. The gargantuan phallic rock sticking out of the sea is just what it appears to be: the only part of the Devil still visible after St. Colmcille banished him to the ocean.

The road east from Glencolmcille to Ardara passes through the spectacular **Glengesh Pass.** Nine hundred feet above sea level, the road tackles the surrounding mountains with hairpin turns. Hitching and biking are ways of life for both tourists and locals in these parts.

Alone in the Husk of Man's Home

The same remoteness that frustrates (and delights) Donegal's visitors has been embraced by some famous artists through the years. The valley next to Port has provided refuge to both poet Dylan Thomas and artist Rockwell Kent. Only two cottages stand in this valley, and even with today's well-paved roads, the area can be reached only by several hours of hiking. Dylan Thomas used his self-imposed isolation in the mind-altering beauty of Port's surroundings to clean the alcoholism out of his system, although locals say that the area's *poitín* smuggling foiled that plan. The locals are sure to break out into grins if you ask them about Rockwell Kent, the "off-kilter" American artist who supposedly came to Port to hide from "government officials who wore white coats" and who never went outside after dark. As many a traveler will tell you, you can certainly lose yourself, both mentally and physically, around Port.

■ Ardara

The origin and former center of the Donegal tweed industry, Ardara (ar-DRAH) now attracts mostly tweed-needers with high credit limits. Other towns have replaced Ardara as the cheapest sources for Aran sweaters in Donegal; better deals can often be found at small "craft centres" in the surrounding area. Ardara has its moment in the sun on the first weekend of June during the **Weavers' Fair,** when weavers from all over Donegal congregate in Ardara to show their weft. Plenty of musicians add further festivity to the weekend.

PRACTICAL INFORMATION Bus Éireann stops in Adara on its **Killybegs-Portnoo** route (2 per day) in front of **Spar Market,** Main St. (tel. 41107; open M-Sa 8:30am-8pm, Su 8:30am-1pm); **McGeehan's** halts in The Diamond at least once a day as part of its **Dublin-Donegal Town-Dungloe** trip. The **Adara Heritage Centre** (tel. 41704) has tourist information (open Jan.-Nov. daily 9:30am-6pm). **Ulster Bank** (tel 41121 or

41201) is on The Diamond (open M-W and F 10am-12:30pm and 1:30-4pm, Th 10am-12:30pm and 1:30-5pm) and has a 24-hour **ATM**. You can rent **bikes** at **Don Byrne's**, West End (tel. 41156), past town on Killybegs Rd. The **Ardara Medical Hall**, Front St., next to the Heritage Centre, is the local **pharmacy** (open M-Sa 10am-1pm and 2-6pm). The **post office** (tel. 41101) is opposite the Heritage Centre (open M-F 9am-1pm and 2-5:30pm, Sa 9am-1pm). The **phone code** is 075.

ACCOMMODATIONS, FOOD, AND PUBS The **Drumbarron Hostel (IHO)**, The Diamond (tel. 41200), does the job cleanly for those seeking shelter. Travelers can get keys at the house across the way from the side entrance (dorms £6; doubles £14; curfew 1am), which also offers pricier but far more aesthetically appealing accommodations in the **Drumbarron B&B**. The rooms have hardwood floors, big fluffy beds, and a modern decor complemented by the owner's semi-abstract paintings. Next door, **Laburnum House**, The Diamond (tel. 41146), has grand rooms and windows stretching to the floor (£13.50). **Charlie's West End Café** (tel. 41656) lacks the trendy atmosphere its name suggests but has its priorities straight. The service is quick and the prices are low for a tourist town—probably because Charlie's is frequented primarily by locals. (Enormous lunch specials £3.75, sandwiches £1-2. Open M-Sa 10am-11:30pm, Su 2-11:30pm.) **Peter Oliver's Central Bar**, Main St. (tel. 41311), has trad every single night June through September. Because it is known as "the place to be," arrive early if you want breathing space. For a quieter pint, head two doors down to the **Corner Bar**. There is actually room for trad sessions six nights per week in this small, pumpkin-colored bar (Tu-Su).

SIGHTS The **Ardara Heritage Centre** (tel. 41704) in the middle of town tells the story of the industry that has united Donegal for hundreds of years. *(Open Jan.-Nov. daily 9:30am-6pm. Free.)* Live weaving demonstrations show the full-bodied dexterity of thousands of hand-loom weavers that creates the richly varied textiles sold in mass quantities throughout the world. Donegal tweeds incorporate dyes made from the county's four elements: lichen, blackberries, heather, and soot. The center also has displays on Ireland's other woolen craftwork. The **tea room** serves food when the center is open (entrees £1-3).

Horse rides around the area start from **Castle View Ranch** (tel. 41212), 2½ well-posted miles from the town center off Glencolmcille Rd. *(£10 per hr., £45 per day, either independent or guided riding.)* To enjoy beautiful walks along the peninsula located east of Ardara, head south toward Glencolmcille through town and turn right at the "Castle View" horse-riding sign toward **Loughros Point** (LOW-crus). At the next horse-riding sign, either turn right for a beautiful view of Ardara Bay or continue straight to Loughros Point to spy the sea (1hr. walk). The **Maghera Caves** 5 mi. from the town center, which once sheltered shipwrecked sailors from the Spanish Armada, make another pleasant excursion from Ardara (1½hr. walk). The six caves vary in size and depth; all require a flashlight. At low tide you can enter the Dark Cave, once the refuge of *poitín* makers. A rising tide, however, could trap you inside. For daily tide times, check the *The Irish Independent*. To reach the caves, follow the main road south past the Loughros turnoff, then follow the signs several miles west on small roads. The road that passes the caves continues across a mountain pass to Dungloe.

■ Glenties

Glenties is best known for being a five-time winner as "Ireland's Tidiest Town" and—rather incongruously—for hosting one of the area's largest discos each Saturday. Dusting and dancing create a spirited beauty in this village, as Brian Friel illustrated in his play about his Glenties aunts, *Dancing at Lughnasa*. Several pleasant walks nearby also recommend the town. It makes a good stop along **Bus Éireann** or **McGeehan's** routes through northwest Donegal.

PRACTICAL INFORMATION In town, the **Bank of Ireland**, Main St., has one of the area's few 24hr. **ATMs** that accept Visa, MC, and Cirrus (bank open M-W and F 10am-12:30pm and 1:30-4pm, Th 10am-12:30pm and 1:30-5pm). **Glentie's Medical Hall**, Main St., provides the usual pharmaceutical goodies (open M-Tu and Th-Sa 9:30am-1pm and 2-6pm, W 9:30am-1pm). The **post office** (tel. 51101), has a narrow little storefront destined to appear on a postcard (open M-Tu and Th-Sa 9am-1pm and 2-5:30pm, W 9am-1pm). The **phone code** is a tidy twist at 075.

ACCOMMODATIONS **Campbell's Holiday Hostel (IHH)** (tel. 51491), just around the bend at the far end of Main St. toward Ardara, provides cheap and clean rooms decorated in primary colors and beds with unusually wide mattresses. The common room has a fireplace, satellite TV, and two fully equipped kitchens. (Dorms £6; doubles with bath £16. Sheets £1. Laundry £2. Wheelchair accessible.) The most convenient and best-priced B&Bs in the area are at the opposite end of Main St. They, too, live up to their town's standards of cleanliness. **Andros B&B** (tel. 51234) has rooms for up to four with plush carpeting (£14). Her daughter-in-law runs **Marguerite's B&B** (tel. 51699) next door in a nearly identical house, although Marguerite's rooms have hardwood floors and TVs (£16).

FOOD AND PUBS The selection of grocery stores is especially large. The town has its own **organic farm** (Thomas Beecht, tel. 51286), reached by heading down Main St. past Glenties toward Columcille and turning left at a sign for the farm, located two miles down Meenahall Rd. There is also a wholefood shop called **Good Earth** (tel. 51794; open M-Sa 9:30am-6pm) and a series of convenience stores along Main St. The sit-down options are fewer. **Jim McGuinness's** offers standard chipper fare to young kids and late-night clubbers (open M-Th noon-midnight, F noon-2am, Sa noon-4am, Su 5pm-midnight). **Pedro's Grill Wagon** (tel. (088) 270 7273) provides delicious middle eastern food from a wagon (open M-F 6pm-1am, Sa 6pm-3am, Su 6pm-1am).

The pubs in town are, where else?, on the main street. **Paddy's Bar** (tel. 51158), though somewhat packaged, is spacious and lively with music performances every night during the summer (trad Wednesday). The **Glen Inn**, a few doors down, is known for its great games of pool and young crowd. It doesn't open until 7pm, though, so don't show up for an afternoon pint. At **John Joe's** (tel. 51333), on the opposite side of Main St., you'll hear the Irish tongue as well as live music bouncing off low ceilings any night of the week (Saturday country and Tuesday trad in July). At the far end of town toward Dungloe, the **Limelight** (tel. 51118) has a ballroom's worth of space, which attracts dancers from all over Donegal to its five bars and splendid discos (Friday ages 14-18, £3; Saturday 18+, £5; open 10pm-2am).

SIGHTS Next to the hostel, the newly opened **St. Connell's Museum and Heritage Centre** (tel. 51227) is probably the best starting point for exploring the area. Its informed staff will introduce you to local history and nearby sites of interest with an assortment of exhibitions and videos, mostly on St. Connell and the remaining markers of his 6th-century missionary in this area; it also has a "study room" for genealogy. They can provide full advice on the walks around the area, in which you can see the sites of historical and religious significance firsthand. *(Open Apr.-Sept. M-F 10am-12:30pm and 2-4:30pm. £2, students 50p.)*

Good walks through the countryside abound. Most of them are signposted from the crossroads next to the Heritage Centre, and a guide to the walks is available from the Heritage Centre. Among the more satisfying explorations is a walk to **Inniskeel Island**, which leads you eight miles past Glenties toward Dungloe; signs point the way from Narin Beach, where drivers can park. The island, where the ruins of **St. Connell's** 6th-century church can be found, is accessible only when the tide is out, so check the *Irish Independent* for times before you set out. A one-hour walk to **Lough Anney**, the reservoir for Glenties and Ardara, is also worthwhile; follow the directions to the organic farm, and the reservoir is a bit farther ahead on your right in the hills. You can reach nice 2½ mi. walk along the **Owenrea River** to the area of Mullantayboyne by following the directions to the organic farm but turning right off the main road at the Meenahalla sign instead of left. The river lies ahead on this side road.

Glenties's big celebrations occur on the 12th of September during the **Harvest Fair,** an annual celebration of local agriculture, industry, and beer drinking, and on the first weekend in October, when fiddlers from all over the world descend upon Glenties for **Fiddler's Weekend.** Call the hostel for information on either.

THE DONEGAL GAELTACHT

Some visitors would tell you that they come here time and again to experience the best aspects of human nature, for the scenery is spectacular and the traditional culture is preserved with a passion. In this part of Ireland, Irish culture—language, music, dance—is lived out, not acted out. Most visitors, whether well-traveled backpackers, students of the Irish language, or the rare tour-bus passenger, come to Donegal with a purist's appetite for Irish culture and leave well satiated, though with a glutton's appetite for more. The Donegal style of music is still fully alive and the Donegal dialect of Irish is distinct from other dialects (like Connemara and Munster). Buses run infrequently, so be sure to plan your schedule—or not, because you may decide to stay. The **phone code** for the whole area is 075.

■ The Rosses

N56 bumps and bounces along the spectacularly beautiful midwest coast from Glenties to Dungloe. The expansive, sandy beaches are isolated by the eerie stillness of the Derryveagh Mountains. To the north and west of Burtonport stretch the Rosses, a haunting, largely untouched area and bog ecologist's paradise jutting into the sea. Stony soil dotted with tiny ponds covers the glacially crumpled ground of this headland. The Rosses is referred to as the broken *gaeltacht,* for its Irish-speaking community also uses some English. The corruptive influence of the English language is hardly to be feared here, though, for locals are likely to tell you that this is the "real" Donegal, where peat cutting and salmon fishing keep the economy and old customs alive.

■ Dungloe and Crohy Head

Dungloe (dun-LO; An Clochan Liath), known locally as the Capital of the Rosses, is a busy market town near Crohy Head where travelers stock up before hurrying on to the mountains.

PRACTICAL INFORMATION Though not on any of the Bus Éireann routes, Dungloe is served regularly by **McGeehan's** (tel. 46150) to **Dublin; Swilly** (tel. 21380) to **Derry; Doherty's** (tel. 21670) to Glasgow via **Letterkenny** and **Belfast; Jim O'Donnell** (tel. 48356) to **Belfast** via **Letterkenny** and **Derry;** and **Feda O'Donnell** (tel. 48114) to **Galway.** The Dungloe **tourist office** (tel. 21297), on a well-marked side street off Main St. toward the shore, has free maps of the town, and it's a good idea to stop in here before heading into the Rosses and Gweedore—it's the last Bord Fáilte you'll find in the area (open June-Sept. M-Sa 10am-1pm and 2-6pm). Main St. sports a **Bank of Ireland** (tel. 21077) and an **AIB** (tel. 21179; both open M-W and F 10am-12:30pm and 1:30-4pm, Th 10am-12:30pm and 1:30-5pm); the Bank of Ireland's 24-hour **ATM** accepts Visa, MC, and Cirrus. **Dennis Brennan** (tel. 21633) provides **taxi** services. Pharmaceuticals proliferate at **O'Donnell's Pharmacy,** Main St. (tel. 21386; open M-Sa 9am-6pm) like philatelists at the teeny **post office,** Quay Rd. (tel. 21179), off Main St. toward the water (open M-F 9am-1pm and 2-5:30pm, Sa 9am-1pm).

ACCOMMODATIONS Greene's Independent Holiday Hostel (IHH), Carnmore Rd. (tel. 21943), is right off Main St. away from the waterfront. Mr. Green offers several dorm rooms with 6 to 8 beds, doubles, a single, and a family room. A well-upholstered common room and a fully equipped kitchen complete this clean, basic hostel. (Dorms £7; singles £8; doubles £16; family room £25-30. **Bike rental** £5 per day. Laundry £3. Curfew Tu-Th 1am, F-M 2am, festival week 3am.) **Park House,** Carnmore Rd. (tel. 21351), across from the Supervalu, has huge, fluffy beds and a kitchen open to guests, an unusual perk for a B&B (singles £20; doubles £32; family rooms available; all with bath). **Hillcrest B&B,** Barrack Brae (tel. 21484), is at the top of the hill on the Burtonport end of town about 100m past the end of Main St. It has views of the water, pretty rooms, and kind proprietors (£16). **Dungloe Camping and Caravan Park** (tel. 21943) is right behind the hostel (£6 per 2-person tent, £1 for each additional person; £3 per car).

FOOD AND PUBS If you're cooking, stop by the **Cope Supermarket,** Main St. (open M-Th 9am-6pm, F 9am-7pm), or the new **SuperValu,** about a half mile down Carnmore Rd. (open M-Th 9am-6:30pm, F 9am-8pm, Sa 9am-7pm). The **Riverside Bistro** softens its posh plaidiness with a rainbow pallet, and the menu offers diverse fare, from enchiladas to curry to home-grown salad (entrees £6-8, fresh seafood £8-10; open daily June-Aug. noon-10pm, Sept.-May noon-3pm and 6-10pm). **Bay View Bar** (tel. 21186) serves a full plate of pub grub for £1-5 and offers snooker and weekend trad, folk, or country music (open daily 10:30am-11:30pm). Weekend trad sessions at spacious **Beedy's,** Main St. (tel. 21219), bring in seasonal musicians from all over Donegal. During the week, a local crowd hangs out here. **Bridge Inn** (tel. 21036) hosts a disco on weekend nights. When the nightclub isn't open, young'uns congregate at the **Atlantic Bar** (tel. 21066) across the street, which is quite large, quite fun, and quite full during its weekend folk and trad sessions. At the other end of town, the **Tirconnail Bar,** Main St. (tel. 21479), has beautiful ocean views that inspire contemplative musings over slow pints.

SIGHTS Hundreds of party-lovers flock to Dungloe in the last week of July for the **Mary from Dungloe Festival** (tel. 48519), named after a popular old song about the tragic love affair between Mary and an American. The population swells to 80,000 during this 10-day celebration, which attracts famous musicians to both trad and modern parties. The highlight of the festival, of course, is the selection of the annual Donegal ambassador, Mary from Dungloe, although many would say that it's the three concerts that Daniel O'Donnell is guaranteed to perform during the week. For festival info and ticket bookings, call the **Festival Booking Office** (tel. 21254), next to the tourist office (open M-Sa 10am-6pm).

Crohy Head, the peninsula 6 mi. southwest of Dungloe, collects strangely shaped rock formations around a jagged coast. **Crohy Head Youth Hostel (An Óige/HI)** (tel. 21950), in an old coast guard station, offers stupendous views over the Atlantic (Apr.-May £5.50, under 18 £4.50; June-Sept. £6.50, under 18 £5; call ahead). To reach the peninsula and the hostel from Dungloe, turn onto Quay Rd. halfway down Main St. and follow the bumpy road along the sea.

■ Burtonport

About 5 mi. north of Dungloe, the fishing village of Burtonport is less a town than a few pubs clustered around a pier. The ferry to Arranmore Island docks here, and the village is also a good base for fishing and boat trips to the many uninhabited islands in the area. The town is so still that it's hard to believe more salmon land here than in any other spot in Ireland or Britain. Intense activity can be observed during July and August, however, when one of its sea angling competitions is taking place (call the Dungloe tourist office for details) or when its weekday **Burtonport Festival** rouses locals up for the following week's Mary of Dungloe Festival with a similar program of endemic trad, dance, and sport. **Sea anglers** are booked from the shop on Burtonport Pier (tel. 42077); be sure to call ahead (open daily 10am-5pm or so; fishing trips £15, rod rental £4.50). The **post office** (tel. 42001) is at the start of town, about 200 yd. from the pier (open M-F 9am-1pm and 2-5pm, Sa 9am-1pm).

The **Cope** (tel. 42004), at the top of the town, is the largest **grocery** on either side of the water, so stock up before boarding the ferry to Arranmore Island (open M-Sa 9am-6pm). The **Harbor Bar and Takeaway** (tel. 42321) next to the pier has a split personality: the restaurant on the right is decorated with nets, buoys, and the scent of fish and chips (soup £1.20; entrees £3-4); the bar on the left has sunlit stone walls and a staff in search of visitors to while away the hours with chat about exotic places. Pink-and-green **O'Donnell's Bar** (tel. 42255), across the street, is the oldest pub in Burtonport and a local favorite. The **Lobster Pot,** Main St. (tel. 42012), is another half-bar, half-restaurant. Irish soccer jerseys and a green fiddle decorate the burgundy walls, as do life-sized models of Humphrey Bogart in a tux and Jaws's head bursting from the wall and clutching a nail-polished hand. (Restaurant open daily 6-10pm; bar open daily 1-10pm.) Finally, **Skippers Tavern** (tel. 42234) rings with trad on the weekends and serves good fishy food during the day (seafood platter £6).

Five miles north of Burtonport on the Coast Road dwells the little village of **Kincasslagh,** birthplace of the sweetheart singer Daniel O'Donnell and the site of his **Viking House Hotel** (tel. 43295); the hotel, though beyond the means of the budget traveler, should be a planned stop for anyone on an O'Donnell pilgrimage, but its attraction is highly specialized and might leave the average traveler feeling left out. A minor road heads west to **Cruit Island,** not really an island at all, but rather a peninsula with nice beaches and a host of thatched cottages. Farther north, the magnificent stretch of sand known as **Carrickfinn Strand** is marred only by the presence of tiny **Donegal Airport** (tel. 48584; flights to **Dublin** and other domestic airports, connections to international destinations).

■ Arranmore Island

Just off the coast lies **Arranmore Island** ("Aran" or "Arran Island" on some maps), where a rocky landscape of grass-covered boulders makes for a good old knee-scraping day-hikes and spooky midnight prowling. The ferry ride out is gentle and passes rocky islands and scenic ruins. About 600 people live in the sheltered southeast corner of the island, and most tourists stay at this end, where there are accommodations and amenities. The smaller population on the other side of the island speaks Irish and feels less influence from the mainland.

PRACTICAL INFORMATION The **ferry** office (tel. 20532) is open daily 8:30am to 7:30pm. The boat from Burtonport takes 20 minutes (July-Aug. M-Sa 8 per day, Su 7 per day; Sept.-June 2-3 per day; £6 return, students £5). A general tourist establishment of note is **Bonner's Restaurant** (tel. 20735), which serves as ferry booking office, B&B, and a take-out shop. Stop in here and you're likely to get all you asked for. (Meals £2-4; open daily noon-7pm.)

ACCOMMODATIONS, FOOD, AND PUBS Along the shore to the left of the ferry port stretches a string of pubs and houses. The house closest to the ferry is **Ward's B&B** (tel. 20511), where life-long residents offer clean rooms with baths and expert advice on exploring the island (£16). One of the island's greatest traditions is its grand summertime nightlife. With 24-hour licenses to serve fishermen returning from sea, some pubs provide "refreshments" into the morning. Accordingly, the list of pubs is a long one for such a small island. Starting just west of the ferry dock to go clockwise around the island, you will find **Phil Bàn's** (tel. 20508). The ocean laps against its foundation at high tide, but it's well-established on the island and attached to the island's only grocery store (store open daily 9am-6pm). **Paddy's** is a mile past the ferry dock; just take the advice of the enormous signpost that reads "have a jar at Paddy's Bar." **Neilly's** is a half mile down the road and has an intimate, local feel. **O'Donnell's Atlantic Bay** offers nightly sessions during the summer and a breathtaking view of the bay. **Boyle's Night Club** is a Saturday night dance party (cover £2) in the ballroom of the **Glen Hotel** (tel. 20505), back on the eastern side of the island. Just above the ferry docks, **Early's Pub** (tel. 20515), where Daniel O'Donnell earned his first gig, is a tiny little space that wouldn't fit an umpteenth of O'Donnell's present following. As a token of thanks to Arranmore's early support, O'Donnell gives an annual concert on the island and brings teary-eyed hordes with him.

SIGHTS Four priceless pearls were a gift to Red Hugh O'Donnell from Philip II for Red Hugh's help in saving Spanish sailors when Armada ships went down off the coast. The pearls were last seen on Arranmore Island in 1905, and people are still searching. Locals can also tell you a less romantic version of the story: the pearls were given by hungry Spanish sailors in exchange for food, tobacco, and booze. The last inheritor put them in Lloyd's Bank in London, where they sit today in their not-so-priceless splendor. Even without pearls, however, the island harbors a beautiful landscape and great hiking opportunities. **The Arranmore Way,** a well-marked footpath, encircles the island and will lead you along three possible paths, the longest of which takes you to the lighthouse at the far tip of the island, high above impressive cliffs and rushing water. A map of trails on the island (50p) is available from Phil Bàn's grocery shop. A full perambulation of Arranmore Way takes a good six hours.

■ Rannafast

In the heart of the Donegal *gaeltacht*, the village of **Annagry** marks the beginning of the **Rannafast** area, famous for its story-telling tradition. *Seanachies,* or storytellers, such as the MacGrianna brothers and Mici Shean Neill, perpetuate the Irish language and narrative tradition. In the summer, Annagry becomes home to Irish teenagers from all over the Republic who come to the area for its total-immersion Irish language camps. About 500 yd. south of the village, on top of a hill to the left of the road, is **Teàc Jack's** pub and restaurant (tel. 48113). The savory food (soup and bread £1.30) and creamy Guinness are well worth a traveler's time, especially on Saturday nights when the local musicians congregate in the pub for fiddle and pipe. About three miles farther down the road is **Leo's Tavern.** Leo is the father of multi-layered voice guru Enya and the family group, Clannad, whose silver, gold, and platinum records decorate the walls of this otherwise modest music hall of a pub. Leo's son Bartely runs the pub these days, while Leo plays his enormous electric piano-accordion on stage and leads a sing-along for a typically international audience in a rousing single voice they probably weren't expecting. Wednesday nights in July through August gather a large company of musicians for trad sessions, which are also likely to occur many other nights during the year.

■ Gweedore

Gweedore, the coastal region northeast of the Rosses, is completely Irish speaking. Crolly is the gateway to this most beautiful, most remote part of Donegal, which features exquisite beaches and the legendary Poison Glen. The crags of Errigal Mountain and waves over Bloody Foreland may make you feel like you're in another country; Tory Island practically *is* another country, with its own elected king and freedom from Irish taxes.

■ Crolly and Tor

The N56 intersects with the coast road at a small bridge. The coastal road twists and bends along the craggy edges where Donegal meets the sea, leading you through ever-varying spectacular scenery dotted with small Irish-speaking villages. The first of these villages is **Crolly,** just past the bridge at N56, where you'd be smart to stop for a pint and groceries. Most of the local buses stop in front of Paddy Oig's at Crolly as part of several routes. **Feda O'Donnell** (tel. 48114) provides a daily coach service to and from **Galway** and **Donegal Town** via **Letterkenny; Swilly** (tel. 21380) travels here on its **Dungloe-Derry** route; **John McGinley Coaches** (tel. (074) 35201) makes Crolly its starting point for a **Dublin** journey; and **O'Donnell Trans-Ulster Express** (tel. 48356) goes all the way to **Belfast.** The postmistress at the Crolly **post office** (tel. 48120) is a good source of information on the area and can point you toward accommodations (open M-F 9am-5:30pm, Sa 9am-1pm). The **shop** next to the post office provides everything from groceries to gasoline to bike repairs at reasonable prices (open M-Sa 9am-11pm, Su 9am-10pm).

Paddy Oig's pub (tel. 31306) has everything a body could need: **camping,** pub grub (sandwiches £1), and Tuesday night trad sessions in the summer. **Coillín Darach Caravan & Camping Park** (tel. 32000), just behind the pub, has modern facilities, a convenience store with the basic commodities (open daily 9am-10pm), and the odd tennis court. (July-Aug. £5-7, Sept.-June £4. Laundry £2.) Just past Paddy Oig's, a weather-beaten sign will point you toward **Screagan an Iolair Hill Hostel** (SCRAG an UH-ler; tel. 48593), which lies 4 mi. up a mountain road at **Tor** in **Glenveagh National Park.** Turn left off the coastal road at the sign and follow Tor Road past breathtaking scenery and climbs; when you pass Lough Keel, the road divides. Hostel-seekers should continue straight ahead to reach what is surely one of the best hostels in Ireland, with a great book collection, ever-changing views of the surrounding crags, and a "meditation room" furnished with mats and Indian tapestries. The hostel hosts frequent trad sessions, poetry readings, and art exhibits. Kind owners Eamon and Mireilla will have you embracing the Irish landscape and culture by the end of the first five minutes of your probably long stay. (Dorms £6.50; private rooms £8.50. Wash £3. Open all year, but call ahead Nov.-Feb.)

Tor Rd. continues past Ashardan Waterfall and Lake and finally into Glen Tor. Crolly and the hostel nearby make a good base for exploring the pristine heath lands of the **Derryveagh Mountains,** inhabited by red deer. Trails for hikers of varying abilities, clearly shown on the *Ordnance Survey Discovery Series I*, begin at the hostel in Tor. As the trails are often hard to follow, hikers should always inform the hostel warden of their plans.

How Poison Glen Got Its Name

According to the Ulster Cycle of Irish mythology, the coast of Donegal was originally inhabited by the Fomarian race of evil tempered devils. The leader of the Fomorians was the giant Balor, a demon famed for his single "evil eye" that would turn the beholder to dust when the eyelid was lifted by two assistants tugging on its chains. Balor ruled the country from his fort on Tory Island until the fateful day when the young Lugh (later to be the god of light) challenged him to battle. Balor accepted the challenge and met Lugh at Dún Lughaidh ("Lugh's Fort," pronounced Dun-LEW-y). Intelligent Lugh took aim for Balor's eye before the eyelid was lifted, then closed his own eyes and let his arrow fly; it struck Balor directly in the Evil Eye and killed him. The poison from Balor's eye supposedly spread across the ground around the battlesite, making it unfit for even animals to browse on. The poisonous plant that today covers the valley is called "spurge," although where that name comes from is anyone's guess. Another theory is that Poison Glen is a mistranslation of the Irish for "Beautiful Glen."

■ Errigal Mountain and Dunlewey

One mile north of Crolly, N56 and the coastal road diverge. N56 turns inland and reaches R251 after about 5 mi. This road leads east through **Dunlewey** past the foot of conical **Errigal Mountain,** Ireland's second highest mountain, and eventually to Glenveagh National Park. The drive is studded with stunning views. A mile from the foot of Errigal Mountain in Denlewy village, the spruce-sheltered **Errigal Youth Hostel (An Óige/HI)** (tel. 31180) is a clean, no frills, hiker's haven (June-Sept. members £6.50, under 18 £5; off-season members £5.50, under 18 £4.50). A few minutes up the road is a turn-off to **Dunlewey Lake** and the **Poison Glen** (see **How Poison Glen Got Its Name**). Within the wooded area of the glen is the manor of the English aristocracy that once held the area. In an open spot next to the lake stands their abandoned church, the decaying black and white, roofless exterior of which makes a spooky addition to the myth-laden glen. If you continue along the paved road around a few curves, you will eventually reach an unmarked car park that signals the beginning of the trail up Errigal Mountain (2466 ft.). You must follow this trail in order to scramble through the loose scree to the summit. Expect the climb to take two to three hours total; an exciting narrow ridge comparable to that at Slieve League must be traversed to reach the summit. Be sure to keep an eye on the clouds—they've been known to congregate suddenly around the mountaintop. The summit is the smallest in Ireland, and the sheer face of the mountain could shorten your journey from one hour to one minute.

Back at the bottom, just before the hostel, the **Ionad Cois Locha Dunlewey,** or **Dunlewey Lakeside Center,** offers boat tours, weaving demos, a craft shop of locals' work, a collection of local animals roaming about, enough info on the area to count as a tourist office, and a fire–warmed café. (Center and café open M-Sa 10:30am-6pm, Su 11am-7pm. Boat trips £2.70, students £2. Thatched weaving cottage town £2.50, students £2. Combined ticket £4.) The center also offers a stunning series of trad concerts during the summer (tickets £3-10, usually £5) and music workshops all year.

■ Bunbeg and Bloody Foreland

Where N56 moves inland, R257 continues along the coast to **Bunbeg.** The coastal route is one continuous strip of raw scenery—perfect for cyclists, since there's little traffic. Hitchers tend to stay on N56, where cars are more common. Bunbeg Harbour, the smallest enclosed harbor in Ireland, was a main port of exit and entry at the height of Britain's imperialism. Relics from that period line the harbor: military barracks, grain stones, and look-out towers. Bunbeg's harbor is one of two docking places for **Donegal Coastal Cruises** (a.k.a. **Turasmara;** tel. 31991), the Tory Island ferry; it leaves daily between 9 and 11am and in the afternoon in summer, weather permitting (£12 return). Halfway from the town to the harbor, a single stone pillar marks a rough path that leads to the gorge through which the Clady River rushes, banks lined by salmon fishermen. **Bicycles** can be rented in Bunbeg from Noel McFadden at the harbor (£7 per day).

If you continue past the Bunbeg turnoff, you will immediately see the irresistible **Hudi Beag's** pub (tel. 31016). Only the truly unmusically inclined could walk past this pub on a Monday night without feeling the pull of the intense session taking place within. A bit farther down the road, delicious lunches and dinners (all-you-can-eat roast lunch £6; dinner entrees £5-9) are available at **Errigal View Hotel** (tel. 31355), which also satisfies vegetarians (open daily noon-2:15pm and 6-9:15pm). A stone's throw away is **An Chisteanoh** (an KEESH-nach), a cozy sit-down deli with stomach-stretching portions for under £4 (open daily 8:30am-7pm).

On the streets of nearby **Derrybeg** are several banks, but only the **AIB** serves the foreign traveler ideally, with both an **ATM** and a **bureau de change** (open M-F 10am-1pm and 2-4:30pm). **Teach Thomais** (tel. 31054), the oldest shop in the parish, sells a delightful collection of English and Gaelic books and crafts (if the shop's locked, knock at the kitchen door to its right). **Gweedore Chemists** (tel. 31254) is housed in a green building across the street from Hudi Beag's. The **post office** is also on the main street (open M-F 9am-1pm and 2-5:30pm).

About 7 mi. north of Bunbeg, **Bloody Foreland,** a short length of red jagged rocks, juts into the sea. At sunset, the sea reflects the deep red hue of the sky and rocks. An old legend holds that the sea is colored with the blood of sailors who perished in the wrecks of Spanish galleons. The headland at **Magheraroarty** farther west offers miles of unspoiled beaches and clear views. A holy well remains full of fresh water despite the twice-daily tidal rush. **Ferries** to Tory Island (tel. (074) 35061) travel from Magheraroarty, but the pier is much more isolated and unpeopled than that at Bunbeg.

■ Tory Island

Visible from the Bloody Foreland, barren Tory Island, named for its *tors* (hills), sits 8 mi. off the coast. The weather-beaten cottages and people of Tory fulfill many visitors' imaginative visions of what "old" Ireland looks like, but visitors are also likely to describe the landscape and the spirit of the people as an otherworldly experience.

Such a description harkens back to the island's mythical status as home of the demonic Fomorians. The Fomarians were the original Tory Island pirates, whose leader in their periodic invasions of the mainland was Balor of the Evil Eye (see **How Poison Glen Got Its Name,** p. 350). Its age-old reputation as a haven for pirates prompted people to equate the word "Tory" with "pirate" or "rascal." The use of "Tory" to mean "Conservative" derives from this Irish slang. (A Whig was originally a Scottish horse thief.) Tory's pirateering reputation existed as recently as the last century, when the island thrived off its *poitín* production, since the inaccessibility of the island thwarted British efforts to control its trade. The present day island is completely exhausted of turf, all six layers of which were burned in *poitín* production, and its soil appears more sandy and grassy than that on the mainland. No trees survive the harsh conditions of the small island's sea-exposed area. The eastern end of the island is broken up into a proliferation of jagged sea cliffs.

This small Irish-speaking community has thus far managed to maintain a strong sense of independence. Islanders refer to the mainland as "the country," and still elect a **"Rí na nOileán"** (king of the island) to a lifetime position, which mainly involves serving as the island's PR man—he'll greet you when you get off the boat and can tell stories of the island's past. Many of the island's unusual traditions remain intact, including the superstition that deters people from rescuing those drowning after having fallen off a boat. Another tradition claims that a stone on one of the island's hills has the power to fulfill wishes. The stone sits on the east end of the island on an unapproachable perch, and if you throw three stones onto it, your wish will come true. Islanders have used the stone to wish shipwrecks on invaders, most recently in 1884, when a gunboat coming to collect taxes was wished to the bottom of the Atlantic. The islanders still pay no taxes (although they pay to maintain a school).

The only way to get out to the island is via the **ferry,** also known as Donegal Coastline Cruises or Turasmara (tel. 31320). The ferry runs boats from **Bunbeg** (tel. 31991; 1½hr., June-Sept. 1 per day, fewer Oct.-May), **Magheraroarty** (tel. (074) 35061; 40min., June 2 per day, July-Aug. 3 per day), and **Portnablagh** (departs July-Aug. W 2pm). All crossings are £14 return (students £12; bicycles free). Be sure to call ahead to check departure times as they depend on tides and weather; storms have stranded travelers here for days in summer or even weeks in winter.

The youth hostel, **Brú Thoraighe, Radharc Na Mara** (tel. (074) 65145) is the best place to stay while exploring the island's bleak, wind-swept scenes (£7; open Apr.-Sept.). To reach it, turn left onto the main street from the pier and left again to reach the strand. The hostel is next door to the small sweet shop where you can inquire about a bed for the night. **Club Thoraighe** (tel. (074) 65121) features Tory Island trad, which beats out a slightly stronger rhythmic emphasis than the mainland music, and nightly *ceìlis* (dances), which everyone on the island is expected to attend. The island's 160 people support a surprising number of businesses, all located along a quarter of a mile stretch of the island's one street: store, hotel and restaurant, craft shop, café/chipper, and **Gailearai Dixon** (Dixon Gallery). The gallery showcases the work of the Tone Primitives, a group of local artists promoted by Derrick Hall of Glebe Gallery fame. Their work usually depicts the natural scenery of the island in color-drenched pigments, evoking the living fury of the sea around Tory or the shadowy ruins of the island's medieval religious past. The island's interesting historical sights include the ruins of the **monastery** that St. Colmcille founded in the 6th century and the **Tau Cross** close to the town center.

NORTHERN DONEGAL

■ Falcarragh and Dunfanaghy

Northeast of the Bloody Foreland, white beaches stretch along the coast with a continuously irregular inland area of rocky hills and fertile valleys. Two welcoming little towns from which you can easily explore the coastal area are Falcarragh and Dun-

"Today We Voted Gildea"

Since the dawn of the Irish Republic, Western Co. Donegal has elected their three Teachta Dála (legislative representatives; TD) from Ireland's largest political parties, Fianna Fail and Fine Gael. In 1997, the region voted in their first independent TD. Thomas Gildea has been a farmer, bachelor, and teetotaler all his life. He entered politics solely to protest the Multi Microwave Distribution System (MMDS), a corporation that the government had contracted to provide television services to the area. Prior to the inception of the MMDS, Donegal inhabitants had paid locals about £5 per year to set up illegal airwave deflectors, which redirected TV programs to community members' antennae. Under the MMDS, they would be paying £200 per year for fewer stations. Even more upsetting was that many of the small valley communities would be unable to receive the hilltop-sent microwave signals. In protest, locals picketed the MMDS headquarters and wrote angry letters to their TDs. Not until Thomas Gildea declared his candidacy, however, did they have a chance of defeating the corporation. On the day of elections, news of Gildea's win spread like wildfire. A week of celebrations ensued, and Gildea for the first time pondered buying a suit.

fanaghy. Falcarragh is Irish-speaking, while Dunfanaghy, about 7 mi. north, still has an Anglo-Irish feel from its days as the administrative center of the region.

Both are resort towns, but **Falcarragh** is today the more major of the two and provides many of the region's basic services. The only **ATM** around (24hr.) is at Falcarragh's **Bank of Ireland** (tel. 35484; open M-W and F 10am-12:30pm and 1:30-4pm, Th 10am-12:30pm and 1:30-5pm). **Flynn's Pharmacy** (tel. 35778) delivers the drugs (open M-Sa 9am-6pm). **McGinley's** supermarket (tel. 35126) provides an amazing array of wholegrain bread, skimmed milk, and veggies as well as the ordinary groceries (open M-Sa 9am-10pm). Falcarragh's **post office,** Main St. (tel. 35110), delivers mail (open M-F 9am-1pm and 2-5:30pm, Sa 9am-1pm). The **phone code** of both towns is 074.

Along the coast, 5½ mi. north of Falcarragh and 1½ mi. south of Dunfanaghy, is the truly amazing **Corcreggan Mill Cottage Hostel (IHH)** (tel. 36507). Owner Brendan has converted an old wooden railway car into comfortable 4-bed dorms and private doubles with mahogany floors and walls. The railway car is sheltered underneath the roof of a house and has exceedingly comfortable common rooms laden with fascinating railroad memorabilia and furniture. More dorms and doubles are available in the equally cool former kiln house. The three kitchens—two for hostelers, one for campers—have been redone using recycled materials to keep the traditional atmosphere. Guests are encouraged to participate in nurturing the owners' extensive organic garden. A Swilly **bus** stops right at the door. (Dorms in kiln £6; dorms in railroad car £8; semi-private double in kiln's loft £8; double in railroad car £10. **Camping** £4. Wash with powder £2.) Hostelers team up at night to hire the services of **John McGinley's Buslines** to travel to and from the pubs (£1 each way regardless of distance). While *Let's Go* does not recommend **hitching,** it is reportedly easy here. Farther on toward Dunfanaghy, **Francis Stewart** provides comfortable, flowery **B&B** (tel. 36560; £12).

Falcarragh lives pub life to the fullest. The **Shamrock Lodge,** or **Lóistín na Seamróige,** in the center of town, is by far the most distinctive. It buzzes with human activity well into the night. The "young room," as owner Mary calls it, has a jukebox, pool table, and comfy leather seats; old folks congregate in the poster-bedecked front bar. The Saturday night trad session (also Wednesday in summer) does full justice to the local talent—and remember that most of Ireland's best trad bands have come out of Northern Donegal (rhythm and blues Friday). On Ballyconnell Rd., just off Main St. at the northern end of town, **The Loft Bar** (tel. 35992) presents a collection of old mugs and flowery upholstery in a cave-dark space, with folk music on summer weekends.

In **Dunfanaghy,** guests peek down the stairs at the revelry in the pub below the small and lively **Shamrock Lodge Hostel (IHH),** Main St. (tel. 35859; dorms £6; doubles £16). Next to the post office, **Patricia McGraddy** (tel. 35145) offers B&B in a modern abode. Guests are invited to "have a bash" on her piano, but please don't take advantage of the proprietress's kindness (£13). You can eat huge portions in seemingly sun-kissed wooden booths at **John's Restaurant** at the top of Main St. (Steaks £7.50-8, seafood and meat entrees £2.30-5, salads £3-4, sandwiches £1-2. Open M-Sa 10am-10pm, Su 2-10pm.) Alternatively, head to **Mighty Mac's** (tel. 65386), next to the post office, for chipper fare in a "take-away/café." The shop is a chipper with a unique pop-inspired decor. (Burgers £1. Open daily 9am-1:30am.) The **Gweedore Bar,** Main St. (tel. (075) 35293), curries the local businessmen's favor with a reasonable lunch menu (lunch served 12:30-2:30pm).

Danny Collins' bar (tel. 36205) stays open from 10:30am until whenever the gardai come to shut it down. Food, however, is only served from 1 to 9:30pm (soup £1.20, meat and vegetarian entrees £4-6). Down the street, **Danann's Restaurant,** Main St. (tel. 36150), specializes in pricier but praiseworthy seafood. (Entrees from £7; early 3-course dinner £10, 6-7pm only. Open June- Aug. daily 6-9pm. Reservations advised.) In the **Arnold Hotel** at the far end of town, the **Whisky Fly** (tel. 36208) hosts a traditional group on Thursday nights in summer. The garden bistro offers gourmet lunches within stone walls (entrees about £5.50). **Michael's Bar** (formerly Molly's, formerly Hugh's) is one of the town's oldest and dearest pubs; it keeps being passed down through the family but never loses its "real men drink here" feel (although they'd say it in Irish). The **Village Shop** is open daily for groceries (9am-11pm).

The **Dunfanaghy Workhouse** (tel. 36540) has created an excellent exhibit on the effects of famine in northwest Donegal. (Open Mar.-Oct. M-F 10am-5pm, Sa-Su noon-5pm. £2, children £1. Art and local history exhibitions free.) It's undergone a miraculous transformation from the days of the famine, when the poorhouse gave minimal shelter and rations to the destitute under prison-like conditions. This former poorhouse hosts numerous community events, including trad sessions, play performances, local art exhibitions, a coffee shop, and a ten-day art festival in the second week of July.

The area around Dunfanaghy and Falcarragh is traversed by a maze of small country roads and boggy hills. One can easily walk, cycle, drive, or hitch to any of the natural attractions within a 5 mi. radius of either town. About 3 mi. outside of Falcarragh are the colossal and isolated dunes of **Back Strand** and **Ballyness** beaches (follow the signs for "Trà," meaning beach, from the southern end of town). The **New Lake**—so called because it was formed in 1912 after a massive storm blocked up this former estuary—features a world-famous ecosystem and lots of otters. **Horn Head,** signposted on the way into Dunfanaghy, invites long rambles around its pristine beaches, megalithic tombs, and gorse-covered hills. Those tireless hikers who make the 3½-hour trek to the far north tip of Horn Head from Dunfanaghy will experience some of the most spectacularly high sea cliffs in Ireland, comparable to those at Slieve League with fewer visitors. **Ards Forest** is a couple of miles past Dunfanaghy and currently features a number of nature trails ranging from 1½ to 8 mi. and pristine beaches accessible only on foot (open July-Aug. daily 10:30am-9pm; Easter-June and Sept. Sa-Su 10:30am-4pm). To experience the water's strength firsthand, call **Marble Hill Windsurfing** (tel. 36231; adult instruction session £20; board hire £8 per hr., £12 per 2hr.). Turning your back to the sea in either Falcarragh or Dunfanaghy will bring the expanse of the Muckish Mountain into view

■ Glenveagh National Park

Fourteen miles northwest of Letterkenny on the eastern side of the Derryveagh Mountains, **Glenveagh National Park** (tel. (074) 37090 or 37262), 37 sq. mi. of forest glens, bogs, and mountains, is justly one of the more popular national parks in Ireland. *(Open Easter to early Nov. daily 10am-6:30pm, Jul.-Aug. Su 10am-7:30pm. £2, students £1, seniors £1.50.)* One of the largest herds of red deer in Europe roams the park and lures travelers to Glenveagh specifically to deer-watch, which is best done at dusk and in the winter months after October, when the deer come down to the valley to forage. Despite Glenveagh's popularity, you probably won't be aware of any other human presence within the enormous pristine area—make sure to hold on to the free map handed out at the visitor's center. The hostels in **Crolly** (p. 349) and **Dunlewy** (p. 350) are most convenient to the park.

Summertime tourists can take the free minibus from the park's entrance to **Glenveagh Castle,** 2½ mi. away (departs every 10-15min., last trip 1½hr. before closing). *(Same hours as park. Last tour 1¼hr. before closing. £2, students and children £1, seniors £1.50.)* Glenveagh Castle is less than 200 years old but looks like a medieval keep with its thick walls, battle-ready rampart, turrets, and round tower. The founder of the Glenveagh estate, John Adair, had a nasty reputation that doesn't suit the beauty of the land. In the cold April of 1861, he evicted 244 tenants on trumped-up charges. Many of them decided to emigrate to Australia while others were forced into the workhouse. The surrounding **gardens** and greenhouse soften the bleak aspect of Adair's lonely castle; not surprisingly, they are the design of a later owner, the American Henry McIlhenry. *(Tours of the garden leave from Castle Courtyard July-Aug. Tu and Th 2pm.)* He planted the gardens around the estate and left it to the government at his death. The areas around the castle are posh and highly cultivated; plots farther away are named after the area of the world to which their species belong (the Dutch garden, for example) and appear almost unkept. Marked nature trails begin at the castle. A 1 mi. walk up the incline behind the castle leads to **View Point,** where the vast expanse of the park can be gluttonously admired. Park rangers lead guided nature walks and more strenuous hill walks. *(Nature walks 1½hr., July-Aug. W 2pm. Hill walks 5-6hr., May-Oct. sometimes Sa 11am.)* The **visitor's center** has more information about these or self-guided hikes. The visitor's center can also prepare you for your hike with a 10-minute video on the park's wildlife and history, several exhibits, and a meal at its cafeteria-style restaurant (most entrees £4-5).

Five miles away from the visitor's center is the **Glebe Gallery** (tel. (074) 37071) in Churchill, art gallery of artist Derek Hill. *(Open Easter week and late May to late Sept. Sa-Th 11am-6:30pm, last tour 5:30pm. £2, students £1.)* Hill fostered the Tory Island school of painters, and their work dominates the gallery's collection, along with work by mainland Donegal artists, international Victorian art, and several pieces by internationally renowned European masters, including Louis de Brocquay and Picasso. On the other side of the lake at the **Glebe House,** a centuries-old family home, the newly opened **St. Colmcille Heritage Center** has a permanent display on the life and times of the saint who brought Christianity to Donegal and changed the face of the land forever. *(Hours and admission same as the Glebe.)* Nearby is St. Colmcille's **Bed of Loneliness,** an enormous horizontal stone slab on which the saint spent the night before leaving the area in exile. Many emigrants have since performed the night of lying on the stone to prevent future loneliness.

■ Rosguill Peninsula

The tiny Irish-speaking village of **Carrigart** sits at the base of one of the more beautiful drives in Donegal, the **Atlantic Drive** around the Rosguill Peninsula. Carrigart provides supplies services necessary for the road. Pull your punts from the **National Irish Bank,** Main St. (open July-Aug. M-F 10am-noon; Sept.-June M-Tu and Th-F 10am-noon). Rent your wheels at **C.C. Cycles** (tel. 55427), half a mile outside Carrigart on Creslough Rd. (£1 per hr., £5 per day; open daily 9am-9pm). **Joy's Cosmetics and Gifts Shop,** Main St. (tel. 55124), has soup and aspirin but not prescriptions. (Open in summer M-Sa 10am-1pm and 2-6:30pm; in winter M-Tu and Th-Sa 10am-1pm and 2-6pm, W 10am-1pm.) The **post office,** Main St. (tel. 55101), includes a **bureau de change** (open M-F 9am-1pm and 2-5:30pm, Sa 9am-1pm). The **phone code** for Carrigart and the peninsula is 074.

Sheephaven Lodge (tel. 55685), on Church Rd. in Carrigart, is around the bend at the end of the Main St. and up to the right on the side road just before the Presbyterian Church. The Gallaghers will treat you to tea and biscuits, invitingly decorated rooms, and all the peace you desire (£17.50). A friendly staff at **Greim-Blasta** ("tasty bites"), Main St. (tel. 55188), serves all-day Irish breakfasts, sandwiches, chips, and pastries (full meal around £2-3, desserts £1-2; open M-Th 9am-6pm, F-Su 9am-10pm). Down the road, upscale but worth it **Weaver's Restaurant** (tel. 55204) specializes in fresh-from-the-ocean seafood (most entrees £8-11; open June-Aug. daily 6-10pm). The **North Star** (tel. 55110) across the way is Carrigart's favorite pub.

The Atlantic Drive leads from Carrigart to the very tip of the peninsula, where **Trá na Rosann Youth Hostel (An Óige/HI)** (tel. 55374) watches from the top of a hill 4 mi. from the tweed-manufacturing town of **Downies.** The view is spectacular. A convenient shop is 50 yd. from the hostel. (Easter-May dorms £5.50, June-Sept. £6.50.) Drink down a draught while the locals mill around at **Singing Pub** 2 mi. down the road, a thatched bar with low ceilings, great grub (sandwiches £1), and trad nearly every night. The **Harbor Bar** (tel. 55920) on the Main St. in Downies calls itself an "old-world style pub" and has trad sessions on Thursday and Saturday nights in July and August. **McNutt's,** Main St. (tel. 55314), is one of the oldest tweed manufacturers in the area. (Open M-Sa 9am-6pm, Su 2:30-5:30pm.) It also features splendid little **coffee shops** (tel. 55961) that serve local dishes (£1.50-4).

■ Fanad Peninsula

The Fanad Peninsula juts into the Atlantic between Lough Swilly and Mulroy Bay. The peninsula's lush greenery makes a striking complement to the sandy beaches. The eastern edge, outlined by the villages of **Ramelton, Rathmullan,** and **Portsalon,** is by far the nicest part of the peninsula, with colorful old houses and sweeping views across Lough Swilly. Ramelton and **Milford** (just on the western edge of the Lough) offer the most services and nightlife. The pretty **Knockalla Mountains** are easy to climb. The lucky few who get to the far reaches of the peninsula will find their efforts rewarded with a bounty of beachscapes. The peninsula favors drivers with beautiful views from remote roads, but the Swilly bus makes only two circular trips out around the end of the peninsula per day. The broad, relatively flat stretches of road from Ramelton to about 4 mi. past Rathmullan are kind to cyclists, but sharp inclines become frequent halfway out the peninsula, and the road becomes narrow, unkept, and poorly paved. The **phone code** for the entire peninsula is 074.

■ Ramelton

A river flanked by stone walls and long-standing trees runs through the pretty, 17th-century town of Ramelton (Rathmelton) at the mouth of the Leannan Estuary, the eastern gateway to the peninsula.

ORIENTATION AND PRACTICAL INFORMATION The Mall runs along the river and contains most of the town's handful of goods and services. The **National Irish Bank,** The Mall (tel. 51028), has a **bureau de change** but no ATM (open M-F 9am-1pm and 2-5:30pm). **Bridge Launderette,** The Mall (tel. 51333), is named after its location, not its proprietor (wash and dry £3.50-£4.50; open M-Sa 9:30am-6pm). **O'Donnell's Pharmacy** (tel. 51080) is also on The Mall (open M-Tu and Th-Sa 9am-1pm and 2-6pm, W 9am-1pm). Mail arrives at the **post office,** Castle St. (tel. 51001), off The Mall (open M-F 9am-5:30pm, Sa 9am-1pm).

ACCOMMODATIONS, FOOD, AND PUBS Just off The Mall and right on the Swilly bus route, **Crammond House,** Market Sq. (tel. 51055), has spacious, pretty rooms with huge bathrooms and high ceilings in a 1760s townhouse (£15, with bath £17; open Easter-Oct.). **Clooney House** (tel. 51125) is set among an expanse of green pastures less than a mile outside Ramelton on the road to Milford (£17, singles £23).

Whoriskey's/Spar Supermarket (tel. 51006) sells groceries (open M-Sa 8:30am-10pm, Su 9am-9pm). Ramelton offers sandwiches and fine dining but little middle ground. Ramelton's "fish house," where salmon were once smoked in Ramelton's salmon heyday, now sells tea and sandwiches along with sweaters and local pottery in the **Fish House Craft Gallery** (tel. 51316; open May-Sept. daily 10am-7pm). Take your sandwich outside and you can dine with the swans along the river. For affordable feasts in a more refined, candlelit setting, cross the street to the posh but reasonably priced **Mirabeau Steak House,** The Mall (tel. 51138), which does have vegetarian meals available. Occasional trad sessions, a good pint, and sheer endurance define 200-year-old **Sweeney's** in the middle of town. At the top of town on the road to Milford, well-established **Bridge Bar** (tel. 51119) knows how to please its customers with music Wednesday through Sunday nights; call to check the flavor of the day. **Conway's** (tel. 51297), an old thatched cottage at the bottom of the hill down Church St., pours proper pints to the beat of trad and ballads every Saturday.

SIGHTS To discover the area's heritage, turn off The Mall and go uphill past Market Sq.; a right at Mary's Bar after Crammond House will bring you to Back Lane and the old **Presbyterian Meetinghouse.** Francis Makemie, who founded the first American Presbytery in 1706, grew up in Ramelton and worshipped here. The building now houses the town library and the paper-pushing **Donegal Ancestry Centre** (tel. 51266). The center, part of Irish Genealogical Project Centres, will help you trace your Donegal ancestors for a fee and provides information on other national heritage centers. (Open M-Th 9am-4:30pm, F 9am-4pm.) Crowds flock to the **Lennon Festival** in early July for a carnival and parade (call the Bridge Bar for info).

■ Rathmullan

Five miles north along the main coastal road, Rathmullan is an ancient town of historical, mythical, and logistical significance as well as of sandy beaches. In 1607, the last powerful Gaelic chieftains, Hugh O'Neill and Red Hugh O'Donnell, fled from Ireland after suffering numerous defeats to British invaders. They and 99 of their retinue set sail from Rathmullan for Spain to gather military support from the Catholic King Phillip II. Their ship blew off course; they landed in France and finally died in Rome while still trying to gain foreign aid. Their departure is known and lamented as the Flight of the Earls. In more recent Anglo-Irish struggles, Wolfe Tone, the famous champion of Irish independence, was arrested in Rathmullan in 1798 (see **History,** p. 55, 57).

Tourist information is gladly dispensed at the Heritage Centre (see below). **Mace Supermarket** (tel. 58148), on the coast road into town, supplies basic gastronomic needs (open July-Aug. daily 9am-10pm; Sept.-May M-Sa 9am-1pm and 2-7pm, Su 9am-1pm and 3-6pm). Quiet **Pier Hotel** (tel. 58178) has multiple personalities, all three with full strength of character; a romantic wooded lane runs parallel to the beach from behind the hotel. First, its **B&B** offers very clean, sunny rooms in an old Georgian home (£15, with bath £22). Second, it serves four-star pub grub, mostly fresh seafood (entrees £4-5; food served 12:30-9:30pm). Finally, the Pier is a quite popular **pub,** with a good mixture of young and old around the simple bar, midweek trad sessions, and live contemporary music Friday and Saturday. Next door to the Heritage Center, the **Beachcomber Bar** (tel. 58125) offers beach access. One wall is taken up by a gigantic view of the water, and a sandy beer garden opens out back in the summer (live music on weekends). The **Water's Edge Inn** (tel. 58182), with newly funky orange walls, is set on the very spot where the Earls set sail, a bit south of the town.

The tales of O'Neill and O'Donnell are very much alive and present at the **"Flight of the Earls" Heritage Centre** (tel. 58229), at the town center on the coast. A helpful staff uses artwork, literature, and wax models to explain Rathmullan's history in detail. The building, a particularly foreboding Martello tower (see p. 58), is a historic monument of the British Admiralty. (Open June-Sept. M-Sa 10am-6pm, Su noon-6pm. £1.50, students and seniors £1, children 75p.) Around the corner, the remains of the **Rathmullan Priory,** a 14th-century Carmelite monastery, lie shrouded in ivy. Overgrown with sometimes blooming weeds, the crumbling priory affords good views across the lough.

■ The Northern and Western Peninsula

North of Rathmullan, the road narrows and winds in synch with the dense wildlife that springs up across the peninsula's tip. The road dips and rises along with the short but frequent inclines of the **Knockalla Mountains.** These remote roads are discouraging to pedestrians and all but the most fit bikers, and hitchhiking is nearly impossible. Beyond this stretch of road, the coast arcs dramatically between mountain and shore and leads through a series of clustered houses called "towns" only because each has a church and a post office. Just before Portsalon, a signposted lane leads from the main road to remote **Bunnaton Hostel,** Glenvar (tel. 50122), high on a hill above the lough, which has a lovely kitchen and pastel rooms with views (dorms £6.50; private rooms £8.50; breakfast £2-4). Continuing north, the main road becomes both mindbogglingly steep and breathtakingly beautiful. Just before Portsalon, the road crests a hill, where **Knockalla Strand** (rated the second best in the world by a British "beach expert") and the tip of the northern peninsula suddenly appear. **Camping** and facilities (including laundry, kitchen, and TV) are available next to Knockalla Strand at the **Knockalla Holiday Centre** (tel. 59108), 3 mi. south of Portsalon (£7 per 2-person tent, £10 per 4-person tent; open Easter-Oct.).

Portsalon (port-SAL-un), on the descent, consists of three shops and a series of homes along the water. It was once a resort town, but the resort hotel burned down three years ago, leaving just the paradise of a beach that needs nothing to recommend it. The **Portsalon B&B** (tel. 59395), next to the post office on the main road, has big, new rooms perfumed by the rosebushes outside (singles £20; doubles £30, with bath £35).

About one hour north of Portsalon by bike, the **Great Arch of Doaghbeg** keeps the **Fanad Lighthouse** company. The arch, a mass of rock over 80 ft. wide detached from seaside cliffs, is visible from above, though not from the main road. It is best reached through the 6-acre **Ballydaheen Gardens,** a seaside array of Japanese and English gardens that blends into the natural landscape amazingly well (open May-Sept. M, Th, and Sa 10am-3pm; £3, children £1). From Fanad Head, the route down the western side of the peninsula winds in and out of the inlets of **Mulroy Bay.** Mrs. Borland's **Avalon Farmhouse** (tel. 59031), on Main St. in tiny **Tamney**—also reachable by a road that cuts across the peninsula from Portsalon—has homemade jam and attractive decor (£15, with bath £17; open Apr.-Sept.). In Kerrykeel (Carrowkeel), farther south at the foot of the Knockalla Hills, you can **camp** right on Mulroy Bay in **Rockhill Park** (tel. 50012), which has complete facilities and a superb view. About 1½ mi. out of Kerrykeel along Glenvar Rd. is a signpost to the **Gortnavern Dolmen,** one of the most spectacular megalithic tombs in the area.

▨ Letterkenny

Letterkenny (Leitir Ceannan) has the most action Donegal ever sees. Several years ago, residents lamented the arrival of a traffic light at the intersection of Main St. and Port Rd., the first in Co. Donegal. Today, Donegal's commercial, academic, and ecclesiastical center has several traffic lights, while cars in the rest of the county still roam freely. Most tourists come to Letterkenny as a connection point for buses to various places in Donegal, the rest of the Republic, and Northern Ireland. Letterkenny's relative urbanity also brings in pub- and club-goers for weekend revelry.

PRACTICAL INFORMATION

Buses: at the junction of Port and Derry Rd. in front of the Quinnsworth Supermarket. **Bus Éireann** (tel. 21309) makes tours of Inishowen Peninsula and Giant's Causeway (£7; call to book). They also run regular service to **Derry** (40min., 3 per day, £3), **Dublin** (5hr., M-Sa 5 per day, Su 3 per day), **Galway** (5hr., 3 per day, £10), and **Donegal Town** (50min.) on the way to **Sligo** (2hr., 3 per day, £6). **Feda O'Donnell Coaches** (tel. (075) 48114 or (091) 761656) drives to **Galway** via **Donegal Town** (2 per day) and to **Crolly** via **Dunfanaghy** (2 per day; more extensive services F and Su). **Lough Swilly Buses** (tel. 29400 or 22863) head north toward the **Fanad Peninsula** (M-Sa 3 per day), to **Derry** (M-Sa 10 per day), and south to **Dungloe** (M-Sa 3 per day); fares run £3-7. **John McGinley Coaches** (tel. 35201) sends at least one bus every day (more M, F, Su) to **Gweedore** via **Dun-**

fanaghy and another to **Dublin** (£8). **McGeehan's Bus** (tel. (075) 46101) goes twice a day to **Killybegs** (£7) and **Glencolmcille** (£6). **Northwest Busways** (tel. (077) 82619) sends buses around Inishowen (M-Sa 2 per day), making stops in **Buncrana** (£3), **Carndonagh** (£4), and **Moville** (£4.30). **Doherty's Travel** (tel. (075) 21105) has buses that leave for **Dungloe** and **Burtonport** from Dunn s Super-maket at 5pm daily (£4).

Local Transportation: Letterkenny Bus Service (Handy Bus; tel. (087) 414714). Extensive city routes (70p).

Tourist Offices: Bord Fáilte (tel. 21160), ¾mi. past the bus station and a good bit out of town on Derry Rd. Pamphlets on Co. Donegal and accommodations booking. Open July-Aug. M-Sa 9am-8pm, Su 10am-2pm; Sept.-June M-F 9am-5pm. **Chamber of Commerce Visitors Information Centre**, 40 Port Rd. (tel. 24866 or 25505), has a much closer though slightly smaller selection of info on Letterkenny and the rest of Co. Donegal. Open M-F 9am-5pm.

Banks: AIB, 61 Upper Main St. (tel. 22877 or 22807). Open M-W and F 10am-4pm, Th 10am-5pm. **Bank of Ireland,** Lower Main St. (tel. 22122). Open M-W and F 10am-4pm, Th 10am-5pm. Both have 24hr. **ATMs.**

Bike Rental: Church St. Cycles (tel. 26204), by the cathedral. £7 per day, £30 per week; deposit £40. Open Tu-Sa 10am-6pm. **Starlight Garage** (tel. 22248), £7 per day.

Laundry: Masterclean, High Rd. (tel. 26880), across from the hostel. £6 wash and dry. Dry cleaning.

Pharmacy: Magee's Pharmacy, Main St. (tel. 21419). Open M-W 9am-6:30pm, Th-F 9am-8pm, Sa 9am-6:30pm.

Counseling and Support: Samaritans, 20 Port Rd. (tel. 27200). 24hr. phone-line; drop in for one-on-one counseling Th-Su 7-10pm. **Letterkenny Women's Aid,** Port Rd. (tel. 26267). Open M-F 9am-5pm.

Post Office: Main St. (tel. 22454), about halfway down. Open M and W-F 9am-5:30pm, Tu 9:30am-5pm, Sa 9am-5:30pm.

Phone Code: 074.

ACCOMMODATIONS

The Manse Hostel (IHH), High Rd. (tel. 25238). From the bus station, head up Port Rd. toward town and turn right up the lane marked "Covehill House B&B." Continue past the playground, through the parking lot, and 50yd. up the road. The hostel is across the street. The longer way around goes farther down Port Rd. and then makes a sharp right onto High Rd. 5min. walk to the town center. Although its interior color scheme seems wearily dated, the beds and couches are as comfy as a traveler could desire. Free coffee. Bunks in clean and tidy 3-,4-, and 6-bed dorms. Dorms £6; private doubles and twins £14. Sheets 50p in dorms.

Riverside B&B (tel. 24907), off Derry Rd 1mi. past Letterkenny. Turn left after the Clan Ree Hotel; signs point the way. Huge rooms with views of the quiet countryside. Full-sized snooker table. £15, with bath £17.

White Gables, Mrs. McConnelogue, Lower Dromore (tel. 22583). Lower Dromore is the 3rd exit from the roundabout 1mi. out on Derry Rd; the house is ½mi. along Lower Dromore around a bend. Call for pick-up from town. Clean and cheery rooms. The upstairs balcony has spectacular views of Letterkenny next to green fields that remind you you're in Donegal. £15.

FOOD

Letterkenny offers a fair share of cheap meals in pleasant, even quirky, café settings. **Quinnsworth** (tel. 22555), in the Letterkenny Shopping Center behind the bus station, is all you could ask for in a grocery store (open M-W 9am-7pm, Th-F 9am-9pm, Sa 9am-6pm, Su noon-6pm). **SuperValu** (tel. 27053), on the lower level of the Courtyard Shopping Centre, is well stocked and more central (open M-W and Sa 8:45am-6pm, Th-F 8:45am-9pm, Su 2-6pm). **The Natural Way,** 55 Port Rd. (tel. 25738), sells wholefood and herbal remedies (open M-Sa 9:30am-6pm).

The Beanery, Main St., next to the Courtyard Shopping Centre. Calls itself a cappuccino and sandwich bar, but offers so much more: full bistro, rich baked goods, delicate pastries, and 2 floors of dining with a view, including outdoor balcony seating. 4-course meals £3-5, sandwiches around £2. Open M-Sa 9am-5:30pm.

Galfees, Main St. (tel. 27173), in the basement of the Courtyard Shopping Centre, assumes different guises throughout the day. It's a carvery 12:15-3pm, a fresh food bar 8:30am-5pm, and a bar/restaurant 5-10pm. The Irish illustrations that bedeck its dark wood walls have a one-of-a-kind, not shopping mall, feel. The evening menu is cheaper than the later dinner (most evening entrees £4-5).

Pat's Too, Main St. (tel. 21761). Hearty take-away meals (pizza, kebabs, burgers) for the budget traveler, with a sit-in option in its highly tiled interior. Always crowded at night. Delivery available. Open M-Th 11am-12:30am, F and Su 11am-1am, Sa 11am-3:30am.

Café Rico, Oliver-Plunkett Rd. (tel. 29808), at the end of Main St. away from the bus station, offers full breakfasts and heaping sandwiches (£2-4) in a mod coffee shop.

Pat's Pizza, Market Sq. The pricier antecedent of Pat's Too, with a spacious Euro atmosphere. Small pizza £4.50; pasta £6-7. Open in summer daily 5-11:30pm; in winter Tu-Su 5-11:30pm.

PUBS

McGinley's, 25 Main St. (tel. 21106). A hugely popular student bar. The upstairs is designed like a chapel, the downstairs is decorated in Victorian style. The mixture creates a pleasingly hectic ambience. Live rock, pop, and blues Th-Su.

McClafferty's, 54 Main St. (tel. 21581). Observed to reverse the effects of aging: in the daytime its patrons are an older, contemplative set; at night they turn young and frisky. Modern ballads and rock Th, Su.

Cottage Bar, Main St. (tel. 21338). A kettle on the hearth, animated conversation around the bar, and nuns drinking Guinness in the corner. Trad Tu, Th.

The Old Orchard Inn, High Rd. (tel. 21615), less than a half mile past the Manse Hostel in a secluded parking-lot setting. Does its best to create a wooden escape out of logwood furniture and ubiquitous leafery. 3 floors that are always busy; the "cellar bar" on the bottom hosts occasional trad and the disco on the top floor is one of the most popular in town (disco £4; open W and F-Sa until 2am).

SIGHTS

Neo-Gothic **St. Eunan's Cathedral,** perched high above town on Church Ln., looks like the heavenly kingdom when floodlit at night. *(Open daily 8am-5pm, except during Sunday masses at 8, 9, 10, 11:15am, and 12:30pm. Free.)* Church Ln. is on your right up Main St. away from the bus station, but you can probably best make your way to the cathedral by looking up for its spire. Proposed as a "resurrection of the fallen shrines of Donegal," the cathedral took 11 years in its construction, all years of economic hardship and depression. Every inch of the cathedral is a piece of art, and they make up a sort of retrospective religious depiction. The arch at the junction of the nave and transcript presents the story of St. Colomb in beautiful carving. The organ is of divine proportions. Although St. Eunan's is less than 100 years old, its burgeoning congregation is already too great for its seating capacity. Out of necessity, a second, modern cathedral has recently been built on the edge of town. Opposite St. Eunan's, the smaller **Parish Church of Conwal** (Church of Ireland) shelters a number of tombstones, some of which date from the 17th century (Sunday services 8 and 10:30am).

Donegal County Museum, High Rd. (tel. 24613), exhibits anything and everything having to do with Co. Donegal. *(Open M-F 10am-12:30pm and 1-4:30pm, Sa 1-4:30pm. Free.)* Artifacts range from the ancient to the very modern.

Heads or Tails

Before he turned to spiritual affairs, Saint Colmcille had been a fearsome swordsman. During these early years, a great monster lurked in the pool at the source of the river that runs through Letterkenny. The local chief, Feardorocha, begged Colmcille to help him kill the monster, called Swileach. When Feardorocha and Colmcille arrived at the pool early one morning, Swileach burst from the water and attacked them. Cowardly Feardorocha fled, leaving Colmcille to fight the monster alone. The brave young man drew his sword and halved the monster with a mighty blow. But only the monster's head was dead. The tail wrapped itself around Colmcille and tried to squeeze the life out of him. Colmcille freed himself from its iron grip and turned the monster into *ciolar coit* (kind of like sushi). Then he chased Feardorocha and caught up with him trying to ford the river. As Colmcille was about to strike the deserter, Feardorocha begged him to at least wash the monster's blood off his blade before exacting revenge. When Colmcille rinsed the metal, he found his wrath abated. He pardoned Feardorocha and named the river whose water could wash away anger Swilly after the monster he had slain.

INISHOWEN PENINSULA

It would be a shame to leave Ireland without seeing the Inishowen Peninsula, an untouristed mosaic of mountains, forests, meadows, and beaches that reaches farther north than "the North." You can have its white beaches to yourself all day and then be welcomed at night by crowds of locals in the pubs, which are filled with trad almost nightly. The peninsula is dotted with many villages and two larger towns, Buncrana and Cardonagh. The winding road that connects all the villages affords views of constantly sublime scenery. It takes two to three days to see the whole shebang properly without a car, and even with a car one would hardly want to spend less time.

The nearest commercial center to Inishowen is Derry, whose residents often vacation here. **Lough Swilly** (head office tel. (01504) 262017; Buncrana depot tel. (077) 61340) runs buses from Derry to points on the Inishowen: **Buncrana** (35min., M-F 10 per day, Sa 12 per day, Su 3 per day), **Moville** (50 min., 4 per day), **Carndonagh** (1hr., M-F 6 per day, Sa 4 per day), **Malin** (1¼hr., M, W, and F 1 per day, Sa 3 per day), and **Malin Head** (1½hr., M, W, and F 1 per day, Sa 3 per day). Swilly also connects **Buncrana** directly to **Carndonagh** (50min., M-Sa 3 per day). Swilly Buses offers an 8-day "rambler ticket" (£18, students £12) and student rates on all individual trips; their return fares are considerably cheaper than two single tickets. **Northwest Buses** (tel. (077) 82619) runs from **Moville** through **Culdaff, Carndonagh, Ballyliffen, Clonmany, Buncrana, Fahan,** and on to **Letterkenny** (M-F 2 per day, Sa 1 per day); from **Shrove** to **Derry** via **Moville** (1hr., M-Sa 3 per day); from **Buncrana** to **Derry** (M-Sa 5 per day); and from **Malin Head** to **Derry** via **Culdaff** and **Muff** (M-Sa 1 per day).

Inishowen's inland landscape is unusual, but the northern and western shores are especially striking. The clearly posted **Inish Eoghin 100** road takes exactly 100 mi. to navigate the peninsula's perimeter. Drivers will find this the best route for seeing Inishowen. Hitchers report having an easy and pleasant time on this road. Cycling, however, can be difficult around Malin Head due to ferocious winds and hilly terrain. Cyclists may want to use the roads that crisscross the peninsula instead to shorten long distances between sights. Most of the inland roads look exactly alike, so good directions and a good map are absolutely necessary. The map published by the Inishowen Tourism Society, available at the Cardonagh tourist office, is the most comprehensive. The **phone code** for all of the Inishowen Peninsula is 077.

■ Grianán Ailigh

Ten miles south of Buncrana at the bottom of the peninsula and three miles west of Derry, the hilltop ringfort Grianán Ailigh (GREEN-in ALL-ya) is an excellent place to start or finish a tour of Inishowen. This site has been a cultural center for at least 4000 years: first as a Druidic temple at the gravesite of Aedh, the son of The Dagda, divine king of the Tuetha De Danoan of pre-Christian Ireland; then as a seat of power for the northern branch of the Uí Néill clan, who ruled Ulster and moved here after the chieftain married Princess Aileach of Scotland; and finally as a Mass rock where Catholics worshipped in secret during the time of the Penal Laws (see **History,** p. 54-57). Much of the present stone structure is a 19th-century reconstruction, but the bottom part of the circular wall is the original. Beyond the fort, a cross marks the site of a healing well holy since pre-Christian times and supposedly blessed by St. Patrick.

The fort figures into many legends and tales, including the naming of Inishowen (the Island of Owen). Owen was the son of **Niall of the Nine Hostages,** the semi-legendary ancestor of the Uí Néill/O'Neill clan. One story claims that Niall slept with an old hag to gain sovereignty over Ireland. Once in charge, he captured young St. Patrick and brought him to Ireland as a slave. Having escaped captivity and begun his missionary work, St. Patrick baptized Niall's son Owen at this very same hillfort, consecrating the Uí Néill fortress as a Christian holy site. The prominence of Grianán Ailigh as the home of rulers ended in the 11th century when Donal McLaughlin, the Prince of Inishowen, was defeated by Brian Ború's grandson, Murtagh O'Brien. Each of O'Brien's men was ordered to carry away one stone from the royal palace of Aileach so that it could never be an outsider's seat of power. The symbolic identity of the fort survived past its physical destruction, and after the Flight of the Earls in 1607 (see **History**, p. 55, and **Rathmullan,** p. 357), Red Hugh O'Neill swore he'd return to Grianán Ailigh as high ruler of Ireland. Legend has it that Red Hugh's soldiers lie slumbering in a cave near the fort, each with one hand on the hilt of his sword and the other on the reins of his also-sleeping horse. When the new ruler of Ireland lands on the island, they will awake.

To reach the fort, turn off Derry Rd. at Bridgend on the way to Buncrana onto N13, which leads to Letterkenny. Two miles up N13 is the Catholic **Burt Circular Chapel,** a modern-day replica of the ancient fort. Just past the Circular Chapel on the N13 is the **Grianán Ailigh Heritage Center** (tel. 68000) inside a former Church of Ireland. The center can prepare you for the 2 mi. journey with informative displays and stomach-bending meals (open daily 10am-10pm; lunch specials £4; no admission charge). The fort is on top of the hill on a path behind the Circular Chapel. The 300-year-old **Burt Woods** are next to the fort. No public transport comes near the fort, so the carless will have to cycle or walk. Travelers who choose to hitch say drivers are particularly nice on the 2 mi. incline. A pleasant 9 mi. shortcut returns to Buncrana: take the first left after Burt Circular Chapel going toward Bridgend.

■ Buncrana

Long Slieve Snaght looms over Buncranca, north of Fahan, while long-sleeve Looms (Fruit of the Looms, that is) dominate the town's economy.

PRACTICAL INFORMATION A brand new **tourist office** (tel. 62600) is on Derry Rd. on the way into town beside the Inishowen Gateway Hotel. It offers maps and brochures for Buncrana and the entire peninsula and books accommodations. (Open June-Aug. daily 10am-1pm and 2-6pm.) **AIB,** 8 Market Sq. (tel. 61087; open M-W and F 10am-12:30pm and 1:30-4pm, Th 10am-12:30pm and 1:30-5pm), and **Bank of Ireland,** Main St. (tel. 61399; open M-W and F 10am-4pm, Th 10am-5pm), both have 24-hour **ATMs. Valu-Clean,** Lower Main St. (tel. 62570), is valued for its washing machines (wash and dry £4.50; open M-Sa 9am-6pm). Its competitor, **Maginn Launderette,** McGinn Ave. (tel. 62718), is nothing shabby either (wash and dry £4; open M-Sa 8:30am-7pm). **E. Tierney Chemist's,** Lower Main St. (tel. 62412), is the local pharmacy (open M-F 9am-6:30pm, Sa 9am-6pm). The **post office,** Main St. (tel. 61010), is also a newsagent (open M-F 9am-1:15pm and 2:15-5:30pm, Sa 9am-1pm).

N

Inishowen
Peninsula

Malin Head · Hell's Hole
Ballyhillion · Slieveban
Knockamany Bens · Crockalough · Glengad Head
Carrickabraghy Castle · Lagg · Glengad
Tullagh Bay · Isle of Doagh · Five Fingers Strand · Malin · Culdaff
Dunaff Head · Trawbreaga Bay · Drumaville · Templemoyle · Culdaff Bay · Dunmore Head · Tremone Bay
Lenan Head · Clonmany · Ballyliffin · Ballymagaraghy · Kinnagoe Bay
Urris · Mamore Hill · Carndonagh Cross · Carrowmena · Inishowen Head
Gap of Mamore · Effishmore · Carndonagh · Gleneely · Craignamaddy · Shroove
Dunree Head · Slieve Snaght · REPUBLIC OF IRELAND · Bredagh Glen · Greencastle
Fort Dunree · Drumfries · Moville · Greencastle Maritime Museum
Slieve Main
Lough Swilly · Tullyarvan Mill · Whitecastle · Redcastle · Lough Foyle
Glenvar · Buncrana
Saltpans · Grainne's Gap · Quigley's Point
Rathmullan · Lisfannon · Iskaheen
Fahan
Inch Island · Muff · NORTHERN IRELAND
Burnfoot · Culmore
Burt · Bridgend · Eglington Airport
Grianan of Aileach · Derry · Eglinton

Inishowen Peninsula · N. IRELAND
REPUBLIC OF IRELAND

0   3 miles
0   3 kilometers

ACCOMMODATIONS, FOOD, AND PUBS

Rattan House, Swilly Terr. (tel. 61222), has hugely comfortable rooms, a great view of Swilly Lough, and a tirelessly hospitable owner. To get there, take Derry Rd. toward the town center, turn onto Swilly Rd. just before the shorefront, then turn left onto Swilly Terr. All rooms have baths, there is a kitchen for B&Bers, and coffee and tea are always accessible (£15). **Golan View B&B,** Ardaravan Rd. (tel. 62644), is closer to Main St. It's up the hill on the right off Maginn Ave., which intersects Main St. Sunny halls complement the cheery proprietor. (Singles £20; doubles £30.)

O'Donnell's Supermarket (tel. 61719), past the bus depot away from the waterfront, sells staples behind a stunning storefront with two cheery murals of Main St. (open M-Sa 7:30am-9:30pm, Su 7:30am-8:30pm). Banks and bars and bikes bump elbows on Main St. The **Ubiquitous,** 47 Upper Main St. (tel. 62530), prides itself on its savory food for every taste, from duck to halibut, in a restaurant-pub atmosphere. The less glamorous but equally scrumptious chicken and vegetarian dishes are the cheapest deals at £7-8. (Open July-Aug. daily noon-11pm, Sept.-June M-Th 5:30-10pm, F-Sa 5:30-11pm, Su 3-10pm.) In the middle of Main St., the **Town Clock Restaurant** (tel. 62146) covers the middle ground extensively in its very typical Irish menu, with all local favorites from toasties to pizza to kebabs (open M-Sa 9am-10pm, Su 10am-10pm). The **West End Bar,** Upper Main St. (tel. 61067), has a copper bar that shines like a lucky penny and live music on weekends. **O'Flaitbeartais,** Main St. (tel. 61305), has a hunting aesthetic, but locals of all trades flock here nightly. **The Millennium Music Box,** in Market Sq. on Main St., is a den of youth culture and pop hits that glows with violet light.

SIGHTS The town's most widely promoted attraction—aside from its shore—is the community owned and operated **Tullyarvan Mill** (tel. 61613), half a mile north of town on Dunree Rd. (Main St.). *(Open Easter-Sept. daily 10am-6pm. £2, students £1.)* This renovated corn mill, which presents a mixture of historical and ecological displays, specializes in textile history, tracing Buncrana's transition from hand-weaving in 1739 to Fruit-of-the-Looming in 1999. Two castles overlook peaceful, pretty **Swan Park:** the stately Queen Anne-era **Buncrana Castle,** in which Wolfe Tone was imprisoned after the French "invasion" of 1798 failed (see **History**, p. 57); and the 1430 **O'Doherty Keep,** a not quite Arthurian castle that looks more like a derelict mansion and is closed to the public. To reach the park, walk up Main St. toward the shorefront. At the cinema crossroads, follow Castle Ave. from the roundabout next to the West End Bar and Cinema. The park is beyond the Castle Bridge, which arcs 100 yd. to the right. A **coastal walk** begins at Castle Bridge, goes past the keep, turns left at the castle, and then ascends the hill. **Ned's Point Fort,** also along the coast, was built in 1812 but is surprisingly (and not very pleasantly) modern looking. The path passes Porthaw Bay and culminates in sandy **Sragill Strand. Friar Hegarty's Rock,** beyond the beach, witnessed the friar's murder during the Penal Times (see **History,** p. 56).

■ West Inishowen

From Buncrana, the Inish Eoghin 100 runs through Dunree Head and the Mamore Gap, while R238 cuts through the interior directly to Clonmany and Ballyliffen.

■ Dunree Head and The Mamore Gap

Fort Dunree and Mamore Gap were the last area occupied in the Republic of Ireland by the British, who passed the fort to the Irish army in 1938. **Dunree Head** pokes out into Lough Swilly 6 mi. northwest of Buncrana. Salt-and-peppered peaks rise up against the ocean buffered by the occasional bend of sandy, smooth beach. At the tip of the head, **Fort Dunree** hides away in the jagged architecture of sea cliffs. *(Open June-Sept. M-Sa 10am-6pm, Su 12:30-6pm. Fort and walks £1.80, students, seniors, and children £1; walks only £2 per car.)* Surely this fort, built by the British army, will be featured as the evil agent's Celtic Tiger headquarters in some future James Bond movie. For the time being, it plays a military museum and a superb vantage point for admiring the sea-carved landscape of the Inishowen and Fanad peninsulas. An example of the Guns of Dunree, one of six built during the 1798 Presbyterian Uprising to defend Lough Swilly against hypothetical Napoleonic invaders, is among the museum's weaponry on display. The fort and five others around Lough Swilly were used in both World Wars as well. The museum's exhibits include copies of German Intelligence maps of the Inishowen Peninsula from World War II. The mammoth searchlights used in World War II have since been used to search for people lost at sea. The fort's coolest feature is its location overlooking Lough Swilly, which especially suits a bird-watcher's fancy. Explore the hills and their history with the help of the "Scenic Walks" map on display in the **coffee shop.** The shop is in a former stable, with troughs still on the wall; staff can provide basic information on the area (sandwiches £1.70; open M-Sa 11am-5pm, Su noon-5pm).

    Farther north along the Inish Eoghin 100 toward Clonmany, a sign points left to the edge of the **Mamore Gap.** This breathtaking pass teeters 800 ft. above sea level between Mamore Hill and Urris. The otherworldly views over the mountains to the Atlantic can be seen on the eastern face of the pass. The steep road through the pass proves difficult, though worthwhile, for hikers and cyclists. It's only a half hour of uphill climbing on foot, but the moderately fit biker might have to walk up this incline. It's easier to drive, although the hairpin turns over the sea are daunting. Queen Mebdh of Connacht, Cú Chulainn's archenemy in the Táin (see **Legends and Folktales,** p. 62), is supposedly buried here (and at Knocknarea, Co. Sligo, and in a few other places).

The road descends from the gap onto wave-scoured northern beaches. The Inish Eoghin 100 proceeds to Urris, Lenan Head, and inviting Lenan Strand. Once, known for its prodigious (even for Donegal) *poitín* production, Urris was the last area in Inishowen to still speak Gaelic. The subdivided flat-bed farms along the road reflect the continued influence of Famine-era farming practices. Heading north, the road passes over Dunaff Head, through Rockstown Harbour, and past Tullagh Bay. Two miles from Clonmany, the road arrives at the **Tullagh Bay Caravan and Camping Park** (tel. 76289) between the mountains and sea. One of the choicest beaches on the peninsula is just outside your tent. (£5 per 2-person tent; 50p per additional person. Showers 20p. Wash £1; dry 50p per 30min. Shop open mid.-June to Aug. daily 9:30am-9:30pm. Park open Easter-Sept. 15.)

■ Clonmany, Ballyliffen, and Doagh Island

North of the Gap, two tiny villages, **Clonmany** and **Ballyliffen,** are separated by one mile. Their combined forces make a wonderful spot to spend the night on a leisurely exploration of the Inishowen peninsula: Clonmany provides the pubs and food, while Ballyliffen has plenty of accommodations and long stretches of sandy beach kissed by crystal-clear, though raucous, ocean water. In Clonmany, grab a big bite to eat at the **Glasbody Center,** Main St. (tel. 76915), which has a friendly staff and serves homecooked meals (full entrees £2-3; open M-Th 9:30am-9pm, F-Su 9:30am-midnight). **McCarron's Pub** (tel. 76415), at the far end of Main St., is your last chance for a pint before the road along the coast, which offers nothing more than incomparably beautiful beaches and mountains. Live music on weekends ranges from country to Irish ballads. More country music and occasional trad fills the weekend air in and around **McFeeley's** (tel. 76122), across the street at Corner House. Both pubs are saturated with trad during the **Clonmany Festival** in the first week of August. **McEleney's Cycles** (tel. 76541), halfway between Clonmany and Ballyliffen, rents brand-new bikes; hours vary widely, but the shop can be easily opened by appointment (£7 per day, £30 per week; deposit £40).

Ballyliffen's highlights are a famous golf course and three long miles of golden sands on Pollan Strand. Grassy dunes connect Ballyliffen with **Doagh Island,** where **Carricksbrahy Castle,** a former seat of the MacFaul and O'Donnell clans, lies in wave-crashed ruins at the end of a 2½ mi. beach walk. Wanderers can stay at the spacious **Castlelawn House** (tel. 76600 or 76977) just behind the Strand Hotel (£18 with bath; singles £19).

Doagh Visitor's Centre (tel. 76493) can be reached by turning left off the road from Ballyliffen to Cardonagh. The way is well signposted along the one road on the land strip. The center is a large reconstruction of famine life, with real sod houses and a fascinating display of the local plants used for sustenance and medicinal purposes. Check out the bogbine, a plant that grows in mossy wetland areas, whose juice is used even today as a last-resort cure for acne. (Open daily 10am-5pm. £2.50, children £1.50. Free cup of tea at tea house.) Guided **pony-trekking** (tel. (087) 280 7334) is also available at the center.

■ North Inishowen

From the southeastern coast, R240 cuts straight up the middle of the peninsula to commercial Carndonagh, a good stop for amenities. North of Carndonagh, R238 veers east to Culdaff. Going north on R242 instead leads to Malin Head, the northernmost tip of all of Ireland.

■ Carndonagh

Two miles south of Trawbreaga Bay, "Carn" is Inishowen's main market town, where the peninsula's farmers pile in on alternate Mondays to sell sheep and cattle. Northern explorers conveniently hit upon all necessary commodities and services in this busy hub of the northern peninsula. **Inishowen Tourism,** Chapel St. (tel. 74933), just off The Diamond, is non-Bord Fáilte and remarkably helpful on the entire peninsula and books accommodations (open July to mid-Sept. daily 9:30-5:30pm, mid-Sept. to June M-F 9:30am-5:30pm). **AIB,** The Diamond (tel. 74388), is the only bank in town with a 24-hour **ATM** (open M 10am-12:30pm and 1:30-5pm, Tu-F 10am-12:30pm and 1:30-4pm). **Carn Cabs,** The Diamond (tel. 74580), provides taxis for late-night jaunts. **Tyres and Cycles,** Pound St. (tel. 74840), rents bikes for further exploration (£6 per day, £30 per week; deposit ID; open M-Sa 9am-6:30pm). **ValuClean,** Bridge St. (tel. 74150), washes and dries (£4.60; open M-Sa 9am-6pm). **McAteer's,** The Diamond (tel. 74120), is the local pharmacy (open M-Sa 10am-6pm). **G&S Supersave** (tel. 74124), in the Carnfair Shopping Centre on Bridge St., sells a full array of foods (open M-F 9am-9pm, Sa 9am-10pm, Su 11am-9pm). Also in the Carnfair Shopping Centre is **The Book Store** (tel. 74389), which offers second-hand books to relax with on the beach and a huge selection for Irish history enthusiasts (open M-Sa 11am-7pm, Su 2-7pm). The **post office,** Bridge St. (tel. 74101), handles mail with care (open M-F 9:30am-1:30pm and 2:30-5:30pm, Sa 9:30am-1pm).

About half a mile from The Diamond, Chapel St. turns into Millbrae when it hits **Dunshenny House** (tel. 74292), where dainty flowered wallpaper sets the mood (£15 with full breakfast, £13 with continental breakfast; book in advance for high season). One mile out of town on Malin Rd., **Ashdale Farmhouse B&B** (tel. 74017) has a peaceful rural setting and an atmosphere that guests rave about; the owners are friendly, the beds are marvelous, and the breakfasts are grand (singles £18, with bath £19; doubles £32, with bath £34). **The Coffee Shop,** The Diamond, is a modest but hugely popular spot where the owner is sure to give a proper welcome to new faces in Carndonagh (open M-Sa 9am-5pm). Tiny **Bradley's Bar,** Bridge St. (tel. 74526), is best known as the local "men's pub." Queen Victoria supposedly used the toilet in the men's room, although the place shows no hint of having been graced by her requisite frills. **The Arch,** The Diamond, attracts a younger clientele to its antique keg-bedecked premises. **The Quiet Lady,** Main Rd. (tel. 74777), gets noisy at night when she plays modern beats for a dance-desiring local crowd (live music W, Sa-Su; DJ Fridays).

Commercial Carn has but one sight to offer, the old Church of Ireland that hulks half a mile down Bridge St. Outside its walls, **Donagh Cross,** a 7th-century Celtic cross, is all that remains of the monastery founded by St. Patrick when he brought Christianity to the peninsula. Two ornamented shorter pillars flank the cross, one of which depicts David playing his harp. Another stands in the graveyard of the church and displays Christ's crucifixion. The church's bell supposedly came from the Spanish Armada ship *Trinidad de Valoencera,* which went down in Kinnagoe Bay.

■ Culdaff

The area surrounding Culdaff on the eastern side of the peninsula holds a variety of ancient monuments. The "Bronze Age triangle" above the Bocan Parochial House, one mile from Culdaff toward Moville, includes the **Bocan Stone Circle,** the **Temple of Deen,** and **Kindroyhead,** where evidence of a prehistoric field and fort system lies. A 4 yd. tall **high cross** stands next to the **Cloncha Church,** signposted 1½ mi. from Culdaff toward Moville. Culdaff hosts the annual **Charles Macklin Festival** (tel. 79104) in the second weekend in October, with performances of the 17th-century playwright's plays, poetry competitions, and a slew of trad sessions. Nearby **Malin Ostriches,** Ballylannon (tel. 70661), farms ostriches for their feathers, meat, and hide (open Sa-Su 1-6pm or by appointment; £1, children 50p).

Anyone on a trad pilgrimage should stop in at **McGrory's** (tel. 79104), where sessions sometimes last until dawn and the fresh food attracts half the town at dinnertime (meat and vegetarian entrees £3-6). McGrory's also does **B&B,** so you can roll out of a firm but fluffy bed and into the pub (£15). Attached to McGrory's is possibly the best live music venue in the northwest of Ireland, **Mac's Backroom Bar,** which has attracted the likes of Altan and Sharon Shannon. Chummy owners Neil and John

McGrory add their personal musical grace by regularly playing in sessions. Wednesday nights are the wildly popular "country jam" (£4; free for B&Bers) where you're likely to hear tongue-in-cheek covers of anything from Al Green to Prince (trad Tu, Th, Sa). **Culdaff Strand,** best seen at daybreak or dusk, is a short walk from McGrory's.

■ Malin Head

Travelers flock to the Inishowen peninsula to reach the northernmost tip of Ireland, although you won't feel anyone's presence among the rocky, wave-tattered coast and sky-high sand dunes of the area. Inish Eoghin 100 from Cardonagh to Malin Head passes through the tiny, tidy town of Malin. It seems as if no man could tame the wind-swept landscape past this point. Five miles from Culdaff, R242 coincides with the Inish Eoghin 100 and winds toward Lagg, where the five standing rocks of **Five Fingers Strand** jut into the dreamy blue ocean. The turquoise water looks tempting but is icy cold and dangerous for swimming. The sand dunes here are reputedly the highest in Europe, towering 100 ft. high in some places. Turn left above the little white church (at the Inish Eoghin 100 signs) to get to the top of this worthwhile detour. High above the beach, **Knockamany Bens** provide fantastic views of the whole peninsula and even Tory Island on a clear day. Clear days are disproportionately likely here; in fact, meteorologist have repeatedly measured Malin Head as the sunniest spot in Ireland.

The scattered town of **Malin Head** includes **Banba's Crown,** the northernmost tip of Ireland, a tooth of dark rock rising up from the ocean spray. Until the 19th century, Malin Head was the site of an annual pilgrimage in which young men and women "frisked and played in the water all stark naked" to celebrate the sea god's affair with the goddess of the land (see **The Wee of All Flesh,** p. 368). On a clear day, the Head offers views of the Paps of Jura in Scotland and perhaps an opportunity to hear the call of the corncrake, one of Ireland's rarest birds. A Lloyds' of London signal tower, built in 1805 by the British Admiralty to catalogue the ships sailing to and from North America, still stands sentry over the point. Written in white-washed stones on a nearby lower cliff and readable from thousands of feet above, "S. S. EIRE" (*Saor Stát Éire;* "Irish Free State") identified Ireland as neutral territory to Nazi would-be bombers. People have removed many of the stones, however, to spell out their own names nearby. A path to the left of the carpark leads to the **Hell's Hole,** a 250 ft. chasm that roars devilishly with the incoming tide. Farther down the coast arcs around the naturally formed **Devil's Bridge.** The bridge is no longer safe to walk on, so the Devil is stuck down in the hole. The raised beaches around Malin Head (the result of glaciers' passage through the region millions of years ago) are covered with semi-precious stones; walkers sifting through the sands may find jasper, quartz, small opals, or amethysts. The 5 mi. circuit of the Inish Eoghin 100 that tours the tip of the peninsula has such stunning views that it is granted the title of the **Atlantic Circle.**

The area around Malin Head teems with affordable accommodations. The **Sandrock Holiday Hostel,** Port Ronan Pier (tel. 70289), is a 15-minute walk from the turnoff from Inish Eoghin 100 by the Crossroads Inn (also a bus stop). This hostel is right on the water and affords huge views of crashing surf, and even seals, dolphins, and puffins. The view is so good that guests are often content simply to lounge in the superbly comfortable common room/kitchen space while others make their way down to the spectacular beach. (Dorms £6.50. Sheets £1. Wash £3, dry £1.50. **Bike rental** £5 per day for guests, £7 per day for non-guests.) Just past the Crossroads Inn on the bus route, the **Malin Head Hostel** (tel. 70309) welcomes guests with an open fire, reflexology, homemade elderflower cordial, and carraigan moss jam (made from a local seaweed). The rooms are impeccably clean, and Mary's garden yields fresh veggies for hostelers to buy cheap and cook in the cozy kitchen. (Dorms £6.50; twins and doubles £17. Sheets £1. Wash £2, dry £1. **Bike rental** £6 per day.) Half a mile south of the Crossroads Inn, Mrs. Doyle at **Barraicín** (tel. 70184) keeps a friendly, comfortable B&B and tends a beautiful garden. A bulletin board with maps and photos of local sights helps plan the day's agenda. If you're traveling by bus, get off at

Malin Head's only phone booth, which stands a bit past the post office. (Singles £18; doubles £30, with bath £32.) Five miles past Malin on the way into Malin Head, the first B&B is **Druin Doo** (tel. 70287), a great escape for weary travelers, especially hitchers who just aren't getting lifts to the Head. You might request their loft room, a carpenter's triumph (£14-16). A broader view recommends Mrs. Anne Hawes's **High-view B&B** (tel. 70283), another 1½ mi. down Malin Rd. past the Crossroads Inn (ask the bus driver to stop at the Parkhouse). The beds are so comfortable that you won't want to get up, and the spacious sitting room boasts a lovely, though incongruous, pastoral view. (Singles £19; doubles £32; all with bath.)

All of Malin Head's pubs have fisherman's late opening licenses and sell groceries. Trad sessions, fishing tackle, and revitalizing brew are all sold at **Farren's,** Ireland's northernmost pub (music nightly July-Aug.). It's imperative that aspiring hipsters and disaffected alike stop in at the **Seaview Bar and Restaurant,** commonly referred to as "ValDoe's." Its 12 ft. by 12 ft. bar pours your pints, while hanging shelves offer a full range of commodities from corn flakes to motor oil. Its fisherman's license means it opens at 8am and closes (supposedly) at 1am. The restaurant next door can also serve you any dish on your mind for around £3-6 (open daily 9am-10pm). **The Cottage** (tel. 70257), located along the Atlantic Circle near Bamba's Crown, provides tea, scones, crafts, and the closet thing to a tourist trap at Malin Head (open June-Aug. daily 11:30am-7pm). They also host trad sessions on Fridays from mid-July to mid-August (9:30pm; £2 per person to bring in your own alcohol). The **Curiosity Shop** (tel. 70236), farther along the Inish Eoghin 100 next to Eskie Bay, sells funky flea market goods that make Malin Head a whole lot hipper than one would think and is really a unique experience (always open). Back toward Malin along R242, **Bree Inn** (tel. 70161) delivers heaping plates of food in front of an open fire (food served daily Easter-Aug. noon-10pm; Sept.-Easter 4-10pm). Back in Malin, lift a pint at **McCleans'** (tel. 70607), a pub/grocery combo popular with the Gaelic Football Association boys.

The Wee of All Flesh

Just past Bree along the right-hand fork of R242 is the "Wee House of Malin" *(Teach na Maíobann)*. This unassuming collection of cave, well, and ruined stone church in a seaside cove epitomizes the uniquely Irish meld of pagan and Christian ritual. The well was once the site of Druidic festivals, but after its blessing by medieval St. Muirdhealach, it became the object of devout Christians' annual pilgrimages on August 15. The pilgrims' behavior, however, might not accord with usual expectations: a 17th-century observer commented that once reaching the well, male and female bathers would wash the sins off each others' naked flesh. The famed "wee house" (actually a cave behind the church) was said to fit an infinite number of people inside. In reality, the cave contains a copper mine; experts speculate that this ancient version of the clowns-in-a-car story developed from the ease with which copper was removed and the cave expanded. The young people of Malin Head still celebrate August 15, but in these prudish days they call it "Sports Day" and participate in only fully-clothed athletic events in broad daylight.

■ East Inishowen

Though overshadowed by its northern neighbor Malin Head, **Inishowen Head** draws beachbathers to the natural beauty of Shroove Strand. The most northern beaches, which look over Lough Foyle to the carnival lights of Portrush, gather small crowds on the handful of hot days in an Irish summer, and all of the beach bays invite visitors traveling by car or foot. A delightful "shore walk" about 6 mi. long runs between the small thumb of Inishowen Head and Moville. Any local can direct you to Port a Doris, a delightful little cove accessible only at low tide, with its share of semi-precious Shroove pebbles. **Tunn's Bank,** a huge sandbank a few hundred yards offshore, is reputedly the resting place of *Manannan McLir,* the Irish sea god whose children were turned into swans.

■ Greencastle and Moville

From Inishowen Head, the road leads south to **Greencastle,** a village that throws some spice (or sea salt, at least) into the one-street Irish-village mix. Institutions associated with a sophisticated fishing industry line its coast, including fishermen's schools, a net weaving factory, a maritime museum, and a fish factory. Greencastle's **castle** was built by the Red Earl of Ulster in 1305 at the center of the in-fighting that brought down the Normans. This ivy-covered ruin next to the sea is a feast for the imagination of the gluttonous Romantic. The Irish government maintains a center for training professional fishing boats next to the ruins. Relics of life on the seas from *curraghs* to trawlers are in the spotlight at the **Greencastle Maritime Museum** (tel. 81363) on the shorefront. Housed in an old coastguard station, the museum's impressive collection includes a traditional-style but newly built Fanad *curragh,* an Armada room, a wildfowling punt complete with swivel gun, a 19th-century rocket cart for rescuing passengers of wrecked ships, and plenty of ship models and photographs. (Open June-Sept. daily 10am-6pm, by appointment during the rest of the year. £2, students, seniors, and children £1.)

In a secluded mansion overlooking Lough Foyle, Mrs. Anna Wright warmly welcomes guests to the high-ceilinged, aristocratic **Manor House** (tel. 81011). To find it, walk along the beach or on the road that leads from Derry to Greencastle (£19). Also on the road from Derry is the **Brooklyn Cottage** (tel. 81087), a modest whitewashed house with all the conveniences of an modern urban apartment. You'll further appreciate its view of Lough Foyle after a conversation with its owner Peter Smith, who is also chairman of the Maritime Museum. (Singles £20, doubles £34; all with bath and TV; open Feb.-Nov.) In a spic 'n' span kitchen behind an inviting neo-Georgian storefront, **Seamy's Fish and Chips** (tel. 81371) does justice to the work of Greencastle's seamen (all meals under £2.25; open M-F noon-1am, Sa-Su 2pm-1am). Next door is **Kealy's Bay** (tel. 81010) where stacked gleaming bottles line the walls to the ceiling. While Kealy's has enough liquor to keep a trawler's worth of fishermen happy, there's only enough seating for Greencastle's tiny population. You'd better grab a seat early on Fridays and Sundays for the trad sessions. The **Greencastle Fort** (tel. 81044), next to the castle, was once a Napoleonic sea fort that housed 160 redcoats and 30 bluecoats to man nine cannons, and it has served the likes of Kaiser Wilhelm and the emperor of Japan. Today, despite extensive renovations, this inn still looks like the sight of militaristic intimidation. The inn's pub, the **Master Gunners Bar,** has great views of Rathlin Island and Giant's Causeway, affordable pub grub (meals £3-6; served daily noon-9:30pm), and spontaneous trad sessions on most summer weekend nights. **The Drunken Duck** (tel. 81362), a few miles north of Greencastle, is a friendly pub so-called because of a local woman whose beer leaked into her ducks' feeding trough—ask the bartender to pour a good pint of Guinness into yours.

A few miles farther south is the grassy, forested seaside promenade of **Moville.** **Peter Bush** at the Coast Guard Station (tel. 82402) 1 mi. out along Derry Rd. rents boats (open M-F 9am-5pm). **Inishowen Adventures** (tel. 82460), at the Moville Boat Club on Front Shore, offers sailing, windsurfing, and snorkeling (open from 2pm F-Su or by appointment; instruction available). An **AIB** (tel. 82050) with a 24-hour **ATM** is on Main St. (open M-W and F 10am-12:30pm and 1:30-4pm, Th 10am-12:30pm and 1:30-5pm). **Hannon's Pharmacy,** Main St. (tel. 82649), cures ills (open M-Sa 9:30am-6pm). The **post office** (tel. 82016) is on Malin Rd., which intersects Main St. (open M-F 9am-1pm and 2-5:30pm, Sa 9am-1pm).

The **Moville Holiday Hostel (IHH)** (tel. 82378), off Malin Rd. about 350 yd. past Main St., was lovingly converted from old stone-walled farm buildings and now emits warmth and cheer. A walk around the hostel's forested grounds will reveal the oldest bridge in Ireland, a mystical Italian ground sculpture, and beautiful land ideal for camping. Large four- and eight-bed dorms, two private rooms with bath, an organic food shop, and a kitchen/eating area with hearth comprise the hostel's pleasing interior. Hostelers get a 50% discount on the standard fare for NorthWest Busways; owners will organize cheap transportation to and from McGrory's Pub in Culdaff. (Dorms

£6; private rooms £11. Key deposit £1. Sheets £1. Towels 50p. **Camping** £4.) Next door and under the same ownership, **Gulladuff House** (tel. 82378) provides sweet, spacious, and well-antiqued rooms in the 18th-century farmhouse that once housed the tillers of the hostel's land (£13, with bath £15). At Mrs. McGuinness's **Dunroman B&B** (tel. 82234), off Derry Rd. across from the football field, breakfast is served in a sunny conservatory overlooking the River Foyle. Great green plants and murals done by the eldest daughter complete the splendid setting. (£16, with bath £17.50.) **Eamon Gillen & Sons,** Main St., will sell you all the groceries you require (open daily 10am-6pm). The local budget traveler's haven is at the **Barron's Café,** Main St. (tel. 82472), which serves heaps of food cooked in the kitchen of the family house behind the storefront. (All-day breakfast £4, burgers around £1.50, entrees £3-5; open daily 9:30am-9:30pm.) There is also a plethora of chippers and tea-shops scattered along the streets leading to the shore. Everyone from fishermen to bikers pass company at the **Hair o' the Dog Saloon** (tel. 82600), at the Lower Pier behind Main St. (live music weekends). No less than 13 other pubs grace the streets of tiny Moville—it makes for a pleasant pub crawl.

NORTHERN IRELAND

The strife that makes the North infamous hides the land's beauty and appeal from international travelers. What they're missing includes the string of seaside villages on the Ards Peninsula; the pockets of green collectively called the Glens of Antrim; the Giant's Causeway, one of the world's strangest geological sights; and the beautiful Fermanagh Lake District. Always a major industrial center, Belfast has recently become a fun, hip destination for a range of travelers and students. Pub culture and urban neighborhoods show everyday life in a divided but generally peaceful society.

The often calm tenor of life in the North has always been obscured overseas by the attention given to politics and bombs. While the North maintains a strong education system and a progressive health insurance policy, unemployment and poor housing are seen as the most pressing problems. Some writers describe the North's conflicts in terms of class. According to these essayists, the moderate middle class wants peace, but the working classes have had less to lose and have therefore historically supported the extremists. Fringe groups on both sides aren't nearly as visible as the huge division in civil society that sends Protestants and Catholics to separate neighborhoods, separate stores, separate pubs, and often separate schools, with separate, though similar, traditional songs and slang. The split can be hard to see on the north Antrim coast, where everyone's on vacation anyhow, but the separation is literally painted on the streets in Belfast and Derry. The widespread support of the 1998 Peace Agreement raises hopes of a resolution to the struggles that have divided the island for centuries.

ESSENTIALS

■ Money

AUS$1 = UK£0.36	UK£1 = AUS$2.74
CDN$1 = UK£0.40	UK£1 = CDN$2.48
IR£1 = UK£0.86	UK£1= IR£1.16
NZ$1 = UK£0.31	UK£1 = NZ$3.25
SAR1 = UK£0.10	UK£ = SAR0.39
US$1 = UK£0.61	UK£1 = US$1.63

> The information in this book was researched during the summer of 1998. Inflation and the Invisible Hand may raise or lower the listed prices by as much as 20%. The European Union's Echo Service posts daily exchange rates on the web (http://www.dna.lth.se/cgi-bin/kurt/rates?).

Legal tender in Northern Ireland and the Isle of Man is the British pound. Northern Ireland has its own bank notes, which are identical in value to English, Scottish, or Manx notes of the same denominations but not accepted outside Northern Ireland. All of these notes, however, are accepted here. U.K. coins now come in logical denominations of 1p, 2p, 5p, 10p, 20p, 50p, and £1. An old "shilling" coin is worth 5p, a "florin" 10p. "Quid," popular slang for pounds sterling, derives from *cuid,* which serves as both the singular and plural cases in Irish. Therefore the plural of quid is "quid," not "quids." Most banks are closed on Saturday, Sunday, and all public

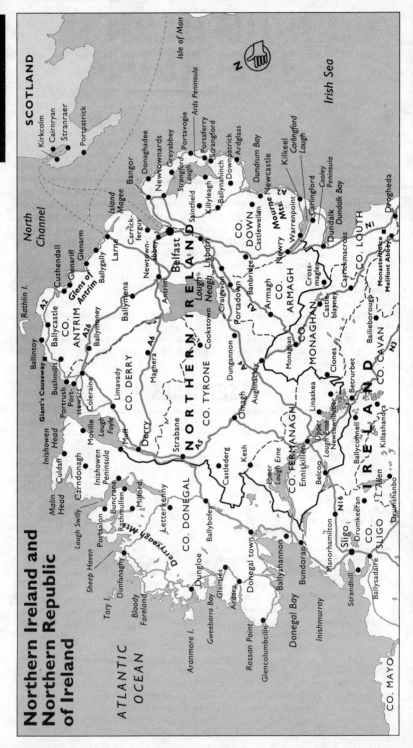

Northern Ireland and
Northern Republic
of Ireland

holidays. On "bank holidays," occurring several times a year in both countries (see **Appendix,** p. 486), most businesses shut down. Usual weekday bank hours in Northern Ireland are Monday to Friday 9:30am to 3:30pm.

For more comprehensive Ireland travel information, see p. 1-50.

■ Safety and Security

Although sectarian violence is dramatically less common than in the height of the Troubles, some neighborhoods and towns still experience turmoil during sensitive political times. It's best to avoid traveling in Northern Ireland during **Marching Season,** from July 4 to July 12 (**Orange Day;** see p. 56). The most common form of violence is property damage, and tourists are not generally targets, but transportation and services may shut down if there are problems—you don't want to be stranded. Vacation areas like the Glens and the Causeway Coast are less affected by the parades. In general, use common sense in conversation, and, as in dealing with any issues of a culture not your own, be respectful of locals' religious and political perspectives. Overall, Northern Ireland has one of the lowest crime rates in the world.

Border checkpoints have been removed and, although it is rare to see armed soldiers and vehicles in Belfast or Derry, it is still generally unsafe to hitch in Northern Ireland. Never take **photographs** of soldiers, military installations, or vehicles; if you do, your film will be confiscated and you may be detained for questioning. Taking pictures of political murals is not a crime, although some people do feel uncomfortable snapping pictures in the close-knit neighborhoods where the murals are. Don't leave your luggage unattended, since it may be viewed suspiciously—but as a savvy traveler, you probably wouldn't do that anyway if you wanted to keep it.

HISTORY AND POLITICS

There's a place called "Northern Ireland," but there are no "Northern Irish." The citizens still identify themselves along religious rather than geographic lines—as Catholics or Protestants. The 950,000 Protestants are generally Unionists, who want the six counties of Northern Ireland to remain in the U.K.; the 650,000 Catholics tend to identify with the Republic of Ireland, not Britain, and many are Nationalists, who want the six counties to be part of the Republic. The conflict between them has seemed intractable. A tentative optimism has descended upon the North since the monumental Peace Agreement of 1998, but challenges remain (see below).

For more information about northern history before the formation of the Republic, see -**Life and Times,** p. 53. Sabine Wichert's *Northern Ireland Since 1945* and Jonathan Bardon's *A History of Ulster* provide comprehensive and relatively unbiased accounts of the Troubles.

BRITISH RULE AND THE DIVISION OF IRELAND

The 17th century's **Ulster Plantation** systematically set up English and Scottish settlers on what had been Gaelic-Irish land and gave Derry to the City of London—hence the name "Londonderry" (see **History,** p. 56). Protestants fleeing France in the late 17th century sought refuge in Ulster, bringing commercial skills to the small linen-manufacturing industry. Over the following two centuries, merchants and working-class immigrants from nearby Scotland settled in northeast Ulster. Their ties to Scotland and proximity to England meant that Cos. Antrim and Down developed an Industrial Revolution economy while the rest of the island remained agricultural. By the end of the 19th century, Belfast was a booming industrial center with thriving textile and ship-building industries, most of which would not hire Catholic workers.

Protestant Unionists in the South made up a small part of the economy, but Ulster Plantation and Scottish settlement, over the course of 300 years, had created a working- and middle-class population in northeast Ulster who identified with the British

Empire and didn't support Irish Home Rule. The **Orange Order,** named after King William of Orange, who had won victories over Catholic James II in the 1690s (see **History,** p. 56), organized the Ulster Protestants and held parades to celebrate their heritage. Its constituency continued to grow long after the Act of Union in 1801 made its original mission obsolete. In the 1830s, the government attempted to dissolve the Order. It quietly gained momentum, however, until its explosive opposition to the first Home Rule Bill in 1886 (see p. 59).

Edward Carson and his ally **James Craig** translated Ulster Unionism into terms the British elite understood. When Home Rule looked likely in 1911, Carson held a mass meeting, and Unionists signed the Ulster Covenant of Resistance to Home Rule (1912). In 1914, when Home Rule appeared imminent, the Unionist **Ulster Volunteer Force (UVF)** armed itself by smuggling guns in through Larne—an act that inspired Nationalists to smuggle their own guns in through Howth. World War I gave Unionists more time to organize and gave British leaders time to see that the imposition of Home Rule on all of Ulster would mean havoc as the UVF fought the **Irish Republican Army (IRA),** who in turn fought the police. The 1920 Government of Ireland Act created two parliaments for North and South. The Act of Union went nowhere in the south and was quickly superseded by the Anglo-Irish Treaty and Civil War (see p. 60), but the measure—intended as a temporary one—became the basis of Northern Ireland's government until 1973. The new Parliament met at **Stormont,** near Belfast.

The new statelet included only six of the nine counties in the province of Ulster. This arrangement suited the one million Protestants there, yet it threatened the several hundred thousand Protestant Unionists living elsewhere on the island and the half million Catholic Nationalists living within the six Northern counties. Carson and Craig had approved these odd borders, hoping to create the largest possible area with a permanent Protestant majority. Craig, as the North's first Prime Minister, his successor **Sir Basil Brooke,** and most of their Cabinet ministers thought in terms, as Brooke put it, of "a Protestant state for a Protestant people." Orange lodges and other strongly Protestant groups continued to control politics, and the Catholic minority boycotted elections. Anti-Catholic discrimination was widespread. The **Royal Ulster Constabulary (RUC),** the new and Protestant police force in the North, filled its ranks with part-time policemen called Bs and **B-Specials,** a major source of Catholic casualties and outrage. The IRA continued sporadic campaigns in the North through the 20s and 30s with little result. The IRA in the Irish State was gradually suppressed.

The depressing 30s sent the Northern economy into the dumps, requiring more and more British subsidies, while the Stormont Cabinet aged and withered. **World War II** gave Unionists a chance to show their loyalty. The Republic of Ireland stayed neutral and stayed out, but the North welcomed Allied troops, ships, and air force bases. The need to build and repair warships raised employment in Belfast, especially among Catholics. The Luftwaffe firebombed Belfast toward the end of the war, making it one of the U.K.'s most damaged cities. In May 1945, Churchill thanked the North and attacked Éire's neutrality in a famous speech.

Over the following two decades, a grateful British Parliament poured money into Northern Ireland. The North's standard of living stayed higher than the Republic's, but discrimination and joblessness persisted. The government at Stormont failed to match social reforms across the water, parliamentary districts were painfully and unequally drawn to favor Protestants, and religious sectarianism frustrated labor activists. Large towns were segregated by religion, perpetuating the cultural separation. After a brief, unsuccessful try at school desegregation, Stormont ended up granting subsidies to Catholic schools. Violence had receded, and barring the occasional border skirmish, the IRA was seen as finished by 1962 and received a formal, eulogy-like farewell in the New York Times. **Capt. Terence O'Neill,** who became the third Stormont Prime Minister in 1963, tried to enlarge the economy and soften discrimination, meeting in 1965 with the Republic's Prime Minister, Sean Lemass. O'Neill may have epitomized the liberal Unionist attitude when he said, "If you treat Roman Catholics with due kindness and consideration, they will live like Protestants."

THE TROUBLES

The economy grew, but the bigotry stayed, as did the Nationalist community's bitterness. The American civil rights movement inspired the 1967 founding of the **Northern Ireland Civil Rights Association (NICRA)**, which tried to end anti-Catholic discrimination in public housing. NICRA tried to distance itself from constitutional concerns, although many Catholics didn't get the message: the Nationalist song "A Nation Once Again" often drowned out "We Shall Overcome" in demonstrations. Protestant extremists included the forceful **Dr. Ian Paisley**, whose **Ulster Protestant Volunteers (UPV)** overlapped in membership with the illegal, paramilitary, resurrected UVF. The first NICRA march was raucous but nonviolent. The second, in Derry in May 1968, was a bloody mess disrupted by Unionists and then by the RUC's water cannons. This incident is usually thought of as the culmination of the Troubles.

Catholic **John Hume** and Protestant **Ivan Cooper** formed a new civil rights committee in Derry but were overshadowed by Bernadette Devlin's student-led, radical **People's Democracy (PD)**. The PD encouraged, and NICRA opposed, a four-day march from Belfast to Derry starting on New Year's Day, 1969. Paisleyite harassment was nothing compared to the RUC's assault on Derry's Catholic Bogside once the marchers arrived. After that, Derry authorities agreed to keep the RUC out of the Bogside, and this area became **Free Derry** to Catholics. O'Neill, granting more civil rights concessions in hopes of calming everyone down, was deserted by more of his hardline Unionist allies. On August 12, 1969, Catholics based in Free Derry threw rocks at the annual Orange parade through the city. The RUC attacked the Catholics, and a two-day siege ensued. Free Derry claimed victory, but the violence showed that the RUC could not maintain order alone. The British Army arrived—and still has not left.

O'Neill quit in 1969. Between '70 and '72, Stormont leaders alternated concessions and crackdowns, to little effect. The rejuvenated IRA split in two, with the Marxist "Official" faction practically fading into insignificance as the new **Provisional IRA**, or **Provos** (the IRA we primarily hear about today), took aim at the Protestants. The British troops became the IRA's main target. While the **Social Democratic and Labor Party (SDLP)** was founded in 1970 and had become, by '73, the moderate political voice of Northern Catholics, British policies of internment without trial outraged Catholics and led the SDLP to withdraw from government. The pattern was clear: any concessions to the Catholic community might provoke Protestant violence, while anything that seemed to favor the Unionists risked explosive IRA response.

On January 30, 1972, British troops fired into a crowd of protesters in Derry; the famous event, called **Bloody Sunday**, and the reluctance of the ensuing British investigation increased Catholic outrage. Thirty-one Catholics were killed: the soldiers claimed they were fired at first, while Catholics say the soldiers shot unarmed marchers in the backs as they fled. Only now is the incident being officially re-examined, with hearings scheduled for February 1999. On February 2, the British embassy in Dublin was burned down. Soon thereafter, the Official IRA bombed a British army barracks. After further bombings in 1973, Stormont was dissolved and replaced by the **Sunningdale executive**, which split power between Catholics and Protestants. This policy was immediately crippled by a massive Unionist work stoppage, and a policy of **direct British rule** from Westminster began. A referendum that year, asking if voters wanted Northern Ireland to remain part of the United Kingdom, showed that voters supported the Union at a rate of 90 to 1—Catholics had boycotted the polls. The verdict didn't stop the violence, which brought an average of 275 deaths per year between 1970 and 1976.

In 1978, 300 Nationalist prisoners in the Maze Prison in Northern Ireland began a campaign to have their special category as political prisoners restored. The campaign's climax was the 10-man H-Block **hunger strike** of '81. The leader, Bobby Sands, was the first to go on hunger strike. He was elected to Parliament from a Catholic district in Tyrone and Fermanagh even as he starved to death. Sands died after 66 days and became a prominent martyr; his face is still seen on murals in the Falls section of Belfast. The remaining prisoners officially ended the strike on October 3.

Sands's election was no anomaly. The hunger strikes galvanized Nationalists, and support for **Sinn Féin,** the political arm of the IRA, surged in the early 80s. British Prime Minister Margaret Thatcher and Taoiseach Garret FitzGerald signed the **Anglo-Irish Agreement** at Hillsborough Castle in November 1985. The Agreement grants the Republic of Ireland a "consultative role" but no legal authority in the governance of Northern Ireland. It improved relations between London and Dublin but infuriated extremists on both sides. Protestant paramilitaries began to attack the British Army, while the IRA continued its bombing campaigns in England. In 1991 and 92, the Brooke Initiative led to the first multi-party talks in the North in over a decade, but they did not include Sinn Féin. In December 1993, the **Downing Street Declaration,** issued by John Major and Taoiseach Albert Reynolds, invited the IRA to participate in talks if they refrained from violence for three months.

THE 1994 CEASEFIRE

On August 31, 1994, the IRA announced a complete cessation of violence. While Loyalist guerillas cooperated by announcing their own ceasefire, Unionist leaders bickered over the meaning of the IRA's statement; in their opinion, it did not go far enough. Nonetheless, **Gerry Adams,** Sinn Féin leader, defended the statement and called for direct talks with the British government. The peace held for over a year.

In February 1995, John Major and John Bruton issued the **joint framework** proposal. The document suggested the possibility of a new Northern Ireland Assembly that would include the "harmonizing powers" of the Irish and British governments and the right of the people of Northern Ireland to choose their own destiny. Subsequently, the British government began talks with both Loyalists and, for the first time, Sinn Féin. Disarmament was the most prominent problem in the 1995 talks—neither the IRA nor Protestant groups would agree to give up its weapons.

A flurry of tragic events left the future of Northern Ireland as tenuous as ever. The IRA ended their ceasefire on February 9, 1996, with the bombing of an office building in London's Docklands. Despite this setback, the stalled peace talks, now chaired by U.S. diplomat George Mitchell, were finally slated for June 10, 1996. Ian Paisley, now leader of the extreme **Democratic Unionist Party (DUP),** objected to Mitchell's appointment, calling it a "dastardly deed," but did not boycott the talks. The talks proceeded sluggishly and precariously. Sinn Féin did not participate in these talks because it did not agree to the **Mitchell principles,** which included the total disarmament of all paramilitary organizations. Despite this exclusion, Sinn Féin's popularity grew in Northern Ireland: in the May elections, they gathered 15% of the vote. The credibility of Sinn Féin, however, was seriously jeopardized on June 15, 1996, when a blast in a busy Manchester shopping district injured more than 200 people.

Violence flared surrounding **Orange Day, 1996,** when the Parades Commission banned an Orange Order march through a Catholic section of Portadown. Protestants reacted by throwing petrol bombs, bricks, and bottles at police, who answered with plastic bullets. After four days of violence, police allowed the marchers to go through, but this time Catholics responded with a hail of debris. Nightly rioting by both sides also took place in Belfast, where RUC policemen were wounded, and in Derry, where Catholic Dermot McShane died after being run over by a jeep.

On October 7, the IRA bombed British army headquarters in Belfast, killing one soldier and injuring thirty, in the first bombing in Northern Ireland in two years. In early 1997, the IRA tried to make Northern Ireland an issue in the upcoming elections in Great Britain by making several bomb threats, including one that postponed the Grand National horse race. No one was injured, but public ire was aroused and John Major condemned Sinn Féin.

In May of 1997, the Labour party swept the British elections and **Tony Blair** became Prime Minister, bringing hope for peaceful change. Sinn Féin made its most impressive showing yet: Gerry Adams and member Martin McGuinness won seats in Parliament but were barred from taking their seats by their refusal to swear allegiance to the Queen. Despite this act, the government ended its ban on talks with Sinn Féin. Sinn Féin, however, refused to join the talks. Hopes for a ceasefire were dashed when the car of a prominent Irish republican was bombed; in retaliation, the IRA shot two members of the RUC.

GOOD FRIDAY AGREEMENT AND RECENT EVENTS

The British government's Northern Ireland Secretary **Mo Mowlam** had a rough introduction to her new job: **marching season** in 1997 was the most violent since before the ceasefire. The Orange Order held a large march through the town of Portadown a week before Orange Day. More than 80 people were hurt in the ensuing rioting and looting, and Mowlam came under scrutiny for allowing the parade to go on without considering the consequences. On July 10, the Orange Order called off and re-routed a number of contentious parades, offering hope for peace. The marches that were held were mostly peaceful; police fired plastic bullets at rioters in Derry and Belfast, but there were no casualties. On July 19, the IRA announced an "unequivocal" **ceasefire** to start the following day.

In September 1997, Sinn Féin joined the peace talks. Members of the **Ulster Unionist Party (UUP),** the voice of moderate Protestants, joined shortly thereafter and were attacked by Ian Paisley and the DUP for sitting with terrorists. David Trimble, leader of the UUP, assured Protestants that he wouldn't negotiate directly with Sinn Féin. Co-founders of the recently formed, religiously mixed **Northern Ireland Women's Coalition,** Catholic Monica McWilliams and Protestant Pearl Sagar brought a human rights agenda and a strong commitment to peace to the talks, where they were subjects of derision by Ian Paiseley.

Some groups still opposed the peace process. In January 1998, another 12 people were killed by sectarian violence, mostly committed by extremist Loyalists against Catholic civilians. After two Protestants were killed by Catholic extremists in early February, Unionist leaders charged Sinn Féin with breaking its pledge to support only peaceful actions toward political change and tried to oust party leaders from the talks. Mitchell, Mowlam, Blair, and Irish Prime Minister Bertie Ahern continued to push for progress, holding the group to a strict deadline in April.

After an interminable week of late-night negotiations, the delegates approved a draft of the **1998 Northern Ireland Peace Agreement** in the early morning after April 10, Good Friday. The Agreement above all emphasized that change in Northern Ireland could come only with the consent of the majority of its people. It declared that the "birthright" of the people is the right to choose whether to personally identify as Irish, British, or both; even as the status of Northern Ireland changes, the Agreement says, residents retain the right to hold Irish or British citizenship.

On Friday, May 22, in the first island-wide vote since 1918, residents of both the North and the Republic voted the Agreement into law. A resounding 71% of the North voted yes, and the Agreement won 94% of the vote in the Republic. Overall, 85% of the island voted yes, meaning that a majority of Protestants voted in favor of the Peace Agreement, which divided governing responsibilities of Northern Ireland into three strands. The main body, a new 108-member **Northern Ireland Assembly,** assigns committee posts and chairs proportionately to the parties' representation. Catholics see this body as an opportunity for reclaiming the political power they were long denied. On June 25, the UUP and the SDLP won the most seats, and Sinn Féin garnered more support than ever before, winning 18 assembly seats and two in the executive. David Trimble of the UUP and Seamus Mallon of the SDLP were elected First Minister and Deputy First Minister, respectively, by the assembly. The second strand, a **North-South Ministerial Council,** serves as the cross-border authority. At least 12 possible areas of focus were under consideration by them in 1998, including social welfare issues such as education, transportation and urban planning, environmental protection, tourism, and EU programs. The final strand, the **British-Irish Council,** approaches similar issues as the North-South Council but operates on a broader scale, concerning itself with the entire British Isles.

The Agreement included two other major provisions: it required the decommissioning of all paramilitary and terrorist groups' arms and called for the early release of political prisoners. Political parties whose military wings did not disarm themselves by the time of the June elections would not be able to assume their seats in the Assembly. Tensions rose out of the **Northern Ireland (Sentences) Bill,** voted against by members of the UUP, the DUP, and the British Conservative Party, splitting the UK Parliament for the first time during the talks. The bill will release all political prisoners, including those convicted of murder, by 2000; the dissenters fear that the bill did not sufficiently link the release of any prisoner to his organization's full disarmament.

While most felt that Northern Ireland was finally on the verge of lasting peace, a few controversial issues remained unresolved. Sinn Féin called for disbanding the still very largely Protestant RUC, which was cited in an April 1998 United Nations report for its systematic intimidation and harassment of lawyers representing those accused of paramilitary crimes. Blair declared that the RUC will continue to exist, but in June appointed Chris Patten, the former governor of Hong Kong, to head a small one-year commission to review the RUC's recruiting, hiring, and training practices, as well as its culture and symbols.

The 1998 marching season brought challenges and tragedy to the newly arrived peace. In the end of May, just a week after the Agreement was voted in, a march by the Junior Orange Order provoked violence on Garvaghy Rd., the Catholic zone in the largely Protestant Portadown where violence had erupted at a 1996 parade. In light of this disturbance, the Parades Commission hesitated in granting the Orange Day marching permits. On June 15, the Parades Commission rerouted the Tour of the North, banning it from entering the Catholic Cliftonville Rd.-Antrim Rd. areas in Belfast. Aside from two short stand-offs with the RUC, the parade proceeded without conflict. The day after the assembly elections, however, violence broke out between Nationalists and policemen at a parade in West Belfast. The beginning of July saw a wave of violence that included hundreds of bombings and attacks on security forces as well as a slew of arson attacks on Catholic churches.

Other parades passed peacefully, but a stand-off began over the fate of the **Drumcree** parade. This Orange parade, which occurs July 4, was not given permission to march down the Catholic section of Garvaghy Rd. in Portadown. Angered by the decision but encouraged by a history of indecision by the British government, thousands of people participated in a week-long standoff with the RUC that affected the whole country. Rioting occurred there and elsewhere, and Protestant marchers were angered by what they saw as the disloyalty of their own police force. Neither the Orangemen nor the Parade Commission would budge, and the country looked with anxiety toward Orange Day, July 12, which would be the climax of the tense situation. On July 11, however, a Catholic home in almost entirely Protestant Ballymoney was firebombed in the middle of the night by local hooligans, and three boys, Richard, Mark, and Jason Quinn, were killed. The Church of Ireland publicly called for the end of the Drumcree protest. The seemingly intractable stand-off, though never officially ended by extreme Protestant leaders, faded away. Although some tried to distance the attack from the events going on at Drumcree, the murders led both to a reassessment of the Orange Order and to a new sobriety about the peace process.

On August 15, 1998, the 29th anniversary of the deployment of British troops in Northern Ireland, a bombing in the religiously mixed town of **Omagh,** County Tyrone, left dozens dead and hundreds injured. Initial analysis blamed a group calling itself the "Real IRA," thought to be the reincarnation of the Official IRA from the early 70s. The obvious motive for the attack, the worst atrocity of the Trouble, was to undermine the Agreement. However, the terrible act could only underline the fact that most people in Northern Ireland, both Catholic and Protestant, had voted for the agreement, and Sinn Féin's Gerry Adams unreservedly condemned the attack. At the time of printing, it remains to be seen whether the acts of extremists will defeat the will of the people of Northern Ireland.

BELFAST

The second-largest city on the island, Belfast (pop. 330,000) is the center of the North's cultural, commercial, and political activity. The surrounding hills appear suddenly at the end of streets filled with a century's worth of industry. Victorian architecture, acclaimed theater, and the annual arts festival in November maintain Belfast's reputation as a thriving artistic center. West Belfast's political graffiti art and famous murals are both informative and truly moving. The burgeoning bar scene—a mix of British pub culture, Irish pub culture, and less traditional international trends—entertains locals, foreigners, and the lively student population. The past few years have brought a chic cosmopolitan edge to this growing city, which, despite a significant visitor presence, seems unlikely to succumb to tourist culture.

Belfast began as a base for "Scots-Irish" Presbyterian settlement in the 17th century and was William of Orange's base during his battles against King James II in 1690 (see **The Protestant Ascendancy,** p. 56). In the 19th century, Belfast became an industrial center with world-famous factories and shipyards. Gathering slums, smoke, flax mills, and social theorists, Belfast continued to grow and by 1900 looked much more British than Irish, especially as the ship-building industry regularly drew Scottish laborers across the channel for jobs. During the Troubles, armed British soldiers patrolled the streets, frequent military checkpoints slowed traffic and pedestrians, and stores advertised "Bomb Damage Sales." The Troubles, however, may have had unintended positive results, from the black taxi services started in response to a bus strike to the prosperous shopping area that grew out of ban of cars downtown—a lesson for urban planners everywhere.

ORIENTATION

Buses arrive at the Europa bus station on **Great Victoria St.** near several landmarks: the Europa hotel, the Crown Liquor Saloon, and the Opera House. To the northeast is the City Hall in **Donegall Square.** A busy pedestrian shopping district extends north four blocks between City Hall and enormous Castlecourt Shopping Centre. Donegall Pl. becomes Royal Ave. and runs from Donegall Square through the shopping area. In the eastern part of the shopping district is the **Cornmarket** area, where several centuries of characteristically Belfast architecture remain in the face of modern establishments. South of the bus station, Great Victoria St. meets Dublin Rd. at **Shaftesbury Sq.** The stretch of Great Victoria St. running between the bus station and Shaftesbury Sq. is known as the **Golden Mile** for its highbrow establishments and Victorian architecture. Botanic Ave. and Bradbury Pl. (which becomes University Rd.) extend south from Shaftesbury Sq. into the **Queen's University area,** where many cafés, students pubs, and budget accommodations await. In this far southern area of the city, the busiest neighborhoods center around Stranmillis, Malone, and Lisburn Rd. The city center, Golden Mile, and university area are quite safe for tourists; Belfast in general is safer than most American cities.

Divided from the rest of Belfast by the Westlink Motorway, working class **West Belfast** is more politically volatile than the city center. There remains a sharp division between sectarian neighborhoods. The Protestant neighborhood stretches along Shankill Rd., just north of the Catholic neighborhood, centered around Falls Rd. The two are separated by the **peace line.** The River Lagan divides industrial **East Belfast** from the rest of the city. The shipyards and docks that brought Belfast fame and fortune extend north on both sides of the river as it grows into **Belfast Lough.**

M1 and M2 motorways join to form a backwards "C" through Belfast. A1 branches off from M1 around Lisburn and heads south to Newry, where it changes to N1 before continuing through Dundalk and Drogheda to Dublin. M2 merges into A6 then heads northwest to Derry. Larne is connected to Belfast by the A8.

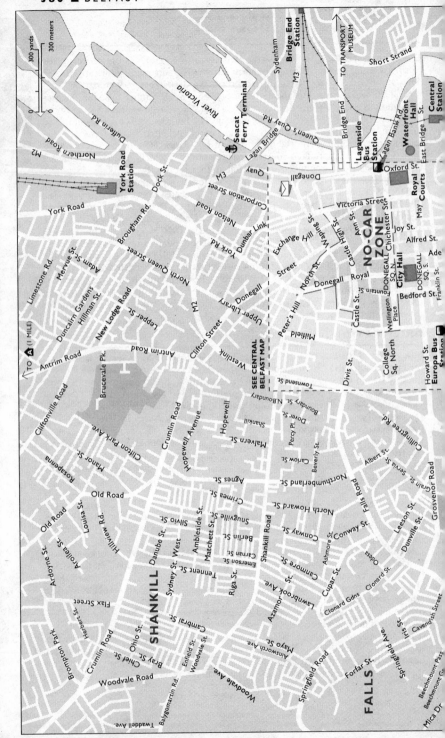

300 yards
300 meters

M2

Northern Road

Dufferin Rd.

River Victoria

York Road Station

York Road

Brougham Rd.

Dock St.

Nelson Road

Corporation Street

M3

Dunbar Link

York Rd.

Seacat Ferry Terminal

Lagan Bridge

Queen's Quay Rd.

Quay

Donegall

Sydenham

M3

Bridge End Station

Bridge End

TO TRANSPORT MUSEUM

Short Strand

Laganside Bus Station

Lagan Bank Rd.

Waterfront Hall

Central Station

East Bridge St.

Oxford St.

Royal Courts

May St.

Victoria Street

Exchange Hill

Street

North St.

Donegall

Waring St.

Castle High St.

Ann St.

Chichester St.

Joy St.

Alfred St.

Ade

NO-CAR ZONE

City Hall

DONEGALL SQ. N.

DONEGALL SQ. S.

Franklin St.

Bedford St.

Royal Ave.

Wellington Pl.

Donegall Place

Castle St.

Fountain St.

Peter's Hill

Millfield

College Sq. North

Howard St.

Europa Bus Station

Divis St.

Townsend St.

SEE CENTRAL BELFAST MAP

Limestone Rd.

Mervue St.

Adam St.

Duncairn Gardens

Hillman St.

New Lodge Road

Lepper St.

North Queen Street

Donegall

Upper Library

M2

Clifton Street

Westlink

Antrim Road

Brucevale Pk.

Cliftonville Road

Clifton Park Ave.

Manor St.

Rosapenna

Old Road

Louisa St.

Ardoyne St.

Agnes St.

Crumlin Road

Hopewell Avenue

Hopewell

Malvern St.

Shankill

Dover St.

Boundary St.

N. Boundary

Percy Pl.

Carlow St.

Beverly St.

Albert St.

Cullingtree Rd.

Grosvenor Road

Leeson St.

Serria St.

Grain St.

Servia St.

Dunville St.

Odeca

Conway St.

Ashmore St.

North Howard St.

Falls Road

Northumberland St.

Crimea St.

Silvio St.

Danube St.

Ambleside St.

Matchet St.

Berlin St.

Caran St.

Emerson St.

Snugville St.

Shankill Road

Conway St.

Cupar St.

Clonard Gdns.

Clonard St.

Clonard St.

Cambrai St.

Tennent St. West

Sydney St. West

Riga St.

Mayo St.

Ainsworth Ave.

Lambrook Ave.

Azamor St.

Cammore St.

Springfield Road

Forfar St.

Iris St.

Cavendish Street

Springfield Ave.

SHANKILL

FALLS

Flax Street

Herbert St.

Brompton Park

Crumlin Road

Chief St.

Bray St.

Ohio St.

Enfield St.

Woodvale St.

Woodvale Ave.

Ballygomartin Rd.

Woodvale Road

Twaddell Ave.

Hillview Rd.

TO A (1 MILE)

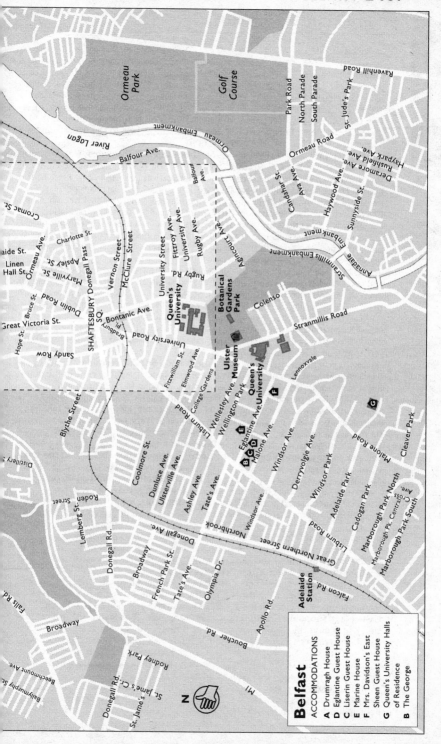

Belfast

ACCOMMODATIONS

- A Drumragh House
- D Eglantine Guest House
- C Liserin Guest House
- E Marine House
- F Mrs. Davidson's East
- Sheen Guest House
- G Queen's University Halls of Residence
- B The George

PRACTICAL INFORMATION

Transportation

Airports: Belfast International Airport (tel. (01232) 422888) in Aldergrove. **Aer Lingus** (tel. (0645) 737747), **British Airways** (tel. (0345) 222111), **Jersey European** (tel. 457200), **British Midlands,** and **Air UK** land here. **Airbus** (tel. 333000) runs to Belfast's Europa/Glengall St. bus station in the city center (M-Sa every 30min. 6:30am-9:30pm, Su about every hr. 7am-8:45pm; £4.50, £7.50 return). **Belfast City Airport,** at the harbor, receives flights by **Manx Airlines** (tel. (0345) 256256) and **Jersey European. Trains** run from the airport to Central Station (M-F 31 per day, Sa 26 per day, Su 2 per day, 60p).

Trains: All trains arrive at Belfast's **Central Station,** East Bridge St. (tel. 899400). Some also stop at **Botanic Station** (tel. 899400), on Botanic Ave. in the center of the University area, or the **Great Victoria Station** (tel. 434424), next to the Europa Hotel. Trains roll in from **Derry** (2½hr., M-F 7 per day, Sa 6 per day, Su 4 per day, £5.50) and **Dublin** (2½hr., M-F 8 per day, Sa 7 per day, Su 3 per day, £15). Call for info on other destinations. To get to Donegall Sq. from Central Station, turn left and walk down East Bridge St. Turn right on Victoria St. then left after 2 blocks onto May St., which runs into Donegall Sq. South. A better option for those disoriented or encumbered with luggage is the **Centrelink** bus service, free with rail tickets (see **Local Transportation,** below).

Buses: There are two main stations in Belfast. Buses traveling to and from the west and the Republic operate out of the **Europa (Glengall St.) Station** (tel. 333000; open for inquiries M-Sa 7:30am-8:30pm, Su 9am-7:30pm). Buses to **Dublin** (M-Sa 7 per day, Su 3 per day, £10.50) and **Derry** (M-Sa 15 per day, Su 6 per day, £6.50). Call for other route info. Buses to and from Northern Ireland's east coast operate out of **Laganside Station** (same tel. and hours as Europa). The **Leaping Leprechaun** bus service (tel. (015047) 42655) takes hostelers to and from IHH hostels on the Antrim coast. Full ticket £18.

Ferries: To reach the city center from the **Belfast SeaCat terminal** (tel. (01345) 523523), you have two options. If you're arriving late at night or early in the morning, a taxi is your best bet; the docks can be somewhat unsafe at night. If on foot, take a left when you exit the terminal on to Donegall Quay. Turn right onto Albert Sq. about 2 blocks down at the Customs House (a big Victorian stone building). After 2 more short blocks, turn left on Victoria St. (not Great Victoria St.). Turn right again at the clock tower onto High St., which runs into Donegall Pl. Here, a left will lead you to the City Hall and Donegall Sq. (at the end of the street), where you can catch a **Centrelink** bus (see **Local Transportation,** below). **Larne ferry terminals** are easily accessible by bus or train from the Belfast city center. (Buses 1hr., M-F 17 per day, Sa 15 per day, Su 3 per day, £2.60.) For information on ferries and hovercraft to Belfast from **England** and **Scotland,** see **By Ferry,** p. 33.

Local Transportation: The red **Citybus Network** (24hr. recorded info tel. 246485), is supplemented by **Ulsterbus** "blue buses" to the suburbs. Travel within the city center 50p, seniors and children 25p. Citybuses going south and west leave from Donegall Sq. East; those going north and east leave from Donegall Sq. West (80p). Money-saving 4-journey tickets £2.70, seniors and children £1.35. 7-day **"gold cards"** allow unlimited travel in the city (£10.50). 7-day **"silver cards"** permit unlimited travel in either North Belfast, West/South Belfast, or East Belfast (£11). All transport cards and tickets can be bought from kiosks in Donegall Sq. and around the city (open M-Sa 8am-6pm). The **Centrelink** green bus connects all of the major areas of Belfast in the course of its cloverleaf-shaped route (Donegall Sq., Castlecourt Shopping Centre, Europa and Langanside Bus Stations, Northern Ireland Rail Station, and Shaftesbury Sq.). The buses can be caught at any of 12 designated stops (every 15 min., M-F 7:15am-8:30pm, Sa 8:35am-8:30pm, 50p, free with bus or rail ticket). Late **Nightline** buses cover 5 extensive routes from Shaftesbury Sq. to various parts of the city. Tickets must be bought in advance from ticket units in Shaftesbury Sq. (open F-Sa until 1 and 2am, £2).

Taxis: Huge **black cabs** run set routes to West and North Belfast, collecting and discharging passengers along the way (standard 60p charge). Cabs heading to Catholic neighborhoods are marked with a Falls Rd., Andersontown, or Irish-language sign; those going to Protestant neighborhoods have a Shankill sign or a red poppy. Yellow-plated black cabs are official City Hall-registered vehicles. Ordinary 24hr. metered cabs abound: **City Cab** (tel. 242000; wheelchair accessible), **Diamond Taxi Service** (tel. 646666), **Fon a Cab** (tel. 233333), and **Jet Taxi** (tel. 323278).

Car Rental: McCausland's, 21-31 Grosvenor Rd. (tel. 333777), is Northern Ireland's largest car rental company. £39 per day, £170 per week. £10 surcharge to drive in the Republic. Ages 21-70. Open M-Th 8:30am-6:30pm, F 8:30am-7:30pm, Sa 8:30am-5pm, Su 8:30am-1pm. 24hr. car return at all offices. Other offices at **Belfast International Airport** (tel. (01849) 422022) and **Belfast City Airport** (tel. 454141). **Budget,** 96-102 Great Victoria St. (tel. 230700). £39-59 per day, £195-395 per week. Drop-off charge for Dublin £50, Galway £75. Ages 23 and over. Open M-F 9am-5:30pm, Sa 9am-1:30pm. **Belfast International Airport Office** (tel. (01849) 23332) open daily 7:30am-11:30pm; **Belfast City Airport** office (tel. (01232) 541111) open daily 8am-9:30pm.

Bike Rental: McConvey Cycles, 10 Pottingers Entry (tel. 330322) or 467 Ormeau Rd. (tel. 491163). £7 per day, £40 per week; deposit £30; panniers £5 per week; locks supplied. Open M-Sa 9am-5:30pm. **ReCycle Bicycle Hire,** 1-5 Albert Sq. (tel. 313113), will pick up cycles M-F from Belfast hostels. F-M £11 per day, Tu-Th £9 per day; £30 per week; £50 or passport deposit; locks and helmets supplied. Open M-Sa 9am-5pm.

Hitching: Notoriously hard in and out of Belfast—most people take the bus out as far as Bangor or Larne before they stick out a thumb.

Tourist and Financial Services

Tourist Office: St. Anne's Court, 59 North St. (tel. 246609). Supplies a great booklet on Belfast, the usual info on the surrounding areas, and an excellent map of the city with bus schedules (free). Staff will get you where you need to go and find you a place to stay (in summer, call until 7:30pm for accommodations), but doesn't have the resources for much more. A 24hr. computerized info bank outside helps travelers arriving at all times. Open July-Aug. M-F 9am-7pm, Sa 9am-5:15pm, Su noon-4pm; Sept.-June M-Sa 9am-5:15pm.

Irish Tourist Board (Bord Fáilte), 53 Castle St. (tel. 327888). Provides info on the Republic and makes reservations for accommodations "south of the border." Open Apr.-Sept. M-F 9am-5pm, Sa 9am-12:30pm; Oct.-Mar. M-F 9am-5pm.

Travel Agency: USIT, 13b The Fountain Centre, College St. (tel. 324073), near Royal Ave. Sells ISICs, European Youth Cards, **TravelSave** stamps (£5.50), and virtually every kind of bus or rail pass imaginable. Books ferries and planes, and compiles round-the-world itineraries. Open M and W-F 9:30am-5pm, Tu 10am-5pm, Sa 10am-1pm. **Additional office** at Queen's University Student Union (tel. 241830). Open M-Tu and Th-F 9:30am-5:30pm, W 10am-5pm.

Youth Hostel Association of Northern Ireland (YHANI): 22 Donegall Rd. (tel. 324733). Books YHANI hostels free, international hostels for £2.80. Sells HI membership cards (£7, under 18 £3). Open M-F 9am-5pm.

Consulates: U.S. Consulate General, Queens House, Queen St. (tel. 228239). Open M-F 1-4pm. **Canada, Australia, Republic of Ireland, South Africa,** and **New Zealand** are not represented.

Banks: Banks and ATMs are a dime a dozen in Belfast; there is at least one on every corner. The major offices are **Ulster Bank,** 47 Donegall Pl. (tel. 244744); **First Trust,** 8 Donegall Sq. South (tel. 324463); **Bank of Ireland,** 54 Donegal Pl. (tel. 244901); and **Northern Bank,** Donegall Sq. West (tel. 245277). UK holders of **Barclays** bank accounts should contact the Barclays office, Water's Edge 25, Clarendon Park (tel. 320105), open M-F 9am-5pm. Most banks are open 9am-4:30pm and have 24hr. **ATMs.**

Currency Exchange: Thomas Cook, 22-24 Lombard St. (tel. 236044). Cashes Thomas Cook traveler's checks with no commission, others with 2% commission. Open M-F 9am-5:30pm. **Belfast International Airport office** (tel. (01849) 422536). Open May-Oct. M 5:30am-11pm, Tu-Th 5am-10pm, F-Su 5:30am-midnight; Nov.-Apr. M-F 7am-8pm, Sa-Su 7am-10pm. **American Express,** Royal Ave. (tel. 242341). Most banks, the YHANI on Donegall Rd., and the post offices also provide bureaus de change and traveler's check cashing services for a minimal fee.

Local Services

Luggage Storage: For security reasons there is no luggage storage at airports, bus stations, or train stations. All three **hostels** will hold bags during the day for those staying there, and the **Ark** will also hold bags during extended trips if you've stayed there (see **Accommodations,** below).

Bookstore: Eason's, Castlecourt Shopping Centre, Royal Ave. (tel. 235070). Large Irish section; lots of travel guides. Open M-W and F-Sa 9am-5:30pm, Th 9am-9pm. **Dillon's,** 44-46 Fountain St. (tel. 240159), has a huge selection of everything from chess to chemistry. Open M-W and F-Sa 9am-5:30pm, Th 9am-9pm. **Queen's University BelfastQueen's University Bookshop,** 91 University Rd. (tel. 666302), offers Irish history textbooks and a world-renowned collection of Beat generation authors and manuscripts. Open M-F 9am-5:30pm, Sa 9am-5pm. There are dozens of second-hand bookstores around; a quick walk (especially in the university area) is sure to turn up several.

Libraries: Linen Hall Library, 17 Donegall Sq. North (tel. 321707). (See **Sights,** p. 391.) Open M-F 9:30am-5:30pm, Sa 9:30am-4pm. Extensive genealogy and information on the Troubles. Free Irish language courses Sept.-May. To get a visitor's pass, you must have a photo ID. **Belfast Central Library,** Royal Ave. Open M and Th 9:30am-8pm, Tu-W and F 9:30am-5:30pm, Sa 9:30am-1pm.

Laundry: Student's Union, Queen's University, University Rd. Wash £1, dry 20p per 5min. Open M-F 9am-9pm, Sa 10am-9pm, Su 2-9pm. Students only. **Duds & Suds,** Botanic Ave. (tel. 243956). Popcorn and TV while you wait. Wash £1.80, dry £1.80. 15% discount for students and seniors. Open M-F 8am-9pm, Sa 8am-6pm, Su noon-6pm. Last load 1½hr. before closing. **YHANI,** 22 Donegall Rd., £3 for wash, dry, and powder (see **Accommodations,** below).

Women's Resources: Ardoyne Women's Centre, Butler St. (tel. 743536).

Bisexual, Gay, and Lesbian Information: Rainbow Project N.I. (tel. 319030). **Lesbian Line** (tel. 238668). Open Th 7:30-10pm. **Belfast Queer Space** (tel. 323419).

Counseling and Support: Samaritans (tel. 664422). 24hr. line for depression. **Rape Crisis Centre,** 29 Donegall St. (tel. 321830). Open M-F 10am-6pm, Sa 11am-5pm. **Contact Youth,** 2A Ribble St. offers a hotline M-F 10am-10pm (tel. 456654 to talk) and one-on-one counseling appointments (tel. 457848 24hr.).

Disability Resources: NI Council on Disability (tel. 491011). Open M-F 9am-5pm.

Camping Equipment: The Scout Shop and Camp Centre, 12-14 College Sq. East (tel. 320580). Ring bell for entry. Vast selection. Open M-Sa 9am-5pm. **Graham Tiso of Scotland,** 12-14 Cornmarket (tel. 231230), offers 3 floors of everything you could possibly need to survive in the great outdoors. Also has notice boards and flyers for people trying to coordinate hiking, climbing, and water-related trips. Open M-Tu and F-Sa 9:30am-5:30pm, W 10am-5:30pm, Th 9am-8pm.

Pharmacy: Boot's, 35-47 Donegall Pl. (tel. 242332). Open M-W and F-Sa 8:30am-6pm, Th 8:30am-9pm, Su 1-5pm.

Emergency and Communications

Emergency: Dial 999; no coins required. **Police:** 65 Knock Rd. (tel. 650222).

Hospitals: Belfast City Hospital, 9 Lisburn Rd. (tel. 329241). From Shaftesbury Sq. follow Bradbury Pl. and take a right at the fork. **Royal Victoria Hospital,** 12 Grosvenor Rd. (tel. 240503). From Donegall Sq., take Howard St. west to Grosvenor Rd.

Post Office: Central Post Office, 25 Castle Pl. (tel. 323740). Open M-Sa 9am-5:30pm. *Poste Restante* mail comes here. **Postal code:** BT1 1NB. Dozens of **branch offices;** two are **Botanic Garden,** 95 University Rd. (tel. 381309), across from the university (**postal code:** BT7 1NG), and **Shaftesbury Square,** 7-9 Shaftesbury Sq. (tel. 326177; **postal code:** BT2 7DA). Open M-F 8:45am-5:30pm, Sa 10am-12:30pm.

Internet Access: Revelations Internet Café, 27 Shaftesbury Sq. £5 per hr. Open M-F 10am-10pm, Sa 10am-8pm, Su noon-10pm.

Phone code: 01232.

ACCOMMODATIONS

Nearly all of Belfast's budget accommodations are located near Queen's University, south of the city center. Convenient to pubs and restaurants, this area is by far the best place to stay in the city. If you have a lot of baggage you may want to catch a

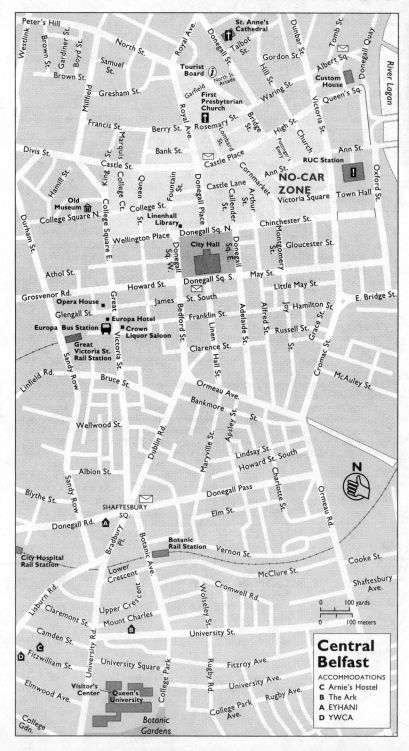

Central Belfast

ACCOMMODATIONS

C Arnie's Hostel
B The Ark
A EYHANI
D YWCA

Centrelink bus to Shaftesbury Sq., or bus #59, 69, 70, 71, 84, or 85 from Donegall Sq. East to areas farther south. A walk to these accommodations takes 10 to 20 minutes from the bus or train station. Hostels and B&Bs are busy in the summer; reservations are recommended. For a list of standard hostel features, see **A Hosteler's Bill of Rights**, p. 40.

Hostels and University Housing

◉**Arnie's Backpackers (IHH),** 63 Fitzwilliam St. (tel. 242867). A 10min. walk from Europa bus station on Great Victoria St. Take a right to head away from the Grand Opera House; at Shaftesbury Sq., take the right fork on Bradbury Pl. then fork left on University Rd. Fitzwilliam St. is on your right across from the university. Relaxed, friendly atmosphere provides a real respite from tiring travels. If people bore you, you'll find ideal companionship in Rosy and Snowy, the Jack Russell proprietors of the hostel. They'll also provide you with tea and toast. Kitchen always open. The **Leaping Leprechaun** stops here (see **Buses,** above). 4- to 6-bed dorms £7.50. Luggage storage during the day.

The Ark, 18 University St. (tel. 329626). Follow the directions to University Rd. given above; University St. is the third left off University Rd. The Ark is the hostel in which guests become resident staff members. Wanted: conversationalists and musicians. 6-bed dorms £7.50; 4-bed dorms £9.50; doubles £28. Kitchen always open, self-service breakfast included. Will keep luggage during weekend trips.

YHANI Belfast Hostel, 22 Donegall Rd. (tel. 324733). Clean, airy, modern rooms of 2-6 beds, some with bath. This hostel is located near Sandy Row, a Loyalist area that has seen violence during marching season (July 4-12). No kitchen. Dorms £8-10. Breakfast £1. Lockers 50p. Linen 50p. Wash, dry, and powder £3. 4-day max. stay. 24hr. reception. Book ahead for weekends. Wheelchair accessible.

YWCA, Queen Mary's Hall, 70 Fitzwilliam St. (tel. 240439). To get here from the bus station, see **Arnie's,** above. Co-ed and always full during the school year. Bright, spic 'n' span doubles and singles with sinks. Limited self-service kitchen open 7am-11pm. 3-bed dorms £9.50, with linen £11, with linen in Aug. £12. B&B £15. Breakfast £3, dinner £6. Wash and dry £3.

Queen's University BelfastQueen's University Accommodations, 78 Malone Rd. (tel. 381608). Bus #71 from Donegall Sq. East or a 25min. walk from Europa. University Rd. runs into Malone Rd.; the residence halls are on your left. An undecorated, institutional dorm: spacious singles or twin rooms with sinks and desks. Strong, reliable showers. 24hr. kitchen; common rooms. Singles £8.80 for U.K. students, £10.36 for international students, £14 for non-students; doubles £22. Open mid-June to mid-Sept. and Christmas and Easter vacations.

Bed and Breakfasts

B&Bs multiply like rabbits between Malone and Lisburn Rd., just south of Queen's University. They tend to be surprisingly similar in price, quality, and decor, and their competitive standards work in the traveler's favor. Calling ahead is generally a good idea; most owners, however, will refer you to other accommodations if necessary.

◉**Mrs. Davidson's East-Sheen Guest House,** 81 Eglantine Ave. (tel. 667149). The best deal in Belfast (if you can get one of their spacious rooms). Sweet Mrs. D. serves up enormous breakfasts and good company. Rooms are bright and clean. £19.50.

The George, 9 Eglantine Ave. (tel. 683212). Spic 'n' span rooms, all with shower and TV. More stained-glass windows than your average Victorian row-house and saloon-appropriate leather couches in the common room. Singles £20; doubles £36, with bath £38. Accepts Visa and MC for a 3% service charge.

Marine House, 30 Eglantine Ave. (tel. 381922). This mansion defies the stereotypes of B&B architecture and overcomes the alienating hotel-like implications of its size. Hospitality and good housekeeping standards as high as the ceilings. Singles £19; doubles £40, with bath £42.

Liserin Guest House, 17 Eglantine Ave. (tel. 660769). Comfy beds and a huge velvet-covered lounge make the Liserin an inviting abode. All rooms have TVs, tea-making facilities, and showers; rooms on the top floor have sky lights. Coffee, tea, and biscuits available all day in the dining room. Singles £20; doubles £38; triples £57.

MCI Spoken Here

Worldwide Calling Made Simple

For more information or to apply for a Card call: **1-800-955-0925**

Outside the U.S., call MCI collect (reverse charge) at: **1-916-567-5151**

International Calling
As Easy As Possible.

The MCI Card
with WorldPhone
Service is designed
specifically to keep
you in touch with the
people that matter
the most to you.

The MCI Card with WorldPhone Service....

• Provides access to the US and other countries worldwide.

• Gives you customer service 24 hours a day

• Connects you to operators who speak your language

• Provides you with MCI's low rates and no sign-up fees

**For more information or
to apply for a Card call:**
1-800-955-0925

**Outside the U.S., call MCI
collect (reverse charge) at:**
1-916-567-5151

Pick Up the Phone, Pick Up the Miles.

You earn frequent flyer miles when you travel internationally, why not when you call internationally? Callers can earn frequent flyer miles if they sign up with one of MCI's airline partners:

- American Airlines
- Continental Airlines
- Delta Airlines
- Hawaiian Airlines
- Midwest Express Airlines
- Northwest Airlines
- Southwest Airlines
- United Airlines
- USAirways

Please cut out and save this reference guide for convenient U.S. and worldwide calling with the MCI Card with WorldPhone Service.

Your MCI Worldphone Access Numbers

COUNTRY	WORLDPHONE TOLL-FREE ACCESS #
#Singapore	8000-112-112
#Slovak Republic (CC)	00421-00112
#Slovenia	080-8808
#South Africa (CC)	0800-99-0011
#Spain (CC)	900-99-0014
#Sri Lanka	(Outside of Colombo, dial 01 first) 440100
#St. Lucia ÷	1-800-888-8000
#St. Vincent	1-800-888-8000
#Sweden (CC) ◆	020-795-922
#Switzerland (CC) ◆	0800-89-0222
#Syria	0800
#Taiwan (CC) ◆	0080-13-4567
#Thailand ★	001-999-1-2001
#Trinidad & Tobago ÷	1-800-888-8000
#Turkey (CC) ◆	00-8001-1177
#Turks and Caicos ÷	1-800-888-8000
#Ukraine (CC) ÷	8★10-013
#United Arab Emirates ◆	800-111
#United Kingdom (CC) To call using BT ■	0800-89-0222
To call using C&W ■	0500-89-0222
#United States (CC)	1-800-888-8000
#Uruguay	000-412
#U.S. Virgin Islands (CC)	1-800-888-8000
#Vatican City (CC)	172-1022
#Venezuela (CC) ÷ ◆	800-1114-0
Vietnam ●	1201-1022
Yemen	008-00-102

Automation available from most locations.
(CC) Country-to-country calling available to/from most international locations.
Limited availability.
÷ Wait for second dial tone.
▶ When calling from public phones, use phones marked LADATEL.
◀ International communications carrier.
■ Not available from public pay phones.
★ Public phones may require deposit of coin or phone card for dial tone.
● Local service fee in U.S. currency required to complete call.
▲ Regulation does not permit Intra-Japan calls.
❖ Available from most major cities

And, it's simple to call home.

1. Dial the WorldPhone toll-free access number of the country you're calling from (listed inside).

2. Follow the voice instructions in your language of choice or hold for a WorldPhone operator.
   - Enter or give the operator your MCI Card number or call collect.

3. Enter or give the WorldPhone operator your home number.

4. Share your adventures with your family!

MCI

The MCI Card with WorldPhone Service... The easy way to call when traveling worldwide.

MCI Calling Card
123 456 7890 1234
J.D. SMITH
WorldPhone

For more information or to apply for a Card call:
1-800-955-0925

Outside the U.S., call MCI collect (reverse charge) at:
1-916-567-5151

Please cut out and save this reference guide for convenient U.S. and worldwide calling with the MCI Card with WorldPhone Service.

COUNTRY		WORLDPHONE TOLL-FREE ACCESS #
American Samoa		633-2MCI (633-2624)
#Antigua	(available from public card phones only)	1-800-888-8000
#Argentina (CC)		#0
#Aruba ÷		800-888-8
#Australia (CC) ◆	To call using OPTUS ■	1-800-551-111
	To call using TELSTRA ■	1-800-881-100
#Austria (CC) ◆		022-903-012
#Bahamas		1-800-888-8000
#Bahrain		800-002
#Barbados		1-800-888-8000
#Belarus (CC)	From Brest, Vitebsk, Grodno, Minsk	8-800-103
	From Gomel and Mogilev	8-10-800-103
#Belgium (CC) ◆		0800-100-12
#Belize	From Hotels	557
	From Payphones	815
#Bermuda ÷		1-800-888-8000
#Bolivia (CC) ◆		0-800-2222
#Brazil (CC)		000-8012
#British Virgin Islands ÷		1-800-888-8000
#Brunei		800-011
#Bulgaria		00800-0001
#Canada (CC)		1-800-888-8000
#Cayman Islands		1-800-888-8000
#Chile (CC)	To call using CTC ■	800-207-300
	To call using ENTEL ■	800-360-180
#China ✦		108-12
	For a Mandarin-speaking Operator	108-17
#Colombia (CC) ◆	Collect Access in Spanish	980-16-0001
		980-16-1000
#Costa Rica ◆		0800-012-2222
#Cote D'Ivoire		1001
#Croatia (CC) ★		0800-22-0112
#Cyprus ◆		080-90000
#Czech Republic (CC) ◆		00-42-000112
#Denmark (CC) ◆		8001-0022
#Dominica		1-800-888-8000
#Dominican Republic	Collect Access	1-800-888-8000
	Collect Access in Spanish	1121
#Ecuador (CC) ÷		999-170
#Egypt (CC) ◆	(Outside of Cairo, dial 02 first)	355-5770
El Salvador		800-1767

--- FOLD ---

COUNTRY		WORLDPHONE TOLL-FREE ACCESS #
#Federated States of Micronesia		624
#Fiji		004-890-1002
#Finland (CC) ◆		08001-102-80
#France (CC) ◆		0800-99-0019
#French Antilles (CC)	(includes Martinique, Guadeloupe)	0800-99-0019
#French Guiana (CC)		0-800-99-0019
#Gabon		00-005
#Gambia		00-1-99
#Germany (CC)		0-800-888-8000
#Greece (CC) ◆		00-800-1211
#Grenada ÷		1-800-888-8000
#Guam (CC)		1-800-888-8000
#Guatemala (CC) ◆		99-99-189
Guyana		177
#Haiti ÷	Collect Access in French/Creole	193
		190
Honduras ÷		8000-122
#Hong Kong (CC)		800-96-1121
#Hungary (CC) ◆		00▼800-01411
#Iceland (CC) ◆		800-9002
#India (CC) ◆	Collect Access	000-127
#Indonesia (CC) ◆		001-801-11
Iran ÷	(SPECIAL PHONES ONLY)	172-1022
#Ireland (CC)		1-800-55-1001
#Italy (CC) ◆		172-1022
#Jamaica ÷	Collect Access	1-800-888-8000
		873
#Japan (CC) ◆	To call using KDD ■ (from public phones)	00539-121▶
	To call using IDC ■	0066-55-121
	To call using ITJ ■	0044-11-121
#Jordan		18-800-001
#Kazakhstan (CC)		8-800-131-4321
#Kenya ✦	Collect Access	*2
#Korea (CC) ◆	To call using KT ■	00729-14
	To call using DACOM ■	00369-14
	Phone Booths÷	Press red button, 03, then ★
	Military Bases	550-2255
#Kuwait		800-MCI (800-624)

--- FOLD ---

COUNTRY		WORLDPHONE TOLL-FREE ACCESS #
#Lebanon	Collect Access	600-MCI (600-624)
#Liechtenstein (CC) ◆		0800-89-0222
#Luxembourg (CC)		0800-0112
#Macao		0800-131
#Macedonia (CC)		99800-4266
#Malaysia (CC) ◆		1-800-80-0012
#Malta		0800-89-0120
#Marshall Islands		1-800-888-8000
#Mexico (CC)	Avantel	01-800-021-8000
	Telmex ▲	001-800-674-7000
	Collect Access in Spanish	01-800-021-1000
#Monaco (CC) ◆		800-90-019
#Montserrat		1-800-888-8000
#Morocco		00-211-0012
#Netherlands (CC) ◆		0800-022-9122
#Netherlands Antilles (CC) ÷		001-800-888-8000
#New Zealand (CC)		000-912
Nicaragua (CC)	(Outside of Managua, dial 02 first)	166
	From any public payphone	★2
#Norway (CC) ◆		800-19912
Pakistan		00-800-12-001
#Panama		108
#Papua New Guinea (CC)	Military Bases	05-07-19140
#Paraguay ÷		00-812-800
#Peru		0-800-500-10
#Philippines (CC) ◆	To call using PLDT ■	105-14
	To call using PHILCOM ■	1026-14
	Collect Access via PLDT in Filipino	1237-77
	Collect Access via ICC in Filipino	00-800-111-21-22
#Poland (CC) ÷		05-017-1234
#Portugal (CC) ÷		1-800-888-8000
#Puerto Rico (CC)		0800-012-77
#Qatar ★		01-800-1800
#Romania (CC) ÷		0808-99
#Russia (CC) ◆ ÷	To call using ROSTELCOM ■ (For Russian speaking operator)	747-3322
	To call using SOVINTEL ■	960-2222
#Saipan (CC) ÷		950-1022
#San Marino (CC) ◆		172-1022
#Saudi Arabia (CC) ÷		1-800-11

If you're stuck for cash on your travels, don't panic. Millions of people trust Western Union to

transfer money in minutes to 153 countries and over 45,000 locations worldwide. Our record of

safety and reliability is second to none. So when you need money in a hurry, call Western Union.

WESTERN UNION | MONEY TRANSFER®

The fastest way to send money worldwide.®

Eglantine Guest House, 21 Eglantine Ave. (tel. 667585). The owner is the sister of the Liserin's proprietor, and their parents taught them to be kind and welcoming to strangers. Small but comfortable. Singles £20; doubles £36; triples £51.

Drumragh House, 647 Antrim Rd. (tel. 773063), several miles north of city center, close to Belfast Castle. Citybuses #123 and 45 stop in front of this house in a quiet residential neighborhood. Large airy rooms and pretty gardens at the foot of Cave Hill. Call ahead; there are only three rooms. £18.

Botanic Lodge, 87 Botanic Ave. (tel. 327682), on the corner of Mt. Charles Ave. This is the place for lazy-bums who want the B&B experience with as short a walk to the city center as possible. Comfortable and tidy. Singles £22; doubles £40.

FOOD

Belfast assumes a cosmopolitan character in its eateries, where you can sample flavors from almost any area of the world. Dublin Rd., Botanic Rd., and the Golden Mile have the highest concentration of restaurants. Bakeries and cafés dot the shopping areas, but nearly all close by 5:30pm. Most convenience stores offer a full supply of groceries, although prices are all fairly high (as with most food in the North). The **Mace Supermarket,** on the corner of Castle and Queen St., sells slightly cheaper food (open M-W and F-Sa 9am-6pm, Th 9am-9pm), and the **Spar Market** at the top of Botanic Rd. is open nearly 24 hours (open M 6am-Su 3am). For fruits and vegetables, plunder the lively **St. George's Market,** East Bridge St., in the enormous warehouse between May and Oxford St. (open Tu and F 6am-3pm). **The Nutmeg,** 9A Lombard St. (tel. 249984), supplies healthy foods, baked goods, and raw ingredients (open M-Sa 9:30am-5:30pm), as does **Canterbury Dyke's,** 66-68 Botanic Ave. (open M-F 7:30am-7pm, Sa-Su 8am-6:30pm). **Lower Lisburn Rd.,** which runs parallel to University Rd., has a good selection of inexpensive bakeries and fruit stands.

Queen's University Area

⊛**Bookfinders,** 47 University Rd. (tel. 328269). Super-cool smoky bookstore/café with mismatched cups and saucers and retro counter-culture paraphernalia. Its beauty is more than skin deep—the relaxed atmosphere would make anyone feel at home. Soup and bread and a variety of sandwiches for around £2. Occasional poetry readings. Art gallery upstairs. Open M-Sa 10am-5:30pm.

⊛**Maggie May's Belfast Café,** 50 Botanic Ave. (tel. 322622). The walls look like brown newsprint sketched with the Belfast of yesteryear. Relax with a cup of tea and a free newspaper; order some food when you feel like it. Sandwiches £2-3. 3-course meals £4. Open M-Sa 8am-10:30pm, Su 10am-10:30pm.

Cloisters Bistro, 1 Elmwood Ave. (tel. 324803), in the Queen's University Student Union. Cafeteria-style food and atmosphere efficiently satiate your hunger with a few frills as well. A hearty meal for about £3. Open M-Th 9:30am-4pm, F 8:30am-3pm in summer; M-F 8:30am-6:30pm during the school year.

Café Clementine, 245 Lisburn Rd. (tel. 611292), 3 blocks south of Eglantine St. Sunburst yellow walls and excellent food in this hot hangout for 20-somethings. Jazz concerts cool things down on weekend nights. Well-conceived sandwich ideas on croissants or baguettes for around £3. Open M-Tu 9am-4:30pm, W-F 9:30am-10pm, Sa 9:30am-10:30pm, Su 10am-5pm.

The Other Side, 79 Botanic Ave. (tel. 236300), at the intersection with University St. A good little restaurant that can fill a gaping hole in your stomach with a heap of food for £3-4.

The Attic Restaurant, 54 Stranmillis Rd. (tel. 661074). A tiny 2nd-floor restaurant that practically spills out the windows to the Victorian balcony. The European menu has light lunch for £4-5 and hearty dinner for £10-12. Open M-Sa noon-3pm and 5-10:30pm, Su noon-3pm and 5-8:30pm.

Mangetous, 30 University Rd. (tel. 315151). Look around and you'll think you're in Italy in the winter. Deliciously inexpensive bistro cuisine is a great deal for lunch. Most entrees around £3-4. 3-course set lunch £4.90. Discount if you're going to Queen's University Film Theatre after dinner. Open M-Th 11am-11pm, F-Sa 11am-7pm, Su 12:30-10pm.

The Golden Mile and Dublin Road

Revelations Internet Café, 27 Shaftesbury Sq. Get connected to cool music and ultra sci-fi art in this rare find—the only privately run internet access center in the area. Internet access £5 per hr., students £4 per hr. Sandwiches £2-3; lots of veggie options. Open M-F 10am-10pm, Sa 10am-8pm, Su noon-10pm.

Café Booth, 40 Dublin Rd. (tel. 310854), in the Salvation Army building. Huge portions of food for the hungry, weary traveler in a flowery, yellow setting. Most entrees around £2.50. Open M-Sa 8am-3:30pm.

Café Mozart, 67 Dublin Rd. (tel. 315200). For a lovely light lunch appropriate to one's experience of the Golden Mile, stop here. Freshly made entrees £3-4 and truly special specialty coffees. Open M-Sa 10am-5pm, Su 10am-4pm.

Pizza Express, 25-27 Bedford Rd. (tel. 329050). One of the few places in town that serves real pizza, and yet the grandeur of its spiral staircase and Hollywood-esque decorations make it more of an exotic find than your typical pizza chain. 1- to 2-person pizzas £4-5; variety of wines available. Open M-Th 11:30am-11:30pm, F-Sa noon-midnight.

Spuds, 23 Bradbury Pl. The menu here accomplishes a remarkable synthesis of the two staples of the Irish diet—meat and potatoes—in fast-food form: a wide variety of meat dishes are placed directly inside an enormous potato for your convenience. Most spuds around £2. Open M-Th and Sa 11am-3am, F 11am-4am, Su 11am-1am.

North of Donegall Square

Roscoff Bakery & Café, 27-29 Fountain St. (tel. 315090). The fast-food cousin of the world-famous Roscoff's Restaurant, this café serves a more affordable feast. Soup and sandwich £2. Divine breads. Open M-W and F-Sa 7:30am-5:30pm, Th 7:30am-8:30pm.

Poiret's Café, Fountain St. Looks and reads French, with granite table-tops and Fauvist artwork, but tastes and sounds Irish, with tons of customers consuming open-faced prawn sandwiches and tea. Most meals around £3, better prices after 2pm. Open M-Sa 9am-5:30pm.

Café Deauville, 58 Wellington Pl. (tel. 326601), at the corner of College Sq. Many notice the intricate mosaic exterior before seeing the café itself. Full breakfast or lunch £3-4. Open M-Sa 8am-4:30pm.

Bewley's, Rosemary St. (tel. 232568), just inside of the Donegall Arcade. For those missing Dublin, this Bewley's is a good replica of the original Japanese tea room, with the same sandwiches (£2.45), salads (£2), and good desserts (£1-3). Newspapers and magazines upstairs. Open M-W and F-Su 8am-5:30pm, Th 8am-9pm.

Windsor Dairy & Home Bakery, 46 College St. (tel. 327157), has a mouth-watering selection of fresh baked goods, sandwiches (£2), stew (95p), and entrees (£1.50). Seating is scarce, but the food is well worth taking out. Open M-Sa 8:30am-5:30pm.

PUBS AND CLUBS

Pubs were prime targets for sectarian violence at the height of the Troubles in the 60s and 70s. As a result, most of the popular pubs in Belfast are new or restored. The *Bushmills Irish Pub Guide,* by Sybil Taylor, relates the history of Belfast's pubs (£7.95 at the tourist office or local book stores). Ask the student staff at the Queen's University Student Centre or the workers at the hostels about current hip night spots. This year, Let's Go is proud to introduce the Belfast Pub Crawl and Pub Crawl Map. We recommend beginning early in Cornmarket's historic entries, visiting the traditional and nontraditional bars of the city center, then partying until close in the university area. If you're staying in the YHANI hostel, you might switch the university area with the Golden Mile for a shorter stumbling-home distance.

Cornmarket

1. **White's Tavern,** Winecellar Entry, off Lombard and Bridge St. Belfast's oldest pub has been serving drinks since 1630. An excellent stop for an afternoon pint.
2. **Morning Star Pub,** Pottinger's Entry (tel. 223976), between Ann and High St. An old wood-paneled pub, hidden in Cornmarket's historic Entries. A glorious Victorian wrought-iron bracket draws all eyes to the sign hanging above its door.

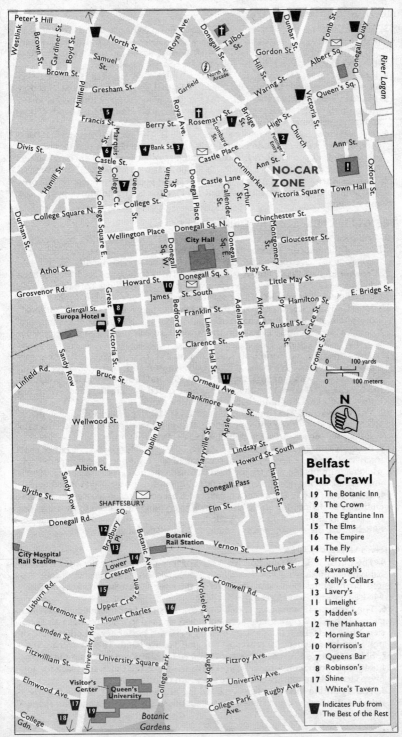

Belfast
Pub Crawl

19 The Botanic Inn
9 The Crown
18 The Eglantine Inn
15 The Elms
16 The Empire
14 The Fly
6 Hercules
4 Kavanagh's
3 Kelly's Cellars
13 Lavery's
11 Limelight
5 Madden's
12 The Manhattan
2 Morning Star
10 Morrison's
7 Queens Bar
8 Robinson's
17 Shine
1 White's Tavern

▼ Indicates Pub from
The Best of the Rest

North of Donegall Square

3. **Kelly's Cellars,** 30 Bank St. (tel. 324835), off Royal Ave. just after the Fountain St. pedestrian area. The oldest pub in Belfast that hasn't been renovated, and that's just as it should be. Make yourself another fixture here. Trad on Th and whenever they feel like it (which is often), folk or rock F-Sa. Cover £1-2.

4. **Kavanagh's Bar,** 24 Bank St. (tel. 249080), next to Kelly's. Like Kelly's, but with a better name and a slightly higher ceiling. Blues, folk, trad, and rock bands W-Sa. No cover.

5. **Madden's Bar,** 74 Berry St. (tel. 244114). Old wooden bar with musical instruments on the walls. Attracts good-sized crowds for its traditional Irish bands (Th-Sa) and traditional blues and folk (Su). No cover.

6. **The Hercules Bar,** 61-63 Castle St. (tel. 324587). This recently rejuvenated bar is completely decked out in green and pulls in the best musicians that the local soil produces. Trad jam sessions F-Sa, blues and jazz other nights. Owners will direct you to other good live music venues. Open until 2am on weekends. No cover.

7. **Queens Bar,** 4 Queen's Arcade (tel. 321347), off Fountain St. Friendly, low-pressure atmosphere in a tiny alley off Donegall Pl. attracts a broad mix of people, gay and straight.

The Golden Mile and The Dublin Road

8. **Robinson's,** 38-40 Great Victoria St. (tel. 247447). Incredibly lively, offering 4 floors of themed bars (varying from a traditional Irish pub to a motorcycle bar in the basement). Live rock on the top floor Th-Sa. Trad sessions nightly.

9. **Crown Liquor Saloon,** 46 Great Victoria St. This carefully restored bar has been bombed 32 times, but you'd never know it. The only National Trust-owned pub. Gilt ceilings, gas lamps, and Victorian snugs make for a very special drink.

10. **Morrisons,** 21 Bedford St. (tel. 248458). Painstakingly reconstructed "traditional" atmosphere, modeled after a bar of the same name in the Republic. It's comforting to think that 2 such places exist in the world. Live bands F and Sa (cover around £3), trad Su after 9pm.

11. **The Limelight** and **Katie Daly's,** 17 Ormeau Ave. (tel. 325968). A truly hip bar/nightclub complex. Live music at Katie Daly's most nights, with a £2 cover to chill out to acid jazz with Sunday's nights "Numb." Tu and Sa are student disco nights at the Limelight (£2 cover) but this place is best visited as a music venue—word has it they have a knack of hiring bands before their time.

12. **The Manhattan,** 23-31 Bradbury Pl. (tel. 233131). Huge 3-story nightclub that is always packed with the younger crowd clad in pop-video fashion. No cover for first-floor bar; cover varies for nightclub (£3-6). Dress to impress.

13. **Lavery's Gin Palace,** 12 Bradbury Pl. (tel. 327159). The popular, if rather unattractive, place to be for all kinds of (cool) people—everyone from bikers to backpackers, from people who try too hard to those who don't try hard enough. Open until 1am. Dancing upstairs on weekends (50p cover for bar; £2.50 for nightclub).

14. **The Fly,** 5-6 Lower Crescent (tel. 235666). This newly reconceived 3-story nightclub tries to define "the scene" by relating everything in it, from the wine to the fireplace, to its pesky namesake. While Bono probably wouldn't buy it, the masses of Belfast are dressing up and swarming to it. Live DJs 7 nights a week.

Queen's University Area

15. **The Elms,** 36 University Rd. (tel. 322106). "It's a scream," as the Munch theme bar is intent on showing you throughout. A nice take on how to deal with your anxiety. Board games, pool, and **Simpsons** on the large screen Sundays at 6pm. Disco F (£1 cover), live band Sa (£2).

16. **The Empire,** 42 Botanic Ave. (tel. 249276). This 120-year old building was once a church, but its 2 stories have been entirely revamped to resemble Belfast's Victorian music halls. Each floor's stage is likely to have a performer, whether hired or not. Sept.-June comedy Tu (cover £3.50), trad Th, live bands Th-Sa (cover £3-5).

17. **Shine,** Queen's University Student Union (tel. 324803), makes it no fun to play hooky from school on Saturday nights. Live DJs make the Union the place for anyone to learn about cutting edge trends in youth culture. Cover £2.

18. **The Eglantine Inn** (the "Egg"), 32 Malone Rd. (tel. 381994). Across the street from the Bot (below), and students maintain the steady flow of white-water rapids

between the two. Trad on W and Th at 10:30pm, Sa 9pm. Disco F and Sa at 9pm (club £2, music free). Open until 1am.

19. **The Botanic Inn** (the "Bot"), 23 Malone Rd. (tel. 660460). Huge and hugely popular student bar. Here, you can rise to the "Yard of Ale Challenge" or just indulge yourself in the annual beer-fest that lasts from late May to early June. Trad on Tu (free), "record club" (60s, 70s, and 80s music) Th-Sa (£2). 21+. Open until 1am.

The Best of the Rest

The Yard of Ale Challenge

Have you ever tried to chug a yard of ale? Not many have—mostly just men who are already "half-pissed" and get egged on by peers celebrating a stag night or birthday. Until recently, The Fly pub in Belfast proudly hosted this English tradition; now only the Botanic Inn has occasional challengers. The trick is to rotate the yard-long glass as you chug; that way, you won't get a rush of beer all at once when you get to the last bits of ale in the bulb at the bottom (if you don't rotate the stem, you're likely to end up covered in ale or sick in the loo). It's easier to chug a yard of ale than a yard of lager, as ale is less fizzy (albeit more filling). Bass Ale tends to be the ale of choice for most challengers, but the brand is up to you. To ask for Guinness, however, would be a *faux pas*—Guinness is never meant to be chugged. And, if you need to, take your time: one 72-year-old man is said to have spent three months—including three falls into his glass, for he was a short little thing—to complete the task.

These pubs are too far north to be feasibly crawled from, but that are still well worth visiting. The Front Page and the Liverpool near the docks are perhaps the best pubs in Belfast, recommended in Dublin and beyond. Besides being rather far from most accommodations, they also warrant evenings of their own. At night, one should take a cab to the pubs farthest north, as the areas are less populated and not as safe as the usually hopping Golden Mile and University areas.

The Front Page, 9 Ballymoney St. (tel. 324924). The tiny box of a building sits alone among the vast vacancies of the docks, but it's the center of the universe when it packs in the locals nightly. Live music on weekends ranges from fine to amazing.

The Liverpool Bar, Donegall Quay (tel. 324796), opposite the SeaCat terminal. This 150-year-old building has also been a lodging house and a brothel. Today it boasts the best trad in the city (W and Su nights; M blues; F sing-song). Occasional cover.

The Parliament Bar, 2-6 Dunbar St. (tel. 234520), around the corner from the Duke. Considers itself the premier gay bar in Northern Ireland. A formerly traditional bar that now looks like it's been transplanted to the Greek Islands, with disco Tu and F-Su (cover £2-7), lives bands on Th (£2), and bingo on M (no cover).

The Duke of York, 11 Commercial Ct. (tel. 241062). An artsy student crowd hangs out in this 2-floor bar and club near the Arts College, and the big collection of beer advertisements on their walls show a discriminating aesthetic taste. F and Sa nightclub upstairs and live bands downstairs. £3 cover for each.

The Crow's Nest, 26 Skipper St. (tel. 325491), off High St. across from the Albert Memorial Clock. It's hard not to notice its stunning yellow and black exterior. The interior is proud to be loud as well, with live music, discos at Flave's 70s Revival Bar upstairs, and karaoke on weekends (cover varies). Don't worry, there's also a lounge for a quiet drink when your legs fail you.

TOURS

One introduction to Belfast is through the **Citybus** (tel. 458484) "Belfast: A Living History" tour, which leaves from Castle Place (in front of the post office). (*June-Sept. tours every Tu, Th, and Su at 10am and 2pm. 2½hr. £8, students £7, seniors and children £5.50. Illustrated souvenir booklet included.*) The tour through the Falls, the Shankill, East Belfast, and Sandy Row is engaging. The **black cab tours** give a more in-depth description and receive rave reviews from both tourists and locals. The hostels can recommend a favorite black cab driver to you; the "Backpackers' Tour" (tel. (0421) 067752) is especially well done (£5 per person for a 6-person tour). Citybus offers a variety of other tours of Belfast and the surrounding area; the tourist office can provide brochures.

SIGHTS

Donegall Square

Belfast City Hall, Donegall Sq. (tel. 320202, ext. 2346), is the administrative and geographic center of Belfast, distanced from the crowded streets by a grassy square. *(1hr. tours June-Sept. M-F 10:30, 11:30am, and 2:30pm, Sa 2:30pm; Oct-May M-Tu and Th-F 2:30pm, W 11:30am. Free.)* Its green copper dome (173ft.) is visible from any point in the city. After Queen Victoria granted Belfast's cityhood in 1888, this symbol of civic pride was built on the site of older linen warehouses. Neoclassical marble columns and arches figure prominently in A. Brunwell Thomas's 1906 design. Inside, a grand marble staircase ascends to the second floor. Portraits of the city's lord mayors somberly line the halls, and glass and marble shimmer in three elaborate reception rooms. The City Council's oak-paneled chambers, used only once a month, are deceptively austere considering the Council's reputation for rowdy meetings that sometimes devolve into fist fights. If you want to see the council in action, a councillor can sign you into the otherwise inaccessible debates with 48-hour notice. Directly in front of the main entrance, an enormous marble Queen Victoria stares down visitors with a formidable grimace as bronze figures representing shipbuilding and spinning curl up at her feet. A more sympathetic sculpted figure of womanhood stands on the eastern side of the garden, commemorating the fate of the *Titanic* and its passengers. An inconspicuous pale gray stone column commemorates the 1942 arrival of the U.S. Expeditionary Force, whose soldiers were stationed here to defend the North from Germany; it was rededicated after President Clinton's visit to Belfast in 1996. The interior of City Hall is accessible by guided tour.

Across the street from City Hall, on the corner of Donegall Sq. North and East Bedford St., the **Scottish Provident Institution,** built in 1902, displays a decadent facade that glorifies virtually every profession that contributed to industrial Belfast. The delusions of grandeur are more palatable when you look down at the building's street level, which is lined with quick-marts. Other decorations depict the loom, ships, and spinning wheel, representing the industries that made Belfast prosperous. The northwest corner of Donegall Sq. shelters one of the oldest establishments around, the **Linen Hall Library,** 17 Donegall Sq. (tel. 321707). *(Open M-W and F 9:30am-5:30pm, Th 9:30am-8:30pm, Sa 9:30am-4pm.)* The library was originally located in the old "Linen Hall" where the City Hall is today; it was moved to its present location in 1894. The red hand of Ulster decorates the top of the street entrance, but the library contains a famous collection of materials for the perusal of people of all political persuasions. Devoted librarians scramble for every Christmas card, poster, hand bill, and newspaper article related to the Troubles that they can get their hands on.

Cornmarket

Just north of the city center, a shopping district envelops eight blocks around Castle St. and Royal Ave. This area, known as Cornmarket after one of its original commodities, has been a marketplace since Belfast's early days. The barricades that prevent cars from entering fall roughly where the old city walls stood in the 17th century. A McDonald's stands on the site of the old city castle (hence Castle St.). Although the Cornmarket area is dominated by modern buildings, relics of old Belfast remain in the tiny alleys, or **entries,** that connect some of the major streets. A drink at any of the pubs along these alleys will have your imagination swimming in nostalgic reverie. Between Ann and High St. runs Pottinger's Entry, which contains the old **Morning Star Pub** in all its wood-paneled traditional splendor. *(Open daily 11:30am-1am.)* Joy's Entry, farther down Ann St., is the alley where the *Belfast News Letter* was printed for over 100 years. The only establishment still in the entry, Globe Tavern, is disappointingly modern inside. Off Lombard and Bridge St., Winecellar Entry is the site of Belfast's oldest pub, **White's Tavern.** *(Open daily 11:30am-11:30pm.)* White's has been serving drinks since 1630. It's still an ideal place for an afternoon pint or a bit of pub grub. The city's oldest public building, **The Old Stock Exchange,** sits on the corner of North and Waring St. Tireless Charles Lanyon designed a new facade for the building in 1845 when the original was deemed not grand enough. The **First Presbyterian Church of Belfast,** the city's oldest church, still stands just a block to the west, on Rosemary St. *(Open W 10:30am-12:30pm.)*

St. Anne's Cathedral Area

Belfast's newspapers all set up shop north of the Cornmarket shopping district, around the still active **Belfast Cathedral** (originally **St. Anne's Church**) on Donegall St. *(Open daily 9am-6pm. Su services: communion 10am, Eucharist 11am, evensong 3:30pm.)* To keep from disturbing regular worship, this Church of Ireland cathedral, begun in 1899, was built around the smaller church already on the site. Upon completion of the cathedral's exterior, the earlier church was removed brick by brick from inside. The mosaic above the Chapel of the Holy Spirit depicts St. Patrick arriving in southeast Co. Down and bringing Christianity to Ireland. The tops of each of the cathedral's 10 interior pillars depict somebody's idea of the 10 basic professions of Belfast: Science, Industry, Healing, Agriculture, Music, Theology, Shipbuilding, Freemasonry, Art, and Womanhood (a nice enough profession, but the pay is lousy). In a small enclave called the Chapel of Peace, the cathedral asks visitors to pray for international peace between noon and 2pm. Until the year 2000, the cathedral will be undergoing restoration as part of a joint appeal with Catholic St. Peter's Cathedral on Falls Rd. The cathedrals remain open to the public during restoration.

The Docks and East Belfast

Although the docks area was once the activity hub of old Belfast, continued commercial development has made the area into a suitable observation point of the activity of industrial machinery, not people. Reminders of the city's ship-building glory days, however, remain in the East Belfast shipyards, surrounded by former employee housing. The most famous of the shipyards is Harland & Wolff, which helped transform Belfast into one of the world's premier shipbuilding centers. Unfortunately, the builders' most famous creation was the *Titanic.* The shipyards figure in numerous poems and novels set in Belfast, notably at the end of Paul Muldoon's "7, Middagh St." Today, the twin cranes nicknamed **"Samson and Goliath"** tower over the Harland & Wolff shipyard and are visible from anywhere across the river.

Other leftovers from Belfast's shipping heyday can be found around Donegall Quay. The stately **Custom House,** built by Charles Lanyon in 1857, stands between Queen and Albert Sq. on the approach to the river from the clock tower. Designed in an imaginative E-shape, it rests on an elaborate pediment of Britannia, Neptune, and Mercury, the god of trade. Belfast also has its own version of the leaning tower of Pisa and Big Ben in one: the **Albert Memorial Clock Tower.** Designed in 1865 by W. J. Barre, the 115 ft. tower leans precariously at the entrance to the docks area, where Oxford St. parallels the Lagan. The Albert is Prince Albert, Queen Victoria's consort.

A bit to the north lies **Sinclair Seamen's Church,** Corporation St. (just down the street from the SeaCat terminal), the church with a theme. *(Su services 11:30am and 7pm; tours W 2-4pm.)* The minister delivers his sermons from a pulpit carved in the shape of a ship's prow, collections are taken in miniature lifeboats, and an organ with port and starboard lights taken from a Guinness barge carries the tune. The exterior was designed by prolific Charles Lanyon, who also designed the Custom House and most other notable mid-19th-century Belfast buildings (except the Albert Memorial Clock Tower, and he was angry about that). Lanyon later became mayor of Belfast.

Farther south along Donegall Quay, across from the Laganside bus station, are the **Lagan Lookout** (tel. 315444) and **Lagan Weir.** The £14-million weir was built to eliminate the Lagan's drastic tides, which used to expose stinking mud flats during ebb; the Lookout offers an interesting room full of displays on the history of Belfast, the purpose and mechanism of the weir, and the harbor's activity. Both structures are part of a huge development project that includes the **Laganside Trail** (along the far side of the river), a road/rail bridge (currently under construction), and the **Waterfront Hall** (tel. 334455), a recently opened concert hall with an uncanny similarity to a sponge cake. *(Lookout open Mar.-Sept. M-F 11am-5pm, Sa noon-5pm, Su 2-5pm; Oct.-Feb. Tu-F 11am-3:30pm, Sa 1-4:30pm, Su 2-4:30pm. £1.50, children 50p, concession £1.)* Also on the western side of the Lagan is the **One Oxford Street Gallery** (tel. 310400), which specializes in the work of contemporary Belfast artists. *(Open M-F 10am-4pm. Free.)*

The Golden Mile

"The Golden Mile" refers to a strip along Great Victoria St. containing many of the jewels in the crown of Belfast's establishment. Belfast's pride and joy, the **Grand Opera House** (tel. 240411), marks its beginning. It was cyclically bombed by the IRA, restored to its original splendor at enormous cost, and then bombed again. The **Grand Opera House Ticket Shop**, 2-4 Great Victoria St. (tel. 241919; 24hr. info line tel. 249129), sells tickets for performances including musicals, operas, ballets, and concerts. *(Open M-W 8:30am-8pm, Th 8:30am-9pm, F 8:30am-6:30pm, Sa 8:30am-5:30pm.)* If the current playbill doesn't float your boat, you can still schedule a daytime tour by calling the booking office. *(Open M-Sa 9:45am-5:30pm.)* Or ask at the stage door on Glengall St.; if there's no rehearsal going on, they'll give you a tour.

Farther down Great Victoria St., the plush **Europa Hotel,** damaged by 32 bombs in its history, has the dubious distinction of being "Europe's most bombed hotel." In March of 1993, the hotel installed shatterproof windows, which seem to have deterred would-be-bombers. Across the street, the **Crown Liquor Saloon,** Great Victoria St., is a showcase of carved wood, gilded ceilings, and stained glass, all fully restored by the National Trust. The box-like snugs fit groups of two or 10 comfortably. Just ring the buzzer when you want another round (see **Pubs,** 390). Great Victoria St. proceeds south to its intersection with Dublin Rd. at **Shaftesbury Square,** which one neon sign allows tourism officials to compare to Piccadilly Circus.

Queen's University Area

Still farther south of the city center, the main building of **Queen's University BelfastQueen's University** sits back from University Rd. in its revival Tudor red brick. Designed by Charles Lanyon in 1849, it was modeled after Magdalen College, Oxford. The **Visitors Centre** (tel. 335252), in the Lanyon Room to the left of the main entrance, offers Queens-related exhibits and merchandise. *(Open May-Sept. M-Sa 10am-4pm, Oct-Apr. M-F 10am-4pm.)*

On warm days, the majority of the student population suns itself behind the university at the **Botanic Gardens** (tel. 324902). *(Open daily 8am-dusk. Tropical House and Palm House open Apr.-Sept. M-F 10am-noon and 1-5pm, Sa and Su 1-5pm; Oct.-Mar. M-F 10am-noon and 1-4pm, Sa and Su 1-5pm. Free.)* Meticulously groomed, the gardens offer a welcome green respite from the traffic-laden Belfast streets. Inside the gardens lie two 19th-century greenhouses, the very hot **Tropical Ravine House,** and the more temperate Lanyon-designed **Palm House.** Amid the Botanic Gardens, the **Ulster Museum** (tel. 381251), off Stranmillis Rd., has developed a variety of exhibits for its huge display halls. *(Open M-F 10am-5pm, Sa 1-5pm, Su 2-5pm. Free, except for some traveling exhibitions.)* Irish and modern art, local history, and antiquities are all subjects for investigation. The treasure salvaged from the *Girone,* a Spanish Armada ship that sank off the Causeway Coast in 1588, is on display here. Visit the Mummy of Takabuti and a Maori war canoe and you'll feel like you just circumnavigated the globe.

South Belfast

There are so many riverside trails, ancient ruins, and idyllic parks south of the city that it is hard to believe that you're only a few miles from the city center. The area can be reached by buses #70 and 71 from Donegall Sq. East. The **Belfast Parks Department** (tel. 320202) and the **N.I. Tourist Board** (tel. 246609) can provide you with maps and tips. The most stunning of the parks, **Sir Thomas and Lady Dixon Park,**

Upper Malone Rd., boasts over 20,000 rose bushes. The gardens were founded in 1836 and include the stud China roses, imported between 1792 and 1824, which provided the foundation for current British roses. Four miles north along the tow path (near Shaw's Bridge) lies **Giant's Ring,** a 4500-year-old earthen ring with a dolmen in the middle. Little is known about the 600 ft. wide circle, but experts speculate that it was built for the same reasons as England's Stonehenge. Those hoping to track down long-lost relatives should head to the **Public Record Office,** 66 Balmoral Ave. (tel. 661621), where you can do just that. *(Open M-F 9:15am-4:15pm.)*

North Belfast

At the bottom of the hills that rise outside the city sits **Belfast Castle,** a relatively new building that was presented to the city by the Earl of Shaftesbury in 1934. *(Open M-Sa 9am-10:30pm, Su 9am-6pm. Free.)* The garden around the castle is landscaped with a kitty-cat theme and looks out at a king's view of Belfast city and the natural environment of Northern Ireland. The castle sits on top of cave hill and has long been the seat of rulers, as the ancient Ulster King Matudan has his **McArt's Fort** here, where the more modern United Irishmen plotted rebellion in 1795. The summit is nicknamed "Napoleon's Nose." Marked trails lead north of the fort to five caves in the area, thought by historians to be ancient mines. Only the lowest is accessible.

WEST BELFAST AND THE MURALS

Separated from the rest of the city by the Westlink motorway, the neighborhoods of West Belfast have historically been at the heart of the political tensions in the North. The Catholic area (centered on Falls Rd.) and the Protestant neighborhood (centered on the Shankill) are grimly separated by the **peace line,** a gray wall that creates peace through physical separation. Along the wall, abandoned houses with blocked-up or broken windows point to a troubled past and an uncertain future. These two neighborhoods embody both the raw sentiment that drives the Northern Irish conflict and the casual calm with which those closest to the Troubles approach daily life. Not a "sight" in the traditional sense, this is not a center of consumer tourism. In fact, the most dominant feature of the neighborhoods is their family community. The streets also contain an occasional political mural, which you will soon come across as you wander among the houses. Be discreet when photographing murals. As the murals in the Falls and Shankill change constantly, the sections below describe only a few. We provide a glossary of some common symbols (see **A Primer of Symbols,** p. 397).

It is best to visit the Falls and Shankill during the day, when the murals can be seen. The Protestant Orangemen's marching season, around Orange Day on July 12 (better known as "the Twelfth"), is a risky time to visit the area, since the parades are underscored by mutual antagonisms that can inspire political violence (see **History and Politics,** 373). Other ceremonial occasions, such as the Catholic West Belfast Cultural Festival (the first or second week in August), may also be less safe times to visit. To see both the Falls and Shankill, the best plan is to visit one then return to the city center before heading to the other, as the area around the peace line is still desolate.

Black cabs are the community shuttles that whisk West Belfast residents to the city center along set routes, picking up and dropping off passengers on the way. For the standard fare (60p), you can ask to be let off anywhere along the route. Black cabs can also reasonably be hired by groups for **tours** of the Falls or Shankill. (£30-50 for up to 6 people). **Catholic black cabs,** identified by signs that read "Falls Rd.," "Andersontown," or "Glen Rd." or are written in Irish, leave the city center from Donegall Sq. and the taxi park on Castle St. **Protestant black cabs,** identified by red poppies or "Shankill" signs, head up and down Shankill Rd. from bases at the top of North and Bridge St. (See **Transportation,** p. 355, and **Tours,** p. 363.)

The Falls

The Falls is much larger than Shankill and, with a younger population, still growing. Farther west on Divis St., a high-rise apartment building marks the site of the **Divis Tower,** an ill-fated housing development built by optimistic social planners in the

1960s. This project soon became an IRA stronghold and experienced some of the worst of Belfast's Troubles in the 70s. The British army still occupies the top three floors, and Shankill residents refer to it as "Little Beirut."

Continuing west, Divis St. turns into the Falls Rd. The **Sinn Féin office** on the right is marked by the wire cage enclosing the building and the surveillance camera outside. The Republican bookstore next door marked *"Sioppa na hEalaine"* (SCHU-pah nah AER-lan) will give you a map that shows the largest groups of murals and other sites of Republican significance in West Belfast. On the side of the bookstore is a large mural with a portrait of Bobby Sands and an advertisement for the Sinn Féin newspaper, *An Phoblacht.* Continuing down the Falls you will see a number of murals characterized by Celtic art and the Irish language. They display scenes of traditional dance and music, or grimmer portraits of Famine victims (usually portrayed in stark black and white in the midst of a colorful Irish landscape). One particularly moving mural, on the corner of the Falls and RPG Ave., shows the 10 hunger strikers who died in 1981-82 above a quote from Bobby Sands: "Our revenge will be the laughter of our children." Murals in the Falls, unlike those of the Shankill, are becoming less militant in nature, though there are a few left in the Lower Falls that refer to specific acts of violence. One shows women banging bin lids on the ground to warn neighbors of British paratroopers. The grim slogan reads: "25 years of resistance—25 more if needs be." Other political graffiti, concerning Sinn Féin, the RUC, and Protestant paramilitary groups, is everywhere.

The Falls Rd. soon splits into Andersontown Rd. and Glen Rd. (the site of Ireland's only urban *gaeltacht*). On the left are the Celtic crosses of **Milltown Cemetery,** the resting place of many Republican dead. Inside the entrance, a memorial to Republican casualties is bordered by a low green fence on the right. Bobby Sands's grave stands here. Another mile along the Andersontown Rd. lies the road's namesake—a housing project (formerly a wealthy Catholic neighborhood)—and more murals. The Springfield Rd. RUC station is the most attacked police station in Ireland and the U.K.; its charred defenses are formidable, as are its eight-story radio tower decked out with directional video cameras and microphones.

The Rape of the Falls

The area stretching from Divis Tower to Cavendish Sq. is known as the **Lower Falls.** This area was sealed off by the British Army for 35 hours in July, 1970, in an episode known as the **Rape of the Falls.** Soldiers, acting on a tip that arms were hidden in some of the houses, searched homes at random while residents were forbidden to leave the area, even for milk or bread. It is estimated that before this event, there were only 50 Republicans in the area. After the incident, however, over 2000 people turned to the IRA. Many regard this raid to be the biggest tactical mistake ever made by the British army in Northern Ireland.

Shankill and Sandy Row

North St., to the left of the tourist office, turns into Shankill Rd. as it crosses the Westlink and then arrives in Protestant Shankill, once a thriving shopping district. There is an age gap of almost a generation between Shankhill and the Falls because of different movement patterns. Streets are wider here than in the Falls and there are fewer houses because of the great migrations out of the area in the 70s. The **peace line** looms at the end of any of the side roads to the left. Many of the neighborhood's murals have been painted on the sides of the buildings that front Shankill Rd. At Canmore St., a mural on the left depicts the Apprentice Boys "Shutting the Gates of Derry—1688" as the Catholic invaders try to get through. Some murals in Shankill tend to glorify the UVF and UFF rather than celebrate any aspect of "Orange" culture. A little farther, also on the left and across a small park, a big, faded mural labeled "UVF—then and now" depicts a modern, black-garbed Protestant paramilitary man and a historical "B-Specials" soldier side-by-side (see **British rule and the Division of Ireland,** p. 350). The densely decorated **Orange Hall** sits on the left at Brookmount St. McClean's wallpaper, on the right, was formerly Fizzel's fish shop, where 10 people died in an October 1993 bomb attack. The side streets on the right guide you to the **Shankill Estate** and more murals. Through the estate, **Crumlin Road** heads back to the city center past an army base, the courthouse, and the jail, which are on opposite sides of the road but linked by a tunnel. The oldest Loyalist murals are found here.

The Shankill area is shrinking as middle-class Protestants leave it, but **Sandy Row,** another Protestant area, has a thriving population. It begins at Donegall Rd. next to Shaftesbury Sq. An orange Arch topped with King William marks the entrance to the Protestant area. Nearby murals show the Red Hand of Ulster, a bulldog, and King William crossing the Boyne (see **The Protestant Ascendancy,** p. 56).

While murals in the more volatile Falls and Shankill areas are often defaced or damaged, better-preserved and more elaborate murals adorn the secure Protestant enclave of East Belfast, across the Lagan. Several line Newtownards Rd. One mural likens the UVF to the ancient hero, Cuchulainn—Ulster's defender. It eerily resembles a mural in Derry that represents the Irish army in these same mythical terms.

A Primer of Symbols in the Murals of West Belfast

Blue, White, and Red: the colors of the British flag; often painted on curbs, signposts, etc., to demarcate Unionist murals and neighborhoods.

The Red Hand: the symbol of Ulster (found on Ulster's crest), usually used by Unionists to emphasize the separateness of Ulster from the rest of Ireland. Symbolizes the hand of the first Norse King, which he supposedly cut off and threw on a Northern Ireland beach to establish his primacy.

King Billy/William of Orange: sometimes depicted on a white horse, crossing the Boyne to defeat the Catholic King James II at the 1690 Battle of the Boyne. The Orange Order was later founded in his honor.

The Apprentice Boys: a group of young men who shut the gates of Derry to keep out the besieging troops of James II, beginning the great siege of 1689. They have become Protestant folk heroes, inspiring an honorary association in their name. The slogan **"No Surrender,"** also from the siege, has been appropriated by radical Unionists, especially Rev. Ian Paisley.

Lundy: the Derry leader who advocated surrender during the siege; now a term for anyone who wants to give in to Catholic demands.

Taig: phonetic spelling of the Irish given name Teague; Protestant slang for a Catholic.

Scottish Flag: blue with a white cross; expresses deep connection Protestants feel with Scots.

Orange and Green: colors of the Irish Republic's flag; often painted on curbs and signposts in Republican neighborhoods.

Landscapes: usually imply Republican territorial claims to the North.

The Irish Volunteers: Republican tie to the earlier (nonsectarian) Nationalists.

Saiorsche: "Freedom." The most common Irish term found on murals.

Éireann go bráth: "Ireland forever," a popular IRA slogan.

Tiocfaidh ár lá: (CHOCK-ee-ar-LA) "Our day will come."

Slan Abnaile: (slang NA-fail) "Leave our streets," directed at the primarily Protestant police force.

Phoenix: symbolizes united Ireland rising from the ashes of British persecution.

Lug: Celtic god, seen as the protector of the "native Irish" (Catholics).

Green ribbon: IRA symbol for "free POWs."

Bulldog: Britain.

ARTS AND ENTERTAINMENT

Belfast's many cultural events and performances are best covered in the monthly *Arts Council Artslink* (free; available at the tourist office and all art galleries). Daily listings appear in the daily *Belfast Telegraph* (which also has a Friday arts supplement) as well as in Thursday's issues of the *Irish News.* For more extensive information on pub entertainment, pick up the free, biweekly, two-page news bulletin *That's Entertainment,* available at the tourist office, hostels, and most pubs. The **Crescent Arts Centre,** 2 University Rd. (tel. 242338), supplies general arts info, but mostly specific news about their own exhibits and concerts, which take place September through May. They also host eight-week courses in yoga, trapeze, writing, trad, ballet, and drawing (classes meet once a week; £28 total) and sponsor art festivals throughout the year. **Fenderesky Gallery,** 2 University Rd. (tel. 235245), inside the Crescent Arts Centre building, hosts contemporary shows all year. *(Open M-Sa 11:30am-5:30pm.)* The **Old Museum,** 7 College Sq. North (tel. 235053 for office; 233332 for tickets), is Belfast's largest venue for new contemporary artwork. *(Open M-Sa 10am-5:30pm. Free.)* Besides art exhibits, it features a large variety of dance, theater, and live music performances as well as workshops on these art forms. *(Most performance tickets around £6, students and concessions £3.)* A word of warning to the summer traveler: July and August are slow months for Belfast arts, and around July 12 the whole city shuts down.

Theater

Belfast's theater season runs from September to June. Some plays are produced in the summer, but most playhouses "go dark" during the tourist season. The truly **Grand Opera House,** Great Victoria St. (tel. 240411), boasts an impressive mix of opera, ballet, musicals, and drama. Tickets for most shows can be purchased either by phone or in person at the box office, 2-4 Great Victoria St. (tel. 241919 for reservations; 24hr. info line tel. 249129). *(Open M-W 8:30am-8pm, Th 8:30am-9pm, F 8:30am-6:30pm, Sa 8:30am-5:30pm. Tickets £8 and up. M-Th 50% student rush tickets available after noon on performance days. Wheelchair accessible.)* The **Arts Theatre,** 41 Botanic Ave. (general inquiries tel. 316901; box office tel. 316900), houses its own company but hosts a wide array of touring troupes and individual performers. *(Open Aug.-June; box office at 23 Botanic Ave. open M-Sa 10am-7pm. Tickets £3-10.)* They produce a variety of genres. The **Lyric Theatre,** 55 Ridgeway St. (tel. 381081), mixes Irish plays with international theater. *(Tickets about £8.50 M-Th, £11 F-Su; student rates M-F.)* The **Group Theatre,** Bedford St. (tel. 329685), produces comedies and farces in the Ulster Hall from September to May. *(Box office open M-F noon-3pm. Tickets £2-6.)* The **Old Museum Art Centre,** 1 College Sq. North (tel. 233332 for tickets), presents avant-garde contemporary works. *(Tickets usually £6, students, seniors, and children £3.)*

Music

Ulster Hall, Bedford St. (tel. 323900), brings everything from classical to pop to town. Try the independent box offices for tickets: **Our Price** (tel. 313131) or the **Ticket Shop at Virgin** (tel. 323744). **The Grand Opera House** (see above) resounds with classical vocal music. **Waterfront Hall,** 2 Lanyon Pl. (tel. 334400), is Belfast's newest concert center, hosting a series of wildly disparate performances throughout the year. *(Tickets £5-35, average £10-12; student discounts available.)* The **Ulster Orchestra** plays concerts at Waterfront Hall and Ulster Hall (tel. 233240; tickets £5-22.50).

Film

There are two major movie theaters in Belfast. Commercial films are shown at **Virgin Cinemas,** 14 Dublin Rd. (tel. 245700 for 24hr. info or (0541) 555176 for credit card bookings); most movies come here three to seven months after their U.S. release. *(£4.25, students and children £3; all seats £3 all day Tu and M-W and Th-F before 5pm.)* **Queen's Film Theatre** (tel. 244857), in a back alley off Botanic Ave., draws a more artsy crowd. *(£2-3.80. "Meal and movie" discounts for certain restaurants.)*

The Belfast Festival at Queen's

Belfast reigns supreme in the art world for three weeks each November when Queen's University holds its annual festival. Over 300 separate performances of opera, ballet, film, and comedy invade venues across the city, drawing groups of international acclaim. Tickets for the most popular events sell out months ahead of time (although there's almost always something to see even if you haven't planned ahead). For advance tickets and schedules (no later than Aug.) write to: Mailing List, Festival House, 25 College Gardens, Belfast BT9 6BS. Ticket sales by mail begin September 15. From October 15 through the festival's end, tickets are available by phone (tel. 667687). Prices range from £2.50 to £25.

■ Near Belfast: Ulster Folk and Transport Museum

In **Cultra,** seven miles east of Belfast on A2 (Bangor Rd.), the Ulster Folk and Transport Museum (tel. (01232) 428428) stretches over 176 acres. *(Open July-Aug. M-Sa 10:30am-6pm, Su noon-6pm; Apr.-June and Sept. M-F 9:30am-5pm, Sa 10:30am-6pm, Su noon-6pm; Oct.-Mar. M-F 9:30am-4pm, Sa-Su 12:30-4:30pm. £4, students and seniors £2.50. Partially wheelchair accessible.)* The three parts of the museum present their subjects in interesting, not brain-tiring ways. The **Folk Museum** contains over 30 buildings, with plenty more to come, from the past three centuries and all nine Ulster counties, including Monaghan, Cavan, and Donegal in the Republic. Some of the buildings are transplanted originals, others exact replicas. All have been successfully placed in the museum's natural landscape to create an amazing air of authenticity. While attendants unobtrusively stand nearby to answer questions, there are no cheesy historical scenes or written explanations to interrupt the visitor's own imaginative role-play. The printer's shop on "Main Street" contains a working original 1844 newspaper press from the *Armagh Guardian*—ask the attendant for a demonstration. The museum also hosts special events, including trad music, dance performances and workshops, storytelling festivals, and textile exhibitions.

The Transport Museum and the Railway Museum are across the road from the Folk Museum. Inside the **Transport Museum,** horse-drawn coaches, cars, bicycles, and trains display the history of moving vehicles. Their motorcycle exhibition is extensive, following the evolution of the genre from the ABC Skootamota, a 1919 gem, to Harley mania with a life-size 1950s diner installation. A *Titanic* exhibit that includes original blueprints traces the Belfast-built ship and its fate. The hangar-shaped **Railway Museum** stuffs in 25 old railway engines, including the largest locomotive built in Ireland. Half a day is just long enough to see the museums here, although spending fewer than two hours would be foolish. Both **Ulsterbuses** and **trains** stop at the park on their way to Bangor.

Down and Armagh

Locals flock to this subtly beautiful area, taking advantage of seaside that the rest of the world has ignored. The coast of Down and the Ards Peninsula are covered with fishing villages, holiday resorts, and 17th-century ruins. The Mourne Mountains, almost directly south of Belfast and just a lough away from the Republic, rise above the town of Newcastle, the largest seaside resort in Down. An inland county surrounded by rivers and lakes, Armagh is set on the rolling hills of Northern Ireland's drumlin belt. The best time to visit Co. Armagh is during apple blossom season in May, when the countryside, known as the "Orchard of Ireland," is covered in pink. Armagh town is an ecclesiastical center of great historical interest; traces of human habitation at Navan Fort date back to 5500 BC. Co. Armagh's other population centers, Craigavon and Portadown near Lough Neagh, are industrial centers of less interest to tourists, although Craigavon does host the Lough Neagh Discovery Centre. The **Ring of Gullion** in South Armagh is a circle of hills containing Slieve Gullion and some astounding volcanic rock formations. Much of the area is privately owned, but visitors can enjoy its amenities at Slieve Gullion Forest Park, which has trails up the mountain as well as an 8 mi. road for cars or bikes. Call the Slieve Gullion tourist office (tel. (01693) 848084) for information.

▓ Bangor

Bangor found a place on early medieval maps of Ireland with its famous Abbey, a center of missionary activity, but this pious era in Bangor's history ended in the 9th century with the Viking raids. By the Victorian era, Bangor had become eminent again, this time as *the* seaside resort for Belfast residents. Today, Bangor caters to families

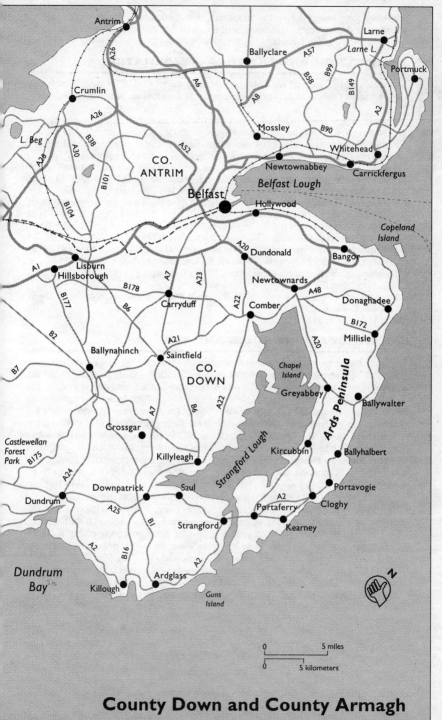

County Down and County Armagh

and older vacationers during the week and hosts busloads of twentysomethings on the weekends. Its location makes it both an inevitable and an enjoyable stop on the way down the Ards Peninsula.

ORIENTATION AND PRACTICAL INFORMATION

The train and bus stations are next to each other at one end of Main St., which runs past the tourist office on its way to the marina. Most sights are near the waterfront.

Trains: Abbey St. (tel. 270141), next to the bus station. Trains chug to **Belfast** (30min., M-F 38 per day, Sa 16 per day, Su 9 per day, £2).

Buses: Abbey St. (tel. 271143). Buses run to **Belfast** (45min., 20 per day, £1.80) and all **Ards Peninsula** towns, including **Donaghadee** (30min., 34 per day, £1.10).

Tourist Office: Tower House, 34 Quay St. (tel. 270069). Great brochures on the Down coast. Will book accommodations. Open July-Aug. M-F 9am-7pm, Sa 10am-7pm, Su noon-6pm; Sept.-June M-F 9am-5pm, Sa 10:30am-4:30pm.

Banks: First Trust, 85 Main St. (tel. 270628). Open M-Tu and Th-F 9:30am-4:30pm, W 10am-4:30pm. **Northern Bank,** 77 Main St. (tel. 271211). Open M 10am-5pm, Tu and Th-F 10am-3:30pm, W 9:30am-3:30pm, Sa 9:30am-12:30pm. **Ulster Bank,** Main St., open M-F 9:30am-4:30pm. All have 24hr. **ATMs.**

Pharmacy: Boot's Pharmacy, 79-83 Main St. (tel. 271134). Open M-Sa 9am-5:30pm.

Emergency: Dial 999; no coins required. **Police:** Castle Park Ave. (tel. 454444).

Counseling and Support: Samaritans, 92 Dufferin Ave. (tel. 464646). Open daily 9:15am-10pm.

Post Office: 143 Main St. (tel. 450150). Open M-F 9am-2:30pm, Sa 9am-12:30pm. **Postal Code:** BT20 482.

Phone Code: 01247.

ACCOMMODATIONS, FOOD, AND PUBS

Although Bangor is without hostel or campground, it teems with B&Bs in the £15-20 range; all of them are listed in the tourist office window. Along coastal Seacliff Rd. (Quay St., which runs by the tourist office, becomes Seacliff) and inland Princetown Rd. (from the train station, take a left on Dufferin Ave., which becomes Princetown), B&Bs are within spitting distance of each other. The **Lisnacree,** 53 Princetown Rd. (tel. 462571), offers sunny colors and tips about Bangor attractions (£16). Next door, **Tara Guesthouse,** 51 Princetown Rd. (tel. 468924), pampers guests with spacious rooms, all with bath, TV, and telephone (singles £25; doubles £40). On the other side of town, **Pierview House,** 28 Seacliff Rd. (tel. 463381), offers hospitality comparable to the charm of its original Victorian decorations (Apr.-Sept. £16; Oct.-Mar. £17). **St. Ives,** 58 Seacliff Rd. (tel. 469444), has frilly and spacious rooms (£15). B&Bs on Seacliff Road are highly recommended for their spectacular views of the sea.

A resort town, Bangor has no shortage of places to eat. Every third shop on Main St. sells baked goods and sandwiches, and every pub in town serves grub during lunch and dinner. **The Diner,** 8 Dufferin Ave., provides good and quite cheap food. (3-course "dinner meal" £3; open M-Sa 8:30am-6:30pm, Su 10am-4pm). A few yards farther along the avenue, **The Cosy,** 28 Dufferin Ave. (tel. 466572), has delicious home-cooked food and a fetish for figurative teapots—the enormous collection competes with customers for seating space (sandwiches around £2, entrees around £4; open M-Th 10am-4:30pm, F-Sa 10am-7pm). **Sandwich Express,** 48 Bingham St. (tel. 462131), just off High St., serves grilled cheese sandwiches (£1.25) to customers at a counter with a view (open M-Sa 8:30am-4pm).

Pubs gather along High St. and the waterfront. **Jenny Watts,** High St. (tel. 270401), is a former Bushmill's "bar of the year." It looks but doesn't feel the part; an older crowd sips pints slowly and sniffs at the debauchery of those with a liking for hard liquor (21+). Just down the street at **Wolseys,** 24 High St. (tel. 460495), regulars enjoy cheap meals (£4-5 from noon on) in green velvet and mahogany snugs with music for the younger crowd upstairs on weekends (live bands Th, decades dances F, disco Sa; cover £1). **Donegan's,** 44 High St. (tel. 270362), decorates its traditional interior with a Fauvist's color palette and has live music six nights a week (no cover), leaving Sunday for rest and good food (2-course lunch £5.25). **The Windsor,** 24 Quay St. (tel. 473943), has pints on the ground floor and DJs above. Check out the marine outside and the great drinks inside the **Steamer Bar,** 30-32 Quay St. (tel. 467699).

SIGHTS

North Down Visitors and Heritage Centre, Town Hall, Castle Park (tel. 271200), is in the "Elizabethan Revival" style house of the Hamilton family, once the owner of all the land around Bangor. *(Open July-Aug. Tu-Sa 10:30am-5:30pm, Su 2-5:30pm; Sept.-June Tu-Sa 10:30am-4:30pm, Su 2-4:30pm. Free.)* The rest of the Hamilton Estate around the center consists of 129 sometimes wooded, sometimes grassy acres that now compose the public **Castle Park.** Nearby, 37-acre **Ward Park** (up Castle St. or Hamilton Rd. from Main St.) entices with tennis courts, bowling greens, and a cricket pitch. A string of lakes down the middle also harbors a wildlife sanctuary. The **North Down Coastal Path** forays for 15 mi. from Holywood through Bangor and Groomsport to Orlock Point. Along the way are abandoned World War II lookouts; Helen's Bay, a popular bathing spot; Crawfordsburn Country Park; an old fort with a massive gun; and a giant redwood. Bicycles are banned from the path. The region is recognized for its colonies of black guillemots, which look like penguins. The most striking Bangor-Holywood portion should take 3½ hours to walk (3mi. northwest of Bangor along A2).

The path also passes through the picturesque village of Crawfordsburn, the home of Ireland's oldest hotel. **The Old Inn,** Main St. (tel. 853255), dates back to 1614 and still maintains many of its original wood decorations. The Inn has been visited by luminaries ranging from Peter the Great of Russia to C.S. Lewis and serves up afford-able food in its "Parlour Bar" (goat cheese tart £2.95; bar open M-Sa noon-7pm, Su noon-9:30pm). The **Crawfordsburn Country Park,** off B20 at Helen's Bay, is another of Northern Ireland's popular forest parks. *(Park open daily 8:30am-dark. Center open daily Apr.-Sept. 10am-6pm; Oct.-Mar. 10am-5pm. Free.)* It offers both coastal paths and green forests. The **Visitors Centre** (tel. 853621) provides plentiful information about the park's natural history and trails. The Bangor **bus** and **train** both run through Craw-fordsburn. In mid-June, the week-long **Bangor and North Down Festival** (sporting a different theme each year) brings in bands, fireworks, and lots of fun. Deep-sea angling and sailing are popular activities (contact the Bangor tourist office for details).

ARDS PENINSULA

The Ards Peninsula is bounded on the west by tranquil Strangford Lough; to its east lies the agitated Irish Sea. The Strangford Lough shore from Newtownards to Porta-ferry is crowded with wildlife preserves, historic houses, crumbling ruins, spectacu-lar lake views, and tourists. On the Irish Sea side of the Ards, each fishing village seems tinier and twice as nice as the one before.

Ulsterbus leaves Laganside Station in **Belfast** to traverse the peninsula, stopping in almost every town. **Trains** roll no farther than **Bangor** (see above). From the south, a **ferry** crosses frequently between **Strangford** and **Portaferry** (see **Portaferry,** 405). The Ards Peninsula can also be seen efficiently by bike.

■ Donaghadee

The fishing villages that line the coast south of Bangor consist of little more than one harbor and a few pubs each. The largest is Donaghadee, famous for its lifeboat and lighthouse. Donaghadee was Ulster's most important passenger port from the 17th century until 1849, when the mail boat began to patronize Larne. Composer Franz Liszt spent several days here waiting for a ship to bring him and his piano to England.

A well-spent morning would include walks along the waterfront or a stroll to the still-operational first electrical lighthouse in Ireland. Past the lighthouse, the **town commons,** formerly communal potato fields, spread along the shore. At the other end of town, an old ruined *motte* (MOTE) towers above the village on Donaghadee's single hill. The former castle's most recent use was holding the ammunition used to blast stone from the hill for building the harbor. Down at Lemons Wharf is the spruced-up and well-loved **RNLB Sir Samuel Kelly.** In 1953, the *Samuel Kelly* rescued scores of passengers when the ferryboat *Princess Victoria* sank just offshore on its way from Scotland to Belfast. Quinton Nelson (tel. (01247) 883403) at the marina skips passenger boats out to the Copeland Islands, a wildlife sanctuary just offshore, from June to September (£4, children £2; frequency depends on demand).

A restful night in Donaghadee can be spent at **The Deans,** 52 Northfield Rd. (tel. (01247) 882204), across from the school playground (singles £19; doubles £33). A handful of pubs and eateries are scattered along High St. Most notable is **Grace Neill's Pub and Bistro,** 35 High St. (tel. (01247) 882553), the oldest pub in Ireland according to the *Guinness Book of World Records.* During its 388-year lifespan, Grace Neill's has supposedly catered to the likes of Peter the Great and Oliver Cromwell. It has recently been renovated (the dark wood bar in the front is the original) and boasts a world-class chef. Lunch specialties from Thai to Italian dishes can delight your fancy (around £5). A few doors to the left, **Boswell's,** 7 High St. (tel. 888001), provides nightly entertainment for the town (9pm-1:30am). In the summer, you can barbecue in the backyard beer garden. If you're not in the mood for pub grub, head to **Alfie's** on High St. Something is certain to please at Alfie's three counters: ice cream, baked goods, and bistro. Combine counters to make a multi-course meal for about £4.

Ulsterbus drives to Donaghadee from **Bangor** (25min., M-F 26 per day, Sa 15 per day, Su 5 per day, £1.40) and **Belfast** (1hr., M-F 24 per day, Sa 17 per day, Su 7 per day, £2.30). South of Donaghadee, gnat-sized fishing villages buzz along the eastern shoreline. **Millisle, Ballywalter, Ballyhalbert, Portavogie, Cloughey,** and **Kearney** make good stops on an afternoon's drive, but none merit a special visit. **Portavogie** is charming, and **Millisle** is home to the **Ballycopeland Windmill.** A2 runs the length of the shore, where hitching a ride is reportedly easy.

■ Mountstewart and Grey Abbey

Roving pheasants greet you at **Mountstewart House and Gardens** (tel. (012477) 88387 or 88487), fifteen miles southeast of Belfast on A20. *(Admission for house, garden, and temple £3.50, children £1.75. Garden and temple £3, children £1.50. Temple £1.)* Held by a string of Marquesses of Londonderry, both house and garden are now National Trust property. They are worth a detour to see, especially if the Ulster Protestant Ascendancy intrigues you. The **gardens,** covering 85 acres, are the main attraction. *(Open Apr.-Sept. daily 11am-6pm; Oct. Sa-Su 11am-6pm.)* Lady Edith was the landscape architect, and she also created a doozy of a **Dodo Terrace,** which contains an interesting menagerie of animal statues meant to display the many rare species that Noah put in his ark. More comprehensive and alive, however, is the plantlife in the garden. Some areas appear wild and untamed, although others, such as the plants in one garden that form the red hand of Ulster, display the heavy hand of human gardeners. Many of the trappings of the stately 18th-century **Mountstewart House** are faded and tattered, but the regal portraits, gilded ceilings, chandeliers, and china still manage to give the place an air of grandeur. *(Open May-Sept. W-M, including bank holidays, 1-6pm; Apr. and Oct. Sa-Su 1-6pm. Last tour 5pm.)* The 22 chairs in the formal dining room, purchased by Lady Edith, the third Marquess of Londonderry, once held the arses of Europe's greatest diplomats at the 1814 Congress of Vienna, where they divvied up the post-Napoleonic continent.

The neo-classical **Temple of the Winds,** once a banquet hall, sits atop a hill with a super view of Strangford Lough. *(Open May-Sept. W-M 2-5pm, Apr. and Oct. Sa-Su 2-5pm.)* To reach the temple from Mountstewart House, turn left on the main road and go about a quarter mile. To reach Mountstewart from **Belfast,** take the Portaferry **bus** from Laganside Station (45min., M-F 20 per day, Sa 15 per day, Su 8 per day, £2.15) and ask the driver to let you off at Mountstewart. Hitchers report success on A20.

Two miles farther south on A20 lies miniscule **Grey Abbey,** whose Main St. comprises four pubs, several antique stores, two art galleries, and the **post office**/newsagent/gift shop. The ruins of the eponymous grey **Cistercian abbey** provide views of neighboring Grey Abbey House and the medieval "physick" herb garden. *(Open Apr. - Sept. Tu-Sa 10am-7pm, Su 2-7pm.)* Only parts of the abbey's foundation walls are intact. The abbey was built in 1193 with the support of Affreca, wife of John de Courcy and daughter of the King of Man, who vowed during a storm at sea to found a monastery if she survived. It was destroyed in 1570 by a native Irishman who wanted to prevent the English from using it in one of the first instances of clear Irish-Anglo conflict. Turn left off A20 onto B5 to reach the abbey—it's about 150 yards ahead on your right. The **bus** from **Belfast** to **Portaferry** also stops in Grey Abbey outside the **police station,** Main St. (tel. (012477) 88222).

■ Strangford Lough

Strangford Lough separates the Ards Peninsula from the mainland. Portaferry and Strangford peer at each other across the teeming, critter-filled depths.

■ Portaferry

Portaferry lies on the southern tip of the Ards Peninsula, on one side of Strangford Lough's narrows. Both residents and tourists prize this quiet seaside village for its aquatic offerings. With a brand-new aquarium and an annual sailing regatta, Portaferry remains one of the more beautiful and charming spots on the peninsula.

PRACTICAL INFORMATION To reach the Lough from the bus stop, head down the hill on Church St., which turns into Castle St., for about 200m, passing several eateries and the Exploris aquarium on the way. **Ulsterbuses** from Belfast drop visitors at The Square in the center of town (1½hr.; M-F 22 per day, less frequently on weekends, £3.30, £5.80 return). **Ferries** (tel. (01396) 881637) leave Portaferry's waterfront at 15 and 45 minutes past the hour for a 10-minute chug to Strangford. (M-F 7:45am-10:45pm, Sa 8:15am-11:15pm, Su 9:45am-10:45pm. 80p, seniors and ages 5-16 40p; cars £4.) The Portaferry **tourist office** (tel./fax 29882) is just behind the castle (follow signs from The Square toward the docks). Besides the usual plethora of brochures, it also offers a **bureau de change,** an exhibit on the maritime features of Strangford Lough, and a 12-minute video on the medieval "tower houses" of Co. Down. (Open July-Aug. M-Sa 10am-5:30pm, Su noon-6pm; Easter-June and Sept. M-Sa 10am-5pm, Su 2-6pm.) If the office is closed, you can call the regional office in Newtownards (tel. 826847). **Northern Bank,** 1 The Square (tel. 28208; open M 10am-5pm, Tu-W and F 10am-3:30pm, Th 9:30am-3:30pm; 24hr. **ATM**) and the **post office,** 2 The Square (tel. 28201; open M-Tu and Th-F 9am-5:30pm, W 9am-1pm, Sa 9am-12:30pm) are both within spitting distance of the bus stop. The **postal code** is BT22 1LN. The **phone code** got an A in Marine Biology 012477.

ACCOMMODATIONS AND FOOD A peaceful stay awaits at the **Portaferry Barholm Youth Hostel,** 11 The Strand (tel. 29598), at the bottom of Castle St. The hostel looks directly out onto the pretty village-scape, and the ferry leaves from just in front. Defying all hostel stereotypes, Barholm is relatively luxurious, with several singles and many doubles. Semi-private bathrooms, a large kitchen, laundry (£2.50), a greenhouse-like dining room, and great views all around add to the atmosphere. Because a Queen's University BelfastQueen's University marine biology lab is nearby, the hostel often hosts groups of students and lecturers; reservations are practically necessary on weekends (£10). Behind the Exploris aquarium is the **Exploris Touring Caravan Park** (tel. 28610), which offers space for up to twelve touring caravans in the midst of the Exploris playground, park, and tennis courts (£6). Campers can also settle across the lough in Strangford (see below).

The **Ferry Grill,** on High St. across from Spar Market, attracts all the local school children come for lunch and serves variations on a burger and fries for less than £2.

The Shambles Bistro and Coffee Shop disperses quick bites on Castle St. (soup and sandwich £1.50). For a slightly pricier meal, wander down to the **Cornstore,** Castle St. (tel. 29779), just before Exploris and the Portaferry castle. Decorated with a sailing motif, this small restaurant specializes in tasty traditional food and seafood on weekends (most meals £5-7). There are also numerous fresh fruit and veggie **markets** and convenient stores scattered around High St. and The Square. At night, everyone stumbles into the **Fiddler's Green,** Church St., where publican Frank leads rowdy traditional sing-alongs and welcomes live folk bands most evenings. A poster on the wall proclaims: "There are no strangers here—just friends who have not yet met." Fiddler's Green also includes a beer garden and a plush **B&B** (mostly doubles; £16). John Wayne paraphernalia covers the walls of **The Quiet Man** across the street. Without the letter from Wayne that until recently hung in a massive frame on the wall, however, the pub is better for a pint than for atmosphere. **M.E. Dunnigan's,** Ferry St., is a tiny pub just up from the waterfront so crammed with locals that craic is guaranteed.

SIGHTS Portaferry's claim to fame is **Exploris,** The Ropewalk (tel. 28062). *(Open Mar.-Aug. M-F 10am-6pm, Sa 11am-6pm, Su 1-6pm; Sept.-Feb. M-F 10am-5pm, Sa 11am-5pm, Su 1-5pm. £3.75, students, seniors, and children £2.60, families £11.75.)* Located near the dock next to the ruins of Portaferry Castle, Exploris houses first-rate exhibits on local ocean and seashore ecology; it is not only Northern Ireland's only public aquarium but also heralded as one of the U.K.'s best. The aquarium takes you on a journey beginning in the shallow waters of Strangford Lough and ending in the depths of the Irish Sea. Within its spooky, cavernous corridors, open tanks teem with sea-rays and nurse sharks, a "touch tank," and interactive displays for children.

Another big tourist attraction in Portaferry, the **Galway Hooker Festival and Traditional Boat Regatta** sails to town each year during the fourth weekend in June. Hookers are traditional fishing boats with thick, black hulls and billowing sails made in the west of Ireland. Hookers are not the only oddly named sailing ships on display: the regatta also includes Nobbies, Prawners, Luggers, and East Coast Smacks. Besides the regatta itself, the festivities include live trad, country, bluegrass, folk, and pipe band music. For general info, call the **Ards Borough Council** (tel. 812215) in Newtownyards; John McAlea (tel. 29532) and Leonard Lawson (tel. 28608) provide sailing information. Book B&Bs months in advance.

Move Over, Tootsie

The remarkable wrasse species of fish is found in various sub-species throughout the depths of the Irish Sea. These fish may be eons ahead of the human species in terms of gender equality. Typically, little difference can be observed between the two sexes of the species in their external appearance, but some wrasse have the far more unusual ability to change sex during courtship. In ballon wrasse and cuckoo wrasse, the dominant female fish of a group becomes male for mating season. The corkwing wrasse bend the sex barrier in an altogether different manner: the males in this sub-species look so like their female counterparts that they manage to mate with the females without other males detecting them. Not all wrasse employ such covert operations. The cuckoo wrasse make quite a statement when the switch happens: the newly male fish's head turns bright blue. When courting, the cuckoo's blue head will alternately turn brilliantly white to catch the females' attention.

■ Strangford

Perhaps the most noteworthy aspect of this Viking village (its name is Norse for "strong waters") is its proximity to the **Castle Ward House and Estate** (tel. 881204). *(House open May-Aug. M-W and F-Su 1-6pm; Apr. and Sept.-Oct. Sa 1-6pm; Easter week daily 1-6pm.)* This 18th-century estate, once owned by the couple Lady Anne and Lord Bangor and now the property of the National Trust, lies atop a hill approximately 2 mi. from Strangford. One wing of the house, built in 1768, is classical, which satisfied

Lord Bangor; the other is Gothic, which was pleasing to Lady Anne. Alas, even exorbitant compromise was not enough, and they split up soon after the house was built. The 700-acre estate features a rectangular lake, a tower house, a restored corn mill, and a "Victorian pastimes center" for children. *(Estate and grounds open year-round dawn to dusk. Free.)* In the summer, the Castle Ward Opera performs here (tel. (01232) 661090 for tickets and info). To get to the estate by car from Strangford, take A25 toward Downpatrick. The entrance to the grounds is about 2 mi. up the road on the right (£3.50 per car).

The **Strangford Lough Wildlife Centre** is located on the estate and provides information on the natural environment of the lough (open July-Aug. M-W and F-Su 2-6pm; Apr.-June and Sept. Sa-Su 2-6pm). If you are walking, you could also follow A25, but turn off the main road at the entrance to the Castle Ward Caravan Park. Follow the driveway to the right fork, and go through the brown gate on your right. This takes you to the **Loughside Walk,** a 30-minute stroll along the coastline to the Wildlife Centre during which you can accumulate scores of observations on the wildlife of the area. In town, a small 16th-century tower house optimistically called **Strangford Castle** stands to the right of the ferry dock as you disembark. Wander into its dark, spooky interior and find a spectacular view from the third floor. (Key to gate available from Mr. Seed, 39 Castle St., across from the tower house's gate, 10am-7pm.)

This tiny harbor village lies just across the Lough from Portaferry, northeast of Downpatrick on A25 and north of Ardglass on A2. **Ferries** leave Strangford for Portaferry every half hour (M-F 7:30am-10:30pm, Sa 8am-11pm, Su 9:30am-10:30pm). **Buses** for Downpatrick leave from in front of the ferry dock (30min., M-F 9 per day, Sa 5 per day, £1.60). Strangford's **phone code** is estranged from 01396.

The **Castle Ward Caravan Park** (tel. 881680), on the Castle Ward National Trust property, charges £7 per tent (open mid-Mar. to Sept.; free showers). Peter McErlean welcomes you to **Cuan Bar and Restaurant,** 6 The Square (tel. 881222), offering pub grub throughout the day (£5-6) and high tea on Sunday (5-7:30pm). Locals nurse their pints at **The Lobster Pot,** 11 The Square (tel. 881288), which also features barsnacks (£1.80-4.25), local seafood (£10), and Sunday high tea (5-8pm; £8). Another popular spot is **The Hole in the Wall Public House** (tel. 881301), on the road to Downpatrick, run by a golf buff and decorated with leaded glass.

ST. PATRICK'S VALE

A stormy gale swept St. Patrick's boat into Strangford Lough in 432, and the famous saint's footsteps lie all over this coastal region. The region has more than just St. Patrick, though; visitors leave enchanted with vivid history, amusing seaside resorts, abundant wildlife, and gorgeous scenery, including the majestic Mourne Mountains.

▓ Downpatrick

Downpatrick lies in the midst of the rolling hills of the Ards Peninsula. Downpatrick's name highlights its two defining characteristics: it is the Down county seat and supposed burial place of St. Patrick. The streets of the town are filled with tradespeople, shoppers, loitering children, and heavy traffic. The countryside around the city is dotted with St. Patrick-related religious and archaeological sites, which are perhaps best seen in a daytrip with a car. Many visitors spend the night in Portaferry (p. 405) or Newcastle (p. 410).

ORIENTATION AND PRACTICAL INFORMATION

The bus station is at the end of Market St., which is the main street in town and connects with all other streets of importance. If you are coming from the station, the first of these streets is St. Patrick's Ave., on the left. At its other end, Market St. meets Irish St. on the right, Church St. straight ahead, and English St. on the left. These streets contain Downpatrick's main features and lead to the countryside's attractions.

Buses: 83 Market St. (tel. 612384). Buses to **Belfast** (45min., M-F 28 per day, Sa 15 per day, Su 6 per day, £3.05), **Newcastle** (20min., M-F 19 per day, Sa 11 per day, Su 6 per day, £2.15), and **Strangford** (25min., M-F 9 per day, Sa 4 per day, £1.60).

Tourist Office: 74 Market St. (tel. 612233), across from the Supervalu. Open July-mid-Sept. M-F 9am-6pm, Sa 10am-6pm, Su 2-6pm, bank holidays 11am-6pm; mid-Sept.-June M-F 9am-5pm, Sa 10am-5pm, bank holidays 11am-6pm.

Banks: Northern Banks, 58-60 Market St. (tel. 614011). Open M 9:30am-5pm, Tu-F 10am-3:30pm, Sa 9:30am-12:30pm. 24hr. **ATM. Bank of Ireland,** 80-82 Market St. (tel. 612911). Open M-Tu and Th-F 9:30am-4:30pm, W 10am-4:30pm.

Local Transportation: Buses run M-Sa 9:55am-4:45pm, 7 per day.

Taxis: 96 Market St. (tel. 614515), run M-Th 10am-1:30 or 2am, F-Su 10am-3:30am.

Pharmacy: Foy's Chemist, 16 Irish St. (tel. 612032). Open M-F 9am-5:30pm. **Beeny Pharmacy,** 30A St. Patrick's Ave. (tel. 613807). Open M-Sa 9am-5:30pm.

Emergency: Dial 999; no coins required. **Police:** Irish St. (tel. 615011).

Hospital: Downe Hospital (tel. 613311).

Post Office: 65 Market St. (tel. 612061), inside the Supervalu near the eggs. Open M-F 9am-5:30pm, Sa 9am-12:30pm. **Postal code:** BT30 6LZ.

Phone code: The up side of Down is 01396.

ACCOMMODATIONS, FOOD, AND PUBS

Although most visitors spend the night in Portaferry or Newcastle, the superb quality of **Hillside,** 62 Scotch St. (tel. 613134), might very well warrant a stay. For £13.50 (with bath £15) Mrs. Murray provides fluffy beds, tasteful Victorian decorations, and a full Irish breakfast. The closest campground is **Castle Ward,** near Strangford (see above); the nearest hostels are in Newcastle and Portaferry.

There seem to be limitless eateries in Downpatrick, and most pubs serve lunch from noon to 2:30pm and bar snacks throughout the evening. The **Daily Grind Coffee Shop,** 21A St. Patrick's Ave. (tel. 615949), offers a wide selection of scrumptuous gourmet sandwiches at a low price (£3; open M-Sa 10am-4:30pm). The **Iniscora Tea Room,** 2-6 Irish St. (tel. 615283), is inside the Down Civic Arts Centre (see **Sights** below). The profit from its simple lunches (sandwiches £1-1.50, baked potato with filling £1.50) goes to the Down Residential Project for the Disabled. **Oakley Fayre's** bakery and sit-down café, 52 Market St. (tel. 612500), provides full meals in the diner-esque seating area behind their traditional bakery (open M-Sa 9am-5:15pm). For picnic food from charming mom-and-pop shops, try **Quinn's Home Bakery,** 10-12 Scotch St. (tel. 612432; open M-Sa 8:30am-5:30pm) or **Hanlon's Deli,** 26 Market St. (open M-Sa 8am-5:45pm).

Good pubs abound in Downpatrick, some of which specially cater to visitors with historical or musical inclinations. **Denvir's Hotel,** 14 English St. (tel. 612012) has housed the likes of Daniel O'Connell and Jonathan Swift and has a bar that dates from 1642. The United Irishmen who fought for home rule in the Rebellion of 1798 met here under the pretext of a literary society (see **Rebellion, Union, and Reaction,** p. 57). When the rebellion failed, the Denvir family was forced to flee to America, where the next generation became the founders of Denver, Colorado. Ponder the scope of history as you enjoy a hearty lunch (£4) in the pub's restaurant (M-Sa noon-2:30pm) or dinner in the bistro (entrees £7-8; Su-Th 6-8pm, F-Sa 7-9pm). Young and old congregate at the **Hootenanny,** 21 Irish St. (tel. 612222), which features a local jam night on Tuesday, live music Saturday and Sunday, and a disco on Friday and Saturday (cover for disco £3). The newly renovated **Forge,** 14 Church St. (tel. 612522), provides an updated version of your traditional Irish pub, with wood paneling, orange walls, and good craic despite an enormous TV screen. On weekends, it becomes a student hangout with disco Thursday and Saturday (cover £1.50) and live bands Friday (cover £2). **The Russell,** 7 Church St. (tel. 614170), claims to serve the best Guinness in town due to the double-cooled tap. Thomas Russell, one of the leaders of the 1803 Presbyterian rebellion for home rule, supposedly haunts the building.

SIGHTS

Down County Museum and Heritage Centre (tel. 615218), at the end of English St. (walk down Market St. away from the bus station and then follow the signs), does regional history with unusual flair. *(Open June-Aug. M-F 11am-5pm, Sa-Su 2-5pm; Sept-May Tu-F and bank holidays 11am-5pm, Sa 2-5pm. Free.)* Housed in the jail where Thomas Russell was hanged, the museum introduces you to St. Patrick, a wax gang of 19th-century prisoners, and the story of Co. Down. Its self-proclaimed goal is to present history as it was, rather than as partisans would like it to be. The **Down Civic Arts Centre,** 2-6 Irish St. (tel. 615283), converted from the old town hall, hosts traveling exhibitions (free) and stages musical performances in autumn. *(Open M and F-Sa 10am-4:30pm, Tu and Th 10am-10pm. Ticket prices vary.)*

Next to the museum, the Church of Ireland **Down Cathedral** (tel. 614922) sits beside the **Mound of Down** (also known as the English Mount or Rathkeltair), originally a Bronze Age hill fort. The medieval illuminated *Book of Armagh*, now cohabiting with its cousins in the Trinity College library, claims that St. Patrick is buried in the hill. A Celtic monastery until the 12th century, the cathedral became a Benedictine monastery under the Norman conqueror John de Courcey and then proceeded to fall to ruin. Rebuilt in 1818, the present cathedral incorporates stone carvings from its medieval predecessor into its walls and houses the only private pew boxes still in use in Ireland. While most foreign tourists know that St. Patrick is the patron saint of Catholic Ireland, the cathedral shows that he is embraced by both major religious groups in Northern Ireland. The entrance of the church proclaims that it proudly represents 1500 years of Christianity, beginning with St. Patrick's settlement in nearby Saul (see below). In the graveyard, a stone commemorates the **grave of St. Patrick;** he is joined by the remains of St. Brigid and St. Colmcille (also known as St. Columba). Although it is uncertain whether the gravestone marks the correct site, it does bring visitors to a beautiful view above Downpatrick and its hilly surroundings.

■ Near Downpatrick: Saul

St. Patrick dominates the landscape and mentality here, and most masterful and famous of all his historical sites is **Saul** (tel. 614922; 2mi. northeast of Downpatrick on Saul Rd.), where St. Patrick is believed to have landed in the 5th century. After being converted to Christianity, the local chieftain Dichu gave Patrick a barn *(sabhal)* which later became the first parish church in Ireland (open daily until 6pm). 1933 replicas of an early Christian church and round tower commemorate the landing. A little more than a mile from Saul, on the summit of Slieve Patrick, stands **St. Patrick's Shrine,** which consists of a huge granite statue of the saint, bronze panels depicting his life, and an open-air temple. Even nonbelievers will appreciate the 360° view of the lough, the mountains, and, on a clear day, the Isle of Man. Another link to St. Patrick lies in the **Struell Wells,** on the Ardglass road to the southeast of Downpatrick. Water runs through underground channels from one well to the next. Belief in their curative powers originated long before Christianity arrived on the scene.

One mile from Downpatrick on the Belfast road (A7) lie the ruins of the **Cistercian Inch Abbey,** the earliest standing Gothic ruins in Ireland. *(Open Apr.-Sept. Tu-Sa 10am-7pm, Su 2-7pm. £1.)* The abbey was founded in 1180 by John de Courcy, Down's Norman conqueror, to make up for his destruction of the Eneragh monastery a few years earlier. The site, located on an island in the Quoile River, makes an excellent backdrop for a picnic. The **Quoile Pondage Nature Reserve** (tel. 615520), off Strangford Rd., offers hiking trails, picnic sites, and birdwatching around a lake created in 1957 when a tidal barrier was erected to prevent the flooding of Downpatrick. The barrier allowed an unusual collection of vegetation, fish, and insect life to grow. The **Quoile Countryside Centre** provides a surplus of information. *(Open Apr.-Sept. daily 11am-5pm; Oct.-Mar. Sa and Su 1-4:30pm.)*

■ Newcastle and the Mournes

Newcastle has all the features of a family seaside resort, with the pleasantly incongruous backdrop of the Mourne Mountains looming over it to the south. Newcastle town is an attractive preliminary to Slieve Donard, the highest point in Northern Ireland. The waterfront is lined with family-run businesses and shops and is fully equipped with carnival goodies including arcades, joke shops, and go-carts. On summer weekends, children crowd the streets and vacationers scramble for places in waterslide lines and spots on the beach. Anyone looking for natural beauty in any season should head up into the hypnotic Mourne Mountains or north along the untrammeled dunes.

The 15 rounded peaks of the Mourne Mountains sprawl across the southeastern corner of Northern Ireland. Volcanic activity pushed up five different kinds of granite beneath a shale crust 50 million years ago. Several million more years of rain and ice created the gray, spotted face of hard acidic granite on the mountains today. No road penetrates the center of the mountains, so hikers are left in welcome solitude. Due to the glaciers of the last Ice Age, the peaks form a skewed figure-eight with two large valleys in the middle. The larger of these valleys holds **Ben Crom** and **Silent Valley,** reservoirs built early this century to supply water to Belfast.

ORIENTATION AND PRACTICAL INFORMATION

The main road in town stretches along the waterfront, changing from Main St. (where it intersects with Railway St., the site of the Ulsterbus stop) to Central Promenade to South Promenade. Those who thumb a ride stand at either end of the main road, south for Kilkeel or north for Downpatrick.

Buses: Ulsterbus, 5-7 Railway St. (tel. 22296), at the end of Main St., away from the mountains. Buses run to: **Belfast** (1¼hr., M-F 25 per day, Sa 18 per day, Su 13 per day, £4.20), **Downpatrick** (20min., M-F 19 per day, Sa 11 per day, Su 6 per day, £2.15), **Kilkeel** (40min., M-F 16 per day, Sa 10 per day, Su 6 per day), **Newry** (1¾hr., M-Sa 4 per day, Su 2 per day, £3.30), and **Dublin** (3hr., M-Sa 4 per day, Su 2 per day, £9.70).

Tourist Office: 10-14 Central Promenade (tel. 22222), in a blue and white building 600yd. down the main street from the bus station. Free map and visitor's guide. Open June-Aug. M-Sa 9:30am-7pm, Su 2-6pm; Sept.-June M-Sa 10am-5pm, Su 2-6pm.

Banks: First Trust Bank, 28-32 Main St. (tel. 23476). Open M-Tu and Th-F 9:30am-4:30pm, W 10am-4:30pm. 24hr. **ATM. Northern Bank,** 60 Main St. Open M 9:30am-5pm, Tu-F 10am-3:30pm. 24hr. **ATM.**

Taxi: Donard Cabs (tel. 24100 or 22823); **Shimna Taxis** (tel. 23030).

Bike Rental: Wiki Wiki Wheels, 10B Donard St. (tel. 23973). On the side of the Xtra-Vision building (left from the bus station). Offers full accessories. £6.50 per day, £30 per week; children £5 per day. Driver's license, passport, or credit card deposit. Open M-Sa 9am-6pm, Su 2-6pm.

Laundry: Dirty Duds, 58A Valentia Pl. (tel. 26190). £2.50 self-service wash, 70p dry. Open M-Sa 9am-6pm.

Camping Equipment: Hill Trekker, 115 Central Promenade (tel. 23842). Trail maps, tips for hiking in the Mournes, info about guided tours, and hiking boots (£2 per day, deposit £10). Owned by knowledgeable hiking enthusiasts. Open Tu-W and Sa-Su 10am-5:30pm, Th 10am-4:45pm, F 10am-6:15pm.

Pharmacy: G. Maginn, 9 Main St. (tel. 22923). Open M-Sa 9am-6pm. **Thornton's Chemist,** 49 Central Promenade (tel. 23248). Open M-Sa 9am-6pm.

Emergency: Dial 999 (including **Mountain Rescue**).

Police: South Promenade (tel. 23583).

Post Office: 33-35 Central Promenade (tel. 22418). Open M-W and F 9am-5:30pm, Th and Sa 9am-12:30pm. **Postal Code:** BT33 ODJ.

Phone code: 013967 is a decent brown ale.

ACCOMMODATIONS AND CAMPING

B&Bs in this summer resort town range in price from affordable to sky high; fortunately, there is a hostel. Of the area's numerous campsites, Tollymore Forest Park is probably the most scenic, but the Mournes themselves are a free and legal alternative.

Newcastle Youth Hostel (YHANI/HI), 30 Downs Rd. (tel. 22133). Follow Railway St. toward the water and take a right onto Downs Rd. at the Percival Arms. The best bet for the budget traveler—central, on the waterfront, and cheap. Quarters are tight even for a hostel, but the cramped conditions matter little, in the face of the prime location and the hospitality of the proprietress. Well-furnished kitchen. Dorms £7.50, under 18 £6; 6-person family penthouse £30. Lockers 50p.

Drumrawn House, 139 Central Promenade (tel. 26847), about a 10min. walk from the bus station. This Georgian townhouse has a marvelous sea view. £16.50.

Castlebridge House, 2 Central Promenade (tel. 23209). Understandably popular, with cozy rooms and an ideal location overlooking the bay. £14.

Arundel, 23 Bryansford Rd. (tel. 22232). Just off the southern end of Central Promenade (after the Anchor Bar). Made-to-order breakfasts, comfy beds, a huge lounge, and a mountain view. £16.

Homeleigh, 7 Slievemoyne Park (tel. 22305), the second left off Tullybrannigan Rd. A strangely pleasing mix of 1970s and Victorian decor greets you in Mrs. McBride's home. £14.

Glenside Farm House, 136 Tullybrannigan Rd. (tel. 22628). This "tourist-approved farmhouse" is a long, if lovely, 1½mi. walk from town (take Bryansford Rd. and follow signs for Tullybrannigan—or take a taxi). Clean, simple rooms. Small single £11; doubles £22.

Tollymore Forest Park, 176 Tullybrannigan Rd. (tel. 22428), a 2mi. walk along A2. Or take the "Busybus" which leaves the Newcastle Ulsterbus station at 10am and noon, more often during the high season (10min., 75p). Excellent **camping** facilities include showers, a café with delicious doughnuts, and 584 hectares of well-marked walks and gardens. Good Friday to Sept. £10 per tent or caravan; Oct. to Thursday before Easter £6.50. Youth groups £1.70 per person plus £10 deposit.

FOOD AND PUBS

The nougat-like density of take-aways, candy stores, and ice cream shops on the waterfront could keep you on a permanent grease and sugar high. **Maud's Coffee Shop,** 139 Main St., at Castlebridge Court, flaunts Pooh Bear (honeycomb and vanilla) ice cream as well as other award-winning flavors. It also serves up heartwarming sandwich entrees (£2-3), breakfast, and full-blooded cappuccino. (Open M-F 9am-9pm, Sa-Su 11am-9pm.) Just down Main St., the **Cookie Jar** makes sandwiches to order (under £2; open M-Sa 9am-5:30pm). The **Cygnet Coffee Shop,** Savoy Ln. (tel. 24758), just off Main St. near the bus station, provides a better-than-usual selection of light fare at less-than-usual prices (sandwiches £1.50, entrees £3-4; open M-Sa 9am-5:30pm, Su 11:30am-5:30pm).

Good meals at reasonable prices are available at most of the hotels in the area. The **Avoca Hotel,** 93 Central Promenade, offers great vegetarian entrees at lunch (£3-4.25, served 12:30-2pm). In the winter, the two-course dinner for senior citizens is a steal (£3.50, served Sept.-Apr. M-F 4:30-7pm). Another Main Street eatery with substantial meals is **Robinson's Restaurant,** run by a proud husband and wife team, which serves bistro platters (sandwiches £2, entrees £5-6).

There are plenty of pubs in Newcastle, but it's quite difficult to find an empty one—Newcastle is not the place for a quiet drink. Especially popular spots include **Quinn's,** 62 Main St. (tel. 26400), where Wellingtons hang from the ceiling and live music shakes the rafters Thursday through Saturday; and century-old **Anchor Bar,** 9 Bryansford Rd. (tel. 23344), which draws large crowds, perhaps because of its stained-glass windows that brilliantly evoke the Irish Sea. The **Central Park Nite Club** (tel. 22487), on the south end of Central Promenade, welcomes live bands to its lounge on weekends and has a disco in the nightclub Friday through Sunday (cover varies). For a classier and dearer drink, head to **Percy French** (tel. 23175) in the Slieve Donard Hotel at the northern end of the beach. Mr. French was a popular Irish songwriter from the last century whose flowery lyrics still appeal to sentimentalists.

SIGHTS: THE MOURNE MOUNTAINS

Before heading for the hills, stop at the **Mourne Countryside Centre,** 91 Central Promenade (tel. (013967) 24059), where the friendly and knowledgeable staff personally leads hikes and offers a broad selection of guides and maps of the mountains. *(Center open July-Aug. M-F 9am-5pm, Sa-Su 10am-5pm; winter hours vary.)* Those planning short excursions can purchase *Mourne Mountain Walks* (£6), which describes 10 one-day hikes. Those planning to stay in the Mournes overnight ought to buy the *Mourne Country Outdoor Pursuits Map* (£5), a detailed topographical map. If the center is closed, ask for maps at the tourist office and advice at Hill Trekker (see **Practical Information,** above). Seasoned hikers looking for company might want to join the **Mourne Rambling Group** (tel. 24315), which sends groups into the Mournes each Sunday. Shuttlebuses run between Silent Valley and Ben Crom (June Sa-Su 1 per day, July-Aug. 3 daily, £2.15). On Wednesdays in July and August, Ulsterbus (tel. (01232) 337004) runs buses from Belfast on tours of the mountains. The trip includes a stop midway for a barbecue meal.

The **Mourne Wall** (built 1904-1923) encircles 12 of the mountains just below their peaks. Following the length of the 22 mi. wall takes a strenuous eight hours; many people break it up with a night under the stars. **The Brandy Pad,** an old path running from Bloody Bridge (2mi. south of Newcastle) right across the mountains, was used in the 1800s to smuggle brandy and tobacco from the Isle of Man. Hiking along the **Glen River** is another attractive option. Locals swim in the crystal-clear (and cold) tiny pools. The Mourne's highest peak, **Slieve Donard** (850m) towers above Newcastle, challenging those below to a tough but manageable day hike to its summit (5hr. return). The record for running up and down is fabled to be 98 minutes. The next peak over, **Slieve Commedagh** ("the mountain of watching"), is 767m high. It is best approached from Newcastle. To reach either peak, head to **Donard Park** on the corner of Central Promenade and Bryansford Rd. Follow the dirt path at the back of the carpark carefully (it crosses two bridges) and you will hit the Mourne Wall. At the wall, turn left for Slieve Donard, right for Slieve Commedagh. A local volunteer **Mountain Rescue** team (tel. 999) is available in case of emergencies. Less avid outdoor enthusiasts might prefer a picnic in Donard Park just off Central Promenade at the foot of the Mournes.

Wilderness **camping** is legal and popular. Common spots include the Annalong Valley, the shores of Lough Shannagh, and near the Trassey River. Hare's Gap and the shore of Blue Lough at the foot of Slievelamagan are also good places to pitch a tent. While camping around the Mourne Wall is allowed, camping in the forest itself is strictly prohibited because of the risk of forest fires. Remember to bring warm clothing since the mountains get cold and windy at night.

■ Nearby Forest Parks

Three parks managed by the Department of Agriculture are just a hop, skip, and a jump from Newcastle. **Tollymore Forest Park** lies just 2 mi. west of town at 176 Tullybrannigan Rd. (tel. (013967) 22428). *(Open daily 10am-10pm. £2, under 17 50p; £3.50 car.)* Within the park are ancient stone bridges, rushing waters, and very well-marked trails suitable for all ages. The Shimna River cuts the park in half from east to west. Four main trails, ranging from one to eight miles in length, afford glimpses of diverse wildlife including deer, foxes, badgers, and, if you're particularly quiet, otters. The "Rivers Trail" hike (3 mi.) encompasses most of the park and is highly recommended. The park is amply equipped with a campground (see **Newcastle: Camping,** above), visitors center, café, and impressive outdoor arboretum. If you're not up for the rambling walk to Tollymore, take one of Ulsterbus's "Tollymore" shuttles (15min., departs 10am and noon year-round, more frequently in July and Aug., 75p).

At the opposite end of town you'll find the **Murlough National Nature Reserve** (tel. (13967) 51467), on Dundrum Rd. to Belfast (A24). Home to sand dunes, heath, and woodlands, Murlough boasts marvelous swimming, as well as seal-watching during the fall moulting season. Plenty of critters can be observed throughout the year, including badgers, foxes, skylark, meadow pipits, and the endangered European insect species of marsh fritillary. To get there, take the Downpatrick or Belfast bus from Newcastle and get off at Murlough. (Beach and walks open in daytime. £2 per car in high season; free other times.) **Castlewellan Forest Park** (tel. (013967) 78664), whose entrance is at the top of the main street in Castlewellan, spreads itself out in the hills just north and east of the Mournes. *(Call the park for info. Open M-F 10am-sunset, Sa-Su 10am-5pm. £3 per car. Call M-F 8:30am-4:30pm for info and site booking. Camping Easter-Sept. £9.50 per tent; Oct.-Easter £6.)* From Newcastle, take A50 past its junction with A25. Inside the park lie many easily accessible attractions: a Scottish baronial castle (now a Christian Conference Centre, not open to the public), an impressive **Sculpture Trail** (with sculptures made of natural materials), and the North's **National Arboretum.** The lake overflows with trout; single-day or seasonal fishing permits are available April to mid-October. **Buses** run from Newcastle to Castlewellan (10min., M-F 26 per day, Sa 20 per day, Su 6 per day, 95p).

■ Carlingford Lough

A few miles down the coast from Newcastle lie **Kilkeel** and **Warrenpoint,** the larger harbor towns on the North's side of Carlingford Lough. Both boast beautiful views of the mountains and sea, but the similarity between the two ends there. Kilkeel is known primarily for its fishing fleet (the largest in Ireland) and proximity to the western peaks of the Mournes, but the town itself contains little. Warrenpoint, in contrast, has plenty to offer the most demanding visitors. The strand, with a marvelous view and various inviting establishments, leaves no need to escape into the mountains. The **phone code** for the region heads to the chipper for some 016937.

■ Kilkeel

There's not much to do in Kilkeel, but there's a great deal to explore around it. A lovely ramble around the natural environment of Co. Down awaits at **Silent Valley,** which is not only Belfast's water reservoir but also a well-managed park with information center, expensive café, and craft shop. *(Reservoir grounds open May-Sept. 10am-6:30pm; Oct.-Apr. 10am-4pm. £3 per car. Information Center open 10am-6:30pm.)* From the park gates, a 3 mi. path runs up the side of Silent Valley to Ben Crom reservoir (see **Newcastle and the Mournes,** p. 410). In the spring and summer, you can travel between the two reservoirs by shuttle bus (July-Aug. daily; May-June and Sept. Sa-Su).

If you take a left onto Hilltown Rd. and follow the signs, you will soon reach **Crocknafeola,** a superb little forest, and the **Spelga Dam.** Best reached by car (though walkable by following B27 from Newcastle), this mirror-like lake offers sublime views of the Mourne and striking quiet. In town, you might explore the waterfront **Cliff Walk.** For the best views, stroll down Knockchree, off Greencastle.

The **tourist office,** 6 Newcastle St. (tel. (016937) 62525), outlines the local attractions (open April-Sept. M-Sa 10am-5:30pm). **First Trust,** 30 Greencastle St. (tel. 62237; open M-Tu and Th-F 9:30am-4:30pm., W 10am-4:30pm) and **Northern Bank,** 42 Greencastle St. (tel. 63797; open M-Tu and Th-F 10am-4:30pm, W 9:30am-5pm) both have 24-hour **ATMs.** The **post office** is at 4 The Square (tel. 62225; open M-W and F 9am-5:30pm, Th 9am-1pm, Sa 9am-12:30pm). The **postal code** is BT34 4AA.

For those searching for a bed, the best choice is **Heath Hall,** 160 Moyadd Rd. (tel. 62612). Tea, sandwiches, advice on seeing the county, and limitless kindness are some of the benefits of staying in this alluring farmhouse (£15-17; call ahead for pickup). The tourist office can give you current B&B options closer to town if you wish; the B&Bs in Kilkeel tend to open and close at a rapid rate. The most popular watering hole, **Jacob Halls,** 8 Greencastle St. (tel. 64751), serves cheap and filling pub grub (most entrees £4; food served noon-7pm). The **Old Mill,** 12 Knockchree Ave. (tel. 65993), poses as both fast-food joint and sit-down restaurant (burgers under £2, most entrees £3-4; open Su-Th 8am-8pm, F 8am-midnight, Sa 8am-2am).

■ Warrenpoint

Farther along the coast on A2 is the pretty harbor town of Warrenpoint, which first gained fame as a resort town in the 1800s. Today it is still quite welcoming to tourists, but a bit more peaceful. On a sunny day, you can sit on the sea wall for hours and watch colorful spinnakers float across the water with the Mournes filling the sky.

ORIENTATION AND PRACTICAL INFORMATION

The bus station is on The Square, with Church St. to the left and the waterfront to the right as you exit; ferries land at the other end of the waterfront.

Tourist Office: Pick up tourist info and free maps at the **Town Hall,** Church St. (tel. 52256), just beyond The Square (open M-Sa 9am-5pm). Tourist info and free maps.

Banks: Ulster Bank, 2 Charlotte St., **Northern Bank** on Queen St., and **First Trust** at The Square all have 24hr. **ATMs.**

Ferries: Red Star Passenger Ferry (tel. 74088). Sporadic service to Omeath, a Republican town across the Lough May-Aug., weather and tides permitting. £2 return.

Bike Rental: Stewart's Cycles, 14 Havelock Pl. (tel. 73565), beside the Surgery Clinic on Marine Parade. Rents bikes and does repairs. £6 per day, £25 per week. Open M-Tu and Th-F 10am-noon and 2-6pm, Sa 10am-6pm.

Taxis: Ace Taxis (tel. 52666). 24hr.

Pharmacy: Walsh's Pharmacy, 25 Church St. (tel. 53661). Open M-Tu and Th-Sa 9am-6pm, W 9am-1pm.

Emergency: dial 999, no coins required.

Post Office: 9 Church St. (tel. 52225). Open M-Tu and Th 8:30am-5:30pm, W 8:30am-1pm, F 9am-5:30pm, Sa 9am-12:30.

Postal code: BT34 3HN.

ACCOMMODATIONS, FOOD, AND PUBS

Mariann's B&B, 18 Upper Dromore Rd. (tel. 52085), on the continuation of Duke St., a 10-minute walk from town (singles £20; doubles £30). If you want a single and would rather be closer to town, stay at the **Whistledown Inn,** 6 Seaview (tel. 52697). This B&B is directly on the waterfront at the end of Church St. on the second floor of an enormous Victorian townhouse (£20). Because B&Bs are a bit pricey here, those with cars might stay in Newcastle.

The B&B situation notwithstanding, Warrenpoint still contains an inviting selection of eating and drinking establishments. **Diamonds Restaurant,** The Square (tel. 52053), is always packed with happy locals devouring burgers (£2.25), pasta (£4), seafood (£3-4), and desserts (open M-Th 10am-7:30pm, F-Su noon-10pm; take-away next door). The **Genoa Café,** next door, boasts that it has served fish and chips to Warrenpoint since 1910. Today the restaurant sports a thoroughly modern decor, but the fish and chips (£1.80 and less) have been in demand this long for a reason. **Bennetts,** 21 Church St. (tel. 52314), is a mellow local favorite for lunch and a pint (lunch daily noon-2:30pm, dinner and bar snacks 5-9:30pm). For a quick bite, try the **Central Café,** 32 Church St. (tel. 52693), across from the tourist office, the closest you'll get to a diner atmosphere (sandwiches under £2), or the **Corn Dolly Coffee Shop & Home Bakery,** 28 Church St. (tel. 53596), which offers buns, biscuits, and sandwiches (£1-3; open M-Sa 8:30am-6pm).

After the shops and eateries around The Square, Warrenpoint's nightlife takes over. The **Crown Entertainment Complex,** The Square (tel. 52917), has two floors of fun: an old-style bar on the first that stages music Wednesday through Sunday (free) and a DJed "fun club" in back. The "Mingles' Nightclub" spews disco on the second floor Friday and Saturday (cover £2-4). Both floors are open and busy daily from 11:30am to 1:30am. Facing the Crown is **Cearnógs** ("the square"), 14 The Square (tel. 74077). Young crowds pour in on weekends for good craic. On the waterfront around the corner from The Square is a string of worthy pubs. **The Marine,** 3-4 Marine Parade (tel. 541477), proudly sponsors live music in its bar and "decades" (60s-90s) music in its nightclub (W and F-Sa 10pm-1:30am; nightclub cover £4).

SIGHTS AND ENTERTAINMENT

Warrenpoint and the surrounding area host several lively festivals during the summer. Thousands of people gather here each August to witness the **Maiden of the Mournes Festival;** maidens from Ireland, Europe, and some parts of the U.S. gather to display their personalities and talents. This event is preceded by the **Fiddler's Green Festival** in sweet and small **Rostrevor** (3 mi. from Warrenpoint along A2). During this late-July extravaganza, fans (and performers) of traditional Irish music, storytelling, and art gather to share good craic (for details, contact Tommy or Sam Sands, tel. 38577). Rostrevor is also known for **Kilbroney Park** which contains Rostrevor Forest, one of the few remaining virgin Irish Oak forests in Ireland, as well as the usual assortment of wildlife, wild walks, and wild picnic facilities (open daily dawn-dusk; free).

■ Armagh

The pagan worshippers who built huge ceremonial mounds at Navan Fort named their city Ard Macha (Macha's Height) after the legendary Queen Macha. According to tradition, St. Patrick came to Armagh (arm-AH) in the 5th century to convert the pagans. Since then, Armagh has become Ireland's ecclesiastical capital, remaining the administrative center for both the Catholic Church in Ireland and the Protestant Church of Ireland. The magnificent cathedrals and monuments amassed over a long history of religious prominence make Armagh worth visiting.

ORIENTATION AND PRACTICAL INFORMATION

English St., Thomas St., and Scotch St. define Armagh's city center. Just to the east lies **The Mall,** a long grassy park that used to be a race course but was converted to an innocent park when betting and racing were deemed inappropriate to the sanctity of the city. Just west of the city center, two cathedrals sit on neighboring hills: the Catholic Cathedral lifts two neo-Gothic spires, the Church of Ireland a medieval-looking tower.

Buses: Buses stop on the west side of The Mall. A new station is being built on Lonsdale Rd. To **Belfast** (1hr., M-F 20 per day, Sa 15 per day, Su 8 per day, £5) and **Enniskillen** (2hr., M-Sa 3 per day, £5.50).

Local Transportation: Intercity buses (tel. 522266) stop at The Mall W. Starting in 1998, two refurbished 40s-style coaches cart tourists from sight to sight in summer.

Tourist Office: Old Bank Building, 40 English St. (tel. 521800). From the bus drop facing The Mall, turn left, walk past The Mall, and turn left up the hill onto College St. The tourist office is 15yd. down the first street on the left. Pick up the *Armagh Visitor Magazine* (free), your one-stop periodical that contains a map and outline of all the major sites. Open M-Sa 9am-5pm, Su 1-5pm. Next door, **Armagh Ancestry,** 42 English St. (tel. (01861) 510033), provides family fun with your distant relatives. Open M-Sa 9am-5pm.

Bank: Northern Bank, 78 Scotch St. (tel. 522004); **ATM.** Open M 9:30am-5pm, Tu-F 10am-3:30pm.

Bike Rental: Brown's Bikes, 21A Scotch St. (tel. 522782). £5 per day, £25 per week. Helmets £1 per day. Open M-Sa 9am-5:30pm.

Pharmacy: J. W. Gray, corner of Russell and English St. Open M-Sa 9am-6pm. Rotating Sunday schedule printed in the Thursday paper.

Emergency: Dial 999; no coins required. **Police:** Newry Rd. (tel. 523311).

Hospital: Tower Hill (tel. 522341), off College Hill.

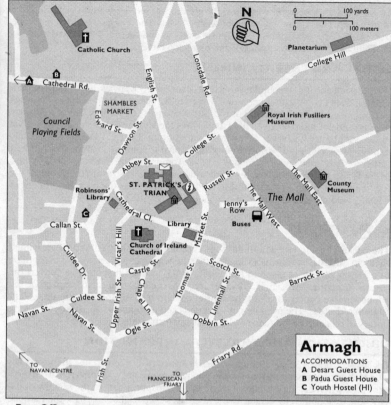

Armagh
ACCOMMODATIONS
A Desart Guest House
B Padua Guest House
C Youth Hostel (HI)

Post Office: 31 Upper English St. (tel. 510313). Mail is held across the street at 46 Upper English St. (tel. 522856). Open M-F 9am-5:30pm, Sa 9am-12:30pm. **Postal Code:** BT61 7BA.
Phone Code: Ecclesiastical ruler of the land of tiny people, 01861.

ACCOMMODATIONS

Armagh's magnificent **hostel (HI)** (tel. 511800) is brand new, spanking clean, and furnished in college dorm style. From the tourist office, turn left twice and follow Abbey St. for two blocks until the hostel appears on your right. It has 6-, 4-, and 2-bed rooms, each with TV and shower. Dinner and breakfast are available, as is the large kitchen. Even your roommates smell good, thanks to the £3 laundry facilities. (Dorms £10, doubles £11.50; £1 off for members. Reception 7:30am-midnight; daytime lockout in winter.) **The Padua Guest House,** 63 Cathedral Rd. (tel. 522039), is just past the Catholic Cathedral (next door to #10). Mrs. O'Hagen and her large doll collection greet guests with a cup of tea. Watch TV in some rooms; hear loud cathedral bells in all of them (£12). Mrs. McRoberts will kindly welcome you to the large and stately **Desart Guest House,** 99 Cathedral Rd. (tel. 522387). Make a right on Desart Road, and turn left 50 yd. down. The rooms are floral and clean (£15). **Gosford Forest Park** (tel. 551277; ranger tel. 552169), off A28, has room for tents 7 mi. southeast of Armagh. Take the #40 bus to Market Hill. (£8.50 per 2-person tent; Oct.-Easter £5.50.)

FOOD AND PUBS

The dearth of restaurants in Armagh and the near extinction of establishments open after 6pm may be the result of formerly soldier-filled streets. What little Armagh has for restaurants are scattered across English and Scotch St. Your best bet may be to pick up groceries at **Emerson's,** 57 Scotch St. (tel. 522846; open M-W 8:45am-5:30pm, Th-F 9am-9pm, Sa 8:45am-6pm), or at **Shambles Market** (tel. 528192), across from the Catholic Cathedral (open Tu and F 9:30am-5pm), for a picnic on The Mall or near the old friary. **The Basement Café** (tel. 524311) sits under the Armagh Film House on English St. next to the library and serves el cheapo meals to hep cats inside its baby blue walls (sandwiches £1.85; open M-Sa 9am-5:30pm). **Rainbow Restaurant,** 13 Upper English St. (tel. 525391), serves standard lunch fare buffet style (4-course lunch special noon-2pm £3.50; open M-Sa 8:30am-5:30pm). **Our Ma's Café,** 2 Lower English St. (tel. 511289), wins the coveted *Let's Go: Ireland 1999* Pun of the Year Award and offers student specials (burger and soda £1; open M-Sa 9am-5:30pm). After Armagh's famous apples blossom in May, **Johnston's Bakery,** 9 Scotch St. (tel. 522995), turns them over into delicious treats (apple turnovers 30p; open M-Sa 9am-6pm). **The Station Bar,** 3 Lower English St. (tel. 523731), looks like a dive but is one of the most popular pubs in town, with trad on Tuesdays and Thursdays at 10pm. **Harry Hoots',** Railway St. (tel. 522103), is another happening hangout. **The Northern Bar** (tel. 527315) across the street provides live entertainment and dancing three nights a week at 9:30pm.

SIGHTS AND FESTIVALS

Armagh's twin cathedrals are its pride and joy. The Church of Ireland **Cathedral of St. Patrick** (tel. 523142) is a 19th-century restoration of a 13th-century structure that enlarged upon the 5th-century original attributed to Patrick himself. *(Open daily Apr.-Sept. 10:30am-5pm; Oct.-Mar. 10:30am-4pm. Tours June-Aug. M-Sa 11:30am and 2:30pm. Free.)* The cathedral is the final resting place of the great Irish King Brian Ború (see **Early Christians,** p. 54). It also contains an Iron Age sculpture of a king with a prosthetic arm. Across town, the **Catholic Church of St. Patrick** raises its spires from Cathedral Rd. *(Open daily 9am-6pm. Free.)* Opened in 1873, the cathedral's imposing exterior and exquisite mosaic interior are marred only by the ultra-modern granite sanctuary, which appears to be a combination of pagan and Martian design. Dark water stains on the lower sections of the cathedral walls are legacies of the Famine, when work on the cathedral halted and the half-completed building was left exposed to the elements.

In the center of town, **St. Patrick's Trian** (tel. 521801) shares a building with the tourist office. *(Open July-Aug. M-Sa 10am-5:30pm, Su 1-6pm; Sept.-June M-Sa 10am-5pm, Su 2-5pm. £3.35, students £2.50.)* Most of the exhibits emphasize St. Patrick's role in

---

Gimme Some Buckfast Love

Buckfast tonic wines, produced by the Benedictine monks of the Buckfast Abbey, are sold in two places: Devon, the abbey's English hometown, and Co. Armagh. While the government warning on the orange label informs the would-be drinker that "Tonic wine does not imply health-giving or medicinal properties," "Bo," as it is popularly termed, has gained near-mythic stature with a certain section of the Armagh community. Though some might pass it off as Bacchus' gift to the wino, those who make the drink a part of their lives know better. Swearing that it's an experience as much like drunkeness as Beamish is like Guinness, aficionados advise restrained consumption for the Buckfast virgin. So what exactly is in this "Bo?" What sweet liquid was once harbored in the tons of broken green bottles you'll find strewn on an Armagh street Sunday morning? Among other things, .009% vanillin, .05% caffeine, .65% sodium glycerophosphate (to keep the drinker very regular), and 15% alcohol. At £5 for .75 liters, it just coincidentally happens to be pretty much the cheapest alcohol for your money.

Armagh, although his link to the town is historically ambiguous. *The Armagh Story* is a walk-through display and audio-visual presentation in which Vikings, priests, and pagan warriors relate the lengthy history of the town. A smaller, fanciful display geared for children recreates Swift's Land of Lilliput. Up College Hill north of The Mall is the **Armagh Observatory,** founded in 1790 by Archbishop Robinson (see below). Would-be astronomers can observe the modern weather station and a refractory telescope dating from 1885. The Robinson Dome (tel. 522928) provides self-guided tours. Celestial wonders await in the **Planetarium,** College Hill (tel. 523689), where a 3cm chunk of Mars is on display. *(£3.50, students £2.50. Call for show times.)* Booking ahead is strongly recommended, as seating is limited.

At the **Armagh County Museum** (tel. 523070), on the east side of The Mall, undiscriminating historians have crammed a panoply of 18th-century objects—old wedding dresses, pictures, stuffed birds, jewelry, and militia uniforms—into huge wooden cabinets. *(Open M-Sa 10am-5pm. Free.)* The **Royal Irish Fusiliers Museum,** The Mall East (tel. 522911), houses the treasure of over 150 years of the business of war. *(Open M-F 10am-12:30pm and 1:30-4pm. £1.50, students £1.)* On Friary Rd., south of the town center, the ruins of the 13th-century **Franciscan Friary,** the longest-standing friary in Ireland, occupy a peaceful green corner of the Palace Demesne. The palace and its chapel and stables were built by the 18th-century Archbishop of Armagh, Richard Robinson, in an effort to rebuild the entire city. Although the palace itself is closed to the public, the **Palace Stables Heritage Centre** (tel. 529629) puts on a slick multimedia show about "A Day in the Life" of the closed palace—July 23, 1776. *(Open Apr.-Sept. M-Sa 10am-7pm, Su 1-7pm; Oct.-Mar. M-Sa 10am-5pm, Su 2-5pm. £2.80, students £2.20.)* Take a peek at an open first edition of *Gulliver's Travels,* covered with Swift's own scrawled comments, at the **Armagh Public Library** (tel. 523142), built on Abbey St. in 1771. *(Open M-F 10am-12:30pm and 2-4pm.)* One might prefer to spend a nice day at **Gosford Forest Park,** 7 mi. southeast of Armagh, which includes a castle, old walled garden, poultry sheds, and miles of nature trails. (See **Accommodations,** above.) *(£2 per car, £1 per person. Open daily 10am-sunset.)*

Armagh holds an annual **Comhaltas Ceoltori Traditional Music Festival** around the first week of June and an arts festival in October. In mid-August, the Ulster **Road Bowls Finals** are held throughout Armagh. In this popular local game, amateurs compete to see who can throw a 28 oz. solid iron ball 4km in the fewest throws. Negotiating the bumps and turns in the road can be quite difficult, injecting an element of brain into this contest of brawn. **The Apple Blossom Festival** (tel. 529600), in the second week of May, brings a number of events to the city and culminates in a lavish May Ball. On March 17, people come from far and near to celebrate St. Patrick's patronage of the city.

■ Near Armagh: Navan Fort

On the outskirts of Armagh, **Navan Fort,** also called Emain Macha (AHM-win maka), was the capital of the Kings of Ulster for 800 years. *(Always open. Free.)* It may look like a grassy mound of dirt, but with a little imagination, historical knowledge, or hallucinogenic drugs, you might see the extensive defensive fortifications and elaborate religious paraphernalia. Where the mound now stands, a huge wooden structure 40 yards in diameter was constructed in 94 BC, filled with stones, promptly burnt to the ground in a religious rite, and covered with soil. In legend, Queen Macha founded the fort, although it is also associated with St. Patrick, who probably chose Ard Macha as a base for Christianity because of its relative proximity to this pagan stronghold. The **Navan Centre** (tel. (01861) 525550), built deep into a nearby hill away, presents an hour-long program of films and interactive exhibits on the archaeological evidence of the hills and the legends associated with the site. *(Open July-Aug. M-Sa 10am-7pm, Su 11am-7pm; Apr.-June and Sept. M-Sa 10am-6pm, Su 11am-6pm; Oct.-Mar. M-F 10am-6pm, Sa 11am-6pm, Su noon-6pm. £3.95, students £3.)* The center is on Killylea Rd. (A28), 2 mi. west of Armagh; the fort is a 10-minute walk from the center.

■ Lough Neagh and Oxford Island

A giant once scooped a heap of prime Ulster real estate out of the ground and chucked it into the sea, creating the Isle of Man (see p. 457-467) and Lough Neagh. The U.K.'s largest lake sits smack in the center of Northern Ireland's industrial heartland, touching five of the North's six counties. Though not yet appreciated in Ireland, the Lough Neagh eel is considered a great delicacy on the continent. Birdwatching, water-skiing, and various aquatic activities are just about the only amusements in the towns around the Lough; its shores are best seen as daytrips from Belfast or Armagh.

On the southeast shore of the Lough, the **Lough Neagh Discovery Centre,** Oxford Island National Nature Reserve, Craigavon (tel. (01762) 322205), contains acres of wooded parkland for exploration, with or without a guided tour. *(Open Apr.-Sept. daily 10am-7pm; Oct.-Mar. W-Su 10am-5pm. Last admission 1hr. before closing. £2.)* The lakeshore hosts hundreds of bird species. Boat rides to the islands run several times daily. Audio-visual displays in the center itself detail the lake's ecosystem and wildlife. The **Kinnego Caravan Park,** Kinnego Marina, Lurgan (tel. (01762) 327573), receives campers (£6 per 2-person tent).

Just off M1, 18 mi. north of Armagh, **Peatlands Park** (tel. (01762) 851102) contains native reserves, an interpretive center with interactive displays on the natural and human history of peat bogs, and a small railroad that was originally used to carry turf out of the bogs. *(Park open daily June-Sept. 9am-9pm; Oct.-May 9am-dusk. Visitor center open June-Sept. daily 2-6pm. Both free; railroad £1.)* Turf-cutting demonstrations take place on busy days. Woo hoo!

Antrim and Derry

The coast of these two counties is fragmented into regions according to the varying geological, commercial, religious, and cultural directions taken by each bit of land; the mismatched pieces are sewn together by a coastal road that can be a fascinating journey. Stodgy and industrial Larne gives way to lovely little seaside towns as the coastal road meanders west. The wooded "nine Glens of Antrim," stomping grounds of the Ulaid dynasty for over a thousand years, sit between the hills behind the villages. Farther west lies the stupendous Giant's Causeway. Most of this area is connected by a flat road that is a cyclist's paradise. Civilization as we know it resumes past the Causeway, however; the garish lights and lively atmospheres of Portrush and Portstewart cause more light-headedness than introspection. The northern coast culminates at Derry, the North's second largest city, whose turbulent history and recent redevelopment demonstrate the messiness of human life compared to these glorious natural landscapes.

■ Larne

The **ferries** that depart for Scotland from here are the only worthwhile reason to pass through industrial Larne, but now that the Hoverspeed SeaCat goes directly to Belfast, it is likely that the popularity of the Larne ferry will decline (see **By Ferry,** p. 33). **P&O Ferries** (tel. (0990) 980777) operates from Larne with passages to Cairnryan in Scotland. Travelers should arrive 45 minutes early, as there are always standby passengers waiting for your seat. The center of **Larne Town** is 15 minutes inland from the harbor. To reach town, take the first right outside of the ferry port. As the road curves left, it becomes Curran Rd. and then Main St.

PRACTICAL INFORMATION The bus and train stations lie adjacent to a roundabout two minutes from the town center; the tourist office and town center are well signposted from the roundabout. **Trains** chug from Central Station in **Belfast** to Larne Town and Larne Harbour. (Belfast office tel. (01232) 899411 or 230671, Larne office tel. (01574) 260604. 50min., M-F 20 per day, Sa 16 per day, Su 6 per day, £3.20.)

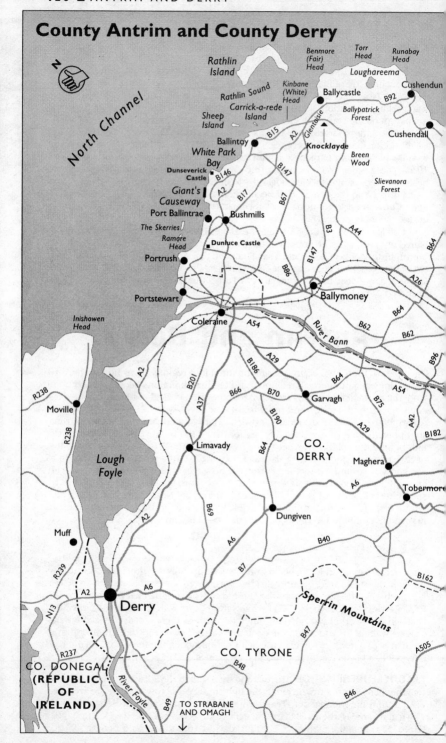

County Antrim and County Derry

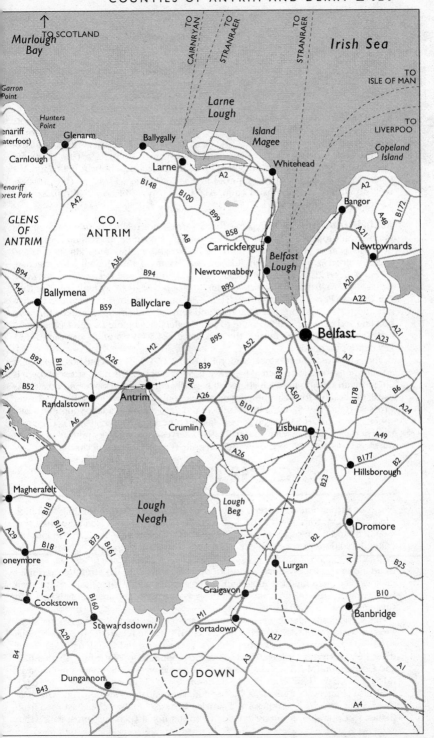

Buses (tel. 272345) leave frequently from Station Rd. for Laganside Station in **Belfast** (1½hr., express 50min., M-F 14 per day, Sa 15 per day, Su 2 per day). Those departing on a ferry from Larne should ensure that their train or bus terminates in Larne Harbour rather than in Larne Town, a 15-minute walk away. The **tourist office,** Narrow Gauge Rd. (tel. 260088), has loads of info, a free town map, and a good geological and historical exhibition. If you're just off the boat, the 20-minute video overview of the sights of Northern Ireland is worth a view. The staff books accommodations in the North, the Republic, and Scotland. (Open July-Aug. M-F 9am-6pm, Sa 9am-5pm; Sept.-Mar. M-F 9am-5pm; Easter-June M-Sa 9am-5pm.) There's a 24-hour computer info point on the outside of the building. All of the major banks are represented in town. **Northern Bank,** 19 Main St. (tel. 276311), has a 24-hour **ATM** that accepts Visa, Mastercard, and Cirrus (open M 9:30am-5pm, Tu-F 10am-3:30pm, Sa 9:30am-12:30pm). **Ulsterbank,** 9 Upper Cross St. (tel. 275757), also has a 24-hour **ATM** (open M-F 9:30am-3:30pm, Sa 9:30am-12:30pm). Larne's **post office,** 98 Main St. (tel. 260489), feels an affinity for the **postal code,** BT4 01RE (open M-F 9am-5:30pm, Sa 9am-12:30pm). The **phone code** is 01574.

ACCOMMODATIONS, FOOD, AND PUBS

Larne's not really the sort of town that people want to stay in. But if you're too weary to move on, there's no shortage of beds. B&Bs most convenient to both the harbor and the bus and train stations and adjacent streets are along Curran Rd. The clean rooms in Mrs. McKane's **Killyneedan,** 52 Bay Rd. (tel. 274943), are stocked with TVs, hotpots, and decorative mugs (£14, with bath £15). Bay Rd. intersects Curran Rd. just before the ferry terminal. **The Curran Caravan Park,** 131 Curran Rd. (tel. 273797 or 260088), midway between the harbor and town, has congested caravan and tent grounds in open greens for lawn bowling and miniature golf. Be sure to pause reflectively before Larne's Ulster-American Memorial Statue just outside the park gates. (£4.50 per tent, £7 per caravan. £5 key deposit for goods.)

The giant **Co-op Superstore,** Station Rd. (tel. 260737), next to the bus station, has an enormous selection (open M-F 9am-9pm, Sa 9am-8pm). The main street of town is littered with cheap sandwich shops, all basically equivalent in value and quality. As usual, the best bet for a cheap sit-down meal is a pub. **Chekker's Wine Bar,** 33 Lower Cross St. (tel. 275305), has a broad selection of bistro food in a take-your-time atmosphere (most meals £3-4; food served daily noon-2:30pm and 5:30-9pm). The cozy, lamp-lit **Bailie,** 111-113 Main St. (tel. 273947), serves congratulatory pints to brave sea travelers. This pub, too, serves lovely pub grub. (Open 11:30am 'til closing.)

GLENS OF ANTRIM

North of Larne, nine lush green valleys, or "glens," slither from the hills and high moors of Co. Antrim down to the seashore. The villages that sit along the coast provide beds and basic sustenance for the glen-wanderer as well as a glimpse into the cultural traditions of song and dance kept alive by the rural people of Northern Ireland. A2 connects the small towns at the foot of each glen to each other. The long flat troad along the rocky shore is kind to cyclists, with long flat stretches and mild inclines. The glens (and the mountains and waterfalls within them) can best be seen by making daytrips inland from one of the seaside towns. The area's only hostel is in Cushendall (see p. 424).

Bus service through the glens is scant but serviceable. Two **Ulsterbus** routes serve the area year-round (Belfast tel. (01232) 320011, Larne tel. (01574) 272345). Bus #162 from **Belfast** stops in **Larne, Ballygally, Glenarm,** and **Carnlough** (M-F 7 per day, Sa 6 per day, Su 3 per day) and sometimes continues to **Waterfoot, Cushendall,** and **Cushendun** (M-F 3 per day). Bus #150 runs between **Ballymena** and **Glenariff** (M-Sa 4 per day) then **Waterfoot, Cushendall,** and **Cushendun** (M-Sa 6 per day). #150 also connects to **Belfast** via **Cushendun, Cushendall, Waterfoot,** and **Glenariff** (M-Sa 3 per day). The summertime **"Antrim Coaster"** follows the coast road from **Belfast** to **Coleraine,** stopping at every town but not at Glenariff Forest Park. (Late

May to early July M-Sa 2 per day; early July to late Sept. 2 daily. Leaves Belfast at 9:10am and 2pm.) **Cycling** is fabulous. The coast road from Ballygally to Cushendun is both scenic and flat; once the road leaves Cushendun, however, it becomes hilly enough to make even motorists groan. The Cushendall hostel rents **bikes.** Hitching is difficult, and the winding, narrow road between cliffs and the sea wall doesn't allow easy stopping. The photo opportunity points and crossroads are the best places to try one's luck.

■ Glenarm

Six flat, winding, coastal miles lead to gradually less polluted and populated skylines and arrive at Glenarm. Glenarm ("glen of the army") was once the chief dwelling place of the MacDonnell clan. The village comprises a short span of centuries-old houses, pubs of the same elderly status, and a wealth of short walks. The **madman's window** appears on the right just before you enter town. While the elements created the formation, an artist supposedly created its name when he jumped to his death from it. A huge arch at the top of Altmore St. is the entrance to **Glenarm Forest,** where trails trace the river's path for miles (open daily 9am-sunset). **Glenarm Castle,** nestled just off the main street behind the trees north of the river, is the current residence of the 13th Earl of Antrim (the first one arrived from Scotland in the 13th century). Its 17th-century gate is visible from Castle St. but is open to the public only on July 14 and 15; the gardens can be explored year-round. Entered by way of the left fork off the Ballymena road on the way out of town. The town also boasts both a heritage trail and a walk along a former water-duct; brochures on both are available at the tourist office or from B&B proprietors. The **Ulster Way** trail also goes through town, if you're up for the hike (a good map is necessary, of course). The **Glenarm Festival** brings this sleepy town to life during the first week of July with events ranging from an eating competition to the multi-categoried Best-Kept Garden/Basket/Windowbox/ Tub Contest.

The **tourist office** (tel. 841087, after hours tel. 841298), in the town council building on the Bridge on Coast Rd., provides friendly advice on the attractions of the area. (Open by demand, but summer hours generally run Tu 9am-3pm, W noon-3pm, Th-F 9am-noon.) Glenarm's **post office** (tel. 841218) is halfway down Toberwine St. (open M-Tu and Th-F 9am-1pm and 2-5:30pm, W and Sa 9am-12:30pm); the **postal code** is BT44 0AP. The **phone code** is 01574.

Nine Glens B&B, 18 Toberwine St. (tel. 841590), looks as well-aged as the town itself with its period furniture and exposed wood beams. The bedrooms, however, are completely modern, each with bath and TV. Fresh fruit and tea available all day (£15). **Margaret's B&B,** 10 Altmore St. (tel. 841307), provides comfortable rooms with 1950s decor (£14). The **Spar Market,** 4 Toberwine St. (tel. 841219), supplies your picnic needs (open M-Tu and Th-Sa 9am-6pm, W 9am-1pm). Across the street, the **Gallery Coffee Shop,** 7 Toberwine St., is a showcase of country home cooking (most meals £3-4; open daily 10:30am-9pm). **Poacher's Pocket,** 1 New Rd. (tel. 841221), serves meaty entrees (£5-7, burgers £3.50; served daily noon-8pm) and live music on summer weekends; the walls are decorated with pictures of pheasants and the seats are filled with patrons of all ages. **The Coast Road Inn,** 3-5 Toberwine St. (tel. 841207), draws a more mature and sedate clientele. The **Bridge End Tavern,** 1-3 Toberwine St. (tel. 841247), is nothing fancy, just drinks and good company.

■ Waterfoot and Glenariff

Nine miles farther up the coast, the village of Waterfoot guards Antrim's broadest glen, Glenariff, often deemed the most beautiful of the nine. Thackeray dubbed Glenariff "Switzerland in miniature," presumably because it was steep and ruggedly pretty; numbered bank accounts and trilingual skiers are rare. It is also commonly known as the "Queen of the Glens." The glen is contained within the very large **Glenariff Forest Park** (tel. (012667) 58769 or 58232), 4 mi. south of the village along Glenariff Rd. (A43 toward Ballymena). The **bus** between **Cushendun** and **Ballymena**

(#150) stops at the official park entrance (M-F 5 per day, Sa 3 per day). If you're walking from Waterfoot, however, you can enter the park 1½ mi. downhill of the official entrance by taking the road that branches left toward the Manor Lodge Restaurant. If you drive, you can park in either the official car park or the Manor Lodge's parking lot, but you'll have to pay pedestrian admission charges if you enter Glenariff from Manor Lodge. (Park open daily 10am-sunset. £2.50 per car or £1 per adult pedestrian, 50p per child pedestrian.)

Once inside the park, you are confronted with a wealth of trails ranging from half a mile to 5 mi. round-trip, all of which will show you the Glenariff and Inver Rivers and the three waterfalls that supply them. The most stunning walk is the **Waterfall Trail**, marked by blue triangles: it follows the cascades and burbles of fern-lined Glenariff River from the park entrance to the Manor Lodge (1 mi. from entrance to lodge, 3 mi. round-trip). This path is most rewarding when walked uphill, that is, starting at the Manor Lodge. Other trails lead to more subtle and less frequented beauty. All of the walks officially begin and end at the car park, where you will also find the **Glenariff Tea House** (tel. (012667) 58769). This bay-windowed restaurant offers fresh snacks (sandwiches £1.75), exotically seasoned meals (£4-5), and free **maps** of the park's trails. (Open daily May-Aug. 11am-8pm; Easter-May and Sept. 11am-5pm.) The entrance to the **Moyle Way**, a 17 mi. hike from Glenariff to Ballycastle, is directly across from the official park entrance. Ask a ranger for details.

You can camp either at **Glenariff Forest Park Camping**, 98 Glenariff Rd. (tel. (012667) 58232; tents £9, off-season £6), or in the fields of one of the many farmers in the area who welcome campers (ask in town). In Waterfoot, closer to the comfort of civilization, **Lurig View B&B**, 4 Lurig View, Glen Rd. (tel. (012667) 71618), is located just off Garron Rd. about a half mile from town along the waterfront and provides big, comfy beds and tasty, enormous breakfasts (£15, off-season £14).

Waterfoot may be a one-street town, but it has two charismatic pubs. **The Mariners' Bar**, 7 Main St. (tel. (012667) 71330), is a life saver, with trad every Sunday and some summer weeknights as well as varied live music on Friday and Saturday nights. Across the street, **Bar-a-Hooley**, 4-6 Main St. (tel. (012667) 72906), swings a good night of craic in the bar and out in the beer garden and serves food from noon to 5pm (bar snacks £1.50-3.50). The **Cellar Bar** downstairs swings to live music on weekends with everything from country to trad. **Angela's Restaurant and Bakery**, 32 Main St. (tel. (012667) 71700), run out of a family home, serves home-cooked meals with cheeky names (Kiss the Blarney Cake) that speak for their surprising culinary sophistication (most meals £3-4, 3-course Sunday lunch £4.50). The back patio has grand views of Lurigethan Hill, to the left, and Garron Point, to the right. (Open M-Sa 9am-7pm, Su 12:30-2:30pm.) **Kearney's Cost Cutter**, 21 Main St. (tel. (012667) 71213), is the place to stock up before your hike through Glenariff (open M-Sa 8am-10:30pm, Su 8am-9pm).

The road from Waterfoot to Cushendall may scarcely be a mile, but it's jam-packed. The **coastal caves** that line the Coast Rd. have served as everything from a school to a blacksmith's shop. The most famous inhabitant of the stretch was "Nanny of the Caves," a *poitín* brewer who lived in her two-compartment cave-home for 50 years. The lucrative business kept Nun Marry, as she was legally known, alive until 1847 at the ripe old age of 100. Just beyond is the unmistakable **Red Arch**, carved out of sandstone by wind and water. On top of the arch lie the ruined walls of Red Bay Castle, believed to have been built by Scottish exiles in the 13th century and currently being renovated.

▦ Cushendall

Cushendall has been nicknamed the capital of the Glens, most likely because its village center is *four* streets instead of just one. The town adds provisions of ideally located goods and services and a lively pub scene to the area's spectacular natural beauty. Moors, hills, and the rough seashore form a triangle with the town at its center. Three of the nine glens (Glenballyeamon, Glenaan, and Glencorp) are closer to Cushendall than to any other human habitation.

PRACTICAL INFORMATION

The busiest section of Cushendall is at a crossroads. From the center of town, Mill St. turns into Chapel Rd. and heads toward Ballycastle; Shore Rd. extends in the other direction toward Glenarm and Larne. Hill St. leads up the hill opposite from Bridge Rd., which becomes Coast Rd. and continues down to the sea toward Waterfoot.

Buses: Ulsterbus #150 runs to **Ballymena** via **Waterfoot** and **Glenariff** (M-F 5 per day, Sa 4 per day). Ulsterbus #162 goes to **Larne** via **Waterfoot, Glenarm,** and **Ballygally** (M-F 3 per day, Sa-Su 1 per day). July-Aug., the **Antrim Coaster** (#252) runs through Cushendall toward Portrush and Larne/Belfast (2 per day).

Tourist Office: 25 Mill St. (tel. 71180), near the bus stop at the Cushendun end of town, has a wealth of info. Open July-Sept. M-F 10am-1pm and 2:30-5pm, Sa 10am-1pm; Oct. to mid-Dec. and Mar.-June Tu-Sa 10am-1pm.

Banks: Northern Bank, 5 Shore St. (tel. 71243). Open M 9:30am-12:30pm and 1:30-5pm, Tu-F 10am-12:30pm and 1:30-3:30pm. 24hr. **ATM** accepts Visa, MasterCard, and Cirrus.

Bike Rental: Ardclinis Activity Centre, 11 High St. (tel. 71340). Mountain bikes £10 per day; deposit credit card, passport, or £50. Wetsuits £6 per day. They also provide guided hill-walking, windsurfing instruction, and other outdoor fun for about £14 per ½day.

Camping Equipment: O'Neill's Country Sports, Mill St. (tel. 72009). Everything from fishing tackle to tents. Open Apr.-Sept. M-Sa 9:30am-6pm, Su 9am-5pm; Oct.-Mar. M-Sa 9:30am-6pm.

Pharmacy: E.L. Gillan Pharmacy, 2 Mill St. (tel. 71523). Open M-Sa 9am-6pm.

Post Office, Mill St. (tel. 71201). Open M and W-F 9am-1pm and 2-5:30pm, Tu and Sa 9am-12:30pm. The **postal code** is BT44 0RR.

Phone Code: 012667.

ACCOMMODATIONS

Cushendall Youth Hostel (YHANI/HI), 42 Layde Rd. (tel. 71344), a well-signposted ½mi. from town, this YHANI hostel doesn't feel compelled to lie miles out of town to claim a lovely spot. Layde Rd. is the left-hand (uphill) fork from Shore Rd.; the pedestrian entrance is marked by a huge "YHA" sign on a stone wall. A recent architectural tune-up generated a gargantuan kitchen and dining area. The two single-sex dorms and the bathroom facilities are huge, while the common room is comfortably intimate. Family run. Dorms £7.50, under 18 £6.50; private room with family capacity has £4 supplementary charge. Non-members pay extra £1.50. Sheets included. Wash £1, dry £1. **Bike rental** £6 per day, £4 per ½day.

Glendale, Mrs. O'Neill's, 46 Coast Rd. (tel. 71495). It's hard to imagine a warmer welcome. Rooms are huge and as soothing to the weary traveler as is the proprietress's company. Tea, coffee, biscuits, and bath in each room. £17.

Shramore, 27 Chapel Rd. (tel. 71610). This snug bungalow has 2 quiet, restful rooms, each with capacity for 3. £14. Open May-Sept.

Cushendall Caravan Park, 62 Coast Rd. (tel. 71699), adjacent to Red Bay Boatyard. Free showers but no kitchen. 2 person tent £4.65; family tent £7.90. Wash £1, dry 10p per 5min.

Glenville Caravan Park, 22 Layde Rd. (tel. 71520), 1 mi. out of town. Showers, toilets, and a splendid view of the ocean. £4 per tent.

FOOD AND PUBS

Spar Market, 2 Coast Rd. (tel. 71763), just past Bridge Rd., is open 365 days per year (366 in leap years) and has a plentiful fruit and veggie selection (open daily 7:30am-10pm). After all those trees in the Glens, it's nice to be around people and pubs again.

Gillan's Home Bakery and Coffee Shop, 6 Mill St. (tel. 71404). Simple food that you could cook yourself, but only for a few pence less. Sandwiches (£1.35) can be polished off with baked goods that you probably couldn't cook yourself. Most meals around £2. Open M-Sa 9am-8pm, Su 11am-8pm.

The Half Door, 6 Bridge St. (tel. 71300). Exotic pizzas with inexplicable North American names (£3-4). Create your own (medium £2.70, large £3.70, toppings 50-70p). Also a take-out chipper (£1-3). Open daily from 5pm until pub closing.

Harry's, 10-12 Mill St. (tel. 72022). The town's pride and joy of a restaurant. Bar snacks break the boundaries of their nomenclature with everything from orange to cointreau sauces on their meats and vegetarian entrees on request (around £5). Restaurant meals are £2-3 more. Food served M-Sa 12:30-3pm and 6-9:30pm, Su 12:30-3pm and 7-9:30pm.

Joe McCollam's, 23 Mill St., a.k.a. "Johnny Joe's." One of the best pubs you'll find on the island. A series of small rooms named after rooms in a house ("the kitchen," "the parlor," etc.) because that's what they originally were. Features impromptu ballads, fiddling, and slurred limericks. All this excitement takes place most nights, but musicians are guaranteed to gather F-Su nights.

Lurig Inn, 5 Bridge St. (tel. 71527). Rough and ready for the young and the restless.

SIGHTS

The sandstone **Curfew Tower** in the center of town on the corner of Mills and High St. was built in 1817 by the eccentric Francis Turley. This landlord of Cushendall made his fortune in China and then enforced his ideals of an orderly village on Cushendall upon his return; the tower features openings for pouring boiling oil on nonexistent attackers and a bell rung every night at "quiet time" for the town (hence the tower's name). Today it is privately owned and closed to the public. The extensive remnants of **Layde Church,** a medieval friary, lie a quarter mile past the hostel along Layde Rd. The ruins of the castle, in use as a Protestant parish church from the 1100s to the 1600s, are now noteworthy for their surrounding graveyard, spectacular seaviews, and pretty cliffside walks that begin at its carpark. *(Always open. Free.)* The graveyard includes **Cross Na Nagan,** a pagan holestone used for marriage ceremonies and Christianized into a Celtic cross by four strokes carved into the hole. **Tieveragh Hill,** a half mile up High St., is known locally as Fairy Hill, where a gate leads to the Otherworld inhabited by ancient "little people." Although locals claim to not believe the legend, they still refuse to cut the hedgerows in which the little people supposedly dwell. **Lurigethan Hill** (1153ft.) would soar above town if its summit weren't flattened on the way up. A climb to the top rewards with up-close access to a virtually intact Iron Age promontory fort. Locals race up the hill for a yearly "Lurigethan Run."

Ossian's Grave molders a few miles away on the lower slopes of Tievebulliagh Mountain. In fact a neolithic burial cairn dating from around 4000 BC, it is linked only by tradition with the Ulster warrior-bard Ossian who, according to legend, was buried here in about AD 300 (see **Literary Traditions,** p. 61). Ossian, while relaying his family's adventures to St. Patrick, allegedly tried to convince the saint that Christianity was far too restrictive for the boisterous Gaels—Young Yeats's first long poem is based on this episode. A2 leads north from Cushendall toward Ballymoney to the lower slopes of Tievebulliagh, where a sign points the way to the grave. The steep walk up the southern slope of Glenaan rewards with views of the lush valley.

More organized outdoor pursuits abound. The Glens of Antrim **Rambling Club** has a series of short and long walks planned throughout the year. Contact the chairman (Liam Murphy; tel. (01266) 656079) or the Cushendall tourist office for details. The annual **Guinness Relay** (third week in July) pits neighbor against neighbor in a race across the Dunn Bridge (all of 100ft.) with a tray of Guinness.

■ Near Cushendall: Cushendun

The tiny, picturesque seaside village of Cushendun, 5 mi. north of Cushendall on A2, was bought by the National Trust in 1954. Since then, Big Brother has protected the town's "olde," quaint, squeaky-clean image from any damaging progress. This whitewashed and black-shuttered set of buildings lies by a vast beach perforated by naturally wonderful, murky **sea caves** that sit inside barnacle-bottomed red sea cliffs. The caves were weathered out of the stone cliffs by the sea when it was much higher than it is now. The largest cave, located just past the Bay Hotel, serves as the only entrance to **Cave House**, which was built in 1820 and is currently occupied by the Mercy religious order and closed to the public. From behind the hotel, an excruciatingly steep path leads to the cliff top. Other, less painful, walks meander around historical monuments in the town and nearby Glendun (free map of walks available in Cushendun Tea Room), a preserved village that is a fine example of Cornish architecture. The relatively unimpressive "Maud Cottages" that line the main street were built by Lord Cushendun for his wife in 1925. Tourist information postings in town warn you against mistaking them for almshouses.

Buses pause at Cushendun's one grocery shop on the main street (open daily 8am-10pm) on their way to **Waterfoot** via **Cushendall** (June-Sept. M-F 10 per day, Sa 5 per day, Su 3 per day; Oct.-May M-F 8 per day, Sa 3 per day, Su 1 per day) and to **Portrush** (June-Sept. M-F 3 per day, Sa 2 per day, Su 2 per day; Oct.-May M-F 8 per day).

The town's most popular attraction is also its only real pub, where you'll find relief in the craic of its local clientele. **Mary McBride's**, 2 Main St. (tel. (012667) 61511), used to be the *Guinness Book of World Records*'s "smallest bar in Europe." Today the original bar is still there, but it has been vigorously expanded to provide a spacious mint-green lounge. Cushendun's characters leave the smallest bar only when trad musicians arrive, usually on Thursday nights in the summer, and start a session in the lounge. McBride's also offers pub grub (steak and Guinness pie £4.95; food served daily noon-9pm). **Cushendun Tea Room** (tel. (012667) 61506), across the street, serves less exciting and less expensive food (burgers and sandwiches £1.50-2, meat around £4). It also passes out some tourist brochures on the town's sights, but you're best off consulting the Cushendall Tourist Office for such information before you hit Cushendun itself. (Open July-Aug. daily 11:30am-7pm; Sept.-June weekends only noon-6:30pm.) One mile toward Cushendall, **Sleepy Hollow B&B**, 107 Knocknacarry Rd. (tel. (01266) 761513), is to your right off the coast road and has flowery, carpeted, well-kept rooms. Mrs. McKay's good humor is sure to improve your own. (Singles £20; doubles £36; all with bath.) Camping at **Cushendun Caravan Site**, 14 Glendun Rd. (tel. (01266) 761254), is cheapest, with a TV/game room and showers but no kitchen (£4.25 per tent; wash £1, dry 50p; open Mar.-Sept.).

CAUSEWAY COAST

Past Cushendun, the northern coast shifts from lyrical into dramatic mode. Six-hundred foot sea-battered cliffs tower over white wave-lapped beaches and then give way to the wondrous Giant's Causeway, for which the region is named. Lying among colossally beautiful scenery, the Causeway itself is a clump of 40,000 black and red hexagonal stone columns formed by volcanic eruptions 65 million years ago. The swarm of visitors who crowd around the columns are easily avoided—few venture more than a mile out from the Visitor's Centre. The western towns are more crowded.

A2, which is suitable for cycling, is the major thoroughfare between the main towns along the Causeway. **Ulsterbus #172** runs between **Ballycastle** and **Portrush** along the coast (1hr., M-F 5 per day, Sa 4 per day, Su 3 per day) and makes frequent connections to **Portstewart**. In good summer weather, the open-topped orange **Bushmills Bus** (Coleraine bus station; tel. (01265) 43334) outlines the coast between **Coleraine**, 5 mi. south of Portrush, and the **Giant's Causeway** (July-Aug. 5 per day). The summertime **Antrim Coaster** bus (Belfast Bus Station, tel. (01232) 333000) runs up the coast from **Belfast** to **Portstewart** via just about every town in *Let's Go* (late June to early July M-Sa 2 per day; early July to late Sept. daily 2 per day). Ulsterbus also runs package **tours** in the area that leave from **Belfast, Portrush,** and **Portstewart** (£3-9). From points farther south along the coast, many take the **express bus** from Belfast (June-Sept. 9 per day). Those hitching along A2 or the marginally quicker inland roads find that the lack of cars and high ratio of tourists slows them down.

■ Cushendun to Ballycastle

There is more than one way to travel this stretch of land, and both options have their merit. The more popular route begins just outside of Cushendall: you can either follow the relatively straight A2, or take the twisty scenic route that first leads to under-explored **Murlough Bay,** protected by the National Trust, where a stunning landscape hides the remains the medieval church of **Drumnakill,** which was also a pagan holy site. Farther west is **Torr Head,** a long peninsula that is Ireland's closest spot to Scotland. The road then bumps and grinds on to **Fair Head,** 7 mi. north of Cushendun and 3 mi. south of Ballycastle. This headland of heather-covered rocks attracts international hikers and winds pass lakes, the most fascinating of which is **Lough na Cranagh.** In the middle of this lake sits a *crannog,* a man-made island built by the Celts in the Bronze Age, and a well-fortified while recreationally equipped dwelling place for the ruling elite. Bikes should be left at home; the hills are so horrific that cyclists will spend more time walking than wheeling, and it's only a 1½-hour hike from Ballycastle. Although those in cars should head straight for this splendid stretch of road, they seldom do. The lack of autos translates into poor hitching conditions. Taking A2 straight from Cushendun to Ballycastle also has its advantages. It is more manageable for cyclists, with one long climb, but an even longer descent from a boggy plain. A2, the official bus route, also leads past its own set of attractions. A few miles northeast of Cushendun, a high hollow contains a vanishing lake, called **Loughareema,** which, in the summer, can appear and disappear into the bog in less than a day. When the lake is full, it has fish in it, but where do they go when it empties? Answer: into the caverns beneath the porous limestone on which the lake lies. The lake stays full only when silt is blocking the pores. The lake is more commonly called Fairy Lough, but there's no scientific explanation for that. Farther along, part of the high plain has been drained and planted with evergreens. The result is secluded **Ballypatrick Forest,** which includes a forest drive and several pleasant, pine-scented walks. Camping is allowed with a permit from the ranger or the Forest Office, 155 Cushendall Rd. (tel. (012657) 62301 or (01266) 631860), 2 mi. toward Ballycastle on A2 (basic facilities; £4.50 per tent; park open daily 10am to sunset). Just before Ballycastle is similar **Ballycastle Forest,** which is most significant for harboring **Knocklayde Mountain** (1695 ft.) in its midst. The mountain is eminently and enjoyably climbable. Its base is approximately 1 mi. into the forest.

▓ Ballycastle

The Glens of Antrim and the Causeway Coast converge upon T-shaped Ballycastle, a bubbly seaside town with a busy beach and great pubs. Warm summer weekends bring carloads of sunbathers to its beaches, and all summer weekends bring plane loads of music-lovers to its pubs. Weekdays are a little less crowded. Although Ballycastle (not to be confused with the town in Co. Mayo) means "town of the castle," don't look for one here: the castle met its demise in 1856.

ORIENTATION AND PRACTICAL INFORMATION

Ballycastle's main street runs perpendicular to the waterfront. It starts at the ocean as Quay Rd., becomes Ann St., and then turns into Castle St. as its passes The Diamond. Most restaurants and shops are found along Ann and Castle St. As Quay Rd. meets the water, the road takes a sharp left onto North St., where more stores and food await, and a right onto Mary Rd., where the tourist office and "leisure facilities" can be found. The "park" along the harbor is a popular meeting place for young and old; to its west is the ferry service, to the east is the town's beach. B&Bs perch on Quay Rd.

Buses: Stop at the Marine Hotel. **Ulsterbus** gives year-round rides to **Portrush** (50min., M-F 6 per day, Sa 3 per day, Su 4 per day), **Cushendall** via **Cushendun** (50min., M-F only, 1 per day), and **Belfast** via **Ballymena** (3hr., M-F 4 per day, Sa 3 per day). In summer, the Ulsterbus **Antrim Coaster** runs through the **Glens of**

Antrim and **Larne** to **Belfast** (full trip 3½-4hr., late May to early July M-Sa 2 per day, early July-late Sept. 2 daily). **McGinn's** (tel. (012656) 63451) also runs trips to **Carrick-a-rede**, the **Giant's Causeway**, and **Bushmills** (leaves harbor daily at 10:15am, £5) and to **Belfast** (1½hr., F 4pm and Su 8pm, £3.50).

Ferries: Argyll and Antrim Steam Packet Co. (tel. (0990) 523523) runs ferries between **Campbeltown, Scotland** (on the Kintryre Peninsula) and Ballycastle (3hr., July-Oct. 19 2 per day in each direction, £23-25, cars and caravans accepted). See **Rathlin Island**, p. 431, for info. on the service to it.

Tourist Office: Sheskburn House, 7 Mary St. (tel. 62024). Super-friendly staff provides information on the entire Antrim coast and books accommodations in the North and in the Republic. 24hr. computerized information outside. Open July-Aug. M-F 9:30am-7pm, Sa 10am-6pm, Su 2-6pm; Sept.-June M-F 9:30am-5pm.

Banks: First Trust Bank, 32-34 Ann St. (tel. 63326). Open M-Tu and Th-F 9:30am-4:30pm, W 10am-4:30 pm; 24hr. **ATM. Northern Bank,** 24 Ann St. (tel. 62238). Open M 9:30am-12:30pm and 1:30-5pm, Tu-F 10am-12:30pm and 1:30-3:30pm; 24hr. **ATM** accepts Mastercard, Visa, and Cirrus.

Taxis: tel. 62822 or 63697 (toll free (0800) 854585).

Bike Rental: Northern Auto Factors, 41 Castle St. (tel. 63748). £6 per day, £30 per week.

Pharmacy: McMichael's, 10 Ann St. (tel. 63342). Open M-Sa 9am-6pm.

Emergency: tel. 999. **Police:** Ramoan Rd. (tel. 62312).

Hospital: Dalriada Hospital, Coleraine Rd. (tel. 62666).

Post Office: 3 Ann St. (tel. 62519). Open M-Tu and Th-F 9am-1pm and 2-5:30pm, W 9am-1pm, Sa 9am-12:30pm. **Postal code:** BT54 6AA.

Phone Code: 012657.

ACCOMMODATIONS

Watch out for the Ould Lammas Fair on the last Monday and Tuesday in August. B&Bs fill almost a year in advance, and even hostel beds fill weeks before the big event. The 35-bed **Castle Hostel (IHH),** 62 Quay Rd. (tel. 62337), centrally located between the promenade and the town center, has a spacious, well-equipped kitchen. The hostel can get crowded because everyone wants the good company of the generous owner as she tends to the open fire—which you need on an Irish summer night at the seaside. (Dorms £6; private rooms £7.50 per person. Wash £1.) The **Ballycastle Backpackers Hostel,** 4 North St. (tel. 63612 or 69458), next to the Marine Hotel, is small (16 beds) and spacious; try to get a room with a sea view (dorms £7.50, off-season £6). At the **Cuchulainn House,** 56 Quay Rd. (tel. 62252), just up the road toward town, you'll breakfast on fresh fruit and local baked goods. Mrs. McMahon outdoes herself with home-made pamphlets on the Ulster myth cycle and immaculate rooms. (£15, with bath £18.50.) A few doors closer to town is **Fragrens,** 34 Quay Rd. (tel. 62168), where friendly Mrs. Greene offers a fruit bowl at breakfast and free tea and coffee in a 17th-century mansion of a cottage that is one of the oldest buildings in Ballycastle. (£15, with bath £17; all rooms with TV.) **Hilsea,** 28 North St. (tel. 62385), is a large, business-like guest house offering bright rooms decorated with watercolors; some have beautiful views of gorgeous Fair Head. Snack on free tea, coffee, and scones in the dining room. (Singles £17.50; doubles £32, with bath £37.)

FOOD AND PUBS

Brady's Supermarket, 54 Castle St. (tel. 62268), the town's biggest and most varied, is a 10-minute walk from the hostels (open M-Sa 9am-9pm, Su 10:45am-9pm). Closer to the harbor are the **Fruit Shop,** The Diamond (tel. 63348), which sells greens (and reds and oranges; open M-Sa 8am-6pm); and **J.F. McLister's Cost Cutter,** 17-19 Ann St. (tel. 62216; open M-Sa 8:30am-6pm). **Herald's,** 22 Ann St. (tel. 69064), realizes the budget traveler's dream: simply great-tasting meals served in huge portions and sold at cheap prices in a clean, cheerful atmosphere. The kind staff is the icing on the cake (all entrees under £2). **The Strand Restaurant,** North St., is next to the sea, but no breeze makes it into the pub walls. The large menu includes several vegetarian dishes and dandy desserts. (Cold platters for less than £5, burgers around £4. Open daily

July-Aug. 11am-10pm; Sept.-June 11am-9:30pm.) **Wysner's,** 16-18 Ann St. (tel. 62372), is the local winner of "healthy eating" awards for its food preparation practices. It is most affordable at lunch (entrees around £4.50), although the fry-free dinner menu offers an affordable main course for £7. (Open July-Aug. M-Sa 8am-9pm; Sept.-June M-Th 8am-5pm, F-Sa 8am-10pm. Only coffee and snacks served 3:30-5pm.) On the other end of the food spectrum is **Flash-in-the-Pan,** 74 Castle St. (tel. 62251); stained-glass window walls decorate this blue-blooded chipper (£1.50-2, other takeout available; open Su-Th 11am-midnight, F-Sa 11am-1am).

Though renowned for its nuttiness during the Ould Lammas Fair, Ballycastle is lively throughout the entire year. Trad is always in vogue here, especially among the young folk, so you'll likely find it starting up in several pubs every night of the week in summer. Tourists usually head for tiny, fire-warmed **House of McDonnell,** Castle St. (tel. 62975), which has the self-proclaimed "best trad on the Antrim Coast" on Fridays; it also features folk on Saturday and an additional Wednesday trad session during the summer. Guinness guzzlers fill the **Boyd Arms,** 4 The Diamond (tel. 62364), to enjoy good company and trad on Friday nights. **McCarroll's Bar,** a.k.a. "Pat's," 7 Ann St. (tel. 62123), is the place to be on Thursdays when it hosts terrific traditional reels and jigs. The trad-bursting **Central Bar,** 12 Ann St. (tel. 63877), has an ebullient owner who can't contain the crowds, which spill out onto the back patio (music W, Sa, sometimes F). **The Harbour Bar,** 6 North St.(tel. 62387), is the least self-conscious of the pubs; locals come to it for strong drinks and good craic rather than for its old-time atmosphere. The **Anglers' Arms,** 12 North St. (tel. 62155), looks neat and tidy, but it booms with popular sing-alongs and lively music in the summer at its **Legends Nightclub,** with a DJed disco on Saturdays (cover £4-5) and summer Tuesdays (£3) and karaoke on Thursdays and Sundays (no cover; closed during the rest of the week; ages 18 and up).

SIGHTS

Just off The Diamond, the Holy Trinity Church of Ireland—better known as the **Boyd Church**—raises its octagonal spire over its plain and proud interior. This edifice, like most of Ballycastle, was built by Hugh Boyd (landlord 1727-1765), who industrialized the area and created the town center, including Quay Rd., Ann Rd. (named after his wife), and the docks where the tennis courts now are. Most of his improvements fell to ruin when his grandsons took over in the days when industry-derived incomes fell out of fashion. Perhaps the town's most impressive sight is the 15th-century **Bonamargy Friary,** which lies in relatively intact ruins in the middle of the golf course a half-mile out of town on Cushendall Rd. You can clamber around some of the rooms in the priory and read the fascinating gravestones surrounding the church. Among the cemetery's more interesting residents are Sorley Boy McDonnell, of Dunluce Castle fame, and "the black nun," a 17th-century recluse who chose to have her grave placed where people would step on her, as a posthumous self-punishment for having turned away her unmarried pregnant sister.

Those with a taste for being on the wild Irish sea should contact **McBride's Boat Trips** (tel. 62637), which runs fishing, diving, and sight-seeing tours from the Ballycastle Harbor around Fair Head, Rathlin, Carrick-a-rede, and Murlough Bay. If you're lacking in sea legs, you could just **fish** off the pier, where pollock, mackerel, colefish, plaice, and cod abound, and then go for a swim on the **strand** to its east. The tourist office sells fishing licenses (£11, 8-day £23.50). Between the harbor and the beach lies the former site of "Boyd's Docks," now filled with silt and covered with 10 grass tennis courts and a bowling green. *(£2 per hr., £1.30 per hr. for juniors. Racket 50p. Ball rental 40p.)*

On the last Monday and Tuesday of August 1999, Ballycastle hosts the 411th **Ould Lammas Fair,** Northern Ireland's oldest and most famous fair. Originally a week-long fiesta, the festival is now crammed into two frenzied days. Continuing the traditions of the ancient Celtic harvest festival, the fair jams Ballycastle's streets with vendors selling cows, sheep, crafts, and baked goods. Trad musicians pack the pubs even tighter. *Dulse* (nutritious seaweed dried on local roofs, reputedly good for the brain) and *yellow-man* (sticky toffee made from a secret recipe) are two curiosities that originated with the fair. Both are worth a try.

■ Rathlin Island

Just off the coast at Ballycastle, bumpy and boomerang-shaped Rathlin Island (Fort of the Sea) is the ultimate in escapism for 20,000 puffins, the odd golden eagle, 100 human beings, and four daily ferries of fresh tourists. Its windy surface supports few trees, but an ecological paradise of orchids, purple heather, and seabirds covers the island. The contrast between the white chalk and black basalt cliffs that encircle the island (both around 200ft. high) caused the novelist Charles Kinglsey to compare Rathlin to a "drowned magpie." Before the Famine ravaged Ireland, more than 1000 people inhabited the island; in just twenty years, the population dwindled to half of that. Most of Rathlin's emigrants set sail for America and created their own community in Maine. Despite the fact that electricity arrived in Rathlin in only 1992, Rathlin has a unique place in the history of science and technology; in 1898, the Italian scientist Marconi sent the first wireless telegraph message, from Rathlin to Ballycastle.

Rathlin makes a beautiful daytrip on a nice day, but there is absolutely nothing to do there in bad weather. **Caledonian MacBrayne** is the only ferry service to the island, connecting it to Ballycastle. The **Ballycastle tourist office** (tel. (012657) 62024) is your best source of information on schedules, since the ferry service is based in Scotland. The ferry runs to the island four times daily from the pier at Ballycastle, up the hill from Quay Rd. on North St. (45min., 4 per day in each direction, £3.60). The small MacBrayne office at the Ballycastle pier (tel. (012657) 62024), open before each departure, sells tickets. A leaflet available at the Ballycastle tourist office, contains a quite good map and description of the island's walks and sights. For a more complete presentation of the island's intricately intertwined history and myths, visit the island's own **Boat House Information Centre** (tel. (012657) 63951) at the opposite end of the harbor from the ferry. Showcasing a wealth of photographs and documents that relay Rathlin's history, the center sells pamphlets on the birds of Rathlin (50p) and West Lighthouse and Rue (South) Lighthouse. (10p each. Open June-Aug. daily 11:30am-4:30pm, other months open on demand. 50p, children free.)

There are three different **minibus** services from the pub to the **Kebble Bird Sanctuary** at the western tip of the island, 4½ mi. from the harbor. (Call Gusty McCurdy; tel. (012657) 63909, Irene McFaul tel. (012657) 63907, or Johnny Curry (tel. 012657) 63905. £4 return.) The buses will usually wait while you take in the area. The **lighthouse** is the best place to view birds, but it's accessible only with the warden's supervision; call Liam McFaul (tel. (012657) 63948) in advance to gain entrance. The minibuses will also make trips to **Rue Point** (£3 return), 2½ mi. from the harbor. Here, visitors marvel at the crumbled remains of **Smuggler's House**, whose wall cavities supposedly hid contraband in the days when pirates and smugglers fueled Rathlin's economy. Ironically, the official tax house is just yards away. The feud between the hated coast guards and the Rathlin residents climaxed when the former filled in the smuggler-popular harbor at Usher Point, the southern tip. The **Richard Branson Dive/Holiday Centre** (tel. (012657) 63915), across from the ferry docks, brings divers to the island. The Holiday Centre is named after the cross-Atlantic hot-balloonist who crashed just short of Rathlin Island in 1987. Rumor has it that the island's lads battled strong currents to save him from drowning but refused to complete the rescue until he promised to donate money to Rathlin. **Fair Head,** where seals frolic freely, looms a few miles away from Rue Point.

The island's few amenities all lie either in the 500 yd. stretch of road to the right of the pier or on the street behind the coast road. If pleased enough with your own company to spend two days on Rathlin, spend the night at tiny **Soernog View Hostel** (tel. (012657) 63954)—that's Sir Nock to you. Take a right from the dock and turn left at the side road before the pub. At the top of the road, turn right; the hostel is 100 yd. ahead on your right. Call ahead for pick-up if you need to. This 6-bed hostel is brand-spanking-new with comfortable beds, but be sure to call from the mainland to make sure there's one left for you and bring groceries with you. (Dorms £8. Tea and coffee included. Wash £1, dry £1.) **McCuaig's Bar** (tel. 012657) 63974) sometimes allows free camping on its grounds. The bar—the single entertainment center for the entire island—takes care of the food (sandwiches and toasties £1.40-2, burgers £1.50-2), pool (20p per game), video games, and, on the off chance that the company's in the mood, discos and karaoke. The head of Duncan, Rathlin's last Highland bull who went loco and had to be shot in 1880, is the showpiece of the pub's otherwise plain interior.

■ Ballintoy and Carrick-a-rede Island

Five miles west of Ballycastle, the modest village of Ballintoy evokes smiles with a picturesque church and a tiny harbor. Two remarkable islands put Ballintoy's name on the map: Sheep Island and Carrick-a-rede Island, both of which are so small in size that they might more aptly be described as giant grass-covered rocks above the ocean. Visible from Ballintoy village, **Sheep Island** is home to puffins, razor bills, shag, kittiwakes, and the largest cormorant colony in Ireland. Its name comes from the 11 sheep that used to be taken to the island each year to graze—10 were thought to be too few (the sheep would get too fat) and 12 were thought too many (they would starve). Access to the island is now restricted year-round to protect the nesting birds.

Smaller and better-known **Carrick-a-rede Island** lies offshore to the east of Ballintoy. Meaning "rock in the road," Carrick-a-rede presents a barrier to migrating salmon returning to their home rivers. Fishermen have set up their nets for over 250 years at the point off the island by which salmon have to pass in their migration westward. To reach the nets, the fishermen annually string a rope bridge between the mainland and the island, where it hangs from April to September. Crossing the shaky, 48 in. wide, 67 ft. long bridge over the dizzying 100 ft. drop to rocks and sea below is now a popular activity for tourists. Be **extremely careful** in windy weather, as the bridge has been known to flip over! Wardens are on site during opening hours to insure visitors' safety, and the bridge is certainly a lot safer than the days when it only had one handrail to cling to. A sign half a mile east of Ballintoy marks the turnoff for the bridge from the coast road, the car park is a quarter mile farther down, and the bridge is three quarters of a mile past the car park.

The walk out to the bridge takes you along the heights of the Larrybane sea cliffs, where a 9th-century fort once stood, the remains of which were destroyed in the 1930s. You'll likely notice at least one of several species of unusual birds, including cliff-nesting, black-and-white razor bills, brown- and white-bellied guillemots, and lots of more mundane gulls. Tiny Carrick-a-rede is as generous to birdwatchers as it is to salmon fishermen. Ask the wardens for the **National Trust's** leaflet on the site, which provides illustrations of the local birds and a map of the area's geological notables. A fishing hut totters on the east side of the island, from which salmon nets stretch out into the sea. On a clear day, you can see the Hebrides. The **tea room** by the parking lot (tel. (012657) 62178) sells snacks, posts information on the site, and offers a bit of local advice. For 50p, they'll give you a certificate stating that you successfully crossed the bridge; you can save your money and use ours instead (see **I am a certified Hero**). (Tea room open Apr.-Sept. daily 11am-7pm.) The **center** is open when the rope-bridge goes up. (Open daily July-Aug. 10am-8pm; Apr.-June and Sept. 10am-6pm. £2 per car, £1 per motorcycle, pedestrians free.) Free **camping** can be arranged with the wardens (tel. (012657) 62178). The cliff walks are always open.

Quiet Ballintoy provides beds and grub to Carrick-a-rede's thrillseekers. The aptly titled **Sheep Island View Hostel (IHH),** 42A Main St. (tel. (012657) 69391 or 62470) is huge, clean, and friendly, with one of the biggest kitchens you'll ever see. All rooms have bath, and one is wheelchair accessible. (Dorms £9. Continental breakfast £2.50; Ulster fry £4. Wash £1, dry £1. Barbecue facilities and hairdryers available.) The two surrounding **camping** greens are as pristine as the hostel, with views of Sheep Island and full separate facilities (£3 per person). Call the hostel for pick-up from anywhere between Cushendall and Portrush. A shop at the entrance to the hostel provides basic groceries and a few delicacies (open daily 8:30am-10pm). In town, the frosted-glass-windowed **Fullerton Arms** (tel. (012657) 69613) and the come-as-you-are **Carrick-a-rede** (tel. (012657) 62241) compete from across the street for locals' business.

I am a Certified Hero

I, _____, *Let's Go: Ireland 1999* reader, am hereby to be referred to as a Hero because I crossed the Bridge to Carrick-a-rede Island. Possession of this here certificate entitles me to all Hero Privileges that may be applicable.

Witness: _____

Date: _____

This certificate is non-transferrable and may not be used in conjunction with any other coupon and all that crap.

Both offer standard pub grub daily from 12:30 to 8:30pm in the £3-5 range and music almost every (rainy) summer night.

Three miles west along the coast road from Ballintoy is **Whitepark Bay Youth Hostel (YHANI)** (tel. (012657) 31745). Its out-of-the-way setting overlooking one of the most famous beaches on the Antrim Coast is either a blessing or a boon, depending on whether or not you have a car. The Portrush-Ballycastle bus (#172) or the Antrim coaster (#252) will drop you off 200 yd. from the hostel, but there are no shops or pubs for miles around. Once there, few of the hostelers visitors spend their precious time complaining, for the natural setting of the hostel will satisfy all contemplative and energetic functions of the human body. Spic 'n' span and pleasingly painted in the most current color scheme, this place is possibly the most mod of all YHANI hostels. All rooms have bath and the private rooms have TV and tea and coffee facilities. In addition to a kitchen, there's a restaurant that sells the most basic food stuffs. (Restaurant open Apr.-Sept.; breakfast £2, dinner £4.50. Dorms £9; twins £22; non-members £1 extra. Oct.-Mar. lockout 11am-5pm. **Bike rental** £6 per day.) There is a splendid 1 mi. **nature trail** along the bay, which the wardens can point you toward.

■ Giant's Causeway

Advertised as the eighth natural wonder of the world, the Giant's Causeway is deservedly Northern Ireland's most famous sight. Be warned that 2000 visitors arrive each day in July and August; such is the life of a wonder. A spillage of forty thousand 60-million year old hexagonal columns of basalt form a honeycomb path from the foot of the cliffs far into the sea. Geologists have decided that the Causeway resulted from an unusually steady cooling of lava that stimulated crystallization, but legend disagrees (see **The Real McCool,** p. 434).

The Causeway is always open and free to pedestrians. **The Giant's Causeway Visitors Centre** (tel. (012657) 31855) sits at the pedestrian entranceway to the Causeway from the carpark. Besides offering the usual tourist information, a bureau de change, and a post office, it sells an excellent leaflet of walks (75p) that will guide you the 8 mi. back to Whitepark Bay or along several shorter circular walks. Every 15 minutes, it runs "Causeway Coaster" minibuses the half mile to the columns (60p, £1 return). An audio-visual show (£1, students 80p) informs about the fact and fiction of the Causeway. (Centre open daily June 10am-6pm; July-Aug. 10am-7pm; Mar.-May and Sept. 10am-5pm; Nov.-Feb. 10am-4:30pm. Parking £2.) Finally, the National Trust operates a gift shop and tea room inside the center (tea room closes 30min. before the visitors center).

Many paths loop to and from the Causeway. Two begin at the visitors center, one passing along the high cliffs and another along the low coast (past the hexagonal columns). The paths meet after 1 mi. and you can return by the road not taken. Both routes make it round to the Causeway, but taking the low road provides more instant

---

The Real McCool

Irish legend states that Finn McCool, the warrior giant, fell in love with a female giant named Una on Staffa Island, off the Scottish coast. The devoted lover built the Causeway to bring her across to Ulster, which explains the existence of similar beehive-esque rock formations on Staffa. The Scottish giant Benandonner, however, followed them to Ireland to defeat Finn and take Una back home with him. When McCool realized how big his Scottish rival was, he realized the folly of his physical confidence and decided to rely on the strength of his wit. The wily Irishman, with the help of his wife Una, disguised himself as an infant. When the Scottish giant saw the size of this Irish "baby," he was terrified by the anticipated proportions of the father. Benandonner quickly fled back to Scotland, destroying the Causeway on his return trip in order to ensure that the huge father McCool would never be able to cross the sea to challenge him.

---

gratification of your desires. The low road also allows something of a downhill walk for a portion of the trail. At the end of this walk, 4½ mi. east of the Causeway's center, you will see the scanty though overwhelmingly romantic ruins of **Dunsverick Castle,** the Iron Age fort of Sobhairce, high above you on a sea cliff. Bus #172 and the Antrim Coaster stop in front of the castle, from where it's 4½ mi. farther to Ballintoy. The well-tended track winds through naturally sculpted amphitheaters and inlets studded with bizarre, creatively named formations (such as the "organ"). Although not essential, the center's trail leaflet contains a helpful map and basic geological and human history.

■ Bushmills

The ardently Protestant town of Bushmills, 2 mi. west of the Giant's Causeway, has been the home of **Bushmills Irish Whiskey** (tel. (012657) 31521) since 1608, making it the oldest functioning whiskey producer in the world. *(Open M-Sa 9:30-5:30pm; last tour 4pm. Tours, with free sample, Apr.-Oct. every 15-20min.; Nov.-Mar. M-F at 10:30, 11:30am, 1:30, 2:30, and 3:30pm. £3, students or seniors £2.50.)* The Bushmills business is all about the aging process, which the distillery uses to produce great whiskey and a selling tale of Ireland's age-old whiskey tradition. The tour guides tell of how Irish monks invented whiskey in the 6th century and called it *uiscebeatha* (is-CAH BAHN-a), "water of life." Travelers have been stopping at Bushmills for some stimulation ever since the ancient days when it was on the route from the castles of Dunluce and Dunseverick to Tara. When the distillery is operating, you get to see whiskey being made. Production stops for three weeks in July for maintenance but (less interesting) tours are still held; around Christmas, neither distilling nor tours occur. An abandoned **Electric Tramway line,** the first of a few hydroelectric-powered tram rails, runs from Bushmills to Portrush and to the Causeway Visitors Center; a walk along it reveals much of the scenery that you miss on the buses and is relatively easy due to the level ground of the former tramway track. For information, contact the Giant's Causeway Visitor's Center or the Portrush Tourist Office.

■ Portrush

By day, the merry-go-rounds, water slides, and arcades of Portrush go full-throttle as bushels of Northern vacationers roam the streets and its two beaches. By night, the young mob creates an MTV beach party on the cold seafront where the thump of the nightclubs competes with the crash of the waves. The Giant's Causeway and Ports-tewart are within easy cycling distance, and Portrush itself has a beach which invites sunset rambles.

PRACTICAL INFORMATION

Trains: Eglington St. (tel. 822395), in the center of town. Carriages from **Belfast** (2hr., M-F 10 per day, Sa 8 per day, Su 4 per day, £5.90) and **Derry** (1hr., M-F 8 per day, Sa 6 per day, Su 4 per day, £4.90).

Buses: Leave from Dunluce St. Regular buses to **Portstewart** (13min., M-F 23 per day, Sa 19 per day, Su 9 per day, £1). Ulsterbus #172 (M-F 8 per day, Sa 6 per day, Su 3 per day) runs along the coast to **Bushmills** (20min.), the **Giant's Causeway** (25min.), **Ballintoy** (40min.), and Ballycastle (1hr.). The open-topped **Bushmills Bus** (#177) goes to **Portstewart, Bushmills,** and the **Giant's Causeway** in good weather (daily 5 per day). The Ulsterbus **Portrush Puffer** runs circles around the town (July-Aug. M-Sa 10am-7pm, Su 2-7pm; Apr.-June and Sept. 10am-6pm, Su 2-6pm; £1.40). **Ulsterbus** has day tours to various scenic spots in the North and the Republic; inquire at tourist office.

Tourist Office: Dunluce Centre (tel. 823333), off Sandhill Dr., just south of the town center. Brochures galore, **bureau de change,** and accommodation bookings. Ulsterbus representative on hand to arrange day tours. Open July-Sept. daily 9am-8pm; Apr.-June M-F 9am-5pm, Sa-Su noon-5pm; Mar. and Oct. Sa-Su noon-5pm.

Banks: First Trust, 25 Eglinton St. (tel. 822726). Open M-Tu and Th-F 9:30am-4:30pm, W 10am-4:30pm. 24hr. **ATM. Northern Bank,** 60 Main St. (tel. 822327). Open M 9:30am-5pm, Tu-F 10am-3:30pm; closed daily 12:30-1:30pm except July-Aug. **Bureau de change.** 24hr. **ATM. Ulster Bank,** 33 Eglinton St. (tel. 823730). Open M-F 9:30am-12:30pm and 1:30-4:30pm.

Taxis: tel. 823483, 822223, or 825013.

Bike Rental: Bicycle Doctor, 104 Lower Main St. (tel. 824340). £7 per day, £30 per week; deposit £40 or passport. Open daily 9am-6pm but bikes can be returned after closing with advance notice. Discount for youth hostel residents.

Surfing Equipment: Troggs Surf Shop, 88 Main St. (tel. 825476). Ireland's largest surf shop, managed by a 6-time Irish National Surfing Champion. Surfboards £5 per day, bodyboards £3 per day, wetsuits £5 per day; deposit credit card. 2hr. lesson £15 (including all equipment). Open daily July-Aug. 10am-10pm, Sept.-June 10am-6pm. **Woodie's Surf-Skate-Snow,** 102 Main St. (tel. 823273). Rent or buy. Surfboards £5 per day, wetsuits £4 per day; deposit credit card. Open daily July-Aug. 10am-6pm, Sept.-June noon-6pm.

Pharmacy: Heron Chemist, 5-9 Main St. (tel. 822324). Open July-Aug. daily 9am-11pm, Sept.-June M-Sa 9am-6pm, Su 2-6pm.

Emergency: Dial 999; no coins required. **Police:** tel. 822721.

Post Office: 23 Eglinton St. (tel. 823700). Open M-Tu and Th-F 9am-12:30pm and 1:30-5:30pm, W 9am-1pm, Sa 9am-12:30pm. **Postal code:** BT56 8DX.

Phone Code: 01265.

ACCOMMODATIONS

Portrush is a convenient place to begin or end a tour of the Giant's Causeway, as most buses that serve the Causeway stop here. When the university sets students free for the summer, plenty of student housing becomes holiday homes. Nearly every other townhouse along Mark St., Kerr St., and Raymore Ave. is a B&B. Most are indistinguishable in size, character, and price (usually £15-20).

Portrush Youth Hostel (formerly known as **Ma Cool's**), 5 Causeway View Terr. (tel. 824845). 5min. walk from the bus stop; turn left onto Dunluce St. and follow it toward the harbor. When you come to a three-pronged fork, take the middle road, which is Mark St. The hostel is a few yards past the intersection of Mark St. and Main St. on Causeway View Terr. From the train station, Mark St. is the second left after turning left out of the station. Relax in the spacious comfort of a homey and accepting common room of carpeted furniture. Owner Joanna's laugh is infectious and Steve's local expertise is a boon to any hiker. Microwave, free tea and coffee, and frequent BBQs. Dorms £7. Laundry £2. Hostelers get discounts at the Bicycle Doctor and at Woodie's Surf Shop.

Rest-a-While Guesthouse, 6 Bath Terr. (tel. 822827). Mismatched neo-Victorian decorations make this hotel-sized B&B cozy. Some rooms overlook East Strand beach. £14.

Atlantis, 10 Ramore Ave. (tel. 824583). Offers an ocean view. Use of the visitor's kitchen and free tea and coffee are added bonuses. Evening meal £5. Singles £16; doubles £28, with bath £34.

Avarest, 64 Mark St. (tel. 823121). Read its name in your best cockney accent and you'll understand its comforts. £14, with bath £17.

FOOD

The proliferation of fast food in Portrush may seem all-encompassing, but a few good restaurants hide amid the neon. If you're not up to the search, stock up on groceries at **Mace,** 58 Main St. (tel. 823715; open daily 9am-10pm).

The Singing Kettle, 315 Atlantic Ave. (tel. 823068). Soothing, lace-curtained relief for tired travelers who need to fill their abyss of a stomach. While in any other town it might seem boring, such wholesomeness is to be appreciated in Portrush. Entrees £3.25-4.25, vegetarian entrees £3-4.25. Open daily July-Aug. 10am-5pm, Sept.-June 11am-5pm.

Donovans, Main St. (tel. 822063), looks and sounds like a trad pub but doesn't taste like pub grub. Typically Irish meals are given zest with worldly seasonings. Most meals £3-6. Music nightly. M-Sa lunch noon-12:30pm, dinner 5-10pm; Su food served 3-9pm.

Don Giovanni's, 9-13 Causeway St. (tel. 825516). Authentic Italian food and owners. Impeccable interior. Pasta platters £5-7. Open daily 5:30-11pm.

The Alamo, Eglinton St. (tel. 822000). Celebrate Ulster-American cultural imperialism with American-style pizza. Free delivery. Open Tu-Su 5pm-midnight.

The Carousel, 6-8 Main St. The best of the quite inexpensive snack-and-ice-cream shops—as spacious as a roller-skating rink with appropriate musical accompaniment. Open daily July-Aug. 9am-10pm, Sept.-June noon-6pm.

PUBS AND ENTERTAINMENT

The **Harbour Bar,** 5 Harbour Rd. (tel. 822430), is a spit-in-the-sawdust sailors' pub popular with locals (music on weekends). The adjacent Harbour Inn also serves good pub grub. The Victorian-fronted **Alpha Bar,** 63 Eglinton St. (tel. 823889), has a diner-like interior and lots of fraternizing. The hippest complex around swallows up one whole corner block on Main St. with the **Atlantic Bar** and the **Retro Bar** (tel. 823693). At the Retro Bar, DJs liven the mix with house, hip-hop, and funk, while customers liven their drinks by sampling one of the 35 different flavors of vodka. Separate from the Retro's orgy is the Atlantic Bar, where brooding pint-sippers win hearts, especially when the bar's guitar player stops in to work his magic (no cover at either). **Shunter's,** in the railway station, powers its engines with live music most nights during the summer (cover varies). Partiers also make tracks for techno-heavy **Traks Nightclub** (tel. 822112) at the railway station (cover £3). **The Rogues,** 51 Kerr St. (tel. 822916), facing the Harbour, is another wiggle-silly night spot that does a good job with everything but the weather in its attempt to plant Palm Beach on the North Antrim coast (cover varies). Finish your evening (or begin your morning) at a Portrush institution, **Beetles Bar and Disco** (everyone calls it **Kelly's;** tel. 466930), just outside Portrush on Bushmills Rd. Kelly's has 11 bars and four discos, including **Lush!** (tel. 822027), voted one of the top ten U.K. clubs by *DJ Magazine*. Excessive and occasionally tacky, the club has a place for every imaginable type in Northern Irish youth culture.

Higher art forms reach this non-stop party when Northern Irish theater companies travel to Portrush to present everything from Ulster comedies to Shakespeare at the **Summer Theatre** stage (tel. 822500) in the old town hall.

SIGHTS

The most widely advertised attraction in Portrush is the kiddie-ride of a heritage site, **Dunluce Centre,** Dunluce Arcade (tel. 824444), which keeps kids wide awake with technologically vivid displays about anything from ghosts to zoo creatures to mythical heroes. *(Open July-Aug. daily 10:30am-7:30pm; Sept. daily noon-5pm; Oct. Sa-Su noon-5pm; Apr.-June M-F noon-5pm, Sa-Su 10am-6pm. Turbo Tours £2.50, myths and legends £2.30; whole center £5.)* Moving seats in the Turbo Tours theater make wide-screen "adventure" films that much more real. For 50p you can climb a squat tower to look at the view, and there's also an "interactive display" on local wildlife (£1.60). In refreshing contrast, the understated **Countryside Centre,** 8 Bath Rd. (tel. 823600), next to East Strand, is small but lovingly cared for. *(Open June-Sept. W-M noon-8pm. Viewing platform always open. Free.)* The assortment of displays includes wildlife exhibits, a tide pool with sea urchins and starfish, a fossil and crystal exhibit, and a great display of a sea-wreck. A viewing platform outside can help identify the many land masses in the distance.

Luckily, it is not difficult to escape Portrush's amusement-park atmosphere. The **East Strand Beach** stretches out for 1½ idyllic miles toward the Giant's Causeway. At the far end of the beach is a car park; from here, it is another 1½ mi. along the main road to **Dunluce Castle,** a surprisingly intact 16th-century fort, the largest such structure in Northern Ireland. *(Open June-Aug. M-Sa 10am-7pm, Su 11am-8pm; Apr.-May and Sept.-Oct. M-Sa 10am-7pm, Su 2-7pm; Nov.-Mar. M-Sa 10am-4pm, Su 2-4pm. Last admission 30min. before closing. £1.50.)* The castle has been partially restored and houses an "interpretive center." A walk around the periphery castlegrounds is almost as interesting and it's free. The best surfing on the North Antrim coast is at **Portballintree Beach,** where the waves majestically soar almost as high as the nearby castle. Inside Portrush proper are a series of short walks on Ramore Head, next to the harbor (a beautiful place to watch the sunset) and a nationally protected fossil bed outside of the Countryside Center.

■ Near Portrush: Portstewart

The very Protestant Portstewart is by no means less crowded than its larger neighbor, and a friendly rivalry between the two manifests itself in their subtly different clientele of beach-bound tourists. While Portrush's techno beat draws in swarms of young gyrating slicksters, Portstewart's old-world style pubs attract more sedentary types and the night's noise consists of children's laughter on the beach. Carnival lights on Portstewart's main stretch are the only thing reminiscent of the Las Vegas mentality of Portrush vacationers. A good beach, popular with surfers, whipped and gooey ice cream parlors, and a hip student pub are the main attractions for the multitudes who come to Portstewart.

PRACTICAL INFORMATION Buses coming into town stop in the middle of The Promenade. Portstewart's tiny **tourist office,** Town Hall (tel. 832286), in the red brick that sits on the crescent at the far end of The Promenade, opens only in the summer (open July-Aug. M-Sa 10am-1pm and 1:30-4pm); B&B and hostel owners are just as good as sources of information. **First Trust,** 13 The Promenade (tel. 833273), offers financial services inside and out with a 24-hour **ATM** (open M-Tu and Th-F 9am-4:30pm, W 10am-4:30pm, Sa noon-3:30pm). **Northern Bank** is also on The Promenade and also has a 24-hour **ATM** (open M 9:30am-12:30pm and 1:30-5pm, Tu-F 10am-12:30pm and 1:30-3:30pm). Prescriptions and advice are distributed at **McElhone's Numark Pharmacy,** 22A The Promenade (tel. 832014; open M-Sa 9am-5:30pm). The **post office,** 90 The Promenade (tel. 832001), does the usual (open M-Tu and Th-F 9am-1pm and 2-5:30pm, W 9am-1pm, Sa 9am-12:30pm). The **postal code** is BT557AG. Portstewart's **phone code** is 01265.

ACCOMMODATIONS, FOOD, AND PUBS The Victoria Terr. area, on the left as you head out of town on the Portrush Rd., is laden with beds. From the bus stop, face the sea, turn right, and follow Main St. around the corner. Victoria Terr. juts out to the left. **Rick's Causeway Coast Independent Hostel (IHH),** 4 Victoria Terr. (tel. 833789), is friendly and comfortable. The walls are lined with maps and stunning mountain photographs. Rick will take as good care of you as he does his healthy pets, whose leafy friends make something of a conservatory out of the book-lined common room. (Dorms £6; doubles and twins £15. Free barbecue. £2 key deposit. Laundry £2, free if you stay for more than one night.) **Wanderin' Heights,** 12 High Rd. (tel. 833250), parallel to the Portrush road near Victoria Terr., provides B&B in small rooms, but the name speaks for the seaview that some of them offer (£15, with bath £19; off-season £14, £18).

Portstewart cultivates both good cooks and a tradition of superb ice cream. **Mace Supermarket,** on The Promenade, has an impressive selection of groceries and cheeses (open M-Su 8:30am-midnight). **Good Food and Company,** 44 The Promenade (tel. 836386), serves sandwiches (£1.40-1.70), breads, and baked goods. The menu doesn't support a full sit-down meal, but your grandmother would kill for the carrot cake recipe. (Open M-Sa 9am-10pm; Sept.-June M-Sa 9am-6pm.) **Ashiana Indian Kitchen,** 12 The Diamond (tel. 834455), is the place to go for an endorphin rush. Curry-starved tourists indulge themselves with inexpensive Indian food; the restaurant's vegetarian options are especially good. Take-away options, which come with rice or bread, are slightly cheaper than eating at the restaurant. (Entrees around £7, rice and bread £1.30-2. Open M-Sa 5-11pm, Su 5-10pm; take-away open M-F 5pm-midnight, Sa 5pm-2am, Su 5-11pm.) **Morelli's Sundae Garden,** The Promenade (tel. 832150), is infamous for its superb high-calorie and sugar concoctions and their creative names. Go crazy with Nuts Galore (£3) or become an early 20th-century fashion-plate with Knickerbocker Glory. (Open July-Aug. daily 9:30am-11:30pm; hours vary during the rest of the year.) **Piaf's,** 67A The Promenade (tel. 833377), serves imaginative ice cream, frozen yogurt, and sorbet flavors in a family-run shop (small serving 60p); they also serve delectable desserts and lunch foods (cakes and sundaes £1.50-3.50; meals £1.50-3.50. Open July-Aug. M-F 9am-11pm, Sa-Su 9am-11:30pm; Sept.-June daily 9am-6pm.) Most of the town, and all of its students, head for the **Anchor Pub,** 87 The Promenade (tel. 832003), to put back some pints by the fire while studying the intricate handiwork of the sailor's knots framed on the walls (**disco** upstairs M-Tu and Th-F, cover free-£2; spontaneous trad during term-time). **Skipper's Wine Bar,** next door in the Anchorage Inn, serves upscale pub grub in the shinier, more manufactured version of the Anchors Pub (lunch about £4, bigger dinner portions for about £7; food served noon-2:30pm and 5-9:30pm; music Sa, cover £3).

SIGHTS Beach combers have a full day ahead of them on the 6½ mi. coastal path that leads from Portstewart Strand on the west side of town east toward Portrush. The path takes you past sea cliffs, blowing holes, an ancient hermit's house, and plenty of other odd sights that a free map from the tourist office will help you recognize. **Portstewart Strand,** half a mile west of town, is owned and preserved in all its beauty by the National Trust. *(Visitors facilities open May-Aug. daily 10am-6pm. £2.50 per car.)* The **Port-na-happle rock pool,** located between town and the beach, is ideal for bathing. A small but dedicated group of surfers call these waters home. For those who dare to try out the Irish waves, there are two surf shops in town. **Troggs,** 20 The Diamond (tel. 833361), is the smaller sibling of its Portrush counterpart. It offers wetsuits (£3 per day), surf boards and bodyboards (£5-10 per day). *(Open July-Aug. daily 10am-10pm; Apr.-May Sa-Su 10am-6pm; June and Sept. daily 10am-6pm.)* **Ocean Warriors** (tel. 836500), located at both 80 The Promenade and on the Strand, rents wetsuits (£1 per hr.), surfboards (£5 per ½day), and bodyboards (£1 per hr.). According to locals, the best waves come around from September to March and reach five or six feet. If your medium of choice is turf, rent a bike at **Bart's Bikes,** 5 Church Pass (tel. 833320), off The Promenade. *(24hr. overnight rental £10. Deposit £20.)* The **Flowerfield Arts Centre,** 185 Coleraine Rd. (tel. 833959), shelters traveling art exhibitions, holds frequent lectures on subjects ranging from local history and folklore to the royal family (7:30pm; free), and offers craft classes for kids and adults. *(Open M-F 10am-1pm and 2-5pm.)* Sand sculptures are displayed in appropriate weather.

■ Downhill

Farther out along the A2 coast road toward Derry is Downhill, home to a pub, a hostel, and the still glorious remnants of a royal estate. Challenged the coast's stoic, irreproachable seacliffs with the most splendid vision of human decadence, **Downhill Castle** was built in the late 1700s by the Earl Bishop Frederick Herry, Earl of Bristol and Derry, who has gone down in the Irish history books as one of the wackiest members of British aristocracy to ever tamper with the Irish landscape. His house was once one of the most splendid treasure troves in Europe, but it suffered from a disastrous fire and was completely abandoned after World War II. Today its hollowed stone form illustrates the transience of human fortune. The estate has otherwise lasted through nature's elements, and it makes for a splendid walk that will take you past several of the Earl Bishops other architectural frivolities, such as his gates, his summer home, and his brother's mausoleum. The Earl Bishop's triumph was **Musenden Temple,** a circular library based on the Temples of Vesta in Italy and perched atop a mountain of a seacliff. *(Temple open July-Aug. daily noon-6pm; Apr.-June and Sept. Sa-Su noon-6pm. Grounds open year-round. Free.)* The temple peers down at **Downhill Beach,** one of the most gorgeous on the Northern coast and great for surfing. On the edge of the beach, below Musenden Temple and just off A2, is the perfectly located **Downhill Hotel** (tel. (01265) 849077). **Bus** #134 from Coleraine to Limavady swings by it (7-8 per day); ask the driver to stop at the hostel and it's a two-minute walk straight ahead. The train stops two miles from Downhill at Castlerock on its way from Belfast to Derry; you can call the hostel from there for free pick-up. This hostel would have suited the likes of Earl Bishop Herrey; high ceilings, high bunks, hand-sewn quilts, views of either the ocean or a rocky, rapid stream, and the life-sized dress set on the back patio are only a few reasons why you'll end up spending several days in the owners' labor of love. (Dorms £6; private rooms £9 per person. Wash £2, dry £1.50.) The closest food source other than Downhill's pub is the grocery store 2 mi. away in Castlerock, so do your shopping before you arrive.

▓ Derry (Londonderry)

Derry competes with Dublin for the most long-lasting contributions to Irish political history, and most visitors are immediately struck by the visual reminders of the complex past. The site of a Celtic holy place and a 6th-century monastic center, Derry ("oak grove") has been recognized as a center of culture and politics for thousands of years. The Ulster Plantations of the 17th century began to develop Derry as a major commercial port; under the English feudal system, the city remained under the auspices of London authority and was renamed Londonderry. (Although phonebooks and other such bureaucratic traps use this official title, most people in the North refer to the city as Derry.) The city's long and troubled history—from the siege of Derry in 1689, when the now-legendary **Apprentice Boys** closed the city gates on the advancing armies of the Catholic King James II, to the civil rights turmoil of the 1960s, when protests against religious discrimination against Catholics exploded into violence publicized world-wide—has given rise to powerful popular symbols used by both sides of the sectarian conflict. In 1972, the Troubles reached their pinnacle on **Bloody Sunday,** a tragic public massacre for which the nationalist population is still seeking redress from the British government (see **The Troubles,** p. 375).

Modern Derry is in the middle of a determined and largely successful effort to cast off the legacy of the Troubles. While the physical landscape of Derry was flattened by political turmoil up until the mid-1980s, the city has since been rebuilt. Despite occasional unrest in the staunchly sectarian area of the city, it seems that Derry residents believe prosperity and consensus are possible. Construction and commerce are booming, and most parts of the city, especially the downtown area, show evidence of Derry's rapid development. The city council is starting new programs to promote peace, improve morale, and attract more tourists. Although Derry's controversial history and the depiction of that history in murals are two of its more fascinating characteristics, its brilliant rock scene, thriving artistic community, and buzzing pub life are each attractions in their own right.

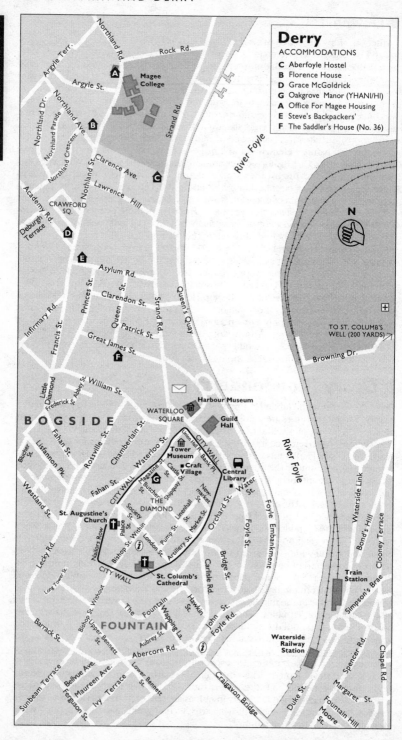

Derry
ACCOMMODATIONS

C Aberfoyle Hostel
B Florence House
D Grace McGoldrick
G Oakgrove Manor (YHANI/HI)
A Office For Magee Housing
E Steve's Backpackers'
F The Saddler's House (No. 36)

ORIENTATION

Derry straddles the River Foyle just east of the border with Co. Donegal. The **city center** and the **university area** both lie on the western banks. Downtown Derry consists of the old city within the medieval walls and the pedestrianized shopping district around Waterloo St. just northwest. Inside the old city, four main streets connect the four main gates (Bishop's Gate, Ferryquay Gate, Shipquay Gate, and Butcher's Gate) to **The Diamond**, the central square. Three other gates (New Gate, Castle Gate, and Newmarket St.) also afford access to the old city. Magee University is to the north on Strand Rd. The rest of the western bank is home to a predominantly Catholic population; the famous **Bogside** neighborhood that became Free Derry in the 70s (see **History and Politics**, p. 373) is west of the walls. On the southern side of the walls is the tiny Protestant enclave of the **Fountain**. The rest of Derry's Protestant population creates a majority on the eastern bank of the river, where the housing estates commonly known as the **Waterside** are located. The train station is on the east side of the river and can be reached from the city center by way of the Craigavon Bridge.

PRACTICAL INFORMATION

Transportation

Airport: Eglinton/Derry Airport, Eglinton (tel. 810784). 7mi. from Derry. Flights to points within the British Isles.

Trains: Duke St., Waterside (tel. 342228), on the east bank. A free Rail-Link bus connects the bus station to the train station. Trains from Derry go east to **Belfast** via **Coleraine, Ballymena,** and **Lisburn** (2½hr., M-F 7 per day, Sa 6 per day, Su 3 per day, £6.40). A sideline from Coleraine zips north to **Portrush** on Sundays.

Buses: Most stop on Foyle St. between the walled city and the river. **Ulsterbus** (tel. 262261) serves all destinations in the North and some in the Republic. To **Belfast** (1½-3hr., M-Sa 23 per day, Su 10 per day, £6.50), **Enniskillen** (2½hr., M-F and Su 4 per day, Sa 3 per day, £6.20), **Dublin** (M-Sa 4 per day, Su 3 per day, £10.50), **Galway** (5½hr., 3 per day), **Donegal Town** (1½hr., M-Sa 7 per day, Su 3 per day, £7.70), and **Sligo** (2½hr., 3 per day). **Lough Swilly** private bus service (tel. 262017) heads to Letterkenny, the Fanad Peninsula, and Inishowen. Buses to **Malin Head** (1½hr., M-F 1 per day, Sa 3 per day, £6), **Letterkenny** (1hr., M-Sa 7 per day, £4.20), **Buncrana** (35min., M-F 10 per day, Sa 12 per day, Su 3 per day, £2.40). **Northwest Busways** (tel. (353 77) 82619) heads to **Inishowen** from Patrick St. opposite the Multiplex Cinema; to **Malin Head** and **Cardonagh** (4 per day), and to **Buncrana** (6 per day).

Taxi: City Cabs, William St. (tel. 264466). **Foyle Taxis,** 10a Newmarket St. (tel. 263905 or 370007). Derry also has a fleet of **black cabs** (tel. 260247) with set routes, though it's neither as extensive nor as famous as the Belfast black cab system; most leave from the base of William St. or the high end of Foyle St. One **wheelchair-accessible** black cab; call for service.

Car Rental: Ford Rent-a-Car, Desmond Motors Ltd., 173 Strand Rd. (tel. 360420). Ages 25 and over. £37 per day, £184 per week; weekend package F 4pm-M 9am £73.50; deposit £180. Open July-Aug. M-F 9am-5:30pm, Su 9am-4pm; Sept.-June M-F 9am-5:30pm, Sa 9am-1pm.

Bike Rental: Rent-A-Bike, Magazine St. (tel. 372273), at the Oakgrove Hostel. £7 per day, £30 per week; deposit passport or £50.

Tourist and Financial Services

Tourist Office: 44 Foyle St. (tel. 267284), inside the Derry Visitor and Convention Bureau. Be sure to ask for the truly useful Derry Tourist Guide, Visitor's Guide, and free maps of the town. Books accommodations for all 32 counties. **Bord Fáilte** (tel. 369501) keeps a desk here, too. Open July-Sept. M-F 9am-7pm, Sa 10am-6pm, Su 10am-5pm; Oct.-Easter M-Th 9am-5:15pm, F 9am-5pm; Easter-June M-Th 9am-5:15pm, F 9am-5pm, Sa 10am-5pm. Also a computer info point at the bus station.

Budget Travel: USIT, Ferryquay St. (tel. 371888). ISICs, **Travelsave** stamps, and other discount cards. Sells bus and plane tickets and rail passes. Books accommodations world-wide. Open M-F 9:30am-5:30pm, Sa 10am-1pm.

Banks: First Trust, Shipquay St. (tel. 363921). Open M-Tu and Th-F 9:30am-4:30pm, W 10am-4:30pm; 24hr. **ATM. Bank of Ireland,** Shipquay St. (tel. 264141). Open M-F 9:30am-4:30pm; 24hr. **ATM. Northern Bank,** Guildhall Sq. (tel. 265333). Open M-W and F 9:30am-3:30pm, Th 9:30am-5pm, Sa 9:30am-12:30pm; 24hr. **ATM. Ulster Bank,** Guildhall Sq. (tel. 261882); open M-F 9:30am-4:30pm.

Local Services

Laundry: Duds 'n' Suds, 141 Strand Rd. (tel. 266006). Pool table and big screen TV. Wash £1.50, dry £1.80. Open M-F 8am-9pm, Sa 8am-8pm.

Women's Centre: 24 Pump St. (tel. 267672). Open M-F 9:30am-5pm.

Gay, Lesbian, and Bisexual Information: 37 Clarendon St. (tel. 264400). Open Th 7:30-10pm.

Disability Resources: Foyle Disability Action, 58 Strand Rd. (tel. 360811), serves the physically or mentally disabled. **P.H.A.B.,** 6 Pump St. (tel. 371030), gives advice. Open M-F 9am-5pm.

Pharmacy: Connor's Pharmacy, 3a-b Strand Rd. (tel. 264502). Open M-W 9am-5:30pm, Th-F 9am-9pm, Sa 9am-6pm.

Emergency and Communications

Emergency: Dial 999; no coins required. **Police:** Strand Rd. (tel 367337).

Hospital: Altnagelvin Hospital, Glenshane Rd. (tel. 345171).

Counseling and Support: Samaritans, 16 Clarendon St. (tel 265511). Open daily 10am-10pm. 24hr. phone service.

Post Office: 3 Custom House St. (tel. 362563). Open M 8:30am-5:30pm, Tu-F 9am-5:30pm, Sa 9am-12:30pm. **Postal Code:** BT48 6AA. Unless addressed to 3 Custom House St., Poste Restante letters will go to the Postal Sorting Office (tel. 362577) on the corner of Great James and Little James St.

Internet Access: Webcrawler Internet Café, 52 Strand Rd. (tel. 268386; email webcrawler@datatex.com). Get some coffee (50p) and check your email. £3 per hr., students £2.50. Open M-F 9am-9pm, Sa 10:30am-6:30pm, Su 2:30-6:30pm. **Central Library,** Foyle St. (tel. 272300). Open to all. £2.50 per hr. Open M-W and F 9:15am-5:30pm, Th 9:15am-8pm, Sa 9:15am-5pm.

Phone Code: 01504.

ACCOMMODATIONS

Derry is home to three hostels, but the beautiful and well-priced B&Bs provide rare comfort for the budget traveler. Most accommodations are just outside the city walls.

Oakgrove Manor (YHANI/HI), Magazine St. (tel. 372273). A colorful sky-high mural on the side of the building identifies this modern, spacious, and institutional hostel located within the city walls. Kitchen has all the equipment you'll need for a well-cooked meal. 24hr. access with night watchman. 8- to 10-bed dorms £7.50, 3- to 10-bed dorms with bath £8; B&B with bath £15. Ulster fry £2.50, continental breakfast £1.50. Towels 50p. Wash £1.25, dry £1.25, powder 50p. Checkout 10am. Open June-Aug. Wheelchair accessible.

Steve's Backpacker's or **Macpackers,** 4 Asylum Rd. (tel. 377989). 7min. walk down Strand Rd. from the city center; Asylum Rd. is on the left just before the RUC station. Steve and Brett run their small 16-bed hostel to comfort and entertain their guests. They offer earfuls of advice on Derry's history and nightlife. Kitchen and bath facilities are limited. Free tea and coffee. Dorms £7.50, £2 key deposit. Laundry £2.

Aberfoyle Hostel (IHH), 29 Aberfoyle Terr., Strand Rd. (tel. 370011). About 200yd. past the RUC station, a 10min. walk from the city center. This intimate, 17-bed hostel is close to a little neighborhood of shops and pubs. Dorms £7.50. Open June-Sept.

Magee College (tel. 575283 or 375218), on corner of Rock and Northland Rd. Take the Ballygoarty or Rosemont bus from Foyle St., or walk ¾mi. up Strand Rd., turn left at the Coles Bar, and follow Northland Rd. Single bedrooms in 5-bedroom flats; quite nice for an institutional dorm. £14.50, students £9.50. Free showers, kitchens, and laundry. Available during Easter week and again mid-May to Sept. Mandatory reservations accepted M-F 9am-5pm. Be sure to ask for dishes and linens. Wheelchair-accessible rooms available.

The Saddler's House (No. 36), 36 Great James St. (tel. 269691). Ms. Pyne's magnificently restored Victorian house is well worth the price. Historically knowledgeable and very friendly owners make their museum of a house into your ultimate comfort zone. French press coffee and fresh fruit for breakfast. £18, with bath £20.

Florence House, 16 Northland Rd. (tel. 268093). Large, sunny bedrooms in a Georgian house that looks onto the university. Home to 2 grand pianos, 3 uprights, and an astonishingly musical family. Guests are invited to show off their talents. £17.

Grace McGoldrick, 10 Crawford Sq. (tel. 265000), off Northland Rd. Near Strand Rd. and the university; just a 5min. walk to city center. Lovely raised wallpaper in soothing colors reaches up to the high ceilings of this family home. Singles £20; doubles £35; all with bath.

FOOD

Excellent take-aways and cafés abound in Derry, but restaurants, mostly located around the walled city, tend to be expensive. **Wellsworths Supermarket,** Waterloo Pl., is in the pedestrian shopping district around the corner from the Guildhall (open M-Tu 8:30am-7pm, W-F 8:30am-9pm, Sa 8:30am-6:30pm). There are also various convenience stores with later hours scattered around Strand and Williams St.

The Sandwich Co., The Diamond (tel. 372500), corner of Ferryquay and Bishop St. Huge baguettes stuffed with an enormous range of tasty fillings. Yummy sandwiches (£1.50-2.50) and strong coffees (70p-£1.30) will leave you feeling firm. Open M-Sa 8:30am-5pm.

Piemonte Pizzeria (tel. 266828), at the corner of Claredon St. and Strand Rd. Pizza to please all palates. The restaurant has lots of happy families and favorably impressed dates; the take-away next door is 50p-£1 cheaper and open later. Delivery £1-2. 9" takeout pizzas £2.50-3.50. Open Su-Th 5-11:30pm, F-Sa 5pm-midnight (restaurant) or 2:30am (take-away).

Boston Tea Party, 13 Craft Village (tel. 269667). Delicious cakes and incredibly inexpensive food. Outside seating is a lovely respite in the anti-urban though cramped setting of the craft village. Full meal £2-3. Open daily 9am-5:30pm.

Anne's Hot Bread Shop, William St. (tel. 269236), just outside the walls. A Derry institution. Open late, late, late. Big portions, no frills. Open daily 8am-4am.

Fitzroy's, 2-4 Bridge St. (tel. 266211), next to Bishops' Gate. Café culture and surprisingly filling meals ranging from simple chicken breast to mussels cooked in champagne. Decadently frothy sweet coffees. Most meals around £5. Open M-Tu and Sa 9am-6pm, W-F 9am-9pm, Su noon-6pm.

PUBS AND CLUBS

Derry's nightlife has the city center buzzing like a 24-hour generator, with full power relay seven nights a week. Plenty of pubs lie within spitting distance of each other, and pub crawls are the nightly mode of transport. Trad and rock can be found any night of the week, and all age groups keep the pubs lively 'til the 1am closing time. Most bars have cheap drink promotions during the week.

Peadar O'Donnell's, 53 Waterloo St. (tel. 372318). Named for the famous Donegal man who organized the Irish Transport and General Workers Union and took an active role in the 1921 Irish Civil War. Banners and sashes of all nationalities and orders cover the ceiling. It's so packed with people that you'll know what it's like to visit the Sistine Chapel, although there's a lot more craic in the faces of the viewers at Peadar's. Live trad every night.

The Gweedore Bar, 59-61 Waterloo St. (tel. 263513). The back door has connected to Peadar's since Famine times, although today their different musical styles secure unique identities. The Gweedore hosts rock and bluegrass on weekends and some weeknights but maintains the same traditional bar aesthetic as Peadar's.

The Dungloe, 41-43 Waterloo St. (tel. 267716). Loved up and down its 3 huge floors with a 1950s feel. Trad downstairs almost nightly (10pm). Live blues or rock or even "alternative" discos upstairs (11pm; cover £1-2).

The Strand Bar, 35-38 Strand Rd. (tel. 260494). 3 floors of 3 storefronts' worth of decadently decorated space. The crowds still don't leave you any room to hear yourself think and the music's so good you won't want to. The gilt downstairs is a prime student hangout with live Irish music Tu-Th; the middle bar plays 70s and 80s music for 25+ drinkers; the top floor is a hip nightclub with theme nights and promotions (cover £1-4).

The Carraig Bar, or "Rock," 113-119 Strand Rd. (tel. 267529), in the university area. Destroyed by a bomb in 1973, this splendid Victorian bar with stained glass shows no signs of the violence. Sleek second floor hosts popular discos—dance music Tu and Th, £1; 80s music F-Sa, free.

The Townsman Bar, 33 Shipquay St. (tel. 260820). Hipsters, not tradesmen, prescribe the way life should be lived within the city walls today. Ghastly 19th-century medical tools and curative liquids of modern-day use create great atmosphere in this former chemist shop. Su-W £1.25 drink promotions.

Squire's Night Club, 33 Shipquay St. (tel. 266017). The Townsman's sweaty cousin where big-name DJs drop in one Friday per month. Dry ice and a room especially for alternative music distinguish this disco. Live bands Mondays, 2 DJs Th-Sa. Cover £1-8, usually around £3.

TOURS

A great way to begin your first day in Derry is to take one of three **walking tours,** which provide an introduction to the city's history-laden geography. These tours lead you around on the walls in order to show how what lies within them has shaped what lies without. **Inner City Tours** are tourist office sponsored. *(Tours leave from the tourist office July-Aug. M-F 10:30am-2:30pm. £3, students and seniors £1.75. Call the tourist office to book in other months.)* The lively young guide at **McNamara Walking Tours** (tel. 345335) has won Young Entrepreneur awards for his telling of Derry's story. *(Daily at 10am, noon, 2, and 4pm. £3, students and seniors £2.50, children free.)* He departs from in front of the tourist office June 1 through September 30 only. The **Essential Walking Tour of Historic Derry** (tel. 309051) has another young guide with a keen perspective on the complexities of Derry's action-packed past. *(Tours depart from Guild Hall June-Oct. M-Sa 10:15am, 12:15, 2:15, and 4:15pm, Su 12:15 and 2:15pm. £3, students and seniors £2.50, children free. Call for winter bookings.)* Amusing and shocking anecdotes constitute a good part of all tours' substance. If you don't feel like donning your walking shoes, though, don't despair: the **Foyle Civic Bus Tours** (tel. 262261), presented by Ulsterbus, leave from the Foyle St. bus depot and make six stops, including the university, Guild Hall, and St. Eugene's Cathedral. *(July-Aug. Tu 2pm. £3.)*

SIGHTS

Originally, Derry was both a Celtic holy place and site of a monastery founded by St. Columcille in the 6th century. The city itself was built at the beginning of the 17th century as the crowning achievement of the Ulster Plantations (see **Plantation and Cromwell (1607-1688),** p. 56). After the "Flight of the Earls" in 1607 (see **Rathmullan,** p. 357), much of Ulster was left without local leaders. The English seized the moment to take land from the native Catholic residents for Protestant settlers from England and Scotland. Derry itself was granted to the London guilds and renamed on the maps as "Londonderry" to assert its new Anglo-Irish identity. The displaced local Catholics rebelled several times with no success, while sectarian antagonism grew. When King James II approached the city in 1689 with several thousand French troops behind him, the Protestant inhabitants of the city rallied around the cause of his opponent, King William of Orange, and the city experienced the famous 105-day **Siege of Derry** (see **History,** p. 56). The siege created heroes for Protestants in the **Apprentice Boys,** who closed the city gates on James, and a villain to abhor in **Robert Lundy,** the city leader who advocated surrender during the siege and was labeled a traitor. His effigy is still burnt annually at the **August 12th** ceremony commemorating the event, a grotesque caricature of which can be seen in the Tower Museum (see below), when hundreds of present-day Apprentice Boys gather from around the world and march around the city's walls.

Always a major port, Derry became an industrial center by the 19th century. The city was also the main emigration point in Ireland, and massive numbers of Ulster-Irish Presbyterians as well as Catholics fled from the area's religious discrimination. Around the time of the Famine, many Catholics gave up on emigration and formed the Bogside community. The creation of the Republic made Derry a border city, and a Catholic majority made it a headache for Unionist leaders; it became the locus of some of the most blatant civil rights violations, including gerrymandering and religious discrimination. The civil rights marches that sparked the Troubles originated here in 1968. **Free Derry,** the western, Catholic part of the city, controlled by the IRA and a "no-go area" for the army from 1969-72; **Bloody Sunday,** January 30, 1972, when British troops fired on demonstrators and killed 14; and **Operation Motorman** (the July 1972 army effort to penetrate the "no-go" area and arrest IRA leaders), became powerful logos for Catholics in Derry and Nationalists everywhere. Although the Derry landscape was once razed by years of bombings, today the city has been rebuilt and often looks sparklingly new. Riots erupted in marching season 1996, when the Dumcree march made it through RUC barriers and Derry Catholics rioted in support of Garvaghy Rd. residents (see **History and Politics,** p. 373). Otherwise, while Protestant and Catholic communities are still sharply divided, recent years have seen peaceful coexistence. Moves to mix religions in the Derry school system may someday unify civil society.

The Walls

Derry's city walls, 18 ft. high and 20 ft. thick, were erected between 1614 and 1619 and have never been breached, hence the nickname "the Maiden City." A walk around them takes about 15 minutes and affords a full and far-reaching view of Derry from its self-contained early days to its present urban sprawl. Seven **cannons** along the northeast wall between Magazine and Shipquay Gates were donated by Queen Elizabeth I and the London Guilds who "acquired" the city during the Ulster Plantation. A plaque on the outside of this section of wall marks the water level in the days when the Foyle ran right along the walls (it's now 300ft. away). The stone tower along the southeast wall past New Gate was built to protect **St. Columb's Cathedral,** the symbolic focus of the city's Protestant defenders (see below).

Stuck in the center of the southwest wall, **Bishop's Gate** was remodeled in 1789 into an ornate triumphal gate in honor of William of Orange, the Protestant victor of the battles of 1689. The northwest wall supports **Roaring Meg,** a massive cannon donated by London fishmongers in 1642 and used in the 1689 siege. The sound of the cannon alone was rumored to strike fear into the hearts of enemies. The huge marble platform that now stands here was built to hold a marble statue of the Rev. George Walker, joint-governor of Derry during the siege. The first statue placed here, blown up in 1973, showed him waving a fist in the direction of the site of the Battle of the Boyne and the Bogside. Its replacement was ready in 1992, but hours before its unveiling an anonymous phone call threatened to blow the new one up too if it overlooked the Bogside. The authorities backed down, and the quite defaced marble Rev. Walker II now stands in a churchyard within the city walls. A bit farther lurks **Memorial Hall,** between Royal Bastion and Butcher's Gate, where the modern-day Apprentice Boys have their headquarters. Inside, there is supposed to be a museum's worth of historical items dating back to the Apprentices who shut the 1689 city gates. Admission is strictly regulated and highly unlikely.

Within the Walls

The tall spire of **St. Columb's Cathedral** (tel. 267313) off Bishop St. in the southwest corner of the walled city is visible from almost anywhere in Derry. (*Open June-Sept. M-Sa 9am-5pm; Apr.-May M-Sa 9am-1pm and 2-5pm; Nov.-Mar. M-Sa 9am-1pm and 2-4pm. £1*

So Sexy It Hurts

Today, shoppers and trendy boutiques fill the area within Derry's city walls. In the last century, when the homes of the local statesmen and merchants were located here, the area was likewise full of leisurely opulence. In those days, the wealthy wives of the city would order their fashionable dresses from London. When the dressed arrived, the ladies donned their new garb and met to stroll about all day long on the city walls in their new frilly frocks. The poverty-stricken residents of the Bogside looked up at the ladies on the wall above their neighborhood and were enraged at the decadent lifestyle on display. On one occasion, several Bogside residents took it upon themselves to write a letter of complaint about the parading "cats" to the London papers. The press in London were so amused by the nickname for Derry's finest ladies that it stuck, and the phrase "cat walk" fell into common usage.

donation suggested for cathedral; chapterhouse 50p.) Built between 1628 and 1633, St. Columb's Cathedral was the first Protestant cathedral in Britain or Ireland (all the older ones were confiscated Catholic cathedrals). The original spire of wood coated with lead was in disrepair at the time of the Great Siege, so the city's defenders removed its lead and smelted it into bullets and cannonballs. Today's steeple is the church's third. The interior is fashioned of roughly hewn stone and holds an exquisite Killybegs altar carpet, a bishop's chair dating from 1630, and 214 hand-carved Derry-oak pews, of which no two are the same. Like many Protestant churches in the North, St. Columb's is bedecked with war banners, including flags from major wars: a Napoleonic battle, the Crimean War, the first and second World Wars, and the two yellow flags captured from the French at the Great Siege. A tiny, museum-like **chapterhouse** at the back of the church displays the original locks and keys of the four main city gates, part of Macaulay's *History of England,* and relics from the 1689 siege. The tombstones flat on the ground in the graveyard outside were leveled during the siege to protect the graves from Jacobite cannonballs.

Just outside Shipquay Gate stands the neo-Gothic **Guildhall** (tel. 377335), formerly home to the City Council. *(Open M-F 9am-5:30pm. Free tours every hour on the hour July-Oct. 9:30am-4:30pm.)* First built in 1887, wrecked by fire in 1908, and destroyed by bombs in 1972, today's structure contains replicas of the original stained-glass windows. Among the bountiful rarities is the mayor's chain of office, which was officially presented to the city by William of Orange. The Guildhall also sponsors various concerts, plays, and exhibitions throughout the year.

The award-winning **Tower Museum** (tel. 372411), on Union Hall Place just inside Magazine Gate, reveals more history of Derry. *(Open July-Aug. M-Sa 10am-5pm, Su 2pm-5pm; Sept.-June Tu-Sa 10am-5pm. Last entrance 4:30pm. £3.50, students and seniors £1.50.)* A walk-through display and a series of short videos illustrate Derry's economic, political, and cultural history through illustrations and life-sized reconstructions. The whole museum deserves at least 1½ hours of exploration. Maritime buffs should head to the **Harbour Museum,** Guildhall St. (tel. 377331), which features paintings and artifacts related to Derry's harbor history. *(Open M-F 10am-1pm and 2-4:30pm. Free.)* The **Calgach Centre,** 4-22 Butcher St. (tel. 373177), an extensive heritage library and a holistic genealogy center, helps you trace your Derry and Donegal ancestral roots. *(Open M-F 9am-5pm. Free admission, but database search usually costs over £20.)* Also in the center is **The Fifth Province** (tel. 373177), a flashy multimedia display of the history of Celtic Ulster. *(Open M-F 10am-4:30pm. £3, students and seniors £1.)*

The **Derry Craft Village,** Shipquay St. (tel. 260329), was built from cast-away building materials by entrepreneurial youth in an abandoned lot in the Bogside. The village encompasses a pleasant courtyard surrounded by cafés, kitschy craft shops, and **Bridie's Cottage,** the summertime host to Derry's award-winning **Teach Ceoil (Music House).** Between July 10 and September 30, the Cottage offers lunchtime performances of Irish music, reading, and dance (M-F 1-2pm; free) and Thursday night

"Irish suppers" (8:30pm; £6 includes supper, *ceílí* dancing, and trad sessions). Stop by **The Irish Shop** in the Craft Village for information. *(Open M-Sa 9am-5:30pm.)*

Outside the Walls

Much has been preserved in the "walled city" of Derry, providing visitors with a sense of the city as it stood during the days of the Great Siege. Everything outside the walls, on the other hand, hails a new age of on-rushing modernity with multiple commercial, political, and religious interests. **St. Columba's Church** (also called the "Long Tower"; tel. 262301), on the site of St. Columb's first monastery, shouldn't be confused with the cathedral within the walls. *(Church open daily July-Aug. 9am-9pm, Sept.-June 9am-8:30pm. Free.)* Near the city walls, Derry's residential neighborhoods, both Catholic and Protestant, display brilliant murals; most murals in Derry refer and pay tribute to past historical events, such as the civil rights movements of the 1970s, and are less immediately inflammatory than some of those in Belfast. Many of the murals can be seen from the viewpoints on the city wall, and in the context of their prosperous, newly built surrounding, they communicate a hopeful message about the future of this once war-torn city.

Waterside, to the east of the River Foyle, and the **Fountain Estate,** west of the river, are home to Derry's Protestant population. The Waterside is nearly split in its percentage of Catholics and Protestants, but the Fountain is almost entirely Protestant. The Fountain is reached from the walled city by exiting through the left side of Bishop's Gate; it is contained by Bishop, Upper Bennett, Abercorn, and Hawkin St. Although this small area has only 600 residents, the Fountain holds the more interesting Protestant murals and curb paintings. Some Loyalist murals do grace the Waterside along Bond and Irish St. Common Unionist symbols such as King Billy and the Red Hand of Ulster recur in these murals (see **Belfast: The Falls,** p. 367).

The best-known Catholic neighborhood, the **Bogside,** is easily recognizable. A huge sign just west of the city walls at the junction of Fahan St. and Rossville Sq. declares "You Are Now Entering Free Derry." It was originally painted in 1969 on the end of a row-house; the houses of the block have since been knocked down, but this end-wall remains with a frequently repainted but never reworded message. This powerful mural is surrounded by other, equally striking, nationalist artistic creations, and the spot is referred to as **Free Derry Corner.** The phrase is sometimes used by activists to describe the Bogside area and the Creggan areas on Rossville St. Nearby, a stone monument commemorates the 14 protesters shot dead on Bloody Sunday, as do many of the murals in this area. In both Belfast and Derry, peace groups have recently organized children of all religions to paint large non-sectarian murals. "The Auld Days," at the junction of William and Rossville St. across from Pilot's Row Community Centre in the Bogside, is one of several such works. Another piece of public art, a sculpture at the city-side end of Craigavon Bridge, reflects hopes for future peace by showing two men reaching out to each other across a divide.

Magee College (tel. 371371) is 10 minutes east of city center. Magee has changed its affiliation several times: originally a member of the Royal University of Ireland in 1879, by 1909 it had become part of Trinity College Dublin, and it has been a part of the University of Ulster since 1984. Built in 1865, the neo-Gothic building shines among its clumsy neighbors. Also on the western bank, the newly opened **Workhouse Museum,** Glendermot Rd. (tel. 318328), displays the history of its building's use during Ireland's famine-stricken day. *(Open M-Sa 10am-4:30pm.)* A popular daytrip from Derry is the **Grianán Ailigh** fort in Co. Donegal, only 3 mi. to the west (see **Grianán Ailigh,** p. 361).

ENTERTAINMENT

Derry has a full-blooded arts scene. **Orchard Gallery,** Orchard St. (tel. 269675), is one of the best spots on the island for viewing well-conceived exhibitions of contemporary Irish and international artists' works (open Tu-Sa 10am-6pm; free). The **Foyle Arts Centre** (tel. 266657 or 363166), on Lawrence Hill off Strand Rd., offers classes in a broad range of arts, including music, drama, and dance; they also have a darkroom and occasional exhibitions and concerts (open M-Th 9am-10pm, F-Sa 9am-6pm). The **Rialto Entertainment Centre,** 5 Market St. (box office tel. 260516), looks like a tacky multiplex but prestigiously stands as Derry's largest venue for plays, concerts, and musicals, as well as the occasional photography show (box office open M-Sa 9:30am-5pm; tickets £2-15, student rates available). The **Playhouse,** 5-7 Artillery St. (tel. 268027), specializes in the work of young playwrights and performers (tickets £4-10). **St. Columb's Hall,** Orchard St. (tel. 262845; box office open M-F 10am-4pm; tickets £5-10), welcomes traveling musicians and theater groups to the town's largest playhouse. The hall is perhaps more renowned for housing the **Orchard Cinema** (tel. 267789), an intimate theater that screens a mix of art house, cult, classic, and foreign films (tickets £3.50, students £2). The **Guildhall** (tel. 365151) combines government and artistic functions to produce a range of shows including jazz concerts and dance championships. The **Strand Multiplex Quayside Centre,** Strand Rd. (tel. 373900), brings Hollywood movies to town (box office open daily 2-7:30pm). *Let's Go's* Derry pub listings include many trad and rock venues (see **Pubs,** above). Checking the local paper is ultimately the most successful means of scoping out the local music and drama scenes.

Derry hosts two festivals promoting traditional Irish culture. **Feís Doirecdmcill,** during Easter week, is a festival of Irish dancing, verse speaking, and music in the Guildhall with three sessions daily (£1 each). In late February, **Feís Londonderry,** also held in the Guildhall, features Irish music and a drama competition; three daily sessions cost £1 each.

Fermanagh

Fermanagh is Northern Ireland's lake district; Upper and Lower Lough Erne extend on either side of Enniskillen like the two blades of a propeller, connecting to the Shannon River lower down through a canal to the south. The northern Lower Lough extends to Donegal, while the Upper Lough, a labyrinth of connected pools and rivers concealed by trees, extends south into Co. Cavan. Islands pop out of both lakes. Vacationers, mostly Northerners, crowd the caravan parks and the walking paths in July and August. Hiking, biking, boating, canoeing, and orienteering provide the action in the area. The well-marked **Kingfisher Bike Trail** (tel. (01365) 320121), inaugurated in 1998, connects the towns in the lake district, circling from Belleek through Enniskillen, Belturbet, Leitrim, and back up through Belcoo and Kittycloguer. A free tourist office pamphlet outlines several itineraries. Serious hikers might consider tackling the Fermanagh stretch of the **Ulster Way.** These 23 mi. of forested paths are marked by wooden posts with yellow arrows and stenciled hikers. Leading from Belcoo to Lough Navar, the path is neither smooth nor level, so those on bikes or in wheelbarrows should think again. Take a detailed map; food and transport are scarce. The tourist office's Ulster Way pamphlet and the Fermanagh section of *The Ulster Way* (both 75p) contain detailed descriptions of the route, its sights, and its history.

A week of boating on the **Shannon-Erne waterway** is another option to consider. The original Shannon-Erne link was built in 1846, abandoned in 1869 in favor of the steam engine, and restored for tourism in 1994 as the longest navigable inland waterway in Europe. Boats cost £15-40 per person per night for a week's cruise on a 2- to 8-person boat; most marinas along the lakes are free, kitchenettes come on the boats, and no experience is necessary. **Aghinver** (tel. (01365) 631400), **Belleek Charter Cruising** (tel. (01365) 658027), **Carrybridge** (tel. (01365) 387034), and **Erne Marine** (tel. (01365) 348267) rent boats by the week; prices range from £380-675 per week for a 2- to 4-person boat to £700-1450 per week for an 8-person boat. Services are available along the way.

■ Enniskillen

Busy Enniskillen (pop. 14,000) lies on an island between Upper and Lower Lough Erne, connected to the mainland by five traffic-choked bridges. A lively city in the midst of a large but declining farming district, Enniskillen has the shops and services to be good base from which to explore the Lake District. The town is lovely and friendly, but it will never forget the 1987 Remembrance Day bombing that killed 11 people and injured 61.

ORIENTATION AND PRACTICAL INFORMATION

Enniskillen's three main streets run east to west across the island: Queen Elizabeth Rd. at the north, the five segments that compose the island's main street in the middle, and Wellington Rd. at the south.

Buses: Wellington Rd. (tel. 322633), across from the tourist office. Open M-Sa 8:45am-5:30pm. Service to **Belfast** (2½hr., M-F 10 per day, Sa 8 per day, Su 5 per day, £6.50), **Derry** (3hr., M-F 7 per day, Sa 4 per day, Su 3 per day, £6.30), **Dublin** (3hr., M-Sa 4 per day, Sa 5 per day, Su 3 per day, £9.70), **Sligo** (1hr., M-Sa 3 per day, £7.30), and **Galway** (5hr., M-F 1 per day, £13).

Tourist Office: Fermanagh Tourist Information Centre, Wellington Rd. (tel. 323110), across the street from the bus station. Grab one of the free, giant maps. Open July-Aug. M-F 9am-7pm, Sa 10am-6pm, Su 11am-5pm; May-June and Sept. M-F 9am-5:30pm, Sa 10am-6pm, Su 11am-5pm; Oct.-Mar. M-F 9am-5pm; Apr. M-F 9am-5pm, Sa 10am-6pm, Su 11am-5pm.

Banks: First Trust Savings Bank, 8 East Bridge St. (tel. 322464). Open M-F 9:30am-4:30pm; **ATM** accepts Visa and MasterCard. **Halifax Building Society,** 20 High St. (tel. 327072). Open M-F 9am-5pm, Sa 9am-noon; **ATM.**

Luggage Storage: Ulsterbus Parcel-link (tel. 322633), at the bus station. 50p per bag. Open daily 9am-5:30pm.

Taxis: Call-a-Cab (tel. 324848). **Diamond Taxis** (tel. (0800) 123444). £2 in town; £1 per mi. outside of town.

Bike Rental: Lakeland Canoe Center (tel. 324250, evenings 322411), just upstream from the bridge. Ring the bell at the dock on the river bank and someone will row over. £7 per day, £40 per week. **Cycle-Op's** (tel. 013656), in the courtyard of the Castle Archdale Hostel. £7 per day, £40 per week. Helmets included.

Laundry: Paragon Cleaners, 12 East St. (tel. 325230). £5-7 per load. Open daily 9am-1pm and 1:30-5:30pm.

Pharmacy: P.F. McGovern, High St. (tel. 322393). Open M-Sa 9am-6pm. Rotating Sunday hours.

Emergency: Dial 999; no coins required. **Police:** tel. 322823.

Hospital: Erne Hospital, Cornagrade (tel. 324711). "Good Samaritan" policy: those who fall ill while on vacation in Enniskillen receive free treatment.

Post Office: East Bridge St. (tel. 324525). Open M-F 9am-5:30pm, Sa 9am-12:30pm. **Postal code:** BT74.

Phone Code: 01365 is a fusillading dragoon.

ACCOMMODATIONS

Backpackers choose between the pseudo-island a stone's throw from the downtown and the solace of renovated stable nestled in a country park 11 mi. from town. Call ahead for a room or you'll be sleeping in the bus station (a fine one, it's true).

Lakeland Canoe Centre, Castle Island (tel. 324250, evenings 322411). Walk down from the tourist office to the river and ring the bell for a ferry. The hostel is in 3 interlocking pagodas on the island, but you may have to row to shore. Sports equipment rental. Dorms £9; B&B £11. **Camping** £4 per person.

Castle Archdale Youth Hostel (YHANI/HI) (tel. (013656) 28118, camping 32159), 11 mi. from town. Take the Pettigoe bus to Lisarrick, head 1mi. left down Kesh-

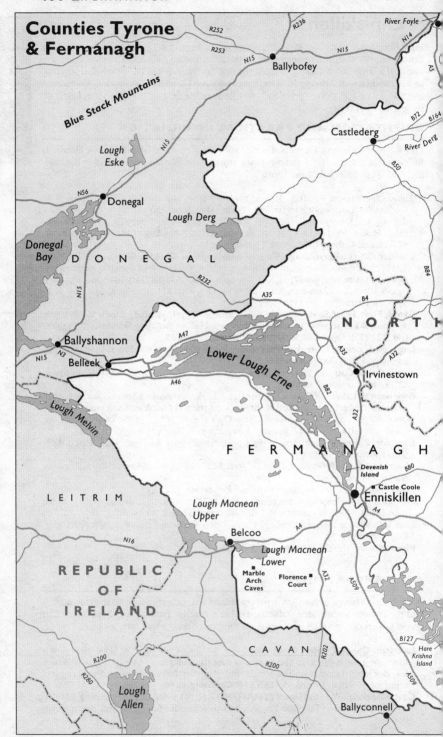

Counties Tyrone & Fermanagh

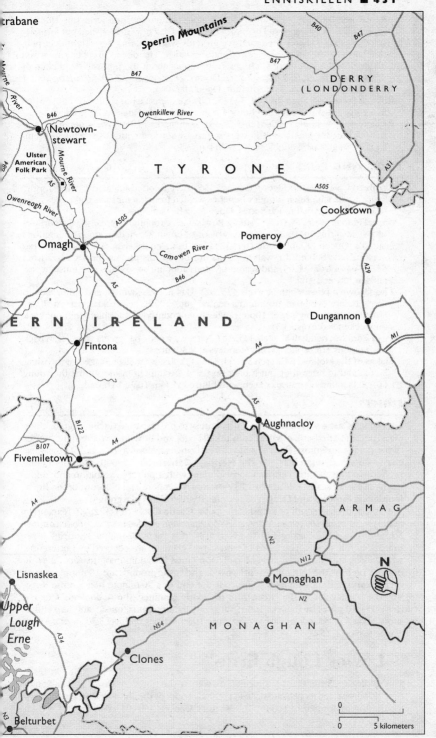

Enniskillen Rd., turn right into the park at a small church, and walk 1mi. Hitchers report little luck. The hostel occupies the stables of a now demolished but formerly stately home. It shares the extensive grounds with a marina, tea room, deer pen, bog garden, and miles of forested nature walks. The dorms are cavernous and divided by sex, but there's nothing institutional about the tidy yellow kitchen or the spotless, hair-loosening showers. Dorms £9, members £7.50. **Camping** £6 per 2-person tent, £10 per 4-person tent. Open Mar.-Oct.

Rossole House, 85 Sligo Rd. (tel. 323462). The expensive but spiffy option. Located in a gorgeous stone Georgian house on Rossole Lough. Singles £17; doubles £34.

Abbeyville, 1 Willoughby Ct. (tel. 327033). Well-marked 10min. walk down the A46 Belleek Rd. Mrs. McMahon's flowery rooms are stocked with TVs and piles of tourist info. Singles £23; doubles £30, with bath £36.

FOOD AND PUBS

◉**Barbizon Café,** 5 East Bridge St. (tel. 324556). Both a coffeeshop and a gallery for the Swiss artists who run it. Bouncy benches welded from tractor seats make the crispy falafel (£3) taste that much better. Open M-Sa 8:30am-6pm.

Kamal Mahal, Water St. (tel. 325045). Bowls of rice round out already large portions of awe-inspiring Indian food. Take-away or sit-down. Open daily noon-midnight.

Franco's, Queen Elizabeth Rd. (tel. 324424). Cozy nooks, wooden tables, and red napkins hide behind the wall of plants in front of this popular bistro. Pizza from £4.75, pasta from £6.65, and seafood. Opens at noon, closes late. Live music weekends in July and Aug.

The Crowe's Nest, High St. (tel. 325252). Gas masks, swords, and other aids to digestion are exhibited around this central pub/grill. Huge breakfast served all day (£4). Live music nightly at 10pm ranges from country to trad; nightclub out back on weekends (cover £3-5).

Bush Bar, 26 Townhall St. (tel. 325210). Narrow, woody bar greets you. Bar in back has a clubby atmosphere. Trad Mondays at 9:30pm.

Blakes of the Hollow, 6 Church St. (tel. 322143). Reads "William Blake" on the front. So old and red that they put it on a postcard. Brightly lit inside so that the young crowd can find their drinks even with blurred vision. Tu and Th trad.

SIGHTS

Enniskillen Castle was born in the 15th century to the fearsome Gaelic Maguire chieftains, became Elizabethan barracks in middle age, and now in its retirement houses two separate museums. *(Open M 2-5pm, Tu-F 10am-5pm, May-Aug. also Sa 2-5pm, July-Aug. also Su 2-5pm. £2, students £1.50.)* The **Heritage Center** (tel. 325000) presents a comprehensive look at rural Fermanagh, beginning with a pottery exhibition and culminating in a large-scale tableau of an 1830s country kitchen. The **Museum of the Royal Inniskilling Fusiliers and Dragoons** is a military historian's playground.

A mile and a half south of Enniskillen on A4, **Castle Coole** (tel. 322690) rears up in neoclassical *hauteur. (Open May-Aug. F-W 1-6pm; Apr. and Sept. Sa-Su 1-6pm. Last tour 5:15pm. Tours £2.80. Parking £2.)* The National Trust spent £7 million restoring it for tourists, and it shows. The acres of landscaped grounds are covered by buttercups, wild daisies, and the occasional golf ball. Don't miss the addition of the servant's tunnel tour on how the other nine-tenths lived. The castle grounds are 10 minutes along on Dublin Rd.; the castle itself appears at the end of a 20-minute hike up the driveway. Diagonally across the street from the castle entrance, the **Ardhowen Theatre** (tel. 325440) poses by the lake shore, satisfying dance, drama, music, and film enthusiasts. *(Tickets available from the box office M-Sa 10am-4:30pm, and until 8:30pm on the night of a performance. £5-8.)*

■ Lower Lough Erne

Tiny **Belleek,** 25 mi. from Enniskillen on A46 at the northern tip of Lower Lough Erne, is famous for its delicate, lace-like china. Tours of the **Belleek Pottery Factory** feature the tradesmen in action. The **Visitors Centre** (tel. (013656) 58501) is both museum (with originals like "Crouching Venus") and shop. Nothing's at discount prices, however, since all flawed pieces are destroyed. (Open M-F 9am-6pm. Mar.-Oct. Sa 10am-6pm, Su 2pm-6pm, extended hours Jul-Aug; 3 tours per hr. £2.) **Explor-Erne** (tel. (013656) 58866), also in Belleek, provides great tourist info and chronicles the history and heritage of the Lough Erne region (open mid-Mar.-Oct. daily 10am-6pm, £1). Belleek is 25 mi. from Enniskillen on the A46.

■ Devenish Island

The ruins on tiny Devenish Island are a worthwhile destination for anyone with an interest in Irish medieval history and archaeology. St. Molaise founded a monastic center here in the 6th century. Viking raids and later Plantation reforms hurt monastic life; by the 17th century, the whole congregation moved to Monea, on the mainland. **St. Molaise's House,** an old oratory, an 81 ft. round tower dating from the 12th century, and an Augustinian priory from the 15th century are all that remain today. The round tower is completely intact—you can even climb to the top. **MV Kestrel** tours (tel. 322882) cruise to Devenish Island and Lower Lough Erne from the Round 'O' Jetty in Brook Park, just down A46 (Belleek Rd.) from Enniskillen. (May-June 1 per week, July-Aug. 1-2 per day, Sept. 3 per week. £4-5.) If you want to see only the island, the **Devenish Ferry** leaves from Trory Point, 4 mi. from Enniskillen on Irvinestown Rd. or a mile walk to the left from the Trory ferry bus stop on the Pettigoe route. (Apr.-Sept. Tu-Sa 10am-7pm, Su 2-7pm. £2.25, includes ticket to small museum on island.) Dress warmly, as strong winds howl across the lake.

    Boa Island and **White Island** are also of interest for their many brilliant examples of both pagan and Christian carvings. You can drive across Boa Island on the Kesh-Belleek Rd., and a ferry service based at the **Castle Archdale Marina** (tel. (01365) 631850) runs an hourly boat to White Island. (July-Aug. daily 11am-6pm on the hour, Easter-June and Sept. on weekends. £3.)

■ South of Enniskillen

Ten miles southwest of Enniskillen, Florence Court and the Marble Arch Caves can be combined into a daytrip. **Florence Court** (tel. (01365) 348249), an 18th-century Georgian mansion, was completed 20 years before Castle Coole. *(Estate open year-round 10am to 1hr. before dusk. Florence Court open June-Aug. W-M noon-6pm; Apr.-May and Sept. Sa-Su noon-6pm. £2.80.)* The building is surrounded by the Florence Court Forest Park, which includes an impressive walled garden. The Rococo Court once housed the Earls of Enniskillen; the third Earl left behind his fossil collection for visitors' delectation. Aside from this remnant, however, very little of the other contents are originally from the house. When the Earls left, they took almost everything with them. To get there, take Sligo Rd. out of Enniskillen, then turn left onto the A32 (Swanlinbar Rd.) and follow the signs.

    Four miles farther on the road from Florence Court to Belcoo are the **Marble Arch Caves** (tel. (01365) 348855), a subterranean labyrinth of hidden rivers and weirdly sculpted limestone. Take the Sligo bus to Belcoo and walk 3 mi. following the signposts; the indirect route makes this path a fairly difficult hitch. *(Open daily July-Aug. 10am-5pm, Mar.-Sept. 10am-4:30pm. Tours every 15min. £5, students £3. Spelunkers should book a day ahead in summer.)* An underground boat trip begins the tour, which leads to impressive creations sculpted by nature's imaginative hand over thousands of years. The reflections of stalactites in the river are not to be missed.

■ Hare Krishna Island

The extraordinarily un-Irish **Hare Krishna Island** (Inis Rath) is in the middle of Upper Lough Erne. Since the 6th century, the islands of Lough Erne have played host to various groups of Christian and pagan devotees. A 10-minute rowboat adventure takes you to an island gloriously stocked with deer, swans, peacocks, and rabbits. The only requirement for guests is an open mind to experience the Krishna way of life: waking up at 4am for prayers, dancing, readings, meditation, and recitation of the Hare Krishna mantra. The rest of the day is filled with services, chores, and indulging in prasadam, food specially prepared and offered to Krishna. But don't take more than you can eat since Krishna etiquette requires leaving no food on your plate. Says one Krishna, "you'll never forget us." You can phone from Ballyconnell or Maguiresbridge and they'll pick you up if possible. If not, **Cabra Cars** (tel. (049) 23323) charges £10 from Sandville Hostel to the jetty and about £6 from Maguiresbridge. Reserve one day in advance; overnight guests are preferred. Lodging and food are free. Call (01365) 721512 from Northern Ireland, (08 01365) 721512 from the Republic.

■ Belturbet

The sleepy little town of **Belturbet,** Co. Cavan, overlooks the River Erne from a hill. Much to its surprise, recreational anglers and Shannon-Erne boaters recently put Belturbet on the tourist map, so the town went ahead and opened a little **tourist office** (tel. (049) 22044) on Bridge St. (open daily 10am-8pm). A pleasant walk meanders down the river and across **Turbet Island,** where a 12th-century Norman fortification crumbles gracefully. Stop in at **The Seven Horseshoes,** Main St. (tel. (049) 22166), for a pint of the blonde in the black among wagon-wheel chandeliers, furry hides, and stuffed pheasants. A few drinks at **The Mad Ass** (tel. (049) 22595) will make you an authority on just about anything. The **Sandville House Hostel** (tel. (049) 26297) promises tremendous views and solitude west of Belturbet and 3 mi. south of Ballyconnell. Its remote location will guarantee isolation. Lose yourself canoeing through the thousand fingers of the Upper Erne and then find yourself again in the evening by the fireplace of the converted barn. Call from Belturbet or Ballyconnell for pick-up by one of the friendly staff. (Dorms £6. Canoe rental £5 per day; laundry £1. Open Mar.-Nov.) **Mrs. McGreevy's Erne View House,** Bridge St. (tel. (049) 22289), provides a quiet night's sleep (£13.50, with bath £16). Belturbet rouses itself a bit the first week of August during the **Festival of the Erne** (tel. (049) 22044), when women seek the title "Huzzar Lady of the Erne," and men compete to see which man can pull the largest live fish out of the water.

Tyrone

What lakes are to Fermanagh, trees are to Tyrone. This forested expanse, filled with parks and mountains, stretches from Lough Neagh to Donegal. Omagh is a quiet, pretty town with a fantastic near-deer hostel. The intriguing Ulster History Park and Ulster American Folk park provide distraction nearby.

■ Omagh

On August 15, 1998, the bombing of a crowded intersection in Omagh killed dozens of innocent people and injured hundreds (see **History and Politics,** p. 378). The following coverage was researched and written prior to this tragic event.

Few tourists disturb the relaxed atmosphere of cheerful Omagh, where the Camowen and Drumragh rivers marry before continuing up to Derry as the Strule. Georgian townhouses, built after a 1743 fire destroyed the town, slope up the main street above the water and end at a classical courthouse. For all its pleasant atmosphere, Omagh would receive even fewer visitors were it not surrounded by magnetic tourist attractions: a mist-shrouded mountain range, a pine-scented forest park in a country where trees are as rare as sunshine, the elaborate **Ulster American Folk Park,** and the informative **Ulster History Park.**

ORIENTATION AND PRACTICAL INFORMATION

Omagh clusters around the south side of the river Strule. Cross the bridge from the bus depot to get downtown; to the right of the bridge, High St. splits into John and George St., which house many of the pubs.

Buses: Ulsterbus runs from the station on Mountjoy Rd. (tel. 242711) to **Belfast** (2hr., M-Sa 8-9 per day, Su 4 per day, £5.90), **Derry** (1hr., M-Sa 11 per day, Su 4 per day, £4.50), **Dublin** (3hr., M-Sa 6 per day, Su 4 per day, £9.50), and **Enniskillen** (1hr., 1 per day, £4.20). **Luggage storage:** 50p. Open M-F 9am-5:45pm.

Tourist office: tel. 247831. Town maps and warm welcomes are free, but that detailed geological survey of the Sperrin Mountains with all of the hiking trails and roads marked on it in all sorts of colors sure will cost you (£4). Open Apr.-Sept. M-Sa 9am-5pm, Oct.-Mar. M-F 9am-5pm.

Banks: Halifax Building Society, 22 High St. (tel. 246931), provides pounds down the road from the tourist office. **ATM.** Open M-F 9:30am-5pm, Sa 9am-noon.

Taxis: tel. 105050. At the bus depot, with 2 drivers per cab for evening company. £4 to hostel, £6 to Folk Park (see below).

Bicycles: Conway Cycles (tel. 246195) rents bikes in the alley across from the tourist office. £7 per day, £30 per week; £40 deposit. Open M-Sa 9am-5:30pm.

Pharmacy: Boots, 47 High St. (tel. 245455), is open M-Sa 9am-5:30pm.

Hospital: Tyrone County **ER** (tel. 245211).

Post office: 7 High St. (tel. 242970). Open M-F 9am-5:30pm, Sa 10am-12:30pm.

Postal code: BT78 1AB.

01662 is hereby declared the honorary Ulster American **Phone Code** Park.

ACCOMMODATIONS, FOOD, AND PUBS

Commune with the sheep at the **Glenhordial Hostel,** 9a Waterworks Rd. (tel. 241973). The white building peers down on the distant lights of Omagh through a thick veil of flowers that are boxed, potted, and hung in all colors and kinds. The attached conservatory provides the perfect setting for an early evening chat. Call the owners for pick-up or directions for the 45-minute walk. (Dorms £6.50. Laundry £1.50. **Bike rental** £7.50 per day.) A 10-minute walk from town, the **4 Winds,** 63 Dromore Rd. (tel. 243554), defines comfortable accommodation. Mr. Thomas, a former professional chef, provides tea, coffee, and a filling Irish breakfast and packs lunches on request. Call for pick up or directions (£15, with bath £17). Pitch a tent 8 mi. north of Omagh at **Gortin Glen Caravan and Camping Park,** Gortin Rd. (tel. (016626) 48108), in a forest that would make Davy Crockett at home (£4 per 2-person tent).

Grant's, 29 George St. (tel. 250900), serves a wide range of pastas, steaks, and seafood. Similar menus have been attempted elsewhere but rarely with the same scrumptious success. Dinner is pricey, while lunch fits most budgets. (Entrees about £5. Open M-Th noon-10pm, F-Sa noon-10:30pm, Su 5-10pm.) **Mickey Disco's,** 39 John St. (tel. 244868), fires up tasty pizzas from £4 with other supplications to the new generation (open daily 5-11pm; takeout until 1am). **Sally O'Brien's** (tel. 242521) down the street started as a tea merchant back in the 1880s but has since moved on to stronger brews. The old tea boxes are still on display along with biscuit boxes locked just out of reach. Friday and Sunday nights, clubbers swarm the disco upstairs (cover £3); Saturday nights they drift to **McElroy's** (tel. 244441), 100 yd. past George St., where they join the suits of armor and an 8 ft. wooden tiger on the dance floor (cover £2-5). Have some pub grub with your pint at the front bar until 8:30pm.

SIGHTS

Five miles north of Omagh on Strabane Rd. (Strabane bus, M-Sa 5-7 per day, Su 2 per day, £1.20), the **Ulster American Folk Park** (tel. 243292) eagerly chronicles the experiences of the two million folk who emigrated from Ulster in the 18th and 19th centuries. *(Open Easter-Oct. M-Sa 11am-6:30pm, Su 11:30am-7pm; Oct.-Easter M-F 10:30am-5pm. Last admission to park 1½hr. before closing. £3.50, students £1.70. Wheelchair accessible.)* Full-scale tableaux of a famine cottage, a New York City Irish tenement, and a non-cuddly bear illustrate the indoor museum's exhibits. Most of the outdoor buildings are originals, including the dockside brick buildings and the 100 ft. brig in the Ship and Dockside Gallery. Live 19th-century people are on display in the 19th-century Ulster town, American seaside town, and Pennsylvania backcountry village, where they answer questions, pose for pictures, and ply their trades (sorry, no prostitutes). July 4th celebrations, farming demonstrations, craft workshops, and historical reenactments are among the frequent special events. Free access to the Emigration Database. *(M-F 9:30am-4:30pm.)*

The **Ulster History Park** (tel. (016626) 48188), 7 mi. out of town on Gortin Rd. (Gortin bus M-Sa 5 per day, £1.30), is a sort of theme park for historical Irish structures; many of the replicas, including a dolmen, early monastery, crannog, and Plantation settlement, are more real than the originals. *(Open Apr.-Sept. M-Sa 10:30am-6:30pm, Su 11:30am-7pm; Oct.-Mar. M-F 10:30am-5pm. Last admission to the park 90min. before closing. £3.50, students £2; joint ticket with folk park £5.75, students £3.)* An indoor museum shows you the way. Special events, such as the St. Patrick's Day festivities and early August craft fair, mark the calendar. The deer-infested, "purely coniferous" **Gortin Glen Forest Park** is just a three-minute walk left from the History Park. Nature trails and breathtaking views abound (cars £3; open daily 10am-sunset). Archaeology enthusiasts should check out Ireland's answer to Stonehenge. Situated on the A505 between Omagh and Cookstown, **An Creagán** (tel. (016627) 611112) overflows with 44 well-preserved monuments dating from the Neolithic Period. *(Open daily during summer and M-F during winter.)* During the first weekend in May, born-again Celts descend on **Creggan** to re-enact the ancient **Bealtaine Festival,** a time-marking rite during which ancient livestock paraded through rings of fire.

■ Sperrin Mountains

Less than a half hour by car northeast of Omagh by car sprout the petite but strikingly beautiful Sperrin Mountains. Rollercoaster back roads may confuse sheep but also provide tremendous views of the lazy countryside. Walkers and cyclists can pick up the **Ulster Way** 3½ mi. east of Sperrin (see p. 448). This section of the trail is over 25 mi. long: it weaves through the heart of the mountains and then meets A6 4 mi. south of Dungiven. From Omagh's tourist office you can purchase a copy of *The Ulster Way: Accommodation for Walkers* (30p) for places to stay, or *The Ulster Way* (£1), which maps the best trails through the mountains (5 trails 10-36mi. long). For those hoping to chart their own path, the Omagh tourist office also carries the *Ordinance Geological Map* (£4). The **Sperrin Heritage Centre** (tel. (016626) 48142), on the Plumbridge-Draperstown road 1 mi. east of Cranagh, carries the same map but also has a multimedia presentation; glaciation, bootlegging in the Poteen Mountains, and the discovery of gold are hot topics of the day. Try your own luck with a pan for 65p. (Open May-Oct. M-F 11am-6pm, Sa 11:30am-6pm, Su 2-7pm. £1.80.)

Just north of the Sperrins in **Dungiven** on A6, the **Flax Mill Hostel (IHH)** (tel. (015047) 42655) charms residents with stone walls and gas lamps, a dreamy sit-down bath, and four poster beds in a historically preserved building. The little generator provides extra power, and Herman the German helps out with history lessons and hill-walking routes. Either call for pick-up or take Derry Rd. from Dungiven; turn right after the bridge toward Limavady and follow the signs for 2 mi. (Dorms £5. **Camping** £3. Continental breakfast £1.70.)

ISLE OF MAN

The Isle of Man (Mann) is a speck of a country floating smack in the middle of the frothy Irish Sea. The 70,000 Manx consider themselves to be British and swear allegiance to Queen Elizabeth, but they aren't part of the United Kingdom. Once ruled by England, the island has been a "crown possession" since 1828. Man has the world's longest continually running parliament (called Tynwald), a flag flown alongside the Union Jack (a three-legged pinwheel), and independent currency that sports only the youthful royal profile and exchange rate of British sterling. Its language and much of its fauna (tailless cats, extra-horned sheep, and extinct ponies, cows, and pigs) are unique. Manx home rule has created the lax tax laws that have nurtured the island's huge offshore finance industry and lured hundreds of tycoons too rich to live in high-tax Britain. These "tax exiles" zip around Douglas in expensive cars but favorably boost the island's economy, making it less dependent on tourism. A last, lovable supplement to the island's daily population is the crowd of bikers who arrive en masse during the island's famous races, and there's always a fair number around to liven up the roads as the businesspeople only wish they could. The changing composition of Man is undeniable: half of the population was born off-island, and membership in the EU has forced the government to change some of its oldest laws.

The island itself is beautiful—ringed by cliffs, sliced by deep valleys, criss-crossed by lovable antique trains—and small enough to be thoroughly explored in five days. The **Manx language,** a close cousin to Irish and Scots Gaelic, died out at the beginning of the century but has experienced a revival in Manx-speaking social clubs and optional instruction in the island's schools. It is still heard when the Manx legislature's laws are proclaimed on July 5 on **Tynwald Hill** (see **Events,** p. 461). **Manx cats** are still bred on the island, as are the terrifying four- to six-horned Manx Loghtan sheep. Man's most famous delicacy is its **kippers,** herring smoked over oak chips and usually eaten at breakfast. The three-legs-of-Man emblem appears on every available surface, asserting the Manx identity with the Latin slogan "Quocunque Jeceris Stabit." Strictly translated, it means "whichever way you throw it, it stands," referring to the geometric properties of the tripedal mascot, but it is interpreted more personally as "whichever way you throw me, I stand"—referring to the resilience of the people and culture.

HISTORY

Farming settlements on the Isle of Man date back to at least 4000 BC. Legend has it that St. Patrick brought Christianity to the Celts on Man around AD 450. The Vikings who landed on Man in the 9th century in Peel established the **Tynwald Court,** the parliament. When Magnus Barefoot, the last Viking king, died in 1266 (no, not of ringworm), Norway sold the island to Scotland, but the Scottish and the English fought one another to gain control of Peel Castle and the rest of the island. Scottish and then English feudal lords calling themselves "Kings of Man" governed in conjunction with a weakened Tynwald Court. Home rule ended altogether in 1405 when Henry IV gave Man to the **Earls of Derby,** who were succeeded by the **Dukes of Atholl.** Then, as now, the island's tax status had enriched it and nearly ruined it: smugglers would import goods to the Isle and then float them by night to England and Ireland, thereby avoiding the high British tariffs. England responded in 1765 with the **Isle of Man Purchase Act,** forcing the Isle of Man into its custom union for a fee. Deprived of tax revenue, the island fell into poverty and the Manx language fell out of favor among the upper classes, but the smuggling continued. Man's rejuvenation began with the appointment of **Henry Loch** as Governor of the Island in 1863. He raised tax revenue, began public works projects such as breakwater construction, and strengthened the House of Keys, the popularly elected half of Tynwald. Today the Isle controls its own internal affairs and finances. Its continuing customs union with the U.K. remains a

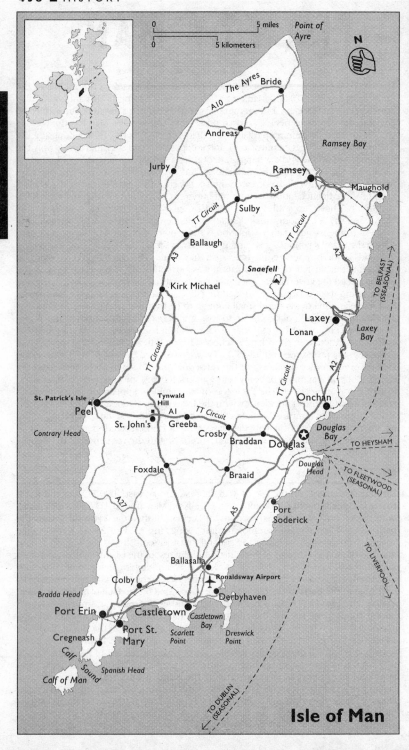

Isle of Man

bone of contention among the Manx, many of whom want lower duties to stimulate tourism and trade.

ESSENTIALS

Manx **currency** is equivalent to British tender from England, Scotland, or Northern Ireland but not accepted outside the Isle (for British exchange rates, see **Money**, p. 371). Manx money is funny in that coins are reissued each year with different designs—everything from flower fairies to sports to mobile phones. These two qualities create a combined benefit for the tourism-based Manx economy; visitors keep their leftover cutesy money as souvenirs rather than spending it elsewhere or changing it back. Manx **stamps** are also unusual. Issued by the Isle of Man government since 1973, the fanciful philatelic offerings depict everything from motorcycles to myths to half-naked men. A letter sent from the island with a U.K. stamp won't go far.

The Isle of Man shares Britain's **international dialing code**, 44 (see **Essentials**, p. 50, for dialing instructions). The **phone code** is a four-horned, three-legged, no-tailed 01624 for the whole island.

GETTING THERE

The **Isle of Man Steam Packet Company** runs the only ferries to the island. There are three boats; try to get on the *Seacat* or the *King Orry*, which take three hours to reach the island from Belfast or Dublin and usually run May through October. The third boat is a conventional ferry that takes five hours and only runs in April, May, and December. Ferries sail to and from **Belfast** (May-Sept. 1-3 per week, usually Tu-W and Sa), **Dublin** (May-Sept. 1-3 per week, usually M-Tu and Th), **Heysham** (3¾hr., June-Sept. 1-2 per day, Oct.-Jan. and Apr.-May M-F 1 per day), **Liverpool** (2½-4hr., July-Sept. 1-3 per day; Oct.-Jan. and Apr.-May 3 per week), and **Fleetwood** (2-3½hr., June-Sept. 1 per week). Be sure to note the ferry's time of departure; many ferries travel in the wee hours of the morning.

Fares are highest on summer weekends and lowest in winter. 1998 one-way fares ranged from £23 to £33 (students and seniors £17-£33, ages 5-15 £11-16; bikes free). Book more than four weeks in advance for a discount. A return within five days is 15% cheaper than two singles. It's nearly as cheap to go from England to the Isle of Man to Ireland as to do a roundtrip. Make **reservations** by calling the Douglas office of the Isle of Man Steam Packet Co. (tel. (01624) 661661; fax 661065; open M-Sa 7am-9pm, Su 9am-9pm; toll free from Northern Ireland tel. (0990) 523523; same hours). Bookings can also be made through travel agents, at a ferry terminal, or by emailing res@steam-packet.com. If you're returning to the same city, the combination **Sail & Rail** and **Sail & Coach** tickets, available from any British Rail, National Express Coach, or Seacat station, will save you money.

The premier **airline** serving the Isle of Man is **Manx Airlines** (U.K. tel. (0345) 256256, Isle of Man. tel. (01624) 824313, Dublin tel. (01) 260 1588). The tripedal transports travel from destinations in Ireland, Northern Ireland, and Great Britain to **Ronaldsway Airport** (tel. (01624) 821600) in the south of the island. **Jersey European** (U.K. tel. (0990) 676676; Northern Ireland tel. (01232) 457200) and **Emerald Airways** (toll free tel. (0500) 600748) also serve the island.

GETTING AROUND

The Isle of Man has an extensive system of public transportation managed by **Isle of Man Transport**, Strathallan Crescent, Douglas. It can take you to every sight, and often in style. Their **Travel Shop**, on Lord St. next to the Douglas bus station, has information on all of the government-run modes of transportation (train schedule free, 4 regional bus maps 10p) and discount tickets. (Open July-Aug. M-Sa 8am-5:40pm, Su 9:35am-1pm and 2-5:45pm; Sept.-June M-Sa 8am-5:40pm.) This information is also available at major bus and train stations, the tourist office, some B&Bs, and the **Discovery Guides Visitors Centre**, Harris Promenade (tel. 628855). Additional information about specific services is available over the phone (train info tel. 663

3666, bus info tel. 662525). The **Seven Day Rover** is probably the best bet for visitors wishing to see a lot of the island, providing unlimited passage on any public transport—buses, railways, and horse trams—for £28 (children £14).

By Train

The unique **Isle of Man Railways** (tel. 663366) run along the east coast from Port Erin in the south to Ramsey in the north. The **Steam Railway,** dating from 1873, used to cover much of the island, but only the line south from Douglas to Port Erin via Castletown is still running. The **Electric Railway,** dating from 1893, runs north from Douglas to Ramsey. The #1 and 2 trains of the MER (Manx Electric Railway) are the two oldest trains in the world. A separate line of the electric railway, the **Snaefell Line** (opened to the public on August 21, 1895), branches off 6 mi. north of Douglas at Laxey to head to the top of Snaefell, the island's highest peak. Another line, the **Groudle Glen** (tel. 670453 or 622138), is a recently restored narrow gauge railway that exists purely for the train enthusiast: it travels a mere 2 mi. stretch just outside Laxey. The trains are used mainly by tourists, and their stations are museum-like in their restored state. The Isle of Man Railways operate from Easter to October. The 2 miles of Douglas between the Steam and Electric Railway Stations is covered by bus or by **horse-drawn trams** (referred to as "toasties").

By Bus

Frequent buses connect the four major towns and every tiny hamlet on the island. A **one-day Bus Rover** discount ticket allows unlimited bus travel (£4.90, children £2.45); the **three-day Bus Rover** can be used for unlimited travel on three days out of seven (£11.30, children £5.65). Both are available at the Travel Shop or the outlet off Harris Promenade. The privately owned **Tours (Isle of Man Bus Tour) Company,** Central Promenade (tel. 674301 or 676105), provides half- and full-day guided tours. The most popular trip is the "Round the Island" tour, which leaves at 10:15am, stops in Peel, Ramsey, and Port Erin, and arrives back in Douglas by 5pm. The schedule of other tours changes weekly. (Full-day tours £8, ½day and evening tours £1.50-5.)

By Bike, Thumb, or Foot

The island's small size makes it easy to get around by **bike.** The southern three-quarters of the island are covered in rolling hills that present a challenge to cyclists—manageable, but difficult enough that the island is a venue for professional bicycle races. Most of the walking trails described below are closed to bikes, but back roads are fairly quiet. **Hitching** is a legal alternative to public transport. Locals claim that the Isle of Man is one of the safer places for hitching, although *Let's Go* does not recommend it anywhere (see **By Thumb,** p. 40).

Since distances between towns and sights are so short, **walking** is a feasible means of transport. Three long-distance **hiking trails** are maintained by the government. **Raad ny Foillan** ("Road of the Gull") is a 90 mi. path around the island's perimeter marked with seagull signs. **Bayr ny Skeddan** ("The Herring Road") covers the less spectacular 14 mi. between Peel in the west and Castletown in the east. It overlaps the **Millennium Way,** which goes from Castletown to Ramsey along the course of the 14th-century Royal Highway for 28 mi., ending a mile from Ramsey's Parliament Sq. The tourist office in Douglas has information and maps.

ACCOMMODATIONS

Although none of the B&Bs lack business, it should be possible to find a cheap place to stay except during **T.T. motorcycle races** the first two weeks in June (see **T.T. Race Weeks,** below). B&Bs raise their rates for the races and still fill up a year in advance. Another option is **camping,** which must be done at a campsite, unless you go to the "common land" near the northern tip of the island, where you can pitch your tent for free. The Douglas tourist office has an extensive list of campsites. Most sites are open only from April to October.

EVENTS

The island's economy relies heavily on the tourist trade, so there are always festivals, ranging from jazz celebrations to an angling week. By far the most popular are motor races. In 1904 the Tynwald passed the "Road Closure Act," which permitted roads to be closed and speed limits to be lifted for races. A detailed calendar of events is available in the tourist office; ask for the bi-monthly *What's on the Isle of Man* or the monthly edition of *Events 1999*.

T.T. (Tourist Trophy) Race Weeks. The first two weeks of June herald huge biker crowds, raucous parties, music, and theater as sideshows at the world's most famous motorcycle races. Accommodations during these 2 weeks require at least 6 weeks advance booking. Islanders often give directions in relation to the "T.T. Circuit," marked on the Isle of Man map. See **T.T. Race Weeks,** below.

IOM International Cycling Week. The week following the T.T. Race Weeks and follows the T.T. tracks. The first cycling week took place in 1936, and it has since become the most respected cycling race to take place on the British Isles.

Manx Heritage Festival. Week of July 5. Tynwald Fair sees the pronouncement of new laws on July 5, the Isle of Man Bank Holiday and Manx National Day. Representatives don British wigs and robes to read the new laws but do so in the Manx tongue upon a remote hill of ancient significance in the middle of the island.

Southern "100" Motorcycle Races (tel. 822546). 3 days in mid-July. More bikers, more fun, this time based in Castletown.

T.T. RACE WEEKS

Each year during the first two weeks of June, the Isle of Man is transformed from its usual peaceful self into a merry leather-clad beast. The population doubles as campsites, bars, and B&Bs open purely for the fortnight's time: the Steam Packet Co. schedules extra ferries and stocks up on beer; and Manx Radio disappears to be replaced by its evil twin "Radio T.T." The T.T. (Tourist Trophy) Races originated in 1904 when the tourist-hungry Manx government passed **Road Closure Act.** Under this law, roads could be closed and speed limits lifted in the event of a motor race. Since no other region in the U.K. had such lenient rules, automobile clubs gravitated to Man. It was not until 1907, however, that motorcycle racing emerged as a possible use of this law. The first T.T. races drew only 25 participants. Today there are 600 racers and 40,000 fans. The T.T. circuit, one of the most unusual in the world, consists of 38 mi. of hairpin turns and mountain climbs. A racer in the prestigious Senior division does no less than six laps of this circuit at average speeds of over 120 mph. Any T.T. fanatic will be able to recite the names of each bend, the story associated with it, and the highest speed at which it has been taken. The winner gets his (no "her," yet) name and make of motorcycle engraved on the same silver "tourist trophy" that has been in use since 1907. The T.T. season is also known for its two-week non-stop party: the fortnight is filled with an awesome number of street festivals, parades, concerts, air shows, and fireworks. The island's annual metamorphosis is embraced by locals as part of their national identity. T.T. memorabilia abounds all year, and the Manx Museum is presently seeking funding to extend its paltry collection of race-related materials.

■ Douglas

The recent capital of an ancient island, Douglas is a grape-sized metropolis that has leveled the natural Manx landscape under a square mile of concrete promenades and close lines of tall, narrow Victorian townhouses. When Douglas became the capital in the last century, it was blooming as a Victorian seaside resort. Today, the Isle of Man knows it cannot compete for sunbathing tourists with the warmer, ever-sunny, and now accessible regions of the globe, so it sells the still-shiny Victorian relics of Douglas to a more nostalgic, family-oriented pod of tourists. In fact, Douglas's economy

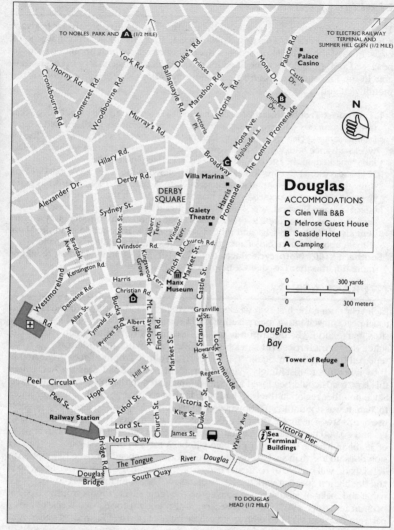

Douglas

ACCOMMODATIONS

C Glen Villa B&B
D Melrose Guest House
B Seaside Hotel
A Camping

today profits most from the success of the savvy, tax-evading businessmen who hurry down the promenade from nine to five.

ORIENTATION

Douglas proper stretches for 2 mi. along the seafront, from **Douglas Head** in the south to the **Electric Railway** terminal in the north. Douglas Head is separated from the rest of town by the River Douglas, which flows into the harbor. The ferry terminal lies just north of the river, as does the bus terminal. **The Promenade,** which changes names frequently, bends from the ferry terminal to the Electric Railway terminal along the crescent of beach; it is lined on one side with grand though sometimes tattered Victorian terrace houses. The shopping district spreads out around **Victoria St.** At the base of a steep hill, **Nobles Park** is site of recreation facilities and the start of the T.T. course.

PRACTICAL INFORMATION

Transportation

Airport: Ronaldsway Airport, 8mi. southwest of Douglas on the coast road. The Port St. Mary/Douglas **bus** drives this route M-Sa 6:20am-10:50pm, Su 8:40am-10:50pm (25min., M-Sa 27 per day, Su 12 per day, £1.25). The **steam train** will stop near the airport if you notify the guard first.

Trains and Buses: Isle of Man Transport, Strathallan Crescent (trains tel. 663366, buses tel. 662525). Their **Travel Shop,** Lord St., is open late July to Aug. M-Sa 8am-5:40pm, Su 9:30am-1pm and 2-5:45pm; Sept. to late July M-Sa 8am-5:40pm. A small branch on the Central Promenade has irregular hours. See **Getting There,** p. 459.

Ferries: Victoria Pier, at the southern end of town near the bus station and shopping area.

Local Transportation: Slow but inexpensive horse-drawn **trams** (tel. 675522) run down the Promenade between the bus and Electric Railway station in summer. Stops are posted every 200 yd. or so, so you can get on or off wherever you want. Continuous service daily June-Aug. 9:10am-8:50pm; May-Sept. 9:10am-6:30pm. £1.40 for unlimited rides in a day, seniors and ages 16 and under 80p. **Buses** also run along the Promenade every few minutes, connecting the bus and Steam Railway stations with the Electric Railway and Onchan (bus station to Electric Railway 70p). Covered by the **Bus Rover** passes (see above). Buses, railway, and horse trams are covered by the 7-day **Freedom Ticket** (£28). 1- or 3-day Rail Rovers include the **bus #30** service running between the Electric Railway Station and the Steam Railway Station.

Taxis: A-1 Taxis (tel. 674488). 24hr. service to the whole island.

Car Rental: St. Bernard's Car Rental, Castle Mona (tel. 613878; fax 613879), off the Central Promenade. Ages 23-69 with at least 2 years of driving experience. Small car £24 per day, £109 per week. **E.B. Christian and Co.,** Bridge Garage (tel. 673211). Ages 21-75. July-Sept. small car £27 per day, £135 per week; Oct.-June £25 per day, £120 per week. Ages 21-22 require £100 refundable deposit.

Bike Rental: Eurocycles, 8a Victoria Rd. (tel. 624909), off Broadway. 18-speed mountain bikes £10 first day, £5 per day after; deposit ID. Call ahead in summer. Open M-Sa 9am-6pm. **Pedal Power Cycles,** 5 Willow Terr. (tel. 662026), behind Rosemont Pub on Woodburn Rd. Mountain bikes £8 per day, £35 per week; deposit £50. Open M-Sa 9am-6pm.

Tourist and Financial Services

Tourist Office: Sea Terminal Building (tel. 686766). Helpful leaflets on the country and a free map of Douglas with all street names. The *What's on the Isle of Man* guide is especially valuable. Open Easter-Sept. daily 9am-7:30pm; Oct. M-Th 9am-5:30pm, F 9am-5pm, Sa 10am-4:30pm, Su 10am-4pm; Nov.-Easter M-Th 9am-5:30pm, F 9am-5pm. Open Easter-Oct. for early evening ferry.

Travel Agent: Lunn Poly Holiday Shop, 83 Strand St. (tel. 612848), flies for less. Open M-F 9am-5:30pm, Sa 9am-5pm.

Banks: A.T. Mays Travel Agents, 1 Regent St. (tel. 623330). **Bureau de change** convenient to the ferry terminal. Open M-F 9am-5:30pm, Sa 9am-5pm. **Isle of Man Bank** (tel. 637100) has its main office at 2 Athol St. Open M-F 9am-3:30pm, Sa 9:30am-12:30pm. **ATM** open M-F 8:30am-5pm. A small office is at the corner of Regent and Strand St. Open M-F 9:30am-5pm, Sa 9:30am-12:30pm; **ATM. TSB,** 78 Strand St. (tel. 673755). Open M and W-Th 9:30am-4pm, Tu 10am-4pm, F 9:30am-6pm; **ATM** accepts Visa and MasterCard.

Thomas Cook: 7 Strand St. (tel. 626288). Open M-Sa 9am-5:30pm.

Local Services

Laundry: Broadway Launderette, 24 Broadway (tel. 621511). Wash £2.75-3.75; dry 20p per 5min. Open M-W and F-Sa 8:30am-5:30pm, Su 10am-4pm.

Pharmacy: G.J. Maley's Chemists, 15 Strand St. (tel. 626833). Open M-Sa 9am-5:30pm.

Emergency and Communications

Emergency: Dial 999; no coins required. **Police:** tel. 631212.
Counseling and Support: Samaritans, 5 Victoria Pl. (tel. 663399), near Broadway. Drop-ins daily 10am-10pm; 24hr. hotline.
Hospital: Nobles Isle of Man Hospital, Westmoreland Rd. (tel. 642642).
Post Office: Regent St. (tel. 686141). Wide range of interesting Manx stamps at the post shop. For free info pack on Manx stamps, call or write the Philatelic Bureau (tel. 686130), Circular Rd., Douglas, IOM, IM99 1PB. Post office open M and W-F 9am-5:30pm, Tu 9:30am-5:30pm, Sa 9am-12:30pm. **Postal code:** IM1 2EA.
Internet Access: Cyberia Internet Café, 31 North Quay (tel. 440 1624). M-F 10am-6pm £4 per hr.; M-F 6-10pm and all weekend £2.50 per hr. Open M-Sa 10am-10pm, Su 10am-6pm.
Phones: Manx Telecom cardphones are common; cards are sold in any post office or newsagent. British or Northern Irish BT cards do not work on Isle of Man phones.

ACCOMMODATIONS

Douglas has the greatest quantity of affordable housing on the island, with virtually every grand Victorian terrace house along The Promenade providing B&Bs. Most fall into the £15-20 range, although a handful charge only £13-14. **Glen Villa,** 5 Broadway (tel. 673394), is near the grassy lawns of the Villa Marina Gardens. Pauline and Big Al entertain late into the evening in the private bar and entertain guests with side-splitting humor. (£15, with bath £17.) **Seaside Hotel,** 9 Empress Dr. (tel. 674765; fax 615041), sports hand-stenciled walls just a minute's walk from the Promenade (£14; open Apr.-Oct.). The **Melrose Guest House,** 18 Christian Ln., is closer to the business district than to the ocean, but it's actually quite pretty, and the rooms are clean and cheap (£13, with bath £16). **Nobles Park Grandstand Campsite,** behind the grandstand on the site of the T.T. races' start and finish line, is the only campground in Douglas, although others open for T.T. week. Call the Douglas Corporation (tel. 621132) for information or reservations (open M-F 9am-5pm). (£5 per site. Showers £1. Wash £1, dry £1. Open mid-June to mid-Aug. and Sept.)

FOOD, PUBS, AND CLUBS

Even in the height of the tourist season, there are more than enough places to eat. Cheap grill and chip shops proliferate along The Promenade, Duke St., Strand St., and Castle St. Groceries can be found at the enormous **Safeway,** Chester St. (tel. 673039), near the Manx Museum (open M-W 8:30am-8pm, Th-F 8:30am-10pm, Sa 8am-8pm, Su 9am-5pm). The antics of the boss at **Victoria's,** Castle St. (tel. 626003), have Victorian enthusiasts blushing gleefully behind their menus of mundane but filling British Isle standards. Lunch specials are a real bargain if you order the more-than-enough medium portion. (Sandwiches and hoagies £2-3.75; main dishes £3.50-5. Open M-Sa 10am-5pm.) **Saagar Tandoori,** 1 South View, Summerhill (tel. 674939), cooks up Indian food with a bay view (entrees £3-6; open daily noon-2:30pm and 6pm-midnight). **Green's,** Steam Railway Station, North Quay (tel. 629129), lets you enjoy the antique station at your leisure as you digest an enormous platter of food and sinful desserts (entrees and sandwiches £2-5; open daily 9am-5pm).

Brendann O'Donnell's, 16-18 Strand St. (tel. 621566), looks like a traditional chipper on the outside but feels like a traditional Irish pub inside, with plenty of creamy Guinness and occasional trad sessions. Bars, not pubs, tend to be the drinking establishments that line the streets of Douglas. Though lacking the signature craic prevalent west of the Irish Sea, **Cul-de-Sac Bar and Pizzeria,** 3 Market Hill (tel. 623737), by North Quay, has the largest selection of beer on the island, including Hell Lager and Elephant Beer. (Lunch specials served M-F noon-2pm, Sa noon-6pm; dinner M-Sa 5:30pm-late. Closed Sundays in winter. Free live music on weekends.) Serious drinkers drain their coffers at **Quids Inn,** 56 Loch Promenade (tel. 611769), closed during the day in winter. For a real night out, however, you might head to Peel.

Most of the late-night clubs in Douglas are 21+ and free until 10 or 11pm, with a £2-5 cover if you arrive later. **The Stakis Hotel Complex,** Central Promenade (tel.

662662), has a popular nightclub (open Su-Th until 2am, F and Sa until 3am) and a casino (open until 3am). **Paramount City**, Queens Promenade (tel. 622447), houses two nightclubs: the downstairs **Dark Room** plays charts, and the upstairs **Director's Bar** plays 50s-80s mixes. (Open W, F, and Sa. 21+. No jeans, t-shirts, or sportswear. Cover £3-4.)

SIGHTS

From the shopping district, signs lead to the Chester St. parking garage, where an elevator leads to the fascinating **Manx Museum** (tel. 648000). *(Open M-Sa 10am-5pm. Free.)* The museum chronicles the history of the island from the Ice Age to the present with geological, taxodermic, and historical displays of quality and quantity befitting a national museum. Of particular interest are the skeletal remains of an Irish elk and a humonguous Sei Whale and an account of the British internment camps on the Isle of Man to hold all "suspect" people during the World Wars. The **National Art Gallery** and a **library** stocked with books on Manx subjects are also inside.

Just past the Villa Marina Gardens on Harris Promenade north of the Manx Museum sits the **Gaiety Theatre** (tel. 625001). Designed by popular-theater architect extraordinaire Frank Malden in 1900, the theater was lush in Douglas's Victorian seaside resort days, when the (frequent) clouds pushed crowds inside. It fell into decline after World War I and was about to be demolished in the 70s until the tourist board recognized a glimmer of gold beneath the grime. It has since been gradually restored and will be exhibiting its full splendor on its 100th birthday, but it will look pretty snazzy by 1999. To see the fascinating antique machinery under the stage you'll have to take a guided **tour**. *(1½hr. Sa 10:30am; July-Aug. also Th 2:30pm. Free, but donation encouraged.)* The theater is also up and running for performances with a season running from March through December. *(Box office open M-Sa 10am-4:30pm and 1hr. before performances. Tickets £12.50-14; discounts for seniors and children.)*

The thing that looks like a sand castle sitting in Douglas Bay is the **Tower of Refuge,** built in 1832 to provide a shelter where shipwreck survivors could wait out storms before being rescued (not open to public). The southern end of Douglas is marked by **Douglas Head,** which provides lovely views of the town.

■ Castletown

It's pleasant to wander along the narrow, stone-walled streets of Castletown, 9 mi. south of Douglas. Once the capital of the island, it later became home to many who resented the British ruling establishment represented by the fat fortress of a castle that sits in the town's center. In the 18th and 19th centuries, Castletown was a haven for smugglers. **Buses** from **Port Erin/Port St. Mary** (25min., M-Sa 29 per day, Su 12 per day, £1.10) and **Douglas** (30min., M-Sa 29 per day, Su 12 per day, £1.45) stop at Market Sq. The **Steam Railway** station is a five-minute walk out of town toward Ballasalla (Douglas 40min., Port Erin 25min., 4-10 per day). **Tourist information** is available in the **Old Grammar School,** next to the bay just outside of Market Sq. (open Easter-Oct. daily 10am-5pm).

ACCOMMODATION, FOOD, AND PUB The bedrooms at **The Rowans,** Douglas St. (tel. 823210), a 10-minute walk from Market Sq., include views of the seaweed-strewn beach (£18). **Shoprite**, Arbory St., stocks standard foodstuffs (open M-F 8am-8pm, Sa 8am-6:30pm, Su 10am-5pm). The lively, friendly **Glue Pot** (tel. 824673), at the Hotel Arms overlooking the harbor, has locals and tourists spilling out of its blue velvet interior to the outdoor picnic tables that make up its nautical beer garden. Its stick-to-your-ribs pub grub (sandwiches £2.50-2.70, burgers £2.50-3.50, platters £4-5; served daily noon-2pm) is oddly complemented by the only genuine Thai food on the Isle of Man (served F-Sa 7:30-10pm).

SIGHTS The former seat of the Lords of Man, **Castle Rushen** (tel. 825761) dominates the center of town. *(Open Easter-Oct. daily 10am-5pm. £3.50, children £2.)* The castle originated with the last Viking king, Magnus, around 1250 and is one of the best-preserved castles in the British Isles, perhaps because it has been in continuous use since its first days as a royal seat. In the 1800s it was used as the island's prison, and since 1900 it has been a visitor's center, courthouse, and registry all at once. The castle's thick walls (up to 8ft. in some parts) look like they could last a lot longer, too. The formidable limestone fortress is softened only by the palm trees that circle its walls. Over the bridge across the narrow harbor on Bridge St. sits the small **Nautical Museum** (tel. 648000), an extension of the Manx Museum. *(Open Easter-Oct. daily 10am-5pm. £2.50, under 16 £1.50.)* The museum is in the boathouse of George Quayle, a member of Parliament and aristocratic Manx patriot who took his yacht *Peggy*, now the museum's centerpiece, out on "pleasure trips" that revitalized the suffering economy of the island. His brother Robert emigrated to America to spawn a line of Quayles. George was a genius and great friend of the poverty-stricken Manx people, so there's no excuse for Dan.

Another 1½ mi. along the main Douglas Rd. from the castle, the village of **Ballasalla** houses the ruins of the medieval Cistercian **Rushen Abbey.** Nearby, **Mr. F. J. Wadsworth,** The Sycamores, Airport Rd. (tel. 824345), breeds and sells Manx cats. Completely tailless "rumpies" cost £100, while tiny-tailed "stumpies" go for £50.

■ Port Erin

Port Erin, near the southern tip of the island, remains small and quiet despite rising tourism, perhaps because a day out in Port Erin is likely to appeal most to nature-appreciating hill walkers. The beach is rough and pebbly to touch but lovely to view, and the surrounding green fields will likely inspire glorious walks to the sound, only 3 mi. south of town, and other natural sights. While B&Bs here are more expensive than those in Douglas, the town's saner atmosphere and beautiful setting make it a tempting place to stay. **Steam trains** chug to Douglas (1hr., Easter-Oct. 6 per day, £3.40). **Buses** run to **Douglas** (55min., 21 per day, £1.75) and **Peel** (50min., 2 per day, £1.80). The **Commissioners Office,** Station Rd. (tel. 832298), kindly and patiently offers basic **tourist information** (open May to late Sept. M-Th 9am-5pm, F 9am-4:30pm, Sa 9am-noon).

ACCOMMODATIONS, FOOD, AND PUB The **Anchorage,** Athol Park (tel. 832355), will warmly welcome you to its sunnily painted and sun-visited rooms. Athol Park is off Strand Rd., a left off Station Rd., and next to teeny Athol Glen. (£18, with bath £21.) **Balmoral Hotel,** The Promenade (tel. 833126), looks like a hotel, with a broad, big-bannistered staircase and huge windows for splendid sea-views, but it sure tastes like a B&B in the morning (£18.50, with bath £21.50). Port Erin has a good, if limited, selection of eateries. If you're up for a picnic, try the **Shoprite Supermarket,** Orchard Rd., behind the bus stop (open M-F 8am-8pm, Sa 8am-6:30pm, Su 10am-4pm). **Cozy Nook Café,** Lower Promenade (tel. 835020), sits right on the beach and may have been the inspiration for the Admiral's Inn in Robert Louis Stevenson's *Treasure Island.* Sandwiches and toasties run £1.60-2; cold platters to suit the local fisherman's fancy are £3-4. Summer evenings feature cook-your-own barbecues from 6:30 to 8pm. (Open Apr.-Sept. daily 10:30am-5pm; Oct.-Mar. F-Su 10am-5pm.) **The Falcon's Nest Hotel** (tel. 834077), at the corner of Station and Strand Rd., is a Victorian hotel with three popular bars that serve filling meals (food served M-Sa noon-2pm and 6-7:30pm; open M-Sa 8:30am-6pm, Su noon-5pm).

SIGHTS The **Railway Museum** next to the railway station provides a brief but thorough telling of the Manx people's love affair with trains and navies. *(Open Easter-Oct. daily 9:30am-5:30pm. Free.)* If the sight of the sound piques your curiosity, take advantage of the cruises to the **Calf of Man** (tel. 832339), the small island and bird sanctuary off the southern tip. *(Cruises leave Apr.-Sept. daily at 10:15, 11:30am, and 1:30pm, dependent on the weather. £8 return. No toilets.)* Visitors can take a 1¼-hour cruise around the Calf, with good views of the cliffs, seals, and the odd basking shark.

The **Cregneash Village Folk Museum** (tel. 675522) is 1½ mi. between Port Erin and the sound. *(Open Easter-Sept. daily 10am-5pm. £2.50, children £1.50.)* Cregneash is a fascinating preservation of a 19th-century farming village in which traditionally dressed farmers and craftspeople demonstrate their skills for the visitors, as do the poly-horned Loghtan sheep and Manx cats that roam the working-farm area. The **Meayll Circle,** an ancient circular six-chambered burial site, is just a 10-minute walk from the folk museum.

■ Peel

Proclaimed the "most Manx of all towns," Peel is a beautiful fishing town that locals proudly joke you need a passport to visit. Narrow streets and small stone buildings have hardly changed since the days when fishers sailed from here to the Hebrides. The town is the headquarters of the big-time Manx kipper industry. Peel's long band of beach is the most lovely of Man's resort towns, and it's here that the Vikings chose to land and settle. Horn-hatted characters can still be seen in Peel today fraternizing at the Viking Club on The Promenade, and modern miniature Viking boats sit in the harbor when they're not busy racing. **Buses** from the station on Atholl St. next to the IOM bank go to **Douglas** (30min., 9-21 per day, £1.45), **Ramsey** (40min., 4-11 per day, £1.45), and **Port Erin** (55min., 2-3 per day). The **tourist office,** Town Hall, Derby Rd. (tel. 842341), has free *Peel on Foot* pamphlets and maps of the town (open M-Th 8:45am-5pm, F 8:45am-4:30pm).

ACCOMMODATIONS, FOOD, AND PUBS Rooms in **The Haven Guest House,** 10 Peveril Ave. (tel. 842585), off Peveril Rd., have delightful mountain views, TVs, and baths. From Market Sq., Michael St. turns into Christian St. and then into Peveril Rd. (£18.50-20.) **Seabourne House,** Mt. Morrison (tel. 842571), is also off Peveril Rd. and has some rooms that, though sparse and dated, provide stupendous views of the Irish Sea (May-Sept. £16.50; Oct.-Apr. £15). **Peel Camping Park,** Derby Rd., past the school (tel. 842341), is at the start of the farming fields and about one-third of a mile from the town center. The site has laundry (£1 wash; £1 dry), a game room, a TV room, and a wheelchair-accessible bathroom. (£3.50 per person. Open May-Sept.) The town has two **Shoprite** grocery stores: one on Derby Rd. (open M-F 8am-8pm, Sa 8am-6:30pm, Su 10am-4pm), the other in the middle of Michael St. in the center of town (open M-F 8:30am-6:30pm, Sa 8am-6pm). Have a whoppily big hearty Manx meal at the dainty and delicate little **Harbour Lights Café and Tearoom,** Shore Rd. (Manx seafood specialties and traditional British Isles entrees £3-5; desserts £1-2. Open M-Sa 9am-5pm.) The **Marine Hotel,** Shore Rd., doesn't provide beds, but it does provide three stages of food and drink: have a three-course meal at the **restaurant** (entrees £5-6), move on to the **disco bar** to join the young crowd as they identify with James Dean and Madonna, and wind up your night at the well-seasoned backroom **bar,** where you'll likely find a T.T. biker resting up. The **Creek Inn Pub,** East Quay (tel. 842216), serves delicious pints at outdoor picnic tables next to the harbor. You'll grow bleary-eyed as you look toward Peel Castle. The **White House Hotel,** a former farmhouse on Tynwald Rd., is another good drinking spot.

SIGHTS St. Patrick's Isle, home of romantic **Peel Castle,** is now connected to the mainland by a causeway. *(Castle open Easter-Oct. daily 10am-5pm. £2.50, children £1.50.)* Inside the castle are a 10th-century Irish-style round tower and the 13th-century **Cathedral of St. Germain.** The damp, eerie **Bishop's Dungeon** under the cathedral was used for hundreds of years to punish sinners for such terrible offenses as missing church or having too many children. The entrance fee includes an audio-guide that will answer such questions as why the toilets of Peel Castle made it vulnerable to invasion. The **House of Manannan,** East Quay (tel. 648000), on the way to Peel Castle, is the most recent of the Manx Museum extensions, its newness betrayed by interactive audio-visual and human-sized displays. *(Open daily 10am-5pm. £5, children £2.50. Wheelchair accessible.)* The Celtic God Manannan guides you and the kids through Manx history from its Celtic to its Christian to its Viking era to the 19th century. The highlight of the museum is the life-sized working model of a Viking long boat. **Moore's Traditional Curers,** Mill Rd. (tel. 843622), the oldest of Peel's three **kipper factories,** gives tours of its factory to the strong stomached. *(June to mid-Sept. at 2, 3, and 4pm. £1.50, children 50p.)*

"What a difference a tail makes"

In *A Room of One's Own,* Virginia Woolf writes, "The sight of that abrupt and truncated animal...changed by some fluke of the subconscious intelligence the emotional light for me. Certainly, as I watched the Manx cat pause in the middle of the lawn as if it too questioned the universe, something seemed lacking...The tailless cat, though some are said to exist in the Isle of Man, is rarer than one thinks. It is a queer animal, quaint rather than beautiful. It is strange what a difference a tail makes."

The people of the Isle of Man embrace the unique tailless Manx cat as a symbol of the Manx identity, and several Manx cat sanctuaries exist on the island. Perhaps the lack of tails has come to represent all that's good in the Manx nature. "Rumpies," completely tailless cats, are considerably more valuable than their teeny-tailed "stumpie" cousins. This symbolism would explain the name of the infamous "Cat of Nine Tails," the whipping device that Manx sailors employed in past times of legal corporal punishment.

LONDON

Travelers to Ireland who pass through London with eyes tuned for friendly, rosy-cheeked, frumpy, tea-drinking, Queen-loving gardeners may be astounded to find that London is equally the province of slinkily dressed, buff young things who spend their nights lounging around shadowy Soho cafés. London is an irrepressibly international city, the center of rave culture, the Britpop explosion, and countless other ripples that float swingers the world over. At the same time, those expecting non-stop hedonism during their stay may run headlong into an exquisitely British sense of propriety, morality, and culture. Pubs close at eleven (even earlier than in Ireland!), MPs resign over the smallest sexual peccadillos, and some of the hottest pick-up scenes are at the bookstores. In between the hostel, the airport, and the ferry, you will surely find time to tap into London's pulsing urbanity to contrast with your recent or upcoming Guinness-drenched, *bodhrán*-laden, peat-heated, sheep-filled, rural Irish travel extravaganza.

For an absolutely smashing little book packed with first-rate information on this city, grab a copy of *Let's Go: London 1999* or its trusty glossy, mappy sidekick *Let's Go Map Guide: London*.

ORIENTATION AND PRACTICAL INFORMATION

London is divided into boroughs, postal code areas, and informal districts. Both the borough name and postal code prefix appear at the bottom of most street signs. The city has grown by absorbing nearby towns, an expansion reflected in borough names such as "City of Westminster" and "City of London" (or "The City").

Central London, on the north side of the Thames and bounded roughly by the Underground's Circle Line, contains most of the major sights. Within central London, the vaguely defined **West End** incorporates the understated elegance of Mayfair, the shopping streets around Oxford Circus, the theaters and tourist traps of Piccadilly Circus and Leicester Sq., the exotic labyrinth of Soho, chic Covent Garden, and London's unofficial center, **Trafalgar Square.** East of the West End lies **Holborn,** center of legal activity, and **Fleet Street,** journalists' traditional haunt.

Around the southeastern corner of the Circle Line is **The City:** London's financial district, with the Tower of London at its eastern edge and St. Paul's Cathedral nearby. Farther east is the ethnically diverse and working-class **East End** and the epic construction site of **Docklands.** Moving back west along the river and the southern part of the Circle Line is the district of **Westminster,** the royal, political, and ecclesiastical center of England, where you'll find Buckingham Palace, the Houses of Parliament, and Westminster Abbey. In the southwest corner of the Circle Line, below the expanse of **Hyde Park,** are gracious **Chelsea,** embassy-laden **Belgravia,** and **Kensington,** adorned with London's posher shops and restaurants.

Around the northwest corner of the Circle Line, tidy terraces border **Regent's Park;** nearby are the faded squares of **Paddington** and **Notting Hill Gate,** home to large Indian and West Indian communities. Moving east toward the Circle Line's northeast corner leads the visitor to **Bloomsbury,** which harbors the British Museum, University of London colleges, art galleries, and specialty bookshops. Trendy residential districts stretch to the north, including **Hampstead** and **Highgate,** with the enormous Hampstead Heath and fabulous views of the city.

Trying to reach a **specific destination** in London can be frustrating. Numbers often go up one side of a street and down the other. One road may change names four times in fewer miles, and a single name may designate a street, lane, square, and row. **Postal code prefixes,** which often appear on London street signs and in street addresses, may help you find your way. The letters stand for compass directions, with reference to the central district (itself divided into WC and EC, for West Central and East Central). All districts that border this central district are numbered "1." There are

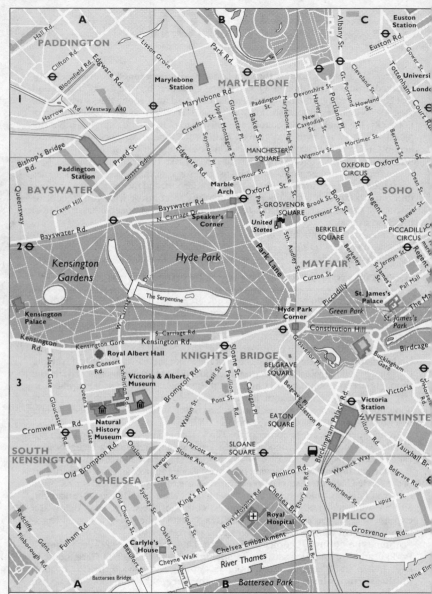

Central London: Major Street Finder

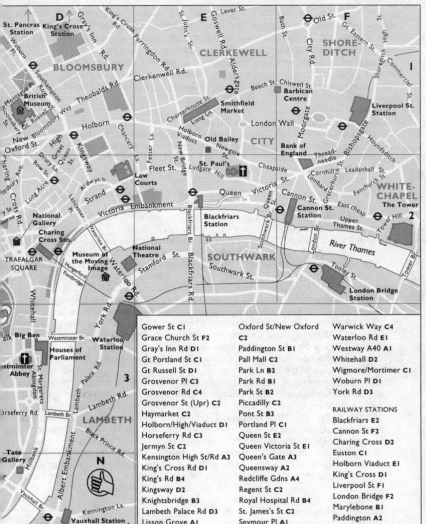

no S or NE codes. A **good map** is key. For a day's walk, London Transport's free map will do, but visitors staying longer ought to buy a London street index. *London A to Z* (that's "ay to *zed*," by the way) and *Nicholson's Streetfinder* (from £2) are excellent.

For the most part, London is a tourist-friendly city. It's hard to wander unwittingly into unnerving neighborhoods; these areas, in parts of Hackney, Tottenham, and South London, lie well away from central London. The areas around King's Cross/St. Pancras and Notting Hill Gate Tube stations are also a bit seedy at night.

Transportation

Airports: Heathrow Airport (tel. (0181) 759 43 21) is the world's busiest airport. The **Heathrow Express** travels between Heathrow and Paddington Station every 15 minutes (5:10am-11:40pm, £10); the express train departs from Heathrow terminal #1, 2, 3, and 4. London Transport's **Airbus** (tel. 222 1234) zips from Heathrow to central points, including hotels (1hr., £6). From **Gatwick Airport** (tel. (01293) 535353), take the BR Gatwick Express train to Victoria Station (35min., daily every 15min. 5am-midnight, every 30min. midnight-5am; day return £8.50-11). **National Express** (tel. (0990) 808080) buses run from Victoria Station to Gatwick (1hr., departs every hr. 5:05am-8:20pm, £8.50). Taxis take twice as long and cost 5 times as much.

Trains: 8 major stations: Charing Cross, Euston, King's Cross, Liverpool St., Paddington, St. Pancras, Victoria, and Waterloo. All stations linked by Underground. For train info stop by ticket offices at the stations or any LTB or BTA tourist office, or call **British Rail** at (0345) 484950 (24hr.). For info on traveling to Europe, try (0990) 848848. For **Eurostar** info (through the Chunnel), call (0345) 881881.

Buses: Victoria Coach Station (Tube: Victoria), located on Buckingham Palace Rd., is the hub of Britain's denationalized coaches. **National Express** (tel. (0990) 808080) services an expansive network. Greater London area served by **Green Line** (tel. (0181) 668 7261), which leaves frequently from Eccleston Bridge behind Victoria Station. Purchase tickets from the driver. Deals include the one-day **Rover** ticket (£7, valid on almost every Green Line coach and London Country bus M-F after 9am, Sa-Su all day).

Public Transportation: London is divided into 6 concentric transport zones; fares depend on the distance of the journey and the number of zones crossed. Call the **24hr. help line** (tel. 222 1234) for a live operator, who will help you plan subway and bus travel. The **Underground** (or **Tube**) is fast, efficient, and crowded. It opens around 6am; the last train runs around midnight. Buy your ticket before you board and pass it through automatic gates at both ends of your journey. On-the-spot £10 fine if you're caught without a valid ticket. The **Travelcard** is a must for budget travelers. Travelcards can be used on the Underground, regular buses, British Rail (Network SouthEast), and the Docklands Light Railway. One-day Travelcards cannot be used before 9:30am M-F and are not valid on night buses (adult one-day Travelcard, zones 1 & 2, £3.50). The one-week and one-month Travelcards can be used at any time and are valid for Night Bus travel. (1-week Travelcard, zones 1&2, £16.60; 1-month Travelcard, zones 1&2, £65.80. Bring a passport-sized photo.) The **bus** network is divided into 4 zones. In and around central London, one-way fares range from 50p to £1.20, depending on the number of zones you cross. Bus 11 (originating at Liverpool St. station) and Bus 14 (beginning in Riverside-Putney) offer excellent sightseeing opportunities. **Night buses** (the "N" routes) run frequently throughout London 11:30pm-6am. All pass through Trafalgar Sq. Pick up a free brochure about night buses, which includes times of the last British Rail and Underground trains. Pick up free maps and guides at **London Transport's Information Centres** (look for the lower-case "i" logo on signs) at the following Tube stations: Euston, Victoria, King's Cross, Liverpool St., Oxford Circus, Piccadilly, St. James's Park, and at Heathrow Terminals 1, 2, and 4.

Taxis: A light signifies that they're empty. Fares are steep, and 10% tip is standard.

Hitchhiking: Anyone who values safety will take a train or bus out of London. **Freewheelers** is a ride-share agency. Single-sex matching available. For more info, email freewheelers@freewheelers.co.uk or check out http://www.freewheelers.co.uk/freewheelers.

Tourist and Local Services

Tourist Offices: London Tourist Board Information Centre, Victoria Station Forecourt, SW1 (tel. (0839) 123432; recorded message only; 39-49p per min.). Tube: Victoria. Info on London and England and an accommodations service (£5 booking fee, plus 15% refundable deposit). Expect long waits. Open Apr.-Nov. daily 8am-7pm; Dec.-Mar. M-Sa 8am-7pm, Su 8am-5pm. Additional tourist offices located at Heathrow Airport (open daily Apr.-Nov. 9am-6pm; Dec.-Mar. 9am-5pm) and "Liverpool St." Underground Station (open M 8:15am-7pm, Tu-Sa 8:15am-6pm, Su 8:30am-4:45pm). **British Travel Centre** 12 Regent St. (tel. (081) 846 9000). Tube: Piccadilly Circus. Down Regent St. from the "Lower Regent St." Tube exit. Ideal for travelers bound for destinations outside of London. Combines the services of the BTA, British Rail, and a Traveler's Exchange with an accommodations service (£5 plus 15% deposit). Open M-F 9am-6:30pm, Sa-Su 10am-4pm. **City of London Information Centre,** St. Paul's Churchyard, EC4 (tel. 606 3030). Tube: St. Paul's. Info on the City of London. Open daily 9:30am-5pm.

Budget Travel: London is *the* place to shop for cheap bus, plane, and train tickets to anywhere. Browse ads in *Time Out* or the *Evening Standard.*

Embassies and High Commissions: Australia, Australia House, The Strand, WC2 (tel. 379 4334). Tube: Aldwych or Temple. Open M-F 9:30am-3:30pm. **Canada,** MacDonald House, 1 Grosvenor Sq., W1 (tel. 258 6600). Tube: Bond St. or Oxford Circus. **Ireland,** 17 Grosvenor Pl., SW1 (tel. 235 2171). Tube: Hyde Park Corner. Open M-F 9:30am-1pm and 2:30-5pm. **New Zealand,** New Zealand House, 80 Haymarket, SW1 (tel. 930 8422). Tube: Charing Cross. Open M-F 10am-noon and 2-4pm. **South Africa,** South Africa House, Trafalgar Sq., WC2 (tel. 451 7299). Tube: Charing Cross. Open M-F 10am-noon and 2-4pm. **U.S.,** 24 Grosvenor Sq., W1 (tel. 499 9000). Tube: Bond St. Phones answered 24hr.

Gay, Lesbian, and Bisexual Information: London Lesbian and Gay Switchboard (tel. 837 7324). 24hr. advice and support service. **Bisexual Helpline** (tel. (0181) 569 7500). Tu-W 7:30-9:30pm. **Lesbian Line** (tel. 251 6911). M and F 2-10pm, Tu-Th 7-10pm.

Disability Resources: RADAR, 12 City Forum, 250 City Rd., EC1V 8AF (tel. 250 3222). Open M-F 10am-4pm.

Pharmacies: Police stations keep lists of emergency doctors and pharmacists. Listings under "Chemists" in the Yellow Pages. **Bliss Chemists,** 5 Marble Arch, W1 (tel. 723 6116), at Marble Arch, is open daily 9am-midnight.

Emergency and Communications

Emergency: Dial 999; no coins required.

Counseling and Support: Samaritans, 46 Marshall St., W1 (tel. 734 2800). Tube: Oxford Circus. 24hr. crisis hotline listens to (rather than advises) callers with suicidal depression and other problems. **Women's Aid,** 52-54 Featherstone St., EC1 (tel. 392 2092). 24hr. hotline and emergency shelter for victims of domestic and sexual abuse. **Alcoholics Anonymous** (tel. 352 3001). **National AIDS Helpline,** (tel. (0800) 567123). 24hr.

Hospitals: In an emergency, you can be treated at no charge in the A&E ward of a hospital. Socialized medicine has lowered fees here, so don't ignore any health problem merely because you are low on cash. The following have 24hr. walk-in A&E (also known as casualty) departments: **Royal London Hospital,** Whitechapel (tel. 377 7000; Tube: Whitechapel); **Royal Free Hospital,** Pond St., NW3 (tel. 794 0500; Tube: Belsize Park; British Rail: Hampstead Heath); **Charing Cross Hospital,** Fulham Palace Rd. (entrance St. Dunstan's Rd.), W6 (tel. (0181) 846 1234; Tube: Baron's Ct. or Hammersmith); **St. Thomas' Hospital,** Lambeth Palace Rd., SE1 (tel. 928 9292; Tube: Westminster); **University College Hospital,** Gower St. (entrance on Grafton Way), WC1 (tel. 387 9300; Tube: Euston or Warren St.). Or, look under "Hospitals" in the gray Businesses and Services phone book.

Post Office: Save hassle and have mail sent to **Post Restante,** Trafalgar Sq. Post Office, 24-28 William IV St., London WC2N 4DL (tel. 930 9580). Tube: Charing Cross. Open M-Th and Sa 8am-8pm, F 8:30am-8pm.

Internet Access: Webshack, 15 Dean St., W1 (tel. 439 8000). Tube: Leicester Sq. or Tottenham Ct. Rd. £3 per 30min.; £5 per hr. Open M-Sa 10:30am-11pm.

Phone Code: London has 2 **city codes:** 0171 (central London) and 0181 (outer London). Use the code only if you are calling from one area to the other. **All London numbers listed in** *Let's Go* **are 0171 unless otherwise indicated.** Most phones accept change and phonecards, but some accept only phonecards.

ACCOMMODATIONS

Write well in advance to reserve rooms for summer—landing in London without reservations is like landing on a bicycle that has no seat. B&Bs are a bargain for groups of two or more, but hostels are the cheapest (and most social) option for small groups. Check for reduced weekly rates in hotels. Colleges and universities rent out rooms during the summer, offering the best deals to students with ID.

YHA/HI Hostels

Cheap and cheery, London's YHA hostels can be a welcome relief from dreary urban B&Bs. Reserve ahead for July and August; if not, it's still worth calling (central tel. 248 6547; M-Sa 9:30am-5:30pm). Bring a padlock to secure your personal locker.

Oxford Street, 14-18 Noel St., W1 (tel. 734 1618; fax 734 1657). Tube: Oxford Circus. Walk east on Oxford St. and turn right on Poland St. As close as possible to the Soho action. Dorms £18.70, under 18 £15.25; doubles £41. Kitchen and laundry. Reception 7am-11pm. Book 3-4 weeks in advance; very few walk-ins accepted. Full payment required to secure a reservation.

Hampstead Heath, 4 Wellgarth Rd., NW11 (tel. (0181) 458 9054 or 458 7096; fax 209 0546). Tube: Golders Green, then bus #210 or 268 toward Hampstead, or on foot by turning left from the station onto North End Rd., then left again onto Wellgarth. More like a hotel than a hostel. Dorms £15.60, under 18 £13.35; doubles £38.50; triples £55; quads £71. Breakfast included. Kitchen, laundry, fax, and **Internet access.** 24hr. security and reception. Reserve ahead.

City of London, 36 Carter Ln., EC4 (tel. 236 4965; fax 236 7681). Tube: St. Paul's. Go left down Godliman St., then take the first right; look for the sign. Sleep in clean and quiet comfort a stone's throw from St. Paul's. Dorms £19-22, under 18 £17-18; singles £25, £21.50; doubles £49, £41; triples £67.50, £90; quads £57, £76. Luggage storage, currency exchange, and laundry. Reception 7am-11pm. Call ahead.

Earl's Court, Earl's Ct., 38 Bolton Gdns., SW5 (tel. 373 7083; fax 835 2034). Tube: Earl's Ct. Exit from the Tube station onto Earl's Ct. Rd. and turn right; it's the 5th street on your left. Very clean townhouse in a leafy residential neighborhood. £18.70, under 18 £16.45. Non-members £1.70 extra; student discount £1. Kitchen laundry, and currency exchange. All rooms single-sex. Reception 7am-11pm. 24hr. security. Meals available in the large, colorful cafeteria 5-8pm.

Holland House, Holland Walk, W8 (tel. 937 0748; fax 376 0667). Tube: High St. Kensington. Handsome 1607 Jacobean mansion nestled in Holland Park offers lovely green views and a multi-lingual staff. HI membership required. Dorms £18.70, under 18 £16.45. Breakfast included. Laundry, kitchen, and luggage storage. 24hr. access.

King's Cross/St. Pancras, 79-81 Euston Rd., N1 (tel. 388 9998; fax 388 6766). Tube: King's Cross/St.Pancras or Euston. Spanking-new 8-story hostel boasts a convenient location and comfortable beds. Ask in advance about A/C. Dorms £18-21.30; doubles £19.40-22.50, with bath £21-24.30; quads £80; quints £97.50. Laundry, kitchen, and luggage storage. Book in advance. 1-week max. stay.

Private Hostels

Private hostels, which do not require an HI card, generally have a youthful clientele and often sport a vaguely bohemian atmosphere. Some have kitchen facilities and curfews are rare.

Ashlee House, 261-65 Gray's Inn Rd., WC1 (tel. 833 9400; fax 833 6777; email ashleehouse@tsnxt.co.uk). Tube: King's Cross/St. Pancras. From King's Cross, turn right onto Pentonville Rd. and right again onto Gray's Inn Rd. Clean, bright rooms within easy walking distance of King's Cross. Large dorms £13; 4- and 6-bed dorms

£17; 2-bed dorms s£22. Breakfast included (served M-F 7:30-9:30am, Sa-Su 8-10am). Kitchens and laundry available. Reception 24hr. Check-out 10am.

Astor's Museum Inn, Montague St., WC1 (tel. 580 5360; fax 636 7948), off Bloomsbury Sq. Tube: Holborn, Tottenham Ct. Rd., or Russell Sq. The prime location compensates for standard dorms. If they're full, they'll direct you to 1 of 3 other Astor's hostels. Co-ed dorms almost inevitable. £14-17; discounts available Oct.-Mar. Breakfast included. Adequate linens provided. Reception 24hr. Book about a month ahead.

Tonbridge School Clubs, Ltd. (tel. 837 4406), Judd and Cromer St., WC1. Tube: King's Cross/St. Pancras. Follow Euston Rd. to the site of the new British Library and turn left onto Judd St.; the hostel is 3 blocks down. Students with non-British passports only. No frills and no privacy, but dirt cheap. Blankets and foam pads provided. Floor space £5. Lockout 9am-9pm. Lights off 11:30pm. No admittance after midnight. Use caution when walking in the area at night.

Quest Hotel, 45 Queensborough Terr., W2 (tel. 229 7782). Tube: Queensway, then turn right onto Bayswater for 2 blocks, and left onto Queensborough. Communal, clean, and sociable. Dorms (co-ed and 1 women-only) £15-18. Breakfast (8-9:45am) and sheets included. Check-out 10am.

Albert Hotel, 191 Queens Gate, SW7 (tel. 584 3019; fax 823 8520). Tube: Gloucester Rd., or bus #2 or 70 from South Kensington. A substantial walk from the Tube, but deliciously close to Hyde Park; take a right on Cromwell and a left on Queen's Gate. Elegant and wood paneled, with sunny balconies. Dorms (single-sex or co-ed) £12-15; singles or doubles £40. Breakfast and sheets provided. Laundry. Reception 24hr. Reserve ahead with 1 night's deposit.

Court Hotel, 194-196 Earl's Ct. Rd., SW5 (tel. 373 0027; fax 912 9500). Tube: Earl's Ct. Sister hostel at 17 Kempsford Gardens (tel. 373 2174). Very clean Australian-managed hostel. All single and double rooms have TV and tea/coffee set. Kitchen. Dorms (single-sex) £15; singles £26; doubles £35. Off-season discounts. Reception 8am-9pm. Reservations not accepted; call for availability.

Hyde Park Hostel, 2-6 Inverness Terr., W2 (tel. 229 5101; fax 229 3170). Tube: Bayswater or Queensway. New and conveniently located. Pool room/lounge. Kitchen, laundry facilities. Dorms £12.50-15. Breakfast included. Reception 24hr.

Victoria Hotel, 71 Belgrave Rd. SW1 (tel. 834 3077; fax 932 0693). Tube: Pimlico. From the station, take the Bessborough St. (south side) exit and go left along Lupus St., then take a right at St. George's Sq. Belgrave Rd. starts on the other side. A clean, friendly, bohemian hostel with cool pool room. Kitchen. Dorms £12.50-15. Continental breakfast included. Luggage storage. Reception 24hr.

University Halls of Residence

London's university residences often accommodate visitors during the summer break (early June to mid-Sept.) and Easter vacations. Many of these halls have box-like rooms and institutional furniture. Most charge £18-25 and contain all singles. Call well in advance (by April for July reservations), as conference groups snatch up rooms early. The **King's Campus Vacation Bureau** (write to 127 Stanford Street, SE1 9NQ; tel. 928 3777) controls bookings for a number of residential halls.

⊛Stamford Street Apartments, 127 Stamford St., SE1 (tel. 873 2960; fax 873 2962). Tube: Waterloo. Take the exit marked "Waterloo Bridge," then the pedestrian subway marked "Subway to York Road," and follow it around the circle to reach Stamford St. 560 spacious singles with bathrooms. Each "apartment" shares a kitchen and TV lounge. Laundry facilities. Use of gym £5 per week. £32.50. 10% discount for stays over 7 days. Reception 24hr. Wheelchair accessible. Open July-Sept.

High Holborn Residence, 178 High Holborn, WC1 (tel. 379 5589; fax 379 5640). Tube: Holborn. An amazing combination of comfort and affordability. Singles are spacious and well furnished. You could eat off the bathroom floors, if so inclined. Lounge and bar. Usually booked far in advance. Singles £27; twins £45, with bath £52; discounts for longer stays. Breakfast included. Laundry facilities. Reception 7am-11pm. Open July to mid-Sept.

Wellington Hall, 71 Vincent Sq., Westminster, SW1 (tel. 834 440; fax 233 7709). Tube: Victoria. Walk 1 block along Vauxhall Bridge Rd.; turn left on Rochester

Row. Charming Edwardian hall on a pleasant, quiet square. Reserve through King's Campus Vacation Bureau (see above). Singles £25; doubles £38.50. English breakfast included. Discounts for longer stays. Book in advance. Rooms generally available June-Sept. and Easter.

John Adams Hall, 15-23 Endsleigh St., WC1 (tel. 387 4086; fax 383 0164). Tube: Euston. Heading right on Euston Rd., take the first right onto Gordon St. and then the first left onto Endsleigh Gdns.; Endsleigh St. is the second right. Elegant Georgian building. Laundry facilities, TV lounge, and 5 pianos. Singles £22; doubles £37. 5 or more days: singles £19; doubles £33. English breakfast included. Reception daily 8am-1pm and 2-10pm. Open July-Aug. and Easter, but a few rooms free all year.

Bed & Breakfasts

The number of B&Bs boggles the mind. Some are dingy and indistinct, others feature unique furnishings and a warm, welcoming atmosphere.

Near Victoria Station

B&Bs around Victoria Station are close to London's attractions as well as transportation connections. In the summer, prudent visitors make reservations well in advance.

@**Melbourne House,** 79 Belgrave Rd., SW1 (tel. 828 3516; fax 828 7120), past Warwick Sq. Tube: Pimlico. Take the Bessborough St. (south side) exit and go left along Lupus St. Turn right at St. George's Sq.; Belgrave Rd. starts on the other side of the square. All of the sparkling rooms come with TV, phone, and hot pot. Singles £30-50; doubles or twins with bath £70; triples £95; quads £110. Winter discounts. English breakfast with cereal option (7:30-8:45am). Book ahead. No credit cards.

@**Luna and Simone Hotel,** 47-49 Belgrave Rd., SW1 (tel. 834 5897; fax 828 2478), past Warwick St. Tube: Victoria or Pimlico. Immaculate and well maintained. Singles £25; doubles £50, with bath £60; triples with shower £75. 10% discount for long-term stays. Winter discount. English breakfast included. Luggage storage.

Georgian House Hotel, 35 St. George's Dr., SW1 (tel. 834 1438; fax 976 6085). Spacious rooms decorated with personality. Ask about the annex (about a block away), which is older but slightly cheaper and quieter. Singles £19-39; doubles £32-55; triples £45-68; quads £54-75. Breakfast included. Reception 8am-11pm.

Eaton House Hotel, 125 Ebury St., SW1 (tel./fax 730 8781). Large, clean, pastel rooms with dark wood chairs, TV, and tea/coffee maker. Singles £35-55; doubles £55-70; triples £70-85. Ask about discounts. English breakfast included.

Earl's Court

The area feeds on the tourist trade: travel agencies, currency exchanges, and souvenir shops dominate. The area also has a vibrant gay and lesbian population. Rooms tend to be dirt cheap, but ask to see a room to make sure the "dirt" isn't literal. Beware of overeager guides willing to lead you from the station to a hostel.

York House Hotel, 27-28 Philbeach Gdns., SW5 (tel. 373 7519; fax 370 4641). Special features include a mod, 60s-style TV lounge and a lovely garden. Extraordinarily clean. Friendly staff, surroundings, and low prices. Singles £30; doubles £47, with bath £66; triples £58, with bath £79; quads £67. English breakfast included.

Mowbray Court Hotel, 28-32 Penywern Rd., SW5 (tel. 373 8285 or 370 3690; fax 370 5693; email mowbraycrthot@hotmail.com). Relatively expensive, but staff this helpful is a rarity in London; wake-up calls, tour arrangements, taxicabs, theater bookings, and dry cleaning are all available. Singles £40-48; doubles £50-60; triples £63-72. Continental breakfast included. Reserve ahead if possible.

Philbeach Hotel, 30-31 Philbeach Gdns., SW5 (tel. 373 1244; fax 244 0149). The largest gay B&B in England, popular with both men and women. Gorgeous garden and an award-winning, upscale restaurant. Singles £45, with shower £55; doubles £58, with bath £75. Continental breakfast. 1-week advance booking recommended.

Kensington and Chelsea

These hotels prove convenient for those who wish to visit the stunning array of museums that line the southwest side of Hyde Park. Prices are a bit higher, but hotels here tend to be significantly more sober and comfortable than many at Earl's Ct.

Abbey House Hotel, 11 Vicarage Gate, W8 (tel. 727 2594), off Kensington Church St. Tube: High St. Kensington. After a series of renovations, the hotel has achieved a level of comfort that can't be rivaled at these prices. Singles £40; doubles £65; triples £78; quads £90; quints £100. English breakfast. Book ahead. No credit cards.

Swiss House, 171 Old Brompton Rd., SW5 (tel. 373 2769; fax 373 4983; email recep@swiss-hh.demon.co.uk). Airy, spacious rooms, most with fireplaces. Singles £42, with bath £59; doubles with bath £75. Continental breakfast included.

Oakley Hotel, 73 Oakley St., SW3 (tel. 352 5599 or 352 6610; fax 727 1190). Tube: Sloane Sq.; Victoria, then bus #11, 19, or 22; or South Kensington. Turn left off King's Rd. at the Chelsea Fire Station. Just steps away from Albert Bridge, Battersea Park, and shopping on King's Rd. Amiable staff and lovely bedrooms. Kitchen. Dorms (women only) £14; singles £32; doubles £48, with bath £58; triples £63, with bath £72; quads £72; quints £80. Breakfast included. Reserve several weeks ahead.

Bloomsbury

Despite its proximity to the West End, Bloomsbury maintains a fairly residential demeanor, with gracious, tree-filled squares and a prime location.

Arosfa Hotel, 83 Gower St., WC1 (tel./fax 636 2115). All furnishings and fixtures are close to new, the rooms are spacious, and the facilities are immaculate. Singles £31; doubles £44, with bath £58; triples £59, with bath £70. MC, V.

Ridgemount Hotel, 65-67 Gower St., WC1 (tel. 636 1141 or 580 7060; fax. 636 2558). Bright rooms with firm beds. **Laundry** facilities, garden in back, free tea and coffee in the TV lounge. Singles £30, with bath £40; doubles £44, with bath £55; triples £57, with bath £72. English breakfast included. Call in advance. No credit cards.

Mentone Hotel, 54-55 Cartwright Gdns., WC1 (tel. 387 3927; fax 388 4671). Pleasantly decorated and newly renovated. Singles £42-60; doubles £60-75; quads with bath £90. Reduced rates Dec.-Apr. English breakfast included. Visa, MC, Amex.

George Hotel, 60 Cartwright Gdns., WC1 (tel. 387 8777; fax 387 8666). Pleasant proprietress manages newly renovated hotel. Singles £44; doubles £60-75; triples £73-87; quads £80. English breakfast included. Visa, MC.

Alhambra Hotel, 17-19 Argyle St., WC1 (tel. 837 9575; fax 916 2476). Singles £30-40; doubles £40-55; quads £90. English breakfast included. Visa, MC, Amex.

Jesmond Dene Hotel, 27 Argyle St., WC1 (tel. 837 4654; fax 833 1633; http://www.scoot.co.uk/jesmond-dene). Newly renovated. Singles £28; doubles £38-55; triples £55-66; quads £75-85; quints £85. English breakfast. Visa, MC.

Paddington and Bayswater

B&Bs of variable quality cluster around Norfolk Square and Sussex Gardens.

Hyde Park Rooms Hotel, 137 Sussex Gdns., W2 (tel. 723 0225 or 723 0965). Tube: Paddington. Family run with airy rooms. An outstanding value. Singles £26, with bath £38; doubles £38, with bath £48; triples £57, with bath £72. English breakfast. Book in advance.

Dean Court Hotel, 57 Inverness Terr., W2 (tel. 229 2961; fax 727 1190). Tube: Bayswater or Queensway. Inverness is the 1st left off Bayswater Rd. Clean rooms with firm mattresses. English breakfast (M-F 7:30-8:30am, weekends 8:30-9:30am). **New Kent** next door offers same rooms, prices, and management. No private facilities. Dorms £14; doubles £38; twins £49; triples £54.

Garden Court Hotel, 30-31 Kensington Gdns. Sq., W2 (tel. 229 2553; fax 727 2749). Tube: Bayswater. From the Tube, make a left onto Queensway, a left onto Porchester Gdns., and then a right onto Kensington Gdns. Sq. A larger hotel in a pleasant, leafy neighborhood. Singles £34, with bath £48; doubles £48, with bath £74; triples £68, with bath £82. English breakfast. £25 deposit required. Check-out 11am.

LONDON

FOOD

London presents a tantalizing range of foreign and English specialties. Indian, Lebanese, Greek, Chinese, Thai, Italian, West Indian, and African food is inexpensive and readily available. If you eat but one meal in London, let it be Indian—London's Indian food is rivaled only by India's. Meals are less expensive on Westbourne Grove (Tube: Bayswater) or near Euston Station than in the West End.

The West End

Mandeer, 8 Bloomsbury Way, W1. Tube: Tottenham Ct. Rd. North Indian food is exceedingly fresh, primarily organic, and all vegetarian. The best deal in the house is the lunch buffet (from £3.50). Open M-Sa noon-3pm and 5-10pm.

West End Kitchen, 5 Panton St. Tube: Picadilly Circus. Perhaps the best deals going in London: a variety of ethnic and English dishes for under £3. 3-course set lunch £3.50. Open daily 7am-11:45pm.

The Stockpot, 18 Old Compton St., W1. Tube: Leicester Sq. or Piccadilly Circus. The cheapest place in Soho to soak up style. Open M-Tu 11:30am-11:30pm, W-Sa 11:30am-11:45pm, Su noon-11pm. Also at 40 Panton St.

The Wren Café at St. James's, 35 Jermyn St., SW1. Tube: Piccadilly Circus or Green Park. Wholefood/vegetarian delights served in the shadow of a Christopher Wren church. Open M-Sa 8:30am-6pm, Su 9am-5pm.

Café Emm, 17 Frith St., W1 (tel. 437 0723). Tube: Leicester Sq. Large portions are served in an unpretentious and soothing atmosphere. A cheap and palatable way to sample Soho café-culture. Open M-Th noon-3pm and 5:30-11pm, F noon-3pm and 5:30pm-1am, Sa 5pm-1am, Su 5:30-11pm. Last order 30min. before closing.

Lok Ho Fook, 4-5 Gerrard St., W1. Busy place with good prices and welcoming atmosphere. Extensive offerings with seafood, noodles, and vegetarian dishes. *Dim sum* (before 6pm) is made fresh when you order. Not to be confused with a nearby (and more expensive) place called Lee Ho Fook. Open daily noon-11:45pm.

Neal's Yard Salad Bar, 2 Neal's Yard, WC2. Take-away or sit outside at this simple vegetarian's nirvana. Tempting salads from £2. Open daily 11am-9pm.

Belgo Centraal, 50 Earlham St. WC2. Second branch, **Belgo Noord,** now open in Camden Town on 72 Chalk Farm Rd., NW1. Waiters in monk's cowls and bizarre 21st century beerhall interior make this one of Covent Garden's most popular restaurants. A fiver buys you wild boar sausage, Belgian mash, and a beer daily noon-5pm. Open M-Sa noon-11:30pm, Su noon-10:30pm. Wheelchair accessible.

City of London and East End

The Place Below (tel. 329 0789), in St. Mary-le-Bow Church crypt, Cheapside, EC2. Tube: St. Paul's. Generous vegetarian dishes served to the hippest of City execs in a church basement. Menu changes daily. Quiche and salad £6. Food much cheaper to take-away and £2 is taken off when you sit in 11:30am-noon. Serves as a café until lunch at 11:30am. Open M-F 7:30am-2:30pm.

Tinseltown 24 Hour Diner, 44-46 St. John St., EC1. Tube: Clerkenwell. All beer is about £1.50 and house wine £4.95. And best of all, it's open 24hr., 7 days a week.

Lahore Kebab House, 2 Umberston St., E1. Tube: Whitechapel. Off Commercial Rd. Some of the best, cheapest Indian and Pakistani cuisine in the city. No dish over £4. Feel free to bring your own beer. Open daily noon-midnight.

Kensington, Knightsbridge, Chelsea, and Victoria

Ciaccio, 5 Warwick Way, SW1. An intimate Italian eatery whose prices and spices make it a giant for budget eaters. Pick a container of pasta and one of about 10 sauces (pesto, veggie, tomato, and meat), and they'll heat it up in the microwave for £1.69-2.85. Open M-F 10am-7pm, Sa 9:30am-6pm.

Apadna, 351 Kensington High St., W8. A 10min. walk from the Tube and an escape from the street's commercial banality. Offers savory kebabs in fresh-baked *naan* (minced lamb kebab £2.80). Open daily 11am-11pm.

Chelsea Kitchen, 98 King's Rd., SW3. 7min. walk from the Tube. Eclectic, filling, and tasty. Breakfast served 8-11:25am. Open M-Sa 8am-11:30pm, Su 9am-11:30pm.

Bloomsbury and North London

Wagamama, 4a Streatham St., WC1. Tube: Tottenham Ct. Rd. Fast food: waitstaff takes your orders on hand-held electronic radios that transmit directly to the kitchen. Noodles £4.50-5.70. Open M-Sa noon-11pm, Su 12:30-10pm.

Diwana Bhel Poori House, 121 Drummond St., NW1. Tube: Warren St. Tasty Indian vegetarian food in a clean and airy restaurant. Many vegetarian and liberal kosher options. Lunch buffet £4 (noon-2:30pm). Open daily noon-11:30pm.

Captain Nemo, 171 Kentish Town Rd., NW1. Tube: Kentish Town. Unassuming Chinese/chipper take-away rocks your world with tangy, delicious chips in curry sauce (£1.40). Open M-F noon-2:45pm and 5:30-11:30pm, Sa-Su 5:30-11:30pm.

Troubador Coffee House, 265 Old Brompton Rd., SW5, near Earl's Ct. and Old Brompton Rd. junction. Whirring espresso machines steam up the windows in this café. Live music. Assorted snacks, soups, and sandwiches under £4. Liquor available with food orders. Open M-Sa 9:30am-12:30am, Su 9:30am-11pm.

Notting Hill, Ladbroke Grove, and Earl's Court

The Grain Shop, 269a Portobello Rd., W11. Tube: Ladbroke Grove. Take-away shop with a large array of tasty foods and a long line of customers. Organic whole grain breads baked daily (80p-£1.40 per loaf). Groceries also available, many organic. Open M-Sa 9:30am-6pm.

Cockney's, 314 Portobello Rd., W10. Tube: Ladbroke Grove. "Traditional pie, mash, and eels," says the sign above the door, and they aren't joking (eels available F-Sa). Cups of liquor for only 30p. Open M-Th and Sa 11:30am-5:30pm, F 11:30am-6pm.

Bistro Benito, 166 Earl's Court Rd., SW5 (tel. 373 66 46). 20-yr. old, family Italian bistro serves good cheer and hearty food in equal helpings. Most pastas £3.95. Good cheer £3.50. Open M-Sa noon-11:30pm, Su noon-11pm.

PUBS

The clientele of London's 700 pubs varies widely from one neighborhood to the next. Avoid touristy pubs near train stations. For the best prices head to the East End. Stylish, lively pubs cluster around the fringes of the West End. Many historic alehouses lend an ancient air to areas swallowed up by the urban sprawl, such as Highgate and Hampstead. Don't be afraid to leave a good pub—doing a crawl lets you experience the diversity of a neighborhood's nightlife.

The Dog and Duck, 8 Bateman St., W1. Tube: Tottenham Ct. Rd. Frequent winner of the Best Pub in Soho award, its size keeps the crowd down. Inexpensive pints (£1.95-2.20). Evenings bring locals, theater-goers, and, yes, some tourists. Open M-F noon-11pm, Sa 6-11pm, Su 7-10:30pm.

The Three Greyhounds, 25 Greek St., W1. Tube: Leicester Sq. This medieval-style pub provides welcome respite from the posturing of Soho. Open M-Sa 11am-11pm, Su noon-10:30pm.

Riki Tik, 23-24 Bateman St., W1. Tube: Leicester Sq., Tottenham Ct. Rd., or Piccadilly Circus. A hyped, hip, and tremendously swinging bar specializing in orgasmic flavored vodka shots (£2.60). Come during happy hour (W-Sa noon-8pm) for near-bargains. Open M-Sa noon-1am. £3 cover after 11pm.

Lamb and Flag, 33 Rose St., WC2, off Garrick St. Tube: Covent Garden or Leicester Sq. A traditional pub, with 2 sections—the public bar for the working class and the saloon bar for the businessmen, although today the classes mix. Live jazz upstairs Su from 7:30pm. Open M-Th 11am-11pm, F-Sa 11am-10:45pm, Su noon-10:30pm.

World's End Distillery, 459 King's Rd., near World's End Pass before Edith Grove. Tube: Sloane Sq. Enjoy pints in the comfy bookshelf-lined booths. Comedy every Su night at 8pm (£3.50). Open M-Sa 11am-11pm, Su noon-10:30pm.

The Old Crown, 33 New Oxford St., WC1. Tube: Tottenham Ct. Rd. A thoroughly untraditional pub with a lively crowd and cool jazz. Homemade food from £2.75. Open M-Sa 10am-11pm.

SIGHTS

London is best explored on foot, but if you have only one day here, a tour may be a good way to intensify your sight-seeing experience. The **Original London Sightseeing Tour** (tel. (0181) 877 1722) provides a convenient, albeit cursory, overview of London's attractions from a double-decker bus. *(Tours daily in summer 9am-7pm; in winter 9:30am-5:30pm. £12, under 16 £6.)* Tours lasting two hours depart from Baker St., Haymarket (near Piccadilly Circus), Marble Arch, Embankment, and near Victoria Station. The route includes views of Buckingham Palace, the Houses of Parliament, Westminster Abbey, the Tower of London, St. Paul's, and Piccadilly Circus. A ticket allows you to ride the buses for a 24-hour period—permitting visitors to hop off at major sights and hop on a later bus to finish the tour. Walking tours can fill in the specifics of London that bus tours run right over. Among the best is **The Original London Walks** (tel. 624 3978), two-hour tours led by well-regarded guides (£4.50, students £3.50).

Mayfair to Parliament

An auspicious beginning to a day's wander is **Piccadilly Circus** and its towering neon bluffs (Tube: Piccadilly Circus). At the center of the Nash's swirling hub stands a fountain topped by a statue everyone calls Eros but actually depicts the Angel of Christian Charity. North are the tiny shops of Regent St. and the renovated seediness of **Soho,** a region that sports a vibrant sidewalk café culture, where pornography once reigned supreme. Outdoor cafés, upscale shops, and slick crowds huddle in **Covent Garden,** to the northeast. Paths across **Green Park** lead to **Buckingham Palace** (tel. 799 2331; http://www.royal.gov.uk), now partially open to tourists. *(Tube: Victoria, Green Park, and St. James's Park. Open daily Aug.-Sept. £9.50, seniors £7, under 17 £5. Tours may be available; call for details.)* The **Changing of the Guard** occurs daily (Apr. to late Aug.) or every other day (Sept.-Mar.) at 11:30am, unless it's raining. Arrive early or you won't see a thing.

    The Mall, a wide processional, leads from the palace to **Admiralty Arch** and **Trafalgar Square.** South of the Mall, **St. James's Park** shelters a duck preserve and a flock of lawn chairs (70p per 4hr.). The center of a vicious traffic roundabout, Trafalgar Sq. (Tube: Charing Cross) centers on Nelson's Column, a 40 ft. high statue astride a 132 ft. column. Political Britain branches off **Whitehall,** just south of Trafalgar. Draped in black velvet, Charles I was led out of the **Banqueting House** (corner of Horse Guards Ave. and Whitehall) and beheaded. *(Open M-Sa 10am-5pm but closed for government functions. Last admission 4pm. £3.50, concessions £2.70.)* The building now hosts less lethal state dinners. The Prime Minister resides off Whitehall at **10 Downing Street,** now closed to tourists. In the middle of Whitehall is the **Cenotaph,** a monument to Britain's war dead. Whitehall ends by the sprawling **Houses of Parliament** (Tube: Westminster). Access to the House of Commons and the House of Lords is extremely restricted since a member was killed in a bomb blast in 1979. Queue up outside when either is in session in order to sit in the upper galleries of the Lords or Commons. You can hear **Big Ben** but not see him; Big Ben is neither the tower nor the clock, but the 14-ton bell, cast when a similarly proportioned Sir Benjamin Hall served as Commissioner of Works. Church and state tie the knot in **Westminster Abbey** (tel. 222 7110), coronation chamber to English monarchs since 1066 and the site of **Poet's Corner,** the **Grave of the Unknown Warrior,** the **Stone of Scone,** and the elegantly perpendicular **Chapel of Henry VII.** *(Abbey open M-F 9am-4:45pm, Sa 9am-2:45pm. Last admission 3:45pm, some W until 7:45pm; call for info. £5, concessions £3, ages 11-18 £2, families £10. Tours £3. Photography permitted W evenings only.)* Britain bestows no greater honor than burial within these walls. The abbey plumber is buried here along with Elizabeth I, Darwin, Dickens, and Newton. Ask about the story surrounding the Stone of Scone.

Hyde Park and Kensington to Chelsea

Hyde Park shows its best face on Sundays from 11am to dusk, when soapbox orators take freedom of speech to the limit at **Speaker's Corner** (Tube: Marble Arch, *not*

Hyde Park Corner). To the west, **Kensington Gardens,** an elegant relic of Edwardian England, celebrates the glories of model yacht racing in the squarish Round Pound. From the gardens, you can catch a glimpse of **Kensington Palace.** Hourly tours of the palace visit uninhabited royal rooms and a collection of regal memorabilia, including Court dresses. (1½hr. tours May-Sept. M-Sa 10am-5pm; call Ticketmaster at 344 4444. £7.50, students £6.) The **Royal Albert Hall,** on the south edge of Hyde Park, hosts the **Proms,** a gloriously British festival of music. Up Brompton Rd. near Knightsbridge, **Harrods** (Tube: Knightsbridge) vends under their humble motto, *Omnia Omnibus Ubique*—*"All things for all people, everywhere."* (Open M-Tu and Sa 10am-6pm, W-F 10am-7pm.) Still-fashionable **King's Road** (Tube: Sloane Sq.), south in **Chelsea,** attempts to do justice to its bohemian past—past residents include Oscar Wilde and the Sex Pistols.

Regent's Park to Fleet Street

Take a break from the city and picnic in the expanse of **Regent's Park,** northeast of Hyde Park across Marylebone (Tube: Regent's Park). The **London Zoo,** in the north end, harbors such exotic animals as mambos, Asian lions, and piranhas. (Open daily Apr.-Sept. 10am-5:30pm; Oct.-Mar. 10am-4pm. Last admission 1hr. before closing. £8.50, concessions £7.) **Camden Town** (Tube: Camden Town), bordering the park to the northeast, sports rollicking street markets. **Bloomsbury**—eccentric, erudite, and disorganized—is known for its literary and scholarly connections, including the **British Museum.** Although nearly all the papers have moved to cheaper real estate, **Fleet Street** is the traditional den of the British press. Close by are the **Inns of Court,** which have controlled access to the English Bar since the 13th century.

City of London & the East End

Once upon a time, "London" meant the square-mile enclave of the **City of London;** the rest of today's metropolis were far-flung towns and villages. The **Tower of London,** the grandest fortress in medieval Europe, was the palace and prison of English monarchs for over 500 years. Inside, the **Crown Jewels** include the Stars of Africa, cut from the enormous Cullinan Diamond, which was mailed third-class from the Transvaal in an unmarked brown paper package. The tower's best-known edifice, the **White Tower,** was begun by William the Conqueror. In 1483, the "Princes in the Tower" (Edward V and his brother) were murdered in the **Bloody Tower** in one of the great unsolved mysteries of British royal history. (Tube: Tower Hill. Open M-Sa 9am-5pm, Su 10am-5pm; last ticket sold at 4pm. £9.50, concessions £7.15.) Two of the wives of jolly King Henry VIII were beheaded in the courtyard, and in 1941 Rudolf Hess was sent to the Tower after his parachute dumped him in Scotland. Next to the tower is **Tower Bridge,** one of London's best-known landmarks. Other fragments of history are scattered throughout the City, among them 24 Christopher Wren churches interspersed among the soaring steel of modern skyscrapers. Wander through smaller churches, such as the Strand's **St. Clement Danes** of "Oranges and Lemons" fame or the superb **St. Stephen Walbrook** near the Bank of England (Tube: Bank). True-blue cockney Londoners are born within earshot of the famous bells of **St. Mary-le-Bow,** Cheapside. In the German Blitz in 1940, **St. Paul's Cathedral** stood firm in a sea of fire. (Tube: St. Paul's. Open M-Sa 8:30am-4pm. Ambulatory and galleries open M-Sa 8:45am-4:15pm. Cathedral, ambulatory, crypt, and galleries £7.50, students £6.50.) Climb above the graves of Wren, Nelson, and Wellington in the crypt to the dizzying top of the dome; the view is unparalleled. The **Barbican Centre** (Tube: Barbican or Moorgate) is one of the most impressive and controversial post-Blitz rebuilding projects.

The **East End** is a relatively poor section of London with a history of racial conflict. A large working-class population moved into the district during the Industrial Revolution, soon followed by a wave of Jewish immigrants fleeing persecution in Eastern Europe; they settled around **Whitechapel.** Notable remnants of the former East End community include the city's oldest standing synagogue, **Bevis Marks Synagogue,** Bevis Marks and Heneage Ln., EC3 (tel. 626 1274; Tube: Aldgate.) From Aldgate High St. turn right onto Houndsditch. Creechurch Ln. on the left leads to Bevis Marks. In

1978, the latest immigration wave brought a large Muslim Bangladeshi community to the East End. At the heart of this community is **Brick Lane** (Tube: Aldgate East), a street lined with Indian and Bangladeshi restaurants, colorful textile shops, and ethnic groceries. *(To reach Brick Lane, head left up Whitechapel as you exit the Tube station; turn left onto Osbourne St., which turns into Brick Lane.)* On Sundays, market stalls selling books, bric-a-brac, leather jackets, and sandwiches flank this street and Middlesex St., better known as **Petticoat Lane.**

The South and Outskirts

Lesser-known but equally rewarding treasures lie south of the river, the area currently experiencing a cultural and economic renewal. **Southwark Cathedral,** a smallish, quiet church, boasts London's second-best Gothic structure and a chapel dedicated to John Harvard (Tube: London Bridge). Not for the squeamish, **London Dungeon** lurks beneath the London Bridge with exhibits on execution, torture, and plague. *(Open daily Apr.-Sept. 10am-6:30pm, last entrance 5:30pm; Nov.-Feb. 10am-5:30pm, last entrance 4:30pm. £9.50, students £7.95.)* West along the riverbank, a reconstruction of **Shakespeare's Globe Theatre** (tel. 902 1400) is used for performances. *(1hr. tours available May-Sept. M 9am-4pm, Tu-Sa 9am-12:30pm, Su 9am-2:30pm; Oct.-Apr. daily 10am-5pm. £5, concessions £4.)*

The genteel Victorian shopping and residential district of Brixton (Tube: Brixton) became the locus of a Caribbean and African community who followed large-scale Commonwealth immigration in the 1950s and 1960s. Most of the activity in Brixton centers around the **Brixton Market** at Electric Ave., Popes Rd., and Brixton Station Rd. Choose from among the stalls of fresh fish, vegetables, and West Indian cuisine, or browse through the stalls of African crafts and discount clothing. Nearby, on the corner of Coldharbor and Atlantic, the **Black Cultural Archives,** 378 Coldharbor Ln., SW9 (tel. 738 4591), mounts small but informative exhibits on black history.

London **Docklands,** the largest commercial development in Europe, is the only section of London built wholly anew—a total break from the city's typically slow architectural evolution. Developers have poured tons of steel, reflective glass, and money onto the banks of the Thames east of London Bridge. The 800 ft. **Canary Wharf** building, Britain's tallest edifice and the jewel of the Docklands, is visible to the east from almost anywhere in London. The best way to see the region is via the **Docklands Light Railway (DLR)** (tel. 918 4000) driverless, totally automatic elevated rail system. All tickets, Travelcards, and passes issued by London Transport, London Underground, and British Rail are valid on the DLR provided they cover the correct zones. The first stop for any Docklands tour should be the **Docklands Visitors Centre** (tel. 512 1111). *(DLR: Crossharbor, then left up the road. Open M-F 8:30am-6pm, Sa-Su 9:30am-5pm.)*

Head by train or boat to red-brick **Hampton Court Palace** (tel. (0181) 781 9500) for a quirky change of pace. *(£8, £12 return. Hampton Court open Mar. to late Oct. M 10:15am-6pm, Tu-Su 9:30am-6pm; late Oct. to Mar. M 10:15am-4:30pm, Tu-Su 9:30am-4:30pm. Last admission 45min. before closing. Gardens open at the same time as the palace, but close at 9pm or dusk, whichever comes first. Free. All-encompassing admission £9.25, concessions £7; only to maze or Privy Garden £2.10.)* Its grounds contain the famous **hedgerow maze** (British Rail: Hampton Ct.). From the Monday before Easter until the end of September, a boat runs from Westminster Pier to Hampton Court, leaving in the morning at 10:30, 11:15am, and noon, and returning from Hampton Court at 3, 4, and 5pm. The trip takes three to four hours one-way.

Windsor Castle (tel. (01753) 868286 or 831118 for 24hr. info line) is the Queen's spectacular country retreat. *(Open daily Apr.-Oct. 10am-5:30pm, last entry 4pm; Nov.-Mar. 10am-4pm; last entry 3pm. £8.80, over 60 £6.20, under 17 £4.60.)* British Rail serves Windsor and Eton Central station and Windsor and Eton Riverside station, both of which are near Windsor Castle.

Just west of central London on the Thames lie the serene and exotic **Kew Gardens** (tel. (0181) 940 1171). Lose yourself in the controlled wilderness of the grounds, or explore the Victorian and modern glasshouses containing thousands of plant species.

(Tube or British Rail: Kew Gardens. Gardens open M-F 9:30am-6:30pm, Sa-Su and bank holidays 9:30am-7:30pm. Last admission 30min. before closing. Conservatories close at 5:30pm. Closing times may vary by season; call ahead. £5, students and seniors £3.50. Daily tours £1. Kew also hosts summer jazz concerts—tickets £18-25. Call Ticketmaster at 344 4444 for details.)

The transport system that encouraged London's urban sprawl blurs the distinction between city and surroundings. If Hyde Park seemed small, **Highgate** and **Hampstead Heath** will prove that there *is* an English countryside. In the Eastern Cemetery, Karl Marx and George Eliot repose in the Gothic tangle of **Highgate Cemetery,** Swains Lane. *(Tube: Archway. Eastern Cemetery open M-F 11am-4:30pm, Sa-Su 10am-4:30pm. £1. Western Cemetery access by guided tour only M-F at noon, 2, and 4pm, Sa-Su every hr. 11am-4pm. £3. Camera permit £1.)*

MUSEUMS

British Museum, Great Russell St., WC1 (info tel. 323 82 99). Tube: Tottenham Ct. Rd. or Holborn. The closest thing to a complete record of the rise and ruin of world cultures. Among the plunder on display are the **Rosetta Stone** (whose inscriptions allowed French scholar Champollion to decipher hieroglyphics) and the Elgin Marbles. Open M-Sa 10am-5pm, Su 2:30-6pm. Free, suggested donation £2.

National Gallery, Trafalgar Sq., WC2 (tel. 839 33 21 or 747 28 85 for recorded info). Tube: Charing Cross, Leicester Sq., Embankment, or Piccadilly Circus. One of the world's best collections of Western paintings. The Micro Gallery can print out a free personalized tour. Open M-Sa 10am-6pm, W 10am-8pm, Su noon-6pm. Free.

National Portrait Gallery, St. Martin's Pl., WC2, opposite St.-Martin's-in-the-Fields. Tube: Charing Cross or Leicester Sq. Mugs from Queen Elizabeth II to John Lennon. Doubles as *Who's Who in Britain.* Open M-Sa 10am-6pm, Su noon-6pm. Free.

Tate Gallery, Millbank, up the Thames from Parliament Sq. (tel. 887 80 00 for recorded info). Tube: Pimlico. The best of British artists, along with Monet, Dalí, Picasso, and Matisse. The best place in London for modern art fans. The vast J.M.W. Turner collection rests in the Clore Gallery. Open daily 10am-5:50pm. Free.

Victoria and Albert Museum, Cromwell Rd. (tel. 938 84 41 for recorded info). Tube: South Kensington. An array of fine and applied arts. Open M noon-5:50pm, Tu-Su 10am-5:50pm. £5, concessions £3, students free.

Madame Tussaud's, Marylebone Rd., NW1. Tube: Baker St. The classic waxwork museum. Might not be worth the wait and the cost. Open in summer M-F 10am-5:30pm, Sa-Su 9:30am-5:30pm; in winter M-F 11am-5:30pm, Sa-Su 9:30am-5:30pm. £9.75, seniors £7.45.

Museum of London, 150 London Wall, EC2 (tel. 600 0807 for 24hr. info). Tube: St. Paul's or Barbican. From Londinium to the 1996 European Soccer Championships. Free lectures W-F; check for times. Open Tu-Sa 10am-5:50pm, Su noon-5:50pm; last entry 5:30pm. £4, concessions £2. Free after 4:30pm. Wheelchair accessible.

Museum of the Moving Image (MOMI), South Bank Centre, SE1 (tel. 401 2636 for 24hr. info). Tube: Waterloo. The entertaining museum charts the development of image-making with light, from shadow puppets to film and telly. Open daily 10am-6pm. Last admission 5pm. £6.25, students £5.25, seniors £4.50.

Science Museum, Exhibition Rd., SW7. Tube: South Kensington. Closet science geeks will be outed by their orgasmic cries as they enter this wonderland of motors, springs, and spaceships. This 5-story collection rivals the best science museums around. Open daily 10am-6pm. £6.50, concessions £3.50. Free 4:30-6pm.

London Transport Museum, Covent Garden, WC2 (tel. 565 7299 for recorded info). Tube: Covent Garden. Although ground floor traffic flows through a maze of historic trains, trams, and buses, the museum offers much more than a history of public transport vehicles. Open M-Th and Sa-Su 10am-6pm, F 11am-6pm; last admission 5:15pm. £4.95, concessions £2.95. Wheelchair accessible.

Imperial War Museum, Lambeth Rd., SE1 (tel. 416 5000). Tube: Lambeth North or Elephant & Castle. The atrium is filled with tanks and planes; gripping exhibits illuminate every aspect of two World Wars in every possible medium. Open daily 10am-6pm. £5, students £4. Free daily 4:30-6pm. Wheelchair accessible.

The Wallace Collection, Hertford House, Manchester Sq., W1 (tel. 935 0687). Tube: Bond St. Outstanding works include Hals's *The Laughing Cavalier,* Delacroix's

Execution of Marino Faliero, Fragonard's *The Swing,* and Rubens's *Christ on the Cross.* Home to the largest armor and weaponry collection outside of the Tower of London. Open M-Sa 10am-5pm, Su 11am-5pm. Guided tours M-Tu 1pm, W 11:30am and 1pm, Th-F 1pm, Sa 11:30am, Su 3pm. Free.

ENTERTAINMENT

On any given day or night, Londoners and visitors can choose from the widest range of entertainment. For guidance consult *Time Out* (£1.80) or *What's On* (£1.30).

Theater, Music, and Film

London **theater** is unrivalled. Seats cost £8-30 and up, and student/senior standby (with an "S," "concessions," or "concs" in newspaper listings) puts even the best seats within reach—£7-10 just before curtain (come two hours early with ID). **Day seats** are sold cheaply (9-10am the day of performance) to all; queue up earlier. The **Leicester Square Ticket Booth** sells half-price tickets on the day of major plays (open M-Sa 11am-6:30pm; long wait; £2 fee; credit cards accepted). Standby tickets for the **Royal National Theatre** (tel. 452 3400; Tube: Waterloo), on the South Bank Centre, sell two hours beforehand (£10-14; students £7.50, 45min. before). The **Barbican Theatre** (24hr. info tel. 382 7272, reservations 638 8891; Tube: Barbican or Moorgate), London home of the Royal Shakespeare Company, has student and senior standbys for £6 from 9am on the performance day. For a mere £5, you can stand as a groundling and watch Shakespearean productions in the meticulously reconstructed **Shakespeare's Globe Theatre** (call 401 9919 for tickets), New Globe Walk, Bankside SE1. (Tube: London Bridge. Box office open M-Sa 10am-8pm.) Exciting cheaper performances are found on the **Fringe,** in less commercial theaters.

Most major **classical music** is staged at the acoustically superb **Royal Festival Hall** (tel. 960 4242; Tube: Waterloo) and the **Barbican Hall. Marble Hill House** has low-priced outdoor concerts on summer Sundays at 2pm (tel. 413 1443). Londoners have been lining up for standing room in the **Royal Albert Hall's "Proms"** (BBC Henry Wood Promenade Concerts; tel. 589 8212) for nearly a century. **Pop music** performers from the world over cannot keep away from London. **Brixton Academy** (tel. 924 9999; Tube: Brixton) is a larger, rowdy venue for a variety of music including rock and reggae (advance tickets £8-25). **Ronnie Scott's,** 47 Frith St., W1 (tel. 439 0747; Tube: Leicester Sq. or Piccadilly Circus), has London's greatest jazz (cover from £15).

The Prince Charles, Leicester Pl., WC2 (tel. 437 8181; Tube: Leicester Sq.), is a Soho institution. The four shows a day (cheerily deconstructed on the recorded phone message) are generally second-runs but also include a sprinkling of classics for only £2-2.50. The **Institute of Contemporary Arts (ICA) Cinema,** Nash House, The Mall, W1 (tel. 930 3647; Tube: Piccadilly Circus or Charing Cross), plays cutting-edge contemporary cinema and an extensive list of classics (£6.50), and the **National Film Theatre (NFT),** South Bank Centre, SE1 (tel. 928 3232; Tube: Waterloo), boggles the mind with its array of film, TV, and video (most screenings £5).

Clubs

London pounds to 100% groovy Liverpool tunes, ecstatic Manchester rave, home-town soul and house, U.S. hip-hop, and Jamaican reggae. Many clubs host a variety of provocative one-night stands (like "Get Up and Use Me") throughout the week. Check listings in *Time Out* for the latest.

Iceni, 11 White Horse St., W1 (tel. 495 5333). Tube: Green Park. Off Curzon St. 3 floors of funk in this Mayfair hotspot. £10-12. Open F 11pm-3am, Sa 10pm-3am.

Ministry of Sound, 103 Gaunt St., SE1. Tube: Elephant and Castle. Night buses #N12, N62, N65, N72, N77, or N78. Mega-club with beefy covers and beautiful people, but beware—bouncers concoct the "most appropriate" crowd. One of the first major rave spots. Open F 10:30pm-6:30am, Sa midnight-9am. Cover F £10, Sa £15.

The Roadhouse, Jubilee Hull, 35 The Piazza, WC2. Tube: Covent Garden. Excellent live cover bands every night (2 bands on Saturday) spice up the place and let you know that everyone is getting what they want, what they really really want—a good time. Open M-Th 5:30pm-3am, F 4:30pm-3am, Sa 6:30pm-3am. Cover £3-10.

The Hanover Grand, 6 Hanover St., W1 (tel. 499 7977). Tube: Oxford Circus. Loud funk atmosphere. W-F 10:30pm-4am, Sa 10:30pm-5am. Cover £5-15, W before 11pm £3.

The Fridge, Town Hall Parade, Brixton Hill, SW2. Tube: Brixton. Night bus #N2. A serious dance dive with a stylish multi-ethnic crowd. Saturday's "Love Muscle," the ultimate London one-nighter, packs in a beautiful and shocking mixed-gay clientele. Open F-Sa 10pm-6am. Cover £10, with flyer £8.

GAY, LESBIAN, AND BISEXUAL LONDON

London has a very visible gay scene, covering everything from the flamboyant to the mainstream. *Time Out* has a section devoted to gay listings, and gay newspapers include *Capital Gay* (free, caters to men), *Pink Paper,* and *Shebang* (for women). *Gay Times* (£3) is the British counterpart to the *Advocate; Diva* (£2) is a monthly lesbian mag. Islington, Earl's Ct., and Soho (especially **Old Compton Street**) are all gay-friendly areas.

Balans, 60 Old Compton St., W1. Tube: Leicester Sq. Another branch at 239 Old Brompton Rd. (tel. 244 8838; open daily 8am-2am). Ruthlessly glamorous ambience for a mostly gay male clientele. Lots of veggie options. Open daily 8am-5am.

The Candy Bar, 4 Carlisle St., W1. Tube: Tottenham Ct. Rd. 3 floors of women (men welcome as guests) at London's first all-lesbian bar. Bar downstairs becomes dance floor W-Sa. Cover £5 F-Sa after 10pm.

Old Compton Café, 35 Old Compton St., W1 (tel. 439 3309). Tube: Leicester Sq. In the geographic epicenter of Soho, this is *the* gay café. Tables and people (predominantly 20- and 30-something males) overflow onto the street. Open daily 7am-5am.

Heaven, Villiers St., WC2, underneath The Arches. Tube: Embankment or Charing Cross. The oldest and biggest gay disco in Europe. Bumping garage music F-Sa 10pm-3am. Cover F £6, after 11:30pm £7.50; Sa £7, after 11:30pm £8.

"G.A.Y.," at London Astoria 1 (Sa), and 2 (Th and M), 157 Charing Cross Rd., WC2. Tube: Tottenham Ct. Rd. Pop extravaganza amid chrome and disco balls. Unpretentious mixed clientele. Open, Th and Sa from 10:30pm, Sa from 11pm. Cover £3-6. Discounts with flyers.

APPENDIX

■ Holidays and Festivals

Time	City or Region	Event
	SPRING	
April 2		Good Friday
April 5		Easter Monday
Late April	Galway	Poetry and Literature Festival
Early May	Creggan	Bealtaine Festival
Early May	Dunarvan	Féile na nDéise
Early May	Cork	Choral Festival
Early May	Glengarriff	Caha Walking Festival
May 4	U.K.	May Day Holiday
Mid-May	Killarney	Killarney Races
Mid-May	Armagh	Apple Blossom Festival
May 25	United Kingdom	Spring or Whitsun Holiday
Late May to Early June	Sligo	Arts Festival
June 1	Republic of Ireland	First Monday in June
Early June	Armagh	Comhietas Collton Traditional Music Festival
Early June	Carlow	Éigse
Early June	Douglas	T.T. (Tourist Trophy) Motorcycle Races
Early June	Ardara	Weaver's Fair
Mid-June	Bangor	The Bangor and North Down Festival
Mid-June	Ballycastle	Fleadh Amhrán agus Rince
Mid-June	Inisheer	St. Kevin's Mass and Festival
Mid-June	Oughterard	Currach racing Championships
June 16	Dublin	Bloomsday
	SUMMER	
Late June	Isle of Man	International Cycling Festival
Late June	The Curragh	Irish Derby
Late June	Cork	Sense of Cork Festival
Late June	Portaferry	Galway Hookers' Regatta
Late June	Athlone	Athlone Festival
Late June	Bantry	West Cork Chamber Music Festival
Late June to Early July	Donegal Town	International Arts Festival
Week of July 5	Isle of Man	Manx Heritage Week
Early July	Glencolmcille	Glencolmcille Folk Festival
Early July	Duncannon	Duncannon Festival
Early July	Killarney	Killarney Regatta
Early July	Galway	Galway Film Fleadh

Early July	Glenarm	Glenarm Festival
Early July	Miltown Malbay	Willy Clancy Summer School
Early July	Ramelton	Lennon Festival
July 4	Galway	Salthill Air Show
July 5	Isle of Man	Tynwald Fair Day
July 12	Northern Ireland	Ancient Order of Hibernians' Parades (Orange Day)
July 15	Ballina	Heritage Day
Mid-July	Kilmore Quay	Seafood Festival
Mid-July	Youghal	Youghal Carnival
Mid-July	Castletown, Isle of Man	Southern "100" Motorcycle Races
Mid-July	Cobh	Seisiún Gis Cuan Festival
Mid-July	Castlegregory	Summer Festival
Mid-July	Drogheda	Samba Festival
Mid-July	Dungarvan	Motorsport Weekend
Mid-July	Killarney	Killarney Races
Mid-July	Ballina	Ballina Street Festival
Mid-July	Boyle	Gala festival
Mid-July	Cushendall	Guinness Relay
July 24	Ardmore	Pattern Day (St. Declan's festival)
Late July	Sligo	Irish National Sheepdog Trials
Late July	Rostrevor	Fiddler's Green Festival
Late July	Boyle	Arts Festival
Late July	Burtonpoint	Burtonpoint Festival
Late July	Dungloe	Mary from Dungloe Festival
Late July	Skibbereen	Welcome Home Week
Late July	Wicklow	Regatta Festival
Late July to Early August	Sligo	Yeats International Summer School
Late July to Early August	Youghal	Youghal Premier Busking Festival
Late July to Early August	Dungloe	Mary from Dungloe International Festival
Mid-Summer	Cong	Midsummer Ball, John Wayne/Maureen O'Hara Look-Alike Contest
August 3	Republic of Ireland	First Monday in August
Early August	Belturbet	Festival of the Erne
Early August	Youghal	Busking Festival
Early August	Castletownbere	Festival of the Sea
Early August	Achill Island	Scoil Acla
Early August	Cahersiveen	Celtic Music Festival
Early August	Clonmany	Clonmany Festival
Early August	Kilkenny	Arts Week
Early August	Kilcar	International Sea Angling Festival, Street Festival
Early August	Kinsale	Kinsale Regatta
Early August	Glencolmcille	Fiddle Festival
Early August	Dingle	Dingle Races

August 10-12	Killorglin	Puck Fair
August 15	Malin Head	Sports Day
Mid-August	Dingle	Dingle Regatta
Mid-August	Bantry	Bantry Bay Regatta
Mid-August	Armagh	Ulster Road Bowls Finals
Mid-August	Kansas	Trash-chucking Day
Mid-August	Miltown Malbay	International "Darlin' Girl from Clare" Festival
Mid-August	Warrenpoint	Maiden of the Mournes Festival
Mid-August	Cobh	Cobh People's Regatta
August 21	Knock	Feast of Our Lady of Knock
Late August	Boyle	Quatrocentennial Celebration
Late August	Clifden	Connemara Pony Show
Late August	Clonmel	Fleadh Ceoil na hÉireann
Late August	Tralee	Rose of Tralee International Festival
Late August	Ballycastle	Oul' Lammas Fair
Late August	Carlingford	Medieval Oyster Fair
Late August	Mullet Peninsula	Feille Iorras
Late August	Balycastle, Co. Antrim	Ould Lammas Fair
Late August	Cape Clear	International Storytelling Festival
Late August	Tralee	Rose of Tralee International Festival
August 31	N. Ireland, Isle of Man, London	Late summer of Holiday
Early September	Monaghan	Jazz and Blues Festival
September	Dublin	All-Ireland Hurling and Football Finals
September	Cork	Folk Festival
September	Lisdoonvarna	Lisdoonvarna Matchmaking Festival
September 12	Glenties	Harvest Fair

AUTUMN

Mid-September	Passage East	Mussel Festival
Late September	Westport	Arts Festival
Late September	Clifden	Arts Week
Late September	Galway	International Oyster Festival
Late September	Waterford	Waterford Festival of Light Opera
Early October	Cork	International Film Festival
Early October	Kildare	Irish National Yearling Sales
Early October	Dublin	Dublin Theater Festival
Early October	Glenties	Fiddler's Weekend
Mid-October	Bundoran	Bundoran Music Festival
Mid-October	Armagh	Arts Festival
Mid-October	Cork	Guinness Jazz Festival
Mid-October	Kinsale	Kinsale Gourmet Festival
Mid-October	Wexford	Wexford Opera Festival
October 26	Republic of Ireland	Last Monday in October
Late October to Early November	Athlone	John McCormack Golden Voice Competition
November	Belfast	Belfast Festival at Queen's

WINTER

December 25		Christmas Day
December 26		St. Stephen's Day/Boxing Day
January 1		New Year's Day
Valentine's Day weekend	Dungarvan	Dungarvan Jazz Festival
Late February	Dublin	Dublin Film Festival
mid-March	Killarney	Guinness Roaring 1920s Festival
March 17		St. Patrick's Day

■ Telephone Codes

Dublin	Belfast	Cork	Derry	Douglas	Galway
01	01232	021	01504	01624	091

Killarney	Letterkenny	London	Limerick	Sligo	Waterford
064	074	0171, 0181	061	071	051

■ International Calling Codes

Australia	Canada	Ireland	New Zealand
61	1	353	64

Northern Ireland from the Republic	South Africa	U.K.	U.S.
08	27	44	1

■ Time Zones

Ireland and the U.K. are on Greenwich Mean Time (GMT), which sets its clock: one hour earlier than (most of) continental Europe; five hours later than Raleigh, North Carolina (EST); six hours later than Winnebago, Illinois (CST); seven hours later than Missoula, Montana (MST); eight hours later than Walla Walla, Washington (PST); 10 hours later than Hilo, Hawaii; eight, 9½, and 10 hours earlier than Australia; and 12 hours earlier than Auckland, New Zealand.

■ Measurements

1 inch (in.) = 25 millimeter (mm)	1mm = 0.04 in.
1 foot (ft.) = 0.30 meter (m)	1m = 3.33 ft.
1 yard (yd.) = 0.91m	1m = 1.1 yd.
1 mile (mi.)= 1.61kilometer (km)	1km = 0.62 mi.
1 ounce (oz.) = 25 gram (g)	1g = 0.04 oz.
1 pound (lb.) = 0.45 kilogram (kg)	1kg = 2.22 lb.
1 lb.= 0.071 stone	1 stone = 14lb.
1 Imperial quart = 1.14 liters (L)	1L = .0.88 Imperial qt.
1 U.S. quart = 0.94L	1L = 1.06 U.S. qt.
1 Imperial gallon = 1.19 U.S. gallons (ga.)	1 U.S. ga. = 0.84 Imperial ga.
1 Imperial pint = 1.19 U.S. pints (pt.)	1 U.S. pt. = .84 Imperial pt.

APPENDIX

■ Glossary

For a brief history and background, see **The Irish Language,** p. 76. The following bits of the Irish language are either used often in Irish English or are common in Irish place names. Spelling conventions do not always match English pronunciations: for example, "mh" sounds like "v," and "dh" sounds like "g."

Irish/British	Pronunciation	(American) English
	USEFUL PHRASES	
Conas tá tú?	CUNN-us thaw too?	**How are you?**
dia dhuit	JEE-a dich	good day, hello
dia's muire dhuit	Jee-as MWUR-a dich	reply to "good day"
fáilte	FAHL-tshuh	welcome
go raibh maith agat	guh roh moh UG-ut	thank you
mór	more	big, great
ní hea	nee hah	no (sort of; it's tricky)
oíche mhaith dhuit	EE-ha woh dich	good night
sea	shah	yes (sort of; it's tricky)
sláinte	SLAWN-che	cheers, to your health
slán agat	slawn UG-ut	goodbye
fok or fook		(for emphasis)
	GEOGRAPHY	
An Lár	on lahr	**city center**
Baile Átha Cliath	BALL-yah AW-hah CLEE-ah	**Dublin**
drumlin		small hill
Éire	AIR-uh	Ireland; official name of the Republic of Ireland
gaeltacht	GAYL-tokt	a district where Irish is the everyday language
inch, innis		island
slieve or sliabh	shleev	mountain
sraid	shrawd	street
strand		beach
trá	thraw	beach
	SIGHTSEEING	
Bord Fáilte	Bored FAHL-tshuh	**Irish Tourist Board**
concession		discount on admission (for students, seniors, etc.)
dolmen		chamber formed by huge stones
dún	doon	fort
gaol	jail	jail
kil	kill	church; monk's cell
queue up, "Q"		waiting line
rath	rath or rah	earthen fort

tumulus		stone burial mound
way out		exit

POLITICS

Dáil	DOY-il	House of Representatives in the Republic
dole, on the dole		welfare or unemployment benefits
DUP		Democratic Unionist Party; right-wing N.I. party led by Ian Paisley
Fianna Fáil	FEE-in-ah foil	"Soldiers of Destiny," political party in Éire
Fine Gael	FINN-eh gayl	"Family of Ireland," political party in Éire
INLA		Irish National Liberation Army, an IRA splinter group
IRA (Provisional IRA)		Irish Republican Army; a Nationalist paramilitary group
Loyalist		pro-British, more extreme than a Unionist
Nationalists		those who want Northern Ireland and the Republic united
Official IRA		less-prominent group that split from the IRA in 1969
Oireachtas	OR-uch-tus	both houses of the Irish Parliament
Orangemen		a widespread Protestant Unionist group
Provisionals, Provos		slang for the IRA
Republican		Nationalist activist
SDLP		Social Democratic and Labor Party; moderate Nationalist Party in the North
Seanad	SHAN-ud	Irish Senate
Sinn Féin	shin fayn	"Ourselves Alone," Northern political party affiliated with the IRA
Taoiseach	TEE-shukh	Irish Prime Minister
teachta dála (TD)	TAKH-ta DAH-lah	member of Irish parliament
the Troubles		the period of violence in the North, starting in 1969
UDA		Ulster Defence Association, an Unionist paramilitary group
UDR		Ulster Defence Regiment, the British Army unit in the North
UFF		Ulster Freedom Fighters (synonymous with UDA)
Unionists		those who want Northern Ireland to remain part of the U.K.
UUP		Ulster Unionist Party, the largest political party in the North

UVF		Ulster Volunteer Force, Unionist paramilitary group

PUBS & MUSIC

bodhrán	BOUR-ohn	traditional drum
busker		street musician
céilí	KAY-lee	Irish dance
craic	krak	good cheer, good pub conversation, a good time
faders		party poopers who go to bed early
fag		cigarette
feis	fesh	an assembly or Irish festival
fleadh	flah	a musical festival
off-license		retail liquor store
pissed		drunk
poitín	po-CHEEN	moonshine; sometimes toxic homemade liquor
pub grub		quality bar food
publican		barkeep
to shift		to chat flirtatiously
to slag		to tease and ridicule
to snog		to kiss
snug		enclosed booth within a pub
to take the piss out		to make fun of
trad		traditional Irish music
uilleann	ILL-in	"elbow," bagpipes played with the elbow
táim	thaw im	I am…
súgach	SOO-gakh	tipsy
ar meisce	uhr MEH-shka	drunk
ar dearg mheisce	uhr jar-eg VEH-shka	very drunk
ólta	OLE-ta	quite drunk
caoch ólta	KWEE-ukh OLE-ta	blind drunk

LITERATURE

aisling	ASH-ling	vision or dream, or a poem or a story about one
Ar aghaidh linn: Éire	uhr EYE linn: AIR-ah	*Let's Go: Ireland*
ogham	Oh-um	early Irish, written on stones
seanachaí	SHAHN-ukh-ee	storyteller

SPORTS

football		Gaelic football in the Republic, soccer in the North
GAA		Gaelic Athletic Association; organizes Gaelic sports
iománaíocht	umauneeakht	hurling
peil	pell	football

snooker		a board game like pool

FOOD

bangers and mash		sausage and mashed potatoes
bap		a soft bun, like a hamburger bun
bill		check (in restaurants)
candy-floss		cotton candy
chips		french fries
chipper		fish and chips vendor
crisps		potato chips
rashers		Irish bacon
take-away		take-out, "to go"

ACCOMMODATIONS AND DAILY LIFE

bedsit		one-room apartment, sometimes with kitchen
biro		ball point pen
caravan		trailer, mobile home
dust bin		trash can
ensuite		with bathroom attached
fir	fear	men
first floor		first floor up from the ground floor (second floor)
flat		apartment
ground floor		first floor
hoover		vacuum cleaner
lavatory, lav		bathroom
lei thras	LEH-hrass	toilets
to let		to rent
loo		bathroom
mná	min-AW	women
self-catering		accommodation with kitchen facilities
torch		flashlight

MONEY

cheap		inexpensive (not shoddy)
dear		expensive
fiver		£5 note
punt		Irish pound
sterling		British pound
tenner		£10 note

CLOTHING

nappies		diapers
pants		underwear
trainers		sneakers

TRANSPORT

coach		bus (long distance)
hire		rental
left luggage		luggage storage
lorry		truck
motorway		highway
petrol		gasoline
return ticket		round-trip ticket
roundabout		rotary road interchange
self-drive		car rental
single ticket		one-way ticket

CIVIC AND CULTURAL

chemist		pharmacist
garda, Garda Siochána	GAR-da SHE-och-ANA	police
OAP		old age pensioner, "senior citizen"
Oifig an Phoist	UFF-ig un fwisht	post office
quay	key	a waterside street
redundancies		job layoffs
RTÉ		Radio Telefis Éireann, the Republic's broadcasting authority
RUC		Royal Ulster Constabulary, the police force of Northern Ireland

Index

About Let's Go

Back in 1960, a few students at Harvard University banded together to produce a 20-page pamphlet offering a collection of tips on budget travel in Europe. This modest, mimeographed packet, offered as an extra to passengers on student charter flights to Europe, met with instant popularity. The following year, students traveling to Europe researched the first, full-fledged edition of *Let's Go: Europe,* a pocket-sized book featuring honest, irreverent writing and a decidedly youthful outlook on the world. Throughout the 60s, our guides reflected the times; the 1969 guide to America led off by inviting travelers to "dig the scene" at San Francisco's Haight-Ashbury. During the 70s and 80s, we gradually added regional guides and expanded coverage into the Middle East and Central America. With the addition of our in-depth city guides, handy map guides, and extensive coverage of Asia and Australia, the 90s are also proving to be a time of explosive growth for Let's Go, and there's certainly no end in sight. The maiden edition of *Let's Go: South Africa,* our pioneer guide to sub-Saharan Africa, hits the shelves this year, along with the first editions of *Let's Go: Greece* and *Let's Go: Turkey.*

We've seen a lot in 39 years. *Let's Go: Europe* is now the world's bestselling international guide, translated into seven languages. And our new guides bring Let's Go's total number of titles, with their spirit of adventure and their reputation for honesty, accuracy, and editorial integrity, to 44. But some things never change: our guides are still researched, written, and produced entirely by students who know first-hand how to see the world on the cheap.

HOW WE DO IT

Our series is completely revised and thoroughly updated every year by a well-traveled set of over 200 students. Every winter, we recruit over 160 researchers and 70 editors to write the books anew. After several months of training, researcher-writers hit the road for seven weeks of exploration, from Anchorage to Adelaide, Estonia to El Salvador, Iceland to Indonesia. Hired for their rare combination of budget travel sense, writing ability, stamina, and courage, these adventurous travelers know that train strikes, stolen luggage, food poisoning, and marriage proposals are all part of a day's work. Back at our offices, editors work from spring to fall, massaging copy written on Himalayan bus rides into witty yet informative prose. A student staff of typesetters, cartographers, publicists, and managers keeps our lively team together. In September, the collected efforts of the summer are delivered to our printer, who turns them into books in record time, so that you have the most up-to-date information available for your vacation. Even as you read this, work on next year's editions is well underway.

WHY WE DO IT

We don't think of budget travel as the last recourse of the destitute; we believe that it's the only way to travel. Living cheaply and simply brings you closer to the people and places you've been saving up to visit. Our books will ease your anxieties and answer your questions about the basics—so you can get off the beaten track and explore. Once you learn the ropes, we encourage you to put *Let's Go* down now and then to strike out on your own. You know as well as we that the best discoveries are often those you make yourself. When you find something worth sharing, please drop us a line. We're Let's Go Publications, 67 Mount Auburn St., Cambridge, MA 02138, USA (email: feedback@letsgo.com). For more info, visit our website, http://www.letsgo.com.

HAPPY TRAVELS!

Researcher-Writers

Kathleen Conroy
Counties Cork, Kerry, Limerick, Tipperary, Waterford
We looked forward to talking to Kathleen every Friday. From her down-to-earth sense of humor and great attitude, we never would have guessed that she was braving the wettest, grayest Irish summer in 10 years. We were happy to hear that she met lots of nice people her own age and even managed to track down a long-lost relative. She got the low-down about agricultural exports from tourist officials and about black pudding from butchers—while making friends with everyone in between and keep us updated on the whole experience. Good job—cheers!

Daniel Horwitz
Counties Armagh, Cavan, Clare, Fermanagh, Galway, Leitrim, Mayo, Monaghan, Roscommon, Sligo, Tyrone
We loved Dan's copy when we downloaded it each week—we wished we could have kept his inside jokes. No p.a.h. he, Dan thoroughly explored every off-the-beaten-track attraction from his coveted left-lane position, turning up such little known gems as the classy Mask & Spear Pub and the awesome, elite river view afforded by the room inside an enchanted red tower. He uncovered the activities of the Ancient Order of Citos, and his extreme lupidity at the unhelpful nature of some tourist offices didn't keep him from turning up tabloid-worthy conspiracies, stigmatic scandals, and strange religious sects. We'll miss those occasional conversations—and we *loved* the flowers! Dan rocked Ireland, T.A.I.S.Y.

Christopher Leighton
Counties Carlow, Dublin, Kildare, Kilkenny, Longford, Meath, Waterford, Westmeath, Wexford, Wicklow
Chris braved his trip to the center of the island with a sharp eye and a sharper wit. As he fearlessly confronted and survived the cross-training lunatic, a herd of crazed sheep, freshly dug graves, and Carrick-on-Suir, we waited breathlessly for his clear, matter-of-fact copy and eloquent commentary on contemporary social issues. His brilliant critque of Irish society broadened our understanding of rural civic development, Irish familial structure, cultural preservation, and the commercial uses of public space. But seriously—Chris's four-color wit about phallic papal crosses, animals on crack, and the throbbing Dublin club scene kept us in stitches. Hell, yeah.

Deirdre O'Dwyer
Counties Antrim, Derry, Donegal, Down, Louth; Isle of Man
Queen Deirdre of Ulster ruled over Donegal and the North. She trekked out to every desolate northern head and every anxious Northern tourist office to give us the most complete, conscientious accounts possible. Her copy revolutionized our coverage of Northern Ireland with careful, sensitive observation laced with wit, and she was, if it's possible, even more in her element in the windswept *gaeltacht*. We hope she'll never stop caring and never stop writing about tricolored (or four-horned) sheep and spectacular scenery wherever she goes. *Go raibh maith agat.*

Shanya Dingle
Editor, London
Rachel Greenblatt, *London*
Ben Jackson, *London*
Tobie Whitman, *London*

Acknowledgments

Team Ireland owes more thanks than it can offer to Lisa Nosal for heavenly guidance through the entire process. Huge thanks to Mapland, especially Dan, for keeping us properly cartographed. Big round of applause for late-night typists Elena and Lano and last-minute proofers Nate, team USA, Tom, and especially Eileen. Thanks to the girl-power pod for spicing up the summer: Shanya for a smashing chunk of London, Olivia in both of her alter egos, Alex for the shroud of energy she cast on her surroundings. Alex, Karen, and Elizabeth crunched for us; Dan, Heath, and Maryanthe took care of the rest. Drew Bryant and Mel gave us installation art. Thanks to the Derry tourist board, Bus Éireann, and others across the ocean for all their help.

Thanks first to Brina, who *almost* kept me down to earth while always cracking me up. Lisa was the only one to walk across the fire for us; just like a prayer, she would appear during any kind of crisis. Dan Visel talked me through those initial editoral qualms and told me to sleep on the final nights. Thanks to Dan, Paul, and Chris for not calling the police when I was gone for days on end, and to Ruby, who I did fortunately get to see. I'm grateful to Nate, Doug, and Ben for the flicks and hospitality; as well as Alex, Sonya, and their metal-jacketed friends. Lastly, thanks to my parents, who have always been the best anyone could hope for. **-JRW**

Big hugs and kisses to Jenny, in part for teaching me the value of peat rental and the beauty of Lullymore. Lisa rocks my party world, which says it all. Thanks to Mum and Da for their thorough inauthenticity and Shira for her p.o.power. None of this would be without the wired inspiration of BSC and the Book of Nells, the good luck of the Blaron Stone, or the music of SRG/SGG, who introduced me to Irish mytholgoy without even knowing it. Other thanks saved for NSS, HDL, and the other BMs. **-BM**

Editor	Jenny Weiss
Associate Editor	Brina Milikowsky
Managing Editor	Lisa M. Nosal
Publishing Director	Caroline R. Sherman
Publishing Director	Anna C. Portnoy
Production Manager	Dan Visel
Associate Production Manager	Maryanthe Malliaris
Cartography Manager	Derek McKee
Design Manager	Bentsion Harder
Editorial Manager	M. Allison Arwady
Editorial Manager	Lisa M. Nosal
Financial Manager	Monica Eileen Eav
Personnel Manager	Nicolas R. Rapold
Publicity Manager	Alexander Z. Speier
New Media Manager	Måns O. Larsson
Map Editors	Matthew R. Daniels, Dan Luskin
Production Associate	Heath Ritchie
Office Coordinators	Tom Moore, Eliza Harrington, Jodie Kirshner
Director of Advertising Sales	Gene Plotkin
Associate Sales Executives	Colleen Gaard, Mateo Jaramillo, Alexandra Price
President	Catherine J. Turco
General Manager	Richard Olken
Assistant General Manager	Anne E. Chisholm

Thanks to Our Readers...

Mano Aaron, CA; Jean-Marc Abela, CAN; George Adams, NH; Bob & Susan Adams, GA; Deborah Adeyanju, NY; Rita Alexander, MI; Shani Amory-Claxton, NY; Kate Anderson, AUS; Lindsey Anderson, ENG; Viki Anderson, NY; Ray Andrews, JPN; Robin J. Andrus, NJ; L. Asurmendi, CA; Anthony Atkinson, ENG; Deborah Bacek, GA; Jeffrey Bagdade, MI; Mark Baker, UK; Mary Baker, TN; Jeff Barkoff, PA; Regina Barsanti, NY; Ethan Beeler, MA; Damao Bell, CA; Rya Ben-Shir, IL; Susan Bennerstrom, WA; Marla Benton, CAN; Matthew Berenson, OR; Walter Bergstrom, OR; Caryl Bird, ENG; Charlotte Blanc, NY; Jeremy Boley, EL SAL; Oliver Bradley, GER; A.Braurstein, CO; Philip R. Brazil, WA; Henrik Brockdorff, DMK; Tony Bronco, NJ; Eileen Brouillard, SC; Mary Brown, ENG; Tom Brown, CA; Elizabeth Buckius, CO; Sue Buckley, UK; Christine Burer, SWITZ; Norman Butler, MO; Brett Carroll, WA; Susan Caswell, ISR; Carlos Cersosimo, ITA; Barbara Crary Chase, WA; Stella Cherry Carbost, SCOT; Oi Ling Cheung, HK; Simon Chinn, ENG; Charles Cho, AUS; Carolyn R. Christie, AUS; Emma Church, ENG; Kelley Coblentz, IN; Cathy Cohan, PA; Phyllis Cole, TX; Karina Collins, SWITZ; Michael Cox, CA; Mike Craig, MD; Rene Crusto, LA; Claudine D'Anjou, CAN; Lizz Daniels, CAN; Simon Davies, SCOT; Samantha Davis, AUS; Leah Davis, TX; Stephanie Dickman, MN; Philipp Dittrich,GER; Tim Donovan, NH; Reed Drew, OR; Wendy Duncan, SCOT; Melissa Dunlap, VA; P.A. Emery, UK; GCL Emery, SAF; Louise Evans, AUS; Christine Farr, AUS; David Fattel, NJ; Vivian Feen, MD; David Ferraro, SPN; Sue Ferrick, CO; Philip Fielden, UK; Nancy Fintel, FL; Jody Finver, FL; D. Ross Fisher, CAN; Abigail Flack, IL; Elizabeth Foster, NY; Bonnie Fritz, CAN; J. Fuson, OR; Michael K. Gasuad, NV; Raad German, TX; Mark Gilbert, NY; Betsy Gilliland, CA; Ana Goshko, NY; Patrick Goyenneche, CAN; David Greene, NY; Jennifer Griffin, ENG; Janet & Jeremy Griffith, ENG; Nanci Guartofierro, NY; Denise Guillemette, MA; Ilona Haayer, HON; Joseph Habboushe, PA; John Haddon, CA; Ladislav Hanka, MI; Michael Hanke, CA; Avital Harari, TX; Channing Hardy, KY; Patrick Harris, CA; Denise Hasher, PA; Jackie Hattori, UK; Guthrie Hebenstreit, ROM; Therase Hill, AUS; Denise Hines, NJ; Cheryl Horne, ENG; Julie Howell, IL; Naomi Hsu, NJ; Mark Hudgkinson, ENG; Brenda Humphrey, NC; Kelly Hunt, NY; Daman Irby, AUT; Bill Irwin, NY; Andrea B. Jackson, PA; John Jacobsen, FL; Pat Johanson, MD; Russell Jones, FL; J. Jones, AUS; Sharon Jones, MI; Craig Jones, CA; Wayne Jones, ENG; Jamie Kagan, NJ; Mirko Kaiser, GER; Scott Kauffman, NY; John Keanie, NIRE; Barbara Keary, FL; Jamie Kehoe, AUS; Alistair Kernick, SAF; Daihi Kielle, SWITZ; John Knutsen, CA; Rebecca Koepke, NY; Jeannine Kolb, ME; Elze Kollen, NETH; Lorne Korman, CAN; Robin Kortright, CAN; Isel Krinsky, CAN; George Landers, ENG; Jodie Lanthois, AUS; Roger Latzgo, PA; A. Lavery, AZ; Joan Lea, ENG; Lorraine Lee, NY; Phoebe Leed, MA; Tammy Leeper, CA; Paul Lejeune, ENG; Yee-Leng Leong, CA; Sam Levene, CAN; Robin Levin, PA; Christianna Lewis, PA; Ernesto Licata, ITA; Wolfgang Lischtansky, AUT; Michelle Little, CAN; Dee Littrell, CA; Maria Lobosco, UK; Netii Ross, ITA; Didier Look, CAN; Alice Lorenzotti, MA; David Love, PA; Briege Mac Donagh, IRE; Brooke Madigan, NY; Helen Maltby, FL; Shyama Marchesi, ITA; Domenico Maria, ITA; Natasha Markovic, AUS; Edward Marshall, ECU; Rachel Marshall, TX; Kate Maynard, UK; Agnes McCann, IRE; Susan McGowan, NY; Brandi McGunigal, CAN; Neville McLean, NZ; Marty McLendon, MS; Matthew Melko, OH; Barry Mendelson, CA; Eric Middendorf, OH; Nancy Mike, AZ; Coren Milbury, NH; Margaret Mill, NY; David H. Miller, TX; Ralph Miller, NV; Susan Miller, CO; Larry Moeller, MI; Richard Moore, ENG; Anne & Andrea Mosher, MA; J. L. Mourne, TX; Athanassios Moustakas, GER; Laurel Naversen, ENG; Suzanne Neil, IA; Deborah Nickles, PA; Pieter & Agnes Noels, BEL; Werner Norr, GER; Ruth J. Nye, ENG; Heidi O'Brien, WA; Sherry O'Cain, SC; Aibhan O'Connor, IRE; Kevin O'Connor, CA; Margaret O'Rielly, IRE; Daniel O'Rourke, CA; Krissy Oechslin, OH; Johan Oelofse, SAF; Quinn Okamoto, CA; Juan Ramon Olaizola, SPN; Laura Onorato, NM; Bill Orkin, IL; K. Owusu-Agyenang, UK; Anne Paananen, SWD; Jenine Padget, AUS; Frank Pado, TX; G. Pajkich, Washington, DC; J. Parker, CA; Marian Parnat, AUS; Sandra Swift Parrino, NY; Iris Patten, NY; M. Pavini, CT; David Pawielski, MN; Jenny Pawson, ENG; Colin Peak, AUS; Marius Penderis, ENG; Jo-an Peters, AZ; Barbara Phillips, NY; Romain Picard, Washington, DC; Pati Pike, ENG; Mark Pollock, SWITZ; Minnie Adele Potter, FL; Martin Potter, ENG; Claudia Praetel, ENG; Bill Press, Washington, DC; David Prince, NC; Andrea Pronko, OH; C. Robert Pryor, OH; Phu Quy, VTNM; Adrian Rainbow, ENG; John Raven, AUS; Lynn Reddringer, VA; John Rennie, NZ; Ruth B.Robinson, FL; John & Adelaida Romagnoli, CA; Eva Romano, FRA; Mark A. Roscoe, NETH; Yolanda & Jason Ross, CAN; Sharee Rowe, ENG; W. Suzanne Rowell, NY; Vic Roych, AZ; John Russell, ENG; Jennifer Ruth, OK; William Sabino, NJ; Hideki Saito, JPN; Frank Schaer, HUN; Jeff Schultz, WI; Floretta Seeland-Connally, IL; Colette Shoulders, FRA; Shireen Sills, ITA; Virginia Simon, AUS; Beth Simon, NY; Gary Simpson, AUS; Barbara & Allen Sisarsky, GA; Alon Siton, ISR; Kathy Skeie, CA; Robyn Skillecorn, AUS; Erik & Kathy Skon, MN; Stine Skorpen, NOR; Philip Smart, CAN; Colin Smit, ENG; Kenneth Smith, DE; Caleb Smith, CA; Geoffrey Smith, TX; John Snyder, NC; Kathrin Speidel, GER; Lani Steele, PHIL; Julie Stelbracht, PA; Margaret Stires, TN; Donald Stumpf, NY; Samuel Suffern, TN; Michael Swerdlow, ENG; Brian Talley, TX; Serene-Marie Terrell, NY; B. Larry Thilson, CAN; J. Pelham Thomas, NC; Wright Thompson, ITA; Christine Timm, NY; Melinda Tong, HK; M. Tritica, AUS; Melanie Tritz, CAN; Mark Trop, FL; Chris Troxel, AZ; Rozana Tsiknaki, GRC; Lois Turner, NY; Nicole Virgil, IL; Blondie Vucich, CO; Wendy Wan, SAF; Carrie & Simon Wedgwood, ENG; Frederick Weibgen, NJ; Richard Weil, MN; Alan Weissberg, OH; Ryan Wells, OH; Jill Wester, GER; Clinton White, AL; Gael White, CAN; Melanie Whitfield, SCOT; Bryn Williams, CAN; Amanda Williams, CAN; Wendy Willis, CAN; Sasha Wilson, NY; Kendra Wilson, CA; Olivia Wiseman, ENG; Gerry Wood, CAN; Kelly Wooten, ENG; Robert Worsley, ENG; C.A.Wright, ENG; Caroline Wright, ENG; Mary H. Yuhasz, CO; Margaret Zimmerman, WA.

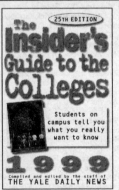